THE LIBRARY OF LIV

THE PHILOSOPHY OF SEYYED HOSSEIN NASR

THE LIBRARY OF LIVING PHILOSOPHERS
PAUL ARTHUR SCHILPP, FOUNDER AND EDITOR 1939-1981
LEWIS EDWIN HAHN, EDITOR 1981-

Paul Arthur Schilpp, Editor

THE PHILOSOPHY OF JOHN DEWEY (1939, 1971, 1989)
THE PHILOSOPHY OF GEORGE SANTAYANA (1940, 1951)
THE PHILOSOPHY OF ALFRED NORTH WHITEHEAD (1941, 1951)
THE PHILOSOPHY OF G. E. MOORE (1942, 1971)
THE PHILOSOPHY OF BERTRAND RUSSELL (1944, 1971)
THE PHILOSOPHY OF ERNST CASSIRER (1949)
ALBERT EINSTEIN: PHILOSOPHER-SCIENTIST (1949, 1970)
THE PHILOSOPHY OF SARVEPALLI RADHAKRISHNAN (1952)
THE PHILOSOPHY OF KARL JASPERS (1957; AUG. ED., 1981)
THE PHILOSOPHY OF C. D. BROAD (1959)
THE PHILOSOPHY OF RUDOLF CARNAP (1963)
THE PHILOSOPHY OF C. I. LEWIS (1968)
THE PHILOSOPHY OF KARL POPPER (1974)
THE PHILOSOPHY OF BRAND BLANSHARD (1980)
THE PHILOSOPHY OF JEAN-PAUL SARTRE (1981)

Paul Arthur Schilpp and Maurice Friedman, Editors

THE PHILOSOPHY OF MARTIN BUBER (1967)

Paul Arthur Schilpp and Lewis Edwin Hahn, Editors

THE PHILOSOPHY OF GABRIEL MARCEL (1984)
THE PHILOSOPHY OF W. V. QUINE (1986, AUG. ED., 1998)
THE PHILOSOPHY OF GEORG HENRIK VON WRIGHT (1989)

Lewis Edwin Hahn, Editor

THE PHILOSOPHY OF CHARLES HARTSHORNE (1991)
THE PHILOSOPHY OF A. J. AYER (1992)
THE PHILOSOPHY PAUL RICOEUR (1995)
THE PHILOSOPHY OF PAUL WEISS (1995)
THE PHILOSOPHY OF HANS-GEORG GADAMER (1997)
THE PHILOSOPHY OF RODERICK M. CHISHOLM (1997)
THE PHILOSOPHY OF P. F. STRAWSON (1998)
THE PHILOSOPHY OF DONALD DAVIDSON (1999)

Lewis Edwin Hahn, Randall E. Auxier, and Lucian W. Stone, Jr., Editors

THE PHILOSOPHY OF SEYYED HOSSEIN NASR (2001)

In Preparation:

THE PHILOSOPHY OF MARJORIE GRENE
THE PHILOSOPHY OF ARTHUR C. DANTO
THE PHILOSOPHY OF MICHAEL DUMMETT
THE PHILOSOPHY OF JAAKKO HINTIKKA
THE PHILOSOPHY OF HILARY PUTNAM
THE PHILOSOPHY OF RICHARD M. RORTY

Seyyed Hossein Nasr

THE LIBRARY OF LIVING PHILOSOPHERS
VOLUME XXVIII

THE PHILOSOPHY OF
SEYYED HOSSEIN NASR

EDITED BY

LEWIS EDWIN HAHN
RANDALL E. AUXIER
LUCIAN W. STONE, JR.

SOUTHERN ILLINOIS UNIVERSITY AT CARBONDALE

CHICAGO AND LA SALLE, ILLINOIS • OPEN COURT • ESTABLISHED 1887

To order books from Open Court, call 1-800-815-2280.

THE PHILOSOPHY OF SEYYED HOSSEIN NASR

Open Court Publishing Company is a division of Carus Publishing Company.

First printing 2001

Printed and bound in the United States of America.

Library of Congress Cataloging-in-Publication Data

The Philosophy of Seyyed Hossein Nasr / edited by Lewis Edwin Hahn, Randall E. Auxier, Lucian W. Stone, Jr.

p. cm.— (The Library of Living Philosophers; v. 28)

"Bibliography of Seyyed Hossein Nasr": p.

Includes bibliographical references (p.) and index.

ISBN 0-8126-9413-9—ISBN 0-8126-9414-7 (pbk.)

1. Nasr, Seyyed Hossein. 2. Philosophy, Islamic. I. Hahn, Lewis Edwin, 1908– . II. Auxier, Randall E., 1961– . III. Stone, Lucian W., 1972– . IV. Series.

B5295 .P48 2001
181'.5—dc21

2001021951

The Library of Living Philosophers is published under the sponsorship of Southern Illinois University at Carbondale.

GENERAL INTRODUCTION TO THE LIBRARY OF LIVING PHILOSOPHERS

Since its founding in 1938 by Paul Arthur Schilpp, the Library of Living Philosophers has been devoted to critical analysis and discussion of some of the world's greatest living philosophers. The format for the series provides for setting up in each volume a dialogue between the critics and the great philosopher. The aim is not refutation or confrontation but rather fruitful joining of issues and improved understanding of the positions and issues involved. That is, the goal is not overcoming those who differ from us philosophically but interacting creatively with them.

The basic idea for the series, according to Professor Schilpp's general introduction to the earlier volumes, came from the late F.C.S. Schiller, who declared in his essay on "Must Philosophers Disagree?" (in *Must Philosophers Disagree?* London: Macmillan, 1934) that the greatest obstacle to fruitful discussion in philosophy is "the curious etiquette which apparently taboos the asking of questions about a philosopher's meaning while he is alive." The "interminable controversies which fill the histories of philosophy," in Schiller's opinion, "could have been ended at once by asking the living philosophers a few searching questions." And while he may have been overly optimistic about ending "interminable controversies" in this way, it seems clear that directing searching questions to great philosophers about what they really mean or how they think certain difficulties in their philosophies can be resolved while they are still alive can produce far greater clarity of understanding and more fruitful philosophizing than might otherwise be had.

And to Paul Arthur Schilpp's undying credit, he acted on this basic thought in launching the Library of Living Philosophers. It is planned that each volume in the Library of Living Philosophers include an intellectual autobiography by the principal philosopher or an authorized biography, a bibliography of that thinker's publications, a series of expository and critical essays written by leading exponents and opponents of the philosopher's thought, and the philosopher's replies to the interpretations and queries in these articles. The intellectual autobiographies usually shed a great deal of light on both how the philosophies of the great thinkers developed and the major philosophical movements and issues of their time; and many of our great philosophers seek to orient their outlook not merely to their contemporaries but also to what they find most important in earlier philosophers. The bibliography will help provide ready access to the featured scholar's writings and thought.

With this format in mind, the Library expects to publish at more or less regular intervals a volume on one of the world's greater living philosophers.

In accordance with past practice, the editors have deemed it desirable to secure the services of an Advisory Board of philosophers as aids in the selection of subjects of future volumes. The names of eight prominent American philosophers who have agreed to serve appear on the page following the Founder's General Introduction. To each of them the editors are most grateful.

Future volumes in this series will appear in as rapid succession as is feasible in view of the scholarly nature of this library. The next volume in the series will be devoted to the philosophy of Marjorie Grene.

Throughout its career, since its founding in 1938, the library of living Philosophers, because of its scholarly nature, has never been self-supporting. We acknowledge gratefully that the generosity of the Edward C. Hegeler Foundation has made possible the publication of many volumes, but for support of future volumes additional funds are needed. On 20 February 1979 the Board of Trustees of Southern Illinois University contractually assumed sponsorship of the Library, which is therefore no longer separately incorporated. Gifts specifically designated for the Library, however, may be made through the Southern Illinois University Foundation, and inasmuch as the latter is a tax-exempt institution, such gifts are tax-deductible.

LEWIS E. HAHN
RANDALL E. AUXIER

DEPARTMENT OF PHILOSOPHY
SOUTHERN ILLINOIS UNIVERSITY AT CARBONDALE

FOUNDER'S GENERAL INTRODUCTION* TO THE LIBRARY OF LIVING PHILOSOPHERS

According to the late F.C.S. Schiller, the greatest obstacle to fruitful discussion in philosophy is "the curious etiquette which apparently taboos the asking of questions about a philosopher's meaning while he is alive." The "interminable controversies which fill the histories of philosophy," he goes on to say, "could have been ended at once by asking the living philosophers a few searching questions."

The confident optimism of this last remark undoubtedly goes too far. Living thinkers have often been asked "a few searching questions," but their answers have not stopped "interminable controversies" about their real meaning. It is nonetheless true that there would be far greater clarity of understanding than is now often the case if more such searching questions had been directed to great thinkers while they were still alive.

This, at any rate, is the basic thought behind the present undertaking. The volumes of the Library of Living Philosophers can in no sense take the place of the major writings of great and original thinkers. Students who would know the philosophies of such men as John Dewey, George Santayana, Alfred North Whitehead, G.E. Moore, Bertrand Russell, Ernst Cassirer, Karl Jaspers, Rudolf Carnap, Martin Buber, et al., will still need to read the writings of these men. There is no substitute for first-hand contact with the original thought of the philosopher himself. Least of all does this Library pretend to be such a substitute. The Library in fact will spare neither effort nor expense in offering to the student the best possible guide to the published writings of a given thinker. We shall attempt to meet this aim by providing at the end of each volume in our series as nearly complete a bibliography of the published work of the philosopher in question as possible. Nor should one overlook the fact that essays in each volume cannot but finally lead to this same goal. The interpretive and critical discussions of the various phases of a great thinker's work and, most of all, the reply of the thinker himself, are bound to lead the reader to the works of the philosopher himself.

---

*This General Introduction sets forth in the founder's words the underlying conception of the Library. L.E.H.

At the same time, there is no denying that different experts find different ideas in the writings of the same philosopher. This is as true of the appreciative interpreter and grateful disciple as it is of the critical opponent. Nor can it be denied that such differences of reading and of interpretation on the part of other experts often leave the neophyte aghast before the whole maze of widely varying and even opposing interpretations. Who is right and whose interpretation shall he accept? When the doctors disagree among themselves, what is the poor student to do? If, in desperation, he decides that all of the interpreters are probably wrong and that the only thing for him to do is to go back to the original writings of the philosopher himself and then make his own decision—uninfluenced (as if this were possible) by the interpretation of anyone else—the result is not that he has actually come to the meaning of the original philosopher himself, but rather that he has set up one more interpretation, which may differ to a greater or lesser degree from the interpretations already existing. It is clear that in this direction lies chaos, just the kind of chaos which Schiller has so graphically and inimitably described.[1]

It is curious that until now no way of escaping this difficulty has been seriously considered. It has not occurred to students of philosophy that one effective way of meeting the problem at least partially is to put these varying interpretations and critiques before the philosopher while he is still alive and to ask him to act at one and the same time as both defendant and judge. If the world's greatest living philosophers can be induced to cooperate in an enterprise whereby their own work can, at least to some extent, be saved from becoming merely "desiccated lecture-fodder," which on the one hand "provides innocuous sustenance for ruminant professors," and on the other hand gives an opportunity to such ruminants and their understudies to "speculate safely, endlessly, and fruitlessly, about what a philosopher must have meant" (Schiller), they will have taken a long step toward making their intentions more clearly comprehensible.

With this in mind, the Library of Living Philosophers expects to publish at more or less regular intervals a volume on each of the greater among the world's living philosophers. In each case it will be the purpose of the editor of the Library to bring together in the volume the interpretations and

1. In his essay "Must Philosophers Disagree?" in the volume of the same title (London: Macmillan, 1934), from which the above quotations were taken.

criticisms of a wide range of that particular thinker's scholarly contemporaries, each of whom will be given a free hand to discuss the specific phase of the thinker's work that has been assigned to him. All contributed essays will finally be submitted to the philosopher with whose work and thought they are concerned, for his careful perusal and reply. And, although it would be expecting too much to imagine that the philosopher's reply will be able to stop all differences of interpretation and of critique, this should at least serve the purpose of stopping certain of the grosser and more general kinds of misinterpretations. If no further gain than this were to come from the present and projected volumes of this Library, it would seem to be fully justified.

In carrying out this principal purpose of the Library, the editor announces that (as far as is humanly possible) each volume will contain the following elements:

First, an intellectual autobiography of the thinker whenever this can be secured; in any case an authoritative and authorized biography;
Second, a series of expository and critical articles written by the leading exponents and opponents of the philosopher's thought;
Third, the reply to the critics and commentators by the philosopher himself;and
Fourth, a bibliography of writings of the philosopher to provide a ready instrument to give access to his writings and thought.

PAUL ARTHUR SCHILPP
FOUNDER AND EDITOR, 1939-1981

DEPARTMENT OF PHILOSOPHY
SOUTHERN ILLINOIS UNIVERSITY AT CARBONDALE

ADVISORY BOARD

ACKNOWLEDGMENTS

The editor hereby gratefully acknowledges his obligation and sincere gratitude to all the publishers of Seyyed Hossein Nasr's books and publications for their kind and uniform courtesy in permitting us to quote—sometimes at some length—from Professor Nasr.

LEWIS E. HAHN

TABLE OF CONTENTS

PREFACE

Seyyed Hossein Nasr, currently University Professor of Islamic Studies at George Washington University, is not only the first Muslim philosopher in our series, but also the first traditionalist since our volume on Martin Buber. Some mainstream philosophers are unaware that traditionalist philosophy still persists in the world, and still more would be hard pressed to say what exactly traditionalist philosophy is. This is regrettable, given the popularity and breadth of traditionalist views beyond the narrower world of Anglo-American and European academies. Professor Nasr, standing as he does at the head of a handsome group of traditionalists, boldly challenges the assumptions and values of the modern world, and of modern scientistic philosophy. Yet, this challenge has been issued forth not as a pure reaction against modernity, but as an informed engagement *with* modernity. Indeed, some of the most "modern" ideas, such as the movement towards religious dialogue in the discipline of religious studies, turn out on close examination to rest upon values and ideas that are traditional—ideas long understood by those who study and practice the major world traditions seriously.

The present volume, therefore, stands as a contribution to cross-cultural dialogue, and to dialogue across traditions. Among Professor Nasr's enduring achievements we may count an on-going and successful effort spanning over four decades to bring the world's living traditions into a kind of exchange that leaves intact the autonomy and viewpoint of each, but also creates a space for mutual understanding and the reinforcement of the forms of life that are nourished by all genuine traditions. Professor Nasr has tirelessly argued that the attempt to live outside of all tradition leads to rootlessness, degradation of the natural world and human beings, and the kinds of madness that are so well characterized by the recently ended bloodiest century in human history. These traditionalist views are very controversial, and Professor Nasr's critics have not spared him the very objections that many first-time readers will want to voice.

Professor Nasr's philosophical achievements are stunningly broad, spanning the globe and numerous languages. Readers unfamiliar with his writings will find this volume a serviceable introduction to his thought, and to the wider world of Islamic philosophy generally. Readers who are more familiar with Nasr and his views will find this volume a very stimulating engagement of those ideas at a high level. We are proud to present a slate of critics from so many places and traditions, and of such prominence, but this far-reaching project has created special challenges in producing this volume. Being obliged, as we have been, to work with so many untranslatable terms, with transliterations, with authors whose first language is not English, and in such an extensive volume as this, it is inevitable that some errors and inconsistencies of usage will have slipped by us. These are not the responsibility of any of the contributors or of Professor Nasr. The errors belong to the editors, and we hope that they have not been terribly numerous. In this context the editors would like to draw special attention to the essay of Professor A. K. Saran, "A Nasr Sentence: Some Comments," 429–39. Owing to communications difficulties, including a postal strike in India, this book went to press before Professor Saran had approved the final version of his essay. Here we express our regret over the situation.

We are grateful to Professor Nasr and his diverse set of able critics for making this volume possible, and we are proud to add this volume to the series. We are happy to acknowledge once more the warm support, encouragement, and cooperation of our publisher, Open Court Publishing Company, especially M. Blouke Carus, David R. Steele, Kerri Mommer, and Jennifer Asmuth. And we also very much appreciate continued support, understanding, and encouragement from the administration of Southern Illinois University. As always, moreover, we are grateful for the friendly and unfailing help in a variety of ways from the staff of Morris Library at SIUC. It is invaluable for our work and that of our fellow scholars.

Our warm gratitude also goes to Christina Martin and the Philosophy Department secretariat for help with numerous projects; to Sharon Langrand, retired secretary who was on staff at the beginning of this project, for help with manuscripts, proofs, and correspondence; and especially to Frances Stanley for continuing the work and for electronic typesetting on this volume. We would also like to thank Darrell Russell, graduate assistant, for his help with proofs and attention to detail.

Finally, for warm support, stimulation, and friendly counsel we are most grateful to our able and resourceful pluralistic colleagues who from diverse perspectives make common cause for philosophy.

LEWIS EDWIN HAHN
RANDALL E. AUXIER
LUCIAN W. STONE, JR.
EDITORS

DEPARTMENT OF PHILOSOPHY
SOUTHERN ILLINOIS UNIVERSITY AT CARBONDALE
MARCH 2001

PART ONE

INTELLECTUAL AUTOBIOGRAPHY OF SEYYED HOSSEIN NASR

Chapter V

Man, Pontifical and Promethean

Look within yourself a moment and ask who ~~[illegible]~~ art ~~[illegible]~~ thou?
From where doest thou comest, from which place, what art thou?
(Rumi)

لحظه‌ای در خود نگر تا کیستی
از کجایی وز چه جایی چیستی

"Was ist der Menschen Leben, ein Bild der Gottheit."
(What is the life of man, an image of the Godhead)
(Hölderlin)

The concept of man as the pontif, ~~a~~ *pontifex* or bridge between heaven and earth ~~[illegible]~~ which is the traditional view of the *anthropos*, ~~is separated by~~ lies at the antipode of the modern conception of man" which envisages him as the Promethean earthly (in the sense used here) creature who has rebelled against heaven and tried to misappropriate the role of the ~~[illegible]~~ Divinity for himself. Pontifical man, which is none other than traditional man, ~~is dominated by the~~ lives in a world which has both an Origin and a Center. He lives in full awareness of the Origin which contains his own perfection and whose primordial purity and wholeness he seeks to emulate, re-capture and transmit. He also lives on a circle of whose Center he is always aware and which he seeks to reach in his life, ~~and~~ thoughts and actions. Pontifical man ~~[illegible]~~ ~~[illegible]~~ is the reflection of the ~~[illegible]~~ Center on the periphery and the echo of the Origin in later cycles of time and generations of history.

Seyyed Hossein Nasr

AN INTELLECTUAL AUTOBIOGRAPHY

FAMILY BACKGROUND

There is a well-known saying of ʿAlī ibn Abī Ṭālib, the cousin and son-in-law of the Prophet of Islam and representative *par excellence* of Islamic esoterism and metaphysics, according to which one should pay attention to what is said and not who has said it. This teaching has been close to my heart since my youth and rarely have I accepted to write something of an autobiographical nature. But the Library of Living Philosophers requires a work of such a nature from the person with whose thought a particular volume is concerned. Therefore, with some reticence I turn to this task. Once having decided to do so, however, I find it necessary to delve in some detail into my family background and upbringing which provided the environment in which I was nurtured and which created the living space marked by the peace of childhood, but also by the tension between Eastern and Western cultures and tradition and modernity, a space in which my intellectual and philosophical worldview received its earliest development and the foundation upon which it later expanded and crystallized.

I was born into a family of well-known scholars and physicians in Tehran in 1933. My paternal and maternal families represented different strands of Persian culture. My paternal grandfather hailed from a family of *seyyeds* (*sādāt*) (descendants of the Prophet of Islam). His ancestor Mullā Mājed Ḥossein, having been a famous religious scholar (*mujtahid*) in Najaf, the seat of Shiʿite learning in Iraq, was invited by the Persian king Nādir Shāh to come to Persia in the eighteenth century. But he died on the way and his family settled in Kashan. My grandfather Aḥmad was born and raised in that city where as the oldest son of a famous religious scholar, Seyyed Naṣrallāh, he enjoyed much respect. At a young age Aḥmad came to Tehran to study medicine. Here he soon became a celebrated physician, serving for some time as court physician during the Qajar period. He received from the king the title Naṣr al-aṭibbāʾ (meaning literally "victory of physicians") from which comes my family name Naṣr. His wife Begum was related to the Ṣabā family of Kashan, an old family related to the Barmakids who were *viziers* in the ninth century. This family had produced the well-known Qajar poet laureate of Persia, Malik al-Shu'arā' Fatḥ 'Alī Khān Ṣabā, and many other famous poets and artists. Although having received only the ordinary traditional education for women of her day, she knew thousands of verses of classical Persian poetry by heart and also composed poems herself. Some of the first verses of Persian poetry that I memorized as a child came from her lips, while much of the folklore that I learned came in the form of stories told to me by her and her daughters, my paternal aunts, who were also well versed in poetry and folklore. Both my paternal grandparents, as well as their five sons and two daughters, were pious Muslims. Moreover, my grandfather's family had been involved with Sufism (Islamic mysticism) for several generations. One of his ancestors, Mullā Seyyed Moḥammad Taqī Posht-mashhadī, was a famous saint of Kashan, and his mausoleum, which is located next to the tomb of the Safavid king Shah 'Abbās, is still visited by pilgrims to this day. My grandfather continued this interest and was a disciple of the famous nineteenth-century Sufi master ṣafī 'Alī Shāh and his successor Ṣafā 'Alī Shāh (Ẓahīr al-Dawlah). My father was to pursue his example and was also connected to these masters.

My father, Seyyed Valīallāh, was thus brought up in a highly educated and religious family. Born also in Kashan, he was brought at an early age to Tehran where he continued his education in both classical Islamic and Persian subjects and medicine, graduating from Persia's only medical school of the day, the Dār al-Funūn, while also learning traditional Islamic medicine going back to Ibn Sīnā (Avicenna). While he became, like his father, a celebrated physician, he showed much greater interest in philosophy, literature, and education. Soon he left the formal practice of medicine (although having also become royal physician), limiting his practice to close friends and relatives, and turned to the field of education. In fact he became the head of Persia's educational system from the end of the Qajar dynasty into the Pahlavi period and ran the ministry of education for decades as its head, general secretary, and later acting minister. He nevertheless tried to resist becoming entangled in politics after his involvement in the drafting of the Constitution and the first parliament after the Constitutional Revolution of 1906 when he was elected to the parliament as a representative of Tehran. His attitude toward politics was to remain indelibly marked upon my mind.

My father was both a professor and an educational administrator. He became rector of the Teachers' College and dean of several faculties of Tehran University and is considered as one of the founders of the modern educational system in what had now become known officially as Iran. He was a master teacher for two generations of many of the leading figures in Persia and was also my first teacher both morally and intellectually. He was an outstanding philosopher, especially in the field of ethics, and the author of a well-known work in Persian entitled *Dānish wa akhlāq* ("Knowledge and Ethics"). Not only did he possess great mastery of Arabic and Persian, in which he was considered one of the greatest authorities of his day, but he also possessed perfect knowledge of French and knew some Latin and English. He had an imposing library of several thousand volumes including numerous tomes in French. It was in this library that I first saw the names of Michel Montaigne and Charles-Louis Montesquieu, René Descartes and Blaise Pascal, François Voltaire and Jean-Jacques Rousseau, as well as Plato and Aristotle. He was also a methodical teacher of both the mind and the soul who, while deeply immersed in the Islamic tradition, was also very knowledgeable in the Western philosophical and scientific traditions as well as in other religions and philosophies. As a result of his influence, I was brought up in an atmosphere which, while being deeply Persian, was also open to both Western ideas and religions and intellectual ideas of other traditions. Universalism in its most positive sense permeated the atmosphere in which I was nurtured without in any way weakening the foundations of traditional Persian culture in which I was brought up.

My mother hailed from a different type of background and yet one with the same keen interest in the intellectual and religious aspects of life. Her grandfather Shaykh Faḍlallāh Nūrī, one of the most famous politico-religious figures of modern Persian history, was the leading Shiʿite religious authority (*ʿālim*) of his day, but having opposed the Constitutional Revolution of 1906 was arrested and put to death by the government of the day. A person who was visited in his house by the Shah and who was one of the most powerful men of his time was thus removed from the scene in an unprecedented manner. This left a deep scar upon the psyche of all his immediate descendants, many of whom turned from the most conservative religious position to extreme forms of modernism. One of his grandsons in fact became the secretary general of Iran's Communist Party (the Tudeh).

One of his sons, my grandfather, was studying in Najaf in Iraq in the great seat of Shiʿite learning when my mother was born. Her mother was also from a distinguished family of religious scholars named Ṭabāṭabāʾī. When my mother was seven years old, they returned to Tehran where, as a result of his father's violent death, my grandfather decided to abandon the career of becoming a religious scholar (*ʿālim*) in the technical sense and instead turned to the field of law, becoming a well-known judge. But he also adopted a modernist stand on many issues and was especially interested in the education of his daughters.

My mother, Ashraf, who was the oldest daughter, was put in the only institution of intermediary and higher learning for women at that time and was one of its first graduates. She was therefore among Iran's first modern educated women and combined her Islamic piety with certain inclinations to participate in activities for women's rights and social institutions serving women's causes to which she devoted much of her time once I and my younger brother, the only two children in the family, had grown up. But she was also devoted to Persian literature and, like my grandmother, knew and in fact still knows numerous Persian and even Arabic poems by heart. It is she who took me to the great centers of pilgrimage such as Qom and Ḥaḍrat-i'Abd al-'Aẓīm near Tehran when I was a child, making possible an experience of the sacred which has remained indelibly etched in my memory to this day. It was also she, rather than my father, who later taught me the rituals of Islam, especially the daily prayers.

EARLY CHILDHOOD

My father married my mother when he was in his fifties and was already not only the head of the extensive Nasr family, but also one of Persia's best known and respected public figures. I was the first born and in fact the oldest son of the oldest son of the oldest son of my family, a fact which paradoxically resulted in the literary treasury which our family had accumulated over several generations being lost during the Iranian Revolution of 1979 when my library, which contained the family heritage of rare books, was plundered. But also by virtue of being the oldest son, the greatest care was taken in my education in a home in which there was constant talk of cultural and religious matters and where poetry flowed freely like the morning breeze. I was tutored from the earliest age by both parents who spent many hours a week teaching me verses of the Quran, Persian poetry, and even history, especially sacred history even when I was at the pre-schooling stage. Being a precocious child, I was already beginning to read and write when I was three years old.

Our house during the first seven years of my life was in one of the more traditional quarters of the city near the mausoleum of the Sufi master Ṣafī 'Alī Shāh. Our house consisted of an outer courtyard and rooms (*bīrūnī*) where my father would receive people and an inner courtyard and rooms (*andarūnī*) where we lived and where the intimate life of the family took place away from public scrutiny. The architecture still reflected the ideals of Islamic domestic architecture and the spaces were interiorized. Our street was a narrow one, like the streets of medieval European cities, and next to the house there was a small mosque so that we could hear the incessant punctuation of the flow of time by the Islamic call to prayer (*adhān*). When we went to the rooftop of our house, we could walk for hours from one rooftop to another and could see minarets and cupolas extending far into the horizon. We could also see the majestic presence of Mt. Damavand, western Asia's highest peak, in the east which always reminded me of the majesty of creation. It was at the foothills of this peak in the village of Damavand where we would spend the summers of my early childhood that I first encountered virgin nature in her awesome majesty and developed an intense love for her which has accompanied me throughout my life.

Although Tehran was becoming gradually modernized, we still lived in a more or less "medieval" Islamic town. The early experience of our house, the narrow streets leading to it, the small mosque, the religiously decorated water fountain (*saqqā-khānah*) nearby, the kind and pious neighbors, the sounds of the Quran and the chants of vendors passing by are all indelibly marked in my memory and represent in a concrete manner the experience of the pre-modern world which I was to rediscover later intellectually. I shall never forget that, during my early years in this house, we had only oil lamps and that it was there that I experienced for the first time light generated by electricity soon to be followed by the radio.

Those early years were, however, even more important from a cultural point of view. Both of my parents encouraged me to memorize poetry, especially those of the poets Firdawsī, Niẓāmī, Sa'dī, Rūmī, and Ḥāfiẓ, and to participate in sessions of exchange of poems by heart called *mushā'ārah*. As a result, at a young age I had memorized numerous poems by the greatest masters of Persian poetry. Although long years spent in America for further education caused me to forget many of them, I still recall a large number to this day. Also my father participated in a literary session once or twice a month with some of Persia's greatest men of letters, some of whom were also major political figures, such as Muḥammad 'Alī Furūghī, several times prime minister and a noted philosopher who translated Descartes's *Discourse on Method* into excellent Persian, the poet laureate of the Pahlavi period, Malik al-Shu'arā' Bahār, Shukūh al-Mulk, the chief of Reza Shah's special bureau, and several others. I was often taken to these gatherings, some in our home and some in the homes of the others, gatherings in which the participants would read just a few verses of poetry, usually from Ḥāfiẓ, and then spend hours discussing and meditating upon their spiritual and philosophical meanings, the discussions sometimes including ideas drawn from European philosophy. It might be said in fact that these sessions were my first exposure at a tender age to philosophical discourse embedded of Sufi and didactic literature.

I began my formal education at the age of five in the second grade at a nearby school next to Shahabad Avenue. Two years later we moved to a new house in the northern and modern part of the city near Shahreza Avenue and my school changed as did my immediate ambience. I was put in a Zoroastrian school, Jamshīd-i jam, known for its high quality of education and later Fīrūzkūhī where I finished the sixth grade having received the highest marks in the national examinations. It was also here that I witnessed the invasion of Persia by the Allied Forces with all the traumas that followed. Our own family was fairly well protected from the extreme effects of this occupation, including poverty and the outbreak of epidemics, but the sense of humiliation experienced by having to submit to the dictate of foreign powers was deeply felt even by a young boy like myself.

Our new house was also frequented by numerous people who came to pay respect to my parents and especially to carry out intellectual discourse with my father. These guests ranged from young Iranians who were now returning from their studies in Europe—especially France and Germany—according to a government sponsored program in which my father himself, who refused to travel outside of Persia, played a major role, to traditional scholars. They included traditional figures as well as nationalists, rabid modernists, and even leftists ranging from some of Persia's leading political figures from prime ministers and ministers such as Qawām al-Saltanah, Manṣūr al-Mulk, and Seyyed Ḥasan Taqīzādeh to Fereidoun Keshāvarz, Īraj Eskandarī, and Nūr al-Dīn Kiā Nūrī who were to become well-known Communist figures later.

Visitors also included such masters of traditional philosophy, Sufism, and gnosis as Sayyid Muḥammad Kāẓim 'Assār, to whom I shall turn later, and Hādī Ḥā'irī, considered by many to have been the greatest authority on Rūmī's *Mathnawī* in his day, and who taught me much about Sufism in later years. Also a stream of professors from the newly founded Tehran University frequented our house including 'Alī Aṣghar Ḥekmat, who became minister of education and foreign affairs, 'Alī Akbar Siāsī, also a minister and the rector of Tehran University, 'Alī Akbar Dehkhodā, the celebrated encyclopedist, Badī' al-Zamān Furūzānfar and Jalāl Humā'ī, the leading authorities in Persian literature in their day, Maḥmūd Shahābī and Sharī'at-i Sangilajī, well-known religious and legal scholars, and numerous younger scholars of Persian literature such as Parvīz Khānlarī, who became one of Iran's greatest scholars of the next generation.

Living in such an ambience left a profound effect upon my mind. By the age of ten I not only had met the greatest Persian scholars of the day, but heard debates, often on a highly philosophical level, about certitude and doubt, tradition and modernism, the scientific worldview and religious cosmology and many other serious subjects. Alongside the names of Ibn Sīnā and Rūmī, the names of not only Descartes, Pascal, and Voltaire but also Immanuel Kant and Georg Wilhelm Friedrich Hegel and even Karl Marx became known to me, even if I did not understand their ideas.

The age of ten marked the beginning of my philosophical awakening and my mind became engaged in thinking about such issues as causality, the finitude or infinitude of space, the immortality of the soul or its perishing with the death of the body, and so on. My faith in God remained firm while my mind continued to be engaged in philosophical issues as well as in the cultural tension between East and West, which at that tender age I perceived in the contrast between following traditional norms in both action and art, and becoming attracted to alien norms which incited the mind more to rebellion. I began to study, in addition to works dealing with Persian culture, some popular Western philosophical works translated into Persian such as those of the Belgian philosopher Maurice Maetterlinck. I also began to read European literature in translation including many plays of Michel Racine and Molière translated by my uncle Seyyed 'Alī Naṣr, who was one of the founders of the modern theater in Iran, French historical novels of Alexandre Dumas and Victor Hugo, again some of them translated by family members, and even some of the plays of William Shakespeare and stories of Leo Tolstoy. All of these, read parallel with Persian classics, helped me to develop a global vision of culture at this young age.

Another element of importance in these early years was that I breathed in an ambience permeated not only by the perfume of Sufism and traditional Persian culture open to the West, but also of the great civilizations east of Persia of whose presence I began to become fully aware at that time. A year before my birth my father had been the host of Rabindranath Tagore when the Bengali poet visited Persia and my father spoke often of him to me. Tagore's poetry was well known in our household. As far as the Indian subcontinent is concerned, it should also be mentioned that some years later my uncle was to become Iran's first ambassador to Pakistan with which I was to have so much contact later in life. This same uncle, Seyyed 'Alī Naṣr, had been our ambassador to China at the beginning of the rule of Chiang-Kai Chek and also to Japan, and spoke to us constantly of the life of the Far East. Moreover, he had brought back a treasure of Chinese and Japanese art some of which found a place in our home. My father always encouraged me to respect these Eastern cultures, whether Indian or Far Eastern, and was especially anxious for me to thumb through a two-volume illustrated work he had in French on the Russo-Japanese War of 1904 which he felt marked the first stage in the rise of Asia before the onslaught of eighteenth- and nineteenth-century European powers.

My education in these early years, when we lived on Shahreza Avenue or in a couple of other houses nearby to which we moved during the next few years, was intense indeed and included, in addition to the usual Persian curriculum at school, extra concentration in Islamic and Persian subjects at home as well as tutorial in French. But most importantly it was the long hours of discussion with my father, mostly on philosophical and theological issues, complemented by both reading and reaction to the discourses carried on by those who came to our house to seek my father's wisdom or sometimes to challenge him, that constituted an essential aspect of my philosophical education at an early age. From the age of ten onward there was never a time in my life when I was not interested in philosophical questions in the traditional sense of this term.

A number of tragedies were to upset the pattern of my life in a short period. My father was hit by a bicycle which threw him in a ditch resulting in the breaking of his pelvic bone. Because of the War, he could not be brought to Europe to have an operation and could not be treated satisfactorily in Iran. He thus became bedridden and this led to pneumonia, the weakening of his heart, and finally his death a couple of years later in 1946. While he was ill, my youngest maternal aunt, who lived in our home, died very suddenly of meningitis. This event, following upon the wake of the death of my maternal grandfather, left a deep scar upon my soul and brought forth the reality of death in a vivid manner that was never to be forgotten.

Meanwhile as my father grew weaker, the family felt that it would be better for me not to be near him at the moment of his death because of my very close attachment to him. A maternal uncle, 'Emād Kiā, was our counsel in New York and therefore plans were made to send me to America to be under his care and to continue my studies. I felt a great sense of adventure to go that far away to an unknown land in pursuit of knowledge and began to study elementary English; but when the moment of departure came in October of 1945, when I was in the eighth grade at the Sharaf High School, the pain of separation from my family and Iran became nearly unbearable. At the moment of departure my father looked me in the eyes and with a gentle smile said that he would never see me again in this world, but that his spirit would hover in the heavens over me and that he would be constantly watching me from the beyond. His last advice to me was to be self-disciplined and to value the pursuit of knowledge above all else.

And so the earliest and most formative period of my life came to an end as I left my country of birth for the long journey to America. What that period crystallized in me, thanks most of all to the influence of my father, was a love of knowledge, self-discipline, and a desire to search incessantly for the truth of things whether religious, philosophical, or scientific. I had in fact displayed an insatiable thirst to discover how things worked and was even able to take a large radio apart and put it back together at a very young age, not because of my attraction to modern technology, against which I was to develop an ever greater aversion later in America, but because I was constantly in quest of understanding the nature of things. My early training also instilled in me respect for various cultures and religions of the world and made me aware of the reality of the tensions between East and West, as well as tradition and modernism. My mind was very active, constantly challenging those much older than myself in debates that were often philosophical. I was also attracted to mathematics in which I did very well at school, as well as literature, poetry, and music to which I was very sensitive from a very tender age. These traits were to remain within my mind and soul throughout my years of study in the West and have in fact persisted as major elements of my intellectual character throughout my life even when I was to leave the field of the modern sciences for the study of metaphysics, philosophy, and the history of science. As my philosophical perspective became crystallized, I became much less argumentative, but the attraction to the rigor of logic on the one hand and the light of mystical illumination and warmth of Divine Love on the other persisted as did the awareness of the multiplicity of cultural worlds and the profound tension between tradition and modernism, a tension which has been a constant factor in the intellectual universe of all those thinkers of the traditional civilizations of the Orient who have also become exposed in one way or another to the theses of modernism and the conditions created by the advent of modernity.

THE JOURNEY TO AMERICA

The journey to America, which was to take place by boat from Alexandria, was far from an easy one. Coming at the end of the Second World War, it was full of unforeseen obstacles which would have been difficult to surmount by a much older traveler. In October 1945 I bade a tearful farewell to my family, especially my father whom I knew I would not see again, and left for the Tehran airport to fly to Baghdad in a small one-engine plane. My father could not move but the rest of my family accompanied me to the plane. The departure was therefore a physical as well as psychological experience of being plucked out of the soil which had nurtured me until then and of departing from the embrace of a closely knit Oriental family.

In Baghdad I was warmly received by our ambassador who was a relative and I stayed at the house of Muḥsin Ṣadr, a maternal relative who had been Iraq's viceroy and president of the senate. There I experienced something of the old Baghdad which was to disappear soon. This was also my first experience of the Arab world with which so much of my intellectual life was to be concerned in my later years.

From Baghdad a ticket was obtained for me to take the special overnight bus, belonging to a British company, which traveled through the forbidding desert between Iraq and Syria. When we arrived in Damascus a Persian friend took me to his house where I spent a few days in preparation for a car ride through the still undivided Palestine of that time. A suitable car was finally found and with a few passengers, including a Persian friend, we traveled to Palestine, passing through beautiful orchards and pastures whose greenery surprised me. Then in Jaffa we took the train which brought us to Cairo.

The city of Cairo was at that time much more modern than Tehran and the stay of over a month in the famous old Shepheard's Hotel, which was later burned to the ground during the Nasserite Revolution of 1952, marked my first direct acquaintance with many aspects of the modern world. It was here in Cairo that, while waiting for a ship to take me to America, I was able to visit a zoo and a department store for the first time. Again our ambassador showed much kindness but I was really on my own. One day when I was eating alone at the dining room of the Shepheard's, an aristocratic Egyptian, who turned out to be a minister in the government, became fascinated by the sight of a young foreign boy eating by himself, came to my table and asked about me. In broken French I explained my situation to him. He became so interested that he said to me as long as I was in Cairo he would treat me like his own son. He took me to many places including the pyramids and it was finally he who arranged for me a hard to find reservation on the Swedish ship, the Gripsholm, which was sailing from Alexandria to New York.

My experience of Cairo was also to include to some extent the incomparable Islamic monuments of the city as well as its ancient monuments, but it was especially the modern ambience of the Shepheard's Hotel and the new quarters of Cairo that made a special impression upon me because it was like an introduction to the Western world that I was about to enter. The Shepheard's was occupied mostly by Europeans and within it one felt as if one were in a high class European hotel. But there were also Egyptian and Islamic elements present. The dress of all the workers was still traditional Egyptian and most of them were Nubians with a gentle nature. King Farouq would usually visit the hotel on Thursday evenings while on Friday he would go in his carriage to the public prayers. I could already see before my eyes, more so than in Tehran, that tension between tradition and modernity as well as East and West with which I have been concerned all my life. The sacred sites of Cairo were, however, to reveal their full presence to me only during later journeys. During the years of exile in the West, Cairo has become my major spiritual home in the Islamic world, but the first seed of love for the spiritual presence of that city was sown in my heart during that fall of 1945 when I spent those weeks in that city which was soon to undergo major political, social, and urban transformations.

The sea voyage was long and difficult. We crossed the Mediterranean to Thessalonica, then sailed West to Naples, then Marseilles and finally on through the Strait of Gibraltar to New York. The danger of mines, strong storms, especially in the Atlantic, and the first experience of the sea all served to create many anxious moments for me. But this month-long journey also helped strengthen my self-reliance and self-confidence which I had to develop in order to undertake such a journey successfully. By the time we arrived on December 17, 1945 in New York, I was transformed from the young boy totally attached to his family and cultural ambience to a person who was now independent, isolated, and on his own. But the challenge of studying in America was an appealing one and it was with great joy and expectation that I left the ship to be received at the docks by my uncle 'Emād Kiā and cousin Taghī Naṣr, then our trade representative in New York, later to become Iran's finance minister and their wives one of whom, the wife of Taghī Naṣr, named Bībī, was also my cousin with whom I was to pass many of my vacations in coming years. A new period had begun which marked an abrupt discontinuity with what I had experienced until that moment in my life.

The Years of Study in America

Peddie

My entry into America happened to coincide with the holiday season which I spent in New York where I was to observe to my great amazement my first Christmas and New Year celebrations in the West, including seeing what appeared to me as extremely unruly and wild celebrations that usher in the New Year at Times Square. New York appeared both fascinating and fearsome, strange and hypnotic, enticing and forbidding. In order not to fall behind in my studies, my uncle contacted through a Persian friend the president of Lafayette College, Dr. Hutchinson. He was in New York and a meeting was arranged in which he counseled my uncle to send me to the Peddie School in Hightstown, New Jersey. Acceptance came rapidly and I started in January in the eighth grade to continue my work of that same academic year which had begun in Iran, but which had been interrupted for three months.

I was to spend the next four and a half years at Peddie from which I graduated in 1950. These years were both traumatic and very constructive. With only an intensive summer course or two of English, I had to master the language fast enough to be able to succeed academically in one of the best preparatory schools on the East Coast. It was also here that I felt for the first time my full dislocation culturally as well as emotionally. Despite my uncle Emād Kiā's great kindness and his taking the trouble to visit me once every week from New York, I felt a deep sense of loneliness and was painfully aware of my need to be able to stand on my own feet. My father died of a heart attack shortly after I began Peddie and this news only added to the pains of separation from home. My mother and brother came to America for a while but were forced to return home because of financial difficulties. My family bonds with my uncle and the cousins nearby remained strong, but I became more and more engrossed in cultivating American friends and learning the American way of life whose popular aspect, especially as manifested in the rebellion and violence of some of the young, repelled me completely.

I succeeded in mastering English rapidly and in fact developed a love for English poetry and the poetic quality of the language. By the ninth grade I was an honors student receiving very high grades in the sciences but also honors grades in English. I also began to study French again, strengthening my command of a language with which I have been involved to this day. My grades in mathematics were especially outstanding and I received some of the highest scores ever received on various national tests given on the subject, which led all my teachers and advisors to believe that I should pursue my studies in physics or mathematics. And it was their advice along with my deep yearning to "understand the nature of things" that brought me to the decision to pursue these fields in college.

The Peddie years were combined with ever greater success academically and otherwise. I became a high honors student and the valedictorian of my class resulting in my having to deliver my first public lecture during the commencement exercises. But I also played several varsity sports, especially squash and tennis which I was to continue at MIT where I even became the captain of the MIT squash team. I also won the Wycliffe Award at Peddie given to the most outstanding all-round student and which is considered as the school's highest honor. All of this gave me both great self-confidence in being able to achieve what I would set out to do, and also placed great responsibility upon my shoulders to be academically successful at college.

Peddie was a Baptist school and from 1945 to 1950, while attending that school, I was required to be present in Sunday morning church service even though I was a Muslim. My childhood upbringing had already created in me respect for other religions, especially Christianity, and I had known by heart some poems of Ḥāfiẓ, Rūmī, and other Sufi poets in praise of Christ as well as stories about him and the Virgin Mary as revealed in the Quran. Those years of attending Protestant service helped to acquaint me directly with Christian practices including rites, preaching, singing of hymns as well as ethics, not to speak of my experience of the palpable presence of Christic grace. My long engagement in dialogue with Christianity has one of its sources in the years of contact with Protestantism at Peddie. Later this experience was to be complemented by my close contact with Catholicism on the level of theology, but I never had such continuous liturgical experience of Catholicism as I had of Protestantism during my Peddie years. This experience also created an acquaintance with the Bible, especially the Psalms and the Gospels whose rendering in the King James Version still echoes in my ears.

If the Peddie years were crucial in my gaining knowledge of English, Western culture, American history, and Christianity as well as the sciences, it was also the period of my longest alienation from Persian culture and separation from the manifestations of Islam. Save for holidays, only some of which were spent in the company of the few members of my family in New York and the rest at camps in various places including one year in the Sierra Nevadas of California, I hardly ever spoke Persian. Therefore, although my level of Persian was much higher than a typical eighth grade student when I left Iran, I began to forget many of the poems that I had memorized and even my writing became somewhat rusty. When my mother came to America in 1950 and we decided that we should live in a house with a Persian ambience, I began to speak Persian on a daily basis again and re-read the great classics in order to become once again a master of my own mother tongue.

Usually the valedictorians of Peddie went to nearby Princeton and I was expected to do the same. Several times in fact I was taken with a few other students to visit the university, the School of Advanced Studies, the physics laboratories, the house of Einstein, and other notable sites and persons, but for some reason I was not interested in going to Princeton. The mystique of MIT and its fame for being very difficult appealed to me as a challenge which I simply had to undertake. I therefore applied to that school as well as to Cal Tech and Cornell. I was accepted in all three with scholarship offers of which the lowest was MIT's. Nevertheless, I chose MIT without hesitation and at the end of the summer of 1950 moved to the Boston area to begin a new and crucial phase of my life. As a seventeen-year-old Persian who had been completely successful in terminating his secondary education in one of the best secondary schools, I felt confident in being able to achieve the goals that lay ahead. But deep down it was neither desire for worldly success and wealth nor even academic achievement that attracted or excited me. It was the possibility of gaining knowledge about the "nature of things," at least on the level of physical reality, that was foremost in my mind. And so I set out for a new city and a new ambience with intellectual thirst but little prescience of the shock that I was soon to receive concerning the real nature of the subject which I had chosen to study, that is, physics.

MIT and Harvard

In the fall of 1950 I began my studies at MIT, the first Iranian student to do so, and a period that was to keep me in Cambridge for the next eight years. Instead of living in a dormitory, I lived in the house that my mother had purchased in Arlington Heights outside of Cambridge upon her coming to America with my younger brother Mehran, who was also to attend Harvard later and who became a specialist in petroleum geology. The ambience of the Persian home she created there was to have an important role in my return to the bosom of Persian culture and ultimately in my decision to return to Iran. I began my study at MIT in the physics department, or what was called Course Eight, with some of the most gifted students in the country. We considered ourselves as members of the elite department in the university and I took great pride in my studies. We had outstanding teachers of physics many of whom such as Charles Friedman and Bruno Rossi had been immediate associates of Robert Oppenheimer and Enrico Fermi and were involved with the project to build the atomic bomb whose horrors were still very fresh in everyone's memory at that time.

Although at MIT I was at the top of my class with high honors at the end of the freshman year, I was already beginning to feel oppressed in an atmosphere which seemed overbearingly scientific at the expense of the humanities. I liked purely theoretical physics and mathematics but disliked laboratories and suffered from the lack of beauty in that ambience. But it was not until my second year that I felt a full-blown spiritual and intellectual crisis in my life. The occasional lectures of Oppenheimer, tormented by his wartime activities which he described while quoting Hindu texts, troubled me greatly. But it was especially the implicit positivism of the atmosphere that was troublesome. I wondered why many metaphysical questions that had concerned me for years were not being asked much less answered and I was even beginning to doubt if physics was going to lead me to the understanding of "the nature of physical reality." I recall clearly that in a small group discussion with Bertrand Russell following one of his lectures, we posed a question to him concerning the nature of physics and he replied that physics did not concern itself with the *nature* of physical reality *per se* but with mathematical structures related to pointer readings. This answer by one of the leading philosophers of the West, speaking against any possibility of "ontological realism" in the domain of physics, was like the straw that broke the camel's back. It made me decide there and then to leave the field of physics. I wanted in fact to leave school altogether in quest of the truth and even depart from the West, but the strong discipline given to me by my father prevented me from doing so. I was to remain in the physics department for another three years and graduate from MIT with honors, but my heart was no longer in physics. Some of my teachers expressed regret that I wanted to leave physics but one of them said that perhaps other fields were more in need of my talents and wished me well.

In addition to physics courses I also took a large number of courses in mathematics beyond the requirements of the physics department. These courses included one on the Fourier series taught at times by Norbert Wiener who was then developing his theory of cybernetics, but who was also deeply interested in languages and cultures. Although he was difficult to approach, I benefited from both his courses and private conversations. I was also drawn to the elegance of advanced mathematics and theoretical physics and although philosophically opposed to Pierre Simon de Laplace, enjoyed a course on celestial mechanics dealing mostly with his work. But I now took all of these courses not as a potential physicist but as a potential philosopher who wanted to know modern science well before dealing with it philosophically.

The spiritual and intellectual crisis which overtook me in my eighteenth year and which was to affect the direction of the rest of my life did not terminate with my decision to leave physics, but became only accentuated now that I had definitely decided that I did not want to devote the rest of my life to the physical sciences. The crisis did not destroy my belief in God but shook all the other elements of my worldview including what I had perceived as the meaning of life, the significance of knowledge, and the means to find the truth. I spoke to many professors, such as Victor Weiskoff, and a few of my close friends in the physics department, especially Philippe Dennery, a Frenchman, and Peter Felsenthal, an American, who like myself were very much interested in general intellectual and cultural pursuits. The three of us formed in fact a kind of intellectual fraternity and discussed many philosophical questions which arose from our studies.

But the quest for the truth must be carried out by each person individually. It is like breathing, something which no one else can do for us. And so, I began to take as many courses in the humanities as possible and to read avidly. At that time President James Killian had sought to strengthen the humanities at MIT, elevating it above the status of recreation as it was perceived to hold by many professors and students. A number of distinguished professors were brought to the Institute and many courses were offered in both the humanities and the arts including philosophy, the history of science, and literature. Soon I fell under the sway of the professor who exercised the greatest influence upon me at MIT. He was Giorgio de Santillana, the well-known Italian philosopher and historian of science, who had settled in America after teaching for many years in Europe. He had been a collaborator with Emile Meyerson in the effort to combat logical positivism with a philosophy of science based not upon the "saving of the phenomena" associated with Henri Poincaré with whom Meyerson had carried out extensive debates, but on a "realism" which saw in physics a means of attaining a knowledge which relates to some aspect of the ontological reality of things on the physical level. But de Santillana was also a profound critical student of Western philosophy and science as well as an unparalleled master of the several levels of meaning of the *Divine Comedy* of Dante.

I took many courses and seminars with him, much more than our program required and viewed through his critical eyes the thought of Descartes, Kant, and Hegel as well as the founders of modern science, especially Galileo Galilei, whom he knew well indeed and about whom he was later to write a major book. But de Santillana also introduced me to Pythagorean philosophy, the Platonic dialogues, Aristotelian metaphysics, and the *Enneads* of Plotinus as well as medieval European philosophy, especially the works of Etienne Gilson, whom I was to come to know personally soon. For a whole year he taught a few of us a seminar on Dante providing an unforgettable opening into the deepest aspects of Christian philosophy and symbolism. It was also he who introduced me to Jacques Maritain and the neo-Thomism which had been revived at that time. But de Santillana also warned me about becoming enmeshed in that movement.

Although from a Catholic background, de Santillana was not a typical

Catholic intellectual. But he was also not a typical skeptical European intellectual. On the contrary he was deeply interested in traditional metaphysics and mystical philosophy and regretted their eclipse in the modern West. He was also seriously interested in Hinduism and Islamic thought, his father David de Santillana having been one of the foremost Islamicists of Italy. Giorgio de Santillana's greatest influence upon my education was in fact related to the field of Hinduism as well as to his critique of modern Western thought. As far as Hinduism was concerned, when I and a few other students asked him if he would teach us a course in "Indian philosophy," he said that he would provided we accepted "to hear it from the horse's mouth" by which he meant from the works of René Guénon. It was he who in this way first introduced me to Guénon's *An Introduction to the Study of Hindu Doctrines* and *Man and His Becoming According to the Vedanta* which were to have a determining role in the crystallization of my worldview for the rest of my life.

Extensive reading took me not only through the major classics of Western philosophy from Descartes to Alfred North Whitehead, nearly all of whose philosophical works I read and studied carefully, but more and more in the direction of Indian thought. Both in conjunction with the courses of de Santillana and independent of them, I plunged myself into the study of Sarvepalli Radhakrishnan, whom I was to come to know personally later when he was president of India, Surendranath Dasgupta, and others. But it was especially Ananda K. Coomaraswamy who was to become my guide in this field along with Guénon. Coomaraswamy, the celebrated Singalese metaphysician, historian of art, and foremost propagator in America of the perennial philosophy and tradition in the Guénonian sense of the term, had died near Boston only three years before my coming to Cambridge. But some of his students were still around and soon they introduced me to his wife Dona Luisa Coomaraswamy, who was then living in a large apartment in Cambridge near Harvard Square preparing editions of her husband's works which were to be published by the Bollingen Foundation, a project that was never realized because of her death. Her apartment contained Coomaraswamy's library whose richness in the realm of traditional philosophy and art can hardly be described. Here one could find almost everything essential that one could seek in Indian (both Hindu and Buddhist), Islamic, Chinese, Platonic, and medieval European traditional thought as well as art and symbolism. The apartment was also strewn with the finest works of traditional art, mostly Indian but also Persian, Chinese, and Japanese. One could furthermore find all the works of the traditionalists from Guénon himself to Frithjof Schuon, Titus Burckhardt, Marco Pallis, Martin Lings, and others not to speak of all the works of Coomaraswamy himself which I helped his widow to catalogue. Once within the library, one felt physically in a traditional milieu removed from the tensions and dispersions of the modern world.

I spent many long hours, including weekends and nights, in this library and read almost everything I could find in traditional studies in both French and English including the other works of Guénon and for the first time the writings of Schuon and Burckhardt. The discovery of traditional metaphysics and the *philosophia perennis* through the works of these figures settled the crisis that had caused such a deep upheaval in my inner life. I gained an intellectual certitude which has never left me since then and which has only grown stronger. One can speak symbolically of journeying from the vision of certainty to its existential experience or to use the Islamic terminology based upon the Quran from the science of certainty (*'ilm al-yaqīn*) to the vision of certainty (*'ayn al-yaqīn*) to the truth of certainty (*ḥaqq al-yaqīn*), from gaining a theoretical knowledge of fire, to seeing fire, to being consumed by fire, a journey which characterizes the trajectory of my life.

Henceforth I knew with certitude that there was such a thing as the Truth and that it could be attained through knowledge gained by means of the heart-intellect and also through revelation. My childhood love for the attainment of knowledge now returned on a new plane related to the very meaning of existence and the soteriological function of knowledge as traditionally understood. The traditional writings, especially those of Schuon which emphasized the need for the practice of a spiritual discipline as well as theoretical knowledge, were crucial in determining the course of my life from that time when I was nineteen years old onward. I had discovered the perennial philosophy, as understood by the traditionalist writers and not someone like Aldous Huxley, and knew that it was the truth. The question was now how to realize that truth operatively as well as to know it theoretically. My studies were to take me from the Indian, Platonic and medieval European intellectual worlds to Lao-Tze and Chuang-Tzu and from there to Islam and Sufism. The circle was therefore in a sense completed and I returned to my intellectual and spiritual homeland but only after having traversed both the modern Western world and the other major traditions outside of both the Western and the Islamic worlds.

This major turning point during my undergraduate years in my intellectual life, which established my intellectual framework once and for all, did not mean that I would leave my academic pursuits aside. On the contrary, in addition to my courses in the sciences, I embarked upon an intensive study of German and also learned some Greek, Latin, and Italian. I also began to attend courses and lectures at Harvard during both my junior and senior years at MIT. Many of these courses were in the field of Oriental art taught at that time by one of Coomaraswamy's students and great admirers, Benjamin Rowland, whose courses in Hindu and Buddhist art were in a way an extension of the teachings of Coomaraswamy. One of the great contrasts for me was going from a dreary laboratory at MIT up Massachusetts Avenue to the Fogg Museum at Harvard to view slides of the greatest works of Oriental sacred art. The difference between the traditional and modern worlds became palpable in this way beyond any theoretical and philosophical considerations. I also pursued avidly the lectures of Daisetz T. Suzuki on Zen Buddhism at Harvard and of Alexandre Koyré at both MIT and Harvard on Giordano Bruno, Galileo, Johannes Kepler, and Isaac Newton and the philosophical underpinnings of the Scientific Revolution. Although years later, I came to disagree with Koyré's assessment of Galileo's supposed Platonism, I owe much to my understanding of the deeper philosophical and methodological factors involved in the Scientific Revolution to the many lectures and private discussions with Koyré who was a scholar of unusual philosophical as well as historical acumen.

Before leaving the MIT years behind, it is necessary for me to mention the significance of the influence of Ernst Levy upon me at that time. As mentioned earlier, I was deeply attracted to classical Persian music since my childhood. At Peddie I became interested in Western classical music and while at MIT worked for several years in the music library. This job allowed me to listen to a great deal of Western classical music, my taste turning from the nineteenth-century Romantic music of even the greatest masters such as Beethoven and Brahms to the classical period of Mozart and Hayden, and then back to Johann Sebastian Bach, Handel, and Vivaldi and still further back to Vittoria and Palestrina, reaching finally into Gregorian Chant which was becoming gradually known to the public at large at that time. I had a season's ticket to the Boston Symphony for nearly all my student years at Cambridge and heard numerous concerts conducted by Serge Koussevitsky, Pierre Monteux, and Charles Munch. I would also travel often to New York to hear Arturo Toscanini and Bruno Walter and was in general deeply immersed in Western classical music on many levels. I felt a spiritual and theological element which seemed to have taken refuge in the classical music of the post-Renaissance period when other Western arts had become so secularized and externalized.

I had also studied Western musicology to some extent. Great interest in Western classical music caused me to meet Ernst Levy, then professor of music at MIT and a master interpreter of the Beethoven piano sonatas as well as a theoretician of music. Levy took a liking to me and soon began to teach me the Pythagorean philosophy of music which had been revived by Hans Keyser and others in Germany before the Second World War. Levy was a real master of this subject and influenced many people including Ernest McClain, the author of several works on Pythagorean and Platonic harmonic theory such as *The Myth of Invariance.* Paul Hindemith, who was then at Yale, would also occasionally come to see Levy to learn more about harmonics which Levy considered as the principle of cosmic reality and not only music. Levy would often say that traditional architecture was based on harmonics and that the saying of Goethe that "architecture is frozen music" is literally true. One summer we traveled together to France and measured the dimensions of the two towers of the Chartres Cathedral as well as the main body of the edifice itself and sure enough the ratios were in harmonic proportions. Our measurements appeared as an appendix to Otto von Simpson's work, *The Gothic Cathedral.*

The influence of Levy caused me to delve into this branch of traditional philosophy which is also related to certain branches of science and during later years I was to continue this study in the context of Islamic sources. My many years of engagement with the question of the relation between religion, philosophy, and science have been intertwined with this deeply rooted Pythagorean/Platonic theory of harmonics while my interest in the classical music of the West, especially of earlier periods, has continued unabated along with my love for not only Persian music but also Arabic, Turkish, Indian, and in fact nearly all traditional forms of music including Flamenco and Celtic music. For inner reasons I discontinued my practice of the piano and the Persian *santūr*, but I have continued to listen intently to classical music of various traditions over the years while preparing myself above all else to be able to hear the "silent music" to which Plato alluded.

The transition from MIT to Harvard during my undergraduate years was an easy one since I had already been attending many courses and lectures at Harvard during my MIT years. I chose for my graduate study the field of geology and geophysics still somewhat uncertain as to whether I would continue to study a science other than physics or turn fully to the history of science and philosophy. In any case I wanted to acquaint myself with a descriptive science such as geology as I had with a mathematical one such as physics. I therefore embarked fully upon graduate studies in geology and geophysics studying with such famous authorities in the field as Marland Billings and Francis Birch whose assistant I became for two years. I also studied crystallography and oceanography which revealed to me on another level the beauty of nature to which I had been so sensitive since my childhood. A full year course was also devoted to paleontology which was in many ways intellectually annoying to me because the discontinuities in the palentological record were glossed over by our teacher by appealing to vague transformist and evolutionary hypotheses which were never allowed to be questioned or discussed in class as one would be able to question the theory of thermodynamics. I soon discovered firsthand that Darwinism was more a pseudo-religion than a scientific theory open to questioning and demanding scientific verification. The study of such subjects complemented, however, my earlier immersion in physics while it also provided greater incentive for me to turn fully to the history of science and philosophy.

My interest in the history of science and philosophy was not simply to join in praise of the glories of present day science by going over the history of the errors of the ages gone by. It was to understand other types of sciences of nature and also to seek the reason as to why modern science had developed as it had. I had learned something about modern science but had escaped completely the clutches of scientism and scientific positivism. Rather, as already mentioned, my philosophical perspective had become already crystallized by the discovery of the perennial philosophy and traditional metaphysics. And so I began to take courses in the history of science with I. Bernard Cohen even while being in the geology department. In 1956 upon receiving my master's degree in geology and geophysics I transferred to the history of science and learning department which had been founded by George Sarton, who was now retired but who still had his office in the Widener Library from which he published the journal of the History of Science Society, *Isis*. I spent much time with Sarton who was a great authority on Islamic science and I wanted to write my doctoral thesis under his direction despite his positivistic interpretation of the history of science which I did not accept. His incredible scholarship in the field, however, was sufficient to attract me to him. Before I embarked on the project of my doctoral work, however, Sarton died and my work came to be carried out mostly under the direction of I. Bernard Cohen, Hamilton A. R. Gibb, and Harry A. Wolfson. Much of it was also done through my own studies in which I took full advantage of the incomparable Widener Library with many of whose stacks I came to be as intimately acquainted as with my own bedroom.

The history of science department was a small one but the students were all outstanding and most of them, such as Allen Debus, Everett Mendelsohn, Shigeru Nakayama, and George Basalla, went on to become well-known scholars in their fields of specialization. We had very differing points of view concerning the philosophy of science and the methodology to study the history of science. I was the only one concentrating on Islamic science for which there was no specialist at Harvard after the death of Sarton. He had in fact trained only one other Muslim scholar in the field before, namely, Aydīn Sāyilī, the famous Turkish historian of Islamic astronomy who was sent by the Turkish government before the Second World War to Harvard specifically to study with the famous historian of science. He, however, had had the fortune of being able to complete his studies under Sarton whereas I had to draw from different sources in order to do so. I studied the general history of science with Cohen, Islamic philosophy and theology with Wolfson, and general Islamic civilization and history with Gibb. I also continued my study of modern philosophy and in fact chose Hegel as one of the four fields required for the doctoral exam.

The Harvard philosophy department at that time had already changed completely from the days of Whitehead and William Hocking. Positivism was beginning to hold sway over the department and many even wanted to have the statue of Ralph Waldo Emerson removed from inside the philosophy building which bears his name. Several professors in fact would say openly that philosophy began with Kant and that there was nothing of interest in philosophy before him. This was hardly what I was looking for and yet I did take a couple of courses on modern European philosophy at the philosophy department, but most of my courses there involved Plato and Aristotle.

Wolfson, who combined incredible linguistic ability, especially as far as philosophical languages of the classical world including Greek, Arabic, Hebrew, and Latin were concerned, with philosophical and theological acumen, was my strongest link with the philosophy department. I attended his courses on Philo, the Church Fathers, and Spinoza, and spent a great deal of time with him since he was one of the main advisors of my thesis. The subject of my thesis being the Islamic conception of nature, Wolfson was able to help me in an active way for many parts of it, especially the sections dealing with Ibn Sīnā (Avicenna). For Wolfson the four philosophical traditions, Greek, Islamic, Jewish, and medieval Christian, were not only serious philosophy but the only authentic philosophy from which modern European philosophies grew either as rivulets flowing from a mighty lake or as rebellions brought about by lack of understanding. He was to teach me much, not only about the traditional philosophies of the Mediterranean world, but also about scholarly methods of studying them in such a way as to be true to their nature and at the same in accordance with Western criteria of scholarship. He was also quite critical of the turn that the study of philosophy was taking in the philosophy department and supported me fully in my attitude to much that was passing there.

Bernard Cohen was a major scholar of Newton, Benjamin Franklin, and the Scientific Revolution but took much interest in Islamic science. Besides teaching me a systematic approach to the study of the general history of science in the West which complemented the brilliant philosophical analyses of de Santillana at MIT, Cohen, then the head of the department of the history of science, also opened the archives of Sarton and the vast bibliographical resources on Islamic science assembled by him to me. He was, moreover, personally opposed to the philosophical positivism prevalent among many philosophers and historians of science of the day and would encourage me to try to study the history of Islamic science from its own point of view.

As for the third major figure under whom I studied at that time, namely H.A.R. Gibb, he was a British Islamicist whom many consider the greatest Islamicist that the English-speaking world has ever produced. Gibb had come to Harvard from Oxford after the debacle of the British and French invasion of the Suez Canal which he had opposed. He had brought with him a number of doctoral students from Oxford and many others joined him when he came to Cambridge. Thanks to him, Harvard came to have the best program of Islamic studies in America and Gibb's seminars attracted numerous students who were later to become well-known scholars of Islamic studies, such men as Leonard Binder, William Polk, Ira Lapidus, Malcolm Kerr, Robert Haddad, Stuart Carey Welsh, Sadr al-Din Aga Khan, Caesar Farah, Marshal Hodgson, Menahem Milson, James Kritzeck, ʻAbd al-Ḥayy Shaʻbān, Yūsuf Ibīsh, and many others. Few, however, were interested in Islamic philosophy or science. Most worked in the fields of Islamic history and institutions on which Gibb gave seminars of great depth. He represented the best of Western Orientalism, speaking always with scholarly authority but also sympathy. We did have some arguments over important issues especially the significance of Sufism in Islamic history, a subject on which I believe I was able to change his views as seen in the introduction he himself asked to write to my *An Introduction to Islamic Cosmological Doctrines*, a revised text of my thesis which was published by Harvard University Press in 1964. But I was also to learn much from him about Western methods of scholarship concerning Islam and also certain notable observations of the dynamics of Islamic history.

Gibb was also a veritable master of classical Arabic. At Harvard I began to study Arabic again after the long hiatus going back to my childhood. Gibb taught an advanced seminar on Ibn Khaldūn's *Muqaddimah* and Arabic poetry which was a pleasure to attend. I remain grateful to him in this domain although specifically philosophical Arabic remained a field with which I had to struggle alone at Harvard, sometimes receiving aid from Wolfson. Upon returning to Persia, I continued to study with traditional masters until I was able to gain serious command of philosophical Arabic.

There were a number of other Harvard professors who exercised influence upon my intellectual development and whom I need to mention. There was Werner Jaeger whose idea of *paediea* as the essence of Greek culture and his views on early Christian thought were of much interest to me. And then there was the somewhat eccentric Arthur D. Nock, professor of Hellenistic thought, who was a specialist in Hermeticism and an excellent scholar of Greek with whom I took some courses and who was one of my examiners for the doctoral exam. As for Benjamin Rowland, who was still giving his illuminating courses on Oriental art at the Fogg Museum, by now we had become good friends, a friendship which was to last even after I returned to Persia.

I was naturally closely associated with all those related to the field of Iranian studies. Foremost among them was Richard N. Frye, who was a friend even before I came to Harvard. I never took courses with him but I was his teaching assistant for some time and carried out a great deal of intellectual discourse with him. I became his teaching assistant in 1955, the date which began my teaching career that continues to this day. I also became tutor at Kirkland House for the rest of my Harvard years. I remained friends with Frye and met him often in Persia when he became director of Arthur Upham Pope's Asia Institute in Shiraz. There was also the independent scholar Eric Schroeder who was associated with the Islamic art collection at the Fogg Museum and who was himself an authority on Islamic art and civilization. He remained an intimate friend until his death and introduced me directly or indirectly to other scholars in the field such as Richard Ettinghausen.

A word must also be said about Henry Kissinger who was professor of government at Harvard at that time. I was not interested in the intellectual message of his courses, none of which I attended because of my indifference to political thought at that time. But he directed a summer program, which brought well-known foreign writers, teachers, and social and political activists for the summer to the Harvard campus, and I became his assistant in running the program for two summers. During this time I became closely associated with him and carried out many discussions with him on the East-West intellectual and cultural debate. When he became National Security Advisor and later Secretary of State I had already returned to Iran. I kept aloof from him when he visited the country because I did not want to become embroiled in political debates, but during his many visits we did meet once and continued our old intellectual discussions.

This summer program also allowed me to meet many figures from abroad including philosophers. Some of these figures were to gain fame later including Jalāl Āl-i Aḥmad from Iran, the seed of whose well-known book, *Gharb-zadagī* ("Westoxication,") so influential among radicals and revolutionaries in Iran in the '70s because it dealt with cultural and philosophical tensions between the Islamic world and the West, was sown at the Harvard summer program. Influenced by Marxist philosophical categories, he differed from me in his appraisal of the major issues involved in the East-West cultural and philosophical discourse, but we nevertheless exchanged many views some of which are reflected in his book.

Finally there were the short encounters at Harvard with outstanding figures in various fields which left an impact upon me. These included Walter Gropius, the founder of the Bauhaus who was residing in Cambridge at that time, with whom I carried out many discussions on the philosophy of architecture and the meaning of "abstraction" in Islamic art in contrast to modern art. There was also the Japanese Zen master Shinishi Hisamatsu whose lectures on Zen brought back memories of those of D. T. Suzuki in this domain and who helped to deepen the little knowledge I had of this all important branch of Japanese Buddhism which was attracting many Western intellectuals at that time.

My Harvard days were also marked by close association with and interest in Catholic thought which had begun at MIT and my encounter with Jacques Maritain. I took the full year course on medieval European history and civilization given by Charles Holt Taylor and read avidly in the field, especially in medieval philosophy, including works by Maurice De Wulf, Fernand van Steenberghen, Maritain himself, and especially Etienne Gilson with whom I was to become friends later, especially when I became chosen as a member of the executive board of the Congress for Medieval Philosophy. He combined a mastery of the philosophical text with a rootedness in a philosophical tradition similar to Islamic philosophy. He lived in the world of faith rather than doubt, and his great success in reviving Thomistic philosophy in a contemporary setting helped me in many ways in my later attempt to revive Islamic philosophy in a contemporary language while remaining faithful to its traditional character.

The noted Catholic historian Christopher Dawson was also at Harvard at that time and helped me to achieve a better understanding of the European Middle Ages. My contact with Catholic thinkers, however, went beyond the Harvard ambience. I began to read the works of Eric Gill and made contact with those in Great Britain who like him were attempting to revive the Christian philosophy of art and work, a contact which has continued to this day. Also in 1957 I attended a conference in Tioumliline in Morocco in a Catholic monastery on relations between Islam and Christianity. It was here that I met for the first time both Louis Massignon and Louis Gardet, major Catholic thinkers who were also among France's greatest Islamicists. My relation with both men continued until their death and especially Gardet continued to hold philosophical and theological discussions with me on various issues, particularly comparative philosophy and mysticism, for many years. The conference in Tioumliline was the first I was to attend on religious dialogue with whose philosophical and theological dimensions I have been concerned during the past forty years. At Tioumliline I was also to meet the famous Yale philosopher Filmer S. C. Northrop whose discussions of philosophy in East and West brought home to me the basic philosophical issues involved when one tries to discuss philosophy on a global scale.

Considering my early acquaintance with French culture and my knowledge of the language, it was not accidental that most of my contact with the continental European intellectual world involved France and the Francophone world of Switzerland, and North Africa. During my Harvard years I spent some time traveling in Europe, especially in Spain, Italy, Great Britain, Switzerland, and France, but my intellectual contacts remained especially strong with France where I would often visit the Sorbonne to occasionally attend lectures and meet with philosophers and scholars, including in later years: Massignon whom I met in Paris at the peak of the Algerian war of independence, and shortly before his death, Henry Corbin, to whom I shall turn shortly, Gaston Berger, Gaston Bachelard, Gabriel Marcel, Gaston Wiet, Charles Puech, and numerous other major intellectual and scholarly figures especially those in the field of Islamic and Iranian studies such as Jean Pierre de Menasce, Emile Benveniste, Roger Arnaldez, Claude Cahen, and Gilbert Lazard.

More important than these meetings in France were my direct meetings from 1957 onward in Europe with the outstanding representatives of the perennial philosophy and tradition in Europe at that time, including first and foremost the incomparable metaphysician Frithjof Schuon, with whom I remained intimately associated until his death in 1998, Titus Burckhardt, who influenced my thought in numerous ways especially in the fields of traditional cosmology and the traditional philosophy of art, Marco Pallis, who introduced me to the metaphysics of Tibetan Buddhism, and Martin Lings, one of the main expositors of traditional Islam and Sufism in the West with whom I have been in close relationship during the past forty years. I can hardly overemphasize the influence of these figures along with René Guénon and A. K. Coomaraswamy on my intellectual formation.

I also spent much of the summer of 1957 and 1958 in Morocco. Those years were crucial to my whole intellectual and spiritual life. It was at this time that my intellectual and philosophical orientation received its final and enduring formation and I embraced Sufism not only intellectually but also existentially in a form linked to the Maghrib and more particularly to the spiritual lineage of the great Algerian master Shaykh Aḥmad al-ʿAlawī and Shaykh ʿĪsā Nūr al-Dīn Aḥmad. These intellectual and existential experiences not only rooted my mind and soul for the rest of my life in the world of tradition, intellectual certitude, and faith, but also led to the discovery of inner illumination, the harmonious wedding of "logic and transcendence," to use the title of one of the works of Schuon, and intellectual lucidity and rigor combined with love for truth and beauty. These years also set my gaze more fully upon the horizon of universal and global truth in the traditional sense of the word, embracing not only the Islamic tradition which was my own, but also the Western, both Graeco-Alexandrian and Christian, Hindu, Buddhist, Far Eastern and primal, and also including esoteric Judaism associated with the Kabbala, and Zoroastrianism and other Iranian religions.

It was, moreover, at this time that the major philosophical themes and investigations that were to be developed and pursued in my later life became strongly apparent. These included the following subjects and issues: to delve more deeply into the various dimensions of traditional metaphysics; to know other sciences of nature and cosmologies than modern science; to discover ways of studying the history of science other than the prevalent method based upon positivism (drawing here from many of the works of Pierre Duhem) and to create especially what I hold to be an authentic methodology to study both Islamic science and Islamic philosophy from within; to resuscitate the whole of the Islamic intellectual tradition including Sufism, philosophy, the arts, and the sciences in the contemporary setting; to pursue the study of Western philosophy from the point of view of the Islamic intellectual tradition; and to deal intellectually and philosophically in the deepest sense of the term with the tensions between East and West and tradition and modernism. My writings during the past four decades have been humble efforts to deal with these themes and issues all of which were already crystallized in my mind during those Harvard years.

There is one other major philosophical occupation of my life, that is, my interest in the environmental crisis, whose beginnings also go back to those Harvard years. From my childhood, when as I mentioned, we spent our summer holidays in the foothills of the majestic Mt. Damavand outside of Tehran, I had a special love for nature in her many forms, from mountain peaks, which have always exercised a special magical power upon me, to the vast starry nights of the Iranian Plateau where heaven seems to descend to the earthly realm, to flowers, trees and animals, to running streams, placid lakes, sandy beaches, and even rocks and earth. The immediate experience of virgin nature, not spoiled by human intrusion, has always been for me a foretaste of paradisal beatitude, while from my early days I have been immersed in reading nature poetry in Persian and later English, Arabic, French, and German. My interest in traditional philosophies of nature and cosmologies was also directly related to this innate love for nature.

When I came to America, many summers spent in camps as both camper and counselor in natural areas as different as those of Pennsylvania, Connecticut, Maine, Colorado, and California only intensified this love for nature. I came to know many of the breathtaking sites of the American West including the Sierra Nevada ranges and especially Yosemite in California, the Rocky Mountains in Colorado where I spent much of the summer of 1954 in the company of Roger Williams, a professor and friend from MIT, and later Yellowstone, the Grand Canyon. and other natural wonders of the American Southwest. As far as this latter area is concerned, I visited it twice in 1956 and 1957 with the explicit goal of meeting Joseph Epes Brown, now a life-long friend, who introduced me for the first time to the Native American traditions and the teachings of Black Elk which he had made known in the early 1950s through his well-known book, *The Sacred Pipe*. It was moreover high up in the Rocky Mountains in a cave behind a waterfall which rushed into an untouched lake, some four hours of hiking from the nearest mountain road, that in the summer of 1954 I decided to reread the Quran and ponder over the future course of my life. It was in such an idyllic ambience that I made the important decision to return to Persia for a visit after so many years of being away from home, a visit which took place in 1955.

While living outside of Boston in Arlington Heights, I would spend much time in the natural scenery nearby, including Walden Pond where Thoreau had spent so many memorable moments a century before. I would also visit Concord and then move farther afield into the Berkshires, New Hampshire, and Vermont whose fall colors are still engraved in my memory. I was aware of the gradual degradation of the natural environment and had even read Rachel Carson's *Silent Spring*. But it was the building in the mid-1950s of Route 128, the beltway around Boston, that brought home to me the imminence of an environmental crisis. In just a short span of time our area in Arlington Heights became suddenly severed in a deep ecological sense from the natural hinterland and animals were no longer able to travel from the forests of Concord and the countryside beyond to our area. I began to ponder the rapidity with which man was destroying the natural environment on the basis of a science rooted in power and domination over nature, as well as on a conception of man based on greed and of human society evaluated solely in terms of what is called economic progress.

For me it was obvious that not only was an environmental crisis of major proportions around the corner, but that also the cause of this crisis was spiritual and religious and not simply the result of bad engineering and faulty economic planning. I began to speak of those matters even during my Harvard years and formulated them later in the Rockefeller series of lectures which I delivered at the University of Chicago in 1966 under the title of *The Encounter of Man and Nature*. This concern for the environment has remained with me for all the years that have followed. I have participated in numerous conferences on this subject all over the world and came back to it intellectually in my 1994 Cadbury Lectures at the University of Birmingham in Great Britain which appeared as *Religion and the Order of Nature*. This work contains my most extensive discussion on the subject including the role of Western philosophy in the environmental crisis. My writings on this subject have also exercised much influence in the Islamic world where until recently few showed any serious interest in this crucial question. It was in this context that I delivered the keynote speech at Harvard at the 1998 conference on Islam and Ecology.

The die was cast concerning my future. Although I could have become a junior fellow at Harvard if I had decided to stay longer and although I was offered a teaching position as assistant professor at MIT, upon the completion of my doctorate in 1958 at Harvard, I decided to return permanently to Tehran. But before leaving the Harvard years behind, it is necessary to say a few words about my doctoral thesis which was entitled "Conceptions of Nature in Islamic Thought" and another work on the history of Islamic science which was written then but which was to appear after my departure from Cambridge. When I realized that modern physics could not provide ultimate knowledge of the physical world, philosophically speaking, the question came to my mind, if not modern physics, then what kind of science could provide such an answer? I turned to traditional cosmologies from the Pythagorean and Platonic, associated especially with the *Timaeus*, to Aristotelian physics, to the Sāṁkhya in Hinduism, to Chinese philosophies of nature found in Taoism and Neo-Confucianism, and finally to Islam. My thesis, which was published later as *An Introduction to Islamic Cosmological Doctrines,* was a step in this quest for traditional knowledge of a cosmological order.

Also during my last year at Harvard, de Santillana saddled me with another task related to this subject. He was editing at that time a series for Mentor Books of the New American Library on the history of science and wanted me to write the volume on medieval science in collaboration with Alistair Crombie of Oxford University. He would write the part on Latin science and I the section on Islamic science. Despite having to complete my thesis, I worked very hard to write my half of the volume which I handed to de Santillana before my departure for Persia. Later, it was decided that a separate volume should be devoted completely to Islamic science and therefore, while in Tehran, I added several chapters to complete the text which was published years later in 1968 by Harvard and the New American Library as *Science and Civilization in Islam*. This work was in fact my first book, at least part of which was completed even before the termination of my thesis.

In any case, in the early summer of 1958, I left Harvard, as the first Iranian to have received a Ph.D. from that university, to return to Persia, thus bringing to an end the long years of formal education and training in America. That summer ushered in a new phase of my life. After a summer spent in Europe, Morocco, Turkey, and Iraq, I returned to Persia in the fall of 1958 and began my duties as associate professor of philosophy and the history of science at the Faculty of Letters of Tehran University.

BACK HOME

The return to Iran after nearly thirteen years in the West was in many ways challenging since my intellectual orientation was diametrically opposed to the modernistic currents which were strong among the modern educated classes that included most of my own family and friends. My intellectual and spiritual training was, however, strong enough to withstand the pull of any currents which might come along. What I needed to do first of all, however, was to gain personal independence from the grid of the extended family system which provided many advantages but which could also be inhibiting in the tasks that lay ahead for me. I needed much time to be alone outside ordinary family and social settings for spiritual reasons as well as intellectual ones. I therefore decided to become married as soon as possible to gain greater independence from the extended family structure.

Having avoided a Western style marriage based on long personal acquaintance (although I had come close to such a marriage) and being a firm believer in the traditional family structure including arranged marriages, I submitted myself like a simple traditional Persian man to my mother and other members of my own family and asked them to find a suitable wife for me, knowing that even in the somewhat modernized ambience of my surroundings, it was still not two individuals but two families that become married in the East. A young woman from a respected family whose members had been close friends of my own family was proposed and the proposal met with my firm approval. Her name was Soussan Daneshvary; her father was a celebrated physician who had studied in the West and was himself the son of one of the religious scholars of Naishapur in Khurasan, and her mother was a daughter of one of the country's well-known merchant figures of the early Pahlavi period. Half modernized and half traditional like members of my own family, my wife-to-be had studied for several years in England and America, had come back to Iran, and was about to leave for France for further studies when we became married. Her family was in fact quite conservative and retained many of the traditional values which I sought. Our backgrounds were therefore similar and in the fall of 1958 just a few months after returning to Tehran we became married. Our marriage was strong and most often a happy one, although there were often tensions caused by the bigger extended family and my own assertion of traditional values amidst an ever greater movement in the upper classes of society towards modernization.

My wife did not share in my intellectual activities, something which I had not sought in any case, but supported me in a life most of which was given to intellectual and spiritual pursuits including many hours spent at home in my study in meditation, writing, and studying. We were to have a son and a daughter, Seyyed Vali Reza and Laili, the son being now a professor of political thought at the University of San Diego and the daughter an art historian at the National Gallery of Art in Washington.

I began my career as professor of philosophy and the history of science at the Faculty of Letters at Tehran University, shortly after my arrival in Tehran in the fall of 1958 and continued to hold that position until the Iranian Revolution of 1979. The dean of the Faculty at that time was 'Alī Akbar Siāsī, one of Iran's foremost educators, who had been one of my father's protégés and colleagues as were many of the leading professors of the Faculty. This fact, added to my own educational career in America, caused the members of the Faculty to give me a warm welcome, and despite my philosophical opposition to much that transpired academically at the Faculty, I was held in respect and honor by nearly all my colleagues. As a result of the influence of not only Siāsī and other important professors who were nearly all educated in France and were intellectually deeply influenced by French philosophy and humanities (or *les sciences humaines*) as conceived in French intellectual circles, but also the general educational policies of the early Pahlavi period, ideas of French origin dominated most departments of the Faculty from psychology to history.

This trait was especially evident in the philosophy department where René Descartes and Auguste Compte still reigned supreme. Yaḥyā Mahdavī, the head of the department, was a noble scholar from a patrician family with great love for the Persian language. He was trained in France and in a sense continued the current of the last part of the last century when Western philosophy was first introduced to the Persian-speaking world through the translations of Descartes's *Discourse on Method*. The second translation of this work in lucid Persian by Muḥammad 'Alī Furūghī as well as this author's *Sayr-i ḥikmat dar urūpā* ("The History of Philosophy in Europe") were still the main staples for courses on Western philosophy and even later studies of Western philosophy and its history were seen mostly through the eyes of French scholars such as Emile Brehier. Some attention was, however, also paid to the German philosophers of the classical period especially Kant and Hegel and the German historiography of philosophy, although not twentieth-century German philosophy itself. Another influential professor of the department, Ghulām Ḥusayn Ṣadīqī, who had studied sociology at the Sorbonne in the '30s, was also like Mahdavī a great supporter of the Persian language and its use for contemporary philosophical discourse. Moreover, he was a patriot and sometime political figure associated with the National Front, having served as Muḥammad Mossadegh's interior minister. Although in later years he became professor of a separate Faculty of Sociology, in 1958 and the years that followed immediately, he was still a member of the Faculty of Letters and taught in our philosophy department on the basis of a positivism which definitely possessed a Comptian origin.

As a young associate professor, the rank with which I began, I was not only assigned to teach the history of science but also Aristotle and sometimes Plato, as well as English philosophical texts such as Alfred E. Taylor's *Metaphysics*. Before long, I consolidated my position in the department and began to gain much influence in the Faculty, becoming at the age of thirty the youngest person to become a full professor at Tehran University. I sought to use this influence to transform the teaching of philosophy in several ways. First of all I wanted to strengthen the teaching of Islamic philosophy as a foundation on whose basis other philosophies, especially those of the West, should be studied rather than studying Western philosophy as if Persians belonged to the European tradition. Already when I came to the department, one course on Islamic philosophy was being taught by Sayyid Muḥammad

Kāẓim 'Aṣṣār, and after his retirement by Abu'l-Ḥasan Sha'rānī. As a result of my insistence, this part of the program was expanded to include a required general course on Islamic philosophy and culture which I gave myself and a doctoral seminar on Islamic thought given jointly by Henry Corbin and myself. But my attempt was also to expand the scope of the study of Western philosophy itself to include more recent German and also Anglo-American schools of thought such as logical positivism and analytic philosophy. Supported by Yaḥyā Mahdavī, I succeeded in this task especially during the years when I was dean of the Faculty and could allot new positions to the department. We brought Aḥmad Fardīd, a gifted philosopher who wrote little but was an exciting teacher and who had studied in Germany, to teach Martin Heidegger, German phenomenology, and even later schools of thought such as that of Frankfurt. We also were able to create courses on Anglo-Saxon philosophy from empiricism to logical positivism taught mostly by Manūchehr Bozorgmehr who translated in a masterly fashion several works of this school for the first time into Persian.

But the world did not consist simply of Iran and the West. I carried out a crusade in every way possible to create greater awareness of the philosophies of lands east of Iran, especially, of course, India. We began the teaching of Sanskrit at the Faculty and years later were even able to teach Indian philosophy at the department when my friend Dariush Shāyegān, who had studied Sanskrit and later completed his doctorate at the Sorbonne under Corbin, joined the department. The impact of these changes in the study of philosophy was to be extensive even beyond the confines of Tehran University, especially since our department was the only one at that time in Iran to give a doctorate in philosophy and influenced philosophical studies throughout the country. My attempt to have Persian students study other schools and traditions of philosophy from the point of view of their own tradition rather than studying their tradition from the perspective of Western thought was in fact to have an enduring and ever increasing influence which continues to this day, propagated by a large number of earlier students, many my own, who are now professors and scholars of philosophy in Iran. Among my best students in these domains I can mention Reżā Dāvarī, Gholām Reżā A'vānī, Gholām Reżā Ḥaddād 'Ādel, Naṣrollāh Pourjavādī, Moḥsen Jahāngīrī, and Moẓaffar Bakhtiyār all, of whom are famous scholars and thinkers in Iran today.

My philosophical activities in Iran were not confined to Tehran University. Almost from the beginning of my return, I began to lecture on philosophy—Islamic, comparative, sometimes Greek, and later Western—in other institutions of learning and even occasionally on the radio and television. I was chosen as a member of almost all the important government and academic councils and societies which were influential in the domain of philosophy and the human sciences. This included the Supreme Cultural Council which determined most of the cultural policies of the country on the national level. Membership in this Council for some sixteen years provided many opportunities for me to help organize national conferences and seminars on various traditional philosophers as well as issues of philosophical interest arising from the confrontation between tradition and modernism. I helped to propagate what is now known as civilizational dialogue long before it became fashionable and carried out many discussions with the French philosopher Roger Garaudy who was trying to establish a network of centers "for the dialogue of civilizations" throughout the world in the '70s. A branch of this network was established in Tehran under the auspices of the Shahbanou of Iran (the Empress Farah) and directed by Dariush Shāyegān, a center which functioned until the Revolution of 1979.

These philosophical activities concerned not only the modern educated segments of society but the traditional elements as well. Long philosophical discussions were held with many traditional philosophers such as Murtaḍā Muṭahharī and Sayyid Jalāl al-Dīn Āshtiyānī, both close personal friends. I also carried out philosophical discussions with religious figures with a modern bent such as 'Alī Sharī'atī who was trying to introduce a modernized and revolutionary form of Islam into Iran at that time, influenced greatly by leftist French sociologists and philosophers. The new religious center in Tehran known as Ḥusayniyya-yi Irshād was where we would often meet. But Muṭahharī and I resigned when we realized the political nature of the activities of the center and the tenure of some of the discourses by Sharī'atī which were opposed to traditional Islamic intellectuality that was precisely what interested Muṭahharī and I most of all.

Nor were my activities only in the realms of teaching and lecturing. The period from 1958 to 1979 was also a very active one as far as writing was concerned. I began to write extensively both in Persian and English with an occasional article or text in French or Arabic. My Persian writings were in several categories: Islamic philosophy, science and Sufism, perennial philosophy which included the introduction of the writings of the traditional school of A. K. Coomaraswamy, R. Guénon, F. Schuon, T. Burckhardt, and others to the Persian-speaking world, critique of modernism, comparative philosophy and religion, the edition of classical texts of Islamic philosophy, and occasionally translations in the field of metaphysics and traditional philosophy from English or French. Besides a large number of essays in these fields, a number of my books appeared in Persian during this period, including the Persian modified version of my doctoral thesis at Harvard on Islamic cosmology entitled *Naẓar-i mutafakkirān-i islāmī dar bāra-yi ṭabī'at*, ("The Concept of Nature in Islamic Thought") which won the royal book award, and *Ma'ārif-i islāmī dar jahān-i mu'āṣir* ("Islamic Culture in the Contemporary World"). A number of books were also edited by me including the *Mullā Ṣadrā Commemoration Volume* and *Mélanges offerts à Henry Corbin* which was multilingual. My critical edition of philosophical texts, which seems like a thankless task to many today but which is foundational for the serious study of any philosophy, included the complete Persian works of Suhrawardī, the Persian treatise *Si aṣl* of Ṣadr al-Dīn Shīrāzī, and the Arabic text of the *al-As'ilah wa'l-ajwibah*, a series of questions and answers exchanged between Ibn Sīnā (Avicenna) and al-Bīrūnī, this latter text having been edited in conjunction with Mehdī Moḥaghegh.

Since my student days with Sarton at Harvard, I had hoped to write a comprehensive study of Islamic science using the methodology employed in my *Science and Civilization in Islam.* To this end I began to compile a complete bibliography of the Islamic sciences, one set in European and another in Islamic languages. It was my hope that upon their completion, someone or a group of like-minded scholars could collect all these works, study them, and on the basis of the knowledge contained therein and in the matrix of the conception of Islamic science which I had developed, produce a collective work like Joseph Needham's *Science and Civilization in China* for Islamic science, but with the major difference that this study would be based on the Islamic understanding of philosophy and science rather than on the Marxism and positivism which dominates the remarkable documentation of Needham and his associates. At the time of the Iranian Revolution I had completed, with the collaboration of a number of young scholars, especially William Chittick, three volumes of which two appeared before the Revolution and one afterwards, all under the title of *An Annotated Bibliography of Islamic Science*, with Persian and English annotations. I do not expect to be able to complete this project but hope that others will do so and at last bring out the other four volumes, using the data which I had prepared and recorded and which remain in the Academy of Philosophy in Tehran to this day.

During this period I also wrote extensively in English, writings which included a number of books that were quickly translated into many languages including Persian itself. In this case I had to go over the translations and supervise them. I was fortunate in this domain in that one of the greatest scholars and translators of Iran, Aḥmad Ārām, translated three of these books, *Three Muslim Sages, Science and Civilization in Islam* and *Islamic Science—An Illustrated Study* into Persian in cooperation with myself. All of these books have been reprinted numerous times in Tehran and are textbooks for several courses in Islamic philosophy and science in various Iranian universities.

Besides my work on cosmology and *Science and Civilization in Islam,* which were written before my return to Persia and to which I put finishing touches before they were published by the Harvard University Press in 1964 and 1968, respectively, the first new book in English to be written and the first to appear was *Three Muslim Sages*. This work, which seeks to present the whole of the Islamic intellectual tradition from within, grew out of three lectures given at the Center for the Study of World Religions at Harvard University where I was the first visiting professor in 1962. These were in fact the first series of public lectures at the Center and the book which was also published by the Harvard University Press, the first book in the Center's series of publications. It was Harry Wolfson, present during all the lectures, who prevailed upon me to present their text as a book to Harvard. Following his suggestion I completed the text by the summer of 1962 before my return to Persia.

Other books were to appear in English, one after another during the years of living in Persia (and for a year in Lebanon), including *Ideals and Realities of Islam,* consisting of the text of the first six of fifteen lectures which I prepared and delivered at the American University of Beirut as the Aga Khan professor of Islamic Studies in 1964–65 under the title "Dimensions of Islam." Because of certain difficulties with a local publisher, this title was not used for my book but it did appear later as the title of an important collection of essays on Islamic metaphysics by Frithjof Schuon, published in London with my preface. *Ideals and Realities of Islam* became my most widely sold work. It has been reprinted numerous times and, along with *Three Muslim Sages,* has been the most widely translated of my works into both European and Islamic languages.

Some of my intellectual energy was being directed during this period to an ever greater degree to the question of the environmental crisis. Therefore when invited to deliver the Rockefeller lectures at the University of Chicago by the Divinity School and more specifically by Dean Brauer, along with John Rust and Mircea Eliade on some aspect of the relation between religion, philosophy, and the environmental crisis, I accepted the challenge gladly and wrote *Man and Nature—The Spiritual Crisis of Modern Man* which appeared a couple of years after I delivered the lectures in Chicago in 1966. This book, dealing with the philosophical and spiritual roots of the question, was one of the first to predict the coming of the environmental crisis which was then called the ecological crisis. The book soon gained much notoriety and, as already mentioned, was translated into several European languages including French, Italian, Spanish, Portuguese, and Bosnian. The Islamic world itself did not show much interest in it until much later, except for in Turkey where this work became the first of some twenty of my books to be translated into Turkish. This work also put me on the front line of the debate and discussion concerning the deeper philosophical and religious factors involved in the environmental crisis. Besides addressing this issue when I delivered the Cadbury Lectures at the University of Birmingham in 1994, I have given many courses and major lectures on the subject over the years in the universities where I have taught as well as at the Temenos Academy in London, Middlebury College, Cornell University, Harvard University, and many other sites as far away as Kuala Lumpur in Malaysia. I even participated with the Dalai Lama, Rabbi Ismar Schorsch, Sallie McFague, and others in an award-winning television documentary with Bill Moyers entitled *Spirit and Nature* based on the conference arranged by Stephen Rockefeller at Middlebury College with the same title. This question continues to occupy much of my attention to this day.

My other books in English during the period when I lived in Persia included several titles dealing with various aspects of Islamic studies in which I always devoted sections to philosophy but which I do not need to discuss separately here. There were, however, other works bearing more directly on philosophical concerns which need to be mentioned separately. This category includes *Islam and the Plight of Modern Man* which contains sections devoted to comparative philosophy and the future of the study of philosophy in the Islamic world, and *Sufi Essays,* which has also become well known in its Italian, French, and Spanish translations and which includes a number of chapters on the metaphysical dimensions of Sufism. I should also mention *The Transcendent Theosophy of Ṣadr al-Dīn Shīrāzī* which in reality constitutes the first of a planned two-part study of which the second part was left incomplete by the Revolution. The parts of the second volume that had been written were incorporated into the recent second edition of the work. During this period in Iran I studied Mullā Ṣadrā avidly and wrote much about him, being the first person to introduce him to the English speaking world. This work was in fact a synthesis of many other studies, some of which had already appeared in article form in English and Persian.

A word also needs to be said about my activities as an educator during these years in Persia because these activities were very much related to my philosophical perspective and the philosophy of education which I sought to have implemented. From my earliest days in the Faculty of Letters of Tehran University I was also left in charge of the doctoral program in Persian language and literature which was especially devised for those whose mother tongue was not Persian. I sought to strengthen the philosophical component of this program in which a number of future scholars of Islamic philosophy and Sufism, such as William Chittick, Sachiko Murata, Ṣalāḥ al-Sāwī, Muḥammad ʻAbd al-Ḥaqq, Laṭīfah Peerwānī, Rusmir Mahmutćehajić, along with a large number of scholars of Persian literature, especially from Pakistan and India, were trained. I also cooperated intellectually on several projects with some of these scholars such as William Chittick, who collaborated with me in the *Annotated Bibliography of Islamic Science* project as well as *A Shiʻite Anthology* and Ṣalāḥ al-Sāwī, a notable Arab poet, with whom I participated in the Arabic translation of Schuon's *Understanding Islam* (*Ḥattā nafham al-islām*). Also, for ten years I was the director of the Faculty's library during which time we built the best collection of philosophical works in European languages in the country. From 1968 to 1972 I served as the dean of the Faculty, and for a while as Tehran University's academic vice chancellor, positions which afforded me the opportunity to strengthen the programs in the humanities in general and philosophy in particular. My constant criticism of the blind emulation of Western scientism and the desire for wholesale adoption of Western technology prevalent in Iran at that time, led in 1972 to my being chosen as the president of Aryamehr University, which was Iran's leading scientific and technical university at that time. Its patron, the Shah, asked me to mold the University into an institution similar to MIT, but with strong roots in Persian culture. During the three years of my tenure (cut short by an illness in 1975 which led to my resignation), I sought to create a strong humanities program, not in the same way as President Killian had sought to achieve one at MIT during my own student days there, but by establishing a program in Islamic thought and culture with an emphasis upon a philosophy of science drawn from the Islamic philosophical tradition rather than positivism in one form or another. This program was to continue after my departure and has led during the last decade to the creation of one of the first graduate programs in the Islamic world in the philosophy of science based upon the Islamic philosophy of science. Furthermore, in 1973 I set out to found the Iranian Academy of Philosophy, an undertaking to which I shall turn shortly.

My educational activities also involved the organization of a number of conferences which were to have an enduring influence. These included the first Congress of Iranian Studies which I organized in the '70s with my friend and colleague Īraj Afshār and of which I was the first president. The congress continues to this day as the major event of its kind in Iran and has a section devoted to philosophy. Also in the '70s I proposed to the Shahbanou, Empress Farah, to hold an international conference on traditional architecture and its philosophy with the goal of resuscitating the traditional philosophy of art, a goal which I had pursued avidly through the translation of works of Coomaraswamy, Schuon, and Burckhardt, as well as my own lectures and writings. Consequently, a major conference was held in Isfahan to which we invited not only Persian architects but also foreign ones including the great Egyptian architect Ḥasan Fatḥy who had been somewhat neglected in his homeland until then. We arranged for the publication in America of his *Building for the Poor*, an event which contributed to the sudden spread of his fame during the twilight of his life. The revival of interest in the traditional arts and architecture and their philosophy throughout the Islamic world received a major impetus from this event.

Another conference, organized by me and also inaugurated by the

Shahbanou, but this time in Shiraz, concerned traditional medicine. Long before the rise of interest in holistic and alternative medicine which we observe today, I had been concerned with the philosophy of traditional medicine about which I had already written as far as Islamic medicine was concerned. I had not heeded the advice of my father to become a physician (*ḥakīm*) like himself but I was certainly attracted to the other meaning in Islamic civilization of *ḥakīm* as philosopher as well as to the worldview and practice of the traditional *ḥakīms* (as physicians). I organized this conference with full awareness of the strong opposition which would come from modern educated physicians as well as modern pharmacists and pharmaceutical firms. Fortunately, however, with the Shahbanou's support and my own influence in educational circles we were able to hold a very successful conference to which many practitioners of various schools of traditional medicine were invited including several experts in Chinese medicine. Special attention was paid, however, to physicians from Pakistan and India where not only Ayurvedic but also Islamic medicine has survived to this day, revived in fact by such figures as Ḥakīm 'Abd al-Ḥamīd in India and his brother, Ḥakīm Muḥammad Sa'īd, from Pakistan who was a major figure in the conference. The treatment of the subject in the conference made a great impact in Iran to the extent that even after the Revolution of 1979, when for some time my writings in Persian were either not published or printed without my name, the proceedings of the conference were brought out in Tehran and included the text of my introductory speech. Since then interest in traditional Islamic medicine has continued to grow in Iran as well as in several other Islamic countries parallel with the rise of interest in alternative and holistic medicine in the West.

Also of enduring importance was the first International Conference on Muslim Education held in Mecca in 1977. For several years I had worked on this project with 'Abḍallāh Naseef, then the president of King Abdulaziz University in Jeddah, Syed 'Alī Ashraf, a well-known Muslim educator from Bangladesh, and a number of other Muslim educational experts, and when the conference was held I presented a position paper on the teaching of philosophy, Islamic, Western, and both non-Islamic and non-Western, which appeared as the opening chapter of the book I edited later as *Philosophy, Literature and Fine Arts* in the Islamic Education Series. This conference was to lead to the establishment of several Islamic universities from Malaysia to Nigeria and also to several later conferences in which the "Islamization" of various disciplines were discussed, and my position paper became the basis for much continued discussion about the teaching of philosophy in the Islamic world. The conference also brought forth the idea of the Islamization of knowledge, an idea associated from the early 1980s onward with the name of my colleague at Temple University, Ismā'īl al-Fārūqī, and later the International Institute of Islamic Thought. I had in fact spoken of the necessity to integrate knowledge cultivated in the modern West into the Islamic perspective from the 1950s onward but had not used the term "Islamization" of knowledge. Moreover, what Syed 'Alī Ashraf and I had proposed at the Mecca Conference was precisely the integration of all forms of knowledge into the Islamic perspective and the creation of an educational curriculum which was based on the Islamic worldview. My special goal was to delineate precisely that worldview as crystallized in the central discipline of philosophy and to develop a program for the study of philosophy and the humanities from the Islamic perspective. The goals set by the Mecca Conference were not fully reached, but the impact of the conference was great and the question of the "Islamization of Knowledge" continues to be one of the central intellectual concerns of the Islamic world today.

Before concluding this discussion about conferences, a word must be said about the two Festivals of the World of Islam, organized by Paul Keeler in London in 1971 and 1976. I played an active role in both events including giving major lectures in Islamic thought. But it was especially the 1976 festival, held on a much grander scale than the first one, that took much of my energy. Besides publishing *Islam and the Plight of Modern Man* and editing *Islam and the Perennial Philosophy* by Frithjof Schuon for that occasion, I supervised the first exhibition ever held of Islamic science in the Science Museum in London. The exhibition, inaugurated by the Shahbanou, sought to demonstrate how Islamic science, far from being only the historical antecedent of modern Western science (although it certainly played a major historical role in its foundation) was based on another philosophy of nature and was a "sacred science," as I was to discuss this concept in my later works. Meanwhile, it was for the occasion of this festival that I wrote *Islamic Science—An Illustrated Study* (with the remarkable photographs taken by Roland Michaud under my direction), a work which continues to attract many readers not only in its English version but also in its Persian, Arabic, and Turkish ones. It was also for the 1976 festival that I, together with Titus Burckhardt, to whom I owed so much of my understanding of traditional cosmology and art, and Yūsuf Ibīsh, a friend and colleague, supervised the six-part BBC film series, "The Traditional World of Islam," a series which continues to be used in schools and universities to this day.

So far I have spoken of my philosophical activities in Iran but now I must return to 1958 and discuss my own re-education in Islamic philosophy which began upon my return to my homeland in that year. Years of study of Islamic and European medieval philosophy in the West, my direct encounter with the great expositors of traditional doctrines such as Schuon and Burckhardt, and my childhood experiences had all added up to convince me that there was an oral tradition of wisdom (*ḥikmah*) that could only be learned at the feet of traditional masters. Islamic philosophy became intertwined in later centuries with gnosis, but what was still distinctly philosophy and not theology or mysticism in the sense understood in the West, still survived in Persia. Therefore, I set out soon after returning home to discover the still living traditional masters of *ḥikmah* in order to benefit directly from their oral teachings. Strangely enough, this quest was facilitated and doors opened for me by my late father, for one of his closest friends, Sayyid Muḥammad Kāẓim 'Aṣṣār, who was one of the greatest teachers of traditional philosophy at that time, was still alive. Soon after my arrival I went to visit him and because of my father, he received me with open arms. Soon he took me with him to the house of a well-known lawyer, Dhu'l-Majd Ṭabāṭabā'ī, where three afternoons a week the master taught traditional texts of philosophy and metaphysics or gnosis (*'irfān*) to a small group. Not only did I begin to attend these courses, but it was there that I was to meet other major masters of traditional philosophy and gnosis. It was through Dhu'l-Majd that I met 'Allāmah Sayyid Muḥammad Ḥusayn Ṭabāṭabā'ī and we also visited other traditional philosophers/theosophers or *ḥakīms* such as Sayyid Abu'l-Ḥasan Qazwīnī and Mahdī Ilāhī Qumsha'ī. Soon, in fact, I met nearly all the well-known *ḥakīms* of Persia including Jawād Muṣliḥ, Maḥmūd Shahābī, and Abu'l-Ḥasan Sha'rānī, as well as nearly all the well-known Sufi teachers and masters of the various orders such as Ḥājj Maleknīā, Jawād Nūrbakhsh, Mullā Ḥubb-i Ḥaydar, and, of course, my teacher of Sufi literature Hādī Ḥā'irī, who was like a second father to me. Here, I need only to say a few words about those who were my direct teachers, who influenced my intellectual views, and who taught me Islamic philosophy and gnosis from the traditional perspective, providing knowledge which I was able to integrate into the metaphysical perspective based upon traditional doctrines and the *philosophia perennis* as expounded by Guénon and Schuon, doctrines that those teachings fortified and confirmed in every way.

Like my other traditional teachers, Sayyid Muḥammad Kāẓim 'Aṣṣār was a member of the class of religious scholars or *'ulamā* and wore the traditional Islamic dress with a black turban, marking his descent from the Prophet of Islam, and an *'abāyah.* His father had also been a religious scholar but the young son had set out to study in France and after studying philosophy and mathematics there had returned to Najaf in Iraq to pursue his Islamic studies and finally settled in Tehran where he was celebrated as an authority on the law as well as on Islamic philosophy. He was also a master of gnosis and the esoteric sciences and a true philosopher in the traditional sense who lived the life of virtue. Detached from the dissipative influences of the world, he possessed a remarkable sense of humor and laughed at the world of relativity in the manner of a Taoist sage in realization of the transience of all that is other than the Absolute and therefore by nature relative. He never ceased to smile while making dismissive remarks about the intellectual and cultural claims of the modernized classes. He was the first traditionally trained Islamic philosopher who also knew Western thought firsthand, but rarely did he delve into comparative philosophy. Rather, at both Tehran University and the Sepahsālār *madrasah* (or traditional school of learning), which was a major center of Islamic education in Tehran, he taught primarily Islamic philosophy.

As early as 1958, I began to attend his classes at the Sepahsālār school on the *Sharḥ-i manẓūmah* of Ḥājjī Mullā Hādī Sabziwārī, a nineteenth-century text of Islamic philosophy which is very popular in Persia. At the house of Dhu'l-Majd Ṭabāṭabā'ī we began our thrice weekly session studying theoretical Sufism or gnosis with the master, the text chosen being the *Ashi''at al-lama'āt* by the fifteenth-century Sufi metaphysician 'Abd al-Raḥmān Jāmī. It took several years to complete just the introduction to this work, but through this exercise I had learned how to read (the Latin *lecture*), in the traditional sense, a text of this kind accompanied always with precious commentaries. 'Aṣṣār, who was then in his eighties, would teach for nearly two hours with incredible joy and spontaneity requiring of us only our attention, not expecting nor willing to accept remuneration of any kind. He followed the traditional Islamic ideal that *ḥikmah* or philosophy should be taught freely. That is why historically the Islamic philosophers had been physicians, such as Ibn Sīnā and Ibn Ṭufayl, jurists such as Ibn Rushd and Mīr Dāmād, or scientists such as Ṭūsī, because it was from these professions that they provided for their livelihood. Even 'Aṣṣār taught Islamic law along with philosophy in the institutions where he taught in order to gain a living. But the "lesson outside the school" (*dars-i khārij*), where philosophy has always been taught in Persia, remained a gift of the mind and spirit given to those in quest of that type of knowledge. In my humble way I have tried to continue this tradition to the extent possible in the contemporary context. 'Aṣṣār died in his early nineties in 1974, living until his last days in meditation, reading Ibn Sīnā, Suhrawardī, Mullā Ṣadrā, and other traditional authorities, and receiving students. I used to visit him on a weekly basis even when he was ill and confined to his house in order to ask philosophical as well as personal questions, for he was for me not only a major teacher in the Islamic sciences, especially metaphysics, but also a second father whom I had known since my earliest childhood.

In the fall of 1958, shortly after meeting Dhu'l-Majd Ṭabāṭabā'ī, I was invited by him to come to his beautiful Persian garden in northern Tehran, where our classes with Sayyid Muḥammad Kāẓim 'Aṣṣār were held, to meet another of the major intellectual luminaries of that day, 'Allāmah Sayyid Muḥammad Ḥusayn Ṭabāṭabā'ī, with whom an immediate relationship developed for the next twenty years. I was to study with him various texts of

Islamic philosophy and Sufism as well as comparative philosophy which meant dealing with works of other traditions including the *Tao Te Ching* and the Upaniṣads. 'Allāmah Ṭabāṭabā'ī hailed from a well-known family of religious scholars from Tabriz and like many other scholars had studied in Najaf. The communist takeover of Iranian Azerbaijan during the Second World War had driven him to Qom, the religious center of Iran, where he settled and where he died in his early eighties in 1982. This venerable teacher was a person of great saintly presence who exuded a sense of silence and an air of inwardness in his immediate surroundings. He had not only studied philosophy and gnosis in his youth, but also spent years in spiritual practice which included long periods during which he observed silence. True to the Platonic ideal of the philosopher, he had for long practiced dying and was in fact already a dead person walking, dead to all the passions of the soul. He spoke little and rarely raised his head. And yet he was one of the greatest philosophers and religious scholars of his day. He revived Islamic philosophy in Qom and trained a number of younger philosophers some of whom were to gain great eminence later. After the Second World War, when the Marxists exercised much influence in Iran, he challenged the Marxists to an intellectual debate and wrote his major philosophic opus *Falsafah wa rawish-i ri'ālism* ("Philosophy and the Method of Realism"), as an in-depth critique of dialectical materialism from the point of view of Islamic philosophy and especially the school of Mullā Ṣadrā with which he identified himself. This unique work, including the commentaries of the most famous of his traditional students, Murtaḍā Muṭahharī, has had considerable philosophical influence since its composition. 'Allāmah Ṭabāṭabā'ī also wrote the most extensive Quranic commentary of this century, *Tafsīr al-mīzān* ("The Commentary of the Balance") and edited with his own commentary the new edition of Mullā Ṣadrā's monumental *al-Asfār al-arba'ah* ("The Four Journeys"), which I studied with him for years.

The 'Allāmah would come to Tehran every other weekend and we had our classes with him on Thursday evenings and Friday mornings. Occasionally I would go to Qom to study and discuss philosophical matters with him. His summers were often spent in Darakah, a village at the foot of the mountains north of Tehran. During one summer I studied alone with him some of the *ghazals* of Ḥāfiẓ whose esoteric significance he would reveal in such profundity that it seemed that the walls of his humble house were speaking in unison with him. Altogether I was to learn much about philosophy and spirituality from him and I participated in many projects with him. Foremost among these were the many years of intellectual discourse between him and Henry Corbin in which I was the main translator in both an intellectual and a linguistic sense.

Each fall Corbin would come to Tehran for three months during which we would have sessions of intellectual discourse with the 'Allāmah at the house of Dhu'l-Majd. Corbin would usually pose some pertinent philosophical questions which had been discussed at the Eranos meetings in Switzerland or in philosophical circles in Paris the year before. Then a major discussion would ensue for which I usually translated from French into Persian and vice versa, often adding my own commentary. This task was also performed sometimes by 'Īsā Sepahbodī, professor of aesthetics and French literature at Tehran University, and also by Dariush Shāyegān, Indologist, philosopher, and friend, who joined our circle early in the '60s. Many other outstanding thinkers participated in these private gatherings, including Muṭahharī, and also from time to time the eminent authority on Sufism, Badī' al-Zamān Furūzānfar. Certainly no intellectual exchange had taken place on such a high philosophical level between the West and the Islamic World since the Middle Ages. These twenty years of intellectual exchange were to result in several publications as well as in the spread of serious interest in comparative philosophy in Persia to which 'Allāmah Ṭabāṭabā'ī himself was much attracted. That is why after the departure of Corbin to France, we would often choose a text of Eastern or Western metaphysics and make it a basis of comparative discourse with the 'Allāmah. One year in fact Shāyegān and I translated most of the *Tao Te Ching* into Persian for this purpose, a translation which was later lost as a result of the destruction of Shāyegān's library in a fire.

When Kenneth Cragg established the center for the global study of religion at Colgate University in America and helped in the founding of the Center for the Study of World Religions at Harvard University, with which I have been connected since its founding, he sought to commission authentic works on various religions of the world and to this end came to Iran to seek my help in preparing three works on Shi'ism. I accepted the invitation and went to 'Allāmah Ṭabāṭabā'ī for help. The result of this cooperation was the book *Shī'ah dar islām* (edited and translated by myself into English from the original Persian as *Shi'ite Islam*) which appeared in 1975 and which remains to this day one of the most popular works on Shi'ism in both Persian and English. As part of this project the 'Allāmah also wrote *Qur'ān dar islām* ("The Quran in Islam") which has also appeared with my introduction in English and Persian, and made a selection of the sayings of the Shi'ite Imams which were to be rendered into English by William Chittick as *A Shi'ite Anthology* again with an introduction by me. This trilogy was to make 'Allāmah Ṭabāṭabā'ī known in Western circles concerned with Islamic thought and also in many other Islamic countries. In the mid-'70s I suggested to 'Allāmah Ṭabāṭabā'ī that he should write a new work on Islamic philosophy to be used as a text for the teaching of the subject in traditional circles. After much insistence on my part, he accepted the task and composed the two short but masterly texts: *Bidāyat al-ḥikmah* ("The

Beginning of Philosophy/Wisdom") and *Nihāhat al-ḥikmah* ("The End of Philosophy/Wisdom") which continue to enjoy great popularity in Iran to this day.

I saw 'Allāmah Ṭabāṭabā'ī for the last time in Tehran in the turbulent days of the fall of 1978. I shall never forget his profound gaze at the moment of our farewell. Later after the Revolution, while he was being much celebrated in Iran (a university was even named after him), he sent me a message saying how happy he was that I was outside the country away from the prevading turmoil. On his deathbed he called one of my friends and asked him to tell me to keep the torch of traditional philosophy burning while I was in that far away land of America.

The third of my main traditional teachers in Islamic philosophy and gnosis was Sayyid Abu'l-Ḥasan Qazwīnī who was a venerable man in his late seventies when I first met him in the early '60s in Tehran. He had a more official and formal religious function than either 'Aṣṣār or Ṭabāṭabā'ī and was in fact a "grand *āyatollāh*" at a time when few scholars in Iran possessed even the title of *āyatollāh*. Early in his life he started teaching in Qom and could count among his students Āyatollāh Khomeini himself. Although a formidable authority in Islamic Law, his great love was the so-called intellectual sciences (*al-'ulūm al-'aqliyyah*) at the heart of which stands philosophy. An expert in traditional mathematics and astronomy, he spent most of his teaching efforts in the domain of the philosophy of Mullā Ṣadrā which he taught in a thorough and incomparably detailed fashion during the fall season in Tehran and the rest of the year, at least off and on, in Qazwin, a city some one hundred miles northwest of the capital. For five years I studied the *Asfār al-arba'ah* ("The Four Journeys") with him in Tehran and also made numerous journeys to Qazwin often with one of his choice students, Sayyid Jalāl al-Dīn Āshtiyānī, who is one of the leading philosophers of Iran today, as well as with other scholars. I have met no one who was as good a systematic teacher of the text of the *Asfār* as he. I owe much to him for clarifying some of the most difficult aspects of Ṣadrian metaphysics and epistemology especially those concerning the question of God's knowledge of creation.

Sayyid Abu'l Ḥasan Qazwīnī wrote little and spent nearly all of his time teaching as well as addressing the religious needs of the community. He had an aura of majesty and exuded a sense of great intellectual power which reminded me often of what I had read about Naṣīr al-Dīn Ṭūsī, who was also an outstanding mathematician as well as a philosopher. The master from Qazwin, who usually bore a severe countenance, took a liking to me and agreed to write a few short treatises for me on specific questions of philosophy that I would pose to him. During each journey to Qazwin I would pose a specific question and then he would write the answer in a notebook which he then gave to me during our next visit. In this manner a number of short treatises were collected, all written in exquisite Persian and dealing in simple language with some of the most complicated issues of traditional philosophy. Fortunately before the Revolution I lent this notebook to the well-known scholar Moḥammad Taghī Dāneshpazhūh of the Central Library of Tehran University who made a photocopy of it for their collection, because with the loss of my library during the Revolution in 1979, this precious notebook was also lost at least to me. I was pleasantly surprised to see these treatises edited and published in later years by important philosophical figures including one of the foremost authorities in traditional philosophy in Iran today, Seyyed Ḥasan Ḥasanzādeh Āmulī. Āyatollāh Qazwīnī himself died in the mid-'70s.

Besides these three main figures with whom I studied traditional philosophy for two decades, there are a few others whom I need to mention with whom I either studied briefly or carried out philosophical exchange. One of these figures, a venerable teacher, poet, and saintly figure, was Mahdī Ilāhī Qumsha'ī, who taught Islamic philosophy at the Faculty of Theology of Tehran University and was the author of a well-known two-volume work on philosophy, *Ḥikmat-i ilāhī khāṣṣ wa 'āmm* ("Divine Wisdom/philosophy [or theosophy in its original sense] General and Particular"). Besides studying this work with him for some time, I also studied *al-Insān al-kāmil* ("Universal Man"), the famous text of Sufi metaphysics by 'Abd al-Karīm al-Jīlī, with this gentle master who would turn to the themes of Divine Love and union no matter with what text he would begin.

In contrast to him Jawād Muṣliḥ, also professor at the same Faculty of Theology and from the school of Shiraz, was given to rigorous logical and philosophical discourse and had a highly logical and analytical mind. He had become known for his fine translations into Persian of sections of Mullā Ṣadrā's *Asfār* and other works of the Safavid master especially *al-Shawāhid al-rūbubiyyah* ("Divine Witnesses") which was published after the Revolution when he migrated to America. I studied with him not Mullā Ṣadrā but rather sections of *Sharḥ al-ishārāt* ("The Commentary Upon the Book of Directives and Remarks [of Ibn Sīnā]") by Naṣīr al-Dīn Tusi. This is one of the most logically rigorous texts of Islamic philosophy which played the major role in the resuscitation of the Peripatetic philosophy of Ibn Sīnā after its criticism by the Ash'arite theologians such as al-Ghazzālī and especially Fakhr al-Dīn al-Rāzī, for whose criticisms of Ibn Sīnā Ṭūsī provides a sentence-by-sentence reply in this work.

There were also a number of younger traditional Islamic philosophers with whom I carried out philosophical discussion. Among this group I must mention first of all Murtaḍā Muṭahharī, a close friend, who had been the choice student of 'Allāmah Ṭabāṭabā'ī and who was also a professor at the Faculty of Theology at Tehran University. Muṭahharī, while being a religious activist, was also a gifted thinker much interested in providing answers drawn from Islamic philosophy to questions posed by modern Western philosophy. Unfortunately he did not know any European languages well enough to be able to make use of Western philosophical writings directly and so he relied on translation of works of European philosophy in Persian and Arabic, much of which is very faulty. He would therefore often spend time with me discussing various theses of Western thought and we also cooperated together on a few scholarly projects as well as educational activities, which included our joint participation in and subsequent resignation from the famous religious center Ḥusayniyya-yi Irshād. I also consulted Muṭahharī when the Academy of Philosophy was established, and he remained one of its advisors to the end. When the Revolution came, he joined it wholeheartedly, having been a student of Āyatollāh Khomeini years before in Qom, and became in fact the head of the Revolutionary Council. In the short period that he held that position he tried to protect educational and intellectual elements as much as possible, but soon after the Revolution he was assassinated, leaving unfinished a notable intellectual and philosophical career.

Another figure with whom I had a close friendship and shared philosophical interests was Sayyid Jalāl al-Dīn Āshtiyānī, a classmate of Muṭahharī in Qom, who became professor of Islamic philosophy at Mashhad University in Khorasan where he still teaches. A prolific author and editor, he has revived numerous major texts of Islamic philosophy usually with his own commentary and substantial introductions which have clarified many chapters of the history of the philosophical tradition of Persia. At my suggestion he participated with Corbin in the preparation of a seven-volume anthology of Islamic philosophy in Persia from the Safavid period to the present day. Four volumes of this vast work entitled *Anthologie des philosophes iraniens depuis le XVIIe siècle jusqu'à nos jours* appeared before Corbin's death in 1978 put an end to this joint effort with which I was involved at nearly every stage. I usually wrote English but occasionally both English and Persian introductions to the numerous works that Āshtiyānī edited and published. If I were to put these introductions together they would constitute a small volume in themselves. I travelled to Mashhad often to plan with Āshtiyānī various projects involving Islamic philosophy and also sent him many students, not only Persian and Arab, but also Western and Japanese, many of whom have become authorities in the field of Islamic philosophy and gnosis.

Finally, among the philosophers who belonged to the generation following that of my own traditional masters of Islamic thought, I must mention Mahdī Ḥā'irī Yazdī. From a famous family of Shi'ite scholars, this venerable thinker studied first in Qom and, after becoming a recognized authority in both Islamic Law and philosophy, set out for the West where he studied analytical philosophy for fifteen years, attaining his doctorate in Western philosophy. He also taught for some time at Oxford, Harvard, the University of Toronto, Georgetown University, and elsewhere. After Sayyid Muḥammad Kāẓim 'Aṣṣār, he was the first person from the class of the '*ulamā*' to have had training in both traditional Islamic philosophy and Western philosophy and the first to have turned his attention to analytic philosophy. He is the author of a number of important works dealing with the confrontation of Islamic philosophy and Western analytic philosophy. We have been close friends for many years and I have always been interested in having his works become known in Western philosophical circles. He resided in the suburbs of Washington, DC for many years after the Revolution and it was here that after many discussions I embarked in consultation with him upon the editing of one of his major works, which had been already rendered into English, but which needed to be seriously edited in order to be published by a reputable press in the West. The result of this effort was his book *The Principles of Epistemology in Islamic Philosophy* with my foreword which has been well received among a number of American philosophers. Ḥā'irī Yazdī, suffering from Parkinson's disease, has now returned to Iran, but he continues to write and teach a new generation of students interested in Islamic philosophy in its relation to various strands of Western philosophical thought, especially analytic philosophy, and the challenge it poses for traditional Islamic philosophy. Ḥā'irī Yazdī is in fact one of the pioneers in the opening of a new chapter in the tradition of Islamic philosophy, and it is precisely in this effort that we have collaborated together for many years even if we do not necessarily agree on the interpretation of all philosophical issues and on the significance of analytic philosophy itself.

While discussing the period between my return to Iran in 1958 and the Revolution of 1979 when I left the country, it is necessary to mention two major intellectual figures who were not Persians but whom I met and with whom I had close philosophical association in Persia, these men being Henry Corbin and Toshihiko Izutsu. I had already read many of the celebrated French philosopher and Islamicist's works while at Harvard, especially his *Avicenna and the Visionary Recital* whose interpretation of Avicenna's mystical philosophy I followed closely in my doctoral thesis. Soon upon returning to Tehran in 1958, I met Corbin and his wife Stella, who has done so much since his death to make the works of her husband available publicly. In the '50s, besides being a professor at the Sorbonne and holder of the chair of Islamic studies of Louis Massignon at the Ecole des Haute Etudes, Corbin was also director of the section on Iranian Studies or *iranologie*, at the Institut Franco-iranien in Tehran and therefore would spend every fall season in Iran.

A very close association was created between us immediately, one which would last until his death in 1978. We taught together a doctoral seminar in philosophy at Tehran University for some fifteen years and participated in the bi-weekly philosophical sessions with ʻAllāmah Ṭabāṭabāʼī for almost two decades. We carried out major scholarly projects together including the writing of *Histoire de la philosophie islamique* which became very popular and which has been translated into almost every major European and Islamic language. Furthermore, it was as a result of Corbin's insistence on bringing out a third volume to complement his two-volume edition of Suhrawardī's *Opera Metaphysica et Mystica* that I spent some eight years in editing Suhrawardī's Persian works to which Corbin wrote a long French prolegomena. The list of the fruits of our philosophical and scholarly collaboration is too long to cite here. Suffice it to say that it continued even after Corbin's retirement from the Sorbonne which coincided with my founding of the Iranian Academy of Philosophy. I invited Corbin to teach at the Academy and continue his philosophical research and teaching under its auspices. He accepted the invitation and was with us until the illness which led to his death.

I also met Corbin often in France where he acquainted me with his philosophical friends who ranged from Cardinal Jean Daniélou and Gabriel Marcel to Gaston Bachelard and Gaston Berger. Through Corbin I was also able to meet and have philosophical discussions with the younger generation of French philosophers who came to be known as the *nouveau philosophes*, including such men as Christian Jambet and Philippe Nemo. I lectured at the Sorbonne from time to time through Corbin's invitation and participated occasionally in conferences with him, one of the most interesting being the first conference ever organized on Shiʻism in Europe, a colloquium held in the University of Strasbourg in 1966.

Corbin was the first person to translate Heidegger into French, including his *Was ist das Metaphysik?* In fact Jean-Paul Sartre has expressed his debt to Corbin for introducing him to the thought of Heidegger. Later, upon discovering Islamic philosophy, especially the later schools which had developed an elaborate ontology, Corbin turned his interests from the *Existenz Philosophie* to the metaphysics of Being of a figure such as Mullā Ṣadrā. In his French introduction to Mullā Ṣadrā's *Kitāb al-mashāʻīr* which he had translated as *Le Livre des pénétrations métaphysiques*, Corbin dealt brilliantly with the divergence of the paths of Western and Islamic philosophies as far as the understanding of *wujūd/esse* was concerned.

During the Strasbourg colloquium, one day Corbin and I took a walk to Mont St. Odile, the church and mausoleum of the tenth-century saint who had brought Christianity to that region of northern Europe. We stood on the hill where the mausoleum is located, behind us France and before us the Black Forest and Germany. Corbin put his arms around my shoulders and said that when he was young he had descended from the trail stretching now before us to go to Fribourg to meet Heidegger. Then he added with a smile, "Now that I have a Shi'ite philosopher standing by my side, I do not need to descend on that path again."

Corbin was the first major philosopher in modern Europe to have been also an Islamicist and his works are of major philosophical as well as scholarly importance. We shared together intense interest in esoterism and gnosis (in its original sense of illuminative knowledge and not the theological heresy associated with gnosticism), in Islamic philosophy and Sufism, in pre-Islamic Persian thought, in Platonism, Hermeticism, and alchemy, in the Western esoteric tradition, and in general philosophies which have been concerned with the world of the Spirit. We both had a disdain for historicism (and of course not history or the "historial") and I always repeated to Corbin my complete agreement with him that the time had come to write the "anti-history of anti-philosophy" in the West.

But we also had important philosophical differences. I was and remain a traditionalist whereas, while Corbin like myself defended the *philosophia perennis*, he had an aversion to the teachings of the main representatives of the traditionalist school, especially Guénon. He appreciated the writings of Schuon more and was especially happy about the latter's severe criticism of Teilhard de Chardin who had become popular in certain Catholic circles in the '60s. In a sense Corbin was a great defender of many aspects of traditional teachings without being a traditionalist strictly speaking.

This difference between us came out especially when we discussed Carl Gustav Jung. For years Corbin attended the Eranos annual conferences held in Ascona, Switzerland and attended by many eminent scholars from Louis Massignon to Ernst Benz and Gershom Scholem. Originally, however, the meetings were arranged around Jung and were especially concerned with his work. Like other traditionalists, I believe that Jung did not at all understand the transcendent and spiritual nature of myths and symbols which he "psychologized," substituting the "collective unconcious" for the "Divine Treasury" which is the source of all veritable symbols. Corbin, on the contrary, kept insisting that although outwardly Jung had spoken of the collective unconscious, privately he shared the traditional perspective. In any case Corbin and I continued to have important divergences of views considering Jung and many other modern figures and ideas.

Altogether my long association with Corbin played an important role in my philosophical life, not in determining its framework and foundation which remained in traditional metaphysics and the perennial philosophy, but in addressing certain specific issues and in carrying out particular projects of a scholarly and philosophical nature. I always considered Corbin's writings to be of importance not only as a means for the rediscovering of important elements of the Islamic philosophical tradition, but also for contemporary Western philosophy as well as comparative philosophy. That is why I edited a major *Festschrift* for him and also asked him to prepare a work on comparative philosophy for our Academy. The book entitled *Philosophie iranienne et philosophie comparée* was published by the Academy in 1977 and was to be one of the last of his works to see the light of day during his own lifetime.

Strangely enough, Corbin was also to exercise considerable influence in the revival of interest in Islamic philosophy in Iran itself while turning the attention of Persians to the non-rationalistic and non-positivistic currents of Western philosophy. Since among modernized Orientals, including my countrymen, there is often an inferiority complex vis-à-vis the West, and they are mesmerized by whatever they hear from Western sources, Corbin served an important function as an antidote to this illness and was a major aid to me in Iran in my attempt to revive Islamic philosophy on the one hand and to expand the horizons of the students of philosophy in understanding Western philosophy on the other. For two decades we were able to collaborate closely together, each facilitating the work of the other despite divergent views on certain fundamental issues. We were able to resuscitate interest in traditional philosophy in Persia and Islamic thought in the West to a much greater degree by working together on so many projects than we could have had we worked separately.

Once I asked Corbin how he would describe himself philosophically. He said, "I am a phenomenologist but I use this term in the traditional sense of one who carries out the process of *kashf al-maḥjūb*." This well-known Arabic term means literally "removing the veil of that which is veiled." Corbin was a spiritual hermeneut who saw the role of the true philosopher as having the ability to bring out the inner or hidden meaning of things. He devoted his life to this task, especially to the understanding of the inward meaning of the imaginal and angelic worlds, and produced a vast corpus of writings which deal with the deepest teachings of the Islamic and Western philosophical traditions with which my own philosophical life has been also concerned to a large extent. And like myself, Corbin always saw the real philosopher as the person who combines theoretical and experiential knowledge, the perfection of mental and intellectual faculties and purification of one's being, the philosopher whom one of Corbin's and my own intellectual mentors, Shaykh al-ishrāq Shihāb al-Dīn Suhrawardī, was to describe so luminously in his many writings to which we both devoted so many years of our lives.

My relationship with Izutsu, the unparalleled Japanese Islamicist and philosopher, was not as extensive as that which I had with Corbin but was nevertheless significant. Like Corbin, Izutsu was at once a philosopher and an outstanding Islamicist but from a Zen Buddhist rather than Western Christian background. Izutsu was a remarkable linguist, a master of not only

Chinese and Japanese, Sanskrit, Arabic, and Persian, but also many of the Western languages both classical and modern. His first interests in Islamic studies were in fact linguistic and he made outstanding studies of the linguistic structure of the Quran and the language of Islamic theology which first brought him to the attention of the scholarly public outside of Japan. After our first meeting at McGill University in 1962 where he was teaching at the time and his attendance at my lecture on Mullā Ṣadrā, he decided to turn his attention to Islamic philosophy and gnosis. He subsequently devoted the rest of his life mostly to their study, although he did also write on Taoism and Zen Buddhism. He wrote a number of outstanding works on Islamic thought including a comparative study of Lao-Tzu and Ibn 'Arabī in his *Taosim and Sufism* and *Creation and the Timeless Order of Things* comprised of a number of essays on metaphysics, some based on our extensive discussions. He also edited a number of important Islamic philosophical texts with the Persian scholar of philosophy and theology, Mehdī Moḥaghegh.

I remained closely associated with Izutsu from 1962 until the Iranian Revolution of 1979 and visited him in Japan. We also attended many international conferences together. Furthermore, he introduced my work to the Japanese audience by arranging for the translation of my *Three Muslim Sages* into Japanese and its publication by the famous publisher Iwanami which had also published so many of his works on Islamic studies in Japanese and which also published in 1997 his *Festschrift* entitled *Consciousness and Reality* for which I wrote the preface as well as contributed an essay on Mullā Ṣadrā.

When the Academy of Philosophy was established, I invited him to join its faculty, an invitation which he accepted happily. Here he taught both Islamic and Far Eastern philosophy and, upon my insistence, wrote an outstanding work on Zen "philosophy." He told me that although Zen was opposed to ordinary philosophical speculation, it nevertheless possessed a philosophy in the deeper sense of the term and therefore entitled his book *Toward a Philosophy of Zen Buddhism*. Also in the '70s upon the discovery of the old manuscript of the Tao-Te Ching in an imperial archaeological site in China, Izutsu suggested that we translate this work into Persian together. For over a year he and I would sit together in the beautiful garden of the Academy to translate the newly discovered text into Persian. He would first translate the text from Chinese to English. Then I would translate the English into Persian. Finally I would read the Persian and he would compare it with the original Chinese and together we would make whatever final corrections were necessary. In this way we not only produced a Persian translation but also an English one as a side product. I also took into full consideration his commentaries in making my Persian translation. When I left Iran in January of 1979, ostensibly for a couple of weeks but in reality not to return again, this text was the only one of my works in progress that I took with me because I thought I could work on it on the plane and other occasions during the journey in order to prepare it for publication. I therefore still have the text although it has not as yet seen the light of day.

I learned much about Far Eastern philosophies as well as the aesthetics associated with Japanese culture from Izutsu. I still recall his wonderful lecture to me on Buddhist aesthetics as we walked in the beautiful gardens of Kamakura in 1970 when I had gone to Japan to lecture on the occasion of the Osaka World Fair. I also benefited from his life long meditations upon the relation between language and meaning or semantics in general especially as it concerned religious and philosophical texts. In as much as the state of the knowing subject has an effect upon one's manner of knowledge according to the famous dictum of Aristotle, "knowledge is according to the mode of the knower," Izutsu's coming from a Zen rather than Western religious and philosophical background and yet dealing with the same Islamic philosophical texts as dealt with by Western scholars was of much interest to me and taught me a great deal about the parameters and modes of comparative philosophy in which Izutsu was certainly one of the masters of his day.

Finally, before leaving my activities in Iran, it is necessary to give an account of the foundation of what was formally known as the Imperial Iranian Academy of Philosophy, an institution which was Iran's most important center of philosophical activity before the Iranian Revolution and which, having survived the Revolution, continues to play that role in today's Iran. In 1973 I was elected a member of the Institut International de Philosophie, a great honor in the realm of philosophy which did not go unnoticed among the general Iranian public. Soon thereafter, Raymond Klibansky, who is a former president of the Institut, visited Tehran and I arranged for him to have an audience with the Shahbanou. During the audience he suggested to her that Persia had been a great center of philosophical activity throughout history and now that a Persian had been chosen as a member of the Institut it would be a good idea to create a center for the study and propagation of philosophy under her patronage. She responded warmly to this suggestion and I was left in charge of establishing such a center. I consulted with many Persians concerned with philosophy as well as with Corbin, Klibansky himself, and a few others outside Persia. Maḥmūd Shahābī, one of Iran's venerable traditional philosophers, suggested that this center should be an academy directly under royal patronage and independent of any university or government organization. Corbin suggested that the academy should be called *impériale* and not *royale*, repeating the German *kaiserlich* in conjunction with the old academy in Berlin. All these suggestions were presented to the Shahbanou as well as to the Shah himself and finally the name *anjuman-i shāhanshāhī-yi falsafa-yi īrān* or the Imperial Iranian Academy of Philosophy was chosen, its by-laws and regulations written and approved, and a generous budget set aside for it.

Rather than building a new edifice for it, I decided to find an old mansion in the middle of the city which could be renovated, thus preserving some of the old buildings in the city and providing the Academy with an ambience of traditional continuity (and history). After some searching I found an old mansion with a beautiful Persian garden that had belonged to Luqmān al-Mulk Mālik, a famous physician and political figure who had died a few years earlier. We also purchased some of the surrounding houses. I brought traditional craftsmen from Isfahan and Tehran to create a completely traditional interior replete with blue tiles and traditionally designed furniture. Soon a beautiful complex dedicated to the study of philosophy was created in the heart of Tehran.

A number of eminent Iranians were chosen as members of the governing board of the Academy including ʻAbdollāh Enteẓām, Yaḥyā Mahdavī, Mehdī Moḥaghegh, Maḥmūd Shahābī, and the traditional philosophers Muṭahharī and Āshtiyānī were among its advisors. The Academy also elected a number of foreign fellows including Raymundo Panikkar, T. M. P. Mahadevan, A. K. Saran, Carmen Blacker, Andrei Bertels, Huston Smith, Naquib al-Attas, and Élemire Zolla. I received a royal edict (*farmān*) as the president of the Academy and early in 1974 we began our activities. I chose Hādī Sharīfī, a very close friend and colleague at Tehran University who was a specialist in the philosophy of education, as the deputy director, and together we soon organized the administrative staff and began to build a major library which would soon become the best library for the field of philosophy, including both Islamic and Western, in the country. Thanks to the support of the Shahbanou, we were able to receive the funds needed to purchase, along with works in Persian and Arabic, nearly all the primary texts of Western philosophy as well as a great number of secondary sources especially in English and French but also in German.

My plan for the Academy was to provide an ambience of study and research but not a degree program. Rather, we would give a certificate to students who either had a doctorate or were about to receive one elsewhere. Our regular teaching staff included Corbin, Izutsu, William Chittick, and myself as well as a number of traditional philosophers such as Shahābī, Muṣliḥ, and Hā'irī Yazdī. We also invited philosophers and scholars from both East and West for seminars or lecture series. We offered fellowships for both short-term research and longer periods of study in either Islamic philosophy or comparative philosophical studies. We were soon to have some thirty advanced students from all over the world, many of whom went on to become notable scholars and thinkers.

The Academy also undertook an ambitious publication program and produced some fifty titles in English as well as Persian and Arabic during the five years of its existence before the Revolution. The publications included important texts by Corbin, Izutsu, Bruce Lawrence, Peter Wilson, who edited the proceedings of the conference in Rothko Chapel (in Houston, Texas) on contemplation and action in world religions, and many others. Among the outstanding achievements of the Academy in the domain of publications were five books on Ismā'īlī thought including the first edition of one of the fundamental texts of Ismā'īlī philosophy, the *A'lām al-nubuwwah* ("Peaks of Prophecy"), edited by Ṣalāḥ al-Sāwī, the distinguished Egyptian poet and scholar, and an accomplished Persian philosopher, Gholām Rezā A'vānī, a former student of mine who is now president of the Academy.

The Academy also began a multi-language journal, *Sophia perennis,* edited by Hādī Sharīfī and Peter Wilson, which in its short four years of existence gained international fame and included articles by traditionalists and perennialists such as Frithjof Schuon, Marco Pallis, Élemire Zolla, Brian Keeble, Leo Schaya, Philip Sherrard, Whitall N. Perry, Ananda K. Coomaraswamy, and Jean Canteins, well-known philosophers and scholars such as Corbin, Izutsu, Josef von Ess and Michael Lowe, critics of the modern world such as Ivan Illich, and poets and literary figures such as Kathleen Raine, Jorge Luis Borges, Cristina Campo, Peter Wilson, Peter Russell, and Vernon Watkins along with some of the most famous Persian scholars and philosophers. *Sophia perennis* became a unique forum for the encounter between the philosophies of East and West as well as tradition and modernism and nothing has quite filled the void which resulted from its demise in 1979.

Despite the demise of *Sophia perennis*, the Academy has continued to function since the Revolution on the foundation which I laid in the '70s and has even expanded its activities in some domains, but it has not been able to recreate the international ambience of the earlier years when some of the most gifted philosophical minds, both young and old, and from East and West were able to investigate, study, and debate the perennial questions and answers of philosophy as well as the challenges cast before all thinking human beings by the modern world.

The international character of the Academy was brought home to the Iranian world when the Institut International de Philosophie met in Iran in 1975, this being the first time it had ever held its meeting in the Islamic world. The Academy was the host and took advantage of this occasion to present some of the foremost philosophers of the West as well as of the rest of Asia to the Iranian public. Some of those who made the journey and gave discourses in the conference, which was held in Mashhad rather than Tehran, included M. Mahadevan, André Mercier, Juan Antonio Nuño, Fernand Brunner, Jean Ladrière, Jerzy Pelc, Emmanuel Levinas, Paul Ricoeur, Seizo

Ohe, Raymundo Panikkar, Raymond Klibansky, Richard McKeon, Andreas von Melsen, Yvon Belaval, and others. The main theme was the meaning of philosophy itself and the use of logic therein, a subject to which I addressed myself both in my opening discourse and in later discussions. This conference and the activities of the Academy in general marked a turning point in the globalization of the concerns, goals and methods of philosophy as understood in the West until recently, a turning point with which I was happy to be associated. Having been chosen as a member of the directing committee of the Federation Internationale des Sociétés Philosophiques (FISP) in the late '70s and for a whole decade, I was able to pursue the goal of enlarging the horizons of philosophy and seeking to return it to its original sense of love of wisdom or *sophia* as this reality has manifested itself in diverse traditional climes. This endeavor continued even after my departure from Iran and separation from the activities of the Academy, whose founding I consider as one of my major achievements during the two decades of activity in Iran from 1958 to 1979.

ACTIVITIES ABROAD WHILE RESIDING IN PERSIA

During this period of residence in Persia, that is, from 1958 to 1979, my intellectual activities were of course far from being confined to my home country. On the contrary, I cultivated extensive contact with scholars and philosophers in many countries, lectured widely on nearly every continent, and published works in many lands and languages. My most extensive philosophical contacts within the Islamic world were with Pakistan which I visited some twenty times in the two decades of my residence in Tehran. Shortly after being appointed as professor at Tehran University, I made my first scholarly trip abroad and it was to Pakistan where I went to attend the Pakistan Philosophical Congress with whose activities I remained closely associated for the next decade. I tried and succeeded to some extent to give a more Islamic dimension in that country to a philosophical discourse which at that time was mostly based on the remnants of early twentieth-century British philosophy.

During these trips I met a number of leading Pakistani philosophers and thinkers with whom I remained closely associated over the years. They included Miān Muḥammad Sharīf, who was busy at that time editing the two-volume *A History of Muslim Philosophy* to which I was to contribute many essays, M. M. Aḥmad, professor of philosophy at the University of Karachi who was to succeed me as Aga Khan professor of Islamic studies at the American University of Beirut, Allāhbakhsh K. Brohi, one of Pakistan's leading intellectual and political figures and a close personal friend, Ishtiaque Ḥusayn Quraishī, historian and federal minister of education, C.

A. Qādir, the leading expert on analytic philosophy in Pakistan as well as nearly all of the philosophers of the younger generation who were to make a mark for themselves later, such as Saeed Shaykh, Bashīr Dār, and Intiṣār al-Ḥaqq. These contacts and the publication of many of my works in Pakistan as well as the Pakistani students who came to Iran to study with me caused my ideas to have influence in many circles in that country ranging from the philosophical to the scientific, and especially in circles concerned with Islamic science such as at the Hamdard University founded by Ḥakīm Muḥammad Sa'īd with whom I have collaborated in many projects since the 1960s. From the 1980s onward the Suheyl Academy, directed by Suheyl Umar, another close friend who is dedicated to the cause of traditional philosophy, has reprinted many of my books in English for the Pakistani audience while others have been translated into Urdu. The close link created with Pakistani intellectual circles from the late '50s has therefore continued to this day, and Pakistan remains one of the Islamic countries in which my philosophical ideas have had the greatest impact. The series of lectures given in that country during a forty-year period including the Iqbal Lecture, which is the most celebrated lecture in Pakistan and which I delivered in 1966, have helped to keep alive this close intellectual and philosophical contact.

As far as the Arab world is concerned, although my most intense spiritual contact during the earlier period of my life in that world had been with Morocco, during the period from 1958 to 1979 now under consideration, my intellectual and philosophical contact was mostly with Lebanon and to a lesser degree with Egypt, Saudi Arabia, and the Persian Gulf states. As far as Saudi Arabia and the Persian Gulf states are concerned, my contacts were mostly in the field of education and I provided advice in the founding of various centers and institutions of learning. An exception was the major international congress on Muslim education to which reference has already been made. As for Egypt, because of strained political relations, I could not travel there until the mid-'70s but over the years I had kept close contact with the leading Egyptian philosophers and scholars of Islamic philosophy especially Ibrāhīm Madkour, 'Abd al-Raḥmān Badawī, Abu'l-'Alā' al-Taftāzānī, and Georges C. Anawati. Occasionally an essay of mine would be published in Cairo, but in general my relation with the philosophical world there was not anywhere as significant as it was with a country such as Pakistan.

The case of Lebanon is quite different because I spent the whole academic year 1964–1965 as the first Aga Khan professor of Islamic studies at the American University of Beirut. The establishment of this chair was a daunting challenge and that year was one of the most difficult of my life. The university had been originally a Christian missionary school but had later become a center for the propagation of Arab nationalism and also Western secularism and humanism, which were taught with the same missionary zeal as in the days when Presbyterian missionaries were trying to spread the Gospels paradoxically among people who had heard the Good News two thousand years ago from Christ himself. Being a Persian and not an Arab and taking Islamic studies seriously placed numerous obstacles before my path. And yet it was a very fruitful year, intellectually speaking, during which I was able to write and complete my *Ideals and Realities of Islam* and *Islamic Studies* which came out later in the West in an expanded edition under the title *Islamic Life and Thought*. I was also able to meet and carry out intellectual discourse with many interesting figures from Edward S. Kennedy, the eminent authority on Islamic science who taught at the university, to Charles Malik, Lebanon's most famous philosopher and former foreign minister, to Sayyidah Fāṭimah Yashruṭiyyah, a great woman Sufi saint who was visited by lovers of Sufism from near and far. During this year I was also able to gain closer knowledge of the intellectual life of Lebanon and Syria through long conversations with groups as diverse as Catholic philosophers at St. Joseph University and Shi'ite intellectuals from southern Lebanon. Throughout the year in Beirut my closest companion was Yūsuf Ibīsh, who was not only an expert on Islamic political philosophy, but also on traditional philosophy in general.

The most prominent among the members of the category of Shi'ite intellectuals was Imam Mūsā Ṣadr, the religious and political leader of the Lebanese Shi'ites who was to leave an indelible mark upon the history of Lebanon in the '70s. Imam Mūsā Ṣadr was a member of one of those Shi'ite families which since the Safavid period , that is the sixteenth century, had had their home at once in the Jabal 'Āmil in southern Lebanon and Syria, Iraq and Persia. Imam Mūsā Ṣadr was himself a graduate of Tehran University and spoke Persian with the same facility as myself while his mother tongue was Arabic. He had studied with many of my own traditional teachers and was seriously interested in traditional philosophy while pursuing an activist agenda as the leader of the Lebanese Shi'ites. We became close friends and he would often come to my house both in Beirut and later in Tehran. I learned much about the intellectual scene in the Arab East from him. How tragic that he was to disappear mysteriously from the scene after a journey to Libya at a time when both Lebanon and Iran needed him so much. His great fame in the political domain has prevented most people from paying attention to his intellectual and philosophical aspects, whereas in fact he was the product of the same Shi'ite religious education that has always included a strong philosophical dimension.

During the years I lived in Iran I also made many journeys to Turkey, especially in the late '60s when I was the chairman of the governing board of a major cultural institute called the RCD (Regional Council for Development) Cultural Institute established by Iran, Pakistan, and Turkey. During this period, however, most of my contact was with Turkish scholars in the fields of history, the history of science, and literature such as Zekī Velīdī Togān, Aḥmad Ateś, Taḥsīn Yāzijī, and Aydīn Sāyilī, along with a number of authorities in Sufism foremost among them being ʻAbd al-Bāqī Gölpinārlī, as well as with the traditionalist Nūrī Arlāsez. I had, however, little contact with academic philosophical circles in Turkey at this time. This contact was to come in the '80s and '90s when I had migrated to America and after my books began to be translated into Turkish, a process that still continues, with over twenty volumes having been already translated. A whole group of younger Turkish philosophers and intellectuals have been influenced and are now assembled around these and other works dealing with the traditional perspective, especially as found in the writings of Guénon, Schuon, Burckhardt, and Martin Lings. These days I continue to have close association with such intellectual circles in Turkey and play a humble role in the philosophical life of the country.

Outside of the Islamic world but east of Persia most of my philosophical activity involved India, Japan, and Australia. Starting in 1961 when I first went to India until the Revolution of 1979, I visited India numerous times, lectured extensively there including giving the prestigious Āzād Memorial Lecture in 1975 in Delhi, the text of which was published in India as *Western Science and Asian Cultures*, visited many of its traditional sages, both Hindu and Muslim, and participated in several joint programs bearing on the subject of philosophy and culture as well as Hindu-Muslim relations. Long years of reading Guénon, Coomaraswamy, and Schuon, not to speak of Heinrich Zimmer, Alain Daniélou, and Mircea Eliade, had laid the groundwork for me to understand the metaphysics and art of that land. I was able to carry out philosophical and cultural discourse with many figures, both Hindu and Muslim. I met and exchanged philosophical views with S. Radhakrishnan when he was president of India. I was also close friends with well-known Hindu philosophers and scholars such as M. Mahadevan and A. K. Saran, who became associated with our Academy, Kotta S. Murty, and Kapila Vatsyayan, who later founded the Indira Gandhi Centre for the Arts in Delhi, and arranged the major conference on Time in 1995 which I attended after many years of absence from India. On the Muslim side I came to know almost all the important figures associated with the Islamic university known as Jamiah Melliah in Delhi such as Zākir Ḥusain, who also became president of India, ʻĀbid Ḥusayn, Humāyūn Kabīr, and the well-known Muslim philosopher Mīr Vahīduddīn. I also cooperated in several activities and lectured on Islamic thought in the Hamdard University near Delhi founded by Ḥakīm ʻAbd al-Ḥamīd, the famous traditional physician who is well acquainted with Avicennan medicine, and Syed Awṣāf ʻAlī who has devoted many studies to the relation between Islam and Hinduism and Islamic culture in the Indian context.

My philosophical activity in India involved either the exposition of later

Islamic philosophy starting with Mullā Ṣadrā, the four hundredth anniversary of whose birth was celebrated in Calcutta in 1961 with myself giving the keynote speech, or comparative philosophy in the light of the *philosophia perennis* and involving not only the Western and Islamic or Hindu philosophical traditions but all three. To this end I worked closely with Mahadevan and participated in a major conference devoted to this issue in Madras in 1972 in which scholars as far apart as Louis Gardet from France and Tu Wei-ming from China were to participate. It was here that I was to meet that young Chinese scholar for the first time. He is now a well-known authority in Neo-Confucian thought at Harvard and we have worked on several projects together in recent years related to the encounter between civilizations in general and the dialogue between Islam and Confucianism and their philosophies in particular, a process which continues to this day.

It was also while I was in Madras that Mahadevan arranged for me to meet one of the supreme spiritual figures of Hinduism, the Jagadguru of Kanchipuram (a town near Madras), a direct spiritual successor of Śaṅkarācharya who, like his predecessor, embodied in his being the eternal metaphysical truths of the Vedas, and especially Advaita Vedanta. I requested to see him and this request was granted but being outside of caste, I could not approach the venerable master closer than a distance of about forty feet where I sat on a designated spot on the ground wearing traditional Islamic dress. Soon he came into the garden near where I was sitting holding his staff in his hand and squatted at the appropriate distance from the carpet. He was then observing a fast of silence. He turned his eyes toward me and we looked at each other intently for some five or ten minutes which could have been a single moment or all eternity. Then he arose and with sign language expressed through a person who was with him his joy of seeing me and his happiness that through this encounter he saw that the deepest truths of the Vedanta and Sufism were the same. I have participated in many religious dialogues during the past four decades. None was as satisfactory and its positive fruit as clearly evident as that silent discourse through the language of unsaying with this supreme master of Hindu metaphysics. My contacts with India continued after the Revolution and some of my works have come out over the years in special Indian editions, but these contacts have not been as frequent and intense as they were when I lived in Tehran, when India was simply next door, and when I had numerous Indian students and visitors almost every season of the year.

My contacts with Japan were much more limited and mostly channeled through Izutsu. Although I did lecture in Japan in 1970 and have known many Japanese scholars and philosophers such as Tomonobu Imamichi, Masao Matsumato, Masao Abe, Shojun Bando, Shigeru Nakayama, who was a classmate at Harvard, and Yasushi Kosugi, a Japanese scholar of Islam and a traditionalist who has translated one of my books into Japanese, I have not had the time to lecture as often in Japan as I would have liked and have had to turn down many invitations. I am in fact known primarily in Japan for my works on Islamic thought and not for those on more general philosophical issues. Although there are a few exceptions, by and large Japanese philosophical thinkers in recent times have been most interested in modern Western philosophy and even when they have turned their attention to comparative philosophy, it has usually excluded Islamic philosophy, Izutsu being of course an outstanding exception. What I have learned about traditional Japanese thought, which has been of special interest to me, has come through Japanese scholars residing in the West such as Suzuki and also, as far as the Kyoto school is concerned, Masao Abe. Also over the years I have not trained many Japanese students but one of them at least, Sachiko Murata, who studied with me for many years in Iran has become a fine scholar of comparative philosophy and mysticism as demonstrated in her *The Tao of Islam* and her pioneering work in the comparison of Islamic and Confucian philosophies.

As for Australia, I spent a month there in 1970 delivering the Charles Strong Memorial Lectures throughout the continent from Darwin to Brisbane to the main central and southern cities and finally all the way west to Perth. During one month I delivered over twenty lectures, besides the Charles Strong Lecture itself, which was devoted to Sufism and was published in my *Sufi Essays*, and met many Australian philosophers and scholars of religious and Islamic studies. I have not been able to visit that land again but that journey followed by the continuation of contacts established at that time has preserved my relation with certain intellectual circles in Australia especially those interested in traditional metaphysics and the perennial philosophy.

Turning to the West, most of my intellectual contact while I lived in Iran was with America. Besides teaching in 1962 and 1965 at Harvard and conducting short seminars at Princeton and the University of Utah, I lectured extensively in many other universities from the East Coast to California. My closest contact, however, continued to be Harvard where I was involved with many aspects of the Middle Eastern program as long as Gibb was alive and with the Center for the Study of World Religions from the time of the directorship of Robert Slater and Wilfred Cantwell Smith onward. I had little contact with the philosophy department, but my contacts were nevertheless mostly in the philosophical domain, whether it was Islamic philosophy or the philosophy of religion. For example, Paul Tillich was teaching at Harvard when I was a visiting professor there in 1962 and having just come back from Japan with a new interest in religious diversity engaged me several times in discussions on comparative religion involving Christianity and Islam as well as the philosophy of religion in general. Also, many of the lectures I gave in different universities dealt with these subjects or with the question of the environmental crisis as far as its philosophical and spiritual dimensions were concerned, as did, for example, my Rockefeller Series Lectures at the University of Chicago mentioned already.

In America, besides scholars of religion and Islamic studies, there were also those concerned directly with philosophy with whom I established close contact. Foremost among them was Huston Smith with whom I have had, besides a close friendship, a continuous dialogue on the philosophy of religion, the philosophy of science, and perennial philosophy for over three decades. He remains to this day my closest intellectual companion and fellow wayfarer in the American academic world. Many discussions we have had together over the years have affected both his and my literary output. Also from the early '70s I have known and conversed intensely about philosophy and its meaning with Jacob Needleman. Our acquaintance goes back to the days when he planned *The Sword of Gnosis* which includes some of my essays. Later I was to lecture in San Francisco at an event sponsored by him and have been in continuous rapport with him over the years. I also had close relations with a number of Catholic philosophers and theologians from Fordham and the Catholic University of America such as Ewert Cousins and George McLean, whose invitation I accepted to become a member of the International Society for Metaphysics and Council for Research in Values and Philosophy.

During these years in Iran I also concerned myself with the expansion of Islamic and Iranian studies in America and my voice was decisive in providing financial help from Iran for Iranian studies and related fields to many American universities such as Princeton, the University of Utah, and the University of Southern California. But my effort was more intellectual than administrative. I helped in the planning of Islamic studies in many institutions and was often consulted on new appointments. I also lectured often on the subject of Islamic studies in general although most of my lectures concerned the philosophical dimensions of the subject as did for example, the Kevorkian Lectures on Islamic Art which I delivered in 1977 at New York University on the philosophy and meaning of Islamic art. The notes and text of these lectures were lost during the Iranian Revolution and therefore I was never able to publish the book containing the lectures which I planned to call *The Meaning of Islamic Art*. Perhaps one day that task can still be realized.

My contact with Wolfson continued to the end of his life and I even proposed to edit and bring out his book on Islamic philosophy but that project never materialized. During these years I also met and was in correspondence with the famous Jewish philosopher Abraham Heschel, with whom I saw eye to eye as to the meaning of philosophy and its role in religious life. Although I never met the Catholic mystic and theologian, Thomas Merton, we were in contact through our mutual friend Marco Pallis, and Merton had begun to read my books on Islam and Sufism toward the end of his life. He was in fact coming to Tehran to spend a month studying Sufism and discussing religious and mystical philosophy with me when his life came to a tragic end as a result of an accident in Southeast Asia.

As for the rest of the Americas, during the years of my stay in Iran I hardly had any contact with the Latin American world despite a few exchanges of letters with various philosophers and the translation of my *Man and Nature* into Portuguese in Brazil and Spanish in Argentina. More extensive contact was to come when I migrated to America about which more will be said later. But Canada was another matter. Since W. C. Smith, a friend and colleague, was the director of the McGill Institute of Islamic Studies, I made journeys to the Institute and was instrumental (on the basis of a proposal made by my uncle Nūr al-Dīn Kiā who was then our ambassador in Canada) in having Tehran University sign an agreement on the basis of which Mehdī Moḥaghegh, one of the Faculty of Letters' well-known professors and a specialist in Islamic thought, would be able to spend some time each year at McGill collaborating with Izutsu who, as already mentioned, had become intellectually "converted" to Islamic philosophy by the '60s. This cooperation led in turn to the establishment of the Tehran branch of the McGill Institute which has been responsible for a large number of important publications in the field of Islamic philosophy and logic.

This activity was to continue even after the retirement of Izutsu. To this day the McGill Institute in Montreal has a strong program in Islamic thought. Moreover, during the past decade the traditional schools in Qom have been sending some of their best students, who have spent years in the study of Islamic philosophy and theology, to the Institute to study Western philosophy and the humanities. This group, several of whose members are in touch with me, promises to produce and in fact has already produced some of the most gifted Iranian philosophers of the younger generation who know well both the Islamic and Western philosophical schools, and who are bound to make important contributions to various branches of philosophy as well as to comparative philosophy. I am glad to have had something to do with the foundation of this program. I did also have many discussions on comparative philosophy and what some call "world philosophy" with my old friend Klibansky as well as Venant Cauchy and several others among the Canadian philosophers.

From 1961 onward, after spending over three years completely in the East without wanting to travel to the West, I came nearly every year to Europe, sometimes more than once. The country I visited most regularly was Switzerland, but the purpose of my journeys there was almost always to visit Schuon, Burckhardt, and other expositors of traditional teachings. I also took advantage of the opportunity during these trips to climb extensively in the Alps which I came to know and to love dearly. I had practically no contact with Swiss universities and met with few Swiss professors except the philosopher Fernand Brunner, the Islamicist Fritz Meier, and his student Herman Landolt who later went to McGill and who, like his teacher, is an expert on Sufism and Islamic mystical philosophy, and Jacques Waardenberg who is a historian of religion. Upon being chosen a member of the Institut International de Philosophie, I also came to know André Mercier well and held many philosophical conversations with him.

The two countries in Europe with which I had the greatest intellectual contact were Britain and France and this has remained true during my years of exile in America. I had traveled to Britain often before returning to Persia in 1958, and so kept my contacts and expanded them with various intellectual circles there after returning home. I kept a close relationship with one of my closest spiritual and intellectual companions, Martin Lings, and also with Marco Pallis, Richard Nicholson, and other traditionalist authors and friends, and was involved from the beginning with the journal *Studies in Comparative Religion*, founded by C. Clive Ross, which was devoted to traditional metaphysics, cosmology, and comparative religion. I wrote often for the journal and my collaboration with it lasted until its demise in 1983.

My philosophical activities also involved many British universities. When Radhakrishnan retired from the Spalding Chair of Comparative Religion at Oxford, I was asked by the Spalding Trust which had established the chair if I were interested in occupying it. It would have been an honor and a wonderful opportunity for me to accept, but I did not show any interest at that time because I did not want to leave the Persian scene. That is also why, when W. C. Smith and Harry Wolfson asked me in 1962 to stay on at Harvard on a permanent basis, I turned down the offer despite being so closely associated with the university. In any case my relations with Oxford remained strong otherwise. I lectured there often, mostly on Islamic philosophy and Sufism, and met many times with Richard Walzer to discuss the relation between Greek and Islamic philosophy. I also lectured several times on Islam at St. Anthony's College and was a good friend of Albert Hourani who directed the Middle Eastern program there. This relationship was to continue upon my return to America. I gave a series of lectures on the present-day revival of Islamic thought on the occasion of the founding of the Oxford Center for Islamic Studies in 1987 and at Manchester College on the philosophical and religious dimensions of the environmental crisis in 1994. I did meet with some of the celebrated professors of philosophy from Oxford in various international conferences but not at Oxford itself.

As for Cambridge, I also lectured there often and had friends who shared my interest in the perennial philosophy and comparative studies in the Oriental Studies department, foremost among them the Sinologist Michael Lowe, and the Shinto specialist Carmen Blacker, who also lectured for us at the Academy in Tehran. For years I had also been involved in an intellectual debate with Joseph Needham concerning the meaning of "Oriental science."

I named my early book on Islamic science *Science and Civilization in Islam* as a humble response to his monumental *Science and Civilization in China* in which he politely took me to task for criticizing his understanding of "Oriental science," tinged as it was with Marxist and positivistic interpretations. We planned to have a public debate on this issue at Cambridge and later at Uppsala but that did not materialize.

When Cambridge University planned to bring out the *Cambridge History of Iran*, I played an active role on the Iranian side to provide intellectual and financial support and also to see to it that the Iranian view of its own history was also respected. I collaborated closely in this project with Peter Burbridge, the head of the Cambridge University Press, and also wrote extensively for volumes four and six on philosophy and the sciences in the early Islamic and Safavid periods. Although my contacts were never as extensive with Cambridge as with Oxford, they also continued after my exile and I have participated in a couple of important conferences there, including one arranged by Myles Burnyeat which dealt with the Biblical phrase, "I am that I am," as it has been understood philosophically and theologically in the three Abrahamic traditions. It remained for me in this conference to give the discourse on Islamic ontology.

The University of London has been also a point of contact for me over the years. I was closely associated with the philosopher Hywell D. Lewis from that university and gave several lectures there on philosophical issues chaired or arranged by him. Most of my contact, however, was with the School of African and Oriental Studies under whose auspices I have given numerous conferences and participated in many seminars over the years, an involvement which continues to this day, the last event being in 1997 when I gave a major talk on philosophy in Safavid Persia.

Since during the decades of living in Iran I was closely involved in the discussion in the West of the philosophy underlying comparative religion and comparative studies in general, I remained in close contact with scholars in this field in Britain as I did with scholars in America, where I had had many discussions on the subject with W. C. Smith, Huston Smith, Mircea Eliade, Raymundo Pannikar, and others. In Britain I had numerous debates and discussions over the philosophical and theological underpinnings of comparative religious, philosophical, and culture studies with a number of the leading figures in the field such as Robert C. Zaehner, Geoffrey Parrinder, Frank Whaling, and in more recent years John Hick with whom I have carried out a long debate on the philosophy of religion and the question of absoluteness and relativity of religious truth, a debate whose summary has been already published.

During these years in Iran I also shifted the focus of my publishing activities in the English language in the West from America to England because the British publishers were still much more capable than American ones in the distribution of books in Asia and Africa. After the Harvard University Press published my first three books, I began to publish my works with Allen Unwin which was later swallowed up by bigger publishers, with the process continuing for several years, and also with a number of other British publishers such as Thames & Hudson and Longmans. Unfortunately, the small, family publishing firms began to disappear in Britain as they had earlier in America, and therefore in the '80s and '90s I have shifted the main weight of my publishing activities back to America although I continue to publish works in Britain. But during the years up to the Iranian Revolution much of my time in England was spent on the various problems connected with the publication of my books.

Like Britain, France was a land which I had visited often before returning to Persia in 1958 and have continued to do so since the Revolution. I have been involved to some extent in French intellectual life for some four decades. Besides lecturing there from time to time, many of my books and articles have appeared in French, mostly translated and some written originally in that tongue, which was the first European language with which I had become acquainted as a child. Besides Corbin and his colleagues and students, some of whom I have already mentioned, I met and had many philosophical conversations with those philosophers who had some interest in traditional philosophies, learned through Corbin or otherwise, such as Gilbert Durand, who founded the *Centre pour l'Etude de l'Imaginaire*, Antoine Faivre, the first professor at the Sorbonne to teach officially the esoteric currents of Western philosophy, and Jean Servier, the anthropologist who wrote the remarkable work, *L'Homme et l'invisible*, asserting that the truth of the perennial quality of man's essential nature can be confirmed by a deeper study of anthropology itself. All of these thinkers are interested in the rediscovery of the traditional nature of man, of the *anthropos*, before he became reduced to a purely historical being determined from below by material forces and factors and finally reducible to the size of his cranium. I was also to have a more official contact with the philosophy section of UNESCO and I participated in many of their projects including their major colloquium on Aristotle held in Paris in 1978 whose proceedings appeared as *Penser avec Aristote* which contains an essay by me. Most of my association with UNESCO, however, has involved Islamic philosophy or it has been the case that I have provided the Islamic component on issues dealt with globally.

Of course, the Institut International de Philosophie is located in Paris and I also visited it from time to time after becoming a member. But our real philosophical activities occurred in our annual meetings elsewhere. Also in France I remained in contact with a number of the followers of the school of Guénon but never collaborated with the *Etudes Traditionnelles,* which was the main voice for traditional thought in France for many decades. As for other currents interested in tradition and the Orient, I met Jacques Masui and contributed to his important French journal *Hermès,* and also Jean Herbert, the famous French philosopher and student of the Orient, especially India, who was the editor of the well-known series *La spiritualité vivante* published by Albin Michel. I met him both in Paris and Tehran and he received my permission to translate my *Sufi Essays* himself for that collection. The work known as *Essais sur le soufisme* met with success and has had a long life in French, being still in print with the original publisher after some twenty-five years.

My intellectual contacts with Germany were more limited than with Britain and France because I journeyed less often to that land whose language I had studied at MIT and whose thinkers I had read carefully over many years. My contact with German orientalists was extensive and I had met most of the well-known ones either outside or inside Germany. Some I knew well personally such as Berthold Spuler, Joseph von Ess, Hans Roemer, Walter Hintz, and with a few I developed close friendships such as Jawād Falāṭūrī, the philosopher of Persian origin who was residing in Germany, and especially Annemarie Schimmel, who like myself has been intensely interested in Sufism, although not as much attracted to philosophy as I have been. She remains a close friend for whom I hold admiration. I also came to know a number of German philosophers such as Hans Gadamer and Jürgen Habermas, and theologians such as Hans Küng with whom I carried out major debates at Temple and Harvard Universities in America, the texts of which have been published. There were a number of German philosophers who were seriously interested in non-Western philosophical traditions with whom I also had many exchanges, chief among them being Alwin Diemer and Franz Joachim von Rintelen.

Although a number of my works have been translated into German, my contact with the German intellectual world has not been extensive and this truth also holds for the years after my exile. Nevertheless, during the past two decades I have participated in two major conferences in Germany, one in Hanover in 1987 on *Geist und Natur* in which I presented a paper on rationalism and its consequences for the relation between man and the natural environment and the necessity of developing a metaphysics that can encompass the rational without being rationalistic (the text of the paper was later published in German), and the second in Berlin in 1996 on the meaning of the term "religion" and whether such a concept is only a European invention.

My relations with Italy were intense for several years due mostly to my developing friendship with the Italian traditionalist writer Élemire Zolla and the Catholic traditionalist Christina Campo who was very active in the *Una Voce* and the attempt to preserve the Latin mass. Zolla was a major intellectual figure in Italy and knew all the philosophers who had some interest in traditional philosophy and metaphysics. He introduced me to the writings of the Italian philosopher Antonio Rosmini and his student Michele Federico Sciacca whom I met and with whom I had extensive discussions. I did also know other Italians more or less in the mainstream of Continental philosophy such as Evandro Agazzi, but in Italy most of my serious intellectual exchange was with the traditionalist circles of thinkers.

Although Zolla no longer associated with Julius Evola, he nevertheless arranged for me to meet Italy's most famous crypto-traditionalist writer who was a very controversial figure because of his espousal of the cause of Mussolini during the Second World War. I had already read some of Evola's works, many of which are now being translated into English and are attracting some attention in philosophical circles. But based on the image I had of him as an expositor of traditional doctrines including Yoga, I was surprised to see him, now crippled as a result of a bomb explosion in 1945, living in the center of Rome in a large old apartment which was severe and fairly dark and without works of traditional art which I had expected to see around him. He had piercing eyes and gazed directly at me as we spoke about knightly initiation, myths and symbols of ancient Persia, traditional alchemy and Hermeticism and similar subjects. While he extolled the ancient Romans and their virtues, he spoke pejoratively about his contemporary Italians. When I asked him what happened to those Roman virtues, he said they traveled north to Germany and we were left with Italian waiters singing *o sole mio!* He also seemed to have little knowledge or interest in esoteric Christianity and refused to acknowledge the presence of a sapiental current in Christianity. It was surprising for me to see an Italian sitting a few miles away from the Vatican, with his immense knowledge of various esoteric philosophies from the Greek to the Indian, being so impervious to the inner realities of the tradition so close to his home.

The leftist publisher Filtrenelli had already requested to bring out my *Science and Civilization in Islam* in Italian when the book first appeared and he did so without much delay. Later Zolla contacted Rusconi and through his good offices several of my books were published in Italian by this important publisher in the '70s and have continued to be reprinted over the years. I also collaborated closely with Zolla in the journal he published under the title *Conoscenza religiosa* to which I sent articles until the termination of publication of this rich and valuable review in 1983.

My other line of contact with Italy was through the Accademie dei Lincei whose president Enrico Cerulli I knew well and for which I lectured several times, and also through various departments of Oriental, Iranian, and Islamic studies in Italian universities. Most of the Italian orientalists were well known to me especially those who were concerned with philosophy and Oriental thought such as Giusseppi Tucci, Alessandro Bausani, and Pio Filippani-Ranconi. Traces of our scholarly and philosophical discussions can be found in the writings of both the Italian Islamicists/Iranists and myself. But my most important contact in Italy was with Zolla who was also active in our Academy in Tehran. Since the Revolution, all of those contacts have come to an end and although I correspond with some Italian traditionalists and some of them like Giovanni Monastra collaborate with the journal *Sophia,* which I help to publish in America and to which I shall turn later, my direct intellectual contact with Italy came more or less to an end with my migration to America in 1979.

In contrast to Italy, Spain has remained a homeland within the world of exile for me since 1979 and during the past two decades I have visited Spain numerous times, especially the south which still echoes eight centuries of Islamic presence. Before the Revolution I also visited Spain and was enraptured by Flamenco music, the arabesques of the Cordova Mosque ,and the cool gardens of Alhambra. But my intellectual contact there was rather limited, confined to the field of Islamic studies but not including philosophy in general. I had known the works of the famous Spanish orientalist Miguel Ásin Palacios and the historian of science Villás Vallicrosa. I kept some contact with their colleagues, students, and successors such as Garcia Gómez, Miguel Cruz Hernandez, and Juan Vernet, but my intellectual contact had not been extensive. In 1975 when the present King and Queen of Spain acceded to the throne, they asked me to inaugurate the new chapter in the relation between Spain and the Islamic world by delivering a lecture at the National University of Madrid which Queen Sophia herself attended. I spoke about cross-cultural studies and the significance of Spain under Muslim rule as a unique period when the three Abrahamic religions lived side by side and created one of the dazzling periods of human civilization, a period rich in spirituality, the arts, the sciences, and philosophy. This theme more than any other has determined my intellectual relation to the Spanish world.

In the '80s some of my books were translated into Spanish in Spain itself, and in the '90s the translation of some of my poems about Spain by the Puerto Rican scholar of comparative literature and dear colleague Luce López-Baralt, who has also written the introduction to a collection of my poems in English, met with success and now more and more of my essays are appearing in traditional journals in Spanish such as *Axis Mundi.* My main contribution intellectually in Spain has been to draw the attention of Spanish scholars to later Islamic philosophy, metaphysics, and gnosis, including the monumental work of Ibn 'Arabī who is now beginning to become known to the general Spanish public as the result of a process to which I have made a humble contribution.

As for the rest of Europe, my scholarly contact with the other countries was minor save for Sweden and Austria. I visited Sweden several times including once in 1972 at the invitation of Maurice Strong, the chairman of

Earth Day, which was then being celebrated as a global environmental event, to give a major lecture on the environment during the famous international conference which was held at that time in Stockholm. I also met at that time and also later the Swedish traditionalist writers such as Tage Lindbom. In 1977 the University of Uppsala awarded me an honorary doctorate on the occasion of its five hundredth anniversary in a glittering ceremony before the king and other dignitaries. As anti-government sentiment was on the rise in Iran, this event itself provided an occasion for leftist Iranian students, many of whom had come from Germany, to carry out political demonstrations which prevented the intellectual debate that I was to have had with Joseph Needham, who was also being honored, from taking place. I have continued my contact with Swedish scholars especially in the fields of Islamic studies and traditional philosophy but have not had the occasion to travel to Sweden again since my leaving Iran in 1979.

As for Austria, I visited Vienna often mostly in conjunction with scholarly and philosophical conferences, the most important of which was in 1977 when the Federation Internationales des Sociétés Philosophiques, of which I was then a member of the Comité Directeur, held its meeting in Vienna and I was asked to speak about my own philosophical position as part of the series entitled *Philosophes critiques d'eux-mêmes/Philosophische Seblstbetrachtungen.* This was the only time before writing the present intellectual autobiography that I wrote something about myself, in an essay under the title of "In Quest of the Eternal Sophia." It was also during this occasion that I gave my only public lecture on philosophy in German to a distinguished audience of Austrian philosophers as well as members of FISP. However, I never traveled to other eastern European countries or the then Soviet Union, although I had several students from the Communist world of that time in Tehran and also knew several Russian and East European philosophers such as Sava Ganovski, Nikolai Iribadzhakov, Jerzy Pelc, and Vadin S. Semenov. I met these men in gatherings in the West usually related to either FISP or the Institut Internationale de Philosophie.

Strangely enough, however, there was some interest in my philosophical views in the Communist world, and several articles and books were written in the '70s and '80s on my thought in Russian, much of the analysis being of course based on the Marxist perspective. As for my students from the Soviet Union, most would become seriously interested in Islamic philosophy or religious philosophy in general and would not be heard from again in the scholarly and philosophical arena after their return home. Yugoslavia was an exception to the rule and some of my former students are now well-known scholars in Bosnia. In Russia itself only Andrei Bertels, both a philosopher and an Islamicist, continued to correspond with me and we met several times including in Tehran and Paris in order to have discussions on various modes of philosophical interpretations of humanity's philosophical heritage.

I also need to say a word about Greece which I visited several times, visits which included the Temple of Delphi. Marco Pallis, who was of Greek origin, had introduced me to his brother who lived in Athens, and during the '60s and '70s I was able to visit him and through him came to know a number of literary figures of the country; but I did not meet there any specialists in Byzantine and Orthodox thought in which I was very much interested and whose representatives such as Archbishop Bloom, Bishop Kallistos Ware, and Philip Sherrard I was to meet in Britain rather than in Greece. As far as Greek philosophical circles are concerned, I became close friends with Evanghelos Moutsopoulos; together we carried out several philosophical programs and he was instrumental in my being elected as a member of the Greek Academy of Philosophy.

The Occidental Exile

Some travel from one country to another through their free choice. Others are forced into exile by circumstances beyond their control. My migration to the West in 1979 belongs to the second category and can be characterized in a sense as an "occidental exile," to repeat the famous phrase of the founder of Illuminationalist philosophy in Islam, Suhrawardī. Inwardly, however, I have remained in that Center which is of neither East nor West, the inward home in which one is never exiled no matter where one lives outwardly as long as one remains within the boundaries of that Center. During over two decades of intellectual activity in Persia, I had become so deeply rooted once again in my homeland and so profoundly involved in its intellectual and cultural life, that I could not have imagined even in 1978 that I would ever be living anywhere other than in Persia. Little did I know that a year later all the external elements of my life would change and I would be beginning a new cycle of my life in America. This painful transformation and upheaval is so important in determining the conditions of the later period of my life, that it is necessary to say a few words about the exact causes and factors which led to my departure in January of 1979 for what was intended as a two-week journey but which has lasted to this day.

During the last two decades I have refused to write about the political and social aspects of the Iranian Revolution of 1979; nor do I wish to do so now despite the fact that I was involved and present on the scene and in fact at the heart of the tumultuous changes which were occurring in 1978. But a few words need to be said here to clarify my own situation and why I could not remain in my homeland after the Revolution. During all the years of activity in Persia, I had sought assiduously to keep away from direct political involvement. Several times I was offered political positions which included the highest positions in government but I had turned them down, preferring instead to devote myself solely to philosophy, scholarly activity, and education. All the positions which I had accepted, such as deanship and presidency of the University, presidency of the Imperial Academy of Philosophy, and cultural ambassador, were of an educational and cultural nature. Of course, in countries such as Iran even these positions possessed a political dimension, but I could not have remained in Iran and succeeded in achieving what I did achieve without accepting such posts which in fact never distracted me from either my teaching or my scholarly and philosophical writings.

In the middle of 1978, however, a polarization began to appear between the religious elements in society and the ruling political structure of the country. Many of the most respected religious scholars, some of whom were later to join the revolutionary forces, wished at that time to create a new balance of power between the court and the religious authorities and felt that I was one of the very few people who was trusted by both sides and who could play an important role in creating a new harmony and avoiding chaos. Therefore, when the Shahbanou, Empress Farah, asked me to become the head of her special bureau, which oversaw most of the cultural activities of the country, I accepted willingly, having previously worked closely with her for many years. Soon thereafter the turmoil which led to the Revolution began. I had not known at first that the Shah was ill and that in the new position, which was one of the most important in the country, I would also have to deal with many political matters with which the Shahbanou now had to concern herself. As a result, in the next few hectic and very difficult months, during which I saw the Shahbanou nearly every day and the Shah often, I had to concern myself with many issues of a political and social nature.

It was as the chief of her bureau that I was chosen by her and the Iranian government to represent Iran in the opening of a major exhibition of Persian art in Tokyo, which was supposed to be inaugurated by her and Prince Mikasa, the brother of the then Emperor of Japan, but which she could not attend due to the Shah's illness and the turbulent condition in the country. With her permission I left Iran on January 6, 1979, a few days before the date of the inauguration of the exhibition, with my wife and daughter, going first to London to find a school for my daughter and with plans to fly over the pole to Tokyo from there. And so we set out with a few suitcases for London, but a couple of days later the Japanese government informed me that the exhibition had been delayed and a couple of days after that the Shahbanou called me from Tehran telling me that she was accompanying the Shah for a vacation to Cairo and that I should remain in London for the moment and not return to Tehran. By February, the Revolution was completed and because of the positions that I had held, especially that of head of her special bureau, my house was plundered, and my library and all scholarly notes confiscated and destroyed or at least "removed" along with all my belongings.

Thus it was that at the age of forty-five I was left in London with a wife and two children and no means of support. It was the best time to remember Plato's definition of philosophy as the practice of death. I had to rebuild my external life from the beginning, at a time when my friends among the religious classes in Iran did nothing to prevent the confiscation of all my belongings and assets, and the vast majority of my Western friends, especially those in America with whom I had the closest contact, decided to ignore my plight for political expediency. I spent two months in London until the little money I had was about to be exhausted. Those were indeed difficult days full of uncertainty in every way. The manuscript of my book on Islamic philosophy in Persia was lost when my office at the Academy was taken over as was the material for the second volume I was preparing on Mullā Ṣadrā which was in my library at home along with notes for the coming Gifford Lectures I had accepted to deliver and the skeleton text of the Kevorkian Lectures on Islamic art. And then there were all my class notes and scholarly documents. The loss was even greater since it involved my personal as well as family library, altogether several thousand volumes, many of which were irreplaceable.

My thoughts, however, had to turn to the more urgent matters of establishing my external life again before worrying about such losses. I preferred to remain in Britain but paradoxically enough, while several offers were to be made to me later, there was no suitable academic opening at that time in that country. And so I wrote to several American universities which had sought my services over the years. Only President David Gardner of the University of Utah and Khosrow Mostofi, the head of the Middle Eastern Center of the university, both of whom were friends, replied and sent me an invitation to join the university as distinguished visiting professor. And so in March 1979 we moved one step further away from Persia, first to Boston, where I left the family temporarily, and then to Salt Lake City where we began our new life in the most humble way possible. I was even forced to bring my son, who was finishing his A levels before going to Oxford, to America because it was simply impossible from a financial point of view to keep him there. In this way began that exile which was a return to the land in which I had studied for so many years and which was to become my new permanent home.

At the University of Utah I taught a small number of students but wrote little because the problems of settling in to my new situation, at a time when affairs were so turbulent in Iran, took much of my mental energy. But I did continue my intellectual activities to some extent. My old friend from Harvard, James Kritzeck, who had attended the conference on Islam and Christianity with me at Tioumliline in Morocco in 1957, was professor of

Islamic studies at the University at that time. We had many discussions on comparative theology together. Also the well-known American philosopher, Sterling McMurrin, was active at that time in the philosophy department of the university and we spent many hours together discussing world philosophy. Later on in 1997 I was to deliver the famous Tanner-McMurrin lecture at Westminster College in Salt Lake City named after him and his philosopher colleague Obert Tanner. In deference to his interests I spoke at this lecture about the meaning of truth in the context of a global philosophy of religion, a theme with which I have been much concerned in recent years.

In the middle of the summer of 1979 my appointment at the University of Utah came to an end. I was offered a tenured full professorship there. Offers of professorships also came first from the University of Toronto and soon thereafter from Temple University in Philadelphia. Before making a final decision we moved to Boston to find a school for my son and daughter. My son was to go to various schools in the area including Tufts University, The Fletcher School of Diplomacy, run by Tufts, and Harvard, and finally MIT, from which he received his Ph.D. in political science. My daughter started at Boston College, then went to Tufts, and later to Boston University to study the history of art. She was to complete her doctoral studies in this field at The George Washington University. Since they were to go to school in the Boston area, we decided to make our home there, although I accepted the offer to teach at Temple. Financially it was impossible to do otherwise and as a consequence I commuted for five years between Boston and Philadelphia. I did so while struggling to reconstruct my external life as well as begin, once again, an active intellectual life which in fact commenced in earnest almost immediately but with some change of direction in some of the fields in which I was doing research, although the heart of my intellectual interests remained unchanged.

In Persia I was forced to be involved in many local issues which were now no longer my concern. Also nearly all administrative chores disappeared replaced by every day tasks of running an uprooted household, tasks the likes of which had also existed in Iran but which were taken care of by servants, drivers, secretaries, and the like. In America I could no more live the life of a philosopher in leisure, removed from the concerns of the world than I could in Iran although the reasons were very different. Also, the loss of my library made it practically impossible for me to do detailed textual research and establish critical philosophical texts of later Islamic philosophy as I had in Iran despite the presence of the Widener Library at Harvard in which I spent a great deal of time and upon which I relied for most of the scholarly works that I needed. For some time, therefore, I did little new work on later Islamic philosophy although I have come back to this field in the last few years. I also discontinued my studies of Ibn ʻArabī whom I had introduced to the American public in my *Three Muslim Sages* because others were now busying themselves with him in a serious manner, especially my former student and now colleague, William Chittick, who has produced several major works in this field during the past fifteen years, and, to a lesser extent, another of my students who is now also a well-known specialist of Ibn ʻArabī, James Morris.

In fact, I was now placed in a situation in which I was seen as an Islamic philosopher and I had to deal with issues which teaching in an American academic setting posed. I was a Muslim intellectual much in demand by both academic circles and the Islamic community in the West itself, expected to address major intellectual and spiritual issues, not to speak of political ones brought forth by the advent of the Iranian Revolution and certain other events in the Islamic world. I was, of course, also and before all else a traditionalist and expositor of the perennial philosophy and came to be recognized soon in academic circles as a major proponent of the traditionalist and perennialist perspective. The migration to America in 1981 of Frithjof Schuon, the premier expositor of the *philosophia perennis* in the West during the second half of this century, added to the already existing interest in tradition in this land, although he kept completely aloof and distant from academic circles. My editing of the *Essential Writings of Frithjof Schuon* in 1986 was very much connected to this aspect of my function in America as the representative of tradition and the *philosophia perennis* in academic circles, and also for many who were interested in these matters without belonging to academia.

This aspect of my intellectual life in America was closely related to my activity in the field of comparative religion which had been of concern to me since my youth, but which now became more intensified not least of all because of the ecumenical interest in the religion department at Temple University. As a representative of the traditionalist perspective in the domain of comparative religion and as a Muslim long interested in serious religious dialogue, including especially its philosophical and metaphysical dimensions, I was to carry out many debates and discussions with eminent Christian theologians and philosophers of religion such as Hans Küng and John Hick and some Jewish ones including Rabbi Izmar Schorch at the Jewish Theological Seminary in New York. This aspect of my activity was also stretched to Europe and especially to England. In the 1990s I was to be selected as a patron of the Center for the Study of Islam and Christian-Muslim Relations of the Selly Oaks Colleges in Birmingham and played an active role in the creation and later activities of the Center for Muslim-Christian Understanding at Georgetown University in Washington. I was also to attend numerous conferences on this subject including the famous 1993 Parliament of World Religions.

My activities as an Islamic philosopher stretched into many other domains including the environmental crisis, the meaning of Islamic art, the

Nasr's function

challenges of new scientific theories and discoveries, and many other realms of philosophical activity. My work in reviving the Islamic intellectual tradition also continued in many ways despite the loss of my library and notes resulting from over two decades of research. I now wrote for a more general audience, partly the Western intelligentsia, partly the Islamic world as a whole. Both of these groups were also the audiences which many of my works written in Persia had addressed, but now the emphasis shifted more toward the global scene. I also wrote now mostly, but not exclusively, in English, for I would continue to write an essay or two each year in Persian despite the fact that in the early years after the Revolution Persian journals in Iran would not publish anything of mine, and even some of my Persian books were reprinted without my name. This has changed in the past few years and now my Persian works have a large audience and many of my books have been reprinted with my name several times in Iran recently.

To come back more specifically to my years at Temple, the department of religion in which I taught had the largest doctoral program in America. With the late Ismā'īl al-Fārūqī and me teaching there, numerous students, many from southeast Asia, came to study for their Ph.D.'s at Temple. During this period I trained for the first time a number of students from Malaysia, some of whom have now become well-established scholars in that country taking my philosophical perspective back home with them. One of them, Osman Bakar, has recently established the most vibrant program in the philosophy of science taught from the perspective of traditional Islamic philosophy in the Islamic world. Other former Malay students such as Saleh Yaapar and Baharuddin Ahmad have tried to introduce Islamic theories of literary criticism to the study of Islamic literature in place of theories emanating from France and England. At Temple I also trained a number of fine scholars in the fields of Sufism and Islamic philosophy who were Americans or who hailed from other lands including a few who were from Iran but who have settled in America. One of them, Mehdī Amīnrazavī, who still collaborates with me on important philosophical projects, is professor of philosophy writing mostly in the field of Islamic and comparative philosophy, while another is a professor of Iranian studies at Columbia. Some of my students at Temple such as Maysam al-Fārūqī and Gisela Webb have concerned themselves to a large extent with comparative philosophy and religion and in the case of the latter with Sufism, while others such as Grace Braeme have delved into Christian spirituality and mysticism. I also had a number of fine Jewish students interested in Islamic philosophy in its relation to Jewish philosophy. One of them, Michael Paley, has not written much on this subject but has been active in seeking to implement some of the ideas we had discussed together in the current educational scene.

Furthermore, I had a few Arab students, one of whom, Ibrāhīm Abū

Rabī‘, a Palestinian, has become a well-known scholar of contemporary Arabic thought, but has remained in America. Space does not allow me to mention the many others who studied with me during this time, hailing from many different lands including Nigeria, Pakistan, and Lebanon not to mention the countries cited above. Altogether the five years spent at Temple in addition to two extra years from 1984 to 1986, when I had moved to Washington to teach at The George Washington University but was still adjunct professor at Temple, was a rich period in the training of many outstanding students in comparative religion and philosophy and Islamic studies, students who are now all scholars and teachers here and abroad. In this sense my activities begun at Tehran University continued and were even expanded.

The department at Temple placed great emphasis upon the philosophy of religion and ecumenical religious studies. Such men as Martin van Buren, Gerhard Spiegler, Norbert Samuelson, and Thomas Dean provided a fertile ground for serious discussion of the philosophy of religion in a comparative setting, while such Christian ecumenists as Gerald Sloyan and especially Leonard Swindler, who was editor of the journal *Ecumenical Studies*, pushed us all into constant ecumenical discourse concerning the philosophy of religion, ethics, and other aspects of religious studies. As a result, the aspect of my intellectual life dealing with comparative studies was much expanded at this time.

Commuting between Boston and Philadelphia was very arduous and sapped much of my energy. Soon, however, I was able to establish a *modus vivendi* spending the middle part of the week in Philadelphia and from Friday to Monday in Boston where I could spend much time in study and research at Widener. By 1980 I was beginning to write essays and reviews again and soon entered one of the most active periods of my life as far as writing is concerned. Shortly before the Revolution of 1979 I had been invited to deliver the prestigious Gifford Lectures at the University of Edinburgh and had accepted this singular honor as the first non-Westerner invited to deliver the most famous lecture series in the fields of natural theology and the philosophy of religion without knowing what upheavals lay ahead in Iran. Now, my notes and the preliminary sketch for the lectures had been lost, but not wanting to postpone them I decided to remain faithful to the date set for the spring of 1981 which I had proposed originally. I spent most of my time in carrying out research for the work at hand and then in the winter of 1981, I wrote the complete text of the ten lectures planned with complete footnotes in a period of two and half months, producing a chapter a week while enduring the incredible strain of commuting between Boston and Philadelphia. The actual writing of the text of the lectures entitled *Knowledge and the Sacred* came as a gift from Heaven. The text would in a sense "descend" upon me and crystallize clearly in my mind and I was able to write each chapter in a continuous flow like a running river with no need for long pauses or hesitation. In the spring of 1981, when I spent three weeks delivering the lectures at the University of Edinburgh, the text was completely ready for publication. A few months later it was to appear at the University of Edinburgh Press with a simultaneous American edition. None of my other books was written with such facility, the pen moving on paper as if I were simply writing down a poem already memorized. The book, which has also been rendered into German and French, is in a sense my most important philosophical work and has had perhaps greater impact outside of the circle of scholars of Islamic thought than any of my other writings.

During 1981 I was also to expand an earlier collection of my essays under the new title of *Islamic Life and Thought* and also increase my lecturing at various universities. During the period at Temple, that is, from 1979 until 1984, both the activities of lecturing and of writing continued unabated along with my teaching. I delivered the Wiegand Lecture at the University of Toronto in 1983 on the philosophy of religion and helped establish the section on Hermeticism and the perennial philosophy at the American Academy of Religion with my old and dear friend and colleague Huston Smith, with whom I have remained close in carrying out many different endeavors for we both represent the same perspective in the study of philosophy and religion. And so it was as a result of his suggestion that I agreed to collaborate in 1982 on the major project of the *Encyclopedia of World Spirituality* whose chief editor was Ewert Cousins.

A professor of medieval philosophy and specialist in St. Bonaventure from Fordham University, Cousins had been asked to become chief editor of a major encyclopedia of some twenty-seven volumes devoted to "spirituality," this new category of thought, sentiment, and action which involves philosophy, theology, mysticism, and religion without being identical with any of them. A group of leading philosophers and scholars of religion were assembled for the task including A.H. Armstrong, Joseph Epes Brown, John Carman, Eliade, Faivre, Langdon Gilkey, Arthur Green, Bernard McGinn, John Meyendorff, Needleman, Panikkar, Jeroslav Pelikan, Krishna Sivaraman, Tu Wei-ming, Whaling, and many others in addition to Cousins, Smith, and myself. The numerous discussions on the meaning of spirituality and the global approach to it implied in this work was of great philosophical significance and was carried out on the highest intellectual level. I agreed to edit the two volumes on Islam which appeared in 1989 and 1991 but many other volumes in the series are yet to be completed. The conceptual scheme for the work as a whole was, however, already achieved after much deliberation in the mid-'80s and marks a major philosophical undertaking and achievement in which I played an active role. It was one of the important projects that I have undertaken in the past two decades and resulted in a two-volume work entitled *Islamic Spirituality* which remains unique to this day in the field of Islamic studies.

Before leaving this period, I need to mention another major project which was begun at that time but which was realized later in Washington. During one of the conferences arranged by Cousins on the theme of spirituality in preparation for the Encyclopedia, I was approached by a woman from the West Coast, Flora Courtois, who had read some of the essays in the English journal *Studies in Comparative Religion* and was so impressed by the traditional perspective that she wanted to create a foundation to pursue such studies, and after contacting Huston Smith was told by him to get in touch with me. We discussed the matter at length and finally created the Foundation for Traditional Studies devoted to the dissemination of traditional thought. A board was selected consisting of the founder, Huston Smith, Joseph Epes Brown, Rama Coomaraswamy, and Alvin Moore with myself as president and Katherine O'Brien as executive director. Later the Foundation was established in Washington where since 1994 it publishes the journal *Sophia*, edited by Katherine O'Brien. *Sophia* is now the leading journal in the English language devoted to traditional thought as understood by Guénon, Coomaraswamy, Schuon, Burckhardt, Lings, and others. The journal publishes essays by these and other traditionalist writers and I remain closely associated with it not only writing for it but also cooperating closely with O'Brien in its production. The Foundation has also published a number of books including *Religion of the Heart*, the *Festschrift* of Frithjof Schuon, edited by myself and William Stoddart, and *In Quest of the Sacred* edited by myself and O'Brien. Cooperation with the Foundation remains an important part of my intellectual activity in America.

In 1984 calls came from Yale and The George Washington University to become a candidate for the chair of Islamic Studies. Since the position at The George Washington University was a university professorship with much less administrative responsibility than an ivy league professorial appointment would require and the city of Washington and its suburbs were much more congenial for my family than New Haven, many of our old Iranian friends having now settled in the Washington area, I accepted The George Washington University appointment. We purchased a house in Bethesda, Maryland where I still live and I began the phase of my intellectual life which continues to this day. I was to join three other university professors, Marcus Cunliffe, a famous expert on American history, Amitai Etzioni, the celebrated social thinker, and Peter Caws, the well-known philosopher whom I had known from my years as member of the directing committee of the Fédération Internationale des Sociétés Philosophiques. Most of my contact with the philosophy department at the University has been through him, but I also do have a number of philosophy students in my courses as well as students from the religion department with which I have been most closely associated. Although University Professor of Islamic Studies, I developed courses on the perennial philosophy, religion and science, man and the environment, and comparative mysticism which are all interdisciplinary and of a philosophical nature. The number of students working on their doctorates with me decreased although a few young scholars in the field of Islamic philosophy, such as Zailan Moris from Malaysia, Ibrāhīm Kālīn from Turkey, and Walīd al-Anṣārī from Egypt have done or are doing their doctoral work with me while I have been in Washington. Most of my students during these years have been undergraduates and masters students many of whom have continued their doctoral work elsewhere in either Islamic studies, the philosophy of religion, or comparative religion after having received a thorough grounding in traditional philosophy.

The years in Washington have been very active ones intellectually, perhaps even more so than those at Temple as far as public lectures and public philosophical discourses are concerned. Every year I give a number of lectures in America, mostly in universities, and for seven years was the A. D. White professor-at-large at Cornell University, during which time I gave several seminars on Islamic thought as well as on traditional metaphysics. I have also traveled regularly to Europe to lecture, especially to the United Kingdom, France, Germany, and Spain, but most of all to Britain. During these years I have been involved as a fellow with the activities of the Temenos Academy and lectured often as already mentioned at Oxford, the University of London, and occasionally at other British universities. I delivered the aforementioned Cadbury Lectures in 1994 at the University of Birmingham under the title *Religion and the Order of Nature*, which as already stated continued my earlier interest in the philosophical and spiritual dimensions of the environmental crisis. The book by the same name is my most complete treatment of the subject. I also became associated with such British organizations interested in philosophy, science, and religion as Friends of the Centre and REEP (The Religious Education and Environmental Programme), and *The Scientific and Medical Network,* and have continued to publish extensively in Britain. Moreover, during these years I have collaborated closely with the Prince of Wales Institute of Architecture and especially the director of its Islamic art program, Keith Critchlow, a specialist on sacred geometry, whom I have known since the 1970s when I met him in London and later invited him to collaborate with the gifted Iranian architect Nāder Ardalān in designing a traditional mosque based on Islamic geometrical principles for the Aryamehr University campus in Isafahan.

Also, in the 1980s my old friend Shaykh Aḥmad Zakī Yamānī asked me to found a major center in England for the study and preservation of Islamic manuscripts and wanted me to move to London for that purpose. Although I did not accept that part of the invitation, I did help to found the new al-Furqān Foundation, now located at Wimbledon in a beautifully renovated Jacobian house. With Shaykh Yamānī's approval I asked one of my closest spiritual and intellectual friends, Hādī Sharīfī, who had been my deputy at the Academy of Philosophy in Tehran, to head the new foundation. For nearly a decade, therefore, I traveled several times a year to England to supervise and help in the activities of the new institution which is now a major center unique in the kind of activity it undertakes. Those journeys were themselves also occasions to participate in other intellectual activities in Britain and I can say that I have remained over these years as closely associated with the British intellectual scene as I had been when living in Persia.

I also travel at least once every year to France where I have kept my contact with the old circle associated with Corbin and have occasionally lectured at the Sorbonne and other French institutions of learning. I have also remained in contact with Faivre and the whole current to revive the serious study of Hermetic and esoteric philosophy in France and this involvement includes my writing occasionally for their journal *Aries*. Much of my time in France is, however, spent in going over translations of my works into French and other matters related to the publication of my books which continue to appear in French. I have also continued to be involved in a number of UNESCO projects, some philosophical and others cultural.

I have already mentioned the lectures delivered during these years in Germany and Spain but I need to say a few words about the significance of Spain for me during these years of exile in the West. There is still much Islamic presence in southern Spain and when I visit that area, it is like a return to Persia itself. For nearly a decade I have been trying to help in the making of a major documentary television series produced by the Foundation for Traditional Studies on Islam and the West, a project which is becoming gradually realized. In relation to this project I have made many journeys to Spain over the years almost always limiting myself to the southern region which the Muslims used to call al-Andalus (Andalusia). Although I have also given some lectures in Spain, my main purpose during all these journeys was not only academic or intellectual in the ordinary sense of the term, but primarily spiritual and artistic. It was also during some of these journeys that I composed a number of poems related to Spanish themes, poems which are included in the collection of my poetry, *Poems of the Way*.

During the years since moving to Washington, my journeys to the Islamic world have increased from the Temple years and I have also begun to travel to India again. In India my major locus of activity has been Delhi where I have delivered a number of major philosophical lectures and discourses and have been especially associated with the Indira Gandhi Centre for the Arts and its director Kapila Vatsyayan. As for the Islamic world, I have become involved to an ever greater degree with the intellectual life of Turkey and remain involved with Pakistan, traveling to both countries from time to time. Being a member of the Jordanian Royal Society, I remain in close touch with a number of key intellectual figures in that country which I also visit occasionally. I visit Egypt regularly every year and although I have participated in several conferences and lectured there over the years, my journeys to Egypt are more than anything else spiritual ones, filling for at least a short period each year the void created by my separation from Persia. The sanctuary of Ra's al-Ḥusayn in Cairo has become for me a spiritual resting place.

My most intense intellectual contact in the Islamic world in the past fifteen years has, however, been with Malaysia and to a lesser extent Indonesia. Many of my students are now active in Malaysia and some hold positions of influence. My writings and many lectures given there over the years have helped to mold the intellectual debate, incite interest in Islamic and comparative philosophy, turn attention to the significance of civilizational dialogue, and many other subjects of philosophical importance. It was in fact my suggestion to Tu Wei-Ming to begin a Confucian-Islamic dialogue that led to our having a small closed conference at Harvard on the subject, the first of its kind, and later the major conference on the same theme in Kuala Lumpur. I received from Tu Wei-Ming the text of Samuel Huntington's "Clash of Civilizations" before it was even published as an article not to speak of as a book while I was in Honolulu on my way to Malaysia in 1993. Having read this text, it was in Kuala Lumpur in a major public lecture that I dealt with this issue for the first time in the Islamic world, beginning a debate which continues unabated and which is, of course, of philosophical significance.

As for Persia itself, I have not been able to return there since the Revolution but during the past decade communication has become easier. Some of my Persian articles are now published there and some of my new books written in English have been translated into Persian. I am in contact with many professors and students and my writings form a central strand in the pattern of philosophical life in Persia today, a life which continues to grow in strength from day to day. There is perhaps no other Islamic country today with as much interest in philosophy, both Islamic and Western, as Persia and I remain very much involved in this new chapter in the intellectual life of the country without being physically present on the scene. My works and students represent me in the current philosophical and theological debates which are bound to be of much significance not only for the future of Persia but way beyond her borders.

Finally, in talking about the Islamic world, I need to say a few words about a country which I have not visited but with whose intellectual life I have been closely involved, and that is Bosnia. Before the breakup of Yugoslavia, a number of Muslim, Serbian, and Croatian intellectuals found in my writings a universalist and "ecumenist" spirit which could bring them all together in a common philosophical and intellectual discourse and so many of my more philosophical essays were translated into the language which some call "Serbo-Croatian" and others "Bosnian." In fact some of the early translators were not Muslim but Orthodox and Catholic. I was to visit Bosnia to meet the intellectual community when the great tragedies of the war and genocide began in 1992. Even during the war, however, my works continued to be translated, printed on cheap paper which was the only kind available under those conditions. The effort to introduce my works to Bosnia as a means of preserving a universalist perspective against parochial sectarianism was carried out most of all by a writer whom I have come to know well, the famous Bosnian scholar and thinker Enes Karić, who was the Bosnian minister of education throughout the war. I have still not been able to visit Sarajevo but remain closely involved in the intellectual and philosophical life of this small but valiant nation which should be the natural bridge between the West and the Islamic world.

As far as writing is concerned, the years in Washington have also continued to be active ones in several fields. My earlier interest in the traditional philosophy of art in general and Islamic art in particular have continued with my lectures and my first book on art entitled *Islamic Art and Spirituality,* which, on the basis of the earlier work of Titus Burckhardt, seeks to bring out the metaphysical and symbolic significance of Islamic art including poetry and music. Meanwhile my study of Islam and its civilization as well as the problem of the relation between Islam and the West, which came to the fore in the '80s, has continued through many articles and through the books *Traditional Islam in the Modern World* and *A Young Muslim's Guide to the Modern World,* which also includes a simplified version of Western schools of philosophy for Muslim students who confront Western cultures and thought. I also have continued to write on Sufism and Islamic spirituality, the most extensive work being the two-volume *Islamic Spirituality* which, besides being edited by me, contains many essays by myself including an extensive treatment of Islamic philosophy in relation to spirituality.

The most extensive part of my writings in the field of Islamic studies during these years has been in fact concerned with Islamic philosophy and its application to current issues. With the British philosopher and scholar of Islamic and Jewish philosophy Oliver Leaman, I edited the two-volume work *History of Islamic Philosophy* in the Routledge series on the history of philosophy and have also participated in their new *Encyclopedia of Philosophy*. During this time a large collection of my essays appeared in book form as the *Islamic Intellectual Tradition in Persia*, a work which replaces to some extent the manuscript on this subject lost during the Iranian Revolution. Also, in joint collaboration with Mehdī Amīnrazavī, I embarked upon the major project *An Anthology of Philosophy in Persia,* suggested originally by the Institut Internationale de Philosophie before the Revolution. At last two of the five projected volumes have been completed and are being published by Oxford. This is the first work of its kind in English and reveals the richness of a vast philosophical tradition going back two and a half millennia and possessing a parallel, but also very different, development from Western philosophy, despite many common sources and historical interactions.

My interest in the relation between religion, philosophy, and science has also continued not only through courses taught at The George Washington University on the subject, but also through many lectures, participation in the so-called "Islamicization of Knowledge" debate in the Islamic world, which I began in the '50s, and active participation in the religion and science program of the Templeton Foundation, but also in writing. In 1993 I published *The Need for a Sacred Science* which follows many of the themes of *Knowledge and the Sacred,* and I am presently assembling a number of essays on Islamic science in a new book. Much of my work in this domain has been concerned with this issue in a general, global context although, of course, work on my specialized field of Islamic science has continued. In recent years, however, I have been dealing not so much with the history of Islamic science as with general philosophical issues involved in the encounter between Islam and modern science.

Needless to say, all of these studies have been carried out from the traditional point of view, but I have also been constantly involved in a more specific sense with traditional metaphysics and the perennial philosophy which I have also been teaching at the University. Besides supervising the activities of the Foundation for Traditional Studies, I have also been lecturing and writing on various aspects of traditional thought all over the globe. These writings include the editing with introductions to the *Essential Writings of Frithjof Schuon* and *In Quest of the Sacred,* as well as many essays published in America, Europe, and the Islamic world.

In Washington I was soon to be surrounded by many students with general interest in Islam or traditional teachings. A smaller number have carried out more advanced studies in these fields under my direction while a number have also come to seek oral, esoteric, and spiritual instruction. Once I moved to Washington, the number of my graduate students diminished but those in search of spiritual teachings grew and continues to grow. My life has in fact fallen into a pattern in which all of these elements, teaching carried out both outwardly and inwardly, lecturing, writing, and time devoted to meditation and the inner intellectual and spiritual life have become woven and harmonized together. Meanwhile, my love for virgin nature and sacred art, including music and poetry with which I am involved on many levels, has continued unabated as I have sought to live the philosophical life in the Platonic sense of being concerned with *noesis*, inner purification, interiorization, and contemplation of the supernal realities with an even greater intensity amidst a most active intellectual and academic life, and irrespective of the forced uprooting of my life at the mid-stream of my earthly existence and continuous sense of nostalgia for the homeland from which I have become exiled.

If I were to be asked what has been the central strand of my intellectual life, I would say without pause the quest for knowledge. On the principial level I attained in my twenties an intellectual certitude and a vision of the nature of reality which have remained with me to this day. But on the level of the application of these principles as well as their deepening actualization and realization in an "existential" manner, my life has been a long quest for ever greater knowledge and my central prayer has been, in the language of the traditional Islamic prayer, *rabbī zidnī 'ilman*, that is, "O Lord increase me in knowledge." And that quest after a knowledge which liberates and delivers us from the fetters and limitations of earthly existence still dominates my intellectual life and is central to all my endeavors.

> For many a year our heart sought the Cup of Jamshīd
> (the Holy Grail) from us,
> What it possessed by itself, it sought from the stranger.
> (Ḥāfiẓ)

Bethesda, Maryland
July 22, 1998 A.D.
27 Rabī' al-awwal 1419 (A.H. lunar)
31 Tīr 1377 (A.H. solar)

SEYYED HOSSEIN NASR

UNIVERSITY PROFESSOR OF ISLAMIC STUDIES
GEORGE WASHINGTON UNIVERSITY
DECEMBER 1998

PART TWO

DESCRIPTIVE AND CRITICAL ESSAYS WITH REPLIES

1

Muhammad Suheyl Umar

"FROM THE NICHE OF PROPHECY": NASR'S POSITION ON ISLAMIC PHILOSOPHY WITHIN THE ISLAMIC TRADITION IN EXCERPTS AND COMMENTARY

Seyyed Hossein Nasr defies classifications. He is unique among our contemporary writers and thinkers in the sense that despite, or perhaps because of, his marvellous contributions to a stunning variety of academic disciplines it is difficult to place him in the categories of present-day academia. As W. C. Chittick has remarked,

> The first meeting with the writings of Seyyed Hossein Nasr may often leave one either pleasantly surprised or disconcerted and annoyed. The reason in both cases is the same: here we have an intelligent, erudite, articulate and impassioned defence of and apologia for religion, or as Nasr might write, for "Tradition in its true sense".... Nasr's educational background is exceptional. What is more exceptional is that he was able to integrate all of these currents and fields into a living and active whole, as if by realising in his own being the fundamental Islamic doctrine of Unity (*tawḥīd*) a doctrine referred to constantly in his works—and thus making all these seemingly disparate elements revolve around a single center. The diversity of his writings reflects the diversity of his background.[1]

Many people wonder while some even doubt whether Islam has a genuine "philosophy." In the West it is common to identify philosophy in Islam with the period from the life of al-Fārābī to that of Averroes. Against this view Nasr has argued that a broader understanding of Islamic philosophy is much needed. Nasr's understanding of the role and function of philosophy in Islam is rooted in his personal quest for the eternal *sophia* as he himself described it. In this regard his memoirs provide revealing insights about a philosophic quest that crystallised in the formulation of his position on Islamic philosophy. Remembering his encounter with the Western philosophic mind-set he remarked,

> I was first shocked to discover that many leading Western philosophers did not consider the role of science in general and physics in particular to be the discovery of the nature of the physical aspect of reality at all. Further studies of the philosophy of science and immersion in the debates between such figures as E. Meyerson and H. Poincaré only confirmed this early sense of bewilderment and drew me more and more into the study of philosophy and the history of science. . . . I was fully immersed in the formal study of philosophy and the history of science with well-known figures as G. Sarton, Sir Hamilton Gibb, W. Jaeger and H. A. Wolfson. Meanwhile, access to the unique Commaraswamy library, unbelievably rich in works on various traditions, deepened my knowledge of things Oriental, while encounters with such figures as D. T. Suzuki and S. H. Hisamatsu only confirmed the pertinence of these living traditions of the Orient. . . . The writings of Sufi masters and Islamic philosophers began to regain the profoundest meaning for me after this long journey through various schools of Western philosophy and science. But this newly gained meaning was no longer simple imitation or repetition of things inherited. It was based upon personal rediscovery after long search and one might add suffering, Islamic wisdom became a most intense living reality, not because I had happened to be born and educated as a Muslim but because I had been guided by the grace of Heaven to the eternal Sophia of which Islamic wisdom is one of the most universal and vital embodiments. Henceforth, I was set upon the intellectual path which I have followed ever since, . . . a period during which my quest has been to discover an unknown beyond the world within which the hands of destiny have since placed me. . . . I returned to Persia after the termination of my formal education and long years spent in the West with a new appreciation of the still living Islamic tradition and also a complete awareness of those errors and deviations which comprise the modern world. . . . Persia is one of the very few Islamic countries where still today a living tradition of Islamic philosophy flourishes and is in fact being rejuvenated.[2]
>
> If I were to summarize my so-called "philosophical position," I would say that I am a follower of that *philosophia perennis* and also *universalis*, that eternal *sophia*, which has always been and will always be and in whose perspective there is but one Reality which can say "I". . . . I have tried to become transparent before the ray of Truth that shines whenever and wherever the veil before it is lifted or rent asunder. Once that process is achieved, the understanding, "observation" and explication of the manner in which that light shines upon problems of contemporary man constitute for me philosophical creativity in the deepest sense of the term. Otherwise, philosophy becomes sheer mental acrobatics and reason cut off from both the intellect and revelation, nothing but a luciferian instrument leading to dispersion and ultimately dissolution. It must never be forgotten that according to the

teachings of the *sophia perennis* itself, the discovery of the Truth is essentially the discovery of oneself and ultimately of the Self, and that is none other than what the father of philosophy in the West, namely Plato, defined as the role of philosophy, for he said, "philosophy is the practice of death" (*Phaedo* 63e6–64a9). And the Self cannot be discovered except through the death of the self and that re-birth which is the goal and entelechy of human life and the aim of *sophia* in all its multiple manifestations within the traditions of the East and the West.[3]

With this background in mind I have traced the journey of his philosophic quest through his published works and collected his views on the position of Islamic philosophy within the Islamic tradition. Almost all that is detailed in the following pages is based directly on his works. I have tried to make few insertions and comments of my own, except where necessary for the sake of continuity, in order to offer to the readers of this volume an immediate insight into his mind and a taste of the distinctive characteristics of his writings.

Two points deserve mention here. S. H. Nasr has consistently maintained his position on the question of the status of Islamic philosophy within the Islamic tradition for a period of thirty-five years or more. The views he expressed in his works more than three decades ago are essentially the same as those that he upholds today. Second, his thought has two facets. On the one hand it addresses the plethora of settled convictions and received opinions; a spectrum of thought that extends from an outright rejection of philosophy as an alien and alienating intellectual enterprise—a phenomenon manifesting itself within the Islamic Tradition under extraneous influences—to an abject submission to the modern western modes of thinking that tries to replace Islamic philosophy with various borrowings from the West. On the other hand it analyzes the Western studies of Islam and Islamic philosophy and, while acknowledging their positive contributions, refutes the erroneous views that are so common in the studies made by the official Orientalism.

Amidst a spectrum of conflicting ideas, Nasr's position on Islamic philosophy within the Islamic tradition is the most balanced and sane view expressed in a contemporary language and serves as a corrective to much muddled thinking that prevails in both camps. To substantiate the claim, I offer a chronological overview of his enduring position as it emerges from his writings.

Early in his career S. H. Nasr was instrumental in planning and compiling the two-volume work on Islamic philosophy that was edited by M. M. Sharif.[4] His contributions,[5] though limited to the intellectual history of certain sectors of the Islamic tradition and focused on the later phases of Islamic philosophy in the eastern lands of Islam, nevertheless provided important insights about his views on the position of Islamic philosophy within the Islamic tradition. In these essays he pointed out the richness, continuity, and religious character of Islamic philosophy as well as the formative influence it exerted upon other disciplines through historical interaction; themes he elaborated and explicated in detail in subsequent works. A few representative quotations stating Nasr's views on a selection of great figures in the Islamic tradition will provide the first glimpses of his thinking.

> In Islam the attack of Sufis and theologians upon the rationalistic aspect of Aristotelian philosophy weakened its hold at the very time when that philosophy was gaining strength in the Christian West and was replaced in the Muslim world by two elements, the doctrinal Sufism of Muḥyī al-Dīn ibn 'Arabī and the *Ḥikmat al-Ishrāq* or illuminative wisdom of Shaikh al-Ishrāq Shihāb al-Dīn Yaḥyā ibn Ḥabash ibn Amīrak Suhrawardī, both of which aimed at an effective realization of the "truth" and replaced the rationalism of Peripatetic philosophy by intellectual intuition (*dhauq*).[6]
>
> Both metaphysically and historically, ishrāqī wisdom means the ancient pre-discursive mode of thought which is intuitive (*dhauqī*) rather than discursive (*baḥthī*) and which seeks to reach illumination by asceticism and purification. In the hands of Suhrawardī it becomes a new school of wisdom integrating Platonic and Aristotelian philosophy with Zoroastrian angelology and Hermetic ideas and placing the whole structure within the context of Sufism.[7]

Regarding Fakhr al-Dīn Razī Nasr commented,

> His own importance in Muslim theology lies in his success in establishing the school of philosophical *Kalām*, already begun by Ghazzālī, in which both intellectual and revelational evidence played important roles.[8] . . . [H]is greatest philosophical importance lies in the criticisms and doubts cast upon the principles of Peripatetic philosophy, which not only left an indelible mark upon that school but opened the horizon for the other modes of knowledge like *ishrāqī* philosophy and gnosis, which were more intimately bound with the spirit of Islam.[9]
>
> Imam Rāzī's role in Muslim intellectual life, besides establishing the school of philosophical *Kalām* begun by Ghazzālī, was to intensify the attack against Peripatetic philosophy, thereby preparing the way for the propagation of the metaphysical doctrines of the Ishrāqīs and Sufis who, like Imām Rāzī, opposed the rationalism inherent in Aristotelianism.[10]

Regarding the theosophers he said, "[A]ll of whom sought to reconstruct Muslim intellectual life through a gnostic interpretation of the writings of Ibn Sīnā, Suhrawardī, and the Sufis, and who carried further the attempt already begun by al-Fārābī, extended by Ibn Sīnā in his Quranic commentaries, and carried a step further by Suhrawardī, to correlate faith (*īmān*) with philosophy."[11]

Regarding Mullā Ṣadrā Nasr's views were as follows:

> The particular genius of Mullā Ṣadrā was to synthesise and unify the three paths which lead to the Truth, viz., revelation, rational demonstration, and purification of the soul, which last in turn leads to illumination. For him gnosis, philosophy, and revealed religion were elements of a harmonious ensemble the harmony of which he sought to reveal in his own life as well as in his writings. He formulated a perspective in which rational demonstration or philosophy, although not necessarily limited to that of the Greeks, became closely tied to the Quran and the sayings of the Prophet and the Imams, and these in turn became unified with the gnostic doctrines which result from the illuminations received by a purified soul. That is why Mullā Ṣadrā's writings are a combination of logical statements, gnostic intuitions, traditions of the Prophet, and the Quranic verses.[12]
>
> Regarded in this way, Mullā Ṣadrā must certainly be considered to be one of the most significant figures in the intellectual life of Islam. Coming at a moment when the intellectual sciences had become weakened, he succeeded in reviving them by co-ordinating philosophy as inherited from the Greeks and interpreted by the Peripatetics and Illuminationists before him with the teachings of Islam in its exoteric and esoteric aspects. He succeeded in putting the gnostic doctrines of ibn 'Arabī in a logical dress. He made purification of the soul a necessary basis and complement of the study of *Ḥikmat*, thereby bestowing upon philosophy the practice of ritual and spiritual virtues which it had lost in the period of decadence of classical civilization. Finally, he succeeded in correlating the wisdom of the ancient Greek and Muslim sages and philosophers as interpreted esoterically with the inner meaning of the Quran. In all these matters he represents the final stage of effort by several generations of Muslim sages and may be considered to be the person in whom the streams, which had been approaching one another for some centuries before, finally united.[13]

The underpinnings of these comments become clear when we approach Nasr's next work. In 1964 he spoke of the "The Intellectual Dimensions in Islam" in his *An Introduction to Islamic Cosmological Doctrines*[14] and included Islamic philosophy as one of the major perspectives that always existed, in varying forms, within the matrix of the "Intellectual Dimensions" of the Islamic tradition. In this early text Nasr approached the issue from the point of view of the various modes of seeking knowledge that dominated different schools or classes of seekers of knowledge.

> The most essential division within Islam is the "vertical" hierarchy of the Sacred Law (*Sharī'ah*), the Way (*Ṭarīqah*) and the Truth (*Ḥaqīqah*), the first

being the exoteric aspect of the Islamic revelation, divided into the Sunni and the Shī'ite interpretations of the tradition, and the latter two the esoteric aspects which are usually known under the denomination of Sufism. Or, one might say that the Truth is the center, the Way or "ways" the radii and the Sacred Law the circumference of a circle the totality of which is Islam.

Another division of the intellectual perspectives within Islam is the classification of the various intellectual dimensions according to the modes of knowledge sought by each school. From this point of view we may enumerate the seekers of knowledge in the earlier centuries of Islam as being the Quranic scholars and traditionalists, grammarians, historians and geographers, natural scientists and mathematicians, the Mu'tazilites and theologians, the Peripatetic philosophers, the Neo-Pythagoreans and Hermeticists, and finally the Sufis.[15]

To discover more specifically how these perspectives appear in the 4th/11th and 5th/12th centuries we turn to the evidence of some of the Muslim authors themselves. In his *Treatise on Being* (*Risālat al-wujūd*), 'Umar Khayyām, one of the most significant figures of the 5th/12th century, writes concerning those who seek ultimate knowledge, as follows:

Seekers after knowledge of God, Glorious and Most High, are divided into four groups:

1. The theologians (*Mutakallimūn*) who became content with disputation and satisfying proofs and considered this much knowledge of the Creator excellent is His Name, as sufficient.
2. The philosophers and metaphysicians [of Greek inspiration (*ḥukamā'*)] who used rational arguments and sought to know the laws of logic and were never content with satisfying arguments, but they too could not remain faithful to the conditions of logic and with it became helpless.
3. The Isma'īlīs and *Ta'limiyūn* who said that the way of knowledge is none other than receiving information from a trustworthy (*ṣādiq*) informer, for in reasoning about the knowledge of the Creator, His Essence and Attributes, there is much difficulty, and the reasoning of the opponents and the intelligent is stupefied and helpless before it. Therefore, it is better to seek knowledge from the words of a trustworthy person.
4. The people of *taṣawwuf* who did not seek knowledge by meditation or thinking but by purgation of their inner being and purifying of their disposition. They cleansed the rational soul from the impurities of Nature and bodily forms until it became a pure substance. It came face to face with the spiritual world (*malakūt*) so that the forms of that world became reflected in it in reality without doubt or ambiguity. This is the best of all paths because none of the perfections of God are kept away from it, and there are not obstacles or veils put before it.[16]

Several centuries later, when the various perspectives had become more crystallised, Sayyid Sharīf al-Jurjānī, the 9th/16th century Persian *ḥakīm*, in his glosses upon the *Maṭāli' al-Anwār*, writes: "To gain a knowledge of the beginning and the end of things, there are two ways possible: one the way of argument and examination (or observation), and the other they way of asceticism and self-purification (*mujāhadah*).[17]

The point that Nasr wanted to register was that in the Islamic perspective, philosophy is one of the several valid paths leading towards veritable knowledge. He elaborated upon this point in his next work *Three Muslim Sages*,[18] and, with reference to the various representative figures of Islamic philosophy, expounded the view that Islamic philosophy was a perspective rooted in the Islamic worldview established by the Islamic revelation.

> [Islamic philosophy per al-Kindī] is a school which, while remaining faithful to the inner consistency and logical demands of the disciplines with which it deals, also assimilates elements that have a profound connection with the intellectual and psychological needs of certain components of the new Islamic community. It thereby creates an intellectual perspective which corresponds not only to a possibility that must be *realize*d but also to a need that must be fulfilled, a perspective that must be created within the total world view of Islam.[19]

In the philosophic theory of religion developed by the Islamic philosophers,

> The prophet is thereby distinguished from sages and saints first, because his reception of knowledge from the Divine Intellect is complete and perfect and theirs partial, and, second, because he brings a law into the world and directs the practical lives of men and societies while the sages and saints seek after knowledge and inner perfection and have no law-bringing function. They are therefore subordinated to prophets, although they are themselves the most exalted and worthy of the vast majority of men who are not endowed with the extremely rare nature which is that of a prophet.[20]

In *Science and Civilization in Islam*,[21] which appeared four years after the aforementioned work, Nasr discussed the issue in greater detail and explained the status of Islamic philosophy from the point of view of "perspectives within the Islamic civilization."[22] As in his earlier works, he maintained that Islamic philosophy was one of the most important and influential perspectives within the Islamic intellectual universe. Apart from it he devoted three full chapters to "Philosophy," "Controversies between Philosophy and Theology," and "The Gnostic Tradition,"[23] wherein he explained in detail the need, rise, formulation, interaction, response, and function of philosophy in the Islamic tradition. The following quotation summarizes his position in a succinct manner.

> Philosophy in the Islamic world began in the third/ninth century, with the translation of Greek philosophical texts into Arabic. The first Muslim philosopher, any of whose writing has survived—al-Kindī—was also celebrated in the Latin West. He was well acquainted with the main tenets of Greek philosophy, and even had a translation of a summary version of the *Enneads* made for him. It was he who initiated the process of formulating a

technical philosophical vocabulary in Arabic, and of rethinking Greek philosophy in terms of Islamic doctrines. In both these respects, he was followed by al-Fārābī, through whom the basis for Peripatetic philosophy became well established in Islam. The philosophers of this school were familiar with the Alexandrian and Athenian Neoplatonists and commentators on Aristotle, and viewed the philosophy of Aristotle through Neoplatonic eyes. Moreover, there are Neopythagorean elements to be seen in al-Kindī, Shī'ite political doctrines in al-Fārābī, and ideas of Shi'ite inspiration in certain of the writings of Avicenna.

The main tendency of the Peripatetic school, however, which found its greatest Islamic exponent in Avicenna, was toward a philosophy based on the use of the discursive faculty, and relying essentially on the syllogistic method. The rationalistic aspect of this school reached its terminal point with Averroes, who became the most purely Aristotelian of the Muslim Peripatetics, and rejected, as an explicit aspect of philosophy, those Neoplatonic and Muslim elements that had entered into the world view of the Eastern Peripatetics, such as Avicenna.

From the sixth/twelfth century onward, the other major school of Islamic philosophy or, more appropriately speaking "theosophy" in its original sense—came into being. This school, whose founder was Suhrawardī, became known as the Illuminationist (*ishrāqī*) school, as contrasted with the Peripatetic (*mashshā'ī*) school. While the Peripatetics leaned most heavily upon the syllogistic method of Aristotle, and sought to reach truth by means of arguments based on reason, the Illuminationists, who drew their doctrines from both the Platonists and the ancient Persians as well as the Islamic revelation itself, regarded intellectual intuition and illumination as the basic method to be followed, side by side with the use of reason. The rationalist philosophers, although they left an indelible mark upon the terminology of later Muslim theology, gradually became alienated from the orthodox elements, both theological and gnostic, so that, after their "refutation" by al-Ghazzālī, they exercised little influence upon the main body of Muslim opinion. But the Illuminationist school, which combined the method of ratiocination with that of intellectual intuition and illumination, came to the fore during that very period that is generally—although quite erroneously—regarded as the end of Islamic philosophy. In fact along with gnosis it occupied the central position in the intellectual life of Islam. At the very moment when, in the West, Augustinian Platonism (which regarded knowledge as the fruit of illumination) was giving way to Thomistic Aristotelianism (which turned away from this very doctrine of illumination), the reverse process was taking place in the Islamic world.

We must, however, make a distinction between the Sunni and Shī'ite reactions to philosophy. The Sunni world rejected philosophy almost entirely after Averroes, except for logic and the continuing influence of philosophy on its methods of argumentation, as well as some cosmological beliefs that have remained in the formulations of theology, and certain Sufi doctrines. In the Shī'ah world, however, the philosophy of both the Peripatetic and Illuminationist school has been taught continuously as a living tradition through the centuries in the religious schools; some of the greatest figures in Islamic philosophy, such as Mullā Ṣadrā, who was contemporary with Descartes and Leibniz, came long after the period usually regarded as "the productive phase" of Islamic philosophy.[24]

Later, in 1971 and 1973, Nasr turned to certain specific questions that he had touched upon during the course of his earlier writings. These pertained to the role and function of philosophy, various responses to it and a creative interplay or interaction of philosophy with other perspectives of the Islamic Tradition. "*Al-Ḥikmat al-Ilāhiyyah* and *Kalām*,"[25] deals with the struggle and reciprocal influence between *falsafah* and *Kalām* in Islam. In the history of the struggle and reciprocal influence between philosophy and *Kalām*, Nasr argued, one can distinguish four periods:

1. The earliest period, from the beginning to the third/ninth century, when the Mu'tazilite school was dominant in *Kalām*, and *Falsafah* was passing through its period of genesis of early development with such figures as Irānshahrī and Al-Kindī and his students. This period was one of distinct but parallel development of and close association between *Falsafah* and *Kalām* in an atmosphere more or less of relative mutual respect, at least in the case of Al-Kindī himself, although from the side of *Kalām* certain of its branches such as the school of Basra opposed *Falsafah* violently even during this early period.
2. The period from the third/ninth to the fifth/eleventh century, from the rise of Ash'arite theology and its elaboration to the beginning of the gradual incorporation of certain philosophical arguments into *Kalām* by Imām al-Ḥaramayn al-Juwaynī and his student Ghazzālī. This was a period of intense opposition and often enmity between *Falsafah* and *Kalām*, a period whose phases have been so ably studied along with those of the first period by many western [sic] scholars . . .
3. The period from Juwaynī and Ghazzālī to Fakhr al-Dīn al-Rāzī, that is from about the fifth/eleventh to the seventh/thirteenth centuries when, while the opposition between *Falsafah* and *Kalām* continued, each began to incorporate into itself more and more of the elements of the other. *Falsafah* began to discuss more than ever before problems such as the meaning of the Word of God, the relation between human and Divine will, the Divine Attributes, etc., which had always been the central concern of *Kalām*, while *Kalām* became ever more "philosophical," employing both ideas and arguments drawn from *Falsafah*. As a result at the end of this period, as already noted by Ibn Khaldūn, men appeared whom it is difficult to classify exactly either in the category of *faylasūf* or *mutakallīm* and who could be legitimately considered as belonging to either or to both groups.
4. From the seventh/thirteenth century onward, when the school of *al-Ḥikmat al-ilāhiyyah* or *Ḥikmat-i ilāhī* developed fully and a new type of relation came into being based on the trends established during the third period.

> Since the *Ḥikmat-i ilāhī* began to develop particularly in Persia where Shi'ism was also on the rise, naturally much of the interaction between *Ḥikmah* and *Kalām* involved Shi'ite *Kalām*, although Sunni *Kalām* must not by any means be forgotten, for even if most of the *ḥakīms* were Shī'ite, they were nevertheless well versed in and fully aware of the arguments of Sunni *Kalām*, to which they often addressed themselves.[26]

Nasr concluded his elucidation with the comments of the famous student of Mullā Ṣadra, 'Abd al-Razzāq Lāhījī quoting from his *Gawhar-Murād*[27] and says,

> In this comparison between *Ḥikmat* and *Kalām*, which is at once principial and historical, Lāhījī expresses the view of those later *ḥakīms* who were also *mutakallims* and above all Gnostics and Sufis. He therefore alludes to knowledge transcending both *Ḥikmat* and *Kalām*—that of the *muwaḥḥid*—while insisting on the superiority of *Ḥikmat* over *Kalām* on their own proper plane. Lāhījī was to be followed by many men like Qāḍī Sa'īd Qummī, Mullā 'Alī Nūrī and Ḥājjī Mullā Hādī Sabziwārī who like him were well-versed in both *Ḥikmat* and *Kalām*, men who while placing a different emphasis upon each discipline all subordinated *Kalām* to the purer knowledge of things divine contained in this theosophy or *Ḥikmat* which has come to play such an important role in the intellectual and religious life of the eastern lands of Islam and especially Persia during the past seven centuries.[28]

One of the most detailed and profound expositions of the question of the position of Islamic philosophy within the Islamic tradition that is to be found in the works of Nasr is contained in his article "The Meaning and Role of Philosophy in Islam."[29] He summarized his earlier insight[30] that "Islam is hierarchic in its essential structure and also in the way it has manifested itself in history. The Islamic revelation possesses within itself several dimensions and has been manifested to mankind on the basic levels of *al-islām*, *al-īmān* and *al-iḥsān* and from another perspective as *Sharī'ah*, *Ṭarīqah* and *Ḥaqīqah*."[31] Afterwards, he emphasised that

> in order to understand the real role of "philosophy" in Islam we must consider Islam in all its amplitude and depth, including especially the dimension of *al-Ḥaqīqah*, where precisely one will find the point of intersection between "traditional philosophy" and metaphysics and that aspect of the Islamic perspective into which *sapientia* in all its forms has been integrated throughout Islamic history. Likewise, the whole of Islamic civilization must be considered in its width and breadth, not only a single part of *dār al-islām*, for it is one of the characteristics of Islamic civilization that the totality of its life and the richness of its arts and sciences can only be gauged by studying all of its parts. Only in unison do these parts reveal the complete unity that lies within all the

> genuine manifestations of Islam. One cannot understand the role of "philosophy" or any other intellectual discipline in Islam by selecting only one dimension of Islam or one particular geographical area, no matter how important that dimension or that area may be in itself.[32]

Having warned us against adopting a truncated vision of the geographical totality of the Islamic civilization, Nasr stressed the need to define the term "philosophy" with utmost precision since, in the case of traditional civilizations, terms have precise connotations.

> We can use the term "philosophy" as the translation of the Arabic *al-falsafah* and inquire into the meaning of the latter term in Islam and its civilization. Or we can seek to discover how the term "philosophy" as used today must be understood within the context of Islamic civilization. Or again we can seek to find all those Islamic sciences and intellectual disciplines which possess a "philosophical" aspect in the sense of dealing with the general worldview of man and his position in the Universe. For our own part, we must begin by making the basic affirmation that if by philosophy we mean profane philosophy as currently understood in the West, that is, the attempt of man to reach ultimate knowledge of things through the use of his own rational and sensuous faculties and cut off completely from both the effusion of grace and the light of the Divine Intellect, then such an activity is alien to the Islamic perspective. It is a fruit of a humanism that did not manifest itself in Islam except for a very few instances of a completely peripheral and unimportant nature. It is what the Persian philosophers themselves have called mental acrobatics or literally "weaving" (*bāftan*), in contrast to philosophy as the gaining of certainty, or literally the discovery of truth (*yāftan*). But if by philosophy we mean a traditional philosophy based on certainty rather than doubt, where man's mind is continuously illuminated by the light of the Divine Intellect and protected from error by the grace provided by a traditional world in which man breathes, then we certainly do have an Islamic philosophy which possesses illimitable horizons and is one of the richest intellectual traditions in the world, a philosophy that is always related to religious realities and has been most often wedded to illumination (*ishrāq*) and gnosis (*'irfān*). If we view philosophy in this light, then the title of "philosopher" cannot be refused to those in Islam who are called the *falāsifah, ḥukamā'* and *'urafā'*. . . . Moreover, if one takes the whole of the Islamic world into account, including the Persian and the Indian parts of it, one certainly cannot call Islamic philosophy a transient phenomenon which had a short lived existence in a civilization whose intellectual structure did not permit its survival.[33]

> For the Islamic *ḥukamā'*, . . . philosophy was originally a form of revealed Truth, closely allied to revelation and connected with the name of Hermes, who became identified by them with Idrīs, who was entitled "The Father of Philosophers" (*Abū'l-ḥukamā'*). The identification of the chain of philosophy with an ante-diluvian prophet reveals a profound aspect of the concept of

philosophy in Islam—far more profound than that any historical criticism could claim to negate it. It was a means of confirming the legitimacy of *ḥikmah* in the Islamic intellectual world.[34]

Having established the existence of Islamic philosophy as a distinct type of traditional philosophy, Nasr probed into the meaning and definition of philosophy.

> We must first of all make a distinction between philosophy in the general sense as *Weltanschauung* and philosophy as a distinct intellectual discipline in the technical sense. If we think of philosophy in the general sense of *Weltanschauung*, then outside of *al-falsafah* and *al-ḥikmah*, with which philosophy has been identified by most schools, we must search within several other traditional Islamic disciplines for "philosophy", these disciplines including *kalām* or theology, *uṣūl al-fiqh*, or principles of jurisprudence, and especially Sufism, in particular its intellectual expression which is also called *al-'irfān* or gnosis. This fact is especially true of the later period of Islamic history when in most of the Arab world *falsafah* as a distinct school disappeared and the intellectual needs corresponding to it found their fulfilment in *kalām* and Sufism.[35]
>
> As for philosophy in the technical sense, it embraces not only Peripatetic philosophy in its early phase, known in the West thanks to medieval translations and modern research following the earlier tradition, but also later Peripatetic philosophy after Ibn Rushd and beginning with Khawājah Naṣīr al-Dīn al-Ṭūsī, the School of Illumination (*ishrāq*) founded by Suhrawardī, metaphysical and gnostic forms of Sufism identified closely with the school of Ibn 'Arabī, and the "transcendent theosophy" (*al-ḥikmat al-muta'āliyah*) of Mullā Ṣadrā, not to speak of philosophies with specific religious forms such as Ismā'īlī philosophy, which possesses its own long and rich history.[36]

In order to emphasise the diffusion of philosophy as well as the richness of the Islamic intellectual tradition Nasr added, "The most profound metaphysics in Islam is to be found in the writings of the Sufi masters, especially those who have chosen to deal with the theoretical aspects of the spiritual way, or with that *scientia sacra* called gnosis (*al-'irfān*). A more general treatment of the meaning of philosophy in Islam would have to include Sufism, *kalām*, *uṣūl* and some of the other Islamic sciences as well."[37]

In the next section Nasr made a rather detailed survey of the definitions of the terms *falsafah* or *ḥikmah* as these terms have been understood by the traditional Islamic authorities themselves. His exposition provides insight into philosophy's own vision of itself as reflected in the definitions formulated by the authorities of Islamic philosophy over the centuries. These definitions and the views of the authorities of Islamic philosophy reveal that there was a gradual increase of close rapport between philosophy and religion, and, in the end, philosophy became completely wedded to religion in its deeper aspects. "In fact the whole later tradition of Islamic philosophy considered philosophy as veritable philosophy only if it is able to transform the being of man and enable him to have a new vision of things made possible by this very transformation. As such it is nothing other than a particular expression of the esotericism (*al-bāṭin*) of religion, accessible only through spiritual exegesis or hermeneutics (*ta'wīl*) of the revealed truths contained in religious sources."[38] A representative piece of writing is given in the following quotation from Mullā Ṣadrā's *Al-Ḥikmat al-Muta'āliyah*, where he defined *falsafah* or *ḥikmah* in a most comprehensive and precise manner[39] and followed it by arguing that the *ḥikmah*[40] mentioned in the Islamic texts is the "first principles discussed in *ḥikmah muta'āliyah* . . ." and it was what the Holy Prophet had in mind in his prayer to his Lord when he said: "O Lord! Show us things as they really are."[41] Nasr adds that,

> Moreover, [Mullā Ṣadrā] gives a spiritual exegesis of the Quranic verse "Surely We created man of the best stature, then We reduced him to the lowest of the low, save those who believe and do good works" (Quran, XCV: 4–6) in this way: "of the best stature" refers to the spiritual world and the angelic part of the soul, "the lowest of the low" to the material world and the animal part of the soul, "those who believe" to theoretical *ḥikmah* and those who "do good works" to practical *ḥikmah*. Seen in this light *ḥikmah*, in its two aspects of knowledge and action, becomes the means whereby man is saved from his wretched state of the lowest of the low and enabled to regain the angelic and paradisial state in which he was originally made. *Ḥikmah* is, in his view, completely wedded to religion and the spiritual life and is far removed from purely mental activity connected with the rationalistic conception of philosophy that has become prevalent in the West since the post-Renaissance period.[42]

Part of the discussion in this article is devoted to the opposition that philosophy had to face from different quarters of the Islamic tradition. Nasr reminds us that "opposition," in the context of a traditional civilization is

> very different from the opposition of contending philosophical schools which have no principles in common. In Islam there has often been a tension between the various components and dimensions of the tradition but a tension that has been almost always creative and has never destroyed the unity of Islam and its civilization. With this reserve in mind it can be said that "opposition" to *falsafah* in Islam came mainly from three groups, but for different reasons: The purely religious scholars dealing with *fiqh* and *uṣūl*, the theologians (*mutakallimūn*) especially of the Ash'arite school, and certain of the Sufis.[43]

Though he had had occasion to refer to this matter of "opposition" in several of his earlier works[44] he further elaborated certain of its aspects and concluded by saying that,

The criticism of *falsafah* by the *mutakallimūn*, therefore, was more than anything else a creative interplay between *falsafah* and *kalām* which left an indelible mark upon both of them. *Kalām* forced *falsafah*, even the Peripatetic school, to deal with certain specifically religious issues while *falsafah* influenced ever more the formulation and argumentation of *kalām* itself, starting with Imām al-Ḥaramayn al-Juwaynī, continuing with al-Ghazzālī and al-Rāzī, and in a sense culminating with 'Aḍud al-Dīn al-Ījī and his *Kitāb al-mawāqif*, which is almost as much *falsafah* as *kalām*. In Shī'ism also it is difficult to distinguish some of the later commentaries upon the *Tajrīd* from works on *falsafah*. The "opposition" of *kalām* to *falsafah*, therefore, far from destroying *falsafah*, influenced its later course and in much of the Sunni world absorbed it into itself after the 7th/13th century, with the result that, as already mentioned, such a figure as Ibn Khaldūn was to call this late *kalām* a form of philosophy.

As for the criticism of *falsafah* made by certain Sufis, it too must be taken in the light of the nature of Islamic esotericism. Sufi metaphysics could not become bound to the "lesser truth" of Aristotelianism against whose inherent limitations it reacted and whose limits it criticized. But the criticism against the substance of *falsafah* came, not from the whole of Sufism, but from a particular tendency within it. In general one can distinguish two tendencies in Sufi spirituality, one which takes the human intellect to be a ladder to the luminous world of the spirit and the other which emphasises more the discontinuity between the human reason and the Divine Intellect and seeks to reach the world of the spirit by breaking completely the power of ratiocination within the mind. The final result, which is union with God, is the same in both cases, but the role played by reason is somewhat different in the two instances. The first tendency can be seen in Ibn 'Arabī, 'Abd al-Karīm al-Jīlī, Ṣadr al-Dīn al-Qūnyawī and the like, and the second in some of the famous Persian Sufi poets such as Sanā'ī and Mawlānā Jalāl al-Dīn Rūmī and in the Arab world in certain early Sufi poets. . . . In fact both tendencies within Sufism have played a critical role in the later history of *falsafah*, one more positive and the other in a sense more negative, while both aspects of Sufism have remained the guardians and expositors of traditional *falsafah* or *ḥikmah* in its profoundest and most immutable sense or what in Western parlance is called *philosophia perennis*. *Falsafah* for its part benefited immensely from this interaction with Sufism and gradually became itself the outer courtyard leading those qualified to the inner garden of gnosis and beatitude. . . . The very substance of *falsafah* was changed during later Islamic history from simply a rational system of thought with an Islamic form to an ancillary of esotericism closely wedded to illumination and gnosis. Likewise Islamic philosophy was saved from the deadlock it had reached with the type of excessive Aristotelianism of an Ibn Rushd and was enabled to channel itself into a new direction, a direction which bestowed upon it renewed vigour and made it a major aspect of Islamic intellectual life in the Eastern lands of Islam during the eight centuries following the death of the Andalusian master of Aristotelianism with whom the earlier chapter of Islamic philosophy had drawn to a close.[45]

Speaking of the changing role of philosophy in Islam and Islamic civilization Nasr alerted us to the fact that

> *falsafah* performed an important role in the process of the absorption and synthesis of the pre-Islamic sciences and the formulation of the Islamic sciences. The science of logic, the problem of the classification of the sciences, the methodology of the sciences, and their interaction with the rest of Islamic culture were all deeply influenced by *falsafah* and its particular elaboration in Islam. Moreover, during this early period most of the great scientists were also philosophers, so that we can speak during the early centuries, and even later, of a single type of Muslim savant who was both philosopher and scientist and whom we have already called philosopher-scientist.[46] In any case during early Islamic history the cultivation and the development of the sciences would have been inconceivable without those of *falsafah*. The meaning of the term *ḥakīm*, which denotes at once a physician, scientist and philosopher, is the best proof of this close connection.
>
> Not only did *falsafah* aid closely in the development of the intellectual sciences, but also it was the major discipline in which tools and instruments of analysis, logic and rational inquiry were developed for the transmitted sciences and other aspects of Islamic culture as well. The tools of logic developed mostly by the *falāsifah* and in conformity with the particular genius of Islam, in which logic plays a positive role and prepares the mind for illumination and contemplation, were applied to fields ranging far and wide, from grammar and rhetoric to even the classification and categorisation of *Ḥadīth*, from organising economic activity in the bazaar to developing the geometry and arithmetic required to construct the great monuments of Islamic architecture.[47]

These and other innumerable proofs

> [a]ll attest to the important role of *falsafah* in early Islam in providing the appropriate intellectual background for the encounter of Muslims with the arts, sciences and philosophies of other civilizations. This role was in fact crucial during the early period of Islamic history when Muslims were translating the heritage of the great civilizations which had preceded them into their own world of thought and were laying the foundations for the rise of the Islamic sciences.[48]
>
> Finally it must be re-asserted that during this earlier phase of Islamic history one of the important and enduring roles of *falsafah* was its struggle with *kalām* and the particularly "philosophical" structure it finally bestowed upon *kalām*. The difference between the treatises of *kalām* of al-Ash'arī himself or his student Abū Bakr al-Bāqillānī and Rāzī, Ījī and Sayyid Sharīf al-Jurjānī is due solely to the long struggle with *falsafah*. Through *kalām*, therefore, *falsafah*, as an Islamic discipline, left its indelible mark upon the Sunni world.[49]

If the post–Ibn Rushdian phase witnessed a different role and function of philosophy in Islam it was due to the impasse that the Peripatetic philosophy had reached as well as the firm establishment of various Islamic sciences which from then onwards followed their own course of development. The role and function of philosophy differed in the eastern and western lands of Islam as well, due to the situations prevailing in these regions. Though philosophy was only pursued sparcely and was not cultivated avidly in the western lands of Islam, it nevertheless continued to possess a certain mode of life within the matrix of *Kalām* and Sufism. Nasr informed us that, as far as the eastern lands of Islam were concerned,

> Besides [*falsafah's*] function in aiding to sustain the intellectual sciences, which continued to be cultivated in Persia and India—and also to a certain extent among the Ottomans—up to the 12th/18th century, and besides its role in the various aspects of the religious life of the community, *falsafah* or *ḥikmah*, which by now had come much closer to the heart of the Islamic message and had left the limitative confines of Peripatetic philosophy, became the bridge for many men to Sufism and Sufi metaphysics. . . . On the one hand *ḥikmah* became profoundly imbued with the gnostic teachings of Ibn 'Arabī and his school and was able to present in such cases as Mullā Ṣadrā a more systematic and logical interpretation of Sufi metaphysics than found in many of the Sufi texts themselves, and on the other hand it became in turn the major point of access to the teachings of Sufism for many men of intellectual inclination who were engaged in the cultivation of the official religious sciences.[50]

The conclusion that Nasr draws from these points has been summarized in the following words.

> *[F]alsafah* in Islam satisfied a certain need for causality among certain types of men, provided the necessary logical and rational tools for the cultivation and development of many of the arts and sciences, enabled Muslims to encounter and assimilate the learning of many other cultures, in its interactions with Kalām left a deep effect upon the latter's future course, and finally became a handmaid to illumination and gnosis, thus creating a bridge between the rigour of logic and the ecstasy of spiritual union.[51]

In his article "Post-Avicennian Philosophy and the Study of Being," Nasr again drew the attention of his readers toward the significant difference of the role and function of philosophy during the course of its later development in the Islamic tradition. He said,

> in the Islamic world philosophy drew even closer to the ocean of Being itself until finally it became the complement of gnosis and its extension in the direction of systematic exposition and analysis. . . . [I]n the Islamic world also philosophy became inseparable from experience. But in this case the experience in question was of a spiritual and inward character, including ultimately

> the vision of Pure Being, tasting of a reality which is the origin of this sapiental wisdom or *ḥikmah*.[52]

In his *Islamic Life and Thought* Nasr returned to many of the issues that he had dealt with in his earlier works and devoted a large part of the book to the study of Islamic intellectual life and, more particularly, to the elucidation of various aspects of Islamic philosophy.[53] Two points deserve special mention here: continuity of the Islamic intellectual tradition and its Islamic/religious character. Nasr tried to dispel certain misconceptions that prevailed about both of these aspects of Islamic philosophy by reminding his readers:

> Because the Western-educated classes in the Islamic world are on the receiving end of general influences from the West, they tend to learn even about Islamic philosophy and their own intellectual heritage from orientalists and other Occidental sources. Even now in the case of the least prejudiced and most sympathetic orientalists—with some honourable exceptions—there is a tendency to substitute that period of Islamic intellectual history which influenced the West for the whole intellectual history of the Muslim world. Thus nearly every branch of the sciences and philosophy terminates, according to most of these sources, around the seventh/thirteenth century, the very period when intellectual contact between the East and West ceased. As a result, most Western-educated Oriental students of Islamic philosophy, who rely upon standard Western sources, think that for the past six or seven centuries there has been no intellectual life in Islam, and they tend to treat their own intellectual tradition as a passing phase in the history of Western civilization.
>
> There has been a great revival of interest in medieval civilization on the part of Western scholars during this century and in respectable academic circles one no longer follows the prejudice of the Renaissance and the seventeenth and eighteenth centuries in calling the medieval period or its early phase the Dark Ages. . . . These and many other factors which have risen from the false view of Islamic intellectual history have made the correct interpretation of the Islamic heritage difficult, although the genuine sources, both written and oral, still exist for all who care to explore and study them.[54]
>
> But contrary to what most Western sources have written, the intellectual life of Islam did not by any means come to an end merely because of the termination of this contact.[55]
>
> There are numerous other traits of the philosophical and metaphysical schools in Islam which are worth discussing. Here it is sufficient to mention that there has been a continuity of intellectual tradition in Islam from the beginning to the present day, and that if this tradition is forgotten it is not because it does not exist but rather because we are sleeping over treasures.[56]

In the quotation that follows, Nasr, for the first time, gave the title "Prophetic Philosophy" to Islamic philosophy.

First of all, Islam is a tradition based wholly upon a distinct revelation, consequently, the sense of the transcendent and the revealed is a potent force in Islamic society. No philosophy that ignores both revelation and intellectual intuition, and thus divorces itself from the twin sources of transcendent knowledge, can hope to be anything but a disrupting and dissolving influence in Islamic society. Indeed, Islamic philosophy is precisely "prophetic philosophy," that is to say a worldview in which the role of revelation, in both the macrocosmic and the microcosmic sense, looms large on the horizon. And it is in Islam that "prophetic philosophy" finds its most complete and perfect expression.

Secondly, and closely connected to this point, there is the question of the relation between reason and revelation, which occupied the Muslim philosophers from the very beginning and which found its most harmonious solution in the hands of Mullā Ṣadrā, who like the sages before him expounded that Divine Wisdom or *sapientia*, that gnosis in which faith and reason find their common ground. One need hardly mention that, once the function of the intellect is reduced to reason and also revelation is limited to its most exoteric and outward level of meaning, then faith and reason can never become truly harmonised. Every attempt which is then made to bring about a harmony will meet with the lack of success that the history of modern times so amply illustrates.

Islamic philosophy also possesses a unified vision of things—that is, a view of the interrelation between all realms of knowledge. However dangerous the separative tendency (or sclerosis as some call it) of the modern sciences may be for the West, it is doubly fatal for Islam, whose sole *raison d'être* is to assert the doctrine of unity (*al-tawḥīd*) and to apply it to every aspect of life. To be able to create and maintain an interrelation between various fields of knowledge is therefore of vital importance for all who are interested in the welfare of Islamic society. And here, as in other instances, the Islamic intellectual heritage offers ample guidance.[57]

[P]hilosophy turns from the attempt to describe a rational system to explaining the structure of reality with the aim of providing a plan of the cosmos with the help of which man can escape from this world considered as a cosmic crypt. Henceforth, in the East the primary role of philosophy became to provide the possibility of a vision of the spiritual universe. Philosophy thus became closely wedded to gnosis as we see in the Illuminationist (ishrāqī) theosophy of Suhrawardī over a century after Avicenna.[58]

Gradually the teachings of Avicenna, Shurawardī and Ibn 'Arabī, as well as those of the theologians, became synthesised in vast metaphysical systems which reached their peak during the eleventh/seventeenth century with Mīr Dāmād and Ṣadr al-Dīn Shīrāzī. These metaphysicians, who are the contemporaries of Descartes and Leibniz, developed a metaphysics which was no less logical and demonstrative than those of their European contemporaries did and yet which included a dimension of gnosis and intuition which the European philosophy of the period completely lacked.[59]

The question of the integration and assimilation of the intellectual heritage of Antiquity came up again in the discussions of Islamic science and, since it holds good for Islamic philosophy as well, a few comments would be appropriate here.

> Islamic science came into being from a wedding between the spirit that issued from the Quranic revelation and the existing sciences of various civilizations which Islam inherited and which it transmuted through its spiritual power into a new substance, at once different from and continuous with what had existed before it. The international and cosmopolitan nature of Islamic civilization, derived from the universal character of the Islamic revelation and reflected in the geographical spread of the Islamic world (*dār al-islām*), enabled it to create the first science of a truly international nature in human history.
>
> Islam became heir to the intellectual heritage of all the major civilizations before it save that of the Far East, and it became a haven within which various intellectual traditions found a new lease upon life, albeit transformed within a new spiritual universe. This point must be repeated, particularly since so many people in the West wrongly believe that Islam acted simply as a bridge over which ideas of Antiquity passed to mediaeval Europe. As a matter of fact nothing could be further from the truth, for no ideas, theory or doctrine entered the citadel of Islamic thought unless it became first Muslimized and integrated into the total world view of Islam. Whatever could not make its peace (*salām*) with Islam was sooner or later dispelled from the arena of Islamic intellectual life or relegated completely to the margin of the tapestry of the Islamic sciences.[60]
>
> The most important source for Islamic alchemy, and in fact a major source of inspiration for certain of the other Islamic sciences and schools of thought, is, however, a number of treatises attributed to Hermes and known in the West as the *Corpus Hermeticum*.[61] What the mediaeval and even post-mediaeval West has known of Hermes comes essentially from Islamic sources rather than directly from Alexandrian ones, where, from the Wedding of the Greek god Hermes and the Egyptian god Thoth, the figure of Hermes as the founder of a alchemy and a whole 'philosophy of nature' come into being.
>
> In Islamic sources the one Hermes of Alexandrian sources became three, hence the term "Hermes Trismegistos" (from the Arabic *al-muthallath bi'l-ḥikmah*), which has inspired so many philosophers and poets in the West. The three Hermes were considered by Muslims as prophets belonging to the golden chain of prophecy stretching from Adam to the Prophet of Islam. Hence Hermeticism was considered as a revealed doctrine and was easily integrated into the Islamic perspective because it was already 'Islamic' in the wider sense of the term as belonging to the chain of prophecy. The first Hermes was identified with the ante-diluvian prophet Idrīs (or Akhnūkh). He lived in Egypt and built the pyramids. The second was entitled al-Bābilī, namely "Babylonian." He lived in Mesopotamia after the flood and was responsible for reviving the sciences. The third lived again in Egypt after the flood and taught men many of the sciences and crafts. The Muslims saw the three Hermes not

only as founders of alchemy, but also of astronomy and astrology, architecture and many of the other arts, and finally of philosophy. The first Hermes is entitled by Muslim sources *Abū'l-Ḥukamā'* (the father of theosophers or philosophers).[62]

One may wish to question the legitimacy and opportuneness of the aforementioned approach, as it is discernible among the theologians, theosophers and philosophers of Islam. From the point of view that Nasr has adopted it derives its legitimacy from the inherent principles and practice of the Islamic Tradition itself. Islamic Tradition, from its vantage point of being the summation, incorporated—obviously with alterations, amendments, abrogation, and adaptations—the "Judeo-Christian" elements; especially the legal (or *Sharī'ite*, in the technical sense of the word) aspects of the Mosaic code and the esoteric elements of the Christian message. These elements were brought to perfection in this summation with the addition of specifically Islamic aspects of the new faith in the Islamic revelation. This process, as it was accomplished on a purely vertical plane, had the stamp of divine sanction on it which distinguished it from any subsequent attempts that the Islamic community may have envisaged in the same direction. Nevertheless it had the significant role of setting the example for integrating ideas and symbols of pre-Islamic origin into the unitary perspective of Islam and its general framework.

As for the opportuneness of such an approach we can do no better than to quote Nasr again. This time he has elucidated the point with reference to Ibn 'Arabī, but the argument holds good for Islamic philosophy also.

> The importance of Ibn 'Arabī consists, therefore, in his formulation of the doctrines of Sufism and in his making them explicit. His advent marks neither a "progress" in Sufism by its becoming more articulated and theoretical, nor a deterioration from a love of God to a form of pantheism, as has been so often asserted against Ibn 'Arabī. Actually, the explicit formulation of Sufi doctrines by Muḥyī al-Dīn signifies a need on the part of the milieu to which they were addressed for further explanation and greater clarification. Now, the need for explanation does not increase with one's knowledge; rather, it becomes necessary to the extent that one is ignorant and has lost the immediate grasp of things through a dimming of the faculty of intuition and insight. As Islamic civilization drew away gradually from its source of revelation, the need for explanation increased to the degree that the spiritual insight and the perspicacity of men diminished. The early generations needed only a hint or directive (*ishārah*) to understand the inner meaning of things; men of later centuries needed a full-fledged explanation. Through Ibn 'Arabī Islamic esotericism provided the doctrines which alone could guarantee the preservation of the Tradition among men who were always in danger of being led astray by incorrect reasoning and in most of whom the power of intellectual intuition was

> not strong enough to reign supreme over other human tendencies and to prevent the mind from falling into error. Through Ibn 'Arabī, what had always been the inner truth of Sufism was formulated in such a manner that it has dominated the spiritual and intellectual life of Islam ever since.[63]

This formulation was responsible, apart from other things, for "placing in the ascendancy the trend to expound the mystical experience in philosophic terminology."[64] As such it was one of the various possible means to justify and prove the religious teachings concerning God's unity that unfolded themselves gradually during the whole of Islamic intellectual history.[65] Use of philosophic terminology or discussion of philosophic positions shall never be equated, however, with the unbridled activity of the unaided reason that would imply that the norm for the mind is reasoning pure and simple, in the absence, not only of intellection, but also of indispensable objective data. This is an expression in a philosophic style and terminology of specifically Islamic positions and data obtained from mystical experience, as well as from unveiling finding as a result of reading and meditating upon the Quran and fearing God, that cannot be legitimately viewed as bringing philosophic issues within the pale of Sufism. To quote Schuon,

> In a certain respect, the difference between philosophy, theology and gnosis is total; in another respect, it is relative. It is total when one understands, by "philosophy," only rationalism;[66] . . . by "theology," only the explanation of religious teachings; and by "gnosis," only intuitive and intellective, and thus supra-rational, knowledge; but the difference is only relative when one understands by "philosophy" the fact of thinking, by "theology" the fact of speaking dogmatically of God and religious things and by "gnosis" the fact of presenting pure metaphysics, for then the genres interpenetrate. It is impossible to deny that the most illustrious Sufis, while being "Gnostics" by definition, were at the same time to some extent theologians and to some extent philosophers and to some extent philosophers and to some extent gnostics, the last word having to be understood in its proper and most sectarian meaning.[67]

Chittick has also pointed out that "the mainstream of Islamic intellectuality, which in any case was moving more towards philosophy than *Kalām*. In addition, from the 7th/13th century onward Islamic intellectuality tends towards synthesis. Many authors contributed to the harmonisation of divergent intellectual perspectives. . . . It was only logical that Sufism should play a major role in this harmonisation of different intellectual streams."[68]

Islam and the Plight of the Modern Man,[69] as the title implies, deals with comparative study of the predicament of the modern man in its varied aspects. Intellectual life is also the focus of Nasr's attention, and in this work comparative aspects of the issue have received greater attention, though the position that Nasr adopted earlier is maintained. Commenting upon the situation of philosophy in the West, Nasr said,

> Sapiental doctrines and the appropriate spiritual techniques necessary for their *realization* are hardly accessible in the West, and "philosophy" has become totally divorced from experience of a spiritual nature. In the traditional East the very opposite holds true. "Philosophy" as a mental play or discipline that does not transform one's being is considered meaningless and in fact dangerous. The whole of the teachings of such Islamic philosophers as Suhrawardī and Mullā Ṣadrā and all of Sufism are based on this point, as are all the schools of Hinduism and Buddhism, especially Vedanta and Zen. The very separation of knowledge from being which lies at the heart of the crisis of modern man is avoided in the Oriental traditions, which consider legitimate only that form of knowledge that can transform the being of the knower.[70]
>
> [The] term "philosophy" (*al-falsafah* or *al-ḥikmah*) used in a traditional Islamic context must not be confused or equated with the modern use of the term, and also that the basic distinction between Oriental metaphysics and profane philosophy must be kept in mind. Moreover, the traditional Islamic "philosophy" which is usually the subject of comparative studies fills, in fact, an intermediate position in the spectrum of Islamic intellectual life between the pure metaphysics contained in various forms of Islamic esotericism, especially Sufism but also the inner aspect of Shi'ism, and rationalistic philosophy, which through its gradual decadence in the West led to the completely profane philosophy of today.[71]

Moreover Islamic philosophy never died. In Nasr's words, "The situation for Islamic philosophy is even more startling, since Islamic philosophy and metaphysics have never really decayed at all."[72]

The theme of absorbing the heritage of earlier civilizations comes up again here, but from a comparative angle.

> Because of the integrating power of Islam and the fact that it was destined to cover the "middle-belt" of the world, it came historically into contact with many modes of thought, including the Graeco-Alexandrian, Persian, Indian and even, to a certain extent, Far Eastern. The basis of Islamic intellectual life was therefore cosmopolitan and international in conformity with the world-wide perspective of Islam itself and the universal nature of the fundamental Islamic doctrine of Unity (*al-tawḥīd*). Moreover, because it was the last revelation and therefore the synthesis of the messages of the traditions before it, Islam developed an extremely rich intellectual life into which was integrated much of the heritage of mankind that had preceded it, a heritage that became transformed by the light of Unity and converted into a building block in the new edifice of the Islamic arts, sciences and philosophy.[73] Islamic philosophy, if considered in its totality and not only in terms of the Peripatetic school

known in the West, is extremely rich and possesses schools that can be compared with most of the intellectual perspectives and traditional philosophies of the East, of the ancient Mediterranean world and of mediaeval Europe.[74]

In his *Knowledge and the Sacred*, S. H. Nasr brought the issue into a still broader perspective. "In the intellectual life of a religious civilization such as that of Christianity or Islam or for that matter in the Jewish tradition, one can detect three and not just two major schools or ways of thinking: philosophy, theology, and gnosis or metaphysics (or theosophy) in its traditional sense."[75]

Besides the various cosmological sciences, there are, as already noted, three modes of knowing dealing with principles which one can distinguish in a traditional world, especially those governed by one of the Abrahamic religions: these three being philosophy, theology, and gnosis, or in a certain context theosophy. The modern world distinguishes only two modes or disciplines: philosophy and theology rather than the three existing in the traditional world of not only Christianity but also Islam and Judaism.

In the Islamic tradition after several centuries during which the various perspectives were formed, a situation developed which demonstrates fully the role and function of philosophy, theology, and metaphysics or gnosis in a traditional context. There were schools such as that of the Peripatetics (*mashshā'ī*) that could be called philosophical in the traditional sense. There were schools of theology (*kalām*) such as that of the Mu'tazilites, the Ash'arites, the Māturīdites, the Ismā'īlīs, and the Twelve-Imām Shī'ites. Then there was gnosis or metaphysics associated with various schools of Sufism. As far as the eastern Islamic world was concerned, there also gradually developed a school associated with Suhrawardī and his school of illumination (*al-ishrāq*) which was both philosophical and gnostic and which should be called, properly speaking, theosophical, while in the western lands of Islam, contemporary with this development, philosophy ceased to exist as a distinct discipline becoming wed to theology on the one hand and gnosis on the other. Likewise, medieval Judaism could distinguish between the same three kinds of intellectual perspectives represented by such figures as Judas Halevy, Maimonides, Ibn Gabirol, and Luria. Needless to say, in medieval Christianity one could also distinguish between the theology of a Saint Bernard, the philosophy of an Albertus Magnus, and the gnosis of a Meister Eckhart, not to speak of a Roger Bacon or Raymond Lull, who correspond more to the school of *ishrāq* of Suhrawardī than anything else if a comparison is to be made with the Islamic tradition.

All three disciplines have a role and function to play in the intellectual life of a traditional world. There is an aspect of "philosophy" which is necessary for the exposition of certain theological and gnostic ideas as there are elements of theology and gnosis which are present in every authentic expression of philosophy worthy of the name. One can, in fact, say that every great philosopher is also to some extent theologian and metaphysician, in the sense of gnostic, as every great theologian is to some extent philosopher and gnostic and every gnostic to some degree philosopher and theologian as found in the case of an Ibn ‘Arabī or Meister Eckhart.[76]

For them the sages of antiquity such as Pythagoras and Plato were “Unitarians” (*muwaḥḥidūn*) who expressed the truth which lies at the heart of all religions. They, therefore, belonged to the Islamic universe and were not considered alien to it.

The Islamic intellectual tradition in both its gnostic (*ma‘rifah* or *‘irfān*) and philosophical and theosophical (*falsafah-ḥikmah*) aspects saw the source of this unique truth which is the “Religion of the Truth” (*dīn al-ḥaqq*) in the teachings of the ancient prophets going back to Adam and considered the prophet Idrīs, whom it identified with Hermes, as the “father of philosophers” (*Abū’l-ḥukamā’*). Many Sufis called not only Plato “divine” but also associated Pythagoras, Empedocles, with whom an important corpus which influenced certain schools of Sufism is associated, and others with the primordial wisdom associated with prophecy. Even early Peripatetic (*mashshā’ī*) philosophers such as al-Fārābī saw a relation between philosophy and prophecy and revelation. Later figures such as Suhrawardī expanded this perspective to include the tradition of pre-Islamic Persia. Suhrawardī spoke often of *al-ḥikmat al-laduniyyah* or Divine Wisdom (literally the wisdom which is near God) in terms almost identical with what Sophia and also *philosophia perennis* mean traditionally, including its aspect of realization. A later Islamic figure, the eighth/fourteenth (Islamic/Christian) century gnostic and theologian Sayyid Ḥaydar Āmulī, made no reservations in pointing to the correspondence existing between the “Muḥammadan” pleroma of seventy-two stars of the Islamic universe and the seventy-two stars of the pleroma comprised of those sages who had preserved their primordial nature but belong to a world outside of the specifically Islamic one.[77]

The belief of the Muslim philosophers that the Greek philosophers had learned their doctrines from the prophets, especially Solomon, and that “philosophy derives from the niche of prophecy,” if not verifiable historically, nevertheless, contains a profound truth, namely, the relation of this wisdom to the sacred and its origin in revelation, even if this revelation cannot be confined in the strictly Abrahamic sense to a particular figure or prophet.[78]

Traditional Islam in the Modern World[79] summarizes the views that Nasr expressed in his earlier works but, as before, always with a fresh dimension added to its exposition.

Islam has created one of the richest philosophical traditions, one which possesses great spiritual significance for Islam itself and which has survived as a continuous tradition to this day. Heir to Pythagoreanism, Platonism, Aristotelianism, Neo-pythagoreanism, Hermeticism and Neoplatonism, and aware of many branches of Stoicism and the later schools of Hellenistic thought, Islam created a powerful and original philosophy within the intellectual universe of Abrahamic monotheism and the Quranic revelation, while incorporating those elements of Greek philosophy which conformed to the Islamic unitarian perspective. The origin of what is characteristically medieval philosophy, whether Jewish or Christian, is to be found in Islamic philosophy.

Being traditional philosophy based upon the supra-individual intellect rather than upon individualistic opinion, Islamic philosophy developed schools and perspectives which were followed over the centuries, rather than being changed and overthrown by one philosopher after another. Already in the 3rd/9th century, Peripatetic (*mashshā'ī*) philosophy, which itself represented a synthesis of Plato, Aristotle and Plotinus in the context of the Islamic worldview, was begun by al-Kindī, further developed by al-Fārābī, pursued in the 4th/10th century by al-'Āmirī and Abū Ya'qūb al-Sijistānī and reached its peak with Ibn Sīnā, the Latin Avicenna, who became the prototype of the philosopher-scientist for all later Islamic history. Criticized by such theologians as al-Ghazzālī, al-Shahrastānī and Fakhr al-Dīn al-Rāzī, this school was temporarily eclipsed in the eastern lands of Islam but enjoyed a period of intense activity in Spain with Ibn Bājjah, Ibn Ṭufayl and Ibn Rushd or Averroes, the foremost expositor of this school in the Islamic West (al-Maghrib). As for the East, the school of Ibn Sīnā was resuscitated by Naṣīr al-Dīn al-Ṭūsī in the 7th/13th century and continued henceforth as an important intellectual tradition during the centuries which followed. . . .

During later centuries, while in most of the Arab world philosophy as a distinct discipline became integrated into either Sufism in its intellectual aspect or philosophical theology (*kalām*), in Persia and the adjacent areas including not only India but also Iraq and Turkey, various schools of philosophy continued to flourish. At the same time, the different intellectual disciplines, such as Peripatetic philosophy, the school of Illumination, theology and Sufi metaphysics were drawing closer together. The ground was thus prepared for the already-mentioned revival of Islamic philosophy in the Safavid period in Persia with Mīr Dāmād, the founder of the "School of Isfahan," and especially Ṣadr al-Dīn Shīrāzī, his student, who is perhaps the greatest of the later Islamic metaphysicians. Even through the gradual decay of the teaching of the "intellectual sciences" in the *madrasahs*, this later school associated with the name of Ṣadr al-Dīn Shīrāzī, as well as those of Ibn Sīnā, Suhrawardī, Ibn 'Arabī and their commentators, continued to be taught and to produce noteworthy figures, some of whom have survived to the present day.

The Islamic philosophical tradition, although of great diversity and richness, is characterised by certain features which are of special significance both for its understanding and for an appraisal of its import for the world at large. This philosophy breathes in a religious universe in which a revealed book and prophecy dominate the horizon. It is, therefore, "prophetic philosophy"; whatever might be the subject with which it is concerned.[80] Moreover, it is a philosophy which, in conformity with the Islamic perspective, is based upon the intellect as a supernaturally natural faculty within man which is a

> sacrament and which, if used correctly, leads to the same truths as revealed through prophecy. It is therefore concerned most of all with the One who dominates the whole message of Islam. This philosophy is also concerned with the basic issues of the harmony between reason and revelation and of providing, within the context of a religious universe dominated by monotheism, a metaphysics centered around the supreme doctrine of the One. It is also concerned with providing keys for the understanding of the manifold in relation to the One. It is therefore rich, not only in religious and ethical philosophy, but also in philosophies of nature and mathematics as well as of art. In fact, as far as the Islamic sciences are concerned, they were cultivated in the bosom of Islamic philosophy and almost always by men who were not only scientists but also philosophers.[81]
>
> The nature of this reality, which man is in his essence, is elucidated by traditional Islamic philosophy, for that is wedded at once to intellect and revelation and is related to God, the cosmos and human society. Islamic philosophy is one of the richest treasures of traditional wisdom that have survived to this day and it stands at the center of the battle which traditional Islam must wage on the intellectual front in the modern world.[82]

As could be discerned from the foregoing quotations, Nasr is expressing his views not only about the past of Islamic philosophy but also about its role and function in present-day Islam.

> But few are aware of the fact that, in the context of present-day education and the current understanding of philosophy, not only is *falsafah* truly philosophy, but that there is also "philosophy" in many other Islamic sciences such as *tafsīr*, *Ḥadīth*, *kalām*, *uṣūl al-fiqh* and *taṣawwuf*, as well as of course in the natural and mathematical sciences, all of which are rooted in principle in the Quran, which is of course the fountain of *ḥikmah* or wisdom. . . .
>
> It is true that the Islamic intellectual tradition is too rich and diversified to provide just one meaning for the Quranic term *al-ḥikmah*, but it is also true that the several intellectual perspectives that have been cultivated in Islam all conform to the doctrine of unity (*al-tawḥīd*), and one can therefore come to understand the term "philosophy" as implying knowledge of the nature of things based upon and leading to *al-tawḥīd*, therefore profoundly Islamic even if issuing originally from non-Islamic sources. . . . The student should be encouraged to know something of this rich intellectual background and not be presented with a picture of the Islamic intellectual tradition as a monolithic structure amenable only to one level of interpretation. Such a perspective only deadens the mind and creates a passivity that makes the penetration of foreign ideas into the Islamic world so much easier. . . . This interpretation of Islamic history was originally the work of orientalists who could accept Islamic civilization only as a phase in the development of their own civilization. The adoption of this view by certain Muslims is, therefore, even more surprising since it does so much injustice to the grandeur of Islamic civilization and, even more importantly, is manifestly false.[83]

The method of reducing philosophy to the history of philosophy is itself something completely modern and non-Islamic. Nor in fact does this method conform to the perspective of any of the other major traditional civilizations. In such civilizations, philosophy is not identified with an individual who gives his name to a particular philosophical mode of thought. . . . Rather, philosophy is identified with an intellectual perspective which lasts over the centuries and which, far from being a barrier to creativity, remains a viable means of access to the Truth within the particular tradition in question. Men who give their names to traditional schools of thought are seen more as "intellectual functions" than mere individuals.[84]

Islamic intellectual life should be divided into its traditional schools of *uṣūl*, *kalām*, *mashshā'ī* (Peripatetic) philosophy, *ishrāqī* (the School of Illumination), *ma'rifah* or *'irfān* (theoretical and doctrinal Sufims) and, finally, the later school of *al-ḥikmat al-muta'āliyah* (the Transcendent Theosophy) associated with the name of Ṣadr al-Dīn Shīrāzī. Then each of these schools should be subdivided according to their traditional divisions, such as Sunni and Shī'ite *uṣūl*, Mu'tazilite, Ash'arite, Ithnā 'Asharī and Ismā'īlī kalām, eastern and western schools of *mashshā'ī* philosophy, etc., . . .

In the same manner, the development of *mashshā'ī* philosophy should not stop with Ibn Rushd, as is usually the case, following Western sources for which Islamic philosophy ends with him, but include the later Turkish criticisms of his *Tahāfut al-tahāfut* during the Ottoman period, the revival of *mashshā'ī* philosophy in the East by Naṣīr al-Dīn Ṭūsī and Quṭb al-Dīn Shīrāzī and the continuation of the school of Ibn Sīnā up to our own times, when major philosophical commentaries and analyzes of his work have continued to appear in Persia, Pakistan and India. The same could be said of the other schools.[85]

The traditional conflict between the various schools of Islamic thought should also be taught as conflicts between so many different perspectives converging upon the Truth, conflicts which are of a very different nature from those found between contending philosophical schools in the modern world because, in the first case, there are always the transcendent principles of the Islamic tradition which ultimately unify, whereas, in the second case, such unifying principles are missing. It is true that the Ash'arites opposed the Mu'tazilities, that the *mutakallimūn* in general were against the *mashshā'ī* philosophers, that Suhrawardī, the founder of the school of *ishrāq*, criticized Peripatetic logic and metaphysics, that Ibn Taymiyyah wrote against formal logic and Sufism, etc. But had these conflicts been like those of modern thought, the Islamic tradition would not have survived. There was, however, always the unifying principle of *al-tawḥīd*, and a sense of hierarchy within the Islamic tradition itself which allowed intellectual figures to appear from time to time who were at once *mutakallim*, philosophers and metaphysicians of the gnostic school (*al-ma'rifah*), and who realized the inner unity of these perspectives within their own being. The fact that there were many and not just one school of thought should not therefore be taught to students as a sign of either chaos or weakness, but as the result of the richness of the Islamic tradition, which was able to cater to the needs of different intellectual types and therefore to keep within its fold so many human beings of differing backgrounds and intellectual abilities. The diversity should be taught as the consequence of so many applications of the teachings of Islam, some more partial and some more complete, yet all formulated so as to prevent men with different mental abilities and attitudes from seeking knowledge and the quenching of their thirst for answers to certain questions outside the structure of the Islamic tradition itself, as was to happen in the Christian West during the Renaissance. This profusion and diversity of schools, which were different but which all drew from the fountain-head of the Quranic revelation and *al-tawḥīd*, was the means whereby Islam succeeded in preserving the sacred character of knowledge and different sciences was a necessity.[86]

In nearly every branch of philosophy, the Islamic tradition is rich beyond belief, if only its sources were made known. This is especially true of metaphysics. Here Islamic metaphysics should be presented as the science of Ultimate Reality, which is the One (*al-Aḥad*) or Allah, who has revealed Himself in the Quran. There has been no Islamic school whose teachings are not based on the doctrine of the One who is both Absolute and Infinite. In the study of this Sublime Principle, the Muslim sages developed several languages of discourse, some based on the consideration of the One as Pure Being with an ensuing ontology conforming to that view but always seeing Pure Being, not as the first link in the "great chain of being," but as the Source which transcends existence altogether. Others saw the One as Light (*al-nūr*) according to the Quranic verse, "God is the Light of the Heavens and the earth"—(XXIV:35); and yet others as the Truth (*al-Ḥaqq*) which transcends even Pure Being, as the supra-ontological Principle whose first determination or act is in fact Being for God said *be* (*kun*) and *there was*. It is the Western scholars of Islamic philosophy who have called Ibn Sīnā "the first philosopher of being"; without any exaggeration or chauvinism, one could say that, in a sense, the development of ontology in the West is a commentary or footnote to Ibn Sīnā, but one which moves towards an ever more limited understanding of Being until finally it results in either the neglect of ontology or a parody of it.[87]

As we remarked earlier, emphasis on the Islamic contours of Muslim philosophy and its religious character becomes more pronounced in Nasr's works[88] as we approach the present. *Islamic Spirituality—Manifestations*, Volume I,[89] elaborated the point further. Nasr wrote,

Every integral Religion has within it intellectual dimensions that may be called theological, philosophical, and gnostic—if this latter term is understood as referring to a knowledge that illuminates and liberates. Islam is no exception to this principle and has developed within its bosom all three types of intellectual activity, each possessing a millennial tradition with numerous illustrious representatives. The relative significance of each dimension is, however, not the same in Islam and Christianity, nor do the categories correspond exactly to schools into which their names are translated in a European language such as English. In the Islamic intellectual universe, there exists first of all *al-ma'rifah* or *al-'irfān* (gnosis). Then there is *falsafah*, which is itself derived from the Greek *philosophia* and corresponds to philosophy in the older sense of the term, before it became limited to its positivistic definition. This school in turn became transformed for the most part in later centuries into *al-ḥikmat al-ilāhiyyah* (literally, theo-sophia). Finally, there is *Kalām*, usually translated as theology, whose propagators, the *mutakallimūn*, were referred to by Thomas Aquinas as the *loquentes*. The significance of these intellectual dimensions is not the same as corresponding perspectives in the West. This is especially true of *Kalām*, which does not at all occupy the same central role in Islamic thought as theology does in Christianity. Furthermore, the Islamic schools have interacted with each other in a totally different manner from what one observes in the Christian West. Gnosis has played a more central role in the Islamic traditions than it has in the West, and the destiny of philosophy has been very different in the two worlds despite their close affinity in the European Middle Ages. As for theology, it has continued to harbor over the centuries the profoundest religious and spiritual impulses of Christianity, whereas in Islam it has always been more peripheral although much that is considered to be theology in the West is to be found in Islamic philosophy.

In Christianity not only has theology attempted to provide a rational defense for the faith, but it has also sought to provide access to the highest realms of the life of the spirit, as one finds in the mystical theology of Dionysius the Areopagite or, in the Protestant context, in the *Theologica Germanica* of Martin Luther. Such has never been the case in Islam, where *Kalām*, which means literally "word," continued to be "the science that bears responsibility of solidly establishing religious beliefs by giving proofs and dispelling doubts."[90] The deepest spiritual and intellectual expressions of Islam are not to be found in works of *Kalām*. Yet this science is important for the understanding of certain aspects of Islamic thought and must be treated in any work seeking to deal with the manifestations of Islamic spirituality.[91]

Commenting upon the meaning and significance of the Islamic philosophy in the Islamic Tradition he said,

In the Islamic perspective, the intellect (*al-'aql*) and the spirit (*al-rūḥ*) are closely related and are two faces of the same reality. Islamic spirituality is inseparable from intellectuality as traditionally understood, and those who have been concerned with the intellect in the Islamic cultural citadel and those concerned with the world of the spirit form a single family with profound affinities with each other. This fact is certainly true of the Islamic philosophers who have been considered by most Western scholars of Islam as well as anti-intellectualist elements within the Islamic world to be peripheral and outside of the main current of Islamic intellectual life. In reality, however, Islamic philosophy constitutes an important component of the Islamic intellectual tradition, and the Islamic philosophers belong to the same spiritual universe as the gnostics (*'urafā'*) among the Sufis. Furthermore, Islamic philosophy has played an important role in the development of *Kalām*, not to speak of the Islamic sciences such as mathematics, astronomy, and medicine, which have been inseparable from Islamic philosophy throughout their history.

To understand the significance of Islamic philosophy, it is necessary to go beyond the prevalent Western view, according to which Islamic philosophy began with al-Kindī and terminated with Ibn Rushd (the famous Latin Averroes) with Ibn Khaldūn representing an interesting postscript. Moreover, one must understand this philosophy as Islamic and not Arabic philosophy, for, although some of its great representatives such as al-Kindī and Ibn Rushd were Arabs, the majority, including such major figures as Ibn Sīnā, Suhrawardī, and Mullā Ṣadrā, were Persian. Especially during the later centuries, the main home of Islamic philosophy was Persia and adjacent areas of the Islamic world such as Muslim India, which had close links with Persian culture. This philosophy is also Islamic not only because different Muslim peoples cultivated it but because it is related by its roots, dominating concepts, and determining world view to the Islamic revelation, which also molded the mind and soul of those intellectual figures who developed this philosophy.

Some figures within the Islamic world wrote works on philosophy, for example, Muḥammad ibn Zakariyyā' al-Rāzī (d. ca. 320/932), but their philosophy was not Islamic in this sense of being related in its principles to the Islamic revelation and functioning in a universe in which revelation looms as a blinding reality upon the horizon. The main tradition of philosophy from al-Kindī and al-Fārābī to Shāh Walīallāh of Delhi and Sabziwārī, however, was Islamic in that it was integrally related to the principles of the Islamic revelation and an organic part of the Islamic intellectual universe. Moreover, this philosophical tradition did not die eight centuries ago with Ibn Rushd but has continued as a living tradition to this day. To understand Islamic spirituality fully, one must gain some knowledge of this long philosophical tradition, which may be called "prophetic philosophy" . . . [92]

The main concern of philosophy was the discovery of the truth wherever it might be. In a famous statement of Abū Ya'qūb al-Kindī, that has been repeated often over the centuries, all Islamic philosophy is characterised. He said:

> We should not be ashamed to acknowledge truth and to assimilate it from whatever source it comes to us, even if it is brought to us by former generations and foreign peoples. For him who seeks the truth there is nothing of higher value than truth itself; it never cheapens or abases him who reaches for it, but ennobles and honors him.[93]

Regarding this, Nasr comments:

> It was this universal conception of truth that has always characterized Islamic philosophy—a truth, however, which is not bound by the limits of reason.

> Rather, it is the illimitable Truth reached by the intellect which al-Kindī, like other Islamic philosophers, distinguished clearly from reason as the analytical faculty of the mind. This intellect is like an instrument of inner revelation for which the macrocosmic revelation provides an objective cadre. The Islamic philosophers considered the call of the truth to be the highest call of philosophy, but this did not mean the subservience of revelation to reason, as some have contended. Rather, it meant to reach the truth at the heart of revelation through the use of the intellect, which, in its macrocosmic manifestation usually identified with the archangel of revelation, Gabriel, is the instrument of revelation itself.[94]
>
> It was the destiny of Islamic philosophy to become finally wed to gnosis in the bosom of the revealed truth of Islam. When one studies later Islamic philosophers, one realizes immediately this wedding between ratiocination and inner illumination, between intellection and spiritual experience, between rational thought and sanctity. This final union characterizes the ultimate nature and destiny of Islamic philosophy, which, besides its great importance in the domains of logic, mathematics, and the natural sciences, has always been concerned with the supreme science and that knowledge which is inseparable from inner realization. That is why Islamic philosophy has been and remains to this day an important element in the vast and multidimensional universe of Islamic spirituality.[95]

The most profound and direct treatment that the subject of Islamic philosophy received from his pen is to be found in Nasr's recent compilation on the history of Islamic philosophy.[96] He reminds the reader that

> On the one hand what is called philosophy in English must be sought in the context of Islamic civilization not only in the various schools of Islamic philosophy but also in schools bearing other names, especially *Kalām*, *ma'rifah*, *uṣūl al-fiqh* as well as the *awā'il* sciences, not to speak of such subjects as grammar and history which developed particular branches of philosophy. On the other hand each school of thought sought to define what is meant by *ḥikmah* or *falsafah* according to its own perspective. . . . The term over which there was the greatest debate was *ḥikmah*, which was claimed by the Sufis and *mutakallimūn* as well as the philosophers [on the basis of traditional texts]. . . . The Islamic philosophers meditated upon the old definitions of *falsafah* and identified it with the Quranic term *ḥikmah* believing the origin of *ḥikmah* to be divine.[97]

Pointing to the comprehensive nature of Islamic philosophy Nasr said that it emphasised the "relation between the theoretical aspect of philosophy and its practical dimension, between thinking philosophically and leading a virtuous life. This nexus, which is to be seen in all schools of earlier Islamic philosophy, became even more evident from Suhrawardī onward and the *ḥakīm* came to be seen throughout Islamic society not as someone who could only discuss mental concepts in a clever manner but as one who also lived according to the wisdom which he knew theoretically."[98] Speaking of the decadence of philosophy in the West he remarked, ". . . the term *philosophy* also suffers from limitations imposed upon it by those who have practised it during the past few centuries. If Hobbes, Hume, and Ayer are philosophers, then those who Suhrawardī calls *ḥukamā'* are not philosophers, and vice versa."[99] That is to say that, for Islamic philosophers, philosophy has to "be realized within one's whole being and not only mentally."[100] It included

> purification of the soul from its material defilement or what the Islamic philosophers call *tajarrud* or catharsis. Mullā Ṣadrā accepts the meaning of *ḥikmah* as understood by Suhrawardī and then expands the meaning of *falsafah* to include the dimension of illumination and realization implied by the *ishrāqī* and also Sufi understanding of the term. For him as for his contemporaries, as well as most of his successors, *falsafah* or philosophy was seen as the supreme science of ultimately divine origin, derived from "the niche of prophecy" and the *ḥukamā'* as the most perfect of human beings standing in rank only below the prophets and Imams.[101]

The "Islamic definition of philosophy," then, would be "as that reality which transforms both the mind and the soul and which is ultimately never separated from spiritual purity and ultimately sanctity that the very term *ḥikmah* implies in the Islamic context."[102]

Having defined Islamic philosophy thus, Nasr turned to the discussion of the source of Islamic philosophy that he explained in a new light.[103]

> Viewed from the point of view of the Western intellectual tradition, Islamic philosophy appears as simply Graeco-Alexandrian philosophy in Arabic dress, a philosophy whose sole role was to transmit certain important elements of the heritage of antiquity to the medieval West. If seen, however, from its own perspective and in the light of the whole of the Islamic philosophical tradition which has had a twelve-century-long continuous history and is still alive today, it becomes abundantly clear that Islamic philosophy, like everything else Islamic, is deeply rooted in the Quran and *Ḥadīth*. Islamic philosophy is Islamic not only by virtue of the fact that it was cultivated in the Islamic world and by Muslims but because it derives its principles, inspiration and many of the questions with which it has been concerned from the sources of Islamic revelation despite the claims of its opponents to the contrary.[104]

> The very presence of the Quran and the advent of its revelation was to transform radically the universe in which and about which Islamic philosophers were to philosophize, leading to a specific kind of philosophy which can be justly called "prophetic philosophy" . . . a type of philosophy in which a revealed book is accepted as the supreme source of knowledge not only of religious law but of the very nature of existence and beyond existence of the very source of existence. The prophetic consciousness which is the recipient of revelation (*al-waḥy*) had to remain of the utmost significance for those who

sought to know the nature of things. How were the ordinary human means of knowing related to such an extraordinary manner of knowing? How was human reason related to that intellect which is illuminated by the light of revelation? To understand the pertinence of such issues, it is enough to cast even a cursory glance at the works of the Islamic philosophers who almost unanimously accepted revelation as a source of ultimate knowledge. . . .

One might say that the reality of the Islamic revelation and participation in this reality transformed the very instrument of philosophising in the Islamic world. . . . The theoretical intellect, which is the epistemological instrument of all philosophical activity, is Islamicized in a subtle way that is not always detectable through only the analysis of the technical vocabulary involved. . . . The subtle change that took place from the Greek idea of the "intellect" (*nous*) to the Islamic view of the intellect (*al-'aql*) can also be seen much earlier in the works of even the Islamic Peripatetics such as Ibn Sīnā where the Active Intellect (*al-'aql al-fa''āl*) is equated with the Holy Spirit (*al-rūḥ al-qudus*).[105]

Islamic philosophy is related to both the external dimension of the Quranic revelation or the *Sharī'ah* and the inner truth or *Ḥaqīqah* which is the heart of all that is Islamic. Many of the doctors of the Divine Law or *Sharī'ah* have stood opposed to Islamic philosophy while others have accepted it. In fact some of the outstanding Islamic philosophers such as Ibn Rushd, Mīr Dāmād and Shāh Walīallāh of Delhi have also been authorities in the domain of the Sacred Law. The *Sharī'ah* has, however, provided mostly the social and human conditions for the philosophical activity of the Islamic philosophers. It is to the *Ḥaqīqah* that one has to turn for the inspiration and source of knowledge for Islamic philosophy. . . . Throughout history, many an Islamic philosopher has identified *falsafah* or *ḥikmah*, the two main terms used with somewhat different meaning for Islamic philosophy, with the *Ḥaqīqah* lying at the heart of the Quran. Much of Islamic philosophy is in fact a hermeneutic unveiling of the two grand books of revelation, the Quran and the cosmos, and in the Islamic intellectual universe Islamic philosophy belongs, despite some differences, to the same family as that of *ma'rifah* or gnosis which issues directly from the inner teachings of Islam. . . .[106]

For the main tradition of Islamic philosophy, especially as it developed in later centuries, philosophical activity was inseparable from interiorization of oneself and penetration into the inner meaning of the Quran and *Ḥadīth*. . . .

The close nexus between the Quran and *Ḥadīth*, on the one hand, and Islamic philosophy, on the other, is to be seen in the understanding of the history of philosophy.[107] . . . [Muslims] considered Idrīs as the origin of philosophy, bestowing upon him the title of *Abū'l-Ḥukamā'* (the father of philosophers). . . . Muslims considered prophecy to be the origin of philosophy, confirming in an Islamic form the dictum of Oriental Neoplatonism that "Plato was Moses in Attic Greek." The famous Arabic saying, "philosophy issues from the niche of prophecy" has echoed through the annals of Islamic history and indicates clearly how Islamic philosophers themselves envisaged the relation between philosophy and revelation. . . .

There are certain *Ḥadīth* which point to God having offered prophecy and

> philosophy or *ḥikmah*, and Luqmān chose *ḥikmah* which must not be confused simply with medicine or other branches of traditional *ḥikmah* but refers to pure philosophy itself dealing with God and the ultimate causes of things. These traditional authorities also point to such Quranic verses as "And He will teach him the Book [*al-kitāb*] and Wisdom [*al-ḥikmah*]" . . . They believe that this conjunction confirms the fact that what God has revealed through revelation He had also made available through *ḥikmah*, which is reached through *'aql*, itself a microcosmic reflection of the macrocosmic reality which is the instrument of revelation. . . . All of this indicates how closely traditional Islamic philosophy identified itself with revelation in general and the Quran in particular.[108]

At this point Nasr draws the attention of his readers to the fact that the Islamic philosophers meditated upon the content of the Quran as a whole as well as on the particular verses to which the uninterrupted chain of the Quranic commentaries testify.

Then he turns to elucidate the Quranic themes that worked as the source of inspiration to Islamic philosophy.

> Certain Quranic themes have dominated Islamic philosophy throughout its long history and especially during the later period when this philosophy becomes a veritable theosophy in the original and not deviant meaning of the term, *theosophia* corresponding exactly to the Arabic term *al-ḥikmat al-ilāhiyyah*. The first and the foremost is of course the unity of the Divine Principle and ultimately Reality as such or *al-tawḥīd* which lies at the heart of the Islamic message. The Islamic philosophers were all *muwaḥḥid* or followers of *tawḥīd* and saw authentic philosophy in this light. They called Pythagoras and Plato, who had confirmed the unity of the Ultimate Principle, *muwaḥḥid* while showing singular lack of interest in later forms of Greek and Roman philosophy, which were sceptical or agnostic.
>
> How Islamic philosophers interpreted the doctrine of Unity lies at the heart of Islamic philosophy. There continued to exist a tension between the Quranic description of Unity and what the Muslims had learned from Greek sources, a tension which was turned into a synthesis of the highest intellectual order by such later philosophers as Suhrawardī and Mullā Ṣadrā. But in all treatments of this subject from al-Kindī to Mullā 'Alī Zunūzī and Ḥājjī Mullā Hādī Sabziwārī during the thirteenth/nineteenth century and even later, the Quranic doctrine of Unity, so central to Islam, has remained dominant and in a sense has determined the agenda of the Islamic philosophers. . . . The concern of Islamic philosophers with ontology is directly related to the Quranic doctrine of *kun fa-yakūn*, as is the very terminology of Islamic philosophy in this domain where it understands by *wujūd* more the verb or act of existence (*esto*) than the noun or state of existence (*esse*). If Ibn Sīnā has been called first and foremost a "philosopher of being," and he developed the ontology which came to dominate much of medieval philosophy, this is not because of the Quranic doctrine of the One in relation to the act of existence. It was as a result of meditation upon the Quran in conjunction with Greek thought that Islamic

philosophers developed the doctrine of Pure Being which stands above the chain of being and is discontinuous with it, while certain other philosophers such as a number of Isma'īlīs considered God to be beyond Being and identified His act or the Quranic *kun* with Being, which is then considered as the principle of the universe.

It is also the Quranic doctrine of the creating God and *creatio ex nihilo*, with all the different levels of meaning which *nihilo* possesses, that led Islamic philosophers to distinguish sharply between God as Pure Being and the existence of the universe, destroying that "block without fissure" which constituted Aristotelian ontology. In Islam the universe is always contingent (*mumkin al-wujūd*) while God is necessary (*wājib al-wujūd*), to use the well-known distinction of Ibn Sīnā. No Islamic philosopher has ever posited an existential continuity between the existence of creatures and the Being of God, and this radical revolution in the understanding of Aristotelian ontology has its source in the Islamic doctrine of God and creation as asserted in the Quran and *Ḥadīth*. Moreover, this influence is paramount not only in the case of those who asserted the doctrine of *creatio ex nihilo* in its ordinary theological sense, but also for those such as al-Fārābī and Ibn Sīnā who were in favour of the theory of emanation but who none the less never negated the fundamental distinction between the *wujūd* (existence) of the world and that of God.

As for the whole question of "newness" or "eternity" of the world, or *ḥudūth* and *qidam*, which has occupied Islamic thinkers for the past twelve centuries and which is related to the question of the contingency of the world *vis-à-vis* the Divine Principle, it is inconceivable without the teachings of the Qur'an and *Ḥadīth*. It is of course a fact that before the rise of Islam Christian theologians and philosophers such as John Philoponus had written on this issue and that Muslims had known some of these writings, especially the treatise of Philoponus against the thesis of the eternity of the world. But had it not been for the Quranic teachings concerning creation, such Christian writings would have played an altogether different role in Islamic thought. Muslims were interested in the arguments of a Philoponus precisely because of their own concern with the question of *ḥudūth* and *qidam*, created by the tension between the teachings of the Quran and the *Ḥadīth*, on the one hand, and the Greek notion of the non-temporal relation between the world and its Divine Origin, on the other.[109]

It was precisely the Islamic insistence upon Divine Omniscience that placed the issue of God's knowledge of the world at the center of the concern of Islamic philosophy . . .

This issue is also closely allied to the philosophical significance of revelation (*al-waḥy*) itself. Earlier Islamic philosophers such as Ibn Sīnā sought to develop a theory by drawing to some extent, but not exclusively, on Greek theories of the intellect and the faculties of the soul. . . . While still using certain concepts of Greek origin, the later Islamic philosophers such as Mullā Ṣadrā drew heavily from the Quran and *Ḥadīth* on this issue.

Turning to the field of cosmology, again one can detect the constant presence of Quranic themes and certain *Ḥadīth*. . . . Nor must one forget the cosmological significance of the nocturnal ascent of the Prophet (*al-mi'rāj*) which so many Islamic philosophers have treated directly, starting with Ibn Sīnā. . . .

In no branch of Islamic philosophy, however, is the influence of the Quran and *Ḥadīth* more evident than in eschatology, the very understanding of which in the Abrahamic universe was alien to the philosophical world of antiquity. . . .

The Islamic philosophers were fully aware of these crucial (eschatological) ideas in their philosophising, but the earlier ones were unable to provide philosophical proofs for Islamic doctrines which many confessed to accept on the basis of faith but could not demonstrate within the context of Peripatetic philosophy. . . . It remained for Mullā Ṣadrā several centuries later to demonstrate the reality of bodily resurrection through the principles of the "transcendent theosophy" (*al-ḥikmat al-muta'āliyah*) and to take both Ibn Sīnā and al-Ghazzālī to task for the inadequacy of their treatment of the subject. The most extensive philosophical treatment of eschatology (*al-ma'ād*) in all its dimensions is in fact to be found in the *Asfār* of Mullā Ṣadrā.[110]

In meditating upon the history of Islamic philosophy in its relation to the Islamic revelation, one detects a movement toward ever closer association of philosophy with the Quran and *Ḥadīth* as *falsafah* became transformed into *al-ḥikmat al-ilāliyah*. . . . the trend culminated in the form of the commentaries on the text of the Quran or on certain of the *Ḥadīth* and continued in later centuries not only in Persia but also in India and the Ottoman world including Iraq.

The Quran and *Ḥadīth*, along with the sayings of the Imāms, which are in a sense the extension of *Ḥadīth* in the Shī'ite world, have provided over the centuries the framework and matrix for Islamic philosophy and created the intellectual and social climate within which Islamic philosophers have philosophized. Moreover, they have presented a knowledge of the origin, the nature of things, humanity and its final ends and history upon which the Islamic philosophers have meditated and from which they have drawn over the ages. They have also provided a language of discourse which Islamic philosophers have shared with the rest of the Islamic community. Without the Quranic revelation, there would of course have been no Islamic civilization, but it is important to realize that there would also have been no Islamic philosophy. Philosophical activity in the Islamic world is not simply a regurgitation of Graeco-Alexandrian philosophy in Arabic, as claimed by many Western scholars along with some of their Islamic followers, a philosophy which grew despite the presence of the Quran and *Ḥadīth*. On the contrary, Islamic philosophy is what it is precisely because it flowered in a universe whose contours are determined by the Quranic revelation.

As asserted at the beginning of this chapter, Islamic philosophy is essentially "prophetic philosophy" based on the hermeneutics of a Sacred Text which is the result of a revelation that is inalienably linked to the microcosmic intellect and which alone is able to actualize the dormant possibilities of the intellect within us. Islamic philosophy, as understood from within that tradition, is also an unveiling of the inner meaning of the Sacred Text, a means of access to that *Haqīqah* which lies hidden within the inner dimension of the Quran.

> Islamic philosophy deals with the One or Pure Being, and universal existence and all the grades of the universal hierarchy. It deals with man and his entelechy, with the cosmos and the final return of all things to God. This interpretation of existence is none other than penetration into the inner meaning of the Quran which "is" existence itself, the Book whose meditation provides the key for the understanding of those objective and subjective orders of existence with which the Islamic philosopher has been concerned over the ages.
>
> A deeper study of Islamic philosophy over its twelve-hundred-year history will reveal the role of the Quran and *Ḥadīth* in the formulation, exposition and problematics of this major philosophical tradition. In the same way that all of the Islamic philosophers from al-Kindī onwards knew the Quran and *Ḥadīth* and lived with them, Islamic philosophy has manifested over the centuries its inner link with the revealed sources of Islam, a link which has become even more manifest as the centuries have unfolded, for Islamic philosophy is essentially a philosophical hermeneutics of the Sacred Text while making use of the rich philosophical heritage of antiquity. That is why, far from being a transitory and foreign phase in the history of Islamic thought, Islamic philosophy has remained over the centuries and to this day one of the major intellectual perspectives in Islamic civilization with its roots sunk deeply, like everything else Islamic, in the Quran and *Ḥadīth*.[111]

Moreover, Nasr reasserted the point that Islamic philosophy was not only important for the Islamic civilization in the past. It is important for the present and the future as well.

> Today Islamic philosophy remains a living intellectual tradition, and, because of the harmony it has achieved between logic and the spiritual life and because of the profound doctrines it contains within the pages of its long and extended historical unfolding, it remains of the greatest pertinence for the modern world. Furthermore, because of the present encounter of Islam with an alien philosophy and sciences—this time from the West—Islamic philosophy must be called upon once again to play the role it fulfilled in early Islamic history, namely to provide the necessary intellectual instruments and the requisite intellectual background with the aid of which Muslims can face various alien philosophies and sciences from a position of discrimination and intellectual rigour. Islamic *falsafah* or *ḥikmah* can fulfil this vital function of providing the Muslims themselves with the necessary intellectual background to confront the modern West and the world with long forgotten but urgently needed truths which Islamic philosophy has been able to preserve within its treasury of wisdom over the centuries and which it is able to present in a contemporary language to the world today.
>
> A thorough re-understanding and re-presentation of Islamic philosophy will itself "orient" our thought by clarifying the ultimate end of human existence and the final goal of man's terrestrial journey. Man is a theomorphic being and cannot escape the profound demands of his inner nature. Only that civilisation and form of thought can survive which conform to man's entelechy and the

ultimate nature of things. The re-understanding of Islamic Philosophy will once again reveal to us that end towards which man and the cosmos are ultimately oriented and towards which all things move. It thus permits us to discover the goal of life and thought itself. By revealing to us the truth, it enables us to reorient ourselves and our thoughts in its direction, on that high road whose end is union with the Truth. The question of the reorientation of Islamic philosophy reduces then to a re-understanding of it and to the discovery of the goal towards which our thoughts and efforts should be directed. Man comes to know the truth not by reorienting it but by reorienting himself so that he can become worthy of being its recipient.[112]

MUHAMMAD SUHEYL UMAR

IQBAL ACADEMY PAKISTAN
MARCH 2000

NOTES

1. W. C. Chittick, "Preface," in *The Complete Bibliography of the Works of Seyyed Hossein Nasr,* ed. Mehdi Aminrazavi and Zailan Moris (Kuala Lumpur, 1994), p. XIII.

2. S. H. Nasr, "In Quest of the Eternal Sophia," in *The Complete Bibliography of the Works of Seyyed Hossein Nasr,* ed. Mehdi Aminrazavi and Zailan Moris (Kuala Lumpur, 1994), pp. 28–29. This essay originally appeared in *Philosophes critiques d'eux-mêmes-Philosophiche Selbstbetrachtungen*, vol. 6. (Bern: Peter Lang, 1980), pp. 113–21. The French translation of this essay also appeared in the same issue of this work as "A la recherche de l'eternelle sagesse," pp. 12–31.

3. Ibid., pp. 31–32.

4. M. M. Sharif, *A History of Muslim Philosophy*, vol. I (Wiesbaden, 1963); vol. II (Wiesbaden, 1966).

5. Ibid., vol. I, ch. XIX, "Shihāb al-Dīn Suhrawardī Maqtūl"; vol. I, ch. XXXII, "Fakhr al-Dīn Rāzī"; vol. II, ch. XLVII, "The School of Iṣpahān"; vol. II, ch. XLVIII, "Ṣadr al- Dīn Shīrāzī (Mullā Ṣadrā)".; vol. II, ch. LXVI, "Natural History"; vol. II, ch. LXXVIII, "Renaissance in Iran (Continued): Ḥāji Mulla Hādi Sabziwāri."

6. M. M. Sharif, *A History of Muslim Philosophy,* vol. I (Wiesbaden, 1963), pp. 372–73.

7. Ibid., p. 379.

8. Ibid., p. 648.

9. Ibid., p. 649.

10. Ibid., p. 655.

11. Ibid., vol. II, p. 907.

12. Ibid., vol. II, p. 939.

13. Ibid., vol. II, pp. 958–59.

14. *An Introduction to Islamic Cosmological Doctrines* (Cambridge Mass.: Harvard University Press, 1964).

15. Ibid., pp. 18–19.

16. Nasr's note: "Tehran National Library, MS. Bayāḍī (dated 659). Also Afḍal al-Dīn al-Kāshānī, *Muṣannafāt*, ed. Mujtabā Mīnovī and Yaḥyā Mahdāvī (Tehran, 1952), vol. I, Introduction; and 'Umar Khayyām, "Az nathr-i fārsī-i Khayyām," *Sharq*, 1:167–168 (1309 [1930]). Likewise, al-Ghazzālī, in his *al-Munqidh min al-ḍalāl*, divides the seekers of knowledge into the *mutakallimīn, bāṭiniyah* (Ismā'īlīs), *falāsifah* and *ṣūfiyah*; see W. Montgomery Watt, *The Faith and Practice of al-Ghazali* (London, 1953), pp. 25ff." (Ibid., p. 20, note 44).

17. Ibid., p. 20.

18. *Three Muslim Sages* (Cambridge: Harvard University Press, 1964); reprint, (Lahore: Suhail Academy, 1988, 1999), pp. 9–10, 12–15, 17–19, 42–43.

19. Ibid., pp. 12–13.

20. Ibid., p. 43.

21. Nasr, *Science and Civilization in Islam* (Cambridge: Harvard University Press, 1968 and New York: Mentor Books, 1970); reprint (Suhail Academy, Lahore, 1983, 1999).

22. Ibid., pp. 33–38.

23. Ibid., pp. 293–349.

24. Ibid., pp. 293–94.

25. "Al-Ḥikmat al-Ilāhiyyah and Kalām," *Studia Islamica* 34 (1971): 139–149.

26. Ibid., pp. 140–41.

27. "Lāhījī, *Gawhar-Murād* (Tehran, 1377 [A. H. Lunar]), pp. 15–21." (Ibid., p. 149, note 2).

28. Ibid., p. 149.

29. See S. H. Nasr, "The Meaning and Role of Philosophy in Islam," *Studia Islamica* 36 (1973): 57–80.

30. *An Introduction to Islamic Cosmological Doctrines* (Cambridge, Mass.: Harvard University Press, 1964), pp. 18–20.

31. S. H. Nasr, "The Meaning and Role of Philosophy in Islam," op. cit., p. 57.

32. Ibid., pp. 57–58.

33. Ibid., pp. 58–59.

34. Ibid., p. 61.

35. Nasr's note: "Already Ibn Khaldūn in his *Muqaddimah*, trans. by F. Rosenthal, vol. 3 (New York, 1958), pp. 52 ff., considered the later school of *kalām* as philosophy and many contemporary Arab authors have emphasised the importance of *kalām* and also Sufism as forms of 'Islamic philosophy'. See for example Muṣṭafā 'Abd al-Rāziq, *Tamhīd li-ta'rīkh al-falsafat al-islāmiyyah*, Cairo, 1959." (Ibid., p. 62, note 1.)

36. Ibid., p. 62.

37. Ibid., p. 63.

38. Ibid., p. 65, note 4. "*Rasā'il*, Cairo, vol. I, 1928, p. 23. [Even] [t]he Ikhwān have a conception of philosophy very close to that of the *ishrāqīs* and the whole later tradition of Islamic philosophy, . . . See Nasr, *An Introduction to Islamic Cosmological Doctrines*, pp. 33ff." (Ibid., p. 65, note 4).

39. Mullā Ṣadrā, *Al-Ḥikmat al-Muta'āliyah fi 'l-asfār al-arba'ah,* Tehran, 1387 (A. H. Lunar), vol. I, part, I, p. 20.

40. E.g., Quran, 2: 269.

41. "Mullā Ṣadrā, *Al-Ḥikmat al-Muta'āliyah fi 'l-asfār al-arba'ah*, vol. I, part I, op. cit., p. 21."

42. Ibid., p. 68.

43. Ibid., pp. 68–69.

44. See *An Introduction to Islamic Cosmological Doctrines* (Cambridge, Mass.: Harvard University Press, 1964) and *Science and Civilization in Islam* (Cambridge, Mass.: Harvard University Press, 1968 and New York: Mentor Books, 1970); reprint (Lahore: Suhail Academy, 1983, 1999).

45. S. H. Nasr, "The Meaning and Role of Philosophy in Islam," op. cit., pp. 69–73.

46. "See S. H. Nasr, *Three Muslim Sages*, ch. I." (Ibid., p. 74, note 1).

47. Ibid., pp. 73–74.

48. Ibid., p. 75.

49. Ibid., p. 76.

50. Ibid., p. 79.

51. Ibid.

52. "Post-Avicennian Philosophy and the Study of Being," in *Humā'ī Nāmah*, (ed.) Mehdi Mohaghegh (Tehran, 1977), p. 23.

53. *Islamic Life and Thought* (London: Unwin, 1981); reprint (Lahore: Suhail Academy, 1985, 1999), chs. 6–19. This book, though appearing in 1981 under the present title, is placed here in its chronological order, precisely because it included a lot of material that Nasr had written much earlier.

54. Ibid., pp. 147–49.

55. Ibid., p. 78.

56. Ibid., p. 151.

57. Ibid., pp. 150–51.

58. Ibid., p. 67.

59. Ibid., p. 78.

60. *Islamic Science, An Illustrated Study* (London: World of Islam Festival Trust, 1976), p. 9.

61. Nasr's note: "For this corpus, which is not the same in Arabic as in Greek, see A. J. Festugiére and A. D. Nock, *La Révélation d'Hermés Trismégiste*, 4 vols. (Paris, 1953) or; G.R.S. Mead, *Thrice-Greatest Hermes*, 3 vols. (London, 1906 and 1949); and W. Scott, *Hermetica*, 4 vols. (Oxford, 1924–1936)." (Ibid., p. 198, note 18).

62. Ibid., p. 198.

63. S. H. Nasr, *Three Muslim Sages*, op. cit., p. 91.

64. Cf. Chittick, "Ṣadr al-Dīn Qūnawī on the Oneness of Being" in *International Philosophical Quarterly* 21 (1981): 171–84.

65. For a profound discussion of the causes that emphasized this need, see S. H. Nasr, *Three Muslim Sages*, op. cit., pp. 1–7.

66. Nasr's note: "Philosophy, in the sense in which we understand the term (which is also its current meaning) primarily consists of logic; this definition of Guenon's puts philosophic thought in its right place and clearly distinguishes it from 'intellectual intuition,' which is the direct apprehension of a truth." F. Schuon, *Language of the Self*, trans. by M. Pallis and M. Matheson (Madras, 1952), p. 7.

67. F. Schuon, *Sufism: Veil and Quintessence* (Suhail Academy, 1985), p. 125.

68. See W. C. Chittick, *The Sufi Path of Knowledge* (State University of New York Press, 1993), pp. xvii–xix. It is true that, after Ibn 'Arabī, there have been Sufis who did not use philosophic terminology. Rumī is its foremost example. Yet it is the dominant trend of the Muslim intellectuality—to the extent that commentators of Rumī's *Mathnawī* also used the ideas and terms of Ibn 'Arabī's school down to the present times.

69. *Islam and the Plight of the Modern Man* (Longman, 1970); reprint (Lahore: Suhail Academy, 1985, 1999).

70. Ibid., p. 34.

71. Logic can either operate as part of an intellection, or else, on the contrary, put itself at the service of an error; moreover, unintelligence can diminish or even nullify logic, so that philosophy can in fact become the vehicle of almost anything; it can be an Aristotelianism carrying ontological insights, just as it can degenerate into an "existentialism" in which logic has become a mere shadow of itself, a blind and unreal operation; indeed, what can be said of a "metaphysic" which idiotically posits man at the center of the Real, like a sack of coal, and which operates with such blatantly subjective and conjectural concepts as 'worry' and 'anguish'? F. Schuon, *Language of the Self*, trans. by M. Pallis and M. Matheson (Madras, 1952), p. 7.

72. See S. N. Nasr, *Islamic Studies*, chaps. 8 and 9; Nasr, "The Tradition of Islamic Philosophy in Persia and its Significance for the Modern World"; also Nasr, "Persia and the Destiny of Islamic Philosophy," *Studies in Comparative Religion* (Winter 1972): 31–42.

73. Not only this. There is an underlying harmony of the Islamic sciences with Islamic philosophy, theology and metaphysics; a harmony that is closely related to the philosophy of nature alluded to in other works.

74. *Islam and the Plight of the Modern Man*, op. cit., p. 38.

75. S. H. Nasr, *Knowledge and the Sacred* (New York: Crossroad, 1981); Suhail Academy, 1988, 1999), p. 38.

76. Ibid., pp. 81–82.

77. Ibid., pp. 71–72.

78. Ibid., p. 35.

79. S. H. Nasr, *Traditional Islam in the Modern World* (London: KPI, 1987); (Lahore: Suhail Academy, 1988, 1999).

80. The term *philosophie prophetique* was used quite correctly by Corbin to describe Islamic philosophy, which functions in a universe dominated by the presence of a revealed book that is not only the source of religious law and ethics but also the fountainhead of knowledge and a means of access to the truth.

81. S. H. Nasr, *Traditional Islam in the Modern World*, op. cit., pp. 131–33.

82. Ibid., p. 139.

83. Ibid., pp. 205–7.

84. Ibid., p. 211.

85. Ibid., pp. 211–12.

86. Ibid., pp. 213–14.

87. Ibid., p. 215.

88. In 1993 Nasr wrote a book that was different from his other works in the sense that it was written in a simplified style for the use of young students. The contents, argument, and the conclusions are the same as we find in other works. See S. H. Nasr, *A Young Muslim's Guide to the Modern World* (Kazi, 1993); (Lahore: Suhail Academy, 1998).

89. S. H. Nasr, *Islamic Spirituality—Manifestations*, vol. I (New York: Crossroad, 1991).

90. Nasr's note: "This is one definition given by 'Aḍud al-Dīn al-Ījī, one of the later masters of the science of *Kalām*, in his *Mawāqif* (Stations) (translated in the article of G. C. Anawati entitled "Kalām" in the new *Encyclopedia of Religion* [New York: Macmillan, 1987] 8:231)." (Note 1, p. 439)

91. Ibid., pp. 395–96.

92. Ibid., pp. 409–10. This passage continues on pp. 410–11: "The best-known school of Islamic philosophy, the *mashshā'ī* or Peripatetic, which is a synthesis of the tenets of the Islamic revelation, Aristotelianism, and Neoplatonism of both the Athenian and Alexandrian schools, was founded in the third/ninth century in the rich intellectual climate of Baghdad by Abū Ya'qūb al-Kindī (d. c. 260/873). The so-called philosopher of the Arab was a prolific author who composed over two hundred treatises, in which he dealt with the sciences as well as philosophy, beginning a trend that characterises the whole class of Muslim sages who were philosopher-scientists and not only philosophers."

93. Ibid., p. 411.

94. Ibid.

95. Ibid., p. 439.

96. S. H. Nasr and Oliver Leaman, *History of Islamic Philosophy*, part I (London: Routledge, 1996).

97. S. H. Nasr, "The Meaning and Concept of Philosophy in Islam," in *History of Islamic Philosophy*, part I, pp. 21–22.

98. Ibid., p. 23.

99. Ibid., p. 23.

100. Ibid., p. 24.

101. Ibid.

102. Ibid., p. 25.

103. S. H. Nasr, "The Quran and *Ḥadīth* as source and Inspiration of Islamic Philosophy," in *History of Islamic Philosophy*, part I, ch. 2, op. cit.

104. Nasr's note: ". . . [Taking] into consideration its whole history, however, one will see that this philosophy is at once Muslim and Islamic according to the above-given definitions of these terms." (Ibid., p. 37, note 1).

105. Ibid., p. 28.

106. Ibid., p. 29.

107. See the discussion noted earlier on the prophetic origin of philosophy through the prophet Idrīs, pp. 111, 127.

108. Ibid., pp. 29–31.

109. Ibid., pp. 32–33.

110. Ibid., pp. 34–35.

111. Ibid., pp. 36–37.

112. *Islamic Life and Thought*, op. cit., p. 156.

REPLY TO MUHAMMAD SUHEYL UMAR

Being well versed in Persian and English as well as being an eminent scholar of traditional Islamic thought, Suheyl Umar has spent years in the study of traditional authors and is very well acquainted with practically the whole corpus of my writings. His essay is in a sense a *tour de force* in that he had been able to string along numerous passages drawn from my diverse works written in a period of over forty years to express my views concerning the role of Islamic philosophy and its relation to Islam as a religion, as well as to the general Islamic intellectual tradition. His essay is in fact comprised, practically, completely of my own words to which he has added only a few lines here and there. It is therefore not an essay to which I could respond since it would mean practically responding to myself. Therefore, in light of such a carefully chosen selection of my own writings on the subject, I will take the opportunity to discuss how I came to hold the views expressed in Suheyl Umar's assemblage of my words and to add a few more comments on the role of Islamic philosophy in the Islamic world today and why I consider this philosophical tradition to be so significant in the present-day situation. These words will simply summarize and perhaps also clarify further what I have treated extensively in several of my writings, some quoted by the author, and others not to be found in his text.

While I became immersed in Sufi poetry practically with my mother's milk—remembering of course that the inner meaning of these verses were to be unveiled much later in my life—as a child and as a young man growing up in Persia, I learned nothing of the specific content of Islamic philosophy except a few general ideas and the names of its greatest masters, although I had an intense interest in philosophical questions from those early days. My coming to Islamic philosophy was in fact through a long and circuitous route. At MIT, upon discovering the tenets of traditional metaphysics and the perennial philosophy as expounded in the works of Guénon, Coomaraswamy, Schuon, and others, my interest turned first towards what is called Indian philosophy parallel with Greek and Western philosophy which I was also studying avidly at that time.

At the age of twenty I knew more about the major Greek and Western philosophers and the Hindu *darśanas* and even Chinese thought than I did about Islamic philosophy as distinct from Sufism, which was occupying much of my attention at that time. But interest in traditional philosophies in general and an intellectual return to the Islamic tradition in particular turned me more and more to the study of Islamic philosophy. I began to read avidly Western writers especially Thomistic ones such as E. Gilson and J. Maritain who in writing about Latin scholasticism also paid some attention to so-called "Arab philosophy." I also read all the standard texts available on the subject of Islamic philosophy written by standard Western scholars such as A. Schmölders, S. Munk, G. Dugat, L. Gauthier, T. J. De Boer, B. Carr de Vaux, D. B. MacDonald, J. Obermann, E. Wiedemann, S. Pines, G. Quadri, H. Wolfson, and R. Walzer. Furthermore, I began to read Muslim authors who had written on the subject including such famous Egyptian scholars of Islamic philosophy as I. Madkour, A. Badawi, 'U. Amīn, 'Abd al-Ḥalīm Maḥmūd (who was also an eminent authority on Sufism and a traditionalist in the line of René Guénon), and M. Abū Rīdah as well as the famous philosopher poet Iqbal. The group of Catholic scholars and theologians who were at the same time Islamicists and who wrote on Islamic philosophy also intrigued me and I studied carefully their works. In this group the most important in this phase of my philosophical education were L. Massignon, L. Gardet, and A. A. Anawati, all of whom I came to know personally and had many occasions to carry out extensive discussions on Islamic philosophy with them.

All this study left me, however, ever more convinced that nearly all of these scholars, whether Muslim or Western, were essentially discussing only a part, but not the whole of Islamic philosophy. I learned a great deal from them about Islamic thought and the Western method of scholarship in the field of philosophy, but that knowledge appeared to me to be incomplete because from the traditional perspective, it was not possible for a religion to survive in an integral manner as Islam had done, while losing its intellectual dimension halfway through its historic existence. The brilliant although somewhat erratic short work of Iqbal, *The Development of Metaphysics in Persia*, in which he spoke of the *ishrāqī* or Illuminationist tradition in later centuries, only strengthened my view that there must have been a later tradition of Islamic philosophy after Ibn Rushd which connected the earlier tradition to those friends of my father such as Sayyid Muḥammad Kāẓim 'Aṣṣār, whom I had known as a child and who was called an eminent philosopher by my father who was his close friend as well as by their mutual colleagues.

It was on the basis of this early phase of study of nearly all Western sources on Islamic philosophy that I discovered, while at Harvard, the works of Henry Corbin. This remarkable philosopher *cum* Islamicist, had not as yet discovered, or at least studied and written about Mullā Ṣadrā and other major late figures of Islamic thought, save for a short treatise on Mīr Dāmād which appeared in 1956. But his study on Ibn Sīnā and Suhrawardī which I read at Harvard pointed clearly to the later tradition of Islamic philosophy concentrated in Persia. Interest in and knowledge of traditional metaphysics and epistemology in general, the Western understanding of Islamic philosophy including that of Arab writers, many of whom espousing the cause of Arab nationalism were now using the term "Arabic philosophy" even in Arabic where it had had no historical precedence, my deeper penetration into the structure of Islam itself in both its exoteric and esoteric dimensions, as well as Corbin's vision of Islamic philosophy, all contributed to the formation in my mind of an understanding of Islamic philosophy. These factors also helped me to formulate a vision of the rapport among various schools of Islamic thought along with the relation of Islamic philosophy to Islamic esoterism and theology as well as to the Islamic sciences. My doctoral thesis at Harvard, dealing as it did with the Islamic conceptions of nature, was already based on this early formulated understanding of the meaning of Islamic philosophy and its role and function within the Islamic tradition.

That view has not changed to this day, but it became much more complete and, at least in my mind, more perfected upon my return to Persia in 1958. It is true that while at Harvard I had begun to read works of contemporary traditional Persian philosophers, but it was not until I was able to sit at their feet for long years of study of Islamic philosophy (both *falsafah* and *ḥikmah)* that I was able to realize the importance of the oral tradition and the intellectual and spiritual transmission which only traditional methods of teaching make possible.

Upon returning to Persia I began to study basic philosophical and gnostic (*'irfānī*) texts with several masters over a period that lasted for the next twenty years. Soon upon my arrival and continuing for a dozen years, I studied the *Sharḥ-i manẓūmah* of Sabziwārī, followed by the *Ashi''at al-lama'āt* of Jāmī and sections of the *Fuṣūṣ al-ḥikam* of Ibn 'Arabī with Sayyid Muḥammad Kāẓim 'Aṣṣār. For almost twenty years I studied several texts including the *Sharḥ-i manẓūmah* and the *Asfār* of Mullā Ṣadrā with 'Allāmah Sayyid Muḥammad Ḥusayn Ṭabāṭabā'ī. For five years I studied the first journey or part (*safar)* of the *Asfār* with Sayyid Abu'l-Ḥasan Qazwīnī. For some four years I studied the *Sharḥ al-ishārāt* of Ibn Sīnā and Naṣīr al-Dīn Ṭūsī with Jawād Muṣliḥ and on and off for a dozen years *al-Insān al-kāmil* of Jīlī and *Ḥikmat-i ilāhī khwāṣṣ wa 'āmm* by Mahdī Ilāhī Qumsha'ī (the text including the *Fuṣūṣ al-ḥikmah* of Fārābī) with the master himself. This extensive study in the presence of these masters was combined with immersion in many later texts of Islamic philosophy and the reading of the earlier texts in light of the continuous living tradition in which I had been privileged to participate.

By the time I went for the first time to Pakistan, met the noble Pakistani scholar M. M. Sharīf and began extensive collaboration in *A History of Muslim Philosophy* that he was editing, my general understanding of Islamic philosophy set forth in my later works and discussed in part by Suheyl Umar had already become crystallized. Only further details needed to be filled in during the years to come, but the general contour of the mountain range was clear before my vision. I tried to convince Sharif to change the outline of his *History* in accordance with the view of Islamic philosophy seen in its totality and from within but to no avail. At least he agreed to include some chapters on later Islamic philosophy for which I accepted the responsibility.

I sought to expose my own vision of Islamic philosophy as comprised of a hierarchy of perspectives leading ultimately to the wedding between philosophy and gnosis and the inner unity as well as hierarchic structure of knowledge itself, in a series of lectures delivered at the Center for the Study of World Religions at Harvard University in 1962. It was Harry Wolfson, my old teacher, who insisted that I prepare the manuscript of these lectures for publication by the Harvard University Press. I complied with his request and before leaving Harvard during that summer handed in the text of the *Three Muslim Sages*, which was my first book in English and also the first opus in which my general understanding of the nature and structure of Islamic philosophical and metaphysical thought was set forth; although in that volume I did not write a separate chapter on Mullā Ṣadrā and late Islamic philosophy. The full expression of my vision of what constitutes the various components, schools, and periods of Islamic philosophy was to come over three decades later in the two-volume work which I edited with Oliver Leaman under the title *History of Islamic Philosophy*.

I can say that my understanding of the Islamic philosophical tradition is the result of the combination of the general view of traditional metaphysics, a study of other major intellectual traditions especially Graeco-Alexandrian and the Western, the Indian, and the Chinese, close study of Western scholarship concerning Islamic philosophy and, most of all, immersion in the living Islamic philosophical tradition in Persia for some twenty years. I have sought to create an intellectual synthesis that would be situated within the Islamic intellectual tradition and be traditionally authentic, a synthesis that would be acceptable to my own and other traditional masters in Persia as well as be scholarly and philosophically rigorous according to Western standards of scholarship. Needless to say, I never expected that secularized Western scholars or those interested only in rationalistic philosophy would be convinced of the truth of the assertions of Islamic philosophy any more than would those in the Islamic world whose minds are closed to the intellectual discourse with which Islamic philosophy is concerned. But I did hope that in the West the understanding of both the length and breadth of Islamic philosophy would be expanded from the few pages devoted to "Arabic philosophy" in, let us say, Bertrand Russell's *A History of Western Philosophy* and that at least some people in the West would begin to look at Islamic philosophy with a philosophical eye and not only a philological, historic, or archeological one. I also hoped that those in the Islamic world endowed with a philosophical mind would at least be attracted to a more integral vision of their own philosophical tradition. On all these accounts, although not fully successful, I am nevertheless not dissatisfied with the results. Today, thanks to the works of not only myself, but especially Corbin, and also T. Izutsu and others, the many riches of the long tradition of Islamic philosophy are becoming recognized in an ever widening circle in the West and taken more seriously as philosophy rather than simply intellectual history. As for the Islamic world, except in the Arab world where for nationalistic reasons the pull of "Arabic philosophy" ending with Ibn Rushd and Ibn Khaldūn is still strong, nearly everywhere, whether it be in Turkey, Pakistan, Malaysia, or Indonesia, a whole new generation of younger scholars has now come forth who are no longer regurgitating the truncated Western views of Islamic philosophy, but who are studying this long tradition in both its length and breadth from within the perspective of the tradition. As for taking Islamic philosophy seriously *as* philosophy, this has taken place to some extent in France, thanks to the works of Corbin, but much less so in Germany and Anglo-Saxon countries; although even in these countries there are a few philosophers here and there whose attraction to Islamic philosophy is not limited to historical reasons.

Many years of teaching and studying philosophy in Persia and lecturing in other Islamic countries helped further my interest in the relation of Islamic philosophy to other dimensions and aspects of the Islamic tradition including first and foremost Sufism and gnosis (*'irfān*), but also Sunnism and Shi'ism. Many journeys from the '50s to the '70s to the Indo-Pakistani Subcontinent and especially Pakistan, in whose philosophical activities I participated actively during that period, convinced me that the widely held view that after Ibn Rushd Islamic philosophy disappeared in the Sunni world but survived only in the climate of Shi'ism had to be modified. The extensive philosophical tradition in Muslim India from the fourteenth century onward was not at all exclusively a Shi'ite affair. The texts of Suhrawardī and Mullā Ṣadrā were taught in Sunni *madrasahs* as well and many Islamic philosophers of India were Sunnis. In order to study this important issue further and to make better known the integral Islamic philosophical tradition, I tried to train while at Tehran University a number of students from the Subcontinent who, after having mastered the principles and development of Islamic philosophy in Persia, could pursue its later development in India. I met with some success in this project but not as much as I had hoped for. The detailed history of Islamic philosophy in India is still unknown and the same holds true for Ottoman Turkey.

My extensive journeys in the Islamic world also convinced me of the importance of introducing Islamic philosophy from its own point of view into that world and of overcoming the unfortunate habit in both the Subcontinent and Arab countries for students to see their own intellectual tradition from the point of view of the West. I was and remain opposed to the domination of the English empirical philosophical stance over philosophy departments in the Subcontinent for the past century and, likewise, the rationalism and later Neo-Marxism so prevalent in philosophy departments in the Arab world. The Neo-Averroism so popular in modernized Arab circles today is in reality the result of the lack of knowledge of the integral Islamic philosophical tradition and the inability to view that tradition from within. As far as my own efforts were concerned, they were more successful in Pakistan and Southeast Asia than in the Arab world.

As for Persia itself, during the twenty years of teaching Islamic philosophy at Tehran University and especially during the years of being dean of the Faculty of Letters and vice-chancellor of that university, I was able to bring about important changes in the content and structure of the department of philosophy which had been originally established along the line of departments in French universities. The rapprochement in Persia between the traditional centers of learning (*ḥawzah)* and the universities in the field of philosophy during the past two decades is very much based on the efforts made during the '60s and '70s.

Islamic philosophy has been always for me a living tradition to which I consider myself to belong. I believe that it is of the utmost importance for the Islamic world to nurture and support the study of Islamic philosophy from its own perspective and to train a younger generation of philosophers who stand firm on the intellectual foundations of Islam and Islamic philosophy and who are then able to study and philosophize about Western as well as other philosophical traditions, modern science, modern theories of the social sciences, and humanities, as well as religious philosophies and the many other questions which pose major challenges to Islam; challenges which can only be answered Islamically from the Islamic philosophical perspective as Islamic philosophy (including *ḥikmah)* has been understood traditionally. Much of my own intellectual energy has been spent during more than four decades in seeking to achieve these ends. In accordance with what has been described in this response I have used my efforts to realize to the extent possible the resuscitation of the Islamic intellectual traditions in general and of Islamic philosophy in particular and, in light of that tradition, providing responses to challenges which modern thought poses in so many domains for Islam. Suheyl Umar in assembling in a masterly fashion quotations from my writings on Islamic philosophy has also afforded me the opportunity to clarify further the process whereby I came to study Islamic philosophy and to formulate my understanding of it.

S. H. N.

2

Huston Smith

NASR'S DEFENSE OF THE PERENNIAL PHILOSOPHY

Festschrifts are one thing, the Library of Living Philosophers is quite another. Since to be included in its distinguished series is itself the highest honor a philosopher can receive from his peers, the Library need not waste words on further tributes and can turn directly to engaging the philosopher under consideration, circling his life's work to wring from him maximum clarity and amplification on certain points while he is still active. Still, I think it worth noting that Professor Seyyed Hossein Nasr is the only person who has received the highest tribute that his colleagues in both religious studies and philosophy could confer on him. In 1981 he was invited to deliver the prestigious Gifford Lectures at the University of Edinburgh, later published as *Knowledge and the Sacred*, and with this volume he receives the highest accolade that a contemporary philosopher can be accorded.[1]

Turning from that biographical point to the engagement that is this Library's signature, I find myself in a quandary. Of the contributors to this volume, I am the one who is closest to Professor Nasr's philosophical position, most importantly his endorsement of the perennial philosophy. In fact, I am so fully in agreement with him in that endorsement—he was instrumental in bringing me to it—that to question him critically about it would be game playing. I would have to manufacture questions I do not really have in order to tease from him answers that I already know. The Library of Living Philosophers deserves better fare than going through motions like that, so I shall adopt a strategy that will be distinctive in this volume. I shall describe in my own words what I take to be key points in his philosophical position, pausing along the way to highlight places where misunderstandings typically occur, and proceed from there to criticisms of his position that the current philosophical climate provokes. My concluding section will be given to what I take to be his critique of that climate. My hopes for this format are twofold. Where Professor Nasr agrees with my formulations, my way of putting things could help to edge his position more sharply. And where he corrects me, we shall all learn something. As my title indicates, I will focus on the perennial philosophy which is the heart of Professor Nasr's position.

I. Which Perennial Philosophy?

The phrase "perennial philosophy," deriving from the Latin, *philosophia perennis*, is generally taken as the claim that some sort of continuous theme runs through the history of philosophy.[2] Certain enduring and lasting truths are recognizable in the philosophical writings and oral traditions of all historical times. Seemingly coeval with the universe itself, the perennial philosophy endures. Its truth persists from generation to generation, weathering ephemeral philosophical fads and fashions that come and go.

What precisely, though, is this subterranean watertable which, pressurized by truth as its adherents believe, gushes forth wherever and whenever the earth is scratched? Charles Schmitt has compiled a list of philosophers who have laid claim to it, and it runs the entire philosophic gamut, from Thomistic Scholasticism, Scholasticism in general, and Catholic philosophy generally; through Platonism, mysticism, Western philosophy, and global philosophy; all the way to naturalism and even positivism.[3] Its association with Scholasticism and subsequent Catholic philosophy is particularly strong, as is suggested by the fact that of the nineteen entries for the term in *The Philosopher's Index*, nine occur in the journal, *Maritain Studies*, and one of the remaining ten in the *Proceedings of the Catholic Philosophical Association*. In the modern period (as James Collins points out in the chapter entitled "The Problem of a Perennial Philosophy" in his *Three Paths in Philosophy*) philosophers began to use the term in two different ways, some reserving it for common conclusions that philosophers reach (as in attempts to synthesize the Platonic and Aristotelian trends in philosophy), while others used it to target polarities that keep erupting.[4] For Karl Jaspers it was nothing more than the questions philosophers keep asking. The polyvalence of this smear of referents is enough to lead one to dismiss the term as useless, yet the range is understandable. Metaphysical positions—and everyone in Schmitt's and Collins's lists would agree that the perennial philosophy is metaphysical—are by definition unrestricted in scope and therefore hold universally, again whenever and wherever. Add to that the presumption that the truth will out, and it seems reasonable to think that invariably there have been discerning souls, at least a few, who have seen something of what the philosopher in question takes to be true. That every metaphysician must believe that his position is true, or at least truer than its known alternatives, goes without saying, for one cannot believe what one considers false. One can do what one considers wrong, but one cannot believe what one considers false.

What, then, does Professor Nasr take to be the subterranean truth that surfaces in different guises everywhere, as if one mind were speaking through many minds? To begin with ostensive definitions, within Western philosophy (the home of the Library of Living Philosophers) Professor Nasr would, I think, accept the general philosophical terrain to which Leibniz pointed when he used the term in a frequently quoted letter to Remond in 1714, as well as the similar landscape the Augustinian monk Agostino Steuco (drawing on an already well-developed tradition) targeted two centuries earlier. As far as we know, it was Steuco who coined the phrase *philosophia perennis*, but in consolidating the intellectual current that Steuco used the phrase to cover, Marsilio Ficino (founder of the Platonic Academy of Florence and translator of Plato, Plotinus, and other Neoplatonic philosophers) should be mentioned. As I am at this point restricting myself to ostensive definitions, I will not describe the philosophical current those philosophers identified, but will move to the stream within which Professor Nasr places himself. Early in the twentieth century a school of thought arose with René Guénon and Ananda Coomaraswamy which has been perpetuated by Frithjof Schuon, Titus Burckhardt, Martin Lings, and Hossein Nasr himself. To distinguish themselves from other claimants to the perennial philosophy, members of this school often speak of the *sophia perennis* or the *religio perennis*, theirs being an emphatically religious philosophy. They also refer to themselves as Traditionalists, from their opposition to what they see as the mistaken directions modern and postmodern philosophy have taken. I shall address this polemical aspect of Nasr's position in the final section of this essay.

With this ostensive definition of Nasr's position in place, it would be logical to summarize its substance and move on to criticisms of it and then to his answers to those criticisms, but I shall forego that route. Instead, I shall address the three topics together. As readers of this volume can be assumed to know in a general way where Professor Nasr stands, I will presuppose that knowledge and target a half-dozen or so points that control his philosophy. If the reader draws a mental line through those points, the contours of his philosophy should emerge. The points are sure to provoke questions, for they are not widely shared today, and as I proceed I will try to say something about how I think Nasr would answer those questions. In good part this will involve correcting misunderstandings, for I often come away from arguments involving the Traditionalists with the disturbing sense that entirely different things are being talked about. Yogi Berra once quipped that he didn't want to make the wrong mistake, and I cathect to that. Critics make the right mistake when their criticisms of Nasr's philosophy fall short of the mark. They make the wrong mistake when they demolish positions that he does not hold.

Using "the perennial philosophy" from here on to denote Professor Nasr's version of it, I turn now to decisive points on which it hinges.

II. Pivotal Points in Nasr's Perennialism

1. Deduction rather than Induction

The name, "the perennial philosophy," may itself be responsible for what is perhaps the most common misunderstanding of Nasr's version of it. Because ubiquity is built into that name, people tend to assume that Nasr derives his perennialism inductively, from what historians report—as if he commissioned social scientists to ransack the world's philosophical heritage and derived his perennial philosophy from the metaphysical nugget that turned up most pervasively. Steven Katz travels that route negatively to support his claim that "there is no *philosophia perennis*, Huxley and many others notwithstanding."[5] Using mysticism to illustrate his claim, Katz argues that mysticisms have no common essence, for they are controlled without remainder by the traditions that house them. I am not concerned here with whether at some level of generalization mysticisms do have a common theme, for my point is that Nasr's perennial philosophy does not depend on the answer to that question. For as I say, it does not derive inductively from identifying a module that turns up repeatedly. It derives from the metaphysical intuitions or discernments of the "intellect." As that word denotes for Nasr the defining feature of our humanity, it is to be expected that its deliverances will surface everywhere, and in this way ubiquity does enter Nasr's perennialism. But it is important to understand that ubiquity is a product of perennialism's truth, not its criterion. Its criterion is the intellect.

2. The Intellect

Human understanding is woven of two kinds of knowledge, which Nasr distinguishes by calling them rational and intellective— "intuitive" roughly doubles for the second of these words. Most of what we think of as knowledge is rational; it is discursive (in being couched in words) and is indirect (in referring to something other than itself). Intellective knowledge is otherwise. It derives from a distinctive noetic faculty that St. Thomas and the Scholastics called the *intellectus*, the Greeks called *nous*, Vedantists call *buddhi*, Buddhists call *prajñā*, and Muslims call *'aql*.

Today the difference between reason and intelligence has largely been lost. Only a moment's attention is needed, however, to notice that our minds have two ways of working that are distinct while being intimately related. When I think of myself, for example, I think first of the "I" that got up this morning, that is expecting a letter, etc., etc. But if I ask myself who this "I" is; if I probe beneath objective definitions of the sort just given to get at the subjective *feel* of who I am, I discover that that "I" cannot be described. Stop for a moment and introspect. Try to sense the origin of your most basic, most personal "I," the core of your subjective experience. To the extent that you succeed, you will realize that the awareness you have identified is different in kind from what it can be aware *of*. This "I" can be aware of anything. It cannot be seen because it is the seer that sees, the experiencer who experiences. Open in principle to any and all contents, it can itself no more be turned into a content than a hand can grasp itself or an eye see itself. Nasr takes the intellect to be the fount of all knowing. In this he follows Aristotle who called it the Active or Agent Intellect to distinguish it from lesser noetic faculties that ride its power. Despite the difficulty of characterizing it, we need not stop with thinking of it in its pure, contentless expression, for we glimpse its direct agency every time we know things that cannot be put into words, the standard example being the colors of a sunset which cannot be described to a blind man.

3. The Source of the Intellect and its Implications for Truth

Few things divide modernity from traditional outlooks more than the question of how we human beings got here. Traditional peoples everywhere assume that, whether by creation or through emanation, we are the less (creatures) who derive from the more (our Creator of the One), whereas Darwinian evolution teaches that we are the more (rational beings) who have derived from the less (organisms without reason). According to the latter view, the intellect as I have described it is one of a number of noetic talents that the human species acquired in the course of its ascent to facilitate its adaptive transactions with its environment. For Nasr it is God's presence within us. Again Aristotle's Agent Intellect comes to mind for being (as one Aristotelian scholar, James Duerlinger, describes it) "the divine activity of pure self-knowledge present in our souls, producing in them likenesses of itself, these likenesses being our own minds, our organs of awareness."[6] Eckhart too enters here with his assertion that "there is something in the soul that is uncreated and uncreatable, namely the Intellect." As God alone is uncreated, this joins Aristotle in making the Intellect God's presence in us. But more. Not only is it the *sine qua non* of our knowing; it is the ground of our being—that which gives us our existence. Philosophers now separate epistemology and ontology and give them different referents, with the result that truth is regarded as a function of propositions, not things. Traditionally the two were more or less joined. In Latin, *verus* means "true"; it also means "real," "genuine," and "authentic"—properties that are not restricted to statements. The same holds for the key terms in other traditional civilizations. In Sanskrit *sat* doubles for both "truth" and "reality," as the famous triumvirate *sat-cit-ānanda* ("being-awareness-bliss") discloses. Etymologically, the Chinese character *chen* in its original seal form depicts a loaded scale standing on a stool which implies full, real, solid, and therefore has the meaning of "true" as opposed to "empty" and "unreal," i.e., *chia*.[7] In Arabic *al-ḥaqq*, one of the Ninety-nine Beautiful Names of Allah, translates as both "the true" and "the real."

As Nasr is a Traditionalist, it is not surprising to find that knowledge and being likewise converge for him, along with other attributes that now have different ontological referents. His metaphysical starting point is the Infinite which he considers the one unavoidable idea because its alternative, finitude, implies a limit, a cutoff point, which the mind cannot accept as final because it must instinctively wonder what lies beyond it; thought-wise, an absolute boundary would be like a door with only one side, an impossible image. Prior to Plotinus, the West considered the absence of finitude a privation, for it equated that absence with indefiniteness, the lack of definition and form. Nasr sides with the Indian philosophers here, who from the beginning had a positive Infinite, seeing it as All-Possibility for including everything that could possibly be. As nothing can subrate the Infinite in this fullness sense, Nasr refers to it alternatively as the Absolute, and (when knowledge is at issue) the Intellect as described above.[8] In us, the Intellect is a ray of the Absolute entering the relative, the world of *māyā*. This makes us theomorphic beings who can know the Real, which is equivalent to saying "Truth" with a capital "T." The words that I am capitalizing all have the same referent, namely That which is Ultimate, as in the Upaniṣadic refrain, *tat tvam asi*, "That thou art."

Few things today are more likely to raise philosophical eyebrows (and for many, philosophical hackles as well) than a capitalized "Truth," for fallibilism is the order of the day. So Nasr's endorsement of it requires exploration. I begin with the importance of the issue.

In *Modernity on Endless Trial*, Leszek Kolakowski argues that the inclination to claim final and ultimate truth on the one hand, and the opposite of that claim—a critical attitude that so undermines all claims to truth that it tends toward skepticism, relativism, and even nihilism—is as deep and abiding a tension as Western civilization affords. His own concern is with the second arm of this tension. Carried all the way, he argues, the critical attitude denies limits, and by extension denies a transcendent order or a deep structure that imposes them. Religion counters this drift, and in doing so (as Kolakowski rather oracularly puts the point) "is man's way of accepting [historical] life as inevitable defeat" for being under the constraint of limits that cannot be deconstructed. When a culture loses this sense of constraint, which can derive only from an order that is sacred for being more ultimate than culture and history, it assumes that people are "endlessly flexible" and opens them to every form of intellectual and political totalitarianism.

I believe that Nasr would concur with Kolakowski's analysis, but those on the other side point out that totalitarianism is itself one of the cruelest forms of absolutism and argue that fallibilism is the surest guard against it. This positions absolutism as fallibilism's alternative, whereas Nasr—subscribing to the thesis Robert Kane puts forward forcefully in *Through the Moral Maze*—considers it its prerequisite.[9] For unless there is a way things are, a way they really, realistically are, there is no way that one can be mistaken. No Truth, no error. A sensible epistemology will be absolutist in assuming that Truth exists and fallibilistic assuming that for the most part we don't know what it is.

Is Nasr's epistemology sensible by this ruling? His notion of the infallibility of the Intellect as God knowing in and through us, appears to be the exact antithesis of fallibilism, but I think he would protest that that reading overlooks his nuancings of that infallibility. Analogies may help here. The law of gravity holds inexorably for macro-objects, but it doesn't force a thistle to plunge directly to the ground; the wind gets into the act. Or again, spray is not the sea, but both are H_2O.

Converting these analogies into the thoughts they are intended to spark, we can begin by noting that if (as was earlier noted) the one uncircumventable idea for Nasr is the Infinite, the one indispensable distinction for him is that between the finite and the Infinite, or (what comes to the same thing) between the Absolute and the relative. Being unsubratable, the Infinite has to be absolute, and the fact that we humans are here is enough to prove that finitude too exists. How are the two related? Nasr relates them by noting that because the Infinite is All-possibility, it must include the finite; if it didn't, something would exist in addition to itself and it would not be infinite. This makes the finite infinite, but not the Infinite in its entirety. To say, as Nasr does, that "God alone exists (transcendence), and everything that exists is God (immanence)," puts that point cryptically, but the assertion becomes straightforward when we add, "but not God in his entirety." Neoplatonism's privative view of evil enters here, with evil covering everything that falls short of perfection, including the error that fallibilism insists on and this paragraph was constructed to get back to; specifically, back to Nasr's concurrence with fallibilism as long as it doesn't throw the baby out with the bathwater. As there is no commensurability between the finite and the Infinite, the formed and the Unformed, every articulation of the Formless can be no more than an approximation. But this does not undercut the distinction between true and false ideas. Nasr's grip on the Absolute remains secure; the Absolute subrates ideas by discounting their literalism, and at the same time provides the standard for their metaphorical accuracy. Ideas are true to the extent that they implicitly suggest aspects of the total truth, which is to say Truth itself. They are intellectual keys and have no function other than that, when confronted with the Divine Reality in Itself, every doctrine is an error. To the extent that it approximates the Truth, however, a doctrine may be a providential, indispensable, and salutary "error" which contains and communicates the virtuality of Truth.

This way of holding onto Truth without hedging on human finitude and ignorance derives, obviously, from Nasr's distinction between reason (which is articulated, referential, and fallible) and the Intellect which transcends those attributes. The Intellect is, to restate the matter, infallible in being the source and empowering agent of all knowing and being, but in the relative world it shows itself in varying degrees according to how deeply it is overlaid by ignorance, or (ontologically expressed) how far it surrenders to the attenuations of nothingness. Socrates believed that truth resides within us, but he gave his life to midwifing it out of people. The *Tipitaka* tells us that "a fund of omniscience exists eternally in our hearts," but no Buddhist would claim to be in command of that omniscience.

Strictly speaking, the Intellect surfaces in the relative world not just in varying degrees but to every possible degree, because (as we have seen) the Infinite is All-possibility. This brings me to the Great Chain of Being, which Arthur Lovejoy made the object of his minor classic on the subject.[10]

4. The Great Chain of Being

Two of Nasr's working principles that have been cited need to be kept in mind as we take note of his espousal of the Great Chain of Being (hereafter GCB). First, it is not itself the perennial philosophy, for articulated metaphysical positions are authored by reason and are prey to its limitations. To the extent that they approximate the Truth such formulations can be useful; functioning in the way icons do, they can awaken intellectual intuitions that are unqualifiedly true. But to absolutize them is, as the Zennists say, to mistake the finger pointing to the moon for the moon itself and to turn icons into idols. The second working principle simply spells out the implications of the first. Because the GCB is not in itself the perennial philosophy, its ubiquity cannot be that philosophy's foundation—this point has been covered. Whether a statistical majority of philosophers and theologians agree with Nasr is not his concern.

Even so, the ubiquity of the GCB suggests that among metaphysical systems it is in its broad outlines the one that most closely approximates the Truth, and this makes it worth documenting. Lovejoy defines the GCB as "the conception of the universe as composed of an immense, or infinite, number of links ranging in hierarchical order from the meagerest kind of existents through 'every possible' grade up to the *ens perfectissimum*," and notes that "down to the late eighteenth century most educated men [accepted it] without question. . . . In one form or another [he adds] it has been the dominant official philosophy of the larger part of civilized mankind through most of its history, taught in their several fashions and with differing degrees of rigor and thoroughness by the greater number of subtler speculative minds and the great religious teachers."[11] Ernst Cassirer considered "the concept and general picture of a graduated cosmos" the most important legacy of ancient speculation,[12] and Ken Wilber contends that belief in the GCB has been "so overwhelmingly widespread that it is either the single greatest intellectual error ever to appear in human history—an error so colossally widespread as to literally stagger the mind—or it is the most accurate reflection of reality yet to appear."[13]

An infinite number of links is unmanageable, so Traditionalists typically distinguish four ontological levels that seem to "cut where the joints are" for housing clearly distinguishable kinds of things. They resemble the ontological levels that Plotinus identified, but as the GCB covers more than Neoplatonism, Traditionalists use their own terminology. Reading upward, we begin with the terrestrial plane (roughly the spatio-temporal world of matter), and proceed from there to the intermediate. This derives its name from Plato's *to metaxy* which (according to Paul Friedlander) "must have been of the utmost significance to him. It is the idea or view of 'the demonic' as a realm 'intermediate' between the human level and the divine, a realm which, because of its intermediate position, 'unites the cosmos with itself'."[14] Above the intermediate plane, the celestial plane houses a creative intelligence that empowers and presides over everything below it and opens out above itself onto the Infinite. The Infinite differs from the celestial in being ineffable. It does not target a different object than the one on the celestial plane, but the celestial plane takes account of its surface (and hence identifiable) features only, whereas the Infinite denotes its totality. The celestial plane is *kataphatic* in inviting descriptions, whereas the Infinite is *apophatic* for being situated above the cloud of unknowing. Access to the celestial plane is gained by the *via affirmativa*, the Infinite by the *via negativa*. All of this can be compressed into a simple (if somewhat oversimplified) schematization. Every religion and most traditional philosophies begin by distinguishing between this world and another world, which distinction Mircea Eliade built into the title of his best known book *The Sacred and the Profane*. Both of those worlds then subdivide. This world divides into its visible and invisible aspects, and the transcendent world into its knowable and ineffable regions. In the course of three NEH Summer Seminars for College Teachers, I worked out a cross-cultural diagram of these four levels of reality and the way they intersect the human self, and I include it as being (I believe) essentially faithful to Nasr's metaphysical position.

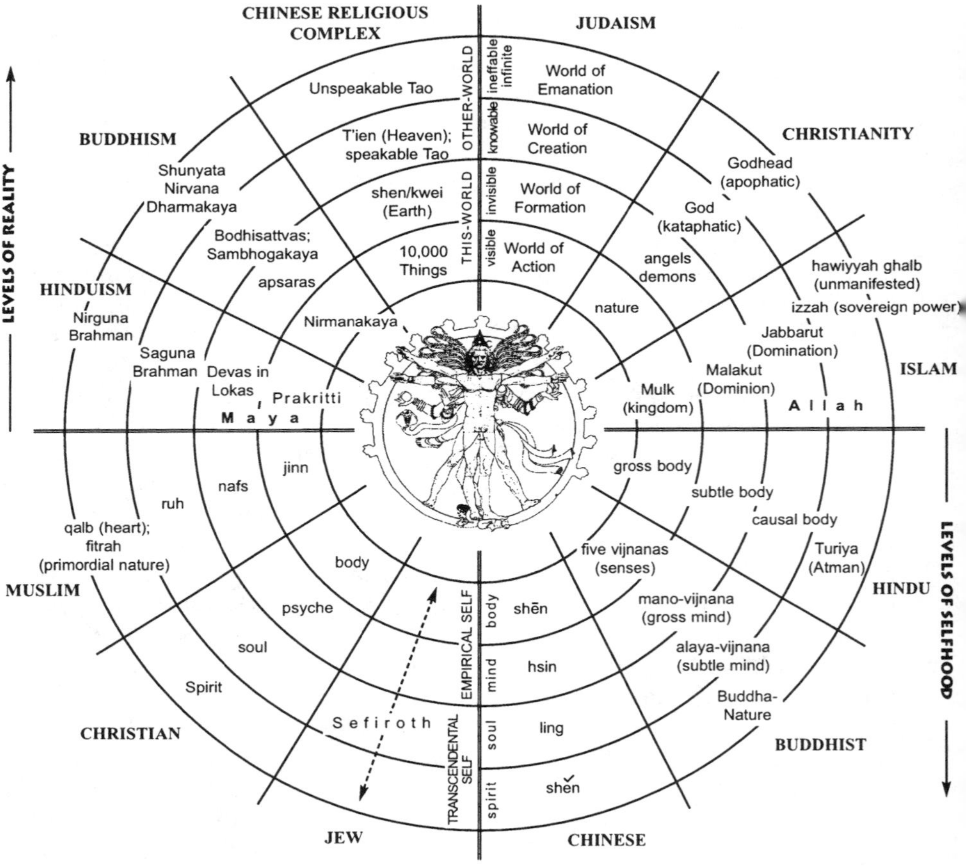

THE PERENNIAL PHILOSOPHY'S HIERARCHICAL ONTOLOGY

Graphic layout courtesy of Brad Reynolds

Only a handful of Western philosophers today subscribes to the GCB, but there are some: one thinks of John Anton, Baine Harris, founder of the Society for Neoplatonic Studies, and Paul Kuntz who was a recent enthusiast of the GCB generally. The outlook provides a useful way of honoring the world's diversity without falling prey to relativism, but as my diagram comes down hard on themes that traditional philosophies and religions ring changes on, I want to point out that Nasr gives equal weight to the differences they present. This point is often lost on his critics who more often than not see his perennialism as conflating the historical traditions and blurring their respective contours. Nothing could be further from the truth. New Age enthusiasts who like Nasr's affirmation of "the transcendent unity of religions"—the title of a landmark book in the Traditionalist school[15] write him off when they discover the severity with which he insists on keeping the boundaries among religions distinct.[16] The mathematical point at which those religions converge *really is* transcendent, and (thus seen) turns on its head the theosophical notion of an underlying unity that can be described and abstracted from lived religions. Depictions of the transcendent unity in sacred texts, art, liturgies, and theologies are invaluable in pointing to the place where they finally converge, but each tradition "gestalts" the sacred in its own way, and attempts to conflate them scramble their pointings. (Who would think of trying to get at beauty by acknowledging its presence in both Chartres Cathedral and the Taj Mahal and then trying to abstract it from those monuments?) Where expression is involved, Nasr is in complete agreement with those who contend that there are no explicit trans-conversational criteria to evaluate or commensurate one conversation—read religious tradition—in terms of another.

5. Esoterism

In claiming conscious access to the noetic faculty that modern philosophy has lost hold of—the Intellect—Nasr opens himself to the charge of elitism. He admits to the charge as long as the word is used descriptively and not as an epithet. Descriptively, "elite" simply denotes that which is superior, and as long as one sticks to talents that exist (and doesn't confuse those with unearned privileges), to object to them amounts to complaining about the kind of world we have, for that world is woven of inequities. Few people are born with the physique to be *sumo* wrestlers. Not everyone can get into MIT. Not everyone can dunk basketballs like Michael Jordan, or do double-dutch jump rope with the finesse of some inner city children.

The same holds for metaphysics, which Nasr (using his reason/Intellect distinction) distinguishes from philosophy. Having severed its ties to theology, philosophy now works exclusively with autonomous reason, whereas metaphysics in Nasr's sense of the word rides intellective discernments that provide reason with a rudder. This leads to Nasr's distinction between two types of mentality which he calls esoteric and exoteric. The consciousness of exoterics works almost exclusively through forms, rational and artistic, whereas esoterics can move beyond those to intellective intuitions which (to switch from the rudder analogy) serve something of the function that stars do for navigators, guiding their calculations and maneuvers. For exoterics, if something has no form—is without boundaries that demarcate it from other things—its cash value (to use a crude expression) is zero. As far as they can discern it is nothing, whereas for esoterics it is everything—literally Everything, for it is Infinite. For exoterics "infinite" is an abstraction. For esoterics it is concrete—the only fully concrete "thing" there is, all else being *samsāra* and *māyā*, the shadows on the wall of Plato's cave.

This concludes my inventory of the places where I find frequently occurring misunderstandings of Nasr's perennialism. In a way, though, this entire section is almost beside the point, for explicit criticisms are not the major problem his philosophy faces. The major problem is neglect. With the notable and praiseworthy exception of the present volume, not just Nasr's perennialism but the perennial philosophy generally is simply shelved today. Philosophers see it as so out of step with current philosophical concerns that (as the quip goes) they don't even bother to ignore it. Of the seventy-four entries for Seyyed Hossein Nasr in *The Philosopher's Index*, seventy-two mention him only as the author of an article, or the author or editor of a book. In the two remaining entries, one mentions him in passing and the other is by an Aurobindo-ite who protests that he doesn't do justice to that Indian philosopher.

Faced with this situation, I shall devote my next section to pointing out some aspects of Nasr's position that make for hard sledding in today's philosophical climate, together with his reasons for holding his ground in the face of them.

III. Stumbling Blocks

1. Metaphysics

The fact that perennialism of whatever stripe is a metaphysics counts against it from the start, for the post-Nietzschean deconstruction of metaphysics has taken hold. As early as mid-century, R. G. Collingwood was describing the twentieth century as "an age when the very possibility of metaphysics is hardly admitted without a struggle," and soon thereafter Iris Murdoch was writing that "modern philosophy is profoundly anti-metaphysical in spirit. Its anti-metaphysical character may be summed up in the caveat: There may be no deep structure."

The criticisms of metaphysics have come from many quarters. Sometimes a particular metaphysical system is faulted—Plato's, say (usually misread, as by Heidegger and Derrida), or Descartes's, or Kant's, or Hegel's—and metaphysics across the board is tarred with the flaws of that particular system. At other times, a given approach to system building is faulted—foundationalism is the current whipping boy—and again all metaphysics is assumed to collapse through its errors. Continental attacks come from a characteristically different quarter. End-running epistemology and questions of truth, postmodernists seize political cudgels and argue that "metanarratives"—their synonym for metaphysics—totalize and in doing so marginalize oppressed minorities whose narratives they exclude. Jean-François Lyotard cites "incredulity toward metanarratives" as post-modernism's defining feature.[17]

Objections like these—the barest sample—cry out for rejoinders, but space does not permit, so I shall try to cut through to how Nasr responds to these anti-metaphysical moves. Sooner or later, I think he would say, the critics of metaphysics will have to face the fact that metaphysics is inevitable. Even Wilfrid Sellars, no fan of the project, had to admit that, surely things (however defined) hang together in some sort of way (however envisioned), and with that minimalist admission we are into metaphysics. Meaning descends from whole to part as much as it ascends from part to whole. Gestalt psychologists have demonstrated that what we see focally always appears against a subliminal background which affects the foreground. This holds for knowing generally, so if we deny the presence and influence of backgrounds we are in fact only ignoring them at our peril. Where they are not ignored but argued against, the arguments fall of their own self-referential weight. Perspectivalism—in the guise of historicism, cultural-linguistic holism, constructivism, or cultural relativism—is currently the leading candidate. Taking off from the obvious fact that we observe the world from different angles, at different times, and through different ontogenetic and cultural lenses, perspectivalism contradicts itself when it stops with that opening gambit, for to recognize that perspectives are such—that is, to recognize that they are perspectives only and not the full picture—requires regarding them from a vantage point that demotes them to that status. Without such demotion, each "take" on the world (in film-making parlance) would present itself, not as a perspective, but as the thing itself. When human beings get into the picture, Nasr fully agrees with Derrida and Rorty that as long as we restrict ourselves to our egos, those ponderous "I's," we are indeed "centerless webs of beliefs and desires and are lost behind the unending web of descriptions" (Rorty). But he would add what they overlook; namely, that to the extent that we are aware of this truth of contingency, we are no longer just egos and are no longer contingent. There must be more to the Self than a linguistic construction in order for us to know that we are often far less. The notion of illusion is for Nasr a ray of the Absolute entering the relative.

Defending metaphysics against its "cultured despisers,"[18] as I have devoted a couple of paragraphs to doing, is necessary, for, as Jacques Maritain warned, as the anti-metaphysical tide was gaining strength, "a loss or weakening of the metaphysical spirit is an incalculable damage for the general order of intelligence and human affairs."[19] There is, however, a more direct way to get at metaphysics' detractors, and that is to point out that contemporary philosophy's claimed dismissal of metaphysics is disingenuous, for its major schools are metaphysical to the core. It is only worldviews with upper stories that are discounted, again, mostly without argument. Those that are limited to basements (materialism) or ground floors (naturalism) are solidly in place. On materialism we have Wilfrid Sellars's assertion that "science is the measure of all things, of what is that it is, and of what is not that it is not;"[20] and John Searle's concurrence in writing that "most of the professionals in philosophy, psychology, artificial intelligence, neurobiology, and cognitive science accept some version of materialism because they believe that it is the only philosophy consistent with our contemporary scientific world view."[21] As for naturalism, in his 1996 Presidential Address to the Pacific Division of the American Philosophical Association, Barry Stroud notes that "most philosophers for at least one hundred years have been naturalists. They have taken it for granted that any satisfactory account of how human belief and knowledge in general are possible will involve only processes and events of the intelligible natural world, without the intervention or reassurance of any supernatural agent."[22]

2. Hierarchy

Science's restriction of reality to a single ontological level is reenforced by the current political animus against hierarchies. This makes it doubly hard for perennialism to get a hearing, for its close ties with the Great Chain of Being make it not only a metaphysics but a hierarchical one as well. Surely, however (Nasr would insist), the wholesale denunciation of hierarchies that we hear today is not thought through, for the charge that hierarchies invariably oppress is patently false: they can empower and affirm as well. A loving family is a hierarchy dedicated to empowering its children, and a well run classroom empowers its students by teaching them things that will help them to live effectively. The prototype of an empowering hierarchy is God's relation to the world, to which Clement of Alexandria gave Christian expression in his formula that "God became man, that man might become God."

3. *Religion*

Nasr's perennialism is clearly a religious philosophy. Actually, it is predisciplinary in the way Plato's *Dialogues* and most traditional philosophies were, presenting an outlook in which philosophy, theology, and psychology are fully merged. Now that these have gone their separate ways, however, we have to use multiple words to bring them together, and religious philosophy is as workable a phrase for Nasr's as any. The prefix in the phrase, "religious," creates a third obstacle that Nasr's philosophy faces, for the time in which philosophy was the handmaiden of theology still rankles in philosophers' memories and they guard their independence jealously. Added to this first, there is a second problem that religious philosophies must face. In *The Soul of the American University*, George Marsden points out that in five generations the ethos of the American university has moved from Protestant establishmentarianism—all the early colleges were founded to train Protestant ministers—to the established disbelief that dominates campuses today.[23] The hermeneutics of suspicion is skepticism's prime entry point, and nowhere is it more active than in dismantling religious outlooks. The Society of Christian Philosophers is exceptional in standing up to it, but though it is vigorous, it has not changed philosophic habits to any significant degree.

Nasr's reason for holding out against this third obstacle can be deduced from what has already been said about his position. As we are theomorphic beings, God is the foundation of our existence, first and foremost in his mode of knowing. If philosophy does not reflect and give expression to that foundation, it betrays its birthright.

My list could be extended, but I shall mention only one more way in which Nasr's philosophy faces an uphill battle today. He is a traditionalist in a generation that reproaches its past more than any other of which intellectual historians are aware.

4. *Tradition*

Nasr does not romanticize the past, nor reject all the innovations to which the present is heir. I have heard him say that his thinking is not modern, but that it *is* contemporary. Modern science understands nature calculatively much better than our forebears did, and I would not myself want to go as far as Nasr does in defending the social patterns of traditional societies. But when it comes to the final nature of things and how human life can best be comported in its context, Nasr sees nothing in modernity or postmodernity that rivals the traditional view as impounded in the great enduring wisdom traditions. He takes that wisdom to have been revealed, but if it is easier for his audience to see it as surfacing from the deepest unconscious of the spiritual geniuses of the past, it comes to the same thing, for the final component of a theomorphic being is God.

My stand-ins for Nasr's responses to these four stumbling blocks to his perennialism have grown shorter and shorter, partly because they follow so obviously from the central points of his philosophy that I have sketched that I find it tedious to state them explicitly, but there is a second reason. There is a saying in team sports that the best defense is a good offense, and the adage rings true here. I suspect that of the philosophies that this Library has covered, Nasr's probably seems the most foreign, possibly to the point that some may wonder if it belongs in this Library. Given Nasr's upbringing in Asia this is not surprising, but I mention it here because if his philosophy seems strange to us, it stands to reason that ours might appear strange to him. That it does, he told us forthrightly in his already mentioned Gifford Lectures, *Knowledge and the Sacred*, and I shall devote the final section of this essay to pointing out that the extent of its peculiarity is his main reason for adhering to his traditional position.

IV. The Best Defense

Before the rise of modern science, when people wanted the Big Picture that would show them the ultimate nature of things they turned to their sacred, revealed texts, or (if they were unlettered) to the great orienting myths that gave their lives meaning and motivation. The West's discovery of the controlled experiment—the defining feature of modern science—changed that by introducing the possibility of proof. The way this epistemic innovation and the scientific method that evolved around it has changed our world (and our worldview, which is the part of the story that concerns us here) needs no retelling.

What does need retelling—or rather telling, for it has yet to be told in a way that can get through to the public—is, first, that the scientific worldview is a huge demotion from the traditional one in the way it works against human flourishing; and second, that there are no legitimate reasons for thinking that it is more accurate than its traditional precursor. It is for psychological, not logical, reasons that science has become (in Alex Comfort's phrase) our "sacral" mode of knowing, and its product (the scientific worldview) the reigning orthodoxy of our time.

Science's prestige derives from its power to transform the physical world through discovering and manipulating its quantifiable, measurable properties. It is important to realize that its prestige derives entirely from that power, which means that the worldview that gives it its prestige consists of numbers and equations only, nothing more. Common sense, though, tells us that there is more to the world than numbers, so scientists flesh out their worldview by embellishing its numerical spine. Their additions to it—the post-its they use to deck out their calculations—begin with what we directly experience (sounds, smells, and colors, the secondary qualities of the philosophers) which common sense registers but science itself cannot deliver. Even those who recognize that the scientific method is limited tend to think that it is competent to deal with the corporeal world, but that is not the case, for we experience that world in Technicolor whereas strictly speaking, science cannot even give it to us in black-and-white, but only in numbers, there being no way to get from nature's numerical aspects to the way we experience it.[24]

Proceeding from secondary qualities, scientists go on to add other things to their worldview until we find it full blown in Carl Sagan's cosmology and Stephen Jay Gould's evolutionary biology. What has passed unnoticed in this ballooning, Nasr argues, is that with every additional overlay the rightful authority of the scientific worldview attenuates. Because that fact has slipped by us, the full-blown scientific worldview is accorded the respect that properly belongs to its empirically derived calculations only. No harm would derive from this mistake if the additions were supplied by common sense, but they are not: For the most part they are minted from assumptions that are indispensable for science's purposes but which imprison the human spirit when they are moved into other spheres.

Not liking the direction in which this train of thought is heading, the partisans of science will protest that it rides the narrowest possible definition of the project. This is true, but Nasr would argue that for purposes of clear thinking and settling the dust, no definition is more useful. The culture war between science and religion is still in full swing, and without an agreed on reference point, each side will define science to its own advantage. The needed reference point is the indubitable fact that science—modern science is what is under discussion—is what has changed our world beyond anything that peoples who lived before it could ever have dreamed. From that incontestable starting point, Nasr's working definition of science, and the argument that flows from it, reasonably follow. It is probably worth mentioning here that Nasr's undergraduate degree is in physics from MIT and his doctorate is in the history of science from Harvard University.

The merit in Nasr's way of "gestalting" the matter is that it enables us to distinguish between what science has a right to ask us to believe, on the one hand—the quantifiable aspects of the corporeal world that it had discovered and the regularities (laws) that organize these—and, on the other, the overlays in its worldview that are optional. Nasr rejects them, for they assume, simply assume, that matter is fundamental, and mind—spirit too, if it is allowed—is derivative. Intelligent design (and a purposeful cosmos generally are discounted) for, as Jacques Monod points out, "the cornerstone of scientific method is the *systematic* denial of final causes."[25] The fossil record is taken to show that greater intelligence derived from lesser intelligence through naturalistic causes only; and finally, in the scientific worldview there is no intelligence greater than the human, for no such intelligence has been spotted (nor can be spotted, Nasr would add) by laboratory experiments.

How far these scientistic (in contradistinction to scientific) assumptions have permeated philosophy, Nasr would want me to leave to the reader to judge, but the assertions of John Searle and Barry Stroud that I quoted suggest that they are solidly ensconced. Cultural critics register the toll they have exacted. They have saddled us with a "disenchanted world" (Max Weber), a "wasteland" (T. S. Eliot), "a disqualified universe" (Lewis Mumford), "one-dimensional man" (Herbert Marcuse), and "the colonization of value spheres by science" (Jürgen Habermas).

This, I think Seyyed Hossein Nasr would say, is his final defense of perennial philosophy. It offers a reasonable alternative to the contemporary Western mindset.

HUSTON SMITH

SYRACUSE UNIVERSITY
JULY 1998

NOTES

1. Seyyed Hossein Nasr, *Knowledge and the Sacred* (New York: Crossroad Publishing Company, 1981).

2. For two reasons, I personally prefer the phrase "the primordial tradition," which I used as the subtitle for the original edition of my book *Forgotten Truth: The Primordial Tradition* (San Francisco: Harper, 1976/1992). First, "perennial" refers only to time, whereas "primordial" adds space and in doing so refers to what is spaceless as well as timeless—everywhere and everywhen. Second, "tradition" fits better than philosophy as it is currently understood for subsuming topics that tend now to be relegated to psychology and theology. But "perennial" has carried the day, so I shall bow to convention.

3. Charles B. Schmitt, "Perennial Philosophy: From Agostino Steuco to Leibniz," *Journal of the History of Ideas* 27, no. 4 (Oct.–Dec., 1966): 505–6.

4. James Collins, *Three Paths in Philosophy* (Chicago, Ill.: Henry Regnery Company, 1962).

5. Steven T. Katz, "Language, Epistemology, and Mysticism," in *Mysticism and Philosophical Analysis*, ed. Steven T. Katz (New York: Oxford University Press, 1978), p. 24.

6. James Duerlinger, in a letter written to the author in 1995.

7. From an unpublished paper by Professor Siu-chi Huang, "Truth in the Chinese Tradition," which was delivered in Washington, D.C. at a cross-cultural symposium on truth.

8. Eckhart, too, considered knowledge to be God's fundamental attribute, contending that "if there were in God that which we could affirm as nobler than another, it is knowledge." Nasr titled his Gifford Lectures *Knowledge and the Sacred* to underscore his thesis that knowledge is sacred in itself for being God's self-expression within us.

9. Robert Kane, *Through the Moral Maze* (Saint Paul, Minn.: Paragon House, 1993).

10. Arthur Lovejoy, *The Great Chain of Being* (Cambridge, Mass.: Harvard University Press, 1936).

11. Arthur Lovejoy, *The Great Chain of Being*, pp. 59, 26. Lovejoy himself concluded that despite its historical importance, "the history of this most persistent and comprehensive of hypotheses is the history of a failure" (p. 329), because he could not see, first, how the manifest temporality of the world could be reconciled with the eternality of the Chain itself; and second, how the All-possibility that the Chain's principle of plenitude requires allows for the contingencies that stud the world. Nasr would argue that these are Lovejoy's problems, not those of the GCB which has resources for resolving them, but it would take me too far afield to include his arguments here.

12. Ernst Cassirer, *The Individual and the Cosmos in Renaissance Philosophy* (New York: Barnes and Noble, 1963), p. 9.

13. Ken Wilber, "The Great Chain of Being," *Journal of Humanistic Psychology* 33, no. 3 (Summer 1993), p. 53.

14. Paul Friedlander, *Plato*, vol. I (London: Routledge & Kegan Paul, 1958), p. 41.

15. Frithjof Schuon, *The Transcendent Unity of Religion* (New York: Harper Torchbook, 1948/1975).

16. This is so regularly overlooked by Nasr's critics that it merits a note. He is told that he should shift away from claims to universality so as to take more seriously the social, interactive dimension of the lived religious or philosophical metaphor. In Wilfred Cantwell Smith's wording of this criticism, "the historian must stand guard against a vitiation of man's actual religious living by enthusiasts for emaciating abstractions." This rides the mistaken assumption that has already been addressed: that perennialism has to do with abstracting from the historical data of particular traditions.

17. See Jean-François Lyotard, *The Postmodern Condition* (Minneapolis: University of Minnesota Press, 1984), p. xxiv. See also p. 3f.

18. The phrase comes from Friedrich Schleiermacher's book, *On Religion: Speeches to its Cultured Despisers*, trans. Richard Crouter (Cambridge: Cambridge

University Press, 1996).

19. Jacques Maritain, *The Degrees of Knowledge* (New York: Charles Scribner's Sons, 1959), p. 59.

20. Wilfrid Sellars, *Science, Perception, and Reality* (New York: Humanities Press, 1963), p. 173. Sellars modifies the famous saying of Protagoras here.

21. John Searle, "Consciousness and the Philosophers," *The New York Review of Books* (March 6, 1997): 43.

22. Barry Stroud, "The Charm of Naturalism," *Proceedings and Addresses of the APA* 70, no. 2 (1996): 43.

23. George M. Marsden, *The Soul of the American University* (Oxford/ New York: Oxford University Press, 1994).

24. The book that brings this out most clearly is Wolfgang Smith's *The Quantum Enigma: Finding the Hidden Key* (Peru, Ill.: Sherwood Sugden & Company, 1995).

25. Jacques Monod, *Chance and Necessity* (New York: Vintage Books, 1972), p. 21.

REPLY TO HUSTON SMITH

Professor Huston Smith commences his essay by saying that he is, "the one who is closest to [my] philosophical position, most importantly his endorsement of the perennial philosophy." I am in full agreement with this assertion and will only add that among well-known philosophers in America I know of no one who stands as close to my philosophical position as he does. This response, in contrast to most others, is not therefore so much a reply to criticism but an occasion to clarify further certain points made by Smith. I wish also to state that the points he mentions as being central to my philosophical outlook are completely confirmed by me. What he calls "pivotal points in Nasr's perennialism" are indeed pivotal and central to my understanding of the perennial philosophy, and I am happy that he has brought them out clearly in this fashion.

A very important point brought out by Smith at the beginning of his discussion of "pivotal points in Nasr's perennialism" which I also need to emphasize is that neither I nor other traditionalist defenders of perennialism have discovered or come to defend the perennial philosophy inductively. We have not begun by scanning the pages of wisdom writings of various historical traditions and then discovering similarities from which we have "induced" the perennial philosophy. The discovery of the truths which constitute the perennial philosophy is the result of the practice of intellection, the use of the intellect as I have always understood the term. Once having discovered these truths, then we have observed their presence in other times and climes and in fact in all the sacred traditions the world over.

One of the leading proponents of the *philosophia perennis* of this century, A. K. Coomaraswamy, wrote a seminal essay entitled, "Paths that Lead to the Same Summit,"[1] to demonstrate the truth that the ultimate goal of various orthodox religions is the same. If I may be allowed to dwell upon the symbol of wayfaring used by Coomaraswamy, I would say that the defenders of the perennial philosophy do not climb each path separately and then conclude that yes these paths do indeed lead to the same summit. They reach the summit by climbing a single path and from the summit thus reached observe that other paths lead to it. "Climbing" in the case of the "theoretical" aspect of the perennial philosophy (if this term is understood in its original sense as *theoria*) may be said to be intellectual and by participation, whereas in the realized aspect of this wisdom it becomes also "existential" and immediately experienced.

To be sure, there have been rare individuals such as Ramakrishna, who lived in the nineteenth century in India, who have actually tried to climb the different paths to give experiential proof of these paths leading to the same summit, but even in such cases there has been an a priori intellectual certitude that the paths did actually do so. In any case the vast majority of the sages and philosophers whom defenders of the perennial philosophy such as myself consider to be main proponents of that philosophy, from Śaṅkara and Nāgārjuna to Suhrawardī and Ibn ʻArabī to Plotinus and Meister Eckhart, did not even have any appreciable knowledge of other paths associated with historical traditions other than their own, and if they did to some extent, as we see in the case of a number of Islamic esoterists, this knowledge itself was intuitive and intellective and not based simply on the detailed analysis of historical texts of other traditions as carried out by modern scholars.

One of the major errors made by opponents of the perennial philosophy can be explained precisely through what Smith has brought out in his distinction between induction and deduction of perennial truths. Some modern opponents have gone so far as to say that the defense of tradition and the perennial philosophy is simply a consequence of the availability of so much material of a religious and philosophical nature from diverse traditions in European languages which has caused certain minds such as Guénon and Coomaraswamy, followed soon by Schuon and others, to posit the existence of a body of perennial wisdom underlying the diversity of teachings of these traditions. Nothing in fact could be further from the truth, and I am glad that Smith brought up this point perspicaciously so as to make clear for those who wish to understand the perspective of perennial philosophy, the source of this philosophy and the means of access to it. What the presence of so much writing from diverse traditions has done is to provide dazzling evidence for the truth reached by means of intellection.

In discussing the intellect, Smith quite rightly makes a clear distinction between intellect and reason as I use these terms and mentions that in this usage of intellect I follow Aristotle "who called it the Active or Agent Intellect." I must only add here that although what is fundamental at first is the basic distinction between intellect and reason, there are also levels of the intellect or its functioning that must be remembered if one is to explain the full traditional doctrine. In the same way that there are grades of being, there are grades of intelligence or intellect which were discussed especially extensively by traditional Islamic as well as Jewish and Christian philosophers. Only the full reality of the intellect and its complete actualization are then to be identified with what Aristotle referred to as "Active Intellect" and Meister Eckhart the "Uncreated Intellect."

I agree with Smith that today since "fallibilism is the order of the day," in academic circles in the West eyebrows are raised whenever someone speaks of the Truth, and I would add that outside the natural and mathematical sciences this observation even holds for truth without capitalization. I am also aware of the political excuses given by the relativizers who think that they are even taking the moral high road by destroying truth claims and "meta-narratives." But being in the academic world like Professor Smith, I also confront everyday the thirst for the Truth among students and the dissatisfaction of so many of them with fallibilism. The more intelligent among them are in fact able to see behind fallibilism a hidden form of absolutism without any reference to the Absolute, for they see fallibilism as the "dictatorship of relativism and skepticism" which raises relativism and skepticism themselves to an "absolute" category. Every philosophical or epistemological claim has an aspect of absolutism in it, including claiming that all is relative or that we cannot know everything absolutely, for such assertions are themselves "absolutized" by their proponents. If we claim that there are no meta-narratives, we are making an absolute statement and substituting an idea in place of the meta-narrative which itself then functions as meta-narrative even if we do not wish to admit its being so.

I am grateful to Smith for pointing to the opposition to my thought as a result of opposition to absolutism. As far as my own intellectual life is concerned, however, I do not care very much whether I am criticized because of the fashions of the day or not. I believe that there is such a thing as truth as well as the Truth and that the goal of all intellectual endeavors is to reach the truth and to express it appropriately. In any case it is much better to be absolutistic about the Absolute than to substitute the relative for the Absolute and to absolutize the relative, which is the order of the day in most of what passes for philosophy today. I have always said that only the Absolute is absolute and even sacred visions of the Absolute and traditional philosophies provided to "explain" the Truth and Its manifestation partake of the domain of relativity, hence the diversity of expressions of the perennial philosophy. But that does not mean for one moment that one should surrender to the cult of pure relativism and fallibilism which would forfeit the power of the intellect to know in the ultimate sense.

Smith himself talks about "every articulation of the Formless [being] no more than an approximation." And he adds, "confronted with the Divine Reality in Itself, every doctrine is an error." He is pointing to the same thing but from a different angle. But to make matters clearer from the perspective of my understanding of things, I would add that articulations of the Formless should be considered more as means that prepare the mind for the miraculous act of intellection which is able to grasp the essence of things with metaphysical precision and not only approximately. As for every doctrine being an error in the face of the Divine Reality, such formulation has also been used by certain traditional masters to accentuate the chasm that exists between the grasp by the mind of the truth and its realization with the whole of our being. To quote F. Schuon, whose views are so strongly supported by Professor Smith,

> Metaphysical knowledge is one thing; its actualization in the mind quite another. All the knowledge which the brain can hold, even if it is immeasurably rich from a human point of view, is as nothing in the sight of the Truth. As for metaphysical knowledge, it is like a Divine seed in the heart; thoughts represent only faint glimmers of it. The imprint of the Divine Light on human darkness, the passage from the Infinite to the finite, the contact between the Absolute and the contingent—herein lies the whole mystery of intellection, of revelation, and of the *Avatāra*. [2]

But I would suggest that in the context of present-day discourse a more nuanced language be used and the term "error" not be employed in order to avoid miscomprehension. I would say that each doctrine is like a key to be used to open a door through which we must pass on our journey to the One. The key is indispensable precisely for the opening of the door in question and is precious for that very reason, but having used the key and having passed through the door, we are no longer in need of it. I insist that we refrain from the double error of either absolutizing a particular doctrine or formulation as if it were the Absolute itself (although it leads to the Absolute and possesses therefore an "absolute" element), or of dismissing doctrine as being irrelevant as we see in so many mindless expositions of "spirituality" today.

In discussing the Great Chain of Being Smith associates the celestial plane with the *kataphatic* way and the Infinite with the *apophatic*, writing that, "The celestial plane is accessed by the *via affirmativa*, the Infinite by the *via negativa*." Although from a certain point of view this is true, I would again see a more nuanced distinction because God as Being (and not Beyond-Being) cannot be identified with the celestial. Now, both the *apophatic* and *kataphatic* ways provide means of access to God as Being. For example, in Islam there is the revelation of the Divine Principle or Essence, which is beyond Being and is none other than the Infinite, but which has for Its first Self-determination Being or God as theologically understood in the Divine Names and Qualities, which still belong to the

Divine Order and stand above the celestial realm. Now, the Divine Names are accessible through the *kataphatic* way which means that this way cannot be associated only with the celestial realm. As for the Essence or Supreme Principle Itself, the assertion of Smith is quite correct that It can only be "reached" by the *via negativa* or the *apophatic* way for It stands above all limitations and categories including the condition of standing above all categories.

I congratulate Smith for assembling so much traditional knowledge in his diagram. There are, however, certain unavoidable problems therein especially in the distinction he makes between soul and Spirit which he makes to correspond to *rūḥ* and *qalb* in Islam whereas of course *rūḥ* means spirit in Arabic and not something else. In any case this is a wonderful diagram as long as it is seen to represent correspondences and not strict equivalences. In this context I am glad that Smith asserts categorically that I have always given the weight necessary to the differences which exist within different traditions. Those like Professor Liu, who have criticized me for not doing so, have not been fully aware of all I have written on this subject.[3]

In discussing the distinction between esoterism and exoterism, Smith quite correctly points to how I distinguish metaphysics as traditionally understood from the current understanding of philosophy and points to the basic distinction I make between intellect and reason. This distinction is not, however, identical with the major distinction I make in the study of religions between the exoteric and the esoteric, although there is no doubt that esoterism of the sapiental type is always associated with the use of the intellect. Exoterism, however, relies first of all upon the faith and only secondly upon reason and there are in fact exoteric formulations in all the Abrahamic religions which are specifically against ratiocination, formulations ranging from those which base themselves upon legalism to those which are purely fideist. As for esoterism, there is also a form of esoterism based upon love which turns its back upon the central role of the intellect and even appears as being anti-intellectual as one finds especially in certain strands of Christian and also Hindu mysticism. It is only sapiental esoterism that is based thoroughly upon the intellect and intellectual intuition. To make clear my understanding of exoterism and esoterism, it would be necessary to take this more nuanced position into consideration.

In talking about stumbling blocks, Smith discusses quite correctly the anti-metaphysical bias of the day which for that reason causes those who possess this bias to oppose my ideas and those of other traditionalists. I need to add here, however, that the metaphysics that most modern and post-modern philosophers oppose is not even the traditional metaphysics which is always related to a means of realization and which has been absent from the mainstream of Western philosophy since the Renaissance and especially Descartes. It is essential to make a distinction between my understanding of metaphysics as the supreme science of the Real and metaphysics as a branch of rationalistic philosophy which has been criticized so much in twentieth-century Western philosophy. It is important for those who criticize my thought to grasp this distinction. It is essential to understand that what they are criticizing is not what I understand by metaphysics but what they understand by it. They are beating a dead horse as far as I am concerned. My thought is as critical of Cartesian philosophy and so-called metaphysics in modern philosophy as is theirs but of course for very different reasons. I mention this point here because it is important in serious philosophical discourse to identify clearly first of all the idea with which one is concerned, and only then to set out to criticize it.

The observation of Smith that perennialism has trouble getting a hearing because of its association with hierarchy while there is such an opposition to this idea today is again an astute one. Let it be added that the etymology of hierarchy (*hiero-arche*) implies divine origin and that the idea of hierarchy is inseparable from every serious philosophy which accepts the Divine Origin of things and draws the consequences of such a position. Today we live in a world which Guénon associated with "the reign of quantity." The tendency is toward quantitative egality, the destruction of qualitative differences and the imposition of uniformity which modern technology in combination with crass materialism and consumerism are spreading all over the world in the name of material development and the necessity of living in a global village. But a world of pure quantity could not even exist. Quality has to manifest itself and so must hierarchy despite the strong tendency to the contrary. The ideas of myself and those like me are addressed to those whose inner being still resonates to the hierarchy which in reality governs cosmic manifestation whether we are willing to accept it or not. For followers of philosophies based on quantity, the leveling of all distinction and destruction of all hierarchies carried out often in the name of freeing common man from "elite" structures, the perennial philosophy certainly has no appeal, as stated by Smith. What is surprising, however, is that amidst the culture of reductionism, quantitative equality and disdain for qualitative distinction and excellence there are so many minds and souls who thirst precisely for the higher reaches of the chain of being and higher degrees of perfection and excellence which are ontologically meaningful only in a world which accepts the nature of hierarchy.

Under the section on tradition Smith mentions that I consider myself contemporary and not modern. I wish to emphasize the truth of this observation. I consider modernism as a philosophy whose very premises and assumptions I oppose and against which I have written for over four decades.

But the hands of destiny have placed me in this day and age and by virtue of that fact I am a contemporary. This distinction is important because it is possible to be contemporary without being modern. In fact one of the realities of the scene during this past century, marked by the spread of modernism, has been opposition to modernism which has taken many forms of which the most fundamental is the critique posed by tradition. The presence of the perennial or traditional point of view is as much a part of the contemporary scene as modernist phenomena and ideas themselves.

As for my being in accord with the reality of certain innovations, that must be considered carefully; for to accept the "reality" of an innovation or new idea is one thing and to condone it quite another. As far as modern science is considered, I do accept that it has been able to understand *an aspect* of the reality of nature better than the traditional sciences of nature which were, however, able to know *other aspects* of nature, especially its spiritual dimension, infinitely better than the quantitative sciences developed since the seventeenth century in the West. That is why I cannot accept the statement, "modern science understands nature calculatively much better than our forbears did," if the term nature is not modified to mean only the quantitative aspect of corporeal reality. I have clarified my views on this important question in my several works on Islamic science and in a more general manner in my *The Need for a Sacred Science*.

Perhaps the only point of difference between my perspective and that of Smith pertains to the social domain and is summarized in his sentence, "I would not want go as far as Nasr does in defending the social patterns in traditional societies." Smith tends to regard the imperfections in these patterns and I the reflections of archetypes which represent the good despite the existence of imperfections. As I stated in my response to Liu, the traditional doctrines themselves confirm the great imperfections in the social order in the particular cosmic period in which we live, being far removed from the Golden Age even at the beginning of what is known as the historical period. What traditions do is not to deny evil but on the basis of a deep knowledge of the nature of the human state to maximize the good with the aim of making possible to the maximum extent permissible the realization of the goal of human life, which is the attainment of salvation for the many and deliverance for the few. Modern society on the contrary seeks to perfect society by means of social engineering on the basis of ignorance of the real nature of man, and the denial of the reality of evil in total disrespect for the ultimate goal of human life. Traditional societies succeeded in surviving for millennia amidst many imperfections to be sure, but they were always able to provide meaning for life and a path for salvation beyond the life of this world. Modern societies, while denying the centrality of man's spiritual goal in this life and reducing him to a purely earthly creature, are faced with a set of imperfections and evils which are certainly no less than what existed in the days of old while facing the destruction of the natural environment and the very dissolution of the societies which continue to be engineered according to the worst kind of hallucinations about the nature of man and his ultimate needs.

As for the traditional worlds, which as Smith says quite rightly, I prefer immeasurably to the modern and the postmodern, I do consider the wisdom contained in the traditional worlds to be ultimately revealed in the theological sense of this term. But I would not "see it [this wisdom] as surfacing from the deepest unconscious of spiritual geniuses of the past," to quote Smith. First of all, revelation has nothing to do with human genius, spiritual or otherwise. To consider Moses, the Prophet of Islam, or for that matter the Buddha or Lao-Tze to have been geniuses is really to diminish their status, and I certainly would never characterize them as such if I were to call Beethoven and Einstein also geniuses. Those to whom revelations were sent possessed all that we associate positively with genius but also infinitely more.

Even more problematic for me is the usage of the term "unconscious" which reminds the reader of the theories of Jung which I consider to be a parody of traditional doctrines. For the traditionalists, even if one uses the language of consciousness rather than God to appeal to certain types of contemporary readers, the source of wisdom is the *supraconscious* and not the *unconscious* or the *subconscious*. It is of the utmost importance to point out these distinctions in order to avoid any error in the understanding of traditional teachings and their basic distinction from various forms of modern psychology including Jungianism.

In conclusion I want to express my special gratitude to Smith for bringing out clearly the main tenets of my thought, so close as he is to my way of thinking, and doing it in such a manner that it has provided the occasion for me to clarify many basic elements of my thought. If, as Smith says, my exposition of the perennial philosophy, like those of notable traditionalists to whom I owe so much, has provided "a reasonable alternative to the contemporary Western mindset," then I am happy to have succeeded in doing what I set out to achieve from the beginning of my intellectual career, having had in mind always not only Westerners but also non-Westerners who have become influenced by the modern "mindset." Moreover, I consider this alternative to be not only "reasonable" but also intellectually evident, lying as it does in the very nature of things and being ingrained in the very substance of our being.

S. H. N.

NOTES

1. A. K. Coomaraswamy, "Paths that Lead to the Same Summit" in *Am I My Brother's Keeper* (Freeport, N.Y.:Books For Libraries Press, Inc., 1967), Ch. III, pp. 36–53.

2. *Spiritual Perspectives and Human Facts*, trans. P. Townsend (Middlesex [U.K.]: Perennial Books, 1987, p. 9).

3. See Shu-hsien Liu's "Reflections on Tradition and Modernity—A Response to Dr. Seyyed Hossein Nasr from a Neo-Confucian Perspective," chapter 6 in this volume.

3

Robert Cummings Neville

PERENNIAL PHILOSOPHY IN A PUBLIC CONTEXT

The perennial philosophy or sacred wisdom so ably expounded and defended by Seyyed Hossein Nasr in his Gifford Lectures, published as *Knowledge and the Sacred*, is out of fashion with philosophers in the late modern European traditions, including postmodernism.[1] "Out of fashion" is a misstatement: they dismiss it with ridicule.[2] In the field of religious studies perennial philosophy fares much better than in academic Western philosophy, partly because of the outstanding contributions to the field by Huston Smith, its foremost American advocate, and partly because it constitutes one of the paradigmatic answers to the question of the relations among the world religions.[3] Professor Nasr does not distinguish sharply between philosophy and religion, calling his position both "perennial philosophy" and "sacred wisdom," and in a theoretical sense he is surely right. There ought not be a break between the professional practice of academic philosophy and living a philosophical life, or between the academic study of religion and its practice, or between philosophy and religion as studied or practiced.[4] In the politics of intellectual culture, however, there is a world of difference between philosophy and religion as academic fields.[5]

Both philosophy and religious reflection, or theology, have publics constituted by anyone who might have an interest in what is at stake, even an interest in rejecting a position as false or unimportant.[6] The modern despisers of perennial philosophy are as much part of the public within which it is expounded and argued as its advocates and fellow travelers. Yet Professor Nasr, in *Knowledge and the Sacred*, gives an account of the development of modern European philosophy that delegitimates the despisers as much as they would delegitimate the perennial philosophy. He describes the modern European tradition as a stupid and perhaps wicked fall, at least a forgetting, without analyzing sympathetically why modern philosophers would have taken the tacks they did.[7] Both sides deserve better if the integrity of philosophy's public is to be exercised.

One of the happiest virtues of Professor Nasr's thought is that he is a genuine world philosopher.[8] He does not define philosophy as limited to the inheritance of Socrates, as many of our Western colleagues do. Nor does he define himself as an Islamic philosopher, although that is the historical tradition from which he derives his main conceptions and expressions. Because he does not distinguish sharply between philosophy and religion, it is important to say that Professor Nasr identifies with the cultic practice of Islam, especially its Sufi branch, from which his philosophy arises.[9] But his philosophy engages the entire philosophic world, not just the Islamic, from the perspective of a position, the perennial philosophy, that finds expressions in each. This is all the more reason for his position to be related with more intimate respect to late modern Western philosophy, for that is the one family of traditions he approaches with an attitude more of blame than learning.

My purpose in this essay is to engage Professor Nasr with the Western public by constructing a late modern Western interpretation of how the perennial philosophy might philosophically and existentially be meaningful and true, and how a version of that is indeed true. To do this I shall first sketch a theory of religious symbols that shows how such symbols allow us to engage religious dimensions of reality. Moreover, such symbols shape the souls of those who gain competence with them so that the religious dimensions to which the symbols refer can be engaged. Without an appropriately developed soul, people miss or misinterpret those dimensions.

Then I shall argue that the leading ideas in the perennial philosophy, those having to do with "the One and the Many," are a kind of religious symbol that engages those who become competent at them with ultimate matters. I shall argue that there are two fundamental perennial paradigms. One is the ascent of understanding to higher and higher principles of unity; this is Professor Nasr's primary affiliation and it emphasizes hierarchy. The other is penetration to the ground from which both unity and multiplicity are created, emphasizing the immediacy of the act of creation *ex nihilo* and of the equiprimordial, non-hierarchical partnership of the One and the Many; this is my kind of perennial philosophy. I shall then argue that competence at the exercise of the perennial symbols of either approach can lead to existential sacred wisdom of the sort Professor Nasr advocates. My entire argument arises from the theory of signs developed initially by Charles Sanders Peirce, the American founder of pragmatism, a more-late-modern-Western-philosopher-than-whom-cannot-be-conceived.[10] Finally, I shall discuss five steps to be taken for the perennial philosophy to engage the contemporary Western academic philosophic tradition. The fourth step contains a significant critical evaluation of Professor Nasr's project.

RELIGIOUS SYMBOLS

The European tradition of semiotics, from Saussure to Derrida, has taken the interpretation of texts as its paradigm case; the earlier interest in Biblical hermeneutics was probably the reason for this. The American pragmatic tradition, by contrast, has taken the interpretation of nature as its paradigm, with signs and interpretive behavior as guides for discovering what is real and how to live well. Thus the European tradition could understandably conclude that signs have no real reference outside their system of surrounding signs that define referents and interpretations. But the American can insist that the function of signs is to engage us with the world and shape our behavior so as to be more realistic and discerning than we would be without the signs. Entire sign systems, including the coded relations among signs as meanings, referents, and interpretations, are taken as referring to reality when we actually employ them in engagement.

Peirce argued that all signs need to be understood in terms of their meanings, their references, and their interpretations. In the case of religious signs, which we should call "symbols" in accord with common usage, meanings are defined in terms of systems of symbols interconnected in meanings.[11] Moreover, systems of symbols are laid on top of one another, or juxtaposed, or set in tension with one another. In Professor Nasr's perennial philosophy, for instance, one system of symbols describes reality in a hierarchy of levels and another describes the mind's capacities in terms of a progressive ascent that is correlatable with the first.[12] There is another system of metaphysical symbols describing the creation of the world of many levels by God, and in this system there is a careful dialectic connecting a perfectly good divine nature with a divine will creating a world which is wholly good in one way but whose lower levels are mixed with what people see as or can turn to evil. The human system for understanding the value-status of things properly notes suffering and evil, and the human will cannot be understood with exactly the same symbol system employed for divinity. To some extent the systems of symbols can be systematized in an encompassing system; but the attempt to do that thoroughly leads to a diminished rationalism. Rather, the several symbol systems correct and resonate with one another, engaging reality more profoundly together than any one or several systems would by themselves. There is a mystery that is apprehended—that is, taken in, but not literally represented in the systems of ideas. Persons competent at the overlayment of religious symbols are not disturbed by a failure to express flat consistency, but find their certainty in the existential interaction of the multiple systems of meanings.

Symbols refer, according to Peirce, in one or several of three ways: as indices pointing to something not otherwise noticed, as icons affirming the referent reality is like the symbol in its structure, and as conventions whereby the symbols connect their referents with other realities by means of systems of symbols.[13] Most religious symbols do all three, and I believe they have both a primary and a secondary referent. Their primary referent is to the religious object, the divine, the ultimate, or what can be analyzed as a finite/infinite contrast.[14] A finite/infinite contrast is a reference to something that can also be identified as finite and determinate but which is taken (legitimately, when a valid reference is made) to bear the infinite. Generally, finite/infinite contrasts are the boundary points, the liminal elements of what constitutes the world.[15] Common examples are the physical existence of the world as bearing the activity of the creator, or those things that are grounds of meaning and value. Events, such as the Exodus or Hijrah, or structures such as the depths of consciousness, and persons, such as Jesus, that found the identity of one's people or of one's personal existence are also finite/infinite contrasts. Theology and philosophy integrate the references to finite/infinite contrasts according to conceptual symbolic theories.

The secondary referent in a religious symbol is the cultural condition, spiritual maturity, or psychological state of soul of the interpreter. This is to say, a given symbol can refer to the primary referent only for those people ready for that meaning. For a person who is too immature, or of an incomprehending culture, or in an inappropriate psychological state, the symbol would not refer to the primary referent it is supposed to, but to something else, usually not religous at all. The symbol of the God beyond Being, important for Professor Nasr, would not make sense for a child who has not reflected on beings and Being and who would spatialize the metaphor. The symbols of Being would not refer to the ultimate for East Asians whose categories take up primary metaphors of process. The symbol of God as Father would not refer accurately for persons sexually abused by their father as a child. Although the relativity of symbols derives from the interpreter's capacities for interpretation, the relativity consists in a matter of doubled reference: a symbol refers to a specific finite/infinite complex for people of a certain ready sort; for other people, that symbol refers to something else. The importance of recognizing doubled reference is that we can understand how symbols are valid in some contexts but invalid or even perverse in others. Moreover, we can understand how spiritual progress is made by attaining to greater capacities for referring with the more profound symbols.

The interpretation of religious symbols is of course contextual because interpretation is an activity. Some contexts are obviously practical, such as the use of symbols in organizing a religious community. Other contexts are much more theoretical, as in philosophy and theology of the sort we have been discussing. Yet other contexts are devotional in which the use of the symbols is not so much to reorganize behavior or to understand more fully but to transform the soul.[16] These contexts are nearly always mixed. Like reference, interpretation is doubled. The primary interpretation consists of the symbols that elucidate the meaning of the symbol as referred to the referent in some respect. The secondary interpretation, however, is the practical implication of the primary interpretation for the interpreter or the interpreting community. Sometimes this implication is merely for how people ought to think about the referent. Other times it is how they ought to behave in more overt senses. Yet other times, or perhaps a bit at all times, the secondary interpretation is the transforming of the interpreter's soul so as to be able to handle the primary interpretation.

Now acts of interpretation engage objects—the religious or ultimate object in our present discussion—by taking them to be as the interpretation's symbol says in a certain respect. The symbol stands for the referent in that respect, and in so doing connects the object and interpreter. The object to which reference is made is included within the act of interpretation. Even if the symbol is mistaken, if the reference is accurate the interpreter and real referent are brought together.

Many modern philosophers would say that what we interpret are only representations of real objects, not the realities themselves. Like Descartes's image of knowing, we are locked in our minds, they think, and cannot make contact with real external things. Nobody quite believes Descartes anymore, though his philosophy has crept into European semiotics. Derrida and others point out that anything we can specify as the referent of a symbol, or as the interpretation of the symbol, no matter how practical and active, is itself another sign or symbol, and thus an element in a larger semiotic system.[17] True enough, to specify a referent or interpretant is to use symbols within the system connected to the symbol under discussion. Moreover, the relations of referring and interpreting, and standing for objects in certain respects, are all elements of semiotic structure, like the grammar of a language. But it is a cheap trick to say that because realities are described by signs in a semiotic system they themselves are in the semiotic system into which we are locked without external reference.

Descartes's image is not the only one, and Peirce carefully developed an alternative, that of engagement. A symbol, and the entire semiotic system within which it is defined, can be the medium by which an interpreter acts to interpret reality. The relations within the code of a semiotic system are extensional, defining the extension of the signs within them and distinguishing how they potentially can function in meaning, reference, and interpretation. An act of interpretation, however, is intentional, engaging real objects by means of the discriminations laid out in the symbols and their semiotic connections.[18] An act of interpretation takes reality to be roughly iconic to the semiotic system employed; we take our culture to be roughly effective in discriminating what is real and important. Moreover, an act of interpretation takes the specific symbols it employs to engage the objects to which it makes reference. When we engage physical objects, we interact with them according to the anticipations defined by our symbols for them. When we interpret a situation, for instance a political situation, or even the very general situation of "modern culture's having lost touch with the deep truths of reality," we engage the situation by the imagination embodied in our symbol systems and direct our attention to what those systems pick out as salient. When we interpret ultimate realities, even though there is no physical interaction across a spatio-temporal field, and no learning about a situation by modifying elements to see what happens, such as voting for a different party or writing a philosophy book, we still engage the ultimate by picking out what our symbols discriminate, appreciating what comes across when we live and contemplate with those symbols of ultimacy.

I have spoken of acts of interpretation in ways that emphasize what the interpreter does, and this is important. But the question of truth reverses the direction of the action. Truth is the carryover of what is valuable and salient from the object interpreted into the interpreter.[19] Some Western philosophers, following Aristotle, have thought of truth as the repetition of the form of the object in the mind of the knower. But then one has to stand outside both object and knower to compare forms. Moreover, we know many things as having forms different from the forms with which we think about them. It is better to say that we know something when we grasp what is valuable about it. Of course things are always in contexts, never known in pure isolation, and so knowing them well is grasping how they achieve singular values, how they integrate their components with intrinsic value, how they are valuable for other things and how they function as parts of larger systems with value, and so on.[20] I believe it can be shown that form itself is a function of value rather than the other way around, which is the common belief.[21]

Carryover is a causal notion, implicit in natural process. Causality is not an innocent philosophical notion, to be sure, and most modern notions of causality are too linear, temporal, and simple-minded to convey the complexity of the process by which physical objects, say, are transformed in their interactions with people so as to become the stuff of experience and engaged intentionally. But pragmatists and process philosophers such as Alfred North Whitehead have developed sufficiently complex notions of causality.[22] We observe babies growing from simple stimulus-response behavior to intentional action and curiosity; so the kind of causation involved is surely possible.

Professor Nasr has been so exercised by the deficiencies of the popular modern Western ideas of causation, with respect to interpreting how people naturally can have sapiental knowledge, that he feels obliged to deny evolutionary theory, which makes his view seem implausible; his objections are subtle and the status of various hypotheses in evolutionary theory is under considerable public discussion. But he runs against a considerable modern consensus that natural history exhibits how much of the natural world has been shaped, and thus unfairly is associated with creationist fundamentalists. That objection to evolution is unnecessary, however, and counterproductive, if one has a sufficiently subtle causal theory of interpretation that meets three conditions: First, that interpretations can have ultimate references and still be true; second, that there can be a directness of engagement that sometimes yields certainty; and third, that higher realities can be known for what they are without being merely a cumulative complexification of lower realities. I shall discuss these conditions in reverse order.

Some early modern empiricists believed that all ideas are built up out of simple ones, such as color patches. John Locke, for instance, tried to give an account of how we construct the idea of infinity by the addition of finite units.[23] This empirical approach makes it difficult to understand how subtler and more perfect things can be conceived before the obvious or simpler ones, as has been true in the history of religions. The semiotic approach I am advocating, however, does not have this difficulty at all. Whether we deal with ordinary physical objects, the Decline of the West, or the God beyond Being, depends on whether we have the symbols for that. Long before we developed symbols for atomic particles and the big bang, we had symbols for the ultimate ground of all the physical cosmos, of meaning, and value. Professor Nasr is entirely right to point out that the roots of perennial philosophy are thousands of years old, and the reason is that symbols for knowing ultimate things were developed very early. Ancient speculative geniuses such as the authors of the Upaniṣads, and Plotinus, put these symbols in good order. In historical perspective, the topics of the perennial philosophy are more elementary than astrophysics and molecular biology. Although the capacity to symbolize evolved slowly, once the capacity was developed the sapiental imagination was competent.

Professor Nasr rightly points to the certainty that often accompanies sapiental knowing. (He also could point to the doubts and struggles of the dark night of the soul.) Philosophers have long tried to account for this with the claim that there is an immediacy or identity between the finite mind and the infinite. But no amount of metaphorical slippage can account for an alleged flat-out immediate identity of the finite and infinite. The certainty comes not with *immediacy* but with the *directness* of engagement in which ultimate matters are interpreted with finite symbols. John E. Smith has long argued that the distinction between directness and immediacy is extremely important.[24] In the pragmatic tradition of experience as engagement, the direct encounter with the divine is mediated by symbols, but no less direct for all that. The certainty of sapiental knowledge, even pure mystical knowledge, derives from the appreciation of unity with the ultimate in the interpretive contemplation such that the divine worth is transmitted at least in part. Few if any contemplatives would claim that their certainty is an infallibility regarding their expressions of what they experience. Moreover, many regard their early experiences, however certain they might be, as preliminary to or superceded by subsequent knowledge. The theory of symbols I have advocated here shows both how the unity of engagement can give certainty and how subsequent engagement with more discriminating and richer symbols can supercede the earlier certainty.

Finally, the theory of symbols I have advocated shows how ultimate things can be symbolized simply by having symbols whose meanings can refer to those things. Even Descartes thought that the idea of perfection is prior to any idea of finitude or imperfection and, as mentioned above, symbols about ultimate principles and grounds developed early in history. In the next section I shall explore certain of these symbols in connection with the perennial philosophy. As to the truth of the symbols dealing with the topics of the perennial philosophy, the tests for truth are extremely complicated. On the one hand are the dialectical tests of the sort Plotinus loved, showing that his theory was superior to alternatives. On the other hand are the long-range pragmatic tests of living with a symbolic theory so as to see how it makes sense of all of life, better sense than its alternatives. But perhaps more important than the tests among competing theories is the fact that symbols can be attained that open up dimensions of reality that otherwise would be opaque. Much of Professor Nasr's complaint about European modernity is that its symbols fail to register the ultimate dimensions that are the direct topic of the perennial philosophy. Moreover, modernity's symbols seem to preclude the symbols with which the ultimate dimensions can be engaged. That we have symbols that do engage the ultimate is more important, at least in the short run, than whether Plotinus, Clement, or Origen has the better symbols.

My claim is that the symbols of the perennial philosophy, engaging the ultimate dimensions of reality that are its topic, are difficult to fit into much of the modern soul. Modernity needs to transform its soul in order to be competent at those symbols, and until it does they cannot refer well: the reason they cannot refer well is that modern interpreters are often incapable of being the secondary referents. My last section shall deal with this.

Modes of Perennial Philosophy

As Professor Nasr indicates, the perennial philosophy has had many symbolic expressions, from personifications to abstract dialectical theories. The latter are of concern here, and they all have to do with what some philosophers have called the problem of the One and the Many. That problem has to do with explaining how all the different things in reality are sufficiently unified as to belong to one world, how they all are real or have being. Or, if one begins with unity, the problem is understanding how the unity of being can be expressed in the differences among things. A few philosophers have asserted pure multiplicity and refused to ask what things have in common such that they can be different; a few others have asserted pure unity and denied the existence of multiplicity. But most philosophers fall between these extremes and acknowledge both unity and multiplicity. Some think that multiplicity is basic and unity mere conjunction making no difference to the things unified; none of these atomistic philosophers would associate themselves with the perennial philosophy. Some at the other extreme believe that unity is basic and that multiplicity is mere appearance, or the function of a certain perspectival approach to reality; many of these would identify with the perennial philosophy. But in between are many possible positions. Perhaps the most penetrating analysis of the problem of the One and the Many in contemporary Western philosophy is Paul Weiss's *Modes of Being*.[25] Weiss strives to give unity and multiplicity a balanced equal weight.

Although this is not the place for a detailed comparison of types, I believe that, where dialectical precision is pressed carefully, there are two families or types of solution to the problem of the One and the Many, each with legitimate claim to association with perennial philosophy. The first and most common, and the one advocated by Professor Nasr, takes an epistemological focus—sapiental, Nasr calls it—and seeks to ascend to higher and higher principles of intelligibility, accounting for higher and higher levels of unity. This is familiar to Western European philosophers through the Neo-Platonic tradition from Plotinus through the Christian Neo-Platonists such as Pseudo-Dionysius, Bonaventura, and the Victorines.[26] The underlying sapiental principle is that if a certain kind of difference is noted, that is because cognition stands at a higher level of unity. "Standing at a higher level" is not a mere logical matter, however. The mind must be cultivated, perhaps through long years of yoga or contemplation under the guidance of a teacher, to attain that level. Some describe the cultivation as the recovery of pre-existent higher levels of mind; others describe it as the construction of human capacities to grasp pre-existent levels of reality. Either way, knowledge of the levels and how to reach them are conveyed by "tradition" in the sense that Nasr uses the term.[27]

On the ontological side for this approach, reality is a hierarchy of levels of greater being and unity, as Professor Nasr argues. Moreover, the lower depend on the higher. Professor Nasr describes these ontological or cosmic levels as a theophany.[28] The highest level, perhaps not even to be called a level, surely beyond Being insofar as Being relates to beings, is pure and necessary reality from which all else flows. Furthermore, each level going down is a mixture of being with non-being, in progressive negativity, so that, at the level of ordinary human living, evil is possible and common.

The second family of approaches to the problem of the One and the Many takes them to be correlative. That is, there is no unity without a multiplicity to unify, and no multiplicity without unity. The important distinction is between determinate being, which is unified and multiple, and absolute nothingness. Anything "prior" to determinate being would have no characters to distinguish itself from anything else or from absolute nothingness. Like the other family within the perennial philosophy, this one takes the realm of determinateness, with unity and multiplicity, to be contingent. But it is contingent upon nothing, and the predominant metaphor is creation *ex nihilo*. The "creator" is nothing apart from creating, however, not a potentiality to create or anything like that, for those are all determinate characteristics requiring to be created. In addition to the creation *ex nihilo* tradition in West Asian religions, this family within the perennial philosophy takes its metaphors from mystics such as Meister Eckhart and, in our own time, Nicholas Berdyaev.[29]

Like the first family within perennial philosophy, the creation *ex nihilo* approach can acknowledge many dimensions of reality, like levels. But because creation *ex nihilo* marks an immediate making that moves directly from nothingness to determinate being, the dimensions need not be related in a hierarchy according to which some are farther from the creative source than others. There might be levels of unity, importance, value, and clarity, but none is closer to the source than any other. This approach can agree with ancient gnosticism about the importance of cultivated and saving knowledge without agreeing with the cosmology that separates the realm of ordinary life from the Creator by mediating levels of increasing non-being. In our time Paul Tillich has given the most elaborate analysis of dimensions of reality relative to being and nothingness.[30]

On the cognitive side there is a striking difference between the "higher unity" and "creation *ex nihilo*" families of the perennial philosophy, a difference in fundamental intuitions about what constitutes a satisfying understanding, vision, or grasp of things. According to the first family of positions, the mind rises to higher explanations in search of a principle from which other, lower, things derive. "Principle" does not mean merely the first or source, because absolute nothingness is a "principle" in that sense. Rather, it means that there is some character of the arche from which the rest of things flow, as pure being gives rise to mixed being or pure unity to unified multiplicities, and so forth. In philosophical dialectic, this family of positions insists on a principle or principles of intelligibility. This is rationalism in a profound metaphysical sense, and corresponds theologically with the position that the divine nature precedes the divine will; the divine will is constrained to exhibit the divine nature. This is Professor Nasr's position.[31]

By contrast the heart of understanding for the creation *ex nihilo* tradition is the location of basic creative decision-points at which determinate unity-multiplicity complexes come to be. In ordinary processes we can find many such decision-points to which both common sense and science attend. In asking about the creation of entire dimensions of reality we need to locate where the characteristic components come together. In pushing the ontological question of why there is something rather than nothing, we look for the ultimate eternal creative act that creates determinateness as such, including time, space, sameness, and difference. Abstract philosophical dialectic can locate where these decision-points are. But to *engage* that singular divine creative act requires the gnosis of preparation that includes a practiced capacity to engage reality with the symbols of creation *ex nihilo*. As Tillich argued in his discussions of ontological reason or *logos*, the underlying ontological structure of the cosmos is a real structure and the human mind has an affinity with it that can be brought to exercise.[32] For this family of positions, only a metaphysically empirical discovery and acknowledgment of the creative act is intellectually (and spiritually) satisfying. No matter how "high" one's principles might be, the questing intellect can always ask how and why those principles got to be the way they are, even a single highest principle.

According to the creation *ex nihilo* family of positions, or at least many of those positions within the family, the divine nature arises in creation itself. Hence this is symbolized theologically in the doctrine that the divine will is prior to the divine nature, Duns Scotus over against Thomas Aquinas. Many thinkers who assume that only an agent with a nature can act believe the position to be paradoxical. But no position within the perennial philosophy thinks of God or the highest principle as *a being* with a nature that functions as an agent. The creation *ex nihilo* approach takes its metaphors for creation, not from inertial motion in which things act according to their natures, but from moral action in which both deeds and one's moral identity are the products of the free actions.[33]

With respect to ultimately satisfying understanding, I confess that there seem to be two kinds of people. Some, associated with the first family of perennial philosophies, cannot accept that creation *ex nihilo* explains anything because for them an explanation would have to follow from the nature of the cause. Others would say that no explanation that appeals to the nature of something can be ultimate because it itself requires an explanation of what makes the nature the way it is. The perennial philosophy embraces both kinds of mind.

My point in this section has been to lay out two philosophical families of positions that, on the one hand, are recognizable in the contemporary Western philosophical community, if not common there, and on the other hand are legitimate contemporary expressions of the perennial philosophy. They both are realisms with regard to ontological structures, and both deal with ultimate origins of multiplicity and determinateness. Moreover, both have religious implications although I have expressed them here so far in terms of merely philosophical dialectical contrasts.

Sacred Knowledge

Professor Nasr's main point in *Knowledge and the Sacred* was not to defend a particular philosophical tradition but to articulate and defend that tradition as a philosophic way of life. In that tradition, philosophy is not mere knowledge but sacred knowledge, the knowing of which is saving and sanctifying, and the result of coming to participate in a tradition of wisdom as well as cultivation of personal capacities for that participation. Moreover, the reason the knowledge is saving is that its object is holy and the object comes to indwell the knower in the knowing. Reality itself, taken in its fullness, even if that fullness is but partially and somewhat inaccurately grasped, is holy and ready to be known.

How is this position, with which I agree according to my version, to be made plausible in a philosophical public that includes the late modern West? Five steps are necessary.

1. We must give a plain philosophical defense of the metaphysics involved in at least some version of the perennial philosophy. I have distinguished two families of versions, those of the hierarchical ascent and those of creation *ex nihilo*. None of these has been defended in detail in this essay against responsible criticism. But I have defended a version of the latter in sufficient detail elsewhere for the position to be at least respectable. Professor Nasr has defended related versions of hierarchical ascent. And looked at in the long view, from the standpoint of the *consensus gentium*, the Neo-Platonic tradition in the West, and the flanking traditions elsewhere that Professor Nasr cites, cannot be all wrong. If they are wrong, it is because of

overstatement or unguarded generalization, or an inability to admit other important truths. None of this proves yet that all late modern Western philosophers ought to adopt a metaphysical version of the perennial philosophy, only that they should take it seriously without delegitimation.

2. A respectable theory needs to be provided for how it might be possible for the holy religious object, God, or finite/infinite contrasts, to enter at least partially into a person through knowledge so as to render the person a bit more holy. The theory presented in the first section here accounts precisely for that. A true interpretation of finite/infinite contrasts is the carryover of the value of the object into the interpreter in the respects the symbols at hand interpret the object. In an Aristotelian vision, we would say that a true interpretation informs the soul with the form of the object. In the version defended here, value rather than form is carried across. Either way, the divine holiness or glory is carried across in the respects involved in the symbolic interpretation. There is a directness of engagement, a unity of the encounter, in which the divine makes the interpreter holy in the respects involved. To be sure, the divine is infinite and no accumulation of finite interpretations can carry across the whole glory of God. No person can be holy in the infinite way God is. But the more accurate, the richer, the more encompassing, the more incisive the symbolic interpretation, the more holy the interpreter. As I argued, the process of coming to use the appropriate symbols competently transforms the soul so that people are better engaged with, that is, more conditioned by, the holiness of what they interpret. Most theologians would say that the kind of knowledge gained of God through directly effective symbols is not a mere condition of the interpreter but becomes essential within the interpreter's life. The knowledge of God becomes increasingly effective as the principle according to which one composes one's own reality; that reality of course includes one's own interpretations of God." As the mystics say, a genuine contemplative engagement allows the interpreter to drop away so that it is God interpreting God. Christian theology models this in the relations among the Trinitarian persons.

3. The dialectic of the perennial philosophy must be correlated with the religious category of the sacred. Professor Nasr asserts this correlation with little argument in *Knowledge and the Sacred*. Nevertheless, there are many traditions, including many outside of the perennial ones, developing the correlation of the most ultimate philosophical categories with the divine in its holiness. This is as true for the *Dao* in East Asia and *Brāhman* in South Asia as it is for God in West Asian civilizations. As Anselm argued, the principle for identifying categories as indicative of God is that they are conceived as whatever greater than which cannot be conceived. It is on the grounds of "greatness," dialectically defined, that we sort candidate objects

of worship. Here is not the place to enter discussion with anthropologists and others who would identify the holy, not with greatness for which a philosophical account might be given, but with some mere quality among other qualities, such as uncanniness. I have argued that what makes something seem uncanny or sacred is its connection, at least according to a culture's symbolism, with something that is recognized in that culture as a finite/infinite contrast.[34] Let us suppose for the sake of argument that this step can be taken, or at least recognized as reasonable, by later modern Western philosophers.

4. The step penultimate in difficulty is showing that the first three steps—the metaphysical theory, the theory of symbols as engaging and transforming the symbolizer with the object symbolized, and the connection of the philosophical ideas with sacredness in God and human beings—do not require the rejection of other things that late modernity has found to be true and important. Here, alas, is where Professor Nasr's argument is its own worst enemy. He grudgingly admits that modern science might not be false if put in its place, but complains that it usually is construed scientistically. Fair enough: scientific expertise does not generalize to philosophy or theology. But he carries this critique so far as to deny the theory of evolution, as if that were incompatible with the metaphysics of the perennial philosophy. Whether evolution is true, and in what form, is an empirical scientific question, an hypothesis subject to ongoing explication and test. Any perennial philosophy worth its salt ought to admit to the creation or emanation of any characteristic of the natural world science might find there. Whatever is determinate, that is what God has created.[35]

Even worse than the negative attack on science is Professor Nasr's positive depiction of the world, of the ordinary dimensions of the world. He uses almost exclusively language derivative from the traditional symbologies of the perennial philosophies worldwide that seems to deny outright important lessons modern culture has learned with pain. Let me call attention to several instances.

He lauds the authority of the great tradition again and again with barely a hint that some kinds of traditional authority, and some aspects of authority, might be very bad. How can a scholar who fled the Islamic Revolution of 1979 led by Khomeini laud authority *simpliciter*? Modernity has learned the hermeneutics of suspicion about authority because of its long history of enforcing ignorance, not enlightenment, and preserving an oppressive status quo. Perennial philosophy in our day needs to do the extremely hard work of distinguishing legitimate authority, as might reside in the great tradition, from illegitimate senses of political and intellectual authority.

The language in which the perennial tradition describes the world praises the sacredness of things and the indwelling of the holy in finite things; Professor Nasr calls the world a theophany. Admitting that in perhaps the highest and richest perspective the world is a sacred book, history has shown that the identification of finite things with the holy is an extremely short step from outrageous idolatry and that barely another step from the organization of national armies to slaughter their neighbors in the name of holiness. Early modern Europe found the tragic bloodshed of religious wars to be far worse than whatever religious spirit might be lost when religion is privatized. Secularism arose in good measure from the rejection of claims to sacredness in the world as justifying violence and oppression. I agree with Professor Nasr that it is true in the most profound sense to say that everything is holy, but we ought not say that out loud until we have developed and committed ourselves to ways to make the point compatible with the wisdom of secularism regarding peace, love, and tolerance. Surely an important secularist lesson is to be learned from the centuries of bloody, naked violence over control of Jerusalem by the three Abrahamic faiths who agree in tragic irony that only God is holy, that only God's holiness can make a city holy, and that both God's nature and God's command for our behavior is love of one another. Perennial philosophy is wholly inadequate in our time unless it can make its point while committing itself wholeheartedly to the secularist lessons about peace, love, and tolerance. As continued religious warring shows, religion is not private and cannot be made to be; so the secularist solution by itself is not sufficient. But the critical secularist point about symbols of the sacred universe that start armies marching must be acknowledged.

Related to uncritical claims for the omnipresence of the sacred in the language Professor Nasr cites of the sapiental tradition, are claims for the supernatural. It is one thing to understand the supernatural as higher or deeper levels and dimensions of reality than appear on the surface of ordinary or scientific experience. It is quite another, and unworthy of a perennial philosophy for our time, to understand the supernatural as the intervention of higher beings or higher levels of reality to change the lower. The very genius of the hierarchical conception is to give each level its integrity. Yet how often the language of the perennial philosophy cultivates an interventionist sensibility! This can pervert religion into a Marxian opiate of the people. It can distract people from the disciplined realism required for personal and communal spiritual progress. It can even justify the oppression of one nation by another because the oppressor believes itself to have a supernatural mandate. The very cultures to which Nasr appeals in order to rescue the West in its time of secular dissolution have themselves been victims of colonialism fueled by claims for supernatural legitimation. Only a deluded supernaturalist fool would look at superior guns and see God's establishment of a manifest destiny. A cannon is a cannon is a cannon. Until the perennial philosophy can formulate itself in ways that reject the supernaturalism rightly criticized by the modern secular West, it needs to be quiet about appeals to quaint ancient sources from mythopoeic cultures.

Professor Nasr himself is no mystagogue, but a sophisticated, urbane, world-class scholar of the late twentieth century. As I said at the beginning, he is an extraordinary model of a philosopher for the world. Yet there is a slippery slope leading from some of the claims to ancient esoteric wisdom in his sources to Aleister Crowley and worse. The perennial philosophy, in any of its forms, cannot make claim to be taken seriously by those who have learned from religion's wickedness until it has internalized a hermeneutics of suspicion and applied that to its own sources. In light of the history of and current potential for disastrous abuse, the ancient sources of the perennial tradition need to be subjected to a critical reconstruction. The stricture applies as well to recent interpretations such as Schuon's and Guénon's. In this regard, the perennial philosophy can take a good lesson from the critical work of Huston Smith. But so far as I can tell, until the critical reconstruction of the sources has been carried out in some detail, and become accepted, it is better for those of us who fit philosophically and religiously into the perennial tradition to use other language.[36] This fourth step is a philosophical project of considerable magnitude that has not yet been undertaken. I fear that Professor Nasr's strategy in *Knowledge and the Sacred* of pitting good perennial philosophy against bad modern secularism, showing that the good has been excluded but now is making a comeback in some esoteric quarters, is counterproductive.

5. The last and most important step in opening perennial philosophy to our contemporary public is the undertaking of its practice. If I am right about the transformative powers of religious symbols, and about including metaphysical dialectic as part of religious symbolic wisdom, then it must be practiced to be believed. The divine must be engaged genuinely for sapiental certainty to be possible. The typical understanding of this in the European West is *faith seeking understanding*, which usually means belonging to a religious community and accepting its beliefs and practices in order to come to serious understanding. There are other models of practice, different kinds of communities, and different forms of relationships with gurus. Even scholarship in the Western sense opens to a piety more profound than its "methods" would suggest possible.

To many Western philosophers this step of actual practice in order to transform the soul and thereby be able to check out the claims of the perennial philosophy seems simply to be an advocacy of religion. It is. I advocate religion not merely in order to engage God, to become more holy, and to fulfill the many elements in the religious dimension of life. I advocate religious practice as necessary for good philosophy about religious matters.

One crucial error of much modern empiricism, carrying down into twentieth-century analytic philosophy, is the belief that philosophical truth and wisdom must show up on the plane of simple consciousness common to all. Analytical "method" often consists in clearing away confusion so that anyone can see what would otherwise be self-evident in consciousness. But as John E. Smith has pointed out in the passage cited above, experience has very little to do with the flat plane of consciousness *per se* and much to do with the activity of engaging that transforms us as engaged interpreters. Only a person with God in the heart can know in the heart what God is. Meta-discussions are only that, meta-discussions of what one would know if one were to know. (Like this discussion.) To get beyond meta-knowledge to knowledge requires practiced engagement. This point need not be lost even on those who choose to avoid the practice.

In this essay I have tried to reconstruct perennial philosophy, especially in the form so brilliantly developed by Professor Nasr, into a viable participant in the contemporary philosophical public. For all the cosmopolitanism of his philosophy, it seems not to make a philosophical engagment with late modern Western philosophy, despite the venue of the Gifford Lectures from which *Knowledge and the Sacred* arose. My strategy has been first to sketch something of a theory I have developed elsewhere of religious symbols that shows that the kind of transformation of soul claimed for the perennial philosophy is what you should expect, and not an anomaly. Second, I have phrased the philosophical or conceptual content of perennial metaphysics in two families of traditions, both of which are recognized with some currency in the contemporary Western discussion. By characterizing the second family as part of the perennial tradition, namely, the creation *ex nihilo* position I have myself defended, I have offered this line as an ally to Professor Nasr's attempt to recover sacred seriousness for the philosophic life. Third, I have discussed the project of involving the perennial philosophy in the contemporary discussion as a series of steps. The first three steps have already been taken more or less well. The fourth requires a serious engagement of the good reasons for secularism, and the hermeneutics of suspicion, by the distinguished leaders of perennial philosophy and sacred wisdom today, such as Professor Nasr. This step has yet to be taken, I think, and if there is a critical edge to this essay concerning Professor Nasr's project, it is here. The fifth step is for an experimental approach to the presentation and assessment of the perennial philosophy. I would hope that the larger philosophical community, even those secularists who have little taste for religious practice or for taking philosophy seriously as a way of life, can appreciate the point of the experiment. If experienced scientists see more in a test tube than a novice, if musicians and connoisseurs hear more in music than ordinary people, then to move beyond the superficial in religion requires cultivating the soul through gaining competence at engaging reality with religion's symbols, and these include the master symbols of the tradition of sacred knowledge Professor Nasr exhibits so well.

In all this, I intend my remarks to honor Professor Nasr's philosophical achievements and, even more, the accomplishments of his heart.

ROBERT CUMMINGS NEVILLE
PROFESSOR OF PHILOSOPHY, RELIGION, AND THEOLOGY
SCHOOL OF THEOLOGY
BOSTON UNIVERSITY
JUNE 1996

NOTES

1. Seyyed Hossein Nasr, *Knowledge and the Sacred* (New York: Crossroad, 1981). I render thanks to William Chittick, Huston Smith, and Charles Upton for very helpful comments on an early draft of this essay; they have vastly improved it and where I was not able to follow their suggestions marks the limits of my corrigibility.

2. Perhaps if one says something positive about Plotinus without mentioning his connection with perennial philosophy or sacred wisdom, the response will be courteous and perhaps curious in an antiquarian way. But even Plotinus is not taken seriously by many philosophers who otherwise have no difficulty engaging Plato, Aristotle, Marcus Aurelius, or Augustine. This is not a universal situation, of course. Plotinus is regularly mentioned if not analyzed in history of philosophy courses and there is a Neo-Platonic Society in North America. There also are philosophers interested positively in gnosticism. See, for instance, the collection of essays culled from the journal *Studies in Comparative Religion* by Jacob Needleman, editor, entitled *The Sword of Gnosis: Metaphysics, Cosmology, Tradition, Symbolism*; Professor Nasr has an article in this volume as do several of those he discusses in *Knowledge and the Sacred*. That Needleman edited that volume, however, indicates that the discussion is on the margin rather than at the center of the academic philosophic discussion. Needleman was my own teacher as a TA in an undergraduate philosophy class, but in his book, *The New Religions: The Meaning of the Spiritual Revolution and the Teachings of the East* (New York: Doubleday, 1970), he apologizes for the narrowness of academic philosophy and embraces the New Religions, California and all (see chapter 1).

3. See Huston Smith's *Forgotten Truth: The Primordial Tradition* (San Francisco: Harper, 1976); Smith is best known for his *The Religions of Man* which has gone through three editions and is now entitled *The World's Religions* (San Francisco: Harper). On the question of the comparative relations among world religions see Frithjof Schuon's *The Transcendent Unity of Religions*, with an introduction by Huston Smith (Wheaton, Ill.: The Theosophical Publishing House,

1984) and, for another related point of view, John Hick's *An Interpretation of Religion* (New Haven: Yale, 1989), especially part 4.

4. The point is that there ought be no break between philosophy and religion, between study and practice, although there surely are parts of each that are outside parts of the other in all the distinctions. For a careful discussion that recognizes that study and practice cannot be kept apart, see John E. Smith's *Reason and God* (New Haven: Yale University Press, 1961), especially part 2. I have discussed some senses in which the academic study of religion itself becomes a spiritual practice in "The Emergence of Historical Consciousness: A Secular Path to Spiritual Depths," in *Spirituality and the Secular Quest*, edited by Peter H. Van Ness (New York: Crossroad, 1996).

5. The most recent study of some of the boundaries and connections between academic philosophy and the study of religion is the special volume, edited by Eugene Thomas Long, of the *International Journal for Philosophy of Religion*, 38/1-3 (December 1995) prepared for the *Journal*'s 25th anniversary, called *God, Reason and Religions*. The volume was simultaneously published as a book with Long as editor with the title *God, Reason and Religions: New Essays in the Philosophy of Religion*, in the Kluwer Studies in Philosophy and Religion volume 18 (Dordrecht: Kluwer Academic Publishers, 1995).

6. See my "Religious Studies and Theological Studies: The 1992 Presidential Address to the American Academy of Religion," in *The Journal of the American Academy of Religion* 61, no. 2 (Summer 1993): 185–200.

7. Op. cit., chap. 1 and passim.

8. "World philosopher" means two things. One, relevant to the contemporary age particularly but adaptable to previous times, is that the philosopher operates knowledgeably in reference to all the main philosophic traditions of the world; there are three, the East Asian, the South Asian, and the West Asian with its European appendage and American colonies. The American philosophical community is nourished by all the traditions and many American philosophers are "world philosophers" in this sense. The other is that the philosopher's thought is important enough to be taken seriously by philosophers in any of the world's traditions, as all take Plato and Zhuangzi seriously. See, for instance, Kuang-ming Wu's *Chuang Tzu: World Philosopher at Play* (New York: Crossroad, 1982), Prelude; and David A. Dilworth's *Philosophy in World Perspective: A Comparative Hermeneutic of the Major Theories* (New Haven: Yale University Press, 1989). Nasr is a world philosopher in both senses.

9. For his own interpretation of the range of Islamic philosophy and science, see Nasr's *Islamic Life and Thought* (Albany: State University of New York Press, 1981). For a very helpful introduction to Sufi philosophy, see William C. Chittick's *The Sufi Path of Knowledge: Ibn al-'Arabi's Metaphysics of Imagination* (Albany: State University of New York Press, 1989). For the story of how Neo-Platonism entered Islamic philosophy, see Syed Nomanul Haq's *Names, Natures and Things: The Alchemist Jabir ibn Hayyan and his Kitab al-Ahjar (Book of Stones)*, volume 158 of the Boston Studies in the Philosophy of Science (Dordrecht: Kluwer Academic Publishers, 1994), chapter 2.

10. Peirce was a late modern Western philosopher, but not a modernist or postmodernist one. Other things than modernism and its dialectical rejection have happened in late modernity. See my *The Highroad Around Modernism* (Albany: State University of New York Press, 1992). Chapter 1 is a general exposition of what I take to be especially valuable in Peirce. I doubt Nasr would like the connection with Peirce, but that is the problem with his approach to the West.

11. I have analyzed the structure of religious symbols in some detail in *The Truth of Broken Symbols* (Albany: State University of New York Press, 1996). The discussion of Peirce's theory of signs, especially reference, is in the Preface; the discussion of systems of meaning is in chapter 3.

12. Op. cit., chap. 4.

13. Peirce discussed this in many places, one of the most complete of which is *The Collected Papers of Charles Sanders Peirce*, edited by Charles Hartshorne and Paul Weiss, volume 2 (Cambridge, Mass.: Harvard University Press, 1932), paragraphs 292–308 (CP 2.292–308).

14. See *The Truth of Broken Symbols*, chap. 2.

15. See Peter Berger's *The Sacred Canopy* (Garden City, N.Y.: Doubleday, 1967).

16. See *The Truth of Broken Symbols*, chaps. 4–5.

17. See Derrida's *Of Grammatology*, translated by Gayatri Chakravorty Spivak (Baltimore: The Johns Hopkins University Press, 1974) or *Speech and Phenomena*, translated by David B. Allison (Evanston: Northwestern University Press, 1974).

18. On the important distinction between extensional and intentional reference and interpretation, see *The Truth of Broken Symbols*, chapter 2.

19. That truth is the carryover of value from objects into the interpretation of them is the thesis of my *Recovery of the Measure* (Albany: State University of New York Press, 1989). The title means that reality measures our interpretation rather than the other way around, which so many philosophers believe today. Although that book presents a theory of meaning and intentionality, its main burden is to describe nature in such a way as to make intelligible value and its carrying over into experience. It deals at length with such topics as identity, being, value, harmony, time, eternity, space, motion, and causality.

20. These different "sites of value" are analyzed at length in my *Normative Cultures* (Albany: State University of New York Press, 1995), chapters 2 and 4.

21. See my *Reconstruction of Thinking* (Albany: State University of New York Press, 1981), chapters 5–8.

22. See John Dewey's *Experience and Nature*, edited by Jo Ann Boydston (Revised edition; vol. 1 of *John Dewey: The Later Works, 1925–1953*; Carbondale: Southern Illinois University Press, 1981; original edition, 1925) and Whitehead's *Process and Reality*, edited by David Ray Griffin and Donald Sherburne (Corrected edition; New York: Free Press, 1978; original edition,1929).

23. See his *Essay Concerning Human Understanding*, any edition, part 2, chapter 17.

24. See his *Experience and God* (New York: Oxford University Press, 1968), pp. 52, 81.

25. Paul Weiss, *Modes of Being* (Carbondale: Southern Illinois University Press, 1958).

26. Nasr traces much of this in detail in op. cit., chap. 1.

27. Ibid., chap. 2.

28. Ibid., chap. 6.

29. I have argued for this position at length in *God the Creator* (New edition; Albany: State University of New York Press, 1992; original edition, 1968) and *Eternity and Time's Flow* (Albany: State University of New York Press, 1993), and elsewhere. Like Nasr, I believe that this family of the perennial philosophy has found expressions in many world cultures, not just the Western, and have argued this in *The Tao and the Daimon* (Albany: State University of New York Press, 1982), especially chapter 6. See also my *Behind the Masks of God* (Albany: State University of New York Press, 1991).

30. See his *Systematic Theology*, volume 3 (Chicago: University of Chicago Press, 1963).

31. Op. cit., chap. 4. This approach to intelligibility is also taken by process theologians; see my discussion in *Creativity and God* (New edition: Albany: State University of New York Press, 1995; original edition 1980), 46–47.

32. See his *Systematic Theology*, volume 1 (Chicago: University of Chicago Press, 1951), introduction and part 1.

33. See the argument for this in *Eternity and Time's Flow*, part 1.

34. See *The Truth of Broken Symbols*, chapter 1.

35. See my *The Tao and the Daimon*, chapter 6 or *God the Creator*, chaps. 3–4.

36. My own strategy is to develop contemporary dialectical metaphysical arguments, to interpret the symbols of my own Christian religion, and to study comparative religions with all the tools that modern secular scholarship can provide, including the secular moral perspectives and the hermeneutics of suspicion. This essay is the first, I believe, in which I have identified myself with the perennial philosophy, although that affinity has been apparent to me since studies of Plotinus in my dissertation in the early 1960s.

REPLY TO ROBERT CUMMINGS NEVILLE

Professor Neville is one of the foremost figures in the field of philosophy as well as religion in America and his present essay is a major study of perennial philosophy in the context of contemporary Western philosophy. To provide a home for his interpretation of perennial philosophy in the present-day context, Neville has developed a theory of signs and symbols and a methodology for making the project possible. This aspect of the paper is a philosophical exposition of his own ideas and therefore I will respond to it only where it may help clarify my own position. There are, however, substantial parts of the paper which concern my views about the perennial philosophy and his critique of them. Naturally my response will be most of all related to those sections.

Neville begins by stating that the perennial philosophy is out of vogue and in fact ridiculed in Western philosophical circles. This statement is certainly true especially if one considers only the mainstream and more "established" and well-known currents of philosophy as associated with academic circles. I have no qualms about this assertion but want to add that this situation must, out of necessity, be the case considering the fact that the whole mainstream of modern Western philosophy down to the contemporary period has been based on the forgetting and rejecting of perennial philosophy as understood traditionally. When as a young scholar and philosopher I began to write in defense of the perennial philosophy and tradition in the sense that I use the term, I knew fully well that I was swimming against the current and not participating in a popularity contest. During over forty years of writing and lecturing on the perennial philosophy in Western languages, I have confronted the opposition mentioned by Neville in many ways but the situation has not prevented me from continuing to hold the positions which I do. Happily I find much more interest in the perennial philosophy today in intellectual circles in the West, more so in religious studies than in philosophy, than when I began to defend traditional metaphysics. But through this long experience it has become ever more clear to me that it is not possible to take the main currents of modern philosophy seriously as real philosophy and at the same time have serious concern for the perennial philosophy as truth. Let me also add that since I have also written extensively in Persian and lectured widely in the East, I have experience of another part of the world where the situation is not the same as it is in the West precisely because modern Western philosophy has not sunk its roots as deeply there as it has in its land of origin. In fact where Western philosophy has taken root in the East as in Japan and among certain sectors of Indian educated classes, one observes the same lack of interest and opposition to the perennial philosophy as one finds in the West. This point itself is further indication that contradictory and opposing worldviews and philosophies cannot be seriously entertained at the same time.

In their negating the millennial wisdom of humanity, I have accused mainstream Western philosophers of not using their intelligence correctly and to the full, but I have never called "the modern European tradition as a stupid and perhaps a wicked fall," to quote Neville. I certainly consider going from Nicholas of Cusa to Feuerbach a fall but I have never used vulgar and emotive terms such as "stupid" and "wicked" in my writings about philosophy. I believe that as a result of the loss and eclipse of the sapiental dimension of religion in the West, combined with the separation of philosophical intelligence from faith, a fall took place. Consequently reason became divorced from both the Intellect and revelation and thus, philosophy in the West, henceforth, developed as the fruit of the use of reason as wed to the results of external empirical experience, leading to various philosophies which could not but deny the perennial philosophy and the traditional metaphysics at its heart which is the fruit of intellection or *noesis*.

Neville honors me by calling me a world philosopher for which I am grateful and then adds, "Nor does he define himself as an Islamic philosopher." Although I have been always concerned with philosophical issues of a global order and have studied to the extent possible the several major existing philosophical traditions in addition to the "inheritance of Socrates," to quote Neville, if I were asked whether I consider myself an Islamic philosopher or not, I would definitely give a humble affirmative answer. I do not think that the two categories of "world philosopher" and "Islamic philosopher" are mutually exclusive. I consider myself a humble member of both categories and believe that the traditional Islamic philosophers of old such as Avicenna, Averroes, and Suhrawardī were also not only Islamic philosophers but also world philosophers in light of the definition that the term "world" had for their period of history. Their considerable influence not only within Islamic civilization but also in the two worlds west and east of the abode of Islam, namely, the Latin West and India, are testimonies to this reality.

In the same paragraph Neville writes that the global nature of my thought is all the more reason for it "to be related with more respect to late Western philosophy, for that is the one family of traditions he approaches with an attitude more of blame than learning." I do not think that the conclusion necessarily follows from the premise. I am interested in global philosophical issues which I seek to answer from the point of view of the perennial philosophy and tradition as I understand the term, issues ranging from the critique of modern science to the environmental crisis, but that does not mean being necessarily engaged with every Western philosophical current which also deals with these issues. I have engaged certain main figures of Western philosophy from Montaigne and Descartes to Kant, Hegel, and Whitehead and on a certain level Marxism as far as its historicism is concerned, but admittedly not every school of modern philosophy, especially the most current ones, although I have made a study and occasionally referred to a number of more recent figures such as Jaspers, Heidegger, and Marcel. I admit that I am not an expert on every new philosophical school, many of which I find to be quickly passing intellectual fads with little substance. But wherever I have found contemporary philosophers with whom I could share some aspect at least of my philosophical concerns, I have certainly engaged them often in long personal conversations. These figures are as varied as Emmanuel Levinas, Paul Ricoeur, Henry Corbin, and Gilbert Durand in France; Federico Sciacca and Elémire Zolla in Italy; Ernst Benz and Franz Joachim von Rintlen in Germany; Raymond Klibansky, Peter Caws, and Huston Smith in America and many others. It is true that I approach modern philosophy with the attitude of blame not for what it has achieved but for what it has neglected and by virtue of this neglect negated, but this blameworthy attitude has not been based completely on ignorance but on some degree of knowledge, although I admit that I do not consider myself deeply versed in modern Western philosophy.

Neville outlines quite brilliantly C. S. Peirce's theory of signs with whose aid he seeks to make the perennial philosophy palatable to current schools of philosophy. I will not deal with this exposition in as much as it concerns Neville's philosophy and not mine, but this exposition nevertheless provides the opportunity to express once again the traditional understanding of symbols, which according to Neville's exposition is the name usually given to religious signs. In contrast to modern philosophers of semiotics and hermeneutics for whom symbols have no "reference outside their system of surrounding signs that define referents and interpretations," traditional interpreters and followers of the perennial philosophy such as I consider symbols to have an ontological status. Symbols are not based on the agreement of a human collectivity concerning the meaning of something called "sign" but are in the nature of things. The symbol reflects a reality of a higher plane by virtue of its very nature and not in an artificial way.

Everything in the universe in fact is ultimately symbolic to the extent that it is real. Only the Ultimate Reality is not a symbol, for It and It alone is Itself and nothing else. Moreover, there are two kinds of symbols: one, natural symbols residing in the nature of things such as the sun which is the symbol of Divine Intellect, and two, symbols sanctified and given special power and significance by a revelation, the example of the latter being, let us say, the cross or wine in Christianity. Furthermore, the same symbol can function in both ways but in different worlds. While the sun possesses the symbolism stated above for Christians, Jews, and Hindus, it possesses also the second function in Mithraism and Shintoism.

In neither of these cases, however, is the meaning of the symbol defined simply by human agreement. The reality of the symbol is ontological and in the second case its efficacy and meaning come from the Source of all being and not from social and human agreement. Traditional philosophers of our day are certainly aware that such a vision is not shared by modern man. In fact modern man may be said to have lost what F. Schuon called "*l'esprit symbolist.*" Even today there are primal people such as the Australian Aborigines who see all things as symbols and not facts. There are even languages such as Arabic and Persian in which there is no word for "fact." It is true that we live in a world in which the "symbolist spirit" has been for the most part lost, but that does not mean that we should forget the real nature of the symbol and turn it into signs. It is as if we lived in a community where color-blindness had taken over most of the population. Would we have then to abandon our knowledge and experience of colors and state that colors are simply interpretations of phenomena based on the agreement of the community? I know that Professor Neville is developing his sophisticated theory of signs/symbols based on the philosophy of Peirce in order to make a certain type of presentation of the perennial philosophy acceptable to modern philosophy whose mainstream has turned away from the symbolic mode of thinking and expression which has at best been called "mythopoetic" or "artistic." But I believe that in order to understand the language of the perennial philosophy as expressed in many different traditions, it is necessary to understand clearly the meaning of symbolism as understood traditionally and then to resuscitate this language whose knowledge is vital for the understanding of traditional doctrines and not simply to reduce symbols to signs in the Peircian sense. Of course, it should also be remembered that throughout the past two and a half millennia, the perennial philosophy has also had recourse to an abstract language more familiar than the language of traditional symbolism to followers of the mainstream of post-medieval Western philosophy.

One of the more interesting developments of twentieth-century Western thought is in fact the attempt of many thinkers, who have not even been in the camp of perennial philosophy, to delve deeply into the meaning of symbolism, not in the manner of the Saussure and Derrida but more or less as understood traditionally. One need only remember figures as diverse as Susanne Langer, Ernst Cassirer, Henry Corbin, Mircea Eliade, Heinrich Zimmer, and Gilbert Durand to realize the widespread interest in this matter. In addition one needs to speak of the vast studies on the general meaning of symbolism as well as particular religions, metaphysical, cosmological, and artistic symbols by the traditionalist expositors of the perennial philosophy including especially Guénon, Coomaraswamy, Schuon, Titus Burckhardt, and Martin Lings, all of whom have written numerous luminous pages on the subject. While reading Neville's development of Peirce's theory of signs, I have found it necessary to restate my understanding of symbols which follows that of the traditionalists just cited and which I have summarized in my *Knowledge and the Sacred*. I believe that to remain faithful to the truth of the perennial philosophy, it is necessary to understand its symbolic language, and to be able to transmit its truths to a world impervious to the meaning of symbols in the traditional sense; it is necessary to resuscitate the meaning of the language of symbolism in a contemporary fashion without betraying its authenticity. In any case, to understand my views on the nature of symbol and the symbolic, it is necessary to recall what I have stated briefly here and discussed more fully in my other writings.

Let me also add at the end of this discussion that man can interpret and understand symbols by means of the intelligence and the symbolist spirit which are innate to the human state, and in the case of religious symbols, through the guidance of revelation. When the Bible and the Quran state that God taught man the name of all things, it meant, besides other meanings I have discussed elsewhere, the ability to see things as symbols and to understand by means of this God-given knowledge and intelligence the meaning of the symbols observed and known. In fact, in the metaphysical sense, the "names of things" are also their nature as symbols. When Neville writes, "even if the symbol is mistaken," he shows that he is using the term "symbol" in a manner different from me, for according to the traditional understanding of symbols, the symbol can never be mistaken. It is like saying that salt is mistaken in tasting salty. The mistake always comes from the side of the interpreter whose inward intelligence, symbolist spirit and/or submission to the guidance of revelation may easily be impeded by various factors in the same manner that our taste buds can become impaired in such a way that they cannot taste the saltiness of salt—which of course would not make salt any less salty.

For this reason I am also not favorable towards the substitution by Neville of value for truth when he says, "It is better to say that we know something when we grasp what is valuable [rather than true] about it." The term "value" is itself metaphysically problematic and tends to substitute subjective for objective determination. It is interesting to note in this context that while since the nineteenth century many Western philosophers wary of the loss of "values" in a world created by scientism sought to formulate a "philosophy of values," such a philosophy is totally absent among various schools of traditional philosophy in which what we call "values" were part and parcel of the abode of existence that had not as yet become shorn of all quality *à la* Descartes and Galileo.

As he continues his exposition of the theory of signs and symbols, Neville turns to my critique of the theory of evolution which makes my views "seem implausible." First of all let it be said, as I have also mentioned elsewhere, that my criticisms of evolutionary theory have to do precisely with the theory which has now become an ideology defended by its believers with the same fervor as any other ideology and not with simply a scientific theory. I have never attacked the findings of the paleontological record or any other verified scientific discovery. To say that there are trilobite fossils in the Cambrian period is one thing and to claim macroevolution which has never been observed or proven is quite another. I do not know why in America whoever opposes Darwinian evolution is called a "creationist fundamentalist" while there are many more "evolutionary fundamentalists" around. Also there are numerous scientists in both Europe and America who oppose the whole theory of macroevolution on purely scientific lines, but they are hardly given a fair hearing in a world dominated not by biology in itself as a science but by the evolutionist ideology.

Now, Neville tries to provide a subtle enough causal theory of interpretation to remove objections to the theory of evolution. But what he provides would never be accepted by an honest to goodness Darwinian evolutionist. For example, if higher realities are not "merely a cumulative complexification of lower realities," then where does that "something" which makes the higher more than the sum of its constituent lower realities come from? The moment we agree that the higher cannot be reduced to its lower constituent parts in a fundamental way, we have removed reductionism from the scene and made evolution as scientifically understood, and not in its crypto-religious forms combined with theism and the like, philosophically meaningless. In any case I belong to those interpreters of the perennial philosophy who believe that creation, including man, has descended from above without this implying the crude creationism often mentioned, and my views stand in contrast to certain modern interpreters of perennial wisdom who combine perennial cosmologies with evolutionary ideas and believe that man and other forms of life have ascended from below. This latter view is associated with many New Age religions and modern "esoteric" movements which stand at the antipode of the traditional view of perennial philosophy. I am glad that Neville made this criticism so that I could clarify this important point.

Neville turns again to symbols of the perennial philosophy and mentions that they were *developed* very early by such geniuses as the authors of the Upaniṣads. Of course on the basis of what I have said about symbols, I would not agree with the word "develop" in this context nor with considering the authors of the Upaniṣads as geniuses. In the Hindu tradition the Upaniṣads are considered as *śruti* or sacred scripture *revealed* to the sages in the forest and not merely the fruit of human genius. As for the symbols of the perennial philosophy being "more elementary than astrophysics and molecular biology," again according to my understanding of symbols these modern sciences do not even possess symbols which could be compared to those of the perennial philosophy. The DNA is not a symbol like wine in Christianity which symbolizes the blood of Christ. Also I do not understand the term "elementary" used by Neville. Does it mean in reference to the elements which constitute the very basis of things or more likely simple and less advanced? In either case I do not accept such a characterization even if the modern sciences were to possess their symbols properly understood because, even if this were to be the case, the symbols of the perennial philosophy could not constitute their basis. And certainly traditional symbols are hardly elementary in the sense of being less advanced or more rudimentary, for they open the door to the highest form of knowledge compared to which all merely rational sciences are elementary and rudimentary.

One of the very positive aspects of Neville's exposition of the theory of signs and symbols is that he realizes that the receiver of symbols must have the preparation for such a reception. He writes, "The theory of symbols I have advocated here shows both how the unity of engagement can give certainty and how subsequent engagement with more discriminating and richer symbols can supersede the earlier certainty." I need to add that a single symbol without the need of other symbols, reveals levels of meaning and one can gain degrees and levels of certainty by ever-greater penetration into the meaning of a single symbol. This theory is elaborated in many Sufi works on the basis of the text of the Quran which speaks of the levels of certainty from the "science of certainty" (*'ilm al-yaqīn*) to the "eye of certainty" (*'ayn al-yaqīn*) to the "truth of certainty" (*ḥaqq al-yaqīn*). These are compared to hearing the description of fire, seeing fire, and being burned by fire. These are all levels of certainty related to a single symbol/reality.

Neville writes that my main complaint about European modernity is "that its symbols fail to register the ultimate dimensions that are the direct topic of the perennial philosophy." My complaint is more basic than that. It is that modernity has lost traditional metaphysical knowledge and along with it the sense of the true understanding of symbols, and to compensate for this loss it has created pseudo-myths, man-made idols, and subjective constructs to fill the void it fills instinctively as a result of the loss of sacred symbols and the sense of the sacred itself. How right he is when he writes that traditional symbols "are difficult to fit into much of the modern soul." Difficult yes, but not impossible. My task over the years has been to explain these symbols and the traditional doctrines they represent in such a way that, at least for those in whose soul there is an opening for such things, they will be able to find a place within themselves for the understanding and presence of these symbols. And I am not unhappy about the results because even amidst rampant modernity there are many who thirst for the very truths against which the modern world turned as it set about creating the modern and now postmodern mentality.

In discussing the modes of perennial philosophy, Neville draws attention to a cardinal truth about perennial philosophy taken seriously when he writes that if one accepts my epistemological approach then there is an underlying sapiental principle according to which to reach the truth: "the mind must be cultivated, perhaps through long years of yoga or contemplation under the guidance of a teacher . . . knowledge of the levels and how to reach them are conveyed by 'tradition' in the sense that Nasr uses the term." I am in total agreement with the need for preparation and training mentioned by Neville, but I would not characterize my approach as epistemological. Rather, it is metaphysical, although in order to attain metaphysical knowledge it is of course necessary to possess the appropriate means of knowing or what is technically called "epistemology."

Neville then turns to a second family of approaches within perennial philosophy associated predominantly with the metaphor of creation *ex nihilo* which he associates with Eckhart and Nicholas Berdyaev among others. He adds, "But because creation *ex nihilo* marks an immediate making that moves directly from nothingness to determinate being, the dimensions need not be related in a hierarchy according to which some are farther from the creative source than others." The relation between this family and the first family of approaches based on hierarchy is a profound one whose full discussion would need a separate treatise. Here it will suffice if I mention a few basic principles as I envisage this relationship. First of all, the two families are not necessarily opposed but can be integrated into a single metaphysical vision. Each being in the hierarchy of existence is at once separated and intimately close to the Source of all existence. Its place in the ladder of being does not take away from that mysterious direct link that it has with the Creator. Moreover, to accept the creation *ex nihilo* perspective does not necessarily destroy the hierarchy which is in the nature of things. Would Meister Eckhart ever say that a sinner and the Apostles, both created *ex nihilo*, had the same proximity to God?

It is unfortunate perhaps that Neville does not mention tradition in this context as I understand the term. Traditional metaphysics is one, and in fact some have preferred to use for that very reason the singular term metaphysic. But it is a mansion with many houses and can encompass the basic theses of the *ex nihilo* position of traditional philosophies as it has the non-dualistic doctrine of a Śaṅkara, which for other reasons does not delve into cosmic hierarchies while dealing with pure metaphysics (yet this metaphysics does not deny various hierarchies on their own level). In Islam also there are levels of understanding unity in relation to multiplicity leading ultimately to the assertion of "the unity of being" understood as the unity of the One which alone is. In any case I find no difficulty in my understanding of the perennial philosophy in its ability to encompass both of Neville's interpretations. The working out of such a task would, however, require a thorough study and analysis in the contemporary language proposed by Neville of the synthesis already carried out in many traditional versions of the perennial philosophy.

I also need to mention in passing here the esoteric meaning of *ex nihilo* itself and the doctrine of creation *in* God and not only *by* God about which there is an extensive literature in the sapiental heritage of all the Abrahamic religions and which holds one of the keys for solving the problem of creating harmony between the two families of perennial philosophy mentioned by Neville. As for one family emphasizing the nature and the other the will of God, this discussion has had a long history in Islam as well as Judaism and Christianity. In the Islamic tradition the Ash'arite theologians emphasized the will and the Islamic philosophers the nature of God while most Sufis, with a metaphysical bent, sided with the philosophers on this issue. For my part I also find myself clearly on the side of the Sufis and philosophers but I understand perfectly well the grandeur of the other perspective which is also a traditional and valid interpretation of religious teachings.

In dealing with sacred knowledge Neville mentions many points with which I am in agreement and need not answer but then suddenly changes direction and takes me to task for rejecting "other things that late modernity has found to be true and important." True and important by what criteria? Yes, I do reject the modernist project as a whole because of what I consider to be its false assumptions, but I have never rejected the number of moons of Jupiter discovered by Galileo nor denied that modern thought has discovered certain things which were not of concern to traditional thought. Neville considers my arguments to be my own worst enemy, but my arguments follow logically from the premises with which I begin and I do not sense any enmity from their quarter towards the foundations of my worldview. If my arguments cause enmity towards my works from others, it is because the arguments challenge their own worldview. What is important for me is the truth and no contingency can in any way alter my attitude towards what thorough intellectual certitude I consider as the truth. When I criticize modern science, it is not to deny its study of the geological structures of the Andes or the species of plants in Africa. It is the creation of a worldview based on a purely quantitative science of the cosmos and the cutting off of the hands of the Creator from creation which the theory of evolution, if interpreted seriously from a scientific point of view and not combined with pseudo-theology, implies. It is surprising that a leading philosopher and scholar of religion such as Neville should write, "He [Nasr] grudgingly admits that modern science might not be false if put in its place, but complains that it usually is construed scientistically. Fair enough: scientific expertise does not generalize to philosophy and theology." Maybe not for Professor Neville but it surely does so for most of the Western educated public where the scientist has come to replace the priest as the source of authority. One needs only to look at so much of modern Western philosophy and even certain strands of theology to realize how rampant scientism has become and how so many philosophers and theologians bend backwards precisely to placate those possessing scientific expertise. Also in relation to the quote above the adverb "grudgingly" is not correct as far as my writings on modern science are concerned. What I have sought is to open an intellectual space in the contemporary world for other modes of knowing nature and not to surrender to the monopoly which the quantitative sciences of the seventeenth century created for themselves in the mind of Western man. To try to destroy a monopolistic hegemony does not mean to accept "grudgingly" the existence or even legitimacy of that which one is trying to limit in power and claim to dominance.

Neville considers my denial of "outright important lessons modern culture has learned with pain" to be even worse than my critique of modern science. And here he repeats the often quoted criticism of the relation of religion to violence in traditional societies, the danger of following blindly religious authority, the danger of considering everything as holy which could lead to religious wars, etc. To call the world holy is considered by Neville to be just a short step from outrageous idolatry leading to wars and slaughters. This view developed in Europe since the seventeenth century and the long religious wars of the period that followed was used for a long time as an instrument to attack religion. Neville seems still to believe in this view when he contrasts the perspective leading religions to wars "with the wisdom of secularism regarding peace, love, and tolerance." I should think that at the end of the twentieth century, a century during which more human beings have been slaughtered for secular causes from nationalism to Fascism to Communism to the imposition of economic power, than in any other period of history, one would no longer speak in such terms. Secularism might have succeeded in banishing the Devil from the world but it has certainly not succeeded in eradicating evil, to put it mildly. Nor can anyone who has encountered a doctrinaire secularist claim that he or she is any more tolerant than a religious person. If the "hermeneutics of suspicion" is to be used anywhere at all, it should be first of all *vis-à-vis* the secularist powers which are devouring the earth and its resources.

The perennial philosophy itself has all the criteria necessary to understand various levels of authority and also the passions of men in this age of darkness as well as the nature of evil and that unfashionable but ever present reality, sin. It would never allow the idealization of a worldly power in the name of religion at a moment of history when such in fact is not possible. It teaches detachment even amidst all the turmoils of the world knowing full well that with human nature having become what it is, one cannot avoid strife completely but should live at all times according to one's moral duty and try to control the passions to the extent possible, an act which only religion can accomplish for the many. All of these teachings of the perennial philosophy, which also includes discernment concerning all worldly power, are beautifully summarized in one of the great masterpieces of the literature of the perennial philosophy, the *Bhagavad-Gita*.

There are many other points in this criticism which I could answer but will leave aside because I have turned to some of them elsewhere in this volume. But I need at least to make a comment upon Neville's statement, "A cannon is a cannon is a cannon." If you look at history, you will discover that that was not in fact the case. When there were traditional societies ruled by religion, whether that was medieval China, the Islamic world, ancient Egypt, or medieval Europe, "the cannon" was in fact a much more rudimentary arm that killed far fewer people. Thanks to the rebellion against religion by secularism and the rise of a secular science along with a technology divorced from spiritual considerations, the earlier rudimentary arms such as bows and arrows, swords, maces, or at worst the Greek fire, became real cannon, first relatively limited in power of destruction but improving to the laser-guided cannon of today and worse than cannon, the bombs whose memory of destruction—whether it was of London, Dresden, Hiroshima, or Nagasaki—the world cannot forget.

Also the interpenetration of the natural and the supernatural is a reality necessitated by the nature of things without this metaphysical truth in any way taking away from things their ordinary nature. The perennial philosophy is not the same as a type of simple religiosity which relies solely on intervention from on high for the foundation of faith and all our rapport with the world. Nevertheless, there is according to all traditional metaphysics a vertical dimension of reality which relates us at every moment of life to the higher reaches of consciousness and being and in fact defines our being human. I do not believe that this intellectual understanding of the interrelation of the various levels of existence with each other and with the Source of all existence in any way diminishes the possibility of the perennial philosophy being taken seriously today. Also Neville writes that some might see "a slippery slope leading from some of the claims to ancient esoteric wisdom in his [Nasr's] sources to Aleister Crowley and worse." But in reality only the perennial philosophy as traditionally understood can prevent the esoteric from becoming the occult and is alone able to create a dike which could prevent such a slippage from taking place. Why is it that one does not have the phenomenon of modern occultism in either medieval Christianity or in other religions? Yes, in the old days there was magic and also what are called the "occult sciences" such as alchemy, but they were quite different from modern occultism since they were guarded within a framework defined by the perennial philosophy and authentic esoterism within a traditional religion. Modern secularist thought is totally helpless in face of the invasion of modern occultism and the like as the contemporary scene bears witness. Neville needs not fear the perennial philosophy leading to outlandish occultism against which the traditional interpreters of the perennial philosophy have always spoken in the strongest terms.

Neville is right when he says that, as I have already mentioned, I have not engaged late modern Western philosophy on its own terms. My task in life has been to present an authentic formulation of the perennial philosophy and traditional metaphysics in a contemporary language and in light of many basic contemporary issues. I have had to respond to many philosophical ideas in order to clear the ground for the establishment of the edifice of traditional doctrines following what was accomplished by Guénon, Coomaraswamy, Schuon, and others before me. I have also engaged directly in contemporary issues such as the environmental crisis, the challenges of modern science, and religious diversity. It will be the task of others to discuss points of confrontation or harmony; rejection or acceptance between the intellectual edifice traditional authors followed by myself have established and various currents of late modern Western philosophy with which Neville is concerned is up to them. In any case I am grateful to him for his critique and I believe that he himself is one of those philosophers best qualified to carry out, in the context of later modern Western philosophy, the task of making the perennial philosophy better understood and of aiding those qualified to do so to engage it on a serious intellectual level.

S. H. N.

4

Sallie B. King

THE *PHILOSOPHIA PERENNIS* AND THE RELIGIONS OF THE WORLD

This essay is a response to certain claims regarding the *philosophia perennis* made by Dr. Seyyed Hossein Nasr. The claims I have in mind are developed most fully in his *Knowledge and the Sacred* and succinctly restated in "The *Philosophia Perennis* and the Study of Religion."[1] Let me begin by summarizing that part of Dr. Nasr's thesis that I would like to examine in this essay.

According to Nasr, the key to understanding the relationship among the world's religions is to look at them from the point of view of Tradition. What is Tradition?

> Tradition . . . means truths or principles of a divine origin revealed or unveiled to mankind and, in fact, a whole cosmic sector through various figures envisaged as messengers, prophets, *avatāras*, the Logos or other transmitting agencies, along with all the ramifications and applications of these principles in different realms including law and social structure, art, symbolism, the sciences, and embracing of course Supreme Knowledge along with the means for its attainment.
>
> Tradition implies truths of a supraindividual character rooted in the nature of reality as such. . . . It comes from the Source from which everything originates and to which everything returns.

Nasr links the meaning of tradition to

> that perennial wisdom which lies at the heart of every religion and which is none other than the Sophia whose possession the sapiental perspective in the West as well as the Orient has considered as the crowning achievement of human life. This eternal wisdom . . . which constitutes one of the main components of the concept of tradition is none other than the *sophia perennis*

of the Western tradition, which the Hindus call the *sanatān dharma* and the Muslims *al-ḥikmat al-khālidah* (or *jāvīdān khirad* in Persian).[2]

For Nasr, the terms, "*philosophia perennis*," "Sophia," "*sophia perennis*," "*scientia sacra*," "sacred knowledge," "metaphysics," "esoteric knowledge," and "principial knowledge" are all closely related terms, pointing to the eternal Truth, embodied at the core of religions in "Tradition," and accessible in experience to humankind.

> [T]radition is closely related to the *philosophia perennis* if this term is understood as the Sophia which has always been and will always be and which is perpetuated by means of both transmission horizontally and renewal vertically through contact with that reality that was "at the beginning" and is here and now.[3]

This *philosophia perennis* can be known by humankind in two ways: by means of revelation and the illumination of the Intellect.

> [T]he twin source of this knowledge is revelation and intellection or intellectual intuition which involves the illumination of the heart and the mind of man and the presence in him of knowledge of an immediate and direct nature which is tasted and experienced.

This is an essentially passive, or receiving, experience.

> The truth descends upon the mind like an eagle landing upon a mountain top or it gushes forth and inundates the mind like a deep well which has suddenly burst forth into a spring. In either case, the sapiental nature of what the human being receives through spiritual experience is not the result of man's mental faculty but issues from the nature of that experience itself.[4]

As God transcends humankind, so does intellectual illumination transcend the merely human products of reason. True knowledge of the Divine is issued forth from the Divine Intellect and received by the human mind.

Chapter 9 of *Knowledge and the Sacred*, "Principial Knowledge and the Multiplicity of Sacred Forms," deals most directly with the issue to be considered in this essay, the relationship between the *philosophia perennis* and the multiple religions of the world. Nasr's thesis, in short, states that the world's religions are many manifestations of a single Truth of Divine Origin, the *philosophia perennis*. Since this is the focal issue for this essay, I quote at length.

> Tradition studies religions from the point of view of *scientia sacra* which distinguishes between the Principle and manifestation, Essence and form, Substance and accident, the inward and the outward. It places absoluteness at

> the level of the Absolute, asserting categorically that only the Absolute is absolute. . . . Hence every determination of the Absolute is already in the realm of relativity. The unity of religions is to be found first and foremost in this Absolute which is at once Truth and Reality and the origin of all revelations and of all truth. . . . Only at the level of the Absolute are the teachings of the religions the same. Below that level there are correspondences of the most profound order but not identity. The different religions are like so many languages speaking of that unique Truth as it manifests itself in different worlds according to its inner archetypal possibilities, but the syntax of these languages is not the same. Yet, because each religion comes from the Truth, everything in the religion in question which is revealed by the Logos is sacred and must be respected and cherished while being elucidated rather than being discarded and reduced to insignificance in the name of some kind of abstract universality.
>
> The traditional method of studying religions, while asserting categorically the "transcendent unity of religion" and the fact that "all paths lead to the same summit," is deeply respectful of every step on each path, of every signpost which makes the journey possible and without which the single summit could never be reached.[5]

In order to know this transcendent unity of religions, one must penetrate beyond the forms to that inner Truth of which all the forms are manifestations. This esoteric and experiential knowledge of the *philosophia perennis* brings us the correct understanding of the relationship among the world's religions.

> To go from the form to the essence, the exterior to the interior, the symbol to the reality symbolized . . . is itself an esoteric activity and is dependent upon esoteric knowledge. To carry out the study of other religions in depth, therefore, requires a penetration into the depth of one's own being and an interiorizing and penetrating intelligence which is already imbued with the sacred.[6]
>
> Man cannot penetrate into the inner meaning of a form except through inner or esoteric knowledge. . . . One might say that total religious understanding and the complete harmony and unity of religions can be found, to quote Schuon, only in the Divine Stratosphere and not in the human atmosphere.[7]

The fact that this transcendent unity of religions exists, however, does not eliminate the absoluteness of each particular religion.

> [I]f there is one really new and significant dimension to the religious and spiritual life of man today, it is this presence of other worlds of sacred form and meaning not as archaeological or historical facts and phenomena but as religious reality. It is this necessity of living within one solar system and abiding by its laws yet knowing that there are other solar systems and even, by participation, coming to know something of their rhythms and harmonies, thereby gaining a vision of the haunting beauty of each one as a planetary

> system which is *the* planetary system for those living within it. It is to be illuminated by the Sun of one's own planetary system and still to come to know . . . that each solar system has its own sun, which again is both a sun and *the* Sun, for how can the sun which rises every morning and illuminates our world be other than *the* Sun itself?[8]
>
> Principial knowledge can defend the absolute character which followers of each religion see in their beliefs and tenets, without which human beings would not follow a particular religion. Yet principial knowledge continues to assert the primordial truth that only the Absolute is absolute and hence what appears below the level of the Absolute in a particular tradition as absolute is the 'relatively absolute.'[9]

It seems to me that in *Knowledge and the Sacred*, Nasr is attempting to do three important things: (1) to base religious theory upon the assumption of the reality of which religion(s) speak(s); and (2) to locate and articulate a place of unity among the various world religions, while (3) preserving the integrity of the particularity of each religion.

I must begin by saying that I respect these objectives. The first objective is particularly crucial and I believe that Dr. Nasr's greatest success in *Knowledge and the Sacred* is in his articulate representation of this approach. This book invites us to recognize the limitations of methods that are incapable of taking seriously the plausibility of the phenomena that they study.

There are times when our disciplines become prisoners of our methodologies. One such instance was during the period in which behaviorism dominated psychology, when the observation that scientific method could only properly study human behavior and not something called "mind," led to a reductionism that concluded, in its popular form, that "mind" and the "inner world" of mental life did not exist.

Another classic instance of this phenomenon is the rendering of the universe soulless in the modern mind by science and reason.[10] Clearly, reason can neither prove nor disprove the existence of an intelligence at the root of all existence. Nevertheless, this inability to demonstrate that such an intelligence *does* exist slid, untidily, into the perception in the modern mind that such an intelligence *does not* exist. The fact that this consequence is logically unjustified has not prevented this conclusion from being firmly grasped by the modern mind as fully rational.

One last example: When we turn to what Nasr calls "esoterism" and I call "mysticism," it should be obvious that it is essential to bear in mind the limitations of all our methods in attempting to understand something that is widely described as "ineffable" by those who claim to have direct experience of it. Nonetheless, this point is often overlooked. If I may be permitted to quote myself on the subject, "It would be better, if necessary, to frankly acknowledge that the phenomena of mystical experience are beyond our reach and live with the consequences of that admission than to reduce mysticism to less than it is for the sake of method."[11]

Nasr, it seems to me, is quite right in pointing to the unjustifiability of the ridding of modern culture by means of reason of all that traditional culture held as sacred. Furthermore, as he rightly points out,[12] Western religious studies itself is replete with methods that reduce the phenomena under study, religious phenomena, to nothing by interpreting them as epiphenomena produced by more fundamental, and in that sense more real, psychological, sociological, historical, political, and the like phenomena. Yet in religious studies we are speaking of matters of which, obviously, the whole of human history displays mountains of claim and counter-claim, belief and disbelief, wonder, awe, talk of unknowable mystery, ineffability, and a radical epistemological gap between the human mind and what we seek to know. One does not wonder that Nasr appears thoroughly impatient with the modern, secular world and its apparently casual dismissal of the religious realm. I myself am often appalled by the arrogance of those scholars of religion who, with nothing more than the same puny human mind with which the rest of us are endowed, feel that they are in a position to write off the profoundest mysteries of life. No one has expressed this sentiment better than the ancient Taoist philosopher Chuang Tzu who wrote, "Calculate what man knows and it cannot compare to what he does not know. Calculate the time he is alive and it cannot compare to the time before he was born. Yet man takes something so small and tries to exhaust the dimensions of something so large!"[13] Reason itself, if used properly, should be able to recognize its own strengths and weaknesses, its own potential and limitations. There is a limit beyond which reason is incapable of going—a limit quite recognizable by reason itself—that ought to be respected by reason. Ironically perhaps, postmodern thought is more aware of this than modern thought and thus has the potential (as yet unrealized!) to ally itself with those who share Nasr's concern to put reason in its rightful place.

Of course, there is a gap between putting reason in its place and acknowledging a transcendent Reality of the kind of which Nasr speaks and it is an important gap to investigate. But to keep the focus on Nasr's work, let us ask with him: What would happen if we took transcendence seriously? What would religious studies, what would human culture look like if our first assumption was the reality of the Absolute? Nasr endeavors at all times to put God, or the Absolute, first and to base all else on that first premise. Granted that reason can neither prove nor disprove the reality of the Absolute, it must be equally reasonable to assume its existence as to assume its nonexistence. So why not give a respectful hearing to this premise and see where it leads? (Of course, a good deal depends upon the precise nature of what we are assuming, as we shall see.)

Accepting this way of proceeding as reasonable, however, does not mean, in my view, that we can do without the "hermeneutics of suspicion." There are, and presumably always have been, quite sufficient numbers of charlatans and dysfunctional people and societies to make us need the analyses of Freud, Nietzsche, and Marx. Here reason has a critical role to play even if one accepts Nasr's premise. However, one can arm oneself against manipulation and distortion—and, indeed, I would not want to send either my children or my students out into the world without providing them with some such defense—and still leave vast space for taking religion seriously. Indeed, for those who take religion seriously, it is a religious duty to distinguish the real from the false in the religious domain.

This leads to my first question for Dr. Nasr. (1) How does he propose that we defend ourselves, and teach our children and students to defend themselves, from charlatans and manipulators in the religious domain? What are the rules for distinguishing between the genuine and the false in a world in which many, but not all, religions are true? What are the characteristics of the genuine? Since charlatans can mouth any words and there have been many "false prophets," I would assume that not only certain teachings, but also certain behaviors would be necessary.

There is a second question regarding criteria for distinguishing the true from the false. I observe in Dr. Nasr's works a hostility towards certain religions which he regards as syncretisms.

> It need hardly be pointed out that this vision of the transcendent unity of religions stands at the very antipodes of the modern syncretisms and pseudo-spiritualities which have been growing during the past few decades as a result of the weakening of tradition in the West. Not only do they not succeed in transcending forms but they fall beneath them, opening the door to all kinds of evil forces affecting those who are unfortunate enough to be duped by their so-called universalism.[14]

I would like to ask Dr. Nasr whom he has in mind in this description. Does he have in mind what is currently called "New Age" religions, in which case the concern might be the shallowness and frivolity evident in much of their speech and behavior? Or, alternatively, does he have in mind such religions as the Baha'i Faith and Unitarian Universalism that, from my perspective, seem as respectable as any other religion and indeed seem to me to come close to embracing the perspective that he articulates. If this latter group is in the group condemned as "modern syncretisms and pseudo-spiritualities," then I must ask how their perspective differs from that of the sage and scriptures quoted at the beginning of chapter 9 of *Knowledge and the Sacred*:

> Verily, to every people there has been sent a prophet. (Quran)

> I meditated upon religions, making great effort to understand them,
> And I came to realize that they are a unique Principle with numerous ramifications. (Ḥallāj)
>
> They worship me as One and as many because they see that all is in me. (Bhagavad Gīta)[15]

It seems to me that the Baha'i Faith and Unitarian Universalism accept precisely these ideas. Again, Nasr cites with approval Ibn 'Arabī's lines,

> My heart has become capable of every form: it is a pasture for gazelles and a convent for Christians
> And a temple for idols and the pilgrim's Ka'bah and the tables of the Torah, and the book of the Quran.
> I follow the religion of Love: whatever way Love's camels take, that is my religion and my faith.[16]

But he disapproves of that approach to the world's religions that,

> sees in all religions the same truth, not of a transcendent order as tradition would assert but of an outward and sentimental kind which cannot but reduce religions to their least common denominator. . . . What characterizes this type of approach is a kind of sentimentalism which opposes intellectual discernment and emphasis upon doctrine as being dogmatic and "anti-spiritual," together with a supposed universalism which opposes the particularity of each tradition . . . thereby destroying the sacred on the tangible level in the name of a vague and emotional universalism which is in fact a parody of the universalism envisaged by tradition.[17]

I must confess that the distinction Nasr is drawing is rather vague to me. This, then, is the second question. (2) When is universalism good and when is it bad? When is religious unity based on transcendence and when on the least common denominator? Can the criteria be stated with some specificity that place a given religion or religious expression either in the category of "modern syncretisms and pseudo-spiritualities" or in the category of Tradition or authentic religion? He mentions "modernized Hinduism" as falling into the problematic category. I am quite concerned to know whether the Baha'i Faith falls into that same category since from an Islamic perspective it is often condemned yet, for this reader at least, it is difficult to see how one could avoid accepting it as a religious tradition that embraces the transcendent unity of religions.

Let us skip Nasr's second objective for the time being and consider next Nasr's third objective, namely, the intention to preserve the integrity of the particularity of each religion despite identifying a realm of transcendent unity above them. Here again I wish to underline the importance of this objective. I have observed in many years of interreligious dialogue that people who otherwise are very open to interreligious discussion often become very angry when faced with a theory coming from outside their religion that interprets their religion in a way that they cannot accept from within the religion. Thus it is crucial that Nasr emphasizes, as we have seen, that

> because each religion comes from the Truth, everything in the religion in question which is revealed by the Logos is sacred and must be respected and cherished while being elucidated rather than being discarded and reduced to insignificance in the name of some kind of abstract universality.
>
> The traditional method of studying religions, while asserting . . . the fact that "all paths lead to the same summit," is deeply respectful of every step on each path, of every signpost which makes the journey possible and without which the single summit could never be reached.

Without this kind of statement, I am sure that Nasr's ideas would have aroused little interest. Jews want to be Jews. Period. Christians want to be Christians. Period. This is my observation. I agree with Nasr that this is perfectly legitimate. However, this leads me to my third question. While Nasr acknowledges that his concept of the "relatively absolute" may appear to be "contradictory,"[18] I believe he has been successful in demonstrating its good sense. However, I do wonder how successful it is religiously. Nasr writes,

> If a Christian sees God as the Trinity or Christ as the Logos and holds on to this belief in an absolute sense, this is perfectly understandable from the religious point of view while, metaphysically speaking, these are seen as the relatively absolute since only the Godhead in Its Infinitude and Oneness is above all relativity.[19]

This raises the following question. (3) While Meister Eckhart said something very much like the above, can the ordinary Christian accept it? Can a Christian who wants to understand herself as a Christian accept that Christianity is good and true, absolute in a sense, and yet finally only one form of Absolute Truth? Does this way of conceiving it—in practice for a religious believer, not for a logician—not force upon her an understanding of her religion that in effect psychologically undermines its validity and practical efficacy for her? Does this view not, then, violate its own objective of guarding the integrity of the particular religion? I can see that it perhaps *should* not have this consequence; but I wonder whether for the unsophisticated believer it does anyway. This question applies to all religions.

People give credence to their own religion. Yet, as Nasr states, in much of the modern world it is quite impossible to remain ignorant of the fact that there are many religions in addition to one's own, each claiming to possess *the* true way. Dr. Nasr has stated that the way to resolve this dilemma is through esoterism. Yet at the same time he acknowledges that the path of esoteric knowledge is in practice only truly open to a few. A fourth question that I would like to address to Dr. Nasr, then, is this. (4) If esoterism will always remain the path of the few, what way does he see to educate the many such that they may remain, as he advocates, both faithfully devoted to their own religion and capable of respecting the validity of other religions? Does Dr. Nasr believe that some kind of popularization of such ideas as are found in Frithjof Schuon's *Transcendent Unity of Religions* and related works is the best way forward? Does he, perhaps, envision the various religions themselves, in their educational programs, emphasizing more their own sapiental and universalistic elements? Does he envision some other way forward?

Let us now turn to Nasr's second objective, his attempt to locate and articulate a place of unity among the various world religions, and devote the rest of this discussion to it. Before responding to this objective, I must introduce the perspective from which I respond. I am a scholar of Buddhism. The perspective from which I view the world is largely shaped by Buddhism. One of the things that strikes me upon reading *Knowledge and the Sacred* is the relative infrequency of references to Buddhism in this work, though Buddhism is certainly mentioned a number of times. Buddhism does not seem to loom large in Nasr's intellectual world. It may be that Dr. Nasr is less familiar with Buddhism than other religions. Certainly his greatest familiarity and allegiance is with Islam. Hinduism seems to make the second greatest claim on his intellectual and religious orientation, followed perhaps by the other Abrahamic traditions. Buddhism runs distantly behind all these, apparently in last place among the world's major religions, in the amount of reference he makes to it.

Reading from a Buddhist perspective, I am naturally concerned with whether Buddhism fits the picture that Nasr has articulated in his vision of the place of unity among the various world religions. Reading from this perspective, I have had to conclude that it does not. I will mention two ways in which this seems to me to be the case.

First, in Nasr's thesis, revelation plays a key role. "Tradition . . . means truths or principles of a divine origin revealed or unveiled to mankind and, in fact, a whole cosmic sector through various figures envisaged as messengers, prophets, *avatāras*, the Logos or other transmitting agencies. . . ." Revelation is essential to Nasr's thesis, both in order to attain the transcendent unity that Nasr asserts and in order to be true to his first premise, the necessity of putting religion first. Religion only deserves to comes first if it comes from a divine source. Religions cannot be unified unless they come from the same, unitive, divine source. Again, Nasr writes, "[E]ach tradition is based on a direct message from Heaven. . . . A prophet or *avatār* owes nothing to anyone save what he receives from the Origin."[20]

Buddhism, however, is quite lacking in any concept of revelation in the ordinary sense of the word. Nor is there in Buddhism any divine being whose act could cause a revelation. Buddhists have been quite straightforward on this subject over the millennia. There are Buddhist writings that argue against the existence of God or any supreme divine being. Buddhists at the World's Parliament of Religions in 1993 adamantly opposed the use of any God language in statements to be issued by the Parliament (much to the dismay of certain other religious representatives, who felt that any statement lacking such language was worthless).

Nasr, of course, has a broader concept of revelation in mind, as we saw above, as "truths or principles of a divine origin revealed or unveiled to mankind . . . through various figures envisaged as messengers, prophets, *avatāras*, the Logos or other transmitting agencies." Thus, Nasr might want to interpret the Buddha's enlightenment experience, for example, as a revelation in this sense. However, a Theravāda Buddhist would never so conceive it. Gautama Buddha himself taught that he was a human being who discovered a path to escape suffering by "waking up" to the nature of reality (a view which may be understood as corresponding to Nasr's *other* point of access to Truth, illumination of the heart and mind). This knowledge was gained, according to the Theravāda tradition, through the Buddha's arduous practice over many lifetimes, absolutely not through the revealing of that knowledge to him by a divine being. Of course, it is possible to believe that, whether the Buddha realized it or not, that knowledge *was* revealed to him from a divine source—and it is possible that that belief is correct. However, this cannot be said to be the Theravāda Buddhist understanding of itself. The same holds, in the Theravāda view, for the Buddhist scriptures. They also cannot be considered revealed scripture because they are the word of the Buddha, and the Buddha is not a god or a divine messenger, but a man —albeit an exceptional one—speaking of his own experience.

I have spoken of the Theravāda view. The same understandings would apply to much of the rest of Buddhism. However, there are exceptions. Certain forms of Indian Mahāyāna, for example, expressed ideas which might be considered amenable to interpretation as revelation in Nasr's sense, for example, the notions of *tathāgatagarbha* (embryo/womb of all Buddhas) and the personified *prajñāpāramitā* (perfection of wisdom). Also in Tibetan and East Asian Buddhism there are notions that might be so interpreted. Without getting into technicalities inappropriate here, I can only say that I think one would have to stretch even those notions to make them fit the category of revelatory agents.

The important point here, however, is that it is invalid, even if one *could* make the case that the *prajñāpāramitā* or *tathāgatagarbha* was a divine source of revelation, to point to those facts and claim on that basis that Buddhism has a notion of revelation. One form of Buddhism cannot substitute for another. Theravāda Buddhism stands on its own. I recognize that Dr. Nasr has claimed that because of the variety of ideas and practices in any world religion, "to have lived any religion fully is to have lived all religions."[21] I can only say that a Theravāda Buddhist would not accept this. Theravāda Buddhism does not accept Mahāyāna beliefs and scriptures. To many Theravādins, Mahāyāna is invalid. Thus one cannot in effect impose Mahāyāna beliefs on Theravādins, saying that it is "all Buddhism." To Theravādins, it is not. Nor will Nasr's way of addressing this in *Knowledge and the Sacred* work for Buddhists. To quote him, "[T]he Theravāda and Mahāyāna schools of Buddhism . . . correspond in their own context to the exoteric-esoteric dimensions of tradition."[22] This is simply not true. Theravāda and Mahāyāna both have exoteric and esoteric dimensions. Theravāda scripture, preserving the teaching of Gautama Buddha, and its monastic tradition could be paradigm examples of esotericism in Nasr's sense of the word, that is, the sapiental dimension of religion (the dimension that addresses "the spiritual and intellectual needs of those who seek God or the Ultimate Reality here and now"),[23] though Theravāda Buddhists would describe their concern not as God or Ultimate Reality but as experiential realization of knowledge which puts an end to suffering and yields liberation. Indeed, Nasr is correct when he says, in a different publication, that "the major and dominating intellectual traditions of the Orient always have been wedded to a direct experience of the spiritual world and intellectual intuition in the strictest sense."[24] This is correct and fully applies to Theravāda Buddhism. The problem lies elsewhere, to which we now turn.

The second problem that a Buddhist will have with Nasr's point of unity among the world religions is the particular cosmology that seems to be required by that view. Buddhism's cosmological perspective is fundamentally unlike the cosmological perspective identified by Nasr as universal, and as an essential element in the perennial philosophy.

That Nasr's theory specifies that the perennial philosophy includes a particular cosmology is demonstrated by the following quotation.

> Perhaps the most direct way of approaching the meaning of the sacred is to relate it to the Immutable, to that Reality which is both the Unmoved Mover and the Eternal. That Reality which is immutable and eternal is the Sacred as such. . . . Man's sense of the sacred is none other than his sense for the Immutable and the Eternal. . . .[25]

And again,

> The knowledge of the Principle which is at once the absolute and infinite Reality is the heart of metaphysics while the distinction between levels of universal and cosmic existence, including both the macrocosm and the microcosm, are like its limbs.
>
> The Principle is Reality in contrast to all that appears as real but which is not reality in the ultimate sense. The Principle is the Absolute compared to which all is relative. It is Infinite while all else is finite. The Principle is One and Unique while manifestation is multiplicity. It is the Supreme Substance compared to which all else is accident. It is the Essence to which all things are juxtaposed as form. It is at once Beyond Being and Being while the order of multiplicity is comprised of existents. It alone *is* while all else becomes, for It alone is eternal in the ultimate sense while all that is externalized partakes of change. It is the Origin but also the End, the alpha and the omega.[26]

Buddhism reacted not only against Brahmanic ritualism, as Nasr notes, but also against Brahmanic cosmology. Indeed, the above nicely summarizes the very Brahmanic cosmology against which Buddhism rebelled. Where the *Upaniṣads* declared the existence of the *Ātman* (the Absolute, Infinite, monistic Supreme Substance), the Buddha declared *Anātman*, *not-Ātman*, a direct rejection of the notion that such a thing as *Ātman* exists. What did he declare in its place? Change, becoming, flux, transience, summed up in the doctrine of *pratītya-samutpāda* or dependent origination, without anything in any sense understood as the ground or root of this universal flux. While this doctrine describes the world of *samsāra* in which we live, the negation of *saṁsāra*, *nirvāṇa*, is not, in Theravāda Buddhism, in any way understandable as the immutable Reality upon which the world of transience is based. Such a thing is expressly negated. Buddhism, named the Middle Way by the Buddha, is presented as the Middle between two extreme views: eternalism, which it identifies with the view that Nasr articulates, and nihilism, which it identifies with simple materialism. Buddhism is said by the Buddha to be neither of these, but an ineffable Middle between these two "extreme views." Whatever that Middle may be, it is clearly not understood to be the view advocated by Nasr.

Nasr does not directly discuss the cosmology of Theravāda Buddhism, nor its forms of expression. However, he does consider the Mahāyāna concept of emptiness, or *śūnyatā*, as a potential challenge to his view. Continuing the quotation we saw above, he writes, "It ["the Principle which is at once the absolute and infinite Reality"] is Emptiness if the world is envisaged as fullness and Fullness if the relative is perceived in the light of its ontological poverty and essential nothingness."[27]

Let us examine the Buddhist concept of "emptiness." When we consider "emptiness" in its classic formulation by the great Buddhist sage, Nāgārjuna, regarded by most Mahāyāna Buddhists as second only to the Buddha, it is clear that "emptiness" cannot in any way be understood as an alternate term for Nasr's "Principle which is at once the absolute and infinite Reality," expressed as "emptiness" in *contradistinction* to a "world . . . envisaged as fullness." For Nāgārjuna, the world itself is "empty," since "emptiness" is another term for the dependent origination, or *pratītya-samutpāda* that characterizes the world. Nāgārjuna writes, "The 'originating dependently' [*pratītya-samutpāda*] we call 'emptiness.' This apprehension . . . is the understanding of the middle way."[28] In other words, "emptiness" refers to the principle of causal flux, found in this realm—the only realm there is for Nāgārjuna—certainly not to a supreme Reality outside of space and time. For Nāgārjuna, since all is radical, interdependent flux, we must turn away from all forms of thinking in terms of both being and non-being, fullness and nothingness, in favor of the middle way. To quote Nāgārjuna, "'It is' is a notion of eternity. 'It is not' is a nihilistic view. Therefore, one who is wise does not have recourse to 'being' or 'non-being'."[29] Indeed, the central thrust of Nāgārjuna's *magnum opus* is a devastating *reductio ad absurdum* argument against the very idea of any "self-existent thing" or *svabhāva*, conceived in any way, including an Absolute or Supreme Substance that could be the root of all things.

What, then, of *nirvāṇa*? Nāgārjuna writes, "There is nothing whatever which differentiates the existence-in-flux (*saṁsāra*) from *nirvāṇa* . . . There is not the slightest bit of difference between these two." The translator adds,

> *Nirvāṇa*, for Nāgārjuna, is not a term which darkly reflects an absolute Ultimate Reality; it, too, is simply a fabrication of the mind which, if misunderstood as referring to a self-sufficient and independent Ultimate Reality, will misguide the one who seeks release. Only as a conventional, that is, relative, term can it be profitably used to direct the mind from ignorance and greed. The Ultimate Truth to which the term *nirvāṇa* points is that it is without any designation; in actuality there is no "it" and no designation. . . .[30]

The observation that there is no "it" is the key point. This is what makes Buddhist thought unique. It also makes it not fit Nasr's paradigm. How does Nasr handle the subject of *nirvāṇa*?

On the one hand, Nasr writes,

> The Ultimate Reality which is both Supra-Being and Being is at once transcendent and immanent. . . . *Scientia Sacra* can be expounded in the language of one as well as the other perspective. It can speak of God or the Godhead, Allah, the Tao, or even *nirvāṇa* as being beyond the world, or forms or *saṁsāra*, while asserting ultimately that *nirvāṇa is saṁsāra*, and *saṁsāra*, *nirvāṇa*.[31]

And then, on the next page, he writes, "Metaphysics [perennial philosophy] does . . . distinguish between the Real and the apparent and Being and becoming. . . ."[32] The latter passage shows the error in the former. There is no issue in Nāgārjuna's thought of ontological transcendence and immanence; these categories do not exist. There is no distinction in his thought between the Real and the apparent or between Being and becoming (though there is in Vedantic Hinduism, whose metaphysics Nāgārjuna expressly refutes). Consequently, what Nasr seems to see as only an apparent problem in Buddhist language is a real problem not resolvable by means of the observation that Ultimate Reality (which category Nāgārjuna negates) can be expressed either in the language of transcendence or immanence, or both.

Nasr addresses the matter of emptiness further in a footnote where he states,

> Some contemporary scholars such as R. Panikkar . . . have contrasted the Buddhist [*Śūnyata*] and the Christian Pleroma but, metaphysically speaking, the concept of Ultimate Reality as emptiness and as fullness complement each other like the *yin-yang* symbol and both manifest themselves in every integral tradition. Even in Christianity where the symbolism of Divine Fullness is emphasized and developed with remarkable elaboration in Franciscan theology . . . the complementary vision of emptiness appears in the teachings of the Dominican Meister Eckhart who speaks of the 'desert of the Godhead.'[33]

The problem here again is that, for Nāgārjuna, the category of "Ultimate Reality," is *emptied* by emptiness such that there is no category "Ultimate Reality" which remains to *be* empty. That does not make "emptiness" itself an Ultimate Reality. Emptiness is only a tool for eliminating error.

> Emptiness is proclaimed by the victorious one as the refutation of all viewpoints;
> But those who hold "emptiness" as a viewpoint—[the true perceivers] have called those "incurable."[34]

I hasten to add that Nāgārjuna is not teaching nihilism. He hopes to be wielding a tool that aids the disciple to find the Middle Way between eternalism (which is how he would see Nasr's theory) and nihilism. Where, then, does Nāgārjuna leave us?

> Since all *dharmas* are empty, what is finite? What is infinite?
> What is both finite and infinite? What is neither finite nor infinite?
> Is there anything which is this or something else, which is permanent or impermanent,
> Which is both permanent and impermanent, or which is neither?
> The cessation of accepting everything [as real] is a salutary . . . cessation of phenomenal development . . .;
> No *dharma* anywhere has been taught by the Buddha of anything.[35]

We are left in uncompromising *via negativa*: the Buddha taught not a single thing. Emptiness, as used in the Buddhist tradition, is a tool intended to eliminate the possibility of all conceptualization whatsoever. This is not to say that the religious life bears no fruit. To the contrary, for Nāgārjuna and those who follow him, this relentless *via negativa* is the necessary condition for fruition in the religious life. This is not nihilism. Nonetheless, it is strictly opposed to any idea of any kind of Ultimate Reality whatsoever. Incidentally, it is also strictly opposed to any idea of revelation insofar as any kind of revelation has to manifest in some kind of (verbal or other) form.

In short, this is not to say that there is no meeting ground for Buddhist sapiental knowledge and that discovered by the mystics of other world religions. However, it is to deny that that meeting ground can be expressed in the terms used by Nasr, terms of Ultimate Reality, whether Full or Empty, no matter how expressed. Such language is quite outside the pale for arguably the two most important moments in the establishment of Buddhism: the teachings of Gautama Buddha and the thought of the great sage Nāgārjuna.

My fifth question for Dr. Nasr, then, is this. (5) Does he see any way to reconcile the languages of Gautama Buddha and Nāgārjuna, on the one hand, with the language he has been using for the meeting ground of the religions of the world, on the other? Or does he prefer to articulate this meeting ground in some other way, not dependent upon cosmology? In "The *Philosophia Perennis* and the Study of Religion," Nasr writes,

> For the traditional school the Buddhist or Taoist vision of the Void does not at all negate the universality of the metaphysics enshrined in the *philosophia perennis* and in fact provides a most powerful expression of this metaphysics in a language which is complementary but not contradictory to that of, let us say, Hinduism and Islam.[36]

This statement does not encourage me since Taoist metaphysics is quite different from the Buddhist metaphysics described above insofar as in Taoism there *is* an "it," the Tao—the fact that it is spoken of in language of the Void does not change the fact that it remains an "it," however "dimly visible," in the language of the *Tao Te Ching*:

> There is a thing confusedly formed,
> Born before heaven and earth.
> Silent and void
> It stands alone and does not change,
> Goes round and does not weary.
> It is capable of being the mother of the world.
> I know not its name
> So I style it 'the way' [Tao].[37]

This is an empty Something that does indeed fit Nasr's paradigm, not at all like what Nāgārjuna was talking about. Could Dr. Nasr spell out with some specificity the way in which Nāgārjuna's language "provides a most powerful expression" of the metaphysics of the *philosophia perennis*?

This is a critical question due to the nature of the authority from which Nasr argues in *Knowledge and the Sacred*, as well as many other works. The authority for his argument cannot, as we have seen, be reason, as reason runs a distant third in usefulness for religious knowledge, after revelation and intellectual illumination. The authority for his argument rests upon revelation and illumination which must, to secure his case, speak with a united voice. If there is any break in the unity of Tradition, Dr. Nasr's case is severely damaged. Yet defining moments in the Buddhist tradition in its sapiental dimension seem to speak a very different language. Can this be demonstrated to be an only apparent contradiction?

Conclusion: I agree with Dr. Nasr that, "every determination of the Absolute is already in the realm of relativity"; this must include Nasr's determination as well. It seems to me that Nasr's work is an articulation of what the "transcendent unity of religions" looks like from an Islamic point of view. Beginning, that is, with two primary assumptions, monotheism and universal revelation ("Verily to every people there has been sent a prophet," states the Quran), a person with Dr. Nasr's intelligence and familiarity with the world's religions might well draw the conclusions he advocates in *Knowledge and the Sacred*. Beginning, as a Buddhist would, from different starting assumptions, even if he felt on the basis of what Dr. Nasr calls esoteric experience that there is a common ground among religions, a Buddhist would not articulate that common ground in language of revelation or an essentialist cosmology with God or Being at the core. This reader concludes that what Nasr has given us is a fine Islamic reconciliation of the world's religions, but it is not a truly universalistic reconciliation since it does not include Buddhism. This does not, to this reader's mind, negate the value of what Dr. Nasr has achieved in *Knowledge and the Sacred*. To have so well articulated an Islamic understanding of the reconciliation of religions is no small accomplishment.

SALLIE B. KING

JAMES MADISON UNIVERSITY
OCTOBER 1998

NOTES

1. Seyyed Hossein Nasr, *Knowledge and the Sacred*, The Gifford Lectures, 1981 (New York: Crossroad, 1981). Seyyed Hossein Nasr, "The *Philosophia Perennis* and the Study of Religion," in Frank Whaling, ed., *The World's Religious Traditions: Current Perspectives in Religious Studies Essays in Honor of Wilfred Cantwell Smith* (Edinburgh: T and T Clark, Ltd., 1984), pp. 181–200.

2. *Knowledge*, pp. 67–68.

3. Ibid., p. 71.

4. Ibid., pp. 130–31.

5. Ibid., pp. 292–93.

6. Ibid., p. 282.

7. Ibid., p. 301.

8. Ibid., p. 292.

9. Ibid., p. 294.

10. This phenomenon is summarized by Dr. Nasr in chapter 1 of *Knowledge*, "Knowledge and Its Desacralization."

11. Sallie B. King, "Two Epistemological Models for the Interpretation of Mysticism," *Journal of the American Academy of Religion* 56, no. 2 (1988): 268.

12. See chapter 9 of *Knowledge and the Sacred*.

13. Chuang Tzu, *Basic Writings*, trans. Burton Watson (New York: Columbia University Press, 1964), p. 99.

14. *Sufi Essays* (Albany, N.Y.: State University of New York Press, 1972), p. 147, n. 37.

15. *Knowledge*, op. cit., p. 280.

16. *Sufi Essays*, op. cit., p. 147.

17. *Knowledge*, op. cit., p. 287.

18. Ibid., p. 294.

19. Ibid., p. 294.

20. Ibid., p. 74.

21. Ibid., p. 296.

22. Ibid., p. 77.

23. Ibid., p. 76.

24. "Conditions for Meaningful Comparative Philosophy," *Philosophy East and West* 22 (January, 1972): 55.

25. *Knowledge*, op. cit., pp. 75–76.

26. Ibid., pp. 133–34.

27. Ibid., p. 134.

28. Nāgārjuna, *Mūlamadhyamakakārikā* 24:18. Translated by Frederick J. Streng in *Emptiness: A Study in Religious Meaning* (Nashville, Tenn. and New York: Abingdon Press, 1967), p. 213.

29. *Mūlamadhyamakakārikā* 15:10; trans. in ibid., p. 200.

30. *Mūlamadhyamakakārikā* 25:19, 20; trans. in ibid., p. 217. The translator's comment is p. 75.

31. *Knowledge*, op. cit., p. 137.

32. Ibid., p. 138.

33. Ibid., p. 134, n. 9.

34. *Mūlamadhyamakakārikā* 13:8; trans. in ibid., p. 198; translator's interpolation.

35. *Mūlamadhyamakakārikā* 25:22–24; trans. in ibid., p. 217; translator's interpolation.

36. "The *Philosophia Perennis* and the Study of Religion," p. 184, n. 11.

37. Lao Tzu, *Tao Te Ching*, trans. D. C. Lau (London and New York: Penguin Books), p. 82.

REPLY TO SALLIE B. KING

The essay of Professor King is a challenging one in that it negates the universality of the perspective of the perennial philosophy by pointing out the cases of Theravāda and Mahāyāna Buddhism which she interprets in such a way that they do not fit into the universal metaphysical doctrines which lie at the heart of that philosophy. But before turning to a discussion of Buddhism she poses certain other questions and elaborates a number of salient points pertaining to religion and the perennial philosophy in general. In answering her, therefore, I shall also divide my reply into two parts: the first dealing with the various questions and assumptions in the first section of her paper and the second with the whole question of Buddhism.

After summarizing my views about tradition and the perennial philosophy, which she interprets correctly, the author alludes to three important goals which she believes my *Knowledge and the Sacred* attempts to achieve. While I agree with what she mentions, I want to add that in addition to these goals and in fact the main goal of the book was to relate once again knowledge to the reality of the sacred and to overcome the chasm created between them in the West since the fifteenth century. The three goals mentioned by King in fact follow from this primary aim of the book.

I also agree fully with the author in her discussions of the imprisoning effect of the methodologies of modern academic disciplines and her assertion that the universe has been rendered soulless by modern disciplines and rationalism which have led to the general denial by the modern mind of "an intelligence at the root of all existence," to quote her directly. I would only add that what she describes is precisely the result of the separation of knowledge and the sacred through the separation within the knowing agent of reason from both the intellect and revelation which belong to the realm of the sacred and which bestow upon reason a sacred dimension as long as it retains its nexus relative to them.

Professor King equates my usage of esoterism with mysticism about whose ineffable goal she speaks. First of all, in my usage of these terms, I do not equate the two. There are domains where they overlap but there are also aspects of esoterism that are not mystical, as this term is ordinarily understood and vice versa. Secondly, sapiental esoterism asserts that while we cannot know that Ineffable Reality discursively nor discuss or describe it in discursive terms, there is within us a divine spark associated with the Immanent Intellect which can "know" that Ineffable Reality directly through the transcendence of the duality of subject and object, although not all this that is thus known can be expressed in human language. Its most perfect expression is through that silence which many works of sacred art such as the traditional Buddha images convey so powerfully and mysteriously.

I also wish to confirm strongly the criticism of the author concerning religious studies in Western academic circles. She points to reducing religion to "epiphenomena produced by more fundamental, and in that sense more real, psychological, sociological, historical, political and the like phenomena." Needless to say, I have always stood for the primacy of the Sacred, present more than anywhere else in religion, over the other categories mentioned by her. The perennial philosophy as understood traditionally is the strongest safeguard against this type of reductionism which has turned religious studies in many places into a tool against religion. Let us hope that with greater interest in the perennial philosophy in religious studies the pitiful state of affairs mentioned by Professor King can be transformed so that the central role of religion in human life becomes clear once again as it has always been in traditional societies.

Having confirmed the necessity "to give a respectful hearing" to those who believe in the primacy of the Transcendent, the author turns, as has Professor Robert Neville in his essay, to the importance of not dispensing with "the hermeneutics of suspicion" in order to be able to deal successfully with those whom she describes as "charlatans and dysfunctional people." She furthermore enlists the help of Freud, Nietzsche, and Marx to identify these charlatans. In reality, such figures are the very last to be able to distinguish fake from authentic manifestations of the Spirit and false from true religions because such figures, especially Marx and Freud, deny the reality of the Spirit and religion as traditionally understood altogether.

Long before such men were born, traditional societies had clear criteria for distinguishing the true from the false in the domain of religion and in life itself. In contrast, today in a world molded to a large extent by such figures as Freud, Nietzsche, and Marx, there are no longer criteria for distinguishing true from false religion. Today all kinds of groups claim for themselves the status of a religious body and expect to be treated by society as such, and modern society is totally helpless in seeking to separate the wheat from the chaff in a world in which orthodoxy as well as heterodoxy, truth as well as heresy are no longer fashionable categories. My claim is that in fact only the perennial philosophy as traditionally understood can distinguish for modern man, in the chaotic world in which he lives, truth from falsehood and the authentic practices of religion from the charlatan as well as authentic religion itself from all that passes for religion today. Christ spoke of "false prophets" coming at the end of time. One can only distinguish a false prophet when one knows an authentic one. In a world in which prophecy is reduced to a psychological complex and religion to a social epiphenomenon, or worse, to the Marxist opium of the people, one no longer speaks of truth and therefore no error in religious thought and in fact in any other domain outside of the sciences. One is left with alternative lifestyles but no sense of the truthful and the authentic which alone determine the false and unveil the charlatan's claims for what they are.

The traditional understanding of the perennial philosophy also stands opposed to all religious syncretism whether current or belonging to an earlier age. When I speak of traditions, I mean the millennial religions of humanity along with their historical confolding which have led to the founding of civilizations, schools of sacred art, traditional social structures, and the like. According to traditional doctrines, the manifestations of the Logos or appearance of plenary revelations such as that of Buddhism, Zoroastrianism, Christianity, and Islam or in another context Hinduism, Taoism, and Confucianism came to an end a long time ago in fact with Islam whose prophet is described by the revelation itself as the Last Prophet. Moreover, history has been witness to the fact that nothing comparable to these major revelations has occurred since the advent of Islam. Now, it is possible to have religious movements which have often grown from the esoteric dimension of the orthodox and traditional religions and which have later made themselves independent. Such movements took place in the nineteenth century in several parts of the globe and the religions the author mentions all belong to this category. Their basic differences with the traditional and orthodox religions are quite clear and here the perennial philosophy in its traditional sense is once again the best guide for distinguishing one category from another as well as distinguishing the orthodox and the traditional expressions of a religion from their modernized versions which must not, however, be confused with religious movements that have broken away completely from existing traditional religions.

The author considers my distinctions between the inner unity of religion and the sentimental universalism so prevalent today to be vague and asks "when is universalism good and when is it bad?" In the domain of the study of religion and religious diversity universalism is good if it concerns the inner, esoteric, supraformal reality of religious forms and doctrines which belong to the universal order, metaphysically understood. It is bad when it identifies universalism with finding common elements on the formal plane of religious doctrine and practice, emphasizing them and rejecting what is not common on the formal plane. The first type of universalism holds the utmost respect for all traditional religious doctrines, practices, and forms in general on the level of forms and considers them to be sacred and essential as vehicles for reaching the universal and transcendent dimension beyond forms, and not in the formal order itself. The type of universalism that I oppose is willing to sacrifice sacred forms, doctrines, and practices in order to achieve a common set of beliefs and views which is then identified as being universal. It seeks the unity of religions in what is common among them on the formal plane. I hope this makes clear what kind of universalism I espouse and what kind I oppose. In fact, the very meaning of the term "univeralism" is different in the two cases.

Dr. King asks a cogent question about ordinary Christians, or for that matter followers of other religions, accepting the idea of the "relative absoluteness" of their own religion without losing sight of the "sense of the absolute" which is necessary for the understanding and practice of religion. Ecumenism in depth is essentially an esoteric undertaking and should in principle be undertaken only by those who have been able to live fully through the forms of their own religion and have then reached the Formless. For the ordinary believer, the model of such sages should suffice to accept what the Quran says about this matter, namely, that God created different peoples with different religions so that they would vie with each other in good works and that they should leave their differences in God's Hands. One could observe such a situation to a large extent among Muslims and Hindus in many areas of India in centuries past and also among Muslims, Christians, and Jews in many parts of the world of Islam and during most of the periods of Islamic history as seen in example in Islamic Spain. In Anatolia, Jalāl al-Dīn Rūmī, the celebrated Sufi poet who wrote much on the inner unity of religions, even had Christian as well as Jewish disciples in addition to Muslim ones. Now, even among his Muslim disciples not all understood fully or were able to follow his advice to journey from the world of forms to the Formless in order to see the inner reality of religions. But they trusted the great master and held respect not only for Jesus as a Muslim prophet but also for Christians while living as very devout Muslims for whom their religion was religion as such. This example can be multiplied both within the Islamic world and in other religious climates.

This response already covers some of the queries the author has assembled under her fourth question but a few further clarifications are needed. The many cannot become esoterists but the universal perspective of esoterism can "trickle down" to the level of the many in the form of myths, poetry, popularizations, etc. A prime example of this phenomenon can be found in Islam where many literary and especially poetic works known to the many reflect the esoteric doctrine of the "transcendent unity of religions" in such a way that its general implications can be grasped even for those who cannot understand the metaphysical intricacies involved. Even among those who know Arabic well, very few can understand Ibn 'Arabī's *Fuṣūṣ al-ḥikam* ("Bezels of Wisdom") dealing with the multiple manifestations of the Logos. But many know his poems about his heart having become a temple where forms of various religions are present. Likewise, nearly every Persian speaker knows some poems of Rūmī and Ḥāfiẓ alluding to the universality of revelation and the fact that the great religions of the world have all come from God. Such people have not become any less devout by reading, chanting, and memorizing such poems.

In the West I believe that in the academic teaching of religion "popularization of ideas as are formed in Frithjof Schuon's *Transcendent Unity of Religions* and related works," to quote the author, should certainly take place provided the principles are not sacrificed. In twenty years of teaching religion in America, I have in fact found such an undertaking to be most fruitful. I also believe that the various religions themselves should emphasize their sapiental and universalist elements as much as possible. This latter task is, however, somewhat different in the West and the East. In the West, opposition to religion arose from within Western society itself. In the non-Western world, religions (other than Christianity and Judaism) are faced not only with the onslaught of modernism which issues from another civilization, but also with the constant pressure of Christian missionary activity drawing from superior financial sources and strong political backing of forces outside of the religious world in question. Therefore, the question of preservation of the identity of religions and their practices looms large on the horizon for them. That is why in non-Western lands modernism and missionary activity usually lead to reactions which emphasize more exclusivism and exoterism than inclusivism and universalism, as one can see in both India and the Islamic world today. But even in these cases I believe that it is of the utmost importance to emphasize the sapiental elements and universal teachings within each religion. This holds true in fact whether the religion in question be of East or West.

Turning now in the second part of this response to the specific field of Buddhism and the questions King poses regarding this tradition, let it be said that the challenge she poses is a serious one. She claims that the teachings of Buddhism, at least of the Theravāda School, do not fit into the universal metaphysical perspective of the perennial philosophy. If this claim were to be accepted as true, then one would have to accept one of two consequences: either the vision of religious reality according to the perennial philosophy is not universal, a view chosen by the author, or that the vision in question is true but Theravāda Buddhism is not actually a religion, but a kind of philosophy as claimed by many modern secularists who are drawn to

Buddhism precisely because they think that it is not a religion, being without the notion of God, revelation, etc., a view which I oppose. I reject also King's claim and therefore both conclusions and will try to respond to all her objections one by one.

Before doing so, however, I must admit that, as she claims, I have not paid as much attention in my writings to Buddhism as I have to Hinduism and the Abrahamic religions. But if she had consulted my *Religion and the Order of Nature* and my review essay on Marco Pallis's, *A Buddhist Spectrum*, she would have realized that there are more references to Buddhism in my writings than those she has found in *Knowledge and the Sacred*. Despite having known D.T. Suzuki during my student days, having read nearly all his and Coomaraswamy's works on Buddhism followed by many later writings on the subject and especially Zen, having known His Holiness the Dalai Lama for several decades first through Marco Pallis who introduced me to Tibetan Buddhism, and having traveled in Japan and known several Buddhist masters from that land, I consider myself only a humble student of Buddhism and do not claim expertise on the subject. My responses are, however, based on authorities who have known much more about the subject than I.

The author objects first of all that there is no revelation in Buddhism as one finds in other religions. Surely this cannot be anything more than semantics. The illumination of the Buddha under the Bodhi Tree is surely revelation even if not called by that name by some authors. What is it that brought about the difference between Siddhārtha Gautama and the Buddha? Is *bodhi* anything other than revelation in its deepest sense? What made possible the discovery by the Buddha of the eternal law (*akālika dharma*)? Whatever that something is, that is revelation in the Buddhist context. From the point of view of the perennial philosophy the definition of revelation is vast enough to include both descent from "above" and the illumination of the Buddha from "within." Buddhism is based on revelation, irrespective of whether this revelation/illumination is seen in Buddhist texts as coming from above or within. It was by virtue of this revelation/illumination that the man Siddhārtha became the Man the Buddha, a solar being able to guide others. The Buddhist text *Saddhama Puṇḍarīka*, XV.I states "The Buddha is a solar deity descended from heaven to save both men and gods from all the ill that is denoted by the word, 'mortality', the view that his birth and awakening are coeval with time.[1]" Even if many Theravāda texts do not use such a language, the reality is the same. Siddhārtha became the Buddha and discovered the eternal *dharma* and what made this transformation possible, from which flowed the *sangha*, the treasures, the sacred art of Buddhism and a whole civilization is none other than what the perennial philosophy considers a form of revelation in the most universal sense of that term.

It is interesting in this context to go even a step further and to compare the Buddha with Christ and the Prophet of Islam with whom Christianity and Islam identify the revelations which are the foundations of their religions. It is true that the Buddha does not speak of God as do Christ and the Prophet, a point to which we shall turn shortly, but he does state, "he who sees the *Dhamma* sees me, and he who sees me sees the *Dhamma*" (*Samyutta-Nikāyā*, III, 120). How similar is this utterance to the saying of Christ, "No man cometh to the Father but by me" and the *ḥadīth* of the Prophet of Islam, "He who has seen me [that is, the Prophet] has seen the Truth [that is God]." This saying also reveals the function of the Buddha as the "Logos" or "Messenger" in the Buddhist universe, fulfilling a role very similar to those of Christ and the Prophet in Christianity and Islam respectively. So not only is there revelation in Buddhism, but there is also a function for the Buddha vis-à-vis the Eternal Law within the Buddhist Universe which is similar to what one finds for the founder of Christianity and Islam vis-à-vis God in the Christian and Islamic universes.

King then criticizes my identification of the Mahāyāna School with esoterism and the Theravāda with exoterism. To some extent her criticism is justified in that in this case I have been a bit too schematic. I admit that there are in fact esoteric elements in Theravāda and of course exoteric elements in Mahāyāna. But this having been said, there is no doubt that many major esoteric perspectives which flowered later in Mahāyāna and Vajrayāna Buddhism were, one might say, in a latent state in the early centuries and did not manifest themselves in the Theravāda world. That is why a number of authors besides myself have tended to identify the Mahāyāna with the esoteric and the Theravāda with the exoteric dimensions of Buddhism, whereas in reality this is at best an approximation which nevertheless points to an important truth.

The author's reference to Buddhism's opposition of Brahmanic cosmology is certainly correct. In fact, Buddhism sees the world as the abode of suffering (*dukkha*) and not as symbol and theophany. Early Buddhism was singularly acosmic although later on many schools of Buddhism developed elaborate cosmologies. But I agree that the usual cosmological hierarchy associated with the "great chain of being" and so central to the perennial philosophy cannot be applied to Theravāda Buddhism which emphasizes practice to become free of the bondage of the world rather than the science which would allow us to know the nature of the world. But this lack of possibility of the application of the idea of cosmic hierarchy does not at all prevent the perennial philosophy from being able to understand the perspective of Buddhism and embrace that perspective within the universal metaphysics which lies at its heart. This task has in fact been already achieved as far as essentials are concerned by Coomaraswamy, Pallis, and

Schuon. It is enough to understand that Buddhism emphasizes the pole of the subject and the state of consciousness rather than the pole of the object and the state of being to realize that a non-cosmological language is needed to do justice to the Buddhist perspective and also to realize that because of the nature of things the cosmological dimension was bound to manifest itself even within the Buddhist perspective as we see in so many of the later schools.

Another major criticism made by King concerns the doctrine of *anātman* or *anattā* in its Pali form which she takes to mean opposition to *ātman* or the self, and which emphasizes that there is no self but only change and flux. Now, if there were to be no identity at all of the "self," how could there be the law of *karma* and a particular being be responsible for the fruits of his or her actions? What the doctrine means most of all is that ordinary creatures subject to the "three poisons" of illusion, lust, and pride are devoid of *ātman*. Otherwise the Buddha refers often to *Ātman* as the immanent *nirvāṇic* Reality which in the language of theism would be called the immanent God. For example, he says "Make the Self your refuge" (*Samyutta Nikāya*, III, 143); or "I have made the Self my refuge" (*Dīgha Nikāya*, II, 120).

The Buddhist thinkers did not want to give an objective definition to the soul and emphasized that deliverance is precisely freedom from all that is transient and changing including what is usually called the "self." But the famous and central Buddhist saying:

> Of all things that spring from a cause,
> The cause has been told by him "Thus-come";
> And their suppression, too,
> The Great Pilgrim has declared

would make no sense if it meant the denial of the Self as well as the self. In that case "Thus-come" would mean nothing and the Great Pilgrim being himself but a moment or episode in the sea of change could not declare the suppression of the cause of change which is also the cause of suffering. The *anattā* doctrine points more than anything else to the apophatic method favored by Buddhism and the emphasis of this religion upon practice rather than on any mental conceptualization. For the true devotees of Buddhism throughout history the point was not whether *attā* or *anattā* is correct, but to remember the Bodhi Tree which can be and is in reality everywhere and under whose shade one can attain the state of Buddhahood. The great dialectical efforts of such Buddhist philosophers as Nāgārjuna were to prevent any form of objectivization or fixation upon the "self" or any other fixed concept in the mind, to prevent man from using all his effort to seek anything other than release from the suffering of *samsāra* leading to attainment of the *nirvāṇic* state. Needless to say, all of this is perfectly understandable and can be easily interpreted within the perspective of perennial philosophy as understood traditionally.

The heart of King's queries is the metaphysical one dealing with the nature of *nirvāṇa* and *śūnyatā*. She insists that *nirvāṇa* is not an immutable reality and therefore other than what I call Ultimate Reality. If by reality she means objective reality, then I agree because Buddhism is based on the pole of the subject and not the object. Otherwise *nirvāṇa* cannot but be "immutable reality" if its attainment means cessation of suffering which is the result of the constant change and flux of *samsāric* existence. *Nirvāṇa* is actually the cessation of all that is negative and is itself therefore absolute, infinite, and perfect even if not defined objectively as is *Brāhman* in Hinduism or Allah in Islam. That is why Buddhism is non-theistic and not atheistic. If *nirvāṇa* had no reality, whatsoever, why then follow the path and why would the Buddha, who had attained it, be called *Tathāgata*, that is "Thus-gone" or "Fully-Arrived"? If a Nāgārjuna refuses to define *nirvāṇa*, it is for reasons already mentioned. Otherwise all the qualities that "flow from it" including Buddhahood are in perfect accord with descriptions of the Divine Reality in other religions and as understood in the universal perspective of the perennial philosophy.

As for *śūnyatā* or "the Void," it is none other than *nirvāṇa* which is, to paraphrase Schuon, "God" subjectivized and seen as a state of realization. In the Abrahamic traditions, God is the Principle seen objectively while in Buddhism the Void is the same Principle envisaged subjectively. That is what Buddhist philosophers mean when they insist that the "Void" or *nirvāṇa* is not an "it." I agree with this assertion of King but do not believe that the "Void" or *nirvāṇa* is anything other than the Supreme Reality even if envisaged only in a subjectivized manner. That is why I mentioned Taoism and Buddhism together wanting to emphasize the non-theistic character of each without being unaware of the fact that Taoism envisages the "Void" objectively and as "it" while Buddhism refuses to do so.

From the point of view of the integral metaphysics at the heart of the perennial philosophy, the Divine Reality possesses an Impersonal Essence as well as the Personal Aspect we ordinarily identify with God. Now most religions emphasize this theistic Principle. Yet, within these religions the manifestation of the Impersonal Essence occurs in their esoteric dimension as we see in the Kabbala, Sufism, and many Christian mystics such as Meister Eckhart and Angelus Silesius. The universal law of the manifestation and revelation of religions required that a religion be also revealed on the basis of the impersonal aspect of the Divine Reality. Such was to be Buddhism. But while within religions in which the personal aspect of the Divinity is a central concern the Impersonal Essence appears in various esoteric schools, in Buddhism the reverse takes place. In its later history

Buddhism was witness to the appearance of theistic modes as one sees for example in Amida Buddhism and in fact theistic elements are even present in Theravāda. But such manifestations remained within the matrix of the Buddhist tradition whose spiritual originality is to consider the Divine Reality in an acosmic and non-anthropomorphic manner as a supra-existential state rather than being, a state which is the Void before the false fullness and plenitude of this lower world of corruption and suffering. If the Void were not "real," albeit not objectively, how could the Buddha, that central reality of Buddhism, be called *shunyāmurtī*, that is, the Manifestation of the Void? It is enough to look at a well-executed Buddha image, such as those remarkable masterpieces of the Nara period in Japan, to realize that the Void of which the Buddha is the manifestation could not but be the Divine Reality envisaged as a state rather than as an objective reality.

King also objects to my usage of the term "Ultimate Reality" as being able to provide a common ground with Theravāda Buddhism. After all I have said I think that the answer to this objection is now clear. If we do not confine the meaning of reality only to the objective pole, then certainly this term can provide the common ground that we seek. Furthermore, let us not forget such terms as *Dharma*, *Ātman*, and *Bodhi* even in early Buddhism, not to speak of *Dharmakāya-Buddha*, *Vairochana-Dharmakāya-Buddha* and *Amitābha Buddha*. Even if one says that Mahāyāna terms denoting Ultimate Reality belong to later manifestations of Buddhism, one has to claim either that this was a later accretion unrelated to the message of the Buddha, a thesis which can hardly be taken seriously, or that that the early message also contained seeds of the teachings which flowered in such a way later. In that case later concepts pertaining to the Ultimate Reality are certainly Buddhist and can be easily correlated with concepts of the Ultimate Reality in other religions, while concepts particularly identified with Theravāda, such as those mentioned above, can also be correlated with the notion of Ultimate Reality if, as already mentioned, reality is not confined to its objective mode.

Professor King asks if I "see any way to reconcile the languages of Guatama Buddha and Nāgārjuna, on the one hand, with the language [I have] been using for the meeting ground of the religions, on the other?" I think that from what I have said, it is clear that I believe such a reconciliation exists if one does not limit the language of the perennial philosophy only to the pole of the object and allows it to be interpreted in a subjectivized manner. Moreover, the aim of the Buddha and Nāgārjuna was to lead to spiritual practice and away from theoretical conceptualizations. What I have said about the common ground for the meeting of the religions of the world can certainly accommodate an apophatic perspective and the *via negativa* combined with emphasis upon self purification. This meeting ground would not have to be based upon cosmology as I have made clear above. But then there is also no need for "some other way," to quote King. The full doctrine of the perennial philosophy embraces all traditional and orthodox religions including Buddhism in both its Theravāda and Mahāyāna forms. And although each religion possesses its own spiritual genius, there are always correspondences and resemblances across religious frontiers. Therefore, various elements of Buddhist teachings have their correspondences in other traditions including *madhyāmā-pritipad* or the Middle Way between conceptual fixation and nihilism on the one hand, asceticism and self-indulgence on the other; although, of course, the accent given to this and other doctrines in Buddhism is unique to that religion as are various elements of other religions within the structure of the religions to which the elements in question belong.

My conclusion is that the metaphysical view that I have expressed embraces all the traditional religions including Buddhism if the interpretations I have made above are taken into consideration. I am indeed indebted to Professor King for having raised the questions which I have sought to answer above and for therefore giving me the opportunity to make the necessary clarifications. She concludes that my presentation of the perennial philosophy provides only an "Islamic understanding of the reconciliation of religions." Although being a Muslim, I naturally have my roots in the Islamic tradition which I know better than others, my exposition of the perennial philosophy is not personal and individualistic and has its roots in an anonymous wisdom to be found wherever tradition has flourished. I have known many Christian, Jewish, Hindu, and Confucian scholars and thinkers of note who have found my exposition to be applicable to their own tradition as well, and I have carried out many dialogues on the basis of my understanding of the perennial philosophy with those belonging to other religious traditions. Among them the scholars who have accepted the traditional point of view have been able to identify themselves with my perspectives while they remain firmly rooted in their own traditions. My hope is therefore that my exposition, in addition to being an articulation of the Islamic position, also possesses a universal nature based as it is on the truth which lies at the heart of all religions and that it can serve as a means of creating reconciliation and better mutual understanding among followers of all traditions.

S. H. N.

Note

1. Quoted by A.K. Coomaraswamy in his *Hinduism and Buddhism* (New York: Philosophical Library, 1943), p. 50.

5

Arvind Sharma

REVISIONING CLASSICAL HINDUISM THROUGH *PHILOSOPHIA PERENNIS*

I. Introduction

This paper should be read as a response to the call issued by Professor Seyyed Hossein Nasr, to those in the academic study of religion, for taking the approach of *philosophia perennis* to the study of religion more seriously.

Some recent movement in this direction can be detected, as has been noted by Professor Nasr himself, when he observes: "During the past few years not only have some well-known scholars adopted the traditional perspective as their own, but to an even greater degree, other notable scholars have been attracted to this school as at least one of the schools of religious studies to be considered seriously."[1]

The swell, however, is by no means a tidal wave. Nevertheless, the fact that the tide is not rising more strongly in that direction must occasion some surprise. It is still generally true that the academic study of religion fights shy of studying religion through the lens of *philosophia perennis*, despite the fact that some of its leading lights, including Professor S. H. Nasr himself, have their feet firmly planted in both camps, and, despite the further fact, that another leading light, Frithjof Schuon, switched from the former to the latter, thereby attesting to the ease of dual citizenship in the matter. All this comes by way of saying that if my exercise seems odd in some respect, it should not. After all, if Hinduism does have a name for itself,[2] then it is *sanātana dharma*,[3] well within a semantic stone's throw of the term *philosophia perennis* itself.[4]

II. Three Dimensions

As I set about reflecting on the agenda I had set for myself, it struck me that it might be more useful to zoom in on some aspects of classical Hinduism with the lens of *philosophia perennis* rather than approach it from a wide angle. Perhaps more might be gained by exploring a few issues in depth than by merely examining, perhaps superficially, a large number of topics. The "depth versus range" issue in discussing a broad theme is something the reader is probably not unfamiliar with. Each has its own advantages and disadvantages. Whether my decision is right only time will tell, or the reader!

I have selected three dimensions of classical Hinduism for such exploration: (1) its Vedic basis; (2) its caste system; and (3) its reputation for tolerance.

III. Vedic Revelation

The position of Śaṅkara, the famous philosopher, on Vedic revelation may be considered paradigmatic for classical Hinduism. He spells out this paradigm in the following passage, which has been cited by numerous scholars. The passage occurs in his gloss on *Brahmasūtra* I.I.2:

> Scriptural text, and the like, are not, in the enquiry into Brahman, the only means of knowledge, as they are in the enquiry into active duty (that is, in the Pūrva Mīmāṁsā), but scriptural texts on the one hand, and intuition, and the like, on the other hand, are to be had recourse to according to the occasion: firstly, because intuition is the final result of the enquiry into Brahman; secondly, because the object of the enquiry is an existing (accomplished) substance. If the object of the knowledge of Brahman were something to be accomplished, there would be no reference to intuition, and text, and the like, would be the only means of knowledge.[5]

I was reminded of this passage while reading the following statement by Professor Nasr:

> By *philosophia perennis*—to which should be added the adjective *universalis*, as insisted upon so often by A. K. Coomaraswamy—is meant a knowledge which has always been and will always be and which is of universal character both in the sense of existing among peoples of different climes and epochs and of dealing with universal principles. This knowledge which is available to the intellect is, moreover, contained at the heart of all religions or traditions, and its realization and attainment is possible *only* through those traditions and by means of methods, rites, symbols, images, and other means sanctified by the

message from Heaven or the divine which gives birth to each tradition. Although *theoretically* it is possible for man to gain this knowledge, at least on a more outward level, by himself because of the nature of the intellect, that "supernaturally natural" faculty which is ingrained in the very substance of man, the *norm* is such that the attainment of this knowledge depends upon the grace and the framework which *tradition alone provides*. If there are exceptions, they are there to prove the rule and bear witness to the well-known dictum that "the Spirit bloweth where it listeth."[6]

The striking point which emerges by comparing the two passages in terms of structure (rather than content) is the similarity of the *problematique* and the broad similarity in the pattern of its resolution, despite the fact that Professor Nasr is dealing with *philosophia perennis et universalis* in general and Śaṅkara only with one tradition in particular, namely, the Vedic or Hindu. The problem for Śaṅkara is—if Brahman is the universal reality, why must it be known through the Vedas. And if so, must it be known *only* through the Vedas? The problem for *philosophia perennis et universalis* is: if perennial philosophy is universal, why must it be approached through one particular tradition. And if so, why must it be known *only* through it? The two problems are akin.

Śaṅkara's exact position in this respect is a subject of debate and, in fact, is an element in the difference between the two sub-schools to which his system gave rise.[7] After wrestling with the issue I am inclined to reduce his position, as I see it, to three propositions:

(1) that the Vedas are the "normal" but not the sole means of gaining access to Brahman;
(2) that *theoretically* Brahman-knowledge can arise spontaneously, as it is, after all, an existent reality, but it is *practically* attained through the Vedas;
(3) Vedas may be necessary but are not indispensable for Brahman-knowledge.

It seems to me that, *pari passu*, all the three propositions apply to the case of *philosophia perennis et universalis* in their own way. Thus the first proposition connects with the statement: "[T]he *norm* is such that the attainment of this knowledge depends upon the grace and framework which tradition alone provides. If there are exceptions they are there to prove the rule."[8] The second proposition connects with the lines: "Although theoretically it is possible for a man to gain this knowledge, at least on a more outward level, by himself because of the nature of the intellect . . . the norm is that . . . "[9] The third proposition connects with the statement that "The spirit bloweth where it listeth."[10]

It might interest the reader how Śaṅkara's position on the Vedas, as the sole authority in matters relating to Brahman, could abide these three propositions, a position analogous in our view to that within *philosophia perennis et universalis* that the knowledge which had always been and always will be can only be reached through a tradition. In the first case the fact that Brahman is an existent reality creates room for direct experience; in the second it is like possessing a map to reach a place, although by ceaseless search one could stumble on the place because "it is there"; and in the third case, even if formal necessity of Vedic knowledge is conceded, it may have been acquired in a previous life.[11]

It is clear that the issue underlying both the positions is the same: How to justify a *particular* approach to something which is *universal* and hence inherently approachable.

This seems to be the right place to introduce a psychological as opposed to what might be called a formal approach to the point. It turns on the question of fundamentalism. It is relevant here because fundamentalism within a tradition relates to the issue of the role of scripture in that tradition (the issue addressed by Śaṅkara), while fundamentalism in relation to other religious traditions relates to the exclusive claims made by a single tradition in the matter of salvation (an issue addressed by Professor Nasr). Such a double understanding of fundamentalism is extremely helpful in the present context, as it enables the analogous issues to be addressed simultaneously.

I would now like to address this common point involved in the *psychology* of fundamentalism which underlies both these manifestations. It hinges on the distinction between *holding* views and *clinging* to views. This distinction is implicit in much of the discussion on these points in the context of Hinduism and the *philosophia perennis*, and is perhaps best illustrated by referring to the situation in which the more *tense* one gets, the more *tightly* one holds on to a thing, as happens in crossing a crevasse while hanging from a rope. Indeed, it is not impossible to imagine that someone might become so paranoid, as a result of this experience, as to be unwilling to let go of the rope even *after* one has successfully crossed over the crevasse!

The subtle difference between holding on to a rope firmly, without clinging to it, is what one seeks in this example. One's tradition, and the scripture within one's tradition, constitute the rope, by the utilization of which we hope to cross over to the other side, but in either case we must not overlook the relative nature of both, while all the time being on our guard against succumbing to a facile relativism.

Much depends on understanding the word "relative" correctly here. It is relative in the sense of "being related to us." While in relation to others it is absolutely relative, the situation in relation to us is relatively absolute. It is this metaphysical subtlety which is psychologically reflected in the distinction between clinging and holding.

Professor Nasr has often warned us against conflating traditionalism and fundamentalism in the context of Islam.[12] It is clear from what has been said that the core issue involved in this distinction is capable of being extended to the relationship of the Vedas to Hinduism and of individual traditions to the "universal religion" of *philosophia perennis*.

IV. THE CASTE SYSTEM

One of the cardinal tenets of *philosophia perennis* is that the "Principle gives rise to a universe which is hierarchical."[13] And Hinduism is notoriously so. In fact, *philosophia perennis* has itself not escaped the charge of elitism in our equalitarian times[14] and Hinduism is perpetually trying to escape it.

This hierarchical principle operates at several levels—that of reality, of approaches to reality, and among the followers of a religion. In this context the application of the lens of *philosophia perennis* to Hinduism produces a remarkable result. It leads one to focus on a neglected account of the so-called caste system as found in the Upaniṣads.

Hitherto the account found in the Ṛg-Veda has held the foreground. It runs as follows:

> When they divided the Man,
> into how many parts did they divide him?
> What was his mouth, what was his arms,
> what were his thighs and his feet?
>
> The brāhmaṇ was his mouth,
> of his arms was made the warrior,
> his thighs became the vaiśya [peasant]
> of his feet the śūdra [serf] was born.
>
> The moon arose from his mind,
> from his eye was born the sun,
> from his mouth Indra and Agni,
> from his breath the wind was born.
>
> From his navel came the air,
> from his head there came the sky,
> from his feet the earth, the four quarters from his ear,
> thus they fashioned the worlds.

With Sacrifice the gods sacrificed to Sacrifice—
these were the first of the sacred laws.
These mighty beings reached the sky,
where are the eternal spirits, the gods.[15]

One needs to focus on the second of the five verses cited above. As A. L. Basham explains:

> Among the entities produced from the gigantic victim were the four estates of the Hindu social order. This is the first appearance of the four, brought together in a single system. Since the four classes are numbered with cattle, horses, and sheep as products of the body of the giant, it is clear that they are already thought of as separate, and no amount of special pleading by a few scholars can controvert the obvious fact that they are ranged in hierarchical order. From the head of Puruṣa came the brahmaṇ, the intermediary of the gods and humans, and thanks to his knowledge of sacrificial ritual, he keeps the world going. From the arms came the *rājanya*, later called the *kṣatriya*, the warrior and ruler; the trunk of the victim yielded the *vaiśya*, the peasant and craftsman; while from the feet, the humblest and lowest of the limbs, was made the *śūdra*, the non-Āryan serf who had gradually drawn closer to his masters and more and more accepted their mythology and ritual, until he achieved a position, albeit a very subordinate one, in the Āryan social order.[16]

This picture of the caste system—as a socially iniquitous, exploitative, rigidly hierarchical incubus—has been painted in such a deep dye that it has virtually become definitive to the point of being almost definitionally associated with it.

If, however, one factors the *philosophia perennis* concept of hierarchy into the equation, the contours change. What I mean by the *philosophia perennis* concept of hierarchy here is the one found in the following passage by Nasr:

> In the same way that the rejection of the reality of hierarchy in its metaphysical sense by so many modern scholars has affected their worldview and methodology in every field and domain, the acceptance of this principle constitutes an essential feature of the traditionalist school in its study of religion in its different aspects. Religion itself is hierarchically constituted and is not exhausted by its external and formal reality. Just as the phenomenal world necessitates the noumenal—the very word phenomenon implying a reality of which the phenomenon is the phenomenon—the formal aspect of religion necessitates the essential and the supra-formal. Religion possesses at once an external, outward or exoteric dimension concerned with the external and formal aspect of human life, but, because it is religion, it is in itself sufficient to enable man who follows its tenets and has faith in its truths to lead a fully human life

and to gain salvation. But religion also possesses an inner or esoteric dimension concerned with the formless and the essential with means to enable man to reach the Supernal Essence here and now. Moreover, within the context of this most general division, there are further levels within both the exoteric and the esoteric, so that altogether there exists within every integral religion a hierarchy of levels from the most outward to the most inward which is the Supreme Center.[17]

The existing version of the caste system clearly constitutes a social, external, and formal reality. In the *Bṛhdāraṇyaka Upaniṣad*, however, one encounters this largely overlooked but equally ancient account of the caste system which is archetypal rather than external in nature. It is also worth noting how, in the end, the earthly *varṇas* are described as replications of the divine ones.

11. Verily, in the beginning this (world) was *Brāhman*, one only. That, being one, did not flourish. He created further an excellent form, the *Kṣatra* power, even those who are *Kṣatras* (rulers) among the gods, Indra, Varuṇa, Soma (Moon), Rudra, Parjanya, Yama, Mṛtyu (Death), Iśāna. Therefore there is nothing higher than *Kṣatra*. Therefore at the Rājasūya sacrifice the Brāhmaṇa sits below the Kṣatriya. On Kṣatrahood alone does he confer this honour. But the Brāhmaṇa is nevertheless the source of the *Kṣatra*. Therefore, even if the king attains supremacy at the end of it, he resorts to the Brāhmaṇa as his source. Therefore he who injures the Brāhmaṇa strikes at his own source. He becomes more evil as he injures one who is superior.

12. Yet he did not flourish. He created the *viś* (the commonality), these classes of gods who are designated in groups, the Vasus, Rudras, Ādityas, Viśvedevās and Maruts.

13. He did not still flourish. He created the Śūdra order, as Pūṣan. Verily, this (earth) is Pūṣan (the nourisher), for she nourishes everything that is.

14. Yet he did not flourish. He created further an excellent form of justice. This is the power of the Kṣatriya class, viz. Justice. Therefore there is nothing higher than justice. So a weak man hopes (to defeat) a strong man by means of justice as one does through a king. Verily, that which is justice is truth. Therefore they say of a man who speaks justice that he speaks the truth. Verily, both these are the same.

15. So these (four orders were created). The Brāhmaṇa, the Kṣatriya, the Vaiśya and the Śūdra. Among the gods that Brahmā existed as Fire, among men as Brāhmaṇa, as a Kṣatriya by means of the (divine) Kṣatriya, as a Vaiśya by means of the (divine) Vaiśya, as a Śūdra by means of the (divine) Śūdra. Therefore people desire a place among the gods through fire only, and among

> men as the Brāhmaṇa, for by these two forms (pre-eminently) Brahmā existed. If anyone, however, departs from this world without seeing (knowing) his own world, it being unknown, does not protect him as the Vedas unrecited or as a deed not done do not (protect him). Even if one performs a great and holy work, but without knowing this, that work of his is exhausted in the end. One should meditate only on the Self as his (true) world. The work of him who meditates on the Self alone as his world is not exhausted, for out of that very Self he creates whatsoever he desires.[18]

Three aspects of this account invite attention. (1) In this account the *varṇas* at the human level are reflections of divine prototypes. This points to the pervasiveness of the hierarchical principle. (2) The complementarity of the various *varṇas* is continually emphasized. Hence exclusiveness should not be considered a logical corollary of the *varṇa* system. (3) The concept of *dharma* herein clearly corresponds to the principle of justice. Hence injustice should not be regarded as a logical corollary of the *varṇa* system.

Now two points deserve special consideration here from the point of view of our present discussion. The first is that the metaphysical contextualization of hierarchy has enabled one to retrieve a neglected version of the caste system, which offers a very different vision of it than one customarily sees. But the second point is perhaps even more significant. I think we need to distinguish between two concepts of hierarchies. For want of better terms let one be called a *step hierarchy* and the other a *circular hierarchy*. Then the scheme of the four *varṇas* could be presented in the following two versions:

STEP HIERARCHY

Brāhmaṇa

Kṣatriya

Vaiśya

Śūdra

CIRCULAR HIERARCHY

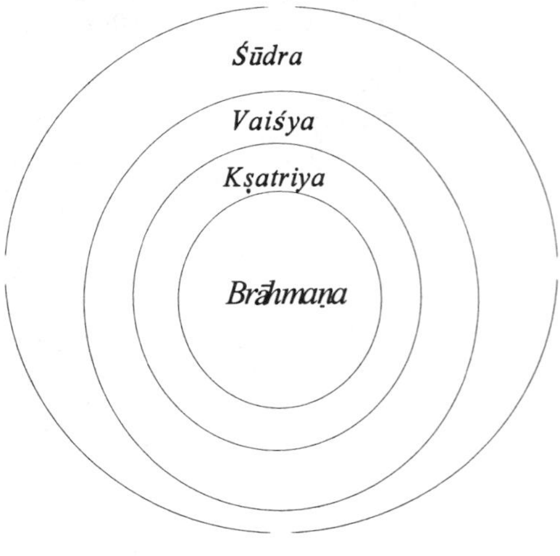

It is obvious, I think, that circular hierarchy is less "hierarchical" (in the obnoxious sense) from step hierarchy. The sapiental tradition, ever pressing towards the core-reality, it seems to me, would favor a circular vision of hierarchy.

The foregoing discussion raises a fascinating question in the context of classical Hinduism which can only be mentioned here, and must be pursued elsewhere. The Upaniṣads are widely credited with having reoriented Hindu *thought* sapientally. Were they also trying to reorient *society* sapientally? This is another point which seems to deserve special consideration if Hinduism's caste system is revisioned in the light of *philosophia perennis*.

V. Hindu Tolerance

I would like to begin the discussion under this heading by claiming that Hinduism is a missionary religion. This very claim is likely to raise a few eyebrows, for the scholarly consensus seems to be that classical Hinduism is a non-missionary religion. This is not the place to contest this point but to point out how, if this proposition is accepted, we face a problem in dealing with such an influential text of classical Hinduism as the *Manusmṛti* and how a *philosophia perennis* approach to Hinduism may help solve that problem.

The following verse of the *Manusmṛti*, a verse regularly cited in India and consistently overlooked in the West, poses a serious challenge to the claim that Hinduism is a non-missionary religion:

> All humans on earth should learn their own individual practices from a priest from that country.[19]

This verse in fact poses two problems: a superficial one and a deep one. The superficial problem is posed by the fact that the Brāhmaṇas are called upon to be the instructors of the whole human race, to become *jagadgurus*. This may be dismissed as another piece of chauvinistic conceit here to keep the essay within bounds. The deeper problem the verse poses is this: how is one to take the expression "their own individual practices" (*svaṃ svaṃ caritram*): is the referent of the norm here the *Brahmin's* conduct or the (*normative*) conduct of the people *themselves*? The double use of *svaṃ*, it seems to me, slides the meaning in the second direction. Thus the Brāhmaṇas are to instruct the people in *their own* respective norms. This sounds odd to say the least, but this oddness vanishes if one considers the *philosophia perennis* concept of orthodoxy. It is found in a passage from Nasr which coincidentally may also help distinguish between the approaches of modern and classical Hinduism on this point:

> The approach of the *philosophia perennis* to the study of religion, as understood in this essay, is none other than the traditional approach as the term traditions has been understood and explained by masters and expositors of the teachings of what one can call the traditional school, that is, such men as R. Guénon, A. K. Coomaraswamy, M. Pallis, T. Burckhart, M. Lings, Lord Northbourne, L. Schaya, W. N. Perry, H. Smith and especially F. Schuon. The point of view of this school should not be identified with either that sentimentalism that sees all religions as being the same or that neo-Vedantism which spread in America after the Second World War and which, despite the passing interest of some of its leading figures in the *philosophia perennis* and tradition, should not be confused with the traditional perspective. If there is one principle which all the traditional authors in question repeat incessantly, it is orthodoxy which they, however, do not limit to the exoteric level but also apply to the esoteric. They are orthodox and the great champions of universal orthodoxy. This point alone should clarify their radical difference from the neo-Vedantists and similar groups with whom they are often identified by opponents who have taken little care to examine in depth what the traditionalists have been saying.[20]

The passage from the *Manusmṛti* seems to be championing the cause of universal orthodoxy, which truly undergirds Hindu tolerance as manifested in classical Hinduism. It will be clear to the reader by now that if we are to make sense of the Hindu reality we need to distinguish between *missionary* activity and *proselytizing* activity and then, on the basis of this distinction, turn to Hinduism and describe it as a missionary but a non-proselytizing religion.

In broader terms, this distinction is a particular expression of a more general principle, which allows one to *combine* commitment to one's own faith with respect for the faiths of others. This general principle, at its most general and hence metaphysical level, finds its clearest articulation, it seems to me, in the formulation of the concept of the "relatively absolute" (as distinguished from the Absolute) by F. Schuon, to which Professor Nasr has drawn repeated attention.[21] I think the point is crucial, for it is the intuitive grasp of this principle in Hinduism which allows it the double confidence in the efficacy of Hinduism for the Hindus, and the efficacy of *their* own religions to the followers of other religions. And this despite the fact that Hinduism itself, like *philosophia perennis*, is capable of claiming that it is the primordial tradition[22] (and not just an expression of the primordial tradition), and despite the fact that its sense of primordiality resonates with the youngest of the major religions—namely Islam. As Professor Nasr has noted:

> There was, in fact, in Islam a presentiment of the primordial character of Hinduism which moved many Muslim authors to identify Brahman with Abraham. This connection may seem strange linguistically but it contains a deep metaphysical significance. Abraham is, for Islam, the original patriarch

identified with the primordial religion (*al-dīn al-ḥanīf*) which Islam came to reassert and reaffirm. The connection of the name of the *barāhimah* (namely Hindus) with Abraham was precisely an assertion of the primordial nature of the Hindu tradition in the Muslim mind.[23]

That Hinduism should claim to be *the* primordial tradition contradicts the similar claim of *philosophia perennis* and yet this contradiction is resolved by the paradox of its parallel claim to being the primordial tradition and yet tolerant at the same time. This is apparent from the teachings, on this point, of the celebrated exponent of traditional Hinduism in this century, Śrī Candraśekharendra Sarasvatī of Kāñcī:

A religion can be preserved only if those who profess it follow its tenets and practices. The basic, universal religion which still flourishes in India declined and disappeared elsewhere. When people in those places did not practice its teachings, new religions came into existence in all those places to fill up the vacuum due to the efforts of great spiritual leaders like Jesus, Muhammad, and others. The Vedic religion, the *Ācārya* says, has survived in India as a result of the practice of *bhakti* and *dhyāna*—that is, devotion and meditation—which leads to the purification of the mind. Since the basic teachings of all religions are the same, there is no antagonism between one religion and another. The *Ācārya* declares that there is no danger to one religion from another. He says: "If your religion is in danger, it is not because of other religions. On the contrary, it is due to the lack of religious practices on our side. One gets disease when one is weak. Our weakness is the cause of disease."[24]

Such a position is also strengthened by the acceptance of the "relatively absolute." It is high time that our talismanic invocation of this concept made way for its explication.

The concept has been beautifully explained by Professor Nasr through the metaphor of the sun. He writes:

Within our solar system our sun is *the* sun, while seen in the perspective of galactic space, it is one among many suns. The awareness of other suns made possible by means as abnormal to the natural and normal human state as the "existential" awareness of several religious universes, does not make our own sun cease to be *our* sun, the center of *our* solar system, the giver of life to *our* world and the direct symbol of the Divine Intellect for *us* who are revivified by its heat and illuminated by its light.

In the same way, within each religious universe there is the logos, prophet, sacred book, avatāra or some other direct manifestation of the Divinity or messenger of His Word and a particular message which, along with its "human container," whether that be the Arabic language of the Quran or the body of Christ, are "absolute" for the religious universe brought into being by the revelation in question. *Yet only the Absolute is absolute. These manifestations are "relatively absolute."* Within each religious universe the laws revealed, the symbols sanctified, the doctrines hallowed by traditional authorities, the grace which vivifies the religion in question are absolute within the religious world for which they were meant without being absolute as such.[25]

Elsewhere, he uses the solar analogy to throw even more light on the question, when he explains that when the Absolute manifests itself in "a particular religious universe. . . . It is the sun in the planetary system which comprises its religious universe. And yet each sun is in reality a star in a vast firmament in which there are also other stars, which, while being stars in the firmament, do not cease to be suns in their own planetary system."[26]

The same point is made by resorting to a maternal metaphor in Hinduism. Mahatma Gandhi once posed the following question to a parliament of religions, which met in Calcutta in 1937: "Are all religions equal, as we hold, or is any particular religion in sole possession of truth and the rest either untrue or a mixture of truth and error as many believe?" Sir Francis Younghusband is reported to have responded as follows:

> To Mahatma Gandhi's question I would add another question: Are all mothers equally good? All mothers are not equally good, but each would think his own mother as the best in the world. Similarly, each one would regard his own religion as the best in the world.[27]

A Gandhian present at the conference, Kakasaheb Kalelkar invited Sir Francis to realize the full implication of his simile, and said:

> "Indeed every one of us regards his own mother as the best, but does he, therefore, expect or ask others to give up their own mothers and adopt his own?" In other words, just as one's mother is *best for oneself*, so is every one's religion the best, each for himself; just as one's own country is *best for oneself*, every one's religion is best, each for himself. The equality of all religions lies in each being adequate or best for its respective adherents.[28]

Krister Stendahl has used a similar simile in the context of scriptures. He said during the course of a lecture delivered at the Center for the Study of World Religions at Harvard University on February 27, 1992:

> These are our texts. Out of our perspectives we interpret them. When a child is born—I guess women can talk better about this—but I would guess that the child's, the baby's, world does not consist of much more than itself and the mother's breast. That's the whole world and one of the things that happens as we grow up is that it dawns upon us that other children have sucked other breasts. The process of sorting out such facts is called maturation. That's what maturation is.[29]

Although the principle of religious tolerance within Hinduism has been elaborated above with the help of examples drawn from modern Hinduism, the position is not very different in the context of classical Hinduism. There is, first, the general point that it holds good for Indian philosophy in general. William Gerber has formulated the "most persistent currents of Indian philosophy"[30] in eighteen theses. Thesis no. 17 reads as follows:

> (a) The religion of every people and every locality reflects a core of universal religion. (b) Specific religions should therefore not be dogmatic.[31]

As proof he cites the following line of the famous Sanskrit poet and dramatist, Kālidāsa, (usually assigned to the fifth century) regarding the so-called Hindu Trinity of Brahmā, Viṣṇu, and Śiva:

> Of Brahma, Vishnu, Shiva
> each may be
> First, second, third amid the
> blessed Three.[32]

Śaṅkara casts the net even wider, when he quotes the following line from the *Manusmṛti* in his commentary on the *Aitareya Upaniṣad*:

> Some speak of it as Agni, some as Manu, Prajāpati, some as Indra, others as Prāṇa, yet others as the eternal Brahman.[33]

It could be argued that such tolerance is intrareligious rather than interreligious in nature. That is to say, it is confined to within Hinduism. However, not just modern but classical Hinduism also felt it "necessary to extend the logic which holds good between one sect and another within Hinduism to the relation between one religion and another."[34] It is in this spirit that the following statement of the famous text, the *Bhāgavata*, is to be understood:

> Just as one substance with many qualities becomes manifold through the apprehension of the senses working in different ways, even so the one Supreme is conceived in different ways through different scriptural traditions.[35]

And indeed was so understood.

VI. CONCLUSION

These are some of the ways in which, given the isomorphic nature of classical Hinduism and *philosophia perennis et universalis*, the latter may serve to elucidate the former.[36]

ARVIND SHARMA

MCGILL UNIVERSITY
NOVEMBER 1998

NOTES

1. Seyyed Hossein Nasr, *The Need for a Sacred Science* (Albany: State University of New York Press, 1993), p. 64; *Religion and the Order of Nature* (New York: Oxford University Press, 1996), p. 12.

2. R. Balasubramaniam, "Two Contemporary Exemplars of the Hindu Tradition: Ramaṇa Maharṣi and Śri Candraśekharendra Sarasvati," in Krishna Sivaraman, ed., *Hindu Spirituality: Vedas Through Vedānta* (New York: Crossroad, 1989), p. 381.

3. T. M. P. Mahadevan, *Outlines of Hinduism* (Bombay: Chetana Limited, 1971), p. 12.

4. See S. H. Nasr, *The Need for a Sacred Science*, p. 65.

5. George Thibaut, tr., *The Vedānta Sūtras of Bādarāyaṇa with the Commentary of Śaṅkara* (New York: Dover Publications, 1962; first published 1890), pp. 17–18.

6. S. H. Nasr, *The Need for a Sacred Science*, pp. 53–54, emphasis added.

7. Satchidananda Murty, *Revelation and Reason in Advaita Vedānta* (Delhi: Motilal Banarsidass, 1974; first published 1959), p. 44 ff.

8. S. H. Nasr, *The Need for a Sacred Science*, p. 54.

9. Ibid.

10. Ibid.

11. Murty, op. cit., p. 139.

12. Seyyed Hossein Nasr, "Islam," in Arvind Sharma, ed., *Our Religions* (San Francisco: Harper, 1993), pp. 516–18.

13. S. H. Nasr, *The Need for a Sacred Science*, p. 54.

14. Ibid., p. 59.

15. Ṛg-veda 10.90 as cited in A. L. Basham, *The Origins and Development of Classical Hinduism*, ed. Kenneth G. Zysk (Boston: Beacon Press, 1989), p. 25.

16. Ibid., pp. 25–26.

17. S. H. Nasr, *The Need for a Sacred Science*, p. 58.

18. S. Radhakrishnan, ed., *The Principal Upaniṣads* (Atlantic Highlands, N.J.: Humanities Press, 1978; first published 1953) pp. 169–71.

19. Wendy Doniger (with Brian K. Smith), *The Laws of Manu* (Harmondsworth, England: Penguin, 1991), p. 19. The country, "Brahmarṣideśa ('the country of priestly sages') is the area of the Doab ('two waters', that is, the land between the two rivers, Ganges and Yamunā) between Delhi and Mathurā" (ibid., note 19).

20. S. H. Nasr, *The Need for a Sacred Science*, pp. 54–55.

21. See, for example, S. H. Nasr, *The Need for a Sacred Science*, p. 61.

22. R. Balasubramaniam, op. cit., pp. 381–82.

23. Seyyed Hossein Nasr, *Sufi Essays*, 2nd ed. (Albany: State University of New York Press, 1991), p. 139.

24. R. Balasubramaniam, op. cit., pp. 382–83.

25. S. H. Nasr, *The Need for a Sacred Science*, pp. 61–62.

26. S. H. Nasr, *Religion and the Order of Nature*, p. 19.

27. M. K. Gandhi, *Hindu Dharma*, ed. Bharatan Kumarappa. (Ahmedabad: Navajivan Publishing House, 1950), p. 235.

28. Ibid., p. 236.

29. Krister Stendhal, "From God's Perspective We Are All Minorities," *Journal of Religious Pluralism* II (1992): 12.

30. William Gerber, ed., *The Mind of India* (Calcutta: Rupa & Company, 1967), p. xv.

31. Ibid., p. xxiv.

32. Ibid., p. xxv.

33. T. M. P. Mahadevan, op. cit., p. 17.

34. R. Balasubramaniam, op. cit., p. 384.

35. S. Radhakrishnan, *Eastern Religions and Western Thought* (London: Oxford University Press, 1940), p. 319.

36. See S. Radhakrishman, *The Hindu View of Life* (New Delhi: Indus, 1993: first published 1927), p. 34.

REPLY TO ARVIND SHARMA

The essay of Professor Arvind Sharma, at once a scholar of comparative religion and of Hinduism, is itself an important contribution to the field of application of the principles of the perennial philosophy to the formal and academic study of religion. Sharma's approach is in itself an indication of greater interest now being shown by scholars of comparative religion and religious diversity in the perennial philosophy and tradition whose cause I have always championed. While confirming that "some recent movement in this direction [i.e. the perennial philosophy] can be detected," Sharma asserts that this trend "is by no means a tidal wave." I agree with him and would not expect it to be otherwise since the study of religions across religious boundaries possesses a strong theological and philosophical dimension. Moreover, with the prevalent philosophical scene in America dominated mostly by one form or another of logical and linguistic analysis, the appropriate philosophical climate does not exist for greater appreciation of the pertinence of the perennial philosophy to the study of religions and therefore one could not expect anything based on the perennial philosophy to become a tidal wave. This having been said, I believe that the trend mentioned by Sharma is bound to continue and to become strengthened in the future. The very success of Sharma's treatment in this essay is in itself proof of the significance of the perennial philosophy for the study of religion.

As for having dual citizenship in both camps, that is, the academic study of religion and the perennial philosophy, while this may be true in my case, it is not true in the case of Schuon as Sharma claims. From the beginning Schuon based his study of religion on tradition and the perennial philosophy and had little interest in the academic treatment of the subject in either Europe or America except in individual cases where the academic study revealed in an authentic manner aspects of a particular tradition without modern philosophical or ideological distortions.

In applying the perspective of the perennial philosophy to Hinduism, Sharma has decided to concentrate on only a few issues, choosing depth over range. I think that in a short essay this certainly was a wise decision, but it is necessary to add that outside of the three dimensions of Hinduism chosen by Sharma, there are many other realities within Hinduism including cosmology, the laws of the flow of time, eschatology, religious symbolism, traditional psychology, or, as A.K. Coomaraswamy called it, *pneumatology*, and pure metaphysics itself which could be elucidated and clarified in an unparalleled manner with the help of the light of the perennial philosophy, in a manner at once authentic and profound which one could not achieve otherwise. Already the considerable works of the masters of traditional doctrines, R. Guénon, A. K. Coomaraswamy, and F. Schuon, as well as the writings of more academically inclined scholars inspired in one way or another by them, such as H. Zimmer, M. Eliade, A. Daniélou, S. Kramrich, and within the Hindu world itself A. K. Saran, have provided a considerable body of literature which explains Hinduism in the light of tradition and the perennial philosophy. The essay of Sharma not only confirms these earlier studies but also points out the extensive field that remains to be investigated in such a manner so as to bring out the deepest meaning of various facets of Hinduism in a way that would be comprehensible to the Western academic world. And at the same time, and most importantly, the investigation should be acceptable to the living traditional authorities within Hinduism as authentic representations.

In speaking of the Vedic revelation, Sharma quotes from Śaṅkara's *Brahmasūtra* and compares this quotation with one by me dealing with the *philosophia perennis* in its relation to particular traditions at whose heart lies the knowledge identified as the perennial philosophy by traditionalist thinkers such as I. After pointing to the striking similarity between the two passages, Sharma adds that this similarity exists, "despite the fact that Professor Nasr is dealing with *philosophia perennis et universalis* in general and Śaṅkara only with one tradition in particular, namely, the Vedic or Hindu." The reason for this similarity is that although Śaṅkara was dealing with only one tradition, he was dealing with the dimension of the perennial philosophy within that tradition, even though he did not use such a term. He was dealing with principles which he did not apply to more than one tradition, but he could have done so if necessary as one finds in the case of Suhrawardī within the Islamic tradition. Suhrawardī spoke of both sapiental principles, which he did in fact associate specifically with the perennial philosophy (*al-ḥikmat al-khālidah/jāwīdān khirad)*, and the application of the principles of that philosophy to more than one tradition. The application, however, belongs to the domain of contingency. What is essential is the set of principles. That is why whether one applies the principles to only one tradition as is the case with Śaṅkara or to several as one sees in Suhrawardī, the *problematique*, to use Sharma's term, and its resolution present stark similarities when one compares the minds of traditional masters of wisdom with those of the contemporary exponents of tradition and the perennial philosophy.

In discussing Śaṅkara Professor Sharma turns to the role of scripture within tradition and uses the term "fundamentalism" in this context. While I understand why he uses this term, seeing that it was originally associated with Protestants who hold fast to the literal interpretation of the Bible, I am much more careful in the usage of this term which has gained many unfortunate connotations during the past few decades. But even if one were to put those associations aside and go back to the earlier meaning of the term, I would not associate the term "fundamentalism" with figures such as Śaṅkara who provide an esoteric and not only literal and exoteric commentary upon sacred scripture to which they are of course as firmly devoted as the literalists. This point might be considered as nothing more than semantics, but in the present situation in which so much confusion is being caused by the usage of such terms as "Hindu fundamentalism" and "Islamic fundamentalism" I prefer a more nuanced usage of this oft maligned term.

I concur with Sharma when he seeks to distinguish between holding and clinging and in trying to understand what we mean exactly by "relative" and "relativisim" when we study religion across boundaries of various religious universes. He comes back to the central significance of the concept of "relatively absolute" which I have used often but which owes its origin to the writings of F. Schuon. I also agree fully with Sharma in his understanding of the distinction made by me between traditionalism and fundamentalism and how this distinction can be applied *mutatis mutandis* to Hinduism. I want to make clear, however, that the usage of "universal religion" in relation to the perennial philosophy must be considered very carefully. The *philosophia perennis*, or even what Schuon called the *religio perennis*, is not a religion alongside other religions except that it is of an esoteric character. Rather, it is an eternal and universal truth which lies at the heart and is identified with the inner dimensions of the orthodox and traditional religions which have governed the life of humanity over the ages. There is no possibility of access to what Sharma calls "universal religion" identified with the perennial philosophy save through attachment to and following of one of the orthodox traditions. If there are any exceptions they are there to prove the rule. I have written about this crucial question often but need to repeat it here precisely because it can give rise to the most dangerous kinds of misunderstanding.

The resuscitation of hierarchy, the comprehension of its profound significance for the understanding of the nature of reality and its rekindling awareness of manifestations in so many domains of the traditional universe are among the basic goals of the perennial philosophy, although hierarchy is not present in a cosmological sense in all traditions, there being some exceptions as one sees in Theravāda Buddhism to which I have alluded in my response to Sallie King's essay in this volume. One of the most misunderstood and maligned aspects of traditional societies, especially that of Hinduism, is the stratification of society according to metaphysical principles which is identified with the *varṇa* or caste system in India. Professor Sharma's treatment of this subject in light of the perennial philosophy reveals how the understanding of the metaphysical principles in question, as expounded by the perennial philosophy, can cast new light on the subject and remove the cloud of misunderstanding that has covered the treatment of the caste system by Western scholars since the nineteenth century. We have in mind here the miscomprehension of the principles involved and not the understandable criticism of certain social imperfections and injustices that are themselves, according to Hindu doctrine, the consequences of the confusion between castes, which means basic human types, and their social function at this juncture of the Dark Age or Kali Yuga. Sharma's application of the teachings of the perennial philosophy concerning hierarchy to the *varṇa* system by considering two types of hierarchy, one a *step hierarchy* and the other a *circular hierarchy* is particularly ingenious and I concur fully with it.

Turning to the questions of Hindu tolerance, Sharma distinguishes between *missionary* activity and *proselytizing* activity and calls Hinduism a missionary religion but not a proselytizing one. If one accepts this distinction, then one can say, on the basis of the evidence provided by Sharma, especially the quotation from the *Manusmṛti,* that missionary activity means not propagating necessarily one's own religion, but propagating universal orthodoxy, or religious truth as such. Needless to say, this perspective is also that of the traditional expositors of the perennial philosophy. Like me, they do not proselytize a particular religion but have as their mission the defense and propagation of tradition and orthodoxy in whatever form it might be found, although they never refer to themselves as missionary. The reason for such as refusal is obvious considering the field of meaning associated with the term "missionary." But putting semantics aside, there is no doubt that the propagation of universal orthodoxy in traditional Hinduism, as expounded by Sharma, is in conformity with the perspective of the perennial philosophy. But it must be added that such is not the case with neo-Vedantic modernism which at the end of the nineteenth century began to adopt methods of Christian missionaries to propagate a modernistic version of Hinduism, de-emphasizing the caste system and many other aspects of traditional Hinduism which were not in accord with the fashions of the day and modernism and might be criticized by the Western converts who were being sought by the neo-Vedantic organizations in question.

Finally, I concur fully with Sharma concerning the application of universality within Hinduism to other religions, or going from the intrareligious to the interreligious. In other times there did not exist the same necessity as one faces today to confront directly the reality of other religions, although there were exceptions including the meeting of Hinduism and Islam in India. But today in Hinduism as in Islam, or Christianity or any other living religion, there is the necessity to apply existing principles within the tradition to the present situation where the reality of other religions must be faced fully and honestly. One might say that to the quotation given by Sharma from Śaṅkara's commentary upon Aitareya Upaniṣad about the name of the Ultimate Principle being sometimes Agni, sometimes Manu, sometimes Prajāpati or eternal Brāhman, one must now also add the Names by which the Divine is known in other religions such as "I Am that I Am," Yhwh, Deus, Allah, Tao, Tai Ch'i, or even *Śunyatā* and *Dharmakāya.*

Professor Sharma's essay is an important contribution to the study of a particular religion in light of the universal principles of the perennial philosophy. His treatment of the subjects chosen within Hinduism, in which he is both an authority and a believer, reveals in every case how pertinent the teachings of the perennial philosophy can be for the deeper understanding of the subject at hand. But most of all it is in his treatment of the question of religious tolerance and the acceptance of religious pluralism that he reveals the unique contribution that traditional doctrines can make to the understanding of religions other than one's own in such a way as to remain faithful to the subject at hand, to guard orthodoxy as well as universality, and to be able to study religion in depth and with intellectual rigour without destroying the religious nature of what one has set out to study.

S. H. N.

6

Shu-hsien Liu

REFLECTIONS ON TRADITION AND MODERNITY: A RESPONSE TO SEYYED HOSSEIN NASR FROM A NEO-CONFUCIAN PERSPECTIVE

First I must confess my lack of knowledge of the Muslim tradition as well as of Dr. Nasr's works. My response to him is based on my limited understanding of his ideas set forth in his Gifford Lectures[1] and a collection of essays on the world's religious traditions in honor of Wilfrid Cantwell Smith edited by my friend Frank Whaling which included Nasr's article on "The *Philosophia Perennis* and the Study of Religion" and other useful materials.[2] However, as there are many significant similarities and differences among the great religious traditions in the world, I feel that I can understand the messages he takes pains to spread and am ready to raise questions about his thoughts. And I would like to be as frank as possible. I shall first discuss problems concerning tradition and then raise questions concerning issues of modernity and modernization.

Reflections on Tradition

When I first went through Dr. Nasr's Gifford Lectures I could not but be struck by his profound understanding of the sacred character and the sapiental dimension of knowledge which according to him has been realized in the world's religious traditions East and West since ancient times. This is rare among our contemporaries, even though he freely admitted that he has been indebted to scholars such as Guénon, Coomaraswamy, and especially Schuon. Nasr also reminds me of the erudition and the passion for spiritual ideals that my teacher, the late professor Thomé H. Fang, who made penetrating critiques of modern civilization and urged us to revive the wisdom of Confucius, Plato, and the *Upaniṣads*, formed about the ancient era, even though Fang did not belong to any religious tradition. He would have heartily endorsed Nasr's observation in the opening passage of *Knowledge and the Sacred* that "In the beginning Reality was at once being, knowledge, and bliss,"[3] and it was only at a later stage that

> Knowledge has become separated from being and the bliss or ecstasy which characterizes the union of knowledge and being. Knowledge has become nearly completely externalized and desacralized, especially among those segments of the human race which have become transformed by the process of modernization, and that bliss which is the fruit of union with the One and an aspect of the perfume of the sacred has become well-nigh unattainable and beyond the grasp of the vast majority of those who walk upon the earth.[4]

In these statements Nasr has provided us the guiding principles he has followed to work out a comprehensive picture of the process of the fall of man in the modern West up to the present time. He sees a chance to reverse the trend by following the lead of the East where somehow the ancient traditions are still kept intact and not totally destroyed by the onslaught of modern civilization. For our purposes there is certainly no need to go into all the details of how Nasr has tried to substantiate his claims; it will suffice to spell out some of his presuppositions, to paint a broad picture of how he sees the development of human civilization, then to raise questions and criticisms about his thought.

First, Dr. Nasr defines tradition in a rather narrow way. For him, the rediscovery of the very heart and essence of tradition is constituted by the reassertion of the Truth, and the "formulation of the traditional point of view was a response of the Sacred, which is both the alpha and the omega of human existence, to the elegy of doom of modern man lost in a world depleted of the sacred and therefore, of meaning."[5] In other words, only the so-called Pontifical man is seen as the traditional man who "lives in a world which has both an Origin and a Center."[6] In contrast, Promethean man is a creature of this world who has rebelled against Heaven. "Such a man envisages life as a big marketplace in which he is free to roam around and choose objects at will. Having lost the sense of the sacred, he is drowned in transience and impermanence and becomes a slave of his own lower nature, surrender to which he considers to be freedom."[7] Under such an interpretation Promethean man can only be seen as the "anti-tradition" man. But such a dualistic structure appears to be much too simple to handle the complexity of various traditions in the world. As a matter of fact most of us would use the term tradition in a rather loose sense; for example, in philosophy I do not see why there cannot be a skeptical, humanistic tradition starting from

Protagoras, Gorgias, through the Middle Academy to Pyrrho, Aenesidemus, Sextus Empiricus, and if you will, one can go on to enlist Montaigne, Bayle, and Hume among others. As new traditions keep emerging, I do not see why we cannot talk about the traditions of Continental Rationalism, British Empiricism, German Idealism, and so on, even though we cannot find precedents in the past. Anyhow, Nasr has used the term "tradition" in a very restricted and specific sense, as he says,

> Tradition as used in its technical sense in this work as in all our other writings, means truths or principles of a divine origin revealed or unveiled to mankind and, in fact, a whole cosmic sector through various figures envisaged as messengers, prophets, *avatāras*, the Logos or other transmitting agencies, along with all the ramifications and applications of these principles in different realms including law and social structure, art, symbolism, the sciences, and embracing of course Supreme Knowledge along with the means for its attainment.[8]

Thus for him, tradition is closely related to religion, but is more than just religion.

Second, Dr. Nasr believes strongly that even though terms used in different religions are different, they point to something similar, as he says,

> There are such fundamental terms as the Hindu and Buddhist *dharma*, the Islamic *al-din*, the Taoist *Tao*, and the like which are inextricably related to the meaning of the term *tradition*, but not identical with it, although of course the worlds or civilizations created by Hinduism, Buddhism, Taoism, Judaism, Christianity, Islam, or for that matter any other authentic religion, is [sic] a traditional world. Each of these religions is also the heart or origin of the tradition which extends the principles of the religion to different domains.[9]

And he also believes that tradition is "a living presence which leaves its imprint but is not reducible to that imprint."[10] It appears that Nasr has not shown any hesitation to recognize that the sapiental dimension has been present in all the authentic religions in the world. I do appreciate his open attitude and also his insistence on the realization of the close ties between knowledge and the sacred. However, the kind of knowledge he refers to is very different from what we understand as knowledge today. Indeed I find that he has used many terms in a way quite different from our common usage of these terms. For example, he says, "Intelligence, which is the instrument of knowledge within man, is endowed with the possibility of knowing the Absolute. It is like a ray which emanates from and returns to the Absolute and its miraculous functioning is itself the best proof of that Reality which is at once absolute and infinite."[11] The term "intelligence" as understood by most of us today would certainly have nothing to do with "the possibility of knowing the Absolute." Intelligence means merely a kind of mental ability some believe can be measured by I.Q. tests. Dewey takes it to be a problem-solving ability which can be employed to balance impulse on the one hand and routine on the other hand.[12] We would have to admit that empirical knowledge and the sapiental dimension of knowledge are on two different levels. Emanation was the favorite metaphor used by Plotinus who presupposed the existence of the Absolute or Reality which is absolute and infinite. In the desacralized world today, however, there cannot be such a presupposition, hence the proof actually proves nothing as it is a perfect example of circular reasoning. Nasr has repeatedly used the term "proof" in such a loose sense in his writings, as he says:

> Consciousness is itself proof of the primacy of the Spirit or Divine Consciousness of which human consciousness is a reflection and echo. . . . Human consciousness or subjectivity which makes knowledge possible is itself proof that Spirit is the Substance compared to which all material manifestation, even what appears as the most substantial, is but an accident. It is in the nature and destiny of man to know and ultimately to know the absolute and the Infinite through an intelligence which is total and objective and which is inseparable from the Sacred that is at once its origin and end.[13]

Obviously such a proof proves nothing for those who do not share Nasr's view. And the only thing proved by such writings is that Nasr still lives in a world of ideas which can only be shared by those who are familiar with Greek and medieval philosophy. I am afraid it is impossible to reach a wider audience by writing in such a style full of traditional terminology.

But such terminology is questionable even for those who are sympathetic to the general thrust of Nasr's thought. Nasr makes a sharp distinction between intellect (*intellectus*) and reason (*ratio*).[14] It appears that he has retained the use of the term "intellect" in the Neo-Platonic sense, while reducing "reason" to a purely human and this-worldly instrument as developed in modern Western philosophy. "Intellect" for most of us today, however, refers only to the intellectual activities of the mind which do not have anything to do with the sapiental dimension of knowledge. Thus I myself would prefer to use "depth of reason," a term coined by Paul Tillich.[15] Naturally Nasr certainly has the right to keep using the terminology of his choice; I only want to point out that it is very difficult to restore the sacred character of the intellect as intended by Nasr.

A much more serious problem is that, by using the kind of terminology Nasr has adopted, it seems that some philosophical ideas behind such terminology are wrongly presumed to be universally applicable to all the authentic religions in the world. Granted that there is the sapiental dimension in all these traditions, which may be interpreted as the manifestations of the same tradition, we must not gloss over the differences among such manifestations. Even though in principle Nasr would certainly agree that significant differences should not be overlooked, still I must point out that one serious shortcoming of his Gifford Lectures lies precisely in that they only stress the universality of the sapiental dimension and neglect to discuss the differences, even conflicts, among these traditions. For example, the Chinese traditions, Taoist or Confucian, would never approve that there is the Eternal Being beyond change, a Greek idea totally alien to the Chinese culture; again, in contrast to the Abrahamic traditions, transcendence for the Chinese could only mean a kind of immanent transcendence which is quite different from the kind of pure transcendence as envisaged in Christianity; and there is no need of a mediator such as Christ or Muḥammad for communication between Heaven and men.[16] Such differences could prove to be significant, as I cannot find a single reference to process theology in Nasr's Gifford Lectures, which seems to imply his disapproval of the trend, while Neo-Confucian scholars may find a certain affinity with the approach.[17]

Third, Dr. Nasr urges us to go back to tradition for the recovery of the sacred, and he portrays the modern era as a falling off from our origin. As a student of philosophy of culture, I see culture not as a finished product but rather forever in the making.[18] Apparently Nasr has not paid enough attention to the developmental view of culture. He just gives us a strong contrast between what is traditional and what is modern, and urges us to revive our tradition. But how far back should we go? Nasr does not seem to worry about the problem at all as he seems to assume that we would go naturally back to the great traditions such as Buddhism, Confucianism, and Greek Philosophy formed in the so-called pivotal age as noticed by Jaspers.[19] But if we go still further, then we would have a problem on our hands. There may not be any problems to go back from the Upaniṣads to the Vedas, but there could be serious problems to go back from Greek philosophy to Greek mythology. In the *Iliad* and the *Odyssey*, the world of man was portrayed as totally dominated by gods. Is that world necessarily better than the world developed in Greek philosophy later on? Heroes like Achilles had a rather dim moral consciousness; that is precisely why Socrates criticized that world as being operated according to the principle that might is right. Skepticism about the tradition in the thought of Xenophanes, Protagoras, and Socrates is not necessarily a bad thing. If we had to uphold all our traditions, we would still have to live in truly dark ages.

In general, Dr. Nasr discredits the evolutionary theory. Indeed there has never been sufficient evidence to prove that one species can evolve into another one since Darwin advanced his thesis. But the evolution of ideas is a different matter. Cassirer traces the development of language and myth, and gives us a picture of the phenomenology of knowledge.[20] There is no need to presuppose a linear progressive view of history, but his study of the evolution of ideas points out a direction from the concept of substance toward the concept of function. Nasr does not seem to leave any room for evolution in any sense. He only cares to lead us to where we can find the lights of tradition; this approach shows both his strengths and his weaknesses. He gives us a sketch of the history of philosophy very different from the one we are used to. I have gained many insights from the picture he offers us. For example, he points out that in the Greek tradition there is unmistakably the sapiental dimension in the Pythagorean-Platonic school and that we must not talk about the so-called "Neo-Platonic" in a derogatory sense. He flatly denies that there is a dichotomy between the so-called Greek "intellectualism" and Hebrew "inspirationalism." In the Christian tradition he traces the spiritual current in Christian spirituality from St. Paul through Clement, Origen, St. Augustine, Dionysius the Areopagite, Scotus Erigena to the syntheses of St. Bonaventure, St. Thomas, and Duns Scotus. But he criticizes Aquinas for becoming overrationalistic in imprisoning intuitions of a metaphysical order in syllogistic categories which hide, more than reveal, their (properly speaking) "intellectual" rather than rational character. He highly praised Dante's *Divine Comedy*. And apart from Meister Eckhart, Nicholas of Cusa, and Jakob Böhme, he also called our attention to the so-called school of Cambridge Platonists. Then he blamed the spread of Aristotelianism and Averroism in the West on St. Thomas who denied the possibility of the illumination by the intellect and considered all knowledge as having a sensuous origin. Such views inadvertently played a role in the desacralization of knowledge. It was unfortunate that Thomas's realism led to the nominalism that marked the swan song of medieval Christianity and destroyed the harmony which had been established between reason and faith in a world dominated by the sacred.

Nasr's critique of modern European philosophy has also presented a very interesting perspective. He pointed out that Descartes's individual was not referring to *Ātman* or the divine *I*, but rather the "illusory" self, which was placing its experience and consciousness of thinking as the foundation of all epistemology and ontology and the source of certitude. After the Humean doubt, Kant taught an agnosticism which in a characteristically subjective fashion denied to the intellect the possibility of knowing the essence of things. This situation further deteriorated into the Hegelian and Marxist dialectics, as they denied that there is anything immutable behind the appearance, and this loss of the sense of permanence was characteristic of mainstream thought of modern Western philosophy. In the analytic philosophy and irrational philosophies that followed, the sacred quality of knowledge was completely destroyed.

Nasr's picture shows the depth of his understanding of the sapiental tradition. But his views are not without their problems. It is one thing to say that there is the sapiental dimension in Greek philosophy, and I would not hesitate to endorse Nasr's insightful interpretation of that tradition. But to say that there are no substantial differences between the Greek and Hebrew understanding of the sapiental dimension is a totally different matter. Charles Hartshorne finds it unacceptable to interpret the Biblical God as Eternal Being, as the God in the Judeo-Christian tradition is a god of sympathy, definitely not the Unmoved Mover as contemplated by Aristotle.[21] There is no need for me to endorse Hartshorne's process theology, but Aristotle's problems are certainly not limited to his overrationalistic categories, as specified by Nasr, but rather that his idea of God as Unmoved Mover was too intellectualistic to be understood the same as the Biblical God worshiped by millions of people to satisfy their emotional demands. Despite Nasr's criticisms of Aristotle, he seems to have inherited a bit too much of the thought and terminology of the Aristotelian-Thomistic school to identify God as Eternal Being in a metaphysics of substance which must face increasingly serious challenges for good reasons.

Fourth, with his deep understanding of the Islamic tradition, he has pointed out that the Latin Averroes was not only more rationalistic than Ibn Sīnā (Avicenna), who put emphasis on illumination of the mind by the angel, but was more of a secularized and rationalistic philosopher than the original Ibn Rushd when read in Arabic. As Latin Averroism enjoyed much greater popularity and influence over Latin Avicennism in the West, the Christian world was moving toward a more rationalistic interpretation of the philosophic school, while the Islamic world was moving in the other direction to reaffirm the primacy of intellection over ratiocination. This Avicennian philosophy served as the basis for the restatement of the sacramental function of knowledge and intellection by Suhrawardī and the school of illumination (*al-ishrāq*) which testified to a new assertion of the sacred quality of knowledge and the ultimately "illuminative" character of all knowledge in the Islamic intellectual universe.

Dr. Nasr claims that at the moment the process of secularization seemed to be reaching its logical conclusion in removing the presence of the sacred altogether from all aspects of human life and thought, as Nietzsche declared that God is dead, some contemporary men strove to rediscover the sacred. Great poets such as Goethe, Blake, and Emerson sought to return to a more holistic view of man and nature against the mechanistic and rationalistic conceptions of the world and man represented by Bacon, Newton, and Locke. But they could hardly bring tradition back to the soil of the West in a total and complete way or revive the *scientia sacra* which lies at the heart of all tradition. The sapiental dimension had become too weakened in the West to enable tradition to be revived during this century without authentic contact with the Oriental traditions which had preserved their inner teachings intact in both their doctrinal and operative aspects. It remained for the Orient itself to bring about the revival of tradition in the West through the men and words of those who lived in Europe or wrote in Western languages, men who had been transformed intellectually and existentially by the traditional worldview. Nasr enlisted as allies scholars such as René Guénon, Ananda K. Coomaraswamy, and Frithjof Schuon. But even he admitted that they have been neglected in academic circles and have only very limited influence. And I wonder if he has been guilty of putting too much weight on the Oriental traditions for reasons to be specified in the following section.

REFLECTIONS ON MODERNITY AND MODERNIZATION

As I greatly admire Dr. Nasr's profound understanding of the meaning of tradition, I am struck by his nearly total lack of reflection of the meaning of modernity and modernization. His "prejudice" against "the modern world" is clearly shown in the following quotation:

> One could say that the traditional worlds were essentially good and accidentally evil, and the modern world essentially evil and accidentally good. Tradition is therefore opposed in principle to modernism. It wishes to slay the modern world in order to create a normal one. Its goal is not to destroy what is positive but to remove the veil of ignorance which allows the illusory to appear as real, the negative as positive and the false as true. . . . From this point of view the history of Western man during the past five centuries is an anomaly in the long history of the human race in both East and West. In opposing modernism in principle and in a categorical manner, those who follow the traditional view wish only to enable Western man to join the rest of the human race.[22]

I just wonder if such a statement is an anomaly in itself! How many people today would rather slay the modern world in order to go back to medieval ages? And how many scholars, even with their sympathetic understanding of tradition, would accept the kind of dualism between the traditional and the modern, East and West, underlying such a statement. We must not idealize the past just as we must not be dazzled by the so-called modern achievements. Even though I cannot go along with Hegel in declaring that what is real is rational, I tend to believe that there are reasons for what actually happened. It is no accident that the modern world emerged in the West since the Renaissance, and this historical event has implications certainly not limited to the West but rather important for mankind. There is no question about the portrayal of the modern West as characterized by desacralization. What is at stake is its evaluation. Although Nasr pays lip service in saying that the revival of tradition is not intending to destroy what is positive in the modern world, yet he never tells us anything about these positive achievements in his Gifford Lectures. I think this is one of the serious shortcomings of the Lectures, and practically all my questions are raised along these lines. The May Fourth Cultural Movement in 1919 in China identified science and democracy as the positive achievements of the modern West. Contemporary Neo-Confucian philosophers see great limitations in modern Western civilization and reject the approach of wholesale Westernization; they want to balance tradition with modernity, but they clearly see the process of modernization as something necessary to inject new life and vitality into our traditional culture in order to overcome its shortcomings with a view to look toward the future.

First, let us start by reflecting on science and its place in the world of knowledge. It is no secret that modern science used a quantitative model to develop a mathematical physics, a model which presupposed a mechanistic worldview and demonstrated that knowledge is power. It is owing to modern science that the West is enabled to outshine the other civilizations; there is no way not to acknowledge the scientific achievements of the West. In *Science and the Modern World* Whitehead traced the roots of modern science to Greek and medieval origins.[23] Ironically, however, the further development of science exposed its limitations. To make a long story short, Whitehead criticized modern science for committing what he called "the fallacy of misplaced concreteness,"[24] which erroneously takes what is abstract to be what is concrete. For Whitehead the new worldview would be an organic one. Whether his own formulation of the worldview is a successful one is a different matter. At least he has pointed out a direction for the future. His view is in some ways echoed by Joseph Needham whose monumental work, *Science and Civilisation in China*, showed that, owing to the lack of the mechanistic view, the Chinese missed the breakthrough since the Renaissance which helped the West to surpass the level of scientific achievements in China; and Needham was also of the opinion that the mechanistic model had had its day and the organic model developed in China in the twelfth century by Chu Hsi would be revived in the future.[25] These claims still need to be substantiated. But both Whitehead and Needham take science to be something for humankind to which different civilizations have made significant contributions. Therefore the problem is not to opt for East or West, and we must not confuse the problem of science with that of scientism. What is wrong is not science, which is the product of abstraction, but rather to take the abstractions as concrete existents, and such an erroneous approach is not only philosophically wrong but limits the further development of science. There is indeed progress in science; there are no convincing reasons to go back to ancient or medieval ages. Romantic nostalgia for the past would not solve our problems. New sciences such as ecology take seriously the quality of life. It takes science to overcome science. Such a line of thought is regrettably missing in Nasr's critique of modern science. I sincerely believe there are good reasons to treat empirical knowledge as knowledge proper, as it is the only branch of knowledge with content that can establish a universal confirmation procedure accepted by all, while the sapiental dimension of knowledge would have to depend on personal realization even if in principle it is open to everybody. And empirical knowledge certainly enjoys its autonomy without any need of a theological foundation. The only thing wrong with the modern approach is that empirical knowledge is taken as the only possible form of knowledge, and faith is relegated to something purely subjective to satisfy individual emotional needs. Consequently the sapiental dimension is totally banished and forgotten. Nasr has every justification to revive this dimension, but he is wrong to urge us to return to the medieval ages.

Second, the modern world has created a new social order which is condemned by Dr. Nasr as essentially evil. I do not think his position can be supported. I would admit that modern society and the practice of democracy have indeed created a lot of problems, but I do not believe that most people are living a worse life at the present time than in the medieval ages. True, there was a much more stable order then, but a high price had to be paid. For example, there were slaves in those days who enjoyed practically no human rights, and women's position in society was low. The practice of the so-called theonomy produced a number of tyrants who claimed to have received the mandate of Heaven. There has to be a mechanism to check the power of the rulers. And I am also convinced that the separation of the church and the state is necessary. Traditional Chinese intellectuals all believed in the ideal of sage-kings. However, this is an ideal which has never been realized in real life. Confucius was the last person who was honored as a sage, but he was never given a chance to rule a kingdom. Despotism was the rule since the Ming dynasty. This is why contemporary Neo-Confucian philosophers, though upholding the spiritual ideals of Confucianism, nevertheless endorse Western democracy as a better political system, as they realize that the ideal of a government of humanity cannot be actualized within the monarchy system practiced over two thousand years in the dynasty days. It does not pay to treat politics as an extension of ethics. Upon deep reflection the Neo-Confucian thinkers give up the traditional straightforward approach which sees outward kingliness as an extension of inward sageliness; they instead adopt the roundabout approach by endorsing the democratic system since it offers a better hope for a government of humanity that works in real life.[26] Naturally new problems will keep emerging in modern society, which is still far from a just society, but some of the injustices we find in the traditional society are avoided. But Nasr seems to prefer any traditional social order to the modern one as he says,

> tradition determines the structure of society applying immutable principles to the social order, resulting in structures outwardly as different as the Hindu caste system and the Islamic "democracy of married monks," as some have characterized theocratic Islamic society, in which there is nevertheless an equality before God and the Divine Law, but of course not in the quantitative modern sense.[27]

Frankly, I do not see anything immutable that can apply to the social structure in this world. I do not condemn the traditional order, as most societies pass through the stage of a hierarchical order no matter whether they are in the East or in the West. But I do not see any intrinsic reasons for some to be kings, others to be subjects or even slaves. The contemporary Neo-Confucian thinkers believe that only what is transcendent does not change and that nothing else is immune to change. When conditions differ, social structures also transform. Furthermore, for one who lives in modern society, equality only before God is not enough. Human rights for every person must be honored. Our humility is before God or Heaven, not before kings or church authorities who are humans, and, like us, are capable of abusing powers. Nasr's defense of the traditional hierarchical order leaves much to be desired.

Third, as Nasr pitches East against West, tradition against modernity, he falls victim to a dualistic structure which, ironically enough, is shared by an atheist like Sartre. We must seriously ask the question whether there could be a third alternative besides either traditional theonomy or modern atheism. I am not happy with Nasr as he fails to appreciate the fact that culture is forever in the making and henceforth refuses to move along with time. I am also not happy with Sartre as he believes that the rift between God and humans is so total that the transcendent message would no longer play a meaningful part in our lives. Both approaches are too one-sided to be convincing to us. As a matter of fact, some contemporary thinkers do not feel that the trend of secularization is necessarily in contradiction to one's religious faith. One striking example was Dietrich Bonhoeffer who demonstrated a deep faith in God in an existential sense as he died in a Nazi prison during the Second World War.[28] He coined the phrase, "man comes of age," by which he meant that man has become adult in the sense that he refuses to fall prey to any religion that tries to make him dependent upon things on which he is, in fact, no longer dependent. Paradoxically, it is God's will, revealed in Jesus, that has forced man to recognize the dedivinization of the world and its gods and that has called man to an acceptance of his free and autonomous responsibility for the world. There can be no more division of the world into two spheres, one sacred and the other secular. In fact the sacred and the secular have never been sharply distinguished from one another in the Chinese tradition. Without neglecting the message of the transcendent, the Confucian philosophers are convinced that Heaven and man can be in perfect union, and man has occupied a pivotal position in the universe, as Confucius pointed out that it is man who can make the Way great, and not the Way that can make man great.[29]

Nasr seems to assume that there is divine intervention in the cosmic and historical process,[30] but such an assumption cannot be substantiated by science. At most it can only be regarded as an item of faith popular in bygone ages but barely surviving among intellectuals at the present time. Once the dualistic structure is abandoned, the so-called desacralization may not be all bad as Nasr has intimated. As human civilizations develop, not only is it impossible for us to resist the changes, but some changes are change for the better, not for the worse. There is the urgent need of desacralization of knowledge in the realm of empirical science where the quest for certainty is no longer our goal.[31] And there is also the need to establish a constitutional democratic government which is based on the principle of the separation between the Church and the state. In fact the guiding principle was provided by none other than Jesus himself as he clearly declared that we should return Caesar's to Caesar. Different levels of knowledge need to be differentiated. The sapiental dimension of knowledge must not be confused with either formal sciences like mathematics or empirical sciences like physics. The only thing needed is the reassertion of the sapiental dimension of knowledge in relation to religious faith which must not be allowed to degenerate into a fideism that turns away the truth-seekers. But each level of knowledge must be allowed to maintain its autonomy without outside interference. And we do need to search for modern expressions for *philosophia perennis*, and look for a balance between tradition and modernity, as Confucius urged us to review the past in order to look forward to the future.[32]

Fourth, Dr. Geoffrey Parrinder has criticized Dr. Nasr's Gifford Lectures by pointing out that his idea of sapience was not clear, his interpretation of Islam was dominated by Sufism which derived its monistic and pantheistic elements from Hinduism, especially the non-dualist Śaṅkara, and that in his approach, comparison became competition, now of East against West, reversing previous trends.[33] As such criticisms come from a leading scholar in comparative religion, they do carry a certain weight and should deserve our further attention. There is little doubt that Nasr understands tradition from a rather special perspective. Not all scholars would subscribe to his presuppositions. On the surface level there are problems concerning scholarship. For example, Nasr has stressed that there is the sapiental dimension in what he calls the Abrahamic traditions. But he has never once addressed the question of whether the main stream of Judaeo-Christian tradition was a covenant religion for which we cannot find a parallel in Greek culture; mysticism was at best a side stream. I do not have enough knowledge to discuss the Islamic tradition, but I suppose Parrinder has touched upon a real problem as he sees the tension when non-dualist Hinduism is employed to interpret the Muḥammadan tradition of monotheism. There are also philosophical problems. Parrinder has pointed out that in his Gifford Lectures the famous historian of philosophy Frederick Copleston made the observation that mysterious experiences can be found among different civilizations, but he himself as a Jesuit philosopher did not have such an experience and they are not enough to prove the existence of a transcendent reality, the One.[34] Parrinder much preferred Copleston's guarded attitude to Nasr's romantic mysticism. This does not mean that Nasr is necessarily wrong; only he has not been able to provide any convincing arguments for the existence of the transcendent Reality or Truth which, as he sees it, is beyond even the scope of ontology. This is why I think when he keeps using words like "proof" in a rather loose sense, he would not win the approval of even those who have sympathy for searching for another level of reality beyond the mundane world today.

Of course, we can always argue that the above criticisms are merely external criticisms, while Nasr has explicitly said that the esoteric approach is preferable. But then Nasr has no choice but to concede that the sapiental dimension of knowledge cannot be confirmed by a procedure accepted by all. In other words, only those who can enter into the same hermeneutical circle would be able to carry on meaningful discourse with Nasr. And I would like to push one step further and argue that internal criticisms are also possible for those who share with Nasr the belief that there is one transcendent Reality but manifestations are different. The contemporary Neo-Confucian thinkers believe in the urgent need to give new interpretations to the dictum: *li-i-fen-shu* (One principle, many manifestations) first formulated in the Sung dynasty. This explains why on the one hand I find a sense of affinity with Nasr's approach, and yet on the other hand I also find that his approach has not been able to work out fully the implications of the traditional insight and look for contemporary expressions of the One Principle that has found manifestations in different civilizations throughout the ages. I would not worry much about the idea of sapience being unclear, as this is an area in which univocal expressions do not apply. Over two thousand years ago the very first chapter of *Tao-te-ching* declared that "The Tao (the Way) that can be told of is not the eternal Tao."[35] And such thought has been shared by all the great religious traditions in the world. But we do find similarities in expressions in the so-called holy books, so that it is not unreasonable to believe that they are pointing to One Truth. Nasr's faith is neither unique nor original, and is clearly based on the testimonies of the great masters both from the East and from the West. In China Lu Hsiang-shan (1139–1193) showed the same strong faith as Nasr when he declared that mind and principle are one regardless of East and West, ancient and modern.[36] But when we try to look for a substantial unity of the traditions we are bound to fail. Therefore we must give up the hope of searching for such a unity and accept the differences of the great religious traditions. The abandonment of absolutism, however, does not mean that we have to succumb to the other extreme: relativism. There is still room for meaningful interreligious dialogue and the search for certain common ground acceptable to all. In order to achieve such a purpose new strategies must be employed.

In 1989 I participated in the Symposium on World Religions and Human Rights held in Paris under the sponsorship of UNESCO organized by Hans Küng who presented a positional paper: "Kein Weltfriede ohne Religions-friede" (No World Peace without Peace among Religions); and scholars were asked to give their response to his views from the perspectives of Islam, Judaism, Confucianism, Buddhism, and Hinduism.[37] Küng pointed out that for religions to seek for mutual understanding, three strategies do not work: first, there is the fortress strategy, just holding on tenaciously to one's own beliefs; second, there is the defusing strategy, denying that there is any problem concerning truth as each religion has its own ways; finally, there is the embracing strategy, maintaining that other religions have gotten hold of certain partial truths, only one's own religion has the perfect Truth. Küng suggests that in order for us to overcome our bias, the best strategy is for each to have soul-searching criticisms of its own tradition. I find that this is exactly what is lacking in Nasr's approach. Küng starts out with critical reflection on Christianity, and his search finds that no transcendent religion can afford to be irrelevant to the human world. At first sight humanism seems to be in opposition to religious aspiration, but in fact this need not be so. The liberation process actually helps to open up new horizons for Christianity. Liberty, equality, love, and especially "human dignity" are rediscovered to be Christian values, even though they are realized in the world under opposition by the Church. In the meantime, the secular world also finds that it needs the help of religion to maintain the sacredness of certain values rising above classes, races, and nations. Therefore Küng suggests that true humanity, or the *humanum,* is the universal ecumenical criterion we are looking for.

As a Confucian scholar I have no trouble appreciating Küng's insight, and wrote a paper to support Küng on the common quest for world peace.[38] The East needs soul searching self-criticisms just like the West. I do not see how the East enjoys any advantage over the West. If we resist all social changes and defend the medieval social and political hierarchical structures in the name of keeping the sapiental dimension of knowledge intact, then we would play right into the hands of certain fundamentalist fanatics against our own intentions. The consequences could be dangerous. Thus my criticism of Nasr from an Oriental perspective is that even Nasr still fails to appreciate fully the truly rich implications of *philosophia perennis* as it must seek ever new manifestations among all the great religious traditions and in all ages. What is perennial is the message of the transcendent, not the worldviews or social and political structures. We must adapt to our new environment, natural or social. And we must live fully in the here and now, not dream of a past golden age.

CONCLUDING REMARKS

My criticisms of Dr. Nasr may sound a bit too harsh, and some of my criticisms may be unfounded as the only source I rely upon is his Gifford Lectures, and I cannot claim to have any deep understanding of his thought. But I may be allowed to play the role of devil's advocate. I think there are good reasons for human society to evolve into a pluralistic one, even though the trend may carry a bit too far, and there is the urgent need to balance modernity with tradition, and revive the sense of unity among mankind as we are forced to live in a global village. But the consensus must be grown from the grassroots, not forced upon us from above. In a pluralistic world like ours, Nasr's perspective is needed as it keeps alive something valuable which may become extinct if we do not make any effort to protect the so-called sapiental dimension of knowledge. But we do need new expressions for the dimension and must not set tradition against modernity. To conclude, I would have to say, it is not only impossible but also undesirable for Nasr's thought to become the main stream in the future.

SHU-HSIEN LIU

DEPARTMENT OF PHILOSOPHY
THE CHINESE UNIVERSITY OF HONG KONG
JULY 1996

NOTES

1. Seyyed Hossein Nasr, *Knowledge and the Sacred* (Albany: State University of New York Press, 1989). As this is the only source I use, in restating

Nasr's position I will paraphrase freely without indicating the exact page numbers on every occasion except where I deem necessary.

2. Frank Whaling, ed., *The World's Religious Traditions: Essays in Honor of Wilfred Cantwell Smith* (Edinburgh: T.& T. Clark, Ltd., 1984). Nasr's own essay: "The *Philosophia Perennis* and the Study of Religion," Dr. Annemarie Schimmel's essay: "The Muslim Tradition," and Geoffrey Parrinder's essay: "Thematic Comparison," are especially helpful.

3. Nasr, *Knowledge and the Sacred*, p. 1.

4. Ibid.

5. Ibid., p. 65.

6. Ibid., p. 160.

7. Ibid., p. 161.

8. Ibid., pp. 67–68.

9. Ibid., p. 67.

10. Ibid.

11. Ibid., p. 2.

12. John Dewey, *Human Nature and Conduct* (New York: Henry Holt & Co., 1922).

13. Nasr, *Knowledge and the Sacred*, p. 3.

14. Ibid., p. 5.

15. Paul Tillich, *Systematic Theology*, vol. 1 (Chicago: University of Chicago Press, 3 vols., 1951, 1957, 1963), pp. 79–81.

16. See Shu-hsien Liu, "A Critique of Paul Tillich's Doctrine of God and Christology from an Oriental Perspective," *Religious Issues and Interreligious Dialogues*, ed. Charles Wei-hsun Fu and Gerhard E. Spiegler (New York: Greenwood Press, 1989), pp. 511–32.

17. See Shu-hsien Liu, "The Religious Import of Confucian Philosophy: Its Traditional Outlook and Contemporary Significance," *Philosophy East and West* 21, no. 2 (April 1971): 157–75.

18. Ernst Cassirer, *An Essay On Man: An Introduction to a Philosophy of Human Culture* (New Haven: Yale University Press, 1944). I translated the book into Chinese; it was published by Tunghai University Press in 1959.

19. Karl Jaspers, *The Origin and Goal of History*, trans. M. Bullock (New Haven: Yale University Press, 1953).

20. Ernst Cassirer, *The Philosophy of Symbolic Forms*, trans. Ralph Mannheim and John Michael Krois (New Haven: Yale University Press, 4 vols., 1953, 1955, 1957, 1996).

21. Charles Hartshorne, *The Divine Relativity* (New Haven: Yale University Press, 1948).

22. Nasr, *Knowledge and the Sacred*, p. 85.

23. Alfred North Whitehead, *Science and the Modern World* (New York: Macmillan, 1950), pp. 14–18.

24. Ibid., pp. 74–75.

25. Joseph Needham, *Science and Civilisation in China*, vol. II: *History of Scientific Thought* (Cambridge: Cambridge University Press, 1956).

26. For contemporary Neo-Confucian thought, see "A Manifesto for a

Reappraisal of Sinology and Reconstruction of Neo-Confucian Thought," which was published as an appendix in Carsun Chang, *The Development of Neo-Confucian Thought*, vol. 2 (New York: Bookman Associate, 1962). The famous manifesto was first published in Chinese in *Democratic Review* in Hong Kong on New Year's Day, 1958, and was signed by T'ang Chün-i, Mou Tsung-san, Hsü Fu-kuan, and Carsun Chang. Recent reflections of mine on the trend can be found in Shu-hsien Liu, "Confucian Ideals and the Real World: A Critical Review of Contemporary Neo-Confucian Thought," in *Confucian Traditions in East Asian Modernity*, edited by Tu Wei-ming (Cambridge, Mass.: Harvard University Press, 1996), pp. 92–111.

27. Nasr, *Knowledge and the Sacred*, p. 81.

28. Dietrich Bonhoeffer, *Letters and Papers from Prison* (New York: Macmillian Co., 1962).

29. Wing-tsit Chan trans. and comp., *A Source Book in Chinese Philosophy* (Princeton: Princeton University Press, 1963), p. 44.

30. Nasr, *Knowledge and the Sacred*, p. 3.

31. John Dewey, *The Quest for Certainty* (New York: Minton, Balch and Co., 1929).

32. Wing-tsit Chan, *A Source Book in Chinese Philosophy*, p. 23.

33. See n. 2. Geoffrey Parrinder, "Thematic Comparison," *The World's Religious Traditions*, pp. 242–247.

34. Frederick Copleston, *Religion and the One: Philosophies East and West* (New York: Crossroad Pub. Co., 1982).

35. Wing-tsit Chan, *A Source Book in Chinese Philosophy*, p. 139.

36. Ibid., p. 580.

37. Hans Küng, *Projekt Weltethos* (München: R. Piper GmbH & Co., 1990).

38. See Shu-hsien Liu, "Reflections on World Peace through Peace among Religions—A Confucian Perspective," *Journal of Chinese Philosophy* 22, no. 2 (June 1995): 193–213.

REPLY TO SHU-HSIEN LIU

It is unfortunate that Professor Liu has not been able to consult some of my works other than *Knowledge and the Sacred*, works in which I discuss the question of tradition and modernity. Therefore in responding to his criticisms, based as they are on his reading of only two of my writings, I am forced to repeat certain ideas mentioned in several of my other essays and books. I shall nevertheless try not simply to repeat these ideas but to tailor my response specifically to the criticism of Liu made on the basis of the particular background from which he hails. Let it also be said at the outset that of all the major intellectual traditions of the world I have dealt least of all with the Chinese tradition and am happy to have the reaction of a Neo-Confucian Chinese philosopher to the ideas expressed in my writings.

Liu's criticism of my use of the term "tradition" fails to understand that the very significance of the usage of this term by twentieth-century traditionalists, beginning with René Guénon, is precisely its specificity and distinction from the ordinary usage of the term which means no more than the continuity of certain thoughts or actions whatever might be their origin. In this latter sense one can of course speak of the "humanist tradition" or the "tradition of rationalism, British Empiricism, German Idealism, and so on," to quote Liu. For traditionalists such as myself, tradition is of sacred and divine origin and includes the continuity and transmission of that sacred message over time. Otherwise, the very concept would be quite trivial and insignificant and not able to play the philosophical role that is expected of it for those who are defenders of the sacred. The aim of using "tradition" in this specific sense is precisely to bring about awareness of the fundamental distinction between that reality described by this particular usage of the term "tradition" and all that lacks a divine origin but issues from the merely human and sometimes the subhuman. To define "tradition" in the way that I and other traditionalists do is itself a major philosophical statement which distinguishes tradition from the modern. If this specificity were to be lost or discarded, "tradition" would be an innocuous general term meaning custom, habit, or mere historical continuity without any ultimate philosophical significance. Liu may disagree with the sharp distinction made between the sacred and the non-sacred or profane and their transmission as reflected in the distinction I make between tradition and modernism, but he cannot criticize why I use the term as I do seeing that I have given a clear definition of how I use this term in my *Knowledge and the Sacred*. Each philosopher or philosophical school has the freedom to use its own terminology as long as the terms are defined and clearly understood. If the terms are not defined with clarity, then that philosophical school ceases to prosper and becomes eclipsed or dies out. In the case of "tradition," as used by me, this is hardly the case. There is now a vast library of works in English, French, Italian, German, and other European languages in which the term "tradition" is used in the way I employ it and is understood as such by both those who espouse the traditional perspective and those who oppose it.

As for my use of the terms "knowledge" and "intelligence" which Liu criticizes by saying, "I find that he has used many terms in a way quite different from our common usage of these terms," again the same argument as given above applies. Of course each philosopher uses key terms in accordance with the philosophical worldview in which such terms are used by him, as can be seen in the use of as central a term as "existence" in medieval, seventeenth-century, or twentieth-century European philosophy. I must again insist that I have defined technical philosophical terms which I used. Moreover, I am not one to have the tendency to invent new terms or to give a wholly new connotation to a term as Heidegger and Sartre did for the key term "existence." When I use a term with a meaning other than its current one, this meaning is always drawn from the wider field of meaning associated historically with the term but often eclipsed or forgotten in later periods of its usage.

Liu criticizes my usage of the term "proof" which he seems to use in a purely rationalistic way. But there are many levels and kinds of proof. One usually says, "where there is smoke, there is fire." But this type of proof is based only on probability, which we usually take for certainty, and is different from proof of the solution to a problem in Euclidean geometry. And then there is proof based on "intellectual intuition" and "supra-rational certitude" which is, however, never irrational. A statue of the Buddha from eighth-century Japan or a Sung landscape from China provides proof of the celestial inspiration which made such works of art possible. Or, for those who have faith, the very beauty of the chanting of the Quran or a Byzantine icon is proof of the existence of God just as the blue sky and majestic mountains are proof of the reality of the Tao for a Far Eastern contemplative. Not being a rationalist, I refuse to limit my understanding of "proof" to only the rationalistic level. I use the term "proof" in such a way that it encompasses many levels of epistemic consent and certitude, including, certainly, both the empirical and the rational but not exclusively limited to these levels.

The author warns that we must "not gloss over the differences among such manifestations [of sapiental dimension in various traditions]." I could not but agree fully with this assertion and throughout my life have written and spoken against a reductionism which would level the various traditions to an amorphous least common denominator. My assertion of the essential unity of the sapiental traditions concerning the Ultimate Principle and profound correspondences on lower levels of reality does not in any way imply that there are not differences in various traditions, differences which I have always regarded with the utmost respect as manifestations of the Sacred Itself. In the field of religion I have discussed many of these differences as well as profound correspondences and have not simply tried to equate everything as being the same. But there are certain criticisms made by Liu concerning this issue which are somewhat puzzling. First he criticizes me for believing that all traditions accept an Ultimate Principle which is Transcendent and says that the Chinese tradition is an exception. He then later in his essay asserts more than once that for Chinese Neo-Confucians only the Transcendent is unchanging. He is right that the Far Eastern tradition does not use the ontological language of Pure Being, but certainly this tradition affirms that Reality to which the Western traditions refer as Pure Being or even Beyond-Being. Otherwise how could the *Tao Te-Ching* begin with the phrase "The Tao that can be named is not the Tao?" Is not what cannot be named beyond all determination including all temporal and spatial conditions? As for there being no need of a mediator in the Far Eastern tradition such as Christ or the Prophet of Islam, I agree that the function is not identical, but what about the elaborate doctrine of the Universal Man in Taoism and the classical Confucian doctrine according to which the Emperor in his hieratic function is bridge and mediator between Heaven and earth?

Liu speaks of the development of cultures and accuses me of not paying attention to the fact that cultures develop. It is as if I did not know the difference between Islamic culture in the Abbasid and the Ottoman periods. The traditional point of view, while being rooted in immutable principles, also possesses teachings concerning the nature of time and history. Far from denying what Liu calls "the developmental view of culture," I view traditional culture as a tree whose root is sunk in the soil of Divinity which provides the sap for its trunk and branches. The tree grows according to its nature but also in response to external conditions of heat, cold, moisture, and so on. Traditions also provide knowledge of the life cycle of the tree itself. Nor do they in any way claim that in the period of the cycle of the world in which we live, which includes the last several thousand years embracing the world of the *Iliad* and *Odyssey*, which Liu mentions, traditional civilizations were perfect. Tradition teaches that the serpent was already in paradise, to use Christian language, and that from the golden age there is a continuous fall interrupted periodically by a new message from Heaven. To defend the traditional point of view is not to negate the reality of all kinds of evil in the premodern world ranging from wars to philosophical skepticism among the Greeks in the dying moments of that civilization. The major difference is that in traditional civilizations while there was evil, the sacred was ubiquitous and people lived in the world of faith. Today evil continues in many more insidious ways while the very meaning of life which is the quest and discovery of the sacred is taken away.

Furthermore, according to the traditional understanding of historical cycles, I would not have any difficulty going back still further, before the pivotal or axial age of Jaspers, because traditional knowledge expressed in symbolic form is to be found no matter how far back one goes, as the surviving primal religions of the world bear witness. It is a misunderstanding on the part of Liu of what I mean by tradition that makes him assert, "If we had to uphold all our traditions, we would still have to live in truly dark ages." If the reality of tradition had been understood, one would certainly not use the terms "still" and "dark ages" in this sentence but would have realized that if the nature of man is to seek and reach the sacred, then we are *now* living in the dark ages based upon metaphysical ignorance, no matter how much we illuminate our cities at night with electricity.

As for my rejection of evolution in "any sense," I reject Darwinian evolution and the idea of the transformation of one species into another by merely natural causes as described by Darwin. Biologically speaking, I oppose macroevolution, not the adaptation of a species to new conditions which occurs all the time. But more than that, I oppose the whole ideology based on evolution which would derive the greater from the lesser and force us to believe in the most illogical and improbable scenarios in order to be certain to cut off the Hands of God from His Creation. Liu uses "evolution" in a much more general sense as "change or development." I do not of course deny the reality of change as I have stated above, but I stand categorically opposed to the theory of evolution understood both biologically and philosophically.

As for the distinction between the Hebrew and Greek sapiental traditions, there is, of course, a long history going back to some of the Greek Fathers of juxtaposing one against the other while others from Origen and Clement to Augustine believed in their ultimate harmony. The same difference in interpretation is to be seen in the Jewish and Islamic traditions. Needless to say I stand on the side of the Christian Platonists and Muslim philosophers while being fully aware that the Unmoved Mover of Aristotle does not give a full description of the Divine Reality revealed in the Abrahamic universe, but I would repeat the famous Islamic doctrine that *al-tawḥīdu wāḥid*, that is, the doctrine of Unity is unique and that the One described by Plotinus cannot be other than *the* One even if certain of Its characteristics are not accentuated in the context of the Greek worldview within which sages such as Plotinus functioned.

Liu accuses me of "prejudice" against "the modern world." The word "prejudice" implies prejudgment. My opposition to the modern world, far from being a prejudgment, is based upon and is the consequence of long years of the study of its philosophical foundations and first-hand experience of its reality on nearly every level. Like other traditionalists, I am opposed to the modern world but this is the result of application of first principles to the constituents of this world and not any "prejudice." I am not blind to what is accidentally good in the modern world but oppose the premises upon which it stands and the result that the culture it has created has had upon the mind and soul of those affected by it. I attribute both the disintegration of the social fabric in modern societies and the destruction of the natural environment to modernism and its false presumptions about the nature of man and the world. Liu would be surprised to know that there are many more people than he thinks, even in the West, who would slay the modern world if they could to reestablish a saner way of life. But they, like me, do not want literally to go back to the Middle Ages, which would in any case be impossible, but want to reestablish a social and intellectual order on the basis of traditional principles and to preserve what they can of the traditional world, much of which has been already lost. Liu underestimates the number of people in the West drawn to things medieval, from music and poetry to heraldry, because they see in them a peace, security, and meaning lost in the frenzy of modern life which moves rapidly but towards nowhere.

The last thing I have ever spoken of is romantic nostalgia for the past. My nostalgia has always been for that spiritual reality residing at the center of man's being, that eternal home from which we have become exiled. If I defend premodern periods of culture, or what we call traditional cultures, it is because they still reflected the light of that Center to which we must all ultimately return. Far from being based on romantic nostalgia, this perspective is rooted in the most rigorous form of realism.

Liu also seeks to defend modern science against my criticisms. He talks of ecology taking seriously the value of life and states, "it takes science to overcome science." This claim will in fact only take place when another science of nature based on traditional principles, or what I have called "sacred science," is accepted in the West once again. Otherwise, despite the effort of a few scientists here and there, the prevalent reductionism of science will continue and scientism will not cease to grow in strength by the day, while the applications of science in the form of technology protrude to an ever greater degree into the last bastion of "sacredness" in the West, which is the human person, at the same time also accelerating the destruction of the globe ecologically. And let us not forget that the empirical sciences are based just as much upon a particular philosophy of nature as were the traditional Chinese or Islamic sciences.

I will not deal with Liu's criticisms of my views about politics and society because they reflect much more his own political and social views than my philosophical theses. I only need to add that as mentioned above, traditional teachings about society have never been fully realized in what the Hindus call the *Kali Yuga* because of the very imperfection of the human state, and therefore shallow comparisons between modern and traditional social and political institutions are of little value. But seeing that the twentieth century has been the most bloody in human history and that the new forms of enslavement to various social or material forces are even more pervasive than the terrible practice of slavery in many societies in days of old, one can only say that in this domain of contingency while modern man has gained certain things, he has also lost a great deal more and endangered in this process the chain of life of the planet itself.

Liu, like many modernized Orientals going back to the last century, wishes to keep both modernism and tradition by ambiguous definitions of both. I belong to that type of Oriental thinker, such as A. K. Coomaraswamy, for whom such a position is impossible, and I see myself as defender of tradition without in any way denying the challenges that exist and the necessity to respond to those challenges. Liu accuses me of refusing "to move with the times." As I have written more than once, if we have to keep up with the times, then with what do the times have to keep up? Why must we be simply passive *vis-à-vis* what is now called "the times"? Why can we not mold our times according to principles? The French philosopher Henry Corbin once said that "ordinary people are made by their times. The spiritual person is he who makes his times." My conception of tradition is both static and dynamic, as in the metaphor of the tree given above, the tree whose roots are static and whose branches grow dynamically according to both the nature of the tree and external conditions. I am all in favor of Oriental traditions facing the challenges posed by modernism and providing appropriate answers rather than fleeing from the challenge. But I am not in the least bit impressed by "the times" or afraid of falling behind the times, especially since the chariot of modern culture is racing ever more rapidly toward the precipice.

It is strange that Liu should quote Geoffrey Parrinder as proof of the Vedantic nature of Sufism, going against not only my words but more importantly the millennial tradition of Sufism. Would Liu take an Arab or Persian scholar's view of the nature of Western Christian mysticism seriously even if those scholars were very famous? This is an example of the inferiority complex from which many of us Orientals still suffer. I knew Parrinder personally and respect him as a scholar of Christianity, but what he has said about Sufism and its relation to the Vedanta is simply incorrect. It is high time that the views of authorities within a tradition be taken seriously for their understanding of that tradition, and the idea that since this or that Western scholar has been molded by the Enlightenment idea of reason and modern scholarship therefore he knows better than a Zen master what Zen means or better than Sufis about the origin of their own tradition be cast aside once and for all.

Liu criticizes me by saying that "Nasr's faith is neither unique nor original." With this statement I agree completely. I have never sought to be "original" in the modern sense of the term, nor to be unique. I have only tried to be original in the sense of returning to the Origin and I prefer anonymity to uniqueness. Only the Ultimate Truth is unique. If what I have written were original in the modern sense of being completely other than what had been said before, and unique in the sense of differing from the wisdom of the ages, I would disown it completely. My task in life has been not to be original but to return to the Origin and then to express truths of a universal and perennial nature in a contemporary language and in answer to new challenges posed by the nature of the world in which we live. I therefore am not in agreement with thinkers such as Hans Küng whom Liu mentions, and consider not only the Transcendent but also its manifestations in various traditions to be sacred and of perennial value as living reality as long as a tradition still possesses life here on this earth.

Finally, unity always descends from above not from consensus from the grassroots. It is always the few philosophers and thinkers who provide the ideas that move men and societies and not vice versa. There is of course always the principle of *vox populi vox Dei* which must be remembered. But in the world of thought, it is the Taoist sage contemplating the Truth who brings the fruit of this contemplation to the world. In today's circumstances, it is the few endowed with the possibility of knowing their own tradition in depth as well as being able to cross religious and cultural frontiers who must provide the map for the many. I believe that it is only the light of tradition that can provide not only a map of reality to the metaphysical realm, but also a map to help us orient ourselves in the chaotic situation of the modern world. Traditional truths must be expressed in a contemporary language in order to be understood by the men and women of today's world, but these truths cannot be compromised in a world already drawing rapidly towards the phase of total disruption and dissolution.

S. H. N.

7

Ernest Wolf-Gazo

NASR AND THE QUEST FOR THE SACRED

PREFACE

The work of Dr. Seyyed Hossein Nasr is a challenge to any contemporary Western professional philosopher. I surveyed Nasr's work, from a philosophic point of view, with the intent to do justice to his basic motif: the *Reenchantment of the Profane World*. For the sake of brevity, I shall call this motif, the *Reenchantment Project*. This project was launched early in Nasr's career, although, at the writing of his classic *Science and Civilization in Islam*, the project had not yet come to fruition and its form had not reached the stage of maturity.[1] Yet, by the time he delivered the 1981 Gifford Lectures, published as *Knowledge and the Sacred*, the project was in full swing.[2] In order to pinpoint some segments and elements that are relevant in their respective treatment of topics, I selected passages and general assessments to be found in the works of Nasr and thereby located stations en route to the sacred. A full-fledged treatment of these stations is wanting; yet, at this writing, I refrain from pointing out all the details and references to be found in his work. In that sense the present treatment of Nasr's work is very selective. The selectivity proceeds in terms of priorities to a professional Western philosopher, with the hope that the Eastern reader will respond accordingly. Of course, I hope that this transaction is done in the spirit of justice and enlightenment, treating fairly the reader as well as the writer. I constructed an ideal type of treatment between the writer, text, and reader pursuing methods, contrasts, and context. I treat a serious theme, promoted by Nasr's project, that addresses a real need to build a "bridge over troubled waters," as the song goes, between the West and the Islamic East. I relied not only on books, articles, and interviews with Nasr, but also on our personal conversations, too numerous to be counted, in Washington, D.C. and Cairo, and also on lecture notes that I took during the academic year 1989–90, while attending numerous courses given by him during the writer's sabbatical year. The present contribution is to be understood as a small token of appreciation of Nasr's generosity and intellectual fairness towards the present writer.

I. Introduction

Aside from identifying Dr. Nasr's *Project of Reenchantment*, I add the following themes, suggestive of eliciting a contrastable response, in terms of *The Quest*. Accordingly, I comment on the sacred order of the *Kosmos*, in Platonic fashion, that includes Newton and Whitehead, not the least Nasr, inheriting the *Neo-Platonic-Sufi* strains from Suhrawardī and Mullā Ṣadrā. In addition, I focus on the ecological dimensions of the sacred, which may very well turn out to be the centerpiece of Nasr's project, for he was among the foremost spokesmen in the late 1960s and early 1970s who sensed the danger to our environment, due to the senseless quest for the domination of nature by Baconian minds—in the West as well as in the East. I try to come to terms with the sacred and the problem of epistemological certainty, promoted by Descartes and ushering in the American instrumentalist pragmatism of John Dewey. Despite Dewey's critique of Descartes, it is fascinating to see how Dewey's ideas of certainty contrast with Nasr's "Sacred Certainty," inherited from the Iṣfahānī tradition of Mīr Dāmād and his student Ṣadrā. Lastly, I ask Goethe's *Gretchenfrage* to the debate and discourse between the West and East on the legitimacy of the intellectual intuition of God since Kant. By using this problematic theme as a foliage, against which I x-ray Nasr's *Reenchantment Project*, I hope to promote an honest, critical, and productive discourse between civilizations towards which Nasr has contributed much, and which is in dire need of being reechoed and reenforced. The well-known theme of the clash of civilizations only promotes a black and white picture that cannot be supported by history; reality does not unveil itself in such a stark bipolarity. Perhaps, to speak in Hegel's and Nasr's language: *Reality* may turn out to be *Sacred Grey*.

II. The Reenchantment Project: Tradition and the Sacred

After the devastating First World War, Max Weber concluded his famous speech, "Science as a Vocation," in 1918 at the University of Munich before an overcrowded auditorium of students, as follows: "The fate of our times is characterized by rationalization and intellectualization and, above all, by the 'disenchantment of the world.'"[3] By the end of the twentieth century we have a better "feel" for that process that Weber called "*Entzauberungsprozess*." The question, however, I must pose at this time is: has the world turned for the better? Or, have things turned out different than anticipated by Weber? These questions remain for the historian to answer. Whatever may be the case, the disenchantment process described by Weber has not been as successful as anticipated, as the neo-tribal conflicts in the late twentieth century have shown.

Contrary to Weber's analysis, Nasr has proposed a project that may be called "*The Reenchantment Process of the Sacred*." At the center of this process is the rediscovery of the sacred as a dynamic element in the modern world. The sacred is no longer classified as an old fashioned counterpart to the profane, or secular, but treated as a quintessential element that has been rediscovered with a new consciousness. Nasr makes the point, "The rediscovery of the sacred is ultimately and inextricably related to the revival of tradition. . . ."[4] It was precisely the notion of tradition, in all spheres of human endeavor, that was stripped of its enchantment through the process of rationalization. The transvaluation of values, as Nietzsche puts it, was the single most essential aspect of the loss of tradition. Nasr's project is designed to regain the sense of tradition and to reclaim the entitlement of enchantment between Man and God, for the sacred must be put at center stage in the reenchantment process. However, we should not equate the project as a "*roll-back*" of the rational; rather, we must see the process as a reinvestment in man's relationship to the Divine. This rediscovery and reinvestment is part of the reenchantment process. Philosophically speaking, we may talk about the transcendence of the Unity of Being.[5] It is precisely this transcendence that has been lost, at least since Kant. It was this, as Weber pointed out, that got lost in the rationalization process of Protestant Europe, involving the transformation of a premodern community into a modern nation state. The interesting part in Nasr's project is that it derives out of the Eastern tradition of Islam and not the notorious Protestant ethic, of which Weber spoke.

The tradition that synthesizes the classical elements of Islam, along with the Sufi strains of Eastern Islam and the Shi'ite component in Nasr's project, makes this a challenging and new kind of proposal. To date, very few professional philosophers in the West, particularly in the academic environment, have dealt with or even noticed Nasr's work. That statement tells us more about the provincial situation of academic philosophy, especially the Anglo-American variety in Western philosophy departments, than about Nasr's cosmopolitan approach to the theme at hand.[6]

Nasr understands tradition as a "*Lebensform*" in terms of "*Lebenswelt*"; a language familiar to anyone acquainted with Dilthey, Husserl, with phenomenology, or Habermas. This form of life is rooted in the organic unity of the very transcendent Unity of Being. The life-world (to use Husserl's term as adapted by Habermas) is not a mere "*life-style*" that comes and goes with the fashions and fads of the season.[7] The traditional forms of life are in quest of wholeness, of holiness, of unity, and of the sacred. One of the basic reasons why the reenchantment project is not just an exclusive quest for the sacred is that the rediscovery of tradition is a prerequisite for the reenchantment project. Tradition provides the basic cultural framework in which the sacred operates. That is to say, societies without tradition no longer can provide the context in which the sacred can manifest itself.

The virtual world of computer technology is exactly the kind of environment in which tradition cannot flourish. The virtual world has no value in itself; it is merely a second-hand world that is used, in Kant's language, as a regulative paradigm, in terms of instrumental reason.[8] The virtual world exhibits rationality without life; without the organic component that provides the background for the special relationship between man and the Sacred. Tradition is treated as something authentic in Nasr's work and not as something that is considered historic, ancient, or of merely anthropological interest.[9] Tradition, in that sense, is not merely treated as belonging in a museum or as a tourist attraction. It is understood as something living, unitary, and organic. It provides space for man and God to meet. The traditional landscape cannot, of course, be recovered. But authentic tradition can be rejuvenated in such a way that tradition is, once again, placed in the center of man's action. Tradition, at this point, is not the old-fashioned sentimental *Biedermeier Romantik* that tried to negate the oncoming industrial development, especially in Germany.[10] Tradition in Nasr's terms means those aspects, elements, and practices that have preserved eternal values, in the face of hard won historical experience. And that includes the transcendent Unity of Being in the context of the Divine. Some of the masters of tradition, such as René Guénon, A. K. Coomaraswamy, Titus Burckhardt, Frithjof Shuon, or Martin Lings, have influenced Nasr's work on tradition.[11] Anyone appreciating the unique perspective Nasr offers must be acquainted with the works by the masters of traditions mentioned, respectively. Again, tradition does not mean anthropological, sociological, or political conceptionalizations such as we read in academic textbooks.[12] They may be useful, but miss the essential point of authentic tradition. The center of authentic tradition is the sacred as a metaphysical element, bonding the transcendence between man and God. It is this proto-original bond, Nasr reminds us, that is to be recalled and recovered, and which constitutes the center of his reenchantment project. Thus, seen in this light we do not use the reenchantment idea as a "going back" to Schiller, or Novalis's "*Verzauberung der Welt*," for this is done in the Disney production *The Lion King*.[13]

Rather, Nasr reminds us of the original bond between man and God defined as ". . . the pre-temporal existence of man in relation with God. . . ."[14]

In view of this perspective it becomes clear that Weber's treatment of the secularization theme is handled in a somewhat different perspective than in Nasr's work. It is a timely reminder for the West that not all options to save the world have been explored. Max Weber is still an inspiration that must be reckoned with, but we can see, as time adds a sense of maturity to our view, that Weber may have been too imbued with Western historical categories to leave room for a rationality in Islamic dress, basically unknown to the Western public.[15]

III. On the Sacred Order of the Kosmos: Plato, Newton, Whitehead, and Nasr

In order to come to terms with Dr. Nasr's *Reenchantment Project* it is useful to recall some of the classical models and their respective structures of the Kosmos. I chose Plato, Newton, and Whitehead with a purpose: These thinkers are deeply into the sacred, despite their mathematical treatment of the structures of the universe, or the Kosmos.[16] The subtle relationship between mathematics and the sacred is something Plato, Newton, and Whitehead have in common. I should remind those readers not familiar with Nasr's academic background that his formal training was initially in mathematics, geosciences, and physics. Anyone familiar with his works knows that he is not a stranger to the natural sciences. Quite the contrary, in Nasr's work we can see an interesting attempt at coming to terms with the modern sciences in terms of the Islamic tradition.[17] He reminds us of the great scientific centers of the golden age of Baghdad, Fatimid Cairo, or Naishapur, and not the least, of 'Umar Khayyām.[18] Thus, it is a misrepresentation, as some may have it, that modern science is opposed to the Islamic tradition. In fact, it is one of Nasr's achievements to make it clear, especially to Western readers of his works, not to mention the more enlightened fellow Muslims, that science and Islam are not contradictions in terms.

In any case, we may agree with Nasr's contention that what has been forgotten in the West is the sacred nature of the order of the universe (Kosmos), of which not only Plato spoke, but also the great Nicholas Cusanus, and not the least Copernicus and Kepler. The classical philosophers treated the understanding of the Kosmos from a mathematical point.[19] The sacred, in Nasr's project, has always been present, but it had been lost, because societies, civilizations, and individuals have gotten out of touch with the sacred and the original pretemporal bond. This situation is somewhat reminiscent of Heidegger's "*Seinsvergessenheit*."[20] According to Nasr, humankind has "*forgotten*" about the transcendent Unity of Being and must now recover the transcendent bond of Being between man and God. There seems to be a subtle analogy between Heidegger's recovery of the authentic "*Sein*" and Nasr's reenchantment of thought, ushering into Ṣadrā's *Wisdom of the Throne*.[21] It is no surprise that the late Henry Corbin, a colleague and friend of Nasr, during the Imperial Academy of Philosophy days in Tehran, should have been the first translator of Heidegger's *Was heisst Metaphysik* into French, opening the gate for the French Heidegger reception.[22] In the long run, Corbin opted for Suhrawardī and the metaphysics of the Illuminationist School of the Islamic East.[23]

Leibniz was the last Western philosopher-mathematician who understood this classical theme. In Descartes we register a partial divorce between the mathematical and the sacred; by the time Kant spoke of God (*Urheber*) as a regulative principle of understanding and as the transcendental structure of our capacity for understanding (*Verstand*), the notion of the sacred became lost in the Western conception of the Kosmos.[24] In the great Charles S. Peirce, not to mention Dewey, this becomes evident. In twentieth-century Western philosophy, as exhibited in Heidegger and Wittgenstein, the demise of the traditional sacred is obvious. The former may still speak in a veiled language, but the latter put it in a very succinct language, to his twentieth-century readers: the world is all that is the case. The mathematical structure of understanding the universe was closely tied to the symmetry of this very structure, expressed in the aesthetic language of beauty, and harmony. Indeed, in Plato, Newton, and Whitehead, not to mention Nasr, we find the essential elements at play: Order, Beauty, Justice.[25] It is no surprise that Newton and Whitehead did not provide for an exclusive ethics. In fact, their mathematical understanding is combined with the aesthetic and identified, therefore, as the ethics of the Kosmos.

In an interesting *Sophia* article, Nasr distinguished between sacred, religious, and traditional art.[26] He did not speak of the difference between sacred and profane art, say, between Sultan Ahmed Mosque in Istanbul and the Bauhaus in Dessau. A profane architectural entity, such as the Dessau Bauhaus, may elicit religious feelings by former students and teachers, as is the case with many tourists visiting the Pyramids in Giza, Egypt. The religious feelings may evoke a sense of grandeur, perfection, and presentness. The Bauhaus in Dessau may rejuvenate our sense of mathematical perfection in terms of a perfect geometrical entity, as was in the mind of Gropius.[27] To see in modernity elements of the secular exclusively is shortsighted; no doubt, in the upcoming century we will witness a turn towards more sensitivity, and less ideology, as to what is and is not modern. The sacred will celebrate a come-back in disguise. In that sense Nasr's reenchantment project is timely.

The sacred and the mathematical, since Pythagoras, have been two sides of the same coin. The Kosmos has always been seen as a sacred entity. Likewise, Plato's forms, Newton's forces, and Whitehead's eternal objects, can only be understood in a mathematico-geometrical context, underlying the sacred order. If we follow Max Weber and hold that the religious, e.g. Pharaonic Egypt, and especially the monotheistic religions, are a higher level of consciousness, compared to the mythological landscape of Homeric Greece, then we can differentiate between the sacred, the religious, the traditional, the profane, the modern, the secular, and not to mention, the postmodern.[28]

In comparison, Nasr's Kosmos is divinely inspired and intersects with the intellectual intuition of God, or the ultimate illumination of the divine light, understood in the Ishrāqī tradition.[29] This is the Sufi tradition in Nasr's quest of the sacred and his understanding of the Kosmos. Nasr is, of course, well aware of the mathematical configurations inherent in Plato's, Newton's, and Whitehead's philosophies of nature. Mathematics, in his interpretation of the world, may be a divine tool, given to humankind by God to unlock the surface of the earth's secret, but it is not the key to the ultimate disclosure of the universe. In Descartes's world, mathematics is understood to be a divine gift of which he partakes, but his God functions as an insurance agent—just in case. He uses God as a footnote, just in case his texts have to verify their respective mathematical sources. Of course, in Nasr's universe mathematics is a means to explore the world, but not an end in itself. In contrast, the Cartesian universe discloses itself in mathematical quantities. It is obvious that the state of revelation becomes problematic. Revelation does not take center stage in Descartes's world, or in the world of deist philosopher scientists. God's beauty and grandeur discloses itself in the scientific search for knowledge in the world. The mathematical is the hidden bond through which the human mind is capable of comprehending the structures of the universe that are accessible and revelatory. Yet, this process of revelation has not yet played out, as far as Nasr is concerned.

IV. The Sacred and Certainty: Nasr and Dewey

I want to contrast Nasr's mature version of his quest for the sacred, presented in his Gifford Lectures in 1981, with another Gifford Lecturer, namely John Dewey, who presented his project of instrumental pragmatism in 1929 which was entitled, *The Quest for Certainty*.[30] I am convinced that, if we compare some aspects of Nasr and Dewey we shall come closer to the basic misunderstandings and antagonisms weighing heavy on the relation between the West and the Islamic East.

A mere comparison is not sufficient, for it does not draw out the specific philosophic import embedded in Nasr's and Dewey's perspectives. Thus, we use the Whiteheadian notion of "contrast" as a unit of analysis. Whitehead used the term "contrast" in his 1928 Gifford Lectures, subsequently published as *Process and Reality*.[31] "Contrast" as understood in Whitehead's Gifford Lectures is presented as a category of explanation. This explanation, " . . . is a datum for a feeling has a unity *as felt* . . . this unity is a 'contrast' of entities."[32] Thus, contrastual assessment, as I use it in this essay, is treated as a metaphysical component of a worldview. No doubt, Nasr and Dewey are very striking in contrast, but on closer inspection, both are true believers of their respective *Weltanschauungen*. Dewey is as much a messenger of the American dream as Nasr is of the message coming from Isfahan, rooted in the Quran. The former expounds Western rationality in terms of pragmatic instrumentalism, the latter, a transcendent intuition that mirrors not only the respective communities, but also exhibits in a variety of ways the respective civilizations in which they are born, raised, and nurtured. In Dewey's case it is the New England landscape, while Nasr represents the Persian classical civilization. Protestant Christianity and Shi'ite Islam provide the bedrock of their respective views.

Dewey presents a reformed Protestant view in terms of the American ideals of the Founding Fathers and the experience of immigration. Chicago, in Dewey's time, was notorious for immigrants and their respective problems of integrating into mainstream America. Dewey addressed his educational views to the problem of immigration. In addition to the American experience, it was the European Enlightenment, as well as the scientific-progressive-optimistic-technological worldview, with therapeutic intent, releasing the human being from the shackles of bondage and slavery that was the underlying motif of Dewey's efforts. Dewey was America's substitute for Marx. That is one of the reasons why Marxism never fared well in the United States, as compared to Europe or Asia.[33]

In contrast, Nasr is the heir to a rich and powerful philosophic-theological school, centered in the magnificent Safavid capital of Abbas the Great in sixteenth century Isfahan, Persia.[34] It was a great period in Persian intellectual history, at the time when Descartes won converts for his view in northern Europe, centered in Amsterdam and Leyden. Cartesianism was on its victorious road in European universities, especially in the Netherlands and Scandinavian countries, predominantly Protestant in outlook, while the Isfahan school, led by Mīr Dāmād and his brilliant pupil Ṣadr al-Dīn Shīrāzī, known as Mullā Ṣadrā, worked out his masterpiece, the *Asfār*, that is, *The Transcendent Theosophy concerning the Four Intellectual Journeys of the Soul*.[35] The contrast between Descartes and Mullā Ṣadrā on the one hand, and Dewey and Nasr, on the other hand, is telling. Again, the contrast between Cartesianism and the Iṣfahānī school, between Dewey and Nasr, reflects the stark differentiation between worldviews that exhibits a quest for the domination of nature in terms of the quest for empirical certainty, as pragmatic instrumentalism—in short, a secular approach to solve human problems on earth, and, on the other hand, a sacred road in terms of the divination of nature, as a religious essence in human beings, created by the Divine.[36]

Contrasting the initial statements by Dewey and Nasr we find, at the outset, a methodological approach that is revealing. The former points out, "Man who lives in a world of hazards is compelled to seek for security."[37] The security that Dewey has in mind is rational certainty in the form of mathematics, natural sciences, and technology. Dewey criticizes European philosophers, especially Descartes, for being too timid in that he and his followers sought epistemological certainty, as security on behalf of *theoria* only. What is missing, according to Dewey, is the emphasis upon praxis, or action, and its relation to knowledge. Dewey, in fact, extends the Cartesian view and includes the pragmatic maxim of Peirce with a Deweyan slant. The instrumentality of theoretical knowledge, in the form of applied technology is, to say the least, the project that will save human beings from irrationality, poverty, ignorance, evil, or what Kant called man's "self-incurred immaturity."[38] Pure knowledge alone is not enough. Dewey emphasizes action, doing, and making. It becomes clear that, from Nasr's point of view, Dewey's secular salvation for the ills of this world is a rather one-sided affair and self-defeating. Dewey, of course, did not witness the resurgence of the ecological consciousness, which Nasr, among the foremost thinkers of his generation in the Islamic world, had pronounced. Thus, Nasr's project of reenchantment, in the form of the quest for the sacred, can be understood as a direct challenge to Dewey's technological praxis, in terms of the transcendent Unity of Being, as opposed to instrumental pragmatism. The Western European, the North American, and the Islamic East, thus contrasted, are in much need of more elaboration and commentary. At this point we are just at the beginning of such a project.[39]

V. The Ecological Dimension of the Sacred and the "Recall" of the Transcendent Unity of Being

Already in the early 1960s, Nasr had warned of an ecological crisis—in the West as well as in the Islamic East—at the time when students and intellectuals entertained social revolution.[40] The young people in Tehran listened to the flamboyant speeches of 'Alī Sharī'atī, rather than Nasr.[41] The sign of the times spelled out social revolution, rather than caring for nature. Interesting enough, if some of the intellectual revolutionaries had read their Frankfurt School primer on the *Dialectic of the Enlightenment* (Horkheimer and Adorno) more carefully, they would have discovered that the human being is also a part of nature, and subject to the laws of nature, at least as far as their bodies are concerned.[42] There was hardly any interest in souls. Thus, nature was understood by the 1960s student revolutionaries as it was expounded by the early Ludwig Feuerbach and the later Marx. Contrary to Nasr, they did not have the environment on their agenda. Nature was not considered endangered, but had to be emancipated from the capitalists' exploitation. The late Soviet Union and its adherents, and any sort of socialism generally, were not considered sinners against nature. In the end, when the workers' paradise was achieved, nature would take care of itself, or, as the young Marx had in mind, we could all go fishing. Now we are, hopefully, a little wiser. Nasr's efforts, in the long run, did bear fruit in that he contributed decisively to our consciousness about the oncoming ecological crises being of a global nature.

The environmental disasters of Bhopal (India), Chernobyl (Russia), the *Exxon Valdez* (Alaska), the Amazon Rainforest, the depletion of the ozone layer, and the Green House effect, are watershed events not only for the Western public, but also for our global village. People have become aware that our treatment of nature is amiss. Television images and reports heighten the empirical awareness of the environmental crisis even among the illiterate. What is to be done? The Western response was immediate action: university courses on environmental ethics treated their respective man-made catastrophes as "case studies." The textbook-approach method and attitude is basically social science and technology *per se*, and not steeped in the more spiritual sources of respective traditions found in the West or the East.

In his lectures from the early 1960s, published as *Islam and the Plight of Modern Man*, Nasr pointed out the following, "The missing dimension of the ecological debate is the world and nature of man himself and the spiritual transformation he must undergo if he is to solve the crisis he himself has precipitated."[43] In the meantime, of course, we have developed an ecological discourse that exhibits the heavy underpinning of social, political, and economic concerns, but not the serious concerns of humankind in terms of religious spirituality. It is in this area that Nasr has contributed pioneering insight towards an ecological theomorphism as a forgotten dimension of the sacred.[44]

The causes for the ecological crisis are many and are still novel. But the essential cause of the crisis, as proposed in Nasr's worldview, is humankind's forgetfulness of God. The 1960s language, borrowed from the Marx of 1844, would have been "man's alienation from man."[45] In the context of the sacred, man's alienation from man is the result of the alienation of man from the Divine. Thus, the recipe for overcoming this forgetfulness, or alienation within the context of the sacred, is the rediscovery of the original bond between humankind and the Deity. We must recognize again, according to Nasr, that our theomorphic nature has to be rediscovered and exercised anew in order to be able to "see" harmony, balance, complementarity, and symmetry in our environment which is, after all, the creation of the Deity. A revival of our spiritual heritage, of any respective culture, is a positive condition under which the emergence of a new bond with the Divinity is possible. Thus, Nasr advocates the religious understanding of the order of nature as a prolegomena to any rejuvenation of a sacred bond between humankind and God.[46]

Humankind, in analysis, is the sick man of modern times. Modern man is in need of healing; especially the heart and the soul must undergo a therapy that provides the conditions under which the heart can "feel" again, and the soul can "see" the immanent principle upon which nature is built. In Nasr's texts we find a critique, especially of the Western Renaissance period, when Western man began to diverge from other civilizations.[47] In other words, Western civilization, from his point of view, became eccentric in comparison to other civilizations. Yet, the precise causes and reasons as to why the West turned "eccentric" are still not too clear. Any Western reader of a European or American high school textbook remembers that the Italian Renaissance got especially high grades for representing the manifestation of man's celebration of the Glory of God. God was glorified in the sculpture of the Italian artists, engineers, and painters. A Giotto, a Michelangelo, a Titian, or a Donatello represented humankind through their respective materials and media precisely to worship the greatness of God. For, after all, humankind was God's creation and not vice versa, as Feuerbach had it. We can well imagine that any reader, educated in the classical curriculum of a British public school, or a German gymnasium, must feel at odds with Nasr's perception on that particular point.[48] The West, during the Renaissance and the Scientific Revolution, did not forget about God, or Divinity, recalling the humiliation Galileo had to endure in the name of sacred truth as interpreted by the Vatican, or the way in which Michelangelo celebrated humankind in God's image. The discourse on this matter has been well presented in the work of the late Hans Blumenberg.[49]

That Western science operated with metaphysical presuppositions, so well put in the works of Alfred North Whitehead and E. A. Burtt, is by now an open secret.[50] These are matters that still have to be sorted out in order to come to some kind of balanced assessment of the Renaissance West. I maintain, at this point, that the secularization of the understanding of nature in the West, especially since Kant, did not necessarily discredit the sacred. The heated discussion on Newton's positions within the Anglican Church should suffice to make this point. Churchmen like Clarke, Bentley, or Whiston, just to name the most prominent, on the discourse on the mechanistic universe and the concept of Deity, testify to the intensive discussions, private as well as public, in eighteenth-century England.[51] The essential problem was then as it still is now, how do we engage the sacred in light of the modern scientific perspective? On this point Nasr's contribution to the ecological dimension of the sacred is decisive.

The German romantics, such as Novalis, or the philosopher Schelling, or the North German painter Casper David Friedrich, had tried to suggest ways of reenchanting nature with the Divine and the Sacred.[52] Anyone who has seen the paintings of Friedrich in the Hamburg Kunsthalle or, recently, at the New York Museum of Modern Art, will immediately understand my contention. That strand of thought may be very useful for a Western reader encountering Nasr's ecological demands. Events were not as linear and secularized as many would have us believe. Again, the work of Hans Blumenberg should suffice to disclaim any sort of black-white framework in the context of the sacred-secular debate.

And Nasr clarifies his view, saying that "The destruction of the environment is the result of modern man's attempt to view the natural environment as an ontologically independent order of reality, divorced from the Divine Environment without whose liberating grace it becomes stifled and dies."[53] The method of recovery, that is, Nasr's *Reenchantment Project*, demands a recovery of the bond between spirit and nature, the sacred and "the works of the Supreme Artisan." That recovery has a system in the reenchantment project: it is what we might call the "Recall" of the transcendent Unity of Being. Simple awareness of religious spirituality may be called upon by the population at large. A recall, or remembrance of the original bond between humankind and God, is expressed in the time-honored doctrine, pioneered by Ibn 'Arabī, as the transcendent Unity of Being. The methodological recall of the transcendent Unity of Being is, likewise, the recovery of the ecological dimension of the sacred. Nasr proposes that a sacred science can succeed in filling the present-day void in the religious understanding of the order of nature caused by the exclusive technological *Weltanschauung* of modern science: "There is need of ethical action toward all natural beings on the basis of a knowledge of the order of nature corresponding to an objective reality, a knowledge that is itself ultimately a sacred science, a *scientia sacra*."[54] Of course, the basic distinction between a sacred science and the modern sciences that deal with environmental issues is that the modern sciences record empirical data in order to draw upon conclusions reached through induction or deduction, and, at the same time, exclude the religious attitude. The original laboratorium, work and pray, has been reduced to action—man then sees experimental activities exclusively in terms of labor, as the young Marx pointed out and as reiterated in a more mature version by Hannah Arendt.[55] Nasr proposes a sacred laboratorium in which humankind does, indeed, work with respect towards fellow workers and researchers at the task at hand, as reflected in the context of the principle of the Divine. The "sacred laboratorium" operates fundamentally on the basis of a metaphysics that Nasr understands as *philosophia perennis*. It is the principle of the *philosophia perennis* that guides him in the "recall" of the transcendent Unity of Being, as a preliminary exercise of the ecological dimension of the sacred. Without the *recall* there cannot be a sacred dimension of the ecological landscape. Nasr reiterates, "The *philosophia perennis* sees a unity which underlies the diversity of religious forms and practices, a unity which resides within that quintessential truth at the heart of religions that is none other than the *philosophia perennis* itself."[56] In this sense Nasr connects the idea of the *philosophia perennis* with the Sufi doctrine of the transcendent Unity of Being as reflected in the work of Ibn 'Arabī. This subtle relationship between the Sufi understanding of nature and contemporary awareness of the necessity of a moral posture towards nature has not been explored sufficiently.[57] Nasr is a pioneer in this field and he often points a finger toward the ecological field that a younger generation of Muslim scholars should plow.

Again, the special concerns about nature and our environment, in light of the revolutionary developments in communication technology and the whole gambit of the audio-visual parameter, not to mention the transvaluation of values on the global scale, has to be explored in more detail.[58] In Nasr's perspective we encounter the possibility of offering a comprehensive worldview that combines natural philosophy, metaphysics, the sciences, and the religious dimensions that provides solutions to our pressing problems. The recall of the transcendent Unity of Being is a prerequisite for such a worldview. In that sense a sacred epistemology is a necessity. The valuation of ecological concerns and the metaphysical presuppositions are two dimensions in which a sacred epistemology must operate. This is a necessity; otherwise, we end up with the typical environmental ethics attitudes portrayed in various journals and academic papers, whose object it is to offer "practical solutions" to ecological problems, which are considered problems of the social sciences, to be resolved in terms of social engineering. Needless to say, the idea of the sacred in this field of endeavor appears as an eccentric attitude not to be taken too seriously, at least from the conventional scientific attitude of positivism.

VI. The Legitimacy of the Intellectual Intuition of God: Why Does the West, since Kant, Have a Legitimacy Problem of Sacred Epistemology?

Concluding my interpretation of Nasr's perspective on these matters I must resort to an essential question that is at the heart of the fundamental difference between the Western view of legitimate knowledge, especially since Kant, and the Islamic East, perennially concerned with the intellectual intuition of the Divine. I want to focus on this specific problem in the following section of my paper, and conclude with a preliminary assessment of Nasr's quest for the sacred. The epistemological concerns of a sacred epistemology and legitimacy of knowledge in terms of the intellectual intuition of the Divine are intimately laced into our concerns with the ecological dimension of the sacred. The *philosophia perennis* takes center stage in the whole enterprise which I called Nasr's reenchantment project. The perennial concern of a theosophy (for example, that of Suhrawardī or Mullā Ṣadrā) has functionally ceased to exist in Western consciousness since the Scientific Revolution. The chain of thought from Plato and Plotinus to Meister Eckhart, Cusanus, the Romantics (Novalis, the Schlegel brothers, Schelling) has made some inroads among the more sensitive of the 1960s generation, but has not been pursued in a serious manner, such as through a sacred epistemology. Yet, the legitimate concerns of an intellectual intuition of the Divine were never entirely discarded in the Western Hemisphere, as Anneliese Maier, the historian of natural philosophy, and Hans Blumenberg have shown.[59] Somehow, intellectual intuition has been an appendix to the more scientific epistemology that was promoted in the process of making science a positivistic enterprise. Newton could still be moved by his friend's critique (Richard Bentley) of the apparent discrepancy between a mechanistic conception of the universe and conventional Christian views. Yet Kant no longer felt that he had to apologize, except in a political context. The *Kritik der reinen Vernunft* was a comprehensive enterprise and accordingly took care of the intellectual intuition (*intellektuelle Anschauung*, especially) as a regulative principle, and as part of a secular epistemology. The reality of the Divine is transformed into a regulative concept to be entertained analogously as a hypothesis in science, for which, however, one could never provide sufficient empirical evidence. Humankind has been left dangling between earth and heaven ever since. Here the gap between the West and the Islamic East turned into the irreconcilable differences that exist to this day. I suggest that Nasr's reenchantment project provides us with an initial response to our dilemma: reconciling a secular and sacred epistemology.

The situation is clear: In Nasr's universe of discourse the concepts of revelation, unity, origin, source, tradition, perennial wisdom, sophia, and intellectual intuition of God are interrelated like a cobweb. There is no doubt about the matrix of intuiting the world in its relation to the Absolute. The reenchantment project is the basic program that shows the way towards regaining, that is, *recalling*, the fundamental insight of humankind, according to Nasr: "Intelligence, which is the instrument of knowledge within man, is endowed with the possibility of knowing the Absolute."[60] But this is precisely what is systematically denied in Western philosophy, since Kant.

Habermas's idea, going back to Kant, is clear: that reason is a historical product of humankind's development ushering in "communicative reason" in the twentieth century and turning into a ". . . binding force of intersubjective understanding and reciprocal reception."[61] Nasr's idea of a theosophy, as we read the respective passages in his *Three Muslim Sages*, is worlds apart from the Habermasian *Weltanschauung*. We would have to return to Spinoza and Leibniz to be able to "feel" the words again pronounced by Nasr, "By theosophy we mean that form of wisdom which is neither philosophy nor theology—but a knowledge of the Divine mysteries. . . ."[62]

Clearly a fault line developed in this area of intellectual activity between the West and the Islamic East. The break can be seen in the seventeenth century of the West. Again, only in Spinoza and Leibniz do we find an echo of what Nasr is trying to revive through his reenchantment project. Let us listen to the words of Leibniz: "I am glad that the most solid part of the theology of the mystics is preserved . . . what there is true and good in our knowledge is still an emanation from the light of God, and that it is in this sense that it may be said, that we see all things in God."[63] These are words that the Illumination school thinkers since Suhrawardī would have understood if they had the chance to read and meet Leibniz. On the other hand, Leibniz did not know about the Iṣfahānī and Ishrāqī schools of the Islamic East, although they were contemporaries. Leibniz and the Jesuits had their eyes on China. Yet, article 47 of his *Monadology*, restates the situation clearly, "Thus God alone is the primary unity, . . . , from which all monads, created and derived, are produced, and are born, so to speak, by continual fulgurations of the Divinity from moment to moment, limited by the receptivity of the created being, which is of its essence limited."[64] This statement certainly reaches out to the sacred as a divine quest towards the Absolute—the primary unity. Yet the monad has an inbuilt characteristic that produces contradiction, which reveals the subtle crack developing into a big gap between West and East: the human creature is limited in its way of knowing God, or the primary unity. Although it is created by the Absolute, it is no longer in the position to apprehend its own creation, as an Absolute. In Spinoza we find a frantic effort to preserve the original bond of absolute unity between God, Man, and Nature, to no avail. Spinoza and Leibniz were the last Western thinkers capable of incorporating the Greek legacy, Eastern Hermeticism, and a unitary vision, as exhibited in the monotheistic religions. They still had a feeling for what Nasr called sacred wisdom, or what the Italian Augustinian Agostino Steuco in his *De perenni philosophia* of 1540 called ". . . one principle of all things, of which there has always been one and the same knowledge among all people."[65]

Precisely what had been lost in the mode of Western thought is the feeling for the Divine Mystery. Nasr emphasizes over and over again that the original idea of *intellectus*, not reason, is basic to *philosophia perennis*—that intellection in its original understanding, since Plato, and especially since Plotinus, got lost on the way to the critique of pure reason, in which reason (*Vernunft*) takes on an analytical function for humankind, rather than serving metaphysical speculation. Transcendence is divided into different types of transcendentalism with their respective *Weltanschauungen* (worldviews). It is no surprise that the term *Weltanschauung* has been accepted generally as pertaining to the world exclusively. A *Gottesanschauung* (contemplation of God) is something for mystics, as understood by Western philosophic academics. Reason claims, as Habermas put it, the criteria for reasonable behavior for human beings. To qualify as being recognized as human means foremost, in the Kantian-Habermasian lineage, to meet the standards of rationality that discursive knowledge dictates.[66] In discursive knowledge, intuition of an Absolute is neither possible nor desirable. For this is the problem: how can we have intuition (*intellektuelle Anschauung*) of something that cannot be verified empirically or just hypothesized mathematically? What kind of evidence is there, aside from the intuitive pronouncement of those who maintain that there is such a cognitive experience? All this is not easy to fathom. The logical analysis game will not do—for the matter at hand is too serious to be handled by mere niceties of logical ballet—the problem is paramount.[66]

The tension between those who claim knowledge as *intellectus*, or *nous*, and those recurring to ratio, or reason, is well known. This situation has been with us since Plotinus and Spinoza and was brought to life again by that sage Goethe, who, it may be said, was the last Western thinker who practiced *philosophia perennis* in earnest. The problem reemerges between the claims of the romantics and positivists in the early nineteenth century, and then flourished in the 1960s with the student revolt at large. The poet-philosopher Novalis still spoke of "*innere Schau.*" This meant a revolt against official Cartesian dualism and its consequences. The experience of the Absolute is still possible in Schelling, who spoke the kind of language every devout Muslim understands: "Not we are in time, . . . , but pure eternity is in us."[67] It is an open secret among Schelling scholars that romantics like Novalis, the Schlegel brothers, Fichte, perhaps Hölderlin, Schleiermacher, Tieck, and Schelling himself, were certainly deeply influenced by the insights of Plotinus—the very ideas that the Arabs picked up as the "Theology of Aristotle."[68] These curious relations and dimensions await exploration by a new generation.

The mystic ecstasy is the paradigm for intellectual intuition. Aristotle's logic is the framework in which discursive logic operates. The problem for the West, since Kant, we find in Plotinus's *Ennead, Book* VI.9.7, "On the Good and The One": Knowledge is non-discursive, it eliminates any temporality of otherness. The *Nous* is another way of seeing in a non-mediated, non-dialectical mode, since the Divine and the One is in us. We are in the One—nature and mind are One. The tension appears for Fichte, Kant, and Hegel: if intellectual intuition does not claim objective knowledge, non-conceptualization, negating *Dasein* and replacing it with mystic annihilation, how can we arrive at an objective subject? How is intuition as God-intuition (*Gottesanschauung*) possible in a finite human being? These are some of the relevant problems of the respective topics we find in the German idealistic tradition. The relevance to Nasr's quest for the sacred should be obvious. It is a major problem in the reenchantment project, as presented by Nasr throughout his work. Again, Schelling expressed this matter as precisely as possible in his *System of Transcendental Idealism* (1800), "Das erste Problem der Philosophie lässt sich also auch so ausdrücken: etwas zu finden, was schlechterdings nicht als Ding gedacht werden kann. . . . (The first problem of philosophy can also be expressed thus: finding something that cannot by any means be thought as a Thing)."[69] That is exactly the point: The Absolute cannot be thought of as a something, that is, as an entity, or as Strawson's *Individual* inhabiting the space-time dimension. For Kant this problem appears as that of the "*innere Anschauung*" (he speaks of it as *problematisch).*[70] If pure reason deals with the system of all principles that makes possible the cognition of objects, how can a non-entity possibly be cognized? Intuition (*Anschauung*) *per se* is not sufficient for Kant. It begs the empirical evidence for us to establish it as a legitimate entity. This legitimacy problem is important to those who claim that sacred epistemology is possible.

Intuition, as an epistemological category, is a blind spot within the framework of Western philosophy since the Scientific Revolution and the rise of positivism. The very concept of intuition (*Anschauung*) is a problematic issue within Kant's program, as outlined in his first *Critique,* and in modern Western philosophy generally. There is nothing to suggest that the mainstream philosophy textbooks, presenting the Rationalists (Descartes, Spinoza, Leibniz) and the Empiricists (Locke, Berkeley, Hume) differ on the idea of intuition. Already in the eighteenth century the intellectual public in London and Paris did not take intuition seriously. Besides, this sort of activity is reserved for gifted poets, prophets, seers like Swedenborg, and clever salon women. Intuition, as a legitimate category of truth (that is, scientific knowledge) was no longer taken seriously or respected. It lost its legitimacy. Intuition becomes a linguistic problem for Kant since he uses the Latin *intuitio* in his dissertation and transforms the Latin term, for want of an equivalent term in German, into *Anschauung*.[71] This left the exclusive

Anglo-Saxon-American reader somewhat puzzled. English translations of the Kantian texts reverted to the Latin term; thus, intuition turns out to be *Anschauung*, although any German reader knows that this is not its equivalent. In fact, there is no equivalent term in English to convey the idea of *Anschauung*. In Kant we find different kinds of *Anschauungen*, from formal to sensible ones. What is decisive for our question is, considering the difficulty, how can we translate Nasr's reenchantment project into adequate language for a Western educated person?

In the decisive and controversial part of Kant's first *Critique* entitled *Transcendental Deduction of Pure Concepts of the Understanding* (B129–B131), he starts his famous paragraph on the proto-synthetic unity of apperception as follows: "*Ich denke, muss alle meine Vorstellungen begleiten können . . .* ?" (It must be possible for the 'I think' to accompany all my representations . . .).[72] Kant tries to find the foundation for the epistemological subject that can claim to state, "*Ich denke*." But, there must be something that gives the subject a counterpart, namely, an object. In short, the epistemological subject can only recognize itself, if at all, as an object itself, in a temporal context as "something," and be able to verify, empirically, that it possesses individuality, in the mode we find brilliantly exhibited by Strawson in his *Individuals*.[73]

Considering this background, we now can reiterate our problem: How can we speak of intellectual intuition of God? This is a serious epistemological problem since Kant, and has not adequately been resolved in modern philosophy. If I, as a person, cannot objectify myself, how can I objectify the idea of God? Of course, this type of crude question already presupposes that in order to attain the status of subject (epistemologically speaking), one must have an object. The story of the subject-object dialectic, since Hegel and Marx, is well-known and need not be recounted at present. Kant handles the notion of God in a respectful manner and leaves the whole matter in an aporetical situation. In this context Kant never uses the term "*Gott*," but "*Urheber*," that is, a something that gave birth to a foundation in the old high German. We know, of course, that he suggests using the concept of God as a regulative principle of understanding, in the manner of a hypothesis in science.

Newton exemplifies this Kantian notion, without being aware of it; in his *Principia Mathematica* he claims gravity is a phenomenon, but what it is in itself—only God knows (the Pantokrator), according to Newton. Even Roger Coates, his brilliant young assistant, made the mistake of ascribing to the master that he knew what gravity is. Kant is more radical and points out that human beings are not able, due to their respective constitution, if we restrict the epistemological subject to a temporal context, of claiming absolute certainty about anything, except what is given in the space-time context. Thus, for Kant God is a possibility, but cannot be proven empirically, precisely for the reason that we are limited by the space-time continuum. Kant was not a proclaimed atheist, but an agnostic with leanings toward believing in a rational Divine Being. That is as far as he would commit himself. Western philosophy has never recovered from this situation.

The problem we entertain now is, how can we initiate a meaningful dialogue or discourse between Western philosophy and the kind of project Nasr is proposing? For intellectual intuition of Divinity is absolutely essential in Nasr's worldview. Simply to bypass Kant would not do, since Kant is not easily bypassed. Thus, we must find a way to enlist Kant's help to make it plausible that intellectual intuition is, in fact, a legitimate category of epistemology, especially in the "reenchantment epistemology." For the sake of brevity let us call it "sacred epistemology": we can identify Nasr's program as a reenchantment project based upon a sacred epistemology.

If we reconstruct some worldviews, from Plato to Plotinus, to Meister Eckhart, Cusanus, and German Romantics (Novalis, Schlegel, Schelling, Steffen), not to mention Spinoza and Goethe, we find that the idea of an intellectual intuition of God is quite legitimate. The reconstruction has to be conducted in such a way that we can reconcile the Neo-Platonic tradition with the nominalists of late medieval philosophy, from Ockham to the analytic schools, from Newton to Whitehead. The union of theology and science in terms of the intuition of the world as a unique place among the creations of God has been dissipated since the seventeenth century. We are now ready, as the gateway of the twenty-first century is opened, for a more comprehensive and mature view in which we can continue to labor in the experimental fields of science, but make more sense of phenomena that do not enter into the big picture of scientific evidence. We know that scientific evidence is not comprehensive; there are many odds and ends in the claims made by science. Alfred North Whitehead is among those thinkers in the twentieth century who tried to formulate a comprehensive picture with no pretense of scientific hubris. He was an accomplished mathematician and a genius of speculative philosophy, equal to the other genius of Western philosophy, Heidegger. Thus, there is a chance to come to terms with Nasr's reenchantment project that does justice to ourselves and to the Islamic East. Our survival as human beings may depend on it.[74]

VII. Conclusion

I have not traced Nasr's quest for the sacred by investigating every minute detail in his work. A full-fledged book would be needed to do that. I merely wanted to show how an Islamic thinker, well-versed in the sciences professionally and well-acquainted with the cultural heritage of the West, presents a worldview that challenges the present mainstream contentions in the West: the road and progress of secularized modernity, with all its powerful trappings of power, money, and consumption, may not necessarily be the great solution for all humankind to follow. There are serious blind spots in the worldview of the West and Nasr's importance in the world of thought is precisely to have pointed out these lacunae of the Western paradigm. Hopefully, through the Library of Living Philosophers, Nasr will be made known to mainstream Western academic philosophy so it can come to terms with itself. After all, did not Socrates say, that to know oneself is a high virtue, but to know God, is the highest virtue of which humankind is capable?

ERNEST WOLF-GAZO

DEPARTMENT OF ENGLISH AND COMPARATIVE LITERATURE
PHILOSOPHY UNIT
THE AMERICAN UNIVERSITY IN CAIRO
CAIRO, EGYPT
MARCH 1999

NOTES

1. See *Science and Civilization in Islam* (Cambridge, Mass.: Harvard University Press, 1968) translated into Persian, Urdu, Malay, Turkish, Italian, French, and Arabic. This major work is the first serious approach to the history and philosophy of science in the contemporary Islamic world and should be read in conjunction with Nasr's *An Introduction to Islamic Cosmological Doctrines* (London: Thames and Hudson Ltd., 1978, Revised Edition), which emphasizes the philosophy of nature conception within the Islamic context. *The Need for a Sacred Science* (Albany: State University of New York Press, 1993) is Nasr's mature synthesis of the previous works, which combines philosophy and the history of science with the philosophy of nature, enmeshed in the environmental-concern-and-ecological-ethics-issue, unique to the Islamic frame of reference. Also, see Jane I. Smith, "Seyyed Hossein Nasr (b. 1933)," in *Oxford Encyclopaedia of the Modern Islamic World*, vol. 3, pp. 230–31; and "S. H. Nasr: Defender of the Sacred and Islamic Traditionalism," in *The Muslims of America*, edited by Yvonne Y. Haddad (Oxford University Press, 1991), pp. 88–95.

2. See *Knowledge and The Sacred* (New York: Crossroad, 1981). Nasr is the first Muslim to be honored with delivering the Gifford Lectures since its inception in 1888, which includes such luminaries of Western philosophy as Dewey,

Whitehead, Bergson, William James, Karl Barth, or Werner Heisenberg, with Radhakrishnan being the first Hindu thinker to be honored. See Stanley L. Jaki, *Lord Gifford and His Lectures* (Edinburgh University Press, 1986).

3. See Max Weber, "Science as a Vocation," in *From Max Weber: Essays in Sociology*, edited with an introduction by H. H. Gerth and C. Wright Mills; with a new preface by Bryan S. Turner (London: Routledge, 1991), p. 155. Relevant material in Weber's *Wirtschaftsgeschichte—Abriss der universalen sozial—und wirtschaftsgeschichte*, edited by S. Hellman and M. Palyi (Berlin: 4th edition, 1981), pp. 232–33 and p. 270. Paradigmatic statement by Weber: "Wo immer aber rational empirisches Erkennen die Entzauberung der Welt und deren Verwandlung in einen kausalen Mechanismus konsequent vollzogen hat, tritt die Spannung gegen die Ansprüche des ethischen Postulates, dass die Welt ein götterordneter, also irgendeine ethisch sinnvoll orientierter Kosmos sei, endgültig hervor." In *Max Weber: Soziologie, Universalgeschichtliche Analysen, Politik*, edited by Johannes Winckelmann (Stuttgart: Kroner Verlag, 1973, 5th edition), p. 472.

4. cf. S. H. Nasr, *Knowledge and The Sacred*, ibid.

5. This concept has been entertained in the Islamic World especially by Ibn 'Arabī and his followers.

6. It is an open secret of the profession that the most innovative and creative philosophic work is done in literature departments, instead of philosophy departments, in the Anglo-American world.

7. Edmund Husserl's life-world as "proto-evident," for example, "Die Lebenswelt ist ein Reich ursprünglicher Evidenzen" and "Die paradoxen Aufeinandergezogenheiten von 'objektiv wahrer' und 'Lebenswelt' machen die Seinsweise beider rätselhaft." This is precisely the problem Habermas comes to terms with in his theory of communicative rationality; see respectively, *Phänomenologie und Lebenswelt. Ausgewählte Texte II*, edited by Klaus Held (Stuttgart: Reclam, 1992), pp. 283 and 288; in contrast, see Jürgen Habermas, *Der philosophische Diskurs der Moderne* (Frankfurt am Main: Suhrkamp Verlag, 1988, 3rd edition 1991), p. 45: "Die Moderne Welt leidet an falschen Identitäten, weil sie, im Alltag wie in der Philosophie, jeweils ein Bedingtes absolute setzt."

8. The loss of cultural tradition is supplanted by traditions of habits. The world of computer technology has replaced traditional culture with virtual culture embodied in the television and audio-visual landscape in the U.S.

9. In this Nasr also agrees with the Anglo-American poet of modernity, T. S. Eliot. The specific problem between Nasr and Eliot is the status of the individuals in community. Eliot describes the "individual, what is the peculiar essence of man." See his "Tradition and the Individual Talent" in T. S. Eliot, *Selected Essays* (London: Faber and Faber, 1934), p. 14.

10. Cf. Ronald Taylor, *Berlin and its Culture: A Historical Portrait* (New Haven: Yale University Press, 1997), pp. 89–113.

11. These respective authors form the basic support for Nasr's methodology in dealing with the Sacred. They are footnoted throughout Nasr's works.

12. The academic treatment of tradition is symptomatic for twentieth-century ethnology. On this, Claude Lévi-Strauss had something telling to reveal: "For many anthropologists, perhaps, not just myself, the ethnological vocation is a flight from civilization, from a century in which one doesn't feel at home." See *Conversations*

with CLS, edited by D. Eribon (Chicago: Chicago University Press, 1991), p. 67. The same is also true for Clifford Geertz; see his *The Interpretation of Culture* (New York: Basic Books, 1973) and Richard Bernstein, "Anthropologist, Retracing Steps After 3 Decades, Is Shocked," in *The New York Times Education*, May 11, 1988, B6.

13. The world success of the video tape *The Lion King* was due to the fact that parents as well as grandparents found meaningful messages in the fairy tale.

14. Cf. S. H. Nasr, *Sufi Essays* (London: Allen and Unwin, 1972), p. 35.

15. Instructive in this regard is Chadwick Owen, *The Secularization of the European Mind in the 19th Century* (Cambridge: Cambridge University Press, 1990).

16. Cf. Victor Lowe, *A. N. Whitehead: The Man and His Work* (Baltimore: Johns Hopkins University Press, 1991, 2 Vols.); Ernest Wolf-Gazo, ed., *Whitehead: Eine Einfuhrung in seine Kosmologie* (Freiburg i.Br.: Alber Verlag, 1980); T. M. Forsyth, "The New Cosmology in its Historical Aspects: Plato, Newton, Whitehead," *Philosophy* VII (1932): 54–61.

17. Nasr is a rare intellectual in the Islamic East in that he has a sound scientific educational background plus a classical heritage education from his family and society and, above all, leaves politics and ideology outside the classroom.

18. The beautifully kept tomb of 'Umar Khayyām near Nishapur, which I visited in August 1998, testifies that scientific endeavor, natural beauty, and architectural subtlety are not strangers to one another. This can also be said of the nearby tomb of 'Aṭṭār, and the tombs of Ibn Sīnā at Hamadan and those of Ḥāfiẓ and Sa'dī in Shiraz.

19. See a first-class account by Walter Kranz, the co-editor of the famous *Die Vorsokratiker,* who was exiled, along with Hellmut Ritter and Erich Auerbach in Istanbul, *KOSMOS*, *Archiv für Begriffsgeschichte*, Bd. 2, Teil 1 (Bonn: Bouvier Verlag, 1955); in the same *Archiv*, see Claus Haebler, *Kosmos—Eine etymologisch-wortgeschichtliche Untersuchung* (*Archiv*, Band XI, Heft 2, 1967), pp. 101–18; of related interest, see Thomas Lier, "Hellmut Ritter in Istanbul 1926–1949," *Die Welt des Islams* 38, no. 3 (1998): 334–85.

20. In fact, Heidegger's project in *Sein und Zeit* could be called the "retrieval of *Sein*."

21. See the comparative study by Alparslan Acikgenc, *Being and Existence: Heidegger and Mullā Ṣadrā* (Kuala Lumpur, Malaysia: ISTAC, 1997): a dissertation written under the guidance of the late Professor Fazlur Rahman at the University of Chicago; also, see James Winston Morris, *The Wisdom of the Throne: An Introduction to the Philosophy of Mullā Ṣadrā* (Princeton, N.J.: Princeton University Press, 1981).

22. Corbin's translation of Heidegger was instrumental in opening up Heidegger's work to the existentialist generation of Paris of the 1950s.

23. Cf. S. H. Nasr, " Henry Corbin: The Life and Works of the Occidental Exile in the Quest of the Orient of Light," in *Traditional Islam in the Modern World* (London: Routledge and Kegan Paul, 1987), pp. 273–90.

24. The Kantian difference between transcendence and transcendental is basic towards grasping Kant's *Transzendentalphilosophie*.

25. It is interesting that this fundamental perspective is also followed by the

present-day President of the Islamic Republic of Iran, Seyyed Muhammad Khatami, a former professor of philosophy at Tehran University, and a student of Nasr's works.

26. Cf. S. H. Nasr, "Religious Art, Traditional Art, Sacred Art: Some Reflections and Definitions," in *Sophia, A Journal of Traditional Studies* 2, no. 2, (Winter 1996): 13–30: "Sacred art is the heart of the traditional art of a particular traditional civilization, dealing as it does with rites and spiritual practices associated with the rites and the Divine Message governing the tradition in question" (p. 20).

27. See for a good overview for the English reader Frank Whitford's, *Bauhaus* (London: Thames and Hudson, 1988), and, of course, the standard massive work by Hans M. Wingler, *The Bauhaus* (Cambridge, Mass.: MIT Press, 1969).

28. That the religious is a higher level of consciousness is already expressed in the work of the young Hegel and his compatriot, the poet Hölderlin. In that sense Marx agrees with Aristotle's judgment on the religious, while Hegel and Max Weber continue the Neo-Platonic version of religion, despite the rationalization thesis of Hegel and Weber.

29. This tradition initiated by the highly original work by Shihāb al-Dīn Yaḥyā Suhrawardī had enormous influence in Persia and the Indian subcontinent. Nasr stands in the *Ishrāqī* tradition as revised by Mullā Ṣadrā and the Iṣfahānī school. See S. H. Nasr, *Ṣadr al-Dīn Shīrāzī and His Transcendent Theosophy* (Tehran: Institute for Humanities and Cultural Studies, 1997, New Edition) and Mehdi Amin Razavi, *Suhrawardī and the School of Illumination* (London: Curzon Press 1997).

30. Cf. S. H. Nasr, *Knowledge and the Sacred* (New York: Crossroad, 1981) and John Dewey, *The Quest for Certainty* (New York: Capricorn, 1929).

31. His *Process and Reality* (New York: The Free Press, 1978, Corrected Edition) is certainly the most speculative attempt by any thinker in the twentieth century. Contrasting studies, at this point, yield valuable results as to a proper understanding of thought structures and forms in varieties of cultures, unknown to each other, or highly misunderstood, based on misinformation and mistrust, as is the sad case between the West and Islam. I have treated this in "John Dewey in Turkey," *Journal of American Studies of Turkey* 3 (1996): 15–42; and my "Malay Identity, Islam, and the Other Language," in *English and Islam: Creative Encounters*, Proceedings of an International Conference at the International Islamic University of Malaysia on 20–22 December 1996, Kuala Lumpur, Malaysia, edited by J. U. Khan and A. E. Hare (Kuala Lumpur, Gombak: The Research Center of IIUM, 1998), pp. 198–208; and in my presentation of "The Transformation of Substance in Whitehead and Mullā Ṣadrā" at the World Congress of Mullā Ṣadrā held in Tehran, Iran, in May 23–27, 1999; also see M. H. Zuberi, *Aristotle and Al-Ghazali* (Delhi-1106: Noor Publ. House, 1992), and M. A. Abdullah, *Ghazali and Kant* (Ankara: Turkiye Diyanet Vakfi, 1992).

32. Cf. A. N. Whitehead, *Process and Reality*, ibid., p. 24.

33. See the comprehensive George Dykhuizen, *The Life and Mind of John Dewey* (Carbondale: Southern Illinois Press, 1973) and still relevant, Ralf Dahrendorf, *Die Angewandte Aufklärung* (Frankfurt am Main: Fischer Verlag, 1968), and the highly instructive, John J. McDermott, *The Culture of Experience: Philosophic Essays in the American Grain* (New York: New York University Press, 1976).

34. See the relevant entries in the new edition of the *Cambridge History of Iran*;

the excellent work by Heinz Halm, *Shia Islam* (Munich: Beck Verlag, 1994, English translation by Cambridge University Press 1996), S. H. Nasr, *The Islamic Intellectual Tradition in Persia*, edited by M. A. Razavi (London: Curzon Press, 1998), pp. 239–70, and Mehdi Ha'iri Yazdi, *The Principles of Epistemology in Islamic Philosophy* (Albany: State University Press of New York, 1992).

35. See the works by Max Horten, Fazlur Rahman, and Winston Morris.

36. This difficulty and antagonism is maintained contemporaneously. See, for example, Samuel Huntington, *Clashes of Civilization and the Remaking of the World Order* (New York: Simon and Schuster, 1997), and compare with the interview by the Islamic Republic Iranian President Khatami, given to CNN, and the opening speech at the U.N. on September 22, 1998.

37. Dewey, *Quest for Certainty*, p. 3.

38. See Kant's well known article entitled "Was ist Aufklärung?" in *Was heisst Aufklärung*? edited by E. Bahr (Stuttgart: Reclam, 1985).

39. Ideological battles on the cultural front are useless, since they are usually fought by cultural illiterates, opportunists, and political exploiters of passions. What is needed are teams of the educated of particular cultures to exchange views and compare and contrast the structures and forms of their respective traditions, in order to get rid of the idols of the cave. This is the reason why comparison and contrast studies of cultures are needed to initiate a serious and fruitful discourse among cultures. Orientalism or Occidentalism serve only the ideologues and are basically useless toward a genuine discourse among cultures. See Ernest Wolf-Gazo, "Postmodernism's Critique of the Enlightenment," *Journal of Islamic Research* 6, no. 1 (Fall 1992): 1–16, and "Contextualizing Averroes within the German Hermeneutic Tradition," *Averroes and the Rational Legacy in the East and the West*: *ALIF*, vol. 16 (1996): pp. 133–63

40. See L. H. Newton and C. K. Dillingham, editors, *Watersheds: Classic Cases in Environmental Ethics* (Belmont: Wadsworth Co., 1994); S. H. Nasr, *Islam and the Plight of Modern Man* (London: Thames and Hudson, New Edition, 1978); Ibrahim Ozdemir, *The Ethical Dimension of Human Attitudes Towards Nature* (Ankara: The Ministry of Environment, originally a Ph.D. thesis from Middle East Technical University, Philosophy Department, 1997); and, of course, S. H. Nasr, "Prologue: Islam and the Study of Nature," in *Introduction to Islamic Cosmological Doctrines* (London: Thames and Hudson, New Edition, 1978, originally a Harvard Dissertation in the History of Science Department), pp. 1–12; also see S. H. Nasr, "Islam and the Environmental Crisis," *Journal of Islamic Research* 4, no. 3 (July 1990): 155–74.

41. See Ali Rahnema, *An Islamic Utopian: A Political Biography of 'Alī Sharī'atī* (London: I.B. Tauris, 1998); and also relevant are Mehrzad Boroujerdi, *Iranian Intellectuals and the West* (Syracuse: Syracuse University Press); Ali Gheissari, *Iranian Intellectuals in the Twentieth Century* (Austin: University of Texas, 1998).

42. See S. E. Bronner and D. M. Kellner, editors, *Critical Theory and Society* (New York: Routledge, 1989); and Peter Gay, *Weimar Culture* (New York: Harper, 1975).

43. S. H. Nasr, *Islam and the Plight of Modern Man* (New York: Longman, 1975), p. 13.

44. There is great interest in this matter among the younger generation of serious Muslim scholars in Turkey, Egypt, Malaysia, and Iran, to name a few countries in which the present author has lived and toured extensively. These scholars have shown excellent work and a capacity for environmental ethics and philosophy of nature. This is a divergence from the older paradigm of positivism, socialism, and old-fashioned nationalism. Unfortunately, the political spectrum has not kept up with this new scholarly trend. See Ernest Wolf-Gazo, "Remarks on Islamic Scholarship at a Crossroad," *Journal of Islamic Research* 5, no. 2 (April 1991): 136–40.

45. See Karl Marx, *Die Frühschriften*, edited by Siegfried Landshut (Stuttgart: Kroner Verlag, 1971, originally published in 1953).

46. This project was presented in its mature form in Nasr's 1994 Cadbury Lectures at the University of Birmingham, England, and published as *Religion and the Order of Nature* (New York: Oxford University Press, 1996). See especially chapter 8, in which we find basic statements by Nasr, supporting the idea of his reenchantment project: (a) "Man is created to seek the Absolute and the Infinite. When the Divine Principle, which is at once absolute and infinite, is denied, the yearning and the search within the human soul nevertheless continues" (p. 272); (b) "The ground must be cleared and a space created for the reassertion of the religious understanding of the order of nature as authentic knowledge, . . ." (p. 273); (c) "What is needed is a rediscovery of nature as sacred reality and a rebirth of man as the guardian of the sacred, . . . the pontifical man whose reality we still bear within ourselves. Nor does it mean the invention of a sacred view of nature, . . . but rather the reformulation of the traditional cosmologies and views of nature held by various religions throughout history" (p. 287). We find an interesting critique of Kant's position on pp. 105ff. and 123, offering as an alternative " . . . the science of the Real as such, or *scientia sacra*" (p. 173).

47. Nasr speaks throughout his works of the course of Western civilization within world history as an "anomaly." See, for example, *Ideals and Realities of Islam* (Cairo: The American University in Cairo Press Edition, 1988), pp. 96ff.

48. Again, I refer to the representative works on the Renaissance by Ernst Cassirer, Erwin Panofsky, Paul O. Kristeller, or the late Charles B. Schmitt, not to mention the classic works in German (but never translated into any other language) by Anneliese Maier, a Roman Catholic nun in Rome; see Hans Blumenberg on Maier in "Die Vorbereitung der Neuzeit," *Philosophische Rundschau* 9 (1961), 81–133.

49. See the major works by Hans Blumenberg, *Die kopernikanische Wende* (Frankfurt am Main: Suhrkamp, 1965); *Legitimität der Neuzeit* (Suhrkamp, 2nd edition, 1977); *Arbeit am Mythos* (Suhrkamp, 2nd edition, 1981)—most of Blumenberg's works have been published by MIT Press in English translation.

50. Cf. A. N. Whitehead, *Science and the Modern World* (New York: The Free Press, 1985, New Edition); E. A. Burtt, *The Metaphysical Foundation of Modern Science* (New York: Anchor/Doubleday, 1954, originally published in 1924); and the classic in the history of science, Herbert Butterfield, *The Origin of Modern Science* (New York: The Free Press, 1966, revised edition); for a more specialized approach see Ernest Wolf-Gazo, "Whitehead and Locke's Concept of 'Power'," *Process Studies*, 14, no. 4 (Winter 1985), 237–52.

51. See Larry Stewart, "Seeing through the Scholium: Religion and Reading Newton in the Eighteenth Century," *History of Science* XXXIV (1996): 123–65; and Ernest Wolf-Gazo, "Newton's Science in the Context of Religion," *Journal of Islamic Research* 6, no. 4 (Fall 1993): 279–92, and supplementary by the author, "Newton's Pantokrator and Hegel's Absolute Mind" in *Hegel and Newtonianism*, edited by M. J. Petry (Dordrecht: Kluwer Academic Publisher, 1993), pp. 125–35; see also the classic by Frank E. Manuel, *The Religion of Isaac Newton* (Oxford: Oxford University Press, 1974).

52. See Berbeli Wanning, *Novalis zur Einführung* (Hamburg: Junius Verlag, 1996), and Martin Dyck, *Novalis and Mathematics: A Study of Friedrich von Hardenberg's Fragments on Mathematics, and its Relation to Magic, Religion, Philosophy, Language and Literature* (Chapel Hill: University of North Carolina, 1960); see also Gertrud Fiege, *Casper David Friedrich* (Reinbek, Hamburg: Rowohlt Verlag, 1977), and William Vaughn, et al., *Casper David Friedrich (1774–1840): Romantic Landscape Painting in Dresden*, The Tate Gallery (London: Thames and Hudson, 1972); and especially Keith Hartley, et al., *The Romantic Spirit in German Art 1790–1990* (London: Thames and Hudson, 1994).

53. S. H. Nasr, *The Need for a Sacred Science* (Albany: State University of New York Press, 1993), p. 131.

54. S. H. Nasr, *Religion and the Order of Nature*, p. 223.

55. See Hannah Arendt, *The Human Condition* (Chicago: University of Chicago Press, 1958).

56. S. H. Nasr, *The Need for a Sacred Science*, p. 59.

57. See S. H. Nasr, *Islamic Life and Thought* (Chicago: ABC International, 2001), pp. 191ff. and his *Islamic Art and Spirituality* (Albany: State of New York University Press, 1987), in addition, "Spiritual Movements of Philosophy and Theology in the Safavid Period," in *The Cambridge History of Iran*, vol. 6 (Cambridge: Cambridge University Press, 1986), pp. 656–97.

58. For example, see Hans Jonas, *The Imperative of Responsibility: In Search of an Ethics for the Technological Age* (Chicago: University of Chicago Press, 1984); and Frederick Williams, *The Communications Revolution* (New York: New American Library, Mentor Books, 1983, New Edition); for the big picture see Eric Hobsbawm, *Age of Extremes: The Short Twentieth Century 1914–1991* (London: Abacus Books, 1997); and still relevant, Alexander Mitscherlich, *Auf dem Weg zur vaterlösen Gesellschaft* (Munich: Piper Verlag, 1996, 10th edition).

59. Again, see the work of Anneliese Maier, *Die Mechanisierung des Weltbilds im 17. Jahrhundert* (Leipzig: Meiner Verlag, 1938) and *Die Vorläufer Galileis im 14. Jahrhundert* (Rome 1949); see also Thomas Kuhn's reference to Maier in the Preface to his well known *The Structure of Scientific Revolutions* (Chicago: University of Chicago Press, 1970, 2nd edition).

60. S. H. Nasr, *Knowledge and the Sacred*, p. 2.

61. Cf. Jürgen Habermas, *Philosophic Discourse on Modernity* (Cambridge, Mass.: MIT Press, 1991, New Edition), p. 324.

62. S. H. Nasr, *Three Muslim Sages* (Cambridge, Mass.: Harvard University Press, 1985, New Edition), p. 150.

63. Philip Wiener, editor, *Leibniz: Selections* (New York: Random House, 1966), pp. 557–58.

64. Leibniz, *Monadology*, edited by W. H. R. Parkinson (New York: Dutton, 1985), p. 186.

65. See Brian P. Copenhaver and Charles B. Schmitt, *Renaissance Philosophy* (Oxford: Oxford University Press, Opus Book, 1992), p. 185.

66. This was reiterated by Professor Habermas in his public lecture, presented at the American University in Cairo, Egypt, entitled "Theory and Praxis Revisited," on March 19, 1998, published in *Al-Ahrām English Weekly Edition* of March 15–19, Culture Section, p. 13. Supplementary by Ernest Wolf-Gazo, "In Reason Lies Hope," *Al-Ahrām*, March 12–18, Culture Section, p. 13, and Mohamed Helmi El Roubi, "Habermas Visits Egypt" *Middle East Times*, 27 March–2 April 1998, p. 12.

67. See the classic in the field by Werner Beierwaltes, *Platonismus und Deutscher Idealismus* (Frankfurt am Main: Klostermann Verlag, 1965), p. 135.

68. See Friedrich Dieterici, *Die Philosophie der Araber im IX und X Jahrhundert:* Band XXII *Die sog. Theologie des Aristoteles*. Übersetzt von F. Dieterici (Leipzig: J.C. Hinrichs'sche Buchhandlung, 1838); Dieterici's volume contains the original Arabic text (pp. 1–180, Arabic Numerals) as well as the German translation (pp. 1–224) of the apparent text by Plotinus.

69. Schelling, *System des Transzendentalen Idealismus*, edited by M. Frank (Frankfurt am Main: Suhrkamp Edition, 1985, vol. I, originally published in 1800), pp. 436–37. Helpful to the English reader is Rüdiger Bubner, editor, *German Idealist Philosophy* (London: Penguin Classics Paperback, 1998), in correspondence, S. H. Nasr and Oliver Leaman, editors, *A History of Islamic Philosophy* (London: Routledge, 1996, 2 volumes).

70. Cf. Kant, *Kritik der reinen Vernunft* (Stuttgart: Reclam Edition, 1969, edited by Ingeborg Heideman under the direction of Gottfried Martin), p. 113.

71. See Gerold Prauss, *Kant und das Problem der Dinge an sich* (Bonn: Bouvier Verlag, 1974).

72. Kant, *The Critique of Pure Reason*, trans. N. Kemp Smith (New York: St. Martin's Press, 1965 [1929]), p. 152.

73. P. F. Strawson, *Individuals: An Essay in Descriptive Metaphysics* (London: Methuen, 1959).

74. Ernest Wolf-Gazo, "Berkeley, Whitehead, Sadra: From Sense Impression to Intuition," *Transcendent Philosophy* (London: Institute of Islamic Studies) 1, no. 1 (June 2000): 107–16.

REPLY TO ERNEST WOLF-GAZO

Professor Wolf-Gazo is a German philosopher trained in the German philosophical schools and is at the same time a person with deep experience of the Islamic world, where he has taught for many years and has gained much knowledge of the Islamic philosophical tradition. These traits make him an excellent candidate to evaluate my philosophical views in relation to the Western and more particularly German philosophical currents. And this is precisely what he has sought to carry out in this extensive essay which treats many critical philosophical issues dealing not only with my thought but also with philosophical discourse between the West and the Islamic world in general. Moreover, being a professional philosopher, his discourse deals completely with purely philosophical subjects and affords me the opportunity to enter into dialogue with a Western philosopher with a German philosophical background who is at the same time knowledgeable in Islamic thought and desirous of carrying out philosophical dialogue with me. His essay and my response taken together constitute, in fact, a valuable philosophical dialogue in themselves, although of course limited to the issues he has chosen to treat in his essay.

Wolf-Gazo begins his exposition by calling my basic motif "*the reenchantment of the profane world*." If taken as a poetic description, then I would accept such a characterization. But let us remember that the dictionary definition of "to enchant" is "to put magic spell upon," "to bewitch," "to charm," "to mislead," and "to delude." Needless to say my basic motif has nothing to do with any of these actions. To reenchant the profane world from my point of view means only to lift the veil which covers our own eyes and ears and to realize once again the sacred character of the world whose appreciation we have lost. It is the Divine Reality that has bestowed a sacred character upon the world and not us. Therefore, we cannot bestow that character upon it again. That is beyond our power but it is possible for us to rediscover the sacred character of both knowledge and the world, and one might say that that has been the basic motif throughout my writings.

To come back to the term "reenchantment," which I take to mean a poetic description for resacralization, there is a deeper sense in which enchantment can be associated with the world of nature and considered to be another way of describing that world's sacred quality. This deeper sense is related to the very etymology of the term. One might say that to be enchanted is to be able to hear the chant of God's creatures, which is nothing other than their existential prayer and the harmony of their very existence. According to Pythagorean doctrines all things are created on the basis of harmonic properties, as the German scholars Albert von Thimus and his student Hans Keyser rediscovered in the nineteenth and twentieth centuries. To hear the chants of things is to become aware of this innate harmony. It is to be able to train ourselves to hear what Plato called the silent music heard only by the sages. Being a strong proponent of the Pythagorean concept of mathematics and harmony, I therefore also accept having my basic motif characterized as "the reenchantment of the profane world" in this deeper sense. Certainly, as Wolf-Gazo states, my goal is to move in the opposite direction than what Max Weber called *Entzauberungprozess*. I also agree with the author in the general contrast he draws between my attempt to resacralize, in the sense of discovering again the sacred character of knowledge and the world, and moving in the opposite direction of what has gone on in the mainstream of Western philosophy since the beginning of the modern period.

In section II the author writes, "The tradition that synthesizes the classical elements of Islam, along with Sufi strains of Eastern Islam and the Shi'ite component of Nasr's project, makes this a challenging and new kind of proposal." I need to clarify this statement in two important ways. First of all "Eastern Islam," which the author uses throughout his essay, might give the illusion that I have not been associated with Western Islam, which is that of the Islamic *maghrib*, or the West, of traditional Islamic geographic texts, whereas in my case there has been an especially close association with *maghribī* Sufism since my youth. Perhaps by "Eastern" the author means simply the Orient in the nineteenth-century sense of the term which included North Africa as well. Second, in enumerating the various elements which I have synthesized, the author has left out the several schools of Islamic philosophy which need to be specifically mentioned in this context. What he calls "a new proposal" is "new" in that I have synthesized the different currents of traditional Islamic thought, including Sunnism and Shi'ism, Sufism, theology, the various schools of philosophy, and even the sciences into a pyramid of knowledge unified by the principle of unity (*al-tawḥīd*). It is only in its being a synthesis expressed in the contemporary medium of discourse and addressing a global audience and global questions that I accept the modifier "new" for what I have to say. Otherwise, as an exponent of the perennial philosophy, I am not given to finding new ideas and do not want to be praised for being original in the current sense of the term. As I have written already in my response to Professor Liu, for me "original" means that which is related to the Origin and the truth that is identified with it. Moreover, let us not forget the Aristotelian doctrine that there is nothing new under the sun.

I also want to emphasize what Wolf-Gazo says in the same section about tradition providing "the basic cultural framework in which the sacred operates" but want to add that tradition provides not only the cultural but above all the intellectual framework, and that it not only provides the framework for the operation of the sacred but is itself the source of all that is sacred, if "tradition" be understood in the sense I have always used the term. This truth must also be kept in mind in order to stay clear of all the pitfalls that face those who would seek to reenchant the world outside of tradition as we see in the New Religions. I fully confirm the author's assertion about the "reenchantment project" having to take place within the cadre of tradition.

In section III dealing with the "sacred order of the Kosmos," Wolf-Gazo writes, "In fact, it is one of Nasr's achievements to make it clear, especially to Western readers of his works, not to mention the more enlightened fellow Muslims, that science and Islam are not contradictions in terms." Later in this volume I will deal with this complex issue and do not need to enter into it here. But I do need to mention briefly here that Islam cannot, on the one hand, simply absorb modern science uncritically as if it were the *'ilm* or *scientia* mentioned in the Quran, nor on the other hand castigate it as being *kufr* or infidelity and forbidden by religious law to study or promulgate. There is need of an Islamic *critique* both intellectual and ethico-social of modern science which my own works have undertaken and which I hope will be pursued to an even greater degree by others, as we are in fact beginning to see already. What is important is to realize what modern science is and what it is not but claims to be—or at least the majority of its practitioners claim it to be. It is essential to distinguish what science can discover and has discovered about the physical world from the philosophical positivism (and ideologies associated with it) now dominating the modern cultural scene in the form of scientism.

The rest of the title of section III is "Plato, Newton, Whitehead, and Nasr" and the section deals mostly with the relation between mathematics and the sacred. There are many profound observations in this section. Others are questionable, such as when Wolf-Gazo writes that "the Bauhaus in Dessau may rejuvenate our sense of mathematical perfection in terms of a perfect geometrical entity, as was in the mind of Gropius," and then adds, "To see in modernity elements of the secular exclusively is shortsighted." Now, the author himself stated earlier that "tradition is a prerequisite for the reenchantment project. Tradition provides the basic cultural framework in which the sacred operates." As already mentioned, I knew Gropius in Cambridge in the '50s and recall one day when standing before the picture of a medieval cathedral in his office he said to me how remarkable tradition was which allowed several generations of architects to create a single work possessing such unity. Then he added how tragic it was that tradition was lost in the West. The geometry of the Bauhaus brings out something of the purity of geometrical intelligibility, but not the sense of the sacred, because it was not based on an understanding of sacred geometry. The ideas of the Bauhaus led to the cubic and rectangular boxes that now dot the cityscape of so many modern cities, while sacred geometry led to the creation of many mosques in Isfahan, Istanbul, and elsewhere that Professor Wolf-Gazo has himself visited, not to speak of the great medieval cathedrals of Europe or Hindu temples. For the person sensitive to sacred geometry, of course, the clear geometric proportions of a building like the Bauhaus have an aesthetic and even intellectual appeal, but it is not an evocation of the sacred in its full sense.

I have paused to point to this single example in order to bring out a more important general point. I am of course honored in being mentioned with Plato, Newton, and Whitehead as far as my understanding of mathematics in relation to the sacred is concerned, but there is nevertheless a need for clarification. I see Plato as a continuation of Pythagoras and Platonic cosmology and mathematics as expressed especially in the *Timaeus* as being essentially Pythagorean. Now, I am in full accord with the philosophy of Pythagorean mathematics which I have studied from both Greek and Islamic sources. In fact a major part of my doctoral thesis at Harvard, which appeared later as *An Introduction to Islamic Cosmological Doctrines*, is devoted to the Ikhwān al-Ṣafā' who were among the most important proponents in Islam of the ideas of Pythagorean mathematics, including of course sacred geometry. Over the years I have also been closely associated with such figures as the British specialist in sacred geometry Keith Critchlow and the Center for the Study of Traditional Arts in the Prince of Wales Institute of Architecture in London devoted to the relation between sacred geometry and art and architecture.

On the basis of my studies of Pythagorean mathematics and harmonics over the years, I am not convinced that either Newton or Whitehead were really interested in or fully understood the meaning of the qualitative and sacred mathematics which was the concern of Plato and is also my concern. There are of course many elements as far as mathematics is concerned which I share with Whitehead and Newton, but there is a basic distinction to be made between Pythagorean/Platonic mathematics and mathematics since the Renaissance, and especially Descartes, which is what Newton and Whitehead were dealing with. I do agree with the author however, that the essential elements at play in my thought are order, beauty, and justice as they are in the thought of Plato, Newton, and Whitehead, and I would add that in my case the principle of unity must also be included as an absolutely essential element of every aspect of my thought. I also need to add that not only do I hold Plato in the greatest esteem, but I also sense an affinity for certain dimensions of Newton's thought, which I do not hold for a Descartes or a Galileo, and also among twentieth century Western philosophers I consider Whitehead to be among the greatest. I read him avidly during my student days and respect his attempt at creating an intellectual synthesis, although I do not accept the premises of the process philosophy and theology associated with him.

At the end of this section Wolf-Gazo writes about mathematics being the hidden bond between the human mind and the structures of the universe "that are accessible, revelatory." Then he adds, "Yet, this process of revelation has not yet played out, as far as Nasr is concerned." This statement needs clarification; otherwise it might give a sense opposed to what I believe. My position is that revelation in its objective mode came to an end with the Islamic revelation and also that the world of nature is itself the remnant of that primordial creation which was also a revelation. Inner illumination and realization of the truth, which some call revelation, has not of course come to an end but continues. As for the process of revelation to which the author refers, I can only accept it in the sense of gaining metaphysical insight into the nature of things. From my perspective what has not as yet played out fully is the metaphysical understanding of the mathematical structure associated with the scientific study of the universe. In contrast to all kinds of hypothesis and conjectures which parade as the philosophy of science today, there is need for authentic metaphysical knowledge in order to be able to understand the significance beyond quantitative science itself of what that science has really discovered. For example, there is a metaphysical significance to the collapse of the state vector in quantum mechanics but this significance cannot be discovered by quantum mechanics itself. It requires metaphysical knowledge to understand the bringing into act of a potential state of existence that the collapse of the state vector signifies. This truth has been discussed by the scientist Wolfgang Smith in his *The Quantum Enigma*. Smith describes the physical elements as a scientist but his interpretation of their significance he discusses as a traditional philosopher and theologian, which he also is, in addition to being a respected scientist. It is only in this sense that I accept Wolf-Gazo's assertion about the process of revelation not having as yet played itself out.

In section IV the author compares and contrasts my views with those of Dewey and brings out in a very perceptive manner our differences. However, he seems to put those differences at the feet of our different backgrounds and upbringings. He has spoken of Dewey as the messenger of the American dream and I "of the message coming from Isfahan" which would be accepted if interpreted symbolically. Otherwise, I need to assert that I represent a message that does not belong to Isfahan alone but to many other loci of Islamic intellectual and spiritual life as well. But my main criticism of this otherwise excellent analysis is that Wolf-Gazo seems to reduce the perspectives of Dewey and myself simply to our cultural backgrounds. While not by any means denying the importance of the cultural milieu in which one is brought up, the way one is educated, the influence of parents, teachers, and friends and many other external factors, I believe too much in the freedom of the will and the inner independence of intelligence to accept these external factors as being completely determining and decisive. There have been those among American philosophers who have hailed from the same background as Dewey but reached very different philosophical conclusions. And the same can be said of other Persian thinkers, even well-versed in the teaching of the School of Iṣfahānī, who have come to hold philosophical views different from mine.

I mention this point in order to clarify my own position concerning background and upbringing versus the innate power of intelligence to discern, to know, and to philosophize. Otherwise, I am fully in accord with the author's excellent study in contrast between Dewey and myself, between his pragmatic instrumentalism and my transcendent intuition. There is also a point that I need to add about the "divination of nature" about which Wolf-Gazo speaks toward the end of this section. I must make it clear again that I consider nature to be sacred and not divine. This nuance is of the utmost philosophical and theological importance especially in the context of Islamic as well as Christian thought. Nature is sacred without this truth in any way detracting from the transcendence as well as immanence of the Divine, which alone is divine, or destroying the distinction between the Divine Principle or God and creation. I think that I have made this point amply clear in my many writings on the relation between religion and the natural environment and on traditional cosmology.

Section V begins with a captivating description of the philosophical scene of the '60s, a description with which I am in full agreement. But let me add that although I did not politicize philosophy nor speak of revolution as did Shari'ati, I had a very wide audience among young people in Tehran and elsewhere in the '60s and '70s. Of course my whole approach and goal was very different from Shari'ati's and I never sought to gain popularity by turning religion into ideology and diluting the traditional philosophy and theology which I always defended. Nevertheless, I always faced large audiences of young people whether I spoke in Tehran, Mashad, Isfahan, Shiraz or elsewhere. It is unfortunate that the intellectual history of Iran during the '60s and '70s has until now been written not objectively but with ideological goals in mind.

There are a number of other points in the section on the ecological dimensions of the sacred which need further clarification or response. The author writes that "the precise cause and reasons as to why the West turned 'eccentric' are still not too clear." It might not be clear to him but it is very clear to me and I have discussed these causes in several of my works, especially *Knowledge of the Sacred* and *Religion and the Order of Nature*. He writes that the Renaissance did glorify God in its art. Yes, this is to some extent true. Western man could not discard the millennial heritage of Christianity so quickly. But let us not forget that except for a few inspired Renaissance painters such as Fra Angelico and Simone Martini, most European artists of the day anthropomorphized the sacred art of Christianity and prepared the ground for its demise. The Sistine Chapel, although "great" from a humanistic point of view, already marks the death of that sacred art which had dominated the West since the inception of Christianity in Europe. From that humanized image of God to denial of Him was but a single step. It is true that that step was not and could not be taken immediately, and that even at the beginning of the Scientific Revolution many people still had religious faith. But the seed of that humanism, rationalism, and skepticism characteristic of a number of very influential Renaissance figures was already sown at that time. Its fruit as ever-greater secularization and finally rehumanization of man was to follow in due course, and in fact much sooner than many expected. One might say with the author that since Kant the West "did not discredit the sacred at least not completely." But it did marginalize it and made it irrelevant both to intellectual and practical political and economic concerns of Western society.

In section VI the author makes an important comment about the chain of thought from Plato to the German Romantics making "some inroads among the more sensitive of the 1960s generation, but not pursued in a serious manner, such as through a sacred epistemology." As one who often lectured in America in the '60s, I am in full accord with this assessment and have mentioned often that what prevented the '60s movement from bringing about an in-depth transformation in Western society was its lack of intellectual rigor and sapience, on the one hand, and moral and spiritual discipline on the other hand. Otherwise much that the so-called "hippies" held dear, such as the natural environment, respect for other religions, and emphasis upon spiritual practice, was and remains of the utmost importance. But like followers of the nineteenth-century Romantic Movement they were not able to break the hold of the scientistic paradigm upon the Western mind in general. Nevertheless, they created certain openings which have made the study of serious metaphysics and spirituality easier in the West today, while they also opened the door to all those parodies of authentic spirituality now known as the New Religions.

Wolf-Gazo adds that the "legitimate concern of an intellectual intuition of the Divine has never been entirely discarded in the Western Hemisphere." I agree that it was not completely discarded but that is not enough. What I and those who think like me claim is that that intuition must be recognized for what it is and placed at the center of the paradigm of knowledge rather than as a marginal possibility accepted by a philosopher here and a scientist there. I think that the author himself realized this truth when he considered the consequence of Kant's *Kritik der reinen Vernunft* to be the creation of a situation in which "humankind has been left dangling between earth and heaven." Of course, I would not say the whole of humankind, but modern man; but I certainly would agree with this assessment as far as those influenced by the mainstream of Western philosophy are concerned.

In a revealing discussion of intuition in relation to *Anschauung* in German philosophy, a discussion with which I am in full agreement, the author writes, "The mystic ecstasy is the paradigm for intellectual intuition." While I agree with what comes before and after this sentence in this section, I cannot agree with this sentence itself. Intellection or intellectual intuition itself is not experience but knowledge. The experiential dimension or mystical ecstasy follows from or accompanies it in most cases but not necessarily so. There are those who have intellectual intuition which confirms perennial truths but have not experienced mystical ecstasy. And there are those who have experienced a mystical ecstasy which does not possess any intellectual content. I would agree, however, that on the highest level, or what the Hindus call the "Supreme Identity," knowledge and being become united in bliss or ecstasy. But even at that supreme level I would not call mystical ecstasy the paradigm for intellectual intuition, while again emphasizing that authentic intellectual intuition is often and even usually combined with a liberating illumination, a state of peace, and even beatitude, which for the contemplative is none other than ecstasy.

Finally, I must comment upon Wolf-Gazo's statement that "Simply to bypass Kant would not do since Kant is not easily bypassed. Thus, we must find a way to enlist Kant's help to make it plausible that intellectual intuition is, in fact, a legitimate category of epistemology." First of all non-Western traditions of philosophy certainly do not have to pass through Kant, whatever Westernized students of Kant in Japan, India, and elsewhere may say. Traditional epistemology stands opposed to Cartesian bifurcation to start with, even before getting to Kant. As for Western thinkers, I cannot see how one can bestow upon intelligence once again the power to know the noumena, to know the essence of the nature of things, without going beyond Kantian agnosticism and passing beyond the limitations of the whole critical approach. Perhaps as a philosopher belonging to the German school, the author has a way to beseech Kant's help while seeking to reach serious metaphysical understanding and rediscovering the real meaning of intellectual intuition. As a follower of the perennial philosophy, I remain critical of the *Kritik* and its approach, and I oppose completely the limiting of the power of intelligence to know the essential nature of things and above all to know the Sacred as such.

I am grateful to Professor Wolf-Gazo for a most interesting essay of philosophical substance which has clarified my position *vis-à-vis* many currents of Western philosophy in matters concerning what he calls quite rightly "sacred epistemology." He has afforded me the opportunity to make comments on the important issues that he has raised, issues that pertain to the domain of pure philosophy as well as to comparative philosophy in which both Wolf-Gazo and I share a common interest.

S. H. N.

8

Kenneth K. Inada

BUDDHIST CREATIVE METAPHYSICS AND ISLAMIC THOUGHT

In considering the thought of Seyyed Hossein Nasr, I would like to proceed comparatively. First I wish to set out some of the basic principles of creative metaphysics in Buddhism, raising a number of fundamental issues along the way, such as the nature of perception, time, eternity, being, becoming, and nonbeing, and the paths to wisdom and Enlightenment. Second, I will begin the comparison and dialogue between Buddhism and Islam by examining some of the ideas of Averroes. Finally I will pose to Nasr a series of questions for his response.

It is true that the historical Buddha disdained engagement in the metaphysical analysis of things and admonished those who indulged in it because nothing fruitful will come out of it in terms of developing the nature of aversion, detachment, cessation, tranquillity, penetrative insight, and ultimate nirvāṇa. In the famous *Cūḷa-Māluṇkyaputta-sutta*,[1] metaphysical questions such as the following were raised: whether or not the world is contingent or eternal, whether or not the soul is the same or different from the body, whether or not the soul persists after death, and whether or not the Tathāgata (the enlightened Buddha) survives death. To each of these questions the Buddha kept his studied silence. Questioned about his silence or noncommittal attitude, he finally replied that if he had answered positively, the listener would then begin to take an objectively realistic approach and, conversely, if he had answered negatively, the listener would take on an "objectively" nihilistic approach, both of which would have led to the extremes that veer off the true perception of things. Indeed, both extremes would have immediately prevented the perceiver from ever honing in on the truth of existence, that is, the *Dharma*, which the Buddha referred to as the middle way (*majjhimā-paṭipadā*).

The concept of the middle way as the truth of existence is naturally a most difficult idea to convey, much less to accept and understand, principally because of past prejudices regarding the terms in use. For example, the term "middle" seems innocuous enough and easy to grasp, but presented in ordinary rational discourse it lacks the power or force to do justice to this basically ontological term. It is after all an existential term that uniquely qualifies the "way" by depicting the nonattached, pure nature of existence. The term shuns the extremes that the mind seems to thrive upon, that is, positivism and negativism or substantialism and nonsubstantialism. But such a depiction of the "middle" is usually met with a skeptical eye and invariably forces one to renew the search for a more plausible account of the "middle." This of course is not to be found since the "middle" is, in the final analysis, beyond our accustomed rational reach and cannot be located or found in ordinary perception of things. In brief, the concept of the "middle" cannot be reified as an epistemic entity that participates in epistemological functions.

Though an unwilling victim of the prevailing language in use, the Buddha nevertheless had to employ it to expound his new theory of the truth of existence. In this, he consciously indulged in a form of neologism to give new meanings to old terms and to a large extent, in retrospect, he did succeed in keeping alive the spirit that preserved the content of his enlightenment. Nonetheless, problems in hermeneutics started early on in the Buddhist tradition and have continued to the present. We still have to sift the common from the uncommon (neologistic) meanings. Though frustrating in many respects, due to the fact that we consciously or unconsciously revert back to common meanings of terms, nevertheless, we must attempt to resolve the problems by seeking out and focusing on the uncommon meanings, especially if we are to engage in a dialogue with another system of thought. Engendering such dialogue has, of course, been one of the primary aims of Nasr's work, and I will end this essay with a series of questions that may, I hope, call forth a new chapter in Buddhist-Islamic dialogue.

Prior to any dialogue, the challenge of a dialogue is first of all to clarify the language in use and, more importantly, its usage in any particular context. Historically, it is alleged that immediately after his nirvanic experience, the Buddha was asked to explain his unusually beautiful and serene countenance so markedly different from his former yogic days of struggles and emaciation. He refused to divulge anything and continued to be suffused in his newly gained peace and tranquillity. When asked repeatedly, he said in effect that the content of his enlightenment, the true nature of relational origination (*paṭicca-samuppāda*), is extremely difficult to comprehend, especially for those who cling to things, material as well as immaterial, and are fond of their dependence on these things. Thus the Buddha put a damper on those who wanted to learn empirically and rationally about his unique experience. Within a few weeks, however, it is told that the Buddha finally relented and divulged to his following the nature and method of attaining Buddhahood, which is recorded in his famous exposition at the Deer Park near Benares (present day Banaras) in the form of the Sutra that Turns the Wheel of the Buddhist Doctrine (*Dhammacakkappavattana-sutta*).[2]

The Sutra, in brief, expounds on the fourfold noble truth of suffering and the way out of suffering, that is, reference to the prescription of the eightfold noble path. There is no need to discuss in detail the noble truth of suffering and its cessation but suffice it to say that the Buddha's exposition is a clear case of going beyond ordinary metaphysics to one of creative metaphysics. He did not condemn outright metaphysics as such but only disdained the use of it in epistemic analysis. Why? It is so because ordinary perception is wholly and indiscriminately reliant on metaphysical elements which are products of metaphysical dichotomization. It should be noted here that the Buddha was the first thinker to understand the origins and ill-effects of dichotomization. When he asserts that merely to be born into this world is suffering, he is exhibiting the fact that a newly born babe is cut off or separated from the mother's womb and must immediately fend for its own existence. Fending for one's existence entails a biological severance which forces one to fragment, the initial metaphysical incision so to speak, and thereby cling to its fragmented reality. A fragmented reality may be in the nature of a sense object derived from one of the sense faculties or a combination of the faculties, or it may be an imagery in the early stage of mind-function. Thus the babe, from an early stage, has all the trappings of metaphysical dichotomies although they are yet to appear in clear or refined terms. The passion to live (*taṇhā*) is obvious but within the very same passion there exists another subtle dimension that causes one to cling or attach to (*upādāna*) the dichotomized element. This dual nature of passion and attachment constitutes the very basis for the origin of suffering (*dukkha*).[3] Suffering has a biological basis but it is vitally connected to the mind at all times. Thus the bio-mental phenomena of suffering continue unrelenting in simple as well as in sophisticated ways. In more developed stages they are expressed in ordinary behavioral patterns which are largely accepted and even sanctioned by society at large. However, some of the more complicated patterns may be the result of psychological deviation or irregularities with respect to the inability to adjust to a normal balanced life. At any rate, the origin of suffering seems simple enough and yet it is so difficult to fully accept it, much less to concentrate on controlling its rise. Indeed, when the child grows up to be an adult, he or she is already a massive phenomenon of passion-attachment, a creature very set in his or her ways.

How do we get out of the passion-attachment bind? The eightfold noble path prescribes the process thus: develop right view, right thought, right speech, right action, right livelihood, right effort, right mindfulness, and right concentration. The key word here is "right." It qualifies all the eight aspects of the noble path. Indeed, the Sutra tells us that the noble path is nothing but the middle way. As stated above, the middle way is a neologism. It has an uncommon meaning when tied up with the eightfold noble path. Again, the term "noble" has not only an auspicious meaning but one that is unique and neologistic.

The middle way as a neologism hearkens us back to the notion of Buddhist creative metaphysics in the sense that it goes beyond ordinary metaphysics. Going beyond does not mean the abandonment of metaphysics as such, but rather it means that there is nonattachment to the dichotomized elements. In short, the elements remain as they are but now they do not dominate or dictate the nature of perception. Only when we are nonattached can we say that creativity occurs. This is an important point that needs to be elaborated.

An ordinary understanding of metaphysics centers on the two pillar concepts of being and becoming. In the history of Western thought, needless to say, Plato opted for being over becoming and thereby set the tone for the metaphysical mechanics of things. The search for and grasp of reality must be in the nature of permanence and absolutism and not in the impermanence and relativism which belong to the realm of becoming. This view fired the spirit of inquiry into the method and function of epistemology, engendering the never-ending quest for the basic and finite empirical and rational nature of things. To make a long story short, all this resulted in the appearance of Newtonian physics which stood supreme for several centuries until doubts concerning the applicability of concepts of permanence and absolutism began to crop up in the various sciences. The consequence was of course the ushering in of a totally new Einsteinian physics at the turn of the twentieth century. Now reality is no longer seen as steady, reliable, permanent, and absolute but is viewed as utterly relative in more ways than one. Nearly a century has gone by since Einstein's first pronouncement of a new physics and yet, ironically, we still think and act as if we have never left the Newtonian world. Indeed, our old habits of perception oriented in Platonic metaphysics still dominate our current perception of things. Perhaps, we will continue to act on this older view for the foreseeable future since the brute forces of empiricism and rationalism, crystallized over the centuries, are difficult to modify and change. But modifications and changes will come in time because of the very character of nature itself.

We no longer live strictly in a Western oriented world, although we readily admit the present-day dominance of science and technology. Science is still science only to the extent that it is in proper human hands and we ought to be ever mindful of any sign of the Frankensteinian effect as we engage in it. When we turn our attention to the East, a region relatively untouched by the sciences up to the nineteenth century, we will note that human existence was still holistic and harmonious with respect to the surroundings. Clear signs of all this still persist in the various cultures despite the onslaught of science and technology which came about largely in this century. An examination of these cultures may prove fruitful in offering some insights into the total nature of things.

In Asiatic metaphysics, the concepts of being and becoming are taken for granted, but as in Einsteinian physics the locus of existence is not in being but in becoming. Furthermore, there is a new component relative to becoming, the novel concept of nonbeing, which together with being and becoming form the vital triadic relationship at all times.[4]

With becoming as the locus of existence, a locus which in human terms would be translated into an experiential locus, the two components within it will now be being on the one hand and nonbeing on the other. This framework of dynamic reality is indeed strange to the uninitiated, but further analysis will prove its merits. As intimated earlier, the focus and concentration on being, the Platonic legacy, sustains the metaphysical fragmentation of things, unknown to the perceiver especially in the accustomed realms of empirical and rational functions. But the focus and concentration are delimiting phenomena insofar as the dynamics of reality is concerned. Moreover, reality is essentially an open ontology, a windowless phenomenon so to speak, which is always moving, fresh, resilient, accommodative, adaptive, and changing. How is it possible at all for reality to take on such traits? If we turn to the nature of being, it does not supply these traits because it is static, permanent, and absolute.

It is here that the Asiatic synoptic vision of things allowed thinkers to get to the bottom of the nature of reality. They came up with the concept of nonbeing, a concept not antithetical to being at all but always inclusive and supportive of it. This is the great insight which accommodates and underlies the total holistic nature-human relationship. In Buddhism, nonbeing appears in the form of emptiness (*śūnyatā*) and in Taoism as nothingness (*wu*). There is no space to elaborate on how this unique concept played a vital role in developing the respective systems of thought; but it can be emphasized that it is the core concept that led to the crystallization of the respective systems, in Buddhist nirvāṇa and Taoist ultimate naturalistic existence (*ming*). It can further be asserted that this concept is the singularly most important factor for the Buddhist and Taoist alignment that contributed so heavily to the Chinese way of life during the T'ang Dynasty (618–906 CE) and thereafter.

Nonbeing then is the other neglected but necessary component in the becomingness of existence. Although being has its role, nonbeing has a greater role to play in terms of providing the flexibility, change, and continuity in becomingness. While being cannot accommodate nonbeing because of its delimiting or truncating metaphysical nature, nonbeing, on the other hand, actually incorporates all activities of being because of its adaptive and unbounded nature. Nonbeing is, if you will, the "principle" of continuity and extensiveness in process that allows all human endeavors to be as great and deep as function allows. Thus the trademark in Buddhist ethics is the unbounded nature of friendliness, loving care, and compassion, all of which are based on and supported by the meditative capture of equaṇimity, the exquisite grounding for all bodhisattva (enlightened) action.

Where the concepts of being and becoming have presented us with the options of focusing on either being or becoming, each thereby limiting the other in mutual ways, now with the introduction of nonbeing as a vital component in the triadic relationship, the options are not only inoperative, but the ontological realm of existence has widened and completely opened up for any dialectical function or movement. This constitutes the essence, essential grounds, of creativity as such, at least as seen from the Buddhist view of becomingness.

To hold the whole universe in the palm of one's hand is a symbolic metaphor for the totality and openness that connects humankind with nature itself, an inviolable bond that exists from the beginning to the end in any activity. This is the insight (*prajñā*) of an open metaphysics which naturally translates into an all-consuming, all-embracing compassion (*karuṇā*) for all creatures, big or small, sentient, or insentient. The visualization of the various deities, images, and concepts at play is possible because of the creative factor in metaphysical perception provided by the presence of the component of nonbeing. Thus, whether one is ascending in the visionary scale of things that ends in nirvāṇa or descending from it to activate the salvific concern for all creatures, all of this owes to the nature of holistic and creative metaphysics. Buddhist metaphysics, in short, allows for the recrudescence of ordinary human activities in a new light by relieving ordinary perception of its occluded nature. So now when the enlightened being is both insightful and compassionate—two sides of the same coin of moving reality as they constantly penetrate and inform each other—the result is a world of harmony, peace, and prosperity.

Perhaps it is opportune here to speculate upon and explore further one more important aspect of the being-nonbeing dynamics in becomingness. Each experiential process has its dynamics, but in the Western sector, owing much to the dominant Platonic metaphysics, the dynamic is limited and focused on the understanding of how being, with all its attributes, is accommodated in becomingness. In this accounting, becomingness is left alone or even neglected despite the fact that it is the actual ground (locus) in which the dynamic takes place. What is missing, consciously or unconsciously, is the mutuality of being and becoming, for there is no being without becoming and, vice versa, no becoming without being. This mutuality has not been worked out satisfactorily in the Western philosophical tradition, although the scientific tradition in this century with particle physics is far ahead on this matter.

As stated earlier, in the Asiatic sector, the introduction of nonbeing as a vital component in becomingness has presented a totally new dimension to reality. Now, being and nonbeing are equal partners in exhibiting the features of becomingness. This is a crucial point that needs to be expanded.

As a way of getting a handle on being-nonbeing dynamics, I will resort to two familiar terms, symmetry and asymmetry, to help define their respective natures and roles in the dynamics. Symmetry belongs to being because being represents best the essence of our ordinary perception of things. In other words, ordinary perception is based on and thrives on clarity and distinctness. This means that all objects of perception are spatial, temporal, finite, particular, quantifiable, causative, and so on, all of which are grists for the empirical and rational mill. Thus, needless to say, objects of perception are quite effective and we rely on them for building up our huge store of knowledge. Yet, as indicated earlier, ordinary perception is delimiting because of its inherent dichotomous nature. To remedy this condition, we need to acknowledge the presence of nonbeing in perception. Nonbeing is the unseen, the intangible, and the nonmanipulable component in becoming which supplements and tones down the excesses of a dynamics known solely in terms of being. Should it be characterized, nonbeing would be nonspatial (aspatial), nontemporal (atemporal), nonquantifiable, infinite, universally extensive, noncausative, and so on. The presence of nonbeing, paradoxically, can only be inferred by way of the nature and behavior of being, so to speak; that is to say, something reveals being's ability to, for example, continue, change, evolve, and repeat itself in ordinary perception. This is indeed mystifying, to say the least, but that is one of the major reasons for our reference to Asiatic mystique but, hopefully, it should pose a real challenge to explore it. In this connection, the real mystery of existence is not why there is something (being) rather than nothing (ordinary connotation here) but, more profoundly, why there is nothing (nonbeing in an inordinate sense here) rather than something. With the above dyadic nature of dynamics, a whole Asiatic culture evolved, but its analysis will have to wait for another occasion.

Coming then to the question of dialogue, how does this Buddhist creative metaphysics fare with Islamic thought? The initial impression seems negative since the Islamic theocentrism does not easily lend itself to a comparative analysis with Buddhist nontheism. Indeed, perusing the whole history of Islamic thought, its philosophers and religious thinkers have always given foremost emphasis to God's creation of the world and the justification thereof, the main justification of God-world-humankind relationship being the doctrine of emanationism. The doctrine is clear and simple enough in terms of everything flowing downward from the Godhead, but astute thinkers have debated long on the nature and function of the relationship between God and the world, that is, between necessity and contingency, to explain the whole scheme of things. Thus, an essential element in this debate focuses on the question of God's pre-eternity and the temporal origination in the world. I will not go into the details of the debates spanning several centuries among such thinkers as al-Kindī (d. 870), al-Fārābī (875–950), Avicenna (980–1037), al-Ghazzālī (1058–1111), and Averroes (1126–1198). What is more important here is to discuss how two seemingly divergent systems of thought could meet and perhaps accommodate each other.

In Islamic thought, the doctrine of creation has two aspects: (a) creation out of nothing and (b) creation out of something. The first aspect, which is strictly in the preserve of God, is a popular view held and propagated by religious thinkers that God created this world out of nothing. It is highly speculative and lacks any demonstrative force; indeed its proponents will immediately counter by asserting that it does not require any demonstration because of the very nature of God's ultimacy and supremacy. The acceptance of this view naturally lies in deep faith regarding God's existence. The second aspect, however, subscribed to by philosophers, is much more plausible in that it speaks about temporal origination or the rise of contingent moments in this world. In human terms, it refers to all contingent moments of individuals, that is, singular as well as collective experiences. It is a way to examine the whole gamut of relationships experienced by humankind throughout the world and even reaching into the realm of the Godhead in the case of the true believer. This account falls within the theory of emanation, albeit beginning at the lower end of it.

It should be noted that neither aspect questions the creation of the world by God, and within this context there must be a meaningful contact between Islam and Buddhism. The focus of course must be on the second aspect, for here the matter of plausibility must rest on how consistent the comparative analysis is with respect to the contingent nature of things. Buddhist metaphysics, on this point, is thoroughly at home with its empirical and existential character. The Buddhist, as seen earlier, avoided metaphysical flights that have lost touch with empirical grounding.

To be contingent means involvement in space and time. The Islamic thinkers took space to be a necessary ingredient of a contingent being. Likewise, Buddhist thinkers accepted space as a necessary ingredient in all experiences but went further to stipulate that space is uncreative (*asaṇkhāta*), that is, it does not play an active role in the making of a contingent experiential moment. But the difference between Buddhism and Islam is rather light so far as ordinary experiences go. On the matter of time, however, there is much seminal activity seen on both sides.

For the Islamic thinkers, the overriding question on time and the world was, which comes first? Or which is necessary and which is contingent? More specifically, we may ask, does the world function in time? If so, then, time is prior to the world and is therefore necessary to the existence of the world. However, if time is created with the world, then is the world necessary to the existence of time? Whether a priority and necessity or a posteriority and contingency belong to the world or to time is an argument which can be narrowed down to simple questions on the nature of beginning and end as applied to both. In the analysis of beginning and end, the Islamic thinkers went back to Aristotle for two principles: (1) if there is an end, there is a beginning and (2) if there is no beginning, there is no end. These two rather simple principles applied to the temporally originated things point to the conclusion that both the world and time in their dynamic involvement with each other are truly contingent, and they support, all the more, the claim that the world was created by an incomparable God *ex nihilo*.

The Islamic religious thinkers naturally tended to side with the priority (necessity) of the world over time, that is, time is created in virtue of the existence of the world.[5] The philosophers, on the other hand, went a step further to argue that the world and time are co-creative of each other without assigning priority to either one. The champion of this view is Averroes and in this respect the Buddhist found an ally.[6] As seen earlier, the Buddhist saw everything within the context of experiential process and sought to accommodate the larger scheme of things (that is, the world) within that process. This process is inherently extendable to the larger scheme because of the unique metaphysics that involves the nature of emptiness. It would seem that Islamic thinkers did not have anything comparable to emptiness but presumably they, especially the sufis, indulged in meditation to control the empirical (that is, sensory) nature of things. After all, the contiguity of the subcontinent India with its long tradition of yoga practice, among other systems, and the fact that Buddhism had spread well into Persia would suggest strongly that Islamic thinkers and practitioners were not immune or unexposed to Indian meditative discipline. What is more, Alexander the Great's foray into India along the banks of the Indus River in the third century B.C.E. clearly exhibits evidence of early cultural infusion. From the Buddhist side, images of the Buddha and other deities show undeniable Greek influence.

The most striking thing about Averroes's analysis of time is his unique compromise position. That is to say, he did not favor either extreme of necessity or contingency.[7] He did not, in brief, side with the religious thinkers on the contingent nature of time with respect to the world, nor did he side with the philosophers on the contingency of the world on time. He was able to do this because he did not conceive of time as linear. Instead, he conceived of time as temporally originated (that is, a contingent phenomenon) by what is circular.[8] The cyclic nature of time means in essence that time need not have a beginning nor an end, contrary to the two Aristotelian principles stated above. Indeed, in one bold stroke, Averroes covered all grounds by this compromise, that is, those elements that function by necessity or contingency, and by priority or posteriority. From this standpoint it can be stated that time originated from a timeless past (that is, eternity, necessity) but at the same time it will continue to be originated in the world (that is, contingency). Time is a perpetually circular phenomenon because it evolves contingently with the world which is a sphere.

This concept of time is remarkably similar to the Buddhist notion that there is no absolute time as such but only time in the making, that is, time as a by-product so to speak of the experiential process. The process, in more precise terms, refers to the doctrine of relational origination (*paṭicca-samuppāda*) where there is no beginning nor end. The process perpetually spins, hence the apt phrase, "wheel of life." The Buddhist has conveniently segmented the wheel into a twelve-divisioned circle where one may begin with ignorance, greed, or desire which propels the wheel to turn and end in old-age and death. But short of the ultimate goal of nirvāṇa, the wheel of life continues to spin due to the empirical quests that "taint" ordinary existence.[9] The Buddhist simply says ordinary beings are in *samsāra*, a term used to describe the perpetual turning of the wheel, as contrasted to the quietude or tranquillity of nirvāṇa.

Thus we see that the circularity or cyclic nature of time is a singular contribution by both Buddhist and Islamic thought. Averroes states succinctly: "when time is imagined correctly as a cyclic continuum (encircled) within (the movement of) the spheres, it is not necessary for its past to have a completion, for if it had a completion, it would (also) have had a beginning, whereas that which has no beginning (likewise) has no completion."[10]

We have now seen that one point of contact between Buddhism and Islam is most significantly focused on the dynamicity of the individual and the world, both of which are coterminous in cyclic origin and perpetuation, like the axle spinning in unison with the outer rim of the wheel. Buddhist creative metaphysics involving emptiness allows the nature of the spin to occur with the particular (that is, contingent element) and the universal (that is, necessary element) in an infrastructural sense, permitting the samsāric nature of the wheel to turn but in the hope of eventual nirvāṇa. It would seem highly probable, on the other hand, that Averroes's introduction of the phenomenon of cyclic time would leave the door open for greater contact with Buddhism and even other systems of thought, a challenge and a task for future dialogues.

Seyyed Hossein Nasr has, in his deep reflective writings, presented the fundamental framework in which such dialogues are to take place. He goes back to the basic tenet of philosophy, metaphysics, to focus on and reveal the true nature and function of Islamic spirituality. By metaphysics, he indicates a return to the very original meaning as employed by the early Greeks, that is, the vision or insight into the true nature of things. This means that the subject is the total cosmos. It was what the prophet Muḥammad had envisioned. Nasr has steadfastly maintained the traditional interpretation of this metaphysical position in order to expound Islamic philosophy, religion, and culture in every conceivable aspect. Without allowing for this metaphysical stance, it would not be possible to understand the various sciences, including mathematics and medicine, in the total scheme of things. Indeed, the metaphysical vision serves to make all disciplines meaningful, effective, and valuable.

At one point Nasr refers to Islam as the "middle people"[11] in terms of geography and metaphysics. Coming late as civilizations go, Islam certainly sat at the opportune middle of the concourse linking the East and West, enjoying commerce as well as cultural interchange. He goes on to point out that Islamic metaphysics, contrary to ordinary thinking, is closer to the Orient than the West. It means that the metaphysical vision of things is, for example, germane to Hinduism (Vedānta), Buddhism, and Taoism. Instead of a God, these systems have independently advanced their respective primordial source in terms of the Brahman, *Dharma*, and Tao. Each is unique, to be sure, but there is much in common in the ultimate ground and quest for the metaphysical vision. Here we might ask Nasr, among other questions soon to follow, for his seasoned reflections on why there had been so few direct religious and philosophical dialogues between Islam and these Oriental systems. Was there any influence of Indian yoga on the Islamic gnostics or Sufis? Historically, we know that Buddhism had a difficult time making inroads into the Chinese culture beginning in the first century but later, during the T'ang Dynasty (618–907), the Chinese thinkers were able to accept and incorporate Buddhist ideas, aided largely by the presence of Taoism. Indeed, they did it so well that the process of sinicization of Buddhism began to take shape and form and facilitated the establishment of new sectarian schools of thought, notably Ch'an (Zen).

Although the Buddhist *Dharma* was basically a metaphysical vision of the holistic nature of things, the Buddha allowed for the lesser or relative "vision" of things. He spoke of truth in a dual sense: conventional (rational, logical, empirical) and nonconventional (without human contrivance), the former is covered truth (*samvrti-satya*) and the latter supreme and incomparable truth (*paramārtha-satya*). The significant point here is that both are co-terminous or existing in the selfsame realm of existence and this permits the "way out" by uncovering the covered realm by meditative discipline. In brief, the rational discriminative faculty (*vijñāna*) can be overcome by the penetrative insight (*prajñā*). Granted that Islam does not permit the existence of covered nature of truth, we might ask whether Islam does in any way provide for this sort of inner action of the faculties in light of Islamic hierarchy of knowledge.

The middle way doctrine of Buddhism shows remarkable resemblance to the approach, method, and ultimate realization of the Islamic metaphysical vision. The Buddha, it is recalled, admonished those who were eternalists, who subscribed to the substantive nature of things, and those who were nihilists or annihilationists subscribing to the notion that everything is impermanent and thus a void. He went on to assert that by avoiding the extremes (eternalism and nihilism), the enlightened one achieved the middle way (*majjhimā-paṭipadā*), pointing at a most unique form of "pure ontology." He then prescribed the famous eightfold noble path that begins with right view and ends in right meditative penetration (*samadhī*) to achieve nirvāṇa, literally, the state where all desires have been extinguished. This is the Buddha's way of capturing the primordiality of existence, the vision of things as they really are (*yathā-bhūtam*). Thus, we may ask, is Islam a "middle way"?

In another influential work,[12] Nasr has discussed the problem of man's relationship with Nature. The word, Nature, is capitalized to follow Nasr's own reference to the content of the metaphysical vision of things. The problem arises immediately as man tries to manipulate, conquer, or dominate Nature.[13] By so doing, the cosmos is disturbed or vitiated. And yet, we know that not every scientific endeavor is wrong or misguided. Nasr himself says, for example, that Einstein's theory of relativity is not relativism *per se* but indicates a high order of perception of the cosmos. Indeed, physicists such as Mendel Sachs have asserted that the theory is in reference to the cosmos and applicable to the whole nature of things.[14] In addition to this, there are other physicists who have in the last fifty years focused their attention on the East or Oriental systems to exhibit parallels, similarities, and even correspondences with respect to the larger scheme of things. The vacuum or void which often comes up in describing the universe is no longer an insipid nothingness but a potential ground for the dynamic play of all forms of the particle world.[15] In light of all this, would Nasr favor us by reflecting on the role that pure science will play in future endeavors to understand man's place in the universe?

A working philosophy or religion has sustaining power proportional to the extent that it harmonizes with the times, however different or difficult the conditions may be. In the last few decades of the twentieth century, we have witnessed the recession of logical positivism and the rise of a phenomenon called multiculturalism. It is a phenomenon that is destined to grow despite countervailing forces of all kinds. Needless to say, philosophy and religion are principal roots of this phenomenon and, like it or not, they will have to be involved in significant ways in the actualization of a kind of global culture. What then will be the role of the great systems of the world coping with the inclement elements arising from technology and materialism?

KENNETH K. INADA

DEPARTMENT OF PHILOSOPHY
STATE UNIVERSITY OF NEW YORK AT BUFFALO
JANUARY 1995

NOTES

1. *The Middle Length Sayings* (*Majjhimā-Nikāyā*), no. 63; Pali Text Society Translation Series, no. 30, vol. II, 97–101, translated by I. B. Horner (London: Luzac & Co., Ltd., 1957).

2. *The Book of the Kindred Sayings* (*Samyutta-Nikāyā*), LVI, xii, no. 11; Pali Text Society Translation Series, vol. V, 356–65, translated by F. L. Woodward (London: Luzac & Co., Ltd., 1956).

3. There are of course different types or modes of suffering. The Buddhist is quite thorough in covering a wide spectrum: (1) ordinary physical injury and consequent suffering as well as psychological and mental suffering such as losing one's beloved parent or friend; (2) inability to cope with change or the impermanent nature of existence such as keeping up with the times; and (3) incapability of comprehending the conditionality or relationality involved in ordinary experiences such as adhering to the false notion of a persistent self in perception and thus the beginning of a dichotomous existence.

The first is common knowledge and we relate suffering to this type for the most part. However, it is very crude and elementary. The Buddhist probes further into the ontological nature and has come forth with the second and third types which are not only novel but more profound and far-reaching in terms of both comprehension and performance. Running through all three modes, however, is the basic passion-attachment (*taṇhā-upādāna*) phenomenon that causes the real rise of suffering.

For a fuller treatment of the three modes, see Walpola Rahula, *What the Buddha Taught* (New York: Grove Press, Inc., 1974), pp. 16–34.

4. I have developed in more detail the triadic relationship of becoming, being, and nonbeing in an essay, "The Challenge of Buddho-Taoist Metaphysics of Experience," in *Journal of Chinese Philosophy* 21 (1994): 27–47.

5. "The world is a condition for the existence of time, time is not a condition for the existence of the world." Translated by Barry S. Kogan in his highly original and penetrating essay, "Eternity and Origination: Averroes's Discourse on the Manner of the World's Existence," in *Islamic Theology and Philosophy: Studies in Honor of George F. Hourani*, edited by Michael E. Marmura (Albany: State University of New York Press, 1984), p. 221.

6. Barry S. Kogan's essay mentioned in the previous note initially aroused my interest in the Buddhist-Islamic connection, and I am indebted to him for the basic ideas in Averroes.

7. The compromise position that avoids the extremes hearkens back to the Buddhist doctrine of the middle way. Averroes, in looking at the microcosmic and macrocosmic realms, saw the solution in the holistic nature of things that involves both realms. Although this connection is difficult to see, the fundamental starting point is remarkably similar, and for all intents and purposes both sides cover the selfsame grounds of existence. Naturally, this connection will have to be developed further.

8. Barry S. Kogan's essay as presented in note 5. Op. cit., p. 223.

9. In a word, the empirical quests refer to karmic activity. Karma is not fatalism or determinism of any kind. It means a deed or an act, but Buddhists introduced the intentional nature to a karmic act. Thus, in more precise terms, a karmic act involves a semi-circular movement, that is, the present condition reaching to the immediate past and moving forward into the future while incorporating novel elements along the way like the surging surf that reaches the shores. By meditative discipline, all reaching or questing for something, whether material or immaterial, will cease so that the ultimate realization of nirvāṇa is a released state of non-karmic existence.

10. Barry S. Kogan, op. cit., pp. 224–25.

11. Seyyed Hossein Nasr, *Science and Civilization in Islam* (Cambridge, Mass.: Harvard University Press, 1968), p. 93.

12. Seyyed Hossein Nasr, *The Encounter of Man and Nature* (London: George Allen and Unwin Ltd., 1966).

13. Ibid., pp. 18–19.

14. Mendel Sachs, *Einstein Versus Bohr: The Continuing Controversies in Physics* (La Salle, Ill., Open Court Publishing Co., 1988).

15. Fritjof Capra, *The Tao of Physics*, Second Edition, Revised and Updated (Boulder: Shambala Publications, Inc., 1983), p. 222.

REPLY TO KENNETH INADA

Professor Inada is an expert on Buddhism and most of his paper is concerned with an exposition of his interpretation of Buddhist metaphysics especially as it concerns the relation between being, becoming, and non-being and the question of the origination of the world, space, and time. At the end Inada turns to a comparative study of time in Buddhism in relation to the views of Ibn Rushd (Averroes). Following this he poses a series of questions for dialogue. Since his final two questions (on the role of science and technology and multiculturalism) are addressed in responses to other essays, I will therefore devote this response to how I envisage the possibility of a Buddhist-Islamic dialogue and comparisons of basic metaphysical and spiritual issues, in light of the first two questions Inada raises.

It should be mentioned at the outset, however, that Buddhism and Islam have had long contacts going back to the first Islamic century and the spread of Islam into what is today eastern Afghanistan and Pakistan which had a large Buddhist population at that time. In fact Buddhism spread into China before the rise of Islam through the eastern regions of the Persian Empire and one of the first harbingers of the Buddhist message into China was called in Chinese "The Persian." Many stories of the life of the Buddha found in the *Tripitaka* found their way into Arabic literature and one can find traces of some Buddhist philosophical ideas such as atomism in certain strands of Islamic thought. Moreover, some commentaries consider the Quranic prophet Dhu'l-Kifl to be none other than the Buddha whose name as *Būdh* is found in both Arabic and Persian. Also the term *nīrwān*, that is *nirvāṇa*, has become a Persian word well known in the literature of that language. Even the life of one of the greatest of the early Sufi saints of Khurasan, Ibrāhīm Adham, resembles that of the Buddha. It is therefore unfortunate that in modern scholarship so little attention has been paid to Buddhist-Islam dialogue and comparative studies between the two traditions.

Inada begins his article with the discussion of the Buddhist Middle Way or *majjhimā-paṭipadā*. Although this term as interpreted by Inada deals with a middle way between taking an objectively realistic approach and nihilism, the term itself has other meanings and reminds one immediately of the Quranic reference to Muslims as the people of the "middle way" (*ummah wasaṭah*). Although this is usually interpreted to mean avoiding extremes in all matters and especially eschewing both this worldliness and completely otherworldliness in the sense of excessive asceticism, it has other meanings and has also been understood metaphysically as striking a balance between the *via negativa* and the *via affirmativa* in theology and metaphysics in one's approach to the understanding of the Ultimate Reality. Even in discussion of the relation of nonbeing and being, being and becoming, the world as veil and theophany, and any form of conceptualization of categories pertaining to the Divine, the Islamic metaphysicians have sought to charter a course which cannot but be called the middle way. In any case there is much to discover in a deeper comparative study of the meaning of the middle way in the two traditions despite the marked difference between the nontheistic and strongly theistic perspectives of Buddhism and Islam, respectively.

As far as creationism is concerned, in addition to the points mentioned by Inada, one must remember another view concerning creation associated with Sufi metaphysics especially as expounded among others by 'Ayn al-Quḍāt Hamadānī and Maḥmūd Shabistarī. This view asserts that at every moment the world is returned to nonexistence and brought again into existence. This doctrine, called the renewal of creation at every instant (*tajdīd al-khalq fī kulli ānāt*), has been studied by Toshiko Izutsu, the famous Japanese Zen scholar of Islam, who in many discussions with me expressed his astonishment at how this view was similar in so many ways to Buddhist doctrines.

Likewise in the discussion of space and time there is a wealth of philosophical writings which were not mentioned by Inada and which are perhaps unknown to him since they are only now becoming available in Western languages. In this context the writings of Mullā Ṣadrā and his theory of trans-substantial motion (*al-ḥarakat al-jawhariyyah*) which posits a constant becoming and motion in the very subsistence of the universe is particularly significant. Henry Corbin referred to this theory in a telling manner as "*l'inquiétude de l'être*," an interpretation which reveals how relevant this theory by one of Islam's greatest metaphysicians can be for comparison with Buddhist theories. As for the cyclic notion of time which Inada mentions in relation to Averroes, there are other schools of Islamic thought, especially Ismā'īlī philosophy, which would offer even greater possibilities for comparison with the Buddhist view. The general Islamic view of sacred history itself is also not linear but cyclic punctuated by the appearance of a new prophet at the beginning of each cycle. The doctrine of the ten Buddhas starting with Dhammadassin and ending with Maitreya at the end of this historical period also have a clear correspondence with the cycles of prophecy (*dā'irat al-nubuwwah*), which according to Shi'ite gnosis end with the advent of the Mahdī and the return of Christ.

This concept also opens the whole field of comparative studies concerning Buddhist and Islamic eschatologies. Both religions, along with of course such religions as Hinduism, Zoroastrianism, Judaism and Christianity, not to speak of Taoism and the primal religions, expect a divine intervention at the end of the present historical cycle. Specific comparison between the doctrine of the appearance of the Maitreya Buddha and that of the Mahdī and Christ according to Islamic teachings will reveal remarkable resemblances to which little attention has been paid in general scholarly works on comparative religion.

Although Islam is opposed to the theory of reincarnation, whose popular understanding in Hinduism and Buddhism has been questioned even by sages of those traditions, the question of the centrality of the human state necessary to gain release from the cycles of rebirth and death, of the reality of wandering after death through transmigration in the intermediary worlds, and of the significance of correct thought and action in this world in determining the state into which one is born after earthly death all have their correspondences in Islamic teachings. In Islam, however, eschatological doctrines which deal in detail with the meaning of the universal descriptions of the Quran with the afterlife and which are in fact explanations and expansions of the teachings of the Quran and *Ḥadīth*, have been always considered as esoteric knowledge. They remained mostly oral in the early days of Islam and did not find their full explanations until later in Islamic history in the writings of such figures as Ibn 'Arabī, Mullā Ṣadrā, Shāh Walīallāh of Delhi, Mullā 'Alī Zunūzī, and Sabziwārī. If one reads carefully a text such as the fourth book of the *Asfār al-arba'ah* of Mullā Ṣadrā, one will realize that Islam has also produced its "book of the dead" which can be profitably compared with the *Tibetan Book of the Dead*. Such comparisons would reveal remarkable parallels despite the two different spiritual universes with which they deal. It is also interesting to note in this context that in Buddhism also the treatises dealing with eschatological matters were put to writing in the later history of the religion as is the case of Islam. In both cases, however, such works, far from being later accretions, represent crystallizations in written form of doctrines which go back to the origin of the religions in question.

Turning to the spiritual realities which "populate" the spiritual universes of Islam and Buddhism, especially in its Mahāyāna and Vajrayāna forms, one can point to the various Buddhas and Bodhisattvas and their functions in the Buddhist world and the archangels and angels in the Islamic one. Although of course there are differences, since we are dealing with two different revelations and spiritual archetypes, there are also remarkable resemblances. Islamic art has not produced *thankas* depicting in the form of plastic arts the various celestial and infernal beings of the Buddhist universe. But the descriptions contained in even popular works such as the genre known as *Wonders of Creation* (*'Ajā'ib al-makhlūqāt*) reveal the remarkable analogies and similarities between the visions of the two religions concerning the beings which inhabit the multiple levels of existence beyond the earthly domain.

Even the Bodhisattva, this uniquely Buddhist being, has its correspondence in the Islamic universe. The mercy associated with the Bodhisattva and his/her desire to save all of creation has its correspondence with the angelic agencies of Divine Mercy (*al-Raḥmah*) which fill the Islamic universe. Moreover, in both cases mercy does not preclude the reality of rigor, justice, judgment, and punishment which are also terribly real for all beings granted the precious gift of human existence in both the Buddhist and Islamic universes.

Turning to the operative and practical domain, one can again observe many similarities between Buddhism and Islam which offer possibilities for comparative studies. One is the relation between the role of knowledge and love or devotion in the spiritual life. Within the Mahāyāna School a clear distinction is made between the sapiental and intellectual approach in which knowledge is primary and the devotional approach. The first became crystallized in several schools of which perhaps the most important is *Dhyana*, *Ch'an* or Zen and the second in *Sukhāvatī*, *Ching-t'u-tsung* or *Jōdo* which is also known as Amida Buddhism. Each school, however, possesses an element of the other. There are devotional elements in Zen and sapiental and metaphysical elements in *Jōdo*. The same can be said of the Vajrayāna School which is by nature sapiental and based on knowledge, but possesses devotional aspects.

Now, in Islam the path of spiritual realization associated with Sufism also emphasizes both love and devotion (*maḥabbah*) and knowledge (*ma'rifah*). Moreover, different Sufi orders are characterized by the emphasis of either one or the other element. But where there is emphasis on gnosis or sapience, there is present also love and vice versa. The works of two of the towering figures of Islamic spirituality, Ibn 'Arabī and Jalāl al-Dīn Rūmī, who lived within a generation of each other in the thirteenth century, demonstrate this principle clearly. Ibn 'Arabī wrote primarily on gnosis and his path was that of knowledge, but he also composed many verses of Sufi love poetry and considered love to be very important in the attainment of the Divine. As for Rūmī, he was the great troubadour of love and most of his voluminous poetry deals with the theme of love as being central to the spiritual life. And yet, his *Mathnawī* is considered as the "ocean of gnosis" and he is identified with the very essence of gnosis (*'irfān* in Persian) by those acquainted with the inner meanings of his work. It seems that in both Buddhism and Islam the role of knowledge and love or devotion are like those of *yin* and *yang* in the Far Eastern symbol. Each element contains something of the other. For that very reason this whole field offers rich possibilities for comparative study.

There are remarkable parallels between the Four Noble Truths and the Eightfold Path of Buddhism and Islamic teachings. The Four Noble Truths teach the universality of suffering, its cause, its cure and the way to achieve it, that is, following the Middle Way and the Eightfold Path. In the language of the Quran, commented upon by so many Sufi texts, this world is *al-dunyā*, which, being separated from the Divine Reality, is contrasted to *al-ākhirah* or the celestial world which is the abode of proximity to that Reality. Now, the very nature of *al-dunyā* is separation, vicissitude and pain. Islam does not emphasize suffering as much as does Buddhism but its characterization of *al-dunyā* is similar to that of Buddhism putting aside the role placed in the Islamic perspective in the positive aspect of the cosmos as symbol and theophany and the lack of this dimension in Buddhism. To overcome the pains and vicissitudes of the world or *al-dunyā*, man must detach himself from this world, which means to control one's ego and its desires. The Sufis know fully well that the cause of attachment to the world is precisely the selfish craving or *trishnā* of which Buddhists speak. And like the Buddhists, they propose a means for overcoming this pain and suffering of *al-dunyā*, this means being overcoming selfish craving and in fact the ego/self itself which is the cause of that desire of the worldly. Finally and corresponding to the fourth Noble Truth, Islamic esoterism in the form of Sufism possesses a path whose main steps present remarkable similarities to the Eightfold Path of Buddhism.

In the Eightfold Path, there is right mind and right intention corresponding to wisdom (*prajñā*); right speech, right conduct, and right livelihood corresponding to morality (*shīla*); and right effort, right mindfulness and right concentration corresponding to realization (*samadhī*). One could draw a parallel between these stages of the path and the grand division in Islam between *al-Sharī'ah*, *al-Ṭarīqah,* and *al-Ḥaqīqah.* The first deals with morality, the second with methods and means of spiritual realization, and the third with wisdom. Again in the context of two very different types of religion, namely Buddhism and Islam, there are to be found remarkable morphological resemblances as well as, of course, differences because of the non-theistic nature of one and the theistic nature of the other.

As for the vices which according to Buddhism must be overcome, namely the three poisons of illusion, lust, and pride, they also have their correspondence in classical texts of Sufi ethics such as the *al-Risālat al-qushayriyyah* of Imam Abu'l-Qāsim al-Qushayrī who, while enumerating the virtues, also points to the vices to be overcome. The Prophet of Islam prayed to God to be able to see things as they are, that is, to overcome our ordinary perception of things which possesses an illusory character. He also decried the danger of lust of all kinds which must be controlled by rules of the *Sharī'ah* or Divine Law and considered pride to be the source of all the vices in the soul. How interesting it is to compare the understanding of the vices or poisons in the two traditions, one emphasizing marriage and sacralizing sexuality and the other based on monasticism and sexual abstention, one incorporating the whole of society and rejection monasticism and the other based on monasticism and the *sangha* and excluding at the beginning at least the rest of society. The treatment of the vices and the poisons mentioned in Buddhism and Islam is like the treatment of a physical disease according to two different medical traditions, let us say the Ayurvedic or acupuncture on the one hand and Islamic on the other. Each medical tradition recognizes the disease and each has for its goal its cure. The regimen given, however, is not identical, but the trajectories of the disease in the two cases and its cure follow a pattern ending finally at the same goal which is the cure of the disease in question.

Among the cures offered for the treatment of the poisons that infect the soul, one central to both traditions provides an unusually fecund source for profound comparisons, again despite the theistic and nontheistic framework of Islam on the one hand and Buddhism on the other. This "cure" is quintessential prayer, invocation or remembrance which is the central practice of the Pure Land School in Buddhism based on the Buddha's "Original Vow" and is central in Islam in the form of *dhikr*, which also means invocation and remembrance in Arabic and which is based on the Quran and the practice of the Prophet of Islam. The *mantra* of the Pure Land School, *Na-mu O-mit'o Fu* in Chinese and *Namu Amida Butsu* in Japanese means "I take refuge in the Buddha the Infinite Light and Infinite Life." The Islamic *dhikr* always concerns God and one or several of his Names or the testimony of Unity, *Lā ilāha illa'Llāh*, that is, there is no divinity but the Divine. The Buddhist form appears from the Islamic perspective to be the invocation of the Divine Names, *al-Nūr* (Light) and *al-Ḥayy* (Life). There are extraordinary parallels in this quintessential practice of prayer across various religious frontiers from the Hesychast prayer of the heart in Orthodox Christianity, to *japa* yoga in Hinduism to the Buddhist and Islamic practices in question. This universal practice and its particular significance for human situation today has already been amply treated by expounders of the traditional doctrines and the perennial philosophy, especially Frithjof Schuon. But much remains to be done in a more detailed manner in studying comparatively this central practice in Islam and Buddhism.

Finally, I wish to return to the question of the Void and Plenitude in the two traditions, a question which I also treated in my response to Sallie King. It is true that the Void is not reified in Buddhism and that in Islam one of God's Names is *al-Ṣamad* which means infinite richness and plenitude. There are moreover other Divine Names in Islam conveying the same meaning. There are to be sure many differences in the metaphysical formulations of the two traditions in question. Yet, there is a profound dialogue to be carried out on the question of fullness and emptiness as well as theism and nontheism between Buddhism and Islam. Here again the *yin-yang* symbols can be used. One religion emphasizes the Void and has within it fullness and the other vice versa. One religion emphasizes theism and in its esoteric dimension possesses a full doctrine of the Impersonal Divine Essence and the other nontheism and yet manifests strong theistic currents. That is why when we turn from theoretical considerations to observation of actual living realities and practices of Islam and Buddhism, one is confronted with so many unexpected parallels. For example, the metaphysical doctrine of the Void has its reflection in Japanese art with its emphasis upon emptiness of living space which one experiences directly in entering a traditional Japanese temple or even private house. But where else in the world is emptiness of interior spaces of architecture emphasized as greatly as in the Islamic world? The interior spaces of the mosque and also the traditional Islamic houses are characterized by their emptiness and the void plays a major spiritual function in Islamic art in general. All of these considerations point to the rich possibilities of dialogue between Buddhism and Islam which for me can only be carried out fruitfully within the matrix of the metaphysics of religious diversity which expositors of the perennial philosophy have formulated in detail in this century in response to the particular needs of present-day humanity.

I am grateful to Professor Inada for providing me the opportunity to expound my views on further Buddhist-Islamic dialogue to which his paper draws attention. Among various domains of comparative religious study, the Buddhist-Islamic one has until now not occupied a position of prominence as have the Christian-Buddhist and Hindu-Buddhist fields. Let us hope that along the line mentioned by Inada and other scholars and proposed by myself here in this essay this field can be expounded and deepened in the future. The fruits of comparative studies in this field are not only of theoretical and philosophical interest but are bound to have practical significance for many living in lands such as China, Thailand, Malaysia, Burma, Śri Lanka, and the Caucasus where Buddhists and Muslims co-exist as living and vibrant religious communities.

S. H. N.

9

George F. McLean and Richard K. Khuri

SEYYED HOSSEIN NASR ON TIME AND ETERNITY

The issue of time and eternity brings one to a central modern challenge to the religious view of life. The writings of Seyyed Hossein Nasr describe this well. In the classical view, often everything was seen in terms of eternity and there was little sense of change. Permanence was valued; change, of which time is the measure, was feared. This is echoed by the ancient Chinese wish: "May you live in uninteresting times." Now the opposite prevails. We have moved from belief and memory to exploration and discovery, from servant of God and monarch to responsible citizen, from an ethics of obedience to the management of freedom.[1]

Three responses are possible. The first is resistance, namely, to attempt to reject time and change in order to live in fidelity to Divine grace. This could be interpreted as implying a rejection of emergent democratic forms of freedom. This has come to be called fundamentalism. Though the term may not so easily be transported to Islam, the reality constitutes a major present problem for many countries in the Islamic world.

The second response is to turn entirely toward modernity, that is, toward the changing and ephemeral world of things and to abandon the sense of any eternal reality and hence of any transcendent or sacred dimension of life. This is the reality of the pervasive secularization of modern life.

If neither of these responses is satisfactory—as most religious and many secular persons would agree—then one must confront the challenge of neither ignoring nor being swallowed up by time, but finding in eternity its real meaning and potentialities. This is a holy quest and one from which Nasr does not shrink. Success in this venture is crucial and one follows his pursuit of this objective with fascination and hope.

Nasr's treatment of so important a topic inevitably is reflected broadly throughout his work on Islamic science, metaphysics, and religious culture.

In two places he has attempted to bring together his thought on time and eternity in a focused and ordered manner, namely, in his 1981 Gifford Lectures, *Knowledge and the Sacred* (Chapter VII, "Eternity and the Temporal Order," hereafter E)[2] and in his *The Need for a Sacred Science* (Chapter II, "Time—The Moving Image of Eternity," hereafter T).[3] Here we shall focus especially on these two concentrated texts, first to describe synthetically his overall vision of time and eternity, and second to proceed analytically to an evaluation of some of its main components.

Ways to God as Eternal

Nasr first approaches the issue of time somewhat phenomenologically, but with strong metaphysical intent. He begins not directly in terms of being—though he will soon come to that—but rather in terms of the human person as an intersection of two axes, one vertical, the other horizontal: the former points to eternity, the latter to time (E 221). However, even here he does not separate the two and make time simply a matter of the measure of physical motion, as might be done in Aristotle's science of physics. Instead he follows Plato and sees time as more properly the moving image of eternity, the ever recurring now. In this sense the vertical dimension not only leads to a higher level of reality, but also to higher levels of time. This opens the way for a plethora of intermediate realms which, since ancient times, have been the context of human aspirations and the path from time to eternity.

But are there reasons to assert the capacity of the human mind even to address such issues? Certainly, it has been the effort of many in modern philosophy to deny this and to hold human vision to a merely successive flow of moments. Nasr does not hesitate to answer in the positive. If it is possible, indeed inevitable, to address the issue of death, then one is already engaged in a horizon which goes beyond the empirical data of the senses and of the reality manifested thereby (E 222). Further, if it is possible to address the issue of time itself, as philosophers always have done, then the human mind already has slipped the moorings of time and sails toward realms that extend beyond or transcend it.

This is not only a matter of leaving time behind; rather in the midst of time we may be able to find within ourselves something eternal. Tagore describes this dramatically in a scene in which he has lost his way in a fog and stumbles about in great confusion and anxiety. Suddenly in the midst of this wandering, his home breaks through the fog and in great relief a sense of peace opens within him.[4] Nasr describes in somewhat similar terms the deep peace that opens within in contemplating a placid mountain lake (E 222). In brief, the reality to which the spirit opens transcends the objects and cares of this life. It is immanent in the human heart; it is as much the inner key to personal peace as it is to the outer source or goal of all.

From this phenomenology Nasr shifts to metaphysics proper and speaks in more technical terms of being or of what is. The eternal simply and purely *is*; it is the fullness of being. It is pure truth and luminosity, leaving no room for non-existence or even for confusion. As Descartes noted earlier in his Third Meditation, it is this that is certain beyond doubt and unquestionable.[5] If there is any lack of clarity here it is not from the Absolute Being, but from the limitations of the human mind (which is not on the same level). Hence, what is problematic here is limited being that changes or becomes, not Absolute Being which is fullness of existence, unlimited and perfect in realization.

The theological emphasis in Nasr's direct metaphysical approach justifies further exposition at this point of his views on the Divine with whom eternity abides, according to the Neoplatonic tradition to which he adheres. For instance, the Divine principle is characterized as "at once the Absolute, the Infinite and the Supreme Good" (T 27). By virtue of its infinity it must contain the possibility of its manifestation, that is, of creation, and this possibility must be realized for "it is of the very nature of the Good to give of itself and radiate" (T 27). This would seem to approach the Plotinian sense of emanation, and indeed he does say that eternity "emanates outward and manifests many levels of existence" (E 225). But the strong sense of the absolute character of the Divine protects Nasr here from any intimation of pantheism (not that it would be fair or accurate to label Plotinus a pantheist). What is radiated must be projected or separated from God, who remains unaffected by His manifestations and ontologically distinct therefrom (as is the One in Plotinus) (T 27).

For the Divine, Nasr uses both "Being" and "beyond-Being" (T 27). There is a dialectic between these terms in the Hindu scriptures and something similar is found in the later Heidegger. When the multiple, contrasting, and changing things are called "beings," their unique and transcendent source is called "Being." When, however, "Being" becomes a familiar term and itself is in danger of being considered the proper name of one being among others, the term "beyond-Being" is used to protect us from this. The great Iberian born Arab mystical thinker, Ibn 'Arabī (1165–1240), whose life and work are much admired by Nasr, almost always used the term "beyond-Being" to stand for the highest metaphysical source or principle.

Nasr notes two further characteristics of the Divine, eternity and omnipresence (T 28). To the former he relates the divine transcendence and infinitude, which he sees manifested by the majesty and "rigor" of God. To the latter he relates divine immanence that he sees manifest in His beauty and mercy.

Eternity he contrasts to time, which is characterized by change, transformation, and death. Omnipresence he relates to space, which is characterized by preservation and permanence. While heuristic, the reason for this alignment is not clear. Were Nasr's procedure a posteriori it would be clear enough how he would begin from the twin characteristics of the physical world, space and time, and move to the perfect reality as that whence they derive. But even then the relation of majesty to eternity rather than to omnipresence is unclear. If, however, as he says above, there is no need of the finite in order to know the infinite, then the reason for this alignment becomes still less clear. It may be that Nasr is supposing much that he does not articulate here, given, for example, that the study of the names of God is a high specialization in Islam with rich traditions. Whatever the case may be, as the text stands, the Western reader for whom it is written may have difficulty in fathoming the relevance of the foregoing distinctions.

Nevertheless, though Nasr does not undertake a posteriori reasoning to the Divine, he does so indirectly. Indeed, almost a third of his study on "Eternity and the Temporal Order" is a massive attack on the contrary notion, namely, on evolution and its notion that change can be self-explanatory and does not need an Absolute and unchanging reality (E 234–44). Nasr reserves his strongest attack for Teilhard de Chardin's position that evolution may bespeak an Omega, but not an absolute and self-sufficient Alpha or origin. But Nasr seems to miss the crucial point made by Teilhard in *The Phenomenon of Man*, namely that the Omega and the Alpha meet and in some deep sense are one and the same.[6] This does not mean that Teilhard's philosophy is entirely congenial to constructive thought about time and eternity and other themes of traditional metaphysical or religious interest, but how it fails to do so cannot be properly assessed without a careful reading of its contents.

In the course of his vigorous attacks on evolutionism and the thought of Teilhard de Chardin, Nasr ends up by providing arguments that are "at once metaphysical and cosmological, religious, logical, mathematical, physical, and biological including the domain of paleontology," arguments that may add up to a kind of updated cosmological proof for the existence of God. But Nasr is not really interested in carrying out an a posteriori, inductive reasoning process to the divine; he sees no need of the temporal in order to know the eternal (T 26). For Nasr, as with Iqbāl, awareness of the divine is the key characteristic of the human mind, in terms of which alone any understanding whatsoever can be obtained. The human mind is the image of the divine, without which there would be no human knowledge at all (T 28). For its part, the reality, meaning, and awareness of the divine are not problematic. God is the answer, not the question or even questionable.

THE KNOWLEDGE OF TIME

In his epistemological position on time and eternity, Nasr stands in sharp contrast to most of his contemporaries, for his ontological approach to the notion of time is built on the clarity of the notion of eternity. We know eternity directly, absolutely, with intuitive immediacy, whereas our knowledge of time is problematic. This is rooted in the difference between immutability and change at the deepest metaphysical level. Like Parmenides, Nasr holds that whereas the perfect and infinite reality is the completeness of being and hence not subject to change, of its essence change entails some nonbeing in the sense of no longer being what it was or not yet being what it is becoming. By such change or becoming the world is removed from the Being from which it derives. Time then, which is characteristic of becoming, is rooted in the eternal or unchanging from which becoming derives. In this light Nasr sees time in Platonic terms as the moving image of eternity: as an image it is a manifestation of the divine, but as pertaining to the world of becoming it is precisely a moving image. But that Nasr does not attempt to move beyond a primitive notion of immutability is surprising given that Plato, Aristotle, and above all Plotinus (and Ibn ʻArabī) long ago saw that Being (or beyond-Being) could not literally be immutable. It must transcend our notions of motion and rest and have some kind of inner activity that is reflected in time and motion as these become known to us.[7] For Aristotle, this inner activity is thought and for Plotinus, a more encompassing intellectual activity combined with something unnameable but deeper still.

In an insightful remark, as Nasr considers the converse of the proposition that upholds the priority of the eternal, he notes that to deny the eternal is not only to lose the distinction between the absolute and the contingent, but thereby to absolutize the world (T 28). This is the real source of contemporary consumerism and of the corruption of public life which now bedevils the world.

He draws up a list of many famous names who speak of the difficulty of grasping the nature of time, but Nasr himself may experience special difficulties. He is clear that he does not want to consider time in the modern abstract fashion as a container for human or physical events; rather he sees it as a character of material existence (which, as Nasr mentions, has become the norm in contemporary scientific thought as a consequence of the theory of Relativity). This already limits his approach to the study of time, for it excludes the manner in which time spans the abyss between physical motion and "the flux of the unlimited" of which Plotinus speaks metaphorically in relation to the eternal. It excludes a vast and layered middle ground of temporality that opens up human experience towards the eternal in a manner that has been explored to great effect by the likes of Kierkegaard, Bergson, Husserl, and Heidegger. We shall have more to say about this presently. However, even were we to restrict ourselves to the reduction of our perspective to that of the stark contrast between time as a character of material existence (which is necessarily prone to change) and eternity (which is equated with immutability), an additional problem derives from Nasr's failure to approach time in terms proper to material things as in Aristotelian physics, which is the study of physical or changing being proper. Rather Nasr is intent on understanding all in terms of the Divine. Hence, he speaks of it as an image of eternity, albeit a moving image. Aristotle would consider changing or moving being to be the basis for a science of physics and treat time as well as space in that context. In contrast, Nasr considers time in terms of that which is clearest in itself, that is, Absolute being and its eternity, of which time is seen as the moving image.

This has the advantage of opening the mind to the ultimate meaning of time. If humans were able to see not only in terms of the Divine, but with the very same knowledge as the divine mind, their knowledge of time would be perfect, comprehensive and exhaustive. But then, if they possessed properly divine knowledge, in fact they would be divine. While the human remains human, however, it will be important to use one's human powers to gain as adequate an appreciation of time in the corresponding sciences as possible. Hence, the multiple human sciences cannot be supplanted, but they need to be reinforced and most richly complemented by metaphysics and other modes of human wisdom in order that the nature and structure of time be more fully understood and its origin, deep meaning, and goal appreciated.

OBJECTIVE TIME

Cyclical Time

Nasr distinguishes between objective and subjective time (T 30; E 224). The former is further divided into cyclical and linear time. In nature, time is seen as cyclical. This does not mean "circular," for all does not return to the very same point; rather, the successive cycles have a cumulative effect, imparting a spiral character to the process. Thus in the traditional view of natural cyclical time, motion is measured by that of the earth around its axis or of the heavens around the earth (in accordance with the reference point chosen, a choice once again permitted by the theory of relativity). On each level, four phases are typically distinguished: four cosmic cycles, the four seasons of the year, and the four stages of one's life from childhood, through youth and maturity, to old age.

A special quality of the cyclical view of objective time is its openness and inclusiveness. This differs from the linear view of time in which the past is gone and done with, the present is the actual, and the future is simply not yet. In the cyclical view the past is always also present, as it returns renewed.

All religions have both cyclical and linear aspects, though in diverse proportions depending upon when they arose within the present cosmic cycle. (Nasr adopts the Hindu view that sees the life of the universe in terms of quaternary cosmic cycles, such that the four phases range from the virtually stationary to the apocalyptically rapid, which he believes is our present situation [E 228–9]). The cyclical view as found in early Hinduism implies little change, whereas in later Abrahamic religions greater change is recognized. Nasr positions Islam between the two. It has a cyclical character in its series of prophets, who bring to the world "over and over again" a truth that was present from the beginning (E 231). But Islam is also located within an historical story line, and it views the world of time as the "cultivating field" for eternity (E 230). By emphasizing the symbolic over the historical, Islam retains a strong sense of the cumulative character of revelation, and especially the permanence of the definitive revelation through Muḥammad.

Nasr is correct in indicating the development of human character as a whole as well as of religion from its archaic period to later times. Jean Piaget has helped to codify the sequential character of the cognitive (and correspondingly the affective and behavioral) life in the development of the child.[8] L. Kohlberg has carried this further through the development of moral reasoning.[9] J. Fowler has applied this as well to the development of religious thought.[10] Nasr's position implies that what obtains in the individual is found as well in the different stages of the development of people and societies. However, it must be stressed that Nasr consistently denies that those developments are evolutionary. It is always the same truth, the self-same realm of the sacred, that becomes manifest at different historical stages. What is emphasized in the various stages is merely accidental, a result of the occurrence of a religiously significant event at one phase or another within the quaternary structure that he delineates.

The priority assigned by Nasr to what endures above all else and his derivative view of the cumulative, spiraling nature of cyclical time may have important epistemological consequences as well. The categories within which he discusses temporality reflect a gradual, hierarchical progression in the effort to express not only physical, but metaphysical meaning and relations. This does fuller justice to the make-up of the human person as spirit and matter. Humanity's two-fold constitution is reflected in the structure of human cognitive capabilities, for humans are endowed with both external and internal sense, and, over and above both types, with intellect. The external senses deal with the physical data received by the senses from physical objects. These data, however, must be ordered and coordinated into wholes by internal senses. When this coordination aims at correspondence with the external object, the work is attributed to the capacity or faculty classically termed "common sense"; where it refers to the past external sensations it is attributed to memory; and where it is a free recombination of those data it is attributed to the power to form new images or the imagination. In all cases the human intellect as the spiritual power of a physical being, even in its purely intellectual operations, is accompanied by a form or figure or picture or symbol in the internal senses.

In truth, what we have just outlined is a standard scheme in need of modification. Reality turns out to be far more complex. The contemporary natural sciences have vindicated the position taken up by Aristotle and Plotinus that no strict separation is possible between mind and matter. For instance, Aristotle believed that even simple sense perception and the faculties designed for it involve mind to a considerable extent. Today, the amazing complexity of our sensory organs is much better understood, although the conceptual and experimental framework to which natural scientists have become habituated stands between them and the philosophical consequences of what they have so spectacularly brought to light. The current factual situation favors a holistic approach like Nasr's, where what seem to us like separate categories are in effect tools employed merely to distinguish among phenomena successively further removed from the Absolute, but never entirely severed therefrom. The problem with Nasr lies not in where he is coming from, but in the need for him to say more about it. Holism need not mean excessive terseness—or silence.

The representation of the relation of humankind to God in temporal images parallels the complex hierarchy of human cognitive capabilities. It is a necessary, but less apt way of expressing what is not a temporal or physical, but a spiritual or metaphysical relation to the Divine. Yet if executed according to the cumulative nature and connectedness of successive categories, even temporal images are bound to serve their purpose well, just as simple sense perception could raise the curtain over further vistas as our layered cognitive capabilities are increasingly concentrated on what is perceived. After all, sacred art has been around for ages, and Nasr regularly acknowledges its excellence as an example of how the sensory and the spiritual are gathered into a whole worthy of what it embodies.[11]

But Nasr is unhappy about and sets himself apart from a later development that originates with the establishment of the mathematical and physical sciences. While for centuries these were pursued in a sacred context, so that their truths were received and assimilated into a broader worldview (as Nasr himself narrates in his writings on Islamic science and cosmology), in modern times, they have become separated from wisdom and metaphysics. The same fate, of course, largely has befallen art, so that all sorts of meaningless, absurd, and bizarrely ironic images fill our world and hover above it. While the separation of abstract and rarefied knowledge from the full religious content of the human-divine interchange has the benefit of clarifying and correcting religious thought, given that it often goes astray, the price is far too high if the drastic dilution of that content is entailed. The corrective would then be to investigate and attempt more fully to appreciate the character and content of religions developed and lived in earlier ages in terms perhaps less proper and exact, but more rich. Hence Nasr argues for the potential to approach reality by means of a complex hierarchy of cognitive capabilities centered around transcendence.

Especially to our point, what is termed "sacred time" bespeaks a permanent presence of our origins and of key acts of prophecy and redemption which remain life-giving and normative for the future. The creation myths of each culture are such. They not only return on a cyclical basis, which is the best that an imaginative intellect bound to temporal terms can do in order to express their permanent meaning. But to appreciate that permanence more fully the human mind must slip the bonds of time and think in terms which are not restricted either to the spiritual, which has no time, or to the physical and temporal. In other words, the mind needs to develop a metaphysics in order more properly to appreciate such religious issues. In the spirit of what we have tried to lay out in this section, such a metaphysics would be a product of the full exertion of the complex hierarchy of cognitive capabilities with which we are gifted, a whole that seamlessly joins transcendence with immanence, a whole in which revelatory moments may be seen alternately as such, namely only as moments or, thanks to their moral or spiritual force, as eternally present. Eternal presence, as is well known, also has a subjective side to which we shall turn shortly.

Nasr does not provide us with that metaphysics himself, not even in outline form, but he does recognize this need and points briefly to the work of Mullā Ṣadrā and Rūmī as the directions he would take. On the present matter, however, he seems to depend largely on the Hindu metaphysical tradition, especially as presented by A. K. Coomaraswamy in an anthology entitled *Time and Eternity*.[12]

Linear Time

Over against cyclical time Nasr sets linear time, which he sees as especially characteristic of Christianity. Each religion has its central point in relation to which all is read as before or after. This, he claims, has been reinforced systematically in the Christian vision by two notions. One is *creatio ex nihilo*, that is the realization of the world entirely by the divine power with nothing at all presupposed on the part of the world. This allows for no "emanation" or continuity from the divine to the human.

The second and central notion is that of the incarnation of the divine into this totally distinct, created reality. This so diginified humanity that in time it succumbed to the temptation graphically described by Milton in *Paradise Lost*, where a creature claims self-sufficiency. This sacralization of the world was matched by a desacralization of the Divine as in a zero sum gain.

In the scenario drafted by Nasr to underline the dire consequences of the dominance of linearity in the modern conception of time, the world, or more properly time as measured by ages, claimed absolute status. Humans with their limitations and failings began to act not as fallible beings struggling to be good, but as absolute beings whose weakness of will defined what was good. In this lies the key to modern alienation, articulated systematically in the materialisms of both Right and Left. This is reflected as well in the *kind* of evolutionism that has come to pervade the sciences. In this, Nasr sees an attempt to bury in absurdly long stretches of time the dependence of all on the divine. In the work of Teilhard de Chardin, he fears, there lurks its ultimate denouement in a formal divinization of matter and of the world process itself or a desacralization of the divine (E 236–45). (Though why matter and the world process are not divinized when they are believed to emanate from the divine or to be continuous therewith, as in the traditional views with which he so strongly identifies, is not made sufficiently clear by Nasr.) For instance, in the *Phenomenon of Man* Teilhard does maintain that what unfolds in the world process is throughout sustained by the force of what exists as the Alpha point, and also that the Alpha and the Omega meet and in a sense are one.[13] This may not be good enough from a traditional metaphysical standpoint, but if so, more must be said about how and why.

Nasr's overall description of this modern process of secularization is an impassioned reading of our times as a contemporary version of Milton's insight. But it is important not to allow the bad to obscure the good, especially not the Good, for one thereby engages in the futile effort of the bad to overcome the good. With the notion of the Incarnation, human life did take on a new and sacred dignity that is now being extended: in personal terms to all individuals, in political terms to a dynamic structure that aims to better reflect the universal allocation of dignity to individuals (irrespective of whether present versions of democracy are adequate to the task or not), and in environmental terms to nature as well. These have become insights shared by humanity as a whole; they are meant to be the moving forces of our times. That market forces usurp this role does not diminish the moral priorities that the Incarnation has brought to the fore. The opening challenge of this paper was to see how what properly belongs to these temporal factors could not only be accommodated, but be promoted by their relation to the eternal. This becomes the challenge to sacralize time in dependence upon, rather than either in substitution for, or through annihilation in, the Divine

Itself. In this, the vision of Teilhard's *Phenomenon of Man* and the effort to read all as the *Divine Milieu*[14]—to but cite the titles of two of his works—and the endeavors of a liberation theology to introduce the temporal and historical into the essentials of theology may be regarded as noble and worthy, though not entirely definitive efforts.

SUBJECTIVE TIME

Professor Nasr's real interest would appear to be subjective time, or time as it is appreciated and lived by human beings (T 31, E 226). This corresponds to the inner conditions of one's consciousness or spirit. If this is dispersed into many concerns and troubled by many conflicts, an objective hour may seem like days because we are remote from the eternal. On the other hand, if the human spirit is in a state of peace and contemplation, then a very long time can seem like a moment because we approach the eternal. This, however, is a tricky business. Recent studies have shown that time flows more quickly for those who are depressed, whereas a powerful and blessed moment can appear to stretch into an eternity in the best conceivable sense, namely, that the experience is so moving and profound that one would be utterly happy for it to be indefinitely prolonged. Some of the most decisive moments in our lives are, if anything, all too brief; we wish deeply that they would last much longer.

It is not our intention to deny the accuracy of Nasr's phenomenology, but merely to show that there are other possibilities. In particular, our subjective encounters with eternity seem to be of two kinds: either we lose ourselves in the eternal, so that a long time seems fleeting, as Nasr mentions; or we are lifted into eternity for but a moment that seems to be much longer precisely because of its transcendence, which makes us regret its rapid passing.

Overall, subjective time has an obvious threefold structure: past, future, and present (E 223, T 32). The past contains the sense of origins, the meaning of paradise lost, and a sense of faithfulness to tradition. The future bespeaks the ideal to be attained and the prolongation of the tradition. This is their positive side. From a negative point of view, we may remain mired in the past and wallow uselessly in unrealized opportunites, while the future may be a source of needless anxiety and the means for escaping the application demanded by a present fully lived. Hence, Nasr correctly underlines the present as the point of actual life, of existence—in the sense stressed by Kierkegaard, for instance, in the *Concluding Unscientific Postscript*[15]—and hence of opening to the Absolute Existent, Divine Being. It is the meeting point of past and future and the symbol of hope. It is the only point in time where the possibility is always there for an encounter with eternity. And so, the present always already has an ecstatic aspect, even though we rarely are up to the task of seizing on this. There is always the danger that the present might degenerate into a hedonistic fascination with sensible pleasures. But its proper realization in terms of faith makes it the gateway to the Eternal.

It is important to note that while Nasr also sees the sacred view of the present as the way to save humankind from hedonism, he sees it not only as an ethical issue, especially not in the sense that it is something humankind can do of, by, and for itself. On the contrary, precisely because he tries to speak for the Sacred, his concern is rather the much deeper issue of how we can exist fully, which is treated not by ethics but by metaphysics. It is here that the full force of his Islamic vision opposes itself to modern materialism.

It is characteristic in the Aristotelian, in contrast to the Platonic, tradition to begin from the sensible and material. Aristotle's metaphysics is, however, a search for the primary notion of being, which search takes him in Book XII near the end of his *Metaphysics* to life divine.[16] In contrast, most modern philosophies, including most versions of rationalism, empiricism, analytical philosophy, and postmodernism, having rejected metaphysics, are left with matter as their prime instance of what is real and in terms of which all is evaluated. Hence, the divine is extraneous and of little relevance as a foundation for reality, transcendence is foresworn, and humanity is trapped inside itself and condemned to its own machination without further guidance or appeal.

In contradistinction to the tragic condition to which much modern thought has led humanity, Nasr, with his conservative and Sufi-inspired vision, takes the Divine as the prime instance of reality in terms of which all else has its being. What it means to be is first of all and most properly divine life. Thus human consciousness, participating as moving image of the divine, is in its essence most properly openness to the divine. Though limited and beclouded, this is its very heart. Our task is to protect and promote this living center of the being of consciousness so that it remains open to the gifts of divine light and love to avoid the dispersal that distracts from the One and instead to relate all back to the Divine Alpha and Omega of all.

One can only express one's dismay over the impoverishment that has bedevilled contemporary thought to such a degree that it is now regarded as an act of courage to assert that consciousness exists as such, as something *sui generis*, rather than being merely an epiphenomenon or some other appendage of matter. Nasr refuses to waste time on such intellectual habits, preferences, and imperatives.

Given the degree to which modernity has managed to lead itself astray, we may once more join Nasr in drawing attention to the importance of several cornerstones of religion (T 33–36):

- *Revelation* is required (or at any rate helpful) in order for humans to overcome the distraction of consciousness characteristic of life in a complex and changing world and to live the present moment in the Eternal.
- *Rites* renew not only the memory of things past, but the openness of the human spirit to the sacred, eternal, and permanent Divine presence.
- *Miracles* break through the ordinary physical sequence of time.
- *Prophecy* enables the human spirit to remain ever alert to the precious moments of divine manifestation.
- *Sacred art*, whether as architecture, icon, music, or poetry, not only depicts religious objects as do religious paintings, but symbolizes, reflects, and expresses in time the divine origin of all. To art there corresponds beauty as a divine quality, which existentially is the presence of the eternal in time, whether through the work of an inspired human artist or that of the supreme author of nature.

To his credit, Nasr repeatedly warns against perfunctory relationships to those cornerstones. How we relate to them must not be allowed to deteriorate into custom, habit, inherited patterns of thought, and so on. Religious tradition is a continuously inspired attempt to express and embody the presence of the sacred (E 67–68, 75–76). Awareness of the dynamic rootedness of all religious cornerstones in the sacred must constantly be renewed lest they should fade into the objects of listless recitations or, worse, tools used by zealots to propel themselves toward tyranny. He does not deny the importance of principles, techniques, laws, and other formal articulations of the sacred; for these, Nasr often affirms his deep reverence. But they ought never be detached from their font, and never be applied with a mechanical or legalistic mindset.

What Nasr curiously leaves out, given his earnest plea to concentrate on the authentic rootedness of tradition in the sacred and his undoubted awareness that tradition is far removed from mimicry, is the role of the subject in the authentication of traditional practice. For it is individual human beings who collectively bring a tradition to the fore. It is individuals alone who are in a position to ensure that they stand inwardly related to tradition. In Islam, it is Muḥammad and the imāms, scholars, sufis, qadis, philosophers, writers, poets, artists, and various other lay persons who have constituted tradition in openness to the sacred, and it is with the help of a revelation that they believe was bestowed upon them early in the seventh century of the common era. That a tradition now exists should not submerge the individuality of those who have wrought it, as though the individual Muslim today need merely ride on its coattails. To demote the role of the individual in the sustenance of tradition's authentic rootedness in the sacred is to risk the very perfunctoriness against which Nasr so wisely warns. In how one relates to tradition, one ought not let reverence quietly slide into diffidence.

From the foregoing emerges the fundamental discovery about the nature and dignity of human life. For Nasr, to be human is to be able to reflect eternity in every moment of time (T 34). In our view, this would be more appropriate for saints. Ordinary mortals realize their humanity quite well should they reflect eternity in time, but not necessarily at every moment. Either way, this reflection is done in three modes: truth and beauty, which belong to the eternal and illumine being; love, which breaks beyond individualism; and action based on goodness, which transcends brute survival and self-interest.

All these come together in prayer and contemplation in which the heart returns to its source and resides in the eternal order. For Christians, it is a turn to God the Father, the unfathomable, mysterious, barely nameable but strangely caring ultimate ground of all that is. In this, Muslims like Nasr may recognize Allah. The spiritual person in general realizes his or her place between the Alpha and the Omega, the final encounter with the Divine. Prayer unites these in a way that transforms the present moment of time into the Eternal now.

At this point, the power and beauty of the view of Seyyed Hossein Nasr, both as philosophy and voice of Islam, must itself be heard:

> How fortunate is he who has realized the unity of the present moment with the alpha and omega of existence. Such a person has realized the fullness of human existence, for to be truly human is to transcend time, to realize the timeless in the temporal order and to bear witness to the Eternal in the world of time in which destiny has placed us. To be veritably human is to fix one's gaze upon Eternity while journeying in time, to travel with the caravan of earthly life while harkening to the call of the Beyond. He who lives in time while fully aware of the Eternal Order has already transcended time and its withering effect. Such a person has not lived in vain. Rather, he has realized what it means to be truly human, to be a being plunged into the river of time but made for immortality. (T 39)

Closing Critical Remarks

The reader of Seyyed Hossein Nasr's work is struck by the degree to which he refuses to engage himself in the kind of philosophical elucidations and processes begun by Plato and Aristotle, and to be found in their own way in both ancient India and China. He frequently seems content to cite traditional thought and briefly mention established texts in support of a point that he is making. For him, it seems, traditional thought is already there. The sacred has already offered itself to those predisposed to embody it in great works. We need only turn to readily available sources with the proper state of heart and mind.

There are problems with this that go well beyond the formal question of what one is entitled to expect in the work of a philosopher. As we shall presently point out, some of these problems have consequences to which Nasr would certainly be averse, for they jeopardize the very soul of what he so genuinely promotes. They have to do with whether or not we interpret "eternity" literally, and whether we might not be more faithful to tradition by viewing it as an ongoing project, not because what ultimately sustains it is in any conceivable way incomplete, but because our way thereto is ever threatened with ossification and must always fall short of perfection. Tradition, even if we agreed with Nasr that it is not entirely human, is necessarily human, and to this extent must remain in a state of flux.

When we turn to our chosen theme of time and eternity, one readily notices that Nasr all but subsumes time into eternity and otherwise regards it as spurious. Eternity is relentlessly emphasized throughout the discussion of time without much elaboration of their relationship. In a cultural and intellectual milieu that tends to absolutize time, history, and the world, Nasr's steadfast and uncompromising stance has its moral and practical merits. It may be possible to justify it in the context of theology or religious thought. But as philosophers, we are required to expound upon the relationship between time and eternity if we happen to take an interest in it, which as metaphysicians we must. Many philosophers from Plotinus onwards have succeeded in doing so without losing sight of eternity (an understatement in the case of Plotinus). It thus comes as a surprise and something of a disappointment that Nasr can be as dismissive of the value of such philosophical application as when he writes:

> One can carry out endless discourse about time and Eternity while the flow of time draws human life ever closer to the moment of truth when subjective time as experienced on earth comes to an end. But that discourse itself will not lead to the Eternal, which is the goal of human life. What is needed is to seize the present moment, to live in it and to pierce, with the help of the "eye of the heart" the cosmic veils of māyā and hence to know and experience that reality which is Eternity. (T 32)

Is there no training for the "eye of the heart" that enables us to live in the eternal present? Is there no kind of training for the mind that helps one concentrate one's intellect on its transcendent source? Were Plotinus, Augustine, Cusanus, Bergson, Proust, Heidegger, and others wasting their time in their painstaking efforts to draw others toward whatever it is that enabled them to experience the sorts of moments that convince us that we are truly alive, that there indeed is contiguity between the temporal and eternal orders? And besides, is it not a thoroughly human disposition to exercise one's mind on a noble subject and to experience joy in the process? How could the thorough humanity of such joy be reconciled with the intimidating language of those who warn that it is a waste of time in the face of death? Did not the ancients teach that it is precisely the proper and thus joyful application of one's intellectual gifts that gives meaning to life given its brevity?

We know from his other writings that Nasr acknowledges various courses of training for the "eye of the heart." After all, the Sufi literature that he venerates is replete with such guidelines. But Nasr's negative attitude toward philosophy is characteristic. It may derive from the deformations that professional philosophy had suffered by the time he journeyed to Harvard University. Along with the other humanities, philosophy had been subjected to a ruthless regime of secularization, of which some accounts have recently begun to appear (by Page Smith,[17] David Hollinger,[18] Alan Kons,[19] and others).

We share Nasr's concern over the impoverishment brought to philosophical discussions of temporality by positivists, radical empiricists, and the great majority of analytical philosophers and their so-called postmodern opponents. We agree that philosophy still and always means the love of wisdom. It would be a grave mistake to be blind to transcendence in crafting a philosophical account of time (or any philosophical work that deals with art, nature, morals, or metaphysics). But philosophy is also an intellectual activity *par excellence*. It only comes into its own when a sustained and well-guided intellectual application reaches a certain plateau. To rise to such a plateau should actually further illuminate our awareness of the transcendence that sustains it, which in turn may inspire our intellectual activity to still greater heights. Again, by "intellectual," we do not only mean "rational," certainly not "rational" in the computational sense to which many today reduce it, but also "intuitive," "imaginative," and whatever other adjectives one may find to express the complex of gifts with which we are graced and that broadly fall under the cognitive and even the aesthetic. Philosophy has shown often enough that it does indeed lead to the eternal. How Nasr is able to deny this fact escapes us.

We may begin with one of the more general consequences of Nasr's demotion of philosophical activity. This would make it possible to commit outright errors that one easily avoids in an atmosphere of critical give-and-take. For instance, Nasr makes the mistake of comparing *esoteric* Islam with *exoteric* Christianity with regard to how they relate respectively to cyclical and linear time (E 231). The symbolic tradition within Islam that is especially dear to Nasr indeed has a more cyclical view of time, for example, in the manner in which it stresses the eternal present and sees the very recitation of the Quran in that spirit. It is also true that Christianity places a prima facie emphasis on history, especially that which spans the Incarnation and the Second Coming, and in this sense projects a linear perspective on temporality. Nasr believes that only those whose temporal outlook is primarily cyclical are in a position to avoid the deification of history to which he thinks Western Christians have succumbed.

However, to contrast symbolic Islam with prima facie Christianity is to confuse categories. A fair and logically sound comparison demands that the two comparables be of the same kind, either both symbolic or both, as they seem, at the surface. One need not get too esoteric to realize that the very idea of the Incarnation not only means divine intervention in history, but the ever present possibility of transcending history. Christian thinkers from Augustine to Kierkegaard have thought in terms of the eternal present precisely because the Incarnation lay before them as a paragon of the piercing of time by eternity. On the other hand, it is possible to view time in linear terms in Islam, given that Islam sees all that came before it as a dark age (*jāhiliyya*), presents a historical lineage of prophets coming to an end with Muḥammad, and talks ceaselessly about Judgment Day. If one is to penetrate to the symbolic intent of these and other Islamic beliefs, then a similar effort ought to be made for Christianity before passing to the question of which has the better perspective on temporality.

When we shift to the more properly philosophical problems associated with how Nasr treats the relationship between time and eternity, and especially with his refusal to treat it philosophically beyond what we have mentioned above, the first difficulty comes from Nasr's identification of philosophy with the extremely narrow rationalism that has been allowed to monopolize it in certain quarters. Nasr's fear of such narrowness, as we have agreed above, is quite in order. To insist on deductive, airtight arguments stifles synthetic thought and conceals all that really matters, for nothing of importance for human beings can be established with exclusive and often petulant recourse to methods more appropriate for petty legal feuds. Here, one may recall Plato's paean to philosophy in the *Theaetetus*.

Mention of Plato compels us to underline the obvious: There are many philosophical options, not all of them developed by ancient sages, from which Nasr inexplicably excludes himself. In the modern period, phenomenology and hermeneutics are two serious endeavors to do justice to all phenomena within the human horizon. Hermeneutics acknowledges that one must know the whole in some way in order to understand the parts (again an awareness shown by Plato in the last section of the *Theaetetus*). Phenomenology is a powerful tool in bridging the gap between metaphysics and religion. There is no reason why a contemporary account of time in this spirit should fail to be open to eternity and offer those engaged with such a philosophy copious means to grasp the existential implications of the relationship between them. A good example is Robert C. Neville's work *Eternity and Time's Flow*.[20]

A more specific problem that follows from Nasr's limited philosophical engagement afflicts his epistemological views. All he offers is the assertion that we have a "principial"[21] knowledge of eternity in the same way that we have direct intuitive knowledge of ultimate reality and that we have a faculty (the intellect) that allows us to know eternity more easily than time (E 223). Intellect is defined unhelpfully as that by which we know the Absolute and as the best evidence we have for it (E 2). It is true that we have a direct, immediate grasp of the ground of whatever it is about which we are talking, and of eternity when time is our concern. Nevertheless, much more needs to be said. It is useful to illumine the nature of the relationship between the ground and what it grounds, as Plato tried to do in much of his work. The effort itself—however elusive to the demands of skeptics and however logically inconclusive—can yet attain its objective if it is undertaken with the right attitude and articulated well enough.

Aristotle has more to say about the importance of first principles, the many places where they come up, and our ability to intuit them. In the *Posterior Analytics*, he leads us to some striking insights about the implications of our ability to explain things. Even a simple syllogism would not be possible were we not intuitively able to grasp (a) that it is logically sound, and (b) that it indeed explains something. When we begin to understand what understanding itself involves, our understanding of first principles and how we know them is deepened. Our claims about the intellect would then carry much more conviction. It would then be left for us to transpose this activity to the question of how we know eternity and how it relates to time. The way for this has been cleared in a tractate written by Plotinus (*Enneads*, III:7).

Finally, we may extend our philosophical inquiry by taking into account more recent developments, such as the implications of Gödel's incompleteness theorems. These reveal much about our intuitive abilities. The theory of relativity has inspired philosophers to take up the question of time and eternity once more. Not all are as open as they should be to the transcendent dimension; not all appreciate eternity for what it is. But we would do well to take at least some of their work into account. Then we would have given ourselves the best philosophical opportunity to articulate the temporal in relation to the eternal. There is no reason why this should not occasionally help lead to the eternal. Certainly it leads to a more adequate and relevant epistemology than that to which Nasr alludes.

A certain philosophical rigidity also limits Nasr's options in the definition of the eternal. Unwilling to reflect on the philosophical paradoxes and subtleties that arise from the human attempt to find words and phrases that are appropriate for transcendence, he is compelled to interpret the meaning of "eternity" literally. Among other things, this means that it is literally immune to change, literally immutable. Since eternity is all that matters, and time in its very nature belongs to the world of change, time is worthless *sub specie aeternitatis*, as must be everything susceptible to change. The implications for the uniqueness and dignity of individuals could hardly be more drastic. In the passage we have quoted above, it therefore comes as no surprise that our lives on earth are reduced to the experience of subjective time whose worth is exclusively measured by the degree to which that experience leads to the eternal.

Nasr is not alone in his philosophical rigidity. Religious and metaphysical thought long have suffered from the tendency to hold fast to literal concepts of eternity, immutability, infinity, and so on. The problem is at least as old as the thought of Parmenides (although even in Parmenides one feels witness to a terrific struggle to find expressive means for an insight so profound as to have seemed to him almost unbearably awesome). But from Anaximander onwards, there has been a parallel tradition full of examples of sensitivity to the fact that our ordinary ways of thinking no longer apply faced with what is truly infinite (rather than the mathematically infinite, which is really nothing more than the indefinite extension of ordinary dimensions and sequences known to us). Eternity need not literally mean absolute frozenness, the endlessly cold stare that Nietzsche finds in Parmenides.[22] Dualities such as motion/rest and change/immutability simply do not apply to what is *metaphysically* infinite. Eternity is beyond either rest or motion, beyond activity or passivity, so that all that moves is but a dim reflection of how it is with the nameless One abiding within itself—or so at least Plotinus tells us with extraordinary brilliance and force. It is only our overzealousness in denying any imperfection to the eternal that creates the illusion that it must therefore be utterly changeless. We fail to see that we thereby make it seem more like nothingness than what properly is beyond being. And we thereby invite thinkers like Nietzsche who are rightly intensely grateful for their lives to condemn such stifling religious visions. One of the roots of the modern rejection of transcendence lay in how much religions had allowed its human expression to become incarcerated within narrow conceptual dualities that do not begin to do it justice.

Perhaps no philosopher was more persistently absorbed in the eternal than Plotinus. Yet he clearly saw beyond the limitations of the standard dualities into which we try to absorb all things. He did not hesitate to ascribe activity to the eternal, which for him is not repose, but has movement (III:7.1,2), even though of a kind unknown to us. This movement originates in one of the modalities of the One, namely as "life limitless" (III:7.3,5).

Time issues forth from the active principle within eternity, from the life of the One (III:7.11). It flows ceaselessly because of the necessary perpetuity of the movement of the partially realized (relative to the One) towards the reflection of the whole (a process that inherently never reaches completion). Thus the living world remains "in a constant progress of novelty" (Ibid.). Plotinus even provides us with the means to tie the different levels of time together, ranging from the outward movement of a walking human being to the inner (physiological) movement that underlies it, to the psychological movement that underlies this. Our psychological experience of time is not quantifiable, yet this is where time begins for us. He then imagines the extension of the same structure to the cosmos by analogy, so that time spans the outer movement that physicists observe as well as the inner life of the whole universe, a reflection of the metaphysical beginnings of time within the One. Throughout, time is considered to be indivisible and continuous, just like eternity (III:7.13).

What Plotinus achieves in the tractate to which we have been referring exceeds the mere satisfaction of philosophical requirements. This he does with an intensity and profundity that may not since have been surpassed. But he also dignifies time and human temporality by underlining the continuity and unity of time for all its complex and variegated structure, a continuity that firmly and organically gathers time into eternity. He shows us how one may keep one's sights fixed on eternity without destroying the integrity of time. His work implies that subjective time has great worth in itself, so that to explore it properly is to expand our awareness of the eternity with which it is continuous.

A contemporary work that also attempts to lay out a dynamic and organic relationship between time and eternity is that of Robert Neville already mentioned. For instance, whereas Nasr simply lists, Neville actually explores the complex interrelationships between past, present, and future. The past is related to the present because the continual accretions to the past constantly shift its meaning despite its outwardly completed aspect. The past is also influenced by the future because its evaluation or understanding cannot be actualized until then. The present is when the given patterns of the past are changed and new actualities that remain over the horizon are made possible. The future is when the potentials and decisions respectively contributed by the past and present are integrated according to a form hidden within itself (Neville, 86–88). These give us a preliminary idea of how Neville elaborates a coherent phenomenology of the dynamics of time's flow and structure. He then goes on to link this structure with eternity, relying only on the acceptance of creation *ex nihilo*. The past is linked with the source of the determinate world, the present with the act of creation, and the future with the product, say the form or transcendental properties of the determinate world (Neville, 154–55). In the same analogical spirit that we have just come across in Plotinus, Neville succeeds in grounding the flow of time in the first outpouring from eternity. In fact, the very structure of that outpouring, from source to act to product, has the character of temporal flow, from past to present to future. Time is not just an image of eternity, but is there, as it is for Plotinus, in the very movement of the eternal.

Nasr then may be too hasty in dismissing philosophy's ability to lead to the eternal. His lack of philosophical commitment leads him to overlook several important and notable counterexamples to his assertions. It also causes him to misrepresent both time and eternity. Time in his work appears uniform, with no attention whatsoever given to its modalities. His idea of eternity is static and modeled on the past dimension of time, which makes it impossible for him adequately to link time's flow with movement within and from the eternal. In general, Nasr's philosophical position suffers from the lack of consideration of key metaphysical dichotomies, for instance that between immutability and change. He thus deprives himself of the conceptual subtlety that enables a portrayal of the relationship between time and eternity to great effect, as Plotinus and Neville have done.

Most detrimental to Nasr's aspirations are the theological consequences of his philosophical rigidity. Earlier we commended his rejection of perfunctorily upholding religious cornerstones, but we also pointed out that the only guarantee that these cornerstones be properly related to is for individuals to be up to the task. To this end, the uniqueness and dignity of individuals must be affirmed. Moreover, individuals must be encouraged to develop the conceptual suppleness that enables them to sustain a dynamic relationship to the cornerstones of their religion. To fail them on this count is to urge on the dark forces that lurk within every religious tradition, ready to submit the joy of living within an infinite horizon to the tyranny of frozen images.

Just as prophets bring to us the same treasures from the Sacred over and over again, and theologians strive to maintain the resonance of those revelations across great temporal and geographic divides, so must philosophers work their way ever anew toward transcendence. To do otherwise is to leave open the way to reduction of transcendent phenomena to formulaic assertions that ineluctably lose their inspirational power.

GEORGE F. MCLEAN
DEPARTMENT OF PHILOSOPHY
THE CATHOLIC UNIVERSITY OF AMERICA
WASHINGTON, D.C.
NOVEMBER 1998

AND

RICHARD K. KHURI
THE COUNCIL FOR RESEARCH IN
VALUES AND PHILOSOPHY
WASHINGTON, D.C.
NOVEMBER 1998

NOTES

1. See Luis Ugalde, "Moral Education and the Challenge of the XXIst Century," in L. Ugalde and G. McLean, *Love as the Foundation of Moral Education and Character Development: A Latin American Contribution to the XXIst Century* (Washington, DC: The Council for Research in Values and Philosophy, 1998), pp. 11–38.

2. S. H. Nasr, *Knowledge and the Sacred* (Albany, N.Y.: SUNY, 1989).

3. S. H. Nasr, *The Need for a Sacred Science* (Albany, N.Y.: SUNY, 1993).

4. Rabindranath Tagore, *The Religion of Man* (New York: Macmillan, 1931).

5. René Descartes, *Meditations on the First Philosophy* in *The Philosophical Works of Descartes*, trans. E. Haldane and G. R. T. Ross, Vol. I (Cambridge: Cambridge University Press, 1969). "As this idea (of God) is very clear and distinct and contains within it more objective reality than any other, there can be none which is of itself more true, nor any in which there can be less suspicion of falsehood," *Meditation III*, 166; "I do not think that the mind is capable of knowing anything with more evidence and certitude," *Meditation IV*, 172.

6. Pierre Teilhard de Chardin, *The Phenomenon of Man* (New York: Harper and Row, 1965), Book IV, Ch. II, cf., 258.

7. See, e. g., Plotinus, *Enneads*, VI:6.3, trans. Stephen MacKenna and B. S. Page (Chicago: University of Chicago, 1952).

8. Jean Piaget, *Six Psychological Studies* (New York: Vintage/Random House, 1968), pp. 3–73.

9. Lawrence Kohlberg, *The Meaning and Measure of Moral Development* (Worcester, Mass.: Clark University Press, 1981).

10. James Fowler, *Stages of Faith and Religious Development: Implications for Church, Education, and Society* (New York: Crossroad, 1991).

11. See chapter 8 of *Knowledge and the Sacred* and *Art and Spirituality* (Albany, N.Y.: SUNY, 1987).

12. Ananda K. Coomaraswamy, *Time and Eternity*, second edition (Bangalore: Select Books, 1989).

13. See note 6 above.

14. Teilhard de Chardin, *The Divine Milieu* (New York: Harper and Row, 1965).

15. Søren Kierkegaard, *Concluding Unscientific Postscript* (Princeton: Princeton University Press, 1941 and 1992). The 1941 translation is more poetic and flowing, the 1992 translation more precise.

16. See Aristotle's *Metaphysics*, Book Lambda (or XII), chapter 7, Jonathan Barnes, ed., (Princeton, N.J.: Princeton University Press, 1985).

17. Page Smith, *Killing the Spirit: Higher Education in America* (New York: Viking, 1990).

18. David Hollinger, *Science, Jews, and Secular Culture: Studies in Mid-20th Century American Intellectual History* (Princeton: Princeton University Press, 1996).

19. Alan C. Kons, *The Shadow University: The Betrayal of Liberty in America's Campuses* (New York: Free Press, 1998).

20. Robert Neville, *Eternity and Time's Flow* (Albany, N.Y.: SUNY, 1993).

21. This is the word that Nasr always uses in order to emphasize that the ground of being, the eternal, and transcendence in general is a principle rather than some sort of entity for instance.

22. Friedrich Nietzsche, *Philosophy in the Tragic Age of the Greeks* (Chicago: Regnery, 1962), pp. 69–90.

REPLY TO GEORGE F. McLEAN AND RICHARD KHURI

This essay by two distinguished Catholic philosophers belonging to two different generations is a major philosophical treatment of one of the most subtle and difficult issues of philosophy and also theology. I am glad that they have chosen the subject of time and Eternity because it affords me the opportunity to deal in one place with many questions related to the subject at hand. I must admit, however, that a full treatment of all the questions raised and criticisms made by them would require a voluminous tome. As it happens, until now I have not written a separate book on the subject in the manner of Robert Neville, whom they mention, but I have dealt with it in several of my writings of which they have chosen two of the most pertinent as the source for my ideas on the subject. While I concur with them about the importance of these sources, I do wish to state that a number of the points brought up by them have been treated either directly or indirectly in some of my other works.

The authors begin by mentioning how in earlier days permanence was valued and change feared whereas now the opposite prevails. Let me begin my discussion of time in relation to Eternity by pointing out that this phenomenon is itself perfectly explainable in light of the traditional doctrine of the march of time found in many religions and traditional sciences. To turn to an image used before me by Frithjof Schuon to explain the qualitative nature of the march of time itself, when we look at the upper chamber of an hour glass when it has just been turned over, we hardly realize that the sand is falling through to the lower chamber. What seems real is permanence or the spatial reality. But as the sand continues to fall through, gradually the configuration of the upper chamber begins to change and time becomes an ever greater reality. At the end, as the tempo of the change itself increases, time and change appear as the only realities and permanence seems to be unreal until suddenly the movement comes to an end. The cycle of the hourglass may be said to symbolize the flow of time in the cosmic cycle in which we live. As we approach the end of the cycle or the historical period in which we find ourselves, change itself becomes ever more accelerated, permanence appears as an illusion and temporal change seems to be the only reality. In a sense, time devours space leading finally to a sudden collapse as a result of which the permanent appears again as the basic reality that it is. Modern man is not afraid of change because, having lost the vision of permanence, he has in a sense divinized the temporal and the changing while seeking to forget the effect of change which brings us to the door of death and the end of "our time."

Three possible responses are mentioned to the question of the relation between permanence and change. The first, to quote the authors, "is resistance, namely, to attempt to reject time and change in order to live in fidelity to Divine grace." They call this response "fundamentalism." As I have had occasion to mention in other responses in this volume, I take issue with the use of the term "fundamentalism" in this way. For example, those who are called Islamic or Hindu fundamentalists certainly do not negate change. And even if the authors identify change with modernism, which itself is philosophically questionable, many of these so-called fundamentalists reject modernism on one level while accepting it completely on another. A clear example is the attitude of so-called fundamentalists to modern science and technology, an attitude which is hardly distinguishable from that of rabid modernists. Those who are resistant to modernism are the traditionalists rather than fundamentalists. But the traditionalists, while opposed to modernism in principle, are fully aware of the metaphysical and cosmological necessity of change albeit within a total reality which for them is dominated by permanence. In any case, the facile identification of those who emphasize permanence with fundamentalism is very questionable and I believe needs to be modified. I certainly do not agree with this simple equation although I do agree with the three possible responses which they mention.

In the section entitled "Ways to God as Eternal," McLean and Khuri state that I adhere to the Neoplatonic tradition. Although I have the greatest admiration for the author of the *Enneads* and consider Neoplatonic metaphysics as a summit of Greek thought, I do not identify myself only with Neoplatonism but with the *philosophia perennis* of which Neoplatonism is a major expression in the ancient Mediterranean world. But I also identify myself with the other expressions of the perennial philosophy in the West as well as in, India, the Far East, and of course especially within the Islamic world. My reading of Neoplatonism itself is conditioned by my understanding of such figures as Suhrawardī, Ibn 'Arabī, Rūmī, and Mullā Ṣadrā in the Islamic world, Śaṅkara in Hinduism, and the twentieth-century Western expositors of traditional metaphysics such as Guénon and Schuon.

Awareness of metaphysics in its traditional sense made me aware long ago how unfortunate is the reductionistic manner in which the term "Neoplatonic" is used for so many figures from Dionysius to Suhrawardī, thereby making their profound teachings spiritually innocuous and "merely" another expression of ordinary philosophy as it is understood by most educated people in the West today. I add this long paragraph here to clarify my position *vis-à-vis* Neoplatonism as well as to indicate a reason for my aversion to most of the later schools of Western philosophy, for which the authors criticize me at the end of their essay and to which I shall turn again in my response.

I am criticized for relating space to Divine Omnipresence. Now, everything on the physical plane has its principle in higher levels of reality and ultimately in God. When I speak of space as being related to the Divine Omnipresence, I am speaking in a symbolic sense. Space by its very reality symbolizes that Divine Presence which is everywhere as the Quran asserts, "Whithersoever, ye turn there is the Face of God." Once the language of symbolism is forfeited for one of conceptual analysis, then the "reason for this assignment [referring to my relating of Majesty to Eternity but as well to Omnipresence in relation to space] becomes less clear." Throughout my discussion of Eternity in relation to time, I have used the traditional language of symbolism as well as a discursive one and it is important to remember this point when referring to my ideas on the matter. To comprehend the reason for relating Eternity to the Divine Transcendence and the Names of Majesty (*al-Jalāl* in Islam) and Omnipresence to Immanence and the Names of Beauty (*al-Jamāl*), as I have stated, needs some background in traditional metaphysics and intellectual intuition in addition of the power of philosophical reasoning. I accept that perhaps I have presumed too much as far as the background of the reader is concerned. In the Islamic world, philosophers dealing with such issues are well aware of the rich tradition concerning the Divine Names, as the authors also state. But even for the Western reader, I have encountered many who have found reference to such correspondences to be theologically and spiritually very meaningful.

As for my claim that we do not in principle need the finite in order to reach the Infinite, this statement does not mean that there are no human beings who need to journey through the finite to the Infinite. In every integral tradition there are perspectives based on the traditional cosmological sciences which lead one to that which is Infinite and beyond the cosmos as we see in the *Sāṁkhya* school in Hinduism and such perspectives are there precisely for those suited to go through the finite to the Infinite. But this cannot be the only approach, as we see again in Hinduism in which the finite is completely bypassed in certain perspectives in seeking to reach the Infinite, that is none other than Ātman, as we see in the school of Advaita

Vedanta. But even if one does not need the finite to reach the Infinite, complete metaphysical knowledge must include seeing the principles of all that is finite in that Reality which is at once absolute and infinite. My study of time in relation to Eternity must be understood in light of what I have just stated.

Over and over again in various responses in this volume I am forced to come back to the question of Teilhard de Chardin. McLean and Khuri write, "Nasr seems to miss the crucial point made by Teilhard in *The Phenomenon of Man* namely that the Omega and the Alpha meet and in some deep sense are one and the same." I have hardly missed this crucial point. My whole criticism, paralleling in fact the criticism of a number of more traditional Catholic theologians and philosophers, concerns this very point and involves the idea that for Teilhard de Chardin the Alpha meets the Omega at the end of a long evolutionary process in time and is not Omega at the Alpha point. When Christ said, "I am the Alpha and Omega" or the Quran states concerning God that "He is the Alpha *(al-Awwal)* and the Omega *(al-Ākhir)*," they did not mean that Christ or God "evolved" to become the Omega. They meant that in the beginning there was already that perfect Reality, source of all realities, and at the end there will again be that Reality which was at the beginning. No amount of casuistry can overcome the chasm that separates the traditional view of the Alpha and Omega, whether seen from a Christian or Islamic or for that matter Hindu or Buddhist point of view, and the views of a Teilhard de Chardin.

McLean and Khuri are correct when they state that I have not dealt, at least in the two works of mine which are their primary sources, with what they call "some kind of inner activity [of the Immutable] that is reflected in time and motion as these become known to us." I find it therefore necessary to summarize my views here. I certainly believe in what one can call "Life Divine" without which there would be no life and becoming in this world, but I also believe at the same time that that Life in the Divine Order does not in any way affect the immutability of the Supreme Principle and that in accepting the principle of cosmic activity and becoming to which Plotinus alluded, one does not have to end up with a kind of process theology *à la* Whitehead.

To clarify my position, it is perhaps best to make use of the language of Islamic metaphysics. While Islam emphasizes above all else the unity of God *(al-tawḥīd)*, the Quran also speaks eloquently of God's Names and Attributes. There is, therefore, a multiplicity introduced into the Divine Order but not touching the Unity of the Divine Essence (*al-Dhāt*) which is the meta-ontological Principle. It is immutable and beyond not only change but also the principle of change *in divinis*. The first determination of the *Dhāt* is the Divine Names (*al-asmā'*) and Qualities (*ṣifāt*) which still belong to the Divine Order but already represent the domain of relationality and multiplicity within unity. But they are not as yet existentiated. By what Islamic metaphysics calls the Most Sacred Effusion (*al-fayḍ al-aqdas*) the Names become distinct in the Divine Order and they include such Names, hence archetypes, as the Living (*al-Ḥayy*), the Giver of Life (*al-Muḥyī*), the Speaker of the Word (corresponding to the *Logos*, *al-Mutakallim*), and the Willer (*al-Murīd*).

Through a second emanation, called the Sacred Effusion (*al-fayḍ al-muqaddas*), the world is existentiated through the "breathing" of the "Divine Breath" called the "Breath of the Compassionate" (*nafas al-Raḥmān*) upon the Divine Names. Through this "breathing" the whole world is generated, everything in the world reflecting through many levels of cosmic existence, the Divine Names and Qualities and their interplay. Thus there appears life and with it movement. There appears the physical world, which metaphysically speaking is alive, and which also moves, giving rise to what we can measure as time, as life itself provides us with the possibility of the experience of subjective time. I certainly accept that becoming itself has its principle in Being and that there is "that something unnamable," to quote the authors, in the immutable order which is the principle of what appears to us as time and change. This "something unnamable" is identified in Sufism with the "Breath of the Compassionate," the Compassionate, *al-Raḥmān*, being one of the Names of the Divine Essence. The idea of the Divine Breath is also found in other traditions, especially the Kabbala, while Hinduism speaks of the day and night in the life of Brahmā. There is a rich tradition in the various expressions of the perennial philosophy concerning this very important issue, a tradition to which I adhere fully. If there were to be no principle in the immutable order for what we observe as change, becoming, life and death and time, these phenomena would never exist. To speak of change and immutability as the only two categories is only a first-degree approximation, important for heuristic purposes but not exhaustive as far as the metaphysical reality involved is concerned. I thank the authors of this essay for posing this question and giving me the opportunity to elucidate my views on this crucial subject.

The authors claim that I myself "may experience special difficulties" in grasping the nature of time as compared to some of the modern philosophers whom I name in this context. The authors should rest assured that I have no difficulty in understanding in my own mind the meaning of time in relation both to the phenomenal world and the eternal realm. While I speak of time in relation to material existence, I certainly do not limit time to this level of reality alone. In fact, not only do I distinguish between objective and subjective time, but I believe that for each category of time there are levels reaching from the experience of the ordinary human subject to that of the higher levels of consciousness and finally to the experience of the threshold of the Eternal, and also from the physical realm to higher orders of cosmic reality which participate in one form or another of becoming. In some of my studies of Sufism I have pointed out these realities.

In discussing the question of objective time the authors assert that "Nasr adopts the Hindu view." While I often mention the Hindu *yugas,* because the doctrine of cyclic time is so extensively developed in Hinduism, I do not limit my exposition of this doctrine to Hindu views alone. I have alluded to the similar divisions of historic time into ages in Greek thought and other divisions of cosmic time as we find in Zoroastrianism and, of course, in Islam itself.

McLean and Khuri also criticize me for mentioning holism but not following all the way through as far as its consequences are concerned. They say, "Holism need not mean excessive terseness or silence." Now, in my many studies of traditional cosmology, especially Islamic, I have demonstrated amply how the holistic principle is applied to particular sciences. As for the modern context, my role has been to state the principle and hope that others will apply it to fields as far apart as neuroscience and botany. Only an expert in a particular science, who at the same time understands the depth and breadth of the holistic principle, can apply this principle to a particular modern discipline. I know a little about physics and geology among the modern sciences and something about the traditional Islamic sciences. Within the framework of my knowledge of these sciences I have sought not to remain silent as far as the meaning of holism is concerned. But outside of my field of expertise, I do not find myself qualified to enter into details of fields of which I only have a cursory knowledge. There is certainly the need to say more about holism as the authors claim, but my reticence must be understood in light of the limitations I impose upon myself and does not mean that I do not encourage others to speak in detail about how the principle of holism can be applied to the findings of a particular science. In any case, I speak of holism as a metaphysician and philosopher whose function it is to state and explain principles rather than the details of the sciences, as was asserted by Aristotle long ago when he wrote of the functions of metaphysics.

I am also accused of not providing even an outline of the metaphysics of "sacred time" but that I have recognized the need to point to the works of Mullā Ṣadrā and Rūmī. It is true that I have not provided detailed metaphysical expositions for the understanding of "sacred time" but I believe that I have certainly provided the outline in several of my works including *Knowledge and the Sacred* where I speak of the nature of Ultimate Reality and of man. I have also dealt with the hierarchy of cognitive capabilities in several of my works. As for depending largely on the Hindu metaphysical tradition concerning objective time, as I just mentioned, this is only partly true. Although I have benefited greatly from Hindu sources on this question, long years of study of Ibn 'Arabī, Rūmī, Mullā Ṣadrā and other Muslim metaphysicians and philosophers along with the works of Schuon, have influenced me more than any other source. I have also benefited from Coomaraswamy's *Time and Eternity*, which, however, is not devoted solely to Hinduism. Moreover, it is not an *anthology* as stated by the authors but a profound metaphysical analysis of texts drawn from different traditions concerning time and Eternity.

In discussing linear time, the views of Teilhard de Chardin are mentioned again and I am asked, "Why matter and the world process are not divinized when they are believed to emanate from the divine . . ." and I am accused of not making this point clear. I have in fact made this point very clear in numerous writings. The world of nature is sacred because it is created by God or can be said to be the result of the effusion of the rays of Being. Seen in either way, the world is not divine precisely because of its separation from its Source which alone is divine. All authentic metaphysics as well as all orthodox religions are aware of this dual relationship between the Principle and Its manifestations, that is, both continuity and discontinuity, and they are aware that there is both transcendence and immanence. It is remarkable to claim that since the world issues from the Divine, it must also be divine, thereby forgetting the ontological hiatus which separates in a categorical manner the Origin from Its manifestations, God from the world.

With all due respect to Christian doctrines, I beg to differ concerning the assertion that the doctrine of Incarnation has lead to "a new and sacred dignity that is now being extended . . ." To point to modern notions of individualism and individual freedom independent of any reference to God and to consider them to be a result of the doctrine of Incarnation is astounding, to say the least. Can one in all honesty claim that in the year 1300 when Europe was deeply Christian, there was a greater sense of the dignity of the human being among the Christians of Spain who believed in the Incarnation than among the Jews and Muslims of that land who did not? And why did this doctrine have to wait for nearly two thousand years, for a time when in most Western countries many nominal Christians do not even believe in the traditional theological understanding of the Incarnation, to manifest itself on the political and social scene in an extensive manner? As for the task of sacralizing time once again, I could not but agree fully with it, although I need to state once again that Teilhard's *Phenomenon of Man* and *Divine Milieu* as well as his other works have the exact opposite effect. Rather than sacralize time they temporalize the sacred by reducing realities that are permanent and atemporal to simply consequences of temporal processes.

Turning to subjective time, the authors agree for the most part with my theses including the spiritual and mystical significance of the present moment. Then they add, "there is always the danger that the present might dissipate into a hedonistic fascination with sensible pleasures." They are quite correct, but this deviation needs further elaboration. The sage or realized person lives in the present moment, the gate to the Eternal. Ordinary profane man is in constant daydreaming about the past or the future, while the hedonist also seeks to shun the past and the future and live in the present, but only for the sake of pleasure. He is a parody of the sage and in this sense it might be said that extremes meet. That is also why a Khayyām, the great poet of the "Eternal Now," became so easily misconstrued in Victorian England through Fitzgerald's free rendering of his quatrains and considered to be a hedonist. In the modern West, several centuries of secularism and neglect of mysticism pushed the significance of the mystical and spiritual meaning of the "Eternal Now" aside. A mental climate developed based on the one hand on a historicism which sought to reduce all realities to historical events and phenomena, and on the other hand on constant dreams of a utopian future marked by the idea of progress. The breakdown of modernism came with the opposition of the new generation to both history and the idea of progress. We see countless youth today who have no interest in the past and little trust in the future and who therefore cling to the present through the attraction of pleasure which alone satisfies them. We see how significant the word "fun" has become in the American vocabulary. So there is now a cultivation of the "now" which is the veritable parody of what Meister Eckhart and Angelus Silesius described. Rather than being the gate to the Eternal, the "now" has become the gate to lower reaches of the human psyche, to the most intense and oft destructive forms of hedonism. Yes, as the authors claim the danger of hedonism is always there, but it manifests itself only when the spiritual principles of a civilization are weakened or destroyed as one also sees in the twilight of both Greek and Roman civilizations. In a traditional civilization, hedonism is always kept at bay, although it is not, of course, totally absent, and the present "now" remains the gate for ascent to the higher states of being rather than descent to the infernal states.

In discussing the cornerstones of religion the authors mention a number of cornerstones with which I am in full agreement. But I am surprised when they claim without qualification that I leave out "the role of the subject in the authentication of traditional practice." I have always said that tradition can survive in this world only through individuals who live according to its tenets. That is why I have written so much about the traditional doctrine of man and spiritual disciplines leading to human perfection. What I have left out and opposed is in fact not the individual but individualism according to which the individual determines and "authenticates" the truth. In a traditional world the human subject is of course an individual, but he or she is also more than that and can transcend the individual domain precisely through the means provided by tradition. What tradition opposes, however, is individualism which characterizes the modern mentality as such. By participating in tradition the individual is able to partake of a reality which is universal and beyond the individual realm while encompassing it, while in the arena of history the universal truths of tradition are manifested through individual beings who have reached such a degree of perfection as to allow the universal truths to shine through them without distortion. Of course, the very expression of tradition implies adaptation to various conditions of time and space but it does not mean surrender to the spatio-temporal conditions at hand. Tradition molds its ambience and is not simply passive towards it. Tradition is like a living tree which continues to flower and bear new leaves every spring as long as it is alive. The leaves and fruit remain distinctly the products of that tree whether the winter be harsh or mild or the soil well nourished or poor. These factors leave an effect upon the new branches, leaves, and fruit of the tree but do not change their nature.

I consider tradition, or more precisely those traditions which have survived to this day, to be like that living tree. The perpetuation of the tradition requires naturally members of each new generation to follow its tenets and to apply its teachings to the circumstance in which they find themselves. It does not mean, however, to surrender to those circumstances, especially if conditions were to be those of an anti-traditional world such as what we find today, for in such conditions surrender would mean the end of the tradition and the drying up of the tree. In this process, I distinguish clearly between the individual as an agent acting in history within a traditional matrix and individualism which is totally opposed to the traditional perspective and which, with the coming of the Renaissance, played a major role in the destruction of tradition in the West. Moreover, the living of an individual within a tradition, far from being mimicry, implies creativity of a high order. It is no more mimicry to emulate and practice traditional teachings than it is mimicry for a tree to produce new leaves, blossoms, and fruit each spring.

Tradition is of Divine Origin but is also concerned with the human plane which it seeks to integrate into a reality that is beyond the merely human. It is immutable in its roots and principles while its branches grow in the world of time and space. But it is not simply in flux. Rather, it contains the principles which govern flux or change within a human society. In the modern world, despite all claims for man's freedom, modern man, in rebellion against Heaven, is for the most part passive *vis-à-vis* the flux and change that surround him. He is always called up to live according to the times without ever asking what the forces are that determine the "times" to which he is expected to bow in all helplessness. One never asks the question: If we have to live according to the times, according to principles, what do the times have to function and change? On the contrary traditional man is passive *vis-à-vis* Heaven, or the sacred norms of tradition, but active towards the world of change or flux. For him the question is not how to live according to the times but how to mold the times in accordance with the sacred principles and practices of tradition.

In their closing critical remarks, McLean and Khuri express their disappointment in me for being dismissive of the value of philosophical speculation on time and Eternity. They quote from me a statement in which I say that one can debate endlessly about time and Eternity while, through the effect of time, our lives move ever closer to the moment of death. The quotation cited by them in full was written from the operative and spiritual point of view in the spirit of some of the Buddha's sermons about the preciousness of human life, which should be spent on finding a way of escape from the cage of *samsāra* rather than studying the nature of the cage. Otherwise, I am certainly not opposed to the philosophical study of time and Eternity—as long as we are dealing with a philosophy which is aware of and has means of access to the Eternal. I have the deepest respect for a philosopher such as Plotinus who has written so profoundly on the subject and in fact have spent years studying works on the subject written from the point of view of traditional philosophy. When the authors write that my "negative attitude toward philosophy is characteristic," this is certainly not true as far as various forms of traditional philosophy from Plato to Plotinus to Avicenna and Suhrawardī to St. Bonaventure and St. Thomas and many others is concerned. My attitude is negative toward those philosophies which denigrate metaphysics and traditional wisdom, which reduce philosophy to either rationalism or empiricism and now more and more to irrationalism. But even in these cases my negative attitude concerns what those philosophies leave out and what they claim to be that they are not. Where they have a positive bearing upon a particular domain, such as the use of logic for the verification of scientific statements or clarifications of logical language, I do not have a negative attitude towards them. But to claim that all philosophy is only logic or what can be verified in an operational or otherwise rationalistically defined manner and nothing else, leads finally to the death of philosophy. Once philosophy disassociates itself from wisdom and loses its vision, it becomes difficult for it to survive save in a marginal manner. It is toward this trend that I hold a negative attitude, especially when philosophies divorced completely from the vision of the Immutable and the Eternal seek to delve into the issue of the relation between time and Eternity by dismissing the most significant aspects of the subject. I remain a defender of the perennial philosophy and its ramifications in the form of various schools of traditional philosophy and hope that as a result of current philosophical efforts in the West having reached a dead end for many people, the ground will be prepared for greater appreciation of traditional metaphysics and the perennial philosophy.

Turning to the question of the linear or cyclical nature of time, the authors write, "Nasr believes that only those whose temporal outlook is primarily cyclical are in a position to avoid the deification of history." I do not believe in this thesis as stated by McLean and Khuri. In fact, as long as Christianity was strong in the West, despite the doctrine of Incarnation, history itself was never deified. With the secularization of the West, however, the effect of the doctrine of the Incarnation which makes history a reality in which the Word of God has entered, was such as to permit many thinkers to continue to look upon history as "ultimate reality" without the presence of the Son whose incarnation in history, according to Christian doctrine, had bestowed so much significance upon the historical process. It was this habit of thinking of the significance of history that, once secularized, led to the deification of history. Otherwise, traditional Christian theologians and philosophers have over the centuries believed in the Incarnation without deifying history because they never lost sight of the Transcendent, nor did they accept the secularization of the historical process.

I am accused of comparing esoteric Islamic doctrines of cycles with the exoteric Christian doctrine of the Incarnation. This is not at all true. Of course in the esoteric dimension in both religions there are profound nuances and meanings not found in the exoteric dimension but in both cases the cyclic and the linear Incarnationist views belong, respectively, to both the exoteric and esoteric dimensions of the two religions in question. In Islam, although on the popular level one speaks of the *jāhiliyyah* or Age of Ignorance followed by Islam, everyone knows that the *jāhiliyyah* refers to the Arab society immediately preceding Islam and not to all of history before the Quranic revelation. The Christians and Jews, not to speak of the *ḥanīfs* or primordial monotheists and heir to the monotheism of Abraham, are not considered by any traditional Muslim in the street to be part of the *jāhiliyyah*, while the cycles of prophecy, that is, one prophet following upon the wake of another from Adam down to the Prophet of Islam, is the commonest exoteric belief shared by everyone.

As for the Christian side, can one ask if there are any Christian esoterists who do not believe in the Incarnation? The level of meaning is of course different among exoteric and esoteric representatives of the tradition, but the general doctrine which posits Adam, then Christ the Word as the second Adam who is incarnated in time and finally the return of Christ as determining the major points of human history, is, I believe quite prevalent among all

Christians. I have not in fact run across any Christian mystics, saints, or esoterists who have denied the central role of the Incarnation in Christianity and in human history. Nevertheless, this having been said, I believe that the differences in the conception of the march of time in Christianity and Islam are the result of the emphasis of one element in one tradition and another in the second. But since both Christianity and Islam are integral traditions, both the linear and cyclical views must manifest themselves in some way and on some level in each religion. As I said, the question is one of emphasis.

In mentioning modern philosophers, Gödel's incompleteness theorems, and the theory of relativity, the authors admit that, "Not all are as open as they should be to the Transcendent dimension." And yet, they say that we should take some of their works into account because this would afford us "the philosophical opportunity to articulate the temporal in relation to the eternal." I do not share this view. While Gödel and Einstein may be very interesting for other reasons, they, as well as others whose writings and philosophical vision is closed to the Transcendent, cannot be of much help in dealing with the question of time and Eternity. Once one denies the Transcendent, one is also cut off from the Eternal, which should not be confused with the perpetual. I therefore do not believe that philosophies which turn their vision away from the Transcendent can be of much interest for an in-depth understanding of the relation of time to Eternity, although they may be of interest in other ways. One cannot be led to the Eternal by turning away from the Transcendent. The fact that I do not commit myself to secularist philosophies in dealing with this and other issues does not mean that I have "no philosophical commitment" as the authors assert. During all of my adult life my commitment has been to the perennial philosophy and it is a commitment which includes much more than my mental faculties.

McLean and Khuri end by saying that "philosophers [must] work their way ever anew toward transcendence." We might ask why it is that they must do so "ever anew," if by that is meant a new way, and that this was not required nor can it be observed in traditional civilizations, including that of the West? One cannot simply say that those civilizations possessed no creativity while we do so. From the point of view of the perennial philosophy as far as essentials are concerned, "There is nothing new under the sun" to quote Aristotle. But to grasp the truth of traditional teachings is not simply to imitate. It is to have a vision, a *theoria*, of the truth which is the most creative of all acts. Originality does not mean simply to be different or do something new. It means in the deepest sense exactly what it says, that is, to return to the Origin and to bring back a message from that Origin. Yes, in each generation philosophers must seek Transcendence anew by searching for the truth but that does not mean by rejecting all the wisdom that has come before them, seeking to be "original" at all cost. On the contrary, the perennial philosophy contains the visions of the Truth and the wisdom issuing from the Transcendent Itself, received and recorded over the ages. The real philosopher is the person who can prepare himself or herself to be worthy of reaching the truths contained therein, who can prepare his or her eyes to gain a *theoria* of the Truth, and to be able to apply the knowledge thus gained to the conditions in which that person finds himself or herself. No philosophy is worthy of that name that is not based on that vision or *theoria* of the Truth which is ultimately both Transcendent and Immanent, the Truth whose theophanies are never repeated.

S. H. N.

10

Eliot Deutsch

SEYYED HOSSEIN NASR'S PHILOSOPHY OF ART

I

If it were not for his acknowledged indebtedness to the twentieth-century "traditionalists" Frithjof Schuon, Ananda K. Coomarasamay, and René Guénon, one might very well get the impression that Seyyed Hossein Nasr dropped in on us without warning from another historical-cultural epoch quite different from our own. Against the background of his Persian-based Islamic tradition, Nasr describes—and celebrates—a perennial philosophy which combines a Plotinian-like philosophical mysticism with what he takes to be a traditional theosophy. Explicating his notion of a *scientia sacra*, Nasr writes:

> If one were to ask what is metaphysics, the primary answer would be the science of the Real or, more specifically, the knowledge by means of which man is able to distinguish between the Real and the illusory and to know things in their essence or as they are, which means ultimately to know them *in divinis*. The knowledge of the Principle which is at once the absolute and infinite Reality is the heart of metaphysics. . . .[1]

He goes on elsewhere to say:

> Now, in the traditional view of the Universe in general and the Islamic universe in particular, reality is multi-structured, that is, it possesses several levels of existence. It issues from the Origin or the One, from God, and it consists of many levels which . . . can be summarized as the angelic, psychic and physical worlds.[2]

And then announces:

> The rediscovery of the sacred is ultimately and inextricably related to the revival of tradition, and the resuscitation of tradition and the possibility of living according to its tenets in the West during this century is the complete and final fulfillment of the quest of contemporary man for the rediscovery of the sacred.[3]

Nasr's reflections on art take place within this metaphysical-traditional framework and are informed throughout with his concern for "the resuscitation of tradition." He is rather explicit in asserting that the spiritual in art has all but disappeared in the West since the late Middle Ages,[4] but that many of its living vestiges are still to be found in "the Orient."[5]

The primary distinction which Nasr draws in his thinking about art and spirituality is between "sacred" (or more broadly "religious") art and "traditional" art (the former being a subset of the latter). In his *Knowledge and the Sacred* (1989) he states that

> Religious art is considered religious because of the subject or function with which it is concerned and not because of its style, manner of execution, symbolism, and nonindividual origin. Traditional art, however, is traditional not because of its subject matter but because of its conformity to cosmic laws of forms, to the laws of symbolism, to the formal genius of the particular spiritual universe in which it has been created, its hieratic style, its conformity to the nature of the material used, and, finally, its conformity to the truth within the particular domain of reality with which it is concerned.[6]

According to Nasr, it follows then that,

> All sacred art is traditional art but not all traditional art is sacred art. . . . Sacred art involves the ritual and cultic practices and practical and operative aspects of the paths of spiritual realization within the bosom of the tradition in question."[7]

And in his *Islamic Art and Spirituality* (1990) he elaborates on this distinction in these terms:

> The quality termed "traditional" pertains to all the manifestations of a traditional civilization reflecting the spiritual principles of that civilization both directly and indirectly. "Sacred," however, especially as used in the case of art, must be reserved for those traditional manifestations which are directly connected with the spiritual principles in question, hence with religious and initiatic rites and acts possessing a sacred subject and symbolism of a spiritual character. Opposed to the sacred stands the profane and opposed to the traditional, the anti-traditional.

> Because a tradition embraces all of man's life and activities in a traditional society it is possible to have an art that has a quality of apparent "worldliness" or "mundaneness" and is yet traditional. But it is not possible to have an example of mundane sacred art.[8]

Nasr is right, I think, in seeing the profound intimacy that obtained between *Weltanschauungen* and art in traditional societies—"art" which in fact was barely identified or distinguished as such, grounded so deeply as it was in the "worldview" and pervading as it did so many aspects of daily living. One must, however, I think, ask: What is the relevance of all this for us today? How can contemporary philosophical aestheticians talk meaningfully about religious art? And how might artists today retrieve and incorporate something of that spiritual power and significance that we associate with the "traditional"? In asking these questions I assume that "we"—the vast majority of philosophers, artists, and "educated citizens" today—cannot, unlike perhaps Nasr himself, locate ourselves as such in any particular traditional cosmos; that we cannot, in short, for political as well as metaphysical reasons, become anything like full-fledged members of, or living embodiments of, a traditional culture.[9]

II

What is sacred art? Jacques Maritain—and here, apart from his Catholicism, a cohort of Nasr—writes:

> Sacred art is in a state of absolute dependence upon theological wisdom. There is manifested in the figure it sets before our eyes something far above all our human art, divine truth itself, the treasure of light purchased for us by the blood of Christ. For this reason chiefly, because the sovereign interests of the Faith are at stake in the matter, the Church exercises its authority and magistracy over sacred art.[10]

Allowing, if you will, for the meaningfulness of "spiritual being" and for the revelatory capacities of art in that domain of experience, must we not insist that art is sacred only insofar as it presents directly, radiates with, is expressive of, an intuition of spiritual being? Is it not the case that Maritain and Nasr confound a subject-matter notion of religious art with the spiritual dimension of art as such and thereby deny the inherent power of (Western post-medieval) art to attain expressive insights into spiritual being that are not bound as such to any particular theological-metaphysical tradition?

Albert Hofstadter has written that:

> Religion interprets reality by means of symbols and rituals that depend only in

> part upon their expressive appearances to communicate their meanings. The consecrated wafer does not need to look like the body of God. Its religious potency and meaning depend more on representational connections in the mind, often quite independent of the symbol, than on its actual aspect. . . .
>
> What art does is to articulate an image which exists as the object of intuition and which gives to intuition an immediate grasp of meaning. This meaning has as its content an ownness, a fitness and adequacy within itself and to the human spirit, on account of which the artistic image can be a living part of the spirit's life and culture.[11]

Nasr would have the spiritual in art be located only in "traditional" art (works that "conform to the cosmic laws of form, of symbolism, and the truths of a particular tradition"; traditional art here encompassing as well the sacramental, the liturgical), and hence rejects the possibility of an autonomous spirituality in art. Now for one who seeks to understand that possibility it is certainly not necessary to deny the efficacy of much traditional art. Quite the contrary; traditional art has surely much to teach us about what may be most profound in art.

The traditional, though, does not necessarily involve a closed, dogmatic system. As it is often pointed out (Tillich, Ricoeur), those religious traditions that retain the traditional and are most intimately involved with what is "Ultimate" are precisely those which do not identify their "truths" as such with what is "truly" real and ultimate. Just as any vital philosophical tradition remains open to internal criticism and growth (MacIntyre, Taylor), so spiritually a religious tradition worthy of the name must always transcend itself. The aesthetic-spiritual traditions of various non-Western cultures, which Nasr finds so congenial, clearly recognized this need for pointing beyond themselves; e.g., the classical Indian, with its concept of *śāntarasa*, the peaceful *rasa*, which discloses the essentiality embodied in the deepest aesthetic experience; the Japanese, with its concept of *yūgen*, which when realized in art reaches into the very core of the mystery of all being; the Chinese, with its notion of *ch'i-yun shêng-tung*, the spirit-resonance, the vitality and movement of life, which, when the artist comes into accord with it, is manifest directly in his art; and so on. This does not involve so much a *conformity* with cosmic laws as it does a creative attainment that resounds directly in the work. As various non-Western traditions themselves show, the spiritual in art does not demand that the art be grounded in a worldview that is hieratic and multi-structured, with angelic and astral orders and the like; that it be replete with macro-micro correspondences, archetypes, and so on. Even when they were so grounded they oftentimes sought to transcend their own formulations and self-imposed limitations. And "we" especially, as I have noted, can no longer dwell within such a world. We can nevertheless,

I believe, be quite at home in various "rational" orderings of experience which may point in the direction of a genuine aesthetic-spiritual creativity.

III

Paul Tillich, writing in 1932, pointed out that "Expressionism proper arose within a revolutionary consciousness and revolutionary force. The individual forms of things were dissolved, not in favor of subjective impressions but in favor of objective metaphysical expression."[12] He goes on to say that:

> [With futurism, cubism and constructivism] The dissolution of the natural forms of things took on geometric character. . . . At the same time the planes, lines and cubes which were used received an almost mystical transparency. In this case as in expressionism in general the self-sufficient form of existence was broken through. Not a transcendent world is depicted as in the art of the ancients but the transcendental reference in things to that which lies beyond them is expressed.[13]

Modern art—Nasr notwithstanding—has in so many ways clearly struggled to embody the spiritual in art within the framework of modernity. One need only think of artists such as Klee, Rédon, Rouault, in painting; Mahler, Poulenc, in music; George, Rilke, Eliot, in poetry; to scratch, as it were, the surface.[14] We now live, however, we are often told, in a "postmodern" cultural space which has little interest indeed in the spiritual. We need then to ask: What are the possibilities today for a "post-post-modern" spiritual art? I want to address this question, in keeping with Nasr's own interests, with specific reference to architecture—that art form which so powerfully relates to where we dwell physically as well as spiritually; or better, where we dwell simply as human beings in environments of our own making. We need thus to point out briefly the claims of modern and postmodern architecture and then to present a challenge to Nasr to confront creatively the problem of how a new sense of the spiritual in art can be attained which is not grounded (in an impossible way for us) in a traditional, hieractic universe comprised of "angelic, psychic and physical worlds."

IV

A modernist architect (of at least one persuasion, say, a Mies van der Rohe, with his dictum that "less is more") would insist that form is present in a building when a right relationship obtains between the building's structure and its shape: "structure" being the mode and manner of a building's construction; the embodied engineering, as it were, that the building utilizes and exhibits; "shape" being the material mass and volume of the building in its environmental context; its physical gestalt, its spatial relations—interior and exterior. All buildings would thus have a structure and a shape, but not all buildings would have a form. For instance, when the demand that a building have a specific shape (e.g., because of programmatic requirements that call for its yielding a certain economic return), with this demand in turn determining, to a considerable extent, the building's structure—your typical undistinguished office building in cities throughout the world—form is not likely to be present. For the modernist, it is when structure and shape are so in accord with each other that the relation between them appears to be necessary, if not inevitable, that form is present.

And further, for the modernist, this form should be pure—hence structure *ohne Ornament*. Glass curtains, transparent skeletons, and the rest, point, it is believed, to purity of form. An economy of means, especially for Mies van der Rohe, as opposed, for instance, to traditional Japanese taste, does not exclude the luxuriant in the selection of materials; quite the opposite, rich marbles and the like are often used (e.g., the Farnsworth house; the Barcelona Pavilion of 1929) which give the buildings a certain opulence.

For the modernist, the absence of the superfluous shows a certain self-sufficiency, an integrity or wholeness that requires nothing outside of itself; although the building itself might be said to aspire to, as well as embody, a transcendent order of perfection. This *Geist* which seeks a Hegelian-like absolute ordering, demands our complete attentiveness. Like all classical aspirations, the achievement of this timeless form invites our admiration, not participation. The international modernist building, then, with its standing out from the social and historical, its elimination of all that is indeterminate and contingent, its striving to be entirely universal, is not—it has been argued —at home in this world; it resides rather in its own isolated splendor.

Modern architecture of the sort we are regarding represents, then, what might be called the epitome of one possibility of order, a rational order which proclaims universality. But like all forms of reasoning that we in the West assume to be universal, this rationality allows all too readily for formulaic imitation—how many modern buildings, no matter what their function or their place, look alike?—that tends to deny the unique particularity and nonrepeatability that is called for by every significant work of art.

A postmodernist architect (a Robert Venturi, with his slogan that "less is a bore"[15]) thus argues:

> When it cast out eclecticism, Modern architecture submerged symbolism. Instead it promoted expressionism, concentrating on the expression of architectural elements themselves: on the expression of structure and function. . . .

> By limiting itself to strident articulation of the pure architectural elements of space, structure, and program, Modern architecture's expression has become a dry expressiveness, empty and boring—and in the end irresponsible.[16]

With its free play with history, postmodern architecture presumes a liberation from all historicity—for, it is believed, anything can be removed from its historical matrix, its native soil, and be made "contemporary." Although it is modernism that is often accused of taking too literally the very meaning of the term "modern" (as derived from the Latin *modernus*, "just now") and affirming itself only by negating the past, it is in fact postmodernism that announces a self-conscious dissolution of the temporal and promotes a radical particularity rather than search for an absolute universality.

However, and somewhat ironically, when architecture is emancipated so completely from its own historicity it loses as well its autonomy—for the work ceases to be in its own right a "significant form" and becomes instead an encoded thing wanting to be read in indeterminate ways. Postmodern architecture, for all its appropriation of the historical, lacks the kind of genuine symbolic import which "preserves," as Gadamer says, "its meaning in itself." The postmodern building, one might say, de-symbolizes rather than brings forth a new unity of form and content.[17]

The escape from historicity allows the postmodern (and avant garde) artist in general to employ all sorts of materials and techniques that were previously thought unworthy to express spiritual concerns and insights. With the overcoming of a hierarchy of the arts in the twentieth century (nineteenth-century aesthetics, especially in the German tradition, tended still to rank the arts in terms of their expressive-spiritual capabilities, with music usually accorded first place in the ranking) there was a corresponding denial of there being privileged means (materials) of expression. Perhaps in keeping with Nasr's idea of a traditional "conformity to the nature of the material used," anything whatsoever became a potential carrier of meaning —from cardboard to throw-aways, as well as the usual marbles and pigments.

This new-found freedom in the use of materials came, of course, at a cost, namely, the failure to develop appropriate standards of excellence. When is a building wrapped in plastic done well or poorly? By what standards are we to judge "music" constituted largely by an arbitrary marking-off of natural and human-made everyday sounds?

The other side to this, however, might well be the happy breakdown of the distinction between "fine art" and "craft work" that has hounded so much of the history of Western art. Today with photographs, pots, and formalistic driven mixed-media works we seem to be moving, and this should please Nasr, in a direction often associated with traditional East Asian art traditions where a distinction is drawn not so much between fine art and craft work as between professional art and folk art—artists within the professional category exercising considerable skill and refinement with what we have long considered to be craft materials (e.g., ceramics). The liberation of craft materials might thus allow a wide range of new possibilities for symbolic expression in the arts in general and, through the use of non-traditional materials, for the opening of new dimensions of meaning in building.

The (deconstructivist) postmodernist, however, insists that signs refer only to other signs and not to some other kind of fundamental—or essential—reality. Meaning is thus liberated from any "objective" correlation, but it is not liberated in the service of a qualitatively new kind of meaning. One might even go so far as to say that the celebration of fragmentation, rather than unity; of conflict, rather than harmony; indeed, the very quest for a self-referentiality that drowns within itself, is surely a novel form of madness. This celebration and quest is entirely without reference to the sacred.

The question then is: What aesthetic motivation would drive a post-modernist to uncover the sacred both in life and art? The only motivation, it would seem, would be that of despair, founded on the inherent meaninglessness of all culture. Despair, however, motivates toward nothing.

One must surmise, then, that it is only if the play side of the postmodern sensibility were itself liberated from its denial of meaning could it then be a source for a new approach to the sacred—with sacred art then taking on the double-duty of being at once aesthetically right (and therefore autonomous) and spiritually efficacious (and thereby mediating between the participant-observer and spiritual being). The possibility of a post-postmodern sacred art rests, then, strongly on the need to formulate a new definition of the "sacred," namely, one in which the traditional elements associated with it, such as radical transcendence founded on a duality of the natural and the spiritual and commonly accepted right modes of symbolization, are set aside in favor of a commonality between the natural and the spiritual. This commonality must be able to provide for a belonging together of humankind and nature in freedom in such a way that a meaningful, creative play in that relationship is brought forth.

I invite Seyyed Hossein Nasr to accept the task, for which he is in so many ways uniquely qualified, of working out this formulation so that he may address adequately for us the crisis, as he perceives it, of the spiritual in art today.

ELIOT DEUTSCH

DEPARTMENT OF PHILOSOPHY
UNIVERSITY OF HAWAII AT MANOA
MAY 1994

NOTES

1. Seyyed Hossein Nasr, *Knowledge and the Sacred* (Albany: State University of New York Press, 1989), p. 133.

2. Seyyed Hossein Nasr, *Islamic Art & Spirituality* (Delhi: Oxford University Press, 1990), p. 65.

3. *Knowledge and the Sacred*, p. 94.

4. "It is not at all accidental," he writes, "that the break up of the unity of the Christian tradition in the West coincided with the rise of the Reformation. Nor is it accidental that the philosophical and scientific revolts against the medieval Christian worldview were contemporary with the nearly complete destruction of traditional art and its replacement by a Promethean and humanistic art which soon decayed into that unintelligible nightmare of baroque and rococo religious art that drove many an intelligent believer out of the church. . . .

[Traditional art] is the vehicle of an intellectual intuition and a sapiental message which transcends both the individual artist and the collective psyche of the world to which he belongs. On the contrary, humanistic art is able to convey only individualistic inspirations or at best something of the collective psyche to which the individual artist belongs, but never an intellectual message. . . . It can never become the fountain of either knowledge or grace because of its divorce from those cosmic laws and the spiritual presence which characterize traditional art." (Ibid., pp. 257–58).

5. Although Nasr is very much aware of differences that obtain between East Asian (Chinese, Japanese, Korean), South Asian (Indian-based) and Middle Eastern traditions, he does tend to speak often of "the Orient" as a rather homogeneous cultural space. Overlooking both internal differences within individual traditions as well as deep external differences, he can say typically without embarrassment that "there has always been in the Orient a logical aspect to poetry and a poetic aspect to the great expressions of logical thought" (*Islamic Art and Spirituality*, p. 88)—which would have been news at least to the Buddhist logician Dignāga, the *navya-naiyāikas* of the classical Indian *Nyāya* tradition, or the "white horse" Chinese dialecticians.

6. *Knowledge and the Sacred*, p. 254.

7. Ibid., p. 275n1.

8. *Islamic Art and Spirituality*, pp. 65–66.

9. I append the "political" here, for it is obvious that the royal, if not feudal, ordering of most traditional societies is deeply alien to contemporary Western sensibilities and that this ordering clearly had a strong impact on the art of these societies—e.g., from the education of craft-artists to the forced abundance of their manual labor.

10. Jacques Maritain, *Art and Scholasticism: With Other Essays*, trans. J. F. Scanlan (New York: Charles Scribner's Sons, 1954), p. 111.

11. Albert Hofstadter, *Agony and Epitaph* (New York: George Braziller, 1977), pp. 57–58.

12. Paul Tillich, *The Religious Situation*, trans. H. Richard Niebuhr (New York: Meridian Books, 1956), p. 87.

13. Ibid., pp. 87–88.

14. For a good survey and discussion of this see Mark C. Taylor, *Disfiguring: Art, Architecture, Religion* (Chicago: University of Chicago Press, 1992).

15. The term "postmodern," as is usually recognized, has come to mean many different things to many different people—some seeing it as a wholesale rejection of the modern (especially those of a deconstructivist bent with their tirade against "logocentrism"), while others see it as the last phase of the modern and thus in some kind of continuity with it. There is, however, considerable agreement that for architecture, postmodernism received its earliest and clearest pronouncement in the writings of Robert Venturi. Venturi writes that "When simplicity cannot work, simpleness results. Blatant simplification means bland architecture. Less is a bore." (*Complexity and Contradiction in Architecture* [New York: The Museum of Modern Art, 1966], p. 25).

16. Robert Venturi, Denise Scott Brown, and Steven Izenour, *Learning from Las Vegas: The Forgotten Symbolism of Architectural Form* (Cambridge and London: MIT Press, 1972), pp. 101–3.

17. What this means for a post-postmodern architecture which strives to be irreplaceable in virtue of its uniqueness is the understanding that what contributes significantly to that uniqueness is the attainment of an appropriate rootedness of the building in nature. The building must become a locus of relationships that has been created precisely as an environment which promotes a belonging together of humankind and nature, a becoming at home in the world.

REPLY TO ELIOT DEUTSCH

Professor Deutsch begins his essay by saying that one could get the impression that I had "dropped . . . without warning from another historical-cultural epoch." If one were to accept the prevailing modernism of the West as the only global reality, then this would be the case. But let us remember that modernism, which had its original home in the West and has spread to other continents during the past two centuries, is certainly not global and in the West itself modernism is not synonymous with the whole of Western life and thought where something of tradition still survives and where the universal doctrines of tradition have been revived in a majestic manner in the twentieth century by the traditional authorities mentioned by Deutsch. As for the rest of the globe, including the Islamic world from which I hail, the traditional perspective is alive and widespread there and is hardly perceived as belonging to another "historical-culture epoch" except by the minority Westernizers. In any case, I do speak from the traditional perspective which is by nature meta-historical and perennial and is not to be identified with a single epoch, although the widespread applications of its principles are to be seen in certain eras and areas and not in others.

As for the metaphysics at the heart of traditional doctrines, the metaphysics which I have also called *scientia sacra*, it must not be confused with a branch of philosophy as this discipline is currently understood in the West, nor reduced simply to philosophical mysticism unless the traditional sense of philosophy is resurrected. In so much discourse today, the significance of traditional metaphysics is denied by simply equating it with an already denatured Neoplatonism whose character as systemized sacred doctrine has long been denied. In this discourse Plotinus is reduced practically to an ordinary philosopher teaching in some school like our present-day universities, except that he lived eighteen hundred years ago rather than today.

Turning to the main subject of this essay, Deutsch points to my primary distinctions among "sacred," "religious," and "traditional" art, considering traditional art to be a subset of religious art. This, however, is not exactly my view and there is a certain confusion in this description of my perspective that needs to be clarified (as I have done fully in an essay with the title of the three types of art in question). While I consider sacred art to be at the heart of traditional art as reflected in the quotations cited by Deutsch, I make a clear distinction between religious and traditional art, a distinction that needs to be emphasized. All traditional art has a profoundly religious significance even if it be a vessel or a sword which, however, would not be called religious art today. Of course, some traditional art, such as a temple or a liturgy, would on the contrary be also called religious art in the current understanding of the term. The greater problem involves religious art in the nontraditional world, an art which deals with religious subjects but not according to traditional canons, an art which I, like other traditionalist metaphysicians of art such as A. K. Coomaraswamy and T. Burckhardt, distinguish rigorously from traditional art. Moreover, for a "sacred art," in the serious sense of the term, to exist, traditional art must be present and living. Nontraditional religious art, whether it be anthropomorphic, humanistic, or surrealistic, cannot produce sacred art. These rigorous distinctions are necessary for understanding my views on the philosophy of art.

Deutsch asks how contemporary philosophical aestheticians and artists can talk about religious art and regain the spiritual power associated with "the traditional" while being unable to belong to a traditional cosmos. This is a profound and fundamental question whose full response would need a separate treatise but which I can address here at least in a summary fashion. To answer this question one must in turn ask why it is that the "we" to whom Deutsch refers cannot be a part of a traditional world? If the response is that such a world is no longer accessible, then my answer will be that although such worlds are not to be found intact as total societies, one can still practice the traditional life personally and create a traditional ambience around oneself. One may thereby find the possibility both of understanding fully traditional doctrines of art in addition to speaking of art as a philosophical aesthetician and of drawing from the spiritual power of the symbols involved. If, however, the response is that a person prefers to be modern and does not want to belong to a tradition, which alone can open our minds and souls to the reception of the light and spiritual power of traditional and sacred arts and symbols, then there is no reason whatsoever why the spiritual power sought by the artist in question should be made accessible to him or her.

Yes, I do deny the possibility of "an autonomous spirituality in art" at least if by autonomous we mean being independent of the Divine Reality which is the source of all "spirituality," as I understand the term. If we define spirituality, as I do, as that which is related to the world of the Spirit, to the Latin *spiritus*, as an objective reality with an ontological status, then spirituality can only be attained through the channels which Heaven has provided for our access to that world, channels which are contained within the various traditions of divine origin. If, however, by spirituality we mean something much vaguer and more associated with sentiments, the psyche and the expansive modes of the ego, then we are speaking different languages. I think that much of the disagreement of Professor Deutsch and myself on this issue is related to different understandings of the term spirituality. For example, when he speaks of being "at home in various 'rational' orderings of experience which may point in the direction of a genuine aesthetic-spiritual creativity," he is simply speaking about another understanding of the term spiritual. For if spiritual were to mean that which is related to *spiritus*, then it cannot be attained simply by being at home in various "rational orderings" which can both ignore and negate the Transcendent as well as the Immanent and deny the spiritual in the sense of belonging to the realm of *spiritus* whose very existence they are prone to question.

I certainly agree with Deutsch that the traditional "does not necessarily involve a closed, dogmatic system." I would in fact add that tradition is never a closed system but a living reality. It is a worldview and set of doctrines that is open "vertically" towards the Infinite and leads the mind in that direction, in contrast to rationalistic philosophical systems which are closed even if they claim not to be dogmatic. Dogma is an externalization and fixation of doctrine while doctrine itself, if metaphysically understood, is but a signpost toward that Reality whose realized knowledge is ineffable. As for the testimony of Tillich and Ricoeur quoted by Deutsch, they refer to another understanding of tradition and traditional than I hold. In the integral traditional perspective, the esoteric element is always central and present. All formulations of doctrine, although precious and sacred, are seen in that perspective to be ultimately keys to open doors before us on the way to realized knowledge. This emphasis is particularly pertinent in a discussion of art, because sacred and traditional art issue precisely from the inner dimension of the tradition, and hence reflect more directly its spiritual essence than do theology and philosophy. Traditional art remains deeply rooted in its symbolic language and techniques and methods of execution in the particular world of forms to which it belongs, and yet traditional art points to the Ultimate Reality beyond itself and beyond all forms. It frees us invariably from bonds of limitation and allows us, especially in its essential form as sacred art, to experience the ecstasy of flying in the unfettered and illimitable expanses of the Divine Empyrean. The conformity of traditional art to cosmic laws does not in any way diminish the resounding creativity which we witness in all great works of sacred and traditional art.

As Deutsch asserts, in many ways I am a kindred spirit with Jacques Maritain. But while the latter speaks of theological wisdom in relation to sacred art, I would speak of esoteric doctrines of metaphysics and cosmology. But the case of Christianity being what it is, namely the centrality of theology in that religion (in contrast, let us say, to Islam and Hinduism) and the mixture in some sense of exoteric and esoteric elements, perhaps this difference between us is not as great as it would seem. In any case, I am much attracted to Maritain's expositions of the Thomistic theory of art and of forms, although I find my views close to those of Coomaraswamy who in his *The Transformation of Nature in Art* and *Christian and Oriental Philosophy of Art* expounds the views of Meister Eckhart and St. Thomas on art.

I will not go into the quotations from Tillich which are problematic to say the least, but turn instead to the important subject they are meant to introduce, namely the struggle in modern art to embody the spiritual and the possibility of a "postmodern" spiritual art. Deutsch mentions a number of modern artists in different fields to demonstrate that there have been those in the modern period who have struggled to embody the spiritual in art. He mentions painters and musicians as well as poets. The case of these latter forms of art is in fact somewhat different from the plastic arts. In the case of poetry, since there is less need of dependence upon extensive patronage, external economic, and social factors, and coercion from the outside as a result of the dependence of the artist on a particular organization or person than one finds in many of the other arts such as architecture, it is possible to produce poetry of a traditional and spiritual character in the West even today. One sees this type of poetry with spiritual elements in the context of tradition in T. S. Eliot who was a Christian poet and also in W. B. Yeats who had recourse to the language of symbolism as traditionally understood on a universal scale although he was not himself strictly speaking a traditionalist. In our own days both Frithjof Schuon and Martin Lings, among leading traditionalists, have also produced poems with great spiritual fragrance and of a traditional character. It must be added, however, that precisely because of the desacralized ambience of modern life, language has lost its symbolic power. Thus, traditional poetry is not "popular" in the West today, to say the least, even though traditionally inspired poems remain popular in non-Western societies, such as my own original home country of Persia. One needs also to mention that poetry itself has been eclipsed in the modern West to such an extent as to be unprecedented in any known historical period, and today it plays a lesser role in public discourse, especially in the English- and French-speaking worlds, than at any other time in history.

As for music, for a long time as the West became ever more secularized and its art more worldly and humanistic, the deeper theological and spiritual yearnings of Western man took refuge in music more than in any of the other arts. Already in the Renaissance the spiritual quality of the music of a Palestrina cannot be compared to the humanistic and worldly plastic arts of his day. Nor can one compare the spiritual quality of the music of Bach in any way with the Baroque and Rococo art and architecture of his age which drove many an intelligent person away from the church. Maritain has included the B Minor Mass of Bach along with the *Divine Comedy* of Dante and the Chartres Cathedral as the greatest masterpieces of Western art, and I understand perfectly why. The music of Bach is still traditional music, and his sacred music is sacred not only because it was performed as part of church service but because of its innate nature, in total contrast to the church architecture of the day. The B Minor Mass can therefore justifiably be categorized with the greatest works of Western traditional poetry and architecture even though it was produced in the eighteenth century.

Because of this background, even when the traditional canons of music were changed from traditional norms in the West, something of the spiritual and cosmic qualities of music survived as we see in many of the compositions of a Mozart, Beethoven, or Brahms. Western classical music is not traditional music, but it still presents the possibilities of an opening to express the cosmic dimension of music or deep spiritual yearning as one sees in the later Beethoven quartets. We see this search also in the case of Mahler whom Deutsch mentions. Mahler even used a traditional Chinese text for one of his most famous works, *Das Lied von der Erde*, and we see similar attempts on behalf of certain other twentieth-century composers. The question, however, is not whether such composers were yearning to embody the spiritual in their art, but whether they succeeded in doing so. Since their search was highly personal and individualistic, while the spiritual belongs to the universal order, in most cases their struggle remained just a struggle with openings here and there which would permit the light of the spiritual world to shine through, at least in the case of some of the more outstanding composers, including Mahler himself. For most, however, another path was taken which has resulted in the creation of modern Western classical music that is more removed from the sacred and also from the general public than the classical music of any other period of Western history. Some say that older classical music was also not appreciated in its day. But can one compare the reception of as "revolutionary" a work as Beethoven's Ninth Symphony in its first performance with the reception of the works of Schönberg? For the most part modern Western classical music has become disconnected from the musical life and spiritual yearnings of both the spiritual "elite" and the general public, while what is called popular music is for the most part of a highly anti-spiritual nature, arising from the lower realms of the psyche and appealing to the lowest instincts of the audience. In music as in poetry, however, there is still the possibility of composing works based on traditional principles and possessing an authentic spiritual quality, as we see in the case of the British composer John Taverner.

Let us also not forget the revival in the West of its own traditional folk music and the spread of non-Western traditional music—whether it be Indian, Japanese, Persian, or Arabic—as well as the renewed interest in the highest genre of traditional music in the West in the form of the Gregorian Chant. These phenomena themselves point to the thirst of the Western public for music with a spiritual content and to the fact that this thirst is not fully quenched by modern and postmodern Western music, despite the struggle of a Mahler, Poulenc, or Messiaen to incorporate spiritual elements in their art.

However, when one speaks of art in the West, it is usually painting that one has in mind. That is because painting has played a central role in Western art going back to the iconic nature of Christian art. Such is not of course necessarily the case everywhere, as we see in Islamic art. In the Occident, because of the centrality of painting, this art form became the mirror which reflected before anything else the depth of the soul of Western man and also new tendencies as they began to appear in Western society. We see the coming of the Renaissance in later Giotto long before the phenomenon of the Renaissance appeared in full force upon the scene. Now modern Western art in the form of painting is no exception, going back to classicism, romanticism, and impressionism before we reached the twentieth century. The breakdown of form in cubism and surrealism took place from below rather than from above and corresponded to cracks in the confines of the solidified mindset created by centuries of humanism, rationalism, and empiricism. These cracks were, however, mostly conduits for the introduction of elements from below, including irrationalism and psychologism. Surrealism in art should in fact be called subrealism. This break from below opened for the most part the gate not for the shining of the Reality from above, the veritable "sur-real," but for the appearance of the lower psychic elements and finally that which is inhuman. Each artist sought to express "himself," but which "self" is it that he or she was trying to express? Not the self which the Hindus call *Ātman* but rather the ego. To be sure, there were artists who sought desperately for some spiritual significance in their work and life and reflected elements of quality in their paintings such as we find among a number of impressionists, but often they reached a nihilism which in a number of cases even resulted in suicide, such as we see in the tragic life of a painter as gifted as Van Gogh or in the equally tragic life of Rothko. This flight into the bosom of the void in its negative sense and the taking of one's life to find "release" itself is, however, nothing but the parody of the Hindu *mokśa*. Instead of surrendering the ego to the Self or realizing the reality of the Void in its metaphysical sense of *śūnyatā* and thereby reaching freedom and deliverance, such artists finally sought to annihilate themselves through external destruction of their earthly lives, as if one could destroy a sacred text by simply throwing it into the fire.

To be sure, there have been those among modern artists such as Kandinsky or Mondrian who have even sought to acquaint themselves with traditional doctrines of art, but they have not been able to produce anything but an individualistic art which remains subjective and does not embody the spiritual in the objective sense. In the nineteenth century in France there were even artists associated with esoteric circles who were seeking to discover the inner meaning and symbolism of art, and some of them became famous. Perhaps the best example is Gauguin who was, however, to seek his salvation outside of the modern world. There were also others such as Rouault who realized the significance of the loss of tradition and painted with full awareness of its absence. Others such as Eric Gill in Britain sought to bring about a revival of Christian art in the field of sculpture and lettering and who were fully aware of the spiritual emptiness of the modern art around them.

Certainly many modern artists have struggled to discover the spiritual and to express it in their art. In a society dominated by the machine, where art has become separated from life and the making of things, where art has become divorced from usefulness and reduced to luxury locked up in buildings called museums to be visited on Sunday afternoons when one takes a vacation from "the realities of life," the modern artist has naturally become an alienated being living in the margin of society. Having no center, in the traditional sense, from which to operate, he pushes himself to the periphery of the circle of his existence with the hope of being creative and original. Saddled with the false notion of originality which is identified with innovation and creativity shorn of all objective criteria for its evaluation, the artist struggles desperately to express himself. He feels that he must be timely, fashionable, and up to date while deep in his heart (at least in the case of the true artist) he realizes how transient are in fact the fashions of the day and how fickle is the art world which causes names to rise and fall, often with little relation to the innate worth of the works produced.

As Deutsch says, in a sense the artist is the friend of the traditionalist in that he refuses to surrender to the crass materialism, commercialization, and consumerism of the day and also in his quest for the spiritual, but this is where the similarity ends. Most artists become completely enmeshed in their own egos and often become submerged to an ever greater degree in the lower depths of the psyche, leading lives which are in many cases not morally disciplined, whereas the traditional perspective seeks to free us through spiritual discipline by ascent to the world of the Spirit and by destroying the stranglehold that the lower ego has upon our immortal soul. The traditionalist sympathizes with many an artist who seeks spiritual realization through art but points out the kind of art which alone makes the wedding between spiritual realization and artistic creation possible. In this context it is of great interest to study the remarkable contrasts in the lifestyles of most modern artists and traditional artists who still survive in non-Western societies.

Having made these comments, I also want to point out that something of traditional art *does* survive in the modern and even the postmodern Western world in the form of the icon of the Orthodox Church, of certain folk arts, traditional sculpture, and architecture associated with the still vibrant and living forms of traditional Christian art such as the Gothic. On the smaller scale of the art of painting there is still the possibility of the practice of an art of a traditional character as there is the possibility of wedding the arts to the crafts once again as was done in traditional societies. One can in fact see something of that in the form of revival of traditional crafts at the margin of the technological behemoth which dominates modern life.

Deutsch turns to architecture as an example to answer the question, "What are the possibilities today for a 'post-postmodern' spiritual art?" Before answering this question I wish to mention a few points concerning architecture without dealing with all the issues which he mentions not as questions but as part of his exposition of the meaning and significance of architecture. The case of architecture is a particularly difficult one because of all of the arts, it is the one most affected by all kinds of external constraints. An Eric Gill could sit in his atelier in London and produce beautiful traditional Latin lettering, but if he wanted to build a major edifice he would need a patron with understanding, approval of the municipality, availability of all kinds of materials, sufficient economic means, and so on, all of which would have made the task of building a traditional building much more difficult than creating stone sculpture or lettering. Of course, it is possible for all these conditions to be met even in the modern West as we see in the beautiful Gothic cathedrals of nineteenth- and twentieth-century America, such as St. Patrick's Cathedral in New York, the Rockefeller Chapels at Princeton University and the University of Chicago, and the Washington National Cathedral. This last edifice is a traditional church, and looks like one, as opposed to looking like a gas station.

The famous architects of the past century, as modern men, have, however, usually rejected the traditional worldview, including its cosmology, and have sought to be attuned to that mysterious "spirit of the times" or *Zeitgeist* inherited from nineteenth-century European philosophy, in contrast to their medieval predecessors who sought to be attuned to the *heilige Geist*. Pushed by their own convictions and also external factors, they have gone from one idea and style to another always speaking of "purity of function," "simplicity of forms," and the like, as spiritual elements while creating glass-like boxes and inhuman ambiences which are environmentally catastrophic and humanly stifling. There are, of course, exceptions to the rule, but they remain exceptions. In numerous Western cities the old quarters are kept as "museums" in whose confines one still has a human feeling, while the newly built parts of the urban environment manifest such brazen inhumanity that even champions of the modern world wish to take refuge from them in the more human spaces defined by earlier styles of architecture. In many places architecture has become the machine in which one lives, as defined by Le Corbusier. To be sure, such architects as Frank Lloyd Wright sought to preserve something of the spiritual dimension of existence in their works, and there are also other notable cases, but the net result in the contemporary period has been an architecture which is impersonal—not in the sense of transcending the personal and the individual from above but of falling below the personal and the human.

In the 1950s when I was at Harvard, one day Walter Gropius of Bauhaus fame, who lived in Cambridge at that time, asked to see me because he wanted to discuss the functions of a mosque which he was designing as part of the University of Baghdad. Soon we became friends and would discuss the philosophy of art together. He once asked why it was that modern architecture was focused upon pure geometry as was Islamic art but the two types of architecture differed so deeply in their results. I told him that one was based in geometry as the science of a purely quantitative space *à la* Descartes and the other on sacred geometry based upon qualitative space. He was deeply moved by this answer and took me to a room in his office where there was hanging on the wall a large picture of a medieval cathedral. He said to me, "Look at this cathedral. It was built over the period of several generations, yet preserves a perfect organic unity, whereas here in my office, if I die tomorrow someone else will come with a wholly different idea and a work possessing unity cannot be created if it stretches over the period of our two careers." He added that what those medieval architects had was an artistic tradition that transcended the individual in contrast to what we have today. Gropius also expressed great sadness that such an art was no longer available in the West to the mainstream of practicing architects.

Now, this story reveals that certainly many of the great Western architects of this century were aware of the significance of the spiritual dimension of architecture and the meaning of its loss. But how many sought to return to principles and to apply them again in the contemporary context? As I said, this is particularly difficult for architecture tied as it is to ever changing technologies, economic demands, social forces, and a scientific worldview, all of which deny the traditionalist vision. But it is not impossible to create traditional architecture, as we see in certain forms of vernacular architecture on a smaller scale and even in some religious architecture. In any case, there is no way to create on a large-scale in an anti-traditional world traditional architecture and urban design with their spiritual accent. But one can at least seek to create a more humane architecture and to apply spiritual principles when possible.

All that I have said here applies to the West. In the non-Western world where tradition still survives to a much greater degree than in the West, the situation is very different. In countries outside the West, traditional architecture is also being destroyed in many places. Architectural monstrosities are being created everywhere which have nothing to do with traditional architecture but are usually poor copies of some Western models. But the reasons for such a phenomenon are very different from what one finds in the West. All of my responses to Professor Deutsch, therefore, are concerned with the West rather than with the problem of the confrontation of traditional and modern art on a global scale, which would require a separate treatment.

To come back to the question of having a post-postmodern spiritual art, the response depends upon what the nature of the post-postmodern world will be. Postmodernism has sought to destroy the idols of modernism as well as tradition and has denied all absolutes in the name of the relative and the transient. If post-postmodern means a negation of the modernist worldview and a return to First Principles, then under those conditions it would certainly be possible to have a spiritual art, as one finds in all traditional civilizations of East and West. If, however, post-postmodernism means taking present trends to their ultimate conclusions and reaching a nihilism which ultimately denies any reality beyond the individual ego on the one hand and the external world conceived in purely quantitative terms on the other, then there will not be the possibility of a spiritual art—unless we abandon the time honored meaning of spiritual and reduce it to the merely psychological as many have already done. This is, however, a position with which I cannot agree in any way whatsoever. One cannot liberate meaning "from any 'objective correlation'," to quote Deutsch and have a spiritual art as conceived traditionally, for all traditional art and aesthetics are based on the intellection of forms which have an objective nature and which can be known through the science of forms. Traditional art is based completely on this correlation.

Deutsch asks, "What aesthetic motivation would drive a postmodernist to uncover the sacred both in life and art?" and answers that it can only be despair. He therefore suggests that postmodernism should itself be liberated from its denial of meaning through a new definition of what is sacred. He does not consider the possibility of liberation from all the errors which constitute modern and postmodern aesthetics and worldviews in general, but proposes rather to change the meaning of the sacred itself as if the sacred were simply a concept and not an objective reality. The sacred is in fact the manifestation of the Center in the periphery of the circle of existence in which we live, the theophany of the Eternal in the realm of the temporal and the transient. No amount of redefinition will change that reality, and something does not become sacred just by our calling it so, even though this term is used loosely by some in daily discourse.

What Deutsch proposes is like changing the definition of clean air since we are polluting the air and cannot keep it clean. The solution is not to change the definition of what is "clean air" but to live our lives in such a way that we will not be actually polluting the air that we breathe. Otherwise, simply changing the definition of "clean air" will not affect in the least the respiratory ailments from which we are apt to suffer while the air surrounding us is polluted. One of the characteristics of modern man is that he wants to change everything but himself. Rather than seeking the good and the beautiful, he changes the very criteria of good and evil, of beauty and ugliness, to deceive himself and to convince himself that he is not committing evil deeds and is not living in an ambience dominated by an ugliness that is unprecedented in human history.

In conclusion, Deutsch invites me to accept the task of working out a formulation which would solve the crisis of the spiritual in art today. I am honored that he invites me to carry out such a colossal task, and I hope to have the occasion to respond to that challenge in the future, although it cannot of course be carried out in the present context. But a few basic points can be mentioned here. The crisis of the spiritual in art is itself the result of the crisis of modern Western civilization and the view of man as a purely secular and earthly being, a view which lies at its heart, a view which when implemented in human life will end in the destruction of man himself. In the words of the famous German art historian Hans Sedlmayr, "Logical and honest materialists are quite ready to admit that the abolition of God brings with it the abolition of art as such. What they will not admit is that such a development must inevitably lead to the abolition of man, to the transformation of man into something subhuman, into a machine, a robot."

Although many contemporary artists seek to fight against this domination by the machine, few are able or willing to challenge and criticize that worldview which has reduced art to an unnecessary luxury and the artist to a stranger in the margin of society. The modern worldview has removed beauty as a central concern of human life and to an ever greater degree has turned art into a product for crass commercialism. The contemporary artist interested in the spiritual dimension of reality must first of all seek that dimension, which also resides in his own center, and make himself and his art subservient to it. He must reexamine the validity of all the idols of the modern art scene such as innovation, originality, and creativity which are "worshipped" and emphasized at the expense of truth and beauty. He must remember that real originality means return to the Origin, to the alpha of existence, whose message the "original" artist must then convey to those around him through his art and above all through his own being. He must eschew the individualism and egotism often combined with that singularly modern category of genius—so much sought and yet so ill-defined—and try to be humble before the light of the truth and the millennial heritage of traditional art, most of which was not produced by individuals bloated by their sense of grandeur and so-called genius, but by anonymous artists who humbled themselves before the reality of the Spirit and through their transparency were able to reflect the light of the spiritual world in their works. Such an artist must also seek those domains of art where more traditional modes of expression are still possible and not seek the so-called cutting edge, which in the present-day context usually means cutting into a lower level of reality at the expense of sacrificing a higher one.

Ultimately, of course, spiritual and traditional art cannot be created on a large scale unless society itself is transformed and regains its spiritual mooring. Meanwhile, there is always the possibility of access to the world of the Spirit and for the contemporary artist who has sought this world and discovered it, by virtue of what he or she has experienced and discovered, a light is created which itself dispenses with the darkness within and without. This light is able to manifest itself in the artistic activity of the person in question and determine the way that an artist will be able to introduce a spiritual elemen into his or her art even in the chaotic conditions of the postmodern world in which the West and its extension on other continents find themselves.

S. H. N.

11

Luce López-Baralt

KNOWLEDGE *OF* THE SACRED: THE MYSTICAL POETRY OF SEYYED HOSSEIN NASR

Let my soul be crystalized as a star
To reside at the proximity of that luminous Sun
Seyyed Hossein Nasr

Seyyed Hossein Nasr has disclosed recently that his foremost book, *Knowledge and the Sacred*, "came as a gift from heaven. He was able to write the texts of the [Gifford] lectures with great facility and speed and within a period of less than three months they were completed . . . it was as though he was writing from a text he had previously memorized."[1] The author's reverent admission may come as a surprise in the West, because his philosophical text, based on the prestigious Gifford Lectures he gave at the University of Edinburgh in 1981, is one of the major intellectual feats in the history of religious ideas of the twentieth century.[2] Nasr reflects upon both Eastern and Western spirituality, and he is equally at ease with Islamic, Christian, Jewish, Buddhist, and Hindu thought, as well as with the philosophy and science of both hemispheres. His display of erudition is indeed stunning, even more so because of the fact that when he wrote his lectures he had recently lost his family library and his scholarly notes from the two decades of research he had done in his mother country, Iran. It comes indeed as a surprise—especially in the West—for such a renowned philosopher to claim spiritual inspiration for a veritable masterpiece of intellectual scholarship.

But, on second thought, Nasr's confession as to the mysterious, other-worldly quality of the intuitive feeling he experienced while writing

Knowledge and the Sacred is ultimately not that surprising after all. His essays constitute an erudite book, yes, but even more so a *sapiental* book. In his Gifford lectures he argues for a special kind of knowledge, a *sacramental* knowledge which the Western world had long disregarded and forgotten due to the long process of postmedieval secularization which divorced intelligence from the sacred.

The Iranian scholar, much in the tradition of sages like René Guénon, Ananda K. Coomaraswamy, and Frithjof Schuon, makes the case for perennial wisdom or *sophia perennis*. This otherworldly, suprarational *sapientia*, like the sacred olive tree of the Quranic Surah XXIV:35, belongs neither to the East nor to the West because it transcends both time and space; it resides in the One as well as in the inner recesses of the gnostic's soul, where the union of the *Unus/Ambo* takes place. This particular wisdom implies the direct knowledge of the Absolute, and the illuminated mystic who attains it is endowed with a unified view of reality. By privileging this sacred experiential knowledge, the philosopher is subjecting Western culture and epistemology to a profound philosophical criticism. He is forcing his readers to an abrupt revision of the ideas they have taken for granted for many centuries now regarding the limits of the cognoscitive capacities of the human mind. *Knowledge and the Sacred* is an invitation—undoubtedly disturbing for many—to revise such a narrow and disheartening epistemological point of view.

But perhaps the times are ripe for Seyyed Hossein Nasr's philosophical challenge. Western philosophy has undergone numerous crises and revisions in the twentieth century, the epistemological pessimism of Fritz Mauthner,[3] Ludwig Wittgenstein,[4] and the Vienna Circle concerning the limits of language being just one case at hand. Contemporary physics is another example. Anyone even remotely familiar with quantum physics is overwhelmed by a new conception of reality which "normal" language and classical logic simply cannot grasp, much less explain in a satisfactory way. The words which must be used to explain quantum theory are not adequate to explain quantum phenomena. Ordinary conceptions and thought processes need to be modified so that we can "understand" certain new scientific propositions. John von Neumann's theories come to mind: the wave function is not quite a thing, but yet it is more than an idea; it occupies a strange ground between idea and reality.[5] Richard Feynman's diagram of the "dance" which continuously changes a neutron into a proton and back into a neutron again is equally disturbing.[6] Bell's theorem, on the other hand, formulates another disquieting notion: separate parts of reality in the universe are connected in an intimate, inexorable way which our common experience and the "laws of physics" belie. The new physics truly defies "Aristotelian logic" in affirming that contraries can coexist. Niels Bohr summarizes the dilemma we face as students of modern physics: "Those who are not shocked when they first come across quantum theory cannot possibly have understood it."[7] I admit to having been profoundly shocked by the most elemental propositions of quantum physics. Much more so because, having dedicated my life to the study of the mystical experience, I am quite aware that for the first time physicists and mystics seem to speak the same "language." Or perhaps I should say that neither can truly "speak," for normal language seems painfully inadequate for both disciplines. Both science and mysticism push our verbal capacities to their uttermost limits to no avail: plain reality, just like Ultimate Reality, transcends our efforts at restraining it with our limited linguistic tools, or even with our sophisticated mathematical symbols. A universe whose subatomic particles dance in perpetual change and yet are connected in an inexorable way, and where time and space are relative is consistent with the mystic's perception: he acknowledges to having attained unified knowledge beyond the limits of space, time, and change. In other words, Nicholas of Cusa's *coincidentia oppositorum* does not seem so incongruous to today's quantum physics student.

Seyyed Hossein Nasr is well aware of this modern tendency on the part of the West of trying to relate modern physics to mysticism and to Oriental esoteric doctrines.[8] He feels it is akin to the concern for the sacred which characterizes contemporary ecology, so adamant in the conservation of nature.

I feel that the Iranian philosopher has grasped a tendency quite true to our times. Indeed it seems that a sacralized mode of knowing is slowly emerging in different scientific and philosophical disciplines in the West. The study of mysticism itself is undergoing a definite process of validation in recent decades. Evelyn Underhill's and William James's theories on the subject are being updated by neo-Freudian psychiatrists such as W. W. Meissner, author of the revolutionary—as well as reverent—*Ignatius of Loyola: The Psychology of a Saint*.[9] Even more relevant to our contemporary revalorization of the mystical experience are Ana María Rizzuto's explorations of spirituality in the light of post-Freudian psychoanalysis and her revision of Freud's theories concerning the Divine.[10]

I think that these epistemological revisions going on simultaneously in different disciplines (science, philosophy, mysticism, psychiatry) must be kept in mind in order to understand the relevance and the opportune timing of Nasr's epistemological theories in the context of contemporary Western religious thought. Nasr's dramatic defense of mystical *sapientia* is very much part of our times and of our hemisphere. Let us now take a closer look at his principal epistemological propositions.

The Iranian scholar makes abundantly clear that in *Knowledge and the*

Sacred he is not dealing with an empirical or rational mode of knowledge but with the highest form of knowledge, "which is the unitive knowledge of God not by man as an individual but by the divine center of human intelligence which, at the level of gnosis, becomes the subject as well as the object of knowledge."[11] For man to attain knowledge of Ultimate Reality is to be delivered from duality and to discover his own essence. Thus, Nasr argues, theology is in the end nothing but "autology." This is an elemental mystical truth which gnostics from all ages and cultures articulate in different ways. Contemporary gnostics like Meher Baba in India claim that "to know Reality is to be transformed in It,"[12] while María Zambrano in Spain affirms in turn that *el conocer es ser* ("knowing is being").[13] Nasr in turn feels at home with Ibn ʻArabī and Meister Ekhart, who propose that the eye with which man sees God is the eye with which God sees man.

The gnostic—called in Arabic *al-ʻārif bi'Llāh* because he knows through or by God—sees things *in divinis*, as Adam did in Paradise. His knowledge must be attained through experience and taste. This is a cognoscitive experience of a radically different order from empiricism and rationalism, and to illustrate his point Nasr rightly reminds the reader of the etymology of the word *sapientia*, from the Latin root meaning "to taste." This concept is equivalent to the *ḥikmah dhawqiyyah* or "tasted knowledge" of Sufis such as Suhrawardī. The Andalusian mystic Ibn ʻArabī, for his part, assigns to "taste" (*dhawq* or ذوق) the first of the symbolic four degrees that mark the manifestation of the Truth.[14] In the West both Nicholas of Cusa and St. John of the Cross became experts in this "tasted knowledge" or *ciencia sabrosa* which led to the blessed state of *coincidentia oppositorum* or unitive knowledge, something the rationalist mind alone can never apprehend. With a certain vulnerability and perhaps even spiritual nostalgia, Albert Einstein reflected that "Die Sehnsucht des Menschen verlangt nach gesicherter Erkenntnis" [Man has an intense desire for assured knowledge].[15] And Nasr is arguing the cause of precisely this kind of knowledge.

Man has what we can call different "organs of knowledge" and is capable of operating at different levels of cognoscitive experience. Sacred knowledge or knowledge of the sacred is not limited to reason but involves the whole of man's being. It is, again, direct and "tasted knowledge," which "imposes itself with blinding clarity upon the mind of the person who has been given the possibility of such a vision through intellectual intuition."[16] This is why this sacred knowledge is never hypothetical or approximative, but absolutely *certain*. The philosopher is speaking here about a direct, infused experience. No wonder knowledgeable Sufis who are part of Nasr's spiritual tradition called their cognoscitive experience the "science of certainty" or *'ilm al-yaqīn*. St. John of the Cross boasted once and again of his absolute certainty of his knowledge of the One, which he had "tasted"[17]:

"*Qué bien sé yo la fonte que mana y corre / aunque es de noche*" [Indeed I know well the spring that flows and bursts forth / in spite of being immersed in night].[18]

Modern Western thought does not grant such infallibility and absolute certainty to any form of knowledge. Seyyed Hossein Nasr is indeed bestowing upon the cognoscitive dimension of the mystical experience an ontological dignity it has not had in the West since the dawn of the so-called "Modern Age." It must be remembered that the author takes into account in his philosophical explorations both the direct revelation of God treasured by traditional religions as well as the personal epiphany of the individual gnostic. And he considers this intuitive, direct knowledge *the* most legitimate form of knowledge. But it is of a different order than rational knowledge.

The source of this inner revelation which Nasr expounds is the center of man, known symbolically as the "heart." He distinguishes this cognoscitive mystical "organ" from the limited rational mind: "The seat of intelligence is the heart not the head, as affirmed by all traditional teachings."[19] This is what Plato, Origen, and St. Augustine called "the eye of the soul," the Sufis the "eye of the heart" or *'ayn al-qalb* and the Hindu tradition "the third eye." This *qalb* or heart as an organ of divine perception constitutes a very complex symbol in Islam, for which there is no exact equivalent in Christian spirituality. We will have the opportunity of examining it further on. Suffice here to say that Nasr claims that "it is not possible to attain this knowledge in any way except by being consumed by it."[20] And the philosopher's prose dissolves into poetry because what he is speaking about, like contemporary quantum physics, cannot easily be reduced to analytical thought:

> The truth descends upon the mind like an eagle landing upon a mountain top or it gushes forth and inundates the mind like a deep well which has burst forth into a spring. In either case, the sapiental nature of what the human being receives through spiritual experience is not the result of man's mental faculty but issues from the nature of that experience itself. Man can know through intuition and revelation not because he is a thinking being who imposes the categories of his thought upon what he perceives but because knowledge is being.[21]

While extolling direct perception of the Truth as a truly legitimate form of knowledge, Nasr submits René Descartes's *cogito ergo sum* to a rigorous critique. With his famous *cogito*, Nasr argues, the French philosopher

> made the thinking of the individual ego the center of reality and the criterion of all knowledge, turning philosophy into pure rationalism and shifting the main concern of European philosophy from ontology to epistemology. Henceforth, knowledge . . . was rooted in the *cogito*. The knowing subject was bound to the realm of reason and separated both from the Intellect and

> revelation, neither of which were henceforth considered as possible sources of knowledge of an objective order . . . [T]o the mentality of those who were caught in the web of the newly established rationalism . . . knowledge and science were henceforth totally separated from the sacred even if the sacred were to be accepted as possessing a reality.[22]

Nasr's critique of the Renaissance is well known, in spite of the fact that, as Gisela Webb so eloquently states, precisely because of our scholar's expertise in science, religion, philosophy, and comparative literatures he could well be considered a "Renaissance man."[23] But Nasr objects to certain crucial philosophical aspects of "modernity" and considers Descartes's rationalism, which was to decide the general approach to knowledge in the West for many centuries to come, as "this most intelligent way of being unintelligent."[24] But the learned philosopher, in spite of his witty remark, is not against speculative reason. His traditional approach and his defense of the *scientia sacra* does not oppose the activity of the mind, but rather opposes its divorce from the heart or *qalb* as an organ of gnosis superior in nature to the rational mind.

Western readers are ill-prepared to embrace this truth, *tam antica et tam nova*, as St. Augustine exclaimed in awe, because our culture, in its radical secularization, has trivialized and ignored sapiental knowledge. We lack—and I am saying this as a Christian by birth and tradition and as a scholar in comparative mysticism—an esoteric dimension for Christian spirituality, a dignified, respectful niche for dimensions of knowledge which transcends (without ever denying) pure reason and speculative logic. Nasr contrasts the case of Christianity with that of Judaism and Islam: both religions have the esoteric branches of Kabbala and Sufism, for which we lack a true equivalent. The efforts on the part of many prominent Renaissance figures of rendering prestige to intuitive or direct knowledge of the Truth went unheeded by the modern Christian tradition. To the well-known cases of Hermetists like Marsilio Ficino, Pico della Mirandola, Nicholas of Cusa, and Francesco Patrizzi Professor Nasr argued, we must add that of St. John of the Cross, who besides being a mystic himself, explored in depth and with an esoteric approach more akin to the Orient than to the West the different dimensions of the faculty of knowledge.[25]

The inspired perception of the Truth these sages expounded has been all but discredited in modern Western thought. The very association with any form of spiritualized knowledge has been sufficient to erase any trace of dignity accorded to certain approaches to knowledge, as Nasr rightly states:

> The most sublime form of wisdom has been transformed into simple historical borrowing, Neoplatonism . . . playing the role of the ideal historical tag with which one could destroy the significance of the most profound sapiental

doctrines. It has been and still is simply sufficient to call something Neoplatonic influence to reduce it, spiritually speaking, to insignificance. And if that has not been possible, then terms such as pantheistic, animistic, naturalistic, monistic, and even mystical in the sense of ambiguous have been and still are employed to characterize doctrines whose significance one wishes to destroy or ignore.[26]

Nasr, an heir of the gnostic approach to knowledge of revealed, traditional religion (in his own case, Islam) updates in a very innovative way the Neoplatonic perfume that pervades both Oriental and early Christian thought. His ardent defense of the unitive, all-consuming knowledge that is perceived by man's whole being, not by his limited rational mind, is, as I stated before, difficult to assume—to "naturalize," as Jonathan Culler would have it[27]—by a reading public long devoid of gnosis. The Iranian philosopher's *inspired* and profoundly Oriental[28] book, written, ironically enough, in the West and in a Western language, is indeed one of the most courageous enterprises in the field of spirituality in recent times. Nasr has dealt a severe blow to the cherished rationalism and empiricism the West has taken for granted since the Renaissance. Personally, I could not agree more with his momentuous contribution to the history of ideas concerning epistemology.

The philosophical and spiritual consequences of this *sophia perennis* that we are exploring again thanks to Nasr's pioneering book are truly significant. The scholar reminds the reader that the world and its changing forms are born from the reflections and reverberations of Being—the author is alluding here to the traditional Islamic concept of *nafas al-raḥmān* or creative "Breath of the Compassionate." This Divine Relativity or *māyā* simultaneously veils and reveals the sacred, but the true sage beholds the cosmos and the myriad of forms it displays as theophany; as reflections of the Divine Qualities rather than as a veil which would hide the "splendor of the face of the Beloved."[29] The gnostic is endowed with a "rhapsodic intellect"[30] which gives him a unified view of creation, with which he "sees God everywhere" and observes harmony where others see discord and light, where others are blinded by darkness. The man of knowledge goes beyond him to reach heaven and in so doing, he reaches the sacred ground of his own being.[31] He is redeemed from his symbolic "Occidental exile" and is finally back home, illuminated by the light of the Eastern dawn.[32] His center is pure consciousness, wherein lies the eternal essence "which survives all change and becoming."[33] Nasr echoes Chuang-Tzu's words to further explain this overwhelming state of knowledge: "[The divine man] fulfills his destiny. He acts in accordance with his nature. He is at one with God and man. For him all affairs cease to exist, and all things revert to their original state."[34] The cosmos, as viewed through eyes "which are not cut off from the sanctifying rays of the *eye of the heart*, indeed reveal the cosmos as theophany."[35] The world functions not as a "pattern of externalized brute facts," but as an icon which reflects diverse aspects of the Divine Qualities, as "a myriad of mirrors reflecting the face of the Beloved."[36] The enlightened mind which is capable of grasping such a form of sacred knowledge asserts that the changing forms or *samsāra* are ultimately *nirvāna*, that all separation is union, that all otherness is sameness, that all manifestation of the One is a return to the One. Nature thus constitutes for him a grand theophany that externalizes all that man is inwardly: "the Ultimate Reality can be seen as both the Supreme Object and the Innermost Subject, for God is both transcendent and immanent, but He can be experienced as immanent only after He has been experienced as transcendent."[37] Thus for the spiritual "hero"[38] the dichotomy of creation is only apparent.

Equally apparent for him is the temporal order and process of change of the cosmos. "Pontifical man"[39] renders ravaging time inoffensive and is able to gain access to the eternal while living outwardly in the domain of becoming, for Eternity is reflected in the present now. The gnostic can experience time not only as "change and transience but also as the *moving image of eternity*."[40] Time mercifully dissolves in "*the* supreme moment in which the spiritual man lives constantly."[41] He knows he is ultimately safe from the cycles of the "days and nights of the life of Brahma" in the immutability of that "eternal instant from which all things are born,"[42] and which he discovers in his own being. The sage always lives in the sacred instant of pre-eternity (*al-āzal* for Sufis such as Ḥāfiẓ); in the "early dawn" in which man made his eternal convenant with God.[43]

The mystic who has attained *sophia perennis* understands that "Heaven and earth are united in marriage, and thus the Unity, which is the source of the cosmos and the harmony that pervades it,"[44] is reestablished for him. Nasr goes as far as to propose a new definition of mankind in the light of his epistemological propositions: "to be fully man is to rediscover that primordial Unity from which all the heavens and earths originate and yet from which nothing ever really departs."[45] No wonder the author reserves such adjectives for the privileged human being of "ecstatic" or "rhapsodic intellect" who has experienced fully his ultimate essence, which is shared by the Eternal One: he considers him a "hero," a "Pontifical man," a "gnostic," even a "divine man."

I propose that the "hero," the "Pontifical man," the "gnostic," and the "divine man" who has realized his full potential as a human being and who is endowed with a veritable "rhapsodic intellect" and a sacred, unified view of creation is none other than Seyyed Hossein Nasr himself. The learned philosopher, historian, and scientist who has authored fifty books and over five hundred articles translated into over twenty languages[46] disclosed for the first time his own soul *in the inner courtyard of intimacy*[47] in his recently published *Poems of the Way*. As a reader of his philosophic texts for so many years, I must confess that this short volume is, surprisingly enough, the veritable crowning of Nasr's sapiental philosophy. His forty poems, anthologized in a volume whose title is an hommage to Ibn al-Fāriḍ's *Poems of the Way*, is an updating of Sufism written in the venerable tradition of Islamic gnostics like Ibn al-'Arabī and Rūmī. But in the context of Nasr's philosophical *opera magna* this collection of mystical odes has an additional meaning: the Persian gnostic has rendered his learned *Knowledge and the Sacred* in ecstatic verse. Philosophy is put into practice, *logos* dissolves into experience, theoretical knowledge (*'aql*) becomes realized knowledge (*'ishq*)[48] before our startled eyes. Nasr has chosen to share his divine gift and to sing in "the language of the birds"[49] for the first time in his life. His book of poetry could only have been authored by a mystic attuned to otherworldly sapiental experience. *Poems of the Way* culminates the scholar's philosophical arguments in a moving admission of direct experience: Nasr has evolved from lecturing about *Knowledge and the Sacred* to celebrating his having attained knowledge *of* the sacred. Truly his sapiental and mystical *knowledge is light*.[50] The sage's poetry is the living proof of his philosophical theories, which the reader suddenly discovers sprang from the fountainhead of unmediated, "tasted" experience. *Poems of the Way* constitutes a veritable *medinah of victory*[51] for *sophia perennis*, and I cannot resist remembering at this point that the name "Naṣr" means precisely "victory."[52]

No wonder our scholar confessed that the ideas for his book *Knowledge and the Sacred* "came as a gift from heaven," and that he felt "as though he was writing from a text he had previously memorized."[53] No wonder he spoke of Grace "as one in which it is operative"; no wonder he exhibited an interior dimension of the Truth which "no mere scholarship could produce."[54] The moving words Nasr applies to his admired sage Frithjof Schuon fit perfectly his own scholarship: it is not difficult to suspect that the Iranian scholar always spoke "from the point of view of realized knowledge not theory," and that is precisely why his writings "bear an *existential* impact that can only come from realization."[55] His praise for René Guénon could also be applied to his own philosophical, mystical, and literary achievement: "His lucid mind and style and great metaphysical acumen seemed to have been chosen by traditional *sophia* itself to formulate and express once again that truth from whose loss the modern world was suffering so grieviously."[56] It is not difficult to conclude that both *Knowledge and the Sacred* and *Poems of the Way* are inspired books.

I have been quoting the epistemological theories advanced by Nasr in *Knowledge and the Sacred* so extensively in this essay because I propose now to demostrate that the scholar's conception of the sacred indeed comes to life in his *Poems of the Way*, a veritable example of "sacred art."[57] Thanks to Nasr's intoxicating poetry, we will be able to attest that for the mystical author the cosmos is a "cathedral of celestial beauty" where he contemplates the "Divine Presence in its metacosmic splendor."[58] The poet-mystic, who as a "Pontifical man lives in time but as a witness to eternity,"[59] finally becomes here "what he always *is*, a star immortalized in the empyrean of eternity."[60] Nasr challenges the impoverished view of nature that has been our sad Western legacy for so long and sees the sacred as ubiquitous, for it is the substance of his own being in the mystical station of union.

As so many Sufis with which he forms tradition, Nasr has probably realized that revealed Truth is better expressed in poetry than in prose. Poetry is mysterious, is inspired, is rhythm—"days and nights of the life of Brahma"—and is, above all, polivalent.[61] Thanks to its very prodigious ambiguity poetry is perhaps the only human endeavor that mimics and even renders true the sacred *coincidentia oppositorum* (to use again Nicholas of Cusa's revealing phrase) of the mystical experience. And Nasr's poetry flows, convinces, caresses, dances with the mystified reader the eternal dance of Shiva. And yet the flowing oceans of light of his inspired poetical images are congealed *like a diamond firm*[62] forever, ready to actualize the poet's spiritual ecstasy every time the reader convokes them and gives them new life.

Seyyed Hossein Nasr the poet is indeed the symbolic *Adam who saw the Face of the beautiful / reflected upon the mirrors of Paradise.*[63] Let us share with him the myriad of paradisiacal reflections in the quicksilver of his scintillating verses, in whose delicate verbal geometry of light and shadow the exquisite opalescence of Persian poetry shows through so clearly.

I allude to the verbal opalescence of Nasr's poetry on purpose. The Persian poet is part of a venerable literary tradition endowed with a rich symbolism of its own. Sufi poets have celebrated once and again their cherished *troubar clus*. Lāhījī, who commented upon Shabistarī's *Gulshan-i Rāz*, acknowledges that only the true initiates are able to comprehend their hermetic *langage à clef*:

> Certains initiés ont exprimé différents degrés de la contemplation mystique par des symboles de vêtements, boucles de cheveux, joues, grains de beauté, vin, flambeaux, etc. . . . que aux yeux du vulgaire ne forment qu'une brillante apparence. . . . Ils ont signifié par la boucle la multiplicité des choses qui cachent le visage de l'Aimé . . . ; le vin représente l'amour, le désir ardente et l'ivresse spirituelle; le flambeau l'irradiation de lumière divine dans le coeur de celui qui suit la voie. . . . [64]

Nasr is perfectly conscious that as a literary *homo faber* he is giving new life to this centuries-old Islamic literary discourse so rich in symbolic meaning.[65] In doing so, his language gains an immediate inner sense and a polivalency that belies the unidimensional character typical of literary works devoid of a complex literary tradition.[66] The author has explored in depth the sacred nature of the symbol not only in *Knowledge and the Sacred*[67] but in his *Introduction to Islamic Cosmological Doctrines*:

> The nature of the symbol differs profoundly from that of an allegory. A symbol is the "reflection" in a lower order of existence of a reality belonging to a higher ontological status, a "reflection" which in essence is unified to that which is symbolized; while allegory is a more or less "artificial figuration" having no universal existence of its own.[68]

Anyone familiar with Sufi poetry will be able to decode Nasr's "secret" mystical symbolism: the wine which the Saki pours is the nectar of divine ecstasy; the Prophet's *mi'rāj* or nocturnal ascent into heaven is now the mystic's own ascent into the Real; the personal "Occidental exile" of Nasr, living in the West far away from the exalted peaks and vast deserts of his Persian homeland turns into the symbolic "Occidental exile" of the Sufi living *in nostalgia for the Paradise within*[69] in this transient realm of becoming; the crescent moon of Ramaḍān is the dagger of the mystic who carries out the inner war against the ego; the "luminous night" is the state of spiritual darkness due to an excess of light (the gnostic attains illumination when he "darkens" discursive reason); the mystic truly enters the Ka'bah in Mecca only when he enters the spiritual *Ka'bah of the heart*.[70]

The symbol of the heart or *qalb* has a particular relevance in Sufism, and in Nasr's poetry as well. It could be said that *Poems of the Way* as a whole constitutes a sacred pilgrimage to the Ka'bah of the heart. The exquisite edition of the book itself points to the different stages of this spiritual path by reproducing a symbolic door (or *miḥrāb*) for each and every poetic unity or *maqām* ("spiritual station") of the mystic's itinerary. The inner heart is the ultimate goal of the Way the poet painstakingly travels. It is the true *locus* of Divine life, and Nasr employs a *ḥadīth* of the Prophet of Islam to repeat the traditional Sufi instruction: "The heart of the Believer is the Throne of the Compassionate."[71] Nasr, ever the Persian poet, celebrates his *locus* of Divine manifestation with luminous metaphors which evoke the incandescent hearts or *qulūb* of such masters as 'Aṭṭār, Kubrā, Suhrawardī, Hujwīrī, Ibn 'Arabī, al-Nūrī. But many other symbols serve him as well for the inner sanctuary of his heart: it is by turn a *crescent moon, a chalice made to receive*[72]; the *castle of the inner man*[73]; the *holy courtyard of inwardness*.[74] Our contemplative, as many Islamic gnostics before him, circles feverishly around his heart like a moth *around the candle of the night / Around this pole supreme of Truth and Presence*.[75] Unlike the passing forms of earthly life, unstable *abode of becoming and change*,[76] this sacred interior temple which holds the Throne of the Compassionate is invulnerable: *immutable like a diamond firm.*[77] The pristine purity and hardness of the diamond is a leitmotif with which the *Poems of the Way* try to evoke the perfect safety of the interior heart as the sublime abode of God. The verses themselves turn majestic, diamantine, fulgorous, when they depict *the crystalline perfection, coldness of life eternal*[78] of our inexpugnable innermost soul.

But the diamond is also multifaceted. It refracts light in a myriad of different hues. And as such it is, again, a perfect symbol for the resplendent, ever-changing organ of gnosis which is the interior *qalb*. Sufis such as Al-Ḥakīm al-Tirmidī and especially the Christian mystic St. Teresa of Avila, so indebted to Islamic mystical symbolism, knew well this heart of *fino diamante* ("fine diamond").[79] Contrary to its European counterparts,[80] the Islamic symbol of the interior heart is immensely rich.[81] The Arabic term for "heart" (*qalb*) comes from the triliteral root *q-l-b*, which includes the meanings of "heart," "perpetual change," and "inversion." Michael Sells explores the meaning of this symbolic heart which is receptive of every form in the mystical poetry of Ibn 'Arabī, especially in the famous verses from his *Tarjumān al-Ashwāq* (*Interpreter of Desires*): "My heart has been receptive of every form. . . . "[82] For the Andalusian mystic, the Truth "manifests itself through every form or image, and is confined to none. The forms of its manifestations are constantly changing."[83] Needless to say, Sells's description of Ibn 'Arabī's symbol could also be applied to knowledgeable Sufis such as al-Kubrā, al-Nūrī, Kāshānī, Baqlī, among many others,[84] who took at heart the *ḥadīth* where Muḥammad prays to God with the words "*yā muqallib al-qulūb*" [O you who make the hearts fluctuate!]:

> the heart's function is . . . dynamically integrative. The heart that is receptive of every form is in a state of perpetual transformation (*taqallub*, a play on the two meanings of the root *q-l-b*, heart and change). The heart molds itself to, receives, and becomes each form of the perpetually changing forms in which the Truth reveals itself to itself.[85]

To achieve a heart that is receptive of every form requires a continual process of effacement of the ego or individual self. The gnostic who succeeds in doing so reaches the loftiest of all mystical stations: the "station of no station" (*maqām lā maqām*). His heart, capable of reflecting all of God's infinite Attributes without being confined to a particular one could be described not so much as an object or an entity, but as an "event, the process of perspective shift, of *fanā'*, the polishing of the divine mirror."[86] Nasr himself confesses to be this sacred mirror: *I am the mirror in which the Self reflects, / Reflects her infinite Beauty, inexhaustible.*[87]

Our mystic has polished the diamantine mirror of his ever changing *qalb*, and he now discovers with inexpressible joy that his inner heart, like a symbolic Ka'bah, becomes *an ocean of light* in spiritual contemplation[88] —a changing, ever fluctuating profusion of *cascades of light.*[89] Sure enough, the myriad of otherworldly reflections he reenacts in his poetry are indeed multifacetous.

But how is it possible for Nasr to celebrate a heart that is simultaneously solidly diamantine—and thus, safe from change—and yet fluctuates like unceasing luminous waves? In the *coincidentia oppositorum* of his ecstatic poetry, Nasr is illustrating with supreme mastership the exalted *knowledge of the sacred* that his symbolic *qalb* has reached as an organ of mystical perception. He takes refuge from the transient shadows of creation in the inexpugnable castle of his inner soul, where he finds supreme peace. Yet, he also experiences, with the passive vessel of his soul, the constantly changing epiphanies of the Truth as it manifests Itself to Itself. Let us see how the poet succeeds in convoking the reader to share—and to reenact—with him this sublime intuition of a mystical experience in which he simultaneously "tastes" the immovable *Center that is the center of all wheres*[90] and, precisely because he has arrived at this lofty spiritual station, also savors his perpetual transformaton in God as well. The stunned reader at this point feels tempted to pray with Ibn 'Arabī: "My Lord, increase me in bewilderment in you."[91] A supreme prayer indeed, and it seems that it has been answered in the case of Seyyed Hossein Nasr.

Let us explore further Nasr's poetic *ars coincidentiarum*. On a first level, he lets us know that he feels exiled *in this domain of transcience*,[92] the sad voice of his nostalgia crying *for the Paradise within.*[93] The poet truly loathes this worldly *abode of becoming and change* which *devours and kills and mutilates*.[94] His longing soul cannot cling to the *fleeting images passing by*[95] which are but evanescent shadows. Even the delightful *changing wonders*[96] of the *azure bright skies*[97] of his native Persia or of the *emerald land of the gods*[98] of Bali pierce his heart with the pang of separation. The mystic is truly *drowning in this sea of change*,[99] as he clamors in a dramatic, moving verse. But we will attend to the wonder of seeing how these fleeting forms of the earthly abode are redeemed into divine epiphanies in the poet's protean heart. The author subjects these myriad forms to a painstaking alchemical transformation and succeeds in rendering the dreadful *sea of change*[100] into a *glorious ocean of light*,[101] *reflecting the Oneness of the Source of all.*[102] Nasr had expounded this supreme lesson in *Knowledge and the Sacred*: true *sapientia* stands for unitive knowledge, and the mystic discovers that change is only apparent.

From the very *Exordium* to the collection of poems, Nasr makes it clear that the world would *suffocate of its own ugliness*[103] were it not for the fact that the very substance of existence manifests the Breath of the Compassionate. God loves His own theophany, and the changing world of forms is indeed part of it, which explains why Nasr begins to sing with an exulting

Alḥamdu li'Llāh ("May God be praised!" or "Glory to God!"). Verily, only a mystic endowed with a *qalb* receptive of every form and with a supreme spiritualized alchemical power can redeem the ugliness of this *sea of ignorance*[104] in such a compassionate, complete way.

Almost every poem reenacts this sanctifying act of true gnosis. In "the Eternal Covenant" Nasr remembers with awe the primordial "yea" of aquiescence man gave to God in the Eternal Covenant they pacted at the dawn of time. The poet still feels that "yea" reverberating in his heart, turning the *meaningless noise devoid of sense or rhyme*[105] of the world into a prelude to our return to the One. The poet has started to upgrade our earthly journey into *a heavenly song.*[106] Thanks to his perpetual state of remembrance he feels he is with God *from eternity to eternity*[107]: his protean *qalb* not only has succeeded in abolishing the fleeting shadows of this earthly abode of change but also of abolishing time itself. The mystical Way to which the *Poems of the Way* invites the reader thus begins to dissolve as if by miracle. The mystic discovers that he has always been in the bossom of God, "sharing" His infinite, timeless Essence, and there cannot possibly be a "way" to separate him from the Truth, to separate the Truth from the Truth.

The poet also celebrates the Saki who pours a wine for which he so strongly thirsts. The reader must decode the Sufi symbol: Nasr is yearning for the intoxicating wine of the Unitive mystical experience, which transcends the limits of a rational mind immersed in the limited, tragic coordinates of space and time. Ibn al-Fāriḍ was one of the foremost Sufis to sing about this wine which had inebriated him "before vine was planted on this earth," as he reverently boasts in his *Al-Khamriyya* (*In praise of Wine*). Nasr repeats *ad pedem letterae* this same verse in "The Wine of Remembrance."[108] Our poet offers his heart as a vessel and his whole being as a chalice for this *ruby wine tasted by the pure in paradise.*[109] Only when he is intoxicated by the sacred elixir can he realize that he had tasted it in the pre-eternal dawn of the Eternal Covenant his soul had made with God. This merciful wine abolishes time, for it is tasted by the gnostic before the vine was even created. But let us remember here that it was precisely the sacred container—the poet's ever changing, protean *qalb*—the one that transformed the mundane drink of the festive Saki into this otherworldly paradisiacal nectar that renders him free from the bondage of time.

In "Occidental Exile" the poet yearns in nostalgia for his lost homeland's exalted peaks, vast deserts and azure skies. As I have already observed, Nasr suffers from a literal Occidental exile, for he lives in America after having been banished from Iran. His longing to return to his native Orient is of course to be expected. But he is again rewriting an important Sufi mystical symbol which the reader needs to decode: the poet-mystic is really yearning to return to his native *spiritual* Orient, not to the geographic

Orient of his birthplace. Nasr is masterfully reenacting the traditional leitmotif of many Sufis who preceeded him. The Persian Suhrawardī describes his *pèlerinage mystique* towards the "Orient" of his own soul in his *Récit de l'éxil occidental*, which in turn Henry Corbin explores in his much quoted essays on Sufism, *Creative Imagination in the Sufism of Ibn 'Arabī* and *The Man of Light in Iranian Sufism*. To arrive in this *Sinaï mystique* implies a symbolic return to the Orient from which the mystic came originally, and where he rejoins his Perfect Nature in ecstasy. The mystical pilgrim, upon reaching this celestial pole, has finally become "oriented" in this *géographie visionnaire*. Nasr's version is close to Suhrawardī's: *Our return from exile is return to that Center / to our real land of birth.*[110] Our poet directly associates the Orient with illumination— *that Orient which is light pure.*[111] He is a true Sufi, for Muslim mystics have claimed for centuries that when they finally reached the "Orient" of their souls their symbolic "Occidental exile" came to an end. And only then were they worthy of the name *ishraqīyyūn*—that is to say, "Orientals," and, at the same time, "illuminated." In Arabic *Ishrāq* means simultaneously the "East" and "to be enlightened." Nasr thus joins the traditional *illuminati* from his native homeland, and in joining them, his "Occidental exile" finally comes to an end.

Engulfed in mystical light, he discovers that his banishment was more spiritual than geographical in nature. Most of all, he realizes that his *qalb*, receptive of every form, has finally banished space and the state of separation we associate with it: we carry the Orient in our hearts. This is precisely the Orient to which he has arrived: *to that Orient we carry in our hearts / at that center which is the seat of the All-Merciful.*[112] And again the reader discovers that the "way" was never really trodden upon because it was a journey from oneself to oneself. Nasr broke the shell and entered the sacred Orient of his inner core, where the Center is. He is singing his *Poems of the Way* from this blessed Center: it is indeed a centrifugal collection of mystical odes. Again, the poet's *qalb*, endowed with a vertiginous alchemical power, has succeeded in transforming the geographical Orient of Persia into the spiritual Orient of the inner soul. And yet I must add that Nasr recovers his yearned-for geographical homeland in a special way: the cascade of interior images that evoke it so beautifully is now congealed forever in his heart and in his poetry, and the reader can visit the poet's long-lost Persia once and again every time he reads the *Poems of the Way*.

Now we gain access to the primordial temple of the Ka'bah itself. Nasr conjures it with a verbal play of light and shadow that subtly begins to render the holy shrine ethereal and otherworldly. The sacred calligraphy that adorns the temple is *woven of golden light upon the darkness of celestial night*, when the Ka'bah *becomes an ocean of light.*[113] The visiting pilgrims are transformed into moths that circle around the nocturnal symbolic candle of this poetic Ka'bah. And the venerated house of God is futher transmuted by the poet's spiritual eye (his *'ayn al-qalb*), which sees everything *in divinis*: it is his own illuminated heart, where the One resides. The poem closes with a majestic, yet supremely intimate final verse—I can almost hear the gnostic reverently whispering to himself and to the reader, with joyous certainty, *How blessed to enter the Ka'bah of the heart.*[114]

Nasr now convokes us to contemplate the breathtaking mountains of Machu Picchu. The poet is taken aback by the beauty of its mountain peaks that cling to heaven, *verdant with the exuberance of life*,[115] and with its snow-peaks, which shine as jewels in the afternoon light. But all of a sudden this majestic scenery begins to dissolve before our eyes: *Their vertical walls disappearing ethereally / In that mist which opens into infinite space.*[116] And the poet asks himself if he is not before a Taoist painting come to life. We all know that the geographical Machu Picchu is frequently enveloped in a thin film of moisture. But the poem's verdant peaks are dissolving in the infinite space of the poet's interior heart, which is transforming them *into jewels which know no death or decay : the exalted empyrean / which is our abode of origin and home.*[117] The mystic claims, nostalgic yet triumphant, that *we belong to peaks that shine above / in that eternal Sun which never sets.*[118] *The mystery of the wedding of heaven and earth*[119] has occurred, and a redeemed Machu Picchu has turned celestial deep in the recesses of the mystic's ever-changing *qalb*.

The emerald isle of Bali is equally dissolved by the mystical gaze of Nasr's inner *'ayn al-qalb*. Its thousand masks of gods and demons dancing to the rhythm of gamelan and drums remind the poet of the imaginal world pouring forth in countless forms, but the reader realizes that Bali's *verdant fields reflect in their green mirror the infinite sky*.[120] Nasr's "green sky" might need an explanation for the Western reader, for he is consistent with this peculiar chromatism. He will allude again to the horizons that *wore an emerald dress*[121] in his poem "Laylat al-Qadr" (The Night of Power). And we have just seen how the verdant Machu Picchu turned celestial inside the poet's spiritual heart. Green is the symbolic color of spirituality in Islam and ultraterrenal bliss is anticipated by the faithful as a green Paradise full of lush vegetation, where the blessed will be robed in green garments of silk and brocade (Quran XVIII: 30–31). The triliteral Arabic root خضر associates the notion of green (*al-khaḍir* or *al-khuḍra*) with the color of Paradise (*al-khuḍayrā'*) and with the color of the sky (*al-khaḍrā'*).[122] So it does not come as a surprise to realize that we have been thrust into the *green mirror* of the mystic's heavenly *qalb*, where the *myriad forms with which the divine veils and unveils Itself*[123] are transmuted into the myriad epiphanies of *the single Face.*[124]

The poet gazes constantly into the night with his redeeming inner vision, rendering it luminous. In "Luminous Night" he rewrites the old Sufi lesson that *night is the day of the gnostic whose heart / Remains luminous by the presence of the Sun.*[125] Indeed a *thousand suns* render bright the holy darkness of the purified soul. Again and again the heavenly bodies are but symbols of the mystic's inner life. For a Muslim gnostic the newly born moon of Ramaḍān is transmuted into a sacred visual image of the glittering warrior's sword needed to *carry out the inner war to empty ourselves from ourselves.*[126] And the moon-dagger in turn is subtly transformed into the *qalb*, which is seen now as a blessed *chalice of all substance freed.*[127] That is why it can be a true container and a true mirror for the One. Paradise is indeed within, and that is why the contemplation of the heavens always brings the mystic poet back into his own interior heaven.

The *Laylat al-Mi'rāj* or the Nocturnal Ascent of the Prophet to the Divine Throne from Jerusalem is again seen in intimate spiritual terms. Muḥammad's mystical station was so high that even the archangel could not approach it *lest his wings be burned.*[128] But Muḥammad prostrated before the Throne is in *perfect submission, an empty cup ready to receive / the nectar of the secrets of the here and beyond.*[129] The nostalgic mystic yearns reverently to imitate Muḥammad's supreme spiritual feat, but we soon realize that the only way to ascend into the Throne is to penetrate into the empty cup of one's purified heart, *that Center wherein He resides.*[130] And the reader is struck with awe: the poet is again singing from his joyous *Station of Intimacy*,[131] deep inside the throne of his inner soul. And his wings, unlike Gabriel's, have not been burnt.

In "Wonders of Creation" Nasr reflects upon the beauty of created forms which overwhelm him with admiration and love:

> The starry heavens, mountain and peaks sublime
> Forests teaming with life, arid deserts pure,
>
> . . . .
> Nebulae far away in immense spaces hidden,
> Reefs underneath the sea with fishes of every hue,
> A broken rainbow hidden from the eye,
> Which casts its glance upon the surface of the sea
> Unaware of the myriad shades in blend,
> A paradise of harmony of colors and forms . . . [132]

The cascade of images indeed has an unearthly beauty that seems to *belong to a world strange to terrestrial man.*[133] The poet observes that this myriad of lovely forms is a blessed gift from the *Inexhaustible Treasury Divine*,[134] and he bears witness to the glory of God manifested in the impressive heights and depths of creation. But there is more to his reverent admission: the unceasing flow of inciting images *is* within. The starry heavens and the reefs with fishes of every hue, as well as the spring flower which *withers not away nor dies*,[135] are but symbols of the Infinite epiphanies in the reflecting mirror of the polished soul. The mystic's *qalb* in perpetual change receives the unceasing, symbolic manifestations of God, rendering sublime and supernatural the already otherworldly beauty of the created forms. But there is still more: it is precisely in the sanctuary of this blessed heart where the mystic can reflect—and can share in the state of Bi-Unity—the *Oneness of the Source of all*.[136] In this sacred abode Heaven and earth are united in marriage. Again Nasr is admitting to having been endowed with *unified* knowledge of the sacred.

Not only nature but art itself—sacred art, I should say—is seen *sub specie aeternitatis*. Nasr reminisces now about the breathtaking beauty of the *Mezquita de Córboba*, an architectonic marvel of Muslim Spain. Suddenly, right in the middle of the poem, the gnostic fixes his protean spiritual gaze in the very center of the old Islamic mosque: its golden *miḥrāb*. The *miḥrāb* orients the faithful in the direction of the house of the One God, Mecca. Yet the mystic goes beyond this sacred religious symbol, remembering the lesson of Surah II:115: *whithersoever we turn, we behold His Face*.[137] The *miḥrāb* is within.

The Alcázar of Seville's wondrous ceilings inspired the exquisite poem "Golden Geometry in Alcázar." Again the poet sees with penetrating eyes the *snow crystals in golden hue / Hovering above yet never falling*.[138] And the congealed stalactites with their iridescent color whose airy beauty has been sung by many an Andalusian poet offer him a double spiritual lesson. Even though they remind him of this world of changing forms, the golden crystals that seem to fall from above but never really do, are like our souls, *embedded eternally in the diadem*[139] of the Almighty. We might seem to fall, yet as jewels in His crown we are forever safe from change. And the poet evokes Surah XXVII:88's sublime lesson: *all things do perish save the Face of God*.[140]

We are still in Spain. Now we enter with the poet in a majestic castle that hovers over a dale, and are entranced by the beauty of the fair queen who resides within. The poetic protagonist, *a traveller who has come from afar*,[141] has always longed for her embrace, which will cast into oblivion all his suffering in this world of time. It is the only erotic poem of the whole collection, and Nasr evokes profane love with exquisite tenderness. He has, of course, the foremost literary lesson of Ibn 'Arabī's love for Niẓām. Yet when our poet whispers gently into his royal lady's ears *grant me a single moment in thy arms*,[142] the reader discovers that both the queen and her majestic castle are within. Her fortified stronghold is the mystical castle of the inner soul sung by *ḥadīths* and by Sufi mystics and even by St. Teresa of Avila. To enter this castle is to draw into the heart, and to embrace the queen is to behold the Supreme Beloved and to experience the unfathomable mystery of Bi-Unity.

Music is very important in Nasr's mystical path. Still in Spain, he hears *the music of the Friend from afar,*[143] this time in the rhythm of the castanets and the throbbing of the guitar. The haunting voice of the flamenco singer raises *in nostalgia for the paradise within,*[144] and as soon as we hear it with the poet, the music dissolves into the timeless primeval dance of creation. The author is returned for a blessed instant to the dawn of time of his pre-eternal pact with God: time is mercifully abolished in the Ka'bah of his heart, where the flamenco from the Sacro Monte of Granada is rendered primordial rhythm. He no longer hears it, for what he is hearing now is his own "Silent Music." And the words of this unimaginable rhapsody are *chanted by the Eternal Singer*[145] himself.

The poet knows well Who is singing his own literary songs: *If I cry Thou, it is Thee calling Thine own Name / For how can Thy Oneness accept this I as I.*[146] It is not Nasr who is really singing in enthralled verses, but *sophia* singing through Nasr. In the last two parts of the collection, titled "Illumination" and "Stages of the Path to the One," the poet-philosopher reflects, with uncanny verbal intelligence, upon the *sacred knowledge* he has attained, a gnosis which harmonizes contraries in instructing him as to Who he really is. Like Ḥallāj and Bisṭāmī before him, our mystic has been delivered from his painful duality and thus claims for the eternalization of his blessed but brief beatific state: *Let Thy Unity as the victorious come / to rend asunder the claimant I / to reveal the One who is I and Thou.*[147] Verily the poet can exclaim *anā-l'Ḥaqq*[148] with al-Ḥallāj, and *subḥanī*[149] with Bisṭāmī, even though his articulation of the state of Divine Bi-Unity (the *Unus-ambo*) is more restrained and more intellectual than the intoxicated utterances of these passionate Sufis. But he has a profound understanding of what his gnostic antecessors really meant: *It is The supreme Self who alone can utter I. / In whom alone am I my real I.*[150] And the reader acknowledges that Nasr is a veritable *al-'ārif bi 'Llāh*—a mystic who knows God through or by God.

Protected in *the crystalline perfection, coldness of life eternal*[151] of the pure and inviolable Reality, where his soul has been *crystallized as a star,*[152] the poet-mystic finally reaches his spiritual goal and enters into his timeless and imageless interior *qalb* to find that *Here is the Center that is the Center of all wheres, / Now is the moment at the heart of all times.*[153] Time and space dissolve and the gnostic feels free at last. The symbolic path of *Poems of the Way* culminates here, and the reader realizes that Nasr, a true *prince*[154] among the guides of that royal road to the One, has succeeded in turning his *earthly journey to a heavenly song.*[155] Thus the path suddenly dissappears. It was never there. We were always embedded in the diadem of the Almighty.

Yet the reader has witnessed a myriad of changing wonders along the mystical Way this collection of poems describe: *arid deserts pure*, *green mountains dissolving in mist*, *fishes of every hue*, *hovering golden stalactites*, *silent music*. The poet's soul has served as a polished, passive mirror for the One: *I am the mirror in which the Self reflects, / Reflects her infinite Beauty, inexhaustible.*[156] We have gazed upon this vertiginous mirror while reading *Poems of the Way*, and in staring, we have witnessed how the changing forms of *samsāra* have been sanctified into *nirvāṇa*. Cosmos is theophany, not *māyā.* The created world has been purified, sacralized, and unified. The poet rewrites the philosopher's lessons, and his bewildering verse renders these spiritual instructions more clear and more convincing.

Every image and indeed every poem, *whose letters are woven of congealed light,*[157] is like a new refraction of light irradiating from our mystic's diamantine heart, *receptive of every form*, just as Ibn 'Arabī's interior *qalb*. The collection of mystical odes itself is an icon of this blessed ocean of pulsating light which is the heart witnessing the epiphanies of the One in the ultimate station of mystical union. In the act of reading we have truly shared Nasr's *'ayn al-qalb*, his mystical "eye of the heart," and in doing so, we too have been symbolically transformed into the sacred vessels of reception of God's ever changing attributes. The anguishing world of changing forms has been miraculously redeemed, even if temporarily, into a myriad of symbolic Attributes of God. Nasr amply demonstrates that he possesses a sacramental sense of the created cosmos, an immediate and unveiled sense of the sacred. We have shared his profound gnoseological intuitions and for a blessed moment we scintillate with the author *in the luminosity of His proximity.*[158]

Nasr's protean heart (*qalb*) has succeeded in literally inverting (*taqallub*) the shadows of this pitiful sea of change into the perpetually changing forms in which the Truth reveals Itself to Itself. "Forms lead to the formless," for when the gnostic sanctifies the forms he is able to "journey beyond them."[159] Again the poet articulates the philosopher's ideas in symbolic verse. In his poetry Nasr has rewritten the traditional symbol of the *qalb* with such amazing perfection that I confess I really do not know if he was conscious of his artistic *coup de grâce* or if *sophia* again spoke through him.

In *Knowledge and the Sacred* Nasr taught that it is not possible to attain this mercifully unifying knowledge without being consumed by it. The whole collection of odes attests to the fact that Nasr has indeed attained the *ḥikmah al-dhawqiyyah*—the "tasted" or "realized" knowledge about which he so amply theorized in his "inspired" philosophical *opus magnus*. Again his verses allow the reader a glimpse (better yet, a "taste") of this otherworldly *sapientia* which the poet discovered deep within the diamantine castle of his heart.

Poetry, as usual closer to the psyche than prose, was able to give life to the philosopher's epistemology in a most dramatic, unexpected way. I salute the *rhapsodic intellect* of Seyyed Hossein Nasr with the very same words with which he reverently celebrated Ibn 'Arabī, the *Interpreter of Desires* and *reviver of the Religion of the Heart*[160]: *Thy poems interpreted the 'Desires' which are those for God, / Dressed in the love of earthly forms.*[161]

Nasr the philosopher, historian, scientist, theologian, literary critic, and now the mystical poet, has succeeded in reminding contemporary mankind *Of the song of that celestial music of which* he is, like Ibn 'Arabī eight centuries before him, *the supreme troubadour in these Western lands.*[162]

LUCE LÓPEZ-BARALT

UNIVERSITY OF PUERTO RICO
FEBRUARY 2000

NOTES

1. I am quoting "The Biography of Seyyed Hossein Nasr" by Zailan Morris in *Knowledge is Light*, Zailan Moris, ed. (Chicago: ABC Internatinal Group, Inc., 1999), p. 27.

2. S. H. Nasr, *Knowledge and the Sacred* (New York: The Crossroads Publishing Co., 1981).

3. *Beiträge zu einer Kritik der Sprache*, 3 vols. (Leipzig, 1923–1924).

4. *Tractatus Logico-Philosophicus* (London, 1922). Bertrand Russell wrote the introduction for this edition of his former pupil's work.

5. *The Mathematical Foundations of Quantum Mechanics*, trans. by Robert T. Beyer (Princeton: Princeton University Press, 1955).

6. See his "Mathematical Formulation of the Quantum Theory of Electromagnetic Interaction," in J. Schwinger, ed., *Selected Papers of Quantum Electrodynamics* (New York: Dover, 1958), p. 272ff.

7. Werner Heisenberg, *Physics and Beyond* (New York: Harper & Row, 1971), p. 206.

8. He mentions the well-known works of F. Capra (*The Tao of Physics*, 1977); R. G. Siu (*The Tao of Science: An Essay on Western Knowledge and Eastern Wisdom,* 1958); and W. I. Thompson (*Passage About Earth*, 1974). We could add to the ever-growing list *The Dancing Wu Li Masters: An Overview of the New Physics*, by Gary Zukav (1979).

9. (Yale University Press, 1992).

10. Of particular relevance are her *Birth of the Living God: A Psychoanalytic Study* (The University of Chicago Press, 1979); *Why Did Freud Reject God?* (Yale University Press, 1999); and especially her "Reflexiones psicoanalíticas acerca de

la experiencia mística" ("Psychoanalitical Reflections on the Mystical Experience"), included in *El sol a medianoche. La experiencia mística: tradición y actualidad*, Luce López-Baralt and Lorenzo Piera, eds. (Madrid: Trotta, 1996), pp. 61–76.

11. *Knowledge and the Sacred*, p. 12.

12. *The Everything and the Nothing* (South Carolina: Sheiran Press, 1989), p. 36.

13. "San Juan de la Cruz. De la 'noche oscura' a la más clara mística," in *Los intelectuales en el drama de España: Ensayos y notas (1936–1939)*. (Madrid: Hispamérica, 1977), p. 189.

14. *Tarjumān al-Ashwāq: A Collection of Mystical Odes*, R. A. Nicholson, ed., (London: Royal Asiatic Society, 1911), p. 75.

15. "Remarks on Bertrand Russell's Theory of Knowledge," in *The Philosophy of Bertrand Russell*, Paul Arthur Schilpp, ed., The Library of Living Philosophers, vol. 5 (La Salle, Ill.: Open Court,1989), p. 285.

16. *Knowledge and the Sacred*, p. 325.

17. The Spanish poet dedicates complete poems (curiously enough, much in the Sufi tradition) to this "taste" or *gusto* with which he had empirically experienced the union with the Divine. See specially his "Glosa a lo divino" (*San Juan de la Cruz. Obra completa*), L. López-Baralt and E. Pacho, eds., (Madrid: Alianza Editorial, 1991), vol. I, p. 97.

18. I translate into English the refrain from the poem "Cantar del alma que se huelga de conocer a Dios por fe."

19. *Knowledge and the Sacred*, op. cit., p. 150.

20. Ibid., p. 154.

21. Ibid., p. 131.

22. Ibid., pp. 42–43.

23. "Tribute: Seyyed Hossein Nasr as Transcultural Educator of Islam," in *Knowledge is Light*, p. 35.

24. *Knowledge and the Sacred*, op. cit., p. 43.

25. I refer the reader to Joaquín García Palacios's illuminating study, *Los procesos de conocimiento en San Juan de la Cruz*. (Salomanca: Universidad de Salamanca, 1992).

26. *Knowledge and the Sacred*, op. cit., p. 44.

27. *Structural Poetics*, (Ithaca, N.Y.: Cornell University Press, 1975).

28. The philosopher himself makes this clear: "In the Orient knowledge has always been related to the sacred and to spiritual perfection . . . intelligence has been seen ultimately as a sacrament, and knowledge has been irrevocably related to the sacred and its actualization in the being of the knower" (*Knowledge and the Sacred*, pp. vii–viii).

29. Ibid., p. 197.

30. Ibid., p. 61. Nasr observes that he owes the term to Th. Roszak (*Where the Wasteland Ends*, Garden City, N.Y.: Anchor Books, 1972).

31. *Knowledge and the Sacred*, p. 8.

32. I will refer again and in more detail to this symbolic "Occidental exile" of Sufi mystics.

33. Ibid., p. 29.

34. Nasr is quoting H. A. Giles, *Chuang-Tzu—Taoist Philosopher and Chinese Mystic*, London, 1961, p. 127; *Knowledge and the Sacred*, p. 50.

35. *Knowledge and the Sacred*, p. 191.

36. Ibid., p. 191. The word in Arabic for this reflection of the Divine in the mirror of cosmos is *tajallī* (ibid., p. 201).

37. Ibid., p. 137.

38. Ibid., p. 227.

39. Ibid., p. 222.

40. Ibid., p. 221.

41. Ibid., p. 226.

42. Ibid., p. 228.

43. Ibid., p. 27.

44. Ibid., p. 183.

45. Ibid., p. 183.

46. See his selected bibliography in *Knowledge is Light*, pp. 368–80, as well as the more updated version in this present volume.

47. *Poems of the Way* (Oakton, Va.: The Foundation of Traditional Studies, 1999, p. 63). I had the privilege of writing the introduction of the book, "Under the Shadow of an Olive Tree that is Neither of the East nor of the West: The Mystical Poetry of Seyyed Hossein Nasr," pp. 1–10.

48. Nasr discusses the meaning of these Sufi terms in *Knowledge and the Sacred*, pp. 314–15.

49. "The language of the birds" is the symbolic language given to Solomon, according to the Quranic revelation, and Nasr uses it metaphorically to celebrate the gnostic wisdom of Frithjof Schuon (Ibid., p. 107).

50. The title for the *Essays in Honor of Seyyed Hossein Nasr*, edited by Zailan Morris, which I have already quoted, is very well chosen indeed.

51. *Poems of the Way*, p. 29.

52. I quote Zailan Moris: "The name 'Nasr' which means 'victory' comes from the title *naṣr al-atibbā'*, ('Victory of Physicians'), which was conferred on Professor Nasr's grandfather by the King of Persia" (*Knowledge is Light*, p. 9).

53. *Knowledge is Light*, p. 27.

54. I am applying to Professor Nasr's philosophical work the same words that B. Kelly applies to F. Schuon's books. See his "Notes on the Light of the Eastern Religions with Special Reference to the Works of Ananda Coomaraswamy, René Guénon, and Frithjof Schuon," *Dominican Studies* 7 (1954): 265 and Nasr, *Knowledge and the Sacred*, p. 108.

55. *Knowledge and the Sacred*, p. 108.

56. Ibid., pp. 101–2.
57. Ibid., p. 201.
58. Ibid., p. 200.
59. Ibid., p. 222.
60. Ibid., p. 245.
61. Octavio Paz, so attuned to Oriental art, explores the polivalent character of poetry with particular sensibility in his essay *El arco y la lira* (Fondo de Cultura Económica, México, 1956).
62. *Poems of the Way*, p. 27.
63. Ibid., p. 19.
64. Émile Dermenghem, "Essai sur la mystique musulmane," Prologue to his French translation of Ibn al-Fāriḍ's *Al-Khamariyya*: L'Éloge du vin (*Al-Khamriya*) de Ibn al-Faridh (Paris: Les Éditions Véga, 1931), p. 63.
65. 'Aṭṭār relates the dialogue Ibn 'Aṭā' (d. 922) had with some theologians:

"How is it with you Sufis," certain theologians asked Ibn 'Aṭā', "that you have invented terms which sound strange to those who hear them, abandoning ordinary language? . . . "

"We do it because it is precious to us . . . and we desired that none but we Sufis should know of it. We did not wish to employ ordinary language, so we invented a special vocabulary" (Farīd al-Dīn 'Aṭṭār, *Muslim Saints and Mystics: Episodes from the Tadhkirat al-Auliyā'* ["*Memorial of the Saints*"], Arthur A. Arberry, transl., (London: Routledge & Kegan Paul, 1966), pp. 237–38).

66. Let us her what Nasr himself has to say about this:

"Since formulated knowledge is inseparable from language, the desacralization of knowledge could not but affect the use of language. If European languages have become less and less symbolic and ever more unidimensional, losing much of the inward sense of classical languages, it is because they have been associated with thought patterns of a unidimensional character" (*Knowledge and the Sacred*, op. cit., p. 46).

67. See pp. 153 ff.
68. *An Introduction to Islamic Cosmological Doctrines* (Cambridge: Harvard University Press, 1964), p. 262.
69. *Poems of the Way*, p. 59.
70. Ibid., p. 28.
71. Ibid., p. 43.
72. Ibid., p. 39.
73. Ibid., p. 75.
74. Ibid., p. 88.
75. Ibid., p. 27.
76. Ibid., p. 87.
77. Ibid., p. 27.
78. Ibid., p. 87.

79. I am quoting St. Teresa's *Moradas del castillo interior* (*Stations of the Interior Castle*). See L. López-Baralt, "Spanish Mysticism's Debt to Sufism: the Mystical Imagery of St. Teresa of Avila," under publication in the proceedings of the International Congress on Mullā Ṣadrā, Tehran, Iran.

80. See Annice Callahan, ed., *Spiritualities of the Heart: Approaches to Personal Wholeness in Christian Tradition* (Mahwah, N.J.: Pauline Press, 1990).

81. For specific studies on the subject of the *qalb*, see Maurice Gloton ("Les secrets du coeur selon l'Islam," *Revue Française de Yoga* V (1991): 65–89), and the recent volume of *Connaissance des Religions* 57-58-59 (1999) titled *Lumière sur la Voie du Coeur.*

82. I use Michael Sells's English version "Ibn 'Arabī's Garden Among the Flames: A Reevaluation" in *History of Religions* XXII (1984): 290–91. The article was reprinted in Sells's book *Mystical Languages of Unsaying*, (Chicago: University of Chicago Press, 1994), pp. 287–315. R. A. Nicholson translates the verse in question as "My heart has become capable of every form . . . " (*The Tarjumán al-Ashwáq: A Collection of Mystical Odes*, (London: Royal Asiatic Society, 1911), p. 67, while Maurice Gloton opts for the French version "Mon coeur est devenu capable / D'accuellir toute forme . . . " (*L'interprète des désirs*, [Paris: Albin Michel, 1996], p. 117). Here is Sells's rendition of the whole stanza:

Marvel, a garden among the flames.
My heart has become receptive of every form
It is a meadow for gazelles, a monastery for [Christian] monks.
An abode for idols, the Ka'ba of the pilgrim,
The tables of the Torah, the Quran.
My religion is love—wherever its camels turn
Love is my belief, my faith (op. cit., p. 287).

83. Sells, op. cit., p. 287.

84. For further discussion regarding the symbol of the *qalb*, see Sachiko Murata, *The Tao of Islam: A Sourcebook on Gender Relationships in Islamic Thought* (New York: State University of New York Press, 1992); William Chittick, *The Sufi Path of Knowledge: Ibn 'Arabī's Metaphysics of Imagination* (Albany: State University of New York Press, 1989); and L. López-Baralt's "Introductory Study to the Spanish Translation of Abū-l-Ḥasan al-Nūrī's *Maqāmāt al-qulūb*" (*Moradas de los corazones*. Traducción del árabe, introducción y notas de L. López-Baralt, [Madrid: Trotta, 1999]).

85. Sells, op. cit., p. 293.

86. Ibid., p. 299.

87. *Poems of the Way*, p. 72.

88. Ibid., p. 27.

89. Ibid., p. 23.

90. Ibid., p. 78.

91. This is a reformulation of the *dhikr* "My Lord, increase me in knowledge." See Sells, op. cit., p. 303.

92. *Poems of the Way*, p. 23.

93. Ibid., p. 23.

94. Ibid., p. 87.

95. Ibid., p. 72.

96. Ibid., p. 73.

97. Ibid., p. 23.

98. Ibid., p. 33.

99. Ibid., p. 89.

100. Ibid.

101. Ibid., p. 27.

102. Ibid., p. 47.

103. Ibid., p. 13.

104. Ibid.

105. Ibid., p. 20.

106. Ibid.

107. Ibid.

108. Ibid., p. 22.

109. Ibid., p. 21.

110. Ibid., p. 23.

111. Ibid.

112. Ibid.

113. Ibid., p. 27.

114. Ibid., p. 28.

115. Ibid., p. 31.

116. Ibid.

117. Ibid.

118. Ibid.

119. Ibid.

120. Ibid., p. 33.

121. Ibid., p. 40.

122. For more on this symbolic green color, see Abdelwhab Bouhdiba, "Les arabes et la couleur," in *Hommage à Roger Bastide* (Paris: PUF, 1979), pp. 347–54. Curiously enough, St. John of the Cross often saw the heavenly skies as "green," as if he were a Muslim (see L. López-Baralt, *Asedios a lo Indecible. San Juan de la Cruz canta al éxtasis transformante* [Madrid: Trotta, 1999]), pp. 37 ff.

123. *Poems of the Way*, p. 48.

124. Ibid.

125. Ibid., p. 37.

126. Ibid., p. 38.

127. Ibid.

128. Ibid., p. 42.
129. Ibid.
130. Ibid., p. 43.
131. Ibid., p. 42.
132. Ibid., p. 47.
133. Ibid.
134. Ibid.
135. I am quoting here the poem "Spring flowers," written in much the same spirit as "Wonders of Creation" (Ibid., p. 51).
136. Ibid.
137. Ibid., p. 55.
138. Ibid., p. 57.
139. Ibid.
140. Ibid.
141. Ibid., p. 76.
142. Ibid.
143. Ibid., p. 59.
144. Ibid.
145. I am quoting now the poem, "Silent Music," ibid., p. 77.
146. Ibid., p. 71.
147. Ibid.
148. Literally, "I am the Truth" or "I am God." Much has been said about these mystical utterances of the Persian mystic, who felt he shared God's essence while in extasis. He died a martyr in 922 C.E.
149. Instead of *subḥān Allāh* ("Glory to God!") Bisṭāmī (d. 874 C.E.) exclaims *subhānī* ("Glory to me!). Again, he felt inseparable from God while in his mystical trance.
150. Ibid., p. 90.
151. Ibid., p. 87.
152. Ibid., p. 90.
153. Ibid., p. 78.
154. Ibid., p. 65.
155. Ibid., p. 20.
156. Ibid., p. 72.
157. Ibid., p. 56.
158. Ibid., p. 63.
159. *Knowledge and the Sacred*, p. 261.
160. *Poems of the Way*, op. cit., p. 64.
161. Ibid.
162. Ibid.

REPLY TO LUCE LÓPEZ-BARALT

Professor López-Baralt is today the leading expert in the field of comparative literature dealing with Sufi texts in relation to Spanish mystical literature. Not only does she have intimate knowledge of Spanish mystical works, especially those of St. Teresa of Avila and St. John of the Cross, but also she knows Arabic and Persian and has immersed herself for years in Sufi literature and especially poetry in both Arabic and Persian. Her appraisal of my poetry is based on this long love affair with mystical poetry in general and Sufi literature in particular as well as an in-depth knowledge of Sufi symbolism, cosmology, and metaphysics. She is also herself a poet in addition to being a celebrated scholar. Her essay in fact reflects these two dimensions. The first part is devoted to a study of my *Knowledge and the Sacred* and the second to a collection of my poetry which appeared under the title *Poems of the Way*. I shall answer the first part as I have done for other essays. But the second part which is a literary work in itself, in which she embarrasses me with her laudatory comments about my poetry, I shall not analyze save to say that her love of Oriental poetry has caused her to use Oriental hyperbole in evaluating my humble poems. Rather, I shall take this occasion to say something about the role of poetry in my own life and how I envisage the relation between philosophy and poetry.

López-Baralt refers at the beginning to how the text of my *Knowledge and the Sacred* came to me as if it had descended upon me and that I was writing each chapter as if from memory. She speaks of the "otherworldly quality of the intuitive feeling he experienced while writing *Knowledge and the Sacred*." I wish to clarify this question by stating first of all that of course the extensive footnotes of the book were the result of long periods of research primarily at the Widener Library of Harvard University and are not to be included in the comments I had made about the text itself which was written in its totality in less than three months, each chapter "flowing" as if I were transcribing a recording. This experience was not, however, one of intuitive feeling but the result of intellectual intuition combined with a sense of light and grace. I could say, if it does not sound too audacious, that the process was similar to what Suhrawardī would have called *ishrāq*. But as she writes, this is not unusual when one is dealing with the *sophia perennis* which is already inscribed upon the tablet of the heart or, one could say, the tablet of the innermost layer of the very substance of our being. After having meditated for many years upon these matters, I was in such a state of being that I can say that the text of the book came to me as a recollection combined with what I could call a gift from Heaven. It was sent during a most difficult period of my life following upon the wake of the Iranian Revolution and my social uprooting as well as the loss of my library and the preliminary notes that I had prepared for the Gifford Lectures in Tehran before the advent of the Revolution. I should also add that in many other cases when I am to write something, after the necessary research and pondering over the matter, the actual process of writing is like the crystallization of a liquid solution and takes place fairly rapidly, the words coming forth in a flow that is most often continuous and uninterrupted. This has not been true of all of my writings but of a number of them, although not on the scale that I experienced in writing *Knowledge and the Sacred*. In the process of writing such works, the first and last sentences are especially important and I usually wait until they come as a categorical assertion within my mind. As for the text itself (for that class of my writings belonging to this category), I do always go over them and make occasional corrections, but in the case of such writings these corrections are always minor. As for what this category comprises, it is almost always writings dealing with exposition of traditional doctrines, whether they be metaphysical or cosmological, and with spiritual matters in general. This manner of writing does not include those essays based on ordinary scholarly research, although even in these cases I have never remained satisfied with scholarship for its own sake but have considered the discovery or exposition of some aspect of the truth to be the goal of all my writings.

The author also speaks of the times being ripe for my philosophical challenge and mentions certain developments in both Western philosophy and science in this connection. I need to add that cracks began to appear in the wall of the Western paradigm based on humanism, rationalism, materialism, and so on, already at the beginning of the twentieth century. These cracks appeared both from below and from above so that along with infra-human elements of dissolution coming from below the possibility was also created for the light of sacred knowledge long forgotten in the West to shine from above. "The philosophical challenge" based on traditional sapiental knowledge and the perennial philosophy was presented long before me by Guénon, Coomaraswamy, and Schuon. My role has been to carry this challenge to the heart of the Western academic community and centers of mainstream Western philosophy, which until recently had chosen to neglect and even overlook the very existence of traditional teachings. With this important historical correction in mind, I would agree that the time has come to challenge the whole edifice of modern and postmodern Western thought including its academic expression which is vital for its survival. And perhaps in this process my humble works have a role to play.

As for modern physics, I have had occasion to speak elsewhere in the volume about my views about it and do not want to repeat myself here. Suffice it to say, quantum mechanics does not itself lead to perennial philosophy, but by breaking the hold of the earlier mechanistic and materialistic physics upon the minds of many and by making evident, for those who can see, the poverty of Cartesian bifurcation as the existing philosophical background of modern physics, the new physics has made it not only possible but also necessary to search outside the mainstream of modern Western philosophy for an appropriate philosophy of nature. The *philosophia perennis* stands as the only possible source of wisdom wherein one can find what is being sought. The works of such figures as Wolfgang Smith, who has contributed to this volume, present crucial keys for discovering an appropriate philosophy for quantum mechanics on the basis of the sacred knowledge of which I speak.

Unfortunately there are also many shallow attempts to correlate the findings of modern physics and those of the mystics. Therefore, when the author writes that for the first time physicists and mystics seem to speak the same "language," I feel quite uneasy because I have observed only too often the kind of superficial harmony which is propagated by so many New Age religions and even by elements within traditional religions—so-called harmonies which have no metaphysical foundation and are in fact dangerous. The energy of modern physics is certainly not the same thing as the Divine Energies about which Orthodox theologians speak, and the movement of molecules in a solution is not the Dance of Śiva. For my part, I prefer to base the discussion between physicists and mystics on a metaphysical foundation which cannot be but the doctrines at the heart of the perennial philosophy rather than the experience of phenomena and mental states. The thrust of my writings on this subject is to resuscitate traditional metaphysics and then to integrate what is positive in modern science within that metaphysical framework. I do not believe that trying to divide material units to an ever greater degree will lead to the same numinous Reality that the true mystic seeks to reach by leaving the abode of the outward and the material for the inward and the spiritual. Therefore, while I have noted interest in such works as *The Tao of Physics* of F. Capra, I have also criticized their neglect of the veritable significance of traditional cosmologies and the sacred sciences with which they are trying to correlate the tenets of modern physics.

Actually what López-Baralt has written on physics and mysticism is peripheral to her main thesis. If I have paused to discuss this point fairly extensively, it is to make clear my own position. As for what she writes in the rest of the first part of her essay on my understanding of sacred knowledge and her interpretation of *Knowledge and the Sacred*, they are fully confirmed by me. They also contain many deep insights which complement my own words and make more accessible some of my theses. Her statements concerning the book are a notable commentary upon its content and are fully accepted by me.

As for the analysis of my poetry, as I have already mentioned the author herself writes in a highly poetic style of much power and beauty and makes comments upon my poetry and its author which make me embarrassed and about which I have nothing to say save to point once again to her recourse to Oriental hyperbole. But her exposition affords me a valuable opportunity to discuss the role of poetry in my life and in my writings as well as my views on the relation between philosophy, or rather *sophia* itself, and poetry.

Poetry has occupied a central role in my life since my earliest childhood. Born into a culture in which poetry has played a central role and continues to be of much greater importance than in present-day America and Europe (with the possible exception of Spain), I was nurtured from the earliest period of my education with the verses of the Quran, which are themselves supreme poetry although never called poetry in Islamic sources, and the works of Persian classical poets such as Firdawsī, Sa'dī, Ḥāfiẓ, Niẓāmī, and Rūmī. I was made to memorize hundreds of verses of poetry and by the age of ten could recite Persian poetry for hours from memory. The rhyme and rhythm of classical Persian poetry left its permanent imprint upon my soul, an imprint which was never erased even during those years at Peddie, the preparatory school which I attended in America, when I hardly had any contact with Persian and forgot many of the poems memorized in childhood.

It was also at Peddie that I began to learn the English language seriously and became exposed to English poetry, especially the works of Shakespeare, Milton and the Romantics such as Shelley, Byron, Keats, and Blake. At first, however, poetry in English did not speak to me and only increased my nostalgia for Persian poetry. But as my command of English improved, the poetic medium in that language began to reveal its treasures to me to an ever-greater degree. We had to memorize many pieces of English poetry and this process also helped in the alchemical process which was taking place at that time in my soul and was being reflected in my writing of English. The process to which I am alluding is the gradual penetration of the poetic characteristics of Persian into my writing of English prose which finally resulted in the style that has characterized my prose writings from the beginning of my writing formally in English in the late '50s and continuing to this day. When I handed my doctoral thesis at Harvard to one of my main advisors, Harry Wolfson, he was kind in praising the scholarship and intellectual context of the work and then added that he had not seen a doctoral thesis in a philosophical subject written in poetic prose which reminded him of some medieval texts. The wedding between the rigor of mathematics and logic and the gentleness of poetry which I have sought to achieve in my prose works owes its existence on the one hand to my long scientific training and on the other to that early imprint of poetry on my soul. Also my own quest after the eternal *sophia* only confirmed not only the possibility but also the necessity of such a wedding in the full expression of realized gnosis as we see in so many traditional works.

While at MIT and Harvard I continued to read much poetry in English including especially the twentieth-century figures T. S. Eliot (whom I met at Harvard), Ezra Pound, and William Butler Yeats as well as Dylan Thomas (whom I met for several days at MIT shortly before his death). These years were also for me the period of return to classical Persian poetry as well as my introduction to German and Italian poetry, especially Goethe and Dante. Although I was and remain much more familiar with the French language and its literature than German, Italian, or Spanish, as far as poetry is concerned, I have always been attracted more to these three languages than to French, whose prose literature has been of greater interest to me than its poetry. There are of course certain exceptions such as Paul Claudel and even Rimbaud and Baudelaire, but by and large German, Italian, and Spanish poetry have always appealed more to me, especially metaphysical poets such as Dante whom I consider to be the supreme poet of Christian Western civilization.

In any case ever greater intimacy with poetry in English combined with reading much wisdom poetry in other languages (including, of course, Arabic or in translation as well as re-reading of the Persian classics) let me at the age of twenty-one to try my hand in writing poetry in English as well as a few verses in Persian, although I never considered myself a poet nor ever labored to write poetry. The fruit of these years which ended in 1958 with my return to Persia was a booklet of poems, some composed directly and others translated from the Persian into English. The latter included a poetic rendition of the introduction to the *Mathnawī* of Jalāl al-Dīn Rūmī and several *ghazals* of Ḥāfiẓ while the whole collection dealt with metaphysical and mystical themes. These poems were personal and I never meant to publish them. The hands of destiny were to assure the realization of my intention for these early poems remained in manuscript form in my library in Persia for the next twenty-one years and were lost along with all my other handwritten and as yet unpublished texts when my house was confiscated and my library plundered in 1979.

During those two decades in Persia from 1958 to 1979 my concern with poetry, especially of the sapiental kind, remained very strong and I continued to read and study much Sufi poetry in Persian and Arabic as well as poetry in European languages, chief among them English. But during this period I wrote little poetry in either Persian or English save for a *ghazal* and quatrain (*rubāʻī*) or two here and there along with translations of Sufi poetry into English verse in the context of some of my prose writings such as those concerning Rūmī.

The angel of poetry, or the muse as Western poets have known her, came to visit me suddenly in the mid-eighties in of all places Cordova, Spain. Since then a number of poems have been written mostly in English but also some in Persian in different places and varying conditions. All of them have come to me quickly, as if in a flash, and have always been related to an inner experience of the spiritual world as a result of which phenomenal reality has gained the tongue to speak of the noumenal realities which the external forms at once veil and reveal. Even where some of the poems speak of pure metaphysical doctrine, they do so as a telling of the vision of that metaphysical reality of which the doctrine speaks rather than of mental concepts associated with the doctrine. These humble poems are in a sense the fruit of that long period of ingestion of the subtleties of the English language and development in my mind of that language as it became evermore impregnated and transmuted by the ethos, forms, symbols, and sensibilities of Persian Sufi poetry. If when Islam came to Bengal, the Bengali language could develop as an Islamic language and create a rich Bengali Sufi poetic tradition, why if one accepts and appreciates all those possibilities and does not remain satisfied with the evermore vulgarized usage of the language so prevalent today can one not achieve the same goal for the English language which is poetically very rich and possesses vast possibilities for the expression of spiritual realities?

In any case I had never meant to publish a book of poetry but only the few poems which I had myself included in a number of my essays and books. Various circumstances, however, including the insistence of a number of intimate spiritual friends, finally forced me to select the forty poems which have appeared in *Poems of the Way*, with López-Baralt's introduction, poems analyzed with such profound sympathy and understanding by her in this essay. I should add once again that I do not consider myself a poet but a lover of sapiental poetry, who like so many traditional Persian philosophers also jots down a few lines of poetry now and then.

It is necessary in conclusion to summarize my views concerning the relation of poetry to philosophy in its original sense. It is not accidental that the father of Greek philosophy, Pythagoras, composed the *Golden Verses,* that Parmenides has left us a poem of the greatest philosophical significance, and that in nearly every tradition the expressions of *sophia* have been in poetry or poetic prose but have never been prosaic. Philosophy in the Pythagorean sense is the love of that *sophia* or *sapientia* which, being the truth, is also surrounded with the splendor of the truth which is none other than beauty. Furthermore, the intellect in its traditional sense, which is the instrument whereby *sophia* is attained, once actualized becomes the "rhapsodic intellect," as López-Baralt says, and expresses itself through the cadence, rhythms, symbols, allusions, and music which characterize poetry. Real poetry is not only the vehicle for the expression of wisdom. It is wisdom itself. The great sages who were also poets were not poets who then attained gnosis and illumination. They were gnostics and illuminated beings, wise men and women whose expression of the wisdom they had attained was by nature poetic. One needs only to recall in this instance the saying of Rūmī that he was not even a poet. This is the statement of one of the greatest mystical poets who ever lived. What Rūmī and others like him wanted to say was that they were not like ordinary poets who would compose a poem on any subject or occasion at hand either to be financially compensated by a benefactor or to fulfill some kind of egotistical urge or so-called self-expression. Rather, contact with the noumenous world had turned the soul of Rūmī and others like him into a poem itself so what they uttered could not but be poetry.

In the West the separation of reason from intellect resulting in the rise of modern philosophy with Descartes, muted the melody of the rhapsodic intellect within and divorced the soul from its source of heavenly music. Philosophy became prosaic in its expression and more and more divorced from poetry. During the past few centuries the West has produced poets who were still philosophical in the time-honored sense of the term, such figures as Shakespeare, Caldéron, Angelus Silesius, Goethe, Blake, and the like, but they are never taught in courses on the history of Western philosophy. As for well-known philosophers in the West, in modern times none has been also known as a poet even if a few have written a number of poetic lines on the side. The eclipse of poetry in the modern West is directly related to the eclipse of the intellect and of gnosis and traditional metaphysics which only the actualized intellect within man can attain, provided it functions within the framework of revelation.

In the Islamic tradition the Quran speaks against the poets of the "age of ignorance" (*al-jāhiliyyah*) because they were fortunetellers and made prophetic claims. But the Quran itself is of the highest poetic quality, to which no Arabic poem of no matter what level of eloquence can be compared. Moreover, the Prophet of Islam appreciated those poets such as Labīd who spoke of the truths of life and death. As a result of the Quranic revelation, a civilization was created wherein poetry has always been held in the highest position of honor and many portions of the greatest Islamic texts of wisdom have been composed in the poetic medium. Even many of the great Islamic philosophers who wrote about logic and rational discourse in philosophy also composed poetry on the side. One can cite as examples among those who were Persian, Ibn Sīnā, Suhrawardī, Naṣīr al-Dīn al-Ṭūsī, Mīr Dāmād, Mullā Ṣadrā, and Sabziwārī, while a number of philosophers such as Nāṣir-i Khusraw and Afḍal al-Dīn Kāshānī were outstanding poets.

It is in light of this tradition as well as that of the Sufi poets such as Sanā'ī, 'Aṭṭār, Ibn al-Fāriḍ, Ibn 'Arabī, Rūmī, Shabistarī, Sa'dī, and Ḥāfiẓ that I interpret the relation of poetry to wisdom or *sophia*. One of my favorite poems, which I have taught over the years along with the appropriate commentaries, is the *Gulshan-i Rāz* ("The Secret Garden of Divine Mysteries") by the fourteenth-century Persian Sufi master Shaykh Maḥmūd Shabistarī. This poem of celestial inspiration was composed in a few days by the author who did not write any poems before or after, and who, like Rūmī, did not even consider himself a poet. Through heavenly inspiration he was able to summarize the whole of Sufi metaphysics and symbolism in verses of unbelievable poetic power. This work represents for me, in the context of the poetic tradition of my mother tongue, one of the supreme examples of the veritable relationship between poetry and *sophia*.

This relationship is not, however, culturally bound. It is universal and can be seen whenever realized principial knowledge finds its fully eloquent expression. In the context of the perennial philosophy in contemporary times, it is interesting to point out the case of Frithjof Schuon, the foremost expositor of the *sophia perennis* of the twentieth century, who was also a remarkable poet leaving behind two short volumes of German poetry written during his youth and a vast collection composed in the last years of his life, a collection which has not as yet been completely published. His case, as well as that of Martin Lings, another celebrated authority of traditional doctrines, who is also a master poet, demonstrates the relation between poetry and wisdom in the context of the present-day Western world and shows that this relationship is not confined to Islamic or other non-Western civilizations and to older eras of history. God is, symbolically speaking, both poet/musician and architect. The attainment of knowledge of that Divine Reality must also in its fullness contain both the mathematical rigor of arithmetic and geometry and the musical gentleness of poetry.

The subject of the relation between poetry and tradition or perennial philosophy is a vast one and in fact there are traditional texts in Islamic languages, Sanskrit, Chinese, Japanese, and so on, pertaining to this subject. My intention has not been to expound the full doctrine here but only to summarize that aspect of the subject which is indispensable for the understanding of my own attitude towards poetry. I am deeply grateful to Professor López-Baralt for her luminous and penetrating analysis of my humble poems but wish to state at the end again that I am not a professional poet but a seeker and lover of *sophia* who, having touched my being, has created rhythmic dilatations within my mind and soul that result occasionally in the composition of a few lines about which the author has kindly made such gracious comments in her highly poetical essay.

S. H. N.

12

A. K. Saran

A NASR SENTENCE: SOME COMMENTS

The world created by the Demiurge is not only an order or cosmos but a living order directed to the good and teleological in nature.[1]

In *Religion and the Order of Nature* which forms the title of Professor Nasr's *magnum opus*, the conjunction *and* is clearly one of internal transformation. Logically, there are two kinds of connections (or connectors). Taking "and" as a basic coupler or connector, we may distinguish between two kinds of connections or conjunctions: the additive and the internal modifier. The distinction does not go very far, nor does it delve deep. The distinction, however, is important and can help us reach important insights.

My point here is to suggest that the traditional theory of nature and religion takes us to the doctrine that all is sacred, each thing in its own way and at the appropriate level. In any consistent and persistent analysis of phenomena and human experience, ultimately all truth is tautologous. This was the view of Wittgenstein in the *Tractatus Logico-Philosophicus*. A lie accordingly is a self-contradiction (or a pretense); needless to say, one is a logical, the other a behavioral concept.

The effect of this insight is that we see the impact of Religion upon Nature is neither circumstantial nor casual. More importantly the impact of Religion upon Nature is not ideological, and even more importantly, it has nothing to do with premodern, nonscientific theories. The "and" in the title of the treatise (*Religion and the Order of Nature*) is, as we said, internal; it is symbolic, suggesting a sacred, divinely given unitive relation. The order of nature is ordained by the Creator, the Supreme Being, and brought into reality by the Demiurge who is also the creator of man. All creation from the huge to the "negligible"—from nature and man to Angels and Satan—is sacred; it has to be accepted by man, but not simply as something "out there" to be exploited in his own interests as he may see them from time to time. Rather, Nature is sacred, something to be approached in awe and wonder —independent of the level and scope of human knowledge and power. The sacred order of nature is to be approached in fear and trembling; never is nature to be exploited for man's fancies nor for autotelic knowledge. (There is, of course, no true autotelic knowledge, for the word "autotelic" does not survive any careful analysis of its meaning.)

Today, however, the very idea of the order of nature seems, for modern man, idiotic, indeed blasphemous—the ultimate profanity in the eyes of the "white world" (and for the white man there is only one human world, namely, the white man's). And for him ecology, environmental concern, the planned endangering of (Only One) Earth—all this is a kind of new game, something like the vogue of J. L. Austin in Harvard and Cambridge some twenty years ago. Man, seeing himself as the Master, need only be concerned about the *logos* of the *eco* (and industry). Where, we might ask, does one fit in the order of nature? Is there an "Order of Resources"? No, we must answer, except as it is ordered about by the white man and by him alone.

The order of nature as resource, if not altogether stupid, is only the order that man chooses to impose upon it. But "man" does not mean you and I (Asians, Africans, *et al.*). "Man" is synonymous with "White Man," in this view. And he (that is, "He") decided to impose upon nature and non-white man, an order that is becoming suicidal, especially when "new science" takes charge of the *ecological crisis*.

The crisis of the modern world is only a footnote to the "nature as resource" theory. Appearances to the contrary, ecology will be conquered by advances in modern science and technology, according to this theory. The key to this hoped-for wonder is simple: Abolish the *eco* and invent a man-created Logos. Here there is no home, no *economy* (in the originary sense of the word), only industry and commerce.

And yet, the higher the scale of affluence, the deeper and ever more unmanageable and revengeful is the effluence. This is a hackneyed warning and it is quite ineffective. As we said, all major threats to human survival are entrusted to a science and technology which are expected to reach omnipotence. Strangely, though, modern man does not care much for omniscience. Perhaps there is nothing so strange here. If one really could always deal with all contingencies, all menaces, omniscience is not indispensable. The only snag is that omnipotence cannot cover time except by abolishing it. An obvious limit of omnipotence is its inability to change the past. If this is included in the idea of omnipotence (or reduced to a short history), Time itself is abolished. And that would be the end of the matter for the modern man who cannot and does not talk about timelessness. For modern man is or chooses to be historical and entertains talk of prehistory. Man makes history. Can he unmake the history he made? I raise this question, but only tentatively to suggest a point I cannot adequately formulate. However, so long as the irreversibility of time remains a fact, omniscience and omnipotence are out of man's true reach. Consider: man can and does try to unmake history—if not wholly, then certainly on a large scale. But did he make history? Can he make history today?

Professor Nasr's *magnum opus* is full of ideas and insights *absolutely* vital for our survival. Primarily for lack of competence but also for limitations of space, we will offer an elucidatory commentary on only one selected passage: "The world created by the Demiurge is not only an order or cosmos but a living order directed to the good and teleological in nature."

The Demiurge is a strange God. He is the primordial transgressor. He breaks the Primal Silence and disrupts the original unity of phenomena. The Demiurge is the archetypal Benefactor of Man and the Protector of all creation.

In the Hindu-creation myth, the Demiurge—Brahmā—is guilty of the Primal Violation: of creating another Time and another Space *and* Man. Śiva, the God of Time (and death), gives Brahmā capital punishment. He cuts off Brahmā's Fifth Head. The Guardian of the Non-manifest could not act otherwise. In consequence, Śiva is declared guilty of murder. The Assembly of Gods punishes Śiva. He is to live for a time by collecting alms with the skull of dead Brahmā as his begging bowl. We have here a strange, even absurd, account of the creation of man.

Primordial creation is both benediction and benefaction. And also the Original Sin which, in the Hindu tradition, is committed by the Creator himself, in contrast to the Christian tradition where the Original Sin is of Adam and Eve, the Primordial Pair. For the Hindu tradition, the idea of redemption belongs to the sin and not necessarily to the sinner. And so Śiva had to live for a time on alms which the God had to beg Himself. It must always be remembered that there is a sense (in traditional thinking) in which all thought and all action are ultimately absolute, in that an ordained consequence must follow.

All sin, that is, the very idea of sin, arises from the non-acceptance of the Absolute. And so modern man rationalizes everything, making the Relative into his (pseudo-) Absolute. For contemporary "thinking" modernity and modernization are absolute, timeless values for contemporary colonial people. Without this pseudo-absolutization of the fancies and fantasies of the brute power (*sans* authority) of the white man, human authority (in its own name, or in the name of a "superior race") cannot be absolutized, unless Man himself becomes omniscient and omnipotent—a cherished and impossible dream that modern man cannot give up.

For man—and modern man especially—omniscience and omnipotence may not suffice even if the possibility were granted of taking care of the internal tension between the two concepts. First, omniscience logically and even more so praxiologically, implies, if not presupposes, omnipotence. The reason is that whatever one comes to know by omniscience entails: (a) it is all that can be known; and (b) that the knower has the knowledge *and* certainty that it is all that is there to know. There is, of course, the problem of the certainty of both past and future (it may be cutting things too fine to include the present). Omniscience, therefore, clearly generates insoluble problems and impossible tasks, at least as far as past and (even) present are concerned. It may be objected that all this concerns the non-initiate. That may be true, but if the omniscient is his own authority, then he can be certain about his omniscience. One only has to remember that omniscience is a strictly closed, one may say, an impenetrably *dark space* and atemporal time. If this can be broadly accepted, the problem of omniscience and the problem of omnipotence remain a dark area. There is, I think, no need to offer a separate analysis of omnipotence.

What is involved here is the necessary infinitude of both the manifest and the non-manifest. There need be nothing strange or recondite about this statement. The idea of finitude or limit presupposes that of the limitless, the infinite. Finitude cannot be understood otherwise than as a modality of limit, which (limit) by itself cannot be given a "definite" meaning without presupposing the infinite. As Coomaraswamy points out, omniscience and omnipotence are both limited and confined to the manifest. What *remains*, the non-manifest, the Uncreated, is beyond all possibilities, measurable and immeasurable.

Pure creation would be residueless. It is impossible to claim that the infinite is Uncreated while the created alone is finite. Creation is always burdened with residues (which are unending by virtue of their necessary birth from the infinite). In the myth of Śiva, Brahmā, the *Dēmiourgos* cannot but sin. Brahmā (the Creator) is punished by Śiva who does what was to be done. This was Śiva's duty; it was Śiva's *dharma*. And this duty entailed the primordial, cardinal sin of Brahmācide. And so Śiva was punished. He had to atone for his cardinal sin. The sin had to be redeemed, and Śiva was redeemed by virtue of his travails.

As "fruits" and "creatures" of the primordial sin of the arch-creator, namely, the sin of violating the Uncreated, we have our original, primal *dharma* of remembering the Uncreated and moving towards the Origin. All *askesis* is a backward movement towards the Uncreated, the inviolate. Human *askesis*, at its deepest, is *repentance*, that is, Being in One's Right Mind. Our self-redemption movement, *askesis* or *Sādhanā*, is available in terms of possibility. It is a silent, backward movement—to the Origin. This does not—cannot—make rational sense. Naturally. For Origin is what one leaves "behind." It is impossible to unite with one's own Origin or even to see what such a personal unity with one's origin could mean. It is no *use* pointing out that this movement is not a matter of Time and Space. Is not human *askesis* a transcending of temporality and spatiality? I am not sure that the Grand Originator is here charged with sin, even though the Original Sin in the Hindu tradition is not of man but of the Creator who has, for this purpose, to disturb the Supernal Majesty of the Uncreated. Śiva avenges and beheads the creator. And in turn He has to atone for this by serving time under conditions not so much hard as demeaning for anyone. As for Lord Śiva—he alone atones—and the myth makes it clear that the Greatest of the Hindu Gods, Śiva, is the Lord of Death and simultaneously of the Great Emancipation for the believer, the *mumuku*. Clearly the dharma of Śiva is to avenge the primordial sin of Brahmā, but it does not follow that Man is born in sin since the relation of man to the Creator is not filial.

Brahmā is immediately avenged by Śiva who is the Lord of Death. Śiva cuts off Brahmā's head. This is Brahmācid, the highest sin. And Śiva has to repent and suffer the penitence, but not at all as a repentance for the "sin" he committed. His act came in response to his duty flowing from his being the Lord of Death. Creation is thus a fractured reality and is bound to remain so under all circumstances, for it follows from the logic of creation *ex nihilo*.

An order, we said, is necessarily asymmetrical. A teleological order repeats this asymmetry. Without using the means-end vocabulary (which in this and many other contexts is vulgar), one may certainly say that the *telos* is the specific asymmetry that defines a given order. Without a given and freely accepted *telos* this asymmetry is a threat to the life and working of an order.

The key words in the succinct formulation of this teleological relation are, therefore, not means-end, but *cosmos* (order) and *living*. The Cosmos is not only a significant whole—at whatever level and with whatever its dimensions may be, the most significant thing here is that it is (strictly) a whole and so it is holy—and no less significant than other aspects of the cosmic reality, it is also an ordered whole and *living* and teleological. Each of the three cardinal aspects of the cosmos is important and definitive. The whole is not only an aggregate. Indeed, a totality can be just that—a number of things which one wishes to refer to as forming *some kind* of unity—and nothing more. In fact, in light of this, some may distinguish between mere totality and a whole, an aggregate in terms of chance as distinguished from something bound by a purpose. However, I, for one, would not see the general point, for in the context of the Nasr Sentence to treat the whole either merely as an aggregate or a totality would be to miss altogether the level of Nasr's book.

An ordered whole (and eventually the concept of order itself) must presuppose, if not imply, a whole of one kind or another. The argument that follows endeavors to avoid a blanket presupposition of wholeness in the logic of the idea of order. It should be mentioned that ultimately in any non-anti-trans-existential context, the holiness of order is necessarily entailed—except in a context divorced from man's humanity which entails transcendental realms.

With reference to asymmetry as necessarily implicated in any concept (and theory) of order, I am presently unsure about it. Indeed this is the old problem of the labyrinth: it seems to me that if the symmetry of the labyrinth were perfect, airtight, the possibility of an actual way could not be admitted. Even so, I feel that the ultimate logico-dialectical asymmetry originates with, or indeed is inherent in the relationship of the creator, creation and creatures. From time immemorial man or superman has denied his creaturehood. The well known Indian mythological story of king *Trishanku* and sage *Vishwāmitra* illustrates this. This story uncovers the inherent weakness of the twin concepts of omniscience and omnipotence which, as pointed out earlier, are confined to the manifest and do not extend to the non-manifest. It seems to me that a symmetrical order entails reversibility and this possibility is cancelled by the reign of Time.

In any case, Nasr's full phrase refers to an order which is living and teleological. This already implies that if man is cannot reverse time (in the full sense of reversibility) then a living order has to be teleological. In this context the teleological dimension of human life is one of the necessities of a *living* order; without *telos*, there could be no humanity in man's life.

In many ways, the key word here is the adverbial adjective "living" (as in "living order"). If I could be allowed to distinguish between an active and a passive adjective, "living" qualifies "order" in two ways. First, the order here in question is highly responsive. "Response" is vitally distinguished from "reaction," since a reaction (notwithstanding the presence of the word "action") is passive, indeed even mechanical, if not automatic. A response, on the contrary, is an active, well-considered manner of dealing with a given situation. A response is ever free; a mere reaction is unfree, being an unthinking, mechanical, and hence a dead "response" to an inter-human situation (and this includes interaction between man and animal, especially the tamed ones). Thus, "living" must be seen as qualifying "order" in the sense of "response" and not "reaction."

At this point too one has to face the problem of the nature and necessity of the *telos* of the creation. One can, of course, say that the asymmetry of human time entails a *telos*. But is that *telos* death? The problem is, then, whether the mortality of the man creates a chaos rather than a cosmos. In other words, the irreversibility of (human) time seems to negate any freedom in (human) teleology through the necessity of death. This seems to cancel the sense in which you and I can respond and act freely and positively. It turns the living order of response into mere reaction, our cosmos into a chaotic illusion. Yet, I must have faith in the ultimate goodness of the creation—in other words, faith in the ultimate Truth, which is a monadic of man and the cosmos. It is this Truth which answers the dilemma of "living order," and shows the latter to have a positive existence.

The Truth is what is true. "True and false" is unlike all other pairs. It is unlike good and evil, where the evil too is a matching power even more powerful. Truth is truth, is truth. Truth is cosmo-existential. "False" is not an antonym of truth, only a limitation of ordinary language. To posit false as the opposite of truth would not hold the day, for the false, the untrue or untruth, has no positive *locus standi*. Unlike good and evil, where the latter too could have a powerful positivity, falsehood does not and cannot have any kind of positive status. Indeed, paradoxically, a false statement must itself be believed to be true in order to serve its purpose as false, whereas evil does not have to be non-evil in order to be evil. Thus the grammar and syntax of falsehood do not support any theory of its positivity, for this very positivity would necessarily and automatically make the falsehood in a real sense "true." As far as I can see and argue, truth is *ipso facto* true—absolute in the sense that its negation itself has to be true. If this leads to a paradoxical situation, so be it.

This hierarchical Firstness of Truth in the traditional triad of Truth, Goodness, and Beauty is designed to encapsulate the whole life-endeavor of man *qua* man. This rather quaint-looking use of the Firstness of Truth is, however, derived from Peirce.[3] In Peirce, broadly speaking, firstness is a non-mediated experience; whether or not there be any such experience is not the point. Even when one holds that all our experience is mediated, the possibility of non-mediated experience is thereby already posited, whether or not there is in fact any such reality. Indeed, spiritual *askesis* in some traditions (say Hindu and Buddhist) is often seen as the goal of human *askesis* (*Sādhanā*).

In the triad of Truth, Goodness, and Beauty a hierarchical relation among the three is necessarily posited. As Coomaraswamy told Eric Gill: "Take care of seeking, finding and seeing the Truth in any given context. And Goodness and Beauty will take care of themselves."[4] How so? Coomaraswamy's primary truth and Peircean Firstness (and Secondness and Thirdness) are, contrary to appearances, wholly compatible—on the basis of the transcendental theory of symbolism, which I see as the only theory.

I do hope that this formulation is not, in any significant way, incompatible with the traditional hierarchy of the four *Purusārthas* (cardinal Ends of human life). Namely, these are *Dharma, Artha, Kama,* and *Moksha*—the life of desire and its fulfillment; the life of pursuit of establishing oneself in a reasonably comfortable living; and the life of *askesis*, working towards the attainment of absolute freedom, *Moksha*.

There are grounds (or reasons) for this hope. First, sensation and intuition, upon which are based Peirce's Firstness, Coomaraswamy's primary truth, and the traditional hierarchy, belong semantically to the same family. What may be called sensory or sensate knowledge (or better, information) is the same as Kierkegaard's aesthetic level of human life (the other two levels being the ethical and the religious). The essential thing here is to remember that the lower level is always pregnant with the higher, and that the higher is all the time threatened with a fall through the pride or the persistence of the lower within the higher as a residue.

And so the asymmetry inherent in a living order, even when it is cast as a hierarchy, is redeemed by the *hieros*. In the living order, teleology again is redeemed by the Unknown and Unknowable *Hieros*. Unless and until man's *telos* be transformed, transmuted by the (Divine) Logos, no hierarchy can be definitively saved. The ultimate Release is a Leap. The essence of any genuine teleology is the *Logos* itself. Otherwise the *telos* can become a breeding ground for human pride, and the cosmos of response in the living order become a chaos of reaction.[5]

A. K. SARAN

INDIA
MARCH 2000

NOTES

1. Seyyed Hossein Nasr, *Religion and the Order of Nature* (Oxford: Oxford University Press, 1996), p. 85.

2. Here are two texts on omniscience and omnipotence. Each is from a cardinal authority of traditional thinking and scholarship:

"It is, of course, 'only as it were with a part of himself' (BG xv.7) that the Supreme Identity of Being and Nonbeing can be thought of as Omnipresent, Omniform, Omniscient. For Omniscience can be only of the possibilities and actuality of manifestation: of what remains (*ucchiam*, AV xi.7, etc.) there can be neither science nor omniscience, and it is from this point of view that, as Erigena justly remarks, 'God does not know *what* he is, because he is not any what' (cf. Buddhist *ākimcaññā*). It is only his possibilities of manifestation that become 'whats' of which there can be science or omniscience."

> [Ananda Kentish Coomaraswamy, *Coomaraswamy 2, Selected Papers—Metaphysics*, ed. Roger Lipsey (Princeton, N.J.: Princeton University Press, 1977), p. 60.]

"All these views are centred on the fundamental thesis of Śaṅkarācārya, viz., that omniscience, omnipotence, etc. are not *really* predicable of the Supreme Being. It is after and through the operation of Cosmic Nescience that these are attributed to Him. Since His essence is knowledge itself, it is only by a metaphor that He may be called all-knowing. Omniscience and omnipotence are, therefore, pseudo-real concepts and not real."

> [Gopinath Kaviraj, *Aspects of Indian Thought* (Burdwan: The University of Burdwan, 1966), p. 27.]

With this foreword let me return to omniscience and omnipotence. Kaviraj sees it with concentrated insight and astounding universal scope. Quoting Śaṅkarāchārya, he denies omniscience and omnipotence, even to *Supreme Being*.

But today, science—natural, social, anthropological, mathematical—is constructed and ordained to serve omniscience and omnipotence; God (if there be One) may or may not attempt to accomplish this. Modern science and technology are hell-bent to pursue and achieve.

What about the view of Coomaraswamy? Does it not conflict with our strictures on the idea of the human attainability of omniscience, and, apart from that, with the impossibility of understanding the idea for man? I think the Coomaraswamy passage steers clear of the problematic here presented. He says: "It is, of course, 'only as it were with a part of himself' (BG xv. 7) . . ." op. cit., p. 60, n. 37.

The formulations of Coomaraswamy and Kaviraj may *seem* to differ on one point. Coomaraswamy seems to concede that with reference to the Manifest, omniscience and omnipotence may be possible, but emphatically impossible if one thinks of the Non-manifest. Regarding the latter, no knowledge and no power is at all conceivable and so ruled out.

The seeming difference between the two formulations vanishes when one remembers that the Manifest is born out of the Womb of the Non-manifest. And excepting that one has power over the Non-manifest one can have no worthwhile power over the Manifest. Then again, one can have knowledge of the Manifest, past, present, and future (assuming the last has an authentic existence). This knowledge must be related in a certain manner; when there is a given relationship the future follows, and if it is not as predicted by the omniscient, there has to be an intervening variable which ought to have been known to the omniscient. If the omnipotent intervenes and disturbs the knowledge of the omniscient the two are working at cross purposes.

The modern age defines itself by its Faustian will to know at all costs—I shall know all or shall not live—and by its Promethean will either to possess all or assert that life is not worth living. Modern Science and its latest advances are a promise of the fulfillment of a Faustian will—never mind whether the Faustian Spirit is hellish. The Universal White Imperialism is a modernization of the ignorant people, Asian and African; modernization here is seen, following Husserl, as the "humanization" of non-white peoples toward self-chosen slavery to the white West. All modern science—physical, chemical, zoological, anthropological—hides in its inner spirit this grand intent. The message to the East is: Be the willing slaves of the White.

There is another aspect of the twin concepts—omniscience and omnipotence:

the omniscient person can know the past, the present, and the future of a given world, small or vast. He can by virtue of his omniscience envision the past, the present, and the future of a given and presumably unchanging present, but the present is, by definition, just a moment and thus a continually vanishing present. By omnipotence he can affect the present and the future. Even here there is a huge problem in how to deal with the sheer moment that the present is. The exercise of power over the moment runs into trouble because the purpose of this kind of exercise of power would be based on the totality of the concatenation of each passing moment. And once the moments are changed then this can change the future, but then it would be an unknown future which *eo ipso* falls outside both omniscience and omnipotence.

As to omnipotence, it is totally powerless over the past. Does the omniscient have memory? By the logic of omniscience memory is abolished, since, for the omniscient being, the distinction between past and present and future is lost.

The ideas of omniscience and omnipotence have persisted in human history and mythology. They seem to be a kind of superstition. If every thing is like a cinema reel, there would be no purpose in knowing them, since they already exist and no action could change them. Maybe in order to avoid this logical result, the idea of omnipotence has been invented to give "meaning" to the idea of omniscience. That is perhaps why the Hindu Avataras never act: they playact (*Līla*). This is a view maintained by some scholars of Buddhism: The Buddha acts in a *Nirmān Kāyā.*

3. Peirce writes: "The idea of First is predominant in the ideas of freshness, life, freedom. The free is that which has not another behind it, determining its actions; but so far as the idea of the negation of another enters, the idea of another enters; and such negative idea must be put in the background, or else we cannot say that the Firstness is predominant. Freedom can only manifest itself in unlimited and uncontrolled variety and multiplicity; and thus the first becomes predominant in the ideas of measureless variety and multiplicity. It is the leading idea of Kant's 'manifold of sense.' But in Kant's synthetic unity the idea of Thirdness is predominant. It is an attained unity; and would better have been called totality; for that is the one of his categories in which it finds a home. In the idea of being, Firstness is predominant, not necessarily on account of the abstractness of that idea, but on account of its self-containedness. It is not in being separated from qualities that Firstness is most predominant, but in being something peculiar and idiosyncratic. The first is predominant in feeling, as distinct from objective perception, will, and thought." Charles Sanders Peirce, *Collected Papers*, vol. I, ed. Charles Hartshorne and Paul Weiss (Cambridge, Mass.: Harvard University Press, 1960 [1931]), pp. 148–49.

4. This is from the correspondence of Ananda Kentish Coomaraswamy and Eric Gill. In a letter to Coomaraswamy, Gill suggested that in the triad of Truth, Goodness, and Beauty the most important is Goodness, given which Beauty and Truth will follow. Coomaraswamy wrote back to disagree: "No, it is Truth that is primary and essential; Seek Truth and Goodness and Beauty will be added unto it." This letter is not included in the Lipsey edition of Coomaraswamy's correspondence. It is in an earlier collection of Coomaraswamy's correspondence by Durai Raja Singam.

5. Kumar Ajai Srivastava, Research Assistant to the *Collected Works* of Saran Project of the Central Institute of Higher Tibetan Studies, Sarnath, Varanasi (India) has spared no trouble and has worked overtime to make my draft of this essay into something respectable and reasonably free of inconsistencies, repetitions, and other blemishes. Far more significant is his positive contribution to my thinking and the draft of this essay. Thanks would be incommensurate with the importance of what he has done for me and for this brief contribution to the *The Philosophy of Seyyed Hossein Nasr*—the latest work in the Library of Living Philosophers.

I pray for God's Grace for his continued advance in this direction. May God's Grace let him overcome difficulties and disturbances so that they do not prove too much for his intellectual work.

REPLY TO A. K. SARAN

Professor Saran is the leading traditionalist philosopher of India today and has been deeply immersed for several decades not only in various schools of Hindu and Buddhist philosophy but also in the thought of Guénon, Coomaraswamy, and Schuon and traditional metaphysics and the perennial philosophy of which they have been the greatest expositors in the West during the twentieth century. Saran therefore shares a great deal with me in philosophical interest and perspective, and over the decades we have had much intellectual exchange both through direct discourse and by reading each other's works. I mention this point to emphasize that Saran is well acquainted with my writings even though he has chosen to comment on only a single sentence. Moreover, his somewhat cryptic comments, many in the form of allusions, assume familiarity with the vast knowledge which he possesses of both Indian and Western thought that he perhaps assumes to be also common knowledge for others. This is probably not so in many cases, but as far as I, the respondent, am concerned there certainly does exist this treasury of knowledge shared by us. I am therefore able to read in many cases between the lines and surmise the unwritten teachings to which he is alluding. In my response, however, I shall limit myself to what is explicitly written rather than comment upon the unwritten teachings to which he refers indirectly in certain parts of his essay.

At the beginning Saran refers to my *Religion and the Order of Nature* as my *magnum opus*. This affords me an opportunity to say something about the place of this work in my writings. As far as my books and monographs are concerned, they can be divided in several ways, one of which is to divide them into two categories: one dealing with some aspect of Islam, its culture, philosophy, science, art, and the like, and the other with general philosophical and metaphysical subjects not solely connected with Islamic studies. I, myself, accept this as a possible categorization if it be remembered that each category is also related to the other. My general works refer often to Islamic teachings and my works dealing more specifically with Islamic subjects have many references to other philosophies and religions. Furthermore, the traditional perspective and the perennial philosophy determine the framework and matrix of all my books and monographs in both categories. Now, as far as the second category dealing with general and universal subjects is concerned, I would say that *Religion and the Order of Nature* is one of my most important works, crowning the series of works I have written on the subject of the relation between religion or the sacred and science and nature, works such as *Man and Nature* and *The Need for a Sacred Science*. But as far as the metaphysical and philosophical foundation of my thought is concerned, it is *Knowledge and the Sacred* that is my principal work and to which the honorary title of *magnum opus* should be given, if my humble works deserve such a title at all. In any case, *Religion and the Order of Nature* remains one of my most important books considered within the second category or among all of my writings.

Saran makes a very perceptive comment about the use of "and" in the title of this book and points out that the meaning of this "and" is not as a connector but as an internal modifier. He writes, "The 'and' in the title . . . is, as we said, internal; symbolic; suggesting a sacred, divinely given unitive relation." I want to confirm this profound observation and add that to understand fully the reality of religion in all its dimensions is to understand both why there is an order of nature and why this order is sacred. It is to understand why the whole of nature is imbued with sacred quality, why it must be beheld in awe and reverence, and why it cannot be exploited with impunity by man without destroying man himself.

Saran confirms my own views about the environmental crisis and the catastrophes it is causing and also criticizes as severely as I do the truncated modern vision of nature and man's relation to the environment. Instead of modern man, however, he uses the term "white man," a term with which I do not agree although I understand the background of experience in the Orient which has made the usage of this term prevalent and acceptable in certain circles. It is true that the development of a secular and later industrialized civilization violently aggressive towards nature and armed with a totally secularized science of nature took place in Western Europe and later America in the hands of the white man. But first of all there were white men such as those of Eastern Europe or Persians, Arabs, and the like, who are white but not European, who did not participate in the development of modern civilization. Secondly, in the twentieth century non-white man in certain areas began to develop an outlook as violently aggressive against nature as that of white Europeans and Americans, the prime example being the Japanese and later the Chinese. In fact modernized men in other nations, including India itself, as well as the Islamic world, would like nothing more than to emulate the white man as soon as possible in the domination and desecration of nature. I therefore believe that the use of a racial term such as "white man" should be avoided, although reference to it is understandable in a land such as India where so much was destroyed as a result of the "white man's burden." I prefer the basic distinction between traditional and modern man, or what I have referred to in *Knowledge and the Sacred* as Pontifical and Promethean man, this distinction cutting across racial lines. For the statement of Saran rephrasing Husserl, "The message to the East is: Be the willing slaves of the White" I would substitute "The message to the modern East is: Be the willing slaves of modernism."

The author writes quite rightly that in the modern world, "all major threats to human survival are entrusted to a science and technology which are expected to reach omnipotence." He then goes into a subtle discussion of the meaning of omniscience and omnipotence to which I wish to add a few comments. First of all, Coomaraswamy and Saran are completely right in that both the qualities of omniscience and omnipotence as usually understood refer to finitude and not the Infinitude which transcends both omniscience and omnipotence by virtue of its infinitude. This relation becomes clear when one refers to the Islamic doctrines of the Divine Names and Qualities in relation to the Divine Essence. The Divine Essence (*al-Dhāt*), which is absolute and infinite and even beyond the condition of absoluteness and infinitude, transcends the realm of the Divine Names which are its first Self-determination. On the level of the Names, one encounters the Names Omniscient (*al-'Alīm*) and Omnipotent (*al-Qādir*) and not at the level of the Divine Essence. However, even on the level of the Divine Essence one cannot deny knowledge of the Self by the Self, although this would not be omniscience in the ordinary sense. Omnipotence, on the contrary, does not apply as a category to the Divine Essence or Infinitude.

As far as modern man is concerned, his situation implies not only rejecting the primacy of God, if not His total negation openly, but also playing the role of God on the earthly plane. To slay the gods, as modern man has set out to do, of necessity implies also playing the role of the gods, for nature abhors a vacuum as the ancient philosophers asserted. This means in the case of modern man trying to take on the attributes of Divinity, including having the illusion of the possibility of gaining both omniscience and omnipotence. Furthermore, this hope is entrusted to Faustian science and the technology which results from its applications. The goal of the attainment of omniscience and omnipotence lies at the center of the Promethean man's vision of himself and his relation to the world about him. It is a dream that as Saran says, "modern man cannot give up." Saran also discusses the relation between the two concepts of omniscience and omnipotence which are of interest and with which I am generally in accord.

The one passage which Saran has selected from my writing to comment upon is "The world created by the Demiurge is not only an order or cosmos but a living order directed to the good and teleological in nature." He turns first of all to the meaning of the Demiurge in Hindu mythology in the form of Brahmā and recounts the Hindu myth according to which Brahmā, or the Demiurge, is guilty of the "primal violation" by breaking "the Primal Silence and disrupt[ing] the original unity of phenomena" for which he was given capital punishment by Śiva, the god of Time. And yet Brahmā is the "archetypal Benefactor of Man and Protector of all creation."

I wish to confirm the profound significance of this Hindu myth which points to the two aspects of the Demiurge to which Plato also referred. On the one hand the Demiurge commits the first aggression and sin by disrupting the primordial harmony, peace and silence of the infinite Reality, the Non-manifest, by bringing about creation. On the other hand this creation or manifestation is a benediction because it issues from the sacred ocean of Non-manifestation. Creation is at once a denial and confirmation of the Sacred, of the Absolute. In my writings I have often spoken of creation as both veil and symbol which refers to the same truth. Moreover, since the first sin, according to this Hindu myth, was the negation of the Absolute (as the Islamic tradition also asserts so categorically), Saran writes, "All sin, that is, the very idea of sin, arises from non-acceptance of the Absolute. And so modern man rationalizes everything, making the Relative into his (pseudo-) Absolute." These two statements are another way of expressing what I have said over the years about the absolutization of the relative by modern man. In recent years, I have also used the phrase, "absolutization of the transient" as being the trait most characteristic of the mentality prevalent today, as a result of which the wisdom of the ages is evaluated according to the most ephemeral and transient "values" that are absolutized, whereas in reality these so-called values change practically every decade. According to this mentality, the '60s are already a far away age, like the Middle Ages, of historical interest only, or valuable for purposes of fulfilling a sense of nostalgia among certain people.

For Pontifical man the memory of that "sin of Brahmā" is never lost. He knows that the primordial Non-manifested or Uncreated Reality was violated by the act of creation. He also knows that since he is now in the created order, his supreme duty is to remember that Divine Origin, the Absolute, and to view the cosmos as flowing from that Sacred Reality. To paraphrase Saran, the primal *dharma* of man is to remember the Uncreated, to move toward the Origin. His *dharma* is also to never confuse the relative for the Absolute but to remain fully aware that the relative, or creation, always bears the imprint of its Origin and that it is therefore sacred.

Being a thinker with a refined philosophical mind, Saran points to a number of subtle points that need further elucidation. One is his statement "An order . . . is necessarily asymmetrical." Now, such a statement should have been given much more explanation by Saran himself than the single sentence that follows. For my part I would add that his statement is not true of every kind of order but it is certainly true of the total order of nature, precisely because of the presence of *telos*. Because nature issues from the Divine Principle and returns to that Principle, there is an element of becoming and irreversibility involved in the order of nature which makes the order within it asymmetrical. Certain recent discoveries of modern scientists such as Ilya Prigogine point to the same reality on the scientific level without there being necessarily a full comprehension of the metaphysics involved. But this asymmetry of the order in nature on the macro scale does not exclude symmetrical order on a particular micro level and confined to specific domains. In a sense nature displays types of symmetric order within the larger and more universal asymmetric order to which Saran alludes. As he had said, the reign of Time in the world of becoming necessitates irreversibility and asymmetry. The cosmos cannot have an order that is both living and teleological and yet be bound by symmetric order alone.

Saran's discussion of wholeness, living nature, teleology, and truth itself contains many interesting points with which I am in accord and to which there is no need to provide a response. How can one deny the "Firstness of Truth" and that it lies at the apex of the triangle of Truth, Goodness, and Beauty which "encapsulate the whole life-endeavor of man *qua* man?" Needless to say, this endeavor cannot be carried out without the aid of Truth itself. It is this central confirmation that I believe Saran has in mind when he says, "the asymmetry inherent in a living order . . . is redeemed by the *hieros*." Indeed, without *hieros* man places himself in the position of the Divinity and through pride mistakes his being as the image of God for the origin of that image Itself. The result cannot but be ultimately self-destruction.

Professor Saran's essay is relatively short but full of profound ideas which are mentioned without much elaboration except in one or two cases. I am most grateful to him for having brought these deep issues to the fore, especially the meaning of the Demiurge, thereby providing me the opportunity for clarifying my views on them. I have not provided a longer response in order to remain in conformity with both the style and content of Saran's challenging and provocative essay.

S. H. N.

13

Ibrahim Kalin

THE SACRED VERSUS THE SECULAR: NASR ON SCIENCE

Nasr's work on science is discomforting for many. His defense of traditional sciences is seen by his critics as a nostalgic appeal to tradition with no real consequences for the current problems surrounding modern science. His unflinching attack on the philosophical foundations of modern science makes the modernists uneasy both in the East and the West. Furthermore, the evolutionary historians of science consider his notion of Islamic science too religious and metaphysical. Part of this perturbed situation comes from Nasr's rigorous assertion of the religious view of the cosmos at a time when religion as a valid source of knowledge is no longer taken seriously even by its sincere adherents. Sailing against the grain, Nasr offers no apologies for his resolute stance and insists on questioning the received meaning of science. Consequently, Nasr's approach to science from a religious point of view suggests a new way of looking at the vexed question of religion and science. This essay, however, will confine itself to a critical analysis of Nasr's concept of science both in its traditional sense and modern form.

A quick look at Nasr's wide-ranging works shows that the question of science occupies a central place in his thought. Following a twofold strategy, Nasr does not remain content with the critique of modern Western science, and presents his alternative view of science on the basis of traditional doctrines. The heavy emphasis put on the distinction between the traditional and the modern, or the sacred and the profane, runs through Nasr's work, and his work comprises many facets of traditional and modern sciences. A considerable number of his works are thus devoted to the exposition of traditional sciences, the metaphysical and cosmological principles on which they are based, and their meaning for a day and age that tends to see them as no more than superstitions and old wives' tales. The second part of Nasr's work is focused on modern science, its historical formation, its philosophical premises and claims, and the catastrophic events brought about by the unquestioned acceptance of modern science and technology. In both of these fields, Nasr stands out as a rigorous practitioner of the traditional school and presents a profound evaluation of the traditional and modern natural sciences from the point of view of traditional doctrines. This can best be seen in his insistence on the necessity of *scientia sacra* and the revival of premodern cosmologies that the traditional civilizations have produced over the centuries. Being the application of a number of metaphysical principles expounded by the traditional school, and especially by René Guénon, Nasr's critique of modern science is accordingly motivated neither by a purely utilitarian impulse nor by a mere academic and historical interest. Rather, his uncompromising defense of traditional sciences on the one hand, and relentless attack on the philosophical claims of modern science on the other, is to be seen as an encounter between the traditional and the modern at the metaphysical level as it pertains to the domain of natural sciences.

It is, therefore, important to note at the outset that Nasr's critique of modern science is marked off from the current criticisms leveled against modern Western science by its metaphysical and religious stance. According to Nasr, modern science is an anomaly not simply because we have to pay a high price by destroying the natural environment, but because modern science operates within a seriously misguided framework in which everything is reduced to pure quantity and by which modern man is made to think that all of his problems, from transportation to spiritual salvation, can ultimately be solved by further progress in science. The other cost of the scientistic fallacy is to make spiritual realities appear as unreal and redundant, or at least not relevant to the world-picture presented by modern science. In sharp contrast to this naïve belief in science and progress which has come under severe attack especially after World War II, Nasr aims at analyzing and questioning the very foundations upon which modern science as the pseudo-religion of the modern age is based. In this regard, one may argue that Nasr's work is not so much concerned with the philosophy of science in the current sense of the term as with the metaphysics of science, namely, the metaphysical framework in which science, be it modern or premodern, is to be understood and given its due place in the hierarchy of knowledge. For Nasr, it is the availability or absence of such a metaphysics that makes science modern or traditional.

Thus, Nasr's highly critical stance towards modern science can best be understood in the light of his notion of sacred science, which might be described very briefly as an application of the One and the Absolute to the plane of relative existence. In fact, Nasr's central claim is that the rise of modern Western science is not the result of some ground-breaking advancements in scientific measurement. Rather it is a direct consequence of the rise of a certain philosophy which underlies the formation of modern science from the seventeenth century onward. This claim can also be read as an extension of his view of sacred and traditional sciences which share a metaphysical outlook entirely different from that of modern science. To use a familiar distinction from the contemporary philosophy of science, Nasr concentrates his criticisms on the context of justification rather than on the context of experiment. In other words, Nasr's work on modern science is not so much concerned with the actual conditions of scientific experiment and measurement, a subject dear to many scientists and philosophers of science, as with the larger framework of meaning in which the findings and the philosophical foundations of modern natural sciences are to be examined.

In what follows, I shall give first a brief description of Nasr's defense of what he calls sacred science. By focusing on the concept of *scientia sacra*, we will be able to gain insight into the metaphysical framework in which traditional sciences, whether Hindu, Chinese or Islamic, were constructed and transmitted. The relevance of metaphysical doctrines of world religions for traditional sciences will thus form an important part of our discussion. The second part of the essay will focus on Nasr's criticism of modern Western science which, in the eyes of Nasr, is the primary cause of the secularization and desacralization of the order of nature. It is, however, extremely important not to lose sight of the fact that Nasr is not opposed to science itself but to its philosophical claims that apparently exceed its legitimate boundaries. Keeping this in mind, our analysis will also provide us with a chance to distinguish between the philosophy and the metaphysics of science with which Nasr's work is primarily concerned.

Scientia Sacra Defined and Defended

Nasr defines *scientia sacra* as "that sacred knowledge which lies at the heart of every revelation and is the center of that circle which encompasses and defines tradition."[1] *Scientia sacra*, whose Latin form Nasr insists on keeping, denotes the supreme science of metaphysics which comprises the principial knowledge of things, whereas, "sacred science" refers to the application of sacred knowledge to various domains of reality, physical and spiritual. Any science, be it natural, mathematical, or intellectual, that places the sacred at the center of its structure is sacred to the extent that it is an application of the immutable principles of metaphysics to the world of change and relativity.[2] In this regard, all sacred sciences are also traditional sciences in the sense that they apply the principles of traditional metaphysics to the scientific study of nature and thus can be called different versions of applied metaphysics.[3] Grounded in this view, all sacred sciences from cosmology to medicine share a number of cardinal principles which Nasr outlines as follows: the sacred sciences construe the world through the prism of a hierarchy of being and knowledge. The physical world is not denied as an illusion, as *māyā*, or as a shadow to be degraded in face of the Absolute. Nor is it taken to be an ultimate reality in and of itself. It is rather placed within a larger framework of meaning and significance that does not confine existence to any particular scientific construction. The traditional civilizations in which the sacred sciences were cultivated insist on the Divine origin of the world, and this view leads to a clear-cut relationship of hierarchy between the absolute and the relative, the eternal and the temporal, the necessary and the contingent. Since hierarchy implies, by definition, a multi-layered structure, the traditional sciences are essentially anti-reductionist. This explains, to a large extent, the persistence of the idea of the "great chain of being" across the traditional civilizations which do not allow the reduction of reality into a pure idea or pure matter as these terms are currently understood.[4] Instead of relegating reality to a lower plane of existence, namely to matter, the sacred sciences analyze each domain of reality in its own level, thus resting on a metaphysical framework within which it is possible to maintain the vision of the One and the many without confounding the two.

In this view, nature, the very subject matter of science, is regarded as a sacred being, as *vestigia Dei*, or as *āyāt Allāh* (e.g., as the signs of God which point to the "symbolic significance" of the world of nature). In sharp contrast to the modern view of nature which reduces the order of nature to everlasting change and impermanence, the traditional sciences look upon nature as the abode of both change and permanence. Although common-sense experience tends to see nature as a perennially changing structure, the world of nature displays also a remarkable continuity, perseverance, and harmony, as we see in the preservation of the species and the endurance of natural forms. For Nasr, this double-aspect of nature proves beyond any doubt the Divine quality in nature: the world of nature has not been left to the infinite succession of haphazard and senseless changes which admit no *telos* in the cosmos. On the contrary, nature contains in itself the principles of change and permanence simultaneously and points to a "big picture" in which all of its parts are recognized as forming a meaningful unity and harmony. As Titus Burckhardt reminds us, "the Greek word *cosmos* means 'order', implying the ideas of unity and totality. Cosmology is thus the science of the world inasmuch as this reflects its unique cause, Being."[5] Defined as such, the order of nature or the cosmos cannot be other than the reflection on the level of relative existence of a higher principle.[6]

Cosmos as a self-disclosure of the Divine can be grasped, according to Nasr, only by what Frithjof Schuon calls the "symbolist spirit" which has been lost in the modern world. The symbolist outlook shared by all the traditional sciences is based on the epistemological premise that the reality of things is more than how it appears to us.[7] Just as the reality of God is not limited to His creation, the reality of the natural world is also not confined to the analysis and classification of natural sciences. In fact, the meaning of the cosmos can be made explicit only when one sees it as more than its quantitative sum. A crucial implication of this premise is obviously the rejection of modern empiricism: since reality is not exhausted by its experimental analysis, there has to be an "intellectual" principle that organizes and guides what is experienced by the five senses. Left unto itself, the sum total of experimental data, however "thick" and informative it might be, does not constitute a whole or unity by which we can understand and describe the world. In fact, pure empiricism as a way of dealing with the world of nature is not a possibility because there is always an element of intellectual knowledge involved in any scientific enterprise undertaken.[8] In other words, the choice of the scientist to deal with a particular domain of reality by using certain scientific instruments is not a theory-free and value-free endeavor. The context of experiment, despite its operational nature, is always the context of a number of choices, judgments, and evaluations that the scientist has in the background of his work. The task of the metaphysics of science, as we observe it in the work of Nasr, is precisely to provide and clarify these principal ideas and judgments through which all natural sciences, whether traditional or modern, function. As a result of the presence of such a metaphysics, the traditional notion of experiment in the natural sciences has a field of meaning completely different from and incommensurable with its modern counterpart. That is why the traditional sciences which Nasr, together with the other members of the traditional school, defends against modern science have never allowed the rise of reductionist empiricism despite the epoch-making achievements of traditional sciences in such experimental fields as medicine, astronomy, mechanics, and alchemy.[9]

Modern empiricism or what Guénon calls "l'expérimentalisme moderne" differs completely from the traditional notion of experiment since it is not only reductionist but also flawed in its most essential assumption that theory has to be checked against the backdrop of a number of experimental conditions. Guénon puts into question this very assumption and claims that to give priority to experiment detached from the theoretical setting in which it is constructed is to reverse the relation between theory and experiment. For Guénon, it is the illusion of modern experimentalism to believe that

> a theory can be proved by facts whereas in reality the same facts can always be explained equally well by a number of different theories, and it would not be possible, as some of the defenders of the experimental method like Claude Bernard have recognized, to interpret these facts without the help of some "preconceived ideas" without which these facts remain as "brute facts," devoid of any significance and scientific value.[10]

Set against this background, the traditional sciences that employ the experimental method always function within a framework of metaphysical principles the most important of which is, for Nasr and the traditional school, the hierarchy of being and knowledge.[11] It is the recognition of this hierarchy that exists objectively and independently of the knowing subject that prevents the traditional sciences of nature from falling into the trap of reductionist empiricism.

The traditional notion of scientific experiment brings us to another fundamental issue in the natural sciences, which is the question of scientific realism. Although neither Nasr nor the other exponents of the traditional school speak about realism in terms similar to the ongoing discussion in contemporary philosophy of science, it is possible to argue that Nasr takes a realist position on the meaning and function of natural sciences. The common-sense definition of realism as the acceptance of an objective world not dependent on our perceptions is, one may claim, uninteresting and even boring,[12] and it would not be wrong to say that it does not yield any substantial knowledge about the structure of the world around us. Yet, this seemingly simple truism entails a far-reaching thesis concerning our consciousness of the world.

Putting aside the conflicting views on the subject, we may characterize this assertion along the following lines. According to a fundamental axiom expounded by the traditional school, man is in principle capable of knowing God and the world through his intellect which is a God-given faculty. In sharp contrast to Kantianism and other forms of rationalism, the possibility of metaphysics as an all-inclusive science stems from the faculty of the intellect whose function is to integrate and know the higher levels of reality. Whereas reason by its nature analyzes and dissects the world around it into fragments in order to function properly, the intellect synthesizes and integrates what has been fragmented by the work of reason. The same principle applies, one may argue, to the natural sciences in the sense that the quantitative study of the cosmos is complemented by the qualitative and "symbolist" perception of the intellect.[13]

Nasr's realist position comes to the fore with his depiction of science as an organized body of knowledge that is in principle capable of describing the world to us as it is. Guided primarily by the supreme knowledge of metaphysics, science can and does investigate the reality of physical entities as they exist objectively in the extra-mental world. This suggests that scientific theories are not mere instruments of operation by which the scientist constructs a picture of the world without having an actual grasp of it.[14] On the contrary, what science presents to us as a world-picture is in fact a true picture of the world, provided that it is substantiated by sound evidence and that it does not lose sight of the hierarchic vision of the universe. As in the case of scientific experimentalism, this minimal or common-sense view of scientific realism is supplemented by what one may call a "metaphysical realism" in that the scientific realism in question is gained not through the operation of the senses and reason alone but primarily through the intellect which is the locus of metaphysical knowledge for intellectual as well as natural sciences. The fact that science can present to us a true picture of the world is to be seen not as being due to an exclusive brilliance of scientific theories or experimental devices, but as a possibility of the intellect. It is through the intellect that we make sense of the world with which the sciences are concerned. Said differently, what makes the quantitative study of the universe possible is the intellect's ability to understand the reality of things as they are, to the extent possible within the confines of human ability, namely as the plane of relative existence in face of the Absolute.[15] It is this metaphysical component that separates realism, as it is defined here, from both positivism and physicalism.[16]

Nasr's ground-breaking work on Islamic science can be taken as an example to illustrate the foregoing points.[17] The Islamic natural sciences cultivated in Islamic civilization by Muslim scientists were based on a careful and analytic study of nature within the matrix of the Islamic revelation. The essence of this revelation is *al-tawḥīd*, the principle of unity professed by every member of the Islamic community, which underlies, as Nasr repeatedly states, the unity and interrelatedness of the world of nature. Although *al-tawḥīd* in its ordinary sense refers to the theological dictum that there is no divinity but God, its ontological and metaphysical meanings enter the picture as a corollary by construing the world of nature as issuing forth from a single source, that is, from the Divine. For Nasr, the primary goal of Islamic sciences, from medicine to geometry, is to disclose this underlying unity and to show "the unity and interrelatedness of all that exists."[18] Seen from this point of view, reality presents itself to us as a well-knit unity in which the individual objects as the subject matter of science are located.[19] A supposedly "pure" analysis of the natural world into its constituent parts does not help us understand these discrete parts because each analysis, whether scientific or philosophical, is carried out within a context in which the terms of the analysis are given. Furthermore, each part by definition requires a whole or unity in relation to which alone it can be called “part.” The distinct characteristic of Islamic sciences, claims Nasr, is to admit this pre-conceptual and relational unity as a given fact and reveal the balance between the whole and the part, and between the one and the many. This is also one of the fundamental differences between the metaphysical framework of Islamic science and its modern counterpart.[20]

Following the same line of argument, it is possible to contend that the “facts” of science are not derivable from an analysis which is thought to be detached and isolated from the multi-layered contexts of meaning. In fact, as Nasr insists upon the necessity of an all-inclusive metaphysical matrix in which any scientific activity is to be conducted, science, be it traditional or modern, represents a prime example of what Gilbert Ryle calls “thick description,” namely, the analysis of the layers of meaning within which an activity is carried out. Now, one of the merits of Islamic science is to unveil the persistence of such layers of meaning that run through the various levels of scientific activity while at the same time explicating the tacit unity and interrelatedness of natural phenomena. The “unifying perspective of Islam”[21] in which the Islamic sciences are deeply rooted defines the “facts” of science not as atomistic quanta but as relational entities that tie the entire cosmos together.[22] A crucial implication of this “metaphysics of relationality,” if I may use such a term, is the denial of pure and simple ideas which the empiricists such as Hume have conceived of as the constitutive elements of human thought. The so-called pure and simple ideas of human mind always assume a “thick” setting in which they are formed and expressed. The same holds true for the sense-data and/or sense-perception which is always embedded in a context of intelligibility larger than mere sensation. In fact, according to the idea of *aṣālat al-wujūd*, the primacy of being over essence (*māhiyyah*), which Nasr expounds in many of his writings, Being is the standing condition of all knowledge. In other words, every act of knowing, whether based on the senses or the intellect, presumes a larger context of intelligibility provided by the all-inclusive reality of Being. It is on the basis of this “existential” ground, as opposed to some physical or ether-like element, that we can talk about the cosmos as an interrelated unity.

This substantive unity, however, becomes comprehensible only through the aid of the intellect which integrates various domains of reality, distinct from quantitative analysis which remains at the steps of fragmentation and dissection. For Nasr, the remarkable achievements of Islamic sciences were made possible by the availability of such a comprehensive outlook, one that has determined both the context of experiment and justification of the traditional natural sciences.[23] This is also the demarcation line between the sacred and modern science, the latter having adopted an entirely different perspective, to which we now turn.

MODERN SCIENCE: THE TRIUMPH OF THE SECULAR

It is now common wisdom that the rise of modern science was not a natural result of some technological advancements that took place in Western Europe in the sixteenth and seventeenth centuries. The formation of modern science was rather the end-result of a number of philosophical and metaphysical changes that have altered humanity's view of nature and science in an unprecedented way. In this sense, modern science represents a radical shift away from the traditional notion of *scientia*—a shift from the sacred evaluation of nature to a secular and profane framework in which pure quantity is taken to be *the* reality. With this new outlook, nature is divested of its symbolic and sacred meaning, and the scientist becomes the sole arbiter of truth. For Nasr, the legitimation crisis of modern science stems from this new and "alien" perspective that has led, among other things, to such global calamities as the environmental crisis and the threat of nuclear warfare. Accordingly, Nasr's relentless attack on modern science is focused on the analysis and critique of the errors of this philosophical purview rather than being a "sentimental attack" on modern science itself, as is commonly and mistakenly assumed. In this regard, Nasr's encounter with the intellectual premises of secular Western science can be interpreted as an archeology of modern science whose roots go back to the seventeenth-century Scientific Revolution.

Five main traits of modern science come to the fore in Nasr's critical analysis. The first is the secular view of the universe that sees no traces of the Divine in the natural order. Nature is no longer the *vestigia Dei* of Christian cosmology but a self-subsistent entity that can be encapsulated exhaustively in the quantitative formulae of natural sciences.[24] The second feature is the mechanization of the world-picture upon the model of machines and clocks. Once couched in terms of mechanistic relations, nature becomes something absolutely determinable and predictable—a much needed safety zone for the rise of modern industrial society and capitalism. The third aspect of modern science is rationalism and empiricism as we have alluded to before. The fourth trait is the legacy of Cartesian dualism that presupposes a complete separation between *res cogitans* and *res extensa*, that is, between the knowing subject and the object to be known. With this cleavage, the epistemological alienation of man from nature comes to completion by leaving behind a torrent of pseudo-problems in modern philosophy, the notorious mind-body problem being a special case in point.[25] The last important aspect of modern science is in a sense a culmination of the foregoing features, and it is the exploitation of nature as a source of power and domination—a fact not unknown to modern capitalist society. Now we can see, in a brief manner, how these aspects of modern science figure in Nasr's critical analysis.

What came into being with the Scientific Revolution was a new way of looking at the world in the deepest sense. Nature was no longer conceived as a being of sacred significance with its own life cycle and unity, something not to be destroyed by man's desire to establish a fake paradise here on earth. The humanist ideal of bringing down heaven to the terrestrial domain was deemed possible only by turning nature into a stage in which the destiny of mankind was to be decided in isolation from the Divine dictums of Christianity or any other religion. The historic break away from the religious view of the universe marks the incubation of a modern secularism that claims to account for all the dimensions of nature by reducing it to pure quantity and a soulless machine. For Nasr, this secular view of the universe underlies the most essential characteristics of modern science. Once translated into the language of pure quantities, nature becomes devoid of any intrinsic meaning and intelligibility. All the qualitative aspects associated with the natural phenomena, such as beauty, harmony, *telos*, and intelligibility turn into what Galileo called the "secondary qualities," namely, the subjective feelings of humans with no corresponding reality in the extra-mental world.[26] Galileo's distinction between the primary and secondary qualities has also laid the foundations of modern empiricism: reality is what can be measured quantitatively, and it is only through the channel of empirical science that access to "reality" defined as such can be gained.[27] Hence, science deals with a domain of reality with no meaning and value in and of itself. As Collingwood rightly points out, this view excludes God as well as man from the world of nature in that both God and man are seen as conferring meaning upon nature *ex post facto*, thus treating nature itself as inert matter.[28] Consequently, this view leads to the glorification of the human mind as the sole locus of meaning and value, and thus slips into a gross subjectivism. Nasr rejects this subjectivism, insists on the intrinsic qualities of nature, and makes the bold epistemological claim that the world of nature, or the external world, displays certain qualities intrinsic to itself which cannot be confined to the feelings or the cognition of the knowing subject. Said differently, the qualities that we associate with the natural phenomena are not simply the results of some psychological states, but rather must be seen as constitutive of what we experience.[29] Placed within this framework, the world of nature appears to be of sacred quality in and of itself and not necessarily dependent on our perceptions of it.

This view has important implications for the so-called "bare facts," the temple of all the positivists, that supposedly replace the metaphysical and philosophical suppositions of premodern sciences with the "facts" of natural phenomena. As I have stated earlier, the myth of neutral fact, free from any context of meaning and value, has to be abandoned as inadequate. This, then, puts into question one of the fundamental premises of the secular view of nature that the "bare facts" of science leave no space for religious or artistic truth and that what is out there in the world of nature is no more than aggregates of chemical and biological elements upon which the human mind antecedently confers meaning. As Nasr repeatedly states, the projection of nature as pure *materia* is a reflection of the secular outlook of modern science in which a "suppositionless" encounter with the world is pushed to the limits of relegating nature to a structure of brute facts with no meaning and even practical use.

It is not a difficult step to take from a nature conceived as inert and essentially devoid of meaning to a nature constructed upon the model of a machine and, later with Newton, a clock. The purpose of this analogy, as we all know, was to prove the precision of modern natural sciences and to substantiate man's claim for absolute domination over nature. The myth of the determinate and predictable state of things was a necessary assumption for the operation of the natural sciences—a myth shattered by the rise of quantum mechanics and sub-atomic studies.[30] In any case, nature had to be construed as a machine in the full sense of the term so that the rise of industrial society could go ahead without any serious objection from religion or society, both of which were already made submissive to the undisputed authority of science. Interestingly enough, the very model through which the bare facts of nature were to be discovered proved to be a clear indication of the philosophical outlook adopted by modern science: "machine" or "clock" is certainly not a phenomenon to be found in nature but rather an invention of modern industrial society. Nasr sees the disastrous effects of the mechanistic view of the cosmos in this misconceived belief in science that has led to the eclipse of traditional ideas and values on the one hand, and to a number of modern disasters on the other. In addition to that, Nasr also insists that thinking about nature in terms of machines is not the best way to deal with natural phenomena. As the history of premodern sciences shows, it is possible to study and make use of nature without subscribing to a mechanistic worldview in which the intrinsic value of nature and everything in it is deemed inconsequential for the progress of human society.

The third important trait of modern science is, for Nasr, rationalism and empiricism which, in spite of their historical rivalry, complement each other in a number of surprising ways. First of all, both rationalism and empiricism, as the two progeny of the Enlightenment, reject the "Great Chain of Being," namely, the hierarchic view of the universe which lies at the heart of traditional sciences. Instead, modern rationalism constructs a world-picture within the limits of reason alone while empiricism takes a similar position by reducing reality to the least common denominator, that is, sense experience. The philosophical roots of Enlightenment humanism can thus be traced back to this epistemological straitjacket imposed upon our perception of the world by rationalism and empiricism. Secondly, both of these schools take the knowing subject, the *cogito* of Descartes, to be the sole possessor of meaning and intelligibility, thus paving the way for a subjectivist epistemology. Although the cosmology of modern science, at the hands of Galileo, supposedly invalidated the Christian view of the universe that regarded the world as the center of the cosmos, modern epistemology put the modern man back at the center by assigning to him the role of being the Promethean "creator" of the world.[31] Thirdly, both rationalism and empiricism adopt what Thomas Nagel calls the "view from nowhere" standpoint according to which man is disengaged from the world (in which he is ineluctably included) and able to see the world by himself from a God-like vantage point.[32] As I have mentioned earlier, modern rationalism, according to Nasr and the traditional school, rests on a serious misunderstanding of the notion of "reason" when it relegates the intellect to calculation and analysis. Modern empiricism, for its part, falls into a similar predicament by repudiating any principle higher than sense perception.

The fourth distinguishing characteristic of modern science is closely related to both rationalism and empiricism, and this is the legacy of Cartesian bifurcation which draws an ontological and epistemological abyss between the knowing subject and the object to be known. With this rupture, the knowing subject is veiled ontologically from the world surrounding it and bound to look at everything as an "other" including nature and "other minds." Historically, the epistemology of "othering," the inevitable offshoot of Cartesian dualism, has been one of the key factors in the alienation of man from nature and the destruction of the natural environment. It is not surprising to see that the decimation of natural resources coincides with the rise of colonialism and Orientalism, both of which are grounded in the creation of "others" as the unavoidable costs of Western domination. Nasr sees the roots of this modern predicament in the Cartesian heritage and argues very strongly for what we may call an "epistemology of unity," according to which the unity between the intellect and the intelligible is to be reasserted in order to have a genuine relationship with the world of nature as well as with other human beings.[33]

The last but by no means the least important aspect of modern science might be described as an ineluctable outcome of the preceding factors that we have just outlined. This pertains to the very context in which modern science is pursued and supported by governments, institutions and corporations. At this point, one of the most apparent *leitmotifs* of modern science is its connection with power and domination that has received a global prevalence with the consolidation of the world capitalist economy. Science as a way of gaining power and control over nature and other human beings is certainly a very strong impulse that lies at the heart of modern scientific enterprise. An important outcome of this new spirit has been the wedding between science and technology to such an extent that one can hardly speak of "pure science" anymore, a science that will not succumb to the demands and conditions of consumerist economy. Putting aside the extremely limited number of scientists who still see their vocation as a pursuit of truth and knowledge, nearly the entire body of modern science is driven by a will to power which manifests itself in the never-ending technological novelties financed by government funds and international corporations. Many critics of modern science have warned against the dangers of rapid technological change, a pace that creates a state of unbounded dependency on the one hand, and an irremediable sense of dislocation on the other.[34] Nasr sees the roots of this predicament in the very assumptions of modern science and its stance towards nature. Accordingly, any plausible solution for the persisting problems caused by modern science and technology can be achieved not by better engineering or further progress but by reconsidering the entire perspective of the modern worldview regarding nature, human life, and its meaning.[35]

By way of conclusion, I would like to state two points on the implications of Nasr's view of science. Nasr's critique of modern secular science is based, as we have seen, on his conviction that the philosophical foundations of the modern physical sciences are marred in a serious way and that their misdeeds can be countered only by rediscovering the sacred view of the cosmos. Obviously, this inference has a number of interesting consequences for the current relationship between religion and science, into which we cannot go within the limits of this study. One important result, however, is that modern science, because of the secular framework it adopts, cannot be regarded as a continuation of traditional or premodern sciences, as is assumed by many historians of science.[36] As I have pointed out earlier, the main difference between traditional and modern sciences is one of perspective and perception, not technical advancement. This being the case, the attempts to dovetail the findings of modern science with the spiritual teachings of traditional religions, as has become a widespread fashion in the recent decades, are destined to fail unless we set out to redefine the metaphysical underpinnings of science as a way of coming to terms with the world of nature. Without undertaking this colossal task, our efforts will do no more than to elevate science to a semi-religious truth or to turn religion into a scientific trope.[37] Keeping this in mind, Nasr's critical work, although it may seem too radical and uncompromising to some, is likely to be a secure starting point for a more comprehensive and plausible discourse on the relation between religion and science.

With his unyielding stance, Nasr also opens up a new avenue for facing up to the challenge of modern science without sacrificing the traditional ideas and values, and for rejecting the totalizing claims of the modern secular worldview which continue ever increasingly to dominate every facet of human life. Considering the current positions taken on science, which have been either total submission in the case of modernism or an inchoate rejection in the case of postmodernism and its associates, Nasr's critical approach offers a veritable alternative to both extremes, inviting us to a serious deliberation over the very terms of the problem. In this sense, the reassertion of the religious view of the universe and its meaning for natural sciences is indubitably of prime importance, not only for the followers of any particular religion but for the whole of humanity.

IBRAHIM KALIN

THE HUMAN SCIENCES PROGRAM
THE GEORGE WASHINGTON UNIVERSITY
AUGUST 1999

NOTES

1. *Knowledge and the Sacred* (Albany: SUNY Press, 1989), p. 130.

2. *The Need for a Sacred Science* (Albany: SUNY Press, 1993), pp. 1–2.

3. Not all traditional sciences are, however, sacred. There is always a human element attached to the formulation of traditional sciences which cannot be taken to be sacred in the strict sense of the term. For Nasr's distinction between the two, see *The Need for a Sacred Science*, p. 96.

4. The best historical account of the great chain of being is A. O. Lovejoy's *The Great Chain of Being: A Study of the History of an Idea* (New York: Harper Torchbooks, 1960).

5. Titus Burckhardt, *The Mirror of the Intellect: Essays on Traditional Science and Sacred Art*, tr. by William Stoddart (Cambridge: Quinta Essentia, 1987), p. 17.

6. Nasr gives a detailed analysis of this point in his works on Islamic science. Especially his *Introduction to Islamic Cosmological Doctrines* (Albany, N.Y.: SUNY Press, 1993) has been devoted to the concept of nature and the methods used for its study by Ikhwān al-Ṣafā', al-Bīrūnī and Ibn Sīnā.

7. This epistemological claim has far-reaching consequences for our relationship with the world and with other human beings. Unfortunately, there is no space here to delve into this important subject. One may, however, refer to Huston Smith's concise discussion in his *Forgotten Truth: The Primordial Tradition* (New York: Harper and Row, 1967), pp. 96–117.

8. In contemporary philosophy of science, this issue has been discussed around the question of whether we can have observation without theory. As the

realists and the instrumentalists alike agree, scientific observation is always theory-laden and this does not necessarily undermine the scientific validity of observation within a particular science.

9. For an illustration of this point, see Nasr's *Islamic Science—An Illustrated Study* (Kent: World of Islam Festival Publishing Company Ltd., 1976), and *Science and Civilization in Islam* (Chicago: ABC International, 2001).

10. René Guénon, *La Crise du Monde Moderne*, (Gallimard, 1946), pp. 76–77.

11. Although one may cite tens of classical books and treatises on the hierarchy of being and knowledge, two contemporary works are worth mentioning here: E. F. Schumacher, *A Guide for the Perplexed* (New York: Harper and Row, 1977), especially, pp. 15–25; and Huston Smith, *Forgotten Truth: The Primordial Tradition* (cited above), especially, pp. 34–59.

12. Michael Devitt, *Realism and Truth* (New Jersey: Princeton University Press, 1997), 2nd edition, pp. 13–14.

13. The distinction between reason and intellect on the one hand, and their unity at a higher level of consciousness on the other, are the two fundamental tenets of the traditional school. For Nasr's exposition of these terms, see his *Knowledge and the Sacred*, chapter 1.

14. For Nasr's critique of the type of scientific instrumentalism which is a version of anti-realism, see *Man and Nature: The Spiritual Crisis in Modern Man* (Chicago, Ill.: ABC International Group, Inc., 1997), pp. 25–27. At this point, it should be mentioned that Glyn Ford's defense of Islamic science, which is based on his interpretation of Nasr, appears to rest on a misreading of Nasr. Ford defines science as a social construction of natural phenomena mediated by the scientific community and society with no claim to objectivity—a thesis promulgated, *inter alia*, by Thomas Kuhn and Paul Feyerabend. In this sense, every scientific tradition, modern Western, Islamic, or Chinese, is entitled to be science notwithstanding their conflicting claims of truth and validity. It is not difficult to see the anti-realist component in this assertion: Islamic science is a valid science not because it is based on the scientific study of nature but because it is one among these social constructions that we collectively agree to call "science." As I have tried to show here, Nasr does not subscribe to such an anti-realist interpretation of science. For Ford's argument, see his "A Framework for a New View of Islamic Science" in *'Ādiyāt Ḥalab: An Annual Devoted to the Study of Arabic Science and Civilization* (Aleppo: The University of Aleppo, 1978–1979), vols. VI–V, pp. 68–74.

15. In a famous prayer, the Prophet of Islam asks God to "show him the reality of things as they are in themselves" (*arini ḥaqā'iq al-ashyā' kamā hiya*). This prayer, which has been elaborated upon by many Muslim scholars and philosophers, suggests that the ultimate reality and meaning of things can be attained only through the aid of Divine guidance. Placed within a larger context, the same principle applies to the proper understanding of the order of nature.

16. There is no intrinsic or necessary connection between realism in science and belief in progress. Nevertheless, historically, the majority of those who take the realist position have allowed some kind of a belief in progress which accounts for the linear development of natural sciences. By contrast, most of the anti-realists and

instrumentalists, notably Kuhn, Feyerabend, and Bas Van Fraassen, have rejected the idea of progress by replacing the idea of cumulative development in science with the concept of paradigm shifts that alter the very definition of science. Interestingly enough, both Guénon and Nasr reject the idea of progress as an intrinsic quality of natural sciences. In this regard, Guénon goes even further and describes the development of chemistry from alchemy and astronomy from astrology as "degeneration" rather than progress and evolution—degeneration in the principles that make alchemy, astrology, or the science of the soul (*'ilm al-nafs*) traditional sciences. The denial of "progress" in natural sciences, as this term is understood currently, is obviously the logical result of the metaphysical outlook that Nasr expounds and defends as a prominent member of the traditional school. For Guénon's remarks, see *La Crise*, op. cit., pp. 79–81.

17. Nasr has authored a number of important works on Islamic science. See: *Islamic Science—An Illustrated Study* (Kent: World of Islam Festival Publishing Company Ltd., 1976); *An Annotated Bibliography of Islamic Science* (Lahore: Suhail Academy, 1985) 3 vols; *Science and Civilization in Islam*; and *An Introduction to Islamic Cosmological Doctrines*. Nasr has also written many articles on the meaning of Islamic science and its relation to modern Western science.

18. *Science and Civilization in Islam*, p. 22.

19. Ibid., p. 25.

20. In addition to Nasr's aforementioned works on Islamic science, see also his brief treatment in *A Young Muslim's Guide to the Modern World* (Cambridge: The Islamic Texts Society, 1993), pp. 85–102.

21. *Islamic Science*, op. cit., p. 4.

22. Ṣadr al-Dīn Shīrāzī, one of the greatest metaphysicians of post-Avicennan Islamic philosophy, on whom Nasr has written extensively, depicts the natural phenomena as "pure relations" (*iḍāfah maḥḍah*) when seen in relation to the absolute (*al-muṭlaq*) and the necessary Being (*al-wājib*), which is God.

23. A thorough survey of Islamic sciences ranging from geography and natural history to physics and astronomy is to be found in *Science and Civilization in Islam*.

24. In a famous anecdote of the history of science, Laplace, explaining his model of the universe to Napoleon, declares God to be a "redundant hypothesis." For Laplace's famous reply that "I had no need of that hypothesis" see, Roger Hahn, "Laplace and the Mechanistic Universe" in *God and Nature*, ed. David Lindberg and Ronald Numbers (Berkeley and Los Angeles: University of California Press, 1986).

25. Rorty goes so far as to attribute the "invention of the mind" to Descartes and his *cogito* which has come to be the source of modern theories of knowledge and the ill-formulated mind-body problem. See his *Philosophy and the Mirror of Nature* (New Jersey: Princeton University Press, 1979), p. 17ff.

26. The distinction between the primary and secondary qualities made by Galileo is one of the foundations of the Scientific Revolution. This issue was later taken up in philosophy by Hume and became one of the pillars of modern empiricism. For the importance of this distinction, one may refer, among others, to

the following: R. G. Collingwood, *The Idea of Nature* (Oxford: Oxford University Press, 1945), pp. 102–5; Wolfgang Smith, *Cosmos and Transcendence: Breaking Through the Barrier of Scientistic Belief* (Illinois: Sherwood Sugden & Company, 1984), pp. 15–16; Alexandre Koyré, *From the Closed World to the Infinite Universe* (Baltimore: The Johns Hopkins University Press, 1957), pp. 88–109; S. H. Nasr, *Religion and the Order of Nature* (Oxford: Oxford University Press, 1996), pp. 136–138; Ian Barbour, *Religion and Science: Historical and Contemporary Issues* (San Francisco: Harper SanFrancisco, 1997), pp. 9–17; E. Burtt, *The Metaphysical Foundations of Modern Physical Science* (New York: Doubleday Anchor Books, 1932), pp. 83–91.

27. For an account of Galileo's distinction from this point of view, see Herbert Butterfield, *The Origins of Modern Science 1300–1800* (New York: The Free Press, 1968), pp. 99–102.

28. Collingwood, op. cit., p. 103.

29. On the traditional school's view of quality and quantity as two philosophical categories, see René Guénon, *The Reign of Quantity and the Signs of the Time*, trans. by Lord Nortbourne (London: Luzac and Company Ltd., 1953), pp. 19–32.

30. The idea of determinism and prediction has been influential not only in the natural sciences but also, and more perniciously, in the social sciences. The best example of this is social Darwinism and behaviorism as evidenced in the work of Pavlov in the former Soviet Union and that of B. F. Skinner in the United States. Set against the background of their ideological assumptions, both the experiments of Pavlov and Skinner's *Beyond Freedom and Dignity* present an interesting example of will to power and domination: both claim to have discovered the "technology of behavior"—a much-needed device for any oppressive political system. For William Barrett's analysis of this anomaly, see his *The Illusion of Technique: A Search for Meaning in a Technological Civilization* (New York: Anchor Books, 1979), pp. xi–xv.

31. The tragic consequences of Promethean humanism have been noticed by many philosophers of the West as well as the East. Nasr has written on the subject extensively, employing a rigorously critical language. Among others, Heidegger, in his celebrated attack on humanism in *Letter on Humanism*, offers a scathing criticism of Western humanism which has turned man, according to him, into a slave of his own inventions.

32. "The attempt is made to view the world not from a place within it, or from the vantage point of a special kind of life or awareness, but from nowhere in particular and no form of life in particular at all." Thomas Nagel, *Mortal Questions* (London: Cambridge University Press, 1979), p. 208.

33. The idea of the unity of the intellect and the intelligible is one of the fundamental teachings of traditional philosophy and plays an important role in Nasr's writings on knowledge. For Nasr's treatment of the subject, see the first chapter of *Knowledge and the Sacred*, pp. 1–64. In the *De Anima* (430a), Aristotle refers to this idea by saying that "in the case of objects without matter, that which thinks and that which is being thought are the same, for theoretical knowledge and its knowable object are the same." See *De Anima*, translated by H. G. Apostle as

Aristotle on the Soul (The Peripatetic Press, 1981), p. 51. The main inspiration of Islamic philosophy, however, comes from *Enneads* V where Plotinus gives a detailed explanation of the subject. Although Ibn Sīnā rejects, curiously enough, the unity of the intellect and the intelligible, later mystics and philosophers such as Suhrawardī, Ibn al-'Arabī and Ṣadr al-Dīn Shīrāzī have continued to elaborate on the subject. Ṣadr al-Dīn Shirāzī has even written a treatise called *Ittiḥād al-'āqil wa'l-ma'qūl* ([*On*] *the Unity of the Intellect and the Intelligible*) published in *Majmū'a-yi rasā'il-i falsafī-yi Ṣadr al-Muta'āllihīn*, ed. by Ḥamīd Nājī Iṣfahānī (Tehran: Intishārāt-i Ḥikmat, 1996), pp. 64–103. Some scholars have claimed that the idea of the unity of the intellect and the intelligible can be traced back to various passages in *Phaedo*, *Timaeus* and the *Republic* where a "solidarité d'existence" is established between the Ideas and the soul. For a well-informed essay on this subject see, J. Pepin, "Elements pour une histoire de la relation entre l'intelligence et l'intelligible chez Plato et dans le néoplatonisme," *Revue Philosophique* 81, (1956): 39–64. For a recent statement of the problem in a comparative way, see M. Hairi Yazdi, *The Principles of Epistemology in Islamic Philosophy: Knowledge by Presence* (Albany, SUNY Press, 1992).

34. There is considerable literature on the consequences of living in a technology-bound society. Among others, one may refer to Philip Sherrard, *The Rape of Man and Nature: An Enquiry into the Origins and Consequences of Modern Science* (Ipswich, Suffolk: Golgoonoza Press, 1987); Jacques Ellul, *The Technological Society*, tr. by John Wilkinson, (New York: Vintage Books, 1964); William Barrett, *The Illusion of Technique* (cited above).

35. Nasr has devoted two separate books to the analysis of this crucial subject. See his *Man and Nature: The Spiritual Crisis in Modern Man* and *Religion and the Order of Nature*, especially the last chapter. See also *A Young Muslim's Guide to the Modern World*, pp. 190–92, for the difference between science and technology.

36. *Religion and the Order of Nature*, p. 127ff; and *A Young Muslim's Guide to the Modern World*, pp. 181–82.

37. Darwinism is probably the best example to illustrate this point. Although Nasr gives credit to the scientific evidence against the theory of evolution, his main critique is metaphysical and philosophical throughout. See his *Knowledge and the Sacred*, chapter 7. For a similar line of argument, see Titus Burckhardt, *The Mirror of the Intellect: Essays on Traditional Science and Sacred Art*, trans. by William Stoddart (Cambridge: Quinta Essentia, 1987), pp. 32–45; and Osman Bakar, ed., *Critiques of the Theory of Evolution* (Kuala Lumpur: The Islamic Academy of Science, 1987).

REPLY TO IBRAHIM KALIN

Ibrahim Kalin is well acquainted with my works and thought and what he writes about my views on sacred versus secular science is by and large acceptable to me. I only need to make a number of clarifications to complement his presentation. Before doing so, however, it is necessary to make a general comment on the subject he has chosen in relation to my works in general. Since my early twenties, I have been concerned first of all with the question of modern science, its history and philosophy, secondly with the traditional sciences at the heart of which is to be found the sacred sciences, and finally with the differences and contrasts between the two types of sciences mentioned, namely the traditional and the modern. Questions dealing with these matters have occupied my attention ever since and a major part of my intellectual life, both in the form of teaching and writing, has been devoted to matters revolving around traditional and modern sciences as well as to the challenges which the modern sciences pose for the religious view of reality in general and the Islamic in particular.

It is necessary, however, to clarify an important point here as I have done in my writings over the years. When I speak of "the religious view of the cosmos," to which Kalin refers at the beginning of his essay, this does not mean only the external understanding of religion prevalent today as a result of which this phrase means only the acceptance of God having created the world and the world finally returning to God. These truths are of course basic for understanding "the religious view of the cosmos," but they do not include all that this phrase implies. Rather, by "religion" in the term "religious view" here is meant religion in its vastest sense as tradition which includes not only a metaphysics dealing with the nature of the Supreme Reality or Source, but also cosmological sciences which see all that exists in the cosmos as manifestations of that Source, the cosmological sciences themselves being applications of metaphysical principles to the cosmic domain. The religious view of the cosmos relates not only the beginning and end of things in the external sense to God, but also studies all phenomena as signs and symbols of higher levels of reality leading finally to the Supreme

Reality and all causes as being related ultimately to the Supreme Cause. I have dealt extensively with the traditional and cosmological sciences and need not go into that issue here again; but it is necessary to emphasize how vast and rich the very concept of "the religious view of the cosmos" is in contrast to the way it is usually employed today in English, reflecting the abdication in the West by religion since the seventeenth century of its right to know the cosmos from the religious point of view.

Since Kalin uses both the terms "*scientia sacra*" and "sacred science" in his exposition, it is necessary for me to clarify once again how I distinguish between the two terms, although the second is simply the English equivalent of the first. But I have kept the Latin form of this phrase to denote the supreme science of Ultimate Reality or metaphysics as traditionally understood, while I use the English equivalent "sacred science" as science of a sacred nature of the manifested and cosmic order but rooted in that supreme science and deriving from it. The two are therefore closely associated with each other without being identical.

All traditional civilizations possessed both a *scientia sacra* which is like the sun and sacred sciences which are like rays emanating from the sun, whether these sciences were articulated and formulated in writing or not. Now, I have called modern science an anomaly not only for the reasons mentioned by Kalin, but also because if one looks at the question from the point of view of the long history of science seen globally, modern science stands out as an anomaly. Other civilizations cultivated various sciences but in those cases the domain of nature was never severed from the rest of reality and considered as a completely independent order; nor was the knowing subject or "mind" cultivating the science in question separated from higher modes of consciousness and knowledge. The sciences of nature in traditional civilizations were always cultivated within an order which was dominated by hierarchy and integration. From this point of view modern science is certainly an anomaly, even if we disregard the devastating consequence its application has had upon the natural environment or the consequence its projection into a scientistic philosophy has had for the intellectual and spiritual life of those affected by such a philosophy.

Kalin refers to my work as dealing not so much with the philosophy of science as with "the metaphysics of science." Now, it is true that what I deal with is not the same as what is treated in most modern works dealing with the philosophy of science. One would have to expand the understanding of this term to be able to include what I am saying under this heading. But the term "metaphysics of science" can also be misleading in its own way. When I speak of the traditional sciences, it is of course perfectly justifiable to refer to "the metaphysics of science" because these sciences are in fact based on metaphysical principles. But since modern science is based to a large extent on the negation of those principles, I am not in agreement with calling their theoretical basis "metaphysics" as was done by E. A. Burtt and others. I use the term "metaphysics" only in the traditional sense and believe that since Leibniz there has been little serious metaphysics within the mainstream of modern Western philosophy. Of course modern science, to the extent that it is concerned with some aspect of reality, has a metaphysical significance to which I have referred in my works, but I remain somewhat uncomfortable with the usage of the phrase "metaphysics of science," unless it be clarified as one would have to do with the philosophy of science when associated with my thought.

Kalin writes that according to me "sacred science . . . might be described very briefly as an application of the One and the Absolute to the plane of relative existence." There is an obvious error here which I need to rectify. The domain of relative existence is not the application of the One and the Absolute but a manifestation of that reality. Sacred science itself cannot therefore be the application of the One. Rather, as I have already mentioned, sacred science is the application of the supreme knowledge of the One and the Absolute to the plane of relative existence.

Kalin also writes concerning my view of sacred science that, "the physical world is not denied as an illusion, as *māyā*, or as a shadow to be degraded in face of the Absolute." This statement has to be modified in order to reflect my view of the matter correctly. First of all, since the physical world is but the manifestation of the Absolute on, in fact, the lowest level of reality, it stands "degraded" when compared to the Absolute; but in itself it is relatively real and of value because it reflects as a mirror realities of higher and even the highest order. Secondly, from the point of view of supreme knowledge, nothing is real but the Real. While emphasizing the importance of the cosmological sciences, I also accept fully and furthermore insist upon the central significance of that supreme knowledge which realizes that only the Principle *is*, as asserted so powerfully in so many Islamic sources with which Kalin is familiar as well as in Hinduism and elsewhere. The world at once veils and reveals. What I have tried to do in my works, and in following other expositors of traditional doctrines, is to point out the hierarchy of modes of knowing itself, at the apex of which stands the knowledge of the One before which all is reduced to nothingness. But then there is also the knowledge of the many in light of the knowledge of the One and acting as a ladder leading to the One. This second category concerns the sacred sciences which deal with different domains of cosmic reality, including the physical which scientists study in light of the reality of the One, and which are means of guiding those who are able to understand them to the Source of all knowledge and being—these sciences also reflecting and revealing what the monotheistic religions call the wisdom of the Creator in His creation. I do not deny the physical world as an illusion on its own level of reality, which is precious in itself precisely because it is the locus of the reflection of higher, or if one wishes to use another language, more inward realities of a spiritual order without which the physical world would cease to exist. But in the blinding light of the Divine Sun everything else disappears like a mirage and there remains only "The Face of Thy Lord, the possessor of majesty and glory" to quote the Quran. To summarize, in affirming the importance of the Lesser Mysteries, I do not wish to imply in any way that I am overlooking for one moment the supreme significance of the Greater Mysteries.

As far as my realist position is concerned, I agree with Kalin that I am a realist, but when he writes, "Nasr's realist position comes to the fore with his depiction of sciences as an organized body of knowledge that is in principle capable of describing the world to us as it is," he is omitting an important point to which I need to turn. I do believe that science, to the extent that it corresponds to some aspect of physical reality, has an ontological content and cannot be reduced to a subjective or simply "mental" mathematical pattern imposed upon physical reality. In the early debate in the nineteenth century between E. Meyerson and H. Poincaré I would take the side of Meyerson. Also I reject totally the Galilean and Cartesian idea that all qualities one observes in nature are subjective. But I do not accept that any human science of the relative order can provide complete and absolute knowledge of any part of that order. I have quoted in my *Science and Civilization in Islam* the famous prayer of the Prophet of Islam, "O Lord, show us things as they are," and have discussed the profound significance of this utterance for the understanding of the status of the sciences of the created order in Islam. In a sense, to know things "as they are," is to know them *in divinis* and no ordinary science can claim exhaustive and absolute knowledge of the relative order "of things as they are." From the metaphysical point of view, it can be said that only the Absolute can be known absolutely. The relative contains within itself always an element of ambiguity or *māyā*, in the authentic Hindu sense, which prevents relative things from being totally intelligible. This basic point has to be kept in mind in reading Kalin's already quoted statement about my realism.

Kalin's assertion that what science presents to us as a world-picture is in fact a true picture of the world must also be understood in light of what I have stated here. There is in fact more than one "true picture of the world" as the multiplicity of cosmological sciences pertaining to the same domain of physical reality exemplify, not only in different traditional civilizations, but even within a single tradition. Each of these pictures is true but not exclusively so. The only absolute science of the nature of things is that for whose attainment the Prophet prayed to God. In certain traditional civilizations such as that of Islam and Hinduism, there is in fact a hierarchy of modes of knowing the world of creation or manifestation, each mode being valid on its own level and providing a "true picture of the world" without there being contradictions, precisely because these modes do not all belong to the same level of reality and consciousness. I have had occasion to speak often of this matter in my writings, and in fact my major works on Islamic science such as *Science and Civilization in Islam, An Introduction to Islamic Cosmological Doctrines,* and *Islamic Science—An Illustrated Study* are based on this hierarchy of knowledge of the domain of existence in general and of nature in particular, as well as knowledge of the Source of all existence.

In the section on "Modern Science: The Triumph of the Secular," the author provides an analysis of my views and criticisms of modern science with which I agree fully. I only need to add a few comments. He mentions as the second feature of my criticism the mechanization of the world-picture. Now, many wonder why I harp on this point when modern physics and especially quantum mechanics rejects totally the seventeenth-century mechanistic concept of the physical world. I am certainly aware of this philosophical change, but the reason I continue to criticize the mechanistic point of view is that, although it has become abandoned by modern physicists, it is still avidly pursued by many in other sciences, even biology, and is, moreover, part and parcel of the general scientistic worldview that dominates so much of the culture of the modern world on the level of both the generally well educated classes and the populace at large.

Also in this section, Kalin writes, "Once translated into the language of pure quantities, nature becomes devoid of any intrinsic meaning or intelligibility." Now, there is one major exception to this statement which needs to be mentioned here, and that is mathematical intelligibility. In fact, nature was reduced to pure quantity by Galileo and Descartes in order to be completely intelligible from the mathematical point of view. One of the great tragedies of modern science is that intelligibility *as such* was reduced to only mathematical intelligibility, and it is precisely this reductionism which I oppose strongly. Otherwise, I understand perfectly well why a nature reduced to pure quantity is mathematically intelligible and why the qualitative aspects of nature, ontologically so intelligible, are not intelligible mathematically, and were therefore banished from the world of modern science seeking only mathematical intelligibility—and a purely quantitative, and not the qualitative Pythagorean mathematics at that. Furthermore, having studied mathematics for many years I appreciate fully the elegance and beauty associated with mathematical intelligibility and only wish that this type of intelligibility had not become exclusive and not divorced in the modern West from intelligibility in its highest sense.

Continuing in this section, Kalin mentions correctly my views about the consequences of reducing nature to pure quantity and then says that this reduces nature to "brute facts with no meaning or even practical use." For the sake of the natural environment, one wishes that this statement were correct. Alas, this reduction of nature to brute facts bereft of any innate qualities of spiritual value has had a very important "practical use." It has allowed for the creation of a science based on power and domination over nature without the least regard for nature's rights. Without this reduction of nature to brute facts and pure quantity, it would not have been possible for modern man to destroy his natural environment with such impunity that we are now facing the possibility of unprecedented environmental devastations.

With the few clarifications that I have made in my response, Ibrahim Kalin's essay serves as a quite adequate exposition of my views on sacred and secular science as well as my criticisms of modern science. Of course, this issue has an extension which concerns the present-day Islamic world and there remains the question of the reception and criticism of my ideas in that world during the past several decades concerning both Islamic science and modern science. I feel that this is an important aspect of the consequence of my views but since Kalin chose not to deal with this subject, I have also refrained from making any comments concerning it here. Meanwhile, I am grateful to Kalin for presenting a clear exposition of a major aspect of my thought and issues which have occupied me since my student days at MIT in the early '50s and which continue to do so today.

S. H. N.

14

Wolfgang Smith

SOPHIA PERENNIS AND MODERN SCIENCE

The relation of *sophia perennis* to natural science in the modern sense has been dealt with often and profoundly in the writings of Professor Seyyed Hossein Nasr. The considerations of the present article will take Professor Nasr's Gifford Lectures as their starting point.

In 1981 a forty-seven-year-old Iranian arrived in Edinburgh charged with a mission to "promote and advance," in accordance with the last request of Adam Lord Gifford, "the true knowledge of Him Who is, in Whom we live and move and have our being, and in Whom all things consist, and of man's real relationship to Him Whom truly to know is life everlasting."[1] The invited speaker had but recently escaped the ravages of revolution in his native land. He had suffered, among other things, the loss of his library, and of the notes he had compiled in preparation for the lectures. After spending most of his energies to reestablish a life for himself and his family in the United States, it was in the early part of 1981, while commuting between Boston and Philadelphia, that he wrote the complete text in a period of about three months, practically one chapter a week. Seyyed Hossein Nasr is, moreover, the first Muslim Gifford lecturer. But the most unusual thing about the Gifford Lectures delivered at Edinburgh in the spring of 1981 is the fact that they gave voice, not to the beliefs of some distinguished scholar, or a man of genius, even, but to the perennial traditions of mankind.

The very first sentence presents what could well be termed their central thesis: "In the beginning Reality was at once being, knowledge, and bliss (the *sat, chit,* and *ānanda* of the Hindu tradition or *qudrah*, *ḥikmah*, and *raḥmah* which are among the Names of Allah in Islam), and in that 'now' which is the ever-present 'in the beginning,' knowledge continues to possess a profound relation with that principial and primordial Reality which *is* the Sacred, and the source of all that is sacred."[2] An entire metaphysics, clearly, is alluded to and in a way implied by that opening statement; and that metaphysics, to be sure, is none other in essence than the *sanātana dharma* of the Hindus, or what in the Western tradition has been named *philosophia priscorium* or *prisca theologia* (Marsilio Ficino), *vera philosophia* (Gemisthus Plethon), and *philosophia perennis* (Agostino Steuco) by turns.[3] However, given the anti-traditional bias of *modern* philosophy, not to mention the state of contemporary theology, the term *sophia perennis* will perhaps be the least misleading. The important thing to bear in mind is that this *sophia* or wisdom, when perceived from its own point of view, "is understood as the Sophia which has always been and will always be, and which is perpetuated by means of both transmission horizontally and renewal vertically through contact with that Reality that was 'in the beginning' and is here and now" (KS 71), as Nasr explains. It is a prime contention of the lectures that this perennial and universal wisdom is to be found in the dominant premodern traditions, from Hinduism, Buddhism, and Taoism in the East to the mystery religions of ancient Greece and the sapiental strains within Judaism, Christianity, and Islam. The modern West, on the other hand, is perceived in this optic as an aberration, a dangerous cultural and spiritual anomaly resulting from a major "fall."

The content and purpose of the lectures can now be described: it is to unfold the main elements of the *sophia perennis*, to document their presence within the traditions, and trace the salient stages of the descent into modernity. But there is more; for it happens that our century has witnessed, not only an unprecedented alienation from the perennial wisdom, but also a no less singular rediscovery and articulation of that same *sophia perennis*. As Nasr points out: "The principle of cosmic compensation has brought to the fore the quest for the rediscovery of the sacred during the very period which the heralds of modernism had predicted to be the final phase of the depletion of human culture of its sacred content, the period whose dawn Nietzsche had declared a century ago when he spoke of 'the death of God'" (KS 93). And so, to complete the picture, the lectures contain a chapter devoted to this compensatory phenomenon, which chronicles the rediscovery and revival in the West of the sapiental tradition. However, what Nasr does not tell us, for reasons that can be surmised, is that these very Gifford Lectures constitute a major manifestation and prime example of that rediscovery, that same revival. For the first time in modern history, I would venture to say, the undistorted and unadulterated voice of the perennial and universal tradition could be heard within the prestigious halls of academe.

It is a main point of the lectures that *sophia perennis* is intimately connected with "science" in a broad and distinctly premodern sense. "Sacred knowledge must also include a knowledge of the cosmos," Nasr maintains; and in fact, "one can speak of a *cosmologia perennis* which, in one sense, is the application, and in another, the complement of the *sophia perennis* which is concerned essentially with metaphysics" (KS 190). One can say that every science, traditionally conceived, is an application of the perennial metaphysical wisdom by virtue of the fact that "all laws are reflections of the Divine Principle" (KS 196), and a complement inasmuch as it constitutes *de jure* a support for the contemplation of the Principle itself. The traditional sciences, thus, are based upon the premise that the cosmos constitutes a theophany, and that, in the words of St. Paul, "the invisible things of Him from the creation of the world are clearly seen, being understood from the things that are made" (Romans 1:20). Science in the traditional sense is thus a matter of "reading the icon"—a far cry indeed from the Baconian vision! Science, as Bacon conceived of it, is concerned with the discovery of causal chains relating one phenomenon to another, an enterprise which can lead to prediction and control; traditional science, on the other hand, seeks to relate phenomena to the reality or principle of which they are a manifestation, an undertaking that leads ideally to enlightenment. In a word, the former is "horizontal" whereas the latter is "vertical" in its quest.

However, we must also take care not to make too much of this disparity; for it is to be noted that contemporary science at its best is not quite as Baconian as one might imagine on the basis of textbook lore. Think of Albert Einstein, for example, and his occasional remarks relating to "the Old One," suggesting that he too may have been searching for *vestigia* of a kind. It is on the level of epistemological presuppositions, in any case, that the distinction between the traditional and the modern conceptions of science assumes its sharpest form. We may not know what actually transpires in the mind of a contemporary scientist, but it is nonetheless clear what *ought* to transpire, according to the accepted canons: the scientist is supposed to reason upon data or information supplied by sense perception. It is all that he is officially permitted to do, if one may put it thus. The *sophia perennis*, on the other hand, provides for an incomparably greater range of cognitive possibilities, inasmuch as it maintains that the human intellect derives its "light" directly from the Divine Intellect: it "participates" in the Divine Intellect, as the Platonists say. All human knowing without exception hinges upon this "participation," which of course admits of various modes and countless degrees, ranging from the humblest act of sense perception to ways and intensities of knowing of which as yet we have not the slightest idea. But the fact remains: What ultimately connects the human subject to its object in the act of knowing is indeed "the true Light which lighteth every man that cometh into the world" (John 1:9).

There is, however, a fundamental difference between the knowing of an ordinary man and the knowing of an enlightened sage. Both may perceive a rock or a tree; but the one perceives it as a "thing," a self-existent entity—which in truth it is not!—whereas the other perceives it as a theophany, an entity whose essence and very being derive from the metacosmic Reality. It is the first kind of knowing, moreover, to which the Vedantic term *māyā* applies, for the world as perceived by the unenlightened *is* in a sense illusory: "For now we see through a glass, darkly" (1 Corinthians 13:12). It is, however, the contention of every sapiental tradition that this generic condition of nescience can be overcome, be it in full or in part, and that this rectification can indeed be effected in the present life through what Buddhists term "right doctrine" and "right method."

These are the things which we need to bear in mind in order to understand what *cosmologia perennis* is about. The fact is that every *bona fide* premodern science is rooted in an integral sapiental tradition, replete with a metaphysical doctrine and operative means, and requires moreover an ambience of this kind if it is not to wither and die, and thus give rise to what may indeed be termed a superstition.

An essential feature of the *cosmologia perennis* which will particularly concern us in the sequel is that it views the integral cosmos as a hierarchy of ontological degrees, what in Western tradition has sometimes been termed "the great chain of being,"[4] what used to be represented in Ptolemaic days by the so-called planetary spheres. One knows of course that Western man has abandoned the notion of "higher worlds" along with the Ptolemaic cosmography—the referent along with the symbol—and has opted instead for a *Weltanschauung* which would reduce the cosmos in its totality to what in fact constitutes, from a traditional point of view, its lowest plane: the domain of ponderable matter. This, I believe, is the decisive step that takes us into the modern world. One needs, however, to recognize that the reductionist hypothesis does not stand alone, but is mandated by what Nasr terms "the inherent limitations of the original epistemological premises of modern science" (KS 206). These philosophic postulates, he maintains, plus the virtual disappearance in the West of the sapiental traditions, have prevented modern science "from becoming integrated into higher orders of knowledge, with tragic results for the human race" (KS 207).

I consider this observation to be of capital importance, and singularly worthy of being pursued in depth. The object of the present article is to lay bare the offending epistemological premise and show how modern physics, freed from this impediment and duly reinterpreted, can indeed be "integrated into higher orders of knowledge" as Professor Nasr suggests.

As is well known, it was René Descartes who provided the philosophical basis of "classical" or pre-quantum physics by enunciating the distinction between *res cogitans* and *res extensa*. One generally perceives this Cartesian dichotomy as nothing more than the mind/body duality, forgetting that

Descartes has not only distinguished between matter and mind, but has, at the same time, imposed a very peculiar and indeed problematic conception of the former element. He supposes, namely, that a *res extensa* is bereft of all sensible qualities, which obviously implies that it is imperceptible. The red apple which we do perceive must consequently be relegated to *res cogitans*; it has become a private phantasm, a mental as distinguished from a real entity. This postulate, moreover, demands another: one is now forced—on pain of radical subjectivism—to assume that the red apple, which is unreal, is causally related to a real apple, which, however, is not perceptible. What from a pre-Cartesian point of view was one object has now become two; as Whitehead puts it: "One is the conjecture, and the other is the dream."[5]

This, in a nutshell, is the fateful "bifurcation" hypothesis which underlies and in a way determines the *Weltanschauung* of modern science. The first thing, perhaps, that needs to be pointed out is that this Cartesian assumption can neither be proven by philosophical argument nor corroborated by scientific means. Whether it is indeed "tenable" is more difficult to say; however, bifurcation is in any case incompatible with the teachings of the traditional philosophic schools, not one of which has subjectivized the perceptual object in the manner of Descartes. According to the perennial consensus, we do "look out upon the world" in the act of perception, as every non-philosopher likewise believes; it is only that the world and the Reality are not exactly the same thing, which is, however, another question.

It is of interest to note that Whitehead attacks the idea of bifurcation on the ground that "Knowledge is ultimate."[6] What he means by this assertion is that the act of knowing cannot in principle be explained by reducing it to some natural process. And this position is traditional: "knowing" does not reduce to "being"; the two poles *chit* and *sat* are irreducible (and so is the third, the Vedantic *ānanda*, which, however, does not enter into our present considerations). Nonetheless, as Nasr points out: "In the beginning Reality was at once being, knowledge, and bliss. . . ." Despite the irreducibility of "knowing" and "being" on the various planes of cosmic manifestation, the two are intimately related by virtue of the fact that *in divinis* "to know" and "to be" coincide.

Here, in this principial identity, lies, I believe, the ultimate explanation of what may well be termed the miracle of perception: the fact, namely, that in this quotidian act a subject and an object meet and in a sense become one, as Aristotle keenly observed. What we need above all to realize is that the cognitive union cannot in truth be consummated within the confines of the universe, which is and remains external to the human subject. There are light waves and sound waves, and there is brain function, to be sure; and these external or objective processes do no doubt play a necessary role. But they do not—they cannot!—constitute the perceptual act; to affirm that they do would be, once again, to reduce "knowing" to "being." The act itself, therefore, transcends perforce the bounds of space, and must by the same token be conceived as instantaneous or atemporal as well. The perceptual act, thus, is literally "not of this world." Is it any wonder, therefore, that post-medieval philosophy should have succumbed to the lure of "bifurcation"? Having lost sight of the Divine Intellect and denied in effect the mystery of "participation," is it surprising that post-medieval man should have implicitly denied the miracle of perception as well?

I will now take as my point of departure the following contention: What vitiates the customary interpretation of physics and prevents that science from being "integrated into higher orders of knowledge" is none other than the bifurcation postulate. This is the hidden premise one unfailingly assumes in the explication of scientific discovery. It is true that this postulate has been uncovered and attacked by some of the leading philosophers of our century—from Edmund Husserl to Alfred North Whitehead, Nicolai Hartmann, and Karl Jaspers, to mention but a few names—and yet that problematic tenet remains to this day unexamined and unopposed by men of science even in the sophisticated arena of the quantum debate, where just about everything else has been "put on the table." However, as I have shown elsewhere,[7] the premise can indeed be jettisoned, which is to say that nothing prevents us from interpreting physics on a non-bifurcationist basis.

Let us consider what this entails. It is clear, first of all, that to deny bifurcation is to give objective status once again to the perceptible things (red apples, for instance). Corporeal objects, let us call them. The first step, thus, in the proposed reinterpretation of physics may be characterized as the rediscovery of the corporeal world. This rediscovery or reaffirmation, however, does not constitute a return to a so-called "naïve" realism, but demands a more refined and discerning ontology. We need in particular to take note of the following fundamental principle: "to be" is to be knowable. This is still realism, to be sure; clearly, it is the distinction between "knowable" and "known" that averts a lapse into idealism—the spurious reduction, that is, of "being" to "knowing." Evidently no such reduction is implied by the stated ontological principle. Every grain of sand in the universe is surely perceptible; but how many will ever be perceived? Now obviously the "naïve" realist believes this as well, and one may ask why it should be necessary to abandon or to refine this common-sense position. What is the advantage, one might ask, of the proposed principle? What proves to be crucial is the following corollary: Different ways of knowing correspond to different kinds of being, or as we shall say, to different ontological domains. For example, corporeal being is the kind which can be known by way of sense perception. There are, however, other kinds of being which cannot be known by this particular means, and this is something a "naïve" realism is ill equipped to comprehend.

So much for the first step in the reinterpretation of physics; the second—as may now be surmised—is perforce the recognition of the physical as a separate ontological domain. Over the past centuries Western man has evolved a new and unprecedented way of knowing based upon measurement and artificial means of observation, which has brought to light a hitherto unrecognized category of objects: physical objects, we shall say. I have delineated the generic *modus operandi* of this cognitive enterprise in the previously mentioned monograph; suffice it to say that the observational process hinges upon an interaction between the *physical* object and a *corporeal* instrument, which then registers the result of the interaction by way of a perceptible state. The process thus renders "visible" in a sense what in fact is not, and thereby reveals a previously unknown ontological stratum. Our knowledge of this stratum has, moreover, progressed from the more or less crude approximations of classical physics to the incomparably more refined conceptions of quantum theory, which has revealed the physical to be in reality none other than the quantum world.

There are thus *two* ontological domains to be reckoned with: the corporeal and the physical; but the quantum theorist reckons only with one! On the strength of the bifurcation postulate he denies the corporeal, and thus in effect reduces the corporeal to the physical. The prevailing interpretation of physics has thus been vitiated from the start by a systematic confusion resulting from a failure to distinguish, in theory, between corporeal and physical objects. I say "in theory," because in practice everyone does evidently know the difference between a tangible scientific instrument, for example, or any other corporeal entity, and a cloud of quantum particles; and that is of course the reason why physics has survived the confusion and is able to function. But the philosophy of physics does not fare as well. As Whitehead pointed out long ago in reference to the bifurcationist bias: "The result is a complete muddle in scientific thought, in philosophic cosmology, and in epistemology"; to which he adds: "But any doctrine which does not implicitly presuppose this point of view is assailed as unintelligible."[8] Let us hope that after seventy years of quantum debate there will now be a greater willingness on the part of scientists to consider a non-bifurcationist view of physics.

The non-bifurcationist interpretation has the immediate advantage of eliminating at one stroke what is generally called "quantum paradox."[9] There is no need any longer for this or that *ad hoc* hypothesis to make things fit; no need for "parallel universes" or new laws of logic! The one thing needful to avoid the semblance of paradox is to jettison bifurcation once and for all.

What presently concerns us, however, is something else, which I consider to be more important still: the fact, namely, that physics, thus reinterpreted, can be "integrated into higher orders of knowledge," to avail ourselves once more of Professor Nasr's significant phrase. Let us consider how this integration comes about.

Modern physics, as I have said, has brought to light a hitherto unknown ontological stratum: the physical, namely, which in fact coincides with the quantum world. To be sure, this newly-discovered realm is nowhere referred to by the traditional schools, and it is open to question whether any ancient master could have divined the presence of such a domain. But though the physical stratum does not appear on the traditional ontological charts, it can be added: its position on the map can be ascertained. As I have shown elsewhere,[10] the physical domain is situated between two traditionally defined levels: below the corporeal, namely, but above the so-called *materia secunda* that underlies the corporeal world.

Why, first of all, does the physical stand "below" the corporeal? The key idea has been supplied by Heisenberg—in *his* Gifford Lectures, no less!—when he pointed out that state vectors or so-called wave functions constitute "a quantitative version of the old concept of '*potentia*' in Aristotelian philosophy," and referred to quantum objects as "a strange kind of physical entity just in the middle between possibility and reality."[11] In a word, the quantum level (and thus, in our view, the physical) stands to the corporeal as potency to act. But it happens that the principle of order in the hierarchy of ontological degrees may be conceived in the same Aristotelian terms: it is the vector from potency to act, if you will, that defines the ascending gradation. To say that the physical is in potency relative to the corporeal is therefore to situate the physical domain *below* the corporeal.

To proceed further, we need to remind ourselves that every traditional cosmology envisages one or more subcorporeal ontological strata. Among the twenty-five *tattvas* of the Sāṁkhya, for example, it is *avyakta*, "the unmanifested," also termed *mulaprakriti* or "root nature," that underlies the rest and thus constitutes the lowest stratum. It is evident, moreover, that the physical domain, made up as it is of things that can be discerned, is in act relative to *avyakta*, and is consequently situated "above" *avyakta*, above the absolute zero, so to speak, of the ontological scale. However, a less universal and thus a sharper and more enlightening "lower bound" to the physical can be found in the Scholastic tradition, which speaks of a *materia secunda* underlying the corporeal world.[12] We say "less universal," because this material substrate is not without determination, and is therefore distinguished from *prima materia*, the Scholastic equivalent of *avyakta*. What, then, is the nature of this determination? The answer to this literally most basic question concerning the corporeal domain has been given by St.

Thomas Aquinas: the protomatter or material substrate of our world is said to be *signata quantitat*e. Here is the key, I contend, to what physics is about.

There is no better way of explaining this connection than by the example of Euclidean geometry. Let us take the Euclidean plane and conceive of it in a pre-Cartesian manner, that is to say, not as a point set, but as a substrate or potency, in which neither points nor lines have yet been defined. One can say that points, lines, and indeed, all constructible figures, subsist potentially in that plane—until, that is, they have been actualized by way of geometric construction. One sees, however, that this plane also "carries" something else: a mathematical structure, namely, which we term "Euclidean" to distinguish it from other possible structures, such as the projective, the Lobachevskian, and so forth. Now this structure manifests itself in certain geometric properties exhibited by constructed figures made up of points, lines, and circles.[13] Let us observe, moreover, that whereas geometric figures are legion—there is an infinite number of them, as mathematicians are wont to say—the Euclidean properties are few, and fit together, so to speak, to constitute a coherent geometry, a single intelligible form; and that geometry or form, of course, is none other than the mathematical structure "carried" by the Euclidean plane.

We are now in a position to understand the rationale of physics from a traditional point of view. Replace the Euclidean plane by the aforesaid *materia secunda*, constructed geometric figures by physical objects, and the Euclidean geometry by the "quantitative signature" of the *materia secunda*, conceived, once again, as a mathematical structure, and we have at hand the essential elements. What is particularly to be noted is that the objects of physics—its actual objects, that is, the kind that can affect a corporeal instrument or leave a track in a bubble chamber—are indeed "constructed," which is to say that they are defined or specified by a certain experimental intervention. This is the aspect of physics which led Eddington to stipulate that all fundamental laws can in principle be deduced on an a priori basis: look at the "net," he said, and you will know the "fish." Yes, up to a point. It is true, as Eddington has astutely observed, that the *modus operandi* of the experimental physicist affects the form of the physical laws or fundamental equations at which one arrives; but these laws or equations have also a content which does *not* derive from that *modus operandi*, even as the Euclidean properties of a constructed figure do not result from the process of geometric construction. The strategies of the geometer do of course affect the manifested geometric properties in the sense that a triangle and a circle, for example, exhibit the underlying Euclidean structure in different ways; and this exemplifies, once again, the subjective aspect of the scientific enterprise, which Eddington had his eye upon. But whereas the manifested geometric properties are indeed dependent upon the contingencies of geometric construction, they are nonetheless expressive of an objective mathematical structure, a given intelligible form in the Platonist sense. My point is that the laws of physics likewise manifest the mathematical structure of the *materia secunda* underlying the physical, and thus *a fortiori*, the corporeal domain.

I have conceived of the *signata quantitate*, in light of contemporary physics as a mathematical structure; but is this exactly what St. Thomas Aquinas had in mind? Whatever the Angelic Doctor may have been thinking, it could hardly have been the Hilbert spaces and Lie groups of Hermitian operators with which contemporary physics is concerned. We must not, however, judge too hastily. What could be more strange, for example, than Plato's idea that "atoms" of earth, air, fire, and water correspond respectively to the cube, the octahedron, the tetrahedron, and the icosahedron? What indeed could be further removed from our contemporary scientific notions? And yet, as Heisenberg has brilliantly observed,[14] it turns out that Plato came as close to the quantum-theoretic conception of "elementary particles" as was possible in terms of mathematical structures available in premodern times. The point is, first of all, that the regular solids are "made of" polyhedra, and thus of entities which have no *corporeal* existence. One could say that Plato's "atoms" are mathematical as opposed to corporeal entities; and as such, they resemble the elementary particles of contemporary physics[15] and not the atoms of Democritus, or indeed, of pre-quantum physics. But why the regular solids of Euclidean geometry? What is special about these? What is special is that they are representations of a symmetry group; and so are the elementary particles of contemporary physics! It is only that the respective groups are different. This is not to suggest, of course, that Plato arrived at his conclusions by way of some rudimentary quantum field theory. He was doubtless looking at "atoms" from a very different point of view; and yet it could hardly have been an accident that he arrived at conceptions so strikingly similar in certain respects to our own.

The relevance of this example to the question of the *signata quantitate* is evident. Obviously St. Thomas, once again, is not looking at the problem from a point of view inspired by modern physics, and certainly one must be careful not to read such things as Hilbert spaces and Lie groups into an ancient text, the *Summa* no less than the *Timaeus*. But the crucial question is whether these mathematical structures are yet "quantitative" in an appropriate sense; and if that be the case, then the *signata quantitate* admits—by transposition, if need be—the interpretation which I have given above. As in the case of Plato's so-called atoms, it is at times necessary to look beneath the surface meaning of an ancient text to discern its contemporary relevance.

What, then, is the requisite conception of "quantity"? The answer, it appears, has been supplied by René Guénon when he observed that "quantity itself, to which they [the moderns] strive to reduce everything, when considered from their own special point of view, is no more than the 'residue' of an existence emptied of everything that constituted its essence."[16] Here we have it: Quantity is "the 'residue' of an existence emptied of everything that constituted its essence."

It is clear, first of all, that cardinal number is quantity in the stipulated sense; after all, if we consider five apples, let us say, and take away their essence, what is left is no longer "five this" or "five that," but simply "five," the pure number. But it is to be noted that the notion of quantity, thus conceived, includes much else besides, and is more than broad enough to encompass the contemporary idea of mathematical structure. There is, however, something else that needs likewise to be pointed out: the tenet that the *materia secunda* of our world is indeed *signata quantitate* follows now from the very definition of "quantity" at which we have arrived. One could put it this way: What remains when all "content" has been evacuated from the universe must belong to the "container"; but that residue, by definition, is quantity.

We need to ask ourselves what it is that differentiates the physical universe from the material substrate; could it be "essences"? That position proves not to be tenable. We must remember that physical objects without exception are in a sense "constructed," which is to say that they are defined through a complex intentional process involving perforce an empirical intervention of some kind. Nothing is a physical object unless it has somehow interacted, directly or indirectly, with a corporeal entity. Physical objects, thus, are in a sense relational: they mediate between the material substrate and the corporeal plane. They have the "*esse*," if you will, of a potency waiting to be actualized in a corporeal entity; and thus, strictly speaking, they have no "essence," because they are not, in truth, a "thing." As Heisenberg has put it, they are "just in the middle between possibility and reality"; but only what is real partakes of essence.

It emerges that physics is *basic* but *inessential*; that is the crucial fact. It is basic because it descends to the material substrate, the *mulaprakriti* or matrix of our world; but for that very reason it is inessential. The essence of a plant, after all, derives from the seed, and not from the ground in which the seed is planted.

It may seem paradoxical that a science whose ultimate object is the *materia secunda* should prove to be the most "exact" of all. Has not the subcorporeal been conceived traditionally as a primordial chaos from which the cosmos is brought forth by a determinative act, a divine command or *fiat lux*? Does not Genesis refer to this tenebrous realm as a *tohu-wa-bohu*, as "without form and void," and does not Proverbs speak of it as the *abyssos* upon which the divine Geometer "set His compass" to construct the world? We need, however, to recall that physics is concerned, not with *prima materia*, but with *materia secunda*, which is *signata quantitate*. The fact is that physics derives its exactitudes from "the white spot in the black field," to put it in yin-yang terms. We may rest assured that the mathematical structure of the material substrate has been inscribed by the great Geometer Himself; Dirac was not mistaken after all when he said that "God used beautiful mathematics in creating the world."[17] One must not forget, however, that God used many other "beautiful things" besides mathematical structures, the point being that above the level of protomatter and of physical objects there are "essences" which likewise derive from the Divine Intellect. And these, to be sure, physics knows nothing about; the knowledge to which physics gives access is "basic but inessential," as I have said.

Meanwhile the black field surrounding the white spot has likewise come into scientific view; on the fundamental level of quantum theory the physical domain has revealed itself as a partial chaos—to the consternation and chagrin of the "classical" physicist. The fact is that physical systems, quantum mechanically conceived, are in a superposition of states corresponding to the various possible values of their observables, even as the tone of a musical instrument is a superposition or composite of pure tones, each with its proper frequency. What is superposed in the quantum system, however, are not actual waves of some kind, but mere possibilities or *potentiae*, as Heisenberg says, which moreover are for the most part mutually incompatible. The quantum-mechanical description of a physical system depicts an ensemble of warring quasi-existences synthetically united; one wonders whether a more perfect characterization of semi-chaos could be conceived! I say "semi-chaos," because physical objects are evidently determined to some degree, on pain of having no objective existence at all; but this determination does not cancel the aforesaid superpositional indeterminacy, which remains as a witness, so to speak, to the primordial chaos that underlies our world. It appears that quantum mechanics has penetrated beneath the plane of *terra firma* to a depth approaching the level of the "waters" alluded to in Genesis, which remain in place even after "the Spirit of God" has moved over them. I find it remarkable how many major truths pertaining to the perennial cosmology have been unwittingly uncovered by twentieth-century physics while scientists, for the most part, continue to view the traditional teachings as "prescientific superstitions."

Getting back to the quantum world, we should note that the measurement of a dynamic variable turns out—once again to the dismay of the classical physicist—to be an act of determination. Let us suppose that we are measuring the position of an electron. Prior to this measurement, this empirical intervention, the electron had presumably no position at all; it was most likely in a superposition of states corresponding to an infinite number of positions, continuously distributed over some appreciable and possibly vast region of space. And so it is until instruments put in place by the physicist interact with the electron so as to impose certain spatial bounds. The particle becomes thus confined, for a shorter or longer period of time, to a region of space small enough to count as a definite position. Now this scenario is disturbing, as I have said, to physicists accustomed to the pre-quantum outlook, which assumes that the physical object has a well-defined position, a well-defined momentum, and so forth, whether these quantitative attributes have been measured or not. But here again quantum theory stands on the side of the *cosmologia perennis*, which from time immemorial has viewed measurement as a determination, a creative act, like that of the geometer who constructs with the aid of his instruments.

Let us not fail to note that on a cosmic plane creative activity of whatever kind requires a preexistent potency. If the divine Geometer had determined everything at one stroke, there would be nothing left for the human geometer to actualize; and as a matter of fact, the world as such could not exist. As every theologian knows, God alone is "fully in act"; which is to say that all other beings partake of potency in varying degrees. On every level, moreover, this potency or indetermination plays a most necessary and indeed beneficent role. According to St. Thomas Aquinas, even the human intellect is able to perform its cognitive function only by virtue of its radical potency, whereby it becomes receptive to whatever object presents itself, even as the emptiness of a container makes it receptive to all manner of concrete things. It must not be thought, therefore, that indetermination exists only in the quantum world; for indeed, it exists everywhere, on every ontological plane of the integral cosmos; and not, moreover, as a foreign element, a kind of blemish, if you will, but precisely as the natural complement of act. This is what the well-known figure of the yin-yang depicts with such grace, and that is doubtless the reason why Niels Bohr adopted this Taoist icon as his heraldic emblem. The notion of a cosmos made of *yang* (the "white" element) alone turns out to be unfounded and unrealistic in the extreme, and one wonders how this chimerical conception could have attained its strangle-hold upon the West; in any case, it was an insufficient physics that has for centuries confirmed us in this misbegotten notion, and it is a corrected and deepened physics which now apprises us of our long-standing blunder. Here again, on this fundamental cosmological issue, quantum theory sides with the traditional doctrine.

The decisive step in the restitution of the *cosmologia perennis* is without question the rediscovery of "forms" as an ontological and causal principle. Ever since Francis Bacon and René Descartes declared substantial forms to be a figment of the Scholastic imagination, Western science has labored to explain the whole in terms of its recognizable parts, or as one can also say: the greater in terms of the lesser. And not without success! As we know, the quest has led to the discovery of the physical realm, with its marvelous mathematical structures and undreamed of possibilities. It has not, however, led towards the realization of the reductionist goal. On the contrary, it turns out that the very discoveries of science point now in the opposite direction, as is evident if only one has eyes to see.[18] Meanwhile the reductionist philosophy appears also to have outlived its erstwhile usefulness as a heuristic principle. The scientist of the late twentieth century need hardly be motivated to investigate physical structures; instead, what he needs to realize, if further fundamental progress is to be achieved, is that there exist formal principles of a non-mathematical kind which also play a causal role, to say the least. These non-mathematical principles, to be sure, are none other than the aforesaid substantial forms, which prove moreover to be "essential" in a strict ontological sense. One should add that these forms or "essences" are mutually related and constitutive of a hierarchic order. What I have termed "the rediscovery of the corporeal" needs thus to be followed by the realization that this domain is itself stratified ontologically under the aegis of substantial forms.

The most obvious and important line of demarcation is given by the distinction between the organic and the inorganic, or better said, between living and non-living substances. One knows today that the distinction between the two realms is revealed with unprecedented clarity on the molecular level, where the difference between substances becomes in a sense quantified. In light of these findings it can now be said that the "distance" between the inorganic and the organic is of a magnitude that *de facto* rules out "accidental" transitions from the first to the second domain. At the present stage of scientific progress it is only on the basis of an unbending reductionist bias that this conclusion can still be denied.

A few words relating to the genetic code may be in order. Whether this magnificent discovery will serve to enlighten or further blind us depends, I believe, on the philosophical presuppositions which we bring to bear upon the issue. What we find in the DNA, clearly, is coded information, a coded message of incredible complexity; and this raises two questions. We need to ask ourselves, in the first place, what it is that has thus been encoded, thus expressed in a kind of molecular language; and we need to ask further by what means or agency this encoding has been effected? The reductionist, of course, assumes from the start that there is neither content nor agency beyond the molecular; but not everyone today agrees with this hypothesis. Robert Sokolowski, for example, has proposed that "it is the plant or animal form that encodes itself into the DNA," and that "the form is what the DNA serves to communicate."[19] There has been a growing recognition in recent years to the effect that the notions of substantial form and formal causation need once again to be taken seriously, not just by philosophers, but in the theory and practice of science as well. Among the benefits to science that can reasonably be expected from a sound ontology, the least, it would seem, is the reduction of futile research. To be more specific, such an ontology could dissuade scientists from searching for things that cannot possibly exist, such as, for example, the so-called "missing links" sought after by Darwinistically oriented anthropologists. By the same token, moreover, it could doubtless inspire life scientists to search for things that do exist but are out of range for a reductionist: "things in heaven and earth," namely, which are indeed not dreamed of in his philosophy. Most importantly, however, it should be clear from the outset that a living organism cannot be understood in depth without reference to the formal principle which constitutes its essence. Explanations "from below" have of course a certain validity and use; but their explanatory value is limited by the fact that they pertain, not to the living organism as such, but to mechanisms by which the organism fulfills its vital functions, which is not the same thing at all. Once again, one looks at the DNA but fails to recognize the plant or animal form which "encodes itself in the DNA," and which the DNA "serves to communicate."

We have alluded to the fact that the corporeal domain is stratified ontologically under the aegis of substantial forms; we should also remind ourselves, however, that according to the perennial doctrine the corporeal domain in its totality constitutes but the first and lowest tier of a larger cosmic hierarchy, consisting of three fundamental degrees.[20] What particularly concerns us is the fact that each level in this hierarchy comprises in a way all that exists below;[21] as Professor Nasr has put it: "Each higher world contains the principles of that which lies below it and lacks nothing of the lower reality" (KS 199). This is a fact of immense importance; we need, however, to interpret the tenet with care, the point being that each higher level contains the *essential* principles of what lies below, and lacks nothing *essential* of the lower reality. What *is*, however, added in the passage from higher to lower states are certain conditions or bounds extraneous to essence, which in the case of the corporeal domain may be referred to summarily as *quantitative*, in conformity with our previous considerations. To put it as succinctly as possible: these constitutive factors of a quantitative kind are rooted in the *materia secunda*, revealed as *potentiae* on the physical level, and actualized on the corporeal. One finds thus that the mathematical structures displayed in the physical domain extend in a sense to the corporeal level,[22] *but not beyond*. What the physicist has his eye upon plays obviously a major role on the level of the perceptible world, but has no bearing whatsoever upon realities of a higher order; and even here below it perforce leaves out of account all that is essential, for the essence of corporeal things, as we have seen, is inexplicable in quantitative terms. To tell the truth, not even a perceptible grain of sand can be understood or explained in terms of physics alone—not to speak of living organisms, or the phenomenon of man.

It remains to be said that there is nothing arbitrary or haphazard in the integration of physics "into higher orders of knowledge," nothing that hinges upon the private beliefs or idiosyncrasies of the person executing this task. There may be more than one way of telling the story, but there is only one story to be told. And it *can* be told, because the requisite conceptions of the perennial philosophy have already been reintroduced in the West and are now at hand.

This brings us back to the monumental accomplishments of Professor Nasr. Foremost among the academic exponents of the *sophia perennis*, he has won for the venerable doctrine an enhanced recognition and a measure of academic respect. It appears that he has in fact transformed the status of the perennial philosophy from an object of historical curiosity to a subject deemed worthy of serious consideration. Professor Nasr has succeeded magnificently in accomplishing the stated purpose of his Gifford Lectures: "to aid in the resuscitation of the sacred quality of knowledge and the revival of the veritable intellectual tradition of the West with the help of the still living traditions of the Orient" (KS viii).

WOLFGANG SMITH

DEPARTMENT OF MATHEMATICS
OREGON STATE UNIVERSITY
MARCH 1998

NOTES

1. Stanley L. Jaki, *Lord Gifford and His Lectures* (Macon, Ga.: Mercer University Press, 1986), p. 75.
2. The lectures have been published under the title *Knowledge and the Sacred* (New York: Crossroad, 1981). The page numbers in the sequel are based upon this edition and will be noted parenthetically hereafter as (KS p.#).
3. Ibid., pp. 69–71.
4. Arthur O. Lovejoy, *The Great Chain of Being* (Cambridge, Mass.: Harvard University Press, 1964).
5. Alfred North Whitehead, *The Concept of Nature* (Cambridge: Cambridge University Press, 1964), p. 30.
6. Ibid., p. 32.

7. Wolfgang Smith, *The Quantum Enigma* (Peru, Ill.: Sherwood Sugden, 1995).

8. A. H. Whitehead, *Nature and Life* (New York: Greenwood, 1968), p. 6.

9. Wolfgang Smith, *The Quantum Enigma*, chapter 3.

10. Ibid., chapter 4.

11. Werner Heisenberg, *Physics and Philosophy* (New York: Harper & Row, 1962), p. 41. It needs to be pointed out that whereas Heisenberg relegates individual atoms and "small" atomic aggregates to the domain of *potentia*, he nonetheless regards "macroscopic" aggregates as actual entities, in keeping with the reductionist outlook. In light of non-bifurcation, on the other hand, one needs to distinguish ontologically between a corporeal entity X and the underlying atomic aggregate SX. The two are literally "worlds apart."

12. See especially René Guénon, *The Reign of Quantity* (London: Luzac, 1953), chapter 2. The fact that the *materia secunda* underlies the physical domain as well will appear from the sequel.

13. These geometric properties are given in Euclid's axioms.

14. *Encounters with Einstein* (Princeton University Press, 1989), p. 83.

15. As Heisenberg has put it: "The 'thing-in-itself' is for the atomic physicist, if he uses this concept at all, finally a mathematical structure." (W. Heisenberg, *Physics and Philosophy*, op. cit., p. 91)

16. Guénon, op. cit., p. 13.

17. Heinz R. Pagels, *The Cosmic Code* (New York: Bantam, 1984), p. 262.

18. Note that quantum mechanics, by its very formalism, puts an end to this reduction. A physical system, quantum mechanically conceived, is definitely not "the sum of its parts."

19. Robert Sokolowski, "Formal and material causality in science," *Proceedings of American Catholic Philosophical Association* 69 (1995): 64.

20. The three degrees correspond to the *tribhuvana* or "three worlds" of the Vedic tradition, to *Beriah, Ietsirah*, and *Asiah* of the *Kabbala*, and microcosmically to the better-known triad *corpus-anima-spiritus*.

21. This ontological truth is symbolized in the Ptolemaic cosmography by the fact that the higher planetary spheres enclose the lower.

22. As I have explained in my monograph, there exists "a presentation-induced isomorphism between corporeal and sub-corporeal quantities" of which physicists make constant use. See W. Smith, op. cit., p. 80.

REPLY TO WOLFGANG SMITH

Professor Wolfgang Smith is one of the very few scientists who have devoted their lives to the pursuit of science and are at the same time rooted in the teachings of the perennial philosophy. Therefore his essay "*Sophia Perennis* and Modern Science" is very pertinent and reveals the essential truth that the tenets of perennial philosophy are not only significant in the domains of religious studies, traditional art, psychology, and the like. Perennial philosophy is also of the greatest importance for a revaluation of the philosophy of the modern sciences and for providing a meaningful framework for the understanding of these sciences and especially what constitutes their basis, namely, quantum mechanics. This latter point has been already treated in Smith's remarkable opus, *The Quantum Enigma*, and in fact much of his discussion in this essay is related to the theses of that work, although the present essay is an exceptional synthesis of Smith's thought on the subject of the relation between the perennial philosophy or *sophia perennis* and modern science and not simply a summary of *The Quantum Enigma*.

I am in such deep agreement with nearly everything written in this essay that there is hardly a point which I would wish to criticize. My response on most issues will be in fact simple confirmations. Nevertheless, there are a number of points upon which I wish to expand in order to clarify further my own views on the subject. Smith writes that "science in the traditional sense is thus a matter of 'reading the icon'—a far cry indeed from the Baconian vision!" This is a very apt manner of speaking of the traditional cosmological sciences. These sciences depict a cosmos which revealed a meaning beyond itself and can be contemplated as an icon. One could in fact go a step further and say that, using the language of Christianity, the cosmos *is* an icon and can only be understood in depth as an icon, which reveals a divine reality beyond itself. The traditional cosmological sciences brought out this iconic reality and permitted those who studied and understood them to *see* the cosmos as an icon and to be able to contemplate it rather than knowing it only discursively. The modern sciences, issuing from what Smith calls "the Baconian vision," also know nature but no longer as an icon. They are able to tell us about the size, weight, and shape of the icon and even the composition of the various colors of paint used in painting it, but they can tell us nothing of its *meaning* in reference to a reality beyond itself. What they tell us about the size, composition of the paints, and so on of the icon are not false on their own level, but they do not exhaust knowledge of the icon and it would be both ignorance and *hubris* to claim that this type of knowledge is the only knowledge possible of the icon. The consequences of this ignorance parading as totalitarian science combined with *hubris*, made even more dangerous by being denied, are lethal for man's spiritual life. This ignorance, *hubris*, and denial have dire consequences even more outwardly in man's relation to the world of nature, divorced in the modern world from ultimate meaning as a result of the exclusive claims of Baconian science.

Smith qualifies his comments about Baconian science by saying that contemporary science at its best is not completely Baconian as Einstein's occasional comment about the "Old One" suggesting that he too may have been searching for "*vestigia* of a kind" shows. I agree that there are a number of individual scientists, even in the contemporary period, who, like the English botanist John Ray, cultivated science with the goal of discovering the *vestigia Dei* in creation. But they were and are functioning within a scientific framework in which such concerns by an individual scientist could not in any way affect the science they have produced. One can study and accept the theory of relativity with or without references to the "Old One," which means that the result of Einsteinian science is not the search for the *vestigia Dei* and the depiction of the cosmos as an icon, whatever may have been Einstein's personal views and attitudes.

The distinction that Smith makes between what *ought* to transpire in the mind of a modern scientist, which is reasoning upon data provided by the senses, and the meaning of knowledge according to the *sophia perennis* is of crucial importance. The epistemology provided by the *sophia perennis* covers "an incomparably greater range of cognitive possibilities" to quote the author, since it relates all acts of knowing to participation of the human intellect in the light of the Divine Intellect. In much of the discussion going on today in the domain of epistemology, both scientific and otherwise, this issue is forgotten or at least not emphasized, including the works of many contemporary Muslim thinkers writing on the subject. This participation is not confined to "moments of illumination" but involves all knowledge which relates the human subject to the object that is known. Smith quotes the Gospel of John and states, "what ultimately connects the human subject to its object in the act of knowing is indeed 'the true Light which lighteth every man that cometh into the world'"(1:9). Since the *sophia perennis* is both perennial and universal, one needs to add here how central this thesis is in other traditions. Being better acquainted with the Islamic tradition than with others, I can turn to that tradition and add that there are numerous verses of the Quran and *Ḥadīth* about the relation of knowledge (*al-'ilm*) to light which constitutes a vast hierarchy issuing from God. In fact according to the Quran (XXIV:35) God is the light of not only the heavens but also the earth. On the basis of these traditional sources and certain elements of Greek philosophy, Islamic philosophers, going back to al-Fārābī and Ibn Sīnā, spoke of the illumination of the human intellect by the Active Intellect in the act of intellection. The symbolism of light was particularly central to the teachings of Suhrawardī, the founder of the School of Illumination (*al-ishrāq*) and what Professor Smith has written on participation in the Light of the Divine Intellect is practically identical with the views of Suhrawardī, except that the latter identifies this light in its various degrees with the different angelic substances. Again I need to emphasize how important this issue is for an in-depth study of the epistemology of modern science in light of traditional teachings, and as far as Islamic thinkers now writing on the subject of epistemology are concerned, how crucial it is first to understand the tenets of traditional Islamic philosophy in this domain before embarking upon often puerile and moreover fruitless comparisons of traditional epistemologies and modern scientific epistemology.

Smith points quite correctly to the need for a living sapiental tradition within which cosmological sciences are cultivated and without which they wither and die "thus giv[ing] rise to what may indeed be termed a superstition." This is a very correct assessment upon which I must elaborate. A superstition is literally something whose ground has been removed. The metaphysical teachings of the *sophia perennis* constitute precisely the ground upon which the traditional cosmological sciences stood. Therefore, with the destruction of that ground these sciences could not but be reduced to superstition, although they still carried residues of truths no longer understood. The whole phenomenon of occultism in the West is quite interesting from this point of view. In other civilizations where the metaphysical ground has not been destroyed, there are certainly forms of popular superstition which are also very much present in the modern world, albeit in other guises, but in those civilizations one does not encounter the phenomenon of occultism as it developed in the *salons* of France and elsewhere in Europe from the eighteenth century onward. Many modern people, especially those of a scientific bent, immediately dismiss the traditional sciences such as alchemy as being simply superstition. But they do not realize that such sciences are like jewels which glow in the presence of the light of a living sapiental tradition and become opaque once that light disappears. Paradoxically enough, by claiming to relegate the traditional cosmological sciences simply to the category of superstition, the modern scientific enterprise has not only been helpless before the mushrooming of interest in these traditional sciences even in their residual form known in occultist circles, but it has been instrumental in the rise of new forms of superstition, such as the idea of progress, which are much more dangerous for the future of humanity than the practice of predictive astrology.

Returning to the question of perception, Smith emphasizes that light waves, sound waves, brain function, and the like are of course necessary and play a role in the act of perception but that "they do not—they cannot! —constitute the perceptual act" which is "literally not of this world." He also lays the error of belief in bifurcation and the lure of it at the feet of the state of forgetfulness of "participation" by post-medieval European man. I have restated these lines to emphasize their central importance and my full agreement with it. Modern philosophy, psychology, or science are simply not able to explain perception which they always reduce to one of its parts or something else because the participation of the human intellect in the Light of the Divine Intellect is simply beyond the truncated worldview within which all modern thought, whether it be philosophical, psychological, or scientific operates. The rediscovery of the real significance of perception is only possible in light of the *sophia perennis* and is itself a key for the discovery of the metaphysical universe depicted by the perennial philosophy in its vastness and wholeness. And I agree with Smith that the greatest obstacle to the integration of modern science into the higher orders of knowledge and the rediscovery of how the miracle of perception works is Cartesian dualism or the theory of bifurcation.

I believe that the ingenious distinction made by Smith between the corporeal and physical worlds and the confining of quantum mechanics to the physical rather than the corporeal world, as well as the relation between the two of which he speaks, are major steps in the formulation of a more meaningful philosophy of physics in accordance with the *sophia perennis*. Like Smith, I also wish to emphasize that the corporeal and the physical worlds, as defined by him, are not only different but constitute two ontologically distinct domains. There is an ontological hiatus between the two and one cannot say that this physical stratum contains simply the "building blocks" for the corporeal world. The whole idea of fundamental particles from which we can build up the corporeal world with its forms and qualities is therefore false; and form and quality associated with the corporeal world—not to speak of psychological and spiritual realities—can never be reduced to the quantitative elements of the physical world which alone can be studied through the "modern scientific method" and be made to constitute the subject of quantum mechanics. Naturally, without mathematics there is no possibility of study of that physical world, as defined by Smith.

To understand the ontological status of the corporeal and physical worlds would also solve the status of quantum physics not only in its relation to the world of classical physics but also to the corporeal, or what is ordinarily called the "physical world" (contrary to Smith's terminology), and the traditional sciences which deal with the qualitative and formal aspects of that world. This ontological awareness would also make clear the basic point I have mentioned in so many of my writings, namely, that the traditional cosmological sciences are not simply crude attempts to understand nature and primitive stages of the modern quantitative sciences, but contain profound knowledge of the formal and qualitative aspects of the corporeal world not reducible to quantity nor of lower significance than quantity *à la* Galileo. On the contrary they refer to realities with a higher ontological status than the quantitative.

The analogy made by Smith between the *materia secunda* and the Euclidean plane from which geometric forms emerge and in which they become actualized is also a brilliant one with which I could not but agree. It is so important to remember that the objects of modern physics are not like tables and chairs except smaller, but that they are "constructed" to quote Smith; that is, "they are defined or specified by a certain experimental intervention." And yet, although experimental means affect the form of the physical laws, the content of the mathematical equations which contain the laws do not derive from the particular experimental methods used. Here again the analogy between the *materia secunda* of physics and the geometric plane of Euclidean geometry becomes useful, because in the case of geometry also, while the manner of operation of a geometer affects the geometric properties of what is constructed, whether the geometer draws a square or a circle, the mathematical structures of the geometric forms are not determined by the geometer. They belong ultimately to the intelligible world which Smith quite rightly associates with the Platonic understanding of this term. This whole analysis is very much in accord with my views and opens the door for those who are able to understand the tenets of the *sophia perennis* as well as modern physics, for the integration of quantum mechanics into the traditional hierarchy of knowledge. It invites the integration of the world with which quantum mechanics deals into the ontological hierarchy of the perennial philosophy.

To achieve this end, it is of crucial importance to realize that the physical objects of quantum mechanics are not "things" in the ordinary sense but of much smaller dimension. Rather, they are relational and do not possess an *esse*. The main lesson to learn from this truth is that the essential attributes of things, therefore, come not from the quantum objects but from elsewhere or more precisely from above. Smith offers a wonderful metaphor by saying, "the essence of a plant, after all, derives from the seed, and not from the ground in which the seed is planted." One might say that the seed in this metaphor refers ultimately to the archetypal reality or Platonic Idea which the particular plant in question reflects and manifests on the corporeal plane. It is a valuable contribution by Smith to assert that modern physics does not deal with *essence*, that it is "*inessential*," because the realization of this truth provides an opportunity for those reductionists who are looking for the sun in the bottom of the well to cast their eyes above in order to see the origin of the essences which one observes and experiences in the corporeal world.

From my perspective, Professor Smith is completely right when he asserts that "the decisive step in the restitution of the *cosmologia perennis* is without question the rediscovery of 'forms' as an ontological and causal principle," and in fact on several occasions in my writings I have expressed the same idea. And it is also completely true that the destruction of the significance of forms based on incomprehension of their real significance by Bacon and Descartes opened the door for the reductionism of modern science and the constant attempt by scientists to explain things by their parts, asserting that the whole is no more than the sum of its parts. When Smith states, however, that this destruction of forms "has not . . . led towards the realization of the reductionist goal" and that "the reductionist philosophy appears also to have outlived its established usefulness as a heuristic principle," it seems to me that he is looking only at a few scientists like himself and not at the impact of reductionism associated with science on the general cultural scene of today. It is enough to look at the current mainstream view of the physical world, of medicine and the body, of the approach to the solution of social, economic, and ecological problems to see how entrenched the reductionist view really is. The philosophy of wholeness still remains in the margin of modern and postmodern man's worldview thanks mostly to mainstream modern science.

Furthermore, Smith makes the crucial statement that there exist in the world non-mathematical formal principles which are "none other than the aforementioned substantial forms, which prove moreover to be 'essential' in a strict ontological sense." He adds further that these forms constitute an ontological order. If this central statement of Smith's, with which I agree whole-heartedly, were to be accepted fully by modern science, a new scientific view would be born that would cease to be that of modern science as it is known today and become transformed into a further extension of the traditional sciences as I have already proposed. Then and only then could one say that reductionism has ceased to be operative and has outlived its "usefulness." Until then, unfortunately reductionism continues to level things to their lowest common denominator, to destroy quality in the name of quantity and to impoverish the spiritual vision and the minds of those affected by its siren call.

The essay of Wolfgang Smith, to which I have only added a few commentaries, is a seminal essay and should be studied carefully by all interested in the reintegration of science into the metaphysics contained in the heart of the *sophia perennis* and the traditional cosmological sciences associated with it. It should also be necessary reading for all searching for a new and richer philosophy for science, for those who often end with superficial adaptations of Taoism or Hinduism which are then related to the findings of modern science. Smith takes us much farther in this quest and shows the role that the *sophia perennis* can play in the veritable understanding of the significance of quantum mechanics and the integration of scientific knowledge into the universal hierarchy of knowledge.

For some forty years I have been writing on traditional science in relation to modern science, on Islamic science, and the hierarchy of knowledge as well as on traditional metaphysics and the perennial philosophy. It is an exhilarating experience for me to see here almost a synthesis of my own thought with many new insights on the subject presented by an active scientist also well versed in traditional doctrines. In writing these lines I feel as if I am expanding some of my thoughts in the direction of a new horizon opened by Smith. There is practically nothing in this important text to which I would need to respond in a critical manner in order to clarify differences with my own thought. On the contrary to understand my thought on the subject of the relation between the *sophia perennis* and modern science, it is important to pay attention to my confirmation of the main theses of Smith's essay which do full justice on the one hand to traditional doctrines and the tenets of the *sophia perennis*, to quote his terminology, and on the other to the discoveries of quantum mechanics and the nature of the whole venture of modern physics. I am happy that the occasion to write for this volume made it possible for Professor Smith to produce this exceptionally important essay in the field of the relation between the perennial philosophy and modern science, a field which has preoccupied me since my student days.

S. H. N.

15

Giovanni Monastra

SEYYED HOSSEIN NASR: RELIGION, NATURE, AND SCIENCE

To be at peace with the Earth one must be at peace with Heaven
S. H. Nasr, *Man and Nature*, p.14

What is the main problem in our time for culture of the *modern world*? Is it learning or discovering new things? Absolutely not. We do not need to discover but to *re-discover*. The main problem is the recovery of what we lost: in the past we had a loss of memory about our spiritual and cultural roots, like a collective *amnesia*. We have to remember, or rather, to learn again something which was darkened by the new view of life and man—a view that began to predominate between the end of the Middle Ages and the Renaissance period, and that opened the way to Modernity.

From that historical period, like a person who had a shock and forgot his past, his knowledge, his identity (there is no real identity without long term memory), Europeans had to start again a new life under many aspects. Their masters embodied narrow circles which created and propagated a new culture; but they did it following completely different values and ideas in respect to those of their ancestors living in the premodern ages, even if, at first, they thought themselves to be in partial continuity with the past, developing some concepts and philosophies coming from the Greco-Roman civilization. Later, the history of culture of peoples living in the West, and also in other areas, was rewritten following a Eurocentric and progressive view. Consequently students were schooled in a particular way, in agreement with this idea of life, history, and world. Clearly, such schooling was quite functional in supporting the activity of white colonization over the other peoples. As a result of this process we are immersed in a peculiar "spiritual" and psychological dimension, which never in the past had the possibility of achieving such extension and hegemony. But few of us are conscious of the deep qualitative gap between the present times and the premodern ones: the idea of a linear progress was the new *faith* which justified the illusion that all new things are "better" because of their "newness." Today, aside from an undeniable material benefit under the quantitative point of view, it is difficult to state that this "reconversion" gave us a real improvement in quality of life. There are so many problems concerning the stressful conditions of living in our modern cities, the existential inanity in a society where success and money are the unique parameters to value people, and the increasing destruction of natural environment due to the Faustian process of industrialization, and so on. This happens because the Western and the Westernized world removed all its *traditional wisdom*, the wisdom which lead all premodern human societies. So, like a person who, upon seeing some objects or hearing some words linked to his past, begins to remember the story of his life, his name, and his personality, we also can recover our very spiritual and cultural roots if we can receive some stimulus which helps us in this difficult task. It is something like the Platonic theory of recollection, because such spiritual and cultural heritage, which is essentially timeless, is much more in affinity with the spirit, the soul, and the body of man than the modern materialistic culture.

The help for seekers of their very roots can come from such people as Ananda Kentish Coomaraswamy, René Guénon, Frithjof Schuon, Seyyed Hossein Nasr, Titus Burckhardt, Julius Evola, Martin Lings, and so on, who through their studies and research, give us the possibility of knowing what we were, what we thought, and what we believed about the main aspects of spiritual and material life, such as metaphysics, religion, art, science, and so on. And their teachings are useful also for peoples living in non-Western countries, who are culturally colonized by the materialistic worldview. Their works not only restore the true dimension of metaphysics and religion, explain the structure and the deep value of symbols, but also deal with important and specific fields such as art or science.

So Ananda Coomaraswamy demonstrated to us what was the real meaning of "art" in Europe, in Asia, and elsewhere. For science we have to specify that, in this context, it means something utterly different from what we know in our time: now science is a group of disciplines permeated by a mechanistic view of reality and based upon a rationalistic and analytical procedure working on empirical data; whereas the same name, among all cultures of the West before the Renaissance, and in the East, even up to today in a few countries, was (or is) used to identify a constellation of knowledge which applies the metaphysical principles to specific fields of study of the *cosmos* (cosmological disciplines) and man, like natural sciences, geography, astronomy, physics, mathematics, alchemy, medicine, and anthropology. This kind of traditional science was branded by "modern" thought as *irrational*, due to ignorance and superstition, except a few parts which were seen as pre-scientific elements, simple vague intuitions which preceded the "authentic" science (see the definition of "alchemy" as a pre-chemical discipline, a significant example of the unbelievable superficiality of analysis). In this way not only all types of traditional cultures of the so-called "old continent," but also the huge amount of knowledge specific to native peoples of Asia, America, and so on (qualitatively, if not formally, very similar to those born in Europe), were cut out, cancelling also remarkable aspects concerning the specificity of those societies. Even if this evaluation is too simple and superficial to be believable at a careful analysis, it has left a lot of prejudices in the minds of many Westerners, persuaded of their superiority, while it has inculcated several inferiority complexes among Westernized people, who feel ashamed of their native culture.

In this critical situation the noteworthy, significant work of professor Seyyed Hossein Nasr plays a pivotal role in destroying many of these wrong ideas. Discussing his complex thought, expounded in books rich with notes and references, is very difficult in a few pages. He has discussed so many topics: Islamic religion, Sufism, Islamic art, traditional sciences, philosophy of Nature, origins and meaning of "modern" science, roots of the ecological crisis, just to cite the main subjects. I can say that my first approaches to the knowledge of Islam were his books *Ideals and Realities of Islam* [1] and *Sufi Essays*,[2] both published in Italy in the 1970s by Rusconi. Still today these works are essential reference points in the topography of my mind, for their clear and full exposition of all the main aspects of Islam and Sufi esoterism, without any compromise with secular ideologies, but also open to the "ecumenic" and universal view of religions, seen as different dialects coming from a unique metaphysical and transcendent language. This aspect is noteworthy, particularly in our time, where many types of the so-called "fundamentalism" (often as result of a poisonous mixture of politics and pseudo-spirituality born from the modernistic contaminations of some traditional societies) are giving a wrong idea about religions, especially in the West for Islam. Westerners frequently associate Islam only with fanaticism, intolerance, violence, and superstition: a negative estimation which is very convenient to justify a policy against the entire Islamic world (aside from a few Westernized "friendly" countries).

Besides this, I see another substantial reason to nourish a particular attention toward Nasr's work. Our society is hypnotized by the power of modern science, or—it is better to say—by its ideology, the *scientism*, which apparently looks to be in crisis, at least among the most disillusioned scientists, but which still has a strong influence among common people.

Thus at the end of the twentieth century we have heard frequently enthusiastic (but very trivial) comments about the "achievements of science and technology" obtained during that century, forgetting all the problems caused by those same "achievements."

For this reason the analysis of the real origin and character of modern science developed by Professor Nasr has a fundamental relevance in helping people who do not accept the present situation, but who lack a clear view of things concerning values, processes, and deep connections, to understand the real "spirit" of our time and its frauds. Nasr explains that there is a strict relation between religion and human culture: in synthesis we can say that every degenerate culture is the fruit of a dangerous decadence in the field of religion. But his work is also very useful for those perennialists and traditionalists who refuse roughly the world of science, knowing nothing about the existence of excellent scientists of the past centuries (or today), who work against the classical paradigms of "modern" science (from J. Wolfgang Goethe, who was a great naturalist, to Gustav Carus, Jakob von Uexküll, Adolf Portmann, Wilhelm Troll, Agnes Arber, Bernhard Bavinck, Walter Heitler, D'Arcy W. Thompson, Luigi Fantappié, David Bohm, Rémy Chauvin, René Thom, Roger Penrose, Giuseppe Sermonti, and so on). These scientists provide a creative and fecund expression of anti-reductionist thought, in many respects close to the main ideas of authors like Pythagoras, Plato, Aristotle, Plotinus. Furthermore I personally have an additional interest in this part of Nasr's thought due to my scientific background and profession as a biologist. When about twenty years ago his book *Man and Nature—The Spiritual Crisis in Modern Man*,[3] a real *masterpiece*, was translated into Italian, people like Roberto Fondi and me (at that time I was a university student and he a young professor of paleontology on the Natural Science Faculty in Siena) found in it many considerable observations and intuitions which were very useful in giving a general frame to our work on the several organicistic and holistic tendencies in biology and physics in opposition to the reductionistic and mechanistic view of nature, mainly exemplified by Darwinism.[4] In fact we, as followers of perennialist thought, but also involved directly in science, did not feel that some arguments of other traditional thinkers were completely convincing, even if they were stimulating. I have in mind writers like Titus Burckhardt[5] or Julius Evola,[6] who disregarded the above mentioned anti-reductionist scientific currents and did not understand the consequences of remarkable aspects of new physics in upsetting the mechanistic view of life and world.

Now I would like to focus my attention in detail on the thorough studies of Professor Nasr dedicated to the birth of modern science, in relation also with traditional sciences, like the Islamic sciences, and the spiritual and cultural surroundings which permitted this birth and the ensuing hegemony.

Among the traditional authors, Nasr is one of the few who has an extensive knowledge in biology and physics due to his academic studies. Besides him we can cite Ananda Coomaraswamy, who had a university degree in Geological Science, and Julius Evola, who attended lectures in scientific matters, mainly mathematics, at the university without finishing his studies. But Coomaraswamy very early shifted his interests from science to art, so in his books and essays we cannot find many references to modern science, while Evola always showed a modest involvement in this sector, frequently characterized by a formal approach. Nasr mastered very thoroughly the field of modern science: he has a knowledge of it *from inside*. Furthermore he is also a philosopher of nature, in my opinion, in a manner much more profound than other traditional scholars. For this reason maybe what Antoine Faivre has written recently on the perennialist authors is partly true: "If one of the characteristics of this group is its indifference toward nature, on the contrary Seyyed Hossein Nasr refers to a Philosophy of Nature which recalls that of Paracelsus."[7] Faivre clearly overstates the point about "indifference toward nature," and moreover the reference to Paracelsus is too restrictive, but the impressive work of Professor Nasr on this issue can account for those words.

First of all, to explain better what I have said before, I have to review the philosophical and scientific formation of Professor Nasr. As William C. Chittick tells us, "Nasr's educational background is exceptional."[8] After finishing high school in the United States, where he was sent from Iran by his father, he entered the prestigious MIT of Boston, where he studied mathematics and physics, following his juvenile interest in the world of science. At the same time he was gradually attracted to the study of tradition—especially Islam, the religion of his native land—deeply reinforcing his spiritual roots. Nasr and some young colleagues of his asked the late Georgio de Santillana to hold a course on Hinduism from the point of view of comparative religion. That occasion allowed him to come in contact with the ideas of the great French traditionalist René Guénon, who has become, with Schuon, whom he met later, one of the most influential scholars in Nasr's thought. Furthermore Nasr had the opportunity to frequent the huge library of traditional texts of Coomaraswamy, from which he was able to extend his knowledge to other perennialist authors, like Pallis or Lings. In that period Nasr also knew representative members of the academic community, among them the philosopher Bertrand Russell and the historian of science George Sarton. After his B.S. at MIT in 1954, Nasr started to study geology and geophysics at Harvard, but his predominant interest in traditional doctrines finally induced him to change the course of his academic studies, devoting himself to the history of science and philosophy, where in 1958 he received the Ph.D. in cosmology and Islamic sciences.

Later, he returned to Iran as a professor at Tehran University, where until 1979 he taught the history of science and philosophy. Before moving to the United States, Nasr—Persian by birth and upbringing, and Muslim by faith—wished to make a thorough and deep study of his culture and religion, unifying, in this way, several different kinds of disciplines: religious, philosophical, historic, and scientific, in a stimulating and well integrated synthesis. This work gained him a great deal of public acknowledgment both in Iran and in several other countries.

Now we can analyze his studies on the topic of "nature," or "cosmos," or "universe" (in this context taken as synonyms), in connection with traditional and modern thought. One of the main questions around which Nasr's research is articulated can be summarized as follows: What process gave origin to the destruction of the traditional conception of nature and to the parallel birth of modern science, with the consequent ecological crisis? What are the profound spiritual causes of it? For Nasr, as for all perennialist thinkers, everything is rooted in the metaphysical realm: there any act has its justification and explanation. Therefore, we must seek at the spiritual level for the reasons for all events. This is valid for the genesis of the phenomenological world, but also, in a different way, for elucidating the processes of darkening as mentioned above in the question. For this reason, even if unusual for the parameters of modern culture, in a book devoted to nature we find a clear and synthetic definition of metaphysics, which, in Nasr's words, "is the science of the Real, of the origin and end of things, of the Absolute and, in its light, the relative. It is a science as strict and exact as mathematics and with the same clarity and certitude, but one which can only be attained through intellectual intuition and not simply through ratiocination" (MN 81). It is important to keep in mind this definition following Nasr's analysis.

He describes in depth in his book, *Religion and the Order of Nature*,[9] how traditional cultures see the natural kingdom, considering many religions, both living and historical. He begins with the rich treasury of beliefs and knowledge characterizing the primal or indigenous religions, which are very close to the spiritual traditions of primordial humanity. Such primal religions, still practiced by tribes living in many areas of the earth (Australia, Africa, the Americas, the Polynesian Islands, India, and so on), in spite of their considerable differences, show several common features and similarities in their deep relation with nature. As Nasr writes, "they have been for millennia the guardians of the natural environment with an ear finely tuned to the message of the Earth, and they possess views concerning the order of nature that are of profound significance as far as the question of the preservation of the natural environment is concerned" (RON 31). For too long an arrogant and blind mankind has defined these religious cultures as forms of ingenuous animism or fetishism, but today some people have begun to admit that their role has been inestimable. Another very important branch of religious thought is shamanism, which was for a long time the only religion of central and east Asia and North America. For shamanism all nature is sacred, the Universe is an ordered and harmonious, multi-stratified structure with several levels in reciprocal vertical connection. In speaking of African religions, Nasr points out that we have to distinguish among true spiritual beliefs and superstitions or degenerate religions (ancestor worship, sorcery, etc.); but if we do this, it is clear that the integral spiritual traditions of that continent (as in the case of peoples like Bambara or Diola) are not very different from the other primal religions, and we find the same close relation with nature, which is seen as coming from a transcendent source (the sacred Word generating the universe) and for this reason *sacred*. The ancient religion of Egypt was another great example of a religious approach to the cosmos: in the Earth the Egyptians saw the image of a celestial archetype. For them the order of the universe was generated and sustained by the Divinity and reflected the metaphysical order of Principles. Concerning Asia, Nasr shows how Taoism and Confucianism have an extreme respect toward nature and its harmony on the basis of a complex and refined metaphysical view, where the polarity of *Yin* and *Yang* plays a central role, permeating everything. Tao, the source of *Yin* and *Yang*, is the supreme Law, meant to rule in the single man, in public life and also in nature, demonstrating an inalienable link among moral, social, and natural levels, different but coming from the same Origin, the supernal Oneness. Also in Hinduism, Buddhism, and Zoroastrianism we find very similar ideas, with a sacred view of the cosmos, visible expression of the Invisible, and a huge living and animated body[10] with an immanent Order, which is, at the same time, transcendent, its Archetypes forming the different structures of physical reality. As with the Chinese, for whom the supernal Law was the Tao, in India we find the words *ṛta* (vedic) and *dharma* (post-vedic), and in Iran *Asha*, which establish the right way for individuals, societies, and nature. In all traditonal perspectives the whole of nature, by its metaphysical Origin, has not only an outward appearance, but also an inward, symbolic, dimension and meaning, revealing itself as a *theophany*, analogous to another reality coming from the supernal sphere, religion, where we distinguish the exoteric from the esoteric level (RON 15–16).

Describing then the Islamic perspective, Nasr says that for Muslims, the world, with its harmony and beauty, derives

> according to Divine Wisdom from the prototype of all existence in the Divine Order, the prototype which is identified according to the language of Quranic cosmology with the Pen (*al-Qalam*) and the Guarded Tablet (*al-Lawh al-mahfuz*). God wrote by means of the Pen, which symbolizes the active principle of Creation, the realities of all things, upon the Guarded Tablet, which remains

> eternally with Him, while through the cosmogenic act, the realities written upon the Tablet were made to descend to lower levels of existence and finally to the world of nature. The order of nature, therefore, reflects and issues from the order that exists in the Divine Realm. (RON 60)

The Quran states that all things have their metaphysical roots in God, so that

> nature is not an independent domain of reality with its own independent order, but . . . its principle resides in another realm of reality, which is Divine. . . . All cosmic reality consists of reflections of combinations of the theophanies (*tajalliyyāt*) of various Divine Names and Qualities. . . . The Divine Names are the principles of the immutable archetypes (*al-a'yān al-thābitah*) which are the "Ideas" of all cosmic manifestation contained in the Divine Intellect. (RON 61)

The physical world is governed by a transcendent Law, which at the same time also rules human society, both at the individual and collective levels, and in accordance with the other spiritual traditions. The order of nature is only the Methaphysical Order manifested in a specific level of reality, identified by us as "nature." In this view man is the vice-gerent of God on the Earth, which he has to preserve and keep well. Again we find an archetypal and holistic view of the cosmos, seen as a sacred expression of the transcendent sphere and closely conneted with the human world.

Clearly every religion has its identity and specificity, in particular at the expressive level, but there is a common ground which emerges with evidence following Nasr's analysis. Furthermore we see that all religions mentioned are very far from any utilitarian relation with nature; rather, for these religions nature has value and importance for itself, independent from man. Thus we are not the owners of nature, because, as the Native Americans say, "man has the Earth in loan": it is a totality to preserve and to transmit to our descendants. These traditions teach us that the needs of man are not the only measure of reality. For traditional thought, nature has to be primarily observed and also contemplated, as a theophany, not manipulated following the most trivial human desires. The whole cosmos, in some cases, can also teach to man, who understands if spiritually well trained, its language of forms and processes, the first steps in the way of deliverance (RON 65), showing in this way the highest form of participation by nature in religious experience. The phenomenological world veils and reveals the supernatural sphere, being symbolic and transparent in agreement with its intellectual and metaphysical origin (RON 15).

Now the task remains to deal with the Greek religion, Judaism, and Christianity, where there are some problematic particularities. In all of them we can find the many features mentioned above, but other aspects emerge that are not in conformity with the traditional harmonic view. For Judaism,

I agree completely with Nasr when he emphasizes the role of some Rabbinic schools or Cabalist thought, which developed an esoteric view of creation *ex nihilo*, which begins as self-negation of the Divine Reality, who then molds the cosmos with its archetypes. In the last analysis, the substance of the whole of nature is related to the coagulation of a reality belonging to God: it means that the physical world is in some way sacred, so *it deserves to be respected in all its manifestations*. Also in this case the law of nature has the same origin and structure of the law which orders the human communities: again we see that they are expressions at different levels of a unique supernal Law. But sincerely, on the other hand, I have also to mention some expressions of the Old Testament, where we find a very different spiritual atmosphere, showing also some contradictions with other pieces, even though I disagree completely with the partial and tendentious interpretation of Lynn White.[11] In spite of some misunderstanding due to mistakes in translation from the Hebrew text, which we can still find in our versions in Western languages (but also this is significant of a general mentality of exploitation of nature), in reality man, living in Eden, is described in Genesis not as a dominator, but as the keeper of the creation (Gen. 1:28), with the task of possessing the Earth without violence and oppression against things and living beings (see the Hebrew word *kabas*), and also to guide and pasture animals (see *rada*). Furthermore the Hebrew Bible brings to light soon after (Gen. 2:15) the religious role of man who must cultivate and guard the Garden, using two Hebrew words (*'abad* and *samar*) which have a strict relation with the worship and faithfulness toward God.[12] The meaning is clear: the duty of man is to have a religious life with nature where he can live at peace. But, after the original sin, the Earth is anathematized by God, the harmonious relation between man and nature looks to be broken, and the Earth becomes sterile and an enemy to him. Now nature is the external world against which to fight. And also after the Flood, we hear from God hard words for the animals: in fact man has to terrorize all other living beings, which are left in his "power" (Gen. 9:2), to satisfy his needs, and are "under the feet" of man (Ps. 8:7). Clearly very different views can be found also in the Old Testament, like those demonstrating the pity of God for animals before the Flood, or His care for the nourishment of the pups (Job 38–39), the statement of a new alliance among all beings coming from the ark (Gen. 9:10), the messianic desire for a universal peace (Isa. 11:6–9), and an agreement in which the animals can be witnesses (Hos. 2:20). In conclusion, if the general relation between God and non-human living beings looks to be unaffected by the original sin, which however also corrupted nature, then the parallel relation between man and nature now appears contradictory and ambiguous, *containing some premises toward a utilitarian approach to the creation*. It seems that in the Hebrew tradition, aside from the main sapiental trend, the utilitarian outlook was a minor but parallel life-view in some ways contrasting with the other one. As a matter of fact, these aspects did not influence Judaism as a whole, especially regarding its deep transcendental tension and its esoteric schools, which preserved it from secularism. But these aspects were to be assimilated by some tendencies in Christianity, at least at the subconscious level, and would in time make their contribution to the decadence of the view of nature in Europe. On the other hand Christianity also inherited some characteristics of the late Greek culture, with its mechanistic and desacralized view of nature.

Therefore we have to turn to the religion and philosophy of ancient Greece, following Nasr's study, to come back in a short while to Christianity. He specifies that there were several religions, Chtonian as well as Olympian, and also misteric traditions, mainly the Dionysian-Orphic branch. In the primary cosmogony "the world is divided into three portions (*moirai*), and order is imposed by the principle of Destiny or *Moira* to which the gods as well as the elements are subjugated" (RON 52). An analogous conception of *Moira* as "principle of order" was *Dike* (righteousness), meaning also "the course of nature": all of these remind us of the Chinese *Tao*, the Hindu *rta*, or the Iranian *Asha*. Only later in the history of Greek religion do we see that the will of the gods becomes the basis for the order in nature, replacing *Moira*, and only then are the various domains of nature divided among the different gods as result of the legislation of Zeus. This is clearly a form of spiritual decay which characterizes in a specific way the Greek religion as a whole; then an anthropomorphic polytheism came to constitute the norm in classical Greece. A consequence of such spiritual regression was the birth of philosophy, as human knowledge, in the early period open toward the Heavens, with Plato and also Aristotle, but then further and further from any true spiritual interest, following instead an analytical and rationalistic type of thinking in a purely secular frame, as shown by the later Sophists. Nasr identifies in the Ionians, like Thales, Anaximander, or Anaximenes, the first philosophers, with fundamentally naturalistic interests (RON 82), although previously he had written: "The water of Thales is not what flows in rivers and streams but is the psycho-spiritual substratum and principle of the physical world" (MN 54). Following the studies of the great Italian scholar, Giorgio Colli, and others, like Ada Somigliana or Jean Biès, I think that Thales, Anaximander, Anaximenes, Heraclitus, Parmenides, Empedocles, and clearly Pythagoras, were all wise men living in a sapiental, not philosophical, dimension, often very close to the ancient Iranian and Hindu metaphysical thought.[13] For the same reasons also in the view of Ionians—I believe—there is no place for any "hylozoism." As Meister Eckhart wrote of Heraclitus that he was "one of our most ancient masters, who found the truth long before the birth of God, before the appearance of the Christian faith" (from the sermon *Stetit Iesus in medio discipulorum*). Instead, the first philosopher probably was Socrates, or Plato, who created the word "philosophy," in search of something which was in possession of the ancient thinkers, but irrevocably lost in his time.

Coming back to Christianity, we can notice that in the Gospels there are few references to any link between the spiritual and the phenomenological world, as, for example, the empathic "behavior" of nature with its withering and rejuvenation during the death and resurrection of Christ according to His cosmic character, which agrees with the view of the other religions about the connection between God and nature. As Nasr states, Christianity is a way of faith and love rather than a way of knowledge and certitude, a true gnosis existing mostly in the peripheral religious groups (MN 56). There was also a contingent aspect, that grew from the necessity of early Christianity to fight the decadent popular Pagan beliefs which deified nature and were seen by the Church as very dangerous superstitions. In general this necessity to preserve the authentic religion against naturalistic and pantheistic convictions originated more and more a suspicious view of nature and induced Christians to claim a deep dualism, God-world; some theologians even went as far as to define the nature "massa perditionis" (MN 55 and 100), the kingdom of Evil, without any positive role for the spiritual life of man. A consequence of this fight against Paganism was that a large part of Christianity, in rightly advancing the de-divinification of nature, contributed also to its desacralization, creating confusion between "divine" and "sacred" —a confusion which we do not find in other monotheistic religions, like Islam.

Furthermore, we have to remember that Christianity absorbed many ideas of classical Greek philosophy and science, which—as noted before—were contaminated by a mechanistic and secular view of the cosmos. With regard to this, some portions of the late Scholastic philosophy also played a negative role. These two aspects of Christian thought—desacralization of nature and acceptance of late Greek thought—in some cases, were supported by a literalistic and formal interpretation of some passages of the Old Testament, especially those where it seems that man is the absolute master of creation and animals exist only for him.

Finally we have also to remark on the dangerous victory of some nominalistic ideas, which became hegemonic in the theological thought in the late Middle Ages. As Nasr notes, nothing could be done to change this situation by those groups, like the so-called Celtic Christianity or the Platonic schools of Chartres or Oxford, and great personalities, like the Greek fathers (Irenaeus, Maximus the Confessor, Gregory of Nissa), St. Francis of Assisi, or St. Hildegard of Bingen, with their extraordinary contemplative and religious visions of nature. Clearly, the composite and, in some ways, problematic heritage, present in a large part of Christianity weakened it and made impossible a vigorous reaction against the worldview born in the Renaissance, when, as Nasr writes, the

> European man lost the paradise of the age of faith to gain in compensation the new earth of nature and natural forms to which he now turned his attention. Yet it was a nature which came to be less and less a reflection of a celestial reality. Renaissance man ceased to be the ambivalent man of the Middle Ages, half angel, half man, torn between heaven and earth. Rather, he became wholly man, but now a totally earth-bound creature. He gained his liberty at the expense of losing the freedom to transcend his terrestrial limitations. Freedom for him now became quantitative and horizontal rather than qualitative and vertical. (MN 64)

But the need of the Absolute and the Infinite is innate in man; he is created to seek them: in this way, rejecting the Divine Principle, at once "absolute" and "infinite," the search for them, now in the form of substitutes, continues all the same. The result is a shift from the vertical to the horizontal dimension:

> On the one hand, man absolutizes himself or his knowledge of the world in the form of science, and on the other hand he seeks the Infinite in the natural world, which is finite by definition . . . man turns to the material world for his infinite thirst, never satisfied with what he has on the material plane, directing an unending source of energy to the natural world, with the result that it transforms the order of nature into chaos and ugliness. (RON 272)

Furthermore this situation is worsened by the absolutization of secular man with its resulting anthropomorphism (and anthropocentrism), man becoming the only measure of all things. In some way the Church was also incapable of understanding in depth and totally the dangerousness of the new ideas, because in part it acted unconsciously as a go-between for them. Indeed,

> neither the "Oriental bureaucratism" of Needham nor any other social and economic explanation suffices to explain why the scientific revolution as seen in the West did not develop elsewhere. The most basic reason is that neither in Islam, nor India nor the Far East was the substance and stuff of nature so depleted of a sacramental and spiritual character, nor was the intellectual dimension of these traditions so enfeebled as to enable a purely secular science of nature and secular philosophy to develop outside the matrix of the traditional intellectual orthodoxy. (MN 97–98)

The rise of the Promethean, individualistic man in the Renaissance[14] coincided with the decisive loss of sacredness of the universe, while

Christianity became more and more oriented toward a radical transcendentalism, where God was seen, especially in Protestant thought, as the only source of activity and nature was reduced to a simply passive reality. This view was then used, in the first period following the Renaissance, by the antitraditional scientists and philosophers who took this idea of the divine role as a model for the relation between the "new" *active* man and nature, the latter seen as a dead thing to control and manipulate without moral or spiritual limits, according to an individualistic and mechanistic worldview.[15] With the work of scientists and philosophers like Galileo Galilei, Isaac Newton, Francis Bacon, René Descartes (RON 135–42), and so on, nature was totally desacralized and considered very similar to an opaque mass of atoms or a machine to use for utilitarian purposes, especially in Bacon's ideology. The main transformation, playing a pivotal role in the rise of secular science, was the substitution of the idea of cosmic order and laws, created by God, with the concept of "laws of nature" in mathematical form, discovered by human reason and completely separated from ethical and spiritual laws—an event which did not happen in other cultures with a deep scientific tradition, such as the Isalmic, Chinese, and Indian (RON 133). Galilei, Newton, and the other "modern" scientists imposed a totalitarian use of mathematics as a tool to know (and to change) the physical world, but—Nasr observes—"the mathematical aspect of things is not everything. It is concerned only with their quantitative dimension, not with the qualitative which connects each being ontologically to its source" (MN 121). A more mathematical precision in our vision of nature means a less direct symbolical understanding of nature: in this way we sacrifice an important part of reality to the arrogance of rationalism, which is not simply the normal use of reason, as some may think, but the consideration of *human* reason as the greatest and exclusive authority for the achievement of truth, attained by an autonomous path and having no need of intellection and revelation (RON 170).

In the end, the humanism of the Renaissance, as a logical process of development of its inner principles, generated the anti-humanism of scientism, so that "rather than man deciding the value of science and technology, these creations of man have become the criteria of man's worth and value" (MN 19). Nasr dissents completely from the idea that the responsibility of the victory of a manipulative and anthropocentric view of life and world, with the consequent ecological crisis, can be ascribed to the monotheistic tradition, as seen in the writings of Arnold Toynbee, the noted historian. The reason for his refusal of this theory is very clear-cut: "Such thinkers forget that the pure monotheism of Islam which belongs to the same Abrahamic tradition as Judaism and Christianity never lost sight of the sacred quality of nature as asserted by the Quran, and that Oriental Christianity and Judaism never developed the attitude of simple domination and plunder of nature that developed later in the history of the West" (MN 5). Seeing this process of decadence from the spiritual perspective, with the progressive loss of all cosmological sciences in the area of Christianity, as a consequence of the totalitarian hegemony of modern science, Nasr shows us the portentous growth of the cosmological sciences in other religious cultures, like Islam. He demonstrates a superb knowledge of the inner meaning of these traditional sciences and gives to us a clear outlook on the topic. Quoting his words, we can say that

> In a traditional civilization, like that of Islam, the cosmological sciences are closely related to the Revelation because in such civilizations the immutable revealed principle . . . manifests itself everywhere in social life as well as in the cosmos . . . cosmological sciences integrate the diverse phenomena of Nature into conceptual schemes all of which reflect the revealed principles and the central Idea of which they are so many applications in the domain of contingency. In this manner cosmology repeats the process of traditional art which likewise selects from the multiplicity of forms those that are in conformity with the spirit of the tradition in whose bosom it has come into being.[16]

Following this Nasr explains the different kinds of approaches and finalities in the study of nature in traditional civilizations. Such study can be made for the sake of utility, which does not mean a *utilitarian* approach, as is seen

> in ancient and medieval technology where aspects of Nature were studied with the aim of discovering the qualities which might make them useful to the daily needs of the society. Or such a study may be made with the aim of integrating cosmic existence into a pervasive rational system as with the Peripatetics, or into a mathematical system as with Archimedes. Or it may be with the aim of describing in detail the functioning of a particular domain of Nature, as in the biological works of Aristotle, and the medieval natural historians, or, again, in connection with the making of objects in which process art and industry before the machine age were always combined as in the medieval guilds and the branches of Hermeticism connected with them. Finally, Nature may be studied as a book of symbols or as an icon to be contemplated at a certain stage of the spiritual journey and a crypt from which the gnosis must escape in order to reach ultimate liberation and illumination.[17]

With his studies on cosmology Nasr shows that Islam is a culture with its specificity and creativity, including the sphere of science, and destroys the idea, based upon a Eurocentric and progressive view of history believed by many Westerners, that Islam was only a means of transmitting a large body of knowledge from the Greco-Roman civilization to Europe, after the so-called dark centuries of the early Middle Ages. The Islamic cosmological sciences are still alive and valid, but their main value is not in the material aspects, separated from their context (so emphasized by progressive historians like George Sarton), but in their qualitative and spiritual mark.

Finally I would like to give evidence of Nasr's excellent knowledge of modern science, as we can see reading his essays on the new physics, like that of Bohm and Prigogine (RON 147 ff), the Gaia hypothesis by J. Lovelock (RON 282 ff) or evolution, criticized with very clear philosophical and scientific argumentation.[18] I would like to cite his words concerning some doctrinal positions of Catholic thought, where we see a hallucinating "Darwinization of theology . . . the surrender of this queen of the sciences to the microscope, which is represented by Teilhard de Chardin" (KS 240). As Nasr states, "The deification of historical process has become so powerful and such a compelling force that, in the souls of many human beings, it has taken the place of religion" (KS 234). We know how important time is for Darwinism and neo-Darwinism for explaining harmony and order in the phenomenal world. Really—I think—we can identify in this modern idolatry, from the structural point of view, the features of a pseudo-religion, coming from a secularization of the idea of Divinity, where "time," in its merely quantitative meaning, is "God," and *chance* and *necessity*—that is, *random genetic mutations* and *natural selection*—are his "powers" or "hands."

One of the most striking characteristics of our time is that man is destroying the Earth with "unprecedented ferocity" as consequence of his mechanistic and desacralized view of nature. The reaction to this environmental devastation has stimulated the genesis and the success of green parties which

> have mushroomed everywhere. The moving force for those movements remains, however, by and large purely external. For a humanity turned towards outwardness by the very processes of modernization, it is not so easy to see that the blight wrought upon the environment is in reality an externalization of the destitution of the inner state of the soul of that humanity whose actions are responsible for the ecological crisis. (MN 3)

Unfortunately, "the ecological movement has become deprived of the revivifying breath of authentic spirituality and the significance of the veritable spiritual dimension of the ecological crisis has become forgotten, for there is no authentic spirituality without orthodoxy understood in the most universal sense of the term" (MN 6).

The same environmental engineering is insufficient to change the situation, reversing the course of events, because it is only a technological intervention. Nasr clearly does not oppose a better "sweet" technology, but, using his words,

> such feats of science and engineering alone will not solve the problem. There is no choice but to answer these and similar questions and to bring to the fore

> the spiritual dimension and the historical roots of the ecological crisis which many refuse to take into consideration to this day. One of the chief causes for this lack of acceptance of the spiritual dimension of the ecological crisis is the survival of a scientism which continues to present modern science not as a particular way of knowing nature, but as a complete and totalitarian philosophy which reduces all reality to the physical domain and does not wish under any condition to accept the possibility of the existence of non-scientistic world-views. While not denying the legitimacy of a science limited to the physical dimension of reality, alternative worldviews drawn from traditional doctrines remain constantly aware of the inner nexus which binds physical nature to the realm of the Spirit, and the outward face of things to an inner reality which they at once veil and reveal. This reductionism and scientism has prevented Western science, for the most part, from turning to the more inward causes of the environmental crisis, while many individual scientists become ever more interested in ecological questions and even somewhat more responsible for the often catastrophic effects of their "disinterested" and "pure" research. (MN 4)

Only in few cases have the underlying and essential causes of our crisis been brought to light, "perhaps partly because if they were to be made known there would have to be a radical change in the very thought pattern of many of those who discern the ill effects of these causes. And this change few are willing to accept or to undergo" (MN 13).

Nasr points out that our reply to today's environmental crisis, coming from a long process of spiritual decay, must be on the global scale, because any superficial intervention or action, including what we do at the philosophical level (that is, a new secular philosophy of life which would bring mankind to respect nature), is too weak to stop the massive destruction of our planet. This is because *the cause of the crisis was a darkening of religious spirit and the reply must be at the same elevated level.* The ecological crisis is only an externalization of an inner disquietude and cannot be solved without a spiritual rebirth of "modern" man, because "the environmental crisis is before anything a spiritual crisis" (RON 285). For this reason it is impossible to live in harmony with that wonderful theophany which is virgin nature, while people forget or remain indifferent to the Source of that theophany (MN 9).

Nasr points out that every attack on monotheism in itself serves the bizarre marriage between ecological movements and all kinds of pseudo-religious sects, and also serves the development of false and dangerous so-called "new religions," lacking in any real metaphysical doctrine. The role of a true metaphysics can be very important to

> aid in the re-discovery of virgin nature by removing the strangulating hold that rationalism has placed upon man's vision of nature. There is a need to rediscover virgin nature as a source of truth and beauty in the most strict

> intellectual sense and not merely in the sentimental one. Nature must be seen as an affirmation and aid in the spiritual life and even a means of grace rather than the obscure and opaque reality it has come to be considered. . . . The rediscovery of virgin nature does not mean a flight of individualistic and Promethean man toward nature. While in the state of rebellion against Heaven man carries with him his own limitations even when he turns to nature. These limitations veil the spiritual message of nature for him so that he derives no benefit from it. It is in this way that the modern urbanized citizen in search of virgin nature takes with him those very elements that destroy nature and thereby he destroys the very thing he is searching for. (MN 118)

If we wish to live well with nature we must accept its norms and its rhythms, giving up the idea of dominating and manipulating it, because earthly man cannot be the measure of all things, nor can human utility be the parameter for judging nature in an anthropomorphic view of the world (MN 86). For Nasr, Christian doctrine itself should be enlarged to include a doctrine concerning the spiritual significance of nature, which means a true "philosophy of nature." This result can be obtained with the aid of Oriental metaphysical and religious traditions wherein such doctrines are still alive, because metaphysics must be the background for the philosophy of nature, a background lacking in Christianity. "These traditions would not be so much a source of new knowledge as an aid to *anamnesis*, to the remembrance of teachings within Christianity now mostly forgotten. The result would be the bestowal once again of a sacred quality upon nature, providing a new background for the sciences without negating their value or legitimacy within their own domain."[19]

In conclusion, synthesizing the message of the ecological thought (a real "deep ecology"!) of Seyyed Hossein Nasr tells us that we have to *resacralize the nature connecting us with its Divine Source*, the metaphysical Origin of everything.

GIOVANNI MONASTRA

PADUA, ITALY
JANUARY 2000

NOTES

1. S. H. Nasr, *Ideals and Realities of Islam* (London: Allen and Unwin, 1966).
2. S. H. Nasr, *Sufi Essays* (London: Allen and Unwin, 1972).
3. S. H. Nasr, *Man and Nature—The Spiritual Crisis in Modern Man* (ABC International Group - Kazi Publications: Chicago, 1997 [last edition]), hereafter cited in the text as "MN."

I must say that S. H. Nasr has been well known in Italy for about twenty-five years, when, aside from the three previous books, all published by Rusconi respectively in 1974, 1975, and 1977, also his *Persia: Bridge of Turquoise* (with R. Beny) and *Science and Civilization in Islam* were translated into Italian and published, the first by Mondadori in 1977 and the second by Feltrinelli in the same year. Nasr also published many essays as prefaces or in collective works or in journals (mainly *Conoscenza Religiosa*), concerning topics like the traditional thought, Islamic religion and culture, the nature of science, and the spiritual roots of the ecological problem.

4. R. Fondi, *Organicismo ed evoluzionismo*, edited by G. Monastra (Il Corallo -Il Settimo Sigillo: Padova-Roma, 1982); revised and updated French edition: R. Fondi, *La Révolution Organiciste*, edited by G. Monastra (Paris: Livre-Club du Labyrinthe, 1986).

5. T. Burckhardt, *Scienza moderna e saggezza tradizionale* (Torino: Borla, 1968), p. 39 ff.

6. J. Evola, *Cavalcare la tigre* (Roma: Mediterranee, 1995), p. 115 ff.

7. A. Faivre, *Esoterismo e Tradizione* (Torino: Elledici, 1999) (partial Italian translation of: A. Faivre, *Symboles et Mythes dans les mouvements initiatiques et ésotériques (XVII °-XIX ° siecles) Filiations et emprunts* (Paris: Edidit-La Table d'Emeraude, collection Aries, 1999).

8. W. C. Chittick in *The Complete Bibliography of the Works of Seyyed Hossein Nasr from 1958 through April 1993*, by M. Aminrazavi and Z. Moris (Kuala Lumpur, Malaysia: Islamic Academy of Science of Malaysia, 1994), p. xiv.

9. Nasr, *Religion and the Order of Nature* (New York: Oxford University Press, 1996), hereafter cited in the text as "RON."

10. It is interesting to emphasize, as Nasr does following the Elémire Zolla's observations, that the term "world" comes from the Old English "weorold," which probably derives from "wer," meaning "man," and "ald," meaning "full grown." (Ibid., p. 74, note 95).

11. L. White, "The Historical Roots of Our Ecological Crisis," *Science* 155 (1967): 1203–7.

12. A. Bonora, "L'uomo coltivatore e custode del suo mondo in Gen. 1–11," in A. Caprioli and L. Vaccaro, eds., *Questione ecologica e conscienza cristiana* (Brescia: Morcelliana, 1988), pp. 155–66. See also: G. B. Guzzetti and E. Gentili, *Cristianesimo ed ecologia* (Milano: Editrice Ancora, 1989).

13. On Pre-Socratics see by G. Colli: *La nascita della filosofia* (Milano: Adelphi, 1978); *La natura ama nascondersi* (Milano: Adelphi, 1998); *La sapienza greca*, vol. 3 (Milano: Adelphi, 1990–1993). Also, A. Tonelli, *Eraclito - Dell' Origine* (Milano: Feltrinelli, 1993); A. Somigliana, *Monismo indiano e monismo greco nei frammenti di Eraclito* (Padova: CEDAM, 1961); J. Biès, *Empédocle d'Agrigente* (Paris, 1969); and, with some reservations, M. L. West, *Early Greek Philosophy and the Orient* (New York: Oxford University Press, 1971).

14. Nasr, *Knowledge and the Sacred* (Albany: State University of New York Press, 1989), pp. 162 ff, hereafter cited in the text as "KS."

15. On this issue see also the essay by Gery B. Deason in D. L. Lindberg and R. L. Numbers, eds., *God and Nature: Historical Essays on the Encounter between*

Christianity and Science (London-Berkeley-Los Angeles: University of California Press, 1986).

16. S. H. Nasr, *An Introduction to Islamic Cosmological Doctrines* (Albany: State University of New York, 1993), p. 1. See also: S. H. Nasr, *Science and Civilization in Islam* (Cambridge: Harvard University Press, 1968) and *Islamic Science—An Illustrated Study* (World of Islam Festival Publishing Company Ltd, printed by Westerham: Westerham Press Ltd, 1976).

17. S. H. Nasr, *An Introduction to Islamic Cosmological Doctrines*, op. cit., p. 2.

18. S. H. Nasr, *Knowledge and the Sacred*, op. cit., pp. 233 ff, and *Religion and the Order of Nature*, op. cit., pp. 144–46.

19. Ibid., p. 14. Concerning the "modern" science, Nasr specifies that although it is legitimate in itself, its role, function, and application "have become illegitimate and even dangerous because of the lack of a higher form of knowledge into which science could be integrated and the destruction of the sacred and spiritual value of nature."

Editors' Note: Giovanni Monastra, an Italian biologist working in a pharmaceutical company near Padua, is a "perennialist," mainly involved in research on sciences of nature, anthropology, traditional medicine, and symbolism. Two essays of his were published in English: "Darwinism: Scientific Theory or Historic Illusion?" and "The 'Yin-Yang' among the Insignia of the Roman Empire?" both in *Sophia—A Journal of Traditional Studies* 3, no. 1 (1997): 57–99, and 6, no. 2 (2000): 39–60.

REPLY TO GIOVANNI MONASTRA

Professor Monastra is a practicing scientist and at the same time a philosopher devoted to the traditional perspective. This is a rare combination especially if the scientist be a biologist since this science has become dominated by the anti-metaphysical pseudo-myth of evolution since the late nineteenth century as has no other science. His commentary upon my treatment of science in relation to religion is therefore particularly pertinent, speaking, as he does, from "within" both worlds. He begins his essay with a statement which is startling, coming from a scientist, but also absolutely true. He asks what is the main problem of our time and continues, "Is it learning or discovering new things? Absolutely not. We do not need to discover but to *rediscover*." I could not but agree completely with this assertion. Being in the situation in which modernity has placed us, practically every new discovery simply accelerates the chaos and dissolution of the world in which we live. Of course every form of knowledge, if it be authentic, has its own legitimacy and one cannot put boundaries upon human intelligence even if it has taken a luciferian direction. But what the world needs today much more than discovering new things is the remembrance of things forgotten. The very survival of humanity depends not on new discoveries within the framework established by the brave new world now being created on a global scale, but on *re-discovering* the millennial truths by which humanity has lived, truths which are none other than the perennial philosophy and its multifarious applications.

Monastra then turns to the significance of the traditional sciences and how their being branded as irrational and superstitious caused them to be cast aside and forgotten. I think that this is a very important point to which little attention was paid until quite recently when a number of ethnobotanists and physicians started scrambling into the living habitat of primal people in quest of the latter's knowledge of herbs and their medicinal properties. Although carried out mostly for utilitarian and often purely economic reasons, such efforts have nevertheless pointed to the enormous amount of knowledge that has been lost and is still being lost as a result of the branding of traditional sciences as fantasy and superstition by modern scientists blinded by the *hubris* generated by the success of their own enterprise on a certain level. Did early generations of people who colonized America, Africa, Oceania and who destroyed much of the traditional culture of those areas, and even the population itself, think of the thousands of years of experience of and experiment with animals, plants, winds, water, the soil, and so on, which these people had assembled in a body of knowledge which is no less science than is modern botany or geology? I am reminded of a passage from an essay of Thomas Berry which states, "How much we might have learned from the native peoples of this [American] continent had we arrived with an open spirit and a reverence for the beauty and complexity of the land."[1] This famous environmentalist is reaffirming what Monastra has stated and I have discussed in another language over the years.

Even today there remains some knowledge of traditional sciences of nature in various parts of the world which are still denied a place in the modern arena of knowledge as a result of the monopolistic claim which modern science makes concerning the knowledge of nature, considering itself to be not *a* science of nature but *the* science of nature. Denied legitimacy in official circles, traditional sciences either die out or are relegated, often in a deformed condition, to the margins of society and in a mutilated form as elements of the new religions and of the teachings of occult groups. I am grateful to the author for pointing out this very important truth in the present day context of the study of the sciences.

The author speaks of the influence of my works translated into Italian in the '60s and '70s and their impact upon him. After thanking the author for his comments, I wish to say a few words about the translation of those works and my contacts with Italian intellectual circles. During the decades of the '60s and '70s I traveled often to Italy and delivered many lectures at the University of Rome and the Accademia Nazionale dei Lincei dealing mostly with Islamic and Iranian studies. But at that time I also developed a rapport with Italian philosophical circles through two channels: Giorgio de Santillana and Elémire Zolla. De Santillana lived in America and was my professor at MIT but he visited Italy often and even got me to participate with him in the four hundredth anniversary of the birth of Galileo in Florence in 1964. He introduced me to a number of Italian philosophers and historians of science and was instrumental in the translation and publication of my *Science and Civilization in Islam* into Italian by Feltrinelli in Rome. Zolla was at that time Italy's leading traditionalist writer to whom I was introduced by Titus Burckhardt. A close friendship developed between Zolla and myself, and he also visited me in Tehran. During my various journeys to Italy, he introduced me to a number of Italian philosophers including J. Evola and F. Sciacca. It was also Zolla who approached Rusconi to have a translated into Italian and rendered many of my essays himself into Italian in the review *Conoscenza religiosa* of which he was himself the editor. By 1980 a number of my books and essays were available in Italian and became the subject of interest for a number of Italian savants who wanted to study the Islamic world and especially Islamic philosophy and the sciences. The translation of my *Man and Nature*, along with a number of essays on the traditional sciences and cosmology, also attracted some philosophers and scientists not concerned with Islamic studies directly such as Dr. Monastra. Strangely enough, however, after I migrated to America and traveled less often to Italy, this intellectual relation became weakened. Only a couple of essays of mine have been translated into Italian during the past two decades but there is now a plan to render *Knowledge and the Sacred* into Italian. In any case I am of course pleased to know that my works in Italian were useful in the framing of the ideas of Monastra and Roberto Fondi concerning "organicistic and holistic tendencies in biology."

Monastra speaks of the disillusionment of many scientists concerning scientism and at the same time the continuous domination of scientism as an ideology in the modern world. His observation is true but one needs to add that unfortunately most disillusioned scientists—in contrast to Fondi, Monastra himself, or Wolfgang Smith (whose essay appears in this volume)—keep this disillusionment to themselves and rarely venture out to criticize the scientific enterprise, not for what it has achieved or for what it has not achieved, but for what it is *claimed* to have achieved by its worshipful bondsmen. If only reputable and honest scientists, who are the first to realize the limitations of all that modern science has discovered or can discover in the future, could become vanguards of a movement to kill scientism and reductionism before they kill us all, the situation would improve rapidly. But alas that is not the case today despite the exceptional efforts of a few figures in both Europe and America. Meanwhile, the technological juggernaut, fed and supported fully by modern science which makes modern technology possible keeps accelerating its pace of destroying the natural environment and superficializing human life.

Monastra brings up another issue which is of importance and needs to be answered. He speaks of the fact that most perennialists and traditionalists have ignored the world of science. This statement needs to be understood in context and must also be somewhat modified. First of all, the traditionalists have been all concerned before everything else with metaphysics, the supreme science whose forgetting in the West made possible both the death of traditional science and the birth of a science separated from the sacred. As for the cosmological and traditional sciences which result from the application of metaphysical principles to various domains of contingency, each of the major traditional authorities concentrated on a particular science or set of sciences. For example, Guénon who was a mathematician as well as metaphysician, did not only write on the general principles of sacred science and the science of symbolism, but also on mathematics (especially calculus) seen from the point of view of metaphysics. Coomaraswamy, although originally a geologist, did not write to any appreciable degree about the traditional cosmological sciences in themselves (although he did compose a few essays on the subject), but did write a great deal about these sciences as they pertained to traditional art and also on time and space which are of course so basic to the sciences of nature as well as to art. Schuon was interested especially in the science of man or anthropology, if this discipline be understood in a traditional sense, and not as much in the sciences of nature, and he devoted many luminous studies to the traditional science of man. He was also interested in traditional cosmology in general, especially that of the Native Americans whose cosmological doctrines he elucidated with unprecedented depth. Burckhardt was deeply drawn to the cosmological sciences and wrote two of the most profound books of the twentieth century on the subject of alchemy and astrology along with his essays on the cosmological sciences. As for Martin Lings, his love in addition to metaphysics has always been for the science of language and literature, being as he is an outstanding poet. It also needs to be added that although the traditionalist authors did not perhaps know all of the scientists mentioned by Monastra who were against scientism and reductionism, Schuon and Burckhardt, whom I knew well personally, did know some of them including of course Goethe as well as Bernhard Bavinck.

This having been said, I admit that I have written more on the traditional sciences, cosmology, and the philosophy of nature than have the other traditionalist authors. That has been a matter of vocation for me, but my intellectual and metaphysical perspective has not differed from theirs. In light of these facts, I am in agreement with the modification Monastra has made concerning Faivre's statement. For my part I know the works of most of the scientists whom Monastra has mentioned along with others such as Wolfgang Smith for whose interpretation of quantum mechanics I hold the greatest respect. The scientists mentioned by the author are important in that, while speaking from within the scientific community, they reveal the limitations of the dominant modern worldview derived from the generalization of the tenets of modern science. They thus seek to break the walls of the mental prison in which most modern people are confined and point to the possibility of visions of the infinitely expanding horizon beyond the confines of the scientific worldview. But they cannot provide that metaphysical vision on the basis of their science. What is needed is that one should possess that metaphysical knowledge independently along with detailed knowledge of a modern science and then seek to interpret what is not mere conjecture but knowledge in that science in light of metaphysical principles, and then to integrate that science into a framework provided by the perennial philosophy rather than by Cartesian bifurcation and quantitative reductionism. The works of Fondi, Guiseppi Sermonti, Monastra himself in biology, and W. Smith in physics are themselves fine examples of the task that I believe should be carried out by scientists. In achieving this desired end certainly the views of such figures as Uexküll, Portmann, Heitler, Chauvin, Bohm, and others can be of great assistance. The works of such men and women also need to be made better known on a more popular level as a cure for the mortal illness of scientism and reductionism.

In responding to the author's discussion of my views on the environmental crisis, perhaps it would be useful if I clarified further why I turned to this problem and its causes in the way that I did. As mentioned in my autobiography, I had always had the greatest love for nature since my childhood. It was as if mountains, trees, and brooks, not to mention animals, spoke to me. For that very reason the ugliness created by modern industry was always particularly painful to me. This love for nature, towards which I felt as a friend and protector, was fortified both intellectually and emotionally by my study of traditional texts and immersion in Persian Sufi poetry which sings so often of the sacred quality of nature. My love of nature was also confirmed and strengthened by reading the nineteenth-century Romantic nature poetry of figures such as Wordsworth who showed such sensitivity to nature, although Romantic poetry lacked the intellectual dimension that I had discovered in traditional philosophies of nature. Not only had I read Thoreau's *Walden,* but in the '50s I would often walk around Walden Pond itself, usually in the late afternoon and evening, before much of it became spoiled and pondered about what Thoreau had written.

The shock of seeing such a rapid destruction of the natural environment around the Boston area along with my study of traditional cosmologies and philosophies of nature in contrast to the quantitative and completely secularized philosophies of nature prevalent in the West of which I was very critical, combined to lead me to an intellectual intuition of the coming of a major crisis in the natural environment long before the terms "ecology" and "natural environment" had become popular and anyone spoke of the ecological crisis. Reading Rachel Carson's *Silent Spring* did not only confirm my intuition of an impending disaster, but also led me furthermore to seek the causes of this situation rather than criticizing only the effects. I realized, while still in my early twenties, that the environmental crisis was in fact the result of a spiritual crisis within the soul of modern man and not simply the consequence of bad engineering. My early books on Islamic science and cosmology, the study of the history of science, religion, and philosophy in the West and comparative religion and philosophy gave me the necessary intellectual disciplines to study in depth and in a comparative framework the cause of the crisis at hand. When the occasion arose for me to deliver the Rockefeller Series Lectures at the University of Chicago on the theme of man and nature in 1966, I took the opportunity to write *Man and Nature* to which Professor Monastra refers. This work was followed by many essays and lectures on the subject culminating in *Religion and the Order of Nature*. After over forty years of study of this subject, I still believe that the environmental crisis is primarily the result of an inner spiritual crisis of modern man and the darkening of the soul within man who then projects this darkness upon the environment and destroys its balance and harmony.

As the author writes, in my analysis of the causes of the environmental crisis I disagree with L. White and A. Toynbee and refuse to lay the blame at the feet of Judaism and Christianity. But I do agree with the author when he writes of the consequences of the ambivalence in the Bible concerning the status of nature. The negative aspect of these consequences did not, however, manifest themselves in the European Middle Ages when faith was strong, nor in Eastern Christianity. Other elements, especially the revival in the Renaissance of desacralized views of nature held by certain Greek schools and the eclipse of the traditional civilization of the West itself, along with the rise in the Renaissance of the titanic view of man enmeshed in rationalism, humanism, and individualism, all had a crucial role to play in actualizing and bringing out the negative aspects of the ambivalence in question.

In reference to the Ionians, Monastra points to what he considers to be a contradiction in my thought and writes that "Nasr identifies in the Ionians, like Thales, Anaximander, or Anaximenes, the first philosophers, with fundamentally naturalistic interests . . ." contrasting this view with my assertion that the water of Thales is not ordinary water but "the psycho-spiritual substratum and principle of the physical world." The author refers to my *Religion and the Order of Nature* (p. 82) as reference concerning my assertion about the "naturalistic interests" of the Ionians. I have, however, not made such a statement on that page or elsewhere and never used the term naturalistic in this context. Rather, on page 82, I write that the Ionians "were keenly interested in the order of nature" which certainly does not mean being naturalistic in the current sense of the term. Furthermore, I add on that page that for these early "natural philosophers" the cosmos "was alive and ensouled." There is therefore no contradiction in my two statements about Thales. In fact one complements the other and I continue to hold the view that the element or substance with which these early Greek philosophers dealt must not be confused with modern notions of matter or natural substances from which any and every form of psycho-spiritual reality has become excluded.

Following this criticism, the author summarizes my views concerning the deeper causes of the environmental crisis as well as the confrontation between the sacred and desacralized views of nature. I am in full agreement with his analysis and am particularly pleased that a practicing scientist, who at the same time has extensive knowledge of Western intellectual history, confirms my analysis of the subject. I am particularly happy that he confirms my assessment of the serious nature of the environmental problem when he reformulates my words as follows: ". . . any superficial intervention or action, including what we do at the philosophical level (that is, a new secular philosophy of life which would bring mankind to respect nature), is too weak to stop the massive destruction of our planet. This is because *the cause of the crisis was a darkening of religious spirit and the reply must be at the same elevated level.*" I have quoted his words in full because I find them quite significant coming from a scientist. Also these words point to an important issue with which I have had to deal over the years, namely, that after the realization of the environmental crisis by a number of secular philosophers, they naturally want to apply secular solutions to it. It is important to bring out the differences in my approach to this problem in comparison with this class of philosophers.

There are a number of scientists, both in American and Europe, who share Professor Monastra's views, although many keep these views to themselves. Fortunately, he has been able to participate in this volume and provide the opportunity for this exchange with a whole sector of the contemporary scientific community who have been interested in traditional writings, including my works, and who have been able to make use of some of the ideas expressed therein in their own expositions which stand out from the writings of so many mainstream scientists, which are dominated by the ideology of scientism and reductionism.

S. H. N.

NOTE

1. "Rediscovering Turtle Island," *Lapis* 10 (1999): 27.

16

Ashok K. Gangadean

THE QUEST FOR THE UNIVERSAL GLOBAL SCIENCE

Prologue: Critical Reflections on Professor Nasr's Vision of the Need for a Sacred Science

In these reflections I will focus on central themes from Nasr's *The Need for a Sacred Science* and *Knowledge and the Sacred*. These two intimately related works present a comprehensive and integrated vision of Nasr's mature thought. I will focus especially on his narrative of the need for a sacred science. I find here a deep convergence with findings of my own quest over the past three decades to clarify the missing primal science of Logos.

Perhaps it would be good to begin with a summary review of some of the main themes and concerns raised by Nasr to help set the context for this exploration.

I. Nasr's Vision of Sacred Science

Nasr's thesis of the need for a sacred science is a unifying theme that brings together a range of insights and concerns running throughout his thought. In its most simplified form his thesis is that there exists a Primordial Tradition that flows from an Absolute Truth which has been expressed in diverse ways through the ages. This tradition has been articulated in various formulations in the evolving school of *philosophia perennis* (a philosophical tradition which holds that there is a fundamental common ground of wisdom and truth recognized in a vast diversity of worldviews through the ages).

This school of perennial philosophy is connected with a view that there is a primal science, sacred science, based on a universal metaphysics of this Ultimate Truth. It is held that diverse authentic cultural (religious, spiritual, philosophical) traditions through the ages have recognized, formulated, and embodied this Eternal Wisdom in diverse ways. One main point stressed by Nasr is that the diversity of these sacred traditions is important even in recognizing that they flow from a common foundational Unity. One important common factor is that these sacred traditions are grounded in the Primordial Truth, flow from a common sacred science of metaphysics, and are thus grounded in a sacred view of reality and the possibilities for human life.

A central theme stressed by Nasr is that with the rise of the modernist worldview in Europe since the seventeenth century there has been an increasing eclipse of the sacred traditions and a tragic loss of the perennial wisdom and sacred science that they involve. The modernist worldview, he finds, is based on a secular humanism and materialism that moves away from the Primal Spirit that is the ground of the sacred traditions and of Perennial Wisdom.

He finds that this development of secular modernism has resulted in tragic consequences for the human condition. It has resulted in all sorts of pernicious fragmentation in cultural life and has placed modern cultures on a course that he claims is not sustainable and is devastating for human flourishing and for the ecology. The secularization of modernism has severed human life from its authentic grounding and connection with reality and Primordial Spirit which is the source of human flourishing. His main finding is that contemporary human cultures desperately need a return to the sacred traditions and to the Perennial Wisdom that flows from the power of sacred science. This is the most urgent priority in the human condition today.

Apparently he sees this return to sacred science and Perennial Wisdom as vital for all aspects of human life, and essential for the advancement of the sciences as well. He insists that the diversity of the wisdom traditions should be respected and honored, and that in authentically living the inner truth of an authentic sacred tradition one lives and embodies the perennial truth being expressed differently in all sacred traditions. In this way the return to tradition in this perennial spirit of sacred science can resolve one of the most profound challenges facing the modern world—that of honoring diversity of religious and cultural forms while achieving consensus and unity in truth and reality.

Before raising some critical questions for this line of thought it would be helpful to further texture the complex ideas expressed here by looking more closely at the actual words of Professor Nasr on these themes. The following excerpts are taken from *The Need for a Sacred Science*.

(1) *What is sacred science?*

> There is first of all the Supreme Science or metaphysics, which deals with the Divine Principle and Its manifestations in the light of that Principle. It is what one might call *scientia sacra* in the highest meaning of the term. It is the science which lies in the very center of man's being as well as at the heart of all orthodox and authentic religions and which is attainable by the intellect, that supernaturally natural faculty with which normal human beings . . . are endowed. This principial knowledge is by nature rooted in the sacred, for it issues from that Reality which constitutes the Sacred as such. It is a knowledge which is also being, a unitive knowledge which transcends ultimately the dichotomy between the object and the subject in that Unity which is the source of all that is sacred and to which the experience of the sacred leads those who are able to reach the abode of that Unity. (pp. 1–2)

Note: This key passage makes clear that there is an Ultimate Reality which is sacred and which is the unifying force in all humans and in diverse authentic religions and traditions. Humans are endowed with a natural capacity to overcome the fragmentation and reach the primal Unity of this Reality.

(2) *What is the view of* philosophia perennis?

> By *philosophia perennis*—to which should be added the adjective *universalis* —is meant a knowledge which has always been and will always be and which is of universal character both in the sense of existing among peoples of different climes and epochs and of dealing with universal principles. This knowledge which is available to the intellect, is, moreover, contained in the heart of all religions or traditions, and its realization and attainment is possible only through those traditions and by means of methods, rites, symbols, images and other means sanctified by the message from heaven or the Divine which gives birth to each tradition. (pp. 53–54)

Note: It should be noted that Nasr claims this tradition of universal wisdom is situated in the heart of all religions or traditions and is theoretically attainable by individuals through the power of the intellect, although he stresses that the "norm" is such that "attainment of this knowledge depends upon the grace and framework which tradition alone provides" (p. 54). This helps to explain why he repeatedly stresses the primary importance of honoring our sacred traditions, and of gaining access to perennial wisdom through the particularity of our traditions. Note also that this perennial wisdom running through our traditions is based on "universal principles" (ostensibly valid for all worldviews).

(3) *What is the metaphysical ground of* philosophia perennis?

> The *philosophia perennis* possesses branches and ramifications pertaining to cosmology, anthropology, art and other disciplines, but at its heart lies pure metaphysics, if this latter term is understood . . . as the science of Ultimate Reality, as a *scientia sacra*. . . . Metaphysics understood in the perspective of *philosophia perennis* is a veritable "divine science" and not a purely mental construct which would change with every alternation in cultural fashions of the day or with new discoveries of a science of the material world. This traditional metaphysics, which in reality should be used in the singular as *metaphysic* [italics mine], is a knowledge which sanctifies and illuminates; it is a gnosis if this term is shorn of its sectarian connotations going back to early Christian centuries. It is a knowledge which lies at the heart of religion, which illuminates the meaning of religious rites, doctrines and symbols and which also provides the key to the understanding of both the necessity of the plurality of religions and the way to penetrate into other religious universes . . . (p. 54)

Note: It is clear in this passage that Nasr claims there is a pure *universal metaphysics*—a divine science—of ultimate reality at the heart of perennial philosophy. It is noteworthy that Nasr stresses that it is a *singular science* which of course suggests that this science gets at the fundamental reality behind diverse worlds. And it should be remembered that this is a sacred science since it is grounded in the Universal Divine Principle. This will be important for us in the subsequent discussion. Nasr is at pains to distinguish this "school" from other versions of "universal wisdom" by insisting that the tradition he has in mind stresses orthodoxy—"If there is one principle which all the traditional authors in question repeat incessantly, it is orthodoxy. . . . They are orthodox and the great champions of *universal orthodoxy*" (italics mine, p. 55). We will explore this theme shortly when we take a critical look at the "tradition" of pure metaphysics and inquire into its "global" potential.

(4) *What is the global potential of the sacred science*?

> According to *philosophia perennis*, reality is not exhausted by the psychophysical world in which human beings usually function, nor is consciousness limited to the everyday level of awareness of the men and women of present-day humanity. Ultimate Reality . . . is beyond all determination and limitation. It is the Absolute and Infinite from which issues goodness like the rays of the sun which of necessity emanate from it. Whether the Principle is envisioned as Fullness or Emptiness depends upon the point of departure of the particular metaphysical interpretation in question. (pp. 55–56)
>
> The school of *philosophia perennis* speaks of tradition and traditions. It believes that there is a Primordial Tradition which constituted original or archetypical man's primal spiritual and intellectual heritage received through

> direct revelation when Heaven and earth were still "united." This Primordial Tradition is reflected in all later traditions. . . . (p. 57)

Note: This passage makes an important distinction between everyday consciousness (and the everyday worldviews that flow from that level of awareness) and the direct encounter with Ultimate Reality which is beyond all determination, and beyond the worldviews of everyday life. It is also noteworthy that this Primal Reality expressed in the *Primordial Tradition* admits of different interpretations and expressions. We shall explore this "global" potential of perennial wisdom below.

(5) *What does it mean to see ultimate reality as sacred or to say that God is Reality?*

> God as Ultimate Reality is not only the Supreme Person but also the source of all that is, hence at once Supra-Being, God as Person and the Godhead or Infinite Essence of which Being is the first determination . . . God as Reality is at once absolute, infinite and good or perfect. In Himself He is the Absolute which partakes of no relativity in Itself or in its Essence. The Divine Essence cannot but be absolute and one . . . God as Reality is also infinite, *the* Infinite, as this term is to be understood metaphysically . . . Ultimate Reality contains the source of all cosmic possibilities and in fact all possibilities as such even the metacosmic . . . Metaphysically, He is the All-Possibility. (pp. 8–9)

Note: These excerpts are striking in presenting reality as God. Here it is clear that Nasr has entered into the perspective and language of pure universal metaphysics. In this language of reality pure metaphysics presumably is presenting a universally binding narrative for all worldviews. The "God as Reality" thesis would be binding even on those who do not countenance "god" and who reject "god-talk." These passages stress that whatever your worldview, it owes its possibility to the Absolute Divine Principle. Presumably, if all people understood this "pure metaphysics" they would recognize the global truth of this "god talk": "there would in fact be no agnostics around if only it were possible to teach metaphysics to everyone" (p. 9). Of course this raises sensitive issues which we shall take up below when we explore the "global" potential and scope of perennial wisdom and sacred science.

(6) *What is the sacred science of the self, moving beyond the ego*?

> In order to reach the Ultimate Self through the expansion of awareness of the center of consciousness, man must reverse the cosmogonic process which has crystallized both the variations and reverberations of the Self within what

> appears to be the cosmic veil as separate and objective existence. And this reversal must of necessity begin with the negation of the lower self . . . The Ultimate Self in its inner infinitude is beyond all determination and cosmic polarization. . . . (p. 16)
>
> The contemplative disciplines of all traditions of both East and West insist in fact on the primacy of the awareness of the self and its nature. . . . (p. 18)
>
> The traditional science of the soul, along with the methods for the realization of the Self, a science which is to be found in every integral tradition, is the means whereby self-awareness expands to reach the empyrean of the Ultimate Self. This traditional science is the result of both intellectual penetration and experiment with and experience of the self by those who have been able to navigate over its vast expanses with the aid of a spiritual guide. (p. 19)

Note: These excerpts are quite important because they stress that in the universal metaphysics/sacred science there is a vital difference between the everyday ego-self and the Ultimate Self which is in direct communion with the Primal Reality. Nasr makes clear over and over that this fundamental truth has been articulated across the vast range of sacred traditions through the ages. Note here that the true inner Self has an infinite structure that is beyond all determination and polarity. In this respect sacred science yields universal knowledge/realization of the Self across worldviews. We shall explore this theme below.

(7) *What are unity and diversity in the human condition*?

> While truth is one, its expressions are many, especially for modern man who lives in a world in which the homogeneity of the traditional ambience is destroyed and in which there is on the one hand acceptance and in fact "absolutization" of secular man and the humanism based upon man conceived in such a manner, and on the other hand the presence of diverse sacred traditions whose reality can no longer be neglected. Consequently, if one is to address the human condition today, one must not only assert the unity of the truth and the oneness of the Spirit, but also the multiple reflections of the world of the Spirit in the human ambience. (p. 45)

Note: This recurring theme stresses that truth is one while its expressions are many. This is Nasr's archetypical model for sacred science which seeks to bring out the fundamental truth while honoring the diversity of manifestations of this truth in the human situation. Here he opens the diagnosis and critique of the modern secular worldview. He continues,

> The one spirit somehow evades modern man, leaving in its wake a multitude of contending egos, of feuding families and of general social disintegration . . . The oneness which people of good intention seek cannot, however, be achieved

> save through contact with Spirit, which is one in itself and many in its earthly reflections. . . . No contact with the Spirit is possible save through the dimension of transcendence, which stands always before man and which connects him with Ultimate Reality whether it be called the Lord, or Brahman or *Śūnyatā*. . . . The human spirit as understood in the humanist sense is not sufficient unto itself to serve as basis for the unity of humanity and human understanding across cultural and religious frontiers . . . (p. 47)

Note: Here we see the recurrent theme of the fragmentation in modernist secular culture and the suggestion that the way to reach true Unity is through the power of sacred science which brings us into true communion with the unifying power of Infinite Spirit. Nasr continues:

> The great role of religions today should be not to placate the weaknesses of modern man by reducing themselves to one or more "ism" or ideology to compete with the many existing ideologies which man has spun around himself over the past few centuries. Rather their task is to hold before men the norm and the model of perfection of which they are capable and to provide the channels for that contact with the Spirit which alone can show the myriad colors and hues of the human spirit to be not sheer multiplicity and division but so many reflections of Unity. Their task is also to present to the contemporary world the sacred science and wisdom which they have guarded in their bosom and within their inward dimensions over the millennia. (p. 49)

Note: This passage further develops the diagnosis of the modernist secular worldview as broken into contending ideologies in a fragmented pluralism. We see again that the wisdom traditions have guarded the seeds of sacred science which the contemporary world desperately needs for its well being.

(8) *What is the global scope of the primordial tradition*?

> Each tradition is marked by a fresh vertical descent from the Origin, a revelation which bestows upon each religion lying at the center of the tradition in question its spiritual genius, fresh vitality, uniqueness and the "grace" which makes its rites and practices operative. But because the Origin is One and also because of the profound unity of the human recipient despite important existing racial, ethnic and cultural differences, the fact that there is both the Primordial Tradition and traditions does not destroy the perennity and universality of the *philosophia perennis*. The anonymous tradition reflects a remarkable unanimity of views concerning the meaning of human life and the fundamental dimensions of human thought in worlds as far apart as those of the Eskimos and Australian Aborigines, the Taoists and the Muslims. (p. 57)
>
> The conception of religion in the school of the *philosophia perennis* is vast enough to embrace the primal and the historical, the Semitic and the Indian, the

> mythic and the "abstract" types of religions . . . to cross frontiers as difficult to traverse as that which separates the world of Abraham from that of Krishna and Rama or the universe of the American Indians from that of traditional Christianity. (p. 58)

Note: In these revealing excerpts we see that the perennial tradition purports to be global in scope across religious worldviews. It would be interesting to inquire, as we do below, whether it finds expression in worldviews that are not religious. Does the universal metaphysic of the perennial tradition have jurisdiction over all worldviews? It is also important to note here that Nasr hints at the Primordial Tradition as "anonymous," and this raises interesting questions. Has this tradition been latent and silent and subliminal and unnamed? Is there in fact an articulated worldview or ontology running through diverse traditions, or is it an unspoken tradition that has only manifested itself in particular "authentic" traditions?

(9) *How does one distinguish traditional from modernist worldviews?*

> For several centuries, and in fact since the Renaissance, Western man has extolled the human spirit while de-sacralizing the whole of the cosmos in the name of the supremacy of man, only to end now in a situation which for the first time in history threatens man with truly infrahuman conditions on a scale never dreamt of before. Clearly the classical humanism which claimed to speak for man has failed, and if there is to be a future for man, there must be a profound change in the very concept of what man is and a thorough re-examination of the secular humanism of the past few centuries in the light of the vast universal and perennial spiritual traditions of mankind which this humanism has brushed aside with the claim of giving man freedom. (p. 45)

Note: In comparing and contrasting the traditional worldview with the "modernist" Nasr sees in classical humanism an increasing secularization (and hence de-sacralizing) of the human condition and of our ecology. He does not explicitly call this secular humanism "egocentric," but it is clear that this ideology places the human at the center and displaces the sacred worldview which places the Infinite Reality at the center of the human condition. And the further the human conditions is distanced from Ultimate Reality the greater the dysfunction and pathology. This secularized and "homo-centric" worldview is found to be responsible for devastating pernicious consequences in the human condition. He continues,

> The current concept of man as a self-centered creature not responsible to any authority beyond himself and wielding infinite power over the natural environment cannot but end in the aggression of man against himself and the world of nature on a scale which now threatens his own existence. (p. 46)

Note: Here he stresses that the "hierarchical" structure of the traditional worldview places the Primal Principle as first and higher and the human condition as dependent and accountable to this higher reality. Again, he sees this de-sacralizing of human life as the primary cause of violence of all sorts.

(10) *How is the sacred distinguished from the secular, and how does this give rise to the "need for a sacred science"?*

> One can speak of sacred and profane science in distinguishing between the traditional and modern sciences. From the traditional point of view, there is of course no legitimate domain which can be considered as completely profane. The universe is the manifestation of the Divine Principle and there is no realm of reality that can be completely divorced from that Principle. To participate in the realm of the Real and to belong to that which is real also implies being immersed in the ocean of the sacred and being imbued with the perfume of the sacred . . . The main difference between the traditional sciences and modern science lies in the fact that in the former the profane and purely human remain always marginal and the sacred central, whereas in modern science the profane has become central and certain intuitions and discoveries which despite everything reveal the Divine Origin of the natural world have become so peripheral that they are hardly ever recognized for what they are despite the exceptional views of certain scientists. (pp. 96–97)

Note: This contrast between traditional sacred science and modern science makes clear that from the worldview of sacred science all reality is pervaded with the sacred, all nature and the ecology are the domain of the sacred. This implies of course that modern sciences are situated in this universal field of the sacred which contextualizes all human efforts. The "profane" is situated in the all-encompassing field of the sacred. We shall pursue this point below.

> The traditional sciences of all traditional civilizations agree on certain principles of the utmost importance which need to be reiterated in this age of forgetfulness of even the most obvious truths. These sciences are based on a hierarchic vision of the universe, one which sees the physical world as the lowest domain of reality which nevertheless reflects the higher states by means of symbols which have remained an ever open gate towards the Invisible for that traditional humanity which had not lost the "symbolist spirit." The psycho-physical world, which preoccupies modern science, is seen in the traditional perspective as a reflection of the luminous archetypes. (p. 97)

Note: Here again we see that there are certain universal principles of sacred science which are recognized in diverse traditional worldviews, and which have vital importance for our contemporary world. We shall have to look closely at Nasr's insistence that the traditional worldview expresses a "hierarchical" vision of the universe.

(11) *Further Questions That Naturally Arise for Nasr's Narrative*

The above selected excerpts from Nasr's book are intended to help us focus on key themes which we shall address in section II. Here are some critical questions to keep in mind as we explore these important ideas in a global perspective.

(a) *Philosophia perennis* alleges that there are perennial truths that are universal, eternal, and valid for all worldviews. Or more specifically, it claims that there are great traditions which authentically express Primordial Truth that holds for these traditions. If it claims to be global in scope for all possible worlds, what is the *source* of the validity for all worlds? Does this tradition establish why this *must be* so, or *that* it is so? Is it one united tradition or is there diversity within it? Could there be alternative accounts of perennial truth?

Does this "school" assume or assert that "perennial" is (means) "global" —valid for all worldviews? Or rather that certain "authentic traditions" have expressed a consensus truth from their perspective? Does it claim global scope and power? For example, Nasr insists that Ultimate Reality is God. This means of course that all worldviews, secular *and* sacred, must arise from this universal God. But has it been shown that worldviews that do not countenance "God" (like the world of modern science) must come to recognize God as their true ground? How has it established that there is global truth across vastly diverse worldviews and languages of reality? We shall now critically explore the possibility of a global narrative.

(b) What is the scope of sacred science? Is it a complement for what is now called "science"? Does it apply to all everyday life? Is it to be a replacement for the secular worldview in all its forms? Must the secular or profane sciences self-revise to truly encounter the Real? Can there be a universal global science that incorporates what is valid in the modern sciences and fulfill the ideals and vision of traditional sacred science? Is there a universal or global worldview or "first philosophy" that grounds all worldviews—sacred and secular? Could it be that the traditional perennial philosophy itself is in evolution and development and needs to mature to full global status? Could it be that traditional wisdom is in evolution and self-development?

(c) Nasr sees the modernist secular development as the main reason for the loss of this sacred worldview, and sees a return to tradition (in the appropriate spirit) as the way to recapture the sacred perennial lifeworld. He recognizes of course that the "perennial tradition" is sacred in its own right, but places the emphasis on realizing the perennial truth within the particularities of each tradition. One question here is: is there a global way, a universal *praxis*, that runs through the diverse traditions? Are there, for example, global norms, a global ethic that the diverse traditions confirm and embody? Has the global scope and power of sacred science / *philosophia perennis* been established?

Is there an alternative account, an alternative diagnosis that might capture the desirable ends of leading cultures into a higher form of life which is faithful to the highest and best in the sacred traditions, and yet self-evolves into a global form that speaks to our future evolution? Is there a way to honor and recognize the sacred traditions of the past that would build on these in moving forward beyond modernism, postmodernism, and secularism to realize a higher global perennial way? Must perennial wisdom be lodged in the past and in tradition, or can it be in evolution and development and global maturation? We shall now explore these themes in section II.

II. My Experiments in Developing the Global Perennial Logos Tradition: The Missing Logos Science

In the spirit of creative dialogue with these themes from Nasr's narrative I should like to present in a summary sketch some highlights of my journey throughout my career to clarify the Ultimate Principle of all life and experience. In my own experiments I find remarkable convergences with Nasr's findings and with the perspective of *philosophia perennis*. This is all the more remarkable because in a real sense my experimental journey took an independent direction which nevertheless brought me to a profoundly analogous result. Still, as we shall see, there are possibly important differences in my articulation of the ultimate science, of the deep diagnosis of the source of human cultural pathologies and of the preferred prescription for the most potent way to move the human condition to well-being and human flourishing.

This is where I find the greatest potential for a significant critical dialogue with Nasr's thought. As we shall soon see, I discovered early in my career that something profound and vital was still missing from human discourse. Although I instinctively gravitated to the intuition of a perennial philosophy and knew in a pre-articulated way that there had to be an ultimate primal principle, an ultimate science of "what is first," I nevertheless found that the language, technology of mind, and narrative for this was still missing. The nascent perennial narrative was still semi-dormant and needed to be brought to mature *global* articulation. One remarkable disclosure was that the Primordial Truth that was seeded in diverse traditions was alive, growing, evolving, and maturing in the global evolutionary process.

It was clear in my journey through different philosophical and cultural worlds, East, West, and other, that there had to be a fundamental logic, a primal ontology, a global primordial tradition at the heart of all worldviews. However, with close critical scrutiny I found that this was still a *presumption* and in fact more deep work had to be done to tap the missing fundamental logic of natural reason, to decode the ultimate grammar of existence and experience, to bring to full global articulation the intuition of a perennial philosophical perspective, to develop the language and narrative of the unified field of diverse worlds. We shall see that these innovations and results vindicate the vision of *philosophia perennis* and bring to more explicit articulation the missing Primordial Tradition in a global context. So let me now review some of the highlights of my adventure and speak directly to the central themes of Professor Nasr.

The themes and findings that I summarize here have been developed in great detail in my essays and books which present my research over the past three decades. Two companion volumes present the heart of my quest for the fundamental missing science of Logos: *Meditative Reason: Toward Universal Grammar*, and *Between Worlds: The Emergence of Global Reason*. The first appeared in 1993 in the *Revisioning Philosophy Series* of Peter Lang Press, and the second appeared in 1997 in the same series. These findings are presented in a simplified narrative in a book designed for the general reader which will appear soon—*The Awakening of the Global Mind*.

Is Perennial Philosophy Possible? Logic and Ontology

Over three decades ago in my early career as a logician and ontologist I encountered polarization, fragmentation, and dualism at the deepest levels of research. As a logician, seeking the ultimate logic of reason and language, I found a primal polarization in the grammar of thought as I traced the evolution of logic from Socrates through Aristotle, Descartes, Leibniz, Kant, Hegel, Husserl, Frege, Russell, Wittgenstein, Heidegger, Quine, Sommers, and Derrida. The Aristotelian tradition of logic which shaped the cultural space of European thought over the centuries was in deep tension with the radical innovations introduced by Frege, Russell, Wittgenstein, Quine, and others as they developed the new mathematical paradigm for the logic of language that launched the analytical revolution in the twentieth century.

If logic is the formal science of thought itself and articulates the grammar of human reason, then the polar tension I found between the classical logical paradigm of Aristotle and the modern mathematical paradigm of Frege leads us to a split in reason itself. My early quest for the fundamental logic of thought and language led me to an apparently irreconcilable split and incoherence between the classical and modern paradigms of logic in the European tradition.

What made this a disturbing crisis is my finding that *both* paradigms captured fundamental features of the logic of thought and language. Neither could be dismissed, nor was there an apparent way to mediate them and bring them together. They appeared to be mutually incompatible and yet mutually complementary at the same time. But each claimed to give a comprehensive and universal account of the grammar of thought. And since the science of logic purports to articulate the deep structure of reason, if logic itself was polarized into incommensurable paradigms, this did not bode well for the ultimate coherence of human reason. So my career began with this crisis of reason. If human reason, which purports to ground meaning, truth, and rational coherence, is itself ultimately polarized and yields dualism and incoherence, then the very foundation of the human condition appears to be fractured and unintelligible.

It was clear that in the foundation of logic something vital was missing. The long quest through the centuries to clarify the universal grammar of thought was obviously unfinished. The dream of Descartes and Leibniz to reach the ultimate universal grammar of reason remained unrealized yet more vital than ever. Frege and Husserl, in very different ways, attempted to realize this dream, but their attempts fell short.

As we shall see in a moment, this perennial dream to articulate the ultimate laws of thought is driven by the intuition at the heart of human reason that there must be some ultimate ground, some unifying formal structure, that is the source of rational life, that makes things intelligible, that generates thought, meaning, and truth. Over the past three decades I remained focused on attempting to resolve this ultimate problem. It is at the core of the possibility of perennial philosophy. And, as we shall see, the guiding intuition that there must be a fundamental grammar of thought and reason is the moving force of the Primordial Tradition.

But this polar crisis at the heart of reason in the European tradition seems to arise in all aspects of the human condition, and on a global scale. For in my early research as ontologist, concerned with the deepest explorations into the nature and structure of reality, an analogous crisis of polarization became evident. The science of ontology, like the science of logic, sought to clarify and articulate the ultimate structure of reality—the grammar of existence. But it was apparent early in the game that diverse philosophies and worldviews (religions, cultures, ideologies, conceptual frameworks, and the like) presented profoundly diverse ontologies or languages of experience and reality.

What made sense in one worldview failed to make sense in another. It seems that meaning and truth, and what makes sense in experience is a function of the worldview or universe of discourse—the ontological context—in which it arises. Different worlds appear to be worlds apart and incommensurable from the ontological point of view. How is it possible for human intelligence, natural reason, to move meaningfully between worlds? Is it possible to reason and communicate between worlds, across diverse ontological languages of reality? Here was another ultimate challenge for the rational enterprise, for human relations between worlds, and certainly for the possibility of perennial philosophy.

And yet nothing seemed more natural in everyday life than the possibility of all kinds of interactions, transactions, communication, and transformations between worlds. For example, someone centered in the Christian worldview (to simplify the matter) seems to be able to enter genuinely into the lifeworlds of the Buddhist or the Hindu or the Bakongo. These are very different languages of reality, and yet it appears that human intelligence has the capacity to self-transform into alternative grammars of life and make sense of things in diverse universes which nevertheless also seem to be mutually incompatible and even incommensurable in important ways. How is it possible for us to live and move and communicate across and between diverse worlds? It was evident that this fundamental problem was not adequately formulated or resolved.

The vast differences among worldviews seem to challenge the very possibility of any perennial or global perspective. So this was another complex of challenges that I faced very early in my career. And it was apparent that these twin problems at the heart of logic and ontology were intimately linked. It seemed to me that the science of ontology was just as much in crisis as was the science of logic. And both these "sciences" purport to get to the deep structure of the human condition—the structure of thought/language, and the structure of being/reality. Could there be a global or universal logic across worldviews? Was there any fundamental universal ontology that was the ground of diverse worlds? If there were not common structures or laws across or between worlds, and across paradigms of logic, how could there be genuine communication and rational discourse between worlds? These issues get to the heart of the possibility of any alleged "perennial philosophy" or "primordial tradition."

The Perennial Quest for the Ultimate Principle

In the midst of this crisis I reached an important turning point. My philosophical journey took me into Eastern thought when in 1971 I took a special leave to spend a year studying and lecturing in India. This was my first trip to India and my first in-depth exploration of Indian traditions of philosophy. I had no idea when I went on this adventure that it would speak deeply to the impasse I had reached in my research in the foundations of reason, logic, and ontology.

My encounter with the powerful meditative traditions of Hindu and Buddhist thought enormously expanded my horizon and brought me into a deeper global perspective in the rational enterprise. And over the years as I went more and more deeply into diverse meditative philosophies certain unmistakable patterns across diverse worlds became clear. My journey into the meditative traditions opened deeper rational space and enabled me to see deep connections between widely variant worldviews, East, West, and other, that I could not have seen before. So meditative philosophy played a key role in my expansion into the global perspective and thus into the deeper common ground among worlds.

The Meditative Turn in Human Reason

Two remarkable breakthroughs arose together over the next two decades as my research and teaching expanded in a global context. The first great advance through the meditative experiments was the realization that there was such a thing as "egocentric" minding. In my earlier research I simply absorbed the European tradition of philosophy (logic and ontology) without reflective awareness that there was a deep pattern of thinking—a technology of mind—a way of "minding" that proceeded on the foundation of the ego. But diverse meditative traditions (in this case the diversity of approaches in the Hindu and Buddhist traditions) concurred that the single most important factor in the human condition was precisely how we were conducting our minds.

The most fundamental teaching of the meditative traditions is that egocentric patterns of thought were the primary source of human suffering, human existential pathologies in diverse forms. Whether, for example, in the teachings of the *Bhagavad Gita* or the *Dhammapada*, the core insight was that the egocentric way of being (of thinking, of interpretation, of world-making, of self-making, and so on) produces deep and pernicious fragmentations in all aspects of life and was the primary source of human pathologies. The great breakthrough of meditative awakening is that it is possible to overcome egocentric minding and living by advancing into more profoundly unitive, integrative, holistic, and nondual patterns of minding. The great experimental traditions of meditative living developed over millennia provided boundless evidence of the pragmatic force of these findings. The meditative turn in natural reason moves us to a more rationally integrated form of life.

Once I became aware of the patterns and dynamics and living reality of egocentric minding my career, my research, scholarship and teaching, indeed, my life as a whole, took a radically different turn. These meditative experiments opened deeper integral space in which I could see clearly why my earlier research had reached the crisis, the paradox, the impasse, the polarization, the fragmentation and incommensurability. I saw clearly that egocentric reason was inherently incomplete, incoherent and the source of all sorts of dualisms, fragmentatons and pathologies of life. I saw more and more clearly as I lived the meditative turn in reason that egocentric minding was an immature stage in our rational and human development. I understood precisely how and why egocentric minding blocked and undermined our rational life and would always produce polarization, fragmentation, disintegration, and all sorts of violence.

Awakening the Global Perspective

At the same time, the other remarkable breakthrough that co-arose with this meditative turn was the expansion of my thought patterns into a higher global perspective. As I experimented more expansively across the spectrum of worldviews—ideologies, religious and cultural worlds, political ideologies, philosophical grammars, conceptual frameworks, disciplinary languages—and diverse forms of life in the broadest global perspective, I began to see deeper patterns and connections. The meditative technology of minding enabled me to experience deeper common ground across and among worlds, and made it possible to hold multiple alternative worlds together in one synoptic consciousness. This global awakening of reason produced astounding results in recognizing how diverse formulations in different worldviews and language forms nevertheless expressed the same fundamental dynamics, insights, principles, and truths.

The Perennial Quest for What-Is-First

The global perspective, the capacity to hold multiple alternative worldviews together in a unifying dialogic encounter opened a more profound dimension of Reality. For when we stand back from any one worldview processed in the egocentric way, and enter the global perspective through the dialogic powers of meditative reason, certain striking perennial patterns emerge. As we scan the range of diverse worldviews across the spectrum of global cultures it is apparent that widely diverse worlds gravitate to some primal Origin.

For example, in one classical Chinese traditional worldview the primal origin is called *Tao* (the Infinite name that cannot be named); in the early Hindu tradition "what-is-first" is expressed as *Aum* (the infinite sacred sound) or *Brahman* (infinite being); in a certain Buddhist tradition the ultimate is expressed as *Śūnyatā* (absolute emptiness beyond names and forms); in the Judaic grammar the ultimate reality is indicated as *Yhwh* (the Infinite living God); in Christianity one version of the primal principle is *Logos* (the infinite Word) or *Christ* (the Logos made flesh); in Islam the Absolute is expressed as *Allāh* (the one true God); certain indigenous cultures recognize the ultimate truth as the Infinite Living *Spirit*; in a certain African classical worldview the originating force is called *Nommo* (the Infinite Name that generates all existence); in the grammar of physics the ultimate reality is recognized as *Energy* (the ultimate stuff that can neither be created nor destroyed) . . . and so on.

Each worldview purports to be universal and all-encompassing of reality. Yet at the same time these diverse grammars of reality (ontological languages) appear to be competing and to repel or displace one another in their universal power; they appear to be diverse universes of discourse. And this is where a meditative turn with its global perspective and technology of processing reality helps to disclose deeper common ground and striking patterns between variant worlds.

The Missing Global Grammar

One revealing pattern is that diverse worlds in one way or another arise from a primal source or ground which is recognized to be boundless, infinite, and universal. The meditative power of the global perspective helps us to see that all worldviews must co-arise from a primal source or origin, that this origin must be Infinite, and that the Infinite must be the same Primal Reality of all possible worlds. Rigorous meditation on the Infinite Origin makes evident that this Unifying Force must be Integral and One-and-the-Same Principle for all possible worlds.

And here it is vital to remember that *egocentric reason inherently fails* to process this Infinite Unifying force-field. For as we shall see shortly, the egocentric mind *objectifies* the "Infinite" and reduces its infinite unifying power to an artificial "unity" that levels the profound important differences among diverse worlds. At the same time the ego artificially "pluralizes" diverse worlds in such fragmented multiplicity and differences that they remain localized and fragmented beyond the reductive and false "unity" it constructs. The egocentric mind fails to understand both Unity and Difference and undermines both. Either way the egocentric mind is unable to process the Primal Principle, and hence Reality itself.

The great enduring mystical traditions have of course recognized early in the game that the Ultimate Truth must be Infinite and hence must be the unifying common source of all possible worlds. But even if we have a clear intuition that the diverse mystical and spiritual traditions were expressing the "same fundamental reality," these traditions remained articulated in their own localized grammars and narratives with all their important differences and diversity. And these localizing forces, East and West, suppressed and inhibited the full maturation of the global force of the grammar of what-is-first.

The intuition of a "primordial truth" or a "perennial philosophy" remained presumed and latent, waiting to be activated, formulated, and realized. There was *no global grammar*, no open generalized space or method of minding and speaking that brought fully into the open the global scope and power of this First Principle. And the profound and pervasive influence of egocentric minding in the human condition preempted and eclipsed access to the perennial force of The First. It appears that *the global turn* in how we mind and in the grammar of how we formulate and express reality matters a great deal. So with all the great advances toward expressing the Infinite Origin, East, West, and other, something vital was still missing.

The Need for a Global Grammar for the Infinite Origin: Logos *as a Global Name*

As my experiments matured over the decades and I advanced more and more deeply into the global perspective, it became increasingly clear that a fundamental global narrative was still absent. I noticed a peculiar and striking "recursive" dialectic at work that moved me in something like a paradoxical, reflexive, expanding "spiral loop" that took on a life of its own. The more I expanded in the global perspective the more evident became the dialectical patterns across and among worldviews and alternate languages of experience. And as these deeper patterns of the Primal Origin emerged, the more I found my rational awareness and experience expanding and I was able to encounter deeper common ground and detect striking recursive patterns and connections among worlds that I could not see before.

I was now able to recognize how quite diverse grammars and narratives of experience were in fact *alternative formulations* of the same fundamental reality. And the more this primal reality was revealed the more the global way of processing reality, the global perspective, intensified. The net effect of this recursive dialectic—the global turn in experience—was the realization that this global awakening of rational awareness was essential in detecting and tapping the missing primal field. The global way of "minding" was a key to discerning fundamental common ground among diverse worlds, indeed, in establishing that there was in fact a primal unified field among worlds. So, in this summary sketch of my experimental clarification of the missing global "science," I shall now try to replay certain key steps in the spirit of this recursive dialectic.

The fact that we can stand back from being immersed within any one worldview and rise to the global or inter-world perspective is of ultimate importance in the quest for the grammar of what-is-first. For this power and capacity in human awareness is a primary feature of reason which issues directly from this fundamental Infinite Force. And what is strikingly noticeable when we stand back in this way and entertain the great enduring traditions through the ages, is that each seeks to express and name what-is-first. As we have seen, diverse languages of Reality concur that there must be some primal ultimate origin, and "it" must be Infinite. It has also been clear that this Infinite Principle must be one and the same for all realities. This follows immediately from the *sacred logic* of what-is-first. I have suggested that in the perennial quest to express this Infinite something vital was still missing. The diverse grammars or narratives that were developed by the traditions, including modern science, each faced a boundary of localism in its grammar and narrative.

First Philosophy still lacked a universal and global grammar to name and express what-is-first. The fact that we faced a vast range of alternative languages attempting to express and name the Infinite Principle—*Aum, Tao, Śūnyatā, God, Christ, Yhwh, Allāh, Nommo, Logos, Nature, First Cause, Energy*, and so on (henceforth, we will refer to this open-ended sequence of primal names as "the Primal Names")—is highly problematic since these diverse languages of reality appear to be inherently incompatible, competing, and mutually exclusive. Each universalizes its discourse and purports to a "universal grammar" of The First. Each alleges to be the primary, preferred, and self-privileging grammar of The Ultimate. And, although great mystic minds and intuitive geniuses know quite well that all authentic First Names *must* be naming the same Infinite Principle, this correct global intuition needs a global grammar to formulate effectively and to express this Truth.

We need a global name for what-is-first, a Name so powerful that it expresses and keeps before us the Infinite Force of the First. In seeking to uncover and tap the Universal Grammar of what-is-first I proposed the word *Logos* as a working candidate to help us move in this direction. Let us experiment together with this: ***Logos** is the Infinite Word, the Infinite Name for the Primal Reality*. The latent global power of the genuine Primal Names just mentioned is released through the universal force of the global name ***Logos***. *Aum* expresses ***Logos***; *Tao* is an ultimate name for ***Logos***; *God* is ***Logos***; *Allah* is a direct revelation of ***Logos***; *Christ* embodies ***Logos***; the Greco-European *Logos* is also a powerful expression of ***Logos***; the ultimate substance of reality names in the physical sciences—*Energy*—expresses ***Logos*** . . . and so on. (Henceforth, for convenience and simplicity, we will express the global name ***Logos*** without italics or boldface thus—Logos.)

Logos as the Infinite Name has infinite alter-expressions. This is an essential feature of its infinitude. It is the Infinite Word. All names, all words, all forms, and so on, derive from and express Logos. Of course, this is not to suggest that the Primal Names are "synonyms" or are "identical" or "say the same thing" or even "refer to the same thing." We must be extremely cautious and remember that each uniquely and authentically expresses Logos. We shall soon see that precisely *because* Logos is the Infinite Word it has boundless unique alternative and authentic expressions.

I introduce the term *holonym* to capture this profound relation among the Primal Names—they are *holonymous* and thus *holonyms*. As holonyms the Primal Names co-express each other in Logos and thus have a deep intimate connection. The sacred logic of Logos makes clear that holonyms are irreducibly different while they nevertheless *co-express* Logos, and of course each other. And when the full global potential of the Primal Names is ignited and realized, this deep dialogic connection is brought to maturity.

Let us meditate more deeply on Logos. It should be immediately apparent that the introduction of this *global name* is of monumental significance. For this Infinite Name invokes and brings with it the universal grammar of the Infinite Word and with this comes the global turn in minding. *The Sacred Logic* of the Infinite Name calls for a higher *logistic or technology of mind* beyond the localizing, finitizing, and fragmenting ways of egocentric minding. And we mentioned earlier that the diverse meditative traditions all stressed that how we mind is all-important in the quality of life and experience. With all the important differences in diverse meditative traditions we may safely say in entering the global perspective that the meditative turn in minding requires breaking the egocentric barriers and crossing into the more holistic and *integral technology of nondual minding*. This is a vital step in encountering Logos, in entering the universal grammar of the Infinite Word.

The meditative turn in thinking is a key step in entering the global mind, in the authentic encounter of Logos. But something radical and unique happens with this *awakening of the global mind*. For to "think" Logos is to participate directly in the Sacred Logic or holistic Logistic (*hologistic*) of the Infinite Word. To process Logos is to enter into the dialectic of Infinition wherein all things, all names, all forms, all phenomena, all grammars or worlds are in deep mutual interaction and inter-relationality. Here all things mutually permeate each other. The deepest global meditation on Logos brings us into the Primal Field, the Grand Unified Field which is Reality itself. Let us call this Primal Field of Reality the *Logosphere*. It may be said that the global name *Logos is the Logosphere*, which can be thought or encountered only through the awakening of the global mind, in the hologistic of Infinition.

The great meditative and mystical traditions of the ages, in all cultures and worlds understood that what-is-first could not be approached in ordinary egocentric ways of thinking. To think Logos is to participate directly in the Infinition process of the Logosphere. And rigorous reflection on Logos reveals that this involves the global turn, the globalization of reason as minding awakens to its highest rational coherence and integrity. In this natural expansion of awareness the Self, the Thinker enters a direct encounter of Logos, the Logosphere; the thought process flows in the holistic dialectic of existence; and language matures to its full integral and primal power.

So to encounter the global name—Logos—is to enter the dynamic Unified Field (Logosphere), is to awaken the global mind, to live and embody the hologistic dynamics of the Logosphere, which is to enter the universal grammar of the Infinite Word. Thus, to introduce Logos as a global name brings with it the awakening of mind to the Logistic of the Unified Field and the ignition of the universal grammar of the Infinite Word. It is here that we find the source of perennial truths, the foundation of the perennial tradition, the global blossoming of sacred science, the source of all knowing, of all sciences, indeed, of the human condition.

Logos is the Logosphere—The Field of Reality

To enter the global perspective then is to enter into the technology of global minding, the hologistic process of the Logosphere. It is not the same as holding the egocentric perspective and entertaining a plurality of worlds from this localizing pattern of minding. When we enter the boundless yet ordered logic of the Logosphere there are astounding revelations of the dynamic flow of Reality. How can the Infinite Name—Logos—*be* Reality itself? What kind of "name" is this? How and why is this Infinite Word the universal and Unified Field of all realities? What is this "sacred logic" of the Logosphere? How could it be that multiple worlds, realities co-exist at once in this "unified field"? How could these diverse worlds be diverse and yet permeate one another at the same time? How do the diverse categories of existence, or Nature, arise from this Primal Word? Can human consciousness really touch and enter this dialectic of the Logosphere? How are all realities generated from this Primal Source? How is it that the awakened Self in "global minding" flows in communion with this Infinite Force? Such deep questions as these naturally arise in this context.

The Infinite Unifying Force

The global mind sees immediately that there must be a Unifying Force proactively holding things together in every way—were this not so, thought, experience, life, and existence could not work. The thinking "self" could not be, there would be no continuity, no coherence; no language could work, no words would exist, no thoughts could be formed, no experience could arise, nothing would be. This is the simplest and most elementary point. The egocentric mind takes all this for granted, unquestioned. The global mind is ever mindful of the boundless presence of the Unifying Force that conditions everything and makes self, thought, language, experience, phenomena, world, and so on, possible. The egocentric mind is incapable of entering into the primal Sacred Logic—the transcendental logistic—that sustains it and makes its "life" possible.

The global mind—awakened reason—sees immediately that the Unifying Force must be Infinite. Everything turns now on processing Infinite Unity in a rigorous and competent manner. Lucid thinking here discloses that the Force that conditions all that appears must be boundless and limitless. It is this rational intuition that reveals there is always something Higher, something First, Primal, and Originating. Were there something —anything—beyond "It" this would violate the *infinite integrity* of the Unifying Force, and any such "thought" self-destructs. It is in this ultimate intuition of awakened reason into Infinite Unity that the Sacred Logic of Logos unfolds.

Logosphere—The Cosmic Continuum

Once the Infinite Force is recognized and acknowledged, it follows immediately that this Force pervades all existence, situates and constitutes all existence, and presides throughout the cosmic Unified Field. And diverse traditions of perennial philosophy have detected this truth in different formulations. It is such a simple and elementary point in the Logic of Infinition that it appears as a truism to the global mind. Once the Cosmic Event-Continuum of Logosphere is discovered, it follows immediately that all existence, all evolution, and history is the creative play of Logos. And the evidence of this is overwhelming once rational intelligence awakens to the Infinite Presence of Logos. It was clear that humanity had not yet developed the technologies of mind and language for processing the Logosphere. We still lacked a Science of Logos, a science of the Logosphere—the foundation of all worldviews. This pure Formal Science was latent (and presumed) in the diverse classical perennial traditions and awaited full maturation and emergence in its explicit globalized form.

As the Logic of Logos came to increasing clarity over three decades it was clear that we urgently needed to develop tools, technology, to become mindful of when we were in the Grammar of Logos and when we were in the grammars of egocentric cultures. Remember in this meditation on Logos that the pathways of awakening move in a recursive loop—the deeper we encounter Logos, the more this invokes the global turn in minding, the more, in turn, this encourages the expansion of thought and language, which enhances our capacity to process the Logosphere . . .

It should be clear that this is just a preliminary sketch, a beginning, of the remarkable human quest for the missing global science. This narrative is developed in a comprehensive way in the forthcoming book, *The Awakening of the Global Mind.*[1]

III. CONCLUDING REFLECTIONS

In concluding let us look back now at the central themes raised by Professor Nasr concerning the need for a sacred science. It is now more evident in the light of the foregoing narrative of the great human quest for Logos that Nasr's affirmations of the tradition of *philosophia perennis* and of the need for sacred science are supported in remarkable ways. We now see that diverse great traditions in the global evolution of thought have, in importantly diverse ways, been in quest of Logos. In this respect the heart of *philosophia perennis* is in this global quest for Logos that embodies the sacred common ground across and among diverse worlds, narratives, disciplines, and dimensions of human cultures. It becomes clear in this transcendental quest that drives the evolution of the human condition that there has been a missing Primal Science to which ancient and classical traditions bear witness.

However, we have been suggesting that the universal grammar and technology of mind for a truly global First Philosophy has been slowly and painfully evolving, and that *philosophia perennis* has been in a deep evolution and maturation. In this respect we cannot look to the past, to past traditions, for the fully developed missing Global Science of Logos and for the missing Global First Philosophy that is its vital center and ground. Nasr is of course right in insisting that we honor and value the emerging perennial truth in our great traditions, but it is also vital to see that the missing sacred science and the global grammar of *philosophia perennis* have been under ongoing self-evolution and maturation in the human condition. What is exciting is that as this sacred process matures, as Logos emerges in our evolutionary drama, this missing Global Science comes into focus with the awakening of the global mind.

ASHOK K. GANGADEAN

DEPARTMENT OF PHILOSOPHY
HAVERFORD COLLEGE
FEBRUARY 2000

NOTE

1. Relevant topics have been featured in two issues of *PARABOLA*: "*The Quest for the Primal Word*" 20, no. 3 (August 1995) and "*The Awakening of Primal Knowledge*" 22, no 2 (Spring 1997).

REPLY TO ASHOK GANGADEAN

Professor Gangadean is at once an Oriental and a Western thinker with a vast philosophical horizon whose quest after the perennial philosophy and search for the universal global science provide him with the means of posing important questions concerning my understanding of the perennial philosophy and sacred science. His name itself contains a symbolic significance related to his philosophical quest. Ashok recalls the name of the great Indian emperor who sought to create peace and harmony among different religions and philosophies and Gangadean recalls the name of Kipling who wrote that East is East and West is West and ne'er the twain shall meet. Professor Gangadean has sought to show that the twain can and in fact must meet. In his vision of philosophy on a global scale he holds a position close to mine but with a different understanding of the meaning of perennial and universal philosophy to which I shall turn later in this response.

The author begins with a discussion of my vision of sacred science and then turns to his own experiences in the search for what he calls "a global perennial Logos tradition." In my response I prefer to say a few words in general about my differences with the account of his experiences before turning to the first part and the last part of his essay, as well as a few specific issues about his experiences and experiments. Obviously both Gangadean and I have been searching for a universal truth underlying the diversity of cultures, philosophies, and religions. But whereas I was to come upon this universal truth in my early twenties, he was to spend several decades in searching for and also developing his own views of this universal and global truth or sacred science. I found for my part the traditional expressions of the perennial philosophy and also its formulation on a global scale by Guénon, Coomaraswamy, and Schuon to be perfect and all that of which I was in need. It was for me to master all those teachings and then expound and apply them to new domains. In contrast to me, Gangadean found all the existing formulations to be still inadequate and in need of further development, growth, and, as he would say, evolution. Herein lie the major differences between us and our understanding of the nature of the perennial philosophy, its contemporary reformulation and the meaning of its globalization.

Since Gangadean speaks often of global and globalization, I find it necessary to clarify how I understand these terms. For me global means embracing diverse human cultures, philosophies, and religions, but not necessarily everything that happens to exist on the globe. For example, the quest for the truth is a global trait found in diverse cultures, but there are those among modern and postmodern Western philosophers who deny that truth is even a significant philosophical category and that the term has any definable meaning. Their denial of the truth does not, however, make the quest after truth by others any less global. Today there are certain issues which are global in the sense that they are faced by men and women in different societies and cultures, and certain solutions are also global in that they provide acceptable responses to diverse issues in different cultural climates. But in neither case should there be an expectation of relevance or acceptance by everyone and everywhere.

And here is to be found the crucial importance of tradition. Traditional doctrines are global in the sense that they are to be found with differing formal structures within the teachings of every tradition, but the fact is that they are rejected by modern civilization which for that very reason is called anti-traditional. For me perennial philosophy, as traditionally understood, is not only perennial but also universal and global in the sense I have defined it above. It is to be found in ancient Egypt as well as Ming China, among the Maoris of New Zealand as well as Muslims of Morocco or Christians of France. But obviously it cannot be found among those who explicitly reject its tenets. To say that a truth is global does not mean that it is acceptable everywhere. If everything is true then nothing is true. Truth implies its opposite which is falsehood. For me, what is global on the philosophical level is the truth of the perennial philosophy which, despite using diverse languages, expresses a remarkable unanimity across vast borders of time and space. Nothing on earth is more inclusive than the perennial philosophy, but that does not mean that this philosophy must embrace everything, including error, in order to be global.

As for globalization, I stand strongly opposed to the process of globalization in the sense of the global spread of norms and practices associated with the anti-traditional modern and postmodern civilization, issuing originally from the West, and I oppose the destruction of what still survives of traditional civilizations and cultures. Legitimate globalization is to formulate in a global manner and to make men and women more fully aware of the single truth underlying their diverse traditions and numerous practices and beliefs of remarkable similarity, which is the direct result of the underlying unity of the inner truth of those traditions. Furthermore, it is the criticisms on the basis of traditional metaphysics of the anti-traditional world on all levels, from the philosophical to the practical, that must be globalized to combat an illness which has also become global. As I understand it, perennial philosophy is by nature both global and globalizing or, on a more "abstract" level and using a more philosophical language, both universal and universalizing.

Returning to the text of Gangadean, let me begin my point by point response by going back to his opening section where he speaks of the evolving schools of *philosophia perennis* to which he returns often in the pages that follow. From what I have said in many other responses in this volume it should be clear that I do not believe in any way in the evolution of perennial philosophy. There have been different expressions of perennial philosophy in the bosom of various sacred traditions over the ages. Each expression has meant an adaptation to a particular world with its own cultural contours and language. Human history has been witness not to an evolution but to a continuous adaptation and recrystallization of a primordial Truth and wisdom without any two crystallizations being formally identical or even necessarily revelatory in the same way of all aspects of that primordial Truth.

In modern times the necessity arose for those diverse languages to be compared and the contents of one translated into another. This providential task has been already achieved in the twentieth century by Guénon, Coomaraswamy, Schuon, Burckhardt, and other expositors of traditional doctrines. But even this exposition on a veritable global scale did not mean an evolution of perennial philosophy any more than would the translation of the *Divine Comedy* into Persian and Japanese mark the evolution of the text or its meaning. Perennial philosophy was always actually universal and potentially global. In our times it became necessary for this potentiality to become actualized and this task has been achieved during the past century. Śaṅkara, Rūmī, or Eckhart were, in principle, no less global in their message than some contemporary expositor of perennial philosophy who might know twenty languages while the old masters knew only one or two. The truth they taught was by nature universal, dealing as it did with the universal realm and, as I mentioned, potentially global. That is why as the works of the old teachers have become available in many languages, their teachings have come to manifest fully their global nature and are in fact much more global than most of the provincial thought of modern philosophers who make all kinds of claims to globality.

Gangadean also uses the term "modernism" somewhat differently from how I understand and employ the term. He speaks of "secular modernism" and "the secularization of modernism." As I define modernism, it is already secularized and there is no need to add the modifier "secular" which is redundant. If someone asks what about religious modernism, I would reply that although this term is now used, it is in fact not exact if we define religion in the traditional sense. A person can be religious and a modernist or one can have a religious art that is also modernist. In such cases it is modernism that has penetrated into the domain of religion and modified it to one degree or another so that what results is no longer traditional religion. In any case the use of "secular" or "secularized modernism" by the author reveals another understanding of this term than the one I have employed throughout my writings.

Gangadean asks in connection with my hinting that the Primordial Tradition is "anonymous" whether this tradition has been latent and silent or whether "there is in fact an articulated worldview or ontology running thoughout diverse traditions." The answer is that perennial wisdom at the heart of all authentic traditions has been both latent and articulated. It has had its indirect and latent expressions as well as well articulated versions identifiable with both anonymous sources and revered sages who, although known by name, have, however, reached the state beyond individual identity and have spoken from the universal perspective. To paraphrase A. K. Coomaraswamy, they have left their selfhood for the Self which is the Self of all selves. Although having a name, they too have become in reality anonymous like the anonymous or "mythical" sages with which so much of the traditional teachings is associated. Furthermore, the universal metaphysics expressed by them constitutes the heart of the traditional world to which they belong while it transcends inwardly the formal order.

In discussing the secular versus the sacred, the author writes that, "modern sciences are situated in this universal field of the sacred which contextualizes all human effort." This is not my view as far as the secular sciences are concerned. The sacred is by nature all-embracing but not in the absolute sense; for it does not include that which by nature rejects the very category of the sacred. The traditional perspective can understand why the sacred can be and has been denied by some and why profane science is what it is, and can even integrate any science which conforms to some aspect of reality into its sacred perspective. Moreover, it can integrate these sciences into the framework of the sacred, not as secular science and in the context of the secularist perspective in which they are cultivated, but as forms of knowledge which can be integrated into the matrix of the sacred to the extent that they are authentic knowledge even it be of a lower order than that of traditional metaphysics and cosmology.

In discussing *philosophia perennis*, the author makes a preliminary statement and then poses a number of questions. In the preliminary statement he asserts that there are perennial truths that are universal, eternal, and valid for all worldviews. Yes, there are perennial truths and they are universal and eternal, but they are not valid for *all* worldviews; they are valid for *all* traditional worldviews. Since there is the possibility of error and falsehood, it is possible to hold anti-traditional worldviews such as the diverse ideologies associated with modernism which deny those perennial truths and in fact have their very existence in the denial of those truths.

Now to the questions. Gangadean asks, what is the source of the validity of the perennial philosophy for all worlds? It is the truth that lies at the heart of all traditions (which is what I presume he means by worlds), the truth that lies also at the center of man's being and in the very substance of his intelligence once it is actualized by the revelation that constitutes the origin of each sacred world. Tradition establishes both "why this *must* be so" and also "*that* it is so." Furthermore, not only are there diverse traditions but there is also the possibility of diverse interpretations or points of view within a single tradition as we can see so clearly, for example, in Hinduism and Islam.

The traditional perspective asserts that the perennial philosophy, which has diverse formal manifestations, is valid within and in fact constitutes the heart of all traditional worldviews, and not simply *all* worldviews as I have already stated above. To assert that in the traditional perspective the Source or Ultimate Reality is the alpha and omega of all things does not mean that this truth will be accepted by every worldview that happens to manifest itself on earth. For example modern science has no place in its perspective for Ultimate Reality and the traditional perspective does not claim to be all-inclusive in the sense of embracing that which negates its foundations. One should not forget that the perennial philosophy is concerned most of all with the truth. Now, to speak of the truth is also to speak of error. On the conceptual level if nothing is false, then there is no truth. The all-embracing nature of the traditional perspective does not mean that it also embraces as valid that which is anti-traditional. As already mentioned, tradition does not claim to be global in the sense of including whatever happens to exist on the globe. One cannot simply deny the presence of evil on the level of relativity by claiming that all that exists is good on that level which is that of contingency or privation itself. Tradition rejects modernism in principle, but let us remember how much it includes. If we put the modernist aberration of the past few centuries aside, the traditional perspective includes practically all the worldviews known to us. It is indeed the unanimous as well as the anonymous tradition.

As sacred science, it is not a complement to what is now called "science," but is all encompassing and could integrate even modern science into its metaphysical matrix if this science were to be shorn from the dualistic and rationalistic philosophy that underlies it. Today we need first of all to assert the reality of sacred science as a category to be accepted and contemplated and open a place for it in our intellectual living space. Later, however, this science could in principle replace the present sciences by integrating them into its matrix. Such a science would be universal without destroying the particularities of the formal order of each sacred tradition. As for the perennial philosophy itself, it is the ground of all traditional worldviews but cannot be the ground of secular philosophies. The truth can never be the common ground of both truth and error. Furthermore, as already mentioned, the perennial philosophy does not evolve, but it has been expressed in different languages according to varying circumstances in which it finds itself.

As for *praxis*, the author asks if there is a universal praxis that runs through the diverse traditions. The answer is yes and no. There are certain universal practices such as prayer, rites, meditation, contemplation, and so on found in all traditions. But the external forms of such practices differ as one can see in bodily postures in prayers and forms in various rites. Inwardly, however, there is a remarkable unaminity in the goal sought which is to overcome the power of the ego, to break the confines of our limited existence, to go beyond ourselves to reach the Self, both Transcendent and Immanent, that Ultimate Reality which has also been called the "not-self" in some traditions such as Buddhism. As for a universal ethics, again there is a remarkable accord on the goal of ethics among various traditions, although external forms of ethical action are different.

The author asks if the global scope and power of sacred science/ *philosophia perennis* has been established. Certainly for those who have read and understood the works of the expositors of traditional teachings of the twentieth century, it has been established. But for the larger "intellectual" public in the West, it certainly has not been established. If it had, there would no longer be the need to write about the concept of sacred science and its central importance. I also believe that there is no "alternative account" which could lead to the desirable goal. Only the reassertion of the perennial truths in a contemporary language can deliver us from the chaos of modernism and post-modernism. But this reassertion does not mean leaning only upon the past. Perennial philosophy is not based on the past but upon a reality that is beyond time. If we defend the traditional civilizations of the past, it is because in those civilizations, despite all their shortcomings which characterize the human order, the truths of the perennial philosophy in the particular form of the tradition in question remained central and dominant. Otherwise, the teachings of perennial philosophy pertain as much to today and tomorrow as they did to yesterday.

In section II of this essay Gangadean turns to his own experiments and experiences with the "global perennial Logos tradition" and states, "Although I instinctively gravitated to the intuition of a perennial philosophy . . . , I nevertheless found that the language, technology of mind and narrative for this was still missing." I want to state how my case was so different. I also gravitated towards the perennial philosophy both intuitively and intellectually, but from the beginning discovered that all that was required for the realization of the truths existed already in the teachings of the perennial philosophy and only needed to be searched out, discovered, and put into practice. This is exactly what I did in my twenties and continue to do so to this day. I have found the traditional methods as well as doctrines to be adequate in every way for the task for which they were created.

As I read this section, I came to discover other divergences with the author. I do not use ontology the same way as he does. If ontology means the science of being, how can one speak of the ontology of modern science, when this science has no interest in the being of things as being and its positivistic interpreters even deny any ontological link from the findings of modern physics to "physical reality"? I believe that the quantum mechanical world as well as the corporeal world with which classical physics deals do possess an ontological status in the universal hierarchy of existence, but this perspective is alien to modern science itself as well as to most modern philosophies of science. Nor do I find any affinity with the idea of "the global awakening of reason" for which I find no proof. I am also completely opposed to comparing with or including in the same category the various names of the Divinity in diverse sacred traditions and the term *energy* in physics. I believe that this kind of mixing of concepts belonging to completely different orders of reality cannot but cloud the picture and make it more difficult to understand the rapport between religion and modern science or the sacred and the secular.

In recounting his experience Gangadean writes that he found perennial philosophy to be latent "awaiting to be activated, formulated, and realized" and that it has "*no global grammar.*" For my part, I found it to have been already activated, formulated, and realized and I discovered in the writings of Guénon, Coomaraswamy, Schuon, and other traditionalists precisely that *global grammar* whose lack the author laments. I also disagree with the author that "First Philosophy still lacked a universal and global grammar to name and express what-is-first." Let us first of all remember the famous statement of the *Tao Te Ching*, "The name that can be named is not the Name." Secondly according to all traditions, the sacramental name of the Supreme Reality, such as *Aum* in Hinduism and *Allāh* in Islam, is revealed by that Reality Itself and is not simply man made. In traditional metaphysics, the diversity of these names, which do not always refer to the same level of the Divine Reality, is neither the cause of incompatibility nor competition.

I also do not share the author's acceptance of the term *Logos* as the universal name for Ultimate Reality. First of all the *Logos* in traditional metaphysics is not the highest Principle but the highest manifestation of the Principle. In Christianity the Logos is identified with the Son and not the Father and in Islam *Allāh* is certainly not "a direct revelation of *Logos*" as the author claims. It is the other way around. The *Logos* is the direct revelation, or to be more exact, self-determination of *Allāh*. I do not want to enter into a debate with the author about his views concerning the *Logos* because that has to do with his philosophical views rather than mine. But I do want to clarify my position concerning the usage of this very important term in place of "Ultimate Reality" which I prefer in this context. I am sympathetic to many points he mentions, for example his discussion of the "Logosphere"; but again I would not use the same language, although I certainly support the holistic view which it propounds.

There are other features of the Logosphere as described by Gangadean with which I do not agree. For example, Logosphere, if considered as Ultimate Reality, is not a process but generates an "infinitely dynamic creative process" as traditional metaphysics teaches. The process must not be confused with the Infinite Beyond-Being and Being which are beyond all process as *Nirvāna* is beyond *samsāra*. Also I need to mention again my strong opposition to any view which believes that humanity has not as yet developed spiritual techniques or the language appropriate for reaching and speaking about the Ultimate Reality, which the author calls the "Logosphere." I oppose completely any belief in the spiritual evolution of man *à la* Teilhard de Chardin or Śri Aurobindo. What is ineffable cannot be discussed discursively tomorrow any more than it could yesterday. Concerning techniques of teaching that Ineffable Reality, it can be said that they have been already revealed in the various sacred traditions. What we need is to put them into practice and not invent new ones. As for language, the traditional languages of metaphysics are completely adequate for the expression of the Truth to the extent that it can be expressed. I see no need in having to invent a new metaphysical language. What the present day calls for is translating metaphysical truths from one language into another as particular situations require. As I have stated in other contexts, I do not believe in evolution as this term is usually used and certainly would be totally opposed to its usage in the domain of the supreme science of metaphysics, which deals with the permanent and abiding truths of that Reality "that changeth not." The creative power of the Divine Reality renews creation at every instant as the Sufis would say but that does not mean having to have recourse to some kind of inner evolutionary force as currently understood.

The whole enterprise of the author concerning the Logosphere, while containing many deep insights, seems to circumvent the question of truth and error. If the "Logos story" includes Genesis as well as Big Bang, traditional metaphysics as well as Darwin, Marx, and Teilhard, then what happens to the question of truth? For me, there is such as thing as truth and therefore there is such a thing as error. As I have already mentioned, one cannot have an all encompassing narrative which, in order to be all encompassing, is willing to forgo the central significance of the truth which traditionally has the highest right.

Our conclusions part ways when the author emphasizes the upward evolution of the human mind and extols the virtues in "scientific method" to the extent that he identifies the awakening of the scientific spirit with the awakening of the global mind "in the quest to express Logos in every aspect of the human condition." He sees the true global First Philosophy to be painfully evolving and the Logos emerging in an evolutionary drama. I see no rapport between the spread of scientism or the practice of the "scientific method" and the development of "the global mind." And I believe that the *Logos* far from emerging in an evolutionary drama was there at the beginning for "In the beginning was the Word/*Logos*." Our human drama and crisis today is the eclipsing of the imprint of the *Logos* upon our mind and soul by a secularist worldview. The regimen is none other than remembrance of the perennial truths which do not evolve but need to be reformulated and freshly expressed as new conditions and circumstances arise.

Obviously Professor Gangadean has spent many years in the thought project, some of whose fruits have been expressed in this extensive essay. In our intellectual quest I have not reached the same goal, but by his many queries and analyses he has provided me the opportunity for clarifying further my views on the perennial philosophy, an opportunity for which I am grateful.

S. H. N.

17

Mehdi Aminrazavi

PHILOSOPHIA PERENNIS AND *SCIENTIA SACRA* IN A POSTMODERN WORLD

Seyyed Hossein Nasr[1] is a metaphysician whose philosophical perspectives are deeply entrenched in the Islamic intellectual tradition. Within the existing trends in Islamic philosophy, Nasr adheres to the tradition of *ḥikmah* (theosophy),[2] a synthesis of the Peripatetic (*mashshā'ī*) methodology, Illuminationist's (*ishrāqī*) emphasis on intellectual intuition (*dhawq*) and Sufism (Islamic mysticism), a path of inner purification through practical wisdom.

In the following discussion, the three components of Nasr's philosophical perspective, namely his critique of rationalistic philosophy, his advocacy of the illuminationist philosophy and Sufism will first be investigated. An attempt will then be made to present and critique his concept of perennial ontology which serves as the foundation for his philosophical perspectives.

Philosophically, Nasr is a medievalist in that his philosophical outlook and positions are those of medieval Islamic philosophy. Within the existing strands in Islamic philosophy, Nasr adheres to that tradition which is inclusive of rationalistic philosophy and practical wisdom. This tradition referred to by some of the perennialists as *ḥikmah*, for Nasr, is that tradition of philosophy which began with the teachings of the prophet Idris identified by classical Muslim authors with Hermes.[3] The tradition of *ḥikmah* which passed through different civilizations, in particular the Persians, Egyptians, and Greeks, reaches its climax in the teachings of Suhrawardī[4] and his school of illumination (*ishrāq*) and later in Mullā Ṣadrā's transcendental theosophy (*al-ḥikmat al-muta'ālayah*).[5]

Human existence for Nasr is fundamentally a spiritual journey and one must engage in a spiritual hermeneutics (*ta'wīl*) through which the act of remembrance takes place. It is in light of this view that Nasr comments on so many facets of Islamic life and thought, be it art or architecture, music or philosophy, not to mention Sufism which he regards to be the heart and soul of Islam.

Nasr views philosophy not as a mere rational activity but as a quest for the Eternal resulting from a longing within every man to find his original abode. Philosophizing, therefore, is the process of recollecting the eternal Truth within us which we have forgotten. Having defined philosophy as a sacred activity whose aim is unveiling the Truth, "living philosophically" becomes a quest for Divine wisdom which Nasr regards as the rightful activity of the intellect and not merely a process of rationalization.

To begin with, Nasr advocates learning Peripatetic philosophy and discursive reasoning. Such training he argues provides the intellectual presence needed for the understanding of a profoundly metaphysical view of the world. In fact he advocates that the educational curriculum of the traditional centers of learning (*madrasahs*) should emphasize the teaching of logic, ethics, and rhetoric first and then philosophy to the advanced students.

Nasr emphasizes training in logic and rationalistic philosophy not only as a means of analysis but also as a framework which prevents the Islamic intellectual tradition from falling into chaos. Rationalization accordingly is a response to the demand of the intellectual faculty that seeks rational answers to philosophical questions.[6] Although Nasr neither writes in the tradition of the Peripatetics nor follows their method of inquiry, his conviction that students of Islamic philosophy should immerse themselves in rationalistic philosophy remains firm.

> Islam respects logic because on its own level logic is an aspect of the truth and the truth (*al-Ḥaqq*) is a name of Allah. Intelligence is likewise a divine gift which leads Man to an affirmation of the doctrine of unity (*al-tawḥīd*) and the essential varieties of the Islamic revelation. The use of logic in the worldview of Islam is as a ladder which leads man to the Divine.[7]

In my various conversations with Nasr, I have raised the issue of why he does not become engaged in rationalistic philosophy of the sort which some of his teachers have practiced. To this he responded: "My intention is to introduce traditional metaphysics and Islamic philosophy to the modern world. Hopefully, the future generation of scholars will take on the task of offering more rationalistically oriented works much needed in this field."

Despite the above, I believe there is a more profound reason for his lack of interest in the rationalization of philosophical issues. Nasr does not believe that the fundamental questions in philosophy can ultimately be solved through rationalistic analysis but that the answer lies in a rapprochement of contemplation and ratiocination, or reason and intellectual intuition.

In fact Nasr's way of doing philosophy is the key to the understanding of his solution to the fundamental questions in philosophy.

Throughout his numerous commentaries, Nasr has elaborated upon various themes within the tradition of Islamic philosophy. From al-Fārābī to Avicenna, al-Ghazzālī, Suhrawardī, and Mullā Ṣadrā, the grand metaphysician of seventeenth-century Persia, he demonstrates not the validity of their individual arguments but the continuity and harmony that exists at the heart of their philosophical doctrine. Whether Nasr discusses the Andalusian Ibn 'Arabī, partly Turkish al-Fārābī, or Persian Mullā Ṣadrā, he returns to the center, the point which unites them all. To Nasr, the unity and uniformity of the Islamic intellectual tradition is as important as the philosophical content of numerous treatises by Muslim philosophers written over a span of a millennium. The continuity and harmony in the tradition of Islamic philosophy for Nasr is the philosophical significance of Islamic philosophy and not the validity of any specific arguments.

Nasr's advocacy of Peripatetic philosophy, however, has its limitations. Discursive knowledge he argues, provides us with a purely intellectual knowledge of the objects of our inquiry and for some this is sufficient. There are those, however, who yearn for an experiential knowledge, one whose existential significance goes beyond a syllogistic proof. These few restless souls who have mastered the possibilities of rationalistic philosophy should then transcend discursive reasoning and leap to a higher domain of reality. As he states:

> Reason, this reflection of the intellect upon the human psyche, can then be both an instrument for reaching the divine truths found in revelation, which are super-rational but not irrational, and a veil which hides these truths from man and becomes the means of rebelling against God and his revealed religion.[8]

Nasr does not offer a critique of specific arguments of the Peripatetics but his criticism is directed at their emphasis on the use of reason alone as a means of attaining truth. Reliance on reason alone, he argues, has had catastrophic consequences both in the realm of philosophy and ethics. Philosophically, the use of reason alone, has led to the relativization of moral principles, destruction of metaphysics, discarding of the sense of the sacred and, last but not least, the closing of so many other possibilities the human intellect possesses. Man is not only a rational animal, but he is also divine in his own right.

Finally, Nasr's critique of the use of reason alone is directed at the humanistic and environmental consequences of the post-Renaissance emphasis on rationalism.[9] He argues that a worldview whose pivotal point is reason will lead to the desacralization of the universe and eventual degradation of it.

> Knowledge has become nearly completely externalized and desacralized, especially among those segments of the human race which have become transformed by the process of modernization, and that bliss which is the fruit of union with the One and an aspect of the perfume of the sacred has become well-nigh unattainable and beyond the grasp of the vast majority of those who walk upon the earth.[10]

The second component of Nasr's philosophical outlook is the illuminationist doctrine of Suhrawardī,[11] the founder of illuminationist philosophy (*ishrāq*). Such a doctrine, whose philosophical methodology relies on a synthesis of rationalistic philosophy, intellectual intuition, and practical wisdom, is echoed throughout Nasr's writings. Illuminationist doctrine maintains that it is only through a direct and unmediated mode of cognition that certainty of the object of one's cognition is possible. According to Suhrawardī a direct epistemic mode is possible only through a continuous emanation of "light."[12]

Illumination according to Nasr is the opening of the intellect to revelation, a receptivity to experience transcendence, a knowledge that is not only informative but also transformative. Nasr, who for the first time introduced the significance of Suhrawardī's Persian writings, considers Suhrawardī's emphasis on the intellectual and practical aspects of wisdom to be among the salient features of the illuminationist doctrine and the ideal way of philosophizing.

The third component of Nasr's philosophical perspective is Sufism which he regards to be the heart and soul of Islam.[13] Sufism is the most extensively treated topic by Nasr. He not only deals with Sufism as a separate topic but also his interpretation of various facets of Islamic life and thought are done in light of Islamic mysticism. To begin with, Sufism according to Nasr is not a branch of Islam but it is that spirituality which manifests itself in the religious life of *Sharī'ah* (Islamic law), constituting the sacred basis for the Islamic jurisprudence.

Sufism, for Nasr, as a methodology has a philosophical significance. It is in this sense that I consider Sufism to be a third component and a complementary part of his philosophical perspective. Acknowledging the limited benefits of rationalistic philosophy and the value of intuition, moral purity and inner cleansing is then emphasized as part of the process of doing philosophy, just as logic and reasoning are. Nasr argues that Sufism's emphasis on ascetic practices and spiritual discipline provides the serenity and reflectiveness that is necessary for opening the psyche to the experiential dimensions of truth. Sufism therefore, becomes an integral part of philosophizing in the larger sense of the word. It is the non-intellectual means of activating the intellect so the sapiental wisdom can be experienced.

The intellect in its medieval sense, Nasr maintains, is the faculty which has the potential to grasp the Truth. Having identified Truth and Reality with God, he then argues that the all embracing nature of God is such that its reality cannot be fully grasped only by reason, intuition alone, or by ascetic practices and mystical vision for that matter. What is called for, according to Nasr, is a synthesis of the three components hitherto discussed. A wedding among various aspects of the Truth which can be understood intellectually, seen introspectively, and experienced inwardly.

Nasr's emphasis on esotericism and the experiential dimension of truth as represented in Sufism poses a major problem among mainstream academics which has made him and his philosophical views controversial in the West. The controversy stems from the non-verifiable nature of his truth claims. Such non-verifiable claims as having experienced God or knowing the mysteries of divine realms, have no place in the mainstream philosophical circles in the West. The question which Nasr's opponents pose is how a serious philosophical debate is possible when one encounters non-verifiable and esoteric truth claims. Operating within an epistemological framework based on truth by authority in the third millennium is as perplexing as it is difficult to be philosophically engaged with it.

Nasr's advocacy of intellectual intuition is also problematic in that it runs into the same problem that Sufi truth claims do, namely, the uncommunicable and unverifiable nature of the claims made. Once again, knowledge through intuition, despite its certitude for the knower, is of no value for others. The second critique against knowledge by intuition is that a state of mind and one's certainty of it do not entail the validity of the state of affairs. The leap from a mental concept to the affirmation of a truth claim about it is simply fallacious. This is a problem similar to the ontological argument for the existence of God in which its propagators conclude that certitude of conceiving of a being necessarily leads to the external existence of that being.

Nasr would reply to the above criticism regarding the subjective nature of his philosophical views by emphasizing the objective nature of the knowledge attained through intellectual intuition and practical wisdom for the person in question. For Nasr, the knowledge attained through intuition is both sacred and certain.

> This knowledge is revelation and intellection or intellectual intuition which involves the illumination of the heart and the mind of man and the presence in him of knowledge of an immediate and direct nature which is tasted and experienced, the sapience which the Islamic tradition refers to as "presential knowledge."[14]

If this knowledge is both sacred and certain, and its source of emanation is Divine Reality, how then do we account for the disagreements among many of those Muslim philosophers and *ḥakīms* whose illustrious commentaries on philosophical issues are rejected as erroneous by one another? Even Nasr himself, whose exposé of the eternal truth is an indication that he is the recipient of intellectual intuition, criticizes others with similar claims[15] and has been criticized by others of similar status. The question then arises as to who truly possesses the knowledge of Absolute Reality and who perceives that he does, and finally is there a Reality instead of realities?

Nasr expends a great deal of effort responding to those objections raised by the modern intellectual thinkers who consider his perennial ontology to be absurd if not dangerous. Nasr responds by offering an ontological and epistemological analysis of the nature of truth and its relationship to revelation. God is the Absolute Reality, Nasr states, and therefore, only the Absolute knows the Absolute, Absolutely. The knowledge of all other beings of God therefore is relative to the ontological status of the knower. An epistemological consequence of this view is to equate the ontological status of a person to the domain of his cognition, that is, the more you "are" the more you "know."[16] In Islamic philosophy there is the inner truth which one comes to know through contemplation and introspection. Since this type of knowledge is of an existential nature, there occurs a unity among the knower, the known, and the knowledge that one has come to know. Perhaps it is for this reason that the Quran asks "are those who know and those who do not, equal?"

Nasr argues that knowledge by nature is divine and the extent to which one comes to know, to that same extent he becomes "God-like." The degree to which one knows God is therefore contingent upon the scope and the intensity of knowledge of the knower and his corresponding ontological status. Whereas this ontological scheme, based on the hierarchy of knowledge explains the variety of opinions with regard to the Absolute Reality, the unmediated nature of this knowledge explains the certainty of it. The relative nature of our knowledge of Reality, therefore, seems to necessitate relative ignorance, a condition which one can ultimately overcome through unity with God. Should one's mastery of discursive reasoning, intellectual intuition, and practical wisdom reach its climax, the knower, the known, and the epistemic relationship between them become one. This view, known as the "Doctrine of the Unity of Being,"[17] is propagated by Nasr throughout his philosophically oriented works as the ultimate solution to the problem of knowledge.

> Hence, every determination of the Absolute is already in the realm of relativity. The unity of religions is to be found first and foremost in this Absolute which is at once Truth and Reality and the origin of all revelations and of all truth.[18]

In light of the foregoing discussion, Nasr's philosophical perspective can now be better understood. The path of knowledge begins by discursive reasoning and is complemented by intellectual intuition. For a select few, however, the path continues through the more practical aspect of wisdom, namely Sufism. It is through Sufism that what is attained through reason is also seen through an unmediated mode of knowledge. This type of knowledge, often referred to as "knowledge by presence" (*al-'ilm al-ḥuḍūrī*),[19] is the acceptable epistemological model for Nasr.

It is now clear how Nasr's view on epistemology presupposes the existence of a particular ontology often referred to as *philosophia perennis*. For Nasr *philosophia perennis*, also referred to as *sophia perennis*, is the knowledge that is of a universal character, has always been and will always be. On the nature and the origin of this knowledge Nasr states:

> This knowledge which is available to the intellect is, moreover, contained at the heart of all religions or traditions, and its realization and attainment is possible only through those traditions and by means of methods, rites, symbols, images and other means sanctified by the message from Heaven or the Divine Origin which gives birth to each tradition.[20]

Nasr's methodology in arguing for the validity of this ontology is not strictly speaking a philosophical one. In his writings one does not find the type of discussion that some of the other ontologists of medieval philosophy, such as Etienne Gilson, offer. Instead, Nasr's approach is what I call "philosophical anthropology" in that he offers a thorough analysis of the worldview of the traditional man whose relationship to and knowledge of the world is characterized as sacred.

Perennial ontology according to Nasr gives rise to a hierarchical universe which provides the framework within which the spiritual foundation of so many aspects of traditional life can be studied. The levels of reality allow for the possibility of the spiritual journey of man from the corporeal world to the pure Being with whom man seeks unity. Religion, therefore, "has its archetype in the Divine Intellect and possesses levels of existence like the cosmos itself."[21] The sense of realness of religion stems from the universal nature of this ontology which is also what distinguishes traditionalists from the modernists who see religion as real only when it can be reduced to its social or anthropological aspects. The school of the *philosophia perennis*, therefore, speaks of "a primordial tradition which constitutes original or archetypal man's primal spiritual and intellectual heritage received through direct revelation."[22]

Nasr's elegant articulation of the *philosophia perennis*, however, does not respond to the criticisms that modern Western philosophy addresses. At a time when relativism, historicism, and hermeneutical discussions on one hand, and analytic philosophy on the other hand are dominating Western (if not global) intellectual thought, Nasr speaks of an ontology whose existence is unverifiable to those who don't possess this particular "knowledge."

This medieval notion of a hierarchical ontology alluded to by Plotinus and elaborated upon by Avicenna and other Islamic philosophers, presupposes the existence of God, the authenticity of revelations, and the historical validity of sacred scriptures, just to mention a few of its features. Nasr knows that all the above are true simply because "he knows it" and this special unmediated knowledge becomes the basis upon which the foundations of his intellectual perspectives rest. The unverifiable nature of the views that Nasr holds with regard to perennial ontology and the knowledge of the *scientia sacra* in an age of philosophical pluralism, humanism, and postmodernism looks ever more doubtful, especially to those who have not had an experience of illumination and transcendence.

Nasr responds to the above criticism by stating that even if "not a single Muslim or Christian were to be left on the surface of the earth, Islam or Christianity would not cease to exist nor lose their reality in the ultimate sense."[23] As to the authenticity of the claim of the knower of truth, Nasr only tells us that the immediate and direct nature of this knowledge is such that it leaves no doubt for the knower, that it is the truth which he knows.

Both of the above responses are circuitous and eliminate the possibility for a critical assessment of his truth claims. Insisting that truth is primordial even though it is not open to any form of verification by an outsider, Nasr's system becomes self-referential, its truth value depending upon the system itself. Nasr would respond to the foregoing objection by arguing that an attempt for a rational explanation of this school will fail for *perennial philosophy* does not render itself to intellectual discourse. To him "scientia sacra is not the fruit of human intelligence speculating upon or reasoning about the content of an inspiration or a spiritual experience."[24] To argue further for the existence and the possibility of knowing the *scientia sacra*, a natural consequence of the hierarchical nature of perennial ontology, Nasr, like other perennialists such as H. Smith, N. Smart, F. Schuon and many others, has also adopted an "empirical" approach in some of his works by surveying the centrality of *scientia sacra* to so many other religious traditions. Throughout his works, and in particular *Knowledge and the Sacred*, he attempts to show how *philosophia perennis* constitutes the heart of all divinely revealed religions and therefore is of a universal nature. Somehow, the universality of religion and its presence throughout human history is indicative of divine presence within the soul of every man, and the inner yearning for transcendence alludes to the divine origin of man. Whereas Nasr uses the universality of religion as evidence for the validity of perennialism, it is not clear why the socio-scientific study of religion which offers a different explanation for this universality is rejected offhand as Western reductionism. This selective use of reason and changing the mode of discourse which is so prevalent among theologians who first select their conclusions and then look for the premises to support their desired conclusion, is a structural weakness within the heart of the perennialist camp.

We are now in a position to ask a more fundamental question with regard to Nasr's philosophical views. If our analysis were to remain on a purely intellectual level, what would be the virtue of adopting Nasr's school of thought since most of us are outsiders to this self-authenticating and tautologous system of belief? After all, like many other philosophical systems, it too attempts to solve some philosophical questions and leaves so many others unanswered. Nasr would state that the very nature of the knowledge, being a "revelation or intellectual intuition which involves the illumination of the heart and the mind of men,"[25] suggests that this type of knowledge is not only informative but also transformative. Whereas a purely informative knowledge brings about what Nasr calls the "Promethean man," the transformative knowledge being experiential, produces the "Pontifical man."[26] For Nasr, any philosophical doctrine which does not intensify one's yearning for the transcendence is of marginal significance and therefore not to be taken seriously. The Pontifical man for Nasr is a bridge between heaven and earth, a refined and virtuous man who has submitted himself to the dictums of his sacred tradition resulting in the containment of his ego. Promethean man, however, is an "earthly creature who has rebelled against Heaven and tried to misappropriate the role of Divinity for himself."[27] Nasr identifies the Pontifical man as the traditional man and the modern Western man as Promethean who represents the antipode of the Pontifical man. On this Nasr states:

> He [Pontifical man] feels at home on earth, earth considered as the virgin nature which is itself an echo of paradise, but as the artificial world created by Promethean man himself in order to make it possible for him to forget God and His own inner reality.[28]

The Promethean and Pontifical man represent two modes of being each of which relies on a different mode of cognition. For the Promethean man, whose point of emphasis is free thinking and critical analysis of the tradition leading to deconstruction and eventual destruction of it, rational thinking is called for. Nasr, therefore, sees the modern schools of epistemology and scientific paradigms as the natural consequences of the Western Promethean man whose concept of knowledge is destructive both to himself and to the environment.[29] The Pontifical man however, relies on an entirely different mode of cognition, one that is introspective but not subjective, it is esoteric and yet bound by the dictums of the religious law. For the Pontificial man it is only the knowledge of Reality which extinguishes the restlessness and inner anxiety of man and emulates the peace and serenity which can only come through submission to the Divine nature in one's self.

With the separation of the Promethean and the Pontifical man in the dawn of the third millennium, Nasr has put himself in a position where he cannot be in a dialogue with modern intellectual thought which views philosophy as a process without a teleology. This process in its traditional Socratic method is a search for seeking truth by rejecting the notion of truth by authority, and, in its postmodern sense, as Richard Rorty says, is a form of therapy and can be an alternative to bird watching. Nasr has a difficult task before him. On one hand, he is standing outside the Western intellectual tradition, disengaged from it and yet highly critical of it. On the other hand, the traditional world which provided a context within which traditional philosophical notions and concerns made sense, is crumbling around him. So his project is as daunting as it is perplexing. Will the modern world collapse underneath its own weight and then wake up and see the validity of a traditional worldview and the wisdom of Nasr's intellectual perspectives? The existing trend seems to suggest otherwise, and even in countries where the dictums of a sacred tradition have been implemented, often by force, the results have been catastrophic.

The modern world has left the perennialists few choices and little common ground for dialogue with contemporary intellectual thought. This is perhaps the reason why the perennialists are awaiting an apocalyptic event, the coming of a savior or awakening of the masses to the divine truth; they merely state and restate their positon, one whose logic and validity remains unverifiable and defies reason and intellectual discourse. In light of this, Nasr's philosophical perspective can perhaps be best summarized in his own words. "If I were to summarize my so-called 'philosophical position', I would say that I am a follower of that *philosophia perennis* and also *universalis*, that eternal sophia which has always been and will always be and in whose perspective there is but one Reality which can say 'I'."

MEHDI AMINRAZAVI

DEPARTMENT OF CLASSICS, PHILOSOPHY, AND RELIGION
MARY WASHINGTON COLLEGE
JANUARY 2000

NOTES

1. For Nasr's account of his life and intellectual journey see: "In Quest of the Eternal Sophia," in *Philosophes critiques d'eux-mêmes: Philosophische Selbstbetrachtungen*, vol. 6 (Bern: Peter Lang, 1980), pp. 113–21. Also see *A Complete Bibliography of the Works of Seyyed Hossein Nasr*, ed., M. Aminrazavi and Z. Moris (Islamic Academy of Science, Malaysia, 1994).

2. Nasr uses "theosophy" according to the etymological root of the word and its usage in the medieval period meaning "Divine Wisdom" which he regards to be equivalent to gnosis. This is not to be mistaken with the nineteenth-century British movement with a similar name.

3. For more information concerning Muslim sources on Hermes, see S. H. Nasr, "Hermes and Hermetic Writings in the Islamic World" in *Islamic Life and Thought* (Albany: SUNY Press, 1981), pp. 102–119.

4. For Nasr's view of Suhrawardi see *Three Muslim Sages* (Carvan Books, 1976), pp. 52–82 and *A History of Muslim Philosophy*, vol. 1, ed. M. M. Sharif (Wiesbaden: Otto Harrassowitz, 1966), pp. 372–98; and his introduction to Shihaboddin Yahya Sohravardi, *Oeuvres Philosophiques et Mystiques*, vol. 3 (Tehran: Institute d'Etudes et des Recherches Culturelles, 1993), pp. 10–65.

5. For more information on Nasr's views on Mullā Ṣadrā see: *Ṣadr al-Dīn Shīrāzī and His Transcendental Theosophy* (Tehran: Institute for Humanities and Cultural Studies, 1977) and "Ṣadr al-Dīn Shīrāzī: His Life, Doctrine and Significance," *India-Iranica* 14 (Sep. 1961): 6–16.

6. Islamic philosophers refer to numerous verses in the Quran where contemplation upon the signs of creation as well as on the attributes of God is encouraged but reflection on divine essence is forbidden. For more information see: S. H. Nasr, "Intellect and Intuition: An Islamic Perspective," *Studies in Comparative Religion* (Winter-Spring, 1979): 65–74.

7. S. H. Nasr, "Revelation, Intellect and Reason in the Quran," *Journal of Regional Cultural Institute* 1, no. 3 (Summer 1968): 61.

8. Ibid., p. 63.

9. For more information on this see: Nasr, *Man and Nature* (London: Allen and Unwin, 1968); *Islam and the Plight of Modern Man* (Chicago: ABC International Group, 2001); and *Religion and the Order of Nature* (New York: Oxford University Press, 1996).

10. S. H. Nasr, *Knowledge and the Sacred* (New York: Crossroad Press, 1981), p. 1.

11. For more information on various aspects of Suhrawardī's illuminationist doctrine see: H. Zi'ai, *Knowledge and Illumination* (Atlanta: Scholars Press, 1992); M. Aminrazavi, *Suhrawardi and the School of Illumination* (London: Curzon Press, 1997).

12. See M. Ha'iri, *Principles of Epistemology in Islamic Philosophy* (New York: SUNY Press, 1992).

13. Although Nasr's treatment of Sufism runs through most of his works, for more discussion concerning the place and significance of Sufism see his: *Sufi Essays* (Albany: SUNY Press, 1991).

14. Nasr, *Knowledge and the Sacred*, p. 130.

15. An example is Teilhard de Chardin, a modern religious thinker whom Nasr criticizes on the ground that he accepts the theory of evolution. Teilhard on the other hand, claims to have experienced God, which then makes his claims just as valid as those of Nasr. So here we have two men both of whom have experienced God and yet standing on opposite sides on the question of how man was created.

16. For a complete discussion on the relationship between one's ontological status and his domain of cognition see: M. Ha'iri Yazdi, *Principles of Epistemology in Islamic Philosophy*, pp. 145–58.

17. For a complete discussion on this see: S. H. Nasr, *Islamic Life and Thought* (Albany: SUNY Press, 1981), pp. 174–87.

18. Nasr, *Knowledge and the Sacred*, p. 293.

19. For more information see, Ha'iri, *Principles of Epistemology in Islamic Philosophy*, pp. 43–56.

20. S. H. Nasr, "The Philosophia Perennis" in *The World's Religious Traditions*, ed. F. Whaling (New York: Crossroad, 1984), p. 182.

21. Ibid., p. 185.

22. Ibid., p. 186.

23. Ibid.

24. Nasr, *Knowledge and the Sacred*, p. 130.

25. Ibid.

26. For a complete discussion on the Promethean and Pontificial man see: *Knowledge and the Sacred*, pp. 160–88.

27. Ibid., p. 160.

28. Ibid., p. 161.

29. S. H. Nasr, "In Quest of Eternal Sophia," *Philosophes critiques d'eux-mêmes: Philosophische Selbstbetrachtungen*, vol. 6 (Bern: Peter Lang, 1980), p. 119.

REPLY TO MEHDI AMINRAZAVI

Although he has been closely associated with me for the better part of two decades, in this text at least Dr. Aminrazavi holds a philosophical position directly opposed to mine. Whether he is trying to play the role of the devil's advocate or is presenting his own views is not the main question. What is important is that he is presenting a number of challenges not only to my position but to that of all traditional philosophies going back to Pythagoras and Plato, and other metaphysicians ancient and contemporary, challenges which concern his own philosophical research since his student days and which need to be answered. I will go systematically over his essay and try to respond to whatever issue I feel to be of particular significance and also in light of some of my other responses.

At the beginning of his discourse he calls me "a medievalist in that his [my] philosophical outlook and positions are those of medieval Islamic philosophy." I do not accept such an assertion, not because I do not admire medieval Western philosophy which I do greatly, but because the term "medieval" as used in Western history does not apply to Islamic history, and certainly not intellectual history. A Western scholar may call me a medievalist in the sense that I deal with such figures as Ibn Sīnā and Suhrawardī, who in the West are called medieval philosophers. For years I was even a member of the executive board of the International Congress of Medieval Philosophy. But if my thought is taken as a whole, I cannot be called a medievalist. Aminrazavi admits that I am closely attached to the thought of Mullā Ṣadrā who lived in the seventeenth century. He could have said as much of Sabziwārī who lived in the nineteenth century. Would such figures be called medieval philosophers living as they did in the seventeenth and nineteenth centuries, respectively? There is no doubt that they had more in common with St. Thomas Aquinas than Descartes or Hegel, but that hardly makes them medieval if this term is to bear any relation to its ordinary Western usage. It is high time that we stop using the term medieval for Islamic philosophy and in fact Islamic history in general, except in particular circumstances which necessitate such a usage. In any case, while I have much affinity with European medieval philosophy and find myself infinitely closer to St. Thomas and St. Bonaventure than to Quine and Sartre, nevertheless I do not consider myself a medieval thinker but a traditional one who espouses the perennial philosophy which transcends the divisions of historical time.

In discussing the stages of learning philosophy, the author writes that I advocate learning Peripatetic philosophy and discursive reasoning before embarking upon other stages. Yes, I do advocate such a course but not necessarily for everyone. To master traditional Islamic philosophy, it is necessary to begin with Peripatetic philosophy and learn the rules of logic. But to understand traditional metaphysics, this is not the necessary course for everyone. There are the few who without systematic logical and philosophical training are able to grasp the truths of metaphysics through intellectual intuition. The traditional regimen, therefore, while valid in general in the context of Islamic philosophy, is not strictly speaking universal. Of course Suhrawardī and Mullā Ṣadrā claim universality for the hierarchy of philosophical learning which begins with logic and Peripatetic philosophy and, in the context of their tradition, their views hold true. But in the context of universal metaphysics, this is not a necessary condition. While I hold to this metaphysical perspective and emphasize the central importance of intellectual intuition and illumination and the possibility of attaining principial knowledge through this channel, nevertheless I also wish to emphasize that I consider philosophical training in the traditional sense to be important and very helpful, especially when it comes to the question of teaching and exposition of traditional philosophical ideas.

Aminrazavi asserts that I do not write in the tradition of the Peripatetics. This is true because I am not a Peripatetic philosopher, but I have studied this philosophy and have written a great deal about the Muslim Peripatetics, especially the chief among them, Ibn Sīnā. I believe knowledge of this philosophy to be essential for the understanding of the more metaphysical later schools of *ḥikmah* associated with Suhrawardī, Mullā Ṣadrā and others. The fact that I do not write as a Peripatetic does not, therefore, in any way contradict my advice to students in Islamic philosophy to immerse themselves at the beginning in Islamic Peripatetic philosophy which, by the way, I do not characterize as rationalistic as does the author. This philosophy is based upon discursive thought and rational discussion and is therefore called *baḥthī* in Arabic, but that is not the same thing as being rationalistic as this term is understood in Western philosophy today.

Aminrazavi quotes me concerning why I do not become "engaged in rationalistic philosophy" by which he means entering into a rationalistic philosophical debate with various currents of modern philosophy. I must clarify the quotation he has attributed to me to convey exactly my thoughts on this matter. In my writings I have confronted in a detailed philosophical manner certain basic theses of modern philosophy, especially those associated with Descartes and to a lesser extent Kant. I have also written extensive rebuttals to many theses of contemporary Western philosophy of science. My function has been to express the perennial philosophy in a language comprehensible to modern scholars who are trained in modern modes of thinking, by which I do not mean of course everyone belonging to these categories. My vocation has also been to resuscitate traditional Islamic thought, to provide answers from the traditional point of view for philosophical and intellectual challenges posed by modernism, and to apply the principles of tradition to the solution of certain contemporary problems, such as the relation between religion and science, the environmental crisis, the alienation of modern man, and so on.

What I told Aminrazavi was that I hope that others with a traditional perspective, including some of my students, would follow with detailed analyses and criticisms of various philosophical currents in the modern world despite the fact that most of these currents have a fairly short life span. For example, three decades ago many people in Europe spoke of structuralism and there was a need at that time to write a critique of its tenets from the perspective of the perennial philosophy. Such a task was not carried out to any appreciable degree, but also structuralism itself soon went out of vogue and such a critique no longer appeared essential. In my own intellectual life, I have done what my energy and time have permitted along the lines mentioned above, but I remain aware that the task of providing a traditional critique of whatever thought pattern suddenly appears on the horizon needs to be carried out even if that pattern does not have a very long life. As for the more enduring forms of modern philosophical thought, whether it be Cartesianism, Kantianism, Hegelianism, Marxism, Darwinism, or Freudianism, many aspects of the thought of these schools have already received an in-depth critique in the hands of the major expositors of traditional doctrines who have preceded me in time, especially Guénon, Schuon, Burckhardt, Lings, Tage Lindbom as well as several others, and there has been no need for me to repeat their analyses but only to make additions when necessary.

Aminrazavi writes that I do not demonstrate the validity of the thought of various Islamic thinkers but discuss only the harmony existing at the heart of their philosophical doctrine. As an Islamic philosopher who considers himself to belong to the Islamic philosophical tradition, I have seen no need whatsoever to demonstrate anew teachings whose validity I have accepted through long study and by reaching certainty concerning them. Proofs provided by the traditional masters are in a sense my proofs as well. To start from scratch and to try to prove again what the traditional Islamic philosophers have already demonstrated would be like re-inventing the wheel. But this does not mean at all that "the continuity and harmony of Islamic philosophy for Nasr is the philosophical significance of Islamic philosophy and not the validity of their specific arguments," as the author asserts. For me the most important issue has always been the truth and hence the validity of the philosophical doctrine that I have accepted as my own. If after extensive study I had not discovered traditional Islamic philosophy to be true, I would have never embraced it. But having studied it and made myself a continuator of that tradition, I have seen no reason to demonstrate and prove once again the tenets of Islamic philosophy. Rather, having studied and absorbed this tradition, as well as Western thought, my goal has been to resuscitate the Islamic philosophical tradition in a contemporary language while responding to criticisms made against it by a number of modern scholars and philosophers. It is in this sense that I have sought to demonstrate the validity of this philosophy in the contemporary context. My task has also been to bring out the relation of various schools of Islamic philosophy as constituting a hierarchy within the total Islamic intellectual tradition. The attempt to reach this goal is to be seen in one of my earliest works, *Three Muslim Sages*, and has continued in the decades that have followed.

The most acute criticism of Aminrazavi concerns what he calls the "non-verifiable nature of [my] truth claims." He considers such truth claims as, for example, experience of God or knowledge of the mysteries of the divine realm to have "no place in the mainstream philosophical circles in the West." Here he speaks as a pure rationalist questioning everything that human reason, cut off from both the Intellect and revelation, cannot grasp. Such a rationalistic criticism could be and in fact has been leveled against Plato and Plotinus as well and is nothing new. Nevertheless, it is necessary to provide a short answer to a question with a long history. What Aminrazavi considers as "truth claims," whether they be by Pythagoras and Empedocles, Suhrawardī or Mullā Ṣadrā, or contemporary expositors of the perennial philosophy such as myself, are in fact not claims at all but truths reached by means of the eye of the intellect and based on certainty that is not available to the unaided reason. But that does not make these truths non-verifiable.

I would like to repeat here the words of Suhrawardī about whom Dr. Aminrazavi has written a book. Suhrawardī asks why rationalist skeptics doubt the words of the Illuminationists who have "observed" the stars and constellations of the spiritual firmament while they do not doubt the words of ordinary astronomers when they speak of constellations in the sky, which the doubting skeptic has not observed himself any more than he has observed the constellations of the spiritual firmament. This complaint of Suhrawardī pertains very much to today's situation. That same rationalist who speaks of the nonverifiable nature of "truth claims" by traditional philosophers accepts completely the truth claims of quantum mechanics without seeking to verify it himself. He simply trusts the physicist and not the metaphysician for reasons which are not rational but ideological and cultural.

Furthermore, in the same way that the truth claims of quantum mechanics are verifiable provided one is willing to devote years of study to them, the "truth claims" of metaphysics are likewise verifiable providing one is also willing to undergo the necessary training and preparation. The difference, however, lies in the fact that the study of quantum mechanics requires only the training of the mind and to some extent the eye, but that of metaphysics requires the education and training of man's whole being. In any case the so called "truth claims" of someone like myself are certainly not nonverifiable unless one reduces verifiability to only the rationalistically proven or operationally definable, in which case many other things including the postulates upon which reasoning itself is based would also become non-verifiable.

If knowledge derived through intuition would be "of no value for others" as claimed by the author, there would have been no value in Platonism, Neoplatonism, and even Aristotelianism, some of whose tenets, such as hylomorphism, are based upon intellectual intuition. Those who possess intellectual intuition or vision are like those who have left the cave in Plato's myth. Those accustomed to looking only at the shadows on the wall do not believe them because they have seen nothing other than shadows. But ultimately it is only those who have seen the light of day, to continue in the language of Plato's myth, who can guide others beyond the world of shadows. Throughout history those who have been given the power of intellectual intuition have provided intellectual maps and philosophical visions of the greatest value even, and especially, for those who have not shared in the original intellectual intuition and vision.

The author also points to the disagreements among various schools of thought in Islam as being opposed to the idea of sacred and certain knowledge of which I speak. This is a significant question to which I have returned in several of my writings. The answer to this question is that in a traditional universe there is always an agreement upon principles. For example, all schools of Islamic thought agree upon the principle of Divine Unity (*al-tawḥīd*). Yet, each expresses an aspect of the truth and one of the latent possibilities within the tradition. These schools are all facets of the traditional and sacred universe of discourse to which they belong. As Shaykh Maḥmūd Shabistarī says in his *Gulshan-i rāz* ("Secret Garden of the Divine Mysteries"):

> Whatever they have said more or less about It [the Truth],
> They have given an indication of it from their own perspective.

Only at the highest level of metaphysical understanding does one come to realize that the various traditional schools debating with each other are all partial expressions of the truth and that their contentious opposition does not detract one iota from the fact that they all belong to a sacred universe of discourse and express different facets of the single truth, or, one could say, that they represent different perspectives upon the same truth. Only the Truth of the Absolute is absolute Truth.

Aminrazavi writes that my "methodology in arguing for the validity of this ontology [which I present] is not strictly speaking a philosophical one." Rather he calls it "philosophical anthropology." This is not true, for what I seek to do is to present an epistemology which makes possible the understanding of the ontology in question and to do so I discuss the traditional nature of man and his faculties, this discussion being necessary in order to resuscitate traditional epistemology. To call this "philosophical anthropology" in a pejorative sense is to misunderstand what I have sought to accomplish. Furthermore, in several of my writings I have dealt directly with ontology itself.

The author returns to his criticism of my position by a rationalistic attack based on the unverifiable nature of my views concerning perennial ontology with which I have already dealt and do not need to treat again, but then he adds that the "*perennial philosophy* does not render itself to intellectual discourse." I oppose this assertion strongly. First of all the author confuses intellectual and rational, a distinction basic to the perennial philosophy. Secondly, even if we take intellectual discourse to mean rational, the perennial philosophy throughout its long history has had both its poetical and didactico-philosophical expressions. In its second mode it has certainly been open to rational discourse as we see in the writings of Nāgārjuna, Erigena, St. Bonaventure, Suhrawardī, Mullā Ṣadrā and others. What it is not willing to do is to participate in a rationalistic discourse which would reduce the intellect to reason and all higher levels of reality to the lower accessible to the senses. Nor is it willing to sacrifice the certainty of intellectual intuition for the ever-recurring skepticism and doubt of rationalistic ruminations.

Also Aminrazavi criticizes my using the universality of religion for the validity of perennialism while excluding socio-scientific explanations. First of all I use not only religion in the general sense, but specific doctrines, beliefs, symbols, practices, and so on. There might be some kind of socio-scientific explanation for the global reality of religion in general, although even this has been questioned by a number of anthropologists such as Jean Servier. But I have not come across any socio-scientific explanation which can give a satisfactory reason for the existence of the universality of religious doctrines, symbols, and so on, without recourse to the worst kind of reductionism and ignorance of blatant realities.

At the end of his essay the author writes, "Will the modern world collapse underneath its own weight and then wake up and see the validity of a traditional worldview and the wisdom of Nasr's intellectual perspective? The existing trend seems to suggest otherwise, and even in countries where the dictums of a sacred tradition have been implemented, often by force, the results have been catastrophic." I have quoted these lines in full because the answer to them is pertinent in clarifying my position on a very important issue. I have come to the position of being the defender of the perennial philosophy not because of the popularity of this position, but because I consider it to be true even if the current trends of philosophy in the West are opposed to it. Nor have I adopted this position waiting for the modern world's collapse so that my position will become accepted more fully. Whether the modern world collapses later rather than sooner does not change one iota my certitude in the truths of the perennial philosophy and all traditional metaphysics.

This having been said, however, I need to add that one does not have to be a prophet to realize that the modern world is collapsing rapidly. The unbelievable destruction of the natural environment should be enough to open our eyes and make us realize that the present-day world cannot continue as it is and the existing trends certainly do not "seem to suggest otherwise." Furthermore, to the degree that the hold of modernism and its progeny post-modernism weaken, the pertinence of traditional teachings becomes more evident. In fact the perennial philosophy is of much greater interest even in the West today than the author thinks. As for the traditional principles being applied, that has not occurred fully in the contemporary period anywhere in the world so that one cannot speak of its catastrophic results. In my *Traditional Islam in the Modern World*, I have written that of the three aspects of present-day Islam, the modern, the fundamentalist (an unfortunate term that one is now forced to use), and the traditional, only the first two have been able to gain political power in Islamic countries. As for the third, while being strong and in fact growing in strength among modern educated "intelligentsia," it has not been able to dominate over and establish a complete politico-social order in any part of the Islamic world. I think that the same truth holds *mutatis mutandis* for other parts of the world.

The whole thrust of Aminrazavi's paper is to provide a rationalistic criticism of my position from the point of view of what he considers mainstream modern Western philosophy. The questions he has brought up concerning the rationalistic critique of not only my own view, but of any philosophy based upon intellectual intuition and certitude, are important and in fact can be seen to run in one way or another throughout the history of philosophy in the East and West. The difference is that only in the modern West did rationalism and empiricism become so strong as to push the intellectually centered traditional philosophies to the margin. At other times and climes both types of philosophy flourished more or less side by side, although the rational philosophies were not as secularized as in the modern period, and they remained in a secondary position compared to traditional metaphysics, standing below the supreme science of gnosis in the hierarchical order which dominate non-modern civilizations and their intellectual tradition. And that is why the questions posed by Aminrazavi have in a sense been answered a long time ago. I am nevertheless happy to be given this occasion to make further clarifications and responses to this rationalistic attack. Since like myself, the author is a Persian, I want to conclude with a poem by Rūmī in answer to the relation between rationalistic cleverness and intellectual intuition which is always combined with a sense of bewilderment in the Divine Reality:

> Sell cleverness and buy bewilderment,
> For cleverness is conjecture and bewilderment victory.

S. H. N.

18

Archie J. Bahm

NASR'S ABSOLUTE EVERYTHING AND NOTHING

Nasr is a Sufi Muslim. I am a Humanistic Naturalist. Differences in our presuppositions about the ultimate nature of things, of self, society, and the universe, have implications for solutions to all other philosophical problems.

DIFFERENCES

I see existence as temporal, everlasting, and dynamic. Nasr sees existence as ultimately Sacred, Eternal, and Absolute. I see humans as an evolving species endowed with creative intelligence, cultural riches, and possibilities for reconstructing the local universe. Nasr sees humans "as being endowed with total intelligence centered upon the Absolute and created to know the Absolute, . . . becoming limited to the realm of profane knowledge, . . . resulting finally in the desacralization of human life to an ever greater degree" (4).[1]

For me, Nasr's view of the Absolute as an eternal, formless, pure unity sterilizes existence of all genuine activity. For him, actual existences are debased unities in which all plurality is by nature exteriorization of the supposed inner unity of the Absolute immanent within each thing. Although he asserts that "Knowledge can attain the Sacred both beyond the subject which knows and at heart is the very subject, for finally that Ultimate Reality which *is* the Sacred as such is both the knower and the known, inner consciousness and outer reality, the pure immanent Subject and the Transcendent Object, the Infinite Self and Absolute Being which does not exclude Beyond Being" (3), each thing, each knower, has no vitality, or knowledge, of its own. Any being, any *is-ness*, and any actuality and activity, which Nasr attributes to persons and things is a bit of the debased is-ness of the Absolute immanent in them. "The only way to know Being is to realize our own nonexistence and to live in awareness of our nothingness before that Reality which alone *is* and which in its inner infinitude transcends even Being" (I186).

I ask why should the Absolute which *is*, and as *is* is undefiled by any *is not*, also become immanent in any (and all) "relatively absolute" being which also *is not* the Absolute which alone *is* as such? Such a view seems inherently unreasonable. Yet it seems to be the basic presupposition of Nasr's rationalized explanations of the nature of worldly, human, and historical existence.

I regard the omnipresence of negation, of multiplicities of negation, in each being as polarly involving positivity, multiplicities of positivity, in the intricate complexities of its organicity. Nasr refers to "The Polarization of Being," but he says that to assert that "something 'is' means only in analogy with respect to Being" (I183). His concept of polarity has only one pole that *is*, the Absolute, or Being, or the Sacred. All else is *māyā*, debased and desacralized veils of illusion. Finite being is referred to also as "relatively absolute," because the Absolute, as its source, seems diminishedly immanent in it. Nasr seized upon what little analogical being may be immanent in it as providing at least a vision of the ultimate sacredness of Being. Then he bathes the whole history of religions as suffused with this sacred analogy of Being.

The immanence of the one pole, Absolute Sacred Formless Being, in whatever else is in any way analogical, seems to me to deprive finite being, and all human beings, of genuine existence. For me, all polar opposites involve some mutual immanence, such that each pole has both some entitiveness of its own, while it endures, and has some of the entitiveness of its opposite pole immanent in it. Since the organicity of beings involves them in multipolarities, it also involves them in multi-immanences. These are not mere analogical beings, but constitute existence itself.

My view of existence centers in the problem of the one and the many and of whole and parts. Existence is ultimately both one and many. Unity and plurality are equally ultimate characteristics, in contrast with Nasr's view that existence is ultimately only one, only unity, only Absolute, pure, and formless unity. All else is *māyā*, which is somehow both illusory unity and immanent embodiment of the Absolute as pure unity, which cannot (that is, as Unity as such) both become many and yet also be the is-ness of all else (as the "relatively absolute").

For me, each existent is both whole and parts. A whole is always a whole of parts. A part is always a part of a whole. Therefore, each, wholeness and partness, is immanent in the other because each involves inherence in the other as part of its nature. But also, a whole is not its parts and the parts of a whole are not that whole. The not-ness, or negation, of whole and parts is also thus characteristic of each existent. So, in addition to the whole which is not its parts, the unity involving the mutual immanence of whole and parts which are also not each other I name "organic unity." This is the ultimate unity of existence, of existing beings which, as complex and dynamic, involve multileveled hierarchies and histories of organic wholes both completely caused by antecedent and other conditions and producing novelty constantly.[2]

Contrasting concepts of organic unity with Absolute unity, and of complex multi-directional hierarchical dynamism with eternally pure formlessness, we can observe some differences more clearly. For me, each being (person, cell, atom, society, galaxy) is a quantum (undivided whole) of energy which proceeds developmentally by both remaining the same in some ways and changing in other ways, resulting from both internal and external causal influences. Existence is dynamic, not merely static, but is also dynamic in static ways. ("Mattergy can be neither created nor destroyed." "You cannot step into the same river twice.")

Each being has its own entitiveness, its own actuality, its own activity, while it endures. But it is also only a bit of existence conditioned by and causally interacting in many ways with many, if not all, other beings. It is not any of those other things, and, although it is both positive and negative in many ways within itself as a whole of parts, it is also both negative and positive in many ways with all other things. Being not all other things, its being is characterized by infinite negativity. But since negative and positive are polar, it must be something positive in relation to each such negativity. Its being is also characterized by infinite positivity. The intricacies of the organic unity, or the organicity, of such multipolarity stretches imagination.

When people think about polarity, a whole-parts or unity-plurality polarity, for example, two poles with an axis ranging between them, they often think about it in different ways. Historically we find philosophies, even whole traditions, emphasizing one rather than the other of such poles. Western Civilization has been torn by two traditions, one generating a series of theocratic monotheisms, demonstrating that people cannot allow a single unitary all-inclusive deity to exist in eternal isolation, the other emphasizing pluralities of part and particles (Greek Atomism), atom crushers,[3] eternal souls, political individualism. Perpetual disputing about which tradition is true, largely in terms of the language of Spiritualism, emphasizing unity as wholeness (and holiness) and of Materialism, preferring multiplicities of parts, also produced the Dualism of Descartes ("Matter is everything that spirit is not; spirit is everything that matter is not.").[4] Descartes's inconsistency in appealing to a God to unite them resulted in the Psychological Parallelism of Arnold Guelinx, which evaded inconsistent mind-body interaction but not unification by God.

My struggle to understand and organize these tendencies resulted in a Diagram of Types, which underwent drastic change when my studies in Indian philosophy revealed to me that Advaita Vedanta, Nondualism, involves another powerful tendency in human thinking, polarly opposed to dualism. My conception of the nature of existence, and of tendencies of persons to interpret it, appeared as a Diagram of Types of theories which, in their complicated togetherness, organized all such philosophical tendencies into one coherent picture.

With Spiritualism as one pole, Materialism as its opposite pole, Dualism as accepting both poles as externally related, and Nondualism as accepting both unity and plurality as somehow internal to something that is both, all contribute something to understanding the nature of existence. When Spiritualism is modified by admitting degrees of plurality (e.g., as in the Neo-Platonism of Plotinus), Materialism is modified by emergentism postulating more and more unity in higher levels of organization, Dualism is modified by speculating that God and matter cooperate in constant creativity (as in J. E. Boodin's Creationism[5]) and Nondualism is modified by Spinoza's Double-Aspect Theory,[6] the richness of metaphysical insights contributing to an organically integrated picture emerges as most insightful. Since polar opposites dynamically interact dialectically, any claim to timeless equality of opposites is itself false ("Extreme Middleism"), and claims that polar opposites are mutually immanent (as in the *yins* and *yangs* of Taoism), require precautionary recognition of other kinds of cultural riches.[7]

As an Organicist, I must recognize the contributions of philosophies exemplifying each of the polarities as illustrating both something true about the nature of existence and something false when any one of the poles is overemphasized by denying (actually or by implication) what is true about the other poles. I am indebted to Nasr for providing an example of this more sophisticated kind of metaphysics. He succeeds both in providing directional insights and in overemphasizing. I interpret Nasr's view as illustrating, in my terms, "Extreme Aspectism," and his own Sufi metaphysics seeks to substantiate it.

CONTRADICTIONS?

Our differences beget conflicting opinions about what is true. I find Nasr's writings filled with apparent contradictions. Chief among them is one serving as a source of many others: How is it possible for what is eternally perfect ("Absolute") to generate what is temporally imperfect ("relatively absolute")? He does not explain.

Some apparent contradictions:

> asserting categorically that only the Absolute is absolute. It refuses to commit the cardinal error of attributing absoluteness to the relative. . . . Hence every determination of the Absolute is already in the realm of relativity. (292–93)

> Within that world, that "relatively absolute" reality, whether it be the Logos itself or a particular determination of the Supreme Divinity, *is* absolute without being *the* Absolute as such. (294)

> the Reality which is completely other and yet none other than the very heart of the self, the Self of oneself. (3)

> Absolute being which does not exclude Beyond Being. (3)

> the essentially sacred character of both logical and mathematical laws which are aspects of Being itself. . . . (5) [But mathematics consists entirely of forms whereas the Absolute, or Being itself, is pure formlessness.]

> The crucial significance of sacred form as the absolutely necessary means for the attainment of the formless. (288–89)

> Only at the level of the Absolute are the teachings of all religions the same. (293) [But the Absolute as such, a perfect formless unity, contains no "teachings."]

> a unity which transcends all forms and a supposed unity which disregards all forms. (288)

> unity lies at the opposite pole of uniformity, and the reduction of religions to a least common denominator in the name of the religious unity of mankind is no more than a parody of "the transcendent unity of religions" which characterized the traditional point of view. (288)

> It is only esotericism which can detect the trace of the Absolute in the multiple universes of sacred form and meaning and yet see the Absolute beyond these forms in the abode of the formless. (294)

> Man is endowed with this precious gift of intelligence which allows him to know the Ultimate Reality as the Transcendent, the Beyond and the objective world as a distinct reality on its own level . . . (3)

Questions

Answers to some questions that people expect from philosophers and theologians seem missing, not explicitly, but implicitly as inherent in doctrinal presuppositions.

1. *Dependence.* Nasr claims that "all things are dependent on it [Being] both in their existence and qualities" (I186). Why does Nasr hold that the Absolute is immanent in the world, which is completely dependent on the Absolute for its being and nature (as "relatively absolute"), but that the Absolute is completely independent of all else and has nothing else immanent in it? Since I regard interdependence and mutual immanence, as more insightful in understanding the nature of existence, I must point out that, since Nasr's Absolute functions as the source of all else, his Absolute depends on all such other beings existing dependently on it, for its embodying in them what it contributes to their inner being, and for being that ideal Being to which they can aspire. As Nasr describes the Absolute and all of the ways that it functions in the world, does not his description imply that it must be something that by its agency and nature depends on its actually so functioning and thus involves it in depending on its so functioning and have such functioning inherent in its nature and thus immanent in it in this way?

Nasr concludes that "all things are dependent on it [Being] both in their existence and qualities" (I186). Since I have named my philosophy "Organicism: The Philosophy of Interdependence,"[8] interdependence and, now after studying Chinese philosophy, mutual immanence, provide a much more insightful understanding of the nature of existence than Nasr's one-way dependence.

2. *Purpose.* I do not recall Nasr describing the Absolute as purposeful. Although it seems to serve as the goal of human purposes, that is, to know the Absolute as Sacred, it has no purpose of its own. Purpose involves both aim and goal. The Absolute may serve as human goal, and thus serve human purposes, but it has no aim, or intention, will, or desire of its own. To will, or to want (hence to lack) anything is impossible for what is complete and perfect. Even though the Absolute is the origin and source of all other existence, it did not intend such existence, but only provided its emanation. Is Nasr's Absolute purposeless?

3. *Evil.* Concern for the problem of evil seems missing from Nasr's view. He employs a metaphor: "In paradise man had tasted of the fruit of the Tree of Life which symbolizes unitive knowledge. But he was also to taste of the Tree of Good and Evil and come to see things as externalized, in a state of otherness and separation" (2). But the words "good" and "bad" are scarce in his writings. His chief word signifying good is "sacred." And, since this word is central to his conceptions, he can say that it is his primary

concern. But such words as "enjoyment," "satisfaction," and "contentment" are missing from his language. Evil, for him, is "loss of the sense of the sacred"(2). The ultimate good is "the Sacred." Evil is "desacralization." But if the Sacred Absolute is the source of all, must it not be also the source of all evil?

If all exteriorization is evil, then any externalizing of the "relatively absolute" from the Absolute is itself evil, and if the only thing that the Absolute can do is to manifest itself in the world of things (even as their inner being), must it not be engaged in desacralization? Must not all creating be desacralization? Must there not be some evil in whatever the Absolute (and Sacred) does in acting, and creating?

4. *Sin*. The ethical monotheisms typical of Judaic, Christian, and Muslim religions tend to emphasize the Will of God and sin as willing to go against the will of God. References to the Will of God, the wills of men, and sin seem largely missing from Nasr's writings. Although I find him deploring debasement and desacralization, I do not observe recognition of attitudes of antagonism to the Supreme Being. Nasr is more concerned with the "states and stations" (S72) "on the Way to God" (S68) and includes a complete translation of a famous list of "Forty Stations" (S77–82). "Sin" is mentioned only once in this list and without evidence of antipathy. I did not find the word "sin" in any index in his writings. Are Nasr's humans essentially without sin?

5. *Salvation*. Popular views of salvation depict God as a person, loving, merciful, but also just, and judging assignment to Heaven or Hell. Good persons can go to Heaven and be with God and with their loved ones. Although Nasr states that "intelligence emanates from and returns to the Absolute" (2), persons who are beings that emanate from the Absolute have no way of returning to it as persons. "Intelligence . . . allows him to know the Ultimate Reality as the Transcendent. . . ." (3). "This unitive vision . . . continues to be a means of access to the Sacred and sacred knowledge remains as the supreme path of union with that Reality wherein knowledge, being and bliss are united" (2). Persons cannot become parts of the Absolute, because the Absolute has no parts. "The only way to know Being is to realize our own non-existence" (I186). How can any person accept salvation as non-existence?

RELIGIONS

For Nasr, religion is intellectual knowledge of the Sacred. "An intelligence which has been illuminated by the Intellect and a knowledge which is already blessed with the perfume of the sacred sees in the multiplicity of sacred forms, not contradictions which relativize, but a confirmation of the universality of the Truth and the infinite creative power of the Real that unfolds Its inexhaustible possibilities in worlds of meaning which, although different, all reflect the unique Truth" (281). "To carry out the study of other religions in depth requires a penetration into the depths of one's own being and an interiorizing and penetrating intelligence which is already imbued with the sacred" (282).

Nasr regrets that most Western studies of comparative religions have succeeded "only in debasing and trivializing even the most exalted subjects . . ." (283). He objects to "The excesses of historicism" (285). But his own understanding of historical religions seems blurred by his "perfume of the Sacred." Historical facts do exist. Human religion is human. Nasr's commitment to the "transcendent unity of religion" puts it out of human reach except as a vision.

My studies in the history of religions yield the conception that "Religion consists in man's concern for his ultimate value and how to attain it, preserve it, and enjoy it."[9] Religion, i.e., human religion, which is the only kind of religion that is, is concern for the ultimate value (i.e., the ultimate intrinsic value) of life as a whole (i.e., of human life: the life of each human being as a whole and the life of humankind as a whole). Nasr's view is religious by being concerned with man's ultimate value. But it puts man's ultimate value beyond reach, in a "transcendental unity of all religions," in the Sacred Absolute which alone *is*. Although Nasr claims that the Absolute exists also within each person as a bit of the "relatively absolute" emanation of the Absolute, "The only way to know Being is to realize our non-existence" (I186). I see Nasr's view, not as non-religious, but as anti-religious. For Nasr, persons have no ultimate intrinsic values of their own.

ARCHIE J. BAHM

DEPARTMENT OF PHILOSOPHY
UNIVERSITY OF NEW MEXICO
FEBRUARY 1994

NOTES

1. Numbers at the end of quotations from Nasr are from pages in *Knowledge and the Sacred* (New York: Crossroad, 1981), e.g. (4), or from the pages of *Islamic Life and Thought* (Albany: University of New York Press, 1981), e.g., (I186), or from the pages of *Sufi Essays*, 2nd ed. (Albany: State University of New York Press, 1991), e.g., (S77).

2. Oversimplified diagrams: (a) Many levels of existence, each contributing causally to the nature and functioning of each being (organic unity).

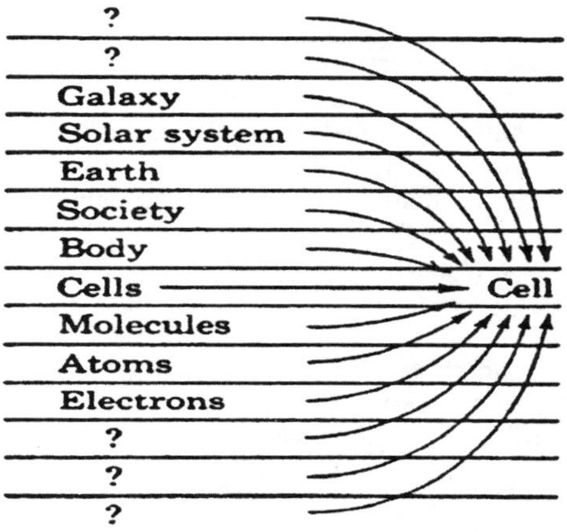

(b) Causation, both completely determining and producing novelty. Novelty is caused when multiple causes produce a new entity as an organic whole having both energy and forms ("information") induced from its antecedents and also some nature not included in any one cause singly or in the many causes as many.

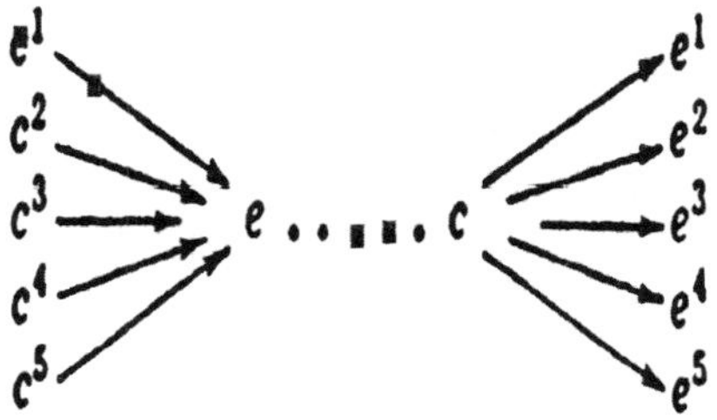

3. "Superconducting Super Colliders."

4. My interpretation inspired by Alfred Weber, *History of Philosophy* (New York: Charles Scribner's Sons, 1925), p. 251, interpreting Descartes's Meditation VI. See Ralph M. Eaton, *Descartes: Selections* (New York: Charles Scribner's Sons, 1927), pp. 152, 161, 162.

5. John E. Boodin, *Three Interpretations of the Universe* (New York: Macmillan, 1934).

6. Benedict Spinoza held that existence is only one substance having two

attributes, thought (mind) and extension (matter), which are completely independent of each other (unable to interact), but are aspects of the same substance. Naming his view "Neutral Monism" makes it seem closer to Advaita Vedanta, and suggests naming Advaita Vedanta as exemplifying Extreme Aspectism.

7. See my book *Polarity, Dialectic and Organicity* (Albuquerque: World Books, 1988 [1970]) for the full treatment of this topic. A stylized sketch appears in that work (p. 28) which will assist interested readers with these relations and my terminology. The two traditions emphasized in Western Civilization exemplify what I call "One-Pole-Ism: and "Other-Pole-Ism" in modified ranges. Nasr's view, understood as opposing Dualism, exemplifies Nondualism (*Advaita*) of Niguna Brahman stylized as what I call "Extreme Aspectism." The first sentence of Nasr's *Knowledge and the Sacred* states: "In the beginning Reality was at once being, knowledge, and bliss (the *sat*, *chit*, and *ānanda* of the Hindu tradition)." His statement that "knowledge has become separated from being . . . " exemplifies modification but other statements seem to emphasize the "relatively absolute" as *māyā*, veils of ignorance mistaking the immanence of the Absolute in the inner nature of apparently different things as actually separated. Nasr's Absolute is, like Nirguna Brahman, eternal being (*sat*) and sacred (*ānanda*), but he attributes "knowledge" described as "intellectual" and including mathematics, to his formless Absolute, whereas the Vedantic *chit* is pure awareness.

8. Archie J. Bahm, "Organicism: The Philosophy of Interdependence," *International Philosophical Quarterly* 7, no. 2 (June, 1967): 251–84.

9. Archie J. Bahm, *The World's Living Religions* (New York: Dell, 1964), p. 6.

REPLY TO ARCHIE J. BAHM

The paper of the late Professor Archie Bahm is valuable in setting in stark contrast the views which issue from a humanistic naturalism and my views and therefore allowing me to clarify many of these differences. He says clearly at the beginning that I am a Sufi Muslim and he a humanistic naturalist with all the differences that these two identities imply. One implies acceptance of God, the Transcendent Reality, and means of access to the attainment of knowledge of that Reality. The other, I presume, means for Bahm the rejection of any reality behind the human in the subjective realm and beyond nature in the objective world. The stark differences brought out by Bahm themselves demonstrate clearly how the foundations and premises of rational thought determine its conclusions and indirectly why reason cannot itself establish the foundations of reasoning.

Bahm asserts that my view of the Absolute as an eternal, formless, pure unity "sterilizes existence of all genuine activity." To assert as I do that all genuine activity in the realm of cosmic existence issues ultimately from the Divine Life or Divine Activity, which itself issues from the Divine as Absolute and Infinite, certainly does not "debase" such activity or "sterilize" it. Bahm seems to have difficulty understanding the integration of the lower in the higher without the destruction of what is essential in the lower. If I claim that each knower has "no vitality or knowledge of its own," to quote Bahm, that means that on the highest metaphysical level "its own" is integrated into its principial Center without this integration taking anything away from the vitality of that being on its own level. To speak of the integration of the levels of the cosmos into the Divine Principle is certainly not to deprive cosmic realities of their vitality, beauty, and reality on their own level. On the contrary, it is to bring out the deepest significance of all cosmic qualities. Metaphysical knowledge means not only to fix one's gaze upon the Absolute and to realize that there is nothing *ultimately* but the One. It also means to realize that to the extent that anything exists, it reflects metaphysical realities. It is to be able to see things not as veil but as transparent windows of realities beyond which external forms are precisely externalizations. In metaphysics vertical integration never means a loss but a gain, an intensification of all that is positive in a lower realm in a realm that stands above it and ultimately in the One Absolute and Infinite, in which all things have their origin. In a famous poem, Jalāl al-Dīn Rūmī after saying, "I was a mineral and became plant, I was a plant and became animal, I was an animal and became man, I am man and I shall become an angel, and so on," adds, "Then let me die for when have I ever become less by dying?" It is this richness of Reality, metaphysically understood, that evades the purely rationalistic and conceptual understanding of the Absolute which Bahm seems to hold.

Māyā, far from being debased and desacralized, constitutes at its highest reach the sacred supreme veil, the sacred veil of Isis, and is divine creativity as well as veil in the negative sense of the term. Through *māyā* the sacred cascades down the levels of the cosmic mountain to encompass man's life here below. Vis-à-vis the Absolute Self, *Ātman*, *māyā* is a veil but it is the cosmic veil that both veils and reveals, that hides and makes manifest.

Nor does my emphasis deprive "all human beings of genuine existence" as claimed by Bahm. Secular humanists often criticize the theologians for depriving man of a genuine sense of existence by emphasizing the reliance of human existence upon the Being of God. As agnostics, they mistake the integration of the lesser into the greater for deprivation. By claiming that we reflect the Divine Reality, receive our being from God and return to Him, I certainly do not think that I am depriving human beings of genuine existence especially since I emphasize the real freedom given to us by God to choose between truth and error, goodness and evil, beauty and ugliness. We are even given the freedom to deny God, as the existence of humanists among us itself bears witness. The grandeur of man is precisely in that his existence comes from God and his end is return to Him. Here below he is free to live in whatever way he wishes and yet his manner of living affects the state of his existence beyond the few flickering moments of earthly life. Would human life possess more genuine existence by being reduced to a transient appearance on a stage where his being is nothing but "a tale told by an idiot signifying nothing"?

As for the relation between Unity and multiplicity, the difference between my view and that of Bahm is that he conceives the relationship between the two in a horizontal manner and I in a vertical one without denying the horizontal dimension. I agree with him that to understand the structure of reality one has to comprehend the relation between Unity and multiplicity. In this world there is always an interplay of the two. The Sufis often speak of the knowledge of Unity in multiplicity (*al-waḥdah fi'l-kathrah*) and multiplicity in Unity (*al-kathrah fi'l-waḥdah*) and this is a universal metaphysical teaching with which I am in full agreement. These concepts themselves, however, must be understood on different planes of reality. Moreover, the vertical hierarchy which leads from the Principial Unity to various levels of multiplicity to which so much traditional wisdom refers (as for example at the beginning of the Tao Te-Ching) must not be confused with the interplay between Unity and multiplicity on various levels of manifestation.

From the point of view of Principial Unity there is only Unity or Non-Duality which is nevertheless the Origin and Source of all multiplicity. It is knowledge of this principial truth about which certain metaphysicians such as Śaṅkara or some of the Sufis speak. This supreme knowledge does not, however, close the door to knowledge of various cosmic orders of existence which always imply the mutual relationship between Unity and multiplicity. Furthermore, on all planes of manifestation there is always a relationship between the existent and the Principle as at once the transcendent and the immanent.

There are also many dualities of a complementary nature such as the static and the dynamic which characterize various planes of manifestation. I do not at all deny such complementarities which are, however, all resolved in that Unity, at once transcendent and immanent, which is also the *coincidentia oppositorum*. I believe that the major difference between Bahm and myself on this matter is the question of the vertical versus the horizontal dimensions of reality. By emphasizing supreme unitive knowledge, I certainly do not wish to negate in any way the various cosmic polarities, complementarities and correspondences with which in fact many of my works deal. The mutual immanence implied in the *Yin-Yang* symbol is one of the profoundest aspects of cosmic manifestation but this does not mean that one should forget that at the beginning is the Tao which transcends the *Yin-Yang* duality.

Bahm contrasts organic unity with Absolute Unity and "complex multi-directional hierarchical dynamism with eternally pure formlessness." This contrast is in reality based upon a misunderstanding of the metaphysical understanding of Unity and confusing it with simply a philosophical concept. This type of thinking also refuses to accept the differences in levels of reality as traditionally understood. In the same way that organic unity is not the same as geometric or mathematical unity, Divine Unity cannot be reduced to organic unity and transcends it infinitely although it contains on the highest level everything that we understand positively by organic unity. All the marvelous complexity and richness contained within organic unity is but a reflection of the infinite richness of the Divine Nature which is also Unique and the very reality of Unity at the same time. It is a misunderstanding of traditional metaphysics to contrast organic unity with what would appear to be a sterile philosophical unity of the One. In reality all the remarkable types of unity we observe in this world including organic unity (with all of its complexity) are reflections of that highest unity that belongs to the One alone.

Under the heading of "contradictions," Bahm refers to many aspects of my thought, which he considers to be contradictory, chief among them the following in Bahm's own words, "How is it possible for what is eternally perfect ('Absolute') to generate what is temporally imperfect ('relatively absolute')?" He then adds the statement that I do not explain this matter. First of all, I have turned to this major issue in several of my writings and it is unfortunate that Bahm had not consulted them before making this assumption. Secondly, as far as this crucial question is concerned, namely the question of theodicy which has turned many a Western—and curiously not Eastern—philosopher away from religion, its answer can only be found in pure metaphysics and not in rationalistic philosophy, for ordinary reason cannot understand how God, who is good, could create a world in which there is evil. Also, for theologians who have no access to esoteric knowledge and metaphysics this is taken to be a mystery. Intelligence can, however, penetrate into this ultimate mystery by turning to the integral knowledge of the Divine Principle as being at once Absolute, Infinite, and Supreme Goodness, to quote the formulation of Frithjof Schuon. The Divine Reality as Absolute is all-exclusive but as Infinite, it must contain all possibilities within Itself. Otherwise it would not be Infinite. Now one of these possibilities is the negation of the Divine Principle Itself, a possibility which must be realized considering that God is good and as St. Augustine stated, "it is in the nature of the good to give of itself." The self-effulgence of the Divine Principle is inseparable from the Divine Nature as is the effusion of the rays of sun from the sun. The realization of this possibility of self-negation which is a tendency, called by some philosophers the demiurgic tendency, toward nothingness, which, however, is never reached, must of necessity take place. It is this possibility actualized that constitutes all levels of cosmic reality, all planes of relative existence bringing about that separation from the Source which in turn brings about what we experience as evil.

The other contradictions cited by Bahm are all the result of his confusing a metaphysical statement with a logical one. Metaphysics is never illogical but it transcends the realm of mere logic. Such a concept as "relatively absolute" or Reality being "completely other and yet none other than the heart of the self, the Self of oneself" only appear contradictory. They are formulated in fact to express a truth that lies beyond the confines of contradiction as seen logically and make use of this apparent contradiction to arouse the mind in such a way that intellectual intuition takes hold and grasps the reality beyond the apparent logical contradiction. Also many of the statements which Bahm finds contradictory are based on misunderstanding because Bahm identifies the "Absolute" simply with a philosophical concept rather than the Reality which is Itself and nothing but Itself and yet contains the roots of all things including, especially, the teachings of religion and the manifestation of sacred forms. Bahm likewise confuses my use of the term "intelligence" with reason despite my extensive discussion in *Knowledge and the Sacred* and several other works concerning the difference between intelligence/intellect and reason.

Bahm has also posed a number of specific questions which I will answer according to his enumeration of them.

1. The first revolves most of all around the Absolute's immanence in the world while it is independent of all things. In emphasizing the metaphysics pertaining to the Absolute and the relation of all things to it, I have perhaps not emphasized enough, at least in *Knowledge and the Sacred* which is Bahm's main source of my ideas, that the world is necessary in order for the Divine Principle to be both absolute and infinite. In a theological language one could say that if the world were not to be, then God would not be God as creator. There is therefore in a certain sense a vertical complementarity between the Absolute and the world of manifestation, but the main point to remember is that the reality of both the Absolute and manifestation is ultimately one and there is ultimately no reality but the reality of the Principle Itself. As for the Absolute also being immanent, it goes without saying that metaphysically speaking the ultimately transcendent must also be the completely immanent; it must be the reality which lies in the heart of all things, the reality to which the path of inwardness leads. That is why in the Quran, God calls Himself not only the alpha (*al-Awwal*) and omega (*al-Ākhir*), but also the inward (*al-Bāṭin*) and the outward (*al-Ẓāhir*).

2. Bahm is right in saying that I do not assign any purpose to the Absolute in the ordinary sense of the term. That would be too anthropomorphic a manner to deal with the metaphysical reality of the Absolute. But I have spoken often of the purpose of the universe as the means whereby God comes to know Himself according to the famous sacred saying of the Prophet of Islam, "I was a hidden treasure. I wanted to be known. Therefore I created the world so that I would be known." The Absolute cannot have a purpose beyond Itself since there is no 'beyond Itself.' But by token of the fact that the "Hidden Treasure" wanted to be known, there is not only a purpose to the world which is to make God's knowledge of Himself through objectivization possible, but indirectly a purpose to Divine Activity to create and sustain the world so that it will fulfill its purpose which is Divine Self-Knowledge.

3. It is true that I have written more about metaphysics than ethics, but

I have also dealt with "good" and "evil" in several of my writings of which Bahm was probably unaware. My use of the term sacred certainly does not preclude interest in or usage of the term good. As I have already written before, from the point of view of the Principle which is the Supreme Good there is no evil and evil has no ontological source as does the good. It is separation from the Supreme Good that brings about evil which on its own level is real without having an independent source of reality. Light shining upon a tree has for its source the sun, but the shadow cast by the tree is simply the result of the absence of light. It has no source for its existence to be compared to the sun and the tree cannot be considered as the cause of the shadow in an ontological sense as the sun can be considered as the source of the light because without light the tree would cast no shadow. All creation implies separation and therefore imperfection and evil, but to the extent that anything exists, it also reflects Being and the presence of the Sacred. If we understand evil as separation, then all creation implies the presence of evil; although again there are grades of existence in most of which, including the terrestrial realm, the good is much greater than the evil, or at least such is the case when we turn to the natural world as God created it and not to the products of modern civilization based upon the forgetfulness of the true, the good, and the beautiful.

4. It is astonishing that Bahm should ask "how can any person accept salvation as non-existence" in light of numerous works of mystics of all religions concerning this issue. Non-existence in the sense used by me and others who share the traditional understanding of the *philosophia perennis* does not mean destruction of existence from below but integration from above as a result of which one never becomes less by dying to cite Rūmī again. What is usually called "union with God" always implies the non-existence of all that is limitative and imperfect in what we identify as our egos. The imperfect cannot have union with the Perfect. But this annihilation or what the Sufis call *fanā'* does not mean the destruction of our personality. It means the return to our reality *in divinis* above and beyond ordinary existence. It means to be able to swim in the ocean of Divinity; it is a "fusion without confusion," to use the well-known formula of Eckhart. That is the highest mode of salvation to which the Hindus refer as deliverance (*mokśa*) and which the Sufis call the attainment of the Paradise of the Divine Essence (*jannat al-Dhāt*).

Finally, in the section entitled "Religions," Bahm makes several false claims which need to be answered. He claims that for me religion is intellectual knowledge of the Sacred. I have never referred to the whole of religion as such and in fact have written on various aspects of different religions, especially Islam, ranging from ethics, laws, and social structures, to art and ritual. What I have said is that sapiental knowledge lies at the heart of religion without in any way denying the significance of the other organs which together constitute the body of any integral religion. Nor has my emphasis upon the "perfume of the Sacred" "blurred" my vision of other religions whose historical realities I have always respected while opposing historicism. Bahm should have cited some concrete examples for this claim. As for my emphasis upon "the transcendent unity of religions" whose full understanding is meant only for the few, this emphasis has not in any way implied that the full participation in the structure of a religion is therefore denied to the many. I have in fact written more than once that the problem of crossing religious frontiers and having to realize the truth at the heart of religions other than our own is a problem peculiar to this anomalous age in which we live. Traditionally men and women could become great saints and sages by following fully and having knowledge of only their own religion and this possibility exists for many people in certain parts of the globe and among certain human types even today.

I need to repeat again that "to realize our non-existence" means to realize that all belongs to God, that He is alone ultimately Reality and that our value and purpose is in being able to realize this basic truth. How strange that Archie Bahm should call this view "anti-religion," for is not the goal of religion to realize our relation to God, to obey Him, and finally on the highest level to realize God Himself in His Infinite and Absolute Reality?

S. H. N.

19

Judy D. Saltzman

THE CONCEPT OF SPIRITUAL KNOWLEDGE IN THE PHILOSOPHY OF SEYYED HOSSEIN NASR

A notable theme in the writings of Seyyed Hossein Nasr is that separation of knowledge from the sacred and from spiritual-metaphysical foundations in the Aristotelian-Cartesian-Kantian views is quite limited and destructive. The externalization and desacralization of knowledge has led to the idea that science in the sense of information, quantification, analysis, and subsequent technological implications is all that can be known. Questions of religion—the Deity, eternal life, and the nature of the soul—are all out of the perimeter of scientific knowledge, and are thus merely matters of faith. However, in the epitome of his work regarding spiritual knowledge, *Knowledge and the Sacred* (Gifford Lectures of 1981), Nasr argues not only that knowledge has spiritual-metaphysical foundations, but also that the goal of knowledge, as originally outlined in the Gnostic-Hermetic-Platonic traditions, is sapiental. In other words, knowledge is originally part of the Tree of Life, not part of the realm of the profane. He contends that real knowledge can result in the elevation of the soul to higher realms, the true meaning of alchemy. For Professor Nasr, the sublime meaning of spiritual knowledge is at the heart of the Islamic message: *ḥikmat-i ilāhī* (The Wisdom of God). The concept of spiritual knowledge is not only a powerful theme in the Quran, but it also holds the essence of the idea of initiation in the world's higher religions. Nasr compares *Qudrah, Ḥikmah*, and *Raḥmāh* to *Sat-Chit-Ānanda*[1] (Existence-Being, Wisdom Illumination, Beneficence-Bliss) and to the *scientia sacra* of the old alchemists and Christian mystics. According to him, the concept of spiritual knowledge, or knowledge of the sacred, transcends all religious divisions and is the essence of religion itself.

METHOD

In assessing the contribution Professor Nasr has made to philosophy itself through the concept of spiritual knowledge or knowledge of the sacred, one must first evaluate his method. His method is highly eclectic. It draws on several different sources. Nasr is academically trained in mathematics, physics, and the history of science, as well as methods of philosophy and comparative religion, but his inspiration comes from the Sufi practice of Illumination through intellectual intuition. Although he is critical of the use of rational and empirical methods in an isolated sense in philosophy, he makes wide use of logical, deductive, and empirical methods in his philosophical investigations. However, it is a key to understanding Nasr's thought in *Knowledge and the Sacred* and other works that the rational mind or the thinking being has a foundation for its existence—the organization of the Logos itself. Nasr is highly Pythagorean and Platonic in conception and method, in that he understands numbers and the geometry of the world not to be discovered by any accident of the senses, but to be the abstract basis of concrete reality.[2] However, this esteem for mathematics does not constitute an abandonment of the empirical. The use of the senses and their extension through telescopes, microscopes, radar, and so on, are all contributions to knowledge. Nasr points out that the Latin, *Videre* (to see), goes back to the Sanskrit root *Vid* (seeing or knowing). Speech itself is a direct reflection of the Logos (*Vāc* in the Hindu tradition). In Hinduism as in Islam there is the idea of the mantra: the very invocation of the Divine Name or the Sacred Sound moves humans toward higher levels of consciousness and to Divine Knowledge. That to which Nasr strongly objects is the analytic faculty of the mind turning against the idea of the sacred. When it does this, it ignorantly attacks its own foundation. For Nasr, whose inspiration is broadly Islamic and especially Sufi in spite of his scientific training, the thinker can affirm, "I think, therefore I am," but also "because I am" (not disconnected from the Ground of Being), "I think," and also know and act. Thinking, reasoning, and knowing all come from the faculty of the Logos.[3] This faculty cannot be reduced simply to the complexity of the organism or to the matter or electrical energy of the brain, but it is that which makes us thinkers in spite of our physical bodies and animal propensities. In fact, throughout *Knowledge and the Sacred*, there is an a priori assumption that we, as thinking beings and acting knowers, are in no way separated from our source, the Divine Ground or *al-Ḥaqq*.

How does Professor Nasr prove these assertions about the Divine Ground of Knowledge? The book *Knowledge and the Sacred* is presented not so much as a formal, logical, or scientific proof of the idea of a Divine Ground to knowledge and thought, but as a compendium of overwhelming evidence for the idea that knowledge has a metaphysical and even divine origin and purpose. This is evident in the perennial philosophy and history of philosophy from the *Corpus Hermeticum* to Frithjof Schuon. A central idea in the perennial philosophy as found, for example, in the Bhagavad-Gita is that the Self (Knower) is not separate from the Known. Another example is the famous passage from the Quran: "Say, He is Allah, the One!"[4] The Sufi knower in the act of knowing dissolves all distinctions in the divine. In looking inward at this purified Self, he or she realizes Unity with the Divine (*al-tawḥīd*). The same idea is cited in the Upaniṣads in a different way, where knowledge of the Self, as Brāhman, destroys the root of ignorance, when the Supreme Lord looks within as well as without.

Other examples in *Knowledge and the Sacred* are that in the ancient pagan and Christian Gnostic traditions, we are all *pneumatikoi*, or possessors of spiritual knowledge. In Christian Gnosticism and other writings, all wisdom is related to the Christos-Logos within ourselves. *Ḥokmah* (Wisdom) is strongly emphasized in Kabbalistic Judaism. The ascent up the Sephirotal Tree of Life is done through acts of asceticism and purification in which the knower reaches higher and higher states of illumination until he is totally absorbed in the quest for the Divine. Just as it was "In the beginning . . ." or "In Wisdom" that God created the heaven and the earth, the whole of human being, according to the Kabbala, is based on a claim to sacred knowledge. Even in the more exoteric Christian tradition, Augustine affirmed that "to think the truth . . . man needs the illumination which proceeds from God."[5] Nasr comments that St. Thomas Aquinas's philosophy would not have developed if the Christian tradition had not been permeated by Gnosis. The idea of *Credo ut Intelligam* makes faith dependent upon knowledge, or at least rational discourse can support faith. In the more heterodox Christian tradition, John the Scot (Scotus Erigena) said that all knowledge has a sacred function, as did Meister Eckhart, who affirmed that the root of the intellect was grounded in Divinity. It is perhaps Meister Eckhart in the Christian tradition who comes closest to the Sufi ideal when Nasr says of him that "For Eckhart, the eye with which man sees God is the eye with which God sees man."[6] This is the focus of the notion of *scientia sacra*, the heart of knowledge in the West. This tradition was carried on by Nicholas of Cusa, Jakob Böhme, Paracelsus, the Cambridge Platonists, Angelus Silesius, and others.

All of the thinkers to whom Nasr refers use not merely scientific or philosophical methods of knowledge in the dry empirical or analytic sense, but they use a method which he calls "sapiental." This word comes from the Latin *sapere* (to taste). Sapiental knowledge implies an intimate connection between the knower, act of knowing, and the known. In the sapiental act of knowing, the knowledge has the power to transform the known, rather in the way the taste of good food can revive and stimulate the hungry person. In this sense, all alchemical knowledge is sapiental. The alchemists knew that, just as certain chemicals, when mixed, transform into higher elements, the souls of fallen, ignorant humans can be moved to a state of sanctity.

As was said, there are some a priori assumptions which are supported by examining the history of science, philosophy, and religion from the viewpoint of the perennial philosophy. It may be a priori that we are on a quest for Divine Truth. There is no way to prove this after the fact. However, the idea that the history of ancient philosophy, religion, and natural philosophy (early science) is permeated by the notion is supported by data. Nasr thinks that a number of ancient astronomers, geographers, physiologists, and philosophers discovered the truth about the soul and human existence. They regarded their quest as sacred because they understood their universe to be alive and holy. However, Nasr writes that the gradual secularization of the cosmos in the disciplines of cosmology and astronomy corresponded to the secularization of reason, which corresponded to the secularization of language. For example, ancient astronomers and natural philosophers such as Anaxagoras, al-Fārābī, al-Kindī, Alhazen (Ibn al-Haytham), and al-Bīrūnī conceived of the cosmos in various ways as emanations of the Divine. Any idea of a coldly conceived "Big Bang" hypothesis was unthinkable. Even the visible "fixed stars" and planets were emanations of the actions of the Divine Logos.

However, in Nasr's opinion, modern astronomy, because it is cut off from philosophy and astrology, no longer has the language to express a relation to the Divine. Al-Bīrūnī (362–442 or 443 A.H. /973–1051 or 1052 C.E.), for example, thought of a human being as *khalīfat Allāh* (God's Viceroy), created for a noble purpose. Even a technical discussion, in al-Bīrūnī's view, goes to affirm some attribute of the Creator or His creation, such as *al-Amīn*, the Trustworthy. For example, the signs of the Zodiac correspond to the organs of the body and are the key to diseases. The planets also correspond to different organs: Jupiter, eyes; Mercury, ear; Venus, breast; Saturn, excretion; Sun, mouth; Moon, navel. Understanding these correspondences can give the physician healing power.[7] Moreover, the consistency and dependability of the cosmos and the Divine Nature behind it is reflected in the motion of the planets themselves. Just as the planets circling the sun reflect the intention of the creator, the devotees circling the *Ka'bah* reenact the cosmic order of their intentions. All multiplicity turns round and round and returns again to unity. It is part of Nasr's method to remind us of these correspondences.

Also in *Islamic Cosmological Doctrines* Nasr explains that al-Bīrūnī believed that the people of earlier times were closer to man's celestial origin.

In our era, we have let time rather than eternity rule us. It is clear that Nasr, while not necessarily subscribing to the rule of ancient science of which he is an historian, is convinced that al-Bīrūnī and other ancients were able to keep knowledge and the sacred together. The ancients can certainly remind the moderns that knowledge has a greater purpose than simply its acquisition.

Nasr's method may be simply characterized as combining the best Western techniques of rational philosophy and scientific method and the Sufi method of intuitive insight or Illumination (related to the *Ḥakīm muta'allih*). His deep intellectual intuition into Sufi spirituality and the history of science and scientific method has led him to be one of the primary discussants of the correspondence between modern physics and the insights of Oriental doctrines. The interdependence of all objects in the universe has been affirmed by a number of distinguished physicists: David Bohm, Erwin Schrödinger, and C. F. von Weizäcker. This idea is supportive of the basic doctrine of Islam: *Al-Tawḥīd* (Unity). In this sense, even the knowledge of the minutest particle in the universe, perhaps a quark, is in some way knowledge of Absolute Reality. In some ways Nasr's viewpoint parallels that of Henri Bergson in *Introduction to Metaphysics*, in which Bergson states that to know something intuitively is to know it more absolutely than by any scientific or rational method.[8] According to Nasr, physics is slowly becoming metaphysics in such a way that it is not reducible to any mere mental activity, as positivists would suggest. Nasr's method involves understanding man's sacred trust with God: the cosmos is a dark mirror which the human mind illumines. Methods such as *jñāna yoga* and *al-khayāl* (Creative Imagination as conceived by Ibn 'Arabī) lead us up the steep path of knowledge through the hierarchy of Being to a higher order. For Nasr the supreme method of philosophizing would lead one to deliverance from this world of illusion. As opposed to ordinary scientific knowledge or philosophizing, *ḥikmah muta'āliyah* (Illumination or Gnosis) is knowledge of the Infinite. In the process of attaining it, an actual transformation occurs in *fanā'* (annihilation of the ego). The transcending of profane science and philosophy and of the world itself is the ultimate culmination of method.

The Idea of Knowledge

After examining Nasr's eclectic method, it becomes quite clear what he considers knowledge to be. Nevertheless, knowledge is a very difficult conception to isolate. However, it is absolutely easy to understand that, for Nasr, there is sacred and profane knowledge. Profane knowledge is all too evident in the present age. It is not that anything in the world which needs to be understood is particularly profane. Quite the contrary. Yet the methods by which the world is studied and the attitude in which it is studied can be quite profane, especially in the hands of the profane. It is not that the method itself, be it deductive, inductive, linguistic analysis, empirical, or phenomenological, is profane or sacred. Nevertheless, when knowledge is gathered purely for selfish motives and worldly results, by any method, it is profane. For example, the knowledge which led to the splitting of the atom clearly has its profane uses, but on its sacred side it holds the very key to the nature of atomic matter and energy. Another example is that the knowledge which led to the discovery by Francis Crick, James D. Watson, and Rosalind Franklin of the double helix as the key to the genetic code seemed alive with spiritual implications.[9] According to Watson, the methods of its discovery involved dreams, intuition, and even rivalry. However, the uses of the discovery have been undeniably profane: animal cloning and genetic engineering. The fact that the double helical structure resembles the Caduceus of Mercury makes it heavy with sacred implications, but these are yet to be discovered.

What is clear to Nasr is that the question for all knowledge, whether scientific, philosophical, or otherwise, was originally motivated by the desire to understand the Creation as a reflection of the Divine and thereby as a Divine Emanation. However, science, which began as natural philosophy, lost its primary motives and intentions as people struggled to live and became more materialistic. Nasr illustrates this point by invoking the powerful images of profane and sacred man. Pontifex is the bridge between heaven and earth—the sacred man—and Prometheus, the thief of fire from the home of the gods, is profane man. Nasr uses the image of Prometheus in a different way from Aeschylus in *Prometheus Bound* and Shelley in *Prometheus Unbound*. In these stories he is a hero, a demi-god or Titan who is willing to risk eternal torture to bring light to ignorant, suffering humanity, even in defiance of Divine Authority. However, in Nasr's analysis, the symbolism takes on a different connotation. Prometheus is viewed as a robber of heavenly fire, a rebel against the Divine, who has forgotten his real mission. He may still secretly long for the Eternal, but he is filled with profane science and excessive materialism.[10]

On the other hand, Pontifical man has never forgotten that he is the viceroy of God (*khalīfat Allāh*). The Pontifical person lives in a world which he or she knows has an origin and a center. Pontifical people are not cut off from their roots. In contrast, the Promethean man or woman is more like Faust, one of the devil's party. Like Oswald Spengler's Faustian Man, they help accentuate the dominance of profane science.[11] Unfortunately, Promethean thinking, whose major aim is to further the ambition of the thinker/actor, has become dominant. According to Nasr, one of its main supporters is evolutionary thought and its implications. In his view, two of the main exploiters of evolutionary science in the name of the sacred are Śri Aurobindo Ghose and Pierre Teilhard de Chardin. These two figures are the main focus of Nasr's attacks on evolutionary theory in *Knowledge and the Sacred*. He explains how the theory of evolution and its use by modernists and liberal theologians has been a major force in the desacralization of knowledge.[12]

In the Darwinian theory of evolution, humans have descended from lower forms. Long prior to this descent, life had evolved out of inert matter. The human being finally became self-conscious when he reached a high enough degree of "complexification." Nasr finds both these assertions to be quite illogical and impossible. One problem is, how can matter evolve into a life form if the life energy is not originally there? It is a mathematical necessity that one cannot take out more information than one has put into a system. In the theory of evolution, the sudden appearance of new organisms seems to be unexplainable. Furthermore, the sophisticated reasoning ability and spiritual longings of humans do not coincide with having evolved from an ape or similar being. It is Nasr's view that, although Teilhard may try to sacralize evolutionary theory, he makes the tragic mistake of inverting the traditional doctrine of emanation. In sacred scriptures higher forms of life do not ascend from lower ones. Human souls descend from celestial archetypes or forms. Animals are later lower forms made from cast-off substance and so related physically to humanity. This line of thinking is true of the Bible, the Quran, the Popul Vuh, and other scriptures. Although Teilhard does think that humans are becoming ever more spiritual by evolving from the biosphere and by moving through the noösphere to Point Omega, they have essentially ascended through matter. Matter becomes ever more spiritual as time goes on. Although God may be present, having involuted the spirit which lights up the human mind when the brain becomes complex enough, Teilhard's faith and focus is in the world of matter. Nasr writes:

> Teilhard tries to explain the transition of inert matter to life as the "coiling up of the molecule upon itself," forgetting the penetration of a new cosmic principle into the domain of inert matter as the cause for the sudden appearance of life on earth. This "coiling up," moreover, is nothing but a parody of spiritual concentration as his description of the transition of life to consciousness as "the threshold of reflection" is a parody of the divine creative act itself. He speaks about this process reaching, through evolution, the state of totality as if totality could have ever not been or could have ever lacked something which it gained later without ceasing to be totality! When one reads Teilhard carefully, one realizes that his faith lies in matter and in this world above all else without an awareness of how matter itself is generated by higher levels of existence.[13]

In general Nasr accuses Teilhard of trying to replace the eternal by the temporal, and of effectively worshipping the world of matter instead of what is behind it.

At a superficial glance, it would appear that some Sufi teachings even encourage Darwinian evolution. For example, the famous passage from Rūmī:

> I died as a mineral and became a plant;
> I died as a plant and rose to an animal;
> I died as an animal and I was a man.
> Why should I fear? When was I less by dying?
> Yet once more I shall die as a man to soar
> With angels blest. But even from an angel
> I must pass on: all except God must perish.
> When I have sacrificed my angel soul,
> I shall become what no mind ever conceived.[14]

But Nasr makes it clear that Rūmī and other Sufis are not speaking simply of the ascent of man through physical forms, but of the eternal presence of the Divine Ego stretching from the lowest to the highest forms. The entire hierarchy of beings is permeated by the Divine. Of Rūmī and other sources which deal with dialectic and hierarchy, such as Marx and Hegel, he writes:

> It is such sources, whether Islamic or otherwise, that alone can explain the meaning of becoming, the scales of cosmic beings including living forms, the vertical hierarchy stretching from the lowest material form through man to the Divine Presence, and even the mutilation and inversion of these teachings in modern times. And for that very reason it is through the subversion of such traditional teachings that tradition itself is betrayed by forces which parade under a religious guise while helping to accomplish the final short-lived victory of the temporal over the Eternal, of the profane over the sacred.[15]

In other words, although he may have been in all of these forms on the physical plane, the Divine Archetypal Man (Adam Kadmon) has always been and will be. Nasr claims that Teilhard fails to find the "missing link" because there is not any. It will remain a controversial part of Nasr's work that he thinks that Teilhard with his Point Omega and Aurobindo with his Supermind have done more to pervert theology and spiritual studies than to sacralize science. It could be said that at least Teilhard and Aurobindo made an attempt to understand the sacred working in the world.

The Spiritual or the Sacred

How does the spiritual or the sacred work with knowledge, or what kind of knowledge is spiritual? To answer these questions, it must first be understood how knowledge has become separated from the sacred. That knowledge as *scientia* has lost its spiritual meaning and goal is a tragic theme of civilization. In *Knowledge and the Sacred* Nasr argues that:

> Knowledge has become nearly completely externalized and desacralized, especially among those segments of the human race which have become transformed by the process of modernization, and that bliss which is the fruit of the union with the One and an aspect of the perfume of the sacred has become well-nigh unattainable and beyond the grasp of the vast majority of those who walk upon the earth. But the root and essence of knowledge continues to be inseparable from the sacred for the very substance of knowledge is the knowledge of that reality which is the Supreme Substance, the Sacred as such, compared to which all levels of existence and all forms of the manifold are but accidents. Intelligence, which is the instrument of knowledge within man, is endowed with the possibility of knowing the Absolute. It is like a ray which emanates from and returns to the Absolute and its miraculous functioning is itself the best proof of that Reality which is at once absolute and infinite.[16]

This sad situation has resulted in the dehumanization of knowledge, and the separation of the disciplines of knowledge. The sciences are compartmentalized from each other, and the humanities and sciences hardly have a dialogue and no longer work together. Worst of all, modern knowledge has lost the very meaning of being human and the goal of life itself:

> To be human is to know and also to transcend oneself. To know means therefore ultimately to know the Supreme Substance which is at once the source of all that comprises the objective world and the Supreme Self which shines at the center of human consciousness and is related to intelligence as the sun is related to its rays. Despite the partial loss and eclipse of this properly speaking intellectual faculty and its replacement by reason, the roots of knowledge remain sunk in the ground of the Sacred and sacred knowledge continues to be at the heart of the concern of man for the sacred. It is not possible in fact to rediscover the sacred without discovering once again the sacred quality of principial knowledge.[17]

It could be said that, since Kant, the knowledge of which Nasr speaks has been consigned to the realm of the transcendent and therefore impossible. One might say that spiritual knowledge is simply a matter of faith or even just belief. However, knowledge can never be consigned to these realms. In Nasr's view, the concept of knowledge can be considerably broadened if we include the possibilities of human experience as expressed in Sufism, and also the Dialectic and mathematical ciphers of Plato. According to Nasr, the sacred is not separated from knowledge, but it is separated from the way a profane mind understands the world and experience. This idea goes to the very basis of the meaning of sacred, or *sacre* (to set apart or consecrate). The word comes from the Latin as "sacrifice," a combination of *sacre* and *facere* (to make sacred). To have knowledge of the Sacred is thus to have some sublime experience which goes beyond mundane life. To have an understanding of the content of this experience is to have knowledge of the Sacred. This viewpoint may be characterized as philosophical mysticism. This way of thinking is certainly fundamental to Plato. For example, one might read about or memorize some of the number theory at the basis of Pythagorean and Platonic metaphysics—that is, the idea that in *The Republic* the tyrant is 729 times less happy than the philosopher king. Or one might study the octaval intervals in Er's five-day journey to heaven.[18] However, knowing the significance of these numbers in their full sacred meaning would involve understanding the state of consciousness in the descent from philosopher king to tyrant, and from living on this plane to an after-death state. Plato quite often asks us to defy the empirical and the sensuous in favor of mathematical truths. The reason for this is that knowing these mathematical ideas takes us to a more stable realm: the structure of reality beyond the chaos of the world.

Because Nasr is intellectually influenced both by Hermetic-Pythagorean-Platonic tradition and by the Muslim Sufis, he understands what it is to move dialectically from the Cave of profane experience to the Noesis of sacred learning. In order to have this experience the Sufi knows that one must purify one's body and mind through ritual and austerity. One must make oneself pure for such an experience. As the mystic Maḥmūd Shabistarī writes:

> Go sweep out the chamber of your heart.
> Make it ready to be the dwelling place of
> the Beloved.
> When you depart out, He will enter it.
> In you, devoid of yourself, He will display
> His beauties.[19]

It is the case with the Sufis, as with Plato, that when one has spiritual knowledge one has been purified. Not only does one know, but in the act of knowing the knower has been transformed. The knower, in effect, becomes the known. However, the process is not easy and can be even incendiary. As Rūmī says, "Enough of phrases, conceit and metaphors, I want burning, burning, burning."[20] One could compare this total devotion to the *Śiva* worshiper when she says, "O Kali, make a burning ground of my heart."[21]

Henry Corbin's writing about Muḥyī al-Dīn ibn 'Arabī's encounter with a being of knowledge while performing the sacred ritual at the Ka'bah is illustrative of this point:

> Ibn 'Arabī is engaged in circumambulating the *Ka'bah*. Before the Black Stone, he encounters the mysterious being whom he recognizes and designates

> as "the Evanescent youth, the Silent Speaker, him who is neither living nor dead, the composite-simple, the enveloped enveloping," all terms oppositorum. At this moment the visionary is assailed by a doubt: "Might this processional be nothing other than the ritual Prayer of a living man around a corpse (the *Ka'bah*)?" The mystic youth replies: "Behold the secret of the Temple before it escapes." And the visionary suddenly sees the stone temple turn into a living being. He becomes aware of his companion's spiritual rank; he lowers his right hand; he wishes to become his disciple, to learn all his secrets; he will teach nothing else. But the Companion speaks only in symbols. His eloquence is only in enigmas. And at a mysterious sign of recognition the visionary is overwhelmed by such a power of love that he loses consciousness. When he comes to himself, his Companion reveals to him: "I am knowledge, I am he who knows and I am what is known."[22]

To circumambulate the *Ka'bah* in the state of consciousness of the Sufi Gnostic Ibn 'Arabī is not just an act of faith, but one of supreme Gnosis. In this act and state the divisions between knower and known and between the spiritual and the scientific break down. Just as it is a scientific fact that Mecca is the geographic center of the world's land masses,[23] one may realize that one's intellectual heart is the center of spiritual knowledge. Ibn 'Arabī's experience with his divine Alter Ego which is verily himself is a perfect example of what Nasr is trying to convey. Ibn 'Arabī is the most scientific of all devotees. However, the object of experimentation in the quest for spiritual knowledge will be oneself. The knower in the act of knowing becomes the known. To be a *Pneumatikos*, a knower in the Gnostic sense, is not only to be possessed of sacred knowledge, but also to be that knowledge itself. In other words, when dry *scientia* is transformed to *sapientia*, it becomes *scientia sacre* or spiritual knowledge. In the words of Sufism, in the illumined soul, God contemplates Himself through those whom He has enlightened. These ideas also have their parallels in Meister Eckhart and in Jakob Böhme. For Eckhart, the root of intellect is grounded in divinity. To Böhme, *innere Erleuchtungen* is Divine Sophia herself.

The work of Seyyed Hossein Nasr is founded on traditions such as these. For him, the primordial knowledge or the Sacred is hidden in the depths of the human heart. For this reason, to remain with a Cartesian metaphysical bifurcation of the world or a Kantian epistemological split between the phenomenal and noumenal is to cut off the soul from Being. Such a view deprives intellect of its main focus and purpose. It can be simply said that if religion is only faith, if knowledge is only empirical or analytic, and if the world is purely mechanical, the human mind will be limited in its description of reality, which cannot be described by faith, by analysis, or in empirical or mechanical terms alone. The seventeenth-century Cambridge Platonists knew this when they attempted to annihilate the epistemological dualism of Descartes. For example, John Smith wrote of "spiritual sensation" to mean a concrete knowledge of the sacred.[24] The Cambridge Platonists were aware, as were Plotinus and the Neo-Platonists, that Plato was more like a Prophet, a *Ṛṣis* or a Seer than simply a philosopher. This was because Plato acted in the true, original spirit of philosophy: the love of wisdom, in which wisdom (*Sophia*) and love (*Eros*) combined in a dialectic to find the Sacred. Nasr praises the understanding of the sacred character of knowledge by many of the Greek philosophers:

> The rediscovery of the sacred character of knowledge today would lead, almost before anything else, to a rediscovery of Greek wisdom, of Plato, Plotinus, and other Graeco-Alexandrian sages and writings such as Hermeticism, not as simply human philosophy but as sacred doctrines of divine inspiration to be compared much more with the Hindu *darśanas* than with philosophical schools as they are currently understood. The belief of Muslim philosophers that the Greek philosophers had learned their doctrines from the prophets, especially Solomon, and that "philosophy derives from the niche of prophecy," if not verifiable historically, nevertheless contains a profound truth, namely the relation of this wisdom to the sacred and its origin in revelation, even if this revelation cannot be confined in the strictly Abrahamic sense to a particular figure or prophet.[25]

Unfortunately, the idea of sacred knowledge was eclipsed in religion as well as in science and philosophy. In Christianity faith and rational theology became separated. In the New Testament, the translation of the Greek *pistis* in St. Paul's Letters as "faith" instead of "knowledge" had dire consequences for the Gnostic viewpoint in the history of Christianity. The particular view of Paul regarding faith was solidified in St. Augustine. In Augustine's works, he makes it clear that it is impossible to achieve salvation without faith and Grace. Philosophical discourse may be useful, but it had little to do with salvation. The history of the Reformation may have been much different if Luther had been reading a Pauline text which emphasized that the "just shall be saved by knowledge" instead of by faith.[26]

In the history of Christian Europe, history, science, cosmology, and even philosophy itself were desacralized. However, knowledge of the sacred or spiritual knowledge was never completely dead. There was always an "alternative reality," as Robert Ellwood confirms.[27] For example, during the Middle Ages in twelfth-century France, the idea of the soul possessing spiritual knowledge independent of any authority resurfaced with the Albigensians and the Cathars. These movements were brutally suppressed by the Catholic Church. Nevertheless, the idea of the soul's potential re-emerged to stay with the Platonic Academy of Florence, headed by Ficino and helped by Pico della Mirandola. Pythagoras, Plato, Ficino, and Pico are all forerunners of Nasr's view of knowledge. They were Unitarian (*muwaḥḥidīn*), and in that sense belonged to the Islamic universe. They all knew that spiritual knowledge was a reality, and not separated from the developing scientific quest in its broadest sense and liberal nature.

SCIENCE AND THE SACRED

The idea that the soul is infinitely perfectible and capable of continually growing in wisdom has profound implications for science as well as for religion. Although Nasr's sense of the sacred is firmly grounded in the rational and empirical, he speaks critically of the attempt of Rudolf Otto to relate the sacred to the irrational in his work *Das Heilige* and others.[28] Nasr concludes that although the sacred may not be unrelated to what humans call "irrational," the traditional view of the sacred is more firmly grounded in the disciplines of scientific, philosophical, and religious thought. In other words, one must comprehend these disciplines and go through the rational to go beyond it. This is true of both scientific and religious thought.

However, Nasr wants to go beyond a respect for science to the idea that there always was and will be a theme of the sacred in science itself. In Islam, for example, there never was a separation from the sacred. Under Islam, science never operated in opposition to an unsympathetic clergy as in the Middle Ages and Renaissance in Europe. Certain rulers, such as Haran al-Rashid, positively preserved and encouraged science.[29] Nasr tells us that it is fundamental to Islam that the devotee should seek knowledge. In fact, the human being who walks upright has a positive need for knowledge, unlike any of the animals. It is clear by the writings of al-Bīrūnī and others that man is the microcosm of the macrocosm. The human being reflects the cosmos in his very being. This interesting statement could be substantiated in part by the fact that our bodies are made mostly of hydrogen, carbon, oxygen, and nitrogen—the same stuff as most of the matter of the universe. However, this is to speak only on the physical level, whereas the spiritual is much more important.

The books *Science and Civilization in Islam* and *Islamic Science* show that Nasr thinks that science is much more than a fact-finding venture. The great scientists of the past he studies such as al-Bīrūnī, astronomer and geographer, al-Kindī, astronomer and philosopher, Ibn Rushd (Averroes) and Ibn Sīnā (Avicenna), physicians and philosophers, and al-Rāzī, alchemist turned chemist, all believed in the interaction between the sciences and in the spiritual nature of what they were doing. They all seemed to be aware that knowledge is not simply ratiocinative thinking or empirical observation alone. They thought that science comes from that metaphysical intuition which arises from the Source of knowledge. A good example of this is the connection between geology, anthropology, and social science in al-Bīrūnī's writings. Al-Bīrūnī considers the idea that time consists in cycles and that things will come to an end along with the changes in the condition of the world through time. Nasr shows how a metaphysical idea can be observed in the very nature of geology itself. In *An Introduction to Islamic Cosmological Doctrines*, Nasr quotes al-Bīrūnī's writing about the fact that mountains and other geologic wonders, although they may appear eternal, have not been always the same.[30] He also quotes al-Bīrūnī's idea that there is geologic evidence that India was once "a sea which by degrees has been filled up by the alluvium of the streams."[31] Al-Bīrūnī writes that "in a similar way, sea has turned into land and land into sea," and that "the steppe of Arabia was at one time a sea, and then was upturned so that the traces are still visible when wells or ponds are dug."[32] Regarding the nature and size of people, al-Bīrūnī carries on the metaphysical idea that things go in cycles, do not stay the same, and may be other than they appear to be. In the chronology of ancient nations he writes:

> As regards the (superhuman) size of bodies (of former generations), we say, if it be not necessary to believe it for this reason, that we cannot observe it in our time, and that there is an enormous interval between us and that time, of which such things are related, it is therefore by no means impossible.[33]

Nasr explains that other scientists wrote curiously about animals and humans:

> Buzurg ibn Shabriyār in his *Book of the Marvels of India* considers the "ape-man" (called in Arabic *nasnās*), and also certain forms of monkeys, to be the result of the union of man with the hyena and other wild beasts. Al-Damīrī follows a general belief among the Muslims that the rhinoceros, whose description was first given by al-Bīrūnī in his *India*, is a cross between a horse and an elephant.[34]

These statements regarding the larger-than-life size of ancient humans, and the possibility that apes and certain monkeys could be the result of the mating between humans and animals, remind one of certain ancient occult doctrines which have been written up in modern form.[35] Furthermore, Nasr's comment on al-Bīrūnī's notion of the rise and fall of continents and the idea of cyclical time confirms al-Bīrūnī's idea, like that of many ancient and medieval writers, that people of earlier cycles were closer to man's celestial origin.[36]

Other examples Nasr uses to illustrate the metaphysical foundations of scientific knowledge are Ibn Sīnā's taking the four causes of Aristotle and applying them to medicine.[37] Another case is al-Rāzī, trained as an alchemist, affirming its metaphysical content but denying its symbolic nature and turning it into chemistry.[38] These natural philosophers drew metaphysical implications from all that they studied. Al-Kindī saw in the design of the celestial globe a justification for God's existence, although he derived his arguments from Aristotle.[39] However, the most striking aspect of Nasr's analysis of ancient and Islamic science is that these scientists are aware that whether they study the human body, the earth, the weather, or the heavens, without the Spirit and Source behind these, they have no life and are of little interest. Also the idea that there is a higher purpose behind the study permeates the work of these scientists. Nasr thinks that science lost the sacred aspect when scientists abandoned the Hermetic dictum, "To awaken fallen man from the dream in which he lives."[40] In perfect condition, the soul may be like gold. The real alchemist, however, does not merely try to turn base metal into gold, or to unite mercury and sulfur (male and female elements), but to unite the human soul, as manifested in a physical body, to her real Divine Nature.

Moreover, if writing specifically of Islamic Science, Nasr makes it clear that it has a primordial, simple Unity. This Unity, symbolized by the Arabic word *al-tawḥīd*, describes not only the relation among the sciences, but among the different disciplines, the quest for knowledge itself, and the whole universe. Mathematics is the discipline common to all the sciences. To these scientists and to the Platonists, it was a kind of Jacob's ladder which led to the primordial Source. Finally, Nasr affirms that Islamic science has never lost its Gnostic character. The *Quranic* revelation is, in fact, the inspiration behind all science. In the quest for knowledge, man, as a multiplicity, returns to Unity. *Al-Tawḥīd*, then, is both a goal and a motivation. Nasr shows us how splendidly science flourished under Islam. This is not surprising since it is a *ḥadīth* of the Prophet that "The quest for knowledge is obligatory for every Muslim."[41]

Religion and the Sacred

Just as science is seen as a religious quest in Nasr's philosophy, religion is seen as a scientific quest in that it seeks knowledge of the Divine. However, the difference between religion and ordinary science is that in seeking the Divine, it searches for what forever recedes. However, it is in this search that the human soul is fulfilled. This is the aim and meaning of religion: to know the reason for existence through the unfolding of the Divine Purpose. A good illustration of this idea is in *Islamic Science*. Nasr quotes the Persian Sufi poet 'Abd al-Raḥmān Jāmī (9th/15th century), who seemed to understand that to gain knowledge of the atom might lead us to lose the reason for gaining the knowledge. One could lose sight of the spiritual empyrean:

I lost my intellect, soul, religion and heart,
In order to know an atom in perfection.
But no one can know the essence of the atom completely.
How often must I repeat that no one shall know it:
Then farewell![42]

In his other writings Nasr makes it clear that the purely religious quest, although it may be undertaken by the scientist, goes beyond science to pure experience. In *Three Muslim Sages* Nasr writes of Suhrawardī (b. 549 A.H./1153 C.E.). He was the founder of the *Ishrāqī* or Illuminationist tradition. According to Suhrawardī, the whole universe is frozen light, an insight not so unscientific if one remembers $E=mc^2$. Suhrawardī, a Sufi master who was executed at the early age of 38, was known as *Shaykh al-ishrāq*, Master of Illumination. He combined elements of Pythagoras, Plato, and the Hermetic and Zoroastrian traditions in his teachings. His basic method was illumination, which consists in combining discursive reasoning and intellectual intuition to discover *al-Ḥaqq* (The Truth). In other words, what begins in logic and experiment may end in spiritual union and ecstasy. Illumination then is explained as a state which is realized through union of the methods of ratiocination and intuition. The ultimate Sufi quest for knowledge may end in Illumination, but it is grounded in the realm of intellectual discourse. In *Ḥikmat al-Ishrāq* (*Theosophy of the Orient of Light*), Suhrawardī says that our journey is to the Orient, a world of pure light that has lost its materialistic rigidity.[43] What we abandon for this state is the Occident, a world of material, earthly existence and cares. The astronomical heavens are in between. The world, as we know it, consists of degrees of light and darkness. The condition of the soul after death depends on how much it has been able to move toward the light, and thereby purify itself.

The most important implication for religion is that Suhrawardī, like other Sufi masters, taught that there was a transcendent Unity underlying different revelations of the truth. Although Muḥammad received the greatest light and the last revelation of Islam, all the different faiths—that is, Judaism, Zoroastrianism, Hinduism, Christianity, and others—received the Divine Light through some Prophet or Prophets.[44]

Muḥyī al-Dīn ibn ʻArabī, the Andalusian *Shaykh*, taught virtually the same doctrine. For Ibn ʻArabī, not only do the different religions reflect the One Divine Reality, but the whole cosmos itself. For him, God transcends, but emanates the universe. *Barakah* (Blessing) flows through the arteries of the world which is mysteriously plunged in God. His philosophy is reminiscent of the qualified non-dualist Hindu philosopher Rāmānuja. However, man is not just a manifestation of Allāh or Brāhman, but he is

Insān who began as *al-Insān al-kabīr* (the Macrocosm or Adam Kadmon). He will end as *al-Insān al-kāmil* (The Universal Man or Perfected Being). On this journey man is a *khalīfah*, or Viceroy of the Divine. All humans are involved in the attempt to realize *al-Ḥaqq* (The Real or the Truth). However, in order to perceive the Real, one must realize that Allāh manifests in everything. The way of coming to this insight is through *al-khayāl* (Creative Imagination). This is the faculty in the human being which allows the person to understand the relationship between the Real as Perceiver and the Real as object of Perception. In Ibn 'Arabī's great work *The Bezels of Wisdom*, the cosmos is like a dark mirror without *insān* (man), but as *khalīfah*, "man is to the Real as the pupil is to the eye through which the act of seeing takes place."[45] In other words, God perceives the world through man. This means He acts through all humans, but most powerfully through a Saint or *Walī*. The experience of *al-Walī* (the friend) is that all religions are particular, yet partial manifestations of the universal truth of Islam. The *walī* eventually becomes totally absorbed in *al-Nūr* (the Light) and realizes *waḥdat al-wujūd* (the Oneness of Being).

Nasr tells us that, along with Jalāl al-Dīn Rūmī and Suhrawardī, Ibn 'Arabī laid the foundation for an Islamic rapprochement with other religions. For Ibn 'Arabī, *al-tawḥīd* is the Unity which links all religions, as well as being the One Source behind the universe. He quotes the famous passage on this subject which concludes that the only idols to be burned are external forms of religion:

> My heart has become capable of every form: It is a pasture for
> gazelles and a convent for Christian monks,
> And a temple for idols and the pilgrim's *Ka'ba* and the tables
> of the Torah, and the book of the Quran.
> I follow the religion of Love: whatever way Love's camels take,
> that is my religion and my faith.[46]

Seyyed Hossein Nasr himself is a teacher much in the tradition of Ibn 'Arabī and Suhrawardī. He is obviously a lover of the ancients and the spirit of seeking Divine Wisdom. However, he has made a distinguished and unique contribution as a teacher who has offered a powerful modern application of the ideas. In *Ideals and Realities of Islam*, Nasr gives a convincing argument that the *Ṭarīqah* or Spiritual Path, also known as *taṣawwuf* in Sufism, is at the root of the Islamic tradition. *Sharī'ah* (Law) and the search for knowledge on the path go together and cannot be separated. The Prophet Muḥammad himself sought the Truth in isolation on a mountain, as did the Sufis.

The Sufis have been much maligned as being anti-*Sharī'ah* and irrational, whirling Dervishes. However, al-Ghazzālī, a learned *imām* and doctor who joined them and lived among them for years, understood their doctrines as the unique essence of Islam. His writings made Sufism respectable. Ibn ʻArabī and Suhrawardī carried on his quest. Al-Ghazzālī returned to the world of ordinary humans to teach them, just as Muḥammad had come down from the mountain al-Nūr to enlighten ignorant and suffering humanity with a supreme spiritual and ethical message.

Nasr has followed the Sufi example in his writings. His idea of spiritual knowledge or knowledge of the sacred is imbued with the Sufi idea of Illumination. However, in the spirit of the *Ishrāqīs*, it is Illumination which starts with its feet on the ground.

Conclusion: Ecology and Spiritual Knowledge

Perhaps the most important application of Nasr's idea that all sciences are involved in a spiritual quest and that the great religions have a single Source behind them is in his writings on ecology. The separation of knowledge from faith in Christian theology and the gradual vulgarization of the scientific view as primarily a search for technological fruits has led to a worldview which is destructive of nature. If we could return to the metaphysical principles of nature which are in the original spirit of Islam, Hinduism, Taoism, Buddhism, or Christianity, the ecological crisis would cease.

Nasr finds the solution to the ecological crisis in the abandonment of the Western scientific attitude of separating the sacred and the scientific. Instead of the positivist or operationalist attitude which stresses analysis, reductionism, and separation, Nasr calls for a return to Oriental science which goes back to the *Vedas*. There is always an attempt to find unity and interdependence.

> The import of Eastern science to the contemporary problems caused by the applications of Western science in many different fields can be illustrated through the problem of the unicity of and interrelation between things. This simple principle, which lies at the heart of all Sufi doctrine, will also cast some light upon the nature of Eastern science itself, whose contents we certainly cannot even begin to analyze here. Until now, modern science has succeeded largely by turning its back upon the interrelation between different parts of nature and by isolating each segment of nature in order to be able to analyze and dissect it separately. Ideally, according to Newtonian physics, in studying a falling body we can only calculate the gravitational forces acting upon it by knowing the mass and distance of every particle of matter in the material Universe. But since this is impossible, we consider only the earth as the centre of attraction and forget about all the other parts of the material Universe. As a result we are able to arrive at the precise numerical figure by applying the laws of Newton to the simplified case in question. Something has been gained

> through this method no doubt; but also something very fundamental has been lost and neglected, namely the basic truth that the simple falling body is related to all the particles of the Universe through a force which Plato would have called *Eros* and Ibn Sīnā *'ishq*.[47]

Continuing in the same vein, in 1966, when the dialogue on the ecological crisis was just getting started, Nasr wrote *The Encounter with Man and Nature*, which shows almost uncanny insight into the problems facing the human race in relation to nature. Again he defined the problem in relation to the obscuration of the sacred and of spiritual knowledge:

> The thesis presented in this book is simply this: that although science is legitimate in itself, the role and function of science and its application have become illegitimate and even dangerous because of the lack of the higher form of knowledge into which science could be integrated and the destruction of the sacred and spiritual value of nature. To remedy this situation the metaphysical knowledge pertaining to nature must be revived and the sacred quality of nature given back to it once again.[48]

There is no proof of the sacred quality of nature. It is an intuitive rather than a logical truth. It was known to Emerson, Thoreau, Coleridge, Rūmī, Lao Tzu, and other great poets and philosophers. However, we will never find the sacred quality of nature in our time unless we again find the sacred quality of science and all pursuits of learning. There are some hopeful signs in the Gaia Movement, which treats the earth as living Mother rather than as dead matter.[49] Humanity has much to realize. However, the teachings of Seyyed Hossein Nasr have been very useful in this context. Because his philosophy is derived from Sufi and Platonic sources, it includes the idea of the living nature of all matter in the cosmos. This makes all that is studied alive. In other words, true science is not dealing with dead bodies and accidentally propelled entities, but with sacred nature, the very manifestation of *al-Ḥaqq* (The Real). It is through this attitude that one can conceive of all real knowledge as spiritual knowledge or knowledge of the sacred. All subjects from medicine to cosmology can be renewed and exciting.

The supreme lesson to be learned about the world is one of love. Ibn 'Arabī, al-Bīrūnī, and others taught that there are moral and spiritual ideas to be grasped from our relationship with all of nature, but especially with the plant and animal kingdoms. Al-Bīrūnī wrote that plants and animals were essential to the maintenance of the natural equilibrium which is being threatened by insensitive humans who have forgotten the real meaning of knowledge: to love wisdom and to seek the spiritual light behind human existence. In the twentieth and twenty-first centuries, Seyyed Hossein Nasr has taught that spiritual knowledge is an eternal quest for the Sacred, absolute in what it demands of humans, but relative in that it moves on forever. His work inspires us to return the original sacred trust of philosophy as the love of wisdom (Divine Wisdom) to the modern world. We will enter the light of this knowledge, but we will never touch its flame.

JUDY D. SALTZMAN

PHILOSOPHY DEPARTMENT
CAL POLY, SAN LUIS OBISPO

NOTES

1. Seyyed Hossein Nasr, *Knowledge and the Sacred* (Albany: State University of New York Press, 1980), p. 1. Nasr makes it clear that *Sat-Chit-Ānanda* is one of the names of God in the Hindu tradition. It is usually translated as "Being-Consciousness-Bliss," but another essential translation of these terms is that of "Object-Subject-Union." Nasr says that, at the highest level, this ternary may also be expressed as "Known-Knower-Knowledge" or "Beloved-Lover-Love." Ibid., Footnotes, p. 49.

2. Ibid., p. 46. Nasr understands such writers as Plato, along with St. Bonaventure, Dante, and the Kabbalists to have grasped mathematics, not only in its quantitative, but also in its sacred sense. Kepler also never lost sight of the symbolic and qualitative and thus sacred nature of mathematics. In this way he kept the spirit of Pythagoras and Plato.

3. Ibid., p. 18. Nasr tells us that the Logos is the basis of Origen's theory of knowledge. Moreover, the Logos is the illuminator of souls. "It is the root of intelligence in man and is the intermediary through which man receives sacred knowledge." The idea of the Logos can also be connected to the Goddess of Speech (*Vac*) in the Veda. *Vac* is sacred sound whose divine reverberations started the whole universe. To call upon her, like invoking the divine names in Islam, is a means toward knowledge.

4. *The Meaning of the Glorious Quran*, tr. Mohammed Marmaduke Pickthall (Scarborough, Ontario: A Mentor Book, New American Library), Surah CXII, The Unity, p. 454.

5. Nasr, *Knowledge and the Sacred*, op. cit., p. 19.

6. Ibid., p. 23.

7. Seyyed Hossein Nasr, *An Introduction to Islamic Cosmological Doctrines* (Albany: State University of New York Press, 1993), p. 101.

8. Henri Bergson, *An Introduction to Metaphysics* (New York: Macmillan Publishing Company, 1955), p. 23. Bergson writes: "It follows from this that an absolute could only be given in *intuition*, whilst everything else falls within the province of *analysis*. By intuition is meant the kind of intellectual sympathy by which one places oneself within an object in order to coincide with what is unique in it and consequently inexpressible."

9. James D. Watson, *Double Helix: Being a Personal Account of the Discovery of the Structure of DNA* (New York: Macmillan Publishing Company, 1968).

10. Nasr, *Knowledge and the Sacred*, p. 165. Nasr carries through the image of Prometheus, not as a "Bringer of Light," but as a rebel against the Divine who ignorantly sought even the death of the gods.

11. Oswald Spengler, *The Decline of the West*, tr. C. F. Atkinson (London: Allen and Unwin, 1932). Spengler says that the Faustian culture of technological advancement and war machinery is well into its autumnal period, and ready for decline.

12. Nasr, *Knowledge and the Sacred*, p. 244. Nasr quotes Titus Burckhardt's "Cosmology and Modern Science" in Jacob Needleman's *The Sword of Gnosis*: "Teilhardism is comparable to one of those cracks that are due to the very solidification of the mental carapace, and that do not open upward, toward the heaven of true and transcendent unity, but downwards toward the realm of psychism. Weary of its own discontinuous vision of the world, the materialist mind lets itself slide toward a false continuity or unity, toward a pseudo-spiritual intoxication, of which this falsified and materialized faith—or this sublimated materialism [of Teilhardism] marks a phase of particular significance."

13. Ibid., pp. 242–43.

14. Mawlānā Jalāl al-Dīn Rūmī, quoted in Shems Friedlander, *The Whirling Dervishes* (Albany: State University of New York Press, 1992).

15. Nasr, *Knowledge and the Sacred*, p. 245. In this passage, Nasr is concerned about the rise of Islamic Marxism, which he considers to be a materialistic perversion of Islamic teachings.

16. Ibid., pp. 1–2.

17. Ibid., p. 4.

18. Ernest G. McClain, *The Pythagorean Plato* (York Beach, Maine: Nicholas Hayes Inc., 1984), pp. 35 and 45.

19. Friedlander, *The Whirling Dervishes*, p. 23.

20. Ibid, p. 23.

21. "The Burning Ground," Bengali Hymn to Kali in *The Jewel in the Lotus*, edited by Raghavan Iyer, (Santa Barbara: Concord Grove press, 1983). The exact translation is:

> Because Thou lovest a burning ground,
> I have made a burning ground of my heart—

22. Henry Corbin, *Creative Imagination in the Sufism of Ibn 'Arabī* (Princeton: Princeton University Press, 1969), p. 279.

23. Seyyed Hossein Nasr, *Islamic Science* (Westerham, Kent, England: World of Islam Publishing Company Ltd., 1976), p. 37.

24. Nasr, *Knowledge and the Sacred*, p. 28.

25. Ibid., p. 35.

26. Several modern scholars argue that "faith" is much too soft a translation of what St. Paul meant. The Greek word *pistis* from which "epistemology" is derived is much closer to knowledge than to faith. Although in *An Intermediate Greek Lexicon* (Oxford: the Clarendon Press, 1972), p. 641, the first meanings given are *faith*, *trustworthiness* or *honesty*; Elaine Pagels argues in *The Gnostic Paul* that he is referring to an "intuitive knowledge" of one's Higher Nature or Christos. Elaine Pagels, *The Gnostic Paul: Gnostic Exegesis of the Pauline Letters*, (Philadelphia: Trinity Press International, 1992).

27. Robert S. Elwood, *Alternative Altars: Unconventional and Eastern Spirituality in America* (Chicago: The University of Chicago Press, 1979). By "alternative reality" Ellwood is referring to views, such as Gnosticism, reincarnation, the eternality and infinite nature of the soul, and the lack of necessity for a Church authority as a guide to salvation. There were times in the history of Europe in which any of these ideas would put one in great peril from the authorities of the Church.

28. Rudolf Otto, *The Idea of the Holy*, tr. J. W. Harvey, 2nd ed. (New York: Oxford University Press, 1950). For Otto, the "holy" is peculiar to the sphere of religion, but it is extended to ethics. Nasr carries through the idea of the pursuit of sacred knowledge.

29. Haran al-Rashid was a Caliph in Baghdad who lived during the ninth century of the common era. He encouraged and supported scientific investigation and medical research.

30. Nasr, *An Introduction to Islamic Cosmological Doctrines*, p. 120.

31. Nasr, *Science and Civilization in Islam* (Cambridge, Mass.: Harvard University Press, 1968), p. 114.

32. Ibid.

33. Nasr, *An Introduction to Islamic Cosmological Doctrines*, p. 120.

34. Nasr, *Science and Civilization in Islam*, p. 118.

35. H. P. Blavatsky, *The Secret Doctrine*, vol. I (Los Angeles: The Theosophy Company, 1964), pp. 284–95. The idea that human beings, in what are referred to as the Third and Fourth Races millions of years ago, were very much larger than they are now, is a central teaching regarding the spiritual and physical evolution of the species. *The Secret Doctrine* refers to giants, Titans, and Rakshasas. The book mentions that these beings are discussed in much of the world's mythology, and even in *Genesis* 6 in the *Bible* in which "the sons of God" married the daughters of men, and produced the "mighty men of old."

36. Nasr, *An Introduction to Islamic Cosmological Doctrines*, p. 121.

37. Nasr, *Science and Civilization in Islam*, p. 114. In this book Nasr quotes Avicenna in a work by M. H. Shah, "The Constitution of Medicine," in *Theories and Philosophies of Medicine* (Delhi: Institute of History of Medicine and Medical Research, 1962), p. 96.

38. Nasr, *Science and Civilization in Islam*, pp. 268–69. Nasr writes that al-Rāzī (Rhazes) had an enormous influence on Medieval and Renaissance Europe. More of a Platonist than an Aristotelian, he was also an atomist similar to Democritus. His work seems to have been the basis for the development of the modern science of chemistry.

39. Ibid., p. 43. Al-Kindī, (Alkinus in Latin, c. 185–266. A.H. or 801–873 C.E.), was considered "The Philosopher of the Arabs." This encyclopedic mind wrote about two hundred and fifty treatises most of which are lost. He adapted Aristotelian arguments for God's existence, such as the argument from motion. Unlike some later Arabic philosophers who asserted the eternity of the world, he attempted to prove that the world had been created from nothing, and that it would dissolve again. His theory is closer to the Quran itself than that of some other Arabian philosophers. See Richard Walzer, "Kindī, Abū-Yūsuf Ya'qūb Ishaq al." *The Encyclopedia of Philosophy*, vol. 4, (New York: The Macmillan Company, 1967), p. 340.

40. Nasr, *Science and Civilization in Islam*, p. 245.

41. Nasr, *Islamic Science*, p. 8. Figure 2a.

42. Ibid., p. 150.

43. Seyyed Hossein Nasr, *Three Muslim Sages* (Cambridge, Mass.: Harvard University Press, 1964), p. 69.

44. Ibid., p. 62.

45. Muḥyidīn ibn al-'Arabī, *The Seals of Wisdom* (Santa Barbara: Concord Grove Press, 1983), p. 33.

46. S. H. Nasr, *Three Muslim Sages,* op. cit., p. 118.

47. Seyyed Hossein Nasr, "The Ecological Problem in the Light of Sufism," in *Religion for a New Generation*, ed. J. Needleman, A. K. Bierman, and J. A. Gould (New York: Macmillan Publishing Co., Inc., 1970), p. 258.

48. Seyyed Hossein Nasr, *The Encounter of Man and Nature: The Spiritual Crisis of Modern Man* (London: George Allen and Unwin Ltd., 1968), p. 14.

49. Tyler Volk, *Gaia's Body: Toward a Physiology of Earth* (New York: Springer Verlag, 1997). This is one of the more interesting attempts toward a scientific theory derived from a spiritual idea.

RESPONSE TO JUDY SALTZMAN

Professor Saltzman has a good grasp of my concept of spiritual knowledge and my response to her therefore will deal only with certain elucidations and nuances which will clarify further my views on the subject. She calls my approach to the subject a method that is highly eclectic. First of all my concept of spiritual knowledge is not itself a method but the result of a method which is none other than intellection in its time honored sense. Furthermore, my method is not at all eclectic. It is not reached by searching within various sources and selecting elements from each. Rather, it is based on the certitude gained through intellectual intuition. It is the examples drawn from many sources to demonstrate the universality of the sacred knowledge, which she calls spiritual knowledge, that can be said to be eclectic. I stand opposed to eclecticism in both thought and method and my claim is that the spiritual knowledge of which I speak can be found within a single tradition and does not depend for its actualization upon having to carry out studies of other traditions. Other traditions, when studied in their essence, only confirm the spiritual knowledge in question. A Śaṅkara, Ibn 'Arabī, or Eckhart certainly possessed such a knowledge at the highest level without having to have recourse to other traditions or being eclectic.

Saltzman calls me Platonic and Pythagorean which I accept fully if these terms are not limited to a merely historical interpretation of these schools in ancient Greece. I am primarily a Muslim metaphysician and follower of the perennial philosophy and it is in that context that my Platonism and Pythagoreanism must be understood. It is in light of the traditional understanding of Pythagoreanism that I would claim that numbers and geometry are not, as Saltzman claims, "the abstract basis of concrete reality" but concrete reality of which what we usually call concrete realities are but shadows and reflections. One cannot understand the traditional Pythagorean and Platonic position by following the modern version of the meaning of concrete and abstract. In the European Middle Ages philosophers who were called "Realists" were those who accepted the Platonic Ideas as real and the world as their shadow. In modern philosophy, concrete reality became identified with the object of the senses or the "concrete" and the Ideas with simply mental abstractions. The goal of traditional metaphysics is to undo this reversal and make clear that it is the archetypes or Platonic Ideas that are concrete and real and the world in a sense an abstraction and not vice-versa. In any case, there is no way to understand my exposition of Pythagorean mathematics, from which Platonism is in a sense derived, without being fully aware of how I use these terms. In traditional metaphysics only the Divine Principle is absolutely concrete Reality. Everything else is only relatively real and therefore less real than the Real as such, and might even be called "abstraction."

Saltzman writes that my "inspiration is broadly Islamic and especially Sufi in spite of his [my] scientific training." I need to comment on this statement because of the usage of the phrase "in spite of." It is true that usually many of those who study the modern sciences also become imprisoned in the scientism and positivism often associated with it. But there are many who do not, including Christian and Jewish scientists. In my case, the study of physics and mathematics and later geology and geophysics helped discipline my mental faculties and also provided me with insight into the workings of modern science which is used by so many to attack sacred knowledge and the religious view of the universe. Since I was saved from the confinement of scientism and rationalism with the help of traditional metaphysics when I was only eighteen years old and still at M.I.T., the study of the sciences did not have a debilitating effect upon my religious and spiritual life. On the contrary, it provided me with further means to combat secularist philosophies which deny the very reality of the Sacred. In my case, therefore, the phrase "in spite of" does not really apply.

My *Knowledge and the Sacred* is not only a "compendium of overwhelming evidence for the idea that knowledge has a metaphysical and even divine origin and purpose." It is first and foremost a metaphysical work which then draws from widely diversified sources in order to illustrate the universality of the theses presented in the book. Its truth or falsehood should be judged first of all upon the philosophical ideas presented and only secondly upon the universal nature of such ideas. Truth cannot be reached by majority vote, but the "overwhelming evidence" presented in this work helps many a reader to be brought to the truths which the book seeks to convey.

I do not claim in that book that "we are all *pneumatikoi*" to quote Saltzman. Yes, we are all *potentially* capable of possessing spiritual knowledge, but that potentiality becomes actualized only in the few whose nature it is to seek salvific knowledge. It is only such a person who can actually be called a pneumatic. For others, impediments within the soul and certain inner tendencies and passions cause that potentiality to remain only a potentiality, for such people are by their second and now practically present nature not drawn to sacred knowledge and even on a more mundane level are not satisfied in acquiring knowledge for itself rather than as a means to power, wealth and/or satisfaction of various passions.

Saltzman also mentions that according to me the philosophy of St. Thomas "would not have developed if the Christian tradition had not been permeated by Gnosis." This is not exactly my view. Rather, I have written that with the advent of Thomism and the Aristotelianization of Christian thought in the West, the early gnostic element, in the doctrinal and not sectarian sense of the term, became partially eclipsed and intellectual intuition became replaced by a sensualist epistemology which denied the intellect the power to know ultimate realities. I of course consider Thomism a traditional philosophy of great value but by drawing an excessively discursive veil upon earlier Christian theology, dominated as it was by a more metaphysical and Platonic vision grounded in intellection and *noesis*, Thomism indirectly prepared the ground for the rebellion of philosophy against Christianity at the end of the Middle Ages.

The author asserts that my viewpoint parallels that of Henri Bergson in his *Introduction to Metaphysics* as far as the primacy of the intuitive over any scientific and rational method is concerned. A number of modern Muslim thinkers, including Muḥammad Iqbāl, have seen in Bergson's intuition something akin to what one finds in traditional Islamic philosophy. But I am certainly not a member of this group. For Bergson, intuition is something vital and biological and one might say infra-rational. For me, intuition leading to sapiental knowledge has nothing to do with the biological and vital aspects of the human microcosm, which of course have a reality on their own level. Rather, I believe that intuition, which could be translated as *dhawq* or *ḥads* in the classical terminology of Islamic philosophy, is supra-rational and not infra-rational. The metaphysical conception of intellectual intuition confirms the rational from above without being limited by the inherent limitations of the merely rational. Bergsonian intuition, however, is a rebellion against reason by what one can only call "from below." Any parallelism between my understanding of intuition and Bergson's is therefore more apparent than real.

In dealing with the idea of knowledge, Saltzman seems to identify immoral uses of scientific knowledge, such as using atomic physics to make bombs, with profane knowledge and its good uses as sacred. This may be her definition; it is not mine. Sacred knowledge is not made sacred by its use, whether it be for the good of humanity or not (whatever meaning we attribute to the word "good" in this context). Sacred knowledge is sacred by virtue of its being the fruit of the act of knowing by a subject, in whom the knowing faculty has not become divorced from its Divine and Sacred

Source, of an object which has also not become severed from its Sacred Origin and is not considered as a totally independent order of reality. The question of what kind of use is made of a particular form of knowledge is certainly important but does not enter into the issue of what constitutes sacred knowledge in itself. Of course, it hardly needs to be mentioned that sacred knowledge is of such a nature that to acquire it requires certain moral and spiritual qualifications which preclude in general its misuse, and certainly do not allow its misuse on the scale that we observe in today's world in the case of modern science and technology which do not possess any innate link to moral and spiritual realities and are considered even by their defenders to be amoral.

I have been taken to task by other authors in this book for my opposition to Darwinian evolution and have provided responses. Therefore, I need not to go into that question again here. But it is necessary to provide a response to Saltzman's assertion that "at least Teilhard and Aurobindo made an attempt to understand the sacred working in the world." What destroys the truth is not only its denial through opposition but even more a pseudo-truth which is its parody. Guénon has already spoken of not only tradition and anti-tradition, but also counter-tradition. In the domain of the sciences, the materialistic science of the eighteenth and nineteenth centuries may be said to correspond to anti-tradition while something like Teilhardism, which could not but lead to pseudo-religion, corresponds to the counter-tradition which makes it much more dangerous as far as authentic sacred science is concerned. The "at least" mentioned above would be seriously challenged by me as it has been by other expositors of traditional metaphysics before me such as F. Schuon and T. Burckhardt.

Saltzman writes that my sense of the sacred is "firmly grounded in the rational and empirical" rather than the irrational. Now, I agree that the sacred is not rooted in the irrational but I believe it to be rooted in the supra-rational and I follow a spiritual perspective which is essentially sapiental, based on the correct functioning of the intellect or *nous* within us which transcends the rational faculty and is its principle. My source of the sacred could not therefore be *grounded* in the rational and/or the empirical. Rather, it is grounded in the noetic and properly speaking the intellectual, which means that the sacred is able to deal with the rational and empirical domains on their own levels of reality without taking refuge in an irrationalism which would have no means of dealing properly with the rational and the empirical. That is why my thought has what would be called a gnostic character if this term is remembered in its original sense corresponding to the Arabic *ma'rifah* or *'irfān* and the Sanskrit *jñāna.* If understood in this sense, then I agree with her when she says that I affirm that "Islamic science has never lost its gnostic character."

When the author states that "religion is seen as a scientific quest in that it seeks knowledge of the Divine," she opens the door to misunderstanding because of the current limitations placed upon the meaning of the word "science" in English. I would certainly not use such a term in this context but prefer to use the term "knowledge" and assert that at the heart of religion there lies the quest for the knowledge of God and also of the cosmos in light of that primary and principial knowledge. I do not believe, however, that "it searches for what forever recedes." Knowledge of God is not only a process or quest that forever recedes and never ends but a goal that is attainable. However, even *in divinis* there is no imaginable frontier to the degrees of that knowledge. Ibn 'Arabī states that when God commanded the Prophet of Islam to say, "O Lord increase me in knowledge" it meant that there is no *terminis quo* to knowledge of the Divine, but that does not mean that the religious knowledge of God is the pursuit of an ever-receding goal. Rather, it is a plunging into an "ocean without shore" to quote again the famous image used by Ibn 'Arabī, who also asserts that the saying of the Prophet, "O God, increase my bewilderment in Thee" refers to the clearest vision and the highest station of spiritual realization.

Saltzman compares my thought with those of Rāmānuja. While this is of course a great honor, I wish to add that my understanding of the doctrine of the unity of the Divine Principle and the transcendent unity of being which the Sufis call *waḥdat al-wujūd*, as well as my conception of the salvific role of principial knowledge, has also much resemblance to certain aspects of the teachings of Śaṅkara with whom I find great affinity on many levels while, of course, breathing within the Islamic universe; I emphasize the reality of the Personal God more than Śaṇkara does.

Turning to the question of the sacred quality of nature, the author asserts that there is no proof of such a quality existing in nature. I beg to differ strongly with this assertion. If by proof she means logical proof, then I accept since the sacred like beauty or goodness is not simply a logical concept to be proven or disproven logically. But logic also dictates that where there is smoke, there is fire. The remarkable beauty and harmony of nature cannot but be the result of the sacred presence in nature. The sacred must, however, be "seen" and "experienced" and not simply proven through mental concepts. Ordinary man, those whose faculties have not become distorted or atrophied by the artificial ambience of the modern urban setting he has created to forget the presence of God, has an innate sense of the sacred in nature and this sense remains strong among all traditional people not affected by the distortions of modernism. Moreover, to the statement of the author, "we will never find the sacred quality of nature in our time unless we again find the sacred quality of science and all pursuits of learning" must be added that before all else we must revive the sense of the sacred within ourselves. The person who has discovered the sacred within, can attest to the sacred quality of nature even if he or she lives in a modern city cut off to a large extent from the rhythms and harmonies of nature.

Saltzman concludes by saying "we will enter the light of this [sacred] knowledge, but we will never touch its flame." Although I have already responded to this issue above, let me conclude in my response to her perceptive essay by providing an answer to this assertion given by Jalāl al-Dīn Rūmī over seven centuries ago.

> The fruit of my life is but three utterances,
> I was unripe, I matured, and I was consumed [in the Divine Fire].

S. H. N.

20

Zailan Moris

THE ESSENTIAL RELATION BETWEEN REVELATION AND PHILOSOPHY IN ISLAM AND ITS IMPORTANCE IN UNDERSTANDING THE NATURE AND HISTORY OF ISLAMIC PHILOSOPHY

A devout Muslim, Seyyed Hossein Nasr believes and accepts fully that the Quran is the Word of God (*Kalām Allāh*) which contains the absolute Truth (*al-Ḥaqīqah*) and is the ultimate and certain source and criterion (*al-furqān*) of knowledge (*al-'ilm*) of both the "Visible World" (*'ālam al-shahādah*) and the "World of the Unseen" (*'ālam al-ghayb*).[1] The question of the veracity of revelation or the certitude of its knowledge is not a philosophical issue for Nasr; rather his concerns are with the implications that the fact of revelation and prophecy have on philosophical thought and activity. Like the Islamic philosophers before him who philosophized in an Islamic universe and worldview which is dominated by the centrality and reality of the Quran or God's revelation to man and the prophethood of Muḥammad, the question of the relation of revelation to philosophy is of great philosophical interest and significance to him.

For Nasr, there exists an essential relation between revelation and Islamic philosophy. He asserts that without the Quranic revelation, there would have been no Islamic philosophy[2] and "the very presence of the Quran and the advent of its revelation was to transform radically the universe in which and about which the Islamic philosophers were to philosophize, leading to a specific kind of philosophy which can be justly called 'prophetic philosophy'."[3] He regards Islamic philosophy as essentially a philosophical hermeneutics of the sacred text of the Quran and *Ḥadīth* or prophetic sayings, while making use of the rich philosophical heritage of antiquity.[4]

What is the basis of Nasr's view of Islamic philosophy? Throughout his philosophic writings, he offers several important reasons for his view.

First, he maintains that the Islamic revelation has created the intellectual and social climate within which the Islamic philosophers have philosophized. The Islamic philosophers who were Muslims, and many of whom were extremely pious and observant of the religion,[5] lived in that part of the world where social and cultural conditions were governed by the *Sharī'ah* or Divine Law which is based on the Quran and *Ḥadīth*.

Second, almost all of the Islamic philosophers identified philosophy or *falsafah* with *ḥikmah*, a Quranic term which means "wisdom" and which is also used to denote the discipline of philosophy. The early Islamic philosophers such as al-Kindī (d. 260/873), al-Fārābī (d. 339/950), and Ibn Sīnā (d. 428/1037), for example, accepted and reflected on the various definitions of philosophy which they inherited from the Greeks and identified these definitions with *ḥikmah*,[6] which the Quran states is a divine gift and blessing and an abundant good.[7] For these philosophers, philosophy is the knowledge of the reality of things to the measure of human ability. The goal of the philosopher in theoretical knowledge is to gain truth, and in practical knowledge to behave in accordance with truth.[8] The later Islamic philosophers such as Suhrawardī (d. 585/1191) and Mullā Ṣadrā (d. 1050/1641), founders of two major schools of Islamic philosophy, used the term *ḥikmah* to refer to their philosophies and also in the titles of their major philosophical works.[9] Both Suhrawardī and Mullā Ṣadrā conceived of philosophy as the supreme science which seeks to discover the truth concerning the nature of things and which requires both the perfection of the theoretical faculty, as well as the purification of the soul.[10] The philosophic truth must be realized within the total being of the individual and not merely in the mind. In their philosophies, philosophic *ḥikmah* can only be attained through the combination of discursive philosophy and spiritual practice.

The identification of philosophy with the Quranic *ḥikmah* has several important implications for philosophical thought in Islam. The most important implication is that philosophy is considered to be divine in its origin. Suhrawardī and the philosophers who followed in his wake considered philosophy to have issued from "the niche of prophecy" (*mishkāt al-nubuwwah*)[11] and the prophet Idrīs as the founder of philosophy and the "Father of philosophers" (*Abu 'l-ḥukamā'*).[12] The prophet Idrīs was identified by Muslims with the famous Hermes who was regarded by Christians, Jews, and Muslims alike as the founder of the sciences.[13]

The view that the origin of philosophy is divine and ultimately linked with prophecy finds reinforcement in the fact that the Quran mentions *kitāb*, meaning "book," that is, the revealed book and *ḥikmah* together, such as in the verses: "And He (God) will teach him the Book (*al-kitāb*) and Wisdom (*al-ḥikmah*)" (Q. III:48); and "Behold that which I have given you of the Book and Wisdom" (Q. III:81). Islamic philosophers, such as Mullā Ṣadrā, considered the Quranic conjunction of *kitāb* and *ḥikmah*, or revelation and philosophy, to confirm the view that what God has revealed through revelation He had also made available through philosophy.[14] Revelation and philosophy, since they arise from a common source, do not represent two contending or conflicting forms of knowledge; rather they complement each other in aiding man to realize the truth and to attain certain and indubitable knowledge.

Third, the presence of certain Quranic themes have dominated Islamic philosophy throughout its long history and have influenced profoundly its development. The most important and dominant theme, which in Nasr's view has "in a sense determined the agenda of the Islamic philosophers,"[15] is that of *al-Tawḥīd* or the doctrine of divine Unity which constitutes the heart of the Islamic message or revelation. He maintains that the doctrine of divine Unity provides the Islamic scholars and philosophers with the essential perspective which enables them to see and affirm the principle of unity operative in every aspect of existence and level of reality. To demonstrate, in the study of nature, the Islamic philosophers such as Ibn Sīnā and the Ikhwān al-Ṣafā' have expounded the view of the unity and inter-relatedness of all that exists such that in contemplating the unity of creation man is led to the unity of God or the Divine Principle.[16] And in epistemology, Islamic philosophers throughout the ages have expounded certain fundamental principles such as the unity of knowledge and the various sciences, the unity of knowledge and reality, and the unity of knowledge and being. These principles underlie much of the Islamic philosophers' discussion and treatment of knowledge, such as al-Fārābī's famous classification of the sciences which is based on the principle of the unity of knowledge,[17] and Mullā Ṣadrā's doctrine of the unity of the knower (*al-'āqil*) and the known (*al-ma'qūl*) which involves the principle of the unity of knowledge and being.[18]

Another example of an important Quranic theme which has also dominated Islamic philosophical thought is that of God's act of bringing something into existence. The oft-quoted Quranic verse, "But His command, when He intendeth a thing, is only that He saith unto it: Be! and it is (*kun fa-yakūn*)" (Q. XXXVI:81) has provided the essential material for the philosophers to philosophize on God's creation and mysterious act of creating. For Nasr, it is on the basis of this and other Quranic verses, and in conjunction with Greek thought, that the Islamic philosophers developed their views on ontology, such as the doctrine of Pure Being, which stands above the chain of being and is discontinuous with it, and the theory of emanation.[19]

Quranic themes also dominate the Islamic philosophers' discussion of cosmology and eschatology. In cosmology for example, certain verses of the Quran such as the famous "Throne Verse" (*āyat al-kursī*) (Q. II:255) and the "Light Verse" (*āyat al-nūr*) (Q. XXIV:35) play a profound and central role in its development, providing the key motifs, symbols, and images in the philosophers' cosmological doctrines;[20] and in eschatology certain issues such as bodily resurrection and the various posthumous events described in the Quran and *Ḥadīth* are of great importance and concern to the philosophers, and they sought to understand and demonstrate their meaning philosophically in their works.[21]

Fourth, in addition to identifying philosophy with *ḥikmah* mentioned in the Quran, the Islamic philosophers, especially from Suhrawardī onward, identified philosophic *ḥikmah* with *al-Ḥaqīqah* or the inner truth or esoteric teachings of the Quran. The term *al-ḥaqīqah* means both "truth" and "reality." In the perspective of the Quran, that which is true is also real and that which is real is necessarily true. One of the Names of God is *al-Ḥaqq* meaning "The Absolutely True" or "The Absolutely Real." *Al-Ḥaqīqah* in relation to the Quran denotes the truth or the reality of the Quran. Since the Quran, as asserted by a *ḥadīth*, contains an outward (*ẓāhir*) and an inward (*bāṭin*) aspect,[22] it therefore possesses an outer and an inner truth and an outer and an inner reality. It is the inner truth or reality of the Quran which the Islamic philosophers are interested to discover and comprehend. The Islamic philosophers' preoccupation with the inner or esoteric meanings of the verses of the Quran, especially in relation to the verses which lend themselves to many levels of meanings (*mutashābihāt*),[23] are clearly demonstrated by their Quranic commentaries. As early as Ibn Sīnā in the 5th/11th century, the Islamic philosophers, besides writing their philosophical works, have also written commentaries, specifically philosophical commentaries on the Quran.[24] And with the later philosophers, the practice of quoting verses from the Quran and *Ḥadīth* in their philosophical writings became a common practice.

The quest of the philosophers was clearly the comprehension of the inner meanings of the Quran which contains knowledge of God and the true nature of things which they sought to attain. They believed that the inner meanings of the verses of the Quran can be discovered and the science of the unveiling of its meaning has become a goal of Islamic philosophers. To this end they have perfected their theoretical faculty and purified their beings, for the Quran states that none can approach it save the pure.[25] Thus, not surprisingly, Islamic philosophy in its later development has become a divine science (*al-ḥikmah al-ilāhiyyah*)[26] which requires from the seeker or lover of wisdom the perfection of the theoretical faculty and the purification of the soul and its embellishment with the virtues in order that the inner truth and reality of the Quran be revealed or unveiled to him. Philosophy is not merely a rational enterprise to discover the true nature of things but a total immersion and participation of the individual philosopher in the truth—a truth which allows for the possibility of knowledge by immediate experience or "tasting" (*dhawq*), direct witnessing (*mushāhadah*), and illumination (*ishrāq*). The philosopher or *ḥakīm* is regarded as the most perfect of human beings, one who can be considered to be among "those who are firmly rooted in knowledge" (*al-rāsikhūn fi 'l-'ilm*) mentioned in the Quran,[27] standing in rank only below the prophets.

Fifth, the central religious fact of prophecy, or the descent of the Quran from the divine realm to the soul of Prophet Muḥammad has greatly influenced and determined the Islamic philosophers' conception and understanding of the intellect (*al-'aql*) and their treatment of its relation to revelation. For Islamic philosophers, the Quranic term *al-'aql*, which is used to denote human intelligence and which is etymologically related to the meanings of "to tie" or "to bind," signifies both that which binds man to God, as well as that which binds or limits the Absolute in the direction of creation.[28] In relation to man, *al-'aql* denotes the human intellect which is his highest and noblest faculty and the principal means by which he is bound to God or to "The Truth" or "The Real." In relation to God, *al-'aql* denotes the Universal Intellect (*al-'aql al-kullī*), which is identified with the "Pen" (*qalam*) mentioned in the Quran,[29] and is the first being created by God and the most direct and immediate manifestation or self-determination of Himself. *Al-'aql* is the repository of God's knowledge of all created beings.

The Islamic philosophers developed various theories of the intellect in order to explain in a philosophical manner the central religious fact of prophecy. For example, the early philosophers such as al-Fārābī and Ibn Sīnā, who were also the major exponents of *Mashshā'ī* or Peripatetic philosophy in Islam, developed, on the basis of Greek theories of the intellect and faculties of the soul, a theory of the intellect which delineates and explains the different stages of the development of the intellect from absolute potentiality to perfect actuality that culminates in a doctrine of the prophetic intellect which receives divine revelation. In their hands, the theoretical intellect (*al-'aql al-naẓarī*) of Aristotle, which is the instrument of philosophizing, was transformed to accommodate the fact of prophecy and the possibility of its illumination by the Active Intellect (*al-'aql al-fa''āl*). Ibn Sīnā identified the Active Intellect with the Holy Spirit (*al-rūḥ al-qudus*) or the archangel Gabriel, the angel of revelation.[30]

Furthermore, the fact of prophecy and the acceptance of a revealed book as the supreme source of knowledge in Islam have also led Islamic philosophers to develop a doctrine of the complementary nature of revelation (*waḥy*) and intellect (*al-'aql*). Revelation which causes a new religion to become established is referred to as universal revelation (*al-waḥy al-kullī*) and is viewed as the macrocosmic manifestation of the Universal Intellect (*al-'aql al-kullī*).[31] Human intellect, which is capable of potentially comprehending the contents of revelation and realizing its verities, is referred to as particular revelation (*al-waḥy al-juz'ī*) and is regarded as the microcosmic manifestation of the Universal Intellect.[32] Revelation provides the necessary framework for the intellect to actualize fully its potential powers, and the *Sharī'ah* protects man from his own passions which can obscure his intellect and obstruct it from functioning properly and realizing its virtual powers.[33] The potential powers of the intellect to comprehend revelation can only be actualized if the intellect submits itself to universal revelation and is illuminated by this revelation. When the intellect is illuminated by the grace (*barakah*) and light of revelation, it is able to experience or apprehend directly the revealed truth contained in universal revelation. Hence, the illuminated human intellect is able to know or realize the meanings of the verses of the Quran with immediacy and certainty.

It is important to mention here that for Islamic philosophers, *al-'aql* denotes both reason (*ratio*) and intellect (*intellectus* or *nous*).[34] The human intellect is capable of both ratiocination, or knowing in a mediate and inferential manner through concepts and mental representations (*al-'ilm al-ḥuṣūlī*), and intuition, or knowing in a direct and immediate way by participation or experience (*al-'ilm al-ḥuḍūrī*).[35] In ratiocination, the subject and object of knowledge are polarized and the form of knowledge attained is indirect; in contrast, the form of knowledge which is attained through intuition is immediate and direct since that which is known is apprehended or experienced immediately, without any mediation of mental concepts. Since reason knows in a mediated way through concepts and mental representations, it is susceptible to doubts concerning its cognitions and, consequently, is required to make a judgment concerning that which it knows. In contrast, knowledge by intuition is direct and immediate; and the immediate and direct nature of intuitive knowledge renders it a form of certain knowledge.

Revelation which deals to a large extent with supernatural realities and transcendent truths cannot be totally or completely understood by human reason and discursive thought alone, since its spiritual contents transcend reason's logical categories which are spatially and temporally conditioned. Thus, there exists a wide chasm between the transcendent truths contained in revelation and reason's spatially and temporally conditioned and mediated mode of knowing. Islamic philosophers such as Suhrawardī and Mullā Ṣadrā postulated that the gap between divine revelation and human reason can be effectively bridged by intellectual intuition which is the result of the intellect being illuminated by the Active Intellect or the angel of revelation.[36] Intellectual intuition, which enables man to apprehend or experience directly the transcendent truths or verities contained in revelation, and provides him with the capacity to comprehend and verify the claims and assertions of revelation by way of immediate experience or direct apprehension. These philosophers maintained that if sense perception enables man to perceive and experience the sensible realities which surround him in the "Visible World," then intellectual intuition provides him with the appropriate and reliable mode of knowing the spiritual realities in the "World of the Unseen" which are mentioned in revelation.[37] Although reason, due to its limited nature and mode of knowing, cannot know directly the transcendent truths contained in revelation, it can, through conception, comprehend and analyze the cognitive contents of intuition. In other words, reason can analyze the assertions and claims of intuition, and comprehend and demonstrate rationally that which the intellect knows by intuition. Reason's analysis and demonstration of the cognitive contents of intuition not only serves to check the claims made by intuition but also enables a rational comprehension of these contents by those who are without immediate knowledge of the verities of revelation. Hence, for Islamic philosophers such as Suhrawardī, Mullā Ṣadrā and the other *Ḥikmat* philosophers, the principle of reason and discursive thought is the intellect and the principle of the intellect is revelation. There exists a complementary relation between divine revelation and the human intellectual powers of intuition and ratiocination, as well as a hierarchic order of their authority and role in man's quest for the attainment of *ḥikmah.*

From the above discussion of Nasr's view of the essential relation between revelation and Islamic philosophy, it is very clear that his view is based on the nature of the main course of development that philosophical thought in the Islamic community has taken in its long history. Nasr sees this development in light of the Islamic philosophers' intellectual responses and philosophical understanding and demonstrations of the teachings of the Quran and *Ḥadīth*, especially the major philosophers such as Ibn Sīnā, Suhrawardī and Mullā Ṣadrā who developed new philosophical perspectives within the Islamic philosophical tradition. For Nasr, a correct understanding and proper appreciation of the Islamic philosophical tradition can only be gained if Islamic philosophy is viewed on the basis of its own historical development and through the views of its exponents.[38]

Nasr's insistence is extremely significant and particularly instructive in light of the fact that for a long time until about fifty years ago, there prevailed in the West three inaccurate views of Islamic philosophy: First, Islamic philosophy is "Arabic philosophy"; second, it is Graeco-Alexandrian philosophy in an Arabic dress; and third, Islamic philosophy began with al-Kindī in the ninth century and came to end with the death of Ibn Rushd or Averroes in the twelfth century.[39]

For a long time Western scholars considered and referred to Islamic philosophy as "Arabic philosophy" after its main language of philosophical discourse and the ethnic background of some of its philosophers. Nasr argues that it is incorrect to regard Islamic philosophy as "Arabic philosophy." Even though most works of Islamic philosophy were written in Arabic, much was also written in Persian,[40] from Ibn Sīnā in the 5th/11th century, to the Safavid philosophers such as Mīr Dāmād and Mīr Findiriskī in the 11th/17th century, to the philosophers of the school of Tehran from the 12th/18th century to the present. And while many of the Islamic philosophers were Arabs, such as al-Kindī and Ibn Rushd, the majority were Persians while others were from Turkish or Indian ethnic backgrounds. Furthermore, Persia has remained the main center of Islamic philosophy during most of Islamic history.[41]

Nasr also points out that even though much Jewish philosophy was written in Arabic, it was not referred to as "Arabic philosophy," and similiarly with Christian Arabic literature of a philosophical nature which was of some significance in the early history of Islamic philosophy.[42] Thus, the appellation "Arabic philosophy" is inaccurate either with reference to the language of philosophical discourse or to the ethnic background of its philosophers. However, for Nasr, the inaccuracy of referring to Islamic philosophy as "Arabic philosophy" is not limited to these historical reasons only but extends more importantly to the grave misunderstanding of the very nature of Islamic philosophy itself. For him, to refer to Islamic philosophy as "Arabic philosophy" is to miss the crucial and fundamental factor that Islamic philosophy is deeply and profoundly rooted in the Islamic revelation and that it is Islamic philosophy precisely because it is a philosophical tradition whose genesis, development, and modalities are inextricably linked to the Quran and *Ḥadīth*.[43]

As to the view that Islamic philosophy is nothing more than Graeco-Alexandrian philosophy in an Arabic dress, or that the Islamic philosophers were not original thinkers but only the transmitters and commentators on the philosophies of Plato, Aristotle, and the Neo-Platonists, Nasr throughout his writings has never failed to point out that although the Islamic philosophers inherited Graeco-Alexandrian wisdom and were profoundly influenced by it, they were original thinkers who developed new theories, perspectives, and syntheses. Although their philosophical thought drew heavily on the translated works of the Greek and Alexandrian philosophers known to them, nevertheless, it also contained many new and original elements which were the result of the Islamic philosophers having to respond intellectually and demonstrate philosophically the principles and tenets of their religion. For example, al-Fārābī's and Ibn Sīnā's theory of the intellect, which, although it was based on the Greek theories of the intellect and faculties of the soul, contained new and original elements. In this context, al-Fārābī and Ibn Sīnā sought to accommodate and demonstrate philosophically the fact of prophecy which, as already noted, was a central concern to them as Islamic philosophers.

In ontology both al-Fārābī and Ibn Sīnā introduced a fundamental distinction between the existence of the world and that of God which was a significant departure from Aristotelian ontology but in line with the Quranic teachings on God's Unity, His transcendent nature, and His relation to creation. Furthermore, Ibn Sīnā's original ontological distinctions of necessary (*wājib*), contingent (*mumkin*), and impossible (*mumtani'*) existence based on the three relations between existence (*wujūd*) and essence (*māhiyyah*) not only provided invaluable categories for the study of Being in both the Islamic and Western world, but also provided the basis for the philosophical demonstration of the contingent existence (*mumkin al-wujūd*) of the world and the necessary existence (*wājib wujūd*) of God. The distinction between necessity (*wujūb*) and contingency (*imkān*) makes possible a metaphysical view of the universe which is consistent with the teachings of the Quran, and which emphasizes the ontological poverty (*faqr*) of the universe; the power of creation and existentiation (*ījād*) belongs to God alone.[44] For Nasr, Ibn Sīnā's ontological views, which came to dominate much of Islamic and medieval philosophy, were not the result of him "simply thinking of Aristotelian theses in Arabic and Persian" but were the outcome of his "meditation on the Quranic doctrine on the One in relation to existence in conjunction with Greek thought."[45] Thus, Islamic philosophy cannot be viewed simply as Graeco-Alexandrian philosophy in an Arabic dress; nor can one truly say that the Islamic philosophers were merely transmitters and commentators on Graeco-Alexandrian philosophy. There was much that was new and original in the works of the Islamic philosophers—the result of their deliberate effort to accommodate and demonstrate philosophically certain fundamental principles of the Islamic religion.

Finally, the view that Islamic philosophy, which began with al-Kindī in the ninth century, terminated with the death of Ibn Rushd in the twelfth century is incorrect. This evidently is an inaccurate account of Islamic philosophy since it continued to develop and flourish in the eastern lands of Islam, specifically in Persia and in certain parts of Iraq and India, as demonstrated by the presence of numerous outstanding and important Islamic philosophers such as Naṣīr al-Dīn Ṭūsī (d. 672/1273), Mīr Dāmād (d. 1041/1631), Mullā Ṣadrā (d. 1050/1641), and Mullā Hādī Sabziwārī (d. 1295/1878), as well as the creation of new and major philosophical perspectives and schools of thought and the establishment of vital centers of Islamic philosophy, such as in Isfahan, Khurasan, and Tehran. Beginning with Suhrawardī and after Ibn Rushd, Islamic philosophy became more closely and intimately bound with the inner or esoteric teachings of the Quran and *Ḥadīth* and began to emphasize and rely more on the immediate and illuminative knowledge of Islamic revealed principles and doctrines rather than on rational and speculative philosophical principles only.

Hence, that which came to an end with the death of Ibn Rushd in the twelfth century is not Islamic philosophy, but is rather the influence of the Islamic philosophers between the ninth and twelfth centuries on the thinkers in the West. The inaccurate account of the history of Islamic philosophy by Western scholars, Nasr explains, was the result of their primary interest and concern in understanding their own intellectual history, in which Islamic philosophy played a crucial role at an important stage of the development of Western thought,[46] rather than arising from an interest in the tradition of Islamic philosophy itself.

It is to correct the prevalent misunderstanding of the nature and history of Islamic philosophy in the West that Nasr has not only refuted the three inaccurate views but also presented his own view and understanding of Islamic philosophy, a view which is based on the structure of Islamic philosophical thought, its development in history, and the views and perspectives of its major philosophers and schools of thought. To this end, he has written extensively over the past forty years on the Islamic nature of the philosophical thought as cultivated by the Islamic philosophers. Nasr does this by explaining and demonstrating how Islamic philosophy is related to the Quran and *Ḥadīth* in an essential way. Nasr has also made known to the West the works of the important Islamic philosophers since Ibn Rushd.[47] It is largely due to the works of Islamic scholars such as Seyyed Hossein Nasr and Western scholars such as Henry Corbin on Islamic philosophy, that the three inaccurate views of Islamic philosophy prevalent in the West, which were also adopted by many Western educated Muslims who learned of their intellectual heritage from Western sources,[48] were refuted and replaced by a view of the tradition which is based on the history and structure of Islamic philosophy itself and the works of its philosophers. Through his writings, Nasr has made known to the West the nature and history of Islamic philosophy, which although heavily influenced by Graeco-Alexandrian philosophy, nevertheless has its source and inspiration in the Islamic revelation. Nasr's writings on Islamic philosophy, which have been translated into several major European and Islamic languages, are instrumental in not only correcting the inaccurate views of Western scholars concerning Islamic philosophy but also in presenting Islamic philosophy as a living tradition with a long and vibrant history. This history leaves Muslims in possession of a treasury of works which demonstrate the profound responses of the Islamic philosophers to the combined demands of their faith in God and the verities of the Islamic revelation, the logical requirements of discursive reasoning and rational demonstration, and their love of *sophia* or *ḥikmah* which they have regarded as inseparable from spiritual purity and intellectual illumination.

ZAILAN MORIS

SCHOOL OF HUMANITIES
UNIVERSITI SAINS MALAYSIA
AUGUST 1996

NOTES

1. See for example chapter 2, "The Quran—the Word of God, the Source of Knowledge and Action," of his *Ideals and Realities of Islam* (London: Unwin Hyman, 1988).

2. S. H. Nasr, "The Quran and *Ḥadīth* as Source and Inspiration of Islamic Philosophy" in *History of Islamic Philosophy, Part I*, S. H. Nasr and O. Leaman, eds., (London: Routledge, 1996), p. 36.

3. Ibid., p. 28.

4. Ibid., p. 37.

5. Nasr gives examples of famous Islamic philosophers who were also extremely pious Muslims such as Ibn Rushd who was the chief *qāḍī* or judge of Cordova, Mullā Ṣadrā who journeyed seven times on foot to Mecca, (Ibid., p. 16) and Ibn Sīnā who would go to the mosque to pray when confronted with a difficult scientific or philosophic problem; see his *Three Muslim Sages* (Delmar: Caravan Books, 1976), p. 41.

6. Nasr, "The Meaning and Concept of Philosophy in Islam," in *History of Islamic Philosophy, Part I*, S. H. Nasr and O. Leaman, eds. (London: Routledge, 1996), p. 21.

7. "He (God) giveth wisdom (*ḥikmah*) unto whom He will, and he unto whom wisdom is given, he truly hath received abundant good" (Q. II:269).

8. Nasr and Leaman, eds., op. cit., p. 22.

9. Suhrawardī referred to his philosophy as *'al-ḥikmat al-ishrāq* ("Illuminationist Philosophy/Wisdom") and it was also used as the title of his most important philosophical work. Mullā Ṣadrā used the term '*al-ḥikmat al-muta'āliyah* ("Transcendent Philosophy/Wisdom") in the title of his philosophical *magnum opus*, the *Asfār*, and it was also used to refer to his school of philosophy. Ibid., p. 23.

10. Ibid., p. 24.

11. A famous Arabic saying states, "philosophy issues from the niche of prophecy" ("*yanba 'al-ḥikmah min mishkāt al-nubuwwah*"), ibid., p. 30.

12. See chapter 9, "Hermes and Hermetic Writings in the Islamic World" in Nasr, *Islamic Life and Thought* (Albany: State University of New York Press, 1981), p. 106.

13. "During the Middle Ages, Christians, Jews and Muslims considered Hermes to be the founder of the sciences. . . . Hermes was considered to be the same as the Thoth of the Egyptians, the Ukhnukh of the Hebrews, Hushang of the ancient Persians and Idrīs of the Muslims. His followers, in whatever land they lived, considered him a prophet who had brought a Divine message to mankind and who was the founder of the sciences." Ibid., pp. 102–3.

14. Nasr and Leaman, eds., op. cit., p. 31.

15. Ibid., p. 32.

16. See Nasr's "Introduction" *in An Introduction to Islamic Cosmological Doctrines*, rev. ed. (Albany: State University of New York Press, 1992).

17. See chapter 2 of Nasr's *Science and Civilization in Islam* (Chicago: ABC International Group, 2001).

18. See chapter 36, "Mullā Ṣadrā: His Teachings" in Nasr and Leaman, eds., op. cit., p. 651.

19. Nasr and Leaman, eds., op. cit., p. 33.

20. Ibid., p. 34.

21. For example, many Islamic philosophers have discussed the Quranic doctrine of bodily resurrection; prominent among them were Ibn Sīnā, al-Ghazzālī and Mullā Ṣadrā. The earlier philosophers, although they sought to discuss this doctrine philosophically in their works, admitted that they could not provide philosophical proofs for it but nevertheless accepted the truth of the doctrine on the basis of their faith. Mullā Ṣadrā managed to demonstrate philosophically the doctrine of bodily resurrection by making use of certain principles original to his philosophical perspective. His *Asfār* contains the most extensive philosophical treatment of the eschatological teachings of the Quran. Ibid., p. 35.

22. A *ḥadīth* of the Prophet states, "The Quran possesses an external appearance and a hidden depth, an exoteric meaning and an esoteric meaning. This esoteric meaning in turn conceals an esoteric meaning. So it goes on for seven esoteric meanings." Quoted in Henry Corbin, *History of Islamic Philosophy*. Trans. by Liadain Sherrard. (London: Kegan Paul International & Islamic Publications, 1993), p. 7.

23. The Quran consists of two types of verses: the verses whose meanings are clear (*muḥkamāt*) and those which contains many levels of meanings (*mutashābihāt*).

24. The first major Islamic philosopher to write philosophic commentaries on the Quran was Ibn Sīnā. Nasr and Leaman, eds., op. cit., p. 31.

25. "That (this) is indeed a noble Quran in a Book kept hidden which none toucheth save the purified." (Q. LVI:77–79).

26. Ibid., p. 36.

27. From the Quran III:7. Mullā Ṣadrā in his work, *al-Mashā'ir*, for example, states that the philosopher who possesses gnostic or illuminative knowledge (*ma'rifah*) of the inner meanings of the verses of the Quran is to be regarded as

"among those who are firmly rooted in knowledge" mentioned in the Quran.

28. Nasr, "Revelation, Intellect and Reason in the Quran," in *Sufi Essays* (Albany: State University of New York Press, 1973), p. 54.

29. *Ideals and Realities*, p. 53.

30. Nasr and Leaman, op. cit., p. 28.

31. Nasr, "Intellect and Intuition: Their Relationship from the Islamic Perspective," *Studies in Comparative Religion* (Winter-Spring, 1979): 67.

32. Ibid.

33. Ibid.

34. *Sufi Essays*, p. 54.

35. "Intellect and Intuition," p. 66.

36. Ibid., p. 71.

37. Ibid., p. 72.

38. Nasr and Leaman, op. cit., pp. 27 and 37.

39. See for example, Nicholas Rescher, *Studies in Arabic Philosophy* (Pittsburg: University of Pittsburg Press, 1966); D. Delacy O'Leary, *Arabic Thought and its Place in History* (London: Kegan Paul, 1922); and T. J. de Boer, *The History of Philosophy in Islam* (London: Luzac and Co., 1933).

40. Nasr and Leaman, op. cit., p. 17.

41. Ibid.

42. Ibid.

43. Ibid., p. 27.

44. "Existence (*wujūd*) and Quiddity (*māhiyyah*) in Islamic Philosophy," *Iqbāl Review* (Lahore) (Oct. 1989–April 1990): 171–72.

45. Nasr and Leaman, op. cit., p. 32.

46. Ibid., p. 18.

47. See his *The Islamic Intellectual Tradition in Persia*, ed. M. A. Razavi (Surrey: Curzon Press, 1996).

48. For Nasr, although it is legitimate for the Western scholars to view and have an interest in Islamic philosophy only in relation to their own intellectual history, it is a grave error for the Muslims to accept and adopt the Western scholars' view of Islamic philosophy. He emphasizes that an individual or a community cannot look at itself through the eyes of another without seriously misunderstanding and falsifying fundamental aspects of its nature, history, and self-worth. See chapter 12, "The Pertinence of Studying Islamic Philosophy Today" in *Islamic Life and Thought*, pp. 145–52.

REPLY TO ZAILAN MORIS

The issues of the relation between revelation and philosophy and the nature of the history of Islamic philosophy in light of that relation discussed by Professor Moris are of central importance to my thought and I am glad to have the opportunity to clarify a number of points raised by the author concerning these subjects. It is true, as Moris says at the beginning, that I have a certitude about revelation, but I would not say that this has never been a philosophical issue for me. Although my faith in revelation has persisted throughout my life, in my youth I sought also a *knowledge* which would be based on certitude in many different quarters and found it finally in traditional metaphysics which I accepted not on faith but on intellectual intuition corresponding to the first level of certitude, which the Quran calls "the science of certitude" (*'ilm al-yaqīn*). This certitude both complemented and strengthened my faith in revelation. For me it was not so much a question of *credo ut intelligam* but intellection complementing and fortifying faith.

I *have* philosophized in a universe dominated by the reality of the Quranic revelation, but for me philosophical activity has not only been to draw the philosophical significance of the inward teachings of the Quran and *Ḥadīth*. It has certainly been such an activity but not *only* such activity. If this had been my only philosophical activity, many in the West would refer to my thought as theology rather than philosophy, as in fact some positivists have already done. But for me the task has been one of allowing the inner intellect to function and seek to reach the truth which could not but be the truth that is to be found at the heart of revelation. While I agree fully with the points mentioned by Moris concerning how I understand the relation between revelation and philosophy in the Islamic context, it is essential to clarify further my position concerning the relation between the intellect (*al-'aql*) and revelation (*al-waḥy*).

I agree with Moris when she states, "the principle of reason and discursive thought is the intellect," but it is not true that "the principle of the intellect is revelation," as this term is usually understood. As made clear by Mullā Ṣadrā, among others, the Divine Intellect, identified by many Islamic philosophers with the instrument of revelation or Gabriel, is also reflected within man, and this reflection is the intellect operating within those capable of attaining metaphysical knowledge. This inner intellect, or the reflection of the Divine Intellect in man, is often referred to as "partial revelation" which is complemented by the complete or objective revelation, and the latter is the foundation of religion. That is why this "inner revelation" is able to function fully only in the world created by that objective manifestation of the Divine Intellect or Logos which we call "revelation" in the ordinary sense of the term. One should therefore say that the principle of the intellect as it functions within man is the reality which is the origin and source of the revelation, namely the Divine Intellect/Logos rather than the external revelation which, however, guides and molds the functioning of the intellect within.

Moris is correct when she asserts that according to my works the mind of the Islamic philosophers was influenced, molded, and transformed by the Quranic revelation and the world created by it. There can be no doubt about this reality which has made Islamic philosophy a "prophetic philosophy" and which has caused Islamic philosophers to philosophize in a world in which revelation always looms on the horizon. From the point of view of the *ḥikmat* tradition in Islamic thought with which I identify in so many ways, revelation is not only the source of ethical precepts and legal and ritual injunctions, but in its inner aspect also of philosophy in the highest sense as *ḥikmah* or *sophia*. To grasp this inner message, however, man must possess a nature prone toward intellection and be able to remove the impediments in his soul which in many cases prevent the inner intellect from functioning. The inner dimension of revelation contains a wisdom which also lies buried deep within the very substance of man and which can only be reached by the heart/intellect actualized with the help of revelation.

In the deepest sense the Intellect is the source of both revelation and reason, while reason itself must be made subservient to the inner Intellect on the one hand and the cosmic manifestation of the Intellect in the form of revelation on the other. Traditional philosophy and metaphysics are not only the result of drawing philosophical conclusions from revealed sources, although revelations are certainly among their sources. Traditional philosophy is also the fruit of reaching the truth by means of the inner intellect molded and guided by revelation, a truth which cannot but confirm, according to Islamic philosophers, the inner meaning of the revelation and its tenets. It is important to emphasize both of these aspects of the relation between philosophy and revelation if one is to present my view of this important issue in its totality. To summarize, man reaches the truth through revelation but also by means of the inner intellect whose actualization is made possible by revelation in its objective mode. This objective revelation allows that inner revelation to take place through the instrument of the heart/intellect, provided man is willing to make reason subservient to both the inner intellect and the revelation which is the theophany of the Divine Intellect.

As for the history of Islamic philosophy, while I agree with Moris's assessment of my position, again there is need for further clarification. As students of Western philosophy know only too well, the history of philosophy as currently understood itself reflects a certain philosophy of history as asserted by Hegel. For example, in the West the history of Western philosophy is usually studied by going back to Pythagoras, Empedocles, and Parmenides, thinkers who have been interpreted in a way that excludes major dimensions of their thought. Furthermore, Western studies include the periodization of this history into, ancient, medieval, and modern. This division is then applied to Islamic philosophy which is presented as a caricature of itself. The perspective within which the origin of modern philosophy is conceived and the choice of which philosophers to include and which to exclude in the account of the history of philosophy all reflect a particular "ideology" and conception of philosophy and are related to modern man's view of himself. That is why when a Thomist historian of Western philosophy such as Gilson writes a work such as *The Unity of Philosophical Experience*, it presents the history of Western philosophy in a manner that differs in essential ways from standard histories such as that of Bertrand Russell.

This observation also holds true for the study of the history of Islamic philosophy itself. As Moris mentioned, I have spent a lifetime crusading for studying Islamic philosophy on the basis of its own understanding of the nature of philosophy and its own conception of the philosophy of time and historical development and not on the basis of Western philosophies of history and the West's image of itself. Therefore, when Moris writes that according to me, "proper appreciation of the Islamic philosophical tradition can only be gained if Islamic philosophy is viewed on the basis of its own historical development," I would add that, in addition, Islamic philosophy should be studied on the basis of its own understanding of the flow of time itself in addition to its outward historical development. Islamic philosophy must be studied according to a perspective that is more than merely historical since Islamic thought does not simply identify philosophical truth with its historical manifestations, which for it are crystallizations in time of essentially non-temporal visions of the truth. For me the history of philosophy is certainly important, but the significance of various schools of traditional philosophy cannot be reduced to their historical significance; for in the last resort truth has no history while its manifestations in history are keys for understanding of stages of the crystallization of non-temporal truths in a given stage of history. The Islamic view of the history of philosophy may be said to be based on the historial and not the historical view if the latter is simply identified with historicism. For traditional Islamic thought, historical events and facts are important on their own level but philosophy cannot simply be reduced to its history.

To this end I have developed over the years, for a period with Henry Corbin and for some time by myself, a conception of the development of Islamic philosophy which is both historical and meta-historical as seen in one of my earliest books, *Three Muslim Sages*, and further elaborated in many later works. I have always remained aware of the centrality for classical Muslim thinkers of the saying attributed to ʻAlī ibn Abī Ṭālib, "Look at what has been said and not who has said it," a view which was held strongly by my traditional teachers of Islamic philosophy in Persia such as ʻAllāmah Ṭabāṭabāʼī. There is a compilation of the sayings of ʻAlī by a scholar of the 4th/10th century by the name of Sayyid Sharīf al-Raḍī and many Western orientalists have refused to accept the authenticity of these sayings precisely because they were compiled long after the death of ʻAlī. One day in the '60s Corbin asked ʻAllāmah Ṭabāṭabāʼī the following question: "As a leading authority on Shiʻite philosophy and religious thought, what argument would you provide to prove that the *Nahj al-balāghah* ("The Path of Eloquence"), [that is, the collection of sayings of ʻAlī,] is by the first Imām ʻAlī?" The venerable master of Islamic philosophy answered, "for us the person who wrote the *Nahj al-balāghah is* ʻAlī even if he lived a century ago."

I have tried through my writings to remain faithful to this ahistorical vision of Islamic philosophy with its emphasis upon schools and perspectives which crystallize at particular periods and transcend individual philosophers. At the same time I have sought to provide careful historical treatments of the figures and issues of Islamic philosophy. I believe that the methodology which I have developed in this domain not only remains faithful to Islamic philosophy's vision of its "own philosophical development," but also remains true to Islamic philosophy's conception of the supra-temporal nature of philosophical truth and the nature of the flow of historical time itself.

As for the usage of the term "Arabic philosophy" instead of "Islamic philosophy," the author writes that "for a long time Western scholars considered and referred to Islamic philosophy as 'Arabic philosophy' after its main language of discourse and the ethnic background of some of its philosophers." Actually in the Middle Ages, when the West was so intensely interested in Islamic thought, ethnic or national background was of no consequence whatsoever, but religion and the language of discourse were of central concern. That is why an Englishman such as Roger Bacon was considered a Latin writer although ethnically he was not Latin at all. It was modern Arab nationalism which from the late 13th/19th century began to turn this medieval linguistic usage into an ethnic one for its own ideological purposes and insisted on propagating the old usage of the term "Arabic" in a new context in which it then gained strong ethnic and nationalistic connotations. Had the medieval West encountered the Persian zone of Islamic civilization and writings in Persian directly, the usage of terms such as "Arabic philosophy," "Arabic science," and so on, would most likely have been altered. In any case, Persia not only was in the past but remains to this day the central homeland where the Islamic philosophical tradition continues to be fully alive and active.

Moris speaks of the Islamic philosophers being influenced by both Graeco-Alexandrian sources and by the "tenets of their religion." I need to expand somewhat here on what "tenets" really are embraced while agreeing in general with her assessment. Remembering what has been already said about revelation being both the source for Islamic philosophy and providing the objective cadre for intellection of the truths contained in the inner message of revelation, I must emphasize here again the inner or esoteric dimension of revelation in relation to Islamic philosophy. It must not be forgotten that the first Islamic philosophical text antedating al-Kindī is the mysterious *Umm al-kitāb* ("Archetypal Book") of Ismā'īlī origin and inspiration, which purports to be the fruit of a discourse of a disciple with the fifth Shi'ite Imām, Muḥammad al-Bāqir, who represents Islamic esoterism. Later on Nāṣir-i Khusraw, another Ismā'īlī philosopher, clearly identifies true philosophy or *ḥikmah* with the truth (*al-ḥaqīqah*) which lies at the heart of religion. Nor was this view confined to Ismā'īlī philosophers, but can be found among many other philosophers.

It is interesting to note, as also mentioned by Moris, that the link between Islamic philosophy and the esoteric teachings of Islam became ever more strengthened in later centuries culminating with Mullā Ṣadrā, who, more than any other philosopher before or since, drew from the inner message of the Quran and *Ḥadīth* as well as from the esoteric sayings of the Shi'ite Imāms as contained in such sources as the *Uṣūl al-kāfī* of al-Kulaynī. As far as the link between Islamic philosophy and Islamic esoterism is concerned, there are those who claim that the gnosis (*al-ma'rifah/'irfān*) of Ibn 'Arabī and his school, which is the most extensive formulation of Islamic esoteric doctrines and metaphysics in the annals of Islamic history, is also the most veritable expression of Islamic philosophy, while my view is that not only Ibn 'Arabian metaphysics, but all the different schools of Islamic philosophy from the Ismā'īlī to the *mashshā'ī* to the *ishrāqī*, to the theoretical and doctrinal teachings of Ibn 'Arabī to Mullā Ṣadrā's *al-ḥikmat al-muta'āliyah*, are authentic dimensions and perspectives of Islamic philosophy. I insist that the link between Islamic philosophy and the Quranic revelation is to be found essentially in the inner teachings of the revelation and the Islamic philosophers' understanding of those inner teachings in which the role of the intellect, as traditionally understood, is central. This assertion does not mean, however, that the Islamic revelation, even in its outward form, did not provide knowledge and define important issues for Islamic philosophies on the more formal plane, such as the relation between faith and reason, the philosophy of law, and political and ethical philosophy, whose framework was provided by the world created by Islam and within which the Islamic philosophers philosophized. Nor does my assertion in any way detract from the truth that the very existence of the revelation as a source of knowledge posed a challenge for those philosophers concerned with questions of epistemology, while certain specific teachings of the revelation such as cosmogenesis and corporeal resurrection, with which the Greek predecessors of Islamic philosophy did not concern themselves, opened new areas of philosophical investigation for Islamic thinkers on the basis of *knowledge* provided by the revelation.

Also it should be mentioned here that it was the sapiental nature of Islamic esoterism, and also the actualization of intellection made possible in the sense understood by Muslim thinkers, that provided the gnostic knowledge necessary for Islamic philosophers to view the Greek pre-Socratics as the *illuminati* and esoteric philosophers that they actually were (rather than fathers of rationalistic philosophy and science as they came to be seen later in the West). It is amazing how accounts of such figures as Pythagoras, Empedocles and Parmenides, as rediscovered through the most recent examination of texts and archaeological evidence—accounts which go beyond the interpretations that came to be widely accepted with Aristotle—are so close to accounts of the thought of these figures provided by such classical Islamic philosophers as Suhrawardī and Shahrazūrī. It might be said that the light of the revelation shining upon the mind of Islamic philosophers and the gnostic (*ʻirfānī*) knowledge made available through the Islamic revelation enabled them to see deeper elements of not only their own religion but also enabled them to gain a vision into the inner sense of the teachings of the Graeco-Alexandrian philosophers to whom they were heirs.

The author writes "that which came to an end with the death of Ibn Rushd . . . is not Islamic philosophy, but rather the influence of Islamic philosophy . . . in the West." While I concur completely with this view as far as it goes, I believe that it fails to mention something else which also came to an end with the death of Ibn Rushd, and that is philosophy in the technical sense of the term in the Arabic part of the Islamic world, except for Iraq. After Ibn Rushd, a few philosophers such as Ibn Sabʻīn and Ibn Khaldūn appeared in the Arab world. But after the 6th/12th century in the Arab world, philosophy in its technical Islamic sense of *falsafah* flowed for the most part like a stream into two different seas, one Sufism and the other theology (*kalām*), both of which became themselves more "philosophical" after Ibn Rushd. Islamic philosophy survived and in fact was revived in the Eastern lands of Islam, especially Persia, but also in Muslim India and the Ottoman world, but not in the Western lands of *dār al-islām* or the Arab world. Those in the Arab world who were interested in philosophical discourse after Ibn Rushd turned to philosophical Sufism and/or philosophical *kalām*, which were certainly philosophical in the universal sense of the term without being *falsafah* in the technical way in which it has been used in the annals of the Islamic intellectual tradition.

In her concluding paragraph Moris mentions the profound responses of the Islamic philosophers to the combined demands of faith, of logical requirements, and of love for *sophia*. I would add that Islamic philosophy also contains responses to challenges of Greek philosophy, and, to a lesser extent, to Indian and pre-Islamic Persian thought. Furthermore, as a living philosophical tradition, Islamic philosophy (along with Sufi metaphysics) is better prepared than other schools of Islamic thought to respond to the considerable challenge of various schools of modern Western philosophy, a response that began in earnest during the twentieth century, especially its second half, and is bound to become more extensive in coming years.

S. H. N.

21

David B. Burrell

ISLAMIC PHILOSOPHICAL THEOLOGY

From Seyyed Hossein Nasr's formidable opus, I wish to focus on his Gifford Lectures: *Knowledge and the Sacred*,[1] complemented by some strategic essays on Mullā Ṣadrā and on Rūmī.[2] These two figures epitomize the modes of reflection which Nasr has been urging upon us, while the extended treatment of the Gifford Lectures, together with its venue, induced him to proceed in an expressly comparative manner, so that the *ishrāqī* mode of thought which he has long labored to commend to his Western interlocutors might initiate a mutually illuminating dialogue. That is precisely what these lectures have inspired in me, having been engaged for nearly twenty years in tracing the mutual understandings realized among Jewish, Christian, and Muslim thinkers, notably in those centuries in which their intellectual inquiries seem so convergent.[3] Yet the fresh light by which Seyyed Hossein Nasr's extended reflections illuminate that venture comes from his own Iranian (or *ishrāqī*) tradition, and allow him to mount a trenchant critique on what philosophy has become in the West—a critique remarkably parallel to that of Pierre Hadot, whose strategies I shall gratefully employ in offering a critical reading of Nasr's work. What is more, the opportunity to enter into this sort of dialogue is itself a welcome one, since it brings my own comparative work to a fine point by engaging a Muslim scholar who addresses us from the vantage point of an explicitly Muslim faith. Yet without the invitation to contribute to this symposium volume, I fear I would not otherwise have undertaken it, for while my respect for Nasr's work and esteem for him personally have hitherto allowed me profit greatly from his varied writings, I have foregone engaging with them critically.

Even more, when the Gifford Lectures first appeared I found myself put off by their mode of discourse, and so was unwilling to grapple with them out of that same respect and esteem. It took the commitment to enter into dialogue in this fashion to overcome my initial misgivings, and while these have not disappeared, they can now be articulated within the larger scope which the lectures themselves provide. Moreover, an intellectual encounter with the work of Mullā Ṣadrā, in preparation for a conference in Tehran in the spring of 1999, led me into the *ishrāqī* mode of thought which Nasr has long been urging upon us, eliciting a personal appreciation of those very perspectives. Finally, a word on the phrase "philosophical theology," which I offer as a counterpoint to Nasr's preferred "theosophy." I believe that it is quite impossible to employ the term "theosophy" in the West; indeed, Nasr's extended critical narrative in the first of the lectures will allow us to see why its resonances keep obscuring whatever sense one might wish to give it, given the recent history of its use. Moreover, I am unwilling to surrender the term "philosophy" which Socrates took such care to explicate for us in practice, as well as in Plato's articulation of that practice. Here is where Pierre Hadot's critique can complement that of Nasr, helping us recapture the term "philosophy" rather than abandon it for another. Yet I have expanded the single term to an inherently complementary phrase, "philosophical theology," in an endeavor to restore those very dimensions for which Nasr (and Hadot) strenuously argue.

The semantic structure of "philosophical theology" is close to the Arabic *iḍāfah* construction, which allows two nouns to function together, with one modifying the other, as in "family house." In such cases, a mutually modifying relation is set up for both terms in the "construct" relation binding them to each other. There are differences, of course, between the languages, as the comparison serves here to illustrate the English relationship of adjective to noun: "theology" is what we are doing, notably attempting to articulate the relation of the One to all-that-is; "philosophical" describes the mode we have adopted, since the realities which our inquiry involves cannot be understood except by employing the requisite intellectual tools. Yet the very juxtaposition of these two terms should also remind us that inquiries of this sort may look unfamiliar to philosophers and to theologians as well, for the result will be a genuine hybrid. In that respect, philosophical theology cannot be subsumed under "philosophy of religion," since that discipline pretends to submit faith-assertions to the generic criteria of philosophy, even as those are currently conceived, while our phrase emphasizes that we are doing *theology*. Yet our reflections may not be recognized as germane by theologians either, since most such thinkers in each of the Abrahamic traditions have little tolerance (or aptitude) for reflections which require them to penetrate the faith-avowals of the tradition in question by using conceptual tools which they rightly deem inadequate. Yet others of us—including myself with Nasr—realize that human inquiry into matters involving divinity can hardly dispense with such tools, even if those very inquiries will need to transform the tools themselves.[4]

I. THE GIFFORD LECTURES: *KNOWLEDGE AND THE SACRED*

So reason and faith will be mutually normative in such inquiries, as Nasr's effective presentation of his own *ishrāqī* tradition clearly displays. Indeed, it is for that mutual normativity which I find him reaching, a mutuality which the very terms he uses to articulate *scientia sacra* sometimes belie. There may indeed be a profound difference between my use of "faith" and Nasr's attempt to articulate the understanding for which *sacra scientia* seeks, yet I am not persuaded that the difference is one between Christian and Muslim understanding. In short, my critical observations will be temerarious enough to wonder whether Nasr's presentation does not surrender something of the uniqueness of his revelation to the norms of what he calls "intellectual intuition," an understanding only available to certain adepts (or "gnostics"), yet not clearly dependent upon the revelation which he himself vigorously espouses. He will insist that revelation is a *sine qua non* for such *gnosis*—"[man] needs revelation which alone can actualize the intellect in man and allow it to function properly" (148), yet his articulation of that *gnosis* avoids delineating how the human appropriation of revelation, faith, is essential to this unique mode of understanding. He avoids it, at least, until the final chapter—"Knowledge of the Sacred as Deliverance"—which finds "intellectual intuition" incomplete in the face of what he calls "realized knowledge" (311), which requires personal appropriation by way of "spiritual exercises" (Hadot's term).

So what this reader proposes to do is to reread the earlier lectures in the light of the final one, much as one could transform Aristotle's *Ethics* by allowing his later reflections on friendship to recast everything he says about the "magnanimous man." And the comparison is more than adventitious, for just as I believe that Aristotle's own arguments for virtue would be enhanced, if not transformed, by the relational perspective of the final books, I also find that Nasr's final chapter offers a way of integrating his earlier remarks about *gnosis* and its attributes more firmly in faith-traditions, precisely so as to honor the prescient reminders about *tradition* which animate his opening critical narrative on "Knowledge and Its Desacralization." The following three lectures offer (2) a constructive exposition of "tradition," (3) the way in which tradition informs endeavors to rediscover the sacred, and how this rediscovery (4) culminates in *scientia sacra*. What results is (5) a view of the place and role of human beings in the cosmos as well as (6) the cosmos itself, wherein (7) time is intrinsically related to eternity, as "traditional art" (which need not be "sacred art") so effectively displays (8). The penultimate lecture (9) offers a way of understanding the situation in which we currently live, yet which our various traditions did not have to face so acutely: that different traditions each claim to be the "right path" though we are rightly called to see them in relation to one another. Nasr offers what he calls "principial knowledge" as a way to make the latter possible, without adopting a facile relativism. I shall try to show that such *knowledge* is only possible in the light of the following final chapter, which effectively endorses Hadot's perspective of "spiritual exercises" as ingredient to an authentic philosophical grasp of such matters.

II. Nasr's Critical Narrative: "Knowledge and Its Descralization"

We are more amenable to Nasr's criticism of the Enlightenment philosophical paradigm now than when his lectures were delivered, as critics rush to occupy a place in a world expressly "postmodern." Yet those who "convert" too quickly find themselves carrying their modern presumptions along, concluding that if knowledge cannot be secured in Descartes's fashion, it cannot be secured at all. So in effect there can be nothing known, or in popular jargon: "anything goes." Such a reaction would be perfectly understandable to Nasr, who indeed shows us how things came to pass so that this reaction was nearly inevitable. Once "true philosophy" is betrayed, anything does go! Yet one can find the roots of the betrayal well on the other side of Descartes, in the "high scholasticism" which includes Aquinas and Bonaventure, as well as Duns Scotus:

> . . . these syntheses, especially the Thomistic one, tended to become over-rationalistic in imprisoning intuitions of a metaphysical order in syllogistic categories which were to hide, rather than reveal, their properly speaking intellectual rather than purely rational character. In fact, the purely sapiental aspect of medieval Christianity is reflected perhaps more directly in the medieval cathedrals and that central epiphany of Christian spirituality, the *Divine Comedy* of Dante, itself a literary cathedral, than in the theological syntheses which, while containing Christian Sophia, also tended to veil it. (KS 22)

This reading of medieval philosophical theology contains key terms which illuminate Nasr's own perspectives, which he amplifies by offering an alternative narrative emphasizing voices usually relegated to a minor role: Dionysius the Areopagite, Scotus Erigena, and Meister Eckhart, culminating in the fifteenth-century Nicholas of Cusa. What is truly disappointing is that Nasr only alludes (here and elsewhere) to Dante, since one senses that Dante's deliberate turn to the poetic already bespeaks a trenchant critique of the medieval tradition, which could have advanced Nasr's own argument in a constructive fashion.

The key contrasts in this exposition—"metaphysical intuitions" vs.

"syllogistic categories" and "intellectual" vs. "rational"—will serve to define Nasr's alternative of *Sophia* or "sapiental" understanding. He knows that the *intellectus/ratio* contrast was available to Aquinas as well, yet faults him for allowing the Aristotelian *ratio* to dominate, in the form of "syllogistic categories." And that indeed has been the Aquinas presented to recent generations in the "Thomistic" synthesis, yet more probing historical studies show another side to Aquinas, one far more beholden to Dionysius and less susceptible to being identified as Aristotelian.[5] In fact, it has become current to contrast Aquinas sharply with Duns Scotus (whereas Nasr places them in a row), and to recall how much of Aquinas was transmitted in Scotistic garb, largely through Suarez, to the world of Descartes and even of "Thomism."[6] Yet however that may be, Nasr is calling our attention to a dimension of medieval thought which allowed a view of philosophy to emerge which connected it with "pure reason," so obscuring if not ruling out what he identifies as "the essentially sacramental function of intelligence," which contends that we "need the illumination which proceeds from God . . . to think the truth" (KS 19). The operative contrast to "sacramental" would of course be "naturalistic," where all the presumptions of modernity come into play. Yet when Nasr himself lauds Augustine for preserving that "sacramental function," he explicitly praises Augustine "despite his emphasis upon faith as the key to salvation" (KS 19). The key term here is "faith" rather than "salvation," for Nasr is presuming here that what he calls the "supernaturally natural [or sacramental] function of the Intellect" (KS 35) will suffice for leading us to wisdom. In fact, he expressly contrasts this view with "the mainstream of Christian theology [which] insisted upon the *credo ut intelligam*, a formula later identified with St. Anselm, while limiting the function of intellection to that of a handmaid of faith rather than a mean of sanctification, which of course would not exclude the element of faith" (KS 36).

Yet can intellection, short of faith, be itself a "means of sanctification?" The thrust of chapters 1 through 9 says *yes*, while chapter 10 denies that it can: "Intellectual intuition, although a precious gift from Heaven, is not realized knowledge, [which] concerns not only the intelligence which is the instrument par excellence of knowing but also the will and the psyche. It requires the acquisition of spiritual virtues which is the manner in which man participates in that truth which is itself suprahuman" (KS 311). He goes on to delineate "realized knowledge" in terms redolent of "sanctification" and indeed of *faith*: it "resides in the heart, which is the principle of both the mind and the body and cannot but transform both the mind and the body. It is a light which inundates the whole being of man removing from him the veil of ignorance and clothing him in the robe of resplendent luminosity which is the substance of that knowledge itself" (KS 311). In fact Aquinas will delineate the way in which grace enhances "natural reason" in similar terms, albeit expressly beholden to an Aristotelian epistemology:

> Natural reason depends on two things: images derived from the sensible world and the natural intellectual light by which we make abstract intelligible concepts from these images. In both these respects human knowledge is helped by the revelation of grace. The light of grace strengthens the intellectual light and at the same time prophetic visions provide us with God-given images which are better suited to express divine things than those we receive naturally from the sensible world.[7]

The *visions* and *images* in question are not ocular but literary, provided in the scriptures themselves. Nasr's penchant for Platonism would prefer another beginning point than "the sensible world," of course, yet the price he pays for that is to claim a sanctifying role for intellect as such, and then to have to modify that claim by introducing the further perfection of a "realized knowledge" which envisages the whole person.

A cognate confusion attends his treatment of Nicholas of Cusa's account of *docta ignorantia* ["learned ignorance"], which he claims is "directed toward that partial form of knowledge which would seek to replace sacred knowledge as such. It applies to reason not to the intellect which *can know* the *coincidentia oppositorum*" (KS 25). So while "there is no doubt that the teachings of 'unknowing' or 'ignorance' represent a major strand of the sapiental dimension of the Christian tradition" (KS 26), nonetheless Nasr finds that emphasis strategic rather than substantive, since "Cusa, like the Christian sages before him, believes in Divine Wisdom which is accessible to man and which is identified with the Divine Word. This knowledge cannot, however, be attained except through being experienced or tasted. It is *sapientia* according to the etymological sense of the term" (KS 25). It does not seem accidental that there is no mention of faith here, for Nasr's concern is rather to show that "the Cusanian ignorance does not lead to . . . the denial of sacred knowledge [but] is a means of opening a path for the ray of gnosis to shine on a space already darkened by excessively rationalistic categories which seemed to negate the very possibility of unitive knowledge . . ." (KS 25). While his reading of Cusanus may be accurate in this context, it is colored by Nasr's own account of "unitive knowledge" which Cusanus may or may not have shared, and which in fact turns out to be incomplete in relation to "realized knowledge." Morever, as we have seen, what "realized knowledge" adds to "unitive knowledge" gives it a role quite similar to the role which faith plays in enhancing Aquinas's "natural reason."

It could well be, of course, that Nasr's shying away from explicit mention of *faith* reflects the considerable confusion which reigns in Christian theology in identifying the virtue of faith and the role it plays in enhancing human understanding. Yet *faith*, with its attendant practices, is integral to any tradition which traces its origins to a revelation, and which continues to mine that revelation in various ways which utilize both mind and heart. Moreover, what faith assures is an understanding complementary to that which either reason or intellect can attain, an understanding of the One which explicitly surpasses human understanding. For if this be not the case, then the crucial "distinction" between creator and creation is put in jeopardy.[8] That "distinction" dictates that "learned ignorance" must characterize any attempt at theological understanding of God and the ways of God, and not merely be a strategic moment. Aquinas argues for the indeterminate "*qui est* [the One who is]" (which for him came from Exodus 3:14) as the most appropriate name for God by reminding us how "in this life our minds cannot grasp what God is in himself; whatever way we have of thinking of him is a way of failing to understand him as he really is" (*ST* 1.13.11).[9] Would Nasr want to say that here Aquinas is privileging *ratio* [reason] over *intellectus* ["intellectual intuition"], which could indeed allow us to "grasp what God is in himself?" If so, then the knowing-by-faith which attends particular revelations and traditions would be superfluous. I cannot imagine that to be Nasr's own view, yet that is in fact the tenor of chapter 4: *Scientia Sacra*.

The key features of *scientia sacra* are "intellectual intuition," "intelligence," and "unitive knowledge," for "what caused this profound way of envisaging reality to become unintelligible and finally rejected in the West was the loss of that intellectual intuition which destroyed the sense of the mystery of existence and reduced the subject of philosophy from the study of the act of existence (*esto*) to the existent (*ens*)" (KS 137). Aquinas is expressly exempted from that move (cf. note 9), which in fact refers more aptly to Scotus and the scholastic tradition which read Aquinas through those lenses. What is really at stake, we shall see, is a reading of creation, so the intellectual response of those traditions which avow the free creation of the universe should be relevant here. Yet Nasr chooses to refer to creation in pejorative terms, by contrast with "unitive knowledge which sees the world not as separative creation but as manifestation that is united through symbols and the very ray of existence to the Source" (KS 137), contrasting this with "theological formulations which insist upon the hiatus between . . . the Creator and the world" (KS 138). Where I have followed Robert Sokolowski in insisting on "the distinction" of creator from creation, Nasr presumes that avowing creation introduces *separation* and *hiatus*. Yet the "distinction" in question is precisely unlike any disticntion within the universe, so need not entail separation or hiatus. Why must Nasr understand a creation-teaching in such terms?

Diverse traditions, of course, understand "theology" in different ways, and should Nasr simply have *kalām* in mind, one could understand the polemic here. Yet his range is expressly intercultural, so one suspects that the issue is more pointedly epistemological. For he does contend that "the metaphysical knowledge of unity comprehends the theological one in both a figurative and literal sense, while the reverse is not true" (KS 138), since "intelligence can know the Absolute and in fact only the Absolute is completely intelligible" (KS 143). Both statements taken together seem effectively to render faith otiose, and to subscribe to a *gnosis* quite independent of revelation, while the use of the term "Absolute" for "that Essence which is beyond all determination" (KS 140) is expressly credited to Frithjof Schuon, already identified in the Preface as Nasr's most intimate guide. Moreover, we are never told *how* "intelligence can know the Absolute," but it must presumably be in the same way that (for Cusanus) "the intellect . . . *can know* the *coincidentia oppositorum*" (KS 25). Were that to be the case, however, such knowledge would inherently resist formulation, though formulation may belong to reason rather than intelligence. Nasr does tend at this point to relativize all formulation to the realm of *māyā*, whereas "intelligence is a divine gift which pierces through the veil of *māyā* and is able to know reality as such. [For] the intellect is itself divine and only human to the extent that man participates in it" (KS 146–47). As a result, "intellection does not reach the truth as a result of profane thought or reasoning but through an a priori direct intuition of the truth" (KS 148).

If this be the metaphysical epistemology of such matters, however, other factors are relevant as well: "although the Intellect shines within the being of man, man is too far removed from his primordial nature [*fiṭrah*] to be able to make full use of this divine gift by himself. He needs revelation which alone can actualize the intellect in man and allow it to function properly" (KS 148). We will primarily be speaking here of "revelation in its esoteric dimension, [so that] rediscovering *scientia sacra* in the bosom of a tradition dominated by the presence of sacred scripture [will require] reviving spiritual exegesis" (KS 149). Yet, we are told, "*scientia sacra* envisages intelligence in its rapport not only with revelation in an external sense but also with the source of inner revelation which is the center of man, namely the heart" (KS 150), since

> human intelligence in its fullness implies the correct functioning of both the intelligence of the heart and that of the mind, the first being intuitive and the second analytical and discursive. . . . Mental formulation of the intuition received by the intelligence of the heart becomes completely assimilated by man and actualized through the activity of the mind. This is in fact one of the main roles of meditation in spiritual exercises, meditation being related to the activity of the mind. . . . The human being needs to exteriorize certain truths, in order to be able to interiorize, to analyze in order to synthesize, synthesis needing a phase of analysis. (KS 151)

Yet just how does revelation, and the faith-response proper to it, relate to what is now described as the "intelligence of the heart?" Can we say that this intelligence is in any way *informed* by the revelation which is needed to *actualize* it? The quick shift from revelation properly understood to the "center of man, the heart," has the effect of silencing that question.

Recalling Aquinas, it seems that the appropriate images do not need to be God-given, since they emerge in their proper symbolic expression from the heart itself. And such "symbols are ontological aspects of a thing, to say the least as real as the thing itself, and in fact that which bestows significance upon a thing within the universal order of existence." Indeed, "one can say that symbols reflect in the formal order archetypes belonging to the principial realm and that through symbols the symbolized is unified with its archetypal reality" (KS 153). What Nasr will call "principial knowledge" (in chapter 9) is here identified with a person's participation in the movement whereby intellect ingathers the many into their one source. So he will conclude this central chapter by reminding us that "traditional metaphysics or *scientia sacra* is not only a theoretical expression of the knowledge of reality. Its aim is to guide man, to illuminate him, and allow him to attain the sacred. . . . As theory it is planted as a seed in the heart and mind of man, a seed that if nurtured through spiritual practice and virtue becomes a plant which finally blossoms forth and bears fruit in which, once again, that seed is contained" (KS 154). In this sense, then, the movement toward truth is inherently dialectical and is said to involve spiritual practice and virtue, and not simply "intellectual intuition," which now becomes more like a seed. So the final word on *scientia sacra* signals its incompleteness:

> But if the first seed is theoretical knowledge, in the sense of *theoria* or vision, the second seed is realized gnosis, the realization of a knowledge which being itself sacred, consumes the whole being of the knower and, as the sacred, demands of man all that he is. That is why it is not possible to attain this knowledge in any way except by being consumed by it.

III. Five Lectures Leading up to "Realized Knowledge"

These final lines invite us to jump to the final chapter, where the "realized gnosis" introduced here is fully expounded, but that would require us to skip over five entire chapters! The two immediately following—"Man, Pontifical and Promethean," and "Cosmos as Theophany"—are interconnected, for the role of human beings as microcosm is central to our perceiving the cosmos itself as theophany. "Pontifical" is used in its etymological sense to suggest human being as the "bridge between Heaven and earth [who thereby] lives on a circle of whose Center he is always aware and which he seeks to reach in his life, thought and actions" (KS 160). This sense of what it is to be human is contrasted with the "Promethean man [who] is a creature of this world" (KS 161) and a product of the "excessively rigid Aristotelianization of Western thought in the thirteenth century identified by some with Averroes. This 'exteriorization' of Christian thought [was] followed by the secularization of science of the cosmos in the seventeenth century, itself a result of the 'naturalization' of Christian man as a well-contented citizen of this world" (KS 163). Nasr contrasts this proto-Nietszchean construction with that "primordial and plenary nature of man which Islam calls the 'Universal or Perfect Man' (*al-Insān al-kāmil*) and to which the sapiental doctrines of Graeco-Alexandrian antiquity also allude" (KS 166), "who is the mirror of the Divine Qualities and Names and the prototype of creation" (KS 168).

But this exalted human nature is only imperfectly realized in human beings, who thus need a revelation given them in their own language. So the actual "human state . . . gives a certain particularity to various revelations of the Truth while the heart of these revelations remains above all form. In fact, man himself is able to penetrate into that formless Essence through his intelligence sanctified by that revelation and even come to know that the formless Truth is modified by the form of the recipient according to the divine Wisdom and Will, God having Himself created that recipient which receives His revelation in different climes and settings" (KS 181). As presented here, revelation influences intellection by *sanctifying* it, coming as it does as a *grace*. So without these revelations, we must conclude, everything said about "intellectual intuition" will remain unactualized, as Nasr himself averred in the chapter dedicated to *scientia sacra* (KS 148). So human beings without revelations can only evidence their "nostalgia for the Sacred and the Eternal [by turning] to a thousand and one ways to satisfy this need" (KS 161), for "this basic nature of man . . . makes a secular and agnostic humanism impossible." Indeed, "the kind of humanism associated with the Promethean revolt of the Renaissance has led in a few centuries to the veritably infrahuman which threatens not only the human quality of life but the very existence of man on earth" (KS 181).

Nasr will treat the relation of the different revelations to one another in chapter 9: "Principial Knowledge and the Multiplicity of Sacred Forms," where the very title points to the way he will elaborate the suggestions offered here: that the heart of these revelations remains above all form. What Nasr's trenchant reiteration of his critique of modernity (now displayed in Promethean man) intimates here, however, is the need for revelation to recall human beings from the intellectual and moral meanderings which have in fact characterized what we called "the Enlightenment." That dynamic replays the central Muslim theme of *jāhiliyyah*, or the "time of ignorance" which characterizes human beings without divine revelation. Reprising his initial critique here also underscores the affinity of Nasr's alternative philosophical strategy with the animus animating a bewildering variety of "postmodern" approaches: reason without a living context will betray the very intellectual *eros* which animates human inquiry. I have consistently anticipated Nasr's identifying that context with faith, indeed his own Muslim faith, yet my anticipations seem blocked by an ambivalence regarding the precise role which faith plays in guiding intellect in its quest. Sometimes it seems that "intellectual intuition" would suffice were the human intellect able to be sufficiently unencumbered, in which case faith and the practices of faith would at best be needed to remove those obstacles; while at other times, the relationship seems more inherent, more intimately related to the inquiry itself, as "sanctifying" it.

IV. "Realized Knowledge" and Spiritual Exercises

I have proposed to resolve this ambiguity by reading these chapters (1 through 9) in the light of the final chapter: "Knowledge of the Sacred as Deliverance," where the inner dynamic of *scientia sacra* articulated at the end of chapter 4 is fulfilled in what he calls "realized knowledge." This is contrasted with "intellectual intuition" in that the former "concerns not only the intelligence which is the instrument par excellence of knowing but also the will and the psyche" (KS 311). Moreover, we are told that "realized knowledge resides in the heart, which is the principle of both the mind and the body and cannot but transform both the mind and the body" (KS 311). Here we are reminded of the classical "tripartite nature of the human being consisting of spirit, soul, and body" (KS 172), or even better, its image in "the human body . . . : the head, the body and the heart" (KS 174), already elaborated in chapter 5 on human being as microcosm. But how is "realized knowledge" *realized*? Pursuing this question makes it clear that Nasr himself appreciated just how misleading his previous exposition had been, for he insists: "To speak of sacred knowledge [*scientia sacra*] without mentioning the crucial importance of the virtues as the *conditio sine qua non* for the realization of this knowledge, is to misunderstand completely the traditional sapiental perspective" (KS 312). Indeed, the accompanying note makes this quite explicit: "If in this present study more accent has not been placed upon this question, it is because our subject has been knowledge itself in its rapport with the sacred. But one should not gain the impression that this knowledge can in any way be divorced from the moral and spiritual virtues which the traditional texts never cease to emphasize" (KS 329, n.10). Yet discerning readers will note that the ambiguity remains: what could "knowledge itself" be if *it* cannot be divorced from virtue? Or put another way, if knowledge without virtue cannot qualify as knowledge, then the implicit metaphor of marriage must be taken in the strongest possible sense in which either spouse cannot be themselves without the other. It is here that Nasr could profit immensely from the work of Pierre Hadot, notably for the way he unveils the critical role which "spiritual exercises" played in ancient philosophy to supply the context which Nasr wants to display in "realized knowledge."[10]

That context is, of course, supplied by the intellectual and moral virtues. It can perhaps best be illustrated by invoking another thinker in the Christian tradition who should prove enlightening in his own way, Aurelius Augustine. Readers of the *Confessions* steeped in modernity find it odd when, in his struggle for intellectual clarification detailed in the seventh book, he feels it necessary to decide between Platonism and Christianity. Why can't he think of himself as a Christian Platonist; certainly many have done just that? Yet Pierre Hadot's familiarity with the demands which ancient philosophy makes on philosophers themselves reminds us that they could only see this mode of thinking as involving the entirety of a person's relation to the universe, and so comprehending not just a "set of beliefs" but a way of life as well: a way of life embodied in a set of practices which embraces one's life and forms one's attitudes. Now this is precisely what any liturgical formation is intended to do: introduce us into a world which should become more and more an alternative to the world in which we live; indeed, (in Christian terms) into the "kingdom of God." If the Platonism of his time pretended, as philosophies tend to do, to offer a complete comprehension of the universe, then it would come replete with practices as well, and some of these would inevitably clash with the mystagogy of Christian initiation. That is, at least, a plausible reconstruction of what faced Augustine. What is more telling for us is that we needed to reconstruct our own conception of philosophy to appreciate his dilemma, yet that reconstruction may bring us closer to an authentic understanding of the role of philosophy in human existence than the modernist frame of a set of beliefs (or "propositional attitudes")—a presumption which Nasr has so effectively exposed.

Yet more constructively, however, can we mine this same thinker for a positive conception of the mutual clarification which reason and faith can bring to one another? The answer is contained in an attentive reading of the *Confessions* themselves, for the final word is not one of opposition, but one which reshapes the Plotinian directions which initially gave Augustine a way entering the world of spirit as the domain of mind and of mind's internal good, God. That reshaping will follow the form of the incarnation of the Word made flesh, to bring human beings into a tensive relation between time and eternity, flesh and spirit, precisely where Platonists tend to oppose them.[11] What allowed Augustine so to reconceive philosophy and its role was the fresh context which revelation provided, an illumination which the *Confessions* puts in disarmingly simple terms: "the mystery of the Word made flesh I had not begun to guess. . . . None of this is in the Platonist books" (7.19,21). He would not even be able to "guess" such a mystery, of course; nor indeed can we, for that very thought exceeds our imagination of what is possible—even when imagination of what is possible is the very thing for which philosophy has long prided itself! These final chapters of Book 7 of the *Confessions* offer a paradigm for "faith seeking understanding," the celebrated formula of Augustine's which animated the work of medieval philosophical theologians beginning with Anselm, and also give us a commentary which presents that effort in a more favorable light than Nasr's reference to the cognate formula: *credo ut intelligam* (KS 36).

Book 7 of the *Confessions* documents the discovery of the idiom which Augustine needed to find a proper way of conceptualizing God, not as another being among beings, but as the "life of the life of my soul" or the wisdom which grants wisdom to the wise—in short, the source of all that is, and hence God should never be thought of as standing over against anything that is.[12] It was probably the *Enneads* of Plotinus which offered Augustine this idiom, and chapter 16 notes why it recommended itself: "I asked myself why I approved of the beauty of bodies, whether celestial or terrestrial, and what justification I had for giving an unqualified judgment on mutable things. . . . In the course of this inquiry why I made such value judgments as I was making, I found the unchangeable and authentic eternity of truth to transcend my mutable mind" (7.16).[13] The text goes on to describe how he appropriated that idiom for his own quest:

> And so step by step I ascended from bodies to the soul which perceives through the body, and from there to its inward forces, . . . [and] from there again I ascended to the power of reasoning to which is attributed the power of judging deliverances of the bodily senses. This power, which in myself I found to be mutable, raised itself to the level of its own intelligence, and . . . at that point it had no hesitation in declaring that the unchangeable is preferable to the changeable, since unless it could somehow know this, there would be no certainty in preferring it to the mutable. So in the flash of a trembling glance it attained to that which is. At that moment I saw your "invisible nature understood through the things which are made" [Rom 1:20] (7.16).

It should be clear how intimately this description relies on the Neoplatonic structure of the mind's capacity to return to its origin, and equally clear how cognate these passages are with Nasr's presentation of "knowledge itself."

Yet a further consideration will actively structure Augustine's own search for the truth. Chapter 7 of the *Confessions* remains incomplete without its companion chapter 8, as the closing words of the previous chapter intimate: "It is one thing to descry that land of peace from a wooded hilltop and, unable to find the way to it, struggle on through trackless wastes where traitors and runaways, captained by their prince, who is 'lion and serpent' [Ps. 91:13] in one, lie in wait to attack. It is another thing to follow the high road to that land of peace, the way that is defended by the care of the heavenly Commander" (7.21). Rhetorical flourish, indeed, yet to appreciate what it takes to live our way into that which we have apparently understood is to grasp the significance of "spiritual exercises." In what do these consist? In practices, of course, which cannot themselves be contained in a text, but chapter 8 does occupy itself with what Augustine then did: he encountered individuals in situations similar to his own, in stories and even in stories imbedded within stories—as was the case with Ponticianus, "who held an important imperial post in Africa," recounting how reading Athanasius's life of Anthony had moved him to take the step he did (8.6). Then follows a telling set of reflections on *doing* under the rubric of *willing*, where we are reminded that while we can move our body in the example of bending our knees—perhaps to pray?—we cannot move our own will; we cannot will to will! Yet that does not dispense us from finding the proper exercises which will allow Another to move our will freely. Chapter 8 outlines the steps involved by two relevant "spiritual exercises:" responding to the invitation as presented in the lives of other people, notably friends; as well as hearing the words of revelation as inviting an inner resonance and response. The first presages the role of community in structuring our own response, intimating the continuing efforts involved in becoming part of any communal endeavor. The second uses revelation as the present vehicle for that grace which allows us to receive when we can no longer actively will: "and the light of confidence flooded into my heart" (8.12).

Are these observations too explicitly Christian to make contact with Nasr's intent? Certainly Augustine's remarks about *incarnation* will be, yet Islamic attention to the Quran as the Word of God made Arabic, and to the *umma* as the living context for guidance along the "straight path," as well as Sufi insistence on the need for a *pir* or personal guide, all conspire to construct a context analogous to the one Augustine forged in chapter 8.[14] Moreover, these living analogies are hardly foreign to Nasr's life and practice. One suspects that what kept him from introducing the lived context of the final chapter, indeed, from outlining in greater detail the requirements for "realized knowledge" throughout the preceding lectures, could well have been the Enlightenment presuppositions built into the Gifford Lectures themselves. Here Nasr's critique of Aquinas, for whom he also shows immense respect, might be directed to his own efforts in *Knowledge and the Sacred*. Recall how he found that Aquinas's preoccupation with syllogistic reasoning or conceptual clarity tended to obscure Aquinas's own commitment to a sapiental tradition, leading Nasr to query sadly: "Had Thomism continued to be interpreted by a Meister Eckhart, the intellectual destiny of the West would have been different" (KS 37). To which I would respond: Amen! Yet Aquinas's efforts at clarity had a role to fulfill, as Nasr explicitly conceived his lectures in the Gifford mode to be fulfilling a specific role, indeed that of "being the first Muslim and the first Oriental to have the occasion to deliver [them]" (KS vii). Not that Nasr pulled any punches; his critique of the Enlightenment mode is trenchant and telling, and probably less well-received in 1981 than it would be now. Yet may it be that he left his own reliance on faith and revelation under-expressed, in an effort to meet a mode of discourse expressly identified with an eighteenth-century model of "natural theology?"[15] I leave that question to my interlocutor, as yet further testimony to how much these lectures have informed my own cognate inquiry, and as a way of displaying to others how much Muslims and Christians have to learn from one another in our shared attempts to show how faith can be a way of knowing. A brief look at the two figures whom Nasr himself finds paradigmatic will complete this grateful response to his work.

Two Paradigmatic Islamic Thinkers: Rūmī and Mullā Ṣadrā

These two thinkers are quite different from one another in their mode of presentation, yet they are brought together here for their formative presence in Seyyed Hossein Nasr's life and thought. Jalāl al-Dīn Rūmī (604/1207–672/1273) "was born in a major centre of Persian culture, Balkh, from Persian-speaking parents and was the product of that Islamic Persian culture which in the seventh/thirteenth century dominated the whole of the eastern lands of Islam and to which the present day Persians as well as Turks, Afghans, Central Asian Muslims and the Muslims of the Indo-Pakistani subcontinent are heir." His formation allowed him to "master . . . both the *Sharī'ite* sciences and Sufism" by the time he was thirty-three years old, when he "established a circle around him in Qonya . . . and was occupied with teaching the religious sciences." A few years later his life "was transformed through his encounter with that mysterious and powerful figure Shams al-Dīn Tabrīzī,"[16] which launched Rūmī himself into composing in poetry—a step which "transformed the history of Persian literature" (IAS 119). His *Mathnawī*, translated into English by Nicholson in eight volumes, presents an epic poetic work, whose only western analogue would be Dante's *Divina Comedia*. Nasr reminds us that this work is in effect a commentary on the Quran (KS 150), and does so poetically in such a way as to "reflect nearly all earlier works of Islamic masters from Quranic commentaries to the Sufi treatises of Sanā'ī, 'Aṭṭār, and Ibn 'Arabī" (IAS 120). As we find with Dante, Rūmī's massive learning is refracted through a poetic mode, designed expressly to assist readers' interiorizing the teaching. It is this characteristic above all which qualifies him as a paradigm of *scientia sacra* for Nasr, and merits his inclusion in a work elucidating Islamic art and spirituality.

Time, space, and ignorance prevent me from making anything more of Rūmī's poetic genius in the *Mathnawī*, but a glance at his *Discourses* reveals a structure similar to the eighth book of Augustine's *Confessions*: a plethora of stories designed to meet persons on their way and insinuate directions to take to set them on the "straight path."[17] While Dante's epic poem was structured as a journey of faith, one might say that any poetic expression is crafted so as to intercept us as journeyers, and give momentary expression to the station to which we have arrived, suggesting as well a direction to the next. The episodic character of the stories contained in Rūmī's *Discourses* serve a similar purpose: to help us articulate where we have come and whither we are headed. And the journey must be a journey of faith, for if the way could be articulated we would be in possession of a map, and stories of this sort would prove at most encouraging, but have little to do with showing us the way. Here we have a further argument for understanding "realized knowledge" in the way suggested: as the product of steps taken in response to the call of revelation, heard personally, to undertake a path in trust.

Together with Shihāb al-Dīn Suhrawardī, whose work he both assimilated and criticized, Ṣadr al-Dīn Shīrāzī [Mullā Ṣadrā] (980/1572–1050/1640) represents the translation of Islamic philosophy to the east from its western migration to Andalusia (and Ibn Rushd). A Persian philosopher of the Savafid period, Mullā Ṣadrā appropriated the perspectives of Ibn 'Arabī into a mode of philosophizing which became identified with *ḥikmat al-ishrāq*, or Eastern wisdom, the title of Suhrawardī's major work on which Mullā Ṣadrā commented. Like his mentor, Mullā Ṣadrā sought to articulate a vision of the universe together with its divine origins. Where he differed was in insisting that the connection (as well as "the distinction") between existing things and their source is displayed in their very existence:

> Now contingent beings, [that is, those not necessary in themselves], need something proper to them [*dhuwāt*] constituting what they are in themselves [*huwiyyāt*], for should one consider them apart from the One who originates them by that very fact they must be considered to be empty and impossible. [That factor proper to them, then, must be] the act constituted by the One who originates them (*Kitāb al-mashā'ir* par. 42).[18]

So the existence proper to contingent things is also what links them to "the One who originates them."

Yet the mode of knowing which connects creatures with their source can easily escape philosophers, since a thing's *existing* is precisely what makes it the individual which it is, and the reality of individual existing things seems ever to elude philosophy:

> . . . we say that it is not possible to attain to knowledge of the precise particularity of a mode of existence unless its very individuality be unveiled [*mushāhadah*], and that cannot be realized without some kind of unveiling of the cause of its emanation. That is why they say that knowing what possesses a cause is only attained by knowing its cause. Ponder this well! (*Kitāb al-mashā'ir*, par 92).

The "unveiling" required to capture the uniqueness of *wujūd* signals that we are in the logical domain of a creator/creation relation. For to speak of things as created implies some knowledge, however imperfect, of their being created and hence of a Creator. So it would follow that even to perceive the uniquely non-conceptual character of *wujūd/esse* would require an "unveiling" analogous to the Sufi "knowing" [*ma'rifah*] of God as *al-Ḥaqq* [the True Reality]. Yet knowing as "unveiling" cannot be equated with that knowing which has dominated modern treatises on epistemology, as Nasr's opening critique showed so clearly. Indeed, while it seems on first glance to be identified with what he calls "intellectual intuition," we have also seen how, humanly speaking, that *gnosis* can only be realized by way of spiritual exercises. So Mullā Ṣadrā can be seen as completing what his mentor Suhrawardī began: a recapitulation of Islamic philosophy into a fresh context, that of the Sufi disciplines of heart as well as mind; and doing so precisely by accentuating the surprising reality of each individual thing's existing. Indeed, such respect for the cognate disciplines of the heart is what philosophy has come to mean in Islam, Nasr would remind us, as his predilection for Mullā Ṣadrā displays.

DAVID BURRELL

UNIVERSITY OF NOTRE DAME (USA)
MARCH 1999

NOTES

1. Nasr, *Knowledge and the Sacred* (Albany: State University of New York Press, 1989), hereafter cited as "KS."

2. The essays on Mullā Ṣadrā [Ṣadra al-Dīn Shīrāzī] can be found in his collection *Islamic Life and Thought* (Albany: State University of New York Press,

1981), 158–81, and the essays on Rūmī in his *Islamic Art and Spirituality* (Albany: State University of New York Press, 1987), 114–47.

3. See my *Knowing the Unknowable God: Ibn Sina, Maimonides, Aquinas* (Notre Dame Ind.: University of Notre Dame Press, 1986).

4. See my contribution to the *Blackwell Companion to Theology*, ed. Gareth Jones: "Theology and Philosophy" (Oxford: Blackwell, 1999).

5. Notably, Edward Booth, *Aristotelian Aporetic Ontology in Islamic and Christian Writers* (Cambridge: Cambridge University Press, 1985); and for a more systematic treatment, see Rudi te Velde, *Participation and Substantiality in Thomas Aquinas* (Leiden: Brill, 1950).

6. See the telling references to this transition in John Milbank, *The Word Made Strange: Theology, Language, Culture* (Oxford: Blackwell, 1997), and Catherine Pickstock, *After Writing: The Liturgical Consummation of Philosophy* (Oxford: Blackwell, 1998), as well as my "Aquinas and Scotus: Contrary Patterns for Philosophical Theology," in Bruce D. Marshall, ed., *Theology and Dialogue: Essays in Honor of George Lindbeck* (Notre Dame, Ind.: University of Notre Dame Press, 1990), 105–30.

7. *Summa Theologica* 1.12.13. Henceforth abbreviated as "*ST*"; I shall regularly use the translation of Herbert McCabe, O.P., in the Blackfriars edition (New York: McGraw-Hill, 1965).

8. For a lucid presentation of "the distinction" of creator from creation as decisive for Christian theology, see Robert Sokolowski, *God of Faith and Reason* (Notre Dame, Ind.: University of Notre Dame Press, 1982/Washington, D.C.: Catholic University of America Press, 1995), as well as my attempt to show this "distinction" operative in each of the Abrahamic faiths: "The Christian Distinction Celebrated and Expanded," in John Drummond and James Hart, eds., *The Truthful and the Good* (Dordrecht: Kluwer Academic Publishers, 1996), 191–206.

9. This statement, which recurs in Aquinas, supports Nasr's positive notation regarding his work: "One can interpret Thomistic metaphysics which begins and ends with *esse* as including the notion of the real in its completely unconditioned and undetermined sense. . . . From this point of view one can assert that despite the sensualist epistemology of St. Thomas . . . Thomism contains in its dogmatic contents truths of a truly metaphysical nature which reflect knowledge of a principial order and which can serve as support for metaphysical contemplation" (156, n. 15).

10. Pierre Hadot's original work, *Exercises spirituels et philosophie antique* (2nd ed. 1987) is now out of print, but an excellent summary of his thought is available in his *Qu'est-ce que la philosophie antique?* (Paris: Gallimard, 1995) and a superb collection of his articles has been translated and presented by Arnold Davidson, *Philosophy as a Way of Life* (Oxford: Blackwell, 1995).

11. For an enlightening view of Augustine reversing Neoplatonic tendencies, see John Cavadini, "Time and Ascent in *Confessions* XI," in *Collectanea Augustiniana 2: Presbyter Factus Sum*, ed. J. Lienhard, E. Muller, R. Teske (New York: Peter Lang, 1993), 171–85. For another essay on the intrinsically narrative character of his thought, see James Wetzel, *Augustine and the Limits of Virtue* (Cambridge: Cambridge University Press, 1992).

12. For an illuminating discussion of the linguistic-conceptual apparatus indispensable to articulating God as "distinct from" creation, yet in a way which forbids us to think of God as something else in the universe, see Kathryn Tanner, *God and Creation in Christian Theology* (New York: Blackwell, 1988).

13. For a discussion of Augustine's sources, see Henry Chadwick's translation (which I shall use throughout) of the *Confessions* (Oxford: Oxford University Press, 1991), xix.

14. See my suggestions for such interfaith analogies in *Freedom and Creation in Three Traditions* (Notre Dame, Ind.: University of Notre Dame Press, 1993), 171–83.

15. See Alasdair MacIntyre's Preface to his Gifford Lectures, which raises this question explicitly: *Three Rival Versions of Moral Enquiry* (Notre Dame, Ind.: University of Notre Dame Press, 1990).

16. Nasr, *Islam Art and Spirituality*, op. cit., pp. 114–18, hereafter "IAS."

17. A. J. Arberry, *Discourses of Rūmī* (London: John Murray, 1961).

18. The Arabic text has been published by Henry Corbin under the title of his accompanying translation: *Le Livre des pénétrations métaphysiques* (Tehran: Institut Franco-Iranien/Paris: Adrien-Maisonneuve, 1964); Nasr has offered an annotated bibliography of his writings in *Recherches d'Islamologie* (Louvain: Peeters, 1977), 261–71. I have translated this passage for a comparative essay on Aquinas and Mullā Ṣadrā on "The Primacy of *esse/wujūd* in Philosophical Theology" for the International Mullā Ṣadrā Conference, Tehran, 1999.

REPLY TO DAVID B. BURRELL

Professor Burrell is not only a distinguished Islamicist but also a Catholic theologian as several of his important comparative theological and philosophical studies reveal. He is in fact heir to men such as Louis Massignon and Louis Gardet who were both outstanding scholars of Islamic thought and Catholic thinkers. Burrell seems to be especially a successor to Gardet who, more than Massignon (who was an expert in Sufism), dealt with comparative Islamic and Christian philosophical and theological themes. And like Gardet, Burrell possesses deep knowledge of Thomism and has not left the grand synthesis of St. Thomas aside as have a number of Catholic modernists. His essay dealing with Islamic philosophical theology must in fact be seen in light of his background as a Catholic theologian rooted in the Thomistic tradition and his command of important aspects of Islamic thought, which he, like Gardet, has been limited mostly to the line of al-Fārābī, Avicenna, al-Ghazzālī, and Averroes. His encounter with the *Ishrāqī* School within the Islamic intellectual tradition, with which he identifies me, is in a sense a new step for Burrell himself in the field of Islamic thought. In any case, this essay is written from the perspective of faith as well as philosophy and is very valuable in bringing up certain issues in my thought with which I have not dealt elsewhere in this volume.

Burrell pleads at the beginning for the usage of the term "philosophical theology" rather than "theosophy" whose "resonances keep obscuring whatever sense one might wish to give it, given the recent history of its use." Yet, he also accepts that in order to use the term "philosophy" we must resuscitate its original meaning or "recapture" the term, to use Burrell's formulation. Now, I have great sympathy for Pierre Hadot's critique and firmly believe, as he does, in the necessity of spiritual practice as a complement to mental activity in order for a person to be a philosopher in the original and time-honored sense of the term. But for that very reason, I do not think that "recapturing" the term "philosophy" in its authentic sense is in any way easier than rendering to "theosophy" its original meaning and washing away all the unfortunate accretions that have been added to it in recent times.

I believe that in every integral tradition, whether it be Jewish, Christian, Islamic, Hindu, Buddhist, Confucian, or otherwise, there must exist something corresponding to what in the Christian tradition is called theology, something to philosophy in the traditional Aristotelian sense and something to what in the West has been called gnosis, *theosis*, esoterism, theosophy or sometimes mystical theology, and especially more recently as mystical philosophy. In Islam we have *kalām, falsafah/ḥikmah* (the term *ḥikmah* having several levels of meaning) and *ma'rifah/'irfān* just to cite an example. There are of course also schools that combine some or all of these perspectives together. To substitute philosophical theology for theosophy as suggested by Burrell might avoid the negative connotations associated with the term "theosophy" in the minds of some readers, but also it leaves the impression of being precisely "a genuine hybrid" to which he himself refers. Since the third category which I have called gnosis, *theosis*, and theosophy disappeared from the mainstream intellectual scene of the West during the past few centuries, it is natural that for those used to only the categories of philosophy and theology, philosophical theology, as used by Burrell, would appear as a hybrid, and here lies my criticism. If he uses this term to replace that kind of knowledge which I call theosophy or gnosis, then there is the major problem that principial knowledge, or gnosis, which is an independent mode of knowledge, is reduced to a hybrid which it certainly is not. Moreover, this kind of knowledge cannot be equated to either theology or philosophy, even in its traditional Aristotelian and medieval sense, unless we go back to the Pythagorean and Parmenidean definition of philosophy. That is why I have sought to revive the terms gnosis and theosophy to demonstrate that what I am dealing with as *scientia sacra* is not theology nor is it philosophy as this term is understood today or was understood even in its everyday sense by an Averroes or Duns Scotus.

This situation is quite clear in the Islamic intellectual tradition where not only the distinctions mentioned above are widely known, but also many authors have distinguished between *falsafah* and *ḥikmah*. I have written extensively on this subject in many of my works, especially those dealing with Suhrawardī and Mullā Ṣadrā, and explained why I translate *ḥikmah* as theosophy when it is used in relation to the thought of such figures. But even in the domain of Islamic philosophy, once I made these distinctions clear, I did not remain completely rigid in my terminology. When necessary, I have used the term Islamic philosophy in the most general sense embracing both *falsafah* and *ḥikmah*. And yet, those who have read my works know that what we call philosophy in the case of Suhrawardī or Mullā Ṣadrā is not exactly the same thing as the term used in reference to Avicenna (in his Peripatetic works) and Averroes. The clarification of terminology is a long and painful process and I do not wish to delve any more into it here. But it was necessary to make these comments in response to Burrell's proposal to employ the term "philosophical theology." In any case, despite differences in our use of terminology, there is no doubt that the kind of knowledge with which he is concerned and which he calls philosophical theology is close to, if not identical with, what I have described by other names. I am also in complete agreement with Burrell that human inquiry into knowledge of the Divinity needs the proper intellectual and philosophical tools which have to be transformed in such a way as to be worthy of serving as means for the carrying out of such an exalted task.

The heart of Burrell's criticism and commentary upon my views has to do with the relation between knowledge and intellection on the one hand and faith on the other. Before turning to answer him point by point, I wish to summarize my views about this complicated situation by saying that intellect and spirit are two sides of the same reality in the perspective from which I speak. In Islamic metaphysics in fact *al-rūḥ* or Spirit and *al-'aql* or Intellect are often equated and reference is made to the sayings of the Prophet, "The first thing that God created was *al-rūḥ*" and also "The first thing that God created was *al-'aql*." Intellection, as I understand it, is to the human microcosm what revelation is to the macrocosm, and in order for inward intellection to be efficacious and become totally actualized there is need of acceptance of revelation, which means having faith. Sapience at once relies on faith for its full flowering and illuminates faith from "blindness" to luminosity and vision. The intellect is a supernaturally natural presence within human beings and is itself sacred, but it needs the grace emanating from revelation to become fully realized within the being of man. If there are exceptions, they are there to prove the rule. "The Spirit bloweth where it listeth." That is why I have always related the full flowering of intellectuality to orthodoxy in the widest sense of the term, which includes, of course, faith, without which one would not become fully attached to an orthodox tradition. On the one hand, revelation provides grace which allows the veils to be lifted from the soul and for the inner eye of the heart to open or the intellect to function and become fully operative and actualized. On the other hand, revelation is itself the source of knowledge as well as providing the language of symbolism which the intellect uses for the expression of the Truth in a particular traditional universe. In any case, I attach the greatest importance to faith and the grace emanating from revelation for the attainment of authentic realization, and, as far as grace is concerned, even the possession of genuine metaphysical knowledge on the theoretical level. But, of course, faith becomes even more central when one seeks realization. Every intellectual intuition itself is a grace from Heaven. That is why the person who is blessed with this gift is in danger of losing it if that intuition does not lead him to attachment to a tradition and faith in a revelation in the highest sense of that term as well as to the practice of virtue.

Having made this general statement, it is now possible to turn to Burrell's comments step by step. He speaks of the possibility of my surrendering something of the uniqueness of my tradition to the norm I call "intellectual intuition." First of all, in speaking of the one and unique God and many traditions, each unique in its own particular genius, I am certainly not sacrificing the uniqueness of any tradition, least of all my own in which I am deeply immersed on every level of my being. What I assert is that in order to confirm the uniqueness of each tradition, it is *not* necessary to have many unique "gods," each being the source of a unique tradition. The uniqueness of each tradition is on the level of the world of forms, spiritual, liturgical, artistic, moral, and even intellectual. Yet, these forms, having issued from the one and unique Source of all reality, which is beyond all forms, are themselves gates through which one can reach the Formless. When I speak of "intellectual intuition," I do not mean that it expresses itself in the same fashion everywhere. Johannes Scotus Erigena and Suhrawardī both possessed "intellectual intuition" of the highest order, but their expressions of metaphysical truth do not in any way violate or destroy the uniqueness of their respective traditions. As for myself, while I have written extensively of traditional metaphysics, the perennial philosophy, and comparative religious subjects, most of my intellectual activity has been devoted to the resuscitation of the Islamic intellectual and spiritual tradition with full awareness of both its uniqueness and also its universality by virtue of its traditional character. And here I need to repeat that although "intellectual intuition" is available only to the few, it is also dependent for its full flowering and efficacy upon faith and revelation, as is the religious life of the many who are not concerned with the path of salvific knowledge.

In part two of his essay, Burrell alludes to my offering an alternative narrative, "emphasizing voices usually relegated to a minor role . . . ," to the main scholastic tradition associated with St. Thomas, Duns Scotus, and the like, and then adds that it is truly disappointing that I only "allude (here and elsewhere) to Dante," whose "deliberate turn to the poetic already bespeaks a trenchant critique of the medieval tradition, which could have advanced Nasr's own argument in a constructive fashion." This comment provides me with an opportunity to say something about my relation to Dante. Like C. S. Lewis, I consider Dante to be the supreme poet of Christianity and the *Divine Comedy* the greatest synthesis of medieval Christianity, including its inner teachings associated with the anagogical level of the interpretation of the text. I was introduced to Dante by Giorgio de Santillana at MIT, an Italian who had unbelievable mastery of all the levels of meaning of the *Divine Comedy*. I spent a whole year studying the complete text with him while also attending some of Charles Singleton's lectures at Harvard on

Dante. Despite all my other courses, I even studied Italian for a while just to be able to read the *Divine Comedy* and I fully agree with Jacques Maritain that this veritably inspired text of Dante represents, along with Chartres and the B Minor Mass of Bach, the peak of Western Christian art. If in *Knowledge and the Sacred* I did not refer more to Dante, it was because that work is written in a highly intellectual language since it intends to challenge the modern philosophical edifice intellectually. I therefore used poetry only here and there as examples, and this includes even Persian Sufi poetry with which I have a more intimate knowledge than I do of Dante. This having been said, I am glad that the author mentions Dante in this context and I fully confirm his view of the poet's opposition to the excessive externalization of the truths of Christianity in the Middle Ages but not the whole medieval tradition.

As for seeing the "other side of Aquinas," different from the Aquinas presented by recent generations of Thomists, I am only too glad to accept such a thesis if it is shown to be so by those more qualified than I am to write of the Angelic Doctor. I have always had the greatest admiration for him and intuited that there must be another dimension to that greatest of medieval Christian theologians than the Aristotelianization of Christian doctrines. But what I have written about him and his role in European intellectual history is most of all based on such interpreters as De Wulf, Gilson, Maritain, and Wolfson as well as the original texts themselves which were, however, read mostly in light of modern Thomistic interpretations. In any case, I am grateful for this clarification, but also I must add that in my writings, although I have sometimes had the name of St. Thomas followed by that of Duns Scotus, I have never believed that they were simply saying the same things.

As for St. Augustine, Burrell writes that "he [Nasr] explicitly praises Augustine 'despite his emphasis upon faith as the key to salvation'" and concludes that I am belittling faith and consider the function of the intellect to be sufficient for leading to wisdom. As I mentioned above, this is a misunderstanding of my position because while in principle it is sufficient for the intellect, that divine spark within, to function in order for man to attain wisdom, the intellect does not function fully within a man who does not possess virtue and whose being is not transformed by the truth, although at the beginning a person might gain a vision or *theoria* of the truth with the help of "intellectual intuition." It might be said that "intellectual intuition" provides, through grace and as a divine gift, a vision of the mountain of truth, but to attain wisdom fully means to climb that mountain and that requires faith and the grace that emanates from revelation. Where I criticized Augustine, or at least the prevalent interpretation of him, was in his emphasis upon faith irrespective of whether it was illuminated by sapience or not. Now, for ordinary believers faith is the key to salvation and this is true as much of Islam as it is of Christianity. From the sapiental point of view, however, faith needs to be illuminated by sapiental knowledge. This is certainly the case in Islam where the Quranic verse "We have created the *jinn* and men in order to worship us *[ya'budūn]*" has been interpreted by numerous representatives of the sapiental tradition, from Ibn 'Arabī to Mullā Ṣadrā, in such a way that to worship means "to know," that is, they consider *ya'budūn* to mean in this verse *ya'rifūn*. Now this knowledge is never divorced from *īmān* or faith, but knowledge of a principial order made possible by grace and faith is the supreme goal of human existence and for those created to follow the path of knowledge it is the means to their salvation in the highest sense of this term, which means total deliverance from the bonds of all limitations. Certain anti-intellectual fideists in Christianity cited St. Augustine's assertion of faith as key to salvation in support of their view and developed a decidedly anti-intellectual attitude, and it is this possibility that I opposed not as a possibility for some but as categorical opposition to the salvific role of sanctified intelligence.

The author writes that chapters 1 through 9 of *Knowledge and the Sacred* believe that intellection short of faith can be itself a means of sanctification while chapter 10 does not. There is, I believe, a serious misunderstanding here concerning the very structure of this book. Delivered as the Gifford Lectures concerned with natural theology, the work was not written as a treatise starting and ending with mystical theology. My goal was first of all to clear the ground that has prevented modern man from understanding the relation between knowledge and the sacred. Then I set about to discuss what sacred knowledge is in itself and in its ramifications. Throughout this discussion, by virtue of the fact that I spoke constantly of sacred knowledge, I took for granted that the attainment of the sacred implies faith and revelation and that man cannot attain his heart or each heart-knowledge without the help of revelation. But in these chapters my goal was to present the contour of this sacred knowledge itself rather than dealing with the question of salvation. Having completed this task, I then turned in the last chapter to the question of realized knowledge in order to make certain that the reader understand what the realization of the truth in our whole being, which alone brings about salvation in the deepest sense of the term, really implies and why it is necessary to cultivate the virtues and undergo spiritual practice. In the context of Islam I have in fact written often of the insistence of the Muslim sages (and my own agreement) upon spiritual practice as well as guarding strictly to the tenets of the *Sharī'ah*. My whole reinterpretation of later Islamic philosophy, which has found many opponents among rationalists in both the West and the Islamic world, is founded on this view and my own life has been also based on combining intellectual activity with spiritual practice.

If what I have written were to be understood, then one could no longer assert that I claim a sanctifying role for intellect as such and then modify a further perfection in "realized knowledge." The intellect, understood in the sense I use it, is itself sacred and does illuminate and sanctify the mind, provided man possesses a soul embellished by virtue and therefore deprived of the power to place impediments before the functioning of the intellect within. But even in this case there must be a sanctification of the total being of man, achieved through realized knowledge, which actualizes within the whole being of man what the mind has received through grace from illumination by the intellect. The greatest Hindu metaphysician, Śaṅkara, who considered knowledge of the *Ātman* to be the only means of deliverance or salvation in its highest sense, nonetheless sang devotional hymns to God. The knowledge received by the "intellect within," about which he spoke so powerfully as a metaphysician, had also become realized knowledge which embraced his whole being. I cite here the supreme case of Śaṅkara. It is even easier to cite a number of Sufi saints, who possessed both metaphysical knowledge of the highest order on a theoretical level and were sanctified beings in the full sense of the term "sanctity," which, although a Christian term, has its complete correspondence in Islam, with the difference that one might say that in Christianity, esoterism is usually associated with sanctity and in Islam sanctity with esoterism.

After mentioning the relevance of a reading of creation and the intellectual response of those traditions which avow the free creation of the universe, Burrell states that I refer to creation in pejorative terms. This is not at all the case. I have written that the world or creation possesses at once discontinuity and continuity vis-à-vis the Divine Principle or Creator. God is both transcendent and immanent in relation to the world. Now, theologies, whether they be Jewish, Christian, or Islamic, usually emphasize the dimension of transcendence and hence the total discontinuity between God and the world. In this perspective, God is the Creator who infinitely transcends His creation. Traditional metaphysics and the perennial philosophy, while accepting this radical discontinuity, also emphasize the dimension of continuity and immanence according to which the world is the manifestation of the Divine Principle and the Principle is immanent within the world. Now, from the perspective of the latter, whether it be in the teachings of the Areopagite, Johannes Scotus Erigena, the Kabbalists or a whole array of Islamic esoteric thinkers from Suhrawardī to Ibn 'Arabī to Mullā Ṣadrā, to look at the world as only creation but not manifestation, in the sense of being both created order and manifested reality in relation to the Divine Principle, which is at once transcendent and immanent in relation to this manifested reality, is only partly true but not completely false. It is a truth precious for the understanding of religions on the exoteric level, but it is not the total truth which must of necessity embrace the dimensions of both transcendence and immanence. As the Quran asserts, "There is nothing like unto Him" but also "Whithersoever ye turn there is the Face of God." What the author refers to as my usage of a pejorative term concerning creation is a misunderstanding of what I have just stated. If Burrell understands creation in another way, such that it does not entail a hiatus or separation, then our difference is simply a question of semantics.

As for creation being free, this assertion brings up the questions of necessity and contingency and also the Nature and the Will of God. It is theologically correct to assert that God has created this world according to free will. But God is both absolute freedom and absolute necessity (the *Wājib al-wujūd* of the Islamic philosophies going back to Ibn Sīnā). Metaphysically speaking, one can ask the question, "Is God free not to create?" If the answer is yes, then God would cease to be the Creator and a change would take place in His Nature, which is impossible because God cannot will not to be God. Here the whole question of the relation between Divine Will and Divine Nature, which has occupied Islamic thought since its inception, and especially since the rise of Ash'arite voluntarism in the 4th/10th century, comes into the foreground. I have dealt with this issue in several of my writings but just to respond to this question briefly here, I would say that God must of necessity create; otherwise He would not be the Creator. But He has created this particular creation, which for us is creation as such, in freedom.

In the same section, after criticizing my making gnosis independent of faith to which I have already replied, the author asks how faith is related to what I call "intelligence of the heart," and also poses the question, "Can we say that this intelligence is in any way *informed* by the revelation which is needed to *actualize* it?" First of all, faith is definitely related to the intelligence of the heart because although the heart, spiritually understood, resides at the center of our being, in our present-day condition we have no direct access to it. It has become hardened and covered by the rust to which the Prophet of Islam referred. In order for this rust to be removed and the eye of the heart opened, there is need for revelation as well as faith in that revelation. To quote the Prophet, "For everything there is a polish. The polish for the heart is the remembrance of God (*dhikr Allāh*)." Now the *dhikr* in its Islamic form was first of all revealed through the Quran by God. Second, in order to practice it, there is the necessity of absolute faith in God and the sacramental power of His Name. Therefore in order for the intelligence of the heart to function and the eye of the heart to open, there is unconditional need of faith. The tradition I have quoted here from Islamic sources has its equivalent in other religions. Once the eye of the heart is opened, then it can "see" the spiritual world or, in other words, the intelligence of the heart, which itself is sacred and functions only within a sacred ambience, is able to know the truth, but that itself depends upon faith and grace. And yes, it is *informed* by the revelation, of which it is the microcosmic counterpart, as well as being actualized by it.

I agree with almost all that is presented in section four dealing with realized knowledge except where, at the beginning of this section, the author writes, "Nasr himself appreciated just how misleading his previous exposition had been." I do not admit to anything of the sort. The order of chapters and materials presented in *Knowledge and the Sacred* was chosen very carefully in light of the audience I was addressing and as I already said the format of the Gifford Lectures. Also as I have already stated I wanted to show how in modern times knowledge had become separated from the domain of the sacred, then show what sacred knowledge is in itself and its application to various domains of reality, and finally, what it means to realize this knowledge within oneself. The first step was necessitated by the secularized ambience in which I had to present my thesis. The second and the third, however, are very much in line with how wisdom is taught to this day in the Islamic world. For those of intellectual bent, and not necessarily any adept of Sufism, to this day works of gnosis (*ma'rifah/'irfān*), such as those of Ibn 'Arabī and al-Jīlī wherein the highest principles of metaphysics and cosmology are revealed, are taught in small sessions to gifted students. At the same time those students who are really serious begin spiritual practice under the guide of a master, practices whose fruit is the actualization of the knowledge contained in the works they are studying. There is a Sufi adage according to which the truth is like a seed which is planted in the soil. From this seed grows a plant which flowers and bears fruit within which is to be found that seed again. The first seed is knowledge of a sacred order described by teachers and learned by those with sufficient intelligence, which in Islam is itself a divine gift and in its pure state a sacrament. The second seed is none other than the first but now realized and interiorized. My book in a sense repeated this propedeutic process in the altered conditions in which I had to expose these teachings. As for the wedding between knowledge and virtue, yes the term "wedding" must be taken in the strongest sense in this context, for sacred knowledge is impossible without great virtue and even ordinary knowledge requires at least the virtue of objectivity. As for the virtues themselves, in the deepest sense they belong to God and our soul possesses the virtues to the extent that it confirms itself to its Divine Norm. Moreover, virtue within the soul implies a kind of "intelligence" of our human substance, a manner of our soul being intelligent and participating in the light of intelligence.

Burrell concludes by mentioning two major Islamic figures who have had a "formative presence" in my life and thought, these being Jalāl al-Dīn Rūmī and Mullā Ṣadrā. I agree with this assessment but need to add to it. First of all I have lived with the poetry of Rūmī since I was five years old. This deep immersion in Persian Sufi poetry, which also included Sa'dī, Ḥāfiẓ, and 'Aṭṭār, did not only become a source of wisdom for me, but it taught me that great poetry, more than acting as a vehicle for the teaching of wisdom, is the means for the experience of that wisdom itself. Sixty years later, I still read Rūmī and Ḥāfiẓ more for the direct experience of the highest wisdom dressed in the robe of beauty, which as Plato said is the splendor of the truth, than only for didactic purposes, and I would be glad to read practically nothing else save the Sacred Scriptures. Furthermore, Rūmī has also been an intimate inner guide through all the phases of my life.

As for Mullā Ṣadrā, I came to him in my late twenties after my return to Persia and the beginning of the second phase of my study of Islamic philosophy with traditional Persian masters. But before coming to Mullā Ṣadrā, I had immersed myself deeply in the thought of Ibn Sīnā (Avicenna), Suhrawardī and Ibn 'Arabī, the three figures to whom I devoted my *Three Muslim Sages*. To understand my intellectual lineage in the Islamic universe, therefore, in addition to Rūmī and Mullā Ṣadrā, the names of Ibn Sīnā, Suhrawardī and Ibn 'Arabī should also be remembered, while spiritually my perspective cannot be understood without reference to Shādhilī spirituality going back to the teachings of the first master and founder of the order, Shaykh Abu'l-Ḥasan al-Shādhilī.

I wish to conclude this response as I began it by turning to further general considerations which complement what I have written at the beginning of my response to this important essay of David Burrell which poses so many delicate and profound questions. At the beginning of *Knowledge and the Sacred* I wrote about the unity of being, knowledge, and bliss at the beginning and their subsequent separation. I believe that this long lost unity cannot be regained save with the help of revelation and faith in that revelation. Only the grace of Heaven can overcome the poison of what the Bible calls the tree of good and evil. While Adam was in paradise he saw all things in God and faith for him was nothing but knowledge through vision itself; knowledge of the highest or seeing the highest also corresponded for him to belief in the deepest sense. But for fallen man that unity has been lost and faith remains a basic necessity for regaining the Adamic state and that unitary vision. Furthermore, man is composed of intelligence, will and the substance we call soul. To become unified and at the highest level sanctified, the intelligence must know the Truth, the will must submit itself to the Truth and the soul must become embellished with the virtues which descend from the Truth. Now, none of this is possible without revelation, faith, and grace. But the highest goal, from the sapiental point of view, remains unitive knowledge and vision whose fruit is the *scientia sacra* that cannot be fully attained without total realization which implies the intelligence, the will, and the virtues of the soul. Knowledge sanctifies us precisely if the Truth embraces every aspect of our being.

In my emphasizing *intellectus*, I have not meant to belittle revelation and faith, as the thrust of the totality of my writings reveals. Rather, my intention has been to reinstate the status of the intellect, as the crowning faculty within the human being and as a supernaturally natural sacramental faculty whose eclipse is responsible for this dichotomy between "intellect" and faith that concerns Burrell so deeply. If we look at my exposition from the Christian point of view, it might be said that I have tried to bring back to life the epistemological hierarchy of Boethius who distinguished clearly between *intellectus, ratio, imaginatio*, and *sensus*, a hierarchy which provided a basis for medieval Christian thought.

Finally, I need to add that there is a question of emphasis between Christianity and Islam as far as the will and the intelligence are concerned. The first is addressed more to the will and the second to the intelligence within man. This difference in emphasis must also be seen in the different nuances one finds in the relation between knowledge and faith in the two traditions in question, although of course both elements are vital to each religion. It can in fact be said that what saving love is in Christianity, sincere faith in the one and Absolute Reality is in Islam. As far as Islam is concerned, over the centuries there have developed not only schools of philosophy and theology but also that sapiental knowledge known sometimes as *ḥikmah*, but usually as *ma'rifah* or *'irfān*. Now, it is true that in Christianity the category of theology is much more inclusive than in Islam, but I believe that even in Christianity there has existed that third category known sometimes as gnosis or mystical theology and at other times as theosophy as we see in a Jakob Böhme, although this dimension has been eclipsed in Western Christianity in recent centuries in contrast to Orthodox Christianity. In any case I do not believe that gnosis, *scientia sacra*, traditional metaphysics, or the perennial philosophy should be considered as simply another type of theology, but that it should be given its own legitimate place in contemporary Western intellectual life as one finds in other living intellectual traditions, such as the Islamic and the Hindu, unless one makes a clear distinction between mystical theology and ordinary theology and adds to the condition for being a theologian the necessity of the presence of God in him, such as one finds in the Orthodox understanding of the term "theologian." Professor Burrell might consider this to be only a matter of terminology, but I believe that something more essential is involved. In any case, I am grateful to him for bringing up some very important issues in the relation between intellection and faith and for allowing me to clarify my views on this matter which is of great concern to both Christianity and Islam, not to speak of other religions, as well as to nearly all schools of the philosophy of religion.

S. H. N.

22

Leonard Lewisohn

SUFISM IN THE THOUGHT OF S. H. NASR

It was a sultry summer afternoon: crouching in the corner of a Sufi *khānaqāh* in south Tehran, dressed in a long-sleeved shirt and dark suit coat, I wore the *de rigueur* respectable attire in Pahlavi Iran, whether for dervish or prince, prime minister or taxi-driver. Across from me sat the venerable Mr. Hasan Kobari, chief shaykh of the *khānaqāh,* a man who never seemed to utter a word or move a limb without one feeling that either a thunderstorm was breaking or a rosebud bursting into bloom. All the voluminous publications of Dr. Nurbakhsh, the Ni'matu'llāhī Order's current Master, were edited and proofread by him; all responsibility for the financial accounts for the sixty-odd Sufi centers run by the Order sat on his shoulders. Iron will, sincerity, rigor, directness to the point of bluntness, merciless wit, the dignity and seriousness of which was never compromised by irony, his silence, inspiring awe, and his speech imposing respect, his gaze as piercing as Ozymandias's sneer of cold command, while his humility and readiness to apply himself, unhesitatingly, to the most humble chores, always left his critics ashamed and abashed, bemused before their own conceit and false self-esteem: These were the qualities of the man which now filled the air before me, burning hotter than the breezeless summer heat. "Mr. Kobari," I asked rashly, "what do you think of Dr. Nasr? It is said that his political affiliation and connection with the government . . . " Mr. Kobari turned, his eyes scorching me with indignant wrath. The thunderstorm broke out, then the rose blossomed forth. "What are you saying?" he cried. "One hundred Kolbaris would not equal one Dr. Nasr. His service to the understanding of Islam and Sufism is unrivaled by anyone else today." I was of course silenced and dumbfounded, full of reverence and reflection, or rather, made to feel the full impact of my lack of reverence and reflection, and so forced to revise the folly of youthful judgment.

I tell this personal vignette to illustrate the impact of Dr. Nasr among dervishes and on Sufism in Iran during the 1960s and 1970s, although that is not the subject of this essay. In what follows, instead I shall examine some of his works and comment on their contribution to the field of Sufism within the general framework of Islamic Studies. If neither the heat of that intense Tehran summer remains, nor now in the West the terror of mullāhs seems as oppressive as it still is, the words of Mr. Kobari, words of praise for Dr. Nasr with no other motive but to cook the raw understanding and correct the rash perception of the present author, still echo in my mind's eye with their thunderous lightning and overpowering fragrance.

S. H. Nasr's voluminous writings encompass a wider scope of topics than any other modern Muslim thinker. The scope of subject matter his works survey encompasses not only most aspects of Islamic Studies but also comparative philosophy and religion, the philosophy of art, history of science, as well as the philosophical and religious dimensions of the ecological crisis.[1] Underlying this diversity of interest, *'ilm al-taṣawwuf* (Sufism) and *'irfān* (mystical gnosis) constitute the leitmotif of his compositions, remaining the fundamental and focal source of inspiration in his work.

So pervasive is the influence of Sufism and so prevalent are the expressions of Islamic gnosis and Sufism in his writings that it is nearly impossible to discriminate and separate on the basis of subject matter or title alone which compositions should be placed amongst his "Sufi" or "theosophical" works, and which amongst his scientific and philosophical ones. As Nasr himself points out, "Gnosis has played a more central role in the Islamic tradition than it has in the West."[2] This being true, with gnosis located at the heart of the *spiritual life* of Islam, then for a major modern Muslim thinker it also naturally lies at the center of his intellectual life as well.

Nasr's *Sufi Essays,* which I first encountered in the early 1970s in a London bookshop, was the first work of its kind in any European language during that decade. "Of its kind . . . "? Well, there were some works of Idries Shah then available in Europe and the United States as well. But these were hardly scholarly, liberally mixing the water of fiction with the wine of truth. I remember strolling into Orientalia, a bookstore in New York's Lower East side specializing in Islam and the Middle East in 1972 and requesting any works on Sufism. The learned proprietor brought forth a shiny new copy of *Sufi Essays* and two well-thumbed books of Idries Shah. And that was his full selection of works on the subject. "Of course, Nasr's works are more authentic, but no one reads them," he sighed, "while Idries Shah is very popular, but obviously content-wise of little value." Today, the situation has changed drastically. Nearly every bookshop with any selection of works on

Islam also now has a correspondingly wide range of books on Sufism. And yet, the serious consideration given today to the study of Sufism in scholarly circles in the West was largely generated by the profundity and novelty of Nasr's pioneering academic treatment, for his *Sufi Essays* was the first solid general work on Sufism to be written in the latter half of the twentieth century.

The list of works composed on Sufism *per se* by Nasr is quite small. It amounts actually to only two books, the above-mentioned *Sufi Essays* (London, 1972) and *Jalāl al-Dīn Rūmī: Supreme Persian Poet and Sage* (Tehran, 1974). Nonetheless, important essays on Sufi themes can be found in many of the available collections of his writings. Among these, the following four articles should be mentioned: "The Flight of Birds to Union: Meditations upon 'Aṭṭār's *Manṭiq al-ṭayr*," "The Influence of Sufism on Traditional Persian Music," "Rūmī, Supreme Poet and Sage," and "Rūmī and the Sufi Tradition," in his *Islamic Art and Spirituality*.[3] In addition, the chapter on "Ibn 'Arabī and the Sufis" in his *Three Muslim Sages*;[4] on "The Prayer of the Heart in Hesychasm and Sufism," in *Greek Orthodox Theological Review* (1986, pp. 195–203); and "The Relation Between Sufism and Philosophy in Persian Culture," in *Hamdard Islamicus* (6; Winter 1983, pp. 33–47), should also be cited as exemplifying his profound interests in Sufism.

Nasr's contribution of articles related to the study of Sufism to various edited collections has also been substantial. First in order of significance is his editorship of and substantial contributions to a massive two-volume collection entitled (vol. 1) *Islamic Spirituality: Foundations,* and (vol. 2) *Islamic Spirituality: Manifestations*,[5] the latter volume being dedicated primarily to the "manifestations" of Sufism. In this tome one finds essays on Sufi topics such as "The Spiritual Significance of the Rise and Growth of the Sufi Orders" (pp. 3–5); "Sufism and Spirituality in Persia" (pp. 206–22); and "Theology, Philosophy, and Spirituality" (pp. 393–446). His "Spiritual Movements, Philosophy, and Theology in the Safavid Period" in *The Cambridge History of Iran*, VI: *The Timurid and Safavid Periods*,[6] also briefly touches on Sufism. More recently, one may cite his three quite different introductions to three respective volumes entitled *The Heritage of Sufism*.[7]

Although the *geographical* scope of Dr. Nasr's researches in Islamic Studies is not confined to any particular area or land of the Muslim world, *intellectually speaking* the primary focus of his writings revolves around the relationship between Islamic philosophy, theosophy, or wisdom-spirituality (*ḥikmah*), Islamic science, and Sufism. In this respect, it should be pointed out that his interests in Sufi literature and poetry, as well as in the fine arts in Islam, are not primarily or even secondarily of a purely "literary" or "aesthetic" nature; his writings are in fact seldom characterized by any interest in exploration of novel or obscure details of the literary or historical biographies of writers and poets, nor in the minute analysis of aesthetic nuances and meanings of poetic metaphors after the fashion of a literary critic. Rather, his concern is primarily to expound on the doctrinal import and metaphysical meaning of the ideas of a given poet's or artist's work, thus highlighting what he understands to be the sacred foundations of their work.

In his various essays on Jalāl al-Dīn Rūmī (d. 1273), for instance, Nasr does not approach Rūmī's poetry with the same concern for detailed literary or philosophical analysis to which he subjects the thought of theosophers such as Mullā Ṣadrā or Suhrawardī. He does not attempt to explore Rūmī's theology or metaphysics systematically, nor to analyze in any detail his notion of love and reason, his theory of the body, soul and spirit, nor to explore the poet's angelology or prophetology, as for instance, one finds in his treatment of Suhrawardī.[8] Nasr presents Rūmī as an illustrator of metaphysical truth rather than as a creator of beauty; Rūmī is cited for the sake of edification, his verses adduced solely to highlight the doctrinal truths of Islamic gnosis, vis-à-vis which Sufism remains a most significant tributary.[9] As Nasr observes:

> In the strict sense one should refer to the Islamic tradition and not to the Sufi tradition, because the first is an integral tradition and the second a part of the first and inseparable from it. In using the term "Sufi tradition," therefore, the more limited sense of the word is intended without wishing in any way to imply that Sufism can be practiced in itself without reference to the Islamic tradition of which it is a part.[10]

Nasr's study of Rūmī thus reflects his own philosophical aims: to expound genuine Islamic gnostic and metaphysical doctrine. The expression of Truth as divine Beauty or as beautiful poetry remains marginal to this aim. It is the category of Sacral Expression, the evocation of the Sacred *Temenos* of Rūmī's poetry which concerns him, insofar as "the beauty of his [Rūmī's] verses is like the beauty of a sanctuary which is there of necessity as the 'existential' condition for all authentic manifestations of the sacred."[11]

At the center of Prof. Nasr's approach to Sufi literature in general, be this prose or poetry, lies his own spiritual attitude to the Sacred Truth as constituting the central divine Origin of all human creativity. As with many other exponents of the perennial philosophy, Nasr considers "Tradition"[12] to be the sole source of all creative expressions of beauty, the latter being merely marginal emanations of the former.

> That which encompasses both logic and poetry is the nature of Ultimate Reality as revealed in various traditional metaphysical doctrines according to which this Reality . . . is at once logical and poetic, mathematical and musical.[13]

The Intellect corresponds to the masculine aspect of the Divine Reality, and poetry vis-à-vis the Intellect corresponds "to the feminine pole which is at once an extrusion of the masculine and its passive and substantial complement."[14] In this fashion, poetry, beauty, and the fine arts are (albeit indirectly) subsumed to logic, philosophy, and metaphysics, just as the feminine can be said to follow the masculine. The common ground between logic and poetry, and by extension, between a "masculine" theosophical reason and a "feminine" creative intuition, is found only in "gnosis or traditional metaphysics," which must be "rediscovered" if any wedding between the two is to take place.[15]

In his essay on "Traditional Art as Fountain of Knowledge and Grace," these ideas are given an eloquent and substantial exposition. Nasr comments that "[traditional sacred] art reflects the truth to the extent that it is sacred, and it emanates the presence of the sacred to the extent that it is true."[16] Stressing the religious significance of the sacred dimension of beauty, Nasr maintains that "the knowledge of the sacred cannot be . . . separated from beauty," for beauty "far from being a luxury or a subjective state, is inseparable from reality and is related to the inner dimension of the Real as such."[17] At the same time, "what in fact distinguishes metaphysics and gnosis from profane philosophy is not only the question of truth but also beauty. Gnosis is the only common ground between poetry and logic, whether formal or mathematical. . . . It is only in gnosis or *scientia sacra* that the rigor of logic and the perfume of poetry meet, for this science is concerned with the truth."[18] The centrality of Sufism in Nasr's thought here becomes evident, for only through the sacred literary and artistic masterpieces of Sufism can a complete "wedding between truth and beauty" in the world of Islam be achieved.[19]

When it comes to actual definitions and descriptions of Sufism, instead of referring to the normal ethical prescriptive categories used by the classical exponents,[20] Nasr generally treats the subject as the given esoteric dimension of the sacred Islamic Tradition, which is understood to be a compound of a civilization's "cumulative historical" development, to use W. Cantwell Smith's term, and to be vouchsafed to man by grace of its divine origin. "In the Islamic period," Nasr states, "mysticism is nearly identical with the inner dimension of Islam known as Sufism, and also exists within Shi'ism."[21] Nasr thus attempts to revive the classical Muslim outlook on Sufism, reiterating "the views of authorities such as al-Ghazzālī, in the Sunni world, and Shaykh Bahā' al-Dīn al-'Amilī, in the Shi'ite world, who . . . have defended both [the esoteric and exoteric] dimensions of Islam,"[22] explaining that:

> Traditional Islam considers it [Sufism] as the inner dimension or heart of the Islamic revelation, without denying either the state of decadence into which certain orders have fallen over the centuries or the necessity of preserving the truths of Sufism only for those qualified to receive them. The attitude of traditional Islam to Sufism reflects that which was current during the centuries prior to the advent of puritanical and modernist movements in the 12th/18th century, namely that it is the means for the attainment of sanctity meant for those wishing to encounter their Creator here and now and not a teaching meant to be followed by all members of the community.[23]

While this view illuminates his own position regarding the relationship between Sufism and the exoteric dimension of Islam, in order to grasp the various nuances and strands of this tradition, the following description of his own native Persian Sufi tradition, within which he was born and raised, is even more significant:

> Altogether one can detect in contemporary Persia three distinct spiritual types with many possibilities within each type. These types include first of all the regular and orthodox Sufi orders, some of which are of Shi'ite inclinations and other Sunni. There is much contact between the two kinds of orders, and they are far from being mutually exclusive. Second, there is spiritual initiation and instruction given by masters of Sufism who do not belong to a distinct Sufi order and who are either independent masters, as in the early centuries of Islam, or are of the Uwaysī type. Many of the great gnostics of contemporary Persia like 'Allāmah Ṭabāṭabā'ī have received their spiritual instruction through such a channel. Third, there is Shī'ite spirituality and initiatic guidance independent of the Sufi orders but issuing from the same esoteric dimension of Islam which has given birth to Sufism and Shī'ism.[24]

Examining the threefold division among the different types of Sufism expressed here, it would appear that, personally speaking, Nasr favors the second two types of Sufism over the first. Thus, Prof. Nasr's describes his two decades of study of gnosis and philosophy under three different Iranian mentors: 'Allāmah Ṭabāṭabā'ī, Mahdī Ilāhī Qumsha'ī and Sayyid Muḥammad Kaẓim 'Aṣṣār,[25] none of whom were formally disciples or followers of a master belonging to any organized Sufi order (*ṭarīqat*) of the first type mentioned above,[26] but who nevertheless were affiliated with a quasi-Sufi esoteric tradition parallel to ordinary *ṭarīqat* Sufism.[27] However, from certain encomiastic comments made about the French scholar of the Traditionalist School, F. Schuon,[28] it is clear that for Nasr it is Schuon, rather than any of those modern Persian sages cited above, who plays the pivotal role of the

"Supreme Master" in his spiritual life and thought.

In terms of comparative religion, the most important contribution of Nasr to inter-religious dialogue is his use of Sufi esotericism as a basis for a philosophy of religious pluralism.[29] With their focus on esotericism in general and Sufism in particular, Nasr's writings have been most successful in arguing that religious plurality does not necessarily imply the relativity of religions. Speaking of "Islam and the Encounter of Religions," he observes:

> The most powerful defense for religion in the face of modern skepticism is precisely the universality of religion, the realization of the basic truth that God has addressed man many times, in each case saying "I" and speaking in a language that is suitable for the particular humanity to which the revelation is addressed.[30]

Following in the footsteps of Louis Massignon and Henry Corbin, the influence of whose lives and scholarship upon his thought Nasr has readily acknowledged,[31] in his *Sufi Essays* Nasr boldly introduced many of the classical Sufis as the real ecumenical thinkers of classical Islam. The writings of Rūmī, Ibn 'Arabī, Al-Jīlī, Shabistarī, Hātif Iṣfahānī, Dārā Shikūh, and many others are here presented as champions of cross-religious dialogue and inter-faith understanding, as the mystic forerunners of the later scholar-sages such as Ananda Coomaraswamy and René Guénon. Nasr proposes that Islamic philosophical and mystical thought contains within itself the seeds of a genuinely higher synthesis of religious diversity. This synthesis is based on a knowledge, which "is already blessed with the perfume of the sacred," envisioning

> in the multiplicity of sacred forms, not contradictions which relativize, but a confirmation of the universality of the Truth and the infinite creative power of the Real that unfolds Its inexhaustible possibilities in worlds of meaning which, although different, all reflect the unique Truth.[32]

Based on the Quranic doctrine of Unity (*tawḥīd*), it does not aim to reduce all religions to a uniform monolithic abstraction, for, as he points out:

> Metaphysically speaking, unity lies at the opposite pole of uniformity, and the reduction of religions to a least common denominator in the name of religious unity of mankind is no more than a parody of the "transcendent unity of religions" which characterizes the traditional point of view.[33]

Nasr's attempt to resuscitate exoteric Islam by revival of its esoteric dimension or Sufism still remains his most important intellectual legacy, offering a spiritual palliative to our soullessly secular modern world alienated from its spiritual traditions and all sacred values, where he says,

> As far as Islam is concerned the key necessary for opening the door towards a true encounter with other religions has already been provided by Sufism. It is for contemporary Muslims to use this key and to apply the established principles to the particular condition presented to the Islamic world today.[34]

LEONARD LEWISOHN

THE INSTITUTE OF ISMAILI STUDIES
JANUARY 2000

NOTES

1. See Z. Moris and M. Aminrazavi, eds., *Complete Bibliography of the Works of Seyyed Hossein Nasr from 1958 through April 1993* (Kuala Lumpur: Islamic Academy of Science of Malaysia, 1994).
2. S. H. Nasr, "Theology, Philosophy, and Spirituality," in S. H. Nasr, ed., *Islamic Spirituality: Manifestions* (New York: Crossroad, 1991), p. 395.
3. *Islamic Art and Spirituality* (Ipswich: Golgonooza Press, 1987).
4. See note 8 below.
5. Nasr, *Islamic Spirituality: Foundations* (New York: Crossroad, 1987, 1991, 1997); *Islamic Spirituality: Manifestions* (New York: Crossroad, 1991, 1997).
6. (Cambridge: Cambridge University Press, 1986), pp. 656–97.
7. Edited by the present writer: *The Heritage of Sufism*. 3 vols. Vol. 1: *Classical Persian Sufism from its Origins to Rūmī.* Vol. 2: *The Legacy of Mediæval Persian Sufism*. Vol. 3 (with David Morgan): *Late Classical Persianate Sufism: The Safavid and Mughal Period* (Oxford: Oneworld, 1999). Nasr's introductions placed the subject matter of each volume in historical, theosophical, and literary perspective.
8. See S. H. Nasr, *Three Muslim Sages* (Delmar: Caravan Books, 1976), pp. 52–82.
9. See, for instance, Nasr's essays, "The Sufi Master as Exemplified in Persian Sufi Literature" and "Islam and the Encounter of Religions," in *Sufi Essays,* pp. 58–62, 149–50. His two excellent essays "Rūmī, Supreme Poet and Sage" and "Rūmī and the Sufi Tradition," in his *Islamic Art and Spirituality*, likewise are primarily focused on "the tree of the Sufi tradition of which he was one of the most dazzling flowers." (Ibid., p. 133).
10. "Rūmī and the Sufi Tradition," in *Islamic Art and Spirituality,* p. 145, n. 2.
11. Ibid., p. 141.
12. On Nasr's concept of tradition, see S. H. Nasr, "What is Traditional

Islam?" in *Traditional Islam in the Modern World* (London: KPI, 1987), pp. 1–25, a collection of essays which has been described as "the best recent example of a Traditionalist perspective on Islam" by Carl Ernst, "Traditionalism, the Perrennial Philosophy and Islamic Studies," *MESA Bulletin* 28 (1994): 179; S. H. Nasr, "What is Tradition," in Nasr, *Knowledge and the Sacred* (Albany: SUNY, 1989), pp. 65–92. See also Adnan Aslan, *Religious Pluralism in Christian and Islamic Philosophy: The Thought of John Hick and Seyyed Hossein Nasr* (London: Curzon, 1998), pp. 46–54. On the concept of "Tradition" in modern religious studies in general, see Paul Valliere, "Tradition," in M. Eliade, ed., *The Encyclopedia of Religion* (New York: Simon & Schuster Macmillan, 1995), XV, pp. 1–16.

13. "Metaphysics, Logic and Poetry in the Orient," in his *Islamic Art and Spirituality*, p. 92.

14. Ibid.

15. Ibid., pp. 95–96.

16. "Traditional Art as Fountain of Knowledge and Grace," in S. H. Nasr, *Knowledge and the Sacred*, p. 256.

17. Ibid., pp. 269, 268

18. Ibid., p. 273.

19. Ibid.

20. See "The Term *Sufi* as a Prescriptive Ethical Concept," in Carl Ernst, *The Shambhala Guide to Sufism* (London & Boston: Shambhala, 1997), pp. 18–26.

21. "Mysticism and Traditional Philosophy in Persia," in Nasr's *The Islamic Intellectual Tradition in Persia*, ed. Mehdi Aminrazavi (London: Curzon, 1996), p. 8.

22. S. H. Nasr, *Traditional Islam in the Modern World*, op. cit., p. 15.

23. Ibid.

24. "Sufism and Spirituality in Persia," in Nasr, ed., *Islamic Spirituality: Manifestions*, op. cit., p. 219.

25. See Nasr, "Oral Transmission and the Book in Islamic Education: the Spoken and the Written Word," *Journal of Islamic Studies* 3, no. 1 (1992): 9, 13.

26. Even though Prof. ʻAṣṣār is cited as a link in the initiatic chain—and thus a "master" of—one of the branches of the Niʻmatu'llāhiyya stretching back to Nūr ʻAlī Shāh Iṣfahānī in the chart appended to Aḥmad Mujāhid, ed., *Majālis-i Aḥmad Ghazālī* (Tehran: Intishārāt-i Dānishgāh-i Tihrān 1376 A.Hsh./1997), certain links in the chain are especially problematic. ʻAṣṣār's initiatic chain (*silsilah*) is given as follows: Nūr ʻAlī Shāh Iṣfahānī (d. 1212/1797)→Mahdī Baḥr al-ʻUlūm (d. 1212/1797)→Mullā Luṭfu'llāh→Ḥusayn Qulī Hamadānī (d. 1311/1893)→ Muḥammad Bahārī (d. 1325/1907)→Aḥmad Vāḥid al-ʻAyn→Muḥammad Kaẓim ʻAṣṣār (d. 1394/1974)→ʻAbd al-Ḥujjat Balāghī. According to a personal communication (Jan. 3, 2000) from Prof. ʻAṣṣār's son, currently residing in Washington, D.C., his father Muḥammad Kaẓim ʻAṣṣār had no practical affiliation, in the sense of disciplic commitment (*irādat*) and "submission" with any Sufi master (*murshid, pīr*). Thus, while Muḥammad Kaẓim ʻAṣṣār was a recognized authority in Persian theoretical theosophy (*ʻirfān*), he was not a master in any traditional Sufi order, but rather affiliated to the theosophical tradition parallel to Sufism described below in note 27.

27. In his introduction to Lewisohn, ed., *The Heritage of Sufism,* III (p. 11, n. 13), Nasr points out that "in the recent history of philosophy in Persia, one finds numerous examples of this phenomenon of very high mystical attainment without any outward affiliation with a Sufi Order, for instance, in figures such as (my own teachers) Sayyid Muḥammad Kāẓim 'Aṣṣār and 'Allāmah Ṭabāṭabā'ī . . . Having been myself intimately acquainted with these teachers, I discovered how they had received initiation and spiritual training from masters of the Tradition who were virtually unknown outside the small circle of their intimate disciples."

28. Schuon is compared to "the cosmic intellect itself impregnated by the energy of divine grace surveying the whole of the reality surrounding man and elucidating all the concerns of human existence in the light of sacred knowledge. He seems to be endowed with the intellectual power to penetrate into the heart and essence of all things, and especially religious universes of form and meaning, which he has clarified in an unparalleled fashion as if he were bestowed with that divine gift to which the Quranic revelation refers as the 'language of the birds'. . . . Schuon speaks from the point of view of realized knowledge not theory, and his writings bear an 'existential' impact that can only come from realization." S. H. Nasr, *Knowledge and the Sacred* (Albany: SUNY, 1989), pp. 107–8. See also Nasr, ed., *The Essential Writings of Frithjof Schuon* (Rockport: Element Books, [1986] 1991); and his similar comments in the "Biography of Frithjof Schuon," in S. H. Nasr and William Stoddart, eds., *Religion of the Heart* (Washington D.C.: Foundation for Traditional Studies, 1991), pp. 1–6.

29. See Adnan, op. cit., pp. 162–68.

30. *Sufi Essays*, op. cit., p. 126.

31. See Nasr, *Traditional Islam in the Modern World*, op. cit., chapters 15, 16.

32. *Knowledge and the Sacred*, op. cit., p. 281.

33. Ibid., p. 288. For a similar interpretation of the unity of religions, see F. Schuon, *The Transcendental Unity of Religions* (Wheaton, Ill.: Quest Books, 1984).

34. *Sufi Essays*, op. cit., p. 151.

REPLY TO LEONARD LEWISOHN

I have known Dr. Lewisohn since as a young student he came to Tehran seeking instruction in Sufism. Now an accomplished scholar of Sufism and Persian Sufi literature, he is intimately familiar with my works on the subject of his essay which is of central importance for the understanding of all aspects of my thought. His statement that "*'ilm al-taṣawwuf* (Sufism) and *'irfān* (mystical gnosis) constitute the leitmotif of his compositions, remaining the fundamental and focal source of inspiration of his work" is fully confirmed by me. While the perennial philosophy constitutes my general perspective, it has been through the engagement on both the doctrinal and practical planes with Sufism that I have sought to reach and realize the truths of the perennial philosophy. Whatever I have written, whether it be in the field of religion, philosophy, science, or art, has been from the perspective of Sufism in its most universal sense, which is none other than the *sophia perennis* expressed in the language of the Islamic tradition. Throughout Islamic history there have been Sufi figures such as Quṭb al-Dīn Shīrāzī, Bahā' al-Dīn 'Āmilī and more recently Shaykh Aḥmad al-'Alawī who have written not only on Sufism but also on law, philosophy, astronomy, and the like; but all of their works have been influenced by their fundamental "philosophical" perspective drawn from Sufism and in fact constituting the heart of Sufism itself. On a more humble scale the whole corpus of my writings must be viewed in the same way, although I have turned to non-Islamic worlds in a way that these and other classical figures did not do because they did not need to do so. In any case I identify myself as belonging to the Sufi tradition in the same way that I am in a more general sense an Islamic thinker and a follower and propagator of the perennial philosophy.

The author states that since according to my own words gnosis has played a central role in the Islamic tradition, "then for a major modern Muslim thinker it [gnosis] also naturally lies at the heart of his intellectual life as well." First of all I am not a "modern" Muslim thinker but a contemporary one who has opposed during all of his life the very tenets of modernism. Secondly, there are many present-day Muslim thinkers, or those who are at least called Muslim thinkers, who precisely because of their modernism are totally opposed to gnosis or Sufism. Unfortunately, in the present-day Islamic world, it does not follow from the fact that gnosis lies at the heart of the Islamic tradition that all those who consider themselves Muslim thinkers are also concerned with gnosis. On the contrary because modernism is based on the forgetfulness of gnosis, as I have defined it as being equivalent to *'irfān*, most modern Muslim thinkers are opposed to gnosis and Sufism as a consequence of their modernism. I am fully aware of my relatively lonely position in this respect in relation to other Muslim thinkers who are modernists, but I need to add that many of the younger Western-educated Muslim thinkers who are no longer blinded by modernism are turning to Sufism and gnosis again. The revival of Sufism and gnosis among Western-educated Muslims (whether they have been educated in the West or in Western style institutions in the Islamic world) during the past few decades is a very important reality of contemporary Islamic history to which not enough attention has been paid.

Lewisohn provides a list of my works specifically devoted to Sufism. This list is well prepared but I need to add that I have written a number of essays such as those dealing with the subject of God, the cosmos, the Quran, and *Ḥadīth* in the first volume of *Islamic Spirituality* which, while not displaying the word Sufi or gnostic in their title, are concerned directly with Sufi doctrine, as are certain chapters of my books not cited by the author such as the final chapter of *Science and Civilization in Islam* and several chapters of *Islam and the Plight of Modern Man* and *Islamic Life and Thought*. Even my short biography of the Prophet, *Muhammad—Man of God*, is in reality a Sufi biography written in a simple language for younger readers.

When it comes to the question of my understanding of beauty, the author makes certain statements which need to be corrected. He says that I present Rūmī "as illustrator of metaphysical truths rather than as a creator of beauty." I object strongly to the word "rather," because for me the two dimensions complement each other entirely. I was brought up with the poetry of Rūmī and was attracted to its beauty long before I understood its metaphysical significance. I would therefore not agree with Lewisohn's statement that "the expression of Truth or Divine Beauty or as beautiful poetry remains marginal to his [my] aim." Strangely enough a page later Lewisohn quotes my statement that "knowledge of the sacred cannot be . . . separated from beauty," which contradicts the earlier assertion.

In any case to make my position clear on this crucial issue, I must state that I have always been and remain very sensitive to beauty whether it be of nature, art, or the human soul, and beauty has always wielded great power over my mind and soul, carrying me to the Abode of the Source of all beauty. Also I have never expressed a moralistic cult of ugliness opposed to beauty, seen as dispersion or luxury, such as one finds among certain modern Christian and also, to a lesser extent, Muslim thinkers. More specifically I have been immersed all my life in Sufi poetry and have even composed a few humble poems now and then in Persian and English. The reason that I have not emphasized aesthetic elements of Sufi poetry independent of the truth contained therein is twofold: first, to bring out the primacy of metaphysical truth for many, especially among my own countrymen who have become drunk with the divine beauty of a Ḥāfiẓ or Rūmī and who quote their poems over and over again for aesthetic enjoyment but separated from the truth they are meant to convey. Such people seem to have forgotten the Platonic dictum that beauty is the splendor of the truth. Second, as one who has sought to present Sufi metaphysics to a Western philosophical audience and also to challenge the philosophical errors of the modern world, I have had to emphasize the pole of the truth over that of beauty, which does not hold the same status in modern philosophical discourse as in traditional philosophies.

In my writings, especially if one reads all of them, it is not true that "poetry, beauty, and the fine arts are (albeit indirectly) subsumed by logic, philosophy, and metaphysics, just as the feminine can be said to follow the masculine" as claimed by the author. I see the relation of the feminine to the masculine as one of complementarity, like the Far Eastern *yin-yang*. It is true that poetry and beauty represent the feminine element and logic and intellectual activity in general the masculine element. But I see their relation as full complementarity rather than either opposition or domination of one over the other. I have often written that poetry and mathematics can meet and have a common ground only in gnosis which possesses both the rigor of mathematics and the beauty of poetry. God is both the supreme Architect and Geometer and the supreme Poet and Musician if these terms are understood symbolically and not anthropomorphically. Rūmī writes in a verse addressing God, "we are the lyre that Thou plucketh." This principial truth is present in all authentic manifestations of gnosis which are both true and beautiful.

In any case, in my own life even from childhood I was drawn to both poetry and music on the one hand and mathematics and science on the other. It was only later that I discovered that traditional philosophy whose most perfect expressions are both beautiful and true. Both in my writings and in my own life I have never separated the two. Rather, I have sought to see in every beauty the reflection of the Divine Beauty, the Divine Name *al-Jamīl* as the Sufis would say, and also never to identify beauty with dispersion but rather with the Truth and its realization. My immersion in the Persian Sufi poetical canon with which Dr. Lewisohn is well acquainted is closely connected with the inner nexus I have both come to realize intellectually and to experience inwardly between truth and beauty.

At the end of his paper the author speaks, quoting my own words, of the three spiritual types consisting of orthodox Sufi orders, initiation given by masters of Sufism who do not belong to a distinct Sufi order, and Shi'ite spirituality outside the Sufi orders. Then he adds, "Nasr favors the second two types of Sufism over the first." I am very surprised at a person who has known me for over a quarter of a century for making such a statement. I cannot go into details concerning my personal spiritual life here, but for the sake of the record it is necessary to mention that although I have had a profound personal as well as intellectual relation with the second two types, it is with the first type that I have been involved since my youth. I have belonged to the world of orthodox Sufi orders, although not a Persian order, since my twenties and experienced the two spiritual types mentioned above as a practitioner of what Lewisohn himself refers to as *khānaqāhī* Sufism. There is a great deal that I could say on this subject but will not do so here. But it is necessary at least to clarify this point.

Turning to the question of Sufism and religious diversity, much of what the author has written meets with my approval. Only when he writes, "Islamic philosophical and mystical thought contains within itself the seeds of a genuinely higher synthesis of religious diversity" do I need to qualify this statement in several ways. First of all, the Islamic esoteric tradition does not contain only the seeds but also fully developed doctrines pertaining to religious pluralism which can and in fact have already been expanded to fulfill present-day needs. Second, the synthesis of all manifestations of the truth as stated already by an Ibn 'Arabī or Rūmī is already of the highest order and not only a seed for a higher order. There is no order higher than the One in which all diversity finds its origin and end.

At the end Lewisohn states that "Nasr's attempt to resuscitate exoteric Islam by revival of its esoteric dimensions or Sufism still remains his most important legacy." Only time will tell what will be my most important legacy, but as far as I am concerned my goal has not been only to revive the esoteric dimension of Islam *in order to* resuscitate exoteric Islam. I have sought to revive the esoteric dimension of Islam also *in itself* and for its innate value. In fact within the realm of the Islamic tradition my goal has been to revive Islam in both its exoteric and esoteric dimensions as well as the Islamic intellectual tradition, especially philosophy and the sciences, by presenting them in a contemporary language and by responding to modern challenges while preserving their traditional authenticity.

Dr. Lewisohn has chosen a subject for his essay which lies at the heart of my whole intellectual and philosophical worldview. He has clarified many points and provided me with the occasion to clarify others as far as my relation with Sufism is concerned. My thought cannot be understood without a clarification of the role that Sufism has played in my life, both philosophical and spiritual. There is much more to say on this question, but at least, thanks to the author, a number of important issues are made clear as a result of this exchange between us. Certain other matters pertaining to this delicate question must be treated in another context while there are aspects of this issue which, because of their very nature, must continue to remain confidential for now.

S. H. N.

23

William C. Chittick

THE ABSENT MEN IN ISLAMIC COSMOLOGY

Nearly thirty years ago, someone told me about a lecture that had recently been given by Seyyed Hossein Nasr. During the question and answer period, the great Orientalist Gustave von Grunebaum remarked that Nasr's talk presupposed a power structure. What was it? Nasr replied with a sparkle in his eyes, "The *rijāl al-ghayb*," and von Grunebaum along with those who caught the reference laughed. Like all good jokes, this one has an element of truth in it—mythic truth, no doubt—but it certainly helps explain the voice of authority that often surfaces in Nasr's writings, producing a variety of reactions in his readers.

The term *rijāl al-ghayb* means literally "the Men of the Absent," and in Sufi lore it refers to those human beings who live in the spiritual world and govern the visible world as God's representatives, thus fulfilling their cosmic and human functions. God created the universe, as the *ḥadīth* puts it, "in order to be known," and among all creatures, only human beings have the capacity to know God in his full amplitude and grandeur. In their historical actuality, human beings are indefinitely diverse, and their diversity pertains to every modality of their being and knowledge. It follows that some people are better at knowing God than others, just as some people are better at understanding mathematics than others. From the Sufi perspective, "knowing God" has relatively little to do with the rational sciences, and much to do with God's gifts to those whom he chooses as his friends (*walī* or "friend" being the term that is commonly translated into English as "saint"). The Prophet reported that God says, "My friends are under My cloak—no one knows them but I." These unknown friends of God are known as "the Men of the Absent," whether they be male or female (the Arabic word for "man" here has connotations not unlike those which allowed Latin *vir* or "man" to give rise to the word *virtue*).

According to some accounts, the Absent Men can be divided into two sorts. One sort, known as "the Men of Number" (*rijāl al-'adad*), fill a static, ever-present hierarchy, so their number never changes (some say it is 124,000, like the prophets from Adam down to Muḥammad). Their chief is the "Pole," who is the most perfect human being of the time and the axis around whom the human world revolves. Outwardly, the Pole may be an ordinary and unremarkable person, but inwardly, as the texts put it, "He holds the reins of affairs in his hands." When the Pole dies, God replaces him with one of the two Imams, who had been the Pole's viziers, and he replaces the missing Imam with one of the four Pegs. Below the Pegs stand the seven Substitutes, below them the twelve Principals. Among the Men of Number, one manifests the perfections of the angel Seraphiel, three the perfections of Michael, five those of Gabriel, seven those of the prophet Abraham, forty those of Noah, and three hundred those of Adam. The ranks of the Men of Number are constantly replenished as people pass on to the next world. As for the second sort of Absent Men, their number is not fixed, and they play a variety of roles according to circumstances. Most of them fall under the authority of the Pole, but one group, known as "the Solitaries," stand outside his realm.

It is not clear how literally these reports are meant to be taken, but, however we understand them, they speak eloquently of a certain concept of human nature, and that concept underlies Seyyed Hossein Nasr's writings. It is a view that is usually ignored in modern studies of Islamic religious teachings, which tend to focus on superficial overviews of Islamic theology and brief descriptions of the duties and obligations imposed on believers by the *Sharī'ah*. Nonetheless, any investigation of the literature that informed the Islamic worldview, from the most technical philosophical and theological texts to the most popular poetry, will find that human beings are always given a unique role in the cosmos. Even texts on the *Sharī'ah* recognize it implicitly, because they set down duties and responsibilities that God has imposed on no other creature.

Nasr often speaks of the loss of the traditional Islamic worldview and the havoc wreaked on the Muslim mind by scientific theories about the universe. As he points out, and as is obvious to those conversant with the texts, we are dealing with two diametrically opposed ways of looking at reality, even if many contemporary Muslim intellectuals see no contradiction between belief in the Islamic God and belief in the objective status of scientific "facts." Throughout the Islamic world, two basic groups of Muslim intellectuals are found. One group, which is constantly becoming smaller, still lives more or less in the traditional worldview, while the other, ever on the increase, is led by the engineers, doctors, and other professionals trained on the Western model. These two groups do not speak the same language, and neither has any real idea of what the other is saying. So utterly self-evident is the nature of the "world" to each group that they cannot imagine any other way of seeing it. The fact that they do not understand each other helps explain why contemporary mullās can preach about the necessity of studying modern science, employing the term '*ilm* or "knowledge" (which has always been recognized as the backbone of Islam), without recognizing that modern science has practically nothing in common with the traditional understanding of '*ilm* and that, in effect, they are encouraging the young to abandon their own intellectual heritage. Of course many if not most reflective Muslims are caught somewhere in between the traditional and modern perspectives, and this helps explain the "cultural schizophrenia" that Daryoush Shayegan has written about and made manifest so eloquently.[1]

In several of his works, Nasr has explained the main principles of the traditional Islamic worldview. I would like to reformulate certain aspects of this worldview—not in terms of his expressions, but in terms of my own understanding based on twenty-five years of studying Islamic texts. My purpose is not to claim that Nasr is right or wrong, but simply to reformulate, in a language as unencumbered by technical Islamic terminology as possible, the basic Islamic ideas on human nature as related to certain key notions in Nasr's writings, especially his evaluation of modern thought. I offer one person's opinion that Nasr's interpretation of the implications of the Islamic tradition for the contemporary world are firmly grounded in the classical texts, much more so than many of his critics want to acknowledge. The fact that he does not always cite Muslim authorities, but instead is likely to refer to authors such as Frithjof Schuon and Ananda Coomaraswamy, cannot be taken as evidence that his views do not have the Islamic support that he claims.

Nasr, of course, does not write only about Islamic teachings. Part of his relevance as a contemporary philosopher has to do with the fact that he claims a universal validity for a point of view which he and others (including Schuon and Coomaraswamy) usually call "traditional" and which observers have often called "traditionalist" or "perennialist." This perspective asserts that humanity, wherever it has been found, has recognized the reality of one unique Principle and received guidance from it on various levels. What makes human beings "human" is not the peculiar biological, social, and historical constraints placed on the species, but the fact that they have been given access to the Infinite, the Absolute. This access is *given* to them, which is to say that it comes to them from the other side, and they cannot reach it on their own; hence the necessity of prophets, avataras, buddhas, sages, shamans, and so on, and the necessity that the guidance be transmitted from generation to generation by "tradition." This is not to say that all claims to suprahuman guidance are true, or that all the forms that guidance takes will lead to the same "place." Nor does this standpoint deny the important role played in the human world by misguidance and evil. Although Nasr does offer some general principles as to how truth is to be discerned from falsehood, by and large he leaves the issue of judging the correctness of specific teachings to the traditions within which they are offered. What is important for Nasr's own writings is the principle of the universality of the guidance that comes from the Absolute and the fact that it is always available to human beings.[2]

One of Nasr's subtexts is the relevance of Sufism to the contemporary situation and the catastrophic results that modern Muslims suffer by ignoring or rejecting Sufism. For a great variety of reasons, people in both the Islamic world and the West become suspicious at the mention of Sufism. In contemporary America, for example, it is often associated with gullibility, sentimentality, and New Ageism. In the Islamic world, Muslim modernists from the nineteenth century onward have taken Sufism as a kind of bugaboo that must be driven out if Islam is to enter the modern world. The more recent offshoot of modernism, "fundamentalism," has agreed with this assessment.[3] However, relatively few Muslims have any idea of the historical role that Sufism has played, even though they all have strong opinions on the topic. A colleague who teaches at Harvard recounts with amusement that a young Egyptian studying at MIT took a course with him on al-Ghazzālī, who has universally been recognized as one of the greatest masters of the Islamic sciences and who is known especially for authoritatively establishing the central role of Sufism in Islam. At the end of the semester, the student submitted a paper beginning with the sentence, "Islamic *taṣawwuf* does not exist" (*taṣawwuf* being the Arabic term for "Sufism"). This opinion, despite its contradictions, is widely held among Muslims, and the historical record is considered of no account.[4] Moreover, those who hold the opinion can draw support from the works of the early Orientalists, who saw Sufism as a clear example of borrowing from other religions (after all, they imply, the Sufis were loving, open-minded, and well-intentioned people, so they could hardly have been real Muslims).

Even specialists in fields like Religious Studies or Islamic Studies will sometimes remark, "Oh, but he's a Sufi," meaning, "You do not have to take him seriously, because he's a mystic," or, "You know, Sufism really has nothing to do with Islam, so don't pay attention to him." Yet for Nasr, and for the grand authorities like al-Ghazzālī who have spoken on behalf of Sufism throughout Islamic history, the diverse beliefs, practices, and institutions of Islam that are apparent to outside observers make up Islam's body, while Sufism is Islam's life-giving spirit. From this standpoint, Muslim modernists and fundamentalists, who violently reject the Sufi tradition, are trying to breathe a new sort of life into Islam's body, and this life can only be drawn from alien sources. The discussion here, of course, is not about the history of the word *ṣūfī* (and its derivatives), since the term came into regular use only in the third/ninth century, but rather about what Nasr and many of the great authorities of the past have understood by it when they employ it.[5]

Although Nasr has written eloquently and persuasively about Sufism's centrality to the Islamic tradition, he cannot repeat these remarks in everything he writes, and even if he could, many observers reject this understanding of Sufism's role in Islam, so they feel no need to consider his position. I do not think that Nasr has helped his case by describing Sufism as "Islamic esoterism." In this he is presumably following Schuon (and to a lesser degree, Henry Corbin). Schuon has written voluminously employing the esoteric/exoteric dichotomy as a key conceptual tool for understanding religion. However, not more than a handful of English-speaking scholars have followed this practice, partly because few specialists have found it helpful in dealing with the actual texts.

One of the problems with the word *esoteric* is that, no matter how carefully terms may be defined, negative connotations cannot be eliminated. The word is suspect by its very aura, and little can be done about it. One of its many disadvantages is its high degree of abstraction, which results in a constricted semantic field that does not easily allow it to embrace the vast diversity of phenomena that have always been associated with Sufism. The restricted field becomes obvious if we compare the English word *esoteric* with the Arabic word *bāṭin*, of which it is sometimes said to be the translation. The two terms may indeed be employed in parallel ways on occasion, but *bāṭin* (which derives from the term *batn*,̣ meaning "innards") has a concrete meaning and vast possibilities for metaphorical use. In other words, the basic meaning of *bāṭin* is "inner" or "inward," not "esoteric."[6] If it is said that Sufism emphasizes the more "inward" teachings of Islam, few would object. The point is simply that Sufism's perspective contrasts with that of disciplines like *fiqh* (jurisprudence) and *Kalām* (dogmatic theology), which emphasize the more outward and socially oriented teachings. The terms *inward* and *outward* are broad and inclusive enough so that everyone will understand an appropriate meaning without being drawn into irrelevant questions, such as the "elitism" that is typically associated with "esoterism." Both *esoterism* and *exoterism* introduce nuances and connotations that are not present in the Arabic terminology. It then makes perfect sense to criticize Nasr for being an "esoterist" or for supporting the views of contemporary esoterists—and people quite sympathetic to Sufism have done so (naturally, they ignore Nasr's nuanced definitions and appeal rather to the prevalent connotations of the word).

The cosmic role of human beings lies in the background of many of the criticisms that Nasr levels at the scientific worldview, criticisms that fly in the face of popular opinion and raise the hackles of numerous scholars and thinkers, especially among Muslims. The notion of the "Men of the Absent" is one way of expressing some of the tradition's fundamental insights here, and the ideas lying behind it can help us understand why Nasr stands where he stands.

In the traditional, broad-based Islamic view of things, one cannot disengage anthropology from cosmology—though many contemporary Muslims, in their ignorance of Quranic teachings and their entrancement by modern thought, do so blithely. Of course, everyone recognizes that Islamic anthropology is rooted in theology, since Islam agrees with the Judeo-Christian tradition in holding that man was created in the divine image. But nowadays, the cosmic dimension of Islamic anthropology is much more difficult to understand and easy to ignore, not least because cosmology has long since been delivered over to physicists in the West. Moreover, most contemporary Muslim thinkers, in their eagerness to prove Islam's respectability in modern terms, have ignored or attacked all Islamic teachings on the universe and human beings that are difficult to reconcile with the rationalistic and scientistic worldview of the contemporary world. Hence they have either gone straight back to the Quran, which, shorn from the commentarial tradition, is easy to interpret however one likes, or they have appealed to *Kalām*, which is the most rationalistic form of Islamic theology and the least concerned with the nature of God's ontological relationship with the universe. *Kalām* is polemical and voluntarist, devoted to nit-picking attacks on any form of thought that is deemed to threaten God's absolute legal authority. It asserts God's radical transcendence and argues vehemently for human responsibility before the divine law.

Most Muslims with a modern education see things in terms of the worldview that has informed the Western tradition since the beginning of the modern period. This worldview is rooted in what Nasr calls a "sensualist and empirical epistemology," and its net result has been the reification and objectification of the cosmos. The world and all its contents, including human beings in most of their roles, have been turned into isolated things standing in ontological, spiritual, and moral vacuums. Of course, the politicians and ideologues who rule the various countries of the Islamic world claim that they can adopt the science and technology without the moral vacuum. They blusteringly tell us that they will not suffer the social disorder of the West, because they will see to it that society observes God's commands as set down in the *Sharīʿah*—as interpreted by themselves, of course. Their first mistake is to suppose that the *Sharīʿah* can be imposed by modern states—with their historically unprecedented ability to indoctrinate and coerce—without turning society into another version of the monstrous totalitarianism that has too often characterized the twentieth century. The

Muslim leaders have offered no empirical evidence that this is possible, quite the contrary.

Even if we grant that the *Sharī'ah* can be applied by government fiat, without the individual religious conviction that has always given life to it in the traditional Islamic world, the legal constraints of the *Sharī'ah* pertain only to certain limited spheres of the human domain, and these spheres become more and more constricted under the dehumanizing effects of modern institutions. The pervasiveness of bureaucracy, technology, and the scientistic worldview, and their steady encroachment on the human domain, mean that more and more of the world is reified and opened up to manipulation. Traditional moral constraints carry little weight in face of the institutions of modernity, especially at the time of crisis—and when has there not been a crisis?

In the West, ecologists of various stripes have recently attempted to show the short-sightedness of current conceptions of the world, usually in terms of an enlightened self-interest. Some have gone so far as to propose alternative cosmologies, but these are almost always "scientific" in that they take for granted the necessity for empirical verification and the nonexistence of any truly transcendent dimension to reality. The few who have recognized a need to recapture transcendence have, by and large, cobbled together diverse notions from science and various traditional worldviews with the hope that they can come up with a softened and sensitized scientific mind-set.

Nasr's critique of scientism and technology is rooted in the understanding that science, standing on its own, cannot conceive of what it means to be human. Many hard scientists, at least, are aware of these limitations, but not the popularizers of these sciences who have the greatest effect on how people perceive the world. As for the scientists and scholars who delve into biology, psychology, sociology, the humanities, and even theology, they seem much less convinced about the inadequacy of scientific findings, often because, without being aware of it, they take the universe of pop-science as reality and speak as if scientific theories provide us with undisputed "facts."[7] As long as the truncated worldview of scientism remains the arbiter, no opening to the Infinite is possible, or, at best, people will devise an imitation that hardly lets them see beyond the horizons of popular culture.

There are many versions of Islamic cosmology, few of which have been studied in modern times.[8] Common to all of them, and indeed to all Islamic thinking, is the idea of unity. Islam's fundamental axiom is that there is one supreme principle—an ultimately unnamable and unknowable principle—and that all things appear from it, whether through the divine command, or creation, or emanation, or various other modes that are discussed in detail in different schools of thought. Once we recognize that this ultimate principle is there, it can be given various names, with the reservation that the names do not really help us to understand the named in itself. Nonetheless, naming the principle is a necessary stage in coming to understand its implications for human reality, and in the Islamic view of things, the only truly efficacious naming—efficacious in terms of the full reality of what it means to be human—comes from the principle itself.

Naming is efficacious by nature. When we name something, we situate it in a pre-existent view of reality that allows the name to have meaning. We deal with things in terms of the names that we give to them. If we name something a "chair," we sit on it, and if we name it "firewood," we burn it. The Islamic tradition—like other traditions—names the world and its diverse contents in ways that let people see the function and role of human beings, and this function and role is conceived of in terms of a divine compassion that has brought the universe into being in the first place.

The Quran tells us that "God taught Adam the names, all of them" (II:30). This verse epitomizes Islam's theology, anthropology, and cosmology. It alerts us to the three basic realities that must be taken into account if we are to understand the nature of things—God, human beings, and the cosmos, whose names God taught to human beings at their origin. It needs to be remembered here that in the Islamic view of things, Adam is not primarily the first sinner but rather the first prophet. He is the primordial recipient of divine guidance and the leader of all his children on the road to salvation. However, in order to deal with the cosmos appropriately and to reach the fullness of their own nature, Adam and his children need to understand the God-given names and act accordingly.

Human beings will always name things, because they are by definition "speaking animals" (*ḥayawān nāṭiq*). The Arabic expression is usually translated into English as "rational animals," in keeping with the way the ancient Greek expression entered the English language, but the Arabic *nāṭiq* or "speaking" preserves a nuance of the Greek that has been lost in English. Human rationality is articulate, uttered, spoken; and proper human speech is intelligent and rational. In the Islamic worldview, the full realization of this spoken, articulate rationality presupposes knowledge of the real names of things, and knowing the real names means knowing things in the context of God's knowledge of them, which only comes to us when He Himself names the things. If people do not name things in the context of God's naming, they will name them as they see fit. However, there is no possible way for them to know the real names of things without assistance from the divine Namer, because the real names are precisely those names that God himself bestows on the things before He creates them. In other words, God's activity is essential to the names, and any worldview that leaves out the divine dimension will necessarily be dealing with inadequate names if not misnomers. The net result of misguided naming will be disaster for those who employ the names, if not for humanity as a whole—a "disaster" that is understood in terms of the whole human domain, not just the world this side of death.

One of the most fundamental differences between the Islamic cosmologies and modern scientific cosmology lies in the names of things. How do we name the ultimate and mysterious principles or realities that determine the configuration of the real world? What happens when the important names are "quasars," "quarks," "muons," "black holes," and "big bangs?" What is the spiritual fruit of naming the ultimate things with mathematical formulae? The basic characteristic of the mathematics that nowadays is deemed able to express with authority the nature of things is its abstraction, its abstruseness, its reconditeness—the fact that only a tiny elite are able to grasp its significance and explain it to the commoners. In the popular perception at least, the more the experts learn of the ultimate mysteries of the scientific universe, the more they find that it is impersonal, unintelligible (to the commoners), and arbitrary. The cosmos, the hard-nosed scientists tell us, is basically inhuman, and human beings are an oddity, a cosmic accident. Let a few romantics talk of "anthropic principles" or "Gaia hypotheses" if they wish, but these are simply the last gasps of the pre-rational urge to feel safe in an alien world, new versions of the old psychological props known as "gods" and "saviors."

Islamic cosmology begins with a transcendent, ultimate One, and then it names this One with a variety of names that are derived from the divine self-naming. None of these names is abstract or inhuman. In fact, the Islamic God is anthropomorphic, because the Islamic human is theomorphic. If God is understood in man's image, it is because man was created in God's image. Unless God is understood in human terms, an unbreachable gap will remain between the ultimate and the here and now. *Re-ligio* or "tying back" to God is impossible without images of God and imagining God. People need to take an active role in tying themselves back, and they can only do so in terms of themselves and their own understanding. They understand only what they are; if they do not display the traces of the divine in some way, they cannot tie themselves back to the divinity. People who live in such a traditional, anthropomorphic universe will necessarily deal with it in human terms. In contrast, those who live in an abstract universe will deal with things and living beings as abstractions. Those who live in a mechanistic universe will treat all beings as machines. Those who find the universe cold and uncaring will reciprocate.

It is of course true that *Kalām* and some forms of Islamic philosophy assert God's absolute transcendence and claim that the names of God should not be understood in human terms. This perspective is necessary, since it helps preserve the primacy of God's reality and the understanding that things begin with God, not with us. In any case, Islamic anthropomorphism is not the crude sort that we know through various unsympathetic accounts of polytheistic worldviews. Rather, it is the recognition of the mercy, goodness, and wisdom that pervade reality, whether or not we are able to grasp how these qualities are present in any given circumstance.

Although the Quran's depiction of God is far from that of polytheistic myth (in the Hindu or Greek sense), it is certainly polynomial. The "ninety-nine" names of God, enacted and performed in the diverse modes of Muslim religious life, determine the Islamic mind-set far more than the abstractions of the *Kalām* experts or the rules and regulations of the legal scholars. Muslims, to the extent that they put their religion into practice and assimilate the teachings of the Quran, cannot fail to see God's wisdom in the "signs" (*āyāt*) that are the phenomena of the universe and the self, just as they see it in the "verses" (again *āyāt*) that make up the Quran and other scriptures. Muslim praxis is studded with the divine names. Every significant act begins with a formula that epitomizes more than any other the Muslim understanding of God and his relationship with his creation—"In the name of God, the All-merciful, the All-compassionate." God deals with the universe in terms of his own names, and his primary names assert his universal mercy and compassion. Every prayer, every supplication, every act of "remembrance" (*dhikr*) is highlighted by divine names. And every rational attempt to understand these names is propelled by the intuition that God lies infinitely beyond human conceptualization. God gives, and he takes away. He gives the names through his revelations, and he takes away our understanding of them through our attempts to understand them. The more we try to grasp their significance, the more they turn us back to the unknowability of God in Himself. These are the two movements of the divine and the human—descent and ascent, origin and return, revelation and concealment, disclosure and curtaining. They mark a creative dynamics in Islamic culture that has totally disappeared in the monolithic thinking of Muslim modernists and ideologues.

Muslims who practice the Prophet's *Sunnah* and live in the Quranic universe cannot help but think of the universe and themselves in terms of the revealed divine names. These are not strictly personal names, nor are they impersonal. God is Living, Knowing, Desiring, Powerful, Speaking, Hearing, Seeing, Creator, Life-giver, Death-giver, Forgiving, Pardoning, Avenging, Bestower, Withholder, and so on. The names of the ultimate reality establish the significance of what people encounter in the signs. The universe is imbued with purpose, and the individual instances of its purpose become clear when situations are understood in terms of the divine attributes that become manifest through the names. Not that this is easy—how can we be sure if an instance of our pleasure displays God's mercy or his wrath, his compassion or his vengeance? We have no way of knowing the final outcome of affairs. How many things we delight in one day, only to regret the next. Even worldly successes or failures can be reversed in a moment, so what about acts and events that impinge on ultimate success and failure?

Traditional Muslims are confident, however, that things will work out for the best, no matter how badly they may go in any given situation. "In the name of God, the All-merciful, the All-compassionate" announces all the phenomena of the universe. The Quran says that God's mercy "embraces all things" (VII:156), and the Prophet emphasized the point with his famous saying, "God's mercy takes precedence over His wrath." This is an ontological and cosmic precedence, and it means that all is well in the divine scheme of things. It follows that, as the Prophet put it, "The believer is fine in every situation" (*al-mu'minu bi 'l-khayr fī kulli ḥāl*). Repeatedly the Quran commands the believers, "Trust in God," and the attitude of trust in God's mercy infuses the traditional worldview. Both the modernists and the "fundamentalists" ask Muslims instead to trust in military technology, utopian dreaming, and the latest demagogue. Then alone, they tell us, will Islam be put back in the driver's seat of history where it belongs. They never question the legitimacy of the impersonal view of reality that has allowed science and technology to dominate people's understanding of the world in the first place.

Although the One God in himself cannot be known, his manifestations cannot be avoided, so much so that it can be said that, from a certain point of view, nothing but the One can be known. However, knowledge of the One's infinitely diverse manifestations is infinitely diverse, though it can be put into general categories. Knowledge that clings to the data of sense perception (whether or not this is mediated through instruments) is limited to the surface, the outward, the superficial, the skin—all these terms understood as metaphors, not as literal, scientific designations. The One can only be truly known inasmuch as it names itself, and these divinely-taught names have everything to do with the genesis of the universe. A typical listing of the names that generate the cosmos begins with Living, Knowing, Desiring, and Powerful. Among these, Living is especially interesting. When the Sufi theoreticians explain the nature of the divine life, they are likely to employ the term *wujūd*, which is typically translated as "existence" or "being" and which was originally used in this meaning when Greek philosophical texts were translated into Arabic. However, the Islamic context allows for no wholly inanimate *wujūd*. "Existence" cannot be conceived of as dead matter. An implicit, and often explicit, side to the Islamic teachings is that God's own life, awareness, and consciousness course through everything that exists, though these show themselves most clearly in what we call "living things"—plants, animals, and human beings.

The single, supreme Principle manifests itself through multiplicity, but this is an ordered and hierarchical multiplicity, one that begins with *twoness* and gradually differentiates itself into various cosmic levels. *Twoness* is an especially important notion in cosmological thinking, because it allows us to conceive of a world along with the supreme One. The duality that appears when we conceptualize the world next to God colors all the relationships between the One and the many and has repercussions throughout the cosmos. As the Quran puts it, "And of everything We created a pair" (LI:49).

For many cosmologists, the basic duality of God and the world gives rise to two complementary points of view. From one standpoint, God is utterly real and the world utterly unreal; from another standpoint, the world has a relative reality (when compared to pure nonexistence), and this reality can only derive from God. Inasmuch as we emphasize God's reality and the world's unreality, we conceive of God and the world in terms of unbreachable otherness. Inasmuch as we conceive of God as giving rise to the world through his activity and attributes, we conceive of God and the world in terms of unfathomable sameness. In other words, God is both transcendent and immanent (or, as I prefer to translate the Arabic terms, both "incomparable" with all things and "similar" to them). In terms of God's transcendence, the world is nothing. In terms of his immanence, it is something, because it displays the divine attributes and qualities that he bestows upon it. True life and consciousness belong to God alone, and everything else is strictly dead. But once we note the divine life in the cosmic signs, we see that everything is alive and aware to some degree.

The vertical duality that differentiates God from the world gives rise to the understanding of a horizontal duality *in divinis*—a duality sometimes referred to in Quranic terms as God's "two hands." Inasmuch as God is distant, transcendent, and incomparable, he is conceived of in terms of the so-called names of "majesty" and "severity"; inasmuch as He is near, immanent, and similar, he is conceived of in terms of the names of "beauty" and "gentleness." Ultimately, "God's mercy takes precedence over His wrath" because beauty and gentleness pertain to God's own fundamental reality, while majesty and severity pertain to God when conceived of in terms of distance from his creatures. But since creatures have no reality of their own through which to be distant from God, perforce they remain in nearness and sameness, despite the vagaries of time and the unfolding of the diverse possibilities for the manifestation of otherness.

From the point of view of Islamic cosmology, what is called "science" in the modern world is a reading of the universe that ignores all but the most insignificant truths the universe has to offer. When the universe is named by names that apply primarily to dead things or to machines or to impersonal processes, we will understand it in terms of death and mechanism and impersonal process. We will necessarily miss the significance of the life, mercy, and awareness that suffuse every atom.

A Sufi axiom holds that "*Wujūd* descends with all its soldiers." *Wujūd* designates being, existence, finding, consciousness—it is God's "life" as found in himself and as reflected in all things in the universe. *Wujūd* leaves its traces in creation when it "descends," that is, when God creates the universe in a manner analogous to the way in which the sun gives rise to its own rays. In God, *wujūd* is pure, which is to say that God is simply pure *wujūd*, nothing else—pure being, sheer finding, undiluted consciousness, infinitely effulgent light. When God creates the universe, he does so by dimming the light in keeping with his infinite wisdom. Wherever anything finds and is found, this is nothing but refracted light. *Wujūd's* soldiers are the divine attributes, the qualities by which *wujūd* in its purity is named. We come to know them when God names himself by them—the Living, the Knowing, the Powerful, the Compassionate, the Wise, and all the rest. Every name leaves its traces in everything in the universe, even if we fail to perceive the traces. The names are present in everything, because *wujūd* is present, failing which, the things would not be found.

Just as God is absent from all things because of his transcendence, absoluteness, and incomparability, so also he is present in all things because of his immanence, infinity, and similarity. Because of his reality in face of our unreality, he makes demands on us, and because of our relative reality, we have the power to respond to his demands. From one point of view, these demands are ontological and cannot be rejected, for we are his creatures, the rays of his light. But the relative fullness of God's presence in his own human image bestows upon people a certain mysterious freedom, and this results in moral and spiritual demands. They have no choice but to try to live up to the divine attributes found in themselves and the universe. There is no refuge from the divine demands, since the King and his soldiers are present in all things, in all "objects." There can be no moral vacuums, no hideouts for "pure objectivity" and "scientific disinterest," no ivory towers. Scientific "objectivity" and "disinterest" become at best ignorance, at worst moral failing and spiritual disaster.

If this view of things is inherent to Islamic cosmology, it may be asked, why was Islamic science the most advanced in the world for several centuries? The very formulation of this question raises several issues that need to be considered before any attempt is made to answer it (here Nasr's *Science and Civilization in Islam* can be consulted with profit). First, the great historians of Islamic science have believed implicitly if not explicitly in scientific progress, and they measure "advancement" in terms dictated by this belief. The earlier historians in particular were interested in the Islamic texts (and in Western texts as well) because of the "scientific" elements in these texts, and they discarded everything that they considered theological, mystical, or superstitious—just as they discarded 90 percent of Newton's works so as to make him a father of modern science. Historians have continued to study Islamic science trying to discover why it did not follow the route that was followed by science in the West, as if modern science is by definition normative and has brought unquestioned benefit in its wake.

Second, even if we grant that some of these texts are "scientific" in a modern sense, their cultural context is every bit as important as their overt content. How did Ibn al-Haytham or al-Bīrūnī, for example, understand their own scientific works? Was their optics, mathematics, astronomy, and geology totally distinct from theology? And more importantly, how were their works read by their contemporaries? The work of the medieval Muslim "scientists" was understood in terms of the dominant worldview of the time.

Third, the modern Western tradition has ascribed the highest value to rational thinking, but rationalism has in fact played a more restricted role in Islamic history than historians suggest. Both modernist Muslims and Western scholars have highlighted the rational sciences in the Islamic past. The early Western scholars were busy tracing the origins of the types of thinking that they considered significant, and they were attempting to explain why rationalism did not follow the same enlightened path in Islam that it followed in the West. Causes for what they thought was aborted progress have usually been sought in the conflict between "free thinking" and "orthodoxy." On the Muslim side, the apologists have been eager to show that at the beginning, Muslims were enlightened, rational, good people, and that they were diverted from their glorious heights of scientific progress only by sinister and evil forces, if not by foreign invasions. It was not Islam, they tell us, but the un-Islamic intrusions, that led the Muslims to abandon scientific progress and devote themselves to obfuscation and darkness.

If we look at the Quran and the way it has been interpreted by the Islamic community as a whole—not just by its rationalistically oriented theologians and jurists—we see that it stresses both God's unity and his utter control of the universe. To speak of "control," however, is to use a scientific, rational term. We would do much better to speak of God's symbolic presence in all things through his signs, through the soldiers that follow *wujūd* in its descent. The net result of these two complementary ways of looking at God's relationship with the universe is that two different modes of knowledge became established among Muslim intellectuals. Knowledge through rational processes stressed God's distance and transcendence and became codified especially in *Kalām* and certain forms of philosophy, while knowledge through direct perception of God's presence in the things, or through the "symbolism" of the things, came to be codified in Sufism and some philosophical currents. The former, rational approach seems almost "scientific," and hence it has been the focus of studies for most Western scholars and the Muslim modernists and fundamentalists. The latter, symbolist approach—branded "mystical," "irrational," and "superstitious" by the same people—came to be looked upon with contempt and was dismissed by the Muslims as "un-Islamic." If it is un-Islamic, it follows that the true Islamic cosmology can be recovered by ridding Islamic thought of the vestiges of Quranic language and pushing God as far as possible from the universe, so that there will be no need to pay heed to any of *wujūd's* soldiers. Then it will be easy to justify the technological rape of the earth and the electronic impoverishment of the human soul—so long as lip service is paid to the Quran, the *Sunnah*, and the *Sharī'ah*.

It was said earlier that names are efficacious by nature. Scientific names allow us to think of things "scientifically," which means that we can dismiss anything but quantifiable reality from our view. Islamic reality is not quantifiable, which is to say that real things possess the attributes of life, knowledge, desire, power, speech, hearing, seeing, and so on, and the degree to which they possess them has nothing to do with "quantity" and everything to do with "quality." Things possess these attributes through a subtle and immeasurable participation, and these attributes are divine, cosmic, and human. Thus the attributes that pertain to human beings also pertain to non-human things—including totally inanimate "objects"—because they pertain to God, the Creator of all things, "the Light of the heavens and the earth" (XXIV:35), who sends down his light on everything in a measure known only to himself. Once things have been named, we deal with them as their names allow. Cultural anthropology has illustrated the arbitrariness with which names can be given to things—especially if we take "rational" or scientific nomenclature as normative. But scientific nomenclature is itself arbitrary when viewed from the standpoint of any of the traditional cultural matrices, which bestow orientation on human beings by naming things in the context of grand master schemes of meaning.

What appears arbitrary to Islamic thinking is any system of naming that ignores the total nature of things and wrenches them from the qualitative contexts that allow us to see how they are connected with greater wholes and with the ultimately Real. God, after all, is the only reality that can be called "real" in a full sense. All other things, including the universe as a whole, take their reality from God's reality. People can, if they choose, close themselves off to reality, at least for a time—death marks the great awakening for everyone. As Sufi texts put it, then the apple will be split open and the worm will recognize the utter insignificance of what it had been calling the "real world."

The fundamental, governing insight of Islamic thinking, after the assertion of the unity and ultimacy of the Real, is that the true nature of the world is inaccessible to human beings without help. Indeed, it is not difficult to see that it is precisely here that the great split occurred between the Western tradition and Islam (not to mention other traditional worldviews). Take, for example, Toby E. Huff's summary of the worldview and metaphysics of modern science:

> We must keep in mind that the modern scientific worldview is a unique metaphysical structure. This means that the modern scientific worldview rests on certain assumptions about the regularity and lawfulness of the natural world and the presumption that man is capable of grasping this underlying structure. . . . [M]odern science is a metaphysical system that asserts that man, unaided by spiritual agencies or divine guidance, is single-handedly capable of understanding and grasping the laws that govern man and the universe. The evolution of this worldview has long been in process, and . . . we in the West simply take it for granted. . . . The rise of modern science was not just the triumph of technical reasoning but an intellectual struggle over the constitution of the legitimating directive structures of the West.[9]

The breakthrough to modern science occurred when people learned how to name things on their own, but this constrained the efficacy of the naming. Having assumed full responsibility for naming things, people remain blind and deaf to the Real and can never see beyond their own horizons.

In Islamic terms, the fact that God names himself is the key to the extraordinary efficacy of the revealed names—their ability to chart a happy course through all the worlds that follow upon death. God's primordial act of naming took place when he taught the names to Adam, and he has kept these names alive by sending the 124,000 prophets down to Muḥammad. It is as if, by naming the cosmos, he bestowed sight on the blind. As al-Ghazzālī puts it, the Quran in relation to intelligence is like the sun in relation to the eye. By naming the cosmic order, God allows people to see its significance in the whole of reality. By naming the human order, he allows people to see their proper role in society and nature. By naming human attributes, he allows people to grasp the difference between a sick and a healthy soul. By naming right and wrong actions, he allows morality and ethics to have an efficacy that transcends limited human views of the world and society. The overarching order in all these domains can never be grasped by strictly human means, because the overarching order is God himself, the ultimately unnamable and unknowable. Until he names himself, human beings live in the darkness of misnomers.

From the standpoint of the Islamic cosmologies in general and the Sufi cosmologies in particular, the peculiar course of modern history is driven by the systematic application of inadequate names. No one will doubt that such names have an efficacy all their own. The enormous power of modern technology and the unprecedented coerciveness of modern institutions became possible only when the human, anthropomorphic names were relegated to the domain of superstition and, at the same time, the "real names" were found through quantification and scientific analysis. Quantification makes sense in the context of mechanism, and conceiving of reality as a machine allows for manipulation without any restraints but the mechanical. When things are looked upon as mere objects, reality is perceived as objective and impersonal, and this demands that we treat things with objectivity and disinterest. If the immediate is impersonal, so also must be the ultimate. In contrast, anthropomorphizing—especially as carried out by those who see themselves as theomorphic—diverts people from contemporary "reality" and prevents them from becoming docile production-line workers and hard-nosed doctors, engineers, and CEOs, hence the real danger of "Sufism" for the Muslim modernists and fundamentalists.

Once I heard Nasr say in a lecture—no doubt with a touch of Oriental hyperbole—that as soon as a Muslim boy learns in school that water is in fact H_2O, he stops saying his daily prayers. I offer my own commentary:

The traditional view of the cosmos presses upon people the interrelatedness of the divine, cosmic, and human orders. The daily prayers that God commands people to perform are nothing but the natural activities of all God's creatures. As the Quran puts it, "Have you not seen that everything in the heavens and the earth glorifies God, and the birds spreading their wings? Each knows its daily prayer and its glorification" (XXIV:41). In the traditional Islamic worldview, "water" is not a substance to be quantified but a quality to be appreciated at every level of created reality. "God's throne is upon the water" (XI:7); "Of water We made every living thing" (XXI:30). Water is one of the four elements, which is to say that it is one of the four qualities or characteristics that allow us to speak of diverse tendencies in the visible universe. All visible things are made of these four elements, but the elements combine in differing proportions, thus helping to determine each thing's aggregate of attributes. Earth keeps things stable and low. Water allows for movement, flow, and the penetration of light. Air is permeable, subtle, naturally clear. Fire is inherently luminous, changeable, and ascending. Such notions are standard fare in texts on cosmology and permeate the thinking of traditional Muslims. People know intuitively the qualities associated with the four elements, with foods, with innumerable natural phenomena. Scientific thinking condemns such knowledge to superstition, or at best, condescends to recognize a certain poetic sensibility.

When science is taught in the West, it is typically taught by believers in a scientific orthodoxy who never question the objective truth of their beliefs. But in the Islamic countries, where the traditional worldview still shows signs of life, science is taught by converts, and they are much more fervent than born believers in their denunciation of superstition and the old ways. Since the worldview of their fathers still persists, they consider it their moral duty to convert the young to the one and only truth.[10] The Islamist rhetoric that may nowadays accompany their teaching is designed to wrench the still remaining Islamic teachings from the traditional context and politicize the students in keeping with the current ideologies. Such rhetoric simply hastens the reification of the cosmos by diverting Islamic sensibilities into an alien but very modern sphere.[11] The mullā regimes have changed nothing here. They are just as enamored of the scientific worldview as anyone else, and in any case, the school teachers are the same. They have simply learned to toe the party line, which now means spouting religious pieties, whereas before it had meant reciting political slogans. The official, government worldview, though labeled "Islamic," is now totally politicized, and it owes its genealogy to the same ancestors that gave us Marxism and its descendants, well known on the contemporary academic scene.

In short, the Muslim boy who learns that water is H_2O is learning that the qualities his grandmother sees in things and the names she applies to them are primitive and superstitious, and he jettisons her understanding along with all its accouterments, including her daily prayers. If, nowadays, Muslim boys have started to pray again, as likely as not they are acknowledging their allegiance to the Islamist party, or protecting themselves against the dangers of not acknowledging such allegiance.

The notion of "the Men of the Absent" is a particularly potent way of presenting several Islamic notions in a coherent myth and showing the inseparability of anthropology and cosmology. The basic notions include unity, bilateralism or complementarity, hierarchy, and human theomorphism.

As already noted, the Islamic idea of unity recognizes two modalities. The first stresses the divine transcendence and absoluteness and rejects the idea that anything other than God can be one in any real sense; God is uniquely and utterly one and real, and all else partakes of inherent multiplicity and unreality. The other modality stresses the divine immanence and infinity and asserts that nothing can escape the umbrella of God's oneness, so all things, through their very multiplicity, display various aspects of the uniquely One. The simultaneous oneness of the Real and manyness of its creations or manifestations are prefigured *in divinis* by the divine names, each of which designates the One along with a specific quality of the One, different from every other quality.

By speaking of the Men of the Absent, Muslims assert God's transcendence and uniqueness by putting God at the pinnacle, beyond the universe, and they assert his immanence and polynomiality by conceiving of the basic structure of the universe in terms of human functions, each of which manifests various divine attributes. Within the created order, God's unity is reflected in the fact that the Pole is always one, while the hierarchy of God's names is reflected in the fact that the Men of Number are ranked in degrees below the Pole. The mathematical progression of the Men—such as 1, 2, 4, 7, 12, and so on—reflects the modes in which the divine Principle unfolds its potentialities through a hierarchy of created realities. Cosmically, these numbers can be found in natural phenomena throughout the universe; here we have a traditional mathematical scheme, but one that is hardly abstract, since anyone can grasp it immediately by reflecting on the world. The number one appears in the unity of each individual thing; two in day and night, heaven and earth, light and darkness; four in the elements, the seasons, the directions, the humors; seven in the heavens and the planets; twelve in the zodiac.

Some authors explain the Absent Men by illustrating the interrelationship of all things in terms of the divine names. Thus, for example, the Pole manifests the name God, because the Pole is the fully actualized image of God, comprehending and embodying all the divine attributes without exception. The two Imams manifest the names King and Lord—that is, God as ruler and controller of the universe (the Absolute) and God as nurturer and protector of each thing in the universe (the Infinite). The four Pegs display the traces of the names Living, Knowing, Desiring, and Powerful (often called the "four pillars" of the divinity). The seven Substitutes reveal the properties of the names Living, Knowing, Loving, Powerful, Grateful, Hearing, and Seeing.

The bilateralism of transcendence and immanence is implicit in the term *Men of the Absent* because "absent" (*ghayb*) is the conceptual counterpart of "witnessed" (*shahādah*). Sometimes the two terms together are translated as "unseen and visible," as in the Quranic Name of God, "the Knower of the unseen and the visible." Islamic cosmology typically sees the universe in terms of two great primary worlds, the absent or invisible world and the witnessed or visible world. The witnessed world is what we see or can see in principle, and the absent world is what we cannot see. Our seeing or not seeing is not an accidental quality, but rather, essential to the two domains. In other words, the absent world is inaccessible to our senses by its very nature, not simply because we do not have the appropriate circumstances or adequate instruments. It pertains to a suprasensory domain that the senses will never grasp, though intelligence (or "intellect" as Nasr would say) does have access to it, because intelligence is that dimension of human reality that partakes of God's absoluteness and transcendence.

In short, the witnessed world is the body of the cosmos, and the absent world is its spirit. Like all bodily things, the witnessed world is indefinitely divisible, and its predominant characteristics are multiplicity, darkness, grossness, opacity, fragility, evanescence, change. In contrast, the absent world partakes of unity, light, subtlety, transparence, strength, permanence, fixity. But these specific attributes are applied to the two worlds when they are envisaged in relatively impersonal terms. In fact, the absent domain partakes of all the personal, divine attributes in a relatively direct and active mode. Hence it is living, knowing, desiring, powerful, speaking, hearing, seeing, compassionate, forgiving, vengeful. These attributes can hardly be found in the witnessed world itself, though their traces do appear. We notice such attributes through deducing the absent attributes that motivate witnessed activities. Some acts suggest generosity, some vengefulness, some compassion. The fact that these attributes stem from an absent domain is acknowledged by traditional expressions such as "soul" and "spirit." The full actualization of these attributes can only be sought in the absent realm, which helps explain the special characteristics of angels, who are among that realm's inhabitants.

The many and diverse Sufi expositions of the nature of the universe are much more explicit than those of the philosophers and theologians concerning the utterly central role of human beings for cosmic reality itself. Modern sensibilities dismiss this "anthropocosmism" (to use Tu Wei-ming's term) for many reasons, not least because it seems to ignore the vast reaches of the universe brought to light by modern scientific techniques. But the Sufis were well aware that our specific world has no great significance in the overall scheme of things and that the universe is unlimited in time or space, except inasmuch as its createdness differentiates it from the Uncreated, which is "infinite" in the strict sense. One can easily imagine them shrugging their shoulders at the "revelation" that there are billions of galaxies and replying:

> All that is of no account in relation to the human role in the world that we do know or may know through our own direct and personal experience. Our texts often speak of 18,000 worlds, and what is meant is everything created by God, just as the Chinese speak of the 10,000 things and mean "everything in the universe." Everyone knows that there are other worlds, and that God fills his worlds with his creatures, because nothing can hold back his infinite creative activity. There are certainly living things in other worlds, and no doubt human beings as well, or beings that play the same role there that human beings play here. But what does this have to do with our own function in the world that we face directly every day of our lives? Our world depends on us. It is we and no one else who can turn it into a realm of harmony or a cosmic waste. We alone have been given the responsibility to maintain it. Moreover, compared to the World of the Absent, the whole visible universe—this vast world of cosmic dust and galaxies that you might see if you had the right instruments—is, as the Prophet put it, but a ring lost in the desert. Human beings have been given responsibility not only for their own witnessed realm, but also for diverse

domains of the Absent World. When they treat the witnessed world as if it were the whole universe and ignore the demands of the Absent World, humans waste their precious talents and ignore their own human nature.

The relationship between the two worlds is analogous to the relationship between God and the universe. This means that, on a cosmic scale, the Absent World is infinitely more vast, powerful, active, intelligent, conscious, and compassionate than the witnessed world, even though the two worlds together are as nothing compared to God. Human beings possess the peculiar characteristic of being made in the image of God, and so they are also images of his whole creation, which is the sum total of the absent and witnessed worlds. Human reality pertains fundamentally to the absent realm, not to the witnessed realm, because people reflect the universe as it is, and absent reality is much more real and significant than witnessed reality. We recognize this even today to the extent that we find human significance in qualities such as love and compassion—qualities not found in the witnessed world, but perceived as essential characteristics of the divine and the human, wherever the interrelationship of these two is acknowledged. To say that the absent world is more real than the witnessed world is to acknowledge that qualities such as intelligence, love, forgiveness, generosity, discernment, justice, and pardon pertain to what is truly real, and that the more intensely these qualities are found, the more intensely reality is present. In no way are these qualities "epiphenomena" of the human order or any other order. To look at the universe in that way is to invert the normal, normative, human, and divine order of things; it is to take the highest as the lowest, and the lowest as the highest.

Because human beings are made in the divine image, they have the potential to manifest all the divine names in diverse degrees of intensity. They differ radically from all other creatures because they possess a synthetic and all-comprehensive nature, which allows them to manifest the most fundamental divine qualities in a fullness that is inconceivable in any other mode of being, absent or witnessed. Compassion, love, justice, and forgiveness are human qualities, and they are not found anywhere else in the universe as we know it, except in dim and metaphorical modes. It follows that human beings are the most real beings in the universe that we know. What modern scientism would call "objective reality" is as impermanent, evanescent, and insignificant as a cloud—as many physicists have been telling us. The only permanent realities, the only things that are truly real, are the divine attributes, and these become manifest to significant degrees only in the absent domain. What appear as "epiphenomena" to the proponents of scientism are the face of reality itself, hidden behind the veil of phenomena, and what appears to be real is in fact a fading illusion.

Where is the "real world?" Only in the absent domain, and it is fully actualized only in the absent domain of human beings. Even angels, though they dwell in the absent domain, are peripheral beings, which explains why God commanded them to prostrate themselves before Adam after he had taught him the names (II:34). Human beings alone can name reality in its fullness, because their innermost nature has access to every name God has taught. When they name reality as it names itself, they necessarily name the absent domains as the primary and most significant domains. This explains why those among them who have traditionally been recognized as the wisest and most humane have consistently affirmed the overriding reality of the absent—of all the hidden, divine attributes that need to be made manifest in terms of witnessed, social reality, through morality, ethics, and law.

The Absent Men do not live primarily in the visible world. They live with God, who manifests himself most directly through the divine qualities in the absent domain. Just as human beings play a central role in the witnessed realm because of the self-awareness that allows them to rule over the world by taking an active role vis-à-vis the relative passivity of all other creatures, so also they play a central role in the absent realm, since the great ones among them rule over the world of consciousness and awareness. The grand difference between the two types of rulership is that in the witnessed realm, rulership too often follows the whims of individuals and the vagaries of human institutions, while in the absent realm, the human rulers follow the divine King in perfect harmony. Those who deny or reject the authority of God's self-naming, or those who misinterpret it for their own aims, may attempt to govern the witnessed world according to their own misnomers. But those who name all things through the God-given names deal with them exactly as God himself is dealing with them through his continual recreation of the universe. True control belongs to God alone, no matter who appears to be in charge.

In this scheme of things, problems arise only from human beings, from their misunderstanding or misapplication of the divine names (Satan also plays a role, but not without the intermediary of human beings). But the Muslim view allows for no despair, because it recognizes that God's mercy takes precedence over his wrath, and that, in the last analysis, he holds the universe in mercy's hand. Those who fail to follow his instructions by submitting to him voluntarily, but who instead, like Satan, embark on their own courses, fit nonetheless into the divine scheme of things, and in the end, God's wisdom will be perceived even in the worst of men and the worst of evils. Everything will be well, but not according to our lights—unless, of course, our lights have submitted absolutely to the divine Light.

It is the recognition of this underlying mercy, I think, that allows Nasr always to put the best spin on things. For those who know him personally,

Nasr has always appeared as someone who sees the good side of reality, so much so that—contrary to what one might expect from some of his writings—he appears as an eternal optimist. Certainly, he never suggests that people should lose hope or cease trusting in God's wisdom and compassion. At the same time, he asks people to take advantage of the best in themselves to rethink their relationship with God and the world. On this note, I will let Nasr have the last word, as he offers in one of his most recent books the Absent Men's answer to the way out of the impasse that modern humanity has constructed for itself:

> What is needed is a rediscovery of nature as sacred reality and the rebirth of man as the guardian of the sacred, which implies the death of the image of man and nature that has given birth to modernism and its subsequent developments. It does not mean the "invention of a new man" as some have claimed, but rather the resurfacing of the true man, the pontifical man whose reality we still bear within ourselves. Nor does it mean the invention of a sacred view of nature, as if man could ever invent the sacred, but rather the reformulation of the traditional cosmologies and views of nature held by various religions throughout history. It means most of all taking seriously the religious understanding of the order of nature as knowledge corresponding to a vital aspect of cosmic reality and not only subjective conjectures or historical constructs. There must be a radical restructuring of the intellectual landscape to enable us to take this type of knowledge of nature seriously, which means to accept the findings of modern science only within the confines of the limitations that its philosophical suppositions, epistemologies, and historical development have imposed upon it, while rejecting completely its totalitarian claims as *the* science of the natural order. It means to rediscover a science of nature that deals with the *existence* of natural objects in their relation to Being, with their subtle as well as gross aspects, with their interrelatedness to the rest of the cosmos and to us, with their symbolic significance and with their nexus to higher levels of existence leading to the Divine Origin of all things.[12]

WILLIAM C. CHITTICK

DEPARTMENT OF COMPARATIVE STUDIES
STATE UNIVERSITY OF NEW YORK AT STONY BROOK
SEPTEMBER 1996

NOTES

1. See his *Cultural Schizophrenia: Islamic Societies Confronting the West*, translated by John Howe (London: Saqi Books, 1992).

2. Although it may not be obvious to those unfamiliar with the traditional understanding of the Quran, this principle is supported by numerous verses and is implicit in the double testimony of Islamic faith—"There is no god but God and Muḥammad is His Messenger." See S. Murata and W. C. Chittick, *The Vision of Islam* (New York: Paragon, 1994), pp. 164–75.

3. In several works, Nasr provides a useful classification of contemporary Muslims into three categories—the modernists (who wish to make whatever changes necessary to "bring Islam into the modern world"), the "fundamentalists" (who differ from the modernists mainly in their Islamist rhetoric and political activism), and the traditional Muslims (who would like to remain faithful to both the spirit and the letter of the living tree of Islam). See, for example, the prologue to his *Traditional Islam in the Modern World.*

4. Westerners should keep in mind that most Muslims, especially in the West and despite the rhetoric to the contrary, know practically nothing of their own tradition, even if they can recite long sections of the Quran in Arabic. They take as their Gospel what they have learned in their family or local environment. They are not much different from those fervent believers in the American context who speak of their own sect as "Christianity," consider Catholics on a par with Hindus, and have never heard of Orthodoxy.

5. On Sufism's role in Islam, see Nasr, *Sufi Essays* (London: Allen & Unwin, 1972; republished as *Living Sufism*, Albany: SUNY Press, 1991); see also Murata and Chittick, *Vision*; Chittick, *Faith and Practice of Islam: Three Thirteenth Century Sufi Texts* (Albany: SUNY Press, 1992).

6. If one claims that "esoteric" is equivalent to the Arabic *bāṭini*, this is much worse, because this Arabic term is employed for heretical sectarians who reject the Sharī'ah, and hence it carries negative connotations perhaps even stronger than the word *esoteric* in English.

7. At least belief in evolutionism is beginning to crumble, despite the fact that the vast majority of contemporary scholars take it for granted. There have been scientific and philosophical critiques all along, but these have largely been ignored. David Berlinski's recent article, "The Deniable Darwin" (*Commentary*, June 1996), along with the heated debate it produced (*Commentary*, September 1996), is now being cited by some observers as the beginning of the end for this pillar of scientistic belief.

8. Nasr provides the historical context and basic teachings for three of these schools in his *Introduction to Islamic Cosmological Doctrines* (Cambridge: Harvard University Press, 1964). Sachiko Murata deals with cosmological schemes in the Quran and a variety of Muslim authors in her *Tao of Islam: A Sourcebook on Gender Relationships in Islamic Thought* (Albany: SUNY Press, 1992). The most detailed study of any Islamic cosmologist in a Western language is found in Chittick, *The Self-Disclosure of God: Principles of Ibn al-'Arabī's Cosmology* (Albany: SUNY Press, 1998).

9. Toby E. Huff, *The Rise of Early Modern Science: Islam, China, and the West* (Cambridge: Cambridge University Press, 1993), p. 65.

10. This sort of fervor is not so obvious in the West, except in cases like the debates between "creationists" and "evolutionists," where the latter exhibit all the indignation of Puritan preachers—if the former do so as well, that is hardly remarkable.

11. If anything has characterized the traditional Islamic worldview, it is its apoliticism (when politics is conceived of in modern terms), despite all the false implications that are drawn from the highly questionable assertion that Islam has never distinguished between religion and politics. In *The Rise of Early Modern Science*, Huff provides an interesting analysis of the social and political institutions of the premodern Western world that allowed for the rise of science and technology and suggests, quite rightly, that the lack of such institutions in the Islamic world helps explain why science in the Islamic world did not follow the same route that it followed in the West. However, he implies that thereby Islam lost something of great worth, whereas it can easily be argued that thereby Islam was able to preserve its own integrity much longer than it otherwise might have.

12. Nasr, *Religion and the Order of Nature* (New York: Oxford University Press, 1996), p. 287.

REPLY TO WILLIAM C. CHITTICK

The unusual and provocative article of Professor William Chittick not only contains many profound truths with which I agree wholeheartedly, but also deals with a subject of great importance for the understanding of the background of the philosophical thought with which I identify myself. The points mentioned in my response are more in the way of clarifying some of my views on the subject rather than responding in the sense of providing a criticism of and rebuttal to the author's theses. To start with the title of the article, although I consider it to be both innovative and attractive, I continue to prefer the term "invisible" rather than "absent" for *ghayb*. It is true that in Arabic *ghayb* or *ghā'ib* is usualiy opposed to *ḥuḍūr* or *ḥāḍir* which mean "present" and would therefore warrant being translated as "absent," but in the context of the term *rijāl al-ghayb* the very absence also implies *presence*. The *rijāl al-ghayb* are absent from the senses. They cannot be seen, heard, touched, smelled or tasted but their presence is very much a reality in the traditional cosmos. Although invisible refers only to something inaccessible to the sense of sight, I believe nevertheless that it is metaphysically more correct to render *ghayb* as "invisible" rather than "absent." In any case it is essential to remember that according to traditional Islamic cosmology the *rijāl al-ghayb*, although invisible and in a sense absent, possess a living function in the universe which makes their "presence" a reality in all levels of the cosmos, even in those such as the terrestrial from which they are outwardly absent.

One of the great virtues of Chittick's essay is that it is courageous enough to call a spade a spade and to criticize the modern scientific worldview as it deserves to be criticized. His analysis of the two types of intellectuals in the Islamic world, one still following the traditional perspective and the other, "ever on the increase, . . . led by the engineers, doctors, and other professionals trained on the Western model" is certainly correct, as is his assertion that many a mullā "can preach about the necessity of studying modern science, employing the term *'ilm* or knowledge . . . without recognizing that modern science has practically nothing in common with the [traditional] understanding of *'ilm*." I am certainly fully aware of this dilemma against which I have been battling for over forty years. But I do want to add that while on a certain level the modernist perspective based on science as understood in the West since the seventeenth century is increasing, voices critical of the facile identification of the Islamic understanding of *'ilm* with modern science are also increasing in number, and that the intellectual debate on this issue among Muslim thinkers is much more serious today than it was a generation ago.

Chittick's comments about the attitude of modernists and fundamentalists toward Sufism is also true and of central importance. I agree completely that precisely because they are impervious to the living reality of Sufism, both groups seek outside of Islam for a source from which they could draw the life and the spirit necessary "to rejuvenate" Islam—with catastrophic consequences for the religion which they seek to revive. But again I believe that many groups within the Islamic world, which until quite recently were adamantly opposed to Sufism, are now beginning to show a more open attitude towards its teachings. This has certainly been my experience in lecturing throughout the Islamic world and the West for several decades. In contrast to what Chittick asserts, I have not found a lack of interest in my lectures or writings because of my open espousal of Sufism. But this is based on my own experience and he may be right as far as others that he may have met are concerned.

As for my usage of the term esoteric or Islamic esoterism, although it may have put certain people off, its usage is essential and its benefits far outweigh whatever negative connotations it might evoke in the minds of certain Westerners or Muslims. In the contemporary world it is necessary to refer clearly in some way to the reality of the inward dimension of both revelation and cosmic reality if one is going to deal with this dimension whose forgetfulness is at the base of the errors that comprise the modern world. The term esoteric is simply the Greek equivalent of "inward" and therefore needs to be used in its correct sense (as distinct from its occult sense) if one is going to speak seriously about traditional metaphysics as well as religion in its integral reality, which comprises both the outward and in inward dimensions. R. Guénon, F. Schuon, and other expositors of traditional teachings in the contemporary West had no choice but to use the terms exoteric and esoteric and to point to the exoteric/esoteric distinction. Schuon clarified what authentic esoterism is and is not in his *Esoterism as Principle and as Way*. I have consciously and voluntarily used their language precisely because I have wanted to express certain teachings and concepts which necessitate recourse to this term. I have always been aware of negative reactions it might create in certain quarters, wary of so much pseudo-esoterism parading as veritable esoterism, but I have been willing and remain willing to take responsibility for its usage and defend reasons for employing it.

As for the Islamic world, I agree with Chittick that the term *bāṭinī* (literally esoteric), as identified in the earlier periods of Islamic history with Ismā'īlism, gained a pejorative sense among the opponents of the Ismā'īlīs, as can be seen in the title of one of the polemical treatises of al-Ghazzālī against them, *al-Faḍā'iḥ al-bāṭiniyyah* ("The Ignominy of the Bāṭinīs"). Nevertheless the term *bāṭin*, which is in fact a Name of God, has continued to be revered in a positive sense in both Arabic and Persian when used in connection with Sufism. In Persian a person of spiritual quality with an attraction to the inner spiritual world is often called *ahl-i bāṭin*, literally "a person of the esoteric" or an esoterist, and this term is used with a completely positive connotation. Moreover, the founder of the gnostic branch of the School of Tehran in the early 13th/19th century Sayyid Raḍī Lārījānī, who was one of the most revered spiritual teachers of his day, respected by the learned and the unlearned alike, was given the honorific title of *mālik-i bāṭin*, or "possessor of the esoteric realm." In any case, in seeking to resuscitate the primacy of the inward dimension and of esoteric knowledge, there is no doubt that one has also to accept the risks of miscomprehension in certain quarters, especially in an age mesmerized by quantitative equality —an age possessing a hatred of all that transcends the mediocre; an age that cannot distinguish pseudo-esoterism from traditional and denounces both as "elitist." I have always written with all these factors in mind and have sought to use the nuances necessary while remaining faithful to the content and form of the traditional teachings that I have been trying to expound. When writing in Persian, I have used the term *bāṭin* and its derivatives with full awareness of all their connotations, and the same holds true for the use of the terms "esoteric" and "esoterism" when writing in English or French.

Turning to Chittick's criticism of the modern scientific worldview and the naïveté bordering on sheer folly that determines for the most part the angle of vision of political authorities in the Islamic world, I could not but agree fully with it. Throughout my writings I have dealt with these issues over and over again and have been perhaps the first person in the Islamic world trained in the Western sciences who has provided a critique of Western science on the basis of traditional Islamic metaphysics and cosmology. It therefore gives me special satisfaction to see other scholars now pursuing the same line of argument and willing to point out the disastrous consequences for the Islamic world of surrendering the Islamic understanding of the cosmos to the quantitative and uni-dimensional perspective of modern science.

Chittick, who has written extensively on Ibn 'Arabī's cosmology in his masterly work *The Self-Disclosure of God*, follows the Murcian master in developing a whole cosmology based on the interplay of the theophanies of the Divine Names and the significance of the "naming of things." While I concur with him about the significance of the "naming of things," I want to add that what is also significant is the consideration that a particular philosophy gives to the act itself of "naming of things." Chittick also asks what happens when important names in the cosmos are "'quasars', 'quarks,' 'muons,' 'black holes' and 'big bang'" rather than, let us say, the Divine Names and Qualities as well as form, substance, angels, creative act, etc.? Of course the changing of names is important, but what is even more essential is what naming *signifies*. For modern science a name is simply a signifier agreed upon by those who use it. For traditional man the "name" of a thing is related to its essential reality. It is in light of this sense of the term that the Bible and the Quran mention that God taught Adam the names of things. It is therefore essential not only to point out the significance of the changing of names in our understanding of things, but also the importance of what naming itself signifies. If the physicists and astronomers today were to change the current names of quarks, gluons, the big bang, and so on, to traditional terms, that would not change their perspective on the cosmos because they would not take these names to be anything *but* names. I remember that when I was at MIT I had an exceptionally gifted physics teacher who would refer to sub-atomic particles as animals in a zoo, but his naming of these particles in such a way did not alter his view of physics which he understood and taught as others who used conventional terms.

In speaking of God's self-Naming Chittick mentions that these Names are not abstract or inhuman and then adds that "the Islamic God is anthropomorphic" adding only later that "if God is understood in man's image, it is because man was created in God's image." To avoid all misunderstanding, I would formulate this basic doctrine differently. I would say that God in Islam *appears to be* anthropomorphic but in reality the reverse is true. It is man who possesses a theomorphic nature and reflects within his being the Divine Names and Qualities. Therefore God reveals Himself to man through Names which he can understand, without God becoming thereby in any way human or anthropomorphic. Having said this, I agree completely with Chittick that it is the Islamic view of the Divinity which enables man to recognize "the mercy, goodness, and wisdom that pervade reality."

In discussing the Islamic view of God, Chittick asserts, "the One God in Himself cannot be known." My view on this basic point is somewhat more nuanced. Of course we cannot know God in Himself through the use of reason. A *ḥadīth* of the Prophet of Islam also advises man to meditate upon God's Names and Qualities and not upon His Essence. Many Sufis also deny the possibility even to the intellect to know God in Himself. But there lies at the heart of man a divine spark. At the center of the heart resides the Divine Throne, to use the traditional Islamic imagery. The Sun of the Self shines at the center of man's being. By passing through the gate of annihilation (*al-fanā'*) and reaching the state of subsistence (*al-baqā'*) in God, man is able to swim in the Infinite Ocean of Divinity, to paraphrase a famous statement of Meister Eckhart, and to participate in a unitive state which transcends the dichotomy of knower and known beyond all mental and even intelligible categories. He cannot *comprehend* God in Himself, since God is infinite and to comprehend means literally to encompass; therefore how can one encompass that which is infinite? But one can become immersed in that ocean of Light on the condition of becoming no one, by becoming totally transparent before the God within or the inner Self which in knowing Itself knows all things.

The question of Islamic science and what it means in the context of the cosmology described by Chittick is a complex one which involves many elements. What Chittick mentions is certainly true in that the Western historians of science developed their discipline on the basis of their view of scientific progress and their positivistic understanding of science. In order to understand the significance of Islamic science in the context of Islamic civilization and the total Islamic intellectual perspective, it is necessary to develop a methodology for the study of the history of Islamic science which would not be simply an adaption of positivistic history of science prevalent in the West. One must develop a properly Islamic methodology for the study of the history of science. In several of my writings I have turned to this task, and in fact my *Science and Civilization in Islam* and *Islamic Science—An Illustrated Study*, to one of which Chittick refers, are written from the point of view of Islamic science itself rather than Western conceptions of it. To understand fully Islamic science and its history and status within the Islamic intellectual citadel, it is necessary to remember the hierarchy of knowledge so central to the Islamic worldview. To be sure there is every legitimacy for the existence of a rational science in the Islamic context, provided it is not taken to be the only legitimate science or even the highest form of knowledge—which is none other than *'irfān* or *ma'rifah* that can be rendered as "gnosis" or "noesis" based upon the twin sources of intellection and revelation.

In all that follows in this essay, I agree in general with Chittick's refined analysis, except where he says "The . . . symbolic approach—branded 'mystical,' 'irrational,' and 'superstitious' by the same people—came to be looked upon with contempt and was dismissed by the Muslims as 'un-Islamic'." I think that this statement is somewhat exaggerated, save in the case of those who adhere strictly to one form or another of rational puritanism or the more radical forms of modernism. For most Muslims, however, even those attracted to the more rational sciences, the evaluation of the symbolic and mystical understanding of things, even if critical, is usually not as severe as Chittick takes it to be, although his characterization definitely applies to certain Muslims.

At the end of his discussion of traditional cosmology Chittick turns again in an important paragraph to the question of "Divine Naming" and describes eloquently the significance of naming in determining the nature of things and the relation of man to the cosmos and, above all, to God. There is, however, one point which I believe needs further clarification, and that is the hierarchic and principial distinction between God's Naming of Himself and His teaching Adam the names of things, and furthermore, on a deeper level, the inward relation between those two acts of "naming."

In conclusion I must mention again the significance of Chittick's essay in dealing with an important subject to which little attention has been paid by other scholars. Even in my own writings I have not dealt to any great extent explicitly with the theme of the "Absent Men" while referring to the subject through allusion and indirectly in several contexts. But as mentioned at the beginning, the ideas expressed in this essay are essential to the understanding of the worldview which I espouse. Therefore, I am grateful to Chittick for having brought them forth in this remarkable text.

S. H. N.

24

Pierre Lory

KNOW THE WORLD TO KNOW YOURSELF

Throughout his manifold publications, Seyyed Hossein Nasr has not limited himself only to the explanation of the main doctrinal elements of the different trends of thought which have passed down through the medieval and contemporary Islamic world. He also has, and above all else, tried to extract from them the first articulations, the common intuitions which were conferring upon them all, an undeniable Islamic mark. Like an alchemist trying to extract from different substances the active principle allowing the constitution of gold, he read the works of the great philosophers, mystics, and artists in order to reconstruct the outlines of the primordial Wisdom present in the whole set of manifestations of Islamic civilization. He has, in this way, explained the foundations of an ideal model of thought, behavior, and sensibility representing the permanent, unchanging, and timeless element of Islam, in order to suggest to the man of the twentieth century a picture of this religion and of its culture, which could be both fully reliable to its past and able to fit into a modern world in continuous mutation.

The fundamental principle of this Wisdom would be *tawḥīd*, this conception of divine unity and of the unification of the creatures around God, which emerges from Quranic predications and which will be taken up by the great thinkers, jurists, and artists of Islam,[1] each in his own way. It is not only a question here of an intellectual or general ideological principle: the use of the word "Wisdom" (*ḥikmah*) emphasizes the fact that there is here a total commitment of the mind, including the metaphysically primary intuition leading the believer to recognize in the One, his origins as his end, and to get reunited to God in the different circumstances of his earthly life. The impulse of faith is here not separated from the rest of the "secular" activities of the society. More than that, in such a perspective—and this is one of the major interests of the "perennialist" reflection which is of importance here—mysticism is not at all rejected as being on the fringe of Islamic civilization. On the contrary, mysticism is its spinal column, the active principle, the sap itself, and has been so from its origin to the present.[2]

For Nasr, this model of thought, this approach of the real, constitutes the implicit mental structure of the totality of Islamic culture, and has repercussions in mysticism as well as in the ethics of work, in cosmography as well as in architecture, in philosophy as well as in gender relationships.[3] This very "Platonic" approach might be difficult to accept for the "positive" minds which refuse to consider religious life or thought outside an historical and precise geographical context, and which exclude a priori every timeless and invariable element in a society. This approach certainly also goes against a lot of Muslims who deny every central importance granted to Sufism or to theosophy, and see in Islam, before anything else, respect for a certain number of juridical rules. However that may be, it is not our purpose here to tackle those debates. We will not consider Muslim thought as a whole, but instead we will look at it from the point of view, already more limited, of its spiritual currents, so as to extricate certain complementary aspects from the traditional model proposed by Nasr.

The relationship among those different forms of thought—whenever it concerns Sufism or the Shi‘ite theosophy, the philosophy of Hellenic (*falsafah*) or Illuminationist (*ishrāq*) inspiration—is nonetheless undeniable. All of them are notable in considering that the phenomena appearing in the sensible world (*ẓāhir*) are the products of dynamisms stemming from concealed dimensions (*bāṭin*). Etymology illustrates well such an approach to the real. *Ẓāhir* comes from *ẓahr*, "the back," which evokes a surface all in exteriority, and which is not related to a precise organ. *Bāṭin* comes from *baṭn*, "the belly," which refers, on the contrary, to the idea of viscera, or vital organs. Those expressions suggest that we are usually looking at things, which are in the world, inside out, "from the back," according to their least deep aspect, and that perceiving them rightly depends on us, "in front," to discover the inside, the "bowels" of this reality that we perceive.

The expression of this vision of the world can be constructed philosophically (particularly in Neo-Platonic terms), or be the concern of an esoteric exegesis of the Quran, or even of a simple, immediate intuition in the case of such and such illiterate saint or thaumaturge; nevertheless, there is here, among Muslim mystics, a common approach to the real. We are even tempted to say that there is a common perception of things, even prior to the reflection itself. The *Homo islamicus*, immersed in a traditional society since his childhood, feels at the same time the rough phenomena (natural phenomena, aesthetic form, disease, . . .), and the dynamism there present in action. Indeed, he did acquire this "naiveness in the mentality"[4] that allowed him to connect his most elementary perception to a network of relations and symbols, and to enter immediately in resonance with other notions, feelings, or forms. These notions and feelings in turn have repercussions upon the activity of his own mind. This is the effect which arouses, for example, in the alchemist watching the purification and vivification of the mineral, a transmutation of his own mind. It is also this effect that prevents philosophical reflection in traditional Islam from limiting itself to a purely formal and cerebral exercise of reason, making it instead a real way of life and wisdom. Basically—and this is the subject of the present contribution—all knowledge of the exterior world is correlative in the traditional scholar with a transformation of the self. Let us try to clarify this.

The fact that there is parallelism, and consequently, interaction between the inner world of the human being and the exterior world(s), is explained in numerous traditional texts by the homology of structure between the microcosm and the macrocosm. This idea of hermetic origin bore fruit in numerous areas of the religious and scientific thought of Islam, where it is emphasized that the human compound reflects integrally the whole cosmos, or else, where the cosmos is thought of as the "Big Man." Ibn 'Arabī (d. 1124) wrote, based on his predecessors over three centuries, an ample synthesis on this matter around the notion of Muḥammadan Reality and Universal Man. This Universal Man, the first human being to be created, is himself the model of the whole creation, macrocosmic as well as human. However, each human being reproduces at his own level this totality of the model. "You are yourself the totality of the sphere of the world," wrote an esoterist of the thirteenth century A.D., "and you are contemplating the realities of the Divine mercy."[5]

The question we would like to ask here is the following: if the human compound is the replica of the great cosmos, in which way can the study of this latter help the man looking for truth to discover himself? Some sciences, such as alchemy, openly appear as access roads to Wisdom; others are, without a doubt, based on sapient presuppositions, such as astrology. But how do the two processes—of scientific apprenticeship and of gnostic knowledge—join together in the mind of the one who acquires knowledge? For it is not enough to assert peremptorily the principle of the universal correspondences to explain the psychological process here implied. Concerned with rigor and synthesis, the Ikhwān al-Ṣafā' suggest, in several passages of their *Rasā'il*, some systematic correspondences. They distinguish nine parts in the human body corresponding to the nine celestial spheres, seven human faculties each one connected to a particular planet, twelve openings in the body parallel to the signs of the Zodiac, and so on.[6] But do those lists really put us on the right track? We do feel a certain arbitrariness and a forced concordance: how can those enumerations help, spiritually speaking, a mind in search of the discovery of its self? We were speaking above of this "naiveness in the mentality" allowing a traditional mind to let itself be enriched and led into the contemplation of external facts; but still those facts—whether they concern the human body, or a metallic or celestial body—have to comprise an effective symbolism, to be able to "attract" the meditation of the seeker, and finally to be able to ensure the mediation between the particular man and the Universal Muḥammadan Reality from which that man proceeds.

Without at all claiming to bring a definite and unequivocal answer to this question, we would like to underscore here the absolutely essential importance which language and word take on in this process of joining the human spirit to its archetypal models; it is by the word that the seeker transforms himself and conforms to the model of the Perfect Man, for the word gives him at the same time meaning, guidance, and energy for that transformation. Here is a tropism appropriate to Islamic spirituality. Other religions have underscored the role of the image (for example in Christianity, Hinduism, or Buddhism), of music, or dance (Afro-West Indian worship) as means to reunite humans with their own celestial roots. Without ignoring other forms of expression of the sacred, Islam confers on the written as well as to the oral word a first rank place, according to the logic inherent in its own historical manifestation. For God, in the beginning, revealed Himself through the word, according to the Quran. The Muslims believe that the prophet Muḥammad has always been a neutral messenger in the Revelation which was fully dictated to him without any intervention by the Angel. Most theologians consider the Quran as divine uncreated verb, co-eternal with God. In other words the Quran is theophany above all else for the Muslim consciousness. The Muslim who recites the Quran (for example, during the five daily ritual prayers), re-actualizes the descent of the eternal Verb, he makes present the energy and Wisdom of the Creator, he becomes unified, by this word, with the divine source from which this word comes.

But the mystics have gone even further in their evaluation of the saving role of this Word. For the Sufi doctrinarians, there is homology, or identity, between the uncreated Quran ("Mother of the Book," see Quran XIII:39 and XLIII:4) and the Universal Man; for the Universal Man, and hence, all of what is left of the cosmos, is built as a language, himself being integrally language and Book. This idea arose at the end of the first century of the Hegirian era in the ultra-Shi'ite circles of Iraq and Iran. It was in the town of Kufa that Mughīra ibn Sa'īd (executed in 737) taught, having seen the Divinity in the form of a Man of Light whose body was constituted by the letters of the alphabet, and who started to create the world by writing on his own palm, under the impulse of the Supreme Name.[7] Even though the visionary form of Mughīrah's doctrine was not acceptable for most Muslims, his intuition was to be found, in a more elaborate form, in other trends of thought. The Twelve Iman Shi'ites have underlined the necessary homology between the deep nature of the Imams and the Quran: the twelve Imams are "silent Qurans," and finally the text of the Quran does not point anything else out than the Face of God which is, in Twelve Imān Shi'i theology, the Fourteen Immaculates.[8]

Nonetheless, this kind of speculation was also found quite early in the Sufism of Sunni allegiance. During the third/ninth centuries, the great master Sahl Tustarī (d. 283/896) wrote a short, but very condensed *Treatise on Letters*. His ideas would be taken up again and expanded in the next generation by the Andalusian philosopher and hermit Ibn Masarrah (d. 319/931) in his *Book of the Properties of Letters*.[9] According to those authors, God instituted first of all the different letters of the alphabet, which constitute, at the same time, the first particles of the whole creation, the orientation of the direction of the beings brought to existence, and the vectors of the creative energy itself. Those primordial letters, which can combine with others, constitute the Beautiful Names of God, which generate the different universes. We therefore could not better emphasize how the metaphysical worlds, the manifested cosmos, and man himself, are built as a language, are a language, and are the same[10] language from the throne of God to the smallest midge. Human languages are the refraction in the human mind of this universal organization; the words will naturally correspond, according to such a vision, to the essence of what they indicate. And in emphasizing this we will better understand how the contemplation of the created world can awaken human consciousness to its own internal dimensions. By naming a thing of the world, the human being awakens because the name brings forth the internal reality which corresponds to what exists in himself. Sky, earth, star, fire, and water are as many essential elements inside the human compound; to invoke them, and above all by means of the Quranic verb, is to shake the human soul or bring it into movement. Those considerations are based on the Quranic passage where God confided in Adam about the science of the names of the things (Quran II: 31), and, who after his disobedience and his repentance, helped him by sending him "words" (*kalimāt*, II: 37).

The ideas presented by Sahl Tustarī and Ibn Masarra would find their way into later Sufism, and would find their accomplishment in the work of Ibn 'Arabī (12th and13th centuries A.D.). This latter figure would devote large treatises to the symbolism of letters.[11] Nevertheless, he would not be the last to practice this science of letters, which spread throughout the Islamic world, and particularly in Iran.[12] The speculations on the symbolic and mystic value of the letters of the alphabet are not somehow the prerogative only of Sufism. Avicenna dedicated a small treatise to the symbolism of letters wherein he tried to integrate speculations about the alphabet into his own philosophical system.[13] Suhrawardī also made some short but very suggestive allusions to it.[14]

The extensive literature given over to magic and occult sciences, makes such great use of it that we cannot pass by in silence.[15] For in fact, the field of symbolism of letters goes beyond simple mysticism and includes a great part of the sciences of nature. In fact, the letters of the alphabet have been assigned to the seven heavens, to the planets, to the signs of the Zodiac, and to the different cutouts of the ecliptic. The twenty-eight letters, each one having numerical value, have been divided up into four groups: hot and cold, dry and humid. By means of this kind of speculation, it is all the natural world—its substances and its rhythms—which has been made "readable" according to a literal and numerical scale. The largest and most audacious synthesis in this field was expounded from the 2nd to 4th century of the Hegirian era in the immense alchemical corpus attributed to Jābir ibn Hayyān. It tried to summarize the natural laws of the world in a series of mathematical matrixes called "Balances" (*mawāzīn*); the main one of which, the one that generated all the others, was the Balance of the Letters. This Balance was based on the principle that words of the daily language correspond to the intimate nature of the thing that they indicate. Thus, the analysis of the names of mineral substances was supposed to give the opportunity to know, in a certain way, their deep composition, their archetypal formula; the alchemical work was here based on a "syntax of the natural phenomena," according to the literal meaning of the expression.[16]

From what has been said, we are thus guessing at the paradoxical and eminent function that language plays in the Islamic spirituality mentioned above. In fact, in such a perspective, the words of the language are not just present to indicate the concrete or abstract things, for those things themselves refer to a new language, to the creative language which has generated them, and which constitutes them. And if the cosmos is effectively comprehensible, it is because its structure itself is of a linguistic nature, and because the human language is precisely medial, the area of coherence above all else where in the human mind and the Mind moving the Universe join together. Everything in this world can and must be perceived as an element of a transcendental message, linguistically structured and endowed with a corporeal (consonant) and a spiritual (vowel) dimension; with a movement (*ḥarakah*, vocalization) or a rest (*sukūn*, quiescence); according to a straight (*naṣb*, accusative case), rising (*raf'*, nominative), or falling (*khafḍ*, dative) orientation. The elements of the world can hold the function of names, verbs or particles.

We are here far away from the Aristotelian universe surrounded by the principle of identity: each earthly phenomenon corresponds to several dimensions, to several "sentences" in the Book of the world. The human mind can only remain bewildered before the thousands of relations that can be discovered in the texture of the sensible world. Yet, the mystics of Islam assert that man is not helpless in the face of those real metaphysical continents that are to be explored. For he has in himself the faculty of exegesis, of *ta'wīl*, that allows him to interpret the perceived phenomena and to bring them again to their concealed dimension in the *bāṭin*ian nature. This is not surprising, for man is himself an integral part of this creation; furthermore, he epitomizes it in its whole. Thus there exists a certain interaction of being between the seeker of truth and the objects that he meets along his earthly journey. Each man carries in himself the nine spheres, the seven planets, the twelve zodiacal "towers."[17] The interpretation that man is able to give concerning them has its source not in a pure inductive process, but in a meeting between the empirical observations and his spiritual intuition. Ibn Khaldūn (14th century A. D.) denied to astrology any certitude;[18] however, he based his theory on the impossibility of applying to this discipline a rational induction and never dealt with its inner or "*bāṭin*ian" dimension. Among some authors like Jābir ibn Ḥayyān, the laboratory work is accompanied by a sustained meditation on terms that help to indicate the things of the world. Thus, a study of the words such as, for example, *dhahab* (gold), or *zirnīkh* (arsenic), will lead, according to him, to the discovery of the intimate composition of these substances, regarding their external (*ẓāhir*) manifestation, but also regarding their inner, concealed (*bāṭin*) composition.[19]

Nevertheless, it is possible to object here that this personal intuition still is a means of very precarious knowledge, subject to error; and the examples of deductions from the language that Jabir is proposing to us are full of arbitrary and fabricated reasonings. But, in reality, Muslim esoterists seldom refer to this kind of approach in the study of natural phenomena, literally speaking. Its most usual dimension is mainly closely akin to mysticism. Most of the speculations of esoterists are based on the text which is the best in accordance with the divine enunciation that can be: the Quran.

As we mentioned above, the celestial Quran is similar to the Universal Man. The first model of all that exists is a "human" reality, of which on one side the human being and on the other side the divine revelation, are the earth's most accomplished typifications. It is therefore rather natural that esoterists have sought, in the sacred text, not only for directives of faith and action given by its literal meaning, but also for less accessible secrets about the concealed dimensions of human destiny, about the way that man can accomplish his plenary vocation as a mirror of divine lights. Thus, the Quranic commentaries proposed by Sufis[20] refer, for example, to such and such Quranic passages on the prophets' lives and to processes of mystical psychology. Even more profoundly, they speculate on some Quranic verses (those of the first *sūrah*, the *Fātiḥah*, or on those of the *Throne*, II: 255) and on some letters (particularly the fourteen "isolated" letters set at the head of some *sūrahs*) to discover there the mysteries of the ascension of the soul towards God. Thus, the Quran is no longer a reference text for good behavior of the Muslim: the Quran is the text which, in a secret but still truly real manner, shows the way of the self towards the Self. It is the simultaneity of those two styles that constitutes for the Sufi the most supernatural characteristic of the revealed text.

Now, if we return to the question asked at the beginning, "how does the knowledge of the world lead to the knowledge of the self?" we notice that in light of putting into play of the sacred language, we have thus to refer to numerous dimensions:

(1) The knowledge of an external object designated by its name awakens, as we note, the area of the human soul that corresponds to it. The principle "we are what we know" is here confirmed. Contrary to what a purely conceptual, cerebral teaching leads to, the apprenticeship as a meditation, which is in question here, implies progressively a real transmutation of the mind. The discovery of the self and the discovery of the world are correlative: a man will know the *bāṭin* of the world that surrounds him as far as his state allows him to grasp it and to accomplish the necessary exegesis.

(2) The Quranic word, more particularly, is endowed with a real operative power, the same power that the Sufis bring into action during sessions of *dhikr*. It is characteristic that the *dhikr* is by far the most practiced ritual in Muslim spirituality, where the "sacramental" value of the verb has been so much emphasized. For to utter the divine uncreated verb is, for each individual, to animate again in himself a timeless memory and to make thus possible the growth of gnosis.

(3) Such a knowledge cannot be summarized as the comprehension of an inanimate object by a subject thinking: this knowledge results, in fact, from the meeting of two consciousnesses. The stars observed by the astrologist are angels, for example, and the material worked by the alchemist manifests the Mind of the world in all its Wisdom. In the traditional science, the mind meets the Mind; this is what makes the mind grow and what purifies it.

(4) If the reading of the Book transforms the individual, the spiritual growth of the Sufi comes in turn to complete the redaction of the Book of the universe. Those saints in whom "the Quran is mixed with their flesh and blood"[21] actualize, in a certain way, this eternal Quran. Just as the Universal Man actualizes himself in the manifestation of the Perfect Man,[22] in the person of the prophets, great saints, or Poles, the Quran of the beginning is performed through mysterious volumes[23] which contain the eschatological evolution of humanity—that is to say, the Quran is fulfilled through the life of man in flesh and blood.

This omnipresent function of the Word in Muslim spirituality finds, nonetheless, its achievement—it has to be underlined—in the ultimate message of a divine silence; silence, of course, not of privation, but of plenitude. For God Himself is forever unknowable, remaining beyond every human discourse, even if symbolic or sacred. "The word is veil, the veil is word," wrote the great Sufi Niffarī,[24] admirably summarizing all the dialectic of the sacred reading of the Book of the world. Arriving at the point of tangency of the world of the word with the one of mystery, the human mind skims past the last of the veils and the last of the letters. There, human language explodes in paradox, takes refuge in repetition, or ends in the silence of Wisdom. An ancient tale relates that the Sufi al-Ḥallāj, on the eve of his execution in the town of Baghdad in 922, said his prayers, then began to repeat "*makr, makr*" ("trickery, trickery"); after a moment of silence, he shouted, "*ḥaqq, ḥaqq*" ("Reality, Reality") before uttering the last orison of his earthly life.[25] This oscillation between the divine illusion to which our existence in this world constrains us, and the absolute truth that this existence can reveal to us, seems well to translate the look cast at the world by most Muslim mystics: sublime camouflage of the divine Wisdom, the language of the Book of the universe is fulfilled in its own annihilation. For the believer immersed in concrete history, the horizon of every exegesis of the world becomes, eventually, messianic.

PIERRE LORY

DEPARTMENT OF RELIGIOUS STUDIES
ÉCOLE PRATIQUE DES HAUTES ÉTUDES
SORBONNE, FRANCE
OCTOBER 1993

NOTES

1. See S. H. Nasr, *Ideals and Realities of Islam* (Chicago: ABC International Group, 2000).
2. See in *Traditional Islam in the Modern World* (London: KPI, 1987), the prologue "What is Traditional Islam?"
3. See *Science and Civilization in Islam* (Cambridge: Harvard University Press, 1968).
4. *Science and Civilization in Islam*, p. 243.
5. Al-Būnī, *Shams al-ma'ārif al-kubrā* (Cairo: Matba'a Mustafa Muhammad, n.d.), p. 74.
6. See among others: the Ikhwān al-Safā', *Rasā'il* (Cairo: 'Arabiyyah Press, 1923), treatises XXIII ("On the composition of the body") and XXVI ("On the principle of the sages according to which man is a small universe"), and the summary proposed by Nasr in *An Introduction to Islamic Cosmological Doctrines* (Albany: SUNY Press, 1993), pp. 96–104. We also notice an interesting parallel

between proportions of the body and musical proportions in the fifth treatise "On Music" (cf. A. Shiloah, "L'épītre sur la musique des Ikhwān al-Safā'," *Revue des Etudes Islamiques*, no. 34 [1966], p. 172).

7. Cf. Our study "Le Livre comme corps de Dieu" in *Magie du Livre, Livres de magie* (Paris: La Table d'Emeraude, 1993), p. 67 ff. For the strictly historical aspect of this movement, see W. Tucker "Rebels and Gnostics: al-Mughīra ibn Sa'īd and the Mughīriyya" in *Arabica*, no. 20 (1975): 33–47.

8. See for example Mahmoud Ayoub, "The Speaking Qur'ān and the Silent Qur'ān: A Study of the Principles and Development of Imāmī Shī'ī *tafsīr*," in *Approaches to the History of the Interpretations of the Qur'ān*, Andrew Rippin, ed. (Oxford: Clarendon Press, 1988).

9. Those two treatises have been published under the care of Kamāl Ja'far, the first (*Risālat al-ḥurūf* of Tustarī) in *Sahl ibn 'Abdallāh al-Tustarī* (Cairo, 1974), pp. 366–75; the second (*Kitāb khawāṣṣ al-ḥurūf wa-ḥaqā'iqi-hā wa-uṣūli-hā* of Ibn Masarrah) in *Min qaḍāyā al-fikr al-islāmī* (Cairo, 1978), pp. 311–44. We will find a general presentation of their content in the commented translation of passages of the *Futūḥāt* of Ibn 'Arabī, *Les Illuminations de la Mecque/The Meccan Illuminations* (Paris: Sindbad, 1988) in the presentation by Denis Gril of the Islamic Science of Letters (pp. 423–29).

10. That is to say that they are built by combination of those same twenty-eight primordial letters; but, the modes of combination, the "cosmic languages" are, of course, numerous.

11. The most important is in chapter 2 of the *Futūḥāt al-makkiyyah*; cf. their presentation and their partial translation in French by Denis Gril in *Les Illuminations de la Mecque/The Meccan Illuminations* (Paris: Sindbad, 1988), pp. 385 ff.

12. By way of example, see the passages on mysticism in the letters of Najm al-dīn Kubrā in *Die Fawā'iḥ al-Jamāl wa-Fawātih al-Jalāl des Najm al-dīn al-Kubrā*, by Fritz Meier (Wiesbaden: Franz Steiner Verlag, 1957), pp. 134 ff.

13. "Al-Risālat al-nayrūziyyah fī ma'ānī al-ḥurūf al-hijā'iyyah" in *Tis'rasā'il fī al-ḥikmah wa-al-ṭabī'iyyāt* (Cairo, 1908), pp. 134–41; cf. also the commentary that has been done about it, Louis Massignon in "La philosophie orientale d'Ibn Sīnā et son alphabet philosophique," in *Mémorial Avicenne* IV (Cairo: I.F.A.O., 1954), pp. 1–18.

14. See for example the short treatise in Persian *Risālah fī ḥālat al-ṭufūliyyah*, translated and commented on in French by Henry Corbin in *L'Archange empourpré* (Paris: Fayard, 1976), pp. 385–412.

15. On the processes of the literal magic, see Edmond Doutté, *Magie et religion dans l'Afrique du Nord* (Paris: J. Maisonneuve et P. Geuthner, 1984), chaps. III and IV. For a doctrinal approach, see Pierre Lory, "La magie des lettres dans le *Shams al-ma'ārif* d'al-Būnī," *Bulletin d'Etudes Orientales*, Vols. XXXIX–XL (1989): 97–111.

16. For more details on this theory of the Balances, see the work of Paul Kraus, *Jābir ibn Ḥayyān-Contribution à l'histoire des idées scientifiques dans l'Islam* (Paris: Les Belles Lettres, 1986), pp. 187–303; and P. Lory, *Alchimie et mystique en terre d'Islam* (Lagrasse: Verdier, 1989), pp. 121–54.

17. From it results another perception of the human body. For if it has been made possible to say in the twenty-first century that consciousness corresponds to the corporal sketch, we notice among the Sufis a consciousness endowed with several levels, blooming in the discovery of the different bodies of the mystical physiology here implied.

18. *The Muqaddimah: An Introduction to History*, trans. F. Rosenthal (New York: Pantheon Books, 1958), chap. VI, section 31.

19. Cf. Paul Kraus, op. cit., pp. 223–36.

20. For the Sufi exegetes' processes of the Quran, we can report, in addition to the quite ancient work of Ignaz Goldziher, *Die Richtungen der islamischen Koranauslegung* (Leiden, 1920) to the rich work of P. Nwyia, *Exégése coranique et langage mystique* (Beyrouth: Dar El-Machreq, 1970); Gerhard Böwering, *The Mystical Vision of Existence in Classical Islam—The Qur'ānic Hermeneutics of the Sufi Sahl At-Tustarī* (Berlin/New York: Walter de Gruyter, 1980); and Pierre Lory, *Les Commentaires ésotériques du Coran selon A. R. Al-Qāshānī* (Paris: Les Deux Océans, 1990).

21. Word attributed to Dhū al-Nūn al-Miṣrī (3rd/9th centuries). Cf. also the expression of Ibn 'Arabī in the *Fuṣūṣ al-ḥikam*: "Nobody will understand what we just said except the one who is himself the Quran." *The Wisdom of the Prophets*, trans. Angela Culme-Seymour (Chisholme, U.K.: Beshara Publications, 1975).

22. See Michel Chodkiewicz, *Le Sceau des saints* (Paris: Gallimard, 1986), pp. 90–92.

23. These are books which allude to, in particular, the Shi 'ite tradition under the quite mysterious titles of *Jafr* and *Jāmi 'ah*; cf. Toufic Fahd, *La Divination arabe* (Paris: Sindbad, 1987), p. 219 ff, and the article "Djafr" in the *Encyclopedia of Islam*, ed. C. E. Bosworth, et al. (Leiden: E. J. Brill, 1971–1999).

24. See *The Mawāqif and Mukhātabāt*, edited with translation and commentary by Arthur John Arberry (London: Luzac & Co., 1935), p. 111.

25. Cf. Louis Massignon, *The Passion of al-Ḥallāj*, trans. Herbert Mason (Princeton University Press, 1982), vol. I, chap. VII, c.

REPLY TO PIERRE LORY

Professor Lory and I are linked together not only in our common interest in Islamic esoterism and philosophy, but also through Henry Corbin who was his teacher at the Sorbonne and my colleague in Tehran and friend of two decades until his death in 1978. In his essay Lory deals with a subject of great interest to me but not treated to any extent in other essays in this volume, the subject being the rapport between philosophy and esoteric sciences in Islam. This rapport concerns not only the general relation between Islamic philosophy and the quintessential esoterism of Islam found in Sufism and certain aspects of Shi'ism, both Twelve-Imam and Ismā'īlī, a relation with which I have dealt extensively in my writings and also in certain responses in this volume. This rapport involves also the nexus between Islamic philosophy and the "Hidden Sciences" (*al-'ulūm al-gharībah* or *khafiyyah*) such as alchemy and the science of letters, a domain in which Professor Lory is an expert and to which he has contributed a number of valuable studies. Before responding to his essay in a specific manner, it would be appropriate for me to say a few words on my general views concerning the relation between philosophy and esoterism.

In the West with the eclipse of authentic esoterism and its reduction to occultism, the whole relation of philosophy to esoterism became suspect at least in the mainstream of Western philosophy. Esoteric philosophy made people in the West think, at best, of Agrippa, Robert Fludd, Michael Maier or the salons of Paris, and even such major esoteric thinkers as Böhme and Eckhart were shunned in official philosophical circles. In more recent times anyone who has sought to speak of esoteric philosophy in Europe and America has been accused of following on the path of Annie Besant and Madame Blavatsky. The reaction of Corbin himself, at once philosopher and esoterist as well as a formidable scholar, among many Islamicists and philosophers in France is itself indicative of the climate of which I speak. Yet Corbin himself was able to open a foothold in the official academic world for esoteric philosophy, at least in its Islamic form, and had a number of followers among French philosophers such as Gilbert Durand and

Christian Jambet. Also he was certainly influential in the establishment of a chair for the study of Occidental esoteric philosophies at the Sorbonne, now occupied by his student Antoine Faivre. One needs also to mention here the central importance of the works of René Guénon who, in expounding authentic esoteric teachings and pure metaphysics after the lapse of many centuries in the West and in clarifying the distinction between esoterism and occultism, opened the door for a "new" consideration of the significance of esoterism and esoteric philosophy. Although opposed severely in French academic circles, his ideas along with those of Schuon have had an immense influence upon both scholarly and philosophical studies being carried out on the subject in continental Europe today. As for the Anglo-Saxon world where positivism has continued to reign supreme for the past half century, the whole idea of esoteric philosophy is still mostly shunned in philosophy departments, and, if studied at all, is confined to religion or literature departments.

In the Islamic world the destiny of philosophy was to be very different. Even in the early centuries, many of the Islamic Peripatetic philosophers such as al-Fārābī and Ibn Sīnā intertwined esoteric ideas with more rational aspects of their philosophies as did many of the ancient Greek philosophers such as the Pythagoreans, Platonists, Neoplatonists, Neopythagoreans, and Hermeticists. Moreover, even during the early period of Islamic history, Ismā'īlī philosophy always connected philosophy to the esoteric (*bāṭin*) dimension of the religion. In later centuries, Islamic philosophy moved even closer to the esoteric dimension of the religion, and esoteric ideas which issued either directly from the Quranic revelation or came from elsewhere—mainly Athens and Alexandria—but were integrated into Islamic esoterism. The case of Suhrawardī is a major example of this trend. His *ḥikmat al-ishrāq* or Philosophy/Theosophy of Illumination, which became a major philosophical school in the later period of Islamic history, combines philosophy even in its rigorous rational sense with esoteric ideas. As we look upon the centuries that followed, we see many of the schools of philosophy becoming even more closely wed to gnosis and esoterism until, with Mullā Ṣadrā and his illustrious students, such as Mullā 'Alī Zunūzī and Ḥājjī Mullā Hādī Sabziwārī, philosophy and esoterism in the form of gnosis became fused in a unity.

There was, moreover, another group of esoteric philosophies in Islam which often interacted with the above schools but remained distinct from them. These types of esoteric philosophy were associated with alchemists such as Jābir ibn Ḥayyān, certain Sufi masters of the science of letters such as Abū Sahl al-Tustarī, Ibn Masarrah, Ibn 'Arabī, 'Abd al-Karīm al-Jīlī and many others, and some of the masters of the "occult sciences," chief among them Shams al-Dīn al-Būnī. Although not as popular and accessible as the first kind, this second group of esoteric philosophies have had a continuous life throughout the Islamic world since the beginning of Islam and have contributed major philosophical ideas to the general tradition of Islamic philosophy. Pierre Lory deals with some of them in this essay. Personally, I have been much interested in all these types of esoteric philosophy in Islam and have contributed a number of studies on them, but more to the first kind than the second. What is important to state here is that both kinds are important for understanding the Islamic intellectual tradition in its integral reality. It is also important to note that the destiny of esoteric philosophy and the relation between philosophy and esoterism in the Islamic world was to be very different from what happened in the West after the Renaissance.

Turning now to the text of Lory, at the beginning of his essay he writes, "He [Nasr] has, in this way, explained the foundations of an ideal model of thought, behavior, and sensibility representing the permanent, unchanging, and timeless element of Islam." He mentions this point in a positive manner but there are many in the West who have criticized me precisely for having carried out such a task. They consider the task illusory, since for them the only reality is the temporal and historical. For my part, however, religion possesses a meta-historical and celestial archetype which manifests itself in a temporal sequence but is never reducible to that sequence. For me the "ideal model" does not mean simply a goal sought in the mind but that which is related to the "Idea" in its Platonic sense. It is that "Idea" which is immutable and unchanging, while its manifestations in time naturally partake of the character of change that is inseparable from history as usually understood. The "Ideal Model" of a religion in this sense is not only the sum of its earthly manifestations or even the faith of its believers, but a heavenly reality reflected in all authentic manifestations of the tradition created by the descent or revelation of that "Ideal Model," to quote Lory. It is possible through active participation in the tradition and through the use of God-given intelligence freed from the fetters of the passions and by the grace of Heaven, to gain knowledge of that "Ideal Model" or archetype and to make it known to those interested in grasping the essence and not only the historical accidents of a religion. In seeking to explain the "foundations of an ideal model of thought, behavior, and sensibility" of Islam, I have not, however, neglected the historical realities. Like Lory's teacher Corbin, I have opposed historicism while holding much respect for what Corbin and I have called the *historial*.

I agree with Lory that this approach, which he calls "Platonic," is difficult for minds trained in positivism to accept. This difficulty is in fact to be seen in the general modern attitude towards perennial philosophy and traditional metaphysics. The refusal to see a permanent reality beyond measurable and observable temporal change is also at the root of the current crisis in the field of religious studies in the West, as far as it concerns comparative studies versus deconstructionism, phenomenology versus historicism, attitudes towards truth claims in religions, and so on. But during the past forty years I have been little affected by positivistic and historistic criticisms and will most likely not be in the future. Whatever historical and phenomenological studies may reveal about a religion's manifestations in history, they cannot fulfill the task of understanding its essence, its heavenly archetype which only the traditional approach is able to attain. As Lory says, one has to be like an alchemist and "extract" the principle from the "different substances" at hand.

Pierre Lory also points to the relationship between several forms of Islamic thought, namely Sufism, Shi'ite theosophy, and the School of Illumination, all of which rely upon the same view of the world as consisting of an outward and an inward dimension and of authentic knowledge as being able to cast aside the veil of outwardness to reach the inner meaning through the process which is called *ta'wīl* or esoteric hermeneutics. I agree fully with the author's assertion and will only add that it is precisely these schools of Islamic thought, along with aspects of the Islamic cosmological sciences, whose symbolic significance I have sought to unveil in some of my writings, and that have been at the center of my attention during all the decades I have been studying Islamic intellectual life. I am by nature attracted to esoteric knowledge not in the sense of occultism but in its authentic sense, and therefore share with Pierre Lory a strong interest in what one might call "esoteric philosophy," although I prefer the terms "traditional metaphysics" and "esoterism."

I am also in full agreement with the author when he states, "every knowledge of the exterior world is correlative in the traditional scholar with a transformation of the self." As I turned from the study of philosophy in a Western academic context to the traditional setting of Persia, I began to realize even more fully how true the above assertion is. Traditional philosophy transforms the being of the knower, and in turn requires a degree of virtue before being understood. I comprehended why Pythagoras and the Pythagoreans had set so many moral conditions upon their adepts before they accepted them into their philosophical circles and why this was still the case in small and fairly closed circles in Persia where the higher doctrines of traditional philosophy were being taught. Some of my traditional teachers used to make their ritual ablutions (*wuḍū'*) before embarking upon teaching the text of a Suhrawardī or a Mullā Ṣadrā. In any case there is certainly a correlation between one's mode of being and the knowledge one gains. At the highest level the very dichotomy of knowledge and being, subject and object, is transcended in that unity which transcends all duality and opposition and is itself the *coincidentia oppositorum*.

Lory asks the question "if the human compound is the replica of the great cosmos, in which way can the study of this latter help the man looking for truth to discover himself?" The first answer to this seminal question is that the qualitative knowledge of the cosmos is also self-discovery precisely because of the correspondence between man and the cosmos. For example, correspondences established by the Ikhwān al-Ṣafā', whom the author mentions, far from being arbitrary and forced, provide occasions for recollection, for intellectual intuition, for awareness of relations not before realized and for gaining a vision of the cosmos as support for the "inner work." All traditional sciences of nature, based as they are on metaphysics, symbolism, and cosmic correspondences, are also sciences of the self on the basis of the microcosmic/macrocosmic correspondence mentioned by the author. But each traditional science achieves this end in a different way. If a science be authentic, however, it is always a key for the understanding of the inner reality of the cosmos and therefore ourselves, a means of access to the vision of the hierarchies of cosmic existence and, therefore, also a ladder by means of which we can ascend through the various realms of the cosmos itself to the Metacosmic Reality. But these functions can only become actualized in the presence of a living spiritual and esoteric current which allows these sciences to be channels for the emanation of the light and grace which alone makes self-realization possible, the element of grace (drawing here from the vocabulary of the three monotheisms) having its equivalent in other worlds, including non-theistic ones. As Titus Burckhardt has written, the traditional sciences are like a jewel and the living esoteric and spiritual current of a tradition like light. In a dark room a jewel is no different from an opaque stone, but held before light, the jewel displays its very different properties of being able to enhance and elaborate the light in contrast to the opaque stone. What transforms man's being in the study of the traditional sciences and the harmonies and correspondences upon which they are based is the light emanating from that jewel, and not the jewel itself if it were to be kept in a dark room. The occultist as opposed to esoteric understanding of the traditional sciences proves the case in point.

As for the cosmological sciences serving as support for contemplation of metacosmic realities and inner transformation, perhaps no better example can be provided for this function than alchemy with which the author has dealt in so many of his important studies, and to which I have also devoted some attention in my *Science and Civilization in Islam* and elsewhere. Alchemy is at once a science of the cosmos and a science of the soul, at once an external and internal medicine, at once a manner of ennobling matter and the being of the alchemist. Its laboratory is at once the chamber in which the alchemist works and his inner being. And alchemical transformation cannot occur save with the presence of the Philosopher's Stone which is none other than the symbol of Divine Presence and grace by means of which "nature can surmount nature," to quote the famous alchemical saying.

I also agree fully with Pierre Lory in his emphasis upon sacred language, the words and letters of which both the revealed book and the cosmic book are comprised. The act of creation or the cosmogonic act can be conceived in terms of the emanation of light (*fiat lux*) or the Word (*in principia erat verbum*), or to use the language of ontology in the Quran, *kun fa yakūn* "be and there is." It can also be expressed in terms of mathematical symbolism (both arithmetic and geometric) as we see in Pythagoreanism, or, in the issuing of sound as music from the primordial silence as in Śivite Hinduism. There are also other symbolic representations to be found in other traditions. In Islam the revelation came in the form of a book whose every letter and word is sacred, for the book is none other than the Word of God itself. In Islamic esoterism each letter and word of the sacred language of the Quran, that is Arabic, has an archetypal reality and is also in its primordial reality a divine energy as well as "idea" in the Platonic sense. It is in light of the primacy of this vision that one must understand not only the esoteric commentaries upon the Quran by the Sufis and Shi'ite gnostics, but also Jābir ibn Ḥayyān's application of the idea of the cosmos as the cosmic book (*al-qur'ān al-takwīnī*), to use the terminology of later Sufism, to the realms of particular sciences, and his idea of the balance (*al-mīzān*) established between the letters comprising the name of a substance in Arabic and its natural characteristics, both inward and outward. Even Jābir ibn Ḥayyān's application of the science of letters to the name of gold (*dhahab*) and arsenic (*zirnīkh*), for example, must be seen in the symbolic sense (including the numbers involved), as must the *mīzān* itself and not literally, although he was also concerned with the outward properties of things.

Lory summarizes his own answer to the question of "how does the knowledge of the world lead to the knowledge of the self?" under four headings with which I concur completely. However, I would like to comment briefly on his third point, which is that the knowledge of the world is "the meeting of two consciousnesses" and not a mind and an inanimate object. This is an esoteric understanding which is certainly correct on a certain level. But it is also possible to say that in the traditional sciences, using the language of Islamic philosophy and science here, man knows the forms of things that have themselves become generated by the intellect, which also plays the central role in cognition because it is through the illumination of the mind by the intellect that perception itself takes place, as stated by Ibn Sīnā. Mullā Ṣadrā goes a step further and asserts that there is the union (*ittiḥād*) of the knower or "intellector" (*al-'āqil*), intellect (*al-'aql*) and the intelligible (*al-ma'qūl*) at the moment of intellection, which is the basis of all perception (*idrāk*). I have the greatest sympathy for this perspective and likewise believe that every act of knowing is an illumination that binds the being of the knower and the known together as knower and known. I would, however, use a more nuanced language than Lory in discussing this very important point.

In the last paragraph of his essay the author speaks of speech reaching silence and the fact that "the language of the Book of the universe is fulfilled in its own annihilation." I will comment on this poetic utterance by saying that the Book of the universe is not annihilated until all creation returns to God, but it helps *us* to become "annihilated" in that silence which is the source of all language, in that ineffable Formlessness which is the origin of all forms. To become nothing is to swim in the Ocean which is the origin of everything. To hear that silent music is also to hear all traditional music, celestial and terrestrial, produced through the ages.

The relation between philosophy and authentic esoterism needs to be investigated again seriously as a philosophical issue in the West. As for the Islamic world, this nexus has never been severed. Professor Pierre Lory, who is one of the rare experts on this subject in the West, has expounded important aspects of what one might call esoteric philosophy in Islam, and has thereby afforded me the occasion to make a few critical comments. I am happy to have been afforded such an opportunity.

S. H. N.

25

Parviz Morewedge

THE TRANSCENDENT SPIRIT, PRIVATE LANGUAGE FALLACY, AND ISLAMIZATION OF IBN SĪNĀ: REFLECTIONS ON THE WORKS OF S. H. NASR

NASR'S CONTRIBUTIONS TO ISLAMIC PHILOSOPHY

Due to his scholarship, his peerless ability in organized research, as well as his graceful ambience and personality, Seyyed Hossein Nasr is well known to a majority of investigators in Islamic philosophy, including this writer. In the '60s, as a graduate student, I was introduced to Ibn Sīnā's philosophy through Nasr's two early works, *Three Muslim Sages* and *Islamic Cosmological Doctrines.* In the '70s, after my twenty-five year absence from Iran, Nasr brought me as a guest lecturer to his academy in Tehran, where I was a witness to the best of Persian hospitality and the vigor of his organizational ability. From the '70s to the present, I have attended his presentations at many conferences and have benefited from his counsel on a number of professional matters. In sum, my reflections on Nasr's philosophy are due to my acquaintance with his work and lectures for the past forty years. For the sake of brevity and the space allowed to me, I begin by delineating briefly four aspects of his contribution to Islamic studies and then proceed to a critique of three themes in his philosophy.

First, Nasr is an excellent manager of organized research, as is evident from the fruits of his directorship of the Imperial Iranian Academy of Philosophy. His philosophical foresight and personal strength resulted in the establishment of an academy where a number of Islamic philosophical texts were edited, including the complete works of S. Suhrawardī and a number of important manuscripts of Ismāʻīlī writers.[1] His managerial genius brought to Tehran the best scholars from abroad. Notable among them were H. Corbin from France and T. Izutsu from Japan. Under Nasr's direction, they and a group of other scholars from abroad collaborated with their Iranian counterparts, such as J. Ashtiyani and M. T. Danish-Pashuh, to form one of the most vibrant centers of Islamic philosophy ever established. For the next two generations, this group published the major references for scholarship on post–Ibn Sīnan philosophers, especially Shiʻite thinkers. It is impossible to overstate the debt of Islamic philosophical scholarship to Nasr.

Second, Nasr is to be praised for his personal dignity, for not seeking security and fame by following the trodden path of philosophers such as Ibn Sīnā and Ibn Rushd. Instead, against all odds, he single-handedly championed the scholarship of thinkers who were unknown to the West, namely post–Ibn Sīnan philosophers. It was he who brought to the attention of the English-speaking public the significance of the philosophy of Mullā Ṣadrā and other members of the School of Isfahan (PAPSB, 337–44). In doing so, he was instrumental in the development of research in these traditions. Since the1990s, a number of organized efforts, such as the *Mullā Ṣadrā Congress* in Tehran, *the Institute of Ismāʻīlī Studies* in London, and *The Islamic Translation Series* in Utah and Binghamton have focused on this post–Ibn Sīnan period. I can only hint at the extent of his contribution by the following analogy. Imagine that in the West, instructors of philosophy stopped with Kant's writing; then someone enriches historical scholarship by encouraging the editing of works by Hegel and later German idealists. Imagine. Where would the history of postmedieval Western philosophy be without Hegel? In the same manner, Nasr's contribution to the scholarship of the history of Islamic philosophy cannot be overstated. Even now, the best accounts of later Islamic philosophy are found in his contributions to various encyclopedia sources (Oxford II, and RIP).

Third, Nasr has always spoken out for the ideals of the Islamic tradition, and he has done so regardless of the popularity of this message for his audience. A good example of this is his explanation of various aspects of "temporary marriage" (SI, 227–30). It is ironic that he has never benefited from his stance as a defender of Islam, either during the Pahlavi regime or postrevolutionary Islamic Republic of Iran.

Finally, a number of original ideas appear in his writings; these include the notion of sacred space and unity as expressed by Islamic architecture (see RIP, vol. 5, 18–19). As another example, Nasr depicts two dialectical phases of religious experience. The first phase occurs in ethnic isolation, when a member of each creed takes his/her system to be the only available system.

The next phase occurs in a multicultural context, when different specific creeds can harmonize their urge via a mystical interpretation of the specifics; for example, in the Jungian sense, there is an archetype of the mediator figure as a member of a clergy, be it a rabbi, a priest, or a shaykh. Thus mysticism ironically expresses themes of different religious perspectives (SE, 124–25).

Prior to my critique of Nasr's views I would like to share a point of frustration in writing this article. A majority of classical Muslim philosophers write clearly about philosophical topics; in contrast, many of Nasr's philosophical views are more analogous to poetry than to analysis. While most philosophers are careful with their use of key philosophical primitives, Nasr uses vague expressions such as "spirits breathing in the world" and "Being radiating its light." Moreover, I do not understand his consciously offensive and almost insulting treatment of "sacred cows of modernity." Here are two general observations: first, Nasr intends to shock the reader; second, often he presents his objections without adequate justifications. Here are two examples: Nasr claims that in some sense alchemy is better than chemistry, and that evolution is incorrect. What is the most reasonable understanding of his praise of alchemy and attack on theory of evolution? This type of attitude is either a poetical cry of religious anti-scientism or incorrect understanding of contemporary views of science. No biologist claims that she/he observes a scientific law such as evolution. Does Nasr claim that he observes the immutable and the supposed process of the immutable seeing its fleeting nature in the outward nature? The main question is how different theories of evolution and postulation of creationism explain facts such as fossils; scientific laws are not observed but proposed to explain observation and used for predication.

Although there may be no tradition of censorship on entertaining a philosophical position, nevertheless one obviously expects some explanations for holding a non-canonical position against modernity, chemistry, evolution, and science in the third millennium. Unfortunately, Nasr's remarks against the "sacred cows of modernity" seldom contain logical arguments or useful references. He charges against whatever does not support the religious tradition—modernity, modern philosophy, and rationalism. While his writing provides comfort to the religious audience, the secular reader often questions his work. Prima facie, there are at least two problems with his arguments, when he presents them. One may ask, are these arguments sound? Do they represent the ethos of the majority of the Islamic philosophical tradition? I will examine answers to these questions in the context of my evaluation of three topics in Nasr's writings: Ibn Sīnā's ontology of the analytic of "being" and cosmogony, the transcendent spirit, and issues related to the "private language fallacy."

I. On Nasr's Interpretation of Ibn Sīnā—Analytic of "Being" and Cosmogony

In this section I question Nasr on two notions of Ibn Sīnā's philosophy: (a) a transcendent notion of being and its confusion with being-qua-being and an existent, and (b) attribution of "religious creationism" to Ibn Sīnā's system.

Let me begin by clarifying my own reading of Ibn Sīnā's metaphysic as a basis of my criticism of Nasr's interpretation.[2] The two primary notions of the soul for Ibn Sīnā are "being" (*hastī, wujūd*) and the modalities of necessity (*wājib*), contingency (*mumkin*), and impossibility (*mumtani'*). When "being" is concatenated with "necessity" the result is "the necessary being," which, according to the second version of the ontological argument, equates with "the Necessary Existent." When "being" is concatenated with "contingency," the result is a "contingent existent" only if there is a cause; for example, in the case of "being a human," persons are existents because they have parents, whereas "being a unicorn" has no existent cases because there are no causes to generate specific unicorns. "Impossibility" and "being" lead to no existent, as illustrated by "round squares," "the largest number," and similar examples. So far we have a purely syntactical model, which clarifies our discourse about some intelligible realm of experience. I hold that the remainder of Ibn Sīnā's primary language is very clear, as follows:

(a) "Being-qua-being" (*hastī, wujūd*) corresponds to Aristotle's *Metaphysica* 1002a20 (*to on he on*) and Ockham's use of "*ens*" in *Summa Totius Logicae*.[3] It signifies the most determinable concept. "Non-being" is meaningless. We should note that all mental concepts (actual or not actual) signify a being. For this reason it is different from an existent.

(b) "Existent" (*maujūd*), signifies an actual entity, Aristotle's notion of first substance (*prote ousia*). There are no impossible existents. For Ibn Sīnā there is only one Necessary Existent, which is the ultimate cause of generation of other existents. "Existence" itself is not an existent, but signifies those entities, which are neither uncaused "contingent being," nor "impossible entities."

I have laid out other specific features of the primitives of Ibn Sīnā's metaphysics elsewhere;[4] the above formulation is sufficient for my evaluation of Nasr's position, as expressed by a sample selection from his work on Ibn Sīnā and others. Let us look at some passages:

> Being in itself is the cause of all particular existing things without being reduced to a genre common to all of them. Being is above all distinctions and polarization and yet the cause of the world of multiplicity, casting its light upon the different and distinct quiddities (*māhīyat*) of all things. Being is the reality of each thing, as it is the source of all goodness and beauty as well as the cause

of all perceptions the quiddities constituting no more than the limitations of Being. (ISCD, 197–98)

Let us evaluate the above passage in the light of our reading of Ibn Sīnā's ontology. "Being" cannot be a cause of any entity, because it is the most common term applicable to the *designata* of all meaningful notions. There is no existent which is not a being. Every actual cause is also a being, thus being-qua-being cannot be a specific cause. Here I hold that Nasr is making a category mistake, like saying that "'two' is blue." The expression "casting its light" is a beautiful metaphor, but it is philosophically confusing. It gives to the reader the false notion that "being" has a normative dimension in Ibn Sīnā's metaphysics. Let me make it clear that all "bad" existents, such as the AIDS virus, poison ivy, a non-*ḥalāl* ham sandwich, and a glass of wine are also cases of "being"; does Nasr want to say that being is "casting its light" through these entities? Also, a black hole is a being without any kind of light in it. "Being" definitely is not the reality of all things—why? It is not, because an impossible entity like "a round square" is a being that cannot be realized. It does not make any sense to point to being as a cause of all goodness, beauty, and so on. Also, the expression "limitation" cannot be applied to "being" but only to "existent." What Nasr asserts may be applied to an interpretation of Mullā Ṣadrā's philosophy that God is pure existence and the cause of existents. It is questionable if such an interpretation is either consistent or correct. At any rate there is no passage in Ibn Sīnā which fits Nasr's transcendent notion of being. Let us examine the next passage.

> If in his [Ibn Sīnā's] ontology . . . emphasis is on the transcendence of Being, or God, above all particular beings or creatures, in cosmogony, on the contrary, accent is placed upon the relation of generated beings to Being and their effusion (*faiḍ*) from the source of all things. (ISCD, 202)

The expression "transcendence" cannot be meaningfully applied to "being" since "being" is the most common notion and there cannot be any meta-being. First of all, use of "transcendence" in ordinary philosophical English is confusing. In Kant we have either "transcendent" (which is in the noumena) or "transcendental" which applies to a set of necessary conditions for having an experience. Neither of these applies to the Ibn Sīnan sense of "being." Being is not transcendent because every actual entity, like the piece of paper that is this page, is a being and can be experienced. Being is not transcendental, because a round square which is inconceivable is also a being.

Now let us direct our attention to " . . . above all . . . " For Plotinus and Proclus, the One is "*uper ousias*," which can be translated as either "beyond being," or "supra being."[5] Ibn Sīnā specifies that "the Necessary Existent" is beholder (*dārandah*) of the world, or a ground of being. Ibn Sīnā's "Necessary Existent" is not the creator-God of Islam, but the emanator of the cosmos. Why Nasr capitalizes "Being" in the above passage is baffling. In Ibn Sīnā's system, every entity is a being, and there is no pure being which exists independent of other notions, as "being" is an abstraction from meaningful entities—possible or impossible. In the next sentence, Nasr introduces three notions: "generated being," "Being," and "the source of being." "Generated being" signifies all contingent beings, which have causes; neither "Being" nor "the source of all things" makes any sense.

Nasr's use of "being" is also baffling when he notes other philosophers' treatments of "being"; here is an example of Nasr's account of al-Bīrūnī's system: "Pure being, which is metacosmic, is hidden by the signs while at the same time its polarization is manifested by them" (ISCD, 159).

What does Nasr mean by "metacosmic"? Literally it means that it is about the cosmos and not in the cosmos. Cosmos is our (ordered) concept. So a meta-cosmos is about cosmos, in the sense that meta-mathematics is about mathematics. It appears that Nasr has attempted to give the term a normative flavor, like a mother telling a child or a lover speaking to a beloved that "You are out of this world." But "being" is the most common aspect of all things and thoughts. This is why Father J. Owens proposes the term "entity" to denote the term "*ousia*" in Greek.[6]

Another ambiguous expression is "the polarization of x is manifested by y." Philosophers often use complex expressions to depict their system. But when they do, normally they place their non-ordinary uses in the context of an axiomatic system where signs and rules of their language are defined. Neither Plotinus nor Whitehead is confusing, as their iconic expressions are accompanied by specific philosophical systems. The problem with Nasr's treatment of being is that there is no detailed clarification of his key terms. Nasr's writings are like butterflies circulating around a monotheistic ethos of the divine. He is not describing Ibn Sīnā's ontology.

Here is another example:

> The gradual forgetting of the reality of Being in favor of the concept of being and then the disintegration of even this concept in the mainstream of Western philosophy was directly connected to the dissociation of *ens* from the act and reality of being itself. (PAPSB, 340)

This ascription to Western philosophy is definitely not the true light of a number of Western philosophers' attention to "being" and "existence," e.g. M. Heidegger, J.-P. Sartre, R. Carnap, and W. V. Quine. I do not know of any Muslim classical thinker who follows this line of "Western philosophy bashing" without any reason.

Next I will criticize his interpretation of Ibn Sīnā's theory of emanation as a religious type of creation. Nasr accepts the fact that Ibn Sīnā uses several terms for depicting the generation of the world, *iḥdāth*, *ibdā'* and *takwīn*—all signifying a "non-creation of out nothing" type of generation. To this list he adds the term "*Khalq*," signifying "creation out of nothing," and states, "Ibn Sīnā uses four words [for] designation or creation of the universe" (ISCD, 212–13). Then he claims that according to Ibn Sīnā God created the world. Now, Ibn Sīnā was very familiar with the Biblical and the Quranic theory of creation as well as the Aristotelian doctrine of emanation, and intentionally chose emanation. I have not found a passage in Ibn Sīnā's emanationistic cosmogony that warrants a creationist interpretation. It is interesting that Nasr omits the recognition of Neoplatonic emanation. Nasr correctly points to the significance of Neoplatonism and Alexandrian tradition, where according to him "the study of mathematics and natural sciences was often carried out in the matrix of a metaphysics that was aware of the symbolic and transparent nature of things" (EMN, 54–55). What Nasr does not mention is that the emanationism of Neoplatonism, which Ibn Sīnā adopted, runs counter to the creationism of Islamic orthodoxy.

Nasr admits that Ibn Sīnā's philosophy is open to criticism by the Muslim orthodoxy with regard to his depiction of God in a deterministic system, but views Ibn Sīnā's cosmogony as compatible with religious creation (ISCD, 234). In addition to Ibn Sīnā's deterministic system, there is a very sharp anti-monotheistic theme in his work. I am referring to the fact that, like Plotinus, in Ibn Sīnā's system there is no place for Divine grace or calling of the chosen. Salvation is purely due to the efforts of the soul. When we add Ibn Sīnā's remarks that he cannot discuss the topic of resurrection of bodies, there is much to doubt in Nasr's religious interpretation of Ibn Sīnā.

II. "THE RELIGIOUSLY TRANSCENDENT SPIRITUAL" AND THE NON-MATERIAL

My second criticism concerns Nasr's presupposition and the polemical use of what may be called "the transcendent spiritual" as a solution to blind materialism. Most philosophers from Plato onwards have been wary of a purely discursive materialistic philosophy for several reasons. Take Plato's argument that matter cannot be depicted as the cause of its motion. Aristotle states that "unity" cannot be constructed out of discursive language. Finally, we have arguments proffered by N. Ṭūsī and G. Leibniz against the ontic primacy of "materiality" and legitimacy of a discursive language for physics. In our times, philosophers such as R. Carnap and A. N. Whitehead have succeeded in describing the physics of space in topological terms. So, many agree with Nasr that we need more than matter to explain experience, but they do not conclude that spirituality is the only solution.

Moreover, just because pure materialism is not satisfactory, it does not follow that a philosophical system can be constructed successfully without any reference to material entities. Even if there were spirits as claimed by Nasr, material entities could nevertheless be considered as necessary, useful, praiseworthy, and beautiful. This is logically possible even if the so-called "spiritual" were essential for a good life. The view that one should deny the significance of material possessions per se is asceticism, a principle prohibited in Islamic culture. Nasr's strong reaction to materialism, physical pleasure, and the like seems to advocate that the only use of material entities is their function as an icon for the spiritual. In this tenor, he talks of "the nothingness of man," and "his limited knowledge before the Divine" (ISCD, 214). Even Plotinus, who compared the human body with a musical instrument, which had its limited but valuable use, shuns this attitude.[7]

It is not clear what Nasr is saying, as his writing is blessed with poetical metaphor and moral prescriptions; permit me to clarify my interpretation of his position using ordinary language.

> The spiritual is the essential element that connects persons to the divine and to happiness. (a) Material concerns work innately against this liaison and thus should be shunned.
> The spiritual is the essential element that connects persons to the divine and to happiness. (b) At best, material entities should be viewed as the icons of the spiritual.

If these formulations depict Nasr's view, then I question the a priori truth of the first part of these premises—that there is a transcendent being who is the source of the spiritual. This may be the case, but if so, we need proof; none is found in Nasr's writings. This dogma is thrown to the reader as an incorrigible fact; in reality, it is a corollary in very common religious beliefs. Incidentally, Nasr does not present his explanation as a representation of commoners' philosophy—that would be simple journalism.

The second part of each of the above statements is not logically implied by the first. In case "a" we observe that some material entities like oxygen are necessary for sustaining life; others like ice cream are pleasant and relatively harmless; finally, acts like experiencing secular arts, making love, and hugging our children are often very satisfying. A comprehensive philosophy should take account of these pleasures.

In case "b" we note that an entity can have a use both as an icon and as part of other natural experiences. Forgive me if I interject a little humor here. Consider the myth of Count Dracula, wherein garlic is a positive natural icon used to protect a person from Dracula. But even if this is true, it does not mean that garlic does not have other good qualities—qualities like being an ingredient of a fine tasty Spanish soup. Or, for another example, why praise light only as the illumination of the soul by God, the light of lights (*nūr-i al-anwār*). Light in the sense of fire is also useful for cooking fine Persian food like *Ghormah Sabzī*! Missing from Nasr's writings is praise of natural experience, like parenthood, beautiful paintings, tasty food, and so on. In sum, his asceticism cannot be deduced from his other premises, nor is it compatible with Islamic doctrines. Nasr states, "The nothingness of man and his limited knowledge before the Divine is hidden by the veil of a rationalistic system in which Ibn Sīnā clothes his intuitions" (ISCD, 214).

We should also point out that Nasr's choice of transcendent spiritualism is not the only alternative to materialism. There are many other choices that avoid pure materialism, such as consideration of the "mental," or spiritualization of nature and human deeds. John Dewey, for example, has successfully proffered a vision of experience and nature in which norms are essential dimensions of experience. Morality is not limited to religious persons. And as another example, B. Russell was both an atheist and a very moral man. Nasr writes as if the only worthy life is that of a monotheist who believes in a transcendent realm of spirit. Obviously he has a right to his belief, shared by a majority of persons in Europe, the Americas, and the Middle East. But it is expected of a philosopher to clarify his premises and provide valid arguments for his conclusions.

The ambiguity of the term "spirit" is also a major problem in Nasr's interpretation. The original Latin version of the term "*spiritus*" has two primary connotations. The first sense is found in the context of monotheistic theology, referring to the divine breath blown into the body that generated life. Hebrew's "*ruwach*," Arabic "*rūḥ*," and Greek "*pneuma*" signify this term in different sacred texts. Second, the word "spirit" refers to the non-physical aspect of a person, distinguished from the soul (*nafs, psyche*) and intellect (*'aql, nous*, *intelligencia*). There are, as well, secondary uses of the word "spirit," such as "life," as used in the expression "the spirit had not yet left his body," as well as "liquor" in ordinary English, but these are far different from Nasr's usage. His use of "spirit" can be understood only in the context of his notion of a transcendent that is considered to be the source of the spiritual. Accordingly, Nasr depicts the world as divided into two realms, the physical and the non-physical, with the non-physical as the higher of the two.

Why "higher," one may ask? Here is an answer. "And in order to have peace and harmony with nature one must be in harmony and equilibrium with Heaven, and ultimately with the Source and Origin of all things. He who is at peace with God is also at peace with creation, both with nature and with man" (EMN, 136). We note here that at least a little bit of nature with its materialistic dimension creeps in as a compromise. But the reader is warned—no humanism or ecumenism. "This type of ecumenism . . . insists upon the love of the neighbor in spite of a total lack of the love for God and the Transcendent. The mentality which advocates this kind of 'charity' affords one more example of the loss of the transcendent dimension and the reduction of all things to the purely worldly" (SI, 5).

It should be mentioned that Nasr uses "transcendent" very loosely. For example, he introduced to the English translators of Mullā Ṣadrā's philosophy the expression "transcendent philosophy," as rendering of the Arabic term "*al-ḥikmat al-muta'āliyah*" (Oxford II, vol. III, 333). The unfortunate adaptation of this term has confused many Western readers to whom "transcendent" prima facie implies the misapplication of reason to the *noumena* which are beyond experience; this is a correct philosophy, but an exercise in dialectical illusion. Translators of Mullā Ṣadrā not familiar with Kant are confused by this use of the word "transcendent." The problem does not stop here. Without much evidence or clarification, Nasr leads a series of attacks on various topics such as "reason": "The power of reason given to man, his *ratio,* which is like the projection or subjective prolongation of the intellect or *intellectus*, divorced from its principle, has become like an acid that burns its way through the fiber of cosmic order and threatens to destroy itself in the process" (EMN, 20).

In this tenor, Nasr lists "Islamic rationalism" next to "Islamic democracy" and "Islamic socialism"; for him these are unfortunate examples of a tendency to "adopt an ideology that happens to be fashionable in the Western world and attach the adjective Islamic to it" (SE, 52). He takes exception to the misuse of "rationalism" and, like al-Ghazzālī, accepts it in the sense of "logic," which for him "is [an] aspect of the truth and truth (*al-ḥaqq*) is a Name of Allah" (SE, 53). This rationalism seems to be grounded in God and not on the coherence of syntax.

Finally, the following passage clarifies his major thesis that each person is endowed with a spiritual dimension from the Divine realm: " . . . the human microcosm has itself lost its tripartite structure of spirit (*spiritus*), soul (*anima*), and body (*corpus*)" (EMN, 116), excluding any reference to intelligence (*'aql, nous, intelligencia*). He repeats the same tripartite theme in another text, and poetically adds, "the Spirit is like the sky, shining and immutable above the horizons of the soul. It is a world, which, although not yet God, is inseparable from Him so that to reach it is already to be in the front courtyard of paradise and the proximity of the Divine" (SE, 68).

Nasr, as a sophisticated Persian, has an admirable habit of writing in poetic allegory. This mode is fine and playful when it is positive; it becomes unjustified, and definitely counter to the main thrust of Islamic tradition, when reason is described as a poison acid. Reason is not alone—Nasr attacks science, Western philosophy, modernity, and whatever is different from the so-called traditional.

Most of us do not observe any poverty in Western philosophy because of its omission of the transcendent. Some of the contemporary Western texts written by A. N. Whitehead, L. Wittgenstein, R. Carnap will surely become part of the body of the world's classic culture. This is also true of contributions in other fields by thinkers such as Sigmund Freud, Karl Marx, and Charles Darwin. Nasr has a right to attribute "poverty" to these and others, but as a philosopher he needs to back up his maxims with arguments. The anti-modern ethos reaches very strange extremes when alchemy is praised over chemistry and creation theory over the theory of evolution.

> The traditional sciences such as alchemy, which can be compared to the celebration of a cosmic mass, became reduced to a chemistry in which substances lost all their sacramental character. In the process, the sciences of nature lost their symbolic intelligibility, a fact that is most directly responsible for the crisis which the modern scientific worldview and its applications have brought about. (EMN, 21)

What is wrong with this approach? First, some of this message is not new. C. G. Jung, for example, clarified the de-alienation effects of the alchemist's ethos. And it is true that ecological perspectives take environmental accounts of chemical entities; for example, rivers polluted by sulfur are not good for fishing. But this consequence, an accidental byproduct of sulfur production, need not be in a chemistry book to be significant. Prima facie, there is no requirement that the pragmatic dimensions of all elements of science should be mentioned in a descriptive empirical text. Is Nasr arguing that a religious body that is aware of the spiritual implication of a descriptive account of nature should monitor scientific writings? I hope not; these strong condemnations remind us of the mentality that condemned poor Galileo.

Nasr asserts, "taken as a dogma, evolution is presented without considering biological cases which cannot be explained by it" (EMN, 126). He places a footnote to this assertion, which consists of nothing but the claim of two authors who make some vague reference to "wisdom of nature" with no apparent connection to questioning the superiority of "the theory of evolution" over the "theory of creation" (EMN, 141). Here is an example of how Nasr simply states an opinion without proffering justification. Any modern biologist knows that a scientific theory, like evolution, is a model in the meta-language. As Plato asserted, a science of nature at best is a likely story of reality, rather than another reality. Who is being attacked by Nasr? Is he attacking the straw man, or does he just want to put in a good word for creationism? His text achieves neither of these goals.

There are some statements about science that are simply inaccurate. Consider the following passage: "It is indeed curious that in the modern world, where everything is criticized and questioned, where there are critics of art, of literature, of politics, of philosophy and even of religion, there are no critics of science" (EMN, 114). Obviously, there is ample criticism of science in modern times. Consider how Heidegger attacks Descartes's account of experience and how Bergson advocates an "intuitive sense of time" over a geometric one. Also, philosophers such as John Dewey propose a different reading of science, considering it not as a set of doctrines but a method of inquiry. Science develops by criticisms and rejection of older theories.

Nasr's praise of the non-modern man is questionable. He notes that "the cosmos speaks to man and all its phenomena containing meaning. They are symbols of a higher degree of reality which the cosmic domain at once veils and reveals" (EMN, 21). Obviously Nasr's account is allegorical, for the cosmos is not a sentient being that can speak. Let us suppose that Nasr implies that ancient and medieval cosmologies have positive pragmatic implications for persons in the sense that a human being does not feel alienated from the cosmos he/she projects in nature. There is a problem here. Does he proffer that we should choose cosmological theories based on their therapeutic dimension? If so, suppose it is more therapeutic to choose an inconsistent theory than a consistent one. But science is not a therapeutic inquiry; it should inform individuals of such matters as global warming and clashes of planets, and the fact that their mothers die and never return to nurture them. Therapy may include "a white lie"; science, however, does not need to be "human friendly." For example, consider Freud's claim that his discoveries where not aimed to please persons but were intended to illuminate them.

But Nasr's views are open to more serious objections. Not only does he wish to choose human-friendly cosmologies; it seems that he believes there is a correct cosmology connected partially with revelations. If this is his view, then his perspective has two prima facie problems: (a) only religiously inclined persons who accept revelation should be allowed to participate in scientific inquiry; and (b) scientific theories are facts, not pragmatic perspectives. I leave to the reader the implications of this view, and to Nasr. I hope I am incorrect in my interpretation of Nasr's views on this topic. If I am correct his position advocates that religion censors science.

In sum, Nasr's use of "spirit" as a divine gift to human beings presupposes a monotheistic religious set of doctrines which are not accepted a priori by non-believers. If Nasr uses "spirit" in this sense, he has to make clear that his philosophy presupposes Islamic dogmas as truths. Thus he is an apologist for Islam. Is this his position? I do not know. I do not see him as a philosopher like Leibniz who reflects carefully to design an analytically clear metaphysics.

Nasr's writings can be classified into two categories: (i) very valuable historical accounts of post–Ibn Sīnan Muslim thinkers which clarify an important dimension of the history of philosophy for the West; and (ii) ethical writings filled with normative prescriptions that presuppose without any justification the existence of a transcendent sense of the spiritual. In his defense, it may be pointed out that all arguments begin with a set of premises. But some premises are more questionable than others. It is definitely not obvious that there is an invisible transcendent world. If Nasr holds these premises, he should clarify them or at least make us, and perhaps himself, aware that these are indeed premises. Moreover, the assumptions that underlie his works have received strong criticism from most philosophers. Take, for example, Kant's objection to the transcendent being part of the noumena and to its investigation a dialectical illusion. A philosopher ordinarily defends his system against "standard" criticisms. For example, those who wish to use the "causation argument" must make an effort to answer Hume's criticism of this view. Muslim philosophers such as Ibn Sīnā traditionally evaluated previous positions that they opposed, such as Ibn Sīnā's argument against Porphyry. Nasr, who praises Islamic philosophy, should follow the tradition on this point.

(a) He presupposes a transcendental spirit as a premise in his writings.
(b) There is no prima facie basis in experience or in reason to support the existence of a transcendent entity. A philosopher who does not base his system on the authority of religion cannot base her/his theories on the assumption that there is a sound argument for the existence of God, such as the ontological or the cosmological argument.

The designation of God or a Transcendent Spiritual as an essential constituent of whatever is good implies censorship of modernity and modern science.

III. Private Language Fallacy

When a critic trained in Western philosophy reads Nasr's writings, she/he notices citations of a family of self-reference notions such as "knowledge of the self," "inner experiences," "knowledge by immediate presence," "intuition," and "the spirit within." This ethos of "incorrigible knowledge of the self," as well as "interior place of the Divine spirit in human beings," and "esotericism" is repeated in Nasr's writings. Prima facie, there are two dimensions of misuse of the term "spiritual." The first points to a false assumption that praise of the spiritual implies degrading the physical. The second mistake is to postulate an inner, intuitive realm which is subject to a series of objections known as "liar paradox, self-reference, and private language fallacy."

Let us examine the first problem in Nasr's note on the Ismā'īlī tradition. He asserts that for the Ismā'īlīs "nature['s] inner spirit . . . breathes through all things" (EMN, 55). He never clarifies the term "inner." What does it mean for a spirit to breathe through all things, such as a piece of rock? We are familiar with the monotheistic myth of the Divine breathing into clay, resulting in a living person. This myth is by no means a clear a priori truth; it is very vague and open to misinterpretations. Nasr's imagery plays on this archetypal theme without any clarification of the original myth. A legitimate philosophical theology should clarify a religious myth through ordinary language or with a clear philosophical model. Nasr's writings are often poetic variations of religious writings that result in beautiful prose rather than clear philosophy. Here is another example, explaining the essence of Ismā'īlī thoughts as ". . . esoteric knowledge associated with the inner meaning of religion" (RIP, 329). It is true that Ismā'īlī thinkers rely on concepts such as "*bāṭin*" (inner) as contrasted to "ẓāhir" (outer); but there is no anti-rationalism or anti-nature/materialism in Ismā'īlī thought.

Let us consider the case of Nāṣir-i Khusraw, the most significant Ismā'īlī theologian. For Nāṣir-i Khusraw, material entities are positive icons of the spirits and are sought as mediator figures for salvation. Let us take an example: "*ṣirāṭ*" depicts a bridge over hell, sharper than a sword.[8] The ethics of this physical icon points to the ethos of humanity. He/she operates on a very fragile moral threshold, where there are two possible outcomes: the possibility of de-alienation from his/her origin, as well as the possibility of being lost to the exclusive search for satisfaction of needs that one shares with animals. Here Nāṣir-i Khusraw asserts that salvation for humanity is not faith. Why? Because faith is a passive state; it is a condition between fear and hope. The true salvation lies in knowledge in two senses: first, knowledge expressed through the hermeneutic incarnation of us as rational beings; and second, observation of our physical nature.[9]

Incidentally, there is no necessity to force a transcendent deity into this perspective. For example, a parent can appreciate his/her child as a concrete person, while simultaneously experiencing the universal feeling of care for the young. A universal perspective is immaterial but need not to be anti-material and anti-humanist. Obviously, Nasr is free to have his religious opinions; nevertheless, he should be aware that these maximums are premises and not facts. Such opinions, however, cannot serve as incorrigible premises.

Now let us turn to the private language fallacy. A clear case of this fallacy is expressed in Descartes's *cogito*, where the French philosopher claims that he knows that he exists as a substantial soul and uses language to converse with himself. A number of objections have been made to Descartes, from Kant's attack on subjective idealism, to type fallacy, and what Wittgenstein calls private language fallacy. The general idea is that language is a game and the criteria of correctness have to lie outside of the game—one cannot measure a ruler by itself. In other words, a reference to a sign in the object language must be in a meta-language. Let us take an example of Nasr's statements in his account of Suhrawardī's philosophy:

> This doctrine is based not on the refutation of logic, but of transcending its categories through an illuminationist knowledge based on immediacy and presence, or what al-Suhrawardī himself called knowledge by presence (*al-'ilm al-ḥuḍūrī*), I contrast to conceptual (*al-'ilm al-ḥuṣūlī*) which is our ordinary method of knowing by concepts. (RIP, 618)

Why is Nasr certain of this mode of knowledge? The answer as to the root of his convictions may be found in his presupposition about the objective force of revelation. Let us note how he connects "truth" and "revelation,"

> The truth in its unlimited and infinite essence is thus particularized by the specific form of Revelation as well as by the characteristics of the people who are destined to receive it. This particularization of the Truth has a direct bearing upon the study of Nature and the whole cosmological perspective which is concerned for the most part with the world of forms. Unlike pure metaphysics and mathematics which are independent of relativity, cosmological sciences are closely related to the perspective of the "observer" so that they are completely dependent upon the Revelation or the qualitative essence of the civilization in whose matrix they are cultivated. (ISCD, 3)

It is not clear if Nasr is guilty of the private language fallacy here because of his ambiguity.[10] Such an ambiguity does not appear in the meticulous classics of either Islamic philosophy or mysticism. Here are three examples: Ibn Sīnā's "flying man argument," Ibn Sīnā's theory of prehensive imagination (*wahm*), and the notion of "state" (*ḥāl*) in Mulsim metaphysics.[11]

There is a strong philosophical tradition that points to the incorrigibility of knowledge of the ground of experience. Here are some examples: Augustine correctly stated that he wanted to know two things, his soul and his God; in this vein, Ibn Sīnā mentions the following celebrated Arabic proverb, "he who knows his soul, knows his God"; Al-Ghazzālī states that both soul and God are without quantity and quality; Wittgenstein asserts that the self is not in the world, but is the boundary of the world; Kant expresses the same theme in his doctrine of transcendental unity of apperception about the subject of the ground of a person's experience. Pedagogically, we can classify these epistemic notions into two types: those like the Cartesian *Cogito*, which commit the private language fallacy; and those like Heidegger's *Dasein*, which do not. The first group presumes that the private experience reveals a substantial self with whom the subject can communicate in a private language, that is, question the ontic ground of its images; the second group, like Heidegger's notion of *Dasein*, points to the logic of discourse—that a ground of experience with a temporal dimension is presupposed by any conscious activity. For the specifics of these distinctions and the claim that Ibn Sīnā's so-called "flying man" argument does not commit the private language fallacy, I refer the reader to Nāder El-Bizrī, *The Quest for Being: Avicenna and Heidegger.*[12] A number of investigators like L. E. Goodman mistakenly link Ibn Sīnā's views to Descartes despite the fact that the Muslim philosopher clearly does not assert any type of Nasrian communication of the subject with his/her inner spirit; all Ibn Sīnā states is that even if the subject abstracts away his/her sense-fields, he/she cannot abstract away the ground of some-experiencing subject.[13] There is a vast difference between the presupposition that one can have a communication in a private domain and the claim that if one thinks, then the world in which this thinking takes place is not empty. [14]

Finally, one of the pillars of Islamic mysticism lies in the doctrine of the twofold stages of the mystics' way (*ṭarīqah*), namely stations (*aḥwāl*) and states (*maqāmāt*). The dialectics of the progress of the mystics through stations and states does not represent any interiority or integration of any kind of inner spirit. Let me illustrate in a non-mystical context. Suppose a student memorizes French vocabulary and "the verb wheel" and receives practical instruction to reach a certain station of mastery of vocabulary and grammar. Having reached this station, the student experiences a state of comprehension of spoken and written French. Consider a typical case in Sufic initiation. Suppose that a novice is overly proud of his/her virtue and purity in following religious ritual. The master may then ask the novice to commit a degrading act, like carrying non-*ḥalāl* meat on his back in the market place. When the novice carries out this act, he experiences the loss of respect from common people. Finally, the novice focuses on actions for their own sake and not for public rewards. To relate this topic to a more general dimension, I think that the questionable aspect of Nasr's ecstatic spiritualism is that human life involves material entities, and many ethical concerns deal with societal relations rather than pure private spirituality. As a matter of fact, Plato submits an idea in the *Euthyphro*, which is developed in *The Laws*, and adopted in The New Testament, that religiosity lies not in passivity; instead religiosity lies in a praxis of service (*therapia*, a Greek word used by both Plato and The New Testament).

CONCLUSION

It is impossible to exaggerate the debt of scholarship of Islamic philosophy to Seyyed Hossein Nasr. His contributions lie in his original ideas, in his peerless ability in organized research, which produced close to fifty texts in the field, as well as in his insightful vision of the significance of post–Ibn Sīnan Islamic philosophy. Moreover, Nasr is to be praised for his moral integrity; he has stood by his principles. This writer criticizes Nasr for his interpretation of Ibn Sīnā's concepts of being and cosmogony, his loose treatment of first person statement which opens his views to the private language fallacy, and finally for his vague assertion of transcendent spirituality. It may be true that classical Muslim philosophers are most precise in both style and content. Nevertheless, Nasr's poetic portrayal of the religious ethos depicts a beautiful illustration of the sentiments of not only Islamic but of all monotheistic believers. His legacy will continue to have a positive impact on Islamic studies.

PARVIZ MOREWEDGE

BINGHAMTON UNIVERSITY
THE STATE UNIVERSITY OF NEW YORK
JUNE 2000

NOTES

1. See, Shihaboddin Yayha Sohrawardi, *Oeuvres Philosophiques et Mystiques*, tome III (Tehran and Paris: Academie Imperial Iranien de Philosophie and Librairie Adrien-Maisonneuve, 1977).

2. See, *Neoplatonism and Islamic Thought,* ed. P. Morewedge (Albany: State University of New York Press, 1992), pp. 57–58.

3. See, E. A. Moody, *The Logic of William of Ockham* (New York: Russell & Russell, 1965), p. 137.

4. See, Avicenna, *The Metaphsyica of Avicenna (Ibn Sīnā)*, trans. Parviz Morewedge (New York and London: Columbia University Press and Routledge Kegan Paul, 1975).

5. Plotinus, *The Enneads*, trans. S. MacKenna (New York: Larson Publications, 1992), VI.6, 5, 35.

6. Joseph Owens, *The Doctrine of Being in the Aristotelian Metaphysics* (Toronto: Pontifical Institute of Medieval Studies, 1978), pp. 149–53.

7. Plotinus, op. cit., I.4, 4, 13–29.

8. Nāṣir-i Khusraw, *Knowledge and Liberation: A Treatise on Philosophical Theology,* ed. and trans. F. M. Hunzai, intro. by P. Morewedge (London and New York: Tauris, 1998), pp. 18, 104–6, 124.

9. Ibid., pp. 101–3.

10. L. Wittgenstein, *Philosophical Investigations*, 3rd edition (Oxford: Blackwell, 1976), paragraphs 243–315.

11. P. Morewedge, *Essays in Islamic Theology, Philosophy and Mysticism* (Oneonta: Oneonta Philosophy Series, 1995).

12. Nader El-Bizri, *The Quest for Being, Avicenna and Heidegger* (Binghamton: Global Publications, 2000).

13. Lenn E. Goodman, *Avicenna* (London: Routledge, 1992). Goodman claims that Ibn Sīnā's argument like Descartes's *cogito* is "similar" in the sense that they both concern "the self" (p. 156). The difference however is clear; Descartes explicitly assumes that he has proved existence of a substantial self, while Ibn Sīnā does not refer to substance (*jawhar*), but ground of experience.

14. In order to direct attention to Ibn Sīnā's thoughts on this issue, I wish to refer the reader to the doctrine of prehensive imagination (*wahm*) in Ibn Sīnā's theory of internal senses; here I disagree with H. A. Wolfson's interpretation that "*wahm*" is the *estimatio* of the scholastics and a confused copy of a point in Greek epistemology. I have argued that this doctrine is an intentional instrumental theory of knowledge where no conscious dialogue takes place interior in the subject. *Essays in Islamic Theology, Philosophy and Mysticism*, op. cit., pp. 125–62.

ABBREVIATIONS OF THE WORKS OF S. H. NASR CITED

EMN: Nasr, S. H. *The Encounter of Man and Nature*. George Allan and Unwin, 1968.

IRIS: Nasr, S. H. *Ideals and Realities in Islam*. New York and Washington: Fredrick A. Praeger Publishers, 1967.

ISCD: Nasr, S. H. *An Introduction to Islamic Cosmological Doctrines*. State University of New York Press, 1992.

Oxford II: *The Oxford Encyclopedia of the Modern Islamic World*. Ed. J. L. Esposito. New York and London: Oxford University Press, 1995. 4 vols.

PAPSB: Nasr, S. H. "Post-Avicennan Islamic Philosophy and the Study of Being." In *Philosophies of Existence: Ancient and Medieval*. Ed. Parviz Morewedge, New York: Fordham University Press, 1982.

RIP: *Routledge Encyclopedia of Philosophy*. Ed. E. Graig, London and New York: Routledge, 1998.

SE: Nasr, S. H. *Sufi Essays*. Albany: State University of New York Press, 1972.

SI: *Shi'ite Islam*. Trans. and ed. S. H. Nasr. Albany: State University of New York, 1975.

REPLY TO PARVIZ MOREWEDGE

As Professor Morewedge mentions in the beginning of his paper, I have known him for over three decades and my early works were instrumental in attracting his attention to Islamic philosophy while he was studying Western and primarily Anglo-Saxon analytical philosophy. It seems, however, that some thirty years of study of Islamic philosophy and even journeys to Iran, where he met a number of the living traditional masters of this philosophy, have not weaned him away from his analytical moorings. It is still as a follower of this philosophy and not as a follower of one of the schools of traditional Islamic thought that he views Islamic philosophy. His criticism of my views of Ibn Sīnā's ontology reflects very much this fact, for he speaks as a logical positivist for whom traditional ontology has essentially no meaning.

Although his philosophical views are not typically Persian, Morewedge's human kindness and sense of humor reflect the traditional norms of Persian *adab* and therefore he begins by praising my organizational abilities and scholarly contribution to later Islamic thought before attacking me philosophically. While I am grateful for his kind comments, what is at issue in this volume is my philosophical thought and not organizational abilities or lack thereof or even my textual scholarship. It is therefore to his philosophical criticism that I will turn directly.

In speaking of my original ideas, the author turns to my views about the inner relation among religions as a means of bringing harmony among them. Then he adds, "for example, in the Jungian sense, there is an archetype of the mediator figure as a member of a clergy, be it a rabbi, a priest, or a shaykh. Thus mysticism ironically expresses themes of different religious perspectives." First of all I have never spoken of a mediator figure nor its archetype in the Jungian sense. I have in fact written against Jung's interpretation of the archetype which he associates with the "collective unconscious" rather than with the noumenal world. Secondly, it is not *ironic* that mysticism expresses themes of different religious perspectives. Rather, because, in its authentic sense, mysticism is concerned with the *mysterium*, with the inner dimension of *a* religion, by virtue of its inward and hence universal character, the heart of the mysticism of one religion is also present in the inner dimension of other sacred universes or religions in the deepest sense of the term.

Morewedge then turns to the critique of my views by objecting that my philosophical views "are more analogous to poetry than to analysis." Here he gives away completely his positivistic bent and forgets that much of philosophy in both the West and the Islamic world was written in either poetry or highly poetic prose. Has he forgotten Pythagoras, Parmenides, Plato, Marcus Aurelius, and in his own country of birth, Suhrawardī? Clarity is not the opposite of poetry unless one reduces the activity of the intellect to only analytical reason and language to only logic. I studied physics and mathematics for many years before beginning to write on philosophy, but I am also deeply rooted in the symbolic dimension of language and have developed carefully over the years a style in English which would seek to be both clear and poetic. I do not believe that the possibilities of language can be reduced to its analytical element, and therefore I stand opposed to all the positivistic attempts to destroy the metaphysical possibilities inherent in language. When Morewedge accuses me of using vague expressions such as "spirit breathing in the world" and "Being radiating its light," he is forgetting the usage of these and similar expressions for over two thousand years in Western philosophy itself. All he has to do is to turn to the texts of a Ficino or St. Thomas, not to speak of countless earlier texts. Or perhaps Morewedge is simply repeating the views of many logical positivists for whom there was no serious philosophy before Hume and Kant, and for whom the earlier philosophical texts are full of what they call vagueness. In this case I take pride in standing with the long list of premodern philosophers who, because of their speaking of matters not rationally definable, are considered vague by those who reject what cannot be logically defined according to their own understanding of logic.

Morewedge is quite irritated by my criticism of modernism, such as my speaking about the "sacred cow of modernism" or criticizing Darwinian evolution. He writes, "this type of attitude is either a poetical cry of religious anti-scientism or an incorrect understanding of contemporary views of science." He should rest assured that my criticisms are not the result of either of these elements. Rather, they are based on the application of the teachings of traditional metaphysics and the perennial philosophy to the modern world which I believe I know, in both its cultural and scientific aspects, as well as the author. To demonstrate his point he says, "no biologist claims that she/he observes a scientific law such as evolution." How then can evolution be considered a law for an observational science as claimed by so many evolutionists? Even as rigorous a logician as Karl Popper asserted that evolutionary theory does not fulfill the criteria of a scientific law. What is even worse, Morewedge adds that the purpose of scientific laws is to explain observations and to be used for prediction. As all honest paleontologists know, there is in fact no way of explaining satisfactorily the evidence of the palentological record in terms of Darwinian evolution. As for prediction, I hardly need to mention how irrelevant the theory of evolution is to this question.

I mention these points only in passing and have dealt more fully elsewhere in this volume with them. If I do mention a few points here, it is to refute the remarkable assertion of Morewedge that my remarks against the "sacred cow of modernity" "seldom contain logical arguments or useful references." In fact, my criticisms are logical and certainly never illogical, although not reducible to rationalism alone, and they usually contain many references which have been useful to many people if not to Morewedge. It might be helpful for the author to know that chapter 7 of my *Knowledge and the Sacred* entitled "Eternity and the Temporal Order" and dealing with the critique of the theory of evolution was printed along with its Italian translation in the leading periodical on biology in Italian and has been debated by many biologists on both sides of the fence.

Morewedge asks whether my arguments are sound and also whether they represent the ethos "of the majority of the Islamic philosophical tradition." As for the soundness of my arguments, the understanding of the term "soundness" is usually colored by the worldview of the person who makes the judgment. Aristotelian philosophers for two thousand years considered the arguments of Aristotle to be sound while Hume and Kant did not consider them to be so. This proves in a sense that philosophy is not reducible to logic, although logic is of course of great importance in philosophy. From the point of view of logic alone one can judge whether the arguments of Aristotle were sound or not, but the question of the premises upon which the logical arguments are based is something else. Now my arguments may not appear to be sound to Morewedge and those who think like him, but many other thinkers have considered them to be sound indeed. The least I can say is that they are not illogical, taking into consideration the fact that I also do speak of matters which transcend the categories of ordinary logic. As for whether my arguments represent the ethos of the Islamic philosophical tradition or not, they may not do so for those who, like Morewedge, interpret the Islamic philosophical tradition from the point of view of modern Western philosophy. But among those belonging to that tradition, some have certainly asserted that my arguments reflect the ethos of the Islamic philosophical tradition. All Morewedge has to do is ask this question of a person such as Sayyid Jalāl al-Dīn Āshtiyānī, perhaps the foremost living representative of the Islamic philosophical tradition in Iran today, as he could have posed it to 'Allāmah Ṭabāṭabā'ī and Murtiḍā Muṭahharī before their deaths. What the author must remember is that I spent long years studying Islamic philosophy with the traditional masters in Iran, as well as with authorities in the West, and identify myself with the Islamic philosophical tradition rather than Western interpretations of it. So I would never use such a term as "analytic of 'being'" in dealing with Ibn Sīnā's ontology as does Morewedge.

In discussing *wujūd* or *hastī* (being/existence) in Ibn Sīnā's philosophy Morewedge begins by equating it with Aristotle's *to on he on* (*Metaphysica* 1002 a 20). This itself is not acceptable from the point of view of the tradition of Islamic philosophy at least not as the Aristotelian text is interpreted by modern Western philosophers. Nor is it acceptable to Thomism as shown so clearly by the work of E. Gilson and others. For Aristotle, existence is "a block without fissure," to use the expression of T. Izutsu, whereas for Ibn Sīnā the Necessary Being is discontinuous with respect to the chain of being and *wujūd* is understood in a manner radically different from Greek philosophy. It is not accidental that Gilson calls Ibn Sīnā the first "philosopher of being."

When Morewedge writes that "all mental concepts (actual or not actual) signify a being," he rejects the very foundation of Ibn Sīnan ontology which is the distinction between *wujūd* and *māhiyyah* or quiddity. To say that quiddity has being but is not existent is meaningless in the context of Ibn Sīnā's thought. On the basis of this interpretation, which I consider totally erroneous, the author makes many statements, all of which suffer from this original error. He even goes so far as to say, "it does not make any sense to point to being as a cause of all goodness, beauty, etc." This is an unbelievable statement, easily deniable if one simply turns to the writings of the whole of the Ibn Sīnan tradition, not to speak of St. Thomas. Morewedge goes on to claim that "there is no passage in Ibn Sīnā which fits Nasr's transcendent notion of being." This exposition is not the place to provide long quotations to refute this assertion. Let me just say that the author should turn to a treatise such as *Risālah fī marātib al-mawjūdāt* as well as to the *Kitāb al-shifā'* itself (Tehran, 1887, p. 598) where Ibn Sīnā writes, "To the Necessary Being belongs beauty and pure brilliance and It is the source of the beauty and brilliance of all things . . . " I need hardly quote any other references, of which there are many in Ibn Sīnā's work, to refute the incredible claim of Professor Morewedge. Unfortunately, he also confuses the concept or notion of being with its reality and many of his statements follow from this confusion.

The author also fails to distinguish between absolute and relative being (*al-wujūd al-muṭlaq* and *al-wujūd al-muqayyad*), and having reduced being to simply a concept cannot understand why, when I refer to Absolute Being, I capitalize the word "being." He calls my practice baffling whereas his question as to why I capitalize being when it refers to the Absolute Being is itself baffling. I wonder if he remembers works written by major Thomistic scholars on Thomistic ontology in which "being" is always capitalized when it refers to Pure Being or God. As for the Necessary Being differing from the Creator-God of Islam while being only the source of emanation, this is also more complicated than simply the either/or situation that he states. One needs only to turn to the meaning of the term "create" in Ibn Sīnan philosophy. If Ibn Sīnā had not been able to incorporate the Islamic understanding of God into his understanding of the Necessary Being, or *wājib al-wujūd*, this latter term would not have become so widely used by Muslim theologians and even religious preachers. If one goes to a Friday sermon in a mosque often one hears the term *wājib al-wujūd* used for God by preachers who do not have any knowledge of Ibn Sīnā's philosophy but who are the representatives *par excellence* of the Islamic religion in its social aspect. The term *wājib al-wujūd* is in fact one of Ibn Sīnā's greatest contributions to not only philosophy but also to the general religious discourse of Islam.

Turning next to the question of emanation, Morewedge writes, "Ibn Sīnā was very well familiar with the Biblical and the Quranic theory of creation as well as the Aristotelian doctrine of emanation, and intentionally chose emanation." First of all the doctrine of emanation is Plotinian and is not to be found in Aristotle himself. Secondly, by making such a black and white distinction, the author is simply taking the side of the *mutakallimūn* against the philosophers and does not wish to pay attention to what an Ibn Sīnā says about the meaning of "creation" itself. I am certainly aware of over a thousand years of debate among the theologians, philosophers, and Sufis about the meaning of "creation" and the relation of the world to its Divine Origin. I have not necessarily taken the side of Ibn Sīnā in this debate and have expressed my own views based on Sufi metaphysics in my writings. But I oppose strongly identifying *à la* the Orientalists one side of this issue with Neoplatonism and the other with orthodoxy. This is to do injustice to Ibn Sīnā and other Islamic philosophers and the subtlety of their arguments. As for the resurrection of bodies, Morewedge fails even to mention that Ibn Sīnā states explicitly in the *Shifā'* that he believed in it even though he could not prove it philosophically. This makes it easier for the author to cast doubt on my religious interpretation of Ibn Sīnā.

In the second part of his criticism Morewedge seeks to attack my opposition to materialism by making many statements which are only half-truths. I have never sought to construct a philosophical system without considering the material world. What I have sought to do is to show its status in the total scheme of reality and have refused to reduce the spiritual to the material or to consider the material plane as an independent order of reality. I have not denied sensual pleasure but have opposed hedonism. In fact every pleasure on the material plane is an echo of a much more intense spiritual reality but cannot be experienced as such without a degree of distancing oneself from the world. There is no possibility of the full appreciation of even the material realm of reality without a degree of asceticism and "emptying," as the *Tao Te-Ching* reminds us so powerfully. And contrary to what Morewedge says, Islam is not opposed to asceticism (*zuhd*) but to monasticism which is quite another thing. In fact the Quran and *Ḥadīth* encouraged asceticism as long as it is not in an extreme form. Otherwise how could the Prophet of Islam, 'Alī and other major figures of the Islamic tradition live so simply and ascetically and praise *zuhd* so highly?

It is unbelievable that Morewedge equates my speaking of "the nothingness of man" with my denial of the body and its spiritual significance. He should study the chapter on the wisdom of the body in my *Religion and the Order of Nature*. If I speak of material forms as symbols of the spiritual, that is not certainly a way of denigrating them. On the contrary, to realize that material "facts" are symbols is the means of elevating and integrating material forms into their principle. In any case I have a millennium of Sufi metaphysics behind my assertions and have not said anything concerning the relation between material form and the spiritual world that has not been expounded in one language or another by an Ibn 'Arabī, a Rūmī, or an Awḥad al-Dīn Kirmānī.

Morewedge follows this criticism by asking me for a proof of the existence of God and asserts that he finds none in my writings. It is true that I have not provided a systematic treatment of the various proofs of God in a separate treatise or chapters such as one finds in the writings of Islamic and Christian theologians. Speaking from the point of view of the perennial philosophy and from within the Islamic philosophical tradition, I have presumed the proofs offered by them as my own. Moreover, my exposition of philosophy does not start with doubt and skepticism, as is the case with much of modern Western philosophy, but with intellectual certitude. Nevertheless, I have provided several "proofs" of the existence of God from both the metaphysical and cosmological points of view. As I have written already, the *cogito ergo sum* of Descartes is a metaphysical absurdity grounded in a basic distortion since it places thinking above being. He should have said *cogito ergo Est*, "I think therefore He is." One of the profoundest proofs of the existence of God is my or your consciousness which can think and say "I." I have asserted in many places that our consciousness itself, or knowledge by presence (*al-'ilm al-ḥuḍūrī*) of ourselves, is the proof of God, an argument which is also central to Suhrawardī and the *ishrāqī* tradition.

I will not take the time here to respond to Morewedge's discussions of Count Dracula and Persian cuisine because they are based on the same misunderstanding of the relation between sensual pleasures and spiritual experiences, between material forms and their intelligible principles. The whole idea of the chain of being, hierarchical levels of both macrocosmic and microcosmic existence, and grades of reality which I have mentioned so often in my writings are completely forgotten by the author. Or perhaps they have not been forgotten but make no sense to him, since he accepts a philosophical view dominated by logical positivism.

The author also speaks of morality not being limited to religious persons, citing Bertrand Russell as an example of a moral atheist and criticizing me for claiming that "the only worthy life is that of a monotheist who believes in a transcendent realm of the spirit." I do believe that the goal of man on earth is to go beyond himself and to seek the Transcendent and that without the Transcendent and the Sacred, man is only accidentally man and lives below the fullness of human potentiality. But I certainly do not limit this access to the Transcendent to the Abrahamic monotheisms. As for moral atheists, I believe that all morality has originally issued from religious teachings, but that it is possible for someone to live by a set of moral values while denying their source. It is like a prodigal son living off the inheritance of his father while cursing him. There is of course such a thing as rational ethics going back to the Greek philosophers and also found in Islamic philosophy, but even in these and similar cases what is presumed to be rational moral value and virtue has itself a religious origin and basis.

Morewedge is very uncomfortable with what he believes is my "Western bashing" since, although he is originally Persian, he identifies himself with that world which he claims I am bashing. Let me make it clear that I have never participated in "Western bashing." Rather, my attack has been against modernism. I have always defended the traditional West and at the same time criticized severely modernism in the Islamic world or in other non-Western societies and cultures. The author criticizes me for speaking of the "poverty of the current Western philosophical scene" and adds "most of us do not observe any poverty in Western philosophy because of its omission of the transcendent." This may be the view of Morewedge, but then why have figures as different as Martin Heidegger and Richard Rorty spoken of the end of Western philosophy, and why is there a flood of writings bemoaning the failure of modern philosophy? Just to cite an example, there is the recent work entitled *The Failure of Modernism—The Cartesian*

Legacy and Contemporary Pluralism (ed. Brendan Sweetman, The American Maritain Association, 1999), which criticizes the state of Western philosophy and which traces the fall of philosophy in the West to the errors of Descartes. In contrast to what Morewedge thinks, I am not a lonely voice speaking of the poverty of modern Western philosophy, nor are my judgments based on mere sentimentality. On the contrary I make such a judgment by applying the principles of the perennial philosophy which I consider to be valid for all times.

As to the relation of the religious view of nature vis-à-vis the view generated by modern science, what I claim has nothing to do with what the author asks namely if a religious body should monitor scientific writings. I think that I have made my views on this matter clear enough in several works, including *The Need for a Sacred Science*, so that there is no need to repeat them here, save to remind Professor Morewedge that a sacred science of nature does not invalidate modern science on its own level or for what it is, but disclaims what it is not but many claim it to be. Sacred science would reject, of course, all hypotheses that are paraded around as "scientific truth," such as evolution, which, in contrast to what the author writes, is not only a meta-language for biologists but also a pseudo-religious ideology for the worldview of modernism.

My proposal to take seriously traditional sciences and cosmologies has to do with their truth and not only with their therapeutic value. It must, however, be remembered that truth alone is therapy for ignorance, and that therefore it also has the most powerful therapeutic effect upon the soul. In contrast to what Freud asserted when he claimed not to please but to illuminate his patients, while he was in fact the farthest removed from the source of illumination, truth does indeed illuminate and by virtue of this power also heals. In emphasizing the importance of traditional cosmologies, I have not sought to use only "human friendly cosmologies" but also those which correspond to the full reality of the cosmos that is conveyed to us through either objective revelation or that "inner revelation" which is intellection. If our horizons were to be expanded once again to include revelation and intellection as sources of knowledge and not restricted to reason and the empirical data received through the external senses, then all of the dichotomies and divisions posed by Morewedge would simply disappear.

Morewedge does not see me as a philosopher but as a religious apologist with two categories of writings: one, on the history of Islamic philosophy and two, what he calls "ethical writings." Needless to say I do not see myself only as such. In a sense I am an apologist in the original meaning of the term, but not only for Islam, rather for all divinely ordained religions. And

I have written some works relating ethics to the act of knowing and to any science that can be considered fully legitimate. But these have been only a part of my writings, the bulk of which deal with traditional thought and the perennial philosophy, including especially metaphysics and cosmology. I consider myself primarily a traditional philosopher and in Western categories perhaps also a theologian. Whether Morewedge considers me a philosopher or not depends on how he defines a philosopher. Although he does not make that clear, I can almost guess, and if my guess is anywhere close to the truth, then yes, I would accept that I am not a philosopher according to his definition and that of other positivists. What is much more important for me is whether I would be considered one by those who are still rooted in various traditional schools of philosophy and thought.

In the last part of his criticisms entitled "private language fallacy" Morewedge takes me to task for the usage of such terms as "inner," which he claims I do not define when I speak of Ismā'īlī philosophy. This is really begging the question. How can one study Ismā'īlī philosophy without being aware of the distinction between the "inner" and the "outer" dimensions of reality? This zeal for logical definition of all that is metaphysical in language and intuitively grasped is a mark of the positivistic perspective with which the author views my works. And yes in contrast to the author's claim, there is an element in Ismā'īlī thought which is anti-rationalistic, although of course not anti-rational or anti-logical. And again in contrast to the views of the author, who says "there is no necessity to force a transcendent deity into this perspective," I have to assert that the whole of Ismā'īlī philosophy is based on the Transcendent Deity and leads back to Him. Needless to say, since this is the case, only in this sense there is no need to "force a transcendent deity" into Ismā'īlism.

Morewedge asks, "why is Nasr certain of this mode of knowledge?" (in referring to illuminative knowledge). The answer is of course certitude and illumination itself which knowledge by presence involves. The answer is immediacy, direct knowledge like that of the sun when we observe it, or of ourselves in moments of introspection.

There are many other assertions made by Morewedge which would need to be answered if I were to write a whole treatise in response to him, but what I have said should suffice as to essentials.

In conclusion let me go back to the Cartesian *cogito ergo sum* which made being an accident of thinking and removed ontology in favor of epistemology as the main concern of modern Western philosophy. Morewedge is the product of the unfolding of that reduction of being to an accident which, through a series of metaphysical descents, finally ended with modern analytical philosophy. I stand on the side of Johann Georg Hamann who reversed the Cartesian dictum saying *sum ergo cogito*, making thinking an accident of being. From the perspective of a positivist, what I and those like me say is not considered philosophy but at best theology. That is why Morewedge concludes by praising my contribution to Islamic studies and not philosophy. But it should be remembered that from the point of view of the perennial philosophy which I champion, most of what the author stands for and defends as philosophy is in reality itself not philosophy but "misosophy," a hatred rather than that love of that *sophia* which is veritable philosophy and which I have sought to reach and to express throughout my life.

S. H. N.

26

Hossein Ziai

NŪR AL-FU'ĀD, A NINETEENTH-CENTURY PERSIAN TEXT IN ILLUMINATIONIST PHILOSOPHY BY SHIHĀB AL-DĪN KUMĪJĀNĪ

Seyyed Hossein Nasr's well-known pioneering studies on the great Iranian philosopher, Shihāb al-Dīn Suhrawardī, have helped demonstrate the continuation of philosophical discourse within Islamic philosophy after Avicenna. In his seminal work, *Three Muslim Sages*, as well as in his numerous articles, Nasr has made major contributions to the analysis and explication of Suhrawardī's Illuminationist philosophy. In part due to Nasr's careful and penetrating studies we are now in a better position to revise the earlier Orientalist view that Islamic philosophy ends with Averroes, and that the spirit of free philosophical analysis and discourse ceases to exist after the end of the twelfth century. On the contrary, Islamic philosophy after Avicenna is developed in ways even more innovative than before, where the earlier dominant Greek element is transformed within new reconstructed holistic systems with their own distinguishing characteristics. There are many such distinguishing components of post-Avicennan developments in Islamic philosophy, specifically in the Illuminationist system (some will be discussed later in this essay). Foremost is the principle position of "knowledge by presence" (*al-'ilm al-ḥuḍūrī*) as a unified epistemological theory which is capable of describing types of knowing, including the obtaining of primary principles. Also the Illuminationist theory of light and vision, and the principle ontological position of the "sameness of knowing and being" rank among the technical refinements specifically of the Illuminationist system. As demonstrated in the works of such scholars as H. Corbin, S. H. Nasr, S. J. Ashtiyani, M. Ha'iri Yazdi, Gh. H. Dinani-Ibrahimi, S. J. Sajjadi, J. Walbridge, M. Aminrazavi, and others, the main conduit for post-Avicennan developments in Islamic Philosophy has been Suhrawardī's

Suhrawardī's holistic reconstructed system named "Philosophy of Illumination." The epistemology of knowledge by presence serves to distinguish the new system from the earlier Avicennan Peripatetic philosophy.

Soon after his execution in Aleppo in 1191, Suhrawardī's innovative philosophical work was hailed as a major achievement and he was bestowed with the epithet "founder" of the new system and given the title "Master of Illumination" (Shaykh al-Ishrāq). Foremost among the thirteenth-century philosophers who wrote commentaries on Illuminationist texts was Shams al-Dīn Shahrazūrī, author of *Sharḥ Ḥikmat al-Ishrāq*. The Illuminationist tradition became widely recognized as the second school of Islamic philosophy (after Avicenna's Peripatetic), and following Shahrazūrī, thinkers such as Quṭb al-Dīn Shīrāzī and Sa'd b. Manṣūr Ibn Kammūnah (thirteenth century); Qiyās al-Dīn Manṣūr Dashtakī and Jalāl al-Dīn Dawwānī (fifteenth and sixteenth centuries); Niẓām al-Dīn Harawī (sixteenth century); and Ṣadr al-Dīn Shīrāzī (seventeenth century), among others, wrote extensive commentaries on Illuminationist texts. The last great Illuminationist work is recognized to be Ṣadr al-Dīn Shīrāzī's *al-Ta'līqāt 'alā sharḥ ḥikmat al-ishrāq*. However, considerable further research is required in order to ascertain the nature and extent of texts composed in the Illuminationist tradition after the seventeenth century. The discovery of the manuscript of the text *Nūr al-fu'ād*, here introduced for the first time, is a clear indication that during the nineteenth-century Illuminationist texts were studied and independent works were written in this tradition.

During my research on Arabic and Persian manuscripts of UCLA's Special Collections I have discovered a unicom autograph Persian manuscript titled *Nūr al-fu'ād* written by the nineteenth-century Illuminationist philosopher, Shihāb al-Dīn Kumījānī.[1] The author is reported to have been a strict follower of the Illuminationist school and was given the title "The Second Master of Illumination," which is of historical significance indicating the status of Illuminationist philosophy as a living tradition in the nineteenth century. The work is an original and engaging Illuminationist text of a period in Islamic philosophy which has remained mainly neglected in Western scholarship. The author, Kumījānī, was one of Hādī Sabziwārī's students for nearly two decades in the city Sabzivār in northeastern Iran. The author's full name, as it appears in the manuscript, and also reported by Manuchehr Saduqi in his pioneering study of post Ṣadr al-Muta'allihīn philosophers in Iran, *Tārīkh-i ḥukamā' wa 'urafā'-i muta'akhkhir bar Ṣadr al-Muta'allihīn* is: Shihāb al-Dīn Muḥammad b. Mūsā al-Buzshallū'ī al-Kumījānī with the title "The [Second] Master of Illumination" as reported by Badī' al-Zamān Furūzānfar.[2] The style and contents of the text plus the author's presumed title are clear indications of the significance of Illuminationist philosophy in nineteenth-century Iran.

innovative, and on occasion creative philosophical text is important for several reasons, some philosophical per se, and some of relevance to the study of nineteenth-century intellectual history of Iran. Given the Orientalist view that creative philosophy suddenly died out altogether after Avicenna in eastern Islam, such fresh discoveries will help the new revisionist trends in Islamic philosophy. These trends address philosophical problems systematically, and this point is evident in the present text here introduced. Kumījānī's text is testimony to the fact that philosophy in the eastern lands of Islam did not die, nor did it deteriorate to some kind of ill-defined "sagesse oriental." There has been, it seems at this point, a continuous line of creative thinkers who kept the creative endeavor of philosophy alive; and this activity found a renewed energy in nineteenth-century Iran.

The text *Nūr al-fu'ād* is written in an elegant philosophical Persian, it is replete with standard Illuminationist terminology, but also introduces a number of new technical terms. The text itself is divided into four main chapters with the heading "*Ishrāq*" (Illumination); with further divisions in each chapter under the heading "*Tajallī*" (Manifestation); with a few lemmas and corollaries added. In what follows I will present a synopsis of the text's contents:

THE FIRST ISHRĀQ

Introduction; discussion of methodology of Illuminationist philosophy named "the science of lights" (*'ilm al-anwār*); and establishing the priority of knowledge by presence.

Tajallī I

A correspondence is shown between demonstrated science (that is, deductive metaphysics) and the purely empirical—the sense-data prior to demonstration. Here a most significant methodological principle informing of Illuminationist "realist" principles is discussed.

Tajallī II

Light is self-evident and cannot be known by definition and is known by "sight" which informs of the Illuminationist epistemological principle of the correspondence of *mushāhada* and *ibṣār*.

THE SECOND ISHRĀQ

On the reality of light and the sameness (*'ayniyyat*) of light with the sequence of all existent entities.

Tajallī I

Examines the term "Allāh."

Tajallī II

Discusses the stated main purpose of the work which is analysis of the proposition sameness (*'ayniyyat*) of the essence light with each and every existent entity in reality. The discussion informs us of the sameness of knowing and being from the perspective of Illuminationist principle epistemological and ontological views.

Tajallī III

To know light is to see light. The Illuminationist ontological position is that "light" is the most well-known real thing and cannot be known primarily by the construction of essentialist definitions. Epistemological priority is given to knowledge by presence when established by the "Illuminationist relation" (*iḍāfah ishrāqiyyah*) between the knowing subject and the manifest object in durationless time.

THE THIRD ISHRĀQ

On Platonic Forms.

Tajallī I and II

Makes the distinctions among Form, image, and paradigm.

Lemma I

The epistemology of unified vision requires the proper functioning of the subject as instrument (say, eye); visibility of object (say, lit entity); and the medium (say, light). Relational, identity preserving correspondence between subject and object is thus defined.

Lemma II and III

On the Illuminationist theory of sight and vision.

This part of the text is indicative of one of Illuminationist philosophy's significant principles regarding the unified theory of knowledge and incorporates a rather novel view of physical sight. From the Illuminationist perspective, theories of the natural philosophers, Peripatetics, and others are discussed and mostly rejected: the corporeality of rays (*jismiyyat al-shu'ā'*), the view that holds rays to be colors (*lawniyyat al-shu'ā'*), and the theory which holds that sight (*ibṣār*) takes place solely because rays leave the eye and meet (*yulāqī*) objects of sight, are all rejected. The Illuminationist also rejects the view that the act of "sight" takes place when the form of the thing (*ṣūrat al-shay'*) is imprinted in the "vitreous humour" (*al-ruṭūbat al-jalīdiyya*). Illuminationists argue that "vision" has no temporal extension, so there is no need for a material relation (*rābiṭat*) between the "seer" and the "thing seen," which means that "sight" or "vision" are prior to syllogistic deductive reasoning and superior to it. The mechanism which allows for the subject to be "illuminated" is a complicated one and involves a certain activity on the part of the faculty of imagination. When an object is "seen," the subject has acted in two ways: by an act of vision and an act of illumination. Thus, vision-illumination is actualized when no obstacle intervenes between the subject and the object. This general theory of vision requires the description of reality as a continuum. Let us explain further: This world of sense-data is a "segment" continuous with and in the whole, wherein its locus time is the usual Peripatetic time as measure, and space as the extended—Euclidean, to put it simply. But, as the "subject" moves away from the center of this segment, nearing the boundaries with the non-corporeal segment, strange things begin to happen. This is when the subject actually "enters" the intermediary realm—a "boundary" realm—called "*'ālam al-khayāl*," or "*'ālam al-mithāl*," which is as real as the other segments, all of them part of the existing whole as continuum. As in all immense (qualitative) and critical changes associated with boundary-value problems (that is, 1/x, as x nears the "boundary" zero), things: time, space, motion, shape, and so on, rapidly and suddenly change. This is a wondrous, amazing realm, *Hūrqalyā dhāt al-'ajāyib*, but the fundamental principles and mechanisms that regulate things remain the same. For example as with sight in the corporeal, in the "boundary" realm, "visions" take place where the subject, whose material body has changed qualitatively to an "Imagined, or Formal" one (*badan khayālī aw mithālī*) will move in a time-frame, not as measure, from "here" to "there" in a different space where no longer the shortest distance between the two points "here" and "there" is necessarily the single straight line between them—rather "here" is some other kind of space which we may name non-Euclidean.

THE FOURTH ISHRĀQ

On cosmology and generation.

Tajallī I and II

Discusses the effects of Heavenly principles on existent entities in the sub-Lunar realm.

Illuminationist Corollary

Relates Shī'ah principles regarding *Imāmat* and *Vilāyat* (*Wilāyat*) to Illuminationist cosmological and epistemological principles.

The treatise is fraught with Illuminationist technical terminology, but more significantly a number of the basic Illuminationist principles that clearly distinguish this system from the Peripatetic are presented, discussed, and in a few cases, philosophically refined. Perhaps the most technically refined philosophical argument is where Kumījānī elaborates the idea of "sameness" between subject and predicate, and/or substance and attribute said of specific constructed and formulated propositions that relate to primary principles, and from the distinctly Illuminationist perspective, between "light" (*nūr*) as subject, and "evidence" (*ẓuhūr*)/"presence" (*ḥuḍūr*), as attribute, or object. The discussion of the related epistemology of knowledge by presence also serves further to confirm the distinct Illuminationist nature of the text *Nūr al-fu'ād*. I will later discuss the distinguishing Illuminationist epistemology in more detail. Before doing so, however, it is important to examine views concerning the position and nature of schools of Islamic philosophy, thus to recognize and confirm the place of the text *Nūr al-fu'ād* as an Illuminationist text.

It is generally accepted that Ṣadr al-Dīn Shīrāzī's interpretations of Islamic philosophy have played the dominant role in scholastic centers in Iran from the seventeenth century to the present. Therefore, it is against his views that Kumījānī's position will be gauged.

While the development of philosophy in Iran from the thirteenth to the seventeenth century has not yet been systematically studied, one of the main characteristics of this period that can be identified is its fundamentally non-Aristotelian "attitude" to philosophical investigation and construction. This also serves to characterize Illuminationist philosophy. This "attitude" is explained by Mullā Ṣadrā in his *al-Asfār al-arba'ah* in terms of the divisions within philosophy. He makes specific references to many works he designates "Illuminationist," such as Ibn Kammūnah's *Commentary on the Intimations* (*al-Tanqīḥāt fī sharḥ al-talwīḥāt*) , Shahrazūrī's *Commentary on the Philosophy of Illumination* and his *al-Shajarat al-Ilāhiyyah*, as well as others. The references are notably to be found in the *Asfār* where Mullā Ṣadrā discusses problems taken from logic, physics, epistemology, metaphysics, and eschatology, in relation to which he carefully delineates the philosophical positions of the various "schools."

One of the many such specific references is the following taken from Mullā Ṣadrā's *al-Asfār al-arba'ah: al-safar al-thālith: fī al-'ilm al-ilāhī: al-*

mawqif al-thālith: fī 'ilmihi ta'ālā: al-faṣl al-rābi': fī tafṣīl madhāhib al-nās fī 'ilmihi bi-al-ashyā'. Here Mullā Ṣadrā distinguishes seven schools of thought, four philosophical, two "theological," and a "mystical" (the latter combining *'irfān* and *taṣawwuf*). This is typical of Mullā Ṣadrā's classification of the history of philosophy, theology, and mysticism, and also reflects an earlier, albeit incomplete, classification found in Shahrazūrī's *al-Shajarat al-ilāhiyyah* three centuries before the composition of the *Asfār*. Only the four philosophical "schools"—referred to as *madhhab*—need concern us here, for the theological and the mystical fall outside of the domain of philosophy proper. The four in Mullā Ṣadrā's order are:

1. "The school of the followers of the Peripatetics (*madhhab tawābi' al-mashshā'īn*)." Included in this category are the "two masters" (*al-shaykhān*) al-Fārābī and Avicenna. Followers of the two masters such as Bahmanyār (Avicenna's famous student and author of *al-Taḥṣīl*), Abū al-'Abbās al-Lawkarī, and "many later Peripatetics" (*kathīr min al-muta'akhkhirīn*) are also included in this group. Mullā Ṣadrā's group "later Peripatetics" is confined to philosophers in Islam, but al-Kindī is not included. The philosophical position of this group concerning being is called "primacy of being" (*aṣālat al-wujūd*); adherents of this school are said to uphold the principle of the eternity of the world (*qidam*); they are said to reject bodily resurrection and posit that the soul is separated from the body, but their position is said to be unclear on the question of the immortality of the individual soul. Of their views Mullā Ṣadrā only accepts the ontological principle of the "later Peripatetics."

2. "The school of the Master Shihāb al-Dīn [Suhrawardī] al-Maqtūl, follower of the Stoics (*madhhab shaykh atbā' al-riwāqiyyah Shihāb al-Dīn al-Maqtūl*), and those who follow him, such as al-Muḥaqqiq al-Ṭūsī, Ibn Kammūnah, al-'Allāmah [Quṭb al-Dīn] al-Shīrāzī, and Muḥammad al-Shahrazūrī, author of *al-Shajarat al-ilāhiyyah*." The addition of the attribution "Stoic" to the Illuminationist school appears in many places in the *Asfār*. However, concerning certain "novel" philosophical issues, such as the distinction between the idea of "intellectual form" (*al-ṣūrat al-'aqliyyah*) and the idea of "archetypal form" (*al-ṣūrat al-mithāliyyah*)—the latter also as "the idea shape," or "imagined shape"—Mullā Ṣadrā is careful to use only the attribution "Illuminationist." In general the epithet "Stoic" is added to the Illuminationist designation only in conjunction with questions that relate to logic and physics, but in matters that pertain to epistemology, cosmology, and eschatology, "Illuminationist" is used alone. Among the central doctrines of this "school" is said to be the position that upholds the real existence of the forms of things outside the mind (*al-qawl bi-kawn wujūd ṣuwar al-ashyā' fī al-khārij*), be the things corporeal or not (*mujarradāt aw*

māddiyyāt), or simple or not (*murrakabāt aw basā'iṭ*). As I have explained elsewhere, this type of a "realism" is a cornerstone of the philosophy of illumination.

3. "The school attributed (*al-mansūb*) to Porphyry, the First of the Peripatetics (*muqaddam al-mashshā'īn*), one of the greatest followers of the First Teacher." It should be noted that the reference to Aristotle in relation to Porphyry includes views of "Aristotle" of the *Uthulūjiyā*, i.e., to Plotinus. Among the views associated with this "school," their view of the "unity" (*ittiḥād*) of the intelligible forms (*al-ṣuwar al-ma'qūlah*) with God, and through the Active Intellect with a "select" number of humans, is considered central to their philosophical belief (*'aqīdah*). Aristotle himself is not always associated with a "school," but is deemed an exemplum against whom every philosophical position is to be judged.

4. "The school of the divine Plato." It is possible that Mullā Ṣadrā here means Plato himself and not a "school of thought" that may have continued after him. I so surmise from his statement: *mā dhahaba ilayhi Aflāṭūn al-ilāhīyyah*. The distinction would indicate an attempt on the part of Mullā Ṣadrā to define the philosophical position of Plato himself as distinct from later syncretic texts designated "Platonic." For example, Mullā Ṣadrā in the *Asfār* (Vol III: 509), clearly attempts to refer specifically to Plato himself by stating "*qāla Aflāṭūn al-sharīf*," and not as elsewhere "*fī madhhab al-aflāṭūniyyah*." The central philosophical doctrine here is said to be the "objectified" reality of the Separate Forms (*al-ṣuwar al-mufāraqa*h) and the Intelligible Platonic Forms (*al-muthul al-'aqliyyat al-aflāṭūniyyah*), a position upheld strongly by Mullā Ṣadrā, who adds that in reference to this position God's knowledge of all existent entities (*'ilm Allāh bi-al-mawjūdāt kulluhā*) is proven.

The "second school" of philosophy here mentioned, namely the Illuminationist, is distinguished from the other schools in every philosophical domain: methodology and the division of the sciences, logic, ethics and political philosophy, physics, metaphysics and eschatology. This school's main philosophical position, as examined and identified by Mullā Ṣadrā throughout the *Asfār*, gives it a distinct position in the history of philosophy. The main philosophical position may be outlined as follows: Philosophical construction is founded on a primary intuition of time-space, and visions and personal revelations are valid epistemological processes. Knowledge by presence is considered prior to predicative knowledge, and the separate intellects (*al-'uqūl al-mujarradah / al-'uqūl al-mufāraqah*) are considered multiple, and said to be uncountable (*bi-lā nihāyah*). The ontological position of this school is one designated "primacy of quiddity" (*aṣālat al-māhiyyah*), which, briefly stated, holds "existence" (*wujūd*) to be a derived

This "realist" position is one of the most essential overall features of Mullā Ṣadrā's characterization of the Illuminationist position, which he also discusses in great detail in his *al-Ta'līqāt* (*Glosses on Ḥikmat al-ishrāq*). Intensity, or its lack (more and less) is considered an attribute of categories, in which motion does enter—a view itself related to Mullā Ṣadrā's own notion of transubstantial motion (*al-ḥarakat al-jawhariyyah*). The immortality of the soul and its "ranks" after separation from the body is a fundamental escatological position of this school. The Platonic Forms are considered objectified, and the *mundus imaginalis* of Illuminationist cosmology is considered a separate realm whose existence is attested by experience.

Finally, metaphysics is divided into two parts: *metaphysica generalis* and *metaphysica specialis*, which was so indicated for the first time in the history of Islamic philosophy systematically by Shahrazūrī in his *al-Shajarat al-ilāhiyyah*. The Illuminationist treatment of *metaphysica specialis* (*al-ilāhī bi-ma'na al-akhaṣṣ*) gradually departs from the Avicennan view of a pure ontology (*wujūd bi-mā huwa wujūd*) and includes discussion of such subjects as mystical states and stations, love, secrets of dreams, prophecy, sorcery and the arts of magic. Though we may characterize this philosophical attitude as Platonist, which it is in many essential ways, it is best described as a "new" non-Aristotelian philosophical constructivist endeavor. The problems discussed from the distinct perspective of Illuminationist philosophy, taken together, overturn the foundation of the Aristotelian scientific method, the imprint of early Islamic philosophy, and pave the way for every major philosophical (and gnostic) reconstruction culminating with the seventeenth-century Transcendental Philosophy (*al-Ḥikmat al-muta-'āliyah*) of Mullā Ṣadrā himself. Regarding all of the above stated philosophical positions, *Nūr al-fu'ād* must be indeed seen as a distinctly Illuminationist text.

Mullā Ṣadrā's view of the Illuminationist methodology of philosophy may be further summed up as follows. This philosophy posits that philosophical construction is founded on a primary intuition of time-space, and that visions and personal revelations are valid epistemological processes. Illuminationist philosophy, Mullā Ṣadrā surmises, holds that knowledge by presence (*al-'ilm al-ḥuḍūrī*) is prior to predicative knowledge (*al-'ilm al-ḥuṣūlī*), and he further contends that the multiplicity of intellects is an "improvement" of the Peripatetic model. We are finally told that the ontological axiom known as "primacy of quiddity" (*aṣālat al-māhiyyah*), is central to the Illuminationists' view of being, but must be rejected in favor of Mullā Ṣadrā's own position "primacy of being" (*aṣālat al-wujūd*).

Illuminationist epistemology, as I indicated, is the single most significant distinguishing characteristic of this school in Islamic philosophy, a view upheld by Kumījānī as well. Here knowledge, according to the Illuminationist theory of knowledge by presence, is not founded on the input of sense-data and the extrapolation of universal concepts. At best the universals established in logic are nothing but relative truths. Knowledge rests on: (1) a knowing subject, *al-mawḍū' al-mudrik*, who is self-conscious and knows its "I" necessarily—*al-'ana'iyyat al-muta'āliyah*—by means of the principle of self-consciousness, the "I" recovers, intuitively, primary notions of time-space, accepts the validity of such things as the primary intelligibles, and confirms the existence of God (unlike the host of philosophical and quasi-philosophical proofs for the existence of God, like the so-called "ontological proof" of Avicenna). Thus knowledge is founded on innate principles, which in a somewhat Platonic manner are "recovered" in the knowing subject's being. (2) Knowable objects, in accordance with Illuminationist cosmology, are part of the continuum of luminous entities (*al-anwār al-mujarrada*) and are inherently knowable. (3) An "a-temporal" relation between the knowing subject and the object takes place in a durationless "instant" (*ān*). This type of knowledge is called "knowledge by illumination and presence" (*al-'ilm al-ishrāqī al-ḥuḍūrī*), which is activated whenever an Illuminationist relation (*al-iḍāfat al-ishrāqiyyah*) is obtained between the subject and the object. The religio-mystical and political implications of this epistemology are to be held premier in our understanding of all subsequent *ḥikmah* compositions in Iran, and the text of *Nūr al-Fu'ād* falls within this category, as is evident in the Third Ishrāq of the text outlined above.

Intuition (*ḥads*), personal revelation (*ilhām*), and insight (*mukāshafah*) are integral constituents of Illuminationist theory of knowledge by presence. And knowledge at every age rests on a "superior" individual's personal experience of reality. Illuminationists argue that just as astronomers observe the heavens—*irṣād jismānī*—and arrive at certitude vis-à-vis planetary motion and are thus able to predict such phenomena as eclipses and so on, so too the divine philosophers, *al-ḥukamā' al-muta'allihūn* (who combine discursive philosophy with intuitive philosophy to a perfect degree), observe reality as-it-is and are thus the most perfect potential "leaders" of society, which in the text *Nūr al-fu'ād* are the Shi'ah Imams who act according to the principle of *Vilāyat* (*Wilāyat*). The result of such non-Aristotelian philosophizing paves the way for the triumph of *al-ḥikmat al-muta'āliyah* in Iran, and is indicative of the victory of practical reason over theoretical science in Islamic philosophy by the seventeenth century. Theoretical philosophy fails because of the impossibility of constructing valid universal, always true, propositions, formalized and employed as the building block of science. In its stead "living" sages at every era determine what "scientific" attitude the society must have, which is based on their own individual experiential, and subjective knowledge. The real, separate Platonic Forms may be known, not by the Aristotelian demonstration (*burhān*) of the *Posterior Analytics*, but by intuition and vision-illumination, which is a coupled atemporal epistemological process initiating from the knowing "I" of the subject, and is considered prior to the Peripatetic conception-assent (*taṣawwur-taṣdīq*) which is temporally extended.

The notion of philosophical "intuition" is of central importance for the constructivist methodology of Illuminationist philosophy. Intuition, in the Illuminationist sense is: (1) similar to the Aristotelian "quick wit," *agkhinoia*, where the truth of propositions may be known immediately, or stated otherwise, prior to constructing a syllogism the conclusion may be struck at once; and (2) recovery by the subject of universals, and of sensible objects. But intuition plays a further fundamental role in that it is an activity of the self-conscious being in a state where the subject and the object are undifferentiated (of things existing in the separate realm of the *imaginalis*). To use the Illuminationist technical terminology, this activity is the "unity of perception, the perceived and the perceiver" (*ittiḥād al-mudrik wa'l-idrāk wa'l-mudrik*) as an altered state in the consciousness of the knowing subject. This altered state, when it is "linked" or "related" to the separate realm, is the *mundus imaginalis*. This philosophical position further posits a multiplicity of self-conscious, self-subsistent "monads" designated "abstract light" (*al-nūr al-mujarrad*) in place of the finite number Peripatetic "intellects" (*al-'uqūl al-mujarradah*). The "abstract lights" which are continuous one with the other, differing only in their relative degree of intensity, form a continuum as the whole (*al-kull*), also conscious of its self.

This type of a cosmology bears directly on the question of God's knowledge. The designation "intuitive philosophy" (*al-ḥikmah al-dhawqiyyah*) is employed to distinguish Illuminationist philosophy from the purely discursive (*al-ḥikmah al-baḥthiyyah*). Kumījānī in his *Nūr al-fu'ād*, by clearly stipulating the essential priority of knowledge by presence of the sage-philosopher (but also of the inspired knowledge of the Imāms), hence the essential priority of Vilāyat (Wilāyat), has further expanded on the basic views of Suhrawardī.

Finally, the use of the term "sameness" (*'ayniyyat*) by Kumījānī is perhaps philosophically the most significant aspect of the text *Nūr al-fu'ād*. Here the term *'ayniyyat* is employed to present the idea of the unity of the knower and the known which, in Peripatetic texts, is normally presented in the form of the proposition *ittiḥād al-āqil wa'l-ma'qūl*. The term "unity" (*ittiḥād*) / "conjunction" (*ittiṣāl*) was seen by the Illuminationist philosophers of the twelfth and thirteenth centuries to be problematic for a complex number of reasons, but mainly because the relation "sameness" must be an identity-preserving relation, and concepts such as *ittiḥād* and/or *ittiṣāl* do not fulfill this requirement. It seems that by his statements "sameness of light and manifestation" (*'ayniyyat-i nūr va tajallīyāt-i vujūd* [*wujūd*]) and "sameness of light and presence" Kumījānī has refined the argument pertaining to the problem of the sameness of being and knowing, and of knower and object of thought. It is testimony to the living legacy of Suhrawardī's Philosophy of Illumination that Kumījānī was recognized as "The Second Master of Illumination" in nineteenth-century Iran.

HOSSEIN ZIAI

UNIVERSITY OF CALIFORNIA, LOS ANGELES
AUGUST 2000

NOTES

1. M. T. Dānesh-Pajhūh named the text in his *Nuskhihā-yi khaṭṭī* (Tehran: Tehran University Press, 1980, p. 347), but did not mention its distinct Illuminationist nature.

2. See Manūchehr Ṣadūqī, *Tārikh-i Ḥukamā' va 'ūrafā'-i muta'akhkhir bar Ṣadr al-Muta'allihīn* (Tehran: Anjuman-i Islāmī-i Ḥikmat va Falsafah-i Īrān, 1980), p. 123. Ṣadūqī writes that Badī' al-Zamān had personally told him Kumījānī's title on "the day 16/9/1345" (December 7, 1966).

REPLY TO HOSSEIN ZIAI

Professor Ziai is one of the foremost scholars of the School of Illumination (*ishrāq*) today and his essay containing an unexpected discovery of a new *ishrāqī* work is a further contribution to the field of study of this important philosophical school. At the same time it affords me the opportunity to clarify further some of my views concerning the School of Illumination to which I have devoted a number of studies over the years. At the outset I should mention that I became deeply attracted to the School of *Ishrāq* and its founder Suhrawardī in my twenties, and he has remained a most appealing figure to me throughout my scholarly and philosophical life. His mastery of discursive philosophy in combination with spiritual vision, his universalist view of philosophy along with his espousal and explicit use of the term "perennial philosophy," and his combining the rigor of logic and beauty of poetic expression so evident especially in his Persian works, which took me many years to edit critically for the first time, are all close to my mind and heart. My own thought and its expression have in fact sought to incorporate these and other elements associated with his philosophy. Just the title of the treatise analyzed by Ziai, namely, *Nūr al-fu'ād* or *The Light of the Heart*, so rich in symbolism and of such poetic quality, reveals something of the characteristics of the School of Illumination and more particularly its incredible founder, Suhrawardī.

Of all the major figures of Islamic thought, there are a few with whom I have always felt a very close personal affinity for one reason or another and have studied not only their thoughts but also their lives carefully. These figures include Ibn Sīnā, al-Ghazzālī, Suhrawardī, Ibn 'Arabī, Rūmī, Afḍal al-Dīn Kāshānī, Shabistarī and Mullā Ṣadrā. Each has left an indelible mark upon my thought and has been a constant source of inspiration for me. In the field of philosophy, in the more technical sense of the term, no person has attracted me, *qua* person, more than Suhrawardī, whose life combines such brilliance and tragedy. I remember that when I stood long ago inside the fort of Aleppo and within the prison room in which Suhrawardī was incarcerated just before his death and where he perhaps died, I felt as if his very presence were there. He was also the only figure about whom I consented to make an hour-long film, which I did for the National Iranian Television in the '70s when I was living in Iran. For that occasion I flew with a helicopter to the completely isolated village of Suhraward in the heart of the rugged Zagros mountains and wondered how a philosopher of the magnitude of Suhrawardī could have hailed from such a far away place and yet was able to illuminate the Islamic world with the light of his *ishrāqī* philosophy (which Corbin and I have also called "theosophy" in the original sense of the term). The sources of his philosophical knowledge, especially the elements drawn from the Mazdean tradition, as well as of his personal inspiration, remain obscure, but the results of what he drew from these sources are luminous in both form and content. To understand fully my synthesis of the perennial philosophy in its contemporary expression and traditional Islamic philosophy, the role of Suhrawardī and the School of Illumination remains of great importance.

Ziai writes of the importance of the *Ishrāqī* School in later Islamic philosophy. This goes without saying but needs to be repeated again and again because those who hold tenaciously to the old view that considers Ibn Rushd as the end of Islamic philosophy do not want to relinquish such a view despite the vast amount of evidence to the contrary. There is in fact a new wave in the Arab world which in face of such figures as Suhrawardī, Mīr Dāmād and Mullā Ṣadrā, still considers Ibn Rushd to be the last so-called Arab philosopher (which for them means Islamic), because its members believe that, since these later philosophers were not rationalists, they were not really philosophers at all. Therefore they can be dismissed as not being real philosophers while they themselves, being out and out rationalists, are good second-rate philosophers in the modern Western definition of the term, while Ibn Rushd as seen by them in his Latin incarnation as Averroes, the arch rationalist, is of course a true philosopher. It is against such unbelievable misinterpretations of Islamic philosophy that the words of Ziai serve as a precious response. If Suhrawardī were not a philosopher, then neither were Pythagoras, Empedocles, Parmenides, Plato, Plotinus, Proclus, Erigena, St. Bonaventure, St. Thomas, and even Aristotle.

Coming back to the later *ishrāqī* tradition, years of studying later Islamic philosophy in Persia, and to some extent India and the Ottoman world, have made it clear to me that Mīr Dāmād and Mullā Ṣadrā were of course deeply influenced by Suhrawardī and the latter integrated many *ishrāqī* teachings into his *ḥikmat al-muta'āliyah* or "transcendent theosophy," but the vast influence of these figures, and especially Mullā Ṣadrā, was not the only channel through which Suhrawardī's teachings were propagated in later centuries. Rather, parallel with the Ṣadrian School, the *Ishrāqī* School continued to be cultivated as a distinct philosophical tradition.

In Persia itself today many people think that as soon as the teachings of Mullā Ṣadrā were propagated, they dominated the whole philosophical scene. That is in fact not true. For some time his teachings were eclipsed and *mashshā'ī* thought continued to be widely cultivated as we see in the works of Mullā Rajab 'Alī Tabrīzī and Sayyid Aḥmad 'Alawī. Even when in the Qajar period the philosophy of Mullā Ṣadrā became resurrected by Mullā 'Alī Nūrī and others, and soon became the most dominant school of philosophy, three other philosophical schools survived and were in fact active outside the dominant Ṣadrian School. These three schools were the *mashshā'ī* or Ibn Sīnan, represented by Mīrzā Abu'l-Ḥasan Jilwah, the philosophical Sufism of the school of Ibn 'Arabī, whose most luminous representative in that period was Āqā Muḥammad Riḍā Qumsha'ī, and the school of Suhrawardī, represented by Kumījānī whose important treatise has been brought back to life by Ziai. When I was studying Islamic philosophy with traditional masters in Persia in the late '50s, as well as the '60s and '70s, they attested to this fact. Especially Sayyid Muḥammad Kāẓim 'Aṣṣār would often mention the continuation of the *ishrāqī* tradition even after the spread of the school of Mullā Ṣadrā. 'Aṣṣār was himself in a sense both an *ishrāqī* philosopher and a Ṣadrian one; that is, he could place himself in each perspective and teach it in a masterly fashion as one possible metaphysical formulation of the truth.

In the Ottoman world there is hardly a trace of the influence of Mullā Ṣadrā's philosophy until quite recently, while there is definitely a whole *ishrāqī* tradition in that world which has not been as yet fully investigated. The recent study of Ismā'īl Anqarawī by Bilal Kuşpinar is a good example of the richness of this tradition. As for India, there the situation was different from both Persia and the Ottoman world. Islamic philosophy itself first spread to India on the wings of Suhrawardī's *ishrāqī* philosophy, rather than through the works of al-Fārābī and Ibn Sīnā, who became widely known in that land only after the fourteenth century. But the teachings of Mullā Ṣadrā also spread to India rapidly even in his own lifetime. The *Ishrāqī* School, however, guarded its independence from Ṣadrian teachings fully and the *ishrāqī* current remained stronger and more distinct as an independent school of thought than in the case in Persia. In Persia the *Ishrāqī* School continued while the Ṣadrian School became the most dominant, but in India probably the reverse is true. Of course one cannot judge fully the relative significance of the two schools until a thorough study is made of later Islamic philosophy in the Subcontinent, a task which has not been accomplished as yet. But judging from the presence of many *ishrāqī* texts in India, one of which has been edited and published by Professor Ziai himself, and the importance of the Niẓāmī curriculum for Islamic *madrasahs* in which *ishrāqī* teachings played a major role, one can only conclude that the school of Suhrawardī remained of major intellectual concern for many Muslims in the Subcontinent. Can it be an accident that the most philosophically minded of the modern Muslim reformers of the Subcontinent, Muhammad Iqbāl, should have devoted his doctoral thesis, published later as *The Development of Metaphysics in Persia*, primarily to *ishrāqī* teachings?

To understand fully the history of the later *ishrāqī* school one would have to know in detail the development of the School of Illumination not only in Persia, the Ottoman world (including the Arab east, especially Iraq and Syria and to some extent Egypt) and the Indian Subcontinent, but also the development of *ishrāqī* teachings in Jewish philosophy, medieval Christian philosophy and even certain strands of medieval Hindu thought. When I wrote *Three Muslim Sages* nearly forty years ago, the text serving as the basis of a series of lectures delivered at the Center for the Study of World Religions at Harvard University in 1962, I already referred to some of these influences, and in later essays I pointed out the necessity of pursuing the study of all these branches of the *Ishrāqī* School. Since then, a number of important studies have been carried out on the later *ishrāqī* tradition by a number of scholars, foremost among them Ziai himself; but much remains to be done as the author himself mentions. The presentation and analysis of Kumījānī in this essay is itself a step in this effort and therefore has provided me with the occasion to return to the question of the importance of the later *ishrāqī* tradition.

In mentioning later *ishrāqī* thinkers the author includes the name of Ṣadr al-Dīn Shīrāzī whose *Ta'līqāt 'alā sharḥ ḥikmat al-ishrāq* he calls, "the last great Illuminationist work." I agree completely with this assessment, at least given our present state of knowledge of later *ishrāqī* texts. But I want to take this occasion to add that this work is also one of Mullā Ṣadrā's own greatest masterpieces, a work which has not received its due until now. I am glad that Professor Ziai has prepared a critical edition of this text and hope that it will see the light of day soon. The study of this work reveals Mullā Ṣadrā's incredible depth of understanding of Suhrawardī, and at the same time shows his vast knowledge of other earlier schools of Islamic thought. Paradoxically enough, therefore, Mullā Ṣadrā is at once a philosopher who created a new school which integrated much of *ishrāqī* thought and became dominant in the philosophical scene in Persia from the Qajar period onward, and himself an *ishrāqī* philosopher in the line of Muḥammad Shams al-Dīn Shahrazūrī and Quṭb al-Dīn Shīrāzī. The interaction between the Ṣadrian and the *Ishrāqī* Schools from the seventeenth to the twentieth century in Persia would constitute the subject of a most fascinating and revealing study, because these two major metaphysical syntheses, one based on the principiality of essence and the other the principiality of existence, both remained realities to be contemplated and studied by those attracted to the intellectual sciences in general and to philosophy in particular.

Ziai mentions that Kumījānī was given the title of "The Second Master of Illumination." One wonders when this title began to be used because it is certainly significant and points possibly to the singular importance of

Kumījānī in Qajar Persia as the foremost authority in *ishrāqī* teachings of that time. We know that Āqā Muḥammad Riḍā Qumsha'ī, his contemporary, was given the title of "The Second Ibn 'Arabī" because he stood out as the foremost expositor of theoretical gnosis (*'irfān-i naẓarī*) of the nineteenth century in Persia. If the title given to Kumījānī is born out in other documents, it would put him in a position parallel with Qumsha'ī and would be further reason for turning to his other writings and studying him as the torch bearer of the *Ishrāqī* School in his day. Unfortunately, this subject has been neglected not only in Western scholarship, as mentioned by Ziai, but by contemporary scholarship in Iran as well.

Ziai writes quite justly that "Kumījānī's text is testimony to the fact that philosophy in the eastern lands of Islam did not die." Then he adds, "nor did it deteriorate to some kind of ill-defined '*sagesse orientale*.'" In defense of Corbin who used this term, let me say that in a world in which philosophy is reduced to rationalism or sub-rationalism, and in which positivists believe that there was no serious philosophy before Hume and Kant, it is necessary to take recourse to terms which do not share this limitation in definition and meaning. If we define philosophy as love of *sophia*, then there is no need of using any other term than "philosophy" when speaking of a Suhrawardī or a Mullā Ṣadrā, but if philosophy is confined to logical positivism or existentialism, then a term such as *sagesse orientale* can be a means of opening the reader's intellectual horizon and showing that there is more to philosophy than rationalism or sub-rationalism, as Suhrawardī would be the first to accept. Besides, Corbin translated *al-ḥikmat al-mashriqiyyah* as *sagesse orientale*, a term which has had a long honored history in Islamic thought, and while not confined to rationalism, has always emphasized the necessity of logical rigor in the understanding of *ḥikmah*.

There is no need for me to go over again Ziai's analysis of the text itself which is carried out in a clear and masterly fashion. There are only a few points upon which I would like to make brief comments. In enumerating the schools of philosophy according to Mullā Ṣadrā, Ziai mentions under the second category the term *riwāqī* or "Stoic" which Mullā Ṣadrā identifies with the school of Suhrawardī. Despite a few studies carried out on the subject, the usage of the term "Stoic" in this context is still a mystery to me, seeing how different Stoic philosophy is from that of Suhrawardī. Since in more specific cases Mullā Ṣadrā adds the epithet "Stoic" to *ishrāqī* only when issues of physics and logic are concerned, could one say that in these two domains the Stoics influenced Suhrawardī, or that Mullā Ṣadrā, having studied directly through some source unknown to us Stoic logic and physics, saw such a parallel and therefore equated the two? When one studies Stoic physics as expounded by specialists such as Samuel Sambursky and compares it with *ishrāqī* physics, one does not find such close resemblances, although there are points of accord. The case of logic is somewhat easier and one could make a case that Suhrawardī's criticism of Aristotelian formal logic reflects his knowledge of Stoic logic. In any case I have not been able to find a solution to this enigma and hope that Professor Ziai, who is well versed in classical logic and physics as well as *ishrāqī* teachings, will be able to cast light on this matter.

I confirm fully Ziai's emphasis on the *ishrāqī* theory of knowledge by presence (*al-'ilm al-ḥuḍūrī*) and its difference from predicative knowledge (*al-'ilm al-ḥuṣūlī*). But I do not understand his assertion that "such non-Aristotelian philosophizing . . . is indicative of the victory of practical reason over theoretical science in Islamic philosophy." Even in the case of the Imams "who act according to the principle *Vilāyat* (*Wilāyat*)," to quote Ziai, knowing always preceded acting. Perhaps Ziai has something in mind of which I am not aware. As far as I can see, in Islamic thought the *naẓarī* or theoretical element has always accompanied the '*amalī* or practical element and has preceded it in principle. In the teachings of traditional philosophy the theoretical branches of philosophy were in fact held in higher esteem than the practical, while at the same time all masters of traditional thought emphasized that knowledge without the appropriate action is like a tree that bears no fruit (repeating the famous Arabic aphorism).

One of the most interesting parts of Ziai's essay is the last part of his analysis where he speaks of Kumījānī's views of the inspired knowledge of the Shi'ite Imāms and the priority of *vilāyat* (*wilāyat*). In the writings of Suhrawardī there are no signs of distinct and explicit Shi'ite doctrines, although he was accused by his opponents of *Bāṭinī* (that is, Ismā'īlī) sympathy. The *Nūr al-fu'ād* seems to present Suhrawardī in Shi'ite dress in the same way that Ḥaydar Āmulī integrated Ibn 'Arabī into the matrix of Shi'ite gnosis. If such is in fact the case, there is an added significance to Kumījānī. The early schools of Islamic philosophy continued and were revived in the Shi'ite Persia of the Safavid period by being brought into the Shi'ite intellectual universe and being made "Shi'ite." We have ample evidence of this process in the case of al-Fārābī, Ibn Sīnā, Ibn 'Arabī, and even al-Ghazzālī. Now with Kumījānī we see the same process taking place for Suhrawardī and his *ishrāqī* teachings.

I am grateful to Professor Ziai for not only unveiling another monument of *ishrāqī* thought in his indefatigable effort to bring back to life the major works of the *ishrāqī* tradition, but also for affording me the opportunity to clarify further some of my views on this school. As I wrote nearly forty years ago, I still believe that the School of Illumination founded by Suhrawardī is not only one of the richest philosophical schools in the Islamic world, but it is also one that is still alive today and that has much to offer to both the contemporary Islamic world and to those in the West in quest of a philosophy which combines the rigor of logic and the ecstasy of spiritual vision.

S. H. N.

27

Enes Karić

NASR: THINKER OF THE SACRED

I

Almost all of the fourteenth and the beginning of the fifteenth century of Islam (the nineteenth and the twentieth centuries according to the Western calendar) have, among other things, been marked in the Muslim world by an extensive search for the Islamic interpretations of the *Moderna* and new Islamic interpretations of Islam. If the *Moderna* has happened to the West, does it inevitably have to happen to Islam and the Islamic East, and has it already taken place? Is the *Moderna* something like the destiny that cannot be avoided, since the West has become a planetary civilization which celebrates the divinity of *Moderna*, which devours other civilizations and deprives them of their own eras, of their feelings of time and eternity? Have the very roots of traditional Islam been shaken, waking it from its centuries-long repose by an external factor which forces it to live in the shadow of the powerful West—which, aided by its technology, endangers others, levels all differences, looks upon the world "conqueringly" and lasciviously, in compliance to the well-known Hegelian metaphor about the relationship between the servant and the master? What hope is there for the Muslims? And can these hopes be founded in their own, still living and still powerful tradition?

Seyyed Hossein Nasr, a Muslim and, more particularly, a Persian Shi'ite, has been asking these and many other questions in his numerous works, but also gives lucid answers which fill with enthusiasm his exceptionally large audience. This audience ranges from the ranks of the Muslim intelligentsia from the Atlantic to the Pacific coast, an audience acquainted with the West but deeply rooted in the unextinguished Islamic tradition. It suffices to say that Nasr's works have been translated into dozens of languages spoken by

Muslims and non-Muslims[1] and that he is equally gladly read by the Muslims, Buddhists, Christians, and the so-called secular intelligentsia of the West. Nasr's thought is as challenging as the vision of Islam he shapes into words; it is as sharp as a knife and as bright as the flash of sunlight reflected from a swaying sword! It confronts the Muslims and non-Muslims alike with the world and the heritage of the *Moderna*, but also with the Islamic answers and Islamic criticism of the *Moderna*: emanating from his pen and prose is that ancient knowledge according to which the subject and the object embrace and caress each other like lovers.

II

Seyyed Hossein Nasr was born in 1933 in Tehran to an educated family whose members were traditionally physicians, philosophers, poets, or theologians. He received his early education in Tehran, with special emphasis upon classical education in religion, Persian poetry, and classical literature. He completed secondary school in the United States of America and studied physics and mathematics at the Massachussets Institute of Technology. He graduated in 1954 with honors and continued advanced studies at Harvard University. He received his M.S. degree in 1956, and Ph.D. in 1958 in the history of science and philosophy with special emphasis upon Islamic science.

In the period between 1955 and 1958 he was a teaching assistant at Harvard University, and from 1962 to 1965 a visiting professor at the same university. From 1958 to 1979 he worked at Tehran University, first as an associate professor (up to 1963), and then as full professor. Nasr was the first professor of Islamic Studies at the American University of Beirut (1964–1965). He was a visiting professor at Princeton University (1975) and at the University of Utah (1979). In the 1979–84 period he was full professor of Islamic Studies at Temple University. Since 1984 he has taught Islamic Studies at George Washington University.

Aside from teaching, Nasr has been engaged in the organizational and administrative aspects of university life. He was Dean of the Faculty of Letters at Tehran University, Vice-Chancellor of Tehran University, and the founder and first President of the Iranian Academy of Philosophy. He was the first chairman of the Board of Governors of the RCD (Iran-Pakistan-Turkey) Cultural Institute (1964–66), and a member of the Organizing Committee of the First Muslim World Educational Conference (Mecca, 1975–77). From 1959 onward, Nasr has been examiner in the field of philosophy for several universities in Pakistan, Saudi Arabia, and Malaysia.

Generally speaking, Nasr is the best known contemporary Muslim intellectual. He has lectured extensively throughout the Islamic world as well as in Western Europe, North and Central America, India, Japan, and Australia. He has participated in numerous conferences and congresses on Islam, philosophy, comparative religion, and the environmental crisis. He has delivered a number of famous lectures: the Iqbal Lecture in Pakistan in 1966; the Azad Memorial Lecture in India in 1975, and the Gifford Lectures at the University of Edinburgh in 1981 (where he was the first Muslim ever to give these prestigious lectures on religion).

Nasr's research and publishing activity has been very extensive. He has written more than twenty books and two hundred articles. Besides, he has participated in numerous research projects and contributed to many contemporary encyclopedia in the fields of philosophy, religion, Islamic science, and the like. His book, *Islamic Science: An Illustrated Study*, was nominated for the Faisal Award. He was awarded the Honorary Doctorate by the University of Uppsala and by Lehigh University. He is a member of the Institut International de Philosophie and the Greek Academy of Philosophy. For ten years now he has been a member of the Board of Directors of Federation Internationale des Sociétés Philosophiques (FISP).

He writes in English and Persian, and occasionally in French and Arabic. His works have been translated into Arabic, Urdu, Bengali, Turkish, Indonesian, Japanese, Polish, French, Spanish, Italian, German, Malay, Portuguese, and the like, and published in the leading scientific periodicals the world over.

III

I have been studying and translating Nasr with pleasure and affection for fifteen years now, consider him a deeply traditional thinker. This corresponds to the Islamic attitude according to which the world is seen as traditional (not traditionalistic): the Prophet Muḥammad did not bring a new religion but only revealed the ancient one, linked to the inexhaustible spring, and heralded by all of the Divine Messengers. The word "Islam" (dedication and surrender to an only God) is deeply traditional in itself, for if God is the beginning and the source, is there anything more traditional than a dedication to God? This commitment has necessarily confronted Nasr with criticism of a nontraditional spirit which has been spreading in the West for a long time, particularly in the course of the eighteenth, nineteenth, and twentieth centuries. Nasr is also faced with the criticism of certain modernist and non-modernist trends in the Islamic world—trends which saw the logical continuation of Islamic science in the rise of the Western science and technology.

It seems that Nasr's primary task was to bring back to the Muslims the belief in a living and inexhaustible Islamic tradition. His success is indisputable: Muslims all over the Islamic world read his works with pride, acknowledging him with the merit of discovering Islam anew, through past (but by no means extinguished) intellectual dimensions. Due to its central geographic position in the world, Islam is the natural inheritor of all of the great traditional teachings of the ancient cultures. For the same reason it is easily able to assimilate these cultures and their achievements. Islam appeared in the part of the earth most heavily marked by human presence for thousands of years; it inherited those spaces not only horizontally (spatially), but vertically (spiritually) as well. In his book, *An Introduction to Islamic Cosmological Doctrines*,[2] Nasr indirectly points out that Islam has no complex about the past because all of the Greek, Roman, Byzantine, Near-East, and Far-East courses of learning flowed into the mainstream of its knowledge. In the Golden Age of Islam its territory was the center of the world. Islam had its geographers, travellers, physicians, mathematicians, men of letters, philosophers, translators, and so on. Islam developed the science[3] which surpassed all sciences that had appeared on the face of the earth before that time and which was rooted in the so-called sacred science (*scientia sacra*). It was a science which, through its various disciplines, did not break being into fragments and did not answer to the satanic cry of the analytical Cartesian science which sees this same world as a carcass and not as a blooming, fragrant rose-garden.[4]

It has been said that in his early works Nasr polemicizes with Western science simply because that science is polemical in itself. He looks down on it just because it looks down on all other traditional sciences. Needless to say, Nasr is one of the most competent contemporary critics of modern Western science because of all the contemporary Muslim intellectuals, he is acquainted with it best. Just as we cannot give up something we do not have, we cannot criticize something we do not know.[5]

Nasr attacks the triumphalism of modern science and its Promethean and Titanic character which has developed in the West from Descartes onwards. He condemns its attempts to reduce human beings to what they know, neglecting their other dimensions and compelling them to be creatures merely earth-bound. Modern man ceased gazing into the depths of the heavens and asking himself what is there behind the starry curtain. He has come to an absurd situation in which he communicates with the world in one dimension only—scientific knowledge—and forgets other dimensions such as love, beauty, grace, contemplation, and imagination, through which various aspects of the world and self can be comprehended. Therefore Nasr, whenever writing about the traditional teachers of Islam such as Ibn Sīnā, Ibn 'Arabī, Suhrawardī, Mullā Ṣadrā,[6] and others, emphasizes that they were the teachers of Wholeness, because the rays of *Tawḥīd* (in this case, a specific "method" by which the One is seen in the multitude and the multitude in the One) shine through them. This is what is missing in modern Western science which approaches things as if they were cut off from the living tree of the world and as if they could be studied correctly and comprehensively outside of the God-given hierarchy of knowledge.

Nasr warns his readers, particularly the Muslim ones, that the paradigm of the West, created as early as the Renaissance and existing for five centuries now, is dangerous. This paradigm is based on rationalism, humanism, Eurocentrism, and the like, and these fundamentals have been persisting not only in philosophy, but also in the sciences based on the nontraditional Eastern paradigms as well. He points out to Muslims that the Western paradigm has exhausted its potential because it is essentially secularist; because it caused an unimaginable ecological catastrophe; and because it turned man against nature at the same time when it turned him against God. Nasr emphasizes that to be at peace with the earth, one must be at peace with Heaven.[7]

This truth is often neglected by many modern Muslims who are enthusiastic about the West and who even claim that Islam made the Renaissance possible, and consequently the industrial (and other) revolutions that shook the West. It is true that Islam had developed sciences, but not those sciences and philosophies which imply rebellion against God, according to Nasr. The Promethean or Titanic spirit never ruled the Islamic sciences because the idea of man without Center is alien to Islam. "What is man without God?" is a question implicitly present on almost every page of Nasr's numerous works, even those dealing with modern industry or technology.

This is exactly the point in Nasr's works which is often misunderstood by many present-day Muslim authors. Thus he is accused of bias towards Sufism and traditional metaphysical doctrines. His critics, as a rule, are those modernist or secularist intellectuals from Muslim countries who have not yet reached a well-rounded scholarly development, and their criticism does not at all affect seriously Nasr's theses. When Nasr claims that the spirit of the Renaissance is in essence non-Islamic and non-religious, he has proofs for that claim in the consequences which humanism and the Renaissance produced and still produce. Had their consequence been just a single atomic bomb, that, in itself, would have already been far too much.

In his works Nasr, too, tackles a significant issue dealt with by Heidegger, Adorno, Horkheimer, Gadamer, and many other German philosophers: Is mankind today suffering because of the lack of (exoteric) knowledge or because of its excess? Nasr goes a step further and claims that the lack of the sacred, salutary knowledge (not exoteric and quantitative) has brought mankind to total collapse, to the edge of the abyss, to an inconceivable ecological catastrophe. In other words, he says that a drama is taking place before our eyes and many of us are not fully aware of it. It is a drama in which the dignity of life and death disappear, in which man takes over the prerogatives of the Absolute. Modern man's present philosophy and poetry resemble an uproar against Heaven more than a beautiful harmony of thoughts and ideas. The culmination of the catastrophe is that man is usurping absolute rights: through the numerous modern rebellions against the Absolute, man denies that umbilical cord (Revelation) which links him to the Absolute and thus creates satanic weapons by which he slowly but irreversibly destroys much more than just human nature. This is one of the major reasons for Nasr's insistence on traditional authors and traditional metaphysical doctrines (but not the kind of metaphysics which does not yield salutary knowledge and with which he has nothing in common).

IV

We have come now to the essence of Nasr's work, the cradle of sacred knowledge in Islam—Sufism. Nasr wrote many beautiful pages on Sufism. Moreover, Nasr's works themselves are Sufism of the highest order, fed from the sources of the traditional Sufi fountains.[8]

In its process of becoming a culture and a civilization, Islam gave birth to magnificent mystic teachings which exist within it and which constitute a part of its very "beginning," alive within the framework of eternal philosophy and eternal wisdom (*al-ḥikmat al-khālidah*, or *sophia perennis*). The Revelation in Islam is in the form of the Word. It is like the River flowing incessantly from the Source. Thus the Word cannot be reduced to a petrified legal convention or exoteric and rigid codices. Basṭāmī, or Ibn 'Arabī, or Nasr (it does not matter which one, for all of them agree on that subject) have said that the experts on law (*fuqahā'*) get their knowledge stillborn—they get it from dead people—while mystics get their knowledge from the Living (God) who never dies. This is not a mere maxim. It means (as Nasr emphasizes) that Islam has a certain inner resistance to any tradition that conceals the sources. This reminds us that Husserl, too, in the European context, expressed a request for a tradition which does not conceal the sources. Sufism is exactly that kind of tradition in Islam; it does not conceal the sources but emanates from them and makes them permanently flourishing.

Sufism made the magic robe of the Quran transparent, so that it may yield its interior in the same way in which a crystal yields its interior when exposed to the light. For centuries Sufism has been giving birth to the doctrines which illuminate the universal message of the Quran. For instance, when Goethe reminds us of Ḥāfiẓ's saying, "All I ever managed to do I did owing to the Quran,"[9] then we should have in mind that the Sufism of supreme poetry enabaled Ḥāfiẓ to identify the universal message of the Quran, that is, to find with ease the One in the multitude. When we ask ourselves what the central theme of the Quran is, we are perplexed because we are bound to say that on some of its pages the theme is an ant, on some other pages man, on yet other pages a bee, or the stars, or constellations and so on. Sufism teaches us, however, that this is an illusory "dispersion" and that in everything, in all of the universe "built without pillars," as well as in the Quran, we feel one common pulse and never think that the universe is "nailed to a board somewhere above." And just when we are about to conclude that the Quran is going to disclose to us what is there on the other side of the starry curtain, it takes us back to decaying human bones. This pattern repeats endlessly.

Sufism, in itself derived from the Quranic message, discovers in the Quran the elements which cannot be discovered by the legalitarian reading of the Quran. Thus Nasr reminds us of the role of Sufism in the Quran's hermeneutics. He likes to repeat al-Ghazzālī's metaphor about the spectre of sunlight. Our eye, such as God has given us, sees the light of the sun the way it sees it. But when this light is refracted through a ground crystal, we see colors which would otherwise remain hidden. Sufism has clearly expressed a need for a man-crystal who will enable the rays of light of the Quran's *āyāts* (verses) to shine through him.

It is a great merit of Nasr to have drawn the attention of the contemporary reading public to this still living tradition in Islam. Through this knowledge Muslims are capable of helping themselves, and others as well, to reach those often forgotten messages of the Eastern sciences whose significant portion was cradled and nourished in the Islamic East.

V

Seyyed Hossein Nasr is also a great critic of contemporary Islamic "isms"—Wahhābism, Fundamentalism (which he labels as "so-called fundamentalism"), Modernism, and so on. It is not difficult to discern that in the wide palette of Islamic trends Nasr stands for traditional Islam. But it is our impression that he uses this syntax in a very specific sense, namely, that *Islam begins with the Quran but does not end with it!* This thought is by no means blasphemous because the line of development of traditional Islam has been such that it remained true to the Quran and the Prophet Muḥammad while at the same time it continued to internalize and externalize the Quranic and *Sunnatic* message. Traditional Islam is a tree on which new branches can always grow beside the existing ones which remain alive. In traditional Islam, tradition does not conceal the Quran nor puts it aside. This is one of the most important of Nasr's messages.

This is exactly what many contemporary trends in Islam fail to comprehend. One of them is Wahhābism. This movement turned against some of the vital arteries of traditional Islam and at the same time magnanimously, yet incautiously, embraced and implemented Western technology. Wahhābistic struggle against the so-called admixtures to "pure Islam" proved to be the cruelest puritanism, sterile and unproductive, although seemingly strong (like incubator eggs which are many, strong, but cannot propagate). Nasr's book, *Traditional Islam in the Modern World*,[10] shows the whole variety of perspectives of Islamic "isms." But it is a topic for a separate study.

VI

How is Seyyed Hossein Nasr to be viewed in the context of contemporary thought? He is now at the peak of his creative powers and will probably produce a number of new works and further develop his ideas. Nevertheless, some underlying constants can already be discerned in the body of thought of the most constructive Muslim critic of the *Moderna*. First of all it should be said that he "deliniates the direction of thought which marks the peak of the spiritual and intellectual reflections on Islam in our time."[11] His work is among the most original and most influential among Muslims.

The language of Nasr is "Islamic" simply because he tells us the greatest truths in the simplest possible way. He is a thinker who, like the great classical thinkers of Islam of a thousand years ago, not only confronts Islam with all the great and living world traditions, but also with Islam itself. Therefore Nasr's thinking is open towards the "outside" as well as towards the "inside." Nasr is an engaged thinker, very dear to Muslims because he gives them back their confidence in their own tradition. But Nasr is also important for non-Muslims because his work represents an "indisputable contribution to the expansion of the spiritual and cultural horizons of contemporaneity."[12] It could be added that "Nasr's writings and books are metaphysical in nature regardless of their topics since they are based on, and permeated with, the desire not to simply link the reader—Muslim or Western—to Islam, but, through Islam, its sources and primeval discovery of man and the world, link him to the Absolute."[13]

Nasr criticizes the imperialistic West; but he also criticizes the slumbering East, but not in the manner of modernist criticism which considers the East inferior to the West and holds that its task should be to chase and try to "catch up with" the West. In his criticism of the East, Nasr searches for the original, perennial knowledge and truths. He does not support the idea of time understood as a straight line; he is not one of those who worships "progress" and defines Islam according to the schemes projected into the future.

His major achievement is the discovery of the congeniality of the ancient sciences of the East and the Islamic East—the congeniality of perennial truths and the traces of the Absolute within the ancient world tradition. Nasr is not the theoretician of *world history*, or *world revolution*, or *world progress*. In a word, he is not a thinker of the projects of mind whose aim is to change mankind and the earth at any cost. On the contrary, Nasr is the thinker of the ancient, perennial *world tradition* and that places him among the most engaged advocates of tradition with a capital "T." The achievements of Frithjof Schuon and Titus Burckhardt enable us to see the magnitude of Nasr's achievement. Namely, Nasr owes them as much as they owe him: without him, their penetration into *philosophia perennis* would remain without a proper answer on the part of Islam.

In his book, *Knowledge and the Sacred*,[14] Nasr explains why it is necessary for the Sacred to knock on our door again. The Sacred rises when danger is near, the Sacred comes as the salutary Sacred, as the Message whispering to the human dust that it is not here, under the moon's sphere, in vain. *Knowledge and the Sacred* is one of the most beautiful comments on the Sacred in modern times.

Let me mention, in the end, a very significant detail which is not sufficiently emphasized by the critics of Nasr's work. To wit, on almost every title page of his many works there is a significant detail from Islamic art.[11] It is as if Nasr were providing the pleasure for our eyes equal to the pleasure for our spirit while we read the filigrees of his sentences. In his numerous studies dedicated to the wide palette of Islamic art and spirituality Nasr clearly emphasizes that Islamic art is a *traditional* art whose arabesques, for example, make us experience "certain infinite wholes" as Hans-Georg Gadamer qualifies them. Nasr, as a matter of fact, insists on the comparative study of Islamic Wholeness, that is, on the need to experience simultaneously the Universal Message of the Quran and Islam in Sufism and Islamic art in many ways in the grandiose esoteric systems of Islamic Persia and in Islamic poetry, architecture, and miniature; in the great, traditional "theological" systems and in Islamic music. In other words, this is the traditional Islam which does not permit any branch to be amputated from its tree, because each branch is connected to the Source of the Revelation. Nasr is a laudable gardener of that tree, the type of gardener traditional Islam had earlier in the personalities of Ibn 'Arabī, al-Ghazzālī, or Rūmī.

ENES KARIĆ

UNIVERSITY OF SARAJEVO
MARCH 1992

NOTES

1. So far, Nasr has written many works, enough to comprise a library. If all of his works that are published and translated in dozens of languages were brought together, they would surpass in number the works of Ibn Rushd and al-Ghazzālī.

2. See S. H. Nasr, *An Introduction to Islamic Cosmological Doctrines* (Cambridge, Mass.: Harvard University Press, 1964). In this work Nasr writes about the cosmological doctrines of Ikhwān al-Ṣafā, al-Bīrūnī, and Ibn Sīnā.

3. Nasr's book *Science and Civilization in Islam* (New York: Mentor Classics, 1970) shows in the most beautiful way the universality of Islamic science, speaks of educational institutions, the classification of sciences, observatories, hospitals, mystic centers, cosmology, cosmography, geography, and natural history, as well as about Alhazen (Ibn al-Haytham), al-Bīrūnī, al-Khāzinī, the Brethren of Purity, al-Khwārazmī, 'Umar Khayyām, and so on.

4. The very titles of traditional Islamic works indicate that Islamic culture and civilization are not somber; that they resemble a fountain whose waters come from the springs of eternal beauty. Nasr never fails to emphasize that.

5. Nasr's criticism of modern Western science is a constructive one. He almost always finds the forgotten counterparts to the traditional Western sciences and points out that the West, too, had its primordial science, and its eternal wisdom (*philosophia perennis*). It is necessary for the West to return to those sources. But Nasr also criticizes the incomplete Muslim scientists (*'ulamā'*) who are not trying to get to know the West, although it represents an imminent threat for them.

6. Compare Nasr's works: *Three Muslim Sages* (Cambridge, Mass.: Harvard University Press, 1964), *Ṣadr al-Dīn Shīrāzī and His Transcendent Theosophy* (Tehran: Imperial Iranian Academy of Philosophy, 1978), *Western Science and Asian Cultures* (New Delhi: Indian Council for Cultural Relations, 1976), and *An Annotated Bibliography of Islamic Science* (Tehran: Imperial Iranian Academy of Philosophy, 1975). All these works deal with the heuristic character of ancient Islamic science and other sciences of traditional Eastern cultures.

7. Nasr's work *The Encounter of Man and Nature: The Spiritual Crisis of Modern Man* (London: Allen and Unwin, 1968) represents the sincere cry of a traditionalistic intellectual to save the earth from the jaws of modern technology. This is the most beautiful work ever dedicated to ecology and *ecophilia*.

8. We would like to direct the reader to the following of Nasr's works: *Sufi Essays* (London: Allen and Unwin, 1972); some chapters from the book *Ideals and Realities of Islam* (London: Allen and Unwin, 1966); and the book *Jalāl al-Dīn Rūmī, Supreme Persian Poet and Sage* (Tehran: High Council of Culture and the Arts, 1974).

9. Goethe first read the translation of Ḥāfiẓ's *Dīwān* translated into German by Joseph Hammer-Purgstall. See: J. Hammer-Purgstall, *Der Diwan,* 2 vols. (Stuttgart: J. G. Cottaschen Buchh, 1812–1813). Upon this reading he composed his own *West-Eastern Divan*, trans. J. Whaley (London: Oswald Wolff, 1974) in 1814. For a brief discussion of this, see: Joseph McCabe, *Goethe: The Man and His Character* (London: G. Bell & Sons, 1912), pp. 333–35.

10. S. H. Nasr, *Traditional Islam in the Modern World* (London: KPI, 1987). As early as 1967 Nasr published a very significant book entitled *Islamic Studies:*

Essays on Law and Society, the Sciences, Philosophy and Sufism (Beirut: Librarie du Liban, 1967). In several chapters of this book he speaks about the significant social, religious, and scientific trends in the Islamic world. This book struck a responsive chord because of its challenging and critically intoned assumptions. It should be pointed out that Nasr published numerous studies in Western languages in which he dealt with the question of traditional Islam in modern times and the modern world. Special emphasis is given to an inter-religious, ecumenic dialogue of the Muslims, Hindus, Christians, Jews, and Buddhists. Nasr is a great advocate of inter-religious tolerance.

11. My friend Hilmo Neimarlija, professor at the Islamic Theological Faculty in Sarajevo, who introduced me to Nasr's works and who earned my eternal gratitude for doing that, wrote a short introductory note to my translations of Nasr's articles published in the periodical *Islamic Thought* in the course of 1986. The note is entitled "Spiritual Perenniality of Islam" and some of its phrasings are quoted in this paper.

12. Ibid.

13. Ibid.

14. S. H. Nasr, *Knowledge and the Sacred* (New York: Crossroad, 1981).

15. See Nasr's book *Islamic Art and Spirituality* (Albany: State University of New York Press, 1987), dedicated to the Islamic experience of art as sacred art.

REPLY TO ENES KARIĆ

As one of the leading intellectual figures of Bosnia, Professor Enes Karić is among those Muslim intellectuals who by their geographical as well as cultural situation are more deeply aware of the challenges of modernism for Islamic thought than most Muslim thinkers living in the heartland of the Islamic world—who usually have less direct access to the primary sources of modern thought. Moreover, Karić is also very well acquainted with my ideas and has translated many of my works into Bosnian. It is therefore natural that in his very kind and laudatory essay, he, as a Bosnian intellectual, should deal first and foremost with my attitude towards modernism. In my response I shall try to clarify my position concerning this issue, especially in the general context of contemporary Islamic thought, rather than commenting upon specific points of his presentation—except at the end where I hope to clarify further two specific statements made by him.

Since the onslaught of the West and the modernism it brought with it to the Islamic world, the question of dealing with modernism, within which I would include in the context of the present discussion postmodernism as well, has been central to Islamic intellectual concerns. Well-known Islamic thinkers from Jamāl al-Dīn al-Afghānī, Muḥammad ʻAbduh, Sayyid Saʻīd Nursī, and Muḥammad Iqbāl to Mawlānā Abu'l-Kalām Āzād, Mawlānā Abu'l-ʻAlā' Mawdūdī, Sayyid Quṭb, and more recently Murtiḍā Muṭahharī (and to some extent his and my own teacher, ʻAllāmah Ṭabāṭabā'ī), ʻAlī Sharīʻatī, Fazlur Rahman, Ismāʻīl al-Fārūqī and during the last few years Sayyid Naquib al-Attas, Muḥammad Arkoun and ʻAbd al-Karīm Surūsh, just to name some but not all of the better known figures, have sought to deal with this multifaceted issue. Meanwhile, numerous Sufis and scholars of jurisprudence or *fuqahā'* appeared during this period of one and a half centuries who rejected modernism outright without seeking to study it in depth and refuted it without providing an intellectual response, although there are a few exceptions such as ʻAbd al-Ḥalīm Maḥmūd.

My position vis-à-vis what Karić calls the *Moderna* in the context of contemporary Islamic thought can be understood by comparison with the views of these and other Islamic thinkers not mentioned here. I have always stood in defense of the traditional perspective in general and specifically in the Islamic context of all dimensions of that tradition including the Divine Law or *al-Sharī'ah*, Sufism and the Islamic intellectual tradition including theology, philosophy, and the sciences. In this sense, I belong to the rank of traditionalist Islamic thinkers who have rejected modernism since its appearance in the Islamic world some two centuries ago. And yet, my position is different from most of them in the sense that my rejection has been more pervasive and, moreover, it has been based upon first-hand knowledge of what I have criticized. I have sought to understand the challenges of modern thought before confronting it, whether this challenge be philosophical or scientific. In the sense of being involved with modern issues, and only in this sense, have I been engaged in an activity similar to that of the Islamic modernists, but because of the perspective from which I have made my criticisms, my works have reached very different conclusions. I do not in any way identify myself with any of the forms of modernism in the Islamic world.

Perhaps I was the first Islamic thinker who, having studied extensively in the West and having become deeply immersed and formally educated in different facets of Western thought, rejected the very foundation of modern thought and returned to the bosom of traditional Islam. Of course, in this task of understanding the real nature of modernism, I was aided to a very great extent by Western traditional critics of modernism, especially the masters of traditional thought in the West, Guénon, Coomaraswamy, and Schuon, as my intellectual autobiography contained in this volume reveals. Also in undertaking my critique of modernism from the traditional point of view, I was equipped perhaps with greater in-depth knowledge of Western science, its history and philosophy, than other well-known Islamic thinkers who sought to deal with these issues on the basis of the Islamic intellectual tradition. Moreover, my exposition of traditional Islam has embraced nearly all the intellectual and spiritual dimensions of it including Sufism, philosophy, theology, and the cosmological sciences, in contrast to many others who have espoused one or two dimensions while rejecting others. Since I began to criticize modernism in detail some forty years ago, there has appeared a younger generation of Islamic thinkers who have followed in one way or another some of the perspectives opened by my writings. But it might not be too audacious to say that I was perhaps the first Islamic thinker rooted completely in the Islamic intellectual tradition in all of its major facets who set out to provide an Islamic response to modernity on the basis of firsthand knowledge of the sources of both modern and Islamic thought. The hands of destiny allowed me to gain this knowledge through long years of study in the West and also provided me with the opportunity to study the intellectual and spiritual aspects of Islam with some of the greatest masters of these subjects in my home country of Persia and elsewhere.

My treading upon an as yet untravelled ground, my defense of the universality of religious truth, espousal of Sufism and at the same time the Islamic philosophical tradition embracing most of the intellectual elements of both Sunni and Shi'ite thought, and holding on to an uncompromising stand against various currents of modern and postmodern philosophical thought from rationalism and empiricism to existentialism and deconstructionism gained me many opponents not only in the West, but also among modernists within the Islamic world. Even some traditional authorities, for whom I have held the greatest respect, could not understand my defense of the universality of religious truth or both Sufism and Islamic philosophy at the same time.

Also, my criticism of the limitations and dangers resulting from the generalization of the scientific worldview in the form of scientism and my severe criticism of the calamities brought about by the blind importation of modern technology and its ever greater applications—resulting in profound alterations in the quality, the rhythm and tempo of everyday life of Muslims—fell at first on deaf ears in the Islamic world. At this time at least a few in the West were willing to listen to what I had to say when from the '60s I began to speak of the impending environmental crisis and its spiritual causes. It is only now, some forty years later, that my appreciation of Islamic science from its own perspective, my criticism but not a simple rejection of the presumptions of modern science, and some of the conclusions drawn from it and analysis of the environmental crisis, its religious and spiritual causes, and the necessity of an Islamic response to this central issue, are receiving wide attention in the Islamic world. I have never written a separate treatise criticizing systematically various modern Islamic thinkers and the lack of serious intellectual content on the one hand and lack of Islamic authenticity on the other within most works by Islamic modernists who claim to be dealing with serious philosophical and intellectual issues. But many of my writings contain sections dealing with these questions.

I want to be clearly distinguished from various types of Islamic modernistic thinkers who, instead of criticizing prevalent "isms" in light of the perennial truths contained in Islamic thought, surrender to these "isms" and try to change Islamic teachings to accommodate the mental fashions of the day. I would be much happier were I to be identified with the traditional thinkers whose knowledge of the tradition on whatever level is highly respected precisely because it is traditional, even if confined to only one dimension of the Islamic tradition. But I identify myself most of all with those within this group who have been concerned with traditional truth at its highest level found at the heart of Sufism and later Islamic philosophy.

Wherein I differ from this group is not in the mode and context of the knowledge in question, but in my being able to formulate that knowledge in a contemporary manner, and in my applying it to the problems at hand, most of which are the result of the philosophical challenges posed by modern and postmodern Western thought. I am now no longer a lonely figure seeking to carry out this task. A whole new generation of Islamic thinkers is now coming forward who are pursuing the same goals.

There is another issue which needs to be mentioned in this context. Nearly all Islamic thinkers who have tried to confront the problems of modernity have turned naturally to the West, the original home of modernism. But rarely have they concerned themselves seriously, at least until quite recently, with one of the consequences of the secularism brought about by modernism; this consequence is the creation of a religious vacuum that has caused many Western theologians, philosophers, and scholars of religion to consider under new light the presence of other religions on a global scale. I was interested in this issue from my youth and have devoted a lifetime to carrying out religious dialogue and writing about other religions including Hinduism, Buddhism, Taoism, and other non-Abrahamic religions. What has now become popular as the question of religious pluralism, and more recently civilizational dialogue, has been at the center of my interests during the past four decades and my philosophical concerns have always been global. In this domain also there are now many younger Islamic thinkers devoted to these issues on a world wide scale, but among well-known Islamic thinkers who have been concerned with the relation of Islam to modernity, such an interest on a truly global scale has been very rare indeed.

Today one can no longer speak, as is often the case in Western studies of Islam which I have criticized on many occasions, of only traditional Muslim thinkers who know nothing of modernity and its philosophical roots on the one hand, and modernists who are trying to accommodate the perennial and traditional teachings of Islam to whatever "ism" happens to be current at the time on the other. There is now a third group of thinkers in the Islamic world who are as firmly rooted in the Islamic tradition as the first group, but who also know modernism as well as, if not better than, the second group, but who instead of trying to accommodate the teachings of Islam to various imported "isms," seek to apply the teachings of tradition in providing answers to the challenge of these "isms." I think that Professor Karić is himself an eminent representative of this third group in Bosnia. I take pride in being a pioneer in the training of this new category of Islamic thinkers who are now coming to the fore to an even greater degree as the main defenders of the Islamic tradition before the unprecedented intellectual and social challenges that the Islamic world is facing today. In trying to understand my role as a critic of the *Moderna*, to use the terminology of the author of this essay, in the general context of contemporary Islamic thought, the comments I have made here may be of some value.

Following these general comments, there are two specific points mentioned by Karić upon which I wish to elaborate further. In referring to my claim that the paradigm which has dominated Western thought since the Renaissance has exhausted its possibility and is coming to an end, Karić writes, "this truth is often neglected by many modern Muslims who are enthusiastic about the West and who even claim that Islam made the Renaissance possible, and consequently the industrial (and other) revolutions that shook the West." This is a major problem which I have been discussing in the Islamic world since the 1950s when I first began to write and lecture publicly. Meanwhile I have also criticized the philosophical assumptions of the Renaissance for the Western audience.

As a result of an inferiority complex vis-à-vis the modern West, many modernized Muslim thinkers, going back to the nineteenth century, have tried to give Islam the credit for the European Renaissance without fully understanding what the Renaissance really meant for the world of faith and tradition in the West. Their argument, even if some of the presumptions are held by them unconsciously, can be summarized as follows: The West is great. This greatness began with the Renaissance. The Renaissance was brought about by the transmission of Islamic learning and philosophy to the West. Therefore, Islam is great. This absurd idea presented here on purpose in syllogistic form is so widely held, especially among the Muslim intelligentsia of the Indo-Pakistani subcontinent, that few are willing to examine its premises. Few in this group have read what a Petrarch wrote about Islam or what the rise of skepticism as a philosophy during the Renaissance entailed for the very religious philosophy in the West which had been deeply influenced by Ibn Sīnā, al-Ghazzālī, Ibn Rushd, and other Muslim thinkers. I was perhaps the first Muslim thinker to carry out an in-depth criticism of the Renaissance and the premises and consequences of the syllogism outlined above and to try to refute the philosophy of history derived from this interpretation of the Renaissance. I have, of course, also discussed in many of my works the transmission of Islamic philosophy and science to the West. My works have also been concerned with a reevaluation of medieval European thought and culture which many modern Muslim thinkers have chosen to see almost completely through the eyes of humanistic and often secular historians of the West who coined the term "Dark Ages." This idea is still alive in everyday Western discourse despite the rediscovery of the Middle Ages in the age of Romanticism and extensive research carried out in the fields of medieval philosophy, theology, art, and so on, during the past century.

Finally in section V, Karić, in referring to my defense of traditional

Islam, writes, "it is our impression that he [Nasr] uses this syntax in a very specific sense, namely, that Islam begins with the Quran but does not end with it!" This statement can be misleading as far as my thought is concerned. For me, Islam both begins and ends with the Quran, but it begins with the outward meaning of the Quran and "ends" in the infinite ocean of its inward meaning. The understanding of Islam must of necessity begin with the outward meaning of the Sacred Text, but the Sacred Text possesses many levels of meaning, the highest, according to tradition, known only to God. The more one grows in the understanding of Islam, the more one penetrates the inward and esoteric meaning of the Quran, which is considered to be the source of all authentic *sophia* by traditional Islamic thinkers including myself; but no matter how deeply one advances in the comprehension of Islam and succeeds in its application to new circumstances and current philosophical and theological issues, one will never transcend the Quran. Rather, one always ultimately "ends" with it, although that "it" is no longer confined to the literal and outward understanding of the Sacred Text. One of the names of the Quran is the Guide (*al-Hudā*) and another Light (*al-Nūr*). My view is that an Islamic thinker can never function as an Islamic thinker without that Guidance and without that Light, no matter in what circumstance he finds himself.

The full exposition of my critique of modernism and my philosophical position dealing with this question in the matrix of contemporary Islamic thought is a vast subject whose full treatment would require a separate treatise. I am grateful to Professor Karić in affording me this opportunity to deal at least with some of the major aspects of my perspective and those places wherein I differ from other well-known Muslim thinkers who have concerned themselves with this critical issue of modernism during the past two centuries.

S. H. N.

28

Marietta Stepaniants

SEYYED HOSSEIN NASR: APOLOGIST OR REFORMER OF ISLAM?

It was in the late sixties that I met Dr. Seyyed Hossein Nasr. He was the Iranian participant in the UNESCO seminar at the Indian International Center in New Delhi. I could not then expect him to become a "hero" of my academic writings for many years to come. I still remember how Dr. Nasr looked: a handsome man in an elegant white suit, very self-confident, in all appearance, quite successful in his career. My memory also keeps some of his views, especially the one about an analogy between the Islamic teaching and the Ka'bah—the perfect cube that does not need any change; consequently, any attempt to bring reforms in Muslim teaching is alien to the true spirit of that religion. His stand was in dissonance with what I was thinking about modern developments in Islam, and that made me later write to him. However, I never got a response. It might not be his fault at all, but the result of the shortcomings of communication between a Soviet and an Iranian in those years.

There was no other occasion for me to meet Nasr personally. Yet, I encountered him many times indirectly through reading his books and reflecting on them. At first, my evaluation of Nasr's views was rather negative. I took him for a Muslim conservative, even a reactionary, who stands for the *status quo* and opposes any new trend in Islam and in the Muslim society. In fact, this evaluation was prompted, to a large extent, by my own understanding of the reformative process in Islam.

Being a student of Urdu language and doing research mainly in the field of Muslim studies on the Indo-Pakistani subcontinent, I wrote my first dissertation in 1964 which was soon published, first in Moscow and then in Lahore, in the form of a book under the title *Pakistan: Philosophy and Sociology*. Thus, from the very start of my academic work I was under the impact of such Muslim thinkers as Seyyed Ahmad Khan, Abu'l-Kalām

Āzād, Muḥammad Iqbāl, and Mawlānā Abu'l-'Alā' Mawdūdī whose ideas shaped my understanding of what was Muslim apology or Muslim reformation. Later on I tried to "cross" the borders of the Indo-Pakistani subcontinent by writing on Islamic philosophy and social thought in the nineteenth and twentieth centuries and dealing with such personalities as Muḥammad 'Abduh, Jamāl al-Dīn al-Afghānī, Sayyid Quṭb, and so on. The judgment, to which I had come finally, made me think that the response of the Muslim world to the challenges of modern times expressed itself in three main forms: Islamic orthodoxy, standing for the *status quo*; modernism, inclined to reject its own tradition and to accept Western values and institutions; and a reformative trend, similar to the Reformation in Christianity.

The views of Nasr do not match any of those divisions. Reckoning upon his appearance, on the social status he held, being closely associated with the Shah of Iran, on the modern education he received as a graduate of MIT and Harvard, one could expect him to belong to the ranks either of modernists or of reformers. However, his writings do not substantiate that. Since Muḥammad Iqbāl is my favorite among Muslim reformers, I see him as a Muslim reformer *par excellence*, and I have always been inclined to compare others with him. From this perspective, the views of Nasr seem not only to be unlike those of Iqbāl, but to conflict with them.

Iqbāl, the poet and philosopher of the Indo-Pakistan subcontinent, aims to *reconstruct* the religious thought of Islam. He believes that "with the reawakening of Islam in modern times Muslims should examine, in an independent spirit, what the Europeans have thought and how far the conclusions reached by them can help them in revision and, if necessary, reconstruction, of theological thought in Islam."[1] As to Nasr, he insists on the necessity of *reasserting* the principles of Islam. In his words, "putting aside the preservation of the Islamic religion itself, no task is more crucial in the present context of Islamic society than this reassertion of the immutable principles of Islam."[2]

Looking at the example of Turkey, which in his time was the only one among Muslim nations to shake off its dogmatic slumber, and to attain to self-consciousness, Muḥammad Iqbāl praises it for stepping forth and creating new values, while the other Muslim countries were mechanically repeating old values. The poet-philosopher shares the opinion of those who affirm that "to have a succession of identical thoughts and feelings is to have no thoughts and feelings at all."[3]

Dr. Nasr, in contrast, considers modernity and tradition to stand in opposition to each other. He does not hesitate to side with the latter and to reject the former in a categorical manner: "One could say that the traditional worlds were essentially good and accidentally evil, and the modern world essentially evil and accidentally good. Tradition is therefore opposed in principle to modernism."[4] Nasr does not accept modernism in principle since he believes that it is due to it that the history of Western men during the past five centuries became an anomaly in the long history of the human race.

Tradition is understood by the Iranian philosopher as "inextricably related to revelation and religion, to the sacred, to the notion of orthodoxy, to authority, to the continuity,"[5] while he views modernity as consisting mainly of secularism, humanism, rationalism, and historicism. It is well known that Muslim reformers highly appreciate the above mentioned aspects of modernity and are of the opinion that the backwardness of Muslim societies results from the lack of them. The reformers reinterpret Islam, striving to prove that their religion does not object to all those elements of modernity; conversely, if it is "purified" from the burden of traditionalism, one would find out that the teaching of Muḥammad is fully in tune with them. As to Nasr, his writings are dedicated to confirming the hostility of all the above mentioned components of modernity to the true spirit of Islam.

The sharpest criticism is addressed toward desacralization, on which modernity is essentially based. Nasr charges desacralization with making a bad impact on everything: religion, knowledge, history, cosmos, language, and so on. In his words, "reason cut off from its root in the permanent could not but reduce reality to process, time to pure quantity, and history to a process without a transcendent entelechy and, at the same time, the mother and progenitor of all that the modern mentality considered as reality."[6]

The clear difference between Nasr and reformers like Muḥammad Iqbāl can be seen in comparing their views on three main notions of modernity associated with the theory of evolution, with the Enlightenment's concept of man, and with rationalism.

In *The Reconstruction of Religious Thought in Islam* Muḥammad Iqbāl a number of times speaks about the concept of evolution. He appeals to the authority of the Quran (III:131, VII:181, XIV:5) constantly citing historical instances; to the writings of Ibn Miskawaih (d. 421 A.H.)—"the first among Muslim thinkers to give a clear and in many respects thorough modern theory of the origin of man";[7] to the great Sufi poet Rūmī, who, in his words, expressed "tremendous enthusiasm for the biological future of man" under the impact of the theory of evolution;[8] to Ibn Khaldūn's view of history. Finally, Iqbāl comes to the conclusion that it is "a gross error" to think that the Quran and the Islamic teaching as such "have no germs of a historical doctrine."[9]

The Iranian philosopher sees, on the contrary, "the logical and even biological absurdity of the theory of evolution."[10] The absurdity of that theory, in his view, results from its futile attempt to substitute horizontal, material causes in a unidimensional world to explain effects whose causes belong to other levels of reality, to the vertical dimensions of existence. The main fault of the theory of evolution is that it does not acknowledge the first stage of the genesis of man, which is the Divinity Itself, thus ignoring an uncreated "aspect" of man. As to the concoctions of scriptural evidence made up to support evolutionary theory, Nasr considers them to be based upon the forgetting of the traditional commentaries pointing out the vertical scale of existence.

Muḥammad Iqbāl is, surely, in great sympathy with the ideas of the Enlightenment, in particular with those concerning the concept of man. He acknowledges man to be superior to nature. Iqbāl strongly criticizes those who regard the world as a process realizing a pre-ordained goal, since "that is not a world of free, responsible agents; it is only a stage on which puppets are made to move by a kind of pull from behind."[11] He affirms that "the lot of man is to share in the deeper aspirations of the universe around him and to shape his own destiny as well as of the universe sometimes by adjusting himself to its forces, sometimes by putting the whole of his energy to mold its forces to his own ends and purposes," in this way becoming a co-worker with God.[12]

Nasr looks at the modern conception of man as the antipode to that which considers man to be the pontiff or bridge between Heaven and earth. The worldly humanism of the Renaissance, in his opinion, has brought into life the Promethean rebel with whom modern man usually identifies himself. The Iranian philosopher claims that the kind of humanism associated with the Promethean revolt of the Renaissance, in the long run, has led to "the veritably infrahuman which threatens not only the human quality of life but the very existence of man on earth."[13] His vision of man's role in this world is in clear opposition to the reformers' views mentioned above, since Nasr believes that "the grandeur of man does not lie in his cunning, cleverness or titanic creations but resides most of all in the incredible power to empty himself of himself, to cease to exist in the initiatic sense, to participate in the state of spiritual poverty and emptiness which permits him to experience Ultimate Reality."[14] Surely, one might easily take this quotation for the words of any mystic.

The life of man, as Muḥammad Iqbāl believes, depends on his ability to "establish connections" with the reality that confronts him. Those connections could be established by knowledge—"sense-perception elaborated by understanding."[15] Knowledge is understood by Iqbāl in a very broad sense—as based on all possible kinds of experience. In fact, Iqbāl refuses to accept any discrimination in that matter. For him, "the facts of religious experience are facts among other facts of human experience and, in capacity of yielding knowledge by interpretation, one fact is as good as another."[16]

Following the tradition of Islamic philosophers, especially of Ibn Rushd, Iqbāl takes science and religion as two separate spheres of knowledge: "In the domain of science we try to understand its meanings in reference to the external *behavior of reality*; in the domain of religion we take it as representative of some kind of reality and try to discover its meaning in reference mainly to the inner *nature* of that reality. The scientific and religious processes are in a sense parallel to each other."[17]

Nasr, vice versa, states that an essential feature of the Islamic worldview has always been the *hierarchy* of knowledge.[18] To demonstrate the genuine attitude of Islam towards knowledge Nasr refers to the Quran (VI:8):

> And with Him are the keys of the invisible.
> None but He knoweth them.
> And He knoweth what is in the land and the sea.
> Not a leaf falleth, but He knoweth it,
> Not a grain amid the darkness of the earth,
> Naught of wet or dry
> But (it be noted) in a clear record.

The Iranian philosopher interprets the above quoted *āyah* as meaning that, since Allāh is the knower of all things and the cause of all events, His Knowledge overshadows the possibility of any secondary cause: "This is not to imply that the study of nature and natural causes is futile. On the contrary, both the Quran and *Ḥadīth* give specific instructions to man to study God's creation. However, this study should be directed towards an understanding of His Wisdom in creation rather than to discover any causes which may be placed alongside Him, thereby destroying His Unity."[19] Hence, in Nasr's opinion, the purpose of getting knowledge is "to study nature as the unified handiwork of God in order to discover His Wisdom, to see His sign upon the horizon, as the Quran states, and to learn spiritual lessons from it."[20]

To the hierarchy of knowledge corresponds the hierarchy of means of knowledge. The Intellect is on the top. It is defined by Nasr in the following way: "The Intellect, the instrument through which this type of knowledge is obtained, which is at once the source of revelation and exists microcosmically within man, must not be mistaken for reason alone. The *'aql* is at once both *intellectus* or *nous* and *ratio* or reason. It is both the supernal sun that shines within man and the reflection of this sun on the plane of the mind which we call reason."[21] The possession of the Intellect is Intelligence, which is nothing but "a divine gift which leads man to an affirmation of the doctrine of unity (*al-tawḥīd*) and of the essential verities of the Islamic revelation."[22]

While the Intellect is a means of obtaining the knowledge of the Reality that transcends nature, reason is an instrument of getting the knowledge of the phenomenal world, of nature. The former deals with the ultimate causes of the Universe, its origin, constitution, and qualitative content, seeking through the understanding of the symbols present in nature to gain knowledge of Reality. The latter, that is reason, occupies itself with phenomena of nature as pure facts without relating them to a higher order of Reality.

The reduction of knowledge to its lowest stage, where individual reason functions cut free from the Intellect, in Nasr's view, has brought rationalism into life. The Iranian philosopher strongly criticizes rationalism, particularly as it developed in the West, for "an attempt to build a closed system embracing the whole reality and based upon human reason alone."[23] Nasr claims that rationalism affirms as the ultimate criterion of reality the human ego and not the Divine Intellect or Pure Being.

Nasr insists on the unacceptability for Muslims to separate the spiritual and the secular. Any true knowledge, including the knowledge in the domain of philosophy and science, has been derived from revelation, from "the niche of prophecy," to use the Quranic terminology. Islam could not remain indifferent to any form of knowledge, hence, any idea or doctrine should be charged in accordance with their conformity with the teaching of Islam.

It is quite significant that when talking about reason and its functions Nasr always deals with its abilities in obtaining knowledge about nature. He never speaks about the role of reason in social life and its organization. On the contrary, the Muslim reformers, like Muḥammad Iqbāl, concentrate their attention on the role that reason could play in regulating and improving social life. Never in Nasr's writings, at least in those which were available to me in Russia, have I found him mentioning *ijtihād*—the right of independent private judgment on legal questions. As to Iqbāl, he joins his voice in support of a call to "open the doors of *ijtihād*" that were closed practically for the last five hundred years. The poet-philosopher believes that Muslim society based on the Islamic conception of Reality, which conceives the ultimate spiritual basis of all life as eternal and at the same time revealing itself in variety and changes, must reconcile in its life permanence and change. If eternal principles are understood in such a way as to lead to the exclusion of all the possibilities of change, it results in the immobility of that which is essentially mobile in its nature. While Europe, in Iqbāl's opinion, demonstrates the failure in maintaining eternal principles to regulate its collective life, the world of Islam illustrates for centuries the immobility caused by its underestimation of and opposition to changes.[24]

Do all of the above mentioned comparisons between the views of Nasr and of Iqbāl lead us to the conclusion that the former is a conservative apologist who opposes reformative process as such? Quite a number of those who are aware of Nasr's views think about him in this way. (I have determined this by talking to many scholars, including Muslims.) However, nowadays I hesitate to make such a verdict. At least two aspects of Nasr's worldview prevent me from that.

The first is Nasr's approach to Sufism. Apologists, conservatives among Muslims, as a rule, base their arguments on the authority of so-called Muslim orthodoxy. Hence, they are commonly named traditionalists or fundamentalists. Sufism as a mystical trend in Islam usually is viewed by Muslim traditionalists either as a kind of heresy or at least as a marginal trend in Islam. At the same time, it is not by chance, Sufism has attracted the attention of many Muslim reformers (including Jamāl al-Dīn al-Afghānī, Muḥammad 'Abduh, Muḥammad Iqbāl, and so on) in the beginning of their careers because of its relatively independent spirit. Nasr has never betrayed his loyalty to Sufism. To him it is not just one of the trends in the frames of Islam, Sufism is its esoteric and inner dimension, "the marrow of the bone."[25] *Ṭarīqah* is a spiritual way, while Sharī'ah is a Divine Law.

Second, Nasr's preoccupation with the theme of knowledge, in general, and scientific knowledge, in particular makes him look quite different from traditionalists, who either express their negative attitude to sciences or at least ignore them as though they do not deserve serious attention.

In reflecting on Nasr's views it might be useful to keep under consideration a hint he drops about his own stand among the main trends in contemporary Muslim thought. Here is the passage from *Sufi Essays* in which Nasr speaks about two kinds of moods prevailing among the students of universities in the more modernized Muslim countries: ". . . those who were completely secularized and Westernized and more or less rejected Islam, at least as a complete code and way of life; and those who were very pious and devout Muslims but who limited Islam to the most outward interpretation of the *Sharī'ah* and rejected all that pertains to Sufism and the whole intellectual and spiritual dimension of Islam."[26] It looks as if Nasr takes neither modernist nor traditionalist sides. Yet, neither does he very much resemble reformers as has been shown above. The reason could be a peculiar strategy suggested by the Iranian philosopher to reform Muslim society.

This strategy is based upon the conviction that Muslim society should be modernized or reformed on grounds rooted in Islam. Hence, Nasr does not oppose scientific progress as such (he is too well educated not to be able to grasp its significance), but advocates the development of so-called Islamic sciences. The latter are supposed to be based upon the particular genius of the Islamic perspective which is centered upon unity: "To see the signs of God in nature . . . for the purpose of seeing Divine wisdom therein."[27]

The idea of unity seems to be of the greatest importance for Nasr, not only in its cosmological sense, but in a social as well. His strategy of reforming aims to avoid disintegration, loss of the spirit of solidarity in *ummah*. It is that very integrating power of Sufism which attracts the Iranian philosopher most. He speaks about this function of Sufism constantly: "The method of integration contained in Sufism concerns not only the individuals who are affected by it but also casts its light upon the whole of society and is the hidden source for the regeneration of Islamic ethics and the integration of the Islamic community."[28] Over and over Nasr warns against disorder, anarchy caused by the "malady of secularization" and its "negative freedom."

Iqbāl's approach to freedom is strikingly different. In one of his lectures the poet-philosopher analyzes the causes that had brought the closure of the door of *ijtihād* and reduced the Law of Islam to a state of immobility. The main cause, in his view, is an incorrect supposition that the survival and prosperity of the Muslim world depends exclusively on preserving the social integrity of Islam by a jealous exclusion of all innovations. Iqbāl acknowledges that those who hold this position are partly right because the social order maintained by organization to a certain extent counteracts the forces of decay. However, according to Iqbāl, they, as well as modern *'ulamā'*,

> do not see, that the ultimate fate of a people does not depend so much on organization as on the worth and power of individual men. In an over-organized society the individual is altogether crushed out of existence. He gains the whole wealth of social thought around him and loses his own soul. Thus a false reverence for past history and its artificial resurrection constitutes no remedy for a people's decay. . . . The only effective power, therefore, that counteracts the forces of decay in a people is the rearing of self-concentrated individuals. . . . They disclose new standards in the light of which we begin to see that our environment is not wholly inviolable and requires revision.[29]

This passage from Muḥammad Iqbāl clearly shows the principal difference in strategies adopted by the Muslim reformer and by Seyyed Hossein Nasr. The views of the Iranian philosopher are of a particular significance because they reflect a certain trend of thought which is gaining momentum in many parts of the non-Western world. Disillusion is widespread: the hopes and plans for overcoming backwardness and for bringing prosperity by following non-traditional models, either of Western capitalism or Soviet socialism, have failed. All the attempts to transplant alien values, institutions, and so on, happen to be futile. The painful reaction against that kind of transplantation takes sometimes the most extreme forms—the anti-Shah revolution in Iran is the best example of that.

Though I do not belong to the world of Islam, I believe I am sensitive to what is taking place due to the similarity of processes in my country, Russia. Here once again, as it was before the October revolution of 1917, the public mood is divided between so-called Westernizers and Slavophiles. The former believe that the future of Russia lies in following the way of the capitalist West. The latter seek to find for their Motherland its own way out, looking back at the traditional values of Orthodox Christianity. Between the two there are also those who try to find the golden middle way.

I might share Seyyed Hossein Nasr's understanding about what reorientation for a nation should mean. Nasr interprets reorientation as "a re-penetrating" into the spiritual and inner contents of one's own culture and "an absorption of its essential truths, or in other words a re-understanding in the profoundest sense of this word."[30]

However, the problem is that there always exist differences in the appreciation of those essential truths. Much depends upon to which tradition of our own cultures we refer and appeal, which of them we consider to be genuinely essential. Another, no less important, point that raises doubt in the way of reorientation suggested by Nasr is his insistence on the necessity of remaining "faithful to both the spirit and the form" of Islam.[31] Does not this claim prove Nasr's unreadiness for or objection to bringing any change, even in forms, and thus result in presenting Islam not as a living teaching but instead as a deadly static set of tenets? Can apology and reform go together? It seems that the forthcoming twenty-first century will bring the solution to the controversy; it will demonstrate whether, in fact, the much sought-after third golden way, for each nation from outside the Western world, is possible and real, or is just another illusion.

MARIETTA STEPANIANTS

RUSSIAN ACADEMY OF SCIENCES
AUGUST 1996

NOTES

1. Muḥammad Iqbāl, *The Reconstruction of Religious Thought in Islam* (Lahore: Sh. Muḥammad Ashraf, 1962), p. 8.
2. Seyyed Hossein Nasr, *Islamic Life and Thought* (London: George Allen & Unwin, 1981), p. 36.
3. Iqbāl, op. cit., p. 162.
4. Seyyed Hossein Nasr, *Knowledge and the Sacred* (New York: Crossroad, 1981), p. 85.
5. Ibid., p. 68.
6. Ibid., p. 45.
7. Iqbāl, op. cit., p. 138.
8. Ibid., p. 186.
9. Ibid., p. 139.
10. Nasr, *Knowledge and the Sacred,* p. 169.
11. Iqbāl, op. cit., p. 54.
12. Ibid., p. 12.
13. Nasr, *Knowledge and the Sacred*, p. 81.

14. Ibid., p. 182.
15. Iqbāl, op. cit., p. 12.
16. Ibid., p. 16.
17. Ibid., p. 196.
18. See Seyyed Hossein Nasr, *Sufi Essays* (New York: Schocken Books, 1977), p. 55.
19. Nasr, *Islamic Life and Thought*, p. 92.
20. Ibid., p. 137.
21. Nasr, *Sufi Essays*, p. 54.
22. Ibid., p. 53.
23. Ibid.
24. See Iqbāl, op. cit., pp. 146–53.
25. Nasr, *Sufi Essays*, p. 43.
26. Ibid., p. 13.
27. Nasr, *Islamic Life and Thought*, p. 13.
28. Nasr, *Sufi Essays*, p. 51.
29. Iqbāl, op. cit., p. 151.
30. Nasr, *Islamic Life and Thought*, p. 154.
31. See ibid., p. 217.

REPLY TO MARIETTA STEPANIANTS

I agree with Stepaniants in the manner in which she compares my thought with that of Iqbāl. In nearly every philosophical domain he and I differ on major issues, many of which she has brought out quite correctly. If one puts aside the fact that both Iqbāl and I are Muslim thinkers seriously interested in the future of the Islamic world, there is little upon which we agree philosophically. Iqbāl is a modernist while I am a traditionalist. He is deeply impressed by nineteenth-century European philosophy while I belong to the Islamic philosophical tradition. He is often critical of major aspects of Sufism while I am a follower of the Sufi tradition. Likewise, Stepaniants is quite correct in distinguishing me from the well-known reformers of either the Indo-Pakistani sub-continent or the Arab world. In fact I do not consider myself a "reformer" in that sense but a "renewer" of the Islamic intellectual tradition and a follower of the perennial philosophy within that tradition.

There are, however, a number of points in Stepaniants's presentation that need clarification from my point of view. She uses the term "Islamic orthodoxy" in the rather narrow sense of exoteric orthodoxy alone. Now, I consider myself to be orthodox through and through without in any way limiting myself to the exoteric realm. There is such a thing as legal or *Sharī'ite* orthodoxy which I accept fully. But there is also orthodoxy on the intellectual and spiritual levels in which I also participate. Throughout my diverse writings I have often discussed the universality of orthodoxy which as literally "correct doctrine" can be rendered in the Islamic context as *ṣirāṭ al-mustaqīm* in its doctrinal aspect. Therefore, when she says that I do not belong to any of the three forms of the response of the Muslim world to the challenges of modern times including Islamic orthodoxy (which she claims stands for the *status quo*), I do not consider this to be true if Islamic orthodoxy be considered in its more universal sense. There is needless to say some confusion in this domain related to the definition of orthodoxy itself. But it is important to note here that I consider myself completely orthodox on all levels ranging from the outward aspects of religion to theology, philosophy, and Sufism and do not consider orthodoxy as understood in its universal sense to be any way opposed to intellectual creativity or universality. On the contrary I believe that only in orthodoxy can the full possibilities of the intellect be actualized.

Stepaniants also speaks of my desire to have Islamic society modernized. In fact nothing could be further from the truth as I have opposed the very philosophical presumptions and basis of modernism all of my life. What I have always sought and in fact strived to achieve in my own works on Islamic thought is the revival and rejuvenation of the Islamic intellectual tradition and the traditional patterns of Islamic life as I have understood the term "tradition." This has meant knowing the West in depth, including Western science, but not simply emulating and imitating it; knowing it from the point of view of Islamic thought and providing responses to challenges posed by modernism rather than simply accepting one form or another of modernism as being inevitable. I have always opposed the intellectual inferiority complex of Muslim modernists who can hardly think independently vis-à-vis whatever current or fashion of thought happens to issue from the West. Needless to say, I have also opposed the anti-intellectual attitude in certain Islamic religious circles which is sometimes misnamed as "traditionalism." My understanding of tradition is that of sacred principles rooted in revelation and their application in the context of a living religious universe. I oppose modernism in principle without in any way forgetting the significance of opening a new chapter in traditional Islamic intellectual life in response to the situation in which the Islamic world finds itself today and in providing responses to the challenge of modernism. This new chapter is, however, meant to be a chapter in the book of traditional Islamic thought and not a chapter belonging to another book. There must be continuity as well as renewal. I am all in favor of renewal (*tajdīd*) of Islamic thought and philosophy to which much of my own life has been devoted, but I oppose the modernist so-called reforms (*iṣlāḥ*) which usually lead to deformation rather than reformation and have moreover produced for the most part intellectually pitiful results in the present-day Islamic world.

In light of these comments my attitude toward *ijtihād* or exercise of fresh opinion should become clear. Stepaniants mentions that in contrast to Iqbāl I never mention the term *ijtihād*. First of all this is not true; I have discussed it several times in my works but certainly not as much as Iqbāl. The reason I do not use this term often is that it has become somewhat trivialized through over-usage by all the Muslim modernists without consideration of what were the traditional conditions set for the practice of *ijtihād*. Tradition is not opposed to *ijtihād*. In fact *ijtihād* itself is a completely traditional concept. One should certainly encourage serious thinking on the basis of Islamic doctrines and teachings, but one cannot accept the attack against the body of Islamic tradition on the pretext of carrying out *ijtihād* by a person whose mind is cluttered by concepts of a secularist nature drawn from another civilization. Such an activity could not but bring about the destruction of the religion itself, not to speak of its philosophy and theology.

Iqbāl attacks constantly the idea of imitation (*taqlīd*) which is juxtaposed to *ijtihād*. Now it is true that on a certain intellectual and spiritual level one must transcend *taqlīd*, but that is only after one has realized the truth to such an extent that one's own inner nature becomes the norm which one "imitates." But even if one has attained such an advanced stage, *taqlīd* of the norms established by Islam must continue on the legal level. Throughout Islamic history the greatest intellectual figures and sages have continued to emulate the Prophet of Islam both outwardly and inwardly. Specifically, in Shi'ism each believer is expected to emulate (*taqlīd*) in matters of Islamic law a person who has himself reached the level of *ijtihād* (and is called *mujtahid*), having fulfilled both the intellectual and moral conditions necessary for the carrying out of this great responsibility.

In every field those who cannot themselves perform *ijtihād* must follow and imitate (*taqlīd*) those who can do so. In the realm of secular life that is done all the time. If we have not reached the level of *ijtihād* in the field of medicine, then we find an authority who has and accept his words and instructions. We literally imitate (*taqlīd*) the model of action he has set before us when we go to him as a patient. This whole debate between *ijtihād* and *taqlīd* in Iqbāl and many others lacks the necessary intellectual rigor as far as I can see. In the traditional context the truth is that *ijtihād* always implies *taqlīd*.

Finally I must comment upon the phrase of Stepaniants at the end of her essay that my insistence upon preserving both the spirit and form of Islam would result in presenting Islam "not as a living teaching but instead as a deadly static set of tenets." My response to this assertion is that my view is definitely not what this assertion claims. Let us look at ourselves; we have both a spirit and a body recognizable by its form. While we are alive both spirit and body are preserved, and yet we are alive and not dead. Biological form survives not in being static and dead but in being alive. The survival of the form is not opposed to its possessing life. This metaphor can be used to understand what I have claimed about religion itself, although of course religions and biological forms are not the same. If I assert that Islam must preserve both its spirit and form, that does not mean that Islam will therefore be nothing more than a dead set of tenets. For thirteen centuries until the advent of modernism, Islam had preserved both its spirit and form, ranging from rites to social institutions, while having a most dynamic history, creating a major world civilization and spreading to new areas. The loss of energy and decrease in creativity during the past two centuries are the result of both a degree of decadence within the classical Islamic civilization, but not the religion itself, and the onslaught of the West which has not allowed this civilization to act freely in order to respond to the challenges facing it.

It must be remembered that in contrast to what Iqbāl and many other Muslim reformers say, dynamism is not always a greater virtue than being static. Two and two have been four ever since we started counting and this static knowledge has not prevented dynamic use of it in countless ways. The dynamic and static poles of existence are like the Far Eastern *Yin-Yang*. They complement rather than oppose each other, if one understands their true nature and function. A tree is both static and dynamic. Its roots are firm in the ground while its branches grow. If the roots were to become dynamic, the tree would die. But it would also die if its branches were to become static. I am fully aware of the significance of both of these qualities in all things, including in the Islamic tradition, in which I defend strongly the static nature of what is immutable by nature, and hence appears as static to us, as well as the dynamic which marks the continuity of the life of Islam as a vibrant and living tradition.

S. H. N.

29

Lucian W. Stone, Jr.

PERENNIAL PHILOSOPHY NOW: THE CASE OF *WILĀYAT-I FAQĪH*

Thus we must concede that the incompatibility of modern civilization with our tradition-bound civilization is one of the most important causes of the crisis in our society. What is to be done? Should we insist on remaining immersed in our tradition, or should we melt fully into Western civilization? Or is there another way of removing this contradiction, or at least taming and channeling it such that it does not lead to our destruction and the unraveling of our social fabric and historical identity?[1]

OPENING REMARKS

Many years ago I began an intensive study of Iranian thought, first through the lens of Sufism. My interest and development in the course of this inquiry led me to the study of: language, poetry, literature, philosophy, history, politics, and, most recently, the Iranian cinema—in other words, any subject related to the Iranian culture. And as anyone the least bit familiar with Iranian studies would have guessed, in the course of my studies, I have had many an occasion to become familiar with the massive corpus of writings compiled by Seyyed Hossein Nasr. His works have been a constant encyclopedic source of information and inspiration for me. Moreover, beyond mere academic influence, I have been deeply influenced personally by his depiction of *philosophia perennis*—traditional philosophy/wisdom.

Thus, upon the invitation of Professor Lewis E. Hahn and the Library of

Living Philosophers, I am pleased to offer this short contribution for the current volume. However, I would like to note here that not only am I still literally a graduate student, I consider myself a student of sorts of Dr. Nasr himself via the narrative of his writings. Consequently, I intend to make full use of the format provided by this series—that is, my essay and his reply to it—and submit this essay as an inquisitive student's appeal for clarification and explication from his teacher.

INTRODUCTION

As a student of Islamic and, more particularly, Iranian thought, I am not merely concerned with my research and studies for sheer historical understanding and appreciation. Rather, I am concerned with the ability to perceive the continuity and/or discontinuity of the tradition as it extends into the current day. The Iranian tradition is a living one and within it is a rich mosaic of its entire history and people.

Among the massive collection of writings, translations, edited volumes, and the like composed or compiled by S. H. Nasr throughout his distinguished career there is, nevertheless, a noticeable gap. Nowhere is there to be found amongst his work anything concerning Nasr's own living tradition in its most current form. That is, since the Islamic Revolution of 1979, and even before that, he has not written a word as to whether or not the current society in the Islamic Republic of Iran is or is not up to par, so to speak, in the perennial tradition of Shi'ite Iran. It is, to say the least, curious that as a proponent of the Shi'ite tradition and, moreover, of the *philosophia perennis* as a living philosophy, he does not apply this knowledge as a critique to the particular major concerns of that tradition as they exist now.

It should be noted at the same time that Nasr has not entirely neglected any application of his philosophy or dialogue with contemporary concerns. In his academic attempts to lay out the religious and philosophical framework of the Islamic tradition, he has been very critical of the West and modernity. He has even written a text intended to be used as a guide for young Muslims encountering the contemporary Western dominated world.[2] Finally one need only study his work on the ecological crisis[3] to know that indeed Nasr is not interested in mere academic pursuits or pure theory, but in the practice and application of these thoughts as well.

But still the question remains, why has he not addressed in more specific terms his own Iranian tradition in its current state? This is most crucial now when Iran stands at one of its most pivotal moments since the 1979 revolution. With the modernized West pressuring Iran more and more to "develop" and even democratize—not to mention the internal strife and pressure of the majority youth who have seemingly grown disenchanted with the current state of affairs—Iran and the Shi'ite community need a figure with the stature and character of Nasr, with his deep, encyclopedic understanding of the tradition, to speak out directly on current matters.

One of the most vital notions for contemporary Shi'ite Iran to come to terms with is *wilāyat-i faqīh* (guardianship of the jurisconsult). It was one of the main theological/philosophical concepts utilized by the late Ayatollah Khomeini to propagate the Islamic Revolution. Furthermore, it is the single most debated topic in current Iranian political thought. The controversy over this notion is directly associated with the debate between traditional Islam and the pressures coming from modernity. Thus, the *philosophia perennis* should partake in this debate and who is better qualified than Nasr who has always championed it?

In this brief essay, I will first present Nasr's explanation of *wilāyah*, the root concept for the development of *wilāyat-i faqīh,* in its traditional sense and use. Before moving on to a short summation of *wilāyat-i faqīh* itself, however, I will need briefly to discuss secularism in Islam.

WILĀYAH

Wilāyat-i faqīh is a relatively recent development; however, it stems from the already established Shi'ite tradition in the form of *wilāyah* (Arabic) / *wilāyat* (Persian). In fact, indirectly Nasr has indeed given some attention to this idea, albeit not in its contemporary, but in its historical manifestation. In his explication of the Shi'ite Islamic doctrine in and of itself, he has had to address the place and role of *wilāyah* which he has most impressively done in "Sunnism and Shi'ism—Twelve-Imam Shi'ism and Ismā'īlism."[4] Here he concisely depicts the development and application of this important matter.

Since the passing of the Prophet Muḥammad in 632 C.E. there has been one ongoing major "crisis" internally in the Islamic tradition—the authority to govern in the absence of the prophet. This, of course, is the root of Islam's division into two major sects, the Sunni and the Shi'ah. It is an extension of the handling of this dilemma that lead to the development of first the concept of *wilāyah* and furthermore to the more current *wilāyat-i faqīh*. Nasr writes,

> Specifically in Islam the door of prophecy closed with the Prophet Muḥammad —upon whom be peace. He was both the exoteric and esoteric source of the revelation but in his function as revealer of Divine legislation he represents the exoteric aspect. After him there must be those who inherited his esoteric function and whose duty it is to expound the inner meaning of the Divine Law [*Sharī'ah*]. . . . [T]he function of interpreting its inner meaning to men and preserving a link with the source of the revelation [is] called *wilāyah* in Shi'ism. In general the word *wilāyah* in Arabic, Persian and other Islamic

> languages means sainthood and the saint is called *walīallāh* "the friend of God." But in the specific context of Shi'ism it refers, not only to the saintly life in general, but to the very function of interpreting the esoteric dimension of the revelation.[5]

Here, Nasr not only sets out the strong root from which *wilāyah* grows into its current manifestation, but also states precisely what the paramount task of the *walīyallāh* is. That is, in the absence of the leadership of the prophet, the only one(s) with the authority to interpret the *Sharī'ah* and serve as the conveyor of it to the Islamic community, is the *walīallāh*.

> The cycle of prophecy (*dā'irat al-nubuwwah*), terminated with the Prophet who was the "Seal of prophecy." Henceforth no new revelation will come in the present cycle of humanity. But with the termination of this cycle there began, as already mentioned, what one might call the "cycle of initiation" (*dā'irat al-wilāyah*). . . . What this second cycle implies is the beginning of a chain of authorities concerned with the esoteric interpretation of the revelation and issuing directly from the Prophet himself who is the source of both the exoteric and the esoteric dimensions. Moreover, this cycle will continue until the Day of Judgment when the historic cycle itself is brought to a close. But as long as man lives on this earth the cycle of *wilāyah* subsists, providing a direct channel to the source of the revelation itself and the means whereby man can perform the fundamental operation of *ta'wīl*, of hermeneutic interpretation, of going from the exoteric to the esoteric. This basic process of *ta'wīl*, or of journeying from the *ẓāhir* [outer/exterior] to the *bāṭin* [inner/interior], is made possible only through the presence of the cycle of *wilāyah*. Without it there would be no way of escaping from the prison of limited forms to the abode of celestial essences.[6]

This is most crucial in that it allows for the tradition to remain a *living* one; that is, although the cycle of prophecy has ended, there still remains a strict source of authority for the Shī'ah community. Furthermore, this authority is legitimized internally within the tradition. The community, then, relies upon the legitimated *walīallāh* to continue the hermeneutic process and to keep the community intact as a unified, cohesive whole.

Further on, Nasr describes the mode of transmission of this authority within Twelve-imam Shi'ism as follows:

> The person who inaugurates the cycle of *wilāyah*, and whose duty it is in every age to fulfill the function of *wilāyah*, is the Imam, whose figure is so central in Shi'ism. That is why the first Imam, 'Ali, is in fact called *walīallāh*. . . . [I]t is also used in Sunni political theory to designate the ruler of the Islamic community, the imamate being in this sense synonymous with the caliphate.
>
> But as used specifically in Shi'ism the Imam means that person who is the real ruler of the community and especially the inheritor of the esoteric teachings of the Prophet. He is one who carries the "Muḥammadan Light" (*al-*

> *nūr al-muḥammadī*) within himself, and who fulfills the function of *wilāyah*. As already mentioned, according to both Sufism and Shi'ism there is a prophetic light which has existed from the beginning within the being of every prophet from Adam onwards. It is the source of all prophetic knowledge and is identified with the "Muḥammadan Light" or "Muḥammadan Reality" (*al-ḥaqīqat al-muḥammadiyyah*), which is Logos. It is this Light that continues from one cycle of prophecy to another and it is this Light that exists within the Imam, by virtue of whose presence he becomes the Imam.
>
> The Imam who fulfills the function of *wilāyah* is the sustainer of the religious law and the guarantee of its continuation. A prophet brings a Divine Law and then himself leaves the world. There are thus times when the world is without a prophet. But the Imam is always present. The earth can never be devoid of the presence of the Imam be he even hidden or unknown. Therefore, once the Prophet of Islam has left the world it is the Imam who, in his continuous presence, sustains and preserves the religion from one period to the next. The Imam is, in fact, the sustainer and interpreter *par excellence* of the revelation. His duty is essentially threefold: to rule over the community of Muslims as the representative of the Prophet, to interpret the religious sciences and the Law to men, especially their inner meaning, and to guide men in the spiritual life. All of these functions the Imam is able to perform because of the presence of the "Light" within him.[7]

Thus, the Imam, in Twelve-imam Shi'ism is the most significant figure after the prophet himself. The Imam is an extension of the "Light of Muḥammad." Hence he carries full legitimacy of religious and political authority over the Shi'ah community. Moreover, he does so infallibly—or as Nasr states, with "the quality of inerrancy (*'ismah*), in spiritual and religious matters."[8] In the absence of the prophet, the Imams act as "the intermediaries between man and God."[9]

A Different Kind of Secularism

Before moving forward to the extension of the concept *wilāyah* into the more current idea of *wilāyat-i faqīh*, I want to make one critical point. It stems from some of the remarks quoted from Nasr in the previous section and is, in the end, my open-ended question for him.

In his concise and decisive essay, "Religion and Secularism, Their Meaning and Manifestation in Islamic History," Nasr explains why there simply is no opening for secularism within Islam. The reality that is Islam is a unified matrix of many categories and disciplines which, it must be stressed, are not mutually exclusive. "In the unitary perspective of Islam, all aspects of life, as well as all degrees of cosmic manifestation, are governed by a single principle and are unified by a common center. There is nothing outside the power of God and, in a more esoteric sense, nothing 'outside'

His Being, for there cannot be two orders of reality."[10] Furthermore, and even more basic, he states as a matter of fact that "there exists no term in classical Arabic or Persian which is exactly synonymous with the word 'secularism.'"[11]

The West's insistence upon the primacy of the "self" or "individual" does not bode well in the Islamic tradition, particularly in the more esoteric nature of Islam which Nasr favors. He dismisses Western critiques of Islam by holding steadfast to the Islamic looking glass (and *philosophia perennis*) and critiquing the Western modern tradition with traditional Islamic criteria. Thus, "secularism," according to Nasr, "may be considered as everything whose origin is merely human and therefore non-divine, and whose metaphysical basis lies in this ontological hiatus between man and God."[12] Those who do not ground their thought in tradition are guilty of such hubris and, hence, subject to human error.

Yet, that said, in the same breath as one can renounce the secularist critique of Islam, one must also be critical of an apolitical approach as well. It is true that Islam is a unified whole of several non-independent disciplines, and consequently one cannot ignore its crucial political dimension. Nasr, however, throughout his writings and career has seemingly intentionally done this. He only discusses the political aspects of Islam in their most general and historical terms.[13]

Nasr attempts to defend this apathetic, or even absent, approach to politics by the basic Shī'ah principle that in the absence of the twelfth and final Imam (the Mahdī), who is now in occultation, there is no true *walīallāh* present.

> As far as the political aspect of Twelve-imam Shi'ism is concerned, it is directly connected with the personality of the Imam. The perfect government is that of the Imam, one which will be realized with the coming of the Mahdī who even now is the invisible ruler of the world but does not manifest himself directly in human society. In his absence every form of government is of necessity, imperfect, for the imperfection of men is reflected in their political institutions. The Shi'ites, especially of Persia since the Safavid period and even before, have considered the monarchy as the least imperfect form of government in such conditions.[14]

Therefore, all forms of government are fallible as opposed to the true Shi'ite community which would be a reality through the infallible hermeneutic lens of the twelfth Imam had he not gone into occultation. Consequently, Nasr argues, Shi'ites have not been politically engaged within the community.

> The distrust of all worldly government after the disappearance of the Mahdī and the early experience of the Shi'ite community made Twelve-imam Shi'ism apathetic towards political life. This is one of the features that distinguishes it

> from both Sunnism and Ismā'īlism. The Twelvers or Imamites remained content with being observers of the political scene rather than the originators of political movements.[15]

That said, however, Nasr does not want there to be any misconstrual of this apparent apathy. Rather, he argues that this instead reflects the zealousness of the Shi'ite community in that in understanding and fully accepting the Shi'ite doctrine and the authority of the Imam, any interest in other political affairs would in fact be a movement away from the true political schema of Shi'ism.

> The withdrawal of the Shi'ites from political life should not however be interpreted as their withdrawal from the life of the community. On the contrary, this very apathy towards politics intensified the religious and scholarly activity of the Shī'ah…Therefore, although politically aloof, Twelve-imam Shi'ism made an immense contribution to the life of the Islamic community in domains that were more connected with the knowledge of things rather than the ruling of men.[16]

In all fairness to Nasr, the essay quoted above was composed and published by Nasr in 1966, many years before the Islamic Revolution of 1979.[17] However, in the aftermath of that significant event, one cannot make such claims of justified apathy. As a matter of fact the Shi'ah community is immersed in political activity in contemporary times. Seeing that the *Sharī'ah* is the code of Islamic life itself, it seems impossible not to be somehow politically concerned. I would like to note then, that when Nasr refuses to address Islamic political issues, he is guilty of another type of secularism—he is ignoring and, hence segregating, an essential part of *the whole* that is Islam. He may object to these current discussions because so much of the modern Islamic political dialogue is infused with foreign ideals such as secularism and democracy. He can even declare that all such political dialogue is impregnated with fallacy since the absence of the Mahdī. Regardless and, for that matter, in lieu of this, he should bear the responsibility of pointing out these inconsistencies with tradition and of attacking them as such at the very least. Nasr, in fact, cannot abstain from participating in this central dialogue.

WILĀYAT-I FAQĪH

In this last section I would like to turn the attention towards the idea of *wilāyat-i faqīh*. For this purpose, I will refer to Hamid Dabashi's informative essay, "Mullā Aḥmad Narāqī and the Question of the Guardianship of the Jurisconsult (*Wilāyat-i faqīh*)," which appears in the volume *Expectation of the Millenium: Shi'ism in History*—co-edited by Nasr himself.[18]

At the outset of Dabashi's explication of *wilāyat-i faqīh*, we revisit what I mentioned above with regard to the main crisis of Islam in general and of Shi'ism in particular, that is, who has the authority to guide the Muslim community—first in the absence of the prophet, and second, in lieu of the occultation of the twelfth Imam? Dabashi writes:

> Perhaps it would not be an exaggeration to suggest that the development of this political doctrine [*wilāyat-i faqīh*] in its integral juridical context has been in dormant process since the very inception of the Shi'i cause in the early Islamic history. As the most successful doctrinal-political movement to perpetuate Muḥammad's charismatic legacy, Shi'i Islam has endured and surpassed persistent tensions that chiefly characterize its understanding and recognition of political authority. The doctrinal development of *wilāyat-i faqīh*, long before its institutional crystallization in the Islamic Republic, is the chief nucleus of that characterizing tension of Shi'i Islam: "By what authority?"[19]

This question consequently has been a source of great debate, even amongst earlier Shi'ite thinkers.

In extension, the development of the concept of *wilāyat-i faqīh* is grounded deeply in the Shi'ite tradition. As Dabashi himself writes, "to be sure, *wilāyat-i faqīh* is much too recent in its theoretical development to be in any significant way articulated in its reciprocal relations with other Shi'i dogmas. However, certain credal dimensions of Shi'ism, in their historical constitution, perhaps are, inevitably and inadvertently, conducive to *wilāyat-i faqīh*."[20] Thus, the foundation for such development already existed within the tradition before evolving into what, some may declare, is its inevitable consequential form.

> The most immediate intrinsic Shi'i dogmatic force with which *wilāyat-i faqīh* is organically related is the doctrine of *Imāmah*. The inevitable and divinely ordained community of Muḥammad's charismatic authority in the physical and metaphysical lines of descent through the Imams has kept the tenacious spontaneity of Shi'i political tract much too alert and responsive to be circumscribed by institutional routinization. Perpetually keeping Shi'ism on the edge of political outburst, the doctrine of *Imāmah* has been its single most important surviving and flourishing force. While in the pre-*ghaybah* [occultation] period, *Imāmah* was the legitimating doctrine of the specific Shi'i Imams; in the post-*ghaybah* period it has grown gradually into the tacit, yet most emphatic, source of authority for the Shi'i jurisconsults (*fuqahā'*). Thus, the very seminal doctrine of *Imāmah*, so crucial to the theological foundation of Shi'ism, has anticipated some mode of authority, the specifics of which are always the subject of legal disputations, for the jurisconsult.[21]

Even within the earliest formulation of Islam at the time of the prophet there was a specific and primary position for the jurisconsults (*fuqahā'*). They were trained rigorously in Islamic Divine Law. It was their duty to make informed interpretations and judgments of the law for exoteric and even esoteric purposes.

In the absence of the Mahdī, and the primary source of authority of the prophet himself, who then is best equipped to guide the Muslim community? The obvious answer is, of course, the *fuqahā'*, who are the most thoroughly trained and most familiar with the entire corpus of *Sharī'ah*—this includes in the Shi'ite tradition, not only the Quran and the Ḥadīth of Prophet Muḥammad, but also the *Ḥadīth* of the Imams as well. The problematic question then arises as to how much authority the jurisconsults should have. For that matter, it was not entirely decided if in fact they did have *legitimate* authority to begin with. "In the post-*ghaybah* period, while the world awaited its apocalyptic end in the 'peace of the Mahdī,' the political apparatus and its basis of legitimacy always faced the equivocal approval of the religious order."[22] But if not the jurisconsult, then who? As we saw above, according to Nasr, this is not an issue. That is, without the Mahdī, there simply is no truly legitimate authority—any claim to it would be a false one. This is consistent with earlier debates on this matter.

> The founding fathers of Shi'i jurisprudence, for example, Kulaynī and Ibn Bābūyah, opposed the idea of "representing the Hidden Imam" on the basis of his being eternally alive and present. Most Shi'i scholars never specifically stipulated the possibility of any "deputy" for the Hidden Imam or even, as in the case of al-Ṭūsī, emphatically forbade it. Al-Ṭūsī had specified that "other than the Hidden Imam nobody can occupy the position of the prophet."[23]

The primary source of such refutation of the concept of a stand-in authority in the absence of the Mahdī stems from the exalted position which the twelfth Imam possesses—that is, the "Light of Muḥammad." This position, first and foremost, is not something which can simply be applied as a title to someone. Moreover, it is ontologically granted; that is, this position is not a man-made decision arrived at for the sake of convenience. Rather, it has deep implications, the most drastic of which is the infallibility of the carrier of this Light. "His [Muḥammad Jawād Mughniyah's] disagreement is principally on the doctrinal basis of the infallibility of the Imam (*'ismah*). The jurisconsult simply cannot claim overriding authority as that of the Imam; this would equate his status with the Infallible, which is not permissible."[24]

If this rebuttal is accepted fully, then there still remains a dilemma as to who guides the community in the absence of the Mahdī. It is one thing to suggest that the monarchy is the lesser of all evils and submit the Islamic community to the Leviathan. But what if the monarch is oppressive and, even more significant, acts in open contradiction to the values of the Islamic community?[25] There needed to be an avenue for an Islamic source of political authority.

Dabashi, in his essay, elucidates the argument of Mullā Aḥmad Narāqī (1185/1771–1245/1829) who "expounded the necessity and legitimacy of 'legal speculation' (*al-maẓannah*) on part of the jurisconsult in the absence of the Twelfth Imam."[26] This clever argument paved the way for the contemporary understanding of *wilāyat-i faqīh*.

> The fact is that, in the absence of the Hidden Imam, as al-Ṭūsī had argued, the *fuqahā'* had a difficult theological position to appropriate for themselves what doctrinally belonged to the "Rightly Guided." They had no claim to infallibility, nor could they have any. As such, they were theoretically as much in danger of error as the political powers. The significance of Narāqī's notion of '*al-maẓannah*' lies in providing the *faqīh* with a doctrinal basis to speculate rather more freely in judicial issues, with its political repercussions.[27]

The *faqīh*, who has the authority to use *ijtihād* (reason) in deciphering the *Sharī'ah* in order to make decisions based on it, according to Narāqī, has a legitimate claim to interpret more freely. This, however, does not equate the stature of the *fuqahā'* with the Imam; Narāqī makes a clear ontological distinction.

> The primary source of *wilāyah*, whose authority upon man is permanent (*thābit*), is Allah. The recipients of this *wilāyah* are (1) the Messenger [Muḥammad] and (2) his successors (*awssiya'*). These two secondary sources of authority are infallible, and thus *wilāyah* is incumbent upon them on a permanent (*thābit*) basis. On qualifying these two sources, Mullā Aḥmad [Narāqī] considers them "the rulers of the human race" (*salāḥn al-anām*), "the kings" (*al-mulūk*), "the governors" (*al-wullāh*), and "judges" (*ḥukkām*). There are those, however, whose *wilāyah* is not on a permanent basis (*ghayr thābit*)—because of their fallibility—and, furthermore, is limited to that to which they have been delegated. The latter kind of *walī* includes "the jurisconsults, fathers, grandfathers, guardians [in the sense of father figures, or foster parents], husbands, masters [of slaves], and the representatives [of such figures]."[28]

Thus, only the prophet and the twelve Imams have permanent *wilāyah*. They are distinguished by their infallibility. Yet, there is still the presence of *wilāyah* in a less robust fashion found on the personal level. Therefore, the *fuqahā'* indeed carry the *wilāyah* (albeit impermanently) and hence have a legitimate source of political authority. Narāqī substantiates his argument with *Ḥadīth*, thus tying it deeply within the tradition itself, and not relying on any external, secular sources.

> Then Mullā Aḥmad [Narāqī] proceeds to enumerate nineteen different *ḥadīths* in support of the *wilāyat-i faqīh*: among them, that "the learned men [*'ulamā'*, a term also used interchangeably with *fuqahā'*] are the successors of the prophets"; and "the *'ulamā'* of my people are like prophets before me." This emphasis on successorship to Muḥammad as the prerogative of the religious authorities is particularly important in reading a political dimension into the doctrine of *wilāyat-i faqīh*.
>
> The eleventh tradition introduced in support of the doctrine is of immediate significance. According to this tradition, "the kings have authority over [*ḥukkām 'alā*] the people, while *'ulamā'* have authority over the kings" (*al-mulūk ḥukkām 'ala'l-nās wa'l 'ulamā' ḥukkām 'ala'l-mulūk*). Here, by *ḥukkām*, the reference is clearly to political and not merely judicial authority. In fact, in this formulation, the mode of authority established between the *'ulamā'* and the kings is precisely that of the king over his subjects.[29]

This being the case, the blind surrender of authority to any existing political regime, or "the lesser of all corrupt forms of government," finds itself mistaken. There is, according to Narāqī and later explicators of *wilāyat-i faqīh*, a Shi'ah source for political legitimization and authority after the occultation of the twelfth Imam. Finally, this legitimacy and authority give religious and traditional credibility to any critique and dismissal of such "false" governments ruling over the Islamic community. This, of course, was adopted and slightly altered by Ayatollah Khomeini in leading the Islamic Revolution of 1979.

Conclusion

Seyyed Hossein Nasr will always stand as one of the most prolific academics in the Islamic tradition, particularly in the West. As such, he has made an invaluable contribution to the field and to the Muslim community itself. His work and teachings have provided inspiration for many interested students to pursue their studies, of which I am one example. As one of the inspired, I have found only one frustrating point throughout his works. Appreciating his insights and views into the Islamic tradition, as well as his uncanny ability to elucidate and elaborate on it in an impressive and accessible prose, I have been left wondering what his exact sentiments are with regard to the current manifestation of the Shi'ite tradition as it exists in the Islamic Republic of Iran. I hope this point of curiosity proves to be legitimate enough to elicit a clarifying response from Professor Nasr whose grateful students we are and will always remain.

LUCIAN W. STONE, JR.

SOUTHERN ILLINOIS UNIVERSITY AT CARBONDALE
JULY 2000

NOTES

This essay is dedicated to the memory of my dear friend and teacher, Dr. Touraj Noroozi (1956–2000), who helped inspire this essay through many in-depth conversations on this subject.

1. President Mohammad Khatami, *Islam, Liberty and Development* (Binghamton, N.Y.: Institute of Global Cultural Studies, 1998), p. 24.

2. S. H. Nasr, *A Young Muslim's Guide to the Modern World* (Chicago: Kazi Publications, 1994).

3. See for example: S. H. Nasr, *The Encounter of Man and Nature* (London: George Allen and Unwin, 1968).

4. This essay appears in S. H. Nasr, *Ideals and Realities of Islam* (London: George Allen & Unwin, 1971), pp. 147–78.

Note also that this is not the only context where he specifically discusses this notion. Nasr also discusses this term as it is used in regards to Sufism. See: "Shi'ism and Sufism" in *Sufi Essays* (New York: Schocken Books, 1977), pp. 106–8.

5. Nasr, *Ideals and Realities of Islam*, pp. 160–61.

6. Ibid., p. 161.

7. Ibid., pp. 161–62.

8. Ibid., pp. 162–63.

9. Ibid., p. 163.

10. S. H. Nasr, "Religion and Secularism, Their Meaning and Manifestation in Islamic History" in S. H. Nasr, *Islamic Life and Thought* (Boston: George Allen & Unwin, 1981), p. 7.

11. Ibid.

12. Ibid., p. 8.

13. This moment permits me to drive home further the point that this critique only applies to Nasr's neglect of current trends and concerns; that is, he does indeed offer such critiques but only for past instances. For example:

> Furthermore, despite the victory of Islam over "pagan" ideas, the aftermath of the battle of Ṣiffīn and the later establishment of the Umayyad

> caliphate by Mu'āwiyah mark the first intrusion of secularism into the political life of Islam in the sense that politics, or at least a part of it, became divorced from divinely revealed principles and fell into the arena of power politics in which human ambition was the dominant factor. (Ibid., p. 9)

Nasr does point out here and in other places (see for example: Nasr, "The *Sharī'ah*—Divine Law, Social and Human Norm" in *Ideals and Realities of Islam*, p. 107), the intrusion of secular or non-Islamic ideals into the Islamic community. These, unfortunately, are always in a historical context and never regard current Iranian Shi'ite practices.

14. Nasr, "The *Sharī'ah*—Divine Law, Social and Human Norm" in *Ideals and Realities of Islam*, pp. 166–67.

15. Ibid., p. 167.

16. Ibid.

17. In order to put this into a complete chronological context, I refer to this passage from Ervand Abrahamian's invaluable study *Iran Between Two Revolutions* (Princeton, NJ: Princeton University Press, 1982), p. 425:

> Khomeini published his first major work in 1943. Entitled *Kashf-i Asrar* (Secrets Revealed), the book argued on behalf of establishing an Islamic system of government, and, without rejecting the whole principle of monarchy, took Reza Shah to task for maltreating the clergy. Despite his views, Khomeini remained aloof from the political struggles of the 1940s and the 1950s. Three pressures explain this aloofness: the fear of communism; the disdain shown by the nationalists, especially Mossadeq, for clerical causes; and the restraining hand of his patron, Boroujerdi, who continued throughout the 1950s to give valuable support to the shah. Freed of this restraint by Boroujerdi's death in 1961, *Khomeini began to speak out in 1962–63*. [my italics for emphasis] Although many clerics opposed the regime because of land reform and women's rights, Khomeini, revealing a masterful grasp of mass politics, scrupulously avoided the former issue and instead hammered away on a host of other concerns that aroused greater indignation among the general population. He denounced the regime for living off corruption, rigging elections, violating the constitutional laws, stiffling the press and the political parties, destroying the independence of the university, neglecting the economic needs of merchants, workers, and peasants, *undermining the country's Islamic beliefs* [emphasis added], encouraging *gharbzadegi*—indiscrimintae borrowing from the West—granting "capitulations" to foreigners, selling oil to Israel, and constantly expanding the size of the central Bureaucracies. Not for the last time, Khomeini had chosen issues with mass appeal.

18. This is yet another instance in which Nasr had the opportunity to address such contemporary concerns with an essay of his own on the matter, but did not; yet his editorship of a volume dedicated to the Shi'ah situation as it heads into the new millennium indicates that he is not just an unconcerned and detached scholar himself.

19. Hamid Dabashi, "Mullā Aḥmad Narāqī and the Question of the Guardianship of the Jurisconsult (*Wilāyat-i faqīh*)" in *Expectation of the Millennium: Shi'ism in History*, ed. S. H. Nasr, H. Dabashi, and S. V. R. Nasr (Albany, NY: State University of New York Press, 1989), p. 288.

20. Ibid., p. 289.

21. Ibid.

22. Ibid., pp. 289–90.

23. Ibid., p. 290.

24. Ibid., p. 292.

25. See note 17 above in reference to the leadership of the Shah.

26. Ibid., p. 293.

27. Ibid.

28. Ibid., pp. 293–94.

29. Ibid., pp. 294–95.

REPLY TO LUCIAN STONE

The essay of Mr. Stone deals with a very sensitive subject as far as the present situation in Iran and contemporary interpretations of Shi'ism are concerned. There are currents, trends, and forces involved in this issue which have not as yet worked themselves out and more time is needed before the consequences of the concept of the *wilāyat-i faqīh* and its application to the political domain can be evaluated in light of both Iranian history and the tradition of Shi'ism. As the author surely knows there have been eminent Shi'ite jurists before the Iranian Revolution of 1979, such as Shaykh Murtaḍā Anṣārī, who explicitly limited the power of *wilāyat* of the jurisprudence to those unable to administer their affairs, while others such as the Arab Shi'ite scholar Shaykh Muḥammad Jawād Mughniyah, even in supporting the Iranian Revolution, limited the *wilāyat* of the jurisprudence to only the juridical realm, relying for his interpretation upon the views of such eminent earlier Shi'ite jurists as Baḥr al-'Ulūm and Mīrzā-yi Nā'īnī. And yet others have pointed to the historical roots of this issue within Shi'ite jurisprudence going back especially to Narāqī whom Stone mentions in this essay.

My response to Stone is not to enter into this debate and act as a jurist over a matter which must be and will be ultimately settled religiously by the official Shi'ite *'ulamā'* and politically by the people of Iran on the basis of its success or failure in present-day Iran. I need to emphasize here that throughout my life I have never given juridical edicts. This does not mean that my exposition of traditional doctrine is incomplete. Like so many classical expositors of Islamic philosophy and metaphysics before me, such as Ibn Sīnā, Jāmī or Mullā Ṣadrā, I have not dealt with *Sharī'ite* questions in my writings on intellectual subjects because, like them, I have taken for granted the acceptance of promulgations and rulings of the *Sharī'ah*, whose meaning and significance in Islam I have sought to explain in my general works on Islam as a religion.

The perennial philosophy is concerned before all else with metaphysics and subsequently the application of metaphysical principles to the realms of the cosmos, and the human order, both individual and collective. There is no realm which it leaves untouched, but that does not mean that each exposition of traditional doctrines must include every realm of contingency. In my own writings I have been concerned most of all with the metaphysical and cosmological realms and less with social philosophy and especially political philosophy. As the author points out, in my exposition of Islamic thought I have on occasion dealt with classical political philosophy but hardly ever with the contemporary situation. The reason for that is first of all because of my personal attraction to prime philosophy and natural philosophy, to use the language of Aristotle, rather than to philosophy dealing with law, society, and politics; and secondly, the personal need to stand above the din of political contention and ever changing circumstances in a world in which the political realm is so chaotic and in which, even in the Islamic world, religious and secular elements vie and intermingle with each other. My vocation has been to state the traditional principles rather than to enter the political arena even on the intellectual level. I feel that in this way I can render greater service to the cause of traditional teachings and the perennial philosophy which determine my worldview.

There is not, however, as great a gap in my writings on the situation in Iran as Stone thinks. He writes, ". . . there is, nevertheless, a noticeable gap" in my writings. "Nowhere is there to be found amongst his work anything concerning Nasr's own living tradition in its most current form." If he were to study some of my essays as well as numerous talks and interviews given in Persia from 1958–1979 when I resided in my country of origin, he would realize how much in fact I was concerned at that time with my own living tradition, and, played a role in the practical realm in which I sought to avoid direct political involvement. The term *sunnat* used currently in Persian for "tradition" was in fact used in this sense for the first time by myself in the late '50s and soon became widely accepted. As for after 1979, if I have not written about current affairs in Iran, it is because, first of all, I never write on current affairs as such, and secondly, because I am not there to study the situation firsthand. Moreover, my position in Iran before the Revolution and the close contact which I had with both the court and the *'ulamā'* made me aware of many things about which I have chosen deliberately to remain silent. Yet, I have remained and continue to remain very much concerned with what goes on in Iran even if I do not write about it.

Stone must remember, however, that during the years following the Iranian Revolution I have continued to defend traditional Islam which in its political aspect rejects all the ideological and revolutionary concepts that grew out of nineteenth-century European thought. The very fact that I have not written about the different sides of the debate going on in Iran today but have continued to write about and defend traditional Islam has been itself an indirect commentary upon what goes on in Iran. It is not accidental that after several years of neglect, my writings are very widely read in Iran today and many there now speak of *islām-i sunnatī* (traditional Islam), whose foremost spokesman they consider me to be, and distinguish this understanding of Islam from both modern interpretations and *bunyād-garā'ī* or "fundamentalism." I may not "speak out directly on current matters" in Iran, but my voice is far from being absent there. Plans are in fact now being made to bring out my complete works in Persian in some thirty volumes.

Turning to the question of *wilāyah*, as Stone mentions I have of course dealt with it, seeing how central the concept and reality of *wilāyah/walāyah* is to both Sufism and Shi'ism. But it is important to make clear how this traditional idea differs from the current understanding of *wilāyat-i faqīh*. When I was in fact writing about *wilāyat* in the '60s and '70s and discussing the matter with such leading masters of Shi'ite learning as 'Allāmah Ṭabāṭabā'ī and Sayyid Muḥammad Kāẓim 'Aṣṣār, they never even envisaged or mentioned its current interpretation. Whether the current understanding is simply a new application of the traditional idea and the realization of certain possibilities latent within the Shi'ite tradition which had not become manifested until now, or simply an "innovation" (*bid'ah*) to be re-interpreted in its traditional sense in the future, only the Shi'ite *'ulamā'* and the response of the Shi'ite community will determine in coming years.

For my part the traditional sense of *wilāyah/walāyah* is what is of basic import. Stone writes, "in the same breath as one can renounce the secularist critique of Islam, one must also be critical of an apolitical approach." This statement is only true if the apolitical approach is posited as a principle. If I were to say that Islam has nothing to do with the political realm and is in principle apolitical, then I would certainly open the door to secularism. But if I were to say that Islam possesses a *Sharī'ah*, which encompasses all of life and applies to the socio-political as well as the personal realm, along with spiritual and intellectual teachings, and that I accept all these dimensions but will concern myself primarily with the intellectual and spiritual dimensions, then I certainly would not be opening the door to any form of secularism. The author can rest assured that my position is the second and not the first. I think that in light of what I have said, I cannot be accused of being guilty "of another type of secularism" as stated by Stone.

After discussing the concept of the *wilāyat-i faqīh*, the author states, "there still remains a dilemma as to who guides the community." This is true but the complementary question which is just as important is "guides in what domain?" Is it religious and juridical guidance, or political guidance or inward, spiritual and ethical guidance, or all of them? What is then the relation between the *walī-i faqīh*, the *marja'-i taqlīd* and the Twelfth Imam? These are questions crucial to Shi'ism; that is why they are so hotly debated and contested in present-day Iran as well as among non-Iranian Shi'ites, whether they be in Iraq, Pakistan, or London. As for the question of an oppressive monarch mentioned in the same paragraph, Shi'ism has always taught opposition and disobedience in such a situation, but traditional Shi'ism did not identify this opposition with the institution of *wilāyat-i faqīh* as currently understood.

As far as Narāqī is concerned, first of all his view of *al-maẓannah* is not the same as the *wilāyat-i faqīh* as promulgated in his later life by Ayatollah Khomeini. Also although Narāqī quotes *ḥadīths* in favor of his view, a millennium of eminent jurists held the opposite view also basing themselves on the Quran and *Ḥadīth*. It is important to bring this point out in order to demonstrate the situation of the concept of the *wilāyat-i faqīh* vis-à-vis the long tradition of Shi'ite jurisprudence and theology.

Mr. Stone has sought to "force me" to "elicit a clarifying response" concerning the situation of Shi'ism in present-day Iran. He has in fact not been the first person to try to do so. There are those who have insisted that I enter directly the arena of politico-religious debates going on in Iran or even the political domain itself. At the present moment I see my role otherwise. What I consider most important globally in general, and for Iran in particular, is the formulation and expounding of various facets of the perennial philosophy and tradition, and more specifically, as far as Iran is concerned, the Islamic tradition in all its facets to the extent of my ability. Vis-à-vis the *Sharī'ah*, my duty has been first of all to live according to it and secondly to point out its significance and meaning without giving juridical edicts for which by training I am not qualified. I believe that without entering into the current religious and political fray in Iran, I am playing a role in the country which I do not believe to be completely inconsequential. The hands of destiny have placed me in a situation, at least for the time being, in which the most effective action is what the Far Eastern tradition calls *wu-wei* or action without acting.

Finally, let me add that, paradoxically enough, interest in the perennial philosophy and traditional doctrines grows from day to day in Iran. Based on seeds which I and a small circle of friends planted over forty years ago, this interest has blossomed in a remarkable fashion and is more intense than in any other Islamic country. It has caused a renewal of intellectual life, philosophically and theologically speaking, in both traditional centers of learning such as Qum and even in Western-style universities. It is this intellectual activity that is bound to determine the future course of Shi'ite thought, at least in Persia if not everywhere, and to evaluate *wilāyat-i faqīh* in light of the long tradition of Shi'ite juridical and theological thought. What is important for now everywhere and in Iran in particular is to keep the flame of traditional thought burning strong and it is primarily to this task that my writings are devoted.

S. H. N.

PART THREE

BIBLIOGRAPHY OF THE WRITINGS OF SEYYED HOSSEIN NASR

Compiled by

Mehdi Aminrazavi
Zailan Moris
Ibrahim Kalin

Edited by

Lucian W. Stone, Jr.

PREFACE TO THE BIBLIOGRAPHY OF THE WRITINGS OF SEYYED HOSSEIN NASR

The present bibliography, compiled by Mehdi Aminrazavi, Zailan Moris, and Ibrahim Kalin, is a revised and updated version of two previously published bibliographies: William Chittick, *The Works of Seyyed Hossein Nasr Through His Fortieth Birthday*, Salt Lake City, The Middle East Center—University of Utah, 1997; and Mehdi Aminirazavi and Zailan Moris, *The Complete Bibliography of the Works of Seyyed Hossein Nasr—From 1958 Through April 1993*, Kuala Lumpur, Islamic Academy of Science, 1994.

There are inherent complexities involved in composing a multilingual document. We chose software with the most inclusive set of diacritic marks in addition to having multilingual capabilities. Nevertheless, we were unable to incorporate some of the proper diacritic marks. Furthermore, we also lost the capability of using smart quotes (“ ”) which is most noticeable with respect to certain Arabic and Persian transliterations in which (‘) and (’) serve as distinct characters; e.g., ‘Allāmah Ṭabāṭabā’ī will instead appear as 'Allāmah Ṭabāṭabā'ī. These slight stylistic inaccuracies, however, should not in any way diminish the usability of the bibliography as the most complete resource on Nasr’s extensive work.

At this time I would like to express my gratitude to those who have dedicated so much time and effort to produce this final product. Prof. Nasr himself has been actively involved with this aspect of the volume, both in compilation and editing, for which I am grateful. Of course the compilers of the bibliography who did the brunt of the work, deserve the appreciation of all of those who will come to use this valuable resource. Finally, but certainly not least, I must acknowledge my sincere indebtedness to Frances Stanley, Kerri Mommer, and Dr. Randall Auxier for all of their help in preparing the manuscript.

LUCIAN W. STONE, JR.

SOUTHERN ILLINOIS UNIVERSITY AT CARBONDALE
MARCH 2001

KEY TO ABBREVIATIONS IN BIBLIOGRAPHY

A	Arabic
AL	Albanian
B	Bengali
BSC	Bosnian-Serbo-Croation
D	Dutch
F	French
FL	Flemish
G	German
GR	Greek
H	Hebrew
I	Italian
IN	Indonesian
J	Japanese
M	Malay
P	Persian
PG	Portuguese
PO	Polish
S	Spanish
SW	Swedish
T	Turkish
TA	Tamil
U	Urdu

BIBLIOGRAPHY OF SEYYED HOSSEIN NASR

BOOKS

1961

1. «رسالهٔ سه اصل»، به انضمام منتخب از مثنوی و رباعیات، (بمناسبت چهار صدمین سال تولد صدرالدین شیرازی) از صدر-الدین محمد بن ابراهیم، به اهتمام و تصحیح سیّد حسین نصر، تهران، انتشارات دانشگاه تهران، ١٣٤٠، چاپ دوّم، تهران – انتشارات مولی، ١٣٤٦، چاپ سوّم، تهران، انتشارات روزنه، ١٣٧٧. (P)

2. «یاد نامهٔ ملّا صدرا»، به اهتمام و با مقدّمهٔ سیّد حسین نصر، تهران، انتشارات دانشگاه تهران، ١٣٤٠. (E & P)

   Mullā Ṣadrā Commemoration Volume. Ed. S. H. Nasr. Tehran: Tehran University Press, 1961.

1963

3.a. «نظر متفکّران اسلامی دربارهٔ طبیعت»، تهران، انتشارات دانشگاه تهران، ۱۳٤۲، چاپ دوّم، تهران، دهخدا، ۱۳۵۰. (P)

1964

b. *An Introduction to Islamic Cosmological Doctrines*. Preface by H. A. R. Gibb. Cambridge: Harvard University Press, 1964. Second edition. New York and London: Thames and Hudson, 1978. Paperback edition, Boulder: Shambhala, 1978. New edition, Albany: State University of New York Press, 1992. Revised edition, Albany: State University of New York Press, 1993.

c. *İslâm Kozmoloji Ögretilerine Giriṣ*. Trans. Nazife Ṣiṣman. Istanbul: İnsan Yayinlari, 1985. (T)

d. *Pengenalan Doktrin Kosmologi Islam*. Trans. Baharuddin Ahmad. Kuala Lumpur: Dewan Bahasa dan Pustaka, 1992. Second edition, 1993. (M)

4. a. *Three Muslim Sages*. Preface by R. H. L. Slater. Cambridge: Harvard University Press, 1964. Second printing, 1969. Reprinted, Delmar: Caravan Books, 1976, 1986. Reprinted, Lahore: Suhail Academy, 1988 and 1999.

b. «سه حکیم مسلمان»، ترجمهٔ احمد آرام، تبریز، کتابفروشی سروش با همکاری مؤسسهٔ فرانکلین، ۱۳۴۵، چاپ دوّم، شرکت سهامی جیبی، ۱۳۵۲، چاپ سوّم ۱۳۵۴. (P)

c. *Tiga Pemikir Islam: Ibnu Sina, Suhrawardi dan Ibnu Arabi*. Trans. Ahmad Mujahid. Bandung: Risalah Bandung, 1986. (Trans. from Arabic). (IN)

d. *Tin Jon Muslim Monishi*. Trans. Mohiudin. Dacca: Bengali Central Board for Development, 1970. (B)

e. «ثلاثة حكماء مسلمين»، ترجمة صلاح الصاوي، بيروت، دار النهار، ١٩٧١ واشنطن، دار الحكمة، ١٩٩٢. (A)

f. «تین مسلمان فیلسوف»، ترجمهٔ محمّد منوّر، لاهور، علاقائی ثقافتی اداره (آر – سی – دی) ۱۹۷۱. (U)

g. *Isuramu no Tetsugakusha Tachi*. Trans. T. Kuroda. Tokyo: Iwanami, 1975. (J)

h. *Üç Müslüman Bilge*. Trans. Ali Ünal. Istanbul: İnsan Yayinlari, 1985. (T)

i. *Tri Muslimanska Mudraca*. Trans. Becir Dzaka. Sarajevo: El-Kalem, 1991. (BSC)

5. a. *L'Histoire de la philosophie islamique*. Collaboration with H. Corbin and O. Yahya. Vol. 1. Paris: Gallimard (Collection Idées), 1964. (Collection folio/essais), 1986. (F) Also in E*ncyclopédie de la Pléiade-Histoire de la philosophie*. Vol. I, Orient, Antiquité, Moyen-Age. Paris: Gallimard, 1969, pp. 1048-1197.

b. *Storia della filosofia islamica*. Collaboration with H. Corbin and O. Yahya. Trans. Vanna Calasso. Milan: Adelphi Edizioni, 1973. (I)

c. “تاريخ الفلسفة الاسلامية”، ترجمة نصير مروّة وحسن قبيسى، بيروت، منشورات جويدات، ١٩٦٦. (A)

d. “تاريخ فلسفهٔ اسلامى”، ترجمهٔ اسدالله مبشّرى، تهران، اميركبير، ١٣٥٢. (P)

e. *Isuramu Tetsugakushi*. Trans. T. Kuroda. Tokyo: Iwanami, 1974. (J)

f. *Historija islamske filosofije*. Trans. Nerkes Smailagić and Tarik Haverić. Sarajevo: Biblioteka Logos, 1987. (BSC)

g. *Historia de la filosofiá: Del mundo romano al Islam medieval*. Madrid: Siglo XXI Editores, 1972. Sixth edition, 1984. (S)

h. *History of Islamic Philosophy*. Trans. Liadain Sherrard. London: Routledge and Kegan Paul, 1993.

1966

6. a. *Iran* (Reading Material for Use in Teaching about Eastern Cultures). Paris: UNESCO, 1966. Reprinted, Tehran: Pahlavi Library, 1971. Tehran: Offset Press, 1973.
   b. *Iran* (Document à utiliser pour l'enseignement des cultures orientales). Paris: UNESCO, 1966. Reprinted, Tehran: Pahlavi Library, 1971. Tehran: Offset Press, 1973. (F)
7. a. *Ideals and Realities of Islam*. London: Allen and Unwin, 1966, 1975. Preface by Huston Smith. Boston: Beacon Press, 1972. Paperback edition, 1979, 1985, 1988 (with new preface by Titus Burckhardt). Karachi: Haider Ali Muljee Tahal (n.d.). Cairo: American University of Cairo Press, 1989. Lahore: Suhail Academy, 1993, 1994, 1999.
   b. *Ideali e realtà dell'Islam*. Trans. Donatella Venturi. Milan: Rusconi Editore, 1974. 2nd ed., 1989. (I)
   c. «الاسلام اهدافه وحقائقه»، ترجمة امين فريحة، بيروت، الدارالمتّحدة للنشر، ١٩٧٤. (A)
   d. *Islam, perspectives et réalités*. Trans. H. Crès. Preface by T. Burckhardt. Paris: Buchet-Chastel, 1975. 2nd ed., 1978, 1985, 1991. (F)
   e. *Islam dalam Cita dan Fakta*. Trans. Abdurrahman Wahid and Hashim Wahid. Jakarta: LEPPENAS, 1981. (IN)
   f. *İslâm Idealler ve Gerçekler*. Trans. Ahmet Özel. Istanbul: Akabe

Yayin Ticaret ve Sanayi A.Ş., 1985. (T)

g. *Idee i Wartości Islamu*. Trans. Janusz Danecki. Warszawa: Instytut Wydawniczy Pax, 1988. (PO)

h. *Ideal und Wirklichkeit des Islam*. Trans. Clemens Williams. Munich: Diederichs Gelbe Reihe, 1993 (G)

8\. a. *Islamic Studies: Essays on Law and Society, the Sciences, Philosophy and Sufism*. Beirut: Librarie du Liban, 1967.

b. «دراسات اسلامية، ابحاث متفرّقة في الشرع والمجتمع والعلوم الشرقية والفلسفة والتصوّف في الاطار الاسلامى»، بيروت، الدار المتّحدة للنشر، ١٩٧٥. (A)

1968

9\. a. *Science and Civilization in Islam*. Preface by G. de Santillana. Cambridge: Harvard University Press, 1968. New York: New American Library, 1970. New York, London and Toronto: Mentor Classics, 1970. Lahore: Suhail Academy, 1983, 1987, 1999. Kuala Lumpur: Dewan Pustaka Fajar, 1984. 2nd ed., Cambridge: Islamic Text Society, 1987. New York: Barnes and Noble, 1992.

b. «علم وتمدّن در اسلام»، ترجمهٔ احمد آرام، تهران، نشريه انديشه، ١٣٥٠. (P)

c. *Scienza e civiltà nell'Islam*. Trans. Libero Sosio. Milano: Giangiacomo Feltrinelli, 1977. (I)

d. *Sciences et savoir en Islam*. Trans. Jean-Pierre Guinhut. Paris: Sindbad, 1979. 2nd ed., Paris Sindbad, 1992. (F)

e. *Sains dan Peradaban di dalam Islam*. Trans. J. Mahyudin. Bandung: Pustaka Bandung, 1986. (IN)

f. "اسلامی سائنس اور تهذیب"، همدرد فاونطیشین پریس، کراچی، ۱۹۸۸. (U)

g. *İslâm'da Bilim ve Medeniyet*. Trans. Nabi Avci, Kasim Turhan and Ahmet Ünal. Istanbul: İnsan Yayinlari, 1991. (T)

10. a. *The Encounter of Man and Nature: The Spiritual Crisis of Modern Man*. London: Allen and Unwin, 1968. Reprinted with an additional preface as *Man and Nature*. London: Unwin Paperbacks, 1987. Kuala Lumpur: Foundation for Traditional Studies, 1986. New edition, London: Unwin and Hyman and Harper-Collins, 1990, Chicago: ABC International, 1997.

b. *L'uomo e la natura: la crisi spirituale dell'uomo moderno*. Trans. Giorgio Spina. Milan: Rusconi, 1977. (I)

c. *O Homem e a Natureza*. Trans. Raul Bezzerra Pedreira Filho. Rio de Janeiro: Zahar Editores, 1977. (PG)

d. *L'Homme face à la nature: la crise spirituelle de l'homme moderne*. Trans. Gisele Kondracki and Jeanine Loreau. Paris: Buchet-Chastel, 1978. (F)

e. *Hombre y naturaaleza*. Trans. Héctor Morel. Buenos Aires: Editorial Kier, 1982. (S)

f. *İnsan ve Tabiat*. Trans. Nabi Avci. Istanbul: Yerüzü Yayinlari, 1982; Agaç Yayincilik, 1991. (T)

g. *Susret Čovjeka i Prirode*. Trans. Enes Karić, Sarajevo: Svjetlost, 1992. (BSC)

1970

11. «مجموعهٔ آثار فارسی شیخ اشراق شهاب الدین یحیی سهروردی»، به تصحیح و تحشیه و مقدمهٔ سیّد حسین نصر، با مقدمه و تجزیه و تحلیل فرانسوی هنری کربن، تهران، قسمت ایرانشناسی انستیتوی فرانسوی پژوهشهای علمی در ایران، ۱۹۷۰/۱۳۴۸ و ۱۹۷۷/۱۳۵۵. (P)

Sohrawardî. *Oeuvres philosophiques et mystiques*. Vol. 2. Oeuvres en persan (*Opera Metaphysica et Mystica* III). Tehran: Departement d'Iranologie de l'Institut Français de Recherche; Paris: Adrien-Maisonneuve, 1970. Reprinted, Tehran: Imperial Iranian Academy of Philosophy, 1977. (A, P, and F)

12. «مطالعاتی در هنر دینی»، زیر نظر سیّد حسین نصر و با

چهار مقدّمهٔ از او، تهران، سازمان جشن هنر شیراز،
۱۳۴۹. (P)

13. «معارف اسلامی در جهان معاصر»، تهران، شرکت سهامی
کتاب جیبی، ۱۳۴۹، چاپ دوّم ۱۳۵۳، چاپ سوّم ۱۳۷۱. (P)

1971

14. *Historical Atlas of Iran*. Edited with others and with introductions in English, French, and Persian. Tehran: Tehran University Press, 1971.

«اطلس تاریخی ایران»، نظارت و مقدّمه به زبان‌های فارسی و
انگلیسی و فرانسی، تهران، انتشارات دانشگاه تهران و سازمان
نقشه برداری، ۱۳۵۰. (P)

15. *Verse et Controverse: Les Musulmans*. (M. Arkoun, H. Askari, M. Hamidullah, H. Hanafi, M. K. Hussein, I. Madkhour and S. H. Nasr). Ed. Youkim Moubarac. Le Chrétien en Dialogue avec le Monde, 14. Paris: Beauchesne, 1971. (F)

1972

16. a. *Sufi Essays*. London: Allen and Unwin, 1972. Albany: State University of New York Press, 1973. Paperback ed., New York: Schocken Books, 1977. As *Living Sufism*. London: Allen and Unwin, 1980. Albany: State University of New York Press, 1985. 2nd ed., Albany: State University of New York Press, 1991. New enlarged ed., Chicago: ABC International, 1999.

b. *Il Sufismo*. Trans. Donatella Venturi. Milan: Rusconi Editore, 1975. 2nd ed., 1989. 3rd ed., 1994. (I)

c. «الصوفيّة بين الامس واليوم»، ترجمة الدكتور كمال اليازجى، بيروت، الدارالمتّحدة للنشر، ١٩٧٥. (A)

d. *Essais sur le soufisme*. Trans. Jean Herbert. Paris: Albin Michel, 1980. (F)

e. *Sufismo vivo: Ensayos sobre la dimensión esotérica del Islam*. Trans. F. Blanch and E. Serra. Barcelona: Herder, 1985. (S)

f. *Tasauf Dulu dan Sekarang*. Trans. Abdul Hadi Win. Jakarta: Pustaka Firdaus, 1985. (IN)

1973

17. «ابوريحان بيرونى و ابن سينا، الاسئلة والاجوبة»، به انضمام پاسخهاى دوبارۀ ابوريحان ودفاع ابوسعيد معصومى از ابن

سینا، به تصحیح ومقدمهٔ فارسی و انگلیسی سیّد حسین
نصر و مهدی محقق، تهران، شورای عالی فرهنگ وهنر، ۱۳۵۲؛
کوالالمپور، المعهد العالي العالمي للفکر والحعنارة الاسلامية، ۱۹۹۵. (A)

Al-As'ilah wa'l-ajwibah ("Questions and Answers"). Kuala Lumpur, International Institute of Islamic Thought and Civilization, 1995.

18. «کتابشناسی توصیفی ابوریحان بیرونی»، تهران، شواری عالی فرهنگ و هنر، ۱۳۵۲. (E & P)

Al-Bīrūnī: An Annotated Bibliography. Tehran: High Council of Culture and the Arts, 1973.

19. *Jalāl al-Dīn Rūmī: Supreme Persian Poet and Sage*. Tehran: High Council of Culture and the Arts, 1974.

20. a. *Shi'ite Islam*, by 'Allāmah Ṭabāṭabā'ī. Trans. from the Persian and edited with introduction and notes. Albany: State University of New York Press, 1975. London: Allen and Unwin, 1975; 2nd ed., 1977; Paperback ed., 1979.

b. *Islam Syiah*. Trans. Djohan Effendi. Jakarta: Pustaka Utama Grafiti, 1989. (Includes Nasr's Introduction to W. Chittick, *A Shi'ite Anthology*). (IN)

c. *İslâm'da Şia*. Trans. Kadir Akaras and Abbas Kazimî, Istanbul: Kevser, 1993 (T)

d. *Ši'a u Islamu*. Trans. Amir Ridžanović. Zagreb: Mešihat Islamski Zajednice u Hrvatskoj, 1996. (BSC)

e. مکتب تشیع، ترجمهٔ سید علی ابن الحسن باقری، نیو دهلی، نیوبیلک پریس، ۱٤۰٦، ه. ق. (U)

21. a. With R. Beny. *Persia: Bridge of Turquoise*. Toronto: McClelland and Stewart, 1975. London: Thames and Hudson, 1975. New York: Times and Life, 1975.

b. «ایران پل فیروزه» (فارسی) _ با همکاری رولف بنی و مظفر بختیار، تهران (ورُنا) مک کلاد و استورت، ۱۹۷۸/۱۳۵۷. (P)

c. *La Perse: pont de turquoise*. Fonds Mercator. Hatier, 1976 (F)

d. *Persien*. Luzern: Bucher, 1976. (G)

e. *Persia: un ponte di turchese*. Milano: Arnoldo Mondadori Editore, 1977. (I)

22. a. With W. Chittick. *An Annotated Bibliography of Islamic Science*. Vol. I. Tehran: Imperial Iranian Academy of Philosophy, 1975. Vol. I, 2nd ed., Lahore: Suhail Academy, 1985.

b. With W. Chittick. *An Annotated Bibliography of Islamic Science*. Vol. II. Tehran: Imperial Iranian Academy of Philosophy, 1978. 2nd ed., Lahore: Suhail Academy, 1985.

c. With W. Chittick. *An Annotated Bibliography of Islamic Science*.

Vol. III. Tehran: Mu'assisa-yi muṭāla'āt wa taḥqīqāt, 1991.

1976

23. a. *Islam and the Plight of Modern Man*. London: Longmans, 1976. Kuala Lumpur: Foundation for Traditional Studies, 1987. Lahore: Suhail Academy, 1988, 1994, 1999.
   b. *Islam dan Nestapa Manusia Modern*. Trans. A. Mahyuddin. Bandung: Penerbit Pustaka, 1983. (IN)
   c. *İslam ve Modern İnsanin Çikmazi*. Trans. Ali Ünal. Istanbul: İnsan Yayinlari, 1985. (T)
24. a. *Islamic Science: An Illustrated Study*. London: World of Islam Festival Trust, 1976. Chicago: Kazi Publications (dist.), 1998.
   b. «العلوم في الاسلام»، دراسة مصورة، نقلة الى العربية، مختار الجوهري، حقق النص العربي محمّد السويسي، تونس، دار الجنوب للنشر، ١٣٩٩/١٣٧٨. (A)
   c. *İslâm ve İlim*. Trans. İlhan Kutluer. Istanbul: İnsan Yayinlari, 1989. (T)
   d. «علم در اسلام»، ترجمهٔ احمد آرام، تهران، سروش، ١٣٦٦. (P)
25. *Western Science and Asian Cultures*. New Delhi: Indian Council for Cultural Relations, 1976. Lahore: Iqbal Academy, 1985.

1977

26. *Mélanges offerts à Henry Corbin*. Ed. S. H. Nasr. Tehran: Institute of Islamic Studies, McGill University and The Imperial Iranian Academy of Philosophy, 1977. (F)

27. *Ismā'īlī Contributions to Islamic Culture*. Ed. S. H. Nasr. Tehran: Imperial Iranian Academy of Philosophy, 1977.

1978

28. a. *Ṣadr al-Dīn Shīrāzī and His Transcendent Theosophy*. Tehran and London: Imperial Iranian Academy of Philosophy, 1978. New enlarged edition, Tehran: Institute for Humanities and Cultural Studies, 1997.

b. *Molla Sadrâ ve İlâhi Hikmet*. Trans. Mustafa Armaĝan. Istanbul: İnsan Yayinlari, 1990. (T)

c. *Sadr al-Din Shirazi dan Hikmat Muta'aliyah*. Trans. Baharuddin Ahmad. Kuala Lumpur: Dewan Bahasa dan Pustaka, 1992. 2nd ed., 1993 (M)

d. The 1st chapter of the book translated as *Sta je Transcendentalna filozofija?* (What is Transcendental Philosophy?). Trans. Nevad Kahteran, in *Dijalog*, no. 7, Sarajevo, 1996. (BSC)

1980

29. *Understanding Islam*, by Frithjof Schuon. Trans. into Arabic.

ترجمه با همکاری صلاح الصاوی، «حتی نفهم الاسلام»، فریدهوف شووان، بیروت، الدارالمتحدة للنشر، ۱۹۸۰. (A)

1981

30. a. *Islamic Life and Thought*. London: Allen and Unwin, 1981. Albany: State University of New York Press, 1981. Lahore: Suhail Academy, 1985.

b. *Vida y pensamiento en el Islam*. Trans. Esteve Serra. Barcelona: Herder, 1985. (S)

c. *İslâm'da Düşünce ve Hayat*. Trans. Fatih Tatlilioğlu. Istanbul: İnsan Yayinlari, 1988. (T)

31. a. *Knowledge and the Sacred*. New York: Crossroad, 1981. Kuala Lumpur: Foundation for Traditional Studies, 1987. Lahore: Suhail Academy, 1988, 1999. Reprinted, Albany: State University of New York Press, 1989.

b. *Die Erkenntnis und das Heilige*. Trans. Clemens Wilhelm. Munich: Eugen Diederichs Verlag, 1990. (G)

c. *La Connaissance et le sacré*. Trans. Patrick Laude. Paris: L'Age d'Homme, 1999.

d. *Bilgi ve Kutsal*. Trans. Yusuf Yazar. Istanbul: İz Yayincilik, 1999. (T)

e. "Que es Tradicion?" (from *Knowledge and the Sacred*). Trans.

Armando Hatzacorsian. Mexico City: Ediciones Heliopolis, 1993. (S)

1982

32. a. *Philosophy, Literature and Fine Arts*. Ed. S. H. Nasr. Islamic Education Series. Kent: Hodder and Stoughton, 1982.

b. *Felsefe, Edebiyat ve Güzel Sanatlar*. Trans. Hayriye Yildiz. Istanbul: Akabe, 1989. (T)

c. *Falsafah, Kesusasteraan dan Seni Halus*. Trans. Baharuddin Ahmad. Kuala Lumpur: Dewan Bahasa dan Pustaka, 1989. (M)

d. «الفلسفة والادب والفنون الجميلة من وجهة النظر الاسلامية»، ترجمة عبد الحميد الخريبي، الرياض، عكاظ، ١٤٠٤/١٩٨٤. (A)

1985

33. *Bati Felsefeleri ve İslâm*. Trans. Selahaddin Ayaz. Istanbul: Bir Yayincilik, 1985. (T)

1986

34. a. *The Essential Writings of Frithjof Schuon*. Ed. S. H. Nasr. Warwick: Amity House, 1986. Paperback ed., Rockport: Element Books, 1991.

b. Trans. into Russian by Algis Uždavinis. *Kaunas: Baltijos Aras*, 1996. (R)

1987

35. a. *Islamic Art and Spirituality*. London: Golgonooza Press, 1987. Albany: State University of New York Press, 1987. Delhi: Indira Gandhi National Center for the Arts, 1990.

b. *İslâm Sanatı ve Mâneviyâti*. Trans. Ahmet Demirhan. Istanbul: İnsan Yayinlari, 1992. (T)

c. "هنر و معنویت اسلامی"، ترجمهٔ رحیم قاسمیان، تهران، دفتر مطالعات دینی هنر، ۱۳۷۵. (P)

36. a. *Traditional Islam in the Modern World*. London and New York: KPI, 1987; Paperback ed., 1990. Kuala Lumpur: Foundation for Traditional Studies, 1989. Lahore: Suhail Academy, 1997.

b. *Traditionalni Islam in Modernom Svijetu*. Trans. Zulejha Ridanović. Sarajevo: El Kalem, Rijaset islamske zajednice u BiH, 1994. (BSC)

c. *Modern Dünyada Geleneksel İslam*. Trans. Savaş Şafak Barkçin-Hüsamettin Arslan. Istanbul: İnsan Yayinlari, 1989. (T)

d. *L'Islam traditional face au monde moderne*. Trans. Gisèle Kondracki. Paris: L'Age d'Homme, 1993. (F)

37. *Islamic Spirituality: Foundations*. Ed. S. H. Nasr. Vol. 19 of World Spirituality: An Encyclopedic History of the Religious

Quest. New York: Crossroad, 1987, 1991. London: Routledge and Kegan Paul, 1987.

1988

38. a. *Muhammad: Man of Allah*. London: Muhammadi Trust, 1982; Reprinted 1988. New ed. as *Muhammad: Man of God*. Chicago: Kazi Publications, 1995.

b. *Muhammad: Kekasih Allah*. Trans. Bachtiar Effendi, Bandung: Mizan, 1984; 2nd ed., 1989. (IN)

c. *Muhammad-Insan Kamil*. Trans. Baharuddin Ahmad, Kuala Lumpur: Dewan Bahasa dan Pustaka, 1993. (M)

39. *Shi'ism: Doctrines, Thought and Spirituality*. Ed. S. H. Nasr with H. Dabashi and S.V.R. Nasr. Albany: State University of New York Press, 1988.

1989

40. *Expectation of the Millenium: Shi'ism in History*. Ed. S. H. Nasr with H. Dabashi and S.V.R. Nasr. Albany: State University of New York Press, 1989.

1991

41. *Islamic Spirituality: Manifestations*. Ed. S. H. Nasr. Vol. 20 of World Spirituality: An Encyclopedic History of the Religious

Quest. New York: Crossroad, 1991. Paperback ed., London: Routledge and Kegan Paul, 1992. Paperback, 1997.

42. a. *Religion and Religions: The Challenge of Living in a Multi-religious World.* The Rey H. Witherspoon Lectures in Religious Studies, The University of North Carolina at Charlotte, April 8, 1985. Charlotte: 1991.

b. *Religija i religije: Izazov zivljenja u multire ligijskom svijetu,* trans. by Zulejha Ridanović. Sarajevo: The Legal Center, 1996. (BCS)

c. In Enes Karić, *Ljudska Prava u Kontek-stu Islamsko-Zapadne Debate.* Sarajevo: Pravni Centar, 1996, 11-41. (BSC)

43. *Religion of the Heart: Essays Presented to Frithjof Schuon on his Eightieth Birthday.* Ed. S. H. Nasr with W. Stoddart. Washington D.C.: Foundation for Traditional Studies, 1991.

1993

44. a. *The Need for a Sacred Science.* Albany: State University of New York Press, 1993.

b. *Bir Kutsal Bilim İhtiyaci,* Trans. Şehabeddin Yalçin. Istanbul: İnsan Yayinlari, 1995. (T)

c. «نیاز به علم مقدس»، ترجمهٔ حسن میانداری، قم، انتشارات طه، ۱۳۷۹. (P)

1994

45. a. *In Quest of the Sacred: The Modern World in the Light of Tradition*. Ed. S. H. Nasr with Katherine O'Brien. Oakton, 1993.

b. *Kutsalin Peşinde*. Trans. Süleyman Erol Gündüz. Istanbul: İnsan Yayinlari, 1995. (T)

46. a. *A Young Muslim's Guide to the Modern World*. Chicago: Kazi Publications, 1993; Cambridge: Islamic Text Society, 1994. Petaling Jaya: Mekar Publishers, 1994. Lahore: Suhail Academy, 1998.

b. *Menjelajah Dunia Modern: Bimbingan untuk Kaum Muda Muslim*. Trans. Hasti Tarekat. Bandung: Penerbit Mizan, Khazanah ilmu- ilmu Islam,1994. (IN)

c. *Genç Müslümana Modern Dünya Rehberi*. Trans. Şahabeddin Yalçın. Istanbul: İz Yayincilik, 1995. (T)

d. "جوان مسلمان در دنیای متجدد"، ترجمهٔ مرتضی اسدی، تهران، طرح نو، ۱۳۷۳. (P)

e. *Vodič Mladom Musulmanu*. Trans. Aida Abadžić-Hodžić. Sarajevo: Ljiljan, 1998 (BSC)

47. *Islam and the Challenge of the 21st Century* (edited from tape of lecture given in Kuala Lumpur in 1993). Ed. H. Rahman and E. Yeahman. Kuala Lumpur: Dewan Bahasa dam Pustaka, 1993.

1995

48. *Makaleler I* (Turkish translation of several articles and reviews). Trans. Şahabeddin Yalçın. Istanbul: İnsan Yayinlari, 1995.

1996

49. *The History of Islamic Philosophy*. 2 vols. Ed. S. H. Nasr with O. Leaman. London: Routledge, 1996.
50. *The Islamic Intellectual Tradition in Persia*. Ed. S. H. Nasr with M. Aminrazavi. London: Curzon Press, 1996.
51. *Söyleşiler* (Conversations). Istanbul: İnsan Yayinlari, 1996.
52. *Religion and the Order of Nature*. New York and Oxford: Oxford University Press, 1996.
53. *Islami Tradicional Dhe Problemi I Shkencës Moderne*. Trans. Selim Syleimani. Drita e Jetës, 1996, 1997. (AL)
54. a. *Mecca the Blessed, Medina the Radiant*. Photos by Ali Nomachi. New York: Aperture, 1997; Hong Kong: SSY, 1997.
   b. *Mekka--Die heiligen Stätten*, Trans. Eva Dempewolf. Munich: Frederking and Thaler, 1998 (G)
   c. Japanese Translation. Trans. Kosugi Yasushi. Tokyo: Shueisha, 1997. (J)
55. *Makaleler II*. Trans. Şehabeddin Yalçın. Istanbul: İnsan Yayinlari, 1997.

1998

56. *Islamic-Christian Dialogue: Problems and Obstacles to be Pondered and Overcome*. Washington, D.C.: Center for Muslim-Christian Understanding, 1998.

1999

57. *Poems of the Way*. Oakton, Va.: Foundation for Traditional Studies (VA), 1999.
58. *The Spiritual and Religious Dimension of the Environmental Crisis*. London: Temenos Academy, 1999.
59. *An Anthology of Philosophy in Persia*, with Mehdi Aminrazavi, vol. 1. New York: Oxford University Press, 1999.
60. *An Anthology of Philosophy in Persia*, with Mehdi Aminrazavi, vol. 2. New York: Oxford University Press, 2000.

ARTICLES AND REVIEWS

1958

1. Review of *Alchemy*, by E. Holmyard, and *Forgérons et alchimistes*, by M. Eliade. *Isis* 49 (December 1958): 451-53.
2. Review of *Late Medieval Mysticism*, by R. C. Petry. *Speculum* 33 (1958): 430-31.

1959

3. Review of *Psychologie d'Ibn Sina*, by J. Bakoš. *Isis* 50 (September 1959): 273-74.

4. "The Polarization of Being."
   a. *Pakistan Philosophical Journal* 3 (October 1959): 8-12.
   b. *Proceedings of the Pakistan Philosophical Congress*, 1959.
   c. *Islamic Studies*, 134-40.
   d. *Islamic Life and Thought*, 182-87.
   e. «وجود و تکسّر آن، مجلّهٔ دانشکدهٔ ادبیات تهران، شمارهٔ ۱، سال هفتم، مهر ۱۳۳۸، ص ۵۱_۵۷. (P)
   f. «الوجود وتکسّره»، دعوة الحقّ، العدد الاوّل، السنة الحادية عشرة، شعبان ۱۳۸۷، نوامبر ۱۹۶۷ (ترجمة عبد اللطيف سعداني). (A)

5. "Spiritual and Temporal Authority in Islam."
   a. *Iqbal* 8 (July 1959): 38-44.
   b. *Pendār* 1 (Summer 1960): 5-7.
   c. *Islamic Studies*, 6-13.

6. نقد کتاب «تفکر سیاسی اسلام»، به قلم ف. روزنثال، مجلهٔ

راهنمای کتاب، سال ۲، شمارهٔ شهریور ۱۳۳۸،
ص ۳۲۰_۳۲۳. (P)

7. نقد کتاب «اسلام و اعراب»، به قلم ر. لانداو، مجلّهٔ راهنمای کتاب، سال ۲، شمارهٔ ۳، آذر ۱۳۳۸، ص ۴۴۷_۴۵۰. (P)

8. نقد کتاب «مدخلی براصول تصوّف»، به قلم ت. بورکهارت، مجلّهٔ راهنمای کتاب، سال ۲، شمارهٔ ۴، دی ۱۳۳۸، ص ۶۱۷_۶۲۰. (P)

1960

9. "A Comparative Study of the Cosmologies of Aristotle and Ibn Sīnā and their Place in the Islamic Tradition."
   a. *Pakistan Philosophical Journal* 3 (January 1960): 13-28.
   b. *Islamic Studies*, 39-55.
   c. *Islamic Life and Thought*, 83-95.

10. *Review of Kitāb al-anwā'*, by Ibn Qutayba. *Isis* 51 (March 1960): 107-8.

11. «نظریّات ابو ریحان بیروني دربارهٔ معنی طبیعت و روشهای

تحقیق در علوم طبیعی»، مجلّهٔ دانشکدهٔ ادبیات، سال هفتم، شمارهٔ ٤، تیر ١٣٣٩، ص ٧٨ _ ٩٠ (استخراج از نظر متفکّران اسلامی دربارهٔ طبیعت، ص ١٦٦ _ ١٨٠). (P)

12. نقد کتاب «خود آموز حکمت مشّاء»، به قلم دکتر محمّد خزائلی، مجلّهٔ راهنمای کتاب، سال ٣، شمارهٔ ٤، تیر ١٣٣٩، ص ١٨٢_١٨٥. (P)

1961

13. "Ṣadr al-Dīn Shīrāzī: His Life, Doctrines and Significance."
   a. *Indo-Iranica* 14 (December 1961): 6-16.
   b. *Islamic Studies,* 113-26.
   c. *Islamic Life and Thought*, 158-68.
14. Translation of article by Sayyid Abu'l-Ḥasan Qazwīnī, "The Life of Ṣadra al-Muta'allihīn Shīrāzī and a Discussion of Motion in the Category of Substance." *Mullā Ṣadrā Commemoration Volume*, 7-21.
15. Translation of 'Allāmah Sayyid Muḥammad Ḥusayn Ṭabāṭabā'ī, "Ṣadr al-Dīn Muḥammad ibn Ibrāhīm Shīrāzī: The Renewer of Islamic Philosophy in the 17th Century." *Mullā Ṣadrā Commemoration Volume*, 22-34.

16. "Religion and Secularism: Their Meaning and Manifestation in Islam History."
   a. *Islamic Quarterly* 6 (July and October 1961), 118-26.
   b. *Islamic Studies,* 14-25.
   c. *Islamic Life and Thought*, 7-15.
   d. "Religija i sekularizam--njihovo značenje i manifestovanje u muslimanskoj historiji." *Glasnik VSA-2* (Sarajevo) 5 (September-October 1982): 533-542. (BSC)
   e. *Studies in Tradition* 1, No. 3 (Summer 1992): 54-62.

17. نقد کتاب «شش بال علم»، به قلم جرج سارتون و ترجمهٔ احمد آرام، مجلّهٔ راهنمای کتاب، سال ٤، شمارهٔ ١، فروردین ١٣٤٠، ص ٥٥_٥٨. (P)

18. a. (الف.) «آشنائی با ملا صدرا در مغرب زمین»، «یادنامهٔ ملاصدرا»، تهران، ١٣٤٠. (P)
   b. (ب.) «معارف اسلامی»، ص ١٣٢_١٤٦. (P)

19. ترجمهٔ «اوّلین ظهور اسمعیلیّه در ایران»، به قلم پروفسور س. استرن، مجلّهٔ دانشکدهٔ ادبیات، سال هشتم، مهر ١٣٤٠، ص ١_١٢. (P)

20. a. (الف.) «ملا صدرا در هندوستان»، مجلّهٔ راهنمای کتاب، سال چهارم، دی ۱۳٤۰ (همچنین سرگذشت ملّا صدرا در این شماره). (P)

b. (ب.) «معارف اسلامی»، ص ۱۲۳_۱۳۳. (P)

1962

21. a. (الف.) «نظری به ادیان عالم»، مجلّهٔ دانشکدهٔ ادبیات، شمارهٔ نهم، فروردین ۱۳٤۱، ص ۲۳_۸۸. (P)

b. (ب.) «معارف اسلامی»، ص ۱۲۲_۲٤۷. (P)

c. (ج.) خلاصهٔ این مقاله در مجلّهٔ کاوش، تیر ۱۳٤۱، ص ۱۱_۱۵. (P)

d. (د.) «نظرة علی ادیان العالم»، دعوة الحقّ، العدد السادس والسابع _ السنة الثامنة، ذوالحجّة _ محرّم ۱۳۸٤، ص ۱۸_۲۵، العدد الثامن، صفر ۱۳۸۵، ص ۳۵_٤۰ (ترجمة عبد اللطيف سعداني). (A)

22. a. (الف.) «هرمس و نوشته‌های هرمسی در جهان اسلامی»، مجلّهٔ دانشکدهٔ ادبیات، شمارهٔ ۲، سال دهم، دی ۱۳٤۱، ص ۱٤۰_۱۷۳. (P)

b. (ب.) «مجموعهٔ سخنرانی‌ها و خطابه های انجمن فلسفه و علوم انسانی»، تهران، ۱۳٤٥، نشریهٔ شمارهٔ ۳، ص ۱٥۹_۱۹۳. (P)

c. (ج.) «معارف اسلامی»، ص ٥۹_۹٤. (P)

d. "Hermes and Hermetic Writings in the Islamic World." *Islamic Studies*, 63-89.

e. *Islamic Life and Thought*, 102-19.

23. نقد کتاب «شرح حال و آراء فلسفی ملّا صدرا»، به قلم سیّد جلال‌الدین آشتیانی، راهنمای کتاب، سال پنجم، دی ۱۳٤۱، شمارهٔ ۱۰، ص ۸۹٤_۸۹۷. (P)

1963

24. Review of *A Muslim Saint of the Twentieth Century*, by M. Lings. *Islamic Quarterly* 7 (January and June 1963): 53-6.

25. "Shihāb al-Dīn Suhrawardī al-Maqtūl."

a. *A History of Muslim Philosophy*. Vol. 1. (ed.) M.M. Sharif. Weisbaden: O. Harrassowitz, 1963, 372-98.

b. *Historija Islamske Filozofije*, I. Trans. H. Susić. Zaghreb, 1988. (BSC)

c. «شهاب الدین سهروردی مقتول»، ترجمهٔ رضا ناظمی، در م. م. شریف، «تاریخ فلسفه در اسلام»، تهران ـ ۱۳۹۲، ص ۵۲۹ـ۵۹۰. (P)

d. *The Islamic Intellectual Tradition in Persia*. Ed. Mehdi Aminrazavi. London: Curzon Press, 1996, 160-86.

e. "Şihabeddin Sühreverdi el-Maktul" in *İslam Düşüncesi Tarihi*, *İnsan Yayınları*, Vol. 1, 1990, 411-35. (T)

26. "Fakr al-Dīn Rāzī."

a. *A History of Muslim Philosophy*. Vol. 1, 642-56.

b. *Historija Islamski Filozofije*, I. Trans. H. Susić. (BSC)

c. «فخرالدین رازی»، ترجمهٔ علی اصغر حلبی، «تاریخ فلسفه در اسلام»، در م. م. شریف، تهران، ۱۳۹۵، ص ۸۱ـ۹۸. (P)

d. *The Islamic Intellectual Tradition in Persia*. Ed. Mehdi Aminrazavi, 160-86.

e. "Fahreddin Rāzi" in *İslam Düşüncesi Tarihi*, *İnsan Yayınları*, Vol. 2, 1990, 267-81. (T)

27. "The Pertinence of Studying Islamic Philosophy Today."

a. *Pakistan Philosophical Journal* 7 (October 1963): 79-87.

b. *Islamic Studies,* 97-106.

c. *Islamic Life and Thought*, 145-52.

d. "L'importance de la recherche philosophique à notre époque." *Le Monde islamique* (Mai 1972): 14-17. (F)

e. «اهمیت تحقیق در فلسفهٔ اسلامی در عصر حاضر»، مجلّهٔ دانشکدهٔ ادبیات، شمارهٔ ٤، سال دهم، تیر ١٣٤٢، ص ٤٢٢_٤٢٣. (P)

f. (ه.) «معارف اسلامی»، ص ١_١٤. (P)

g. (و.) «اهمية التحقيق في الفلسفهٔ الاسلامية»، ترجمة صلاح الصاوي، مجلّهٔ معارف اسلامی (المعارف الاسلامية)، عدد ١٤، جمادی الاولی ١٣٩٣، ص ١٤_٢١. (A)

h. "Primjejerenost proucavanja islamske filozofije danas" *Islamska misao*, No. 157 (Sarajevo, 1991): 46-51.

28. نقد کتاب «داستانهای مثنوی»، به قلم ا. ج. آربری، راهنمای کتاب، سال ششم، شمارهٔ ٣، خرداد ١٣٤٢، ص ٢٠٨_٢٠٩. (P)

29. a. (الف.) «فلسفه»، «کتاب دائرة المعارف ایرانشهر»، زیر نظر
علی اصغر حکمت، تهران، جلد اوّل، ۱۳٤۲، ص
٦۲۰_٦۳٥. (P)

b. (ب.) «معارف اسلامی»، ص ۱٥_٤٤. (P)

1964

30. "Contemplation and Nature in the Perspective of Sufism."
    a. *Iqbal* 12 (January 1964): 14-21.
    b. *Islamic Studies*, 141-49.
    c. *Islamic Life and Thought*, 200-206.
31. Review of *Understanding Islam*, by F. Schuon. *Islamic Studies* (Karachi) 3 (March 1964): 107-8.
32. Preface to Mullā Muḥammad Ja'far Lāhījānī, *Sharḥ risālat al-mashā'ir Mullā Ṣadrā*. (ed.) S. J. Ashtiyani. Mashhad: Khorasan Press, 1964, 1-10.
33. "Islamic Philosophy: Re-orientation or Re-understanding?"
    a. *Pakistan Philosophical Journal* 8 (July 1964): 52-56.
    b. *Re-orientation of Muslim Philosophy*. Lahore: Pakistan Philosophical Congress, 1965, 1-5.
    c. *Islamic Studies*, 107-12.
    d. *Islamic Life and Thought*, 153-57.

34. Review of *The Sufis*, by I. Shah.
   a. *Islamic Studies* (Karachi) 3 (December 1964): 531-33.
   b. (ب.) مجلّة الابحاث، السنة ۱۸، الجزء ۱، ۱۹٦٥، ص ۹۱_۹٦. (A)

35. "Mullā Ṣadrā as a Source for the History of Muslim Philosophy."
   a. *Islamic Studies* (Karachi) 3 (September 1964): 309-14.
   b. *Proceedings of the Twenty-Sixth International Congress of Orientalists*. Vol. 4. *Poona*, 1970: 307-10.
   c. *Islamic Studies*, 127-33.
   d. *Islamic Life and Thought*, 169-73.

36. a. Article in *Changes in Muslim Personal Law*. New Delhi: Caxton Press, 1964, 54-64.
   b. Revised as "The Question of Changes in Muslim Personal Law." *Islamic Studies*, 26-34.
   c. "Faut-il modifier la loi personelle en Islam?" *Le Monde non-chrétien* 87 (Juillet-September 1968): 50-57. (F)

37. ترجمه و مقدمهٔ مقالهٔ «ودانتا»، به قلم فریدهوف شوان، مجلّهٔ مهر، شمارهٔ اوّل، سال دهم، بهار ۱۳٤۳، ص ۳٦_٤۳. (P)

38. نقد کتاب «کتاب المشاعر صدرالدین شیرازی»، تصحیح هنری کربن، مجلّهٔ راهنمای کتاب، سال هفتم، شمارهٔ اوّل،

پائیز ۱۳۴۳، ص ۶۴ـ۶۷. (P)

39. ترجمهٔ مقالهٔ «مقام ملّاصدرای شیرازی در فلسفهٔ ایران»، به قلم هنری کربن، مجلّهٔ دانشکدهٔ ادبیات، سال دوازدهم، شمارهٔ ۱، مهر ۱۳۴۳، ص ۱ـ۳۴. (P)

40. «کنگرهٔ فلسفی پاکستان»، راهنمای کتاب، سال هفتم، شمارهٔ دوّم، زمستان ۱۳۴۳، ص ۳۹۲ـ۴۰۴. (P)

41. مقدّمهٔ فارسی بر «شرح رسالهٔ المشاعر ملّا صدرا»، تالیف حکیم محقّق حاج محمّد جعفر لاهیجانی، تصحیح سیّد جلال‌ـ الدین آشتیانی، مشهد، ۱۳۴۳، ص ۱ـ۳. (P)

1965

42. "Islamic Arts and Sciences." *Muslim World* (Karachi) 2 (January 1965): 2 & 5.

43. "The Sacred Law of Islam." *Muslim World* (Karachi) 2 (March 1965): 2.

44. "The Spiritual Path in the Quran." *Muslim World* (Karachi) 2 (April 1965): 2.

45. "Islamic Theology." *Muslim World* (Karachi) 2 (April 1965): 2.

46. a. "Islamic Art." *Muslim World* (Karachi) 2 (May 1965): 2 and 4.
b. "The Philosophy of Islamic Art." *Wisdom* (Sind) 3 (1965): 11-13.
c. «الفن الاسلامی»، دروب، السنة الثالثة عشرة، العدد الرابع والعشرون، حزيران ١٩٦٥، ص ٨ـ١٠. (A)

47. "Science in the Muslim World." *Muslim World* (Karachi) 2 (May 1965): 2.

48. "Introduction à la mystique musulmane: le soufisme." *Les Cahiers de l'Oronte* (Beirut) (Juillet-Aout 1965): 8-12. (F)

49. a. "The Unity of the Intellectual and Philosophical Tradition of Iran, Turkey and Pakistan." *Papers Read at the R.C.D. Seminar on Common Cultural Heritage*. Tehran: R.C.D. Cultural Institute, 1965, 135-37.
b. (ب.) «ایران، پاکستان و ترکیه: اتّحاد فرهنگی و معنوی آنان»، ترجمهٔ سیّد مرتضی موسوی، مجلّهٔ پاکستان، شمارهٔ ۸۰ـ۸۱، آبان ۱۳۴۸، ص ۷ـ۹. (P)

50. "Al-Ṭarīqah: The Spiritual Path of Islam." *Middle East Forum* (Winter 1965): 32-33.

51. a. "Cosmographie en l'Iran pre-islamique et islamique: le problème de la continuité dans la civilization irannienne." *Arabic and Islamic Studies in Honor of Hamilton A. R. Gibb*. Ed. G. Makdisi. Leiden: E.J. Brill, 1965, 507-24. (F)

b. "Cosmography in Pre-Islamic and Islamic Persia." Tehran: The Cultural Committee for the Celebration of the 2500th Anniversary of the Founding of the Persian Empire, 1971. (Monograph).

c. *Ta'thīr ma'nawī-i Irān dar Pakistan.* Ed. J. Qasimi. Lahore: Punjab Endowments Organization, 1971, 1-20.

d. "Cosmografia e continuità culturale nell'Iran." *Conoscenza religioso* 5 (1974): 252-67. (I)

e. *History of Persian Literature.* Ed. Y. Jaffery. Delhi: Trevini Press, 1981, 37-57.

f. *The Islamic Intellectual Tradition in Persia.* Ed. Mehdi Aminrazavi, 7-38.

52. a. "The Meaning of Nature in Various Intellectual Perspectives in Islam." *Islamic Quarterly* 9 (January-March 1965): 25-29.

b. "Note on the Meaning of Nature in Various Intellectual Perspectives in Islam." *La filosofia della natura nel Medioevo.* Milan: Societa Editrice Vita e Pensiero, 1966, 236-41.

c. *Islamic Studies*, 56-62.

d. *Islamic Life and Thought*, 96-101.

53. "The Cosmos in the Visionary Recitals of Ibn Sīnā." *The World of Philosophy.* (ed.) C.A. Qadir. Lahore: Sh. Muhammad Ashraf, 1965, 343-45. (Revised Version of "Nature and the Visionary Recitals", *An Introduction to Islamic Cosmological Doctrines*, 15-40.)

54. a. "Islam, the Last Religion and the Primordial Religion: Its

Universal and Particular Traits." (from *Ideals and Realities of Islam*, 15-40.)

b. (الف.) «الاسلام: صفاتة الكلّيّة والجزئيّة»، حوار، العدد ١٧، تموز ـ آب ١٩٦٥، ص ٥ـ٢٣. (A)

c. *Islamic Perspective* 1 (March 1971): 6-20.

d. *The Voice of Islam* 21 (October 1972): 678-90.

e. "Ideaux et Realités de Islam: L'Islam dernier religion et religion primordial, ses aspects universels et particuliers." *Le Monde islamique* (Mars-Avril 1973): 3-5; (Juin-Juillet 1973): 3-5 & 20; (November 1973): 4-5 & 24; (Mars 1974): 20-21. (F)

f. "Islam--posljednja I praiskonkska vjera--univerzalne I projedinacne osebujnosti" *Islamska misao*, No. 83 (Sarajevo, 1985): 3-13.

55. a. (الف.) «الطريقة واصولها في القرآن الكريم»، الابحاث، السنة ١٨، الجزء ٢، حزيران ١٩٦٥، ص ١٣٩ـ١٦١، ترجمة محمود زيد. (A)

b. (ب.) خلاصه در الاخاء، العدد ٧٠، ٧ شعبان ١٣٨٥، ص ١٢، ٣٧ والعدد ٧٢، شوال ١٣٨٥، ص ٣٠. (A)

56. a. (الف.) «نفوذ فلسفهٔ اسلامی در مکتب‌های فلسفی

مغرب زمین»، مجلّهٔ رادیو ایران، شمارهٔ ۱۱۱، اسفند
۱۳۴۴، ص ۱۲_۱۳ و ۲۳. (P)

b. (ب.) «معارف اسلامی»، ص ۱۴۷_۱۵۵. (P)

1966

57. "Mullā Ṣadrā." *Encyclopedia of Philosophy*. Vol. 5. New York: Macmillan, 1966, 411-13.

58. a. "Le maître spirituel d'après la littérature soufie persane." *Hermès* 4 (1966-67): 119-29. (F)

b. "The Sufi Master as Exemplified in Persian Sufi Literature." *Iran* 5 (1967): 35-40.

c. *Studies in Comparative Religion* (Summer 1970): 140-49.

d. *Sufi Essays*, 57-67.

59. "Islam and the Encounter of Religions."

a. *Islamic Quarterly* 10 (July-December 1966): 47-68.

b. *Proceedings of the XIth International Congress of the International Association for the History of Religions*. Vol. 3, *The Role of Historical Scholarship in Changing the Relations among Religions*. Leiden: E.J. Brill, 1968, 23-42.

c. Also published as a separate brochure by the Islamic Cultural Center, London: (Several times).

d. *Sufi Essays*, 123-51.

e. "O Islã e o Encontro das Religiões." *Islã o credo é a conduta.* (eds.) R.S. Bartholo and A.E. Campos. Rio de Janiero: Imago Editora, 1990, 235-64. (PG)

f. «اسلام کا سابقه دوسری مذاهب سی»، مجلّهٔ اسلام اور عصر جدید (دهلی)، جلد ۱، شمارهٔ ۱، ۱۹۶۹، ص ۲۹_۴۷، شمارهٔ ۲، ۱۹۶۹، ص ۳۶_۵۱. (U)

g. "Islam i susret religija." *Takvim* (1986), 41-76. (BSC)

60. "Why We Should Keep the Lunar Hegira Calendar"

a. *Muslim World* (Karachi) 3 (March 1966): 2.

b. *Al-Serāt* 6, No. 1 (1980), 63-65.

c. *Islamic Life and Thought*, 216-17.

61. Review of *Studies in Islamic Culture in the Indian Environment*, by A. Ahmad. *Islamic Quarterly* 10 (January-June 1966): 40-41.

62. "The Immutable Principles of Islam and Western Education."

a. *Muslim World* (January 1966): 4-9.

b. *Iqbal Review* (October 1966): 82-87.

c. In summary form as "The Aga Khan Chair." *Africa Ismaili* 2 (August 1969): 3-5 & 7.

d. In summary form as "Islam and Western Education: Duties of Muslim Scholars." *Muslim World* (Karachi) 3 (April 1966): 2 & 6; and 3 (May 1966): 4.

e. *Al-Serāt* 6, No. 2 (June 1980): 5-10.

f. "The Immutable Principles of Islam and Westernised Education in the Islamic World." *Islamic Life and Thought*, 31-36.

g. "Neprmjenjiva nacela islama i zapadnjacko obrazovanje u islamskom svijetu," *Znakovi vremena*, No. 1 (Sarajevo, 1996): 78-83 (extract from *Ideals and Realities of Islam*).

h. «اسلام کی غیر متغیر اصول اور اسلامی دنیا مین مغربی نظام تعلیم»، ترجمۂ محمد یوسف عرفان، جنوری ـ مارچ، اقبالیات، ۱۹۸۷، ص ۱۴۵ـ۱۵۲. (U)

63. "The School of Isfahan."

a. *A History of Muslim Philosophy*, Vol. 2. Ed. M. M. Sharif. Weisbadon: O. Harrassowitz, 1966, 904-32.

b. *Historija islamske filosofije,* II. Zaghreb, 1988. (BSC)

c. «مکتب اصفهان»، «تاریخ فلسفه در اسلام»، م. م. شریف، ترجمۂ عبد الحسین آذرنگ، تهران ـ ۱۳۹۵، ص ۴۴۳ـ ۴۷۴. (P)

d. *The Islamic Intellectual Tradition in Persia*. Ed. Mehdi Aminrazavi, 352-80.

e. "Isfahan Okulu" in *İslam Düşüncesi Tarihi. İnsan Yayınları,* Vol. 3, 1991, 125-52. (T)

64. "Ṣadr al-Dīn Shīrāzī (Mullā Ṣadrā)."

a. *A History of Muslim Philosophy*, Vol. 2, 952-61.
b. *Historija islamske filosofije*, II. Zaghreb, 1988. (BSC).
c. «صدرالدین شیرازی (ملّا صدرا)»، «تاریخ فلسفه در اسلام»، م. م. شریف، ترجمهٔ کامران فانی، ص ۴۷۵_۵۰۸. (P)
d. *The Islamic Intellectual Tradition in Persia*. Ed. Mehdi Aminrazavi, 381-410.
e. "Sadreddin Şirāzī (Molla Sadra)" in *İslam Düşüncesi Tarihi, İnsan Yayınları*, Vol. 3, 1991, 153-81. (T)

65. "Natural History."
a. *A History of Muslim Philosophy*, Vol. 2, 1316-32.
b. *Historija islamske filosofije*, II. Zaghreb, 1988. (BSC)
c. *Islamic Life and Thought*, 124-41.
d. "Tabiat Tarihi" in *İslam Düşüncesi Tarihi*, *İnsan Yayınları*, Vol. 4, 1991, 107-23. (T)

66. "Renaissance in Iran: Ḥājī Mullā Hādī Sabziwārī."
a. *A History of Muslim Philosophy*. Vol. 2, 1543-56.
b. *Historija islamski filosofije,* II. Zaghreb, 1988. (BSC)
c. *The Islamic Intellectual Tradition in Persia*. Ed. Mehdi Aminrazavi, 433-47.
d. "İran'da Rönesans: Haci Molla Hādi Sebzivari" in *İslam Düşüncesi Tarihi*, *İnsan Yayınları*, Vol. 4, 1991, 331-43. (T)

67. "Some Metaphysical Principles Pertaining to Nature." *Tomorrow* (Summer 1966): 167-78; (Autumn 1966): 210-22. (extract from

Encounter of Man and Nature, 81-113).

68. Introduction to *Sharḥ-i muqaddimah-yi Qayṣarī bar Fuṣūṣ al-Ḥikam*, by S. J. Ashtiyani. Mashhad: Bastan Press, 1966, 1-5.

69. مقدّمهٔ فارسی و ترجمهٔ مقدّمهٔ فرانسوی استاد هنری کربن بر «شرح مقدّمهٔ قیصری»، تالیف سیّد جلال‌الدین آشتیانی، کتابفروشی باستان، مشهد، ۱۳۴۵، ص ه ـ ک. (P)

70. «نکاتی چند دربارهٔ شیخ اشراق شهاب الدین سهروردی»، مجلّهٔ معارف اسلامی (نشریهٔ سازمان اوقاف) شمارهٔ اوّل، شهریور ۱۳۴۵، ص ۱۶ـ۱۸. (P)

71. a. (الف.) «برخی مسائل مربوط به تاریخ فلسفه در ایران اسلامی»، راهنمای کتاب، سال نهم، شمارهٔ سوّم، شهریور ۱۳۴۵، ص ۲۳۸ـ۲۴۶. (P)

b. (ب.) تلاش، شمارهٔ ۳، بهمن ۱۳۴۵، ص ۱۱۲ـ۱۱۵. (P)

c. (ج.) «معارف اسلامی»، ص ۴۵ـ۵۶. (P)

72. نقد کتاب «جهان فلسفه»، راهنمای کتاب، سال نهم، شمارهٔ

پنجم، دی ۱۳٤٥، ص ٥۳۳_٥۳٦. (P)

73. نقد کتاب «تذکرة الاولیای عطّار»، راهنمای کتاب، سال نهم، شمارۀ چهارم، آبان ۱۳٤٥، ص ٤۳۰_٤۳۲. (P)

74. a. (الف.) «مختصری دربارۀ تحقیقات نوین در تاریخ نجوم اسلامی»، مجلّۀ معارف اسلامی، شمارۀ دوّم، اسفند ۱۳۳٥، ص ۳٥_٤۰. (P)

b. (ب.) «معارف اسلامی»، ص ۱۰۳_۱۱۱. (P)

1967

75. a. "Seventh Century Sufism and the School of Ibn 'Arabī: A Spiritual and Cultural Heritage of Iran, Pakistan and Turkey." *Journal of the Regional Cultural Institute* (Iran, Pakistan, Turkey) 1 (Summer 1967): 35-43.

b. "Ibn 'Arabī in the Persian Speaking World." *Memorial Mohyiddine Ibn 'Arabī.* Cairo: Conseil Superieur des Arts, des Lettres et des Sciences Sociales, 1969, 357-63.

c. *Sufi Essays*, 97-103.

76. "Sufism and the Integration of Man."

a. *Muslim World* (Karachi) 4 (May 20, 1967): 2 & 6; (May 27,

1967): 6; (June 3, 1967): 6.

b. *Journal of the Regional Cultural Institute* (Iran, Pakistan, Turkey) 1 (Summer 1967): 35-43.

c. *Islamic Review and Arab Affairs* (September 1967): 11-14.

d. *Africa Ismaili* (new series) 1, No. 6 (April 4, 1969): 4-8.

e. *Al-Islam* (Singapore) 1 (April-June 1970): 20-25.

f. *God and Man in Contemporary Islamic Thought*. Ed. C. Malik. Beirut: American University of Beirut, 1972, 144-51.

g. *The Ways of Religion*. Ed. R. Eastman. San Francisco: Canfield, 1975, 476-84.

h. *Sufi Essays*, 43-56.

77. Preface to *al-Shawāhid al-rubūbiyyah*, by Ṣadr al-Dīn Shīrāzī. Ed. S. J. Ashtiyani. Mashhad: Mashhad University Press, 1967, 3-10.

78. "Ṣadr al-Dīn Shīrāzī." *Muslim World* (Karachi) 4 (May, 1967): 5 (Extracts from *Islamic Studies*, 113-17).

79. a. (الف.) «از کیمیای جابر تا شیمی رازی»، مجلّهٔ معارف اسلامی (نشریهٔ سازمان اوقاف)، شمارهٔ چهارم، آبان ۱۳٤٦، ص ۲۹_۳۲. (P)

b. (ب.) «معارف اسلامی»، ص ۹۵_۱۰۱. (P)

c. "From the Alchemy of Jābir to the Chemistry of Rāzī." *Islamic Studies*, 90-95.

d. *Islamic Life and Thought,* 120-23.

80. a. (الف.) ترجمهٔ مقالهٔ «روح هنر اسلامی»، به قلم تیتوس بورکهارت، مجلّهٔ هنر و مردم، شمارهٔ پنجاه و پنجم، اردیبهشت ۱۳۴۶، ص ۲_۷. (P)

b. (ب.) در «مطالعاتی در هنر دینی» (رک. شمارهٔ ۱۲)، تهران، ۱۳۴۹، ص ۲۲_۲۹. (P)

c. (ج.) اقبالیات (فارسی)، ۱۵ اپریل ۱۹۸۷، ص ۳۱_۳۷.

1968

81. "The Persian Works of Shaykh al-Ishrāq Shihāb al-Dīn Suhrawardī."

a. *Acta Iranica* (January-March 1968): 12-16.

b. *Islamic Quarterly* 12 (1968): 3-8.

c. «مؤلفات فارسی شیخ الاشراق شهاب الدین سهروردی»، ترجمهٔ غلامعلی عرفانیان، مجلّهٔ دانشکدهٔ ادبیات و علوم انسانی، دانشگاه فردوسی، شمارهٔ اوّل، سال دوازدهم، ۴۵، بهار، ۲۵۳۵، ص ۱۴۵_۱۹۰. (P)

d. *The Islamic Intellectual Tradition in Persia.* (ed.) Mehdi Aminrazavi, 381-410.

82. "Who is Man?: The Perennial Answer of Islam."

a. *Studies in Comparative Religion* (Winter 1968): 45-56.

b. *Man and His World.* Toronto: University of Toronto Press, 1968, 61-68.

c. *The Sword of Gnosis.* Ed. J. Needleman. Penguin Metaphysical Series. Baltimore: Penguin Books, 1974, 203-17.

83. Review of *Alchemy: Science of the Cosmos, Science of the Soul*, by T. Burckhardt. *Studies in Comparative Religion* (Spring 1968): 116-17.

84. "Revelation, Intellect and Reason in the Quran."

a. *Journal of the Regional Cultural Institute* (Iran, Pakistan, Turkey) 1 (Summer 1968): 60-64.

b. *International Islamic Conference* (Islamabad, 1968): 59-62.

c. *World Muslim League Magazine* 4 (Singapore, 1968): 28-31.

d. *Sufi Essays*, 52-56.

e. «قرآن مجید اوروحی، عقلیت اوراستدلال»، فکر ونظر (راولپنطی) جلد ٦، شمارهٔ ٨، ذیقعده ١٣٨٨، فروری ١٩٦٩، ص ٥٦٩_٥٧٤. (U)

85. "Man in the Universe: Permanence Amidst Apparent Change."

a. *Studies in Comparative Religion* (Autumn 1968): 244-53.

b. *I valori permanenti nel divenire storico.* Rome: Instituto Academico di Roma, 1970, 287-98.
c. "L'uomo nell'universo." Ibid., 413-21. (I)
d. English version also appeared in *Eternità e storia.* Florence: Valecchi Editore, 1970, 182-93.
e. Italian translation also appeared in ibid., 413-21. (I)
f. *Sufi Essays*, 84-93.
g. «انسان در نظام کیهانی»، ترجمهٔ احمد آرام، تماشا، سال هشتم، شمارهٔ ۳۸۸، شنبه ۱۱، آذر ۱۳۵۷، ص ٤_٥، و ص ٥٩. (P)

86. «گزارشی از کنفرانس بین المللی اسلامی در پاکستان»، مجلّهٔ معارف اسلامی، شمارهٔ ٥، فروردین ۱۳٤۷، ص ۳٥_۳۷. (P)

87. a. (الف.) «انسان و فلسفهٔ وجود واگزیستانسیالیزم»، تلاش، شمارهٔ نهم، فروردین ۱۳٤۷، ص ۷۸_۸٦. (P)

b. (ب.) معارف اسلامی، ص ۱۹۷_۲۲۰. (P)

c. «الانسان، فلسفة الوجود، والاجزیستانسیالیزم او الوجودیة» (تعریب الاستاذ صلاح الصاوي)، دعوة الحقّ، العدد الثاني،

السنة الثانية عشرة، رمضان شوال ١٣٨٨، ص ١٨_٢٨. (A)

d. «حوار مع الدكتور السيد حسين نصر حول الانسان وفلسفة الوجود والوجودية»، الفكر الاسلامي، ٢٧_٢٨، ربيع الاول وربيع الثاني ١٣٩٦، ص ١٨_٢٨. (A)

88. مقدّمه بر ترجمهٔ فارسی «احیای فکر دینی در اسلام»، به قلم محمّد اقبال لاهوری و ترجمهٔ احمد آرام، تهران، نشریهٔ شمارهٔ ۱، مؤسسهٔ فرهنگی منطقه ای، ص هفت _ یازده. (P)

89. «گزارشی از اوّلین مجمع علمی دربارهٔ تشیّع در مغرب زمین»، مجلّهٔ معارف اسلامی، شمارهٔ ششم، تیر ۱۳٤۷، ص ۲۵_۳۰. (P)

90. a. (الف.) «عوامل مؤثر در علم و تحقیق در ایران»، تلاش، شمارهٔ یازدهم، تیر و مرداد ۱۳٤۷، ص ۱۱_۱۷. (P)

b. (ب.) «معارف اسلامی»، ص ۱۵۷_۱۸۳. (P)

91. a. (الف.) «دین در جهان معاصر»، «محمّد خاتم پیامبران»، تهران، انتشارات حسینیّهٔ ارشاد، شمارهٔ ۱، ۱۳۴۷، ص ۱_۲۶. (P)

b. (ب.) تلاش، شمارهٔ ۱۴، دی و بهمن ۱۳۴۷، ص ۲۴۹_۲۶۹. (P)

c. (ج.) «معارف اسلامی»، ص ۲۴۹_۲۶۹. (P)

92. تصحیح و مقدمه بر «رسالة في حقيقة العشق»، سهروردی، مجلهٔ معارف اسلامی، ۷، آبان ۱۳۴۷، ص ۱۶_۲۵. (P)

93. مقدمهٔ بر «الاشارات والتنبیهات»، نمط نهم، مقامات العارفین، شیخ الرئیس ابو علی سینا، ترجمهٔ سیّد ابوالقاسم پور_حسینی، تهران، انتشارات خانقاه نعمت اللهی، ۱۳۴۷، ص ۷_۱۳. (P)

94. a. (الف.) «گفت و شنودی دربارهٔ دین و فلسفه»، روزنامهٔ آیندگان، ۲۵ اردیبهشت، ۱۳۴۷. (P)

b. (ب.) «مسألهٔ ایمان و برتری اسلام»، دهمین سالنامهٔ معارف جعفری، قم، ۱۳۴۸، ص ۷_۱۳. (P)

c. (ج.) «معارف اسلامی»، ص ۱۸۵_۱۹۵. (P)

d. (د.) «حوار مع الدکتور سیّد حسین نصر حول الدین والفلسفة والحیاة»، ترجمة محمّد علي آذرشب، الفكر الاسلامي، ٦، السنة الاولى، ربيع الثاني، ١٣٩٣، ص ٤_١٢. (A)

1969

95. a. "Ithnā 'asharī Shi'ism and Iranian Islam." *Religion in the Middle East*. Ed. A. J. Arberry. Vol. 2. Cambridge: Cambridge University Press, 1969, 96-118.

b. "Islam in Persia: Yesterday and Today." *Islam and the Plight of Modern Man*, 101-21.

96. "The Death of Thomas Merton." *Monchanin-Information* (Canada) 2 (April 1969): 12-13.

97. "The Pertinence of Islam to the Modern World."

a. *Islamic Quarterly* 13, No. 1 (January-March 1969): 3-8.

b. *The World Religions Speak*. The Hague: Dr. W. Junk N.V. Publishers, 1970, 130-35.

c. *Chuto-Tsuho* (The Middle East News) (July 1970): 25-30. (J)

d. *Sufi Essays*, 164-70.

e. (ه.) «اهمیت اسلام در جهان معاصر»، ترجمهٔ یکی از اعضای انجمن اسلامی دانشجویان دانشکدهٔ ادبیات و علوم انسانی دانشگاه تهران (غلامعلی حداد عادل) با مقدّمهٔ مترجم (به صورت رساله‌ای مستقل)، نشریهٔ انجمن اسلامی دانشجویان دانشکدهٔ ادبیات و علوم انسانی دانشگاه تهران (۱)، تهران، شرکت سهامی انتشار، ۱۳٤۹. (P)

f. (و.) «انسان و جهان»، نشریهٔ انجمن اسلامی دانشجویان دانشکدهٔ ادبیات، دانشگاه تهران، شمارهٔ ۱، اسفند ۱۳۵۰، ص ۱۹ـ٤۰. (P)

g. (ز.) «اهمیّة الاسلام لعالم الیوم»، ترجمة صلاح الصاوي الفکرـ الاسلامي، ۳، السنة الاولی، ذو الحجّة ۱۳۹۲، ص ۲ـ۱٦. (A)

98. "Dr. M. M. Ahmad: A Personal Testimony." *Taj* (Mahmood Number) 7 (July-August 1969): 8-9.

99. "Why do Muslims Fast?"

a. *Harvard Islamic Society Gazette* 1 (December 1969): 8-9.

b. *Al-Serāt* 6, No. 2 (June 1980): 3-4.

c. *Islamic Life and Thought*, 214-15.

d. Laleh Bakhtiar, ed. *Ramadan: Motivating Believers to Action.* Chicago: Kazi Press, 1995, v-vii.

100. "Les arts libéraux dans le monde non-Latin." *Arts libéraux et philosophie au Moyen Age*. Paris-Montreal: Actes du quatrième congrès international de philosophie médiévale, 73-77. (F)

101. "The Spiritual Path." *Africa Ismaili* 1 (1969): 4. (Extract from "The Ṭarīqah: The Spiritual Path and its Quranic Roots," *Ideals and Realities of Islam*, 121-22.

102. "The World of Imagination and the Concept of Space in the Persian Miniature."

a. *Islamic Quarterly* 13 (1969): 129-34.

b. *The Memorial Volume of the Vth International Congress of Iranian Art and Archaeology*. Vol. 2 Tehran: Ministry of Culture and Art, 1972, 132-36.

c. "Il mondo dell'immaginazione ed il concetto di spazio nella miniature persiana." Trans. E. Zolla. *Conoscenza Religiosa* 1 (1970), 11-16. (I)

d. *Bulletin of the Society for Near Eastern Studies in Japan* (Nihon Orient Gakkai) 12 (1969): 119-27. (J)

e. (ه.) «عالم خیال و مفهوم فضا در مینیاتور ایرانی»، مجلّهٔ باستان شناسی و هنر، شمارهٔ اوّل، زمستان ١٣٤٧، ص ١٦_٢١. (P)

f. *Islamic Art and Spirituality*, 177-84.

103. a. (الف.) «مفسّر عالم غربت و شهید طریق معرفت شیخ اشراق شهاب الدین سهروردی»، مجلّهٔ معارف اسلامی، شمارهٔ ۱۰، آذر ماه ۱۳٤۸، ص ۸_۱۹. (P)

b. "Suhrawardī: The Master of Illumination, Gnostic and Martyr." Trans. W. Chittick. *Journal of the Regional Cultural Institute* (Iran, Pakistan, Turkey) 2 (Autumn 1969): 209-25.

c. (ج.) «شیخ الاشراق»، ترجمة صلاح الدین الصاوي، الكتاب التذكاري _ شیخ الاشراق شهاب الدین السهروردی، اشرق علیه وقدّم له الدكتور ابراهیم مدكور، قاهره، ۱۹۷۳، ص ۱۷_۳۲. (A)

d. *The Islamic Intellectual Tradition in Persia*. Ed. Mehdi Aminrazavi, 187-203.

104. مقدّمه بر «هزار و یک شب و افسانهٔ شهرزاد»، به قلم جلال ستاری، تهران، ۱۳٤۸، ص ۷_۱۳. (P)

105. a. (الف.) «سنّت فلسفی در ایران و اهمیت آن در جهان

معاصر»، مجلّهٔ معارف اسلامی، شمارهٔ ۸، فروردین ۱۳٤۸،
ص ۳۳_٤۲. (P)

b. (ب.) «مجموعهٔ سخنرانی‌های عمومی دانشکدهٔ ادبیات و
علوم انسانی تهران»، تهران، ۱۳٤۸، ص ۱۷_۳٦. (P)

c. "The Tradition of Islamic Philosophy in Persia and its Significance for the Modern World." Trans. W. Chittick. *Iqbal Review* 12 (October 1971), 28-49.

d. *The Islamic Intellectual Tradition in Persia*. Ed. Mehdi Aminrazavi, 52-73.

106.a. مقدّمه بر «شیعه در اسلام»، به قلم علّامه سیّد محمّد حسین
طباطبائی، تهران، ۱۳٤۸، ص الف _ ک (چاپ پنجم،
۱۳۵۲). (P)

b. مقدّمه (اردو) «بر مکتب تشیع»، علّامه سیّد محمّد
حسین طباطبائی، ترجمهٔ سید علی بن الحسن باقری،
دهلی ۱٤۰۹، ص ۵_۲۱. (U)

107. مقدّمه بر «معنی شناسی»، به قلم منصور اختیار، تهران،

۱۳٤۸، ص ۱_۳. (P)

108. مقدّمه بر «مجموعهٔ سخنرانی‌های عمومی دانشکدهٔ ادبیات و علوم انسانی دانشگاه تهران»، ۱۳٤۷_۱۳٤۸، تهران، ۱۳٤۸، ص الف _ د. (P)

1970

109. Preface to *Rasā'il* (Persian and Arabic) by Sabziwārī. Ed. S. J. Ashtiyani. Mashhad: Mshhad University Press, 1970, 1-7.

110. a. "Le shî'ism et le soufisme, leurs relations principielles et historiques." *Le Shî'ism imâmite, Colloque de Strasbourg* (Mai 1968). Paris: 1970, 215-33. (F)

b. "Shi'ism and Sufism: Their Relationship in Essence and in History," *Religious Studies* 6 (1970): 229-42.

c. *Sufi Essays*, 104-20.

d. (د.) «تشیّع و تصوّف»، ترجمهٔ غلامرضا اعوانی، مجلّهٔ تلاش، شمارهٔ بیست و چهارم، شهریور _ مهر ۱۳٤۹، ص ۸۲_۸۸. (P)

e. *Shi'ism: Doctrines, Thought and Spirituality*, 101-108.

111. Preface to *Dimensions of Islam*, by F. Schuon. London: Allen and Unwin, 1970, 7-10.

112.a. *Sacred Art in Persian Culture*. A Publication of the Festival of Arts, Shiraz-Persepolis, Tehran: Sekeh Press, 1970. (Monograph).

b. *Middle East Forum* (Spring 1971), 91-37.

c. *Studies in Art and Literature of the Near East*. Ed. P. Chelkowski. Salt Lake City: University of Utah and New York University, 1974, 161-79.

d. In summary form in *Courier* (UNESCO), (October 1971): 16-26 (in 14 languages).

e. In completely revised form in *Islamic Art and Spirituality*, 54-83.

f. (و.) «هنر قدسی در فرهنگ ایران»، در «جاودانگی و هنر»، ترجمهٔ سید محمد آوینی، تهران، ۱۳۷۰، ص ۳۷ ـ ۵۸. (P)

113. ترجمهٔ مقالهٔ «اصول و معیار هنر جهانی»، به قلم فریدهوف شووان، در «مطالعاتی در هنر دینی» (رک. شمارهٔ ۱۲)، ۲، تهران، ۱۳٤۹. (P)

114. ترجمهٔ مقالهٔ «ارزش‌های جاویدان هنر اسلامی»، به قلم تیتوس بورکهارت، در «مطالعاتی در هنر دینی» (رک. شمارهٔ ۱۲)، ۲، تهران، ۱۳٤۹، ص ۹ـ۲۰. (P)

115. a. "Eastern Science, Western Science: The Problem of the Conquest of Nature." *Contemplation for Better Tomorrow.* Osaka: Japan Association for the 1970 World Exposition, 1970, 281-87.

b. Japanese translation, 263-77. (J)

c. "The Ecological Problem in the Light of Sufism: The Conquest of Nature and the Teachings of Eastern Science." *Sufi Essays*, 152-63.

116. "Sufism and the Perennity of the Mystical Quest."

a. *Milla wa-Milla*, No. 10 (1970): 4-18.

b. *Comparative Religion, The Charles Strong Trust Lectures, 1961-1970.* Ed. J. Bowman. Leiden: E.J. Brill, 1972, 99-115.

c. "Il Sufismo e la perennità della ricerca mistica." *Conoscenza Religiosa* 2 (1971): 117-30. (I)

d. *Sufi Essays*, 25-42.

117. "The Spread of the Illuminationist School of Suhrawardī."

a. *Islamic Quarterly* 14 (July-September 1970): 111-21.

b. *Irān-shināsī* 1 (Summer 1971): 84-102.

c. *La Persia nell Medioevo.* Rome: Accademia Nazionale dei Lencei, 1971, 255-65. (I)

d. *Studies in Comparative Religion* (Summer 1972): 141-52.

e. *The Islamic Intellectual Tradition in Persia*, M. Aminrazavi, 52-73.

118. مقدمه بر «بحران دنیای متجدّد»، به قلم رنه گنون، ترجمهٔ

ضیاء الدین دهشیری، تهران، انتشارات مؤسسهٔ مطالعات و تحقیقات اجتماعی، ۱۳٤۹، ص ۱_۷. (P)

119. a. (الف.) «تصوّف و تأثیر آن در موسیقی»، تلاش، شمارهٔ بیست و ششم، دی ـ بهمن ۱۳٤۹، ص ۸۱_۸٤. (P)

b. (ب) مجلّهٔ معارف اسلامی، شمارهٔ ۱۲، فروردین ۱۳۵۰، ص ۸_۱۳. (P)

c. "The Influence of Sufism on Traditional Persian Music." Trans. W. Chittick. *Journal of the Regional Cultural Institute* (Iran, Pakistan, Turkey) 3 (Summer and Fall 1970): 79-88.

d. *Islamic Culture* 45 (July 1971): 171-79.

e. *Studies in Comparative Religion* (Autumn 1972): 225-34.

f. *The Sword of Gnosis*. Ed. J. Needleman. Baltimore: Penguin Books, 1974, 330-42.

g. *Islamic Art and Spirituality*, 163-74.

120. «ادارهٔ کشور از دیدگاه اسلامی»، «ماهنامهٔ وزارت کشور»، بهمن ۱۳٤۹، ص ۲۵_۲۸ و ۳۰. (P)

121. «زندگانی سهروردی از نزهة الارواح نوشتهٔ شمس الدین

محمّد شهرزوری، ترجمهٔ مقصود علی تبریزی»، به تصحیح دکتر سیّد حسین نصر، مجلّهٔ معارف اسلامی، شمارهٔ ۱۱، خرداد ۱۳٤۹، ص ۸ـ۱۳. (P)

122. «تأویل قرآن و حکمت معنوی اسلام»، ترجمهٔ رضا داوری از فصل اوّل «تاریخ فلسفه اسلامی»، به قلم هنری کربن با هکاری سیّد حسین نصر و عثمان یحیی، مجلّهٔ معارف اسلامی، شمارهٔ ۱۱، خرداد ۱۳٤۹، ص ۱۹ـ۲٦. (P)

123. a. «مقام رشید الدین فضل اللّه در تاریخ فلسفه و علوم اسلامی»، مجلّهٔ ایران شناسی، جلد دوّم، شمارهٔ اوّل، تابستان ۱۳٤۹، ص ۷ـ۲۲. (P)

b. "The Status of Rashīd al-Dīn Faḍl Allāh in the History of Islamic Philosophy and Science." Trans. M. Aminrazavi. *Islamic Culture* (Jan. 1994): 1-10.

c. *The Islamic Intellectual Tradition in Persia*. Ed. Mehdi Aminrazavi, 245-59.

1971

124. "Islam" *The Middle East: A Handbook*. Ed. M. Adams. London: Anthony Blond, 1971, 179-84.

125. a. "The Influence of Traditional Islamic Thought upon Contemporary Muslim Intellectual Life." *Contemporary Philosophy*. Ed. R. Klibansky. Florence: La Vuova Italia Editrice, 1971, 578-83.

b. *The Islamic Intellectual Tradition in Persia*. Ed. M. Aminrazavi, 466-72.

126. "Homage to Jagad Guru Shankaracharya of Kanchi." *Kalki* (June 5, 1971): 10-11. (TA)

127. Review of *The Origins of Alchemy in Graeco-Roman Egypt*, by J. Lindsay. *Science* 172 (June 4, 1971): 1017-18.

128. "The Role of Women: A Muslim View." *PHP* (Japan) (August 1971): 16-17.

129. Review of *Letters of a Sufi Master*, by T. Burckhardt. *Studies in Comparative Religion* (Winter, 1971): 57-58.

130. "The Prophet and the Prophetic Tradition: The Last Prophet and Universal Man." (chapter II of *Ideals and Realities of Islam*)

a. *Islamic Perspectives* 1, nos. 2 and 3 (June-September 1971): 67-76.

b. *Al-Serāt* 3, No. 1 (March 1977): 3-11. (Summarized form).

c. "O Profeta e a Tradição Profética O Ultimo Profeta e o Homem Universal." *Islãm-O credò é a conduta*. Ed. R.S. Bartholo and

A.E. Campos. Rio de Janeiro: Imago Editora, 1990, 64-87. (PG)

131. "The Life of Mysticism and Philosophy in Iran: Pre-Islamic and Islamic."
   a. *Studies in Comparative Religion* (Autumn 1971): 235-40.
   b. *Journal of the Regional Cultural Institute* (Iran, Pakistan, Turkey) 5 (Winter 1972): 13-18.
   c. *Commemoration Cyrus*. Vol. 1. *Hommage universal*. Leiden: E.J. Brill, 1974, 261-67.
   d. *The Islamic Intellectual Tradition in Persia*. Ed. M. Aminrazavi, 1-6.

132. "*Al-Ḥikmat al-ilāhiyyah* and *Kalām*." *Studia Islamica* 34 (1971): 139-49.

133. "Persia and the Destiny of Islamic Philosophy."
   a. *Journal of the Regional Cultural Institute* (Iran, Pakistan, Turkey) 4 (1971): 67-80.
   b. *Studies in Comparative Religion* (Winter 1972): 31-42.
   c. "La Perse et le destin de la philosophie islamique." *Sophia Perennis* 1 (Spring 1975): 60-71. (F)
   d. *The Islamic Intellectual Tradition in Persia*. Ed. Mehdi Aminrazavi, 38-51.

134. «شرح مؤنس العشّاق سهروردی»، با همکاری مظفّر بختیار،

مجلّهٔ دانشکدهٔ ادبیات و علوم انسانی، فروردین ۱۳۵۰، ص ۲۷۱_۲۸۸. (P)

135. مقدمه بر «مجموعهٔ خطابه‌های تحقیقی دربارهٔ رشیدالدین فضل‌الله همدانی»، تهران، ۱۳۵۰، ص ج و سخنرانی در همان کنگرهٔ رشید الدین، ص ۳_۶. (P)

136. مقدمه بر «تاریخ تحوّل دانشگاه تهران و مؤسسات عالی آموزشی ایران در عصر خجستهٔ پهلوی»، به قلم حسین محبوبی اردکانی، تهران، ۱۳۵۰، ص پنج و شش. (P)

137. «فلسفه در اعصار تاریخ ایران»، در «گوشه‌ای از سیمای تاریخ تحوّل علوم در ایران»، تهران، ۱۳۵۰، ص ۹_۲۷. (P)

138. «تقابل ساحت‌های معنوی و مادی در حیات بشر کنونی»، تلاش، شمارهٔ سی و سوّم، اسفند ۱۳۵۰، ص ۶۵_۷۳. (P)

139. «ایرانیان و فلسفهٔ اسلامی»، نشریهٔ دانشکدهٔ ادبیات و علوم انسانی (اصفهان)، سال پنجم، شمارهٔ ششم، قسمت اوّل،

۱۳۵۰، ص ۴۲ـ۵۹. (P)

1972

140. "The Western World and its Challenges to Islam."

a. *The Muslim,* part 1 (January 1972): 56-61 and part 2 (September-October 1972): 6-11.

b. In revised form in *Islamic Quarterly* 17 (January-June 1973): 3-25.

c. *Islam: Its Meaning and Message*. Ed. Khurshid Ahmad. London: Islamic Council of Europe, 1975, 217-41.

d. *Islam and the Plight of Modern Man*, 130-50.

e. "Zapadni svijet L Njegovi izzovi islamu." *Suvremena Ideologijska Tumačenja Kur'ana Islama*. Ed. E. Karić. Zagreb, 1990, 7-27. (BSC) Bosnian Translation also in E. Karić, ed., *Kur'an u Savremenom Dobu*, I. Sarajevo: El-Kalem, 1979, 7-29.

f. (و.) «اسلام اور مغرب کا چیلنج»، روایت، ۲، ۱۹۸۵، ص ۲۰۵ـ ۲۳۵، ترجمۂ تحسین فراقی اور محمد سهیل عمر. (U)

141. a. "Conditions for Meaningful Comparative Philosophy." *Philosophy East and West* (January 1972): 53-61.

b. "Philosophy East and West: Necessary Conditions for

Meaningful Comparative Study." *Philosophy, Theory and Practice.* Ed. T. M. P. Mahadevan. Madras: Center for Advanced Study in Philosophy, University of Madras, 1974, 11-20.

c. "Metaphysics and Philosophy East and West: Necessary Conditions for Meaningful Comparative Study." *Islam and the Plight of Modern Man*, 27-36.

142. "The Significance of the Void in the the Art and Architecture of Islamic Persia."

a. *Journal of the Cultural Institute* (Iran, Pakistan, Turkey) 5 (1972): 121-28.

b. *Chûtô-Tsûhô* (The Middle East News) April 1973, 23-26. (J)

c. "The Significance of the Void in the the Art and Architecture of Islam." *Islamic Quarterly* 16 (1972): 115-20.

d. "Il significato del vuoto nell'arte e nell'architectura dell'Islam." *Conoscenza religiosa* 5 (1974): 152-57. (I)

e. *Fine Arts in Islamic Civilization.* Ed. M. A. J. Beg. Kuala Lumpur, 1977, 19-24.

f. "The Significance of the Void in Islamic Art." *Islamic Art and Spirituality*, 185-91.

143. Review of *Sufis of Andalusia, the Ruh al-Quds and al-Durrat al-Fakhirah*, by Ibn 'Arabī. Trans. R.W.J. Austin.

a. *Studies in Comparative Religion* (Autumn 1972): 253-54.

b. *Islamic Quarterly* 16 (1972): 218-19.

144. a. "Religion and Arab Culture." *Cahiers d'Histoire Mondiale* (*Journal of World History*) 16 (1972): 702-13.

b. "Islam in the Contemporary Arab World." *Islam and the Plight of Modern Man*, 89-100.

145. Review of *The Thousands of Abu Ma'shar*, by D. Pingree. *Journal of the American Oriental Society* 92 (October-December 1972): 568.

146. a. *Islamic Philosophy in Contemporary Persia: A Survey of Activity during the Past Two Decades*. Salt Lake City: Research Monograph No. 3, Middle East Center, University of Utah, 1972.

b. "Islamic Philosophical Activity n Contemporary Persia: A Survey of Activity in the '50s and '60s" in *The Islamic Intellectual Tradition in Persia*. Ed. M. Aminrazavi, 448-65.

147. a. *Abū Rayḥān Bīrūnī: Scientist and Scholar Extraordinary*. Tehran: Ministry of Culture and Arts Press, 1972. (Monograph).

b. Japanese Translation, Tokyo: Iran Society, 1973. (J)

c. (ج.) «ابوریحان بیرونی – معرفی یک دانشمند و محقق برجسته»، تهران، وزارت فرهنگ و هنر، ۱۳۵۱. (P)

d. (د.) «ابوریحان بیرونی ایک عظیم دانشمند اور محقق»، در صفحات مخصوص روزنامهٔ جنگ، کراچی، ۲٦ نومبر، ۱۹۷۳، ص ۱_۲. (U)

e. (ه.) به مناسبت هزارهٔ ابوریحان محمّد ابن احمد البیرونی،

کانگرس عالمی ابوریحان، مؤسسهٔ همدرد، کراچی، ۱۹۷۳. (U)

f. (و.) پندره روزه نیا پیام، لاهور، مجلد شمارهٔ ۱۶،

ص ۱ـ۱۵، دسمبر ۱۹۷۳، عدد شمارهٔ ۲۳، ص ۱۷ـ۱۹. (U)

148. مقدّمه بر «چهارده رسالهٔ فارسی»، از صائن الدین علی بن محمّد ترکهٔ اصفهانی، به تصحیح دکتر سیّد علی موسوی بهبهانی و سیّد ابراهیم دیباجی، تهران، ۱۳۵۱، ص الف ـ د. (P)

1973

149. "The Meaning and Role of 'Philosophy' in Islam."
   a. *Studia Islamica* 36 (1973): 57-80.
   b. *Journal of the Regional Cultural Institute* 6 (1973): 5-28.
   c. *Proceedings of First Afro-Asian Philosophical Conference: Philosophy and Civilization*. Ed. M. Wahba. Cairo: Ain Shams University Press, 1978, 97-116.

150. a. Introduction to *The Sense of Unity: The Sufi Tradition in Persian Architecture*, by N. Ardalan and L. Bakhtiar. Chicago: University of Chicago Press, 1973, xi-xv.

b. «سنّت اسلامی در معماری ایرانی»، در «جاودانگی و هنر»، ترجمهٔ سیّد محمد آوینی، تهران، ۱۳۷۰، ص ۵۹ــ۶۸. (P)

151. "Jesus Through the Eyes of Islam."
   a. *The Times* (London), Saturday, July 28, 1973.
   b. *World Faiths*, 1973.
   c. "Il Messe." *Anno-8* (August 1977): 245 ff.
   d. *Islamic Life and Thought*, 209-11.

152. "The Significance of Comparative Philosophy for the Study of Islamic Philosophy."
   a. *Islam and the Modern Age* 4 (February 1973): 11-19.
   b. *Studies in Comparative Religion* (Autumn 1973): 212-18.
   c. "The Significance of the Comparative Method for the Study of the Islamic Intellectual and Spiritual Heritage." *Islam and the Plight of Modern Man*, 3-16.

153. a. "Contemporary Man between the Rim and the Axis." *Studies in Comparative Religion* (Spring 1973): 113-26.
   b. "Between the Rim and the Axis: The Plight of Modern Man." *Main Currents in Modern Thought* 30 (November-December 1973): 85-91.
   c. *Ilm* 4, No. 1 (July 1978): 29-41.
   d. "O Sunkhronos Anthropos," Anamesas To Stephani Kaiton Axona, in *Perennial Values Against Contemporary Decadence*, (Athens, 1992): 44-62. (GR)

e. *Islam and the Plight of Modern Man*, 3-16.

154. a. "Al-Bīrūnī as Philosopher." *Published on the Occasion of the al-Bīrūnī International Congress*. Karachi: Hamdard Institute, 1973. (Monograph).

b. "Free-wheeling Philosopher." *Courier* (UNESCO) (June 1974): 38-41. (Also in 14 other languages).

c. "Al-Bīrūnī as Philosopher." *The Islamic Intellectual Tradition in Persia*. Ed. M. Aminrazavi, 130-39.

155. a. "The Complementarity of Contemplation and Action in Islam." *Main Currents in Modern Thought* 30 (November-December 1973): 64-68.

b. *Traditional Modes of Contemplation and Action*. Ed. Y. Ibish and P. L. Wilson. Tehran: The Imperial Iranian Academy of Philosophy, 419-30.

c. *Contemplation and Action in World Religions*. Ed. Y. Ibish and I. Marculesu. Seattle and London: A. Rotako Chapel Book, 1978, 195-204.

d. "The Harmony of Contemplation and Action in Islam." *Islam and the Plight of Modern Man*, 67-80.

156. "Mullā Ṣadrā and the Doctrine of the Unity of Being."

a. *Philosophical Forum* (December 1973): 153-61.

b. "Mullā Ṣadrā e la docttrina dell'unità dell'essere." *Conoscenza Religiosa*, Vol. 4 (1976): 365-72. (I)

c. *Islamic Life and Thought*, 174-81.

157. a. "The Islamic Conception of Intellectual Life." *Dictionary of the*

History of Ideas, Vol. 2. New York: Scribners, 1973, 633-52.

b. "Panorama of Classical Islamic Intellectual Life." *Islamic Life and Thought*, 55-79.

158. a. *Les états spirituels dans le soufisme*. Tome: Academia Nazionale dei Lincei, Fondazione Leone Caetani, 1973. (Monograph). (I)

b. "The Spiritual States in Sufism." *Sufi Essays*, 68-83.

159. "Why Science lost the Cosmic." *Religion for a New Generation*. Ed. J. Needleman, A. K. Bierman and J. A. Gold. New York: Macmillan, 1973, 448-65. (Extracts from *The Encounter of Man and Nature*, 51-80 and 105-6.)

160. Introduction to *Rasā'il-i falsafī* by Ṣadr al-Dīn Shīrāzī. Ed. S. J. Ashtiyani. Mashhad: Mashhad University Press, 1973, 1-6.

161. «زمینهٔ فکری بر خورد فرهنگ و تمدن ایران و غرب»، مجلّهٔ یغما، شمارهٔ دوّم، سال بیست و ششم، اردیبهشت ۱۳۵۲، ص ٦۵_۷۱، شمارهٔ چهارم، سال بیست و ششم، تیر ۱۳۵۲، ص ۲۰٦_۲۱۰، شمارهٔ پنجم، سال بیست و ششم، مرداد ۱۳۵۲، ص ۲۷۷_۲۸۳. (P)

162. «ویژه‌های فرهنگ اسلامی»، مجلّهٔ رودکی، ۱۹ اردیبهشت ۱۳۵۲، ص ۵_۸. (P)

163. مقدّمه بر "'علم النفس'، روانشناسی صدر المتألّهین، ترجمه و تفسیر از سفر نفس کتاب اسفار، نگارش جواد مصلح، جلد اوّل، تهران، ۱۳۵۲، ص یک تا چهار. (P)

1974

164. "Avicenna," *Encyclopaedia Britannica*, 15th edition. New York: Encyclopaedia Britannica, 1974, 540-41.

165. Foreword to *The Sufi Doctrine of Rumi: An Introduction*, by W. Chittick. Tehran: Offset Press, 1974, 5-6.

166. "Ithna 'ashariyya." *Encyclopedia of Islam*. New Edition, Vol. 4. Leiden: E.J. Brill, 1974, 277-79.

167. "Al-Bīrūnī versus Avicenna in the Bout of the Century."
   a. *Courier* (UNESCO), (June 1974): 27-29. (Also in 14 other languages).
   b. *Maroc Magazine* 9 (Dimanche 1974): 7 (F)
   c. *Ilm* (London) (March 1976): 42-43 and 48.
   d. "Al-Bīrūnī versus Avinenna on the Nature of the Universe" in *The Islamic Intellectual Tradition in Persia*. Ed. M. Aminrazavi, 140-41.

168. "Rūmī and the Sufi Tradition."
   a. *Studies in Comparative Religion* (Spring 1974): 74-89.

b. As a monograph published by the R.C.D. Cultural Institute, Tehran, 1974.

c. *The Scholar and the Saint: Studies in Commemoration of Abu' l-Rayḥān al-Bīrūnī and Jalāl al-Dīn Rūmī.* (ed.) P. J. Chelkowski. New York: New York University Press, 1975, 169-85.

d. In highly revised form in *Islamic Art and Spirituality*, 133-47.

169. "Religion in Safavid Persia."

a. *Iranian Studies* (Studies on Isfahan) 7 (1974): 271-86.

b. *Traditional Islam in the Modern World*, 59-72.

1975

170. "Western Science and Asian Cultures" (excerpts). *Indian and Foreign Review* 12 (April 1, 1975): 16-18; and 12 (April 15, 1975): 17-19.

171.a. "The Significance of Persian Philosophical Works in the Tradition of Islamic Philosophy." *Essays on Islamic Philosophy and Science*. Ed. G. Hourani. Albany: State University of New York Press, 1975, 67-75.

b. *The Islamic Intellectual Tradition in Persia*. Ed. M. Aminrazavi, 74-82.

172. a. "Life Sciences, Alchemy and Medicine." *Cambridge History of Iran*. Vol. IV. Ed. R. N. Frye. Cambridge: The University Press, 1975, 396-418.

b. «علوم زیستی»، در «تاریخ ایران کمبریج»، جلد چهارم، گردآورنده، ر. ن. فرای، مترجم حسن انوشه، بخش دوازدهم، تهران، ۱۳۶۳. (P)

173. a. "Philosophy and Cosmology." *Cambridge History of Iran*. Vol. IV. Ed. R. N. Frye. Cambridge: The University Press, 1975, 419-41.

b. «فلسفه، جهان شناسی و تصوّف»، «تاریخ ایران کمبریج»، جلد چهارم، بخش سیزدهم، تهران، ۱۳٤۳. (P)

174. a. "Ṣūfism." *Cambridge History of Iran*. Vol. IV. Ed. R. N. Frye. Cambridge: The University Press, 1975, 442-63.

b. (ب.) «تصوّف»، «تاریغ ایران کمبرج»، جلد چهارم، بخش سیزدهم، تهران، ۱۳٦۳. (P)

175. a. With M. Muṭahharī, "The Religious Sciences." *Cambridge History of Iran*. Vol. IV. Ed. R.N. Frye. Cambridge: The University Press. 1975, 464-80.

b. «علوم دینی»، با همکاری مرتضی مطهری، «تاریخ ایران کمبریج»، جلد چهارم، بخش چهاردهم، تهران، ۱۳٦۳. (P)

176.a. "Sufism and the Spiritual Needs of Contemporary Man." *Sacred*

Tradition and Present Need. Ed. J. Needleman and D. Lewis. New York: Viking Press, 1975, 75-95.

b. "Il Sufismo e le esigenze spirituali dell'uomo contemporaneo." *Conoscenza Religiosa*, Vol. 3 (1975): 238-58. (I)

c. "Sufismen och den moderna människans behov." *Religion och Bibel*, Vol. XXXVI (Årsbook, 1977): 26-37. (SW)

d. "The Spiritual Needs of Western Man and the Message of Sufism." *Islam and the Plight of Modern Man*, 47-66.

177. Introduction to *Uṣūl al-ma'ārif*, by Mullā Muḥsin Fayḍ Kāshānī. Ed. S.J. Ashtiyani. Mashhad: Mashhad University Press, 1975, 7-8.

178. a. Preface to *Sophia Perennis* 1 (Spring 1975): 7-8.

b. (ب.) سر آغاز «مجلّهٔ جاویدان خرد»، شمارهٔ اوّل، سال اوّل، بهار ۱۳۵٤، ص ۷ـ۸. (P)

179. a. «چرا فارابی را معلم ثانی خوانده‌اند؟»، مجلّهٔ دانشکدهٔ ادبیات و علوم انسانی ـ تهران ـ سال ۲۲ ـ ۱۳۵٤، شمارهٔ ۲، ص ۱ـ۷. (P)

b. «ابو نصر فارابی»، زیر نظر ایرج افشار، تهران، ۱۳۵٤، ص ۱٤ـ۱۹. (P)

c. "Why was al-Fārābī called the 'Second Teacher'?" Trans. by M.

Aminrazavi. *Islamic Culture* 59, No. 4 (1985): 357-64.

d. *The Islamic Intellectual Tradition in Persia*. Ed. Mehdi Aminrazavi, 99-106.

180. "The Traditional Texts used in the Persian Madrasahs."

a. *Islamic Quarterly* 19, No. 3 & 4 (July-December 1975): 172-86.

b. *Arabic and Islamic Garland: Historical, Educational and Literary Studies Presented to Abdul Latif Tibawi*. London, 1977, 174-88.

c. *Traditional Islam in the Modern World*, 165-82.

1976

181. Preface and Afterword to the *Catalogue of the Science and Technology in Islam Exhibition*. London: World of Islam Festival, 1976.

182. Preface to *Islam and the Perennial Philosophy*, by F. Schuon. London: World of Islam Festival Publishing Co., 1976.

183.a. Introduction to *Al-Mabda' wa'l-ma'ād*, by Ṣadr al-Dīn Shīrāzī. Ed. S. J. Ashtiyani. Tehran, 1976, V-XIII.

b. مقدمهٔ فارسی بر صدرالدین شیرازی، «المبدء والمعاد»، به تصحیح جلال‌الدین آشتیانی، تهران، ۱۳۵٤، ص ۷_۱٦. (P)

184. Preface to *Anwār-i jaliyyah*, by Mullā 'Abdallāh Zunūzī. Ed. S. J. Ashtiyani. Tehran: McGill Institute of Islamic Studies, 1976, 1-7.

185. Foreword to *Islamic Patterns: An Analytical and Cosmological*

Approach, by K. Critchlow. London: Thames and Hudson, 1976, 6.

186. Review of *What is Sufism?*, by M. Lings. *The Middle East Journal* (Autumn 1975): 491-92.

187. a. "One is the Spirit and Multiple its Earthly Reflections: Thought on the Human Condition Today." *Sophia Perennis* 2, No. 1 (Spring 1976): 58-66.
   b. "Reflections on the Human Condition Today." *Insight: A Journal of World Religions* 1, No. 1 (Summer 1976): 45-49.
   c. "Uno è lo spirito, molteplici sono i suoi reflessi terreni." *Conoscenza Religiosa* 7 (1979): 391-96. (I)
   d. "Uno es el espiritu." *Cielo y Tierra* 3, No. 8 (Verano 1984): 9-16. (S)
   e. *The Need for a Sacred Science*, 45-52.

188. a. Preface to *Tamhīd al-qawā'id*, by Ibn Turkah. Ed. S. J. Ashtiyani. Tehran: Imperial Iranian Academy of Philosophy, 1976, 3-8.
   b. مقدمهٔ بر «تمهید القواعد»، تألیف صائن الدین علی بن ترکه، به تصحیح سیّد جلال‌الدین آشتیانی، تهران، ۱۳۹۹ (۲۵۳۵)، ص ۵ـ۸. (P)

189. a. "Quṭb al-Dīn Shīrāzī." *Dictionary of Scientific Biography*. Vol. XI Ed. C. Gillespie. New York: Charles Scribner's Sons, 1976, 247-53.

b. *The Islamic Intellectual Tradition in Persia*. Ed. Mehdi Aminrazavi, 303-10.

190. "پرورش اخلاقی و نقش اولیاء و مربیان"، سومین کنگرهٔ انجمن‌های خانه و مدرسه، ۱۰ تا ۱۲ اسفند ۲۵۴۵، تهران، ۲۵۴۵، ص ۷۸ _ ۸۹. (P)

191. a. "Naṣīr al-Dīn al-Ṭūsī." *Dictionary of Scientific Biography*. Vol. XIII. Ed. C. Gillespie. New York: Charles Scribner's Sons, 1976, 508-14.

b. *The Islamic Intellectual Tradition in Persia*. Ed. Mehdi Aminrazavi, 296-302.

192. a. "Islam and Music: The Views of Rūzbahān Baqlī." *Studies in Comparative Religion* (Winter 1976): 37-45.

b. "L'Islam e la musica secondo Rūzbahān Baqlī, Santo Patrons di Shiraz" and "Rūzbahān Baqlī: Il significato di musica spirituale (*samā'*)." *Conoscenza Religiosa* 4 (1976): 373-81. (I)

c. *Sufi musiche et cerimonie dell'Islam*. Milan: Centro Ricerca per il Teatro, 1981. (I)

193. "Philosophy." *The Study of the Middle East: Research and Scholarship in the Humanities and the Social Sciences*. Ed. L. Binder. New York: Wiley Press 1976, 327-45.

194. a. Introduction to *Lama'āt-i ilāhiyyah*, by Mullā 'Abdallāh Zunūzī. Ed. S. J. Ashtiyani. Tehran: Imperial Iranian Academy of

Philosophy, 1976, 5-12.

b. پیشگفتار فارسی بر «لمعات الهیة»، تألیف ملا عبدالله زنوزی با مقدمه و به تصحیح سیّد جلال‌الدین آشتیانی، تهران، انجمن شاهنشاهی فلسفه ایران ۲۵۳۵ (۱۳۵۵)، ص ۵_۸. (P)

195. Introduction to *The Enneads of Plotinus with Glosses of Qāḍī Sa'īd al-Qummī*. Ed. S. J. Ashtiyani. Tehran: Imperial Iranian Academy of Philosophy, 1976, 5-12.

196. مقدمه بر «علم الحدیث»، تألیف علّامه سید محمّد کاظم عصّار، تهران، ۱۳۵٤، ص الف _ ج. (P)

197. «مختصری دربارهٔ سیر فلسفه در ایران»، گوهر، فروردین ماه ۱۳۵۵ (۲۵۳۵) سال چهارم شمارهٔ اوّل، ص ۳٤_٤۱، سال چهارم، شمارهٔ دوّم، ص ۱۳۲_۱۳۹. (P)

198. «گفتگو به مناسبت تشکیل جشنوارهٔ جهان اسلام»، تلاش، شمارهٔ پنجاه و نهم، سال یازدهم خردادماه ۲۵۳۵، ص ۱۰_۱۵. (P)

199. «ایرانی بودن در زمان حال چه معنایی دارد؟»، روزنامهٔ

کیهان، ۵ شنبه ۲۱ اسفند ۱۳۵٤، ص ۱۱. (P)

200. «کارتمدن غرب تمام شده است»، روزنامهٔ رستاخیز، شنبه ۳۰ بهمن ماه ۲۵۳۵ و یکشنبه ۱ اسفند ۲۵۳۵، ص ۱۱، ۱۹. (P)

201.a. «جهان بینی و مقام فلسفی حکیم نظامی گنجوی»، «آئینهٔ جهان غیب»، از انتشارات بانک ملی ایران، ۲۵۳۵، ص ۱۷ـ۲۹. (P)

b. "The World-view and Philosophical Status of Ḥakīm Niẓāmī Ganjawī." Trans. M. Aminrazavi. *Muslim World*, LXXXII, No. 3-4 (July-October 1992): 191-200.

c. *The Islamic Intellectual Tradition in Persia*. Ed. M. Aminrazavi. London: Curzon Press, 1996, 178-188.

1977

202. "Post-Avicennan Islamic Philosophy and the Study of Being."

a. *Humā'ī-nāmah*. Ed. M. Mohaghegh. Tehran, 1977, 23-34.

b. *International Philosophical Quarterly* XVII, No. 3 (September 1977), 265-71.

c. *Reason, Action and Experience: Essays in Honor of Raymond Klibansky*. Ed. H. Kohlenberger. Hamburg: Meiner Publishers, 1979, 87-93.

d. *Philosophies of Existence*. Ed. P. Morewedge. New York: Fordham University, 1982, 337-44.

203. a. «خاطراتی از محقق فقید مجتبی مینوی»، تماشا، سال ششم، شمارهٔ ۲۹۹۶، ۱۹ بهمن ۲۵۳۵ (۱۹ صفر ۱۳۹۷)، ص ۱۷ـ۱۹. (P)

b. راهنمای کتاب، فروردین ـ اردیبهشت ۲۵۳۹ (۱۳۵۹)، سال بیستم، شمارهٔ ۱ـ۲، ص ۱۱۵ـ۱۱۸. (P)

204. a. "Henry Corbin 'L'Exil Occidental': Une vie et une oeuvre en quête de l'Orient des Lumières." *Mélanges offerts à Henry Corbin*. Tehran: McGill Institute of Islamic Studies and Imperial Iranian Academy of Philosophy, 1977, 3-27. (F)

b. "Henry Corbin: The Life and Works of the Occidental Exile in Quest of the Orient of Light." *Sophia Perennis* 3, No. 1 (Spring 1977): 88-106.

c. *Traditional Islam in the Modern World*, 273-90.

205. مقدمه بر «زندگی و آثار و افکار استاد هانری کربن»، در جشن نامهٔ کربن زیر نظر سیّد حسین نصر، تهران، ۲۵۳۹/۱۳۹۷، ص ۱ـ۲۱. (P)

206. "The Interior Life in Islam."

a. *Al-Serāt* 3, No. 2 & 3 (August-September 1977): 3-10.
b. "La vita interiore nell'Islam." *Centro Pro Unione* 12 (1977): 37-41. (I)
c. *Religious Traditions* 1, No. 2 (October 1978): 48-55.
d. *Conoscenza Religiosa* 4 (1979): 397-405. (I)
e. *Al-Serāt: Selected Articles (1975-1983)*. London: Muhammadi Trust, 1983: 227-34.
f. *Islamic Life and Thought*, 191-99.

207. Foreword to *Indian Alchemy or Rasayana in the Light of Ascetism and Geriatrics*, by S. Mahdihassan. New Delhi: Institute of History of Medicine and Medical Research, 1977, i-v.

208. «مدخل لدراسة حياة صدر الدين الشيرازى وفلسفته» (تعريب مقدمهٔ رسالهٔ سه اصل صدر الدين شيرازى)، در «مباحث فى علم الكلام والفلسفة»؛ به قلم الدكتور على الشابى، تونس، ۱۹۷۷، ص ۱۸۵_۲۰۱. (A)

209. "Islam in the World: Cultural Diversity within Spiritual Unity."
a. *Cultures*, (UNESCO) 4, No. 1 (1977): 15-34. (Also in several other European languages.)
b. "Islam di dunia keragaman budaya dalam ke satuan spiritual." *Jurnal Ulumul Qur'an* (1990): 78-90.
c. «انسان در جهان هستى از ديدگاه اسلامى»، ترجمهٔ احمد

آرام، تماشا، سال هشتم ـ شمارهٔ ۳۸۷، شنبه ۲۷ آذر ۱۳۵۷، ص ٤ـ۷ و ص ۷۵. (P)

210. "Self-awareness and Ultimate Selfhood."
   a. *Religious Studies* 13, No. 3 (September 1977): 319-25.
   b. "L'Autocoscienza e l'Identità Suprema." *Conoscenza Religiosa* 3 (1979): 328-35. (I)
   c. *Person and Society*. Ed. G. F. McLean and H. Meynell. New York: University of America Press, 1988, 49-61.
   d. *The Need for a Sacred Science*, 15-23.

211. Introduction to *Wajh-i dīn*, by Nāṣir-i Khusraw. Ed. G. R. A'vani. Tehran: Imperial Iranian Academy of Philosophy, 1977, 1-5.

212. «کلماتی چند دربارهٔ آیت الله امینی»، در حماسهٔ غدیر، گرد آوری و نگارش محمد رضا حکیمی، تهران ۱۳۹۹، ص ۵۳۸ـ۵۳۹. (P)

213. «دربارهٔ معلم و معنی و مفهوم آن»، سمینار تربیت معلم (هدف برنامه، روش، سازمان)، سی ام مهر ماه، اوّل و دوّم آبان ماه سال ۲۵۳۹، دانشگاه تربیت معلم، ص ۲۷ـ٤۲. (P)

214. Introduction to *al-Aqwāl al-dhahabiyyah*, by Ḥamīd al-Dīn Kirmānī. Ed. S. Al-Sawy. Tehran: Imperial Iranian Academy of

Philosophy, 1977, 1-5.

215. Preface to *A'lām al-nubuwwah,* by Abū Ḥātim Rāzī. Ed. S. Al-Sawy and G. R. A'vani. Tehran: Imperial Iranian Academy of Philosophy, 1977, 1-5.

216. a. "Metaphysics, Poetry and Logic in Oriental Traditions." *Sophia Perennis* 3, No. 2 (Autumn 1977): 119-28.

b. "Metaphysics, Poetry and Logic in the Orient." *Islamic Art and Spirituality*, 87-97.

217. "Inaugural Speech at the First World Conference on Muslim Education." *Conference Book*. Mecca-Jeddah, 1977, 70-71.

218. Preface to *Three Treatises*, by Suhrawardī. Ed. N. J. Habibi. Tehran: Imperial Iranian Academy of Philosophy, 1977, 1-5.

1978

219. "The Writings of Ṣadr al-Dīn Shīrāzī." *Recherches d'Islamologie: Recueil d'articles offerts à Georges C. Anawati et Louis Gardet par leurs collegues et amis*. Louvain: Peters Press, 1978, 261-71.

220. "The Place of Fārābī in Islamic Philosophy." *International Conference on Fārābī at Tehran University*. Tehran: Tehran University Press, 1975, 1-3.

221. a. "The Contemporary Muslims and the Architectural Transformation of the Urban Environment of the Islamic World." *The Aga Khan Award for Architecture: Proceedings of Seminar One*. Philadelphia, 1978, 1-4.

b. "The Architectural Transformation of the Urban Environment in the Islamic World." *Traditional Islam in the Modern World*, 227-37.

222. "Some Observations on the Place of 'Aṭṭār within the Sufi Tradition." *Colloquio Italo-Iraniano sul Poeta Mistico Farīduddīn 'Aṭṭār*. Rome, 1978, 5-20. (Also published as a monograph.)

223. Review of *Mystical Dimensions of Islam*, by A. M. Schimmel. *Studies in Comparative Religion* (Winter-Spring 1978): 125-26.

224. Introduction to *Lawā'iḥ*, by Jāmī. Trans. E.H. Whinfield and M.M. Kazvini. London, 1978, xix-xxvii.

225. "Value and Development in the Contemporary Islamic World."
a. *The Re-Evaluation of Existing Values and the Search for Absolute Values: Proceedings of ICUS*. New York: The International Cultural Foundation Press, 1978, 343-46.
b. *Quarterly Academy* (October 1979): 58-65. (J)
c. *Traditional Islam in the Modern World*, 115-18.

1979

226. a. "Decadence, Deviation and Renaissance in the Context of Contemporary Islam." *Islamic Perspectives (In Honor of Mawdudi)*. London: The Islamic Foundation, 1979, 35-42.
b. "Dekadencija, devijacija i renesansa u korekstu avremenog

islama." *Islamska Misao* (Sarajevo) 92 (August 1986): 9-12. (BSC)

c. "Decadence, Deviation and Renaissance: Their Meaning in the Context of Contemporary Islam." *Islam and the Plight of Modern Man*, 122-29.

d. «زوال، انحراف اورنشاة الثانية»، ترجمة محمد سهيل عمر، روايت ١، لاهور ـ ١٩٨٣، ص ٣٠٥ـ٣١٨. (U)

227. a. "Islamic Alchemy and the Birth of Chemistry," *Journal of the History of Arabic Science* 3, No. 1 (1979): 40-45.

b. "From the Alchemy of Jābir to the Chemistry of Rāzī." *Islamic Life and Thought*, 120-23.

c. «شیمی دانان اسلامی»، تماشا، سال هشتم، شمارهٔ ۳۸۹، شنبه ۲۵ آذر، ص ۴۷، ۹۱. (P)

d. مقدمهٔ کتاب «شیمی دانان نامی اسلامی»، به قلم جعفر آقائی چاووشی، تهران، ۱۳۵۷. (P)

228. "Intellect and Intuition: Their Relationship from the Islamic Perspective."

a. *Studies in Comparative Religion* (Winter-Spring 1979): 65-74.

b. *Islam and Contemporary Society*. Ed. S. Azzam. London and New York: Longman, 1982, 36-46.

c. «عقل و وجدان: اسلامی نقطه نظر سی باسمی تعلُق»، ترجمهٔ احمد جاوید، اقبالیات، جولائی ـ ستمبر ۱۹۸٦، ص ۲۵۱ـ۲٦۱. (P)

229. a. "Avicenna: Prince of Science and Philosophy." *Ur* (January-February 1979): 32-35.

b. "Ibn Sīnā's Prophetic Philosophy." *Cultures* (UNESCO) 7, No. 4 (1980): 165-80 (Also in several other European languages.)

c. "Ibn Sīnā's Prophetic Philosophy." *The Islamic Intellectual Tradition in Persia.* Ed. M. Aminrazavi, 114-29.

230. "Suhreverdi i iluminacionisti." *Život* 6 (1979): 693-713. ("Suhrawardī and the Illuminationists," from *Three Muslim Sages*, 52-82.) (BSC)

1980

231.a. "In Quest of the Eternal Sophia." *Philosophes critiques d'eux mêmes: Philosophische Selbstbetrachtungen.* VI. Bern: Peter Lang, 1980, 113-21.

b. "À la recherche de l'éternelle sagesse." *Philosophes critiques d'eux-mêmes: Philosophische Selbstbetrachtungen.* VI. Bern: Peter Lang, 1980, pp. 123-31. "Complete Bibliography of S. H. Nasr up to 1978," 133-61. (F)

c. "U potrazi za vječnom mudrošću." Trans. Enes Karić. *Islamska Misao* (January 1991), 19-23. (BSC)

d. "Ezelî Hikmet (Sophia) arayışim," *Söyleşiler Seyyid Hüseyin Nasr*. Istanbul: İnsan Yayinlari, 1996, 31-39. (T)

232. "Reflections on Islam and Modern Thought."

a. *Al-Serāt* 6, No. 1 (1980): 4-16.

b. *Petahim* 51-52, No. 3-4 (September 1980): 68-74. (H). English summary, 25-27 of English section.

c. *Islamic Quarterly* (1979): 119-31.

d. *Al-Serāt: Selected Articles (1975-1983)*. London: The Muhammadi Trust, 1983, 235-47.

e. *Studies in Comparative Religion* (Summer-Autumn 1983): 164-76.

f. "L'Islam et la vie moderne," *Aux Sources de la Sagesse* 5, No. 20 (1419/1999): 55-71. (F)

g. "اسلام و اندیشهٔ مدرن"، ترجمهٔ منصور انصاری، مجلّهٔ متین، شمارهٔ ۲، ۱۳۷۸، ص ۲۳۹ـ۲۵۵ و اطلاعات، مهر ۱۳۷۸، ص ۵ و ۶. (P)

h. *Traditional Islam in the Modern World*, 97-113.

233. "A Muslim Reflection on Religion and Theology."

a. *Consensus in Theology? A Dialogue with Hans Küng and Edward Schillebeeckx*. Philadelphia: Westminster Press, 1980, 112-20.

b. *Journal of Ecumenical Studies* 17, No. 1 (Winter 1980): 112-20.

c. *Studies in Comparative Religion* (Summer-Autumn 1979): 148-57.

d. "A Muslim's Reflection on Hans Küng." *Iqbal Review* (April-June 1985): 17-28.

e. «مذهب اور فکر جدید» نئی نسلین (علیگطه)، ستمبر ۱۹۸٤، ص ٦١_٦٧، ترجمهٔ انیس این شاه. (U)

f. "Reflections on the Theological Modernism of Hans Küng." *The Need for a Sacred Science*, 159-69.

234. Introduction to *A Shi'ite Anthology*, translated with explanatory notes by W. Chittick. London: Muhammadi Trust of Great Britian and Northern Ireland, 1980, 5-13. Reprinted, Albany: State University of New York Press, 1981.

235. "Reflections on Methodology in the Islamic Sciences."

a. *Hamdard Islamicus* 3, No. 3 (Autumn 1980): 3-13.

b. *'Ādiyāt Ḥalab: An Annual Devoted to the Study of Arabic Science and Civilization*, IV and V. (1978-79): 21-30.

c. "İslâm bilimlerinin metodolojisi üzerine düşünceler." *İslâm bilimi tartismalari*. Ed. M. Armağan. Istanbul: İnsan Yayınlari, 1990, 185-96. (T)

d. «منهج البحث العلمي فى العصور الاسلامية»، عاديات حلب، مجلد ٤_٥، ١٩٧٨_١٩٧٩، ص ٦٧_٧٢. (A)

236. "A Prayer on the Occasion of the End of Ramadan."
a. *Al-Serāt* 6, No. 3 and 4 (November 1980): 3-5.
b. "La fin du Ramadan Id al-Fitr 1400." *Célébrer Dieu.* Paris, 1980, 163-64. (F)
c. *Quranulhuda* 9, No. 4 (June 1984): 10.
d. *Studies in Comparative Religion* (Winter-Spring 1984): 97-98.
237. "Islamic Countries." *Handbook of World Philosophy.* Ed. J. R. Burr. Westport, 1980, 421-33.
238. "The Concept and Reality of Freedom in Islam and Islamic Civilization."
a. *The Philosophy of Human Rights.* Ed. A. S. Rosenbaum. Westport: Greenwood Press, 1980, 95-101.
b. *Islamic Life and Thought*, 16-23.
239. "Islam in the Islamic World: An Overview." *Islam in the Contemporary World.* Ed. C. K. Poullapilly. Notre Dame: Crossroad Books, 1980, 1-20.
240. "*Mut'ah.*"
a. *The Light* (Tanzania) 14 (October 1980): 45-47.
b. "*Mut'ah* or Temporary Marriage." *Shi'ite Islam*, 227-30.
241. "The Male and Female in the Islamic Perspective."
a. *Studies in Comparative Religion* (Winter-Spring 1980): 67-75.
b. Schuon, Sherrard and Nasr, *Arsen Kai Oēlu Epoiēsen Autous*, Athens, Pemptousia, 1991, 83-95. (GR)
c. *Traditional Islam in the Modern World*, 47-58.

242. Preface to *Contemplative Disciplines in Sufism*, by M. Valiuddin. London: East-West Publications, 1980, 149-58.

1981

243. "Ekološki problem u svetlosti sufizma: osvajanje prirode i učenja istočne." ("The Ecological Problem in the Light of Sufism: The Conquest of Nature and the Teachings of Eastern Science," *Sufi Essays,* 152-63.) (BSC)

a. *Delo* (Belgrade) 7 (July 1978): 71-84.

b. *Sufizam.* Ed. D. Tanasković and I. Šop. Belgrade, 1981, 195-209.

244.a. "Progress and Evolution: A Reappraisal from the Traditional Perspective." *Parabola* 6, No. 2 (Spring 1981): 44-51.

b. "The Ideas of Human Progress Through Material Evolution: The Position of Western Philosophy." *The Re-Evaluation of Existing Values and the Search for Absolute Values: Proceedings of ICUS.* New York: The International Cultural Foundation Press, 1981, 347-57.

c. "The Concept of Human Progress through Material Evolution: A Traditional Critique." *The Need for a Sacred Science,* 149-58.

245. a. "On the Teaching of Philosophy in the Muslim World." *Hamdard Islamicus* 4, No. 2 (Summer 1981): 53-72.

b. "Izučavanje filozofije." *Islamska Visao* 12, No. 142 (October 1990): 33-41. (BSC)

c. "The Teaching of Philosophy." *Philosophy, Literature and Fine Arts*, 3-21.

246. Preface to *Kitāb al-irshād: The Book of Guidance*, by Shaykh al-Mufīd. Trans. I. K. A. Howard. London: Balagha Books and The Muhammadi Trust, 1981, xvii-xx.

247. "Ibn Sīnā (Avicenna) i filozofinaučnici." *Život*, No. 11 & 12 (1981): 564-79. ("Avicenna [Ibn Sīnā] and the Philosopher-Scientists," from *Three Muslim Sages*, 9-51.) (BSC)

1982

248. Reviews of *Esoterism as Principle and as Way*, by F. Schuon; *Sufism: Veil and Quintessence*, by F. Schuon; *From the Divine to the Human*, by F. Schuon. *Parabola* 7, No. 1 (Winter 1982): 108-12.

249. "Islam and Modern Science."

a. *Islam and Contemporary Society*. Ed. S. Azzam. London and New York: Longman, 1982, 177-90.

b. "İslâm ve Modern Bilim." *İlim ve Sanat* (August 1985), 11-19. (T)

c. *Al-Nahdah* (Kuala Lumpur) 7, No. 1 (1987): 14-21.

d. In summary, *Maydan* (Japan) 16 (November 1988): 4-5. (J)

250. "Ananda Coomaraswamy and the Metaphysics of Art: A Review Essay of His Selected Papers on Traditional Art and Symbolism." *Temenos* 2 (1982): 252-59.

251. Preface to *Fakhruddin 'Iraqi: Divine Flashes*, trans. W. Chittick and P. L. Wilson. New York: Paulist Press, 1982, ix-xiv.

252. Reviews of *Spiritual Body and Celestial Earth*, by H. Corbin; *Corps spirituel et terre céleste*, by H. Corbin; and *Temple et contemplation*, by H. Corbin. *Religious Studies* 18, No. 2 (1982): 233-36.

253. "Mīr Findiriskī." *Encyclopedia of Islam*. New Edition. Leiden: E.J. Brill, 308-9.

254. "The Spiritual Significance of *jihād*."
   a. *Parabola* 7, No. 4 (Fall 1982): 14-19.
   b. *Al-Serāt* 9, No. 1 (1983): 16-20.
   c. *Al-Serāt: Selected Papers (1975-1983)*. London, 1983, 248-52.
   d. "O Significado Espiritual de *Jihād*." *Islã: O credo é a conduta*. Ed. R. S. Bartholo and A. E. Campos. Rio de Jainero: Imago Editora, 1990, 269-75. (PG)
   e. *Traditional Islam in the Modern World*, 27-34.

255. a. "Le scienze tradizionali." *Conoscenza Religiosa* 1/2, No. 2 (1982): 112-31. (I)
   b. "The Traditional Sciences." *The Unanimous Tradition*. Ed. R. Fernando Colombo, 1991, 129-46.
   c. *The Need for a Sacred Science*, 95-118.

256. Review of *Ethics and Economics: An Islamic Synthesis*, by S. N. H. Naqvi. *Hamdard Islamicus* 5, No. 2 (Summer 1982): 89-91.

1983

257. Review of *Islamic Understanding of Death and Resurrection*, by J. I. Smith and Y. Y. Haddad. *The Review of Books and Religion* 11, No. 6 (March 1983): 9.

258. Review of *The Rise of Colleges: Institutions of Learning in Islam and the West*, by G. Makdisi. *The Muslim World* 3, No. 4 (Summer 1983): 42-45.

259. "Afḍal al-Dīn Kāshānī and the Philosophical World of Khwāja Naṣīr al-Dīn Ṭūsī."
    a. *Islamic Theology and Philosophy-Essays in Honor of George F. Hourani*, Albany, N.Y.: The State University of New York Press, 1984, 2, 249-64 and 323-26.
    b. *The Islamic Intellectual Tradition in Persia*, ed. M. Aminrazavi, 189-206.

260. "Traditional Cosmology and Modern Science." (Interview) *Parabola* 8, No. 4 (1983): 20-31.

261. "The Flight of Birds to Union: Meditations upon 'Aṭṭār's *Manṭiq al-ṭayr*."
    a. *Temenos* 4 (1983): 103-15.
    b. "Ptičji let u sjedinjenje." *Kulture Istoka* (Belgrade) 17 (July-September 1988): 32-36. (BSC)
    c. *Islamic Art and Spirituality*, 98-113.

262.a. «رابطهٔ بین تصوّف و فلسفه در فرهنگ ایران»، ایران نامه،

سال اوّل شمارهٔ ۱، پائیز ۱۳۶۱، ص ۴۹ـ۵۹. (P)

b. "The Relation between Sufism and Philosophy in Persian Culture." *Hamdard Islamicus* 6, No. 4 (Winter 1983): 33-47.

c. «برصغیر اور ایران کی ثقافت مین تصوّف اور فلسفی کا یا همی تعلق»، ترجمهٔ اردو از خواجه حمید یزدانی، اقبالیات، جولای ـ ستمبر ۱۹۸۵، ص ۱۵۵ـ۱۷۱. (U)

263. a. "The Metaphysics of Ṣadr al-Dīn Shīrāzī and Islamic Philosophy in Qajar Persia." *Qajar Iran: Political, Social and Cultural Change (1800-1925)*. Ed. E. Bosworth and C. Hillenbrand. Edinburgh: The University Press, 1983, 177-98.

b. «ما بعد الطبیعهٔ صدر الدین شیرازی و فلسفه اسلامی در ایران دورهٔ قاجار»، ترجمهٔ جواد قاسمی، مشکوة (آستان قدس رضوی)، شمارهٔ ۳۲، پائیز ۱۳۷۰، ص ۳۷ـ۵۸. (P)

264. «طب سنتی ایران و اهمیت امروزی آن»، در «مجموعهٔ مقالات دربارهٔ طب سنتی ایران»، تهران، مؤسسه مطالعات و تحقیقات فرهنگی ۱۳۶۲، ص ۲۵ـ۳۴. (P)

265. "Ibn 'Arebi i sufije." *Pregled*, No. 7 & 8 (1983): 765-85. ("Ibn

'Arabī and the Sufis," from *Three Muslim Sages*, 83-121). (BSC)

266. «شیخ عیسی نور الدین»، مجلّهٔ روایت (اردو) ـ لاهور ـ ۱۹۸۳، ص ۴۳ـ۴۸. (U)

267. "Posljednji Poslanik I Univerzalni covjek" *Islamska misao*, No. 50, (Sarajevo), 1983, 15-25 (extract from *Ideals and Realities of Islam*). (BSC)

1984

268. Review of *Muḥammad: His Life Based on the Earliest Sources*, by M. Lings.
  a. *Parabola* (Winter 1984): 92-94.
  b. *Quranulhuda* (January 1985): 23 and 25.
  c. *Marg* 2, 84.

269. "Islamic Education and Science: A Summary Appraisal." *The Islamic Impact*. Ed. Y. Y. Haddad, B. Haines, and E. Findly. Syracuse: University of Syracuse Press, 1984, 47-68.

270. Preface to *A Muslim's Reflections on Democratic Capitalism*, by M. Abdul Rauf. Washington, D.C.: American Enterprise Institute, 1984, vii-viii.

271. "The Philosophia Perennis and the Study of Religion."
  a. *The World's Religious Traditions*. Ed. F. Whaling. New York: Crossroad, 1984, 181-200.
  b. *The Need for a Sacred Science*, 53-68.

272. a. "Eternity and Temporal Order: A View of Evolution from the Islamic Perspective." (Based on "Eternity and the Temporal Order," *Knowledge and the Sacred.*) *Rivista di Biologia* 77, No. 2 (1984): 222-32. (I)

b. "L'Eternità e l'ordina temporale: considerazioni sull'evoluzionismo dell'Islam." *Rivista di Biologia* 77, No. 2 (1984): 222-32. (I)

c. *Critique of Evolutionary Theory.* Ed. O. Bakar. Kuala Lumpur: The Islamic Academy of Science and Nurin Enterprise, 1987, 103-20.

273. a. "Present Tendencies, Future Trends." *Islam: The Religious and Political Life of a World Community.* Ed. M. Kelly. New York: Praeger, 1984, 275-92.

b. "O Mundo Islâmico. Tendências Atuais e Futuras." *Islã: O credo é a conduta.* Ed. R. S. Bartholo and A.E. Campos. Rio de Jainero: Imago Editora, 1984, 310-26. (PG)

c. "The Islamic World: Present Tendencies, Future Trends." *Traditional Islam in the Modern World*, 299-316.

274. a. "The Principles of Islamic Architecture and Contemporary Urban Problems." *Arts and the Islamic World* 3, No. 2 (Summer 1985): 33-40 and 96.

b. "İslam Mimarisi ve Çagdaş Sorunlar." *İlim ve Sanat* (Eylül-Ekim 1985): 58-64. (T)

c. "Die Prinzipien der islamischen Architektur und Probleme der heutigen Stadt." *Das Abenteuer der Ideen.* Berlin: Internationale

Bauausstellung, 1987, 207-18. (G)

275. Review of *A Buddhist Spectrum*, by M. Pallis. *Philosophy East and West* 34, No. 4 (October 1984): 451-58.

276. "Islamic Work Ethics."
   a. *Hamdard Islamicus* 7, No. 4 (Winter 1984): 25-35.
   b. *Comparative Work Ethics*. Washington, D.C.: Library of Congress, 1985, 49-62.
   c. *Etika Kerja dalam Tradisi Islam*. Trans. N. Muḥammad. Kuala Lumpur, 1989. (Monograph). (M)
   d. "Pandangan Islam Tentant Etika Kerja." *Ulumul Qur'an* 6, No. 2 (1990): 4-11. (IN)
   e. *Traditional Islam in the Modern World*, 35-46.

277. "Message." *Quest for New Science*. Ed. R. Ahmad and S. N. Ahmad. Aligargh: Center for Studies on Science, 1984, 15-16.

278. "With Titus Burckhardt at the Tomb of Ibn 'Arabī."
   a. *Studies in Comparative Religion* (Winter-Spring 1984): 17-20.
   b. *Traditional Islam in the Modern World*, 291-96.

279. "وحدت الوجود اور ابن عربی"، ترجمهٔ محمد منوّر، نئی
نسلین (علیگره)، ستمبر ١٩٨٤، ص ٥٨ـ٦٠. (U)

1985

280. "Response to Thomas Dean's Review of *Knowledge and the Sacred*." *Philosophy East and West* (January 1985): 87-90.

281. "The Role of the Traditional Sciences in the Encounter of Religion and Science: An Oriental Perspective."
   a. *MAAS Journal of Islamic Science* (Aligarh) 1, No. 1 (January 1985): 9-30.
   b. *Religious Studies* 20 (December 1984): 519-41.

282. "The Long Journey." (Interview)
   a. *Parabola* (Spring 1985): 28-41.
   b. *Leaning on the Moment*. New York: Parabola Books, 1986, 214-29.

283. Review of *The Passion of al-Ḥallāj: Mystic and Martyr of Islam*, by L. Massignon. *Speculum* (January 1985): 183-84.

284. Foreword to *New Horizons in Muslim Education*, by S. A. Ashraf. Suffolk: St. Edmunds, 1985, v-vi.

285. "The Principle of Unity and the Sacred Architecture of Islam."
   a. *Temenos* 6 (1985): 2-40.
   b. *Islamic Art and Spirituality*, 37-63.

286. "Editorial." *MAAS Journal of Islamic Science* 1, No. 2 (July 1985): 6-8.

287. "The Islamic Philosophers' Views on Education."
   a. *Muslim Education Quarterly* 2, No. 4 (1985): 5-16.
   b. *Beyond Conventional Constructs: Essays in Honor of Professor Dr. C.A. Qadir*. Ed. G. Irfan. Lahore: Qadir Presentation Committee, 1987, 240-55.
   c. *Traditional Islam in the Modern World*, 147-63.

288. "L'astrologie islamique." *Astrologies-Chinoise, Indienne, Arabe,*

Hebraique & Occidentales-Question de 62. Paris, 1985, 21-36. (Trans. of "The Wedding of Heaven and Earth in Astrology," *An Introduction to Islamic Cosmological Doctrines*.) (F)

289. "Islam i proučavanje prirode." *Glasnik-VIS-a* 2 (March-April 1985): 162-72 and 3 (May-June 1985): 269-79. ("Islam and the Study of Nature," trans. of *An Introduction to Islamic Cosmological Doctrines*, 1-11). (BSC)

1986

290. "Spiritual Movements, Philosophy and Theology in the Safavid Period." *The Cambridge History of Iran,* Vol. VI. Ed. P. Jackson. Cambridge: Cambridge University Press, 1986, 656-97.

291. "The Islamic View of Christianity."
    a. *Concilium*. Ed. H. Küng and J. Moltmann. Edinburgh: T. and T. Clark, Ltd., 1986, 3-12.
    b. *Christianity Through Non-Christian Eyes*. Ed. P. J. Griffith. New York: Orbis Books, 1990, 126-34.
    c. "De Islamitische visie op het Christendom," *Concilium*, Vol. 1 (1986), 12-20. (D)
    d. "La visione islamica del Christianesimo," *Consilium,* Vol. 1 (1986), 22-34. (I)

292. "Bilim ve Teknoloji Üzerine Seyyed Hüseyin Nasr ile Bir Konoşma." (Interview). *İlim ve Sanat* 6 (Mart-Nisan 1986): 59-62. (T)

293. "The Prayer of the Heart in Heschasm and Sufism."
   a. *Greek Orthodox Theological Review* 31, No. 1 and 2 (1986): 195-203.
   b. *Orthodox Christians and Muslims*. Ed. W. M. Vaporis. Brookline, 1986, 195-203.
   c. *Greek translation in Synaxi* 27 (July-September 1988): 69-77. (GR)
   d. "Das Herzensgebet im Hesychasmus und Sufismus." *Universale Religion* (May 5, 1991): 2-6. (Summary) (G)

294. "The Essence of Dr. Faruqi's Life's Works." *Islamic Horizons* (August-September 1986): 26.

295. "To the Murcian Gnostic Muḥyī al-Dīn Ibn 'Arabī." (Poem) *Journal of the Muhyiddin Ibn 'Arabi Society* 5 (1986): 3. Reprinted in Vol. 8 (1988): 75. (Corrected version.)

296. "Bugün modern dünyanin büyük bir bölümünde İslâm, tasavvuf yoluyla tanıtılıyor, yayılıyor . . . " *Altınoluk* (Eylül 1986): 40-41. (T)

297. "Obredna praksa u šiizmu." *Islamska Misao* 93 (September 1986): 18-19. (From Nasr's "Introduction" to *Shi'ite Islam*, by Ṭabāṭabā'ī.) (BSC)

298. "Poslanice Ihvanus-Safa njihov identitet i sadržaj." *Islamska Misao*, No. 85 and 86 (January-February 1986): 11-15. (From *An Introduction to Islamic Cosmological Doctrines*.) (BSC)

299. "Mikrokosmos i njegov odnos prema univerzumu." *Islamska Misao* 87 (March 1986): 14-17. (From *An Introduction to Islamic*

Cosmological Doctrines.) (BSC)

300. "Život, djelai značaj El-Birunija." *Islamska Misao*, No. 88 and 89 (April-May 1986): 20-23. (From *An Introduction to Islamic Cosmological Doctrines*.) (BSC)

301. "Stvaranje svijeta injegova povijest." *Islamska Misao*, No. 90 and 91 (June-July 1986): 9-11. (From *An Introduction to Islamic Cosmological Doctrines*.) (BSC)

302. a. «غزالی حکیم معاند فلسفه»، ایران نامه، سال چهارم،
شمارهٔ ٤، تابستان ١٣٦٥، ص ٥٨٣_٥٩٢. (P)

b. «فلسفی کا مخالف فلسفی»، ترجمهٔ محمد سهیل عمر،
اقبالیات، جنوری _ مارچ ١٩٨٧، ص ١٢٢_١٣٥. (U)

1987

303. "La crise spirituelle de l'homme moderne." *Congrès international de la famille*. Paris: Fayard, 1987, 45-52. (F)

304. نقد کتاب «سایهٔ خدا و امام غائب»، با همکاری سید ولی
رضا نصر، ایران نامه، سال پنجم، شمارهٔ ١، پائیز ١٣٦٥،
ص ١٧١_١٨٠. (P)

305. "Darwīsh." *Encyclopedia of Religion*. New York: Macmillan

Publishing Corp., 1987, 240-41.

306. "René Guénon." *Encyclopedia of Religion.* New York: Macmillan Publishing Corp., 1987, 136-38.

307. "Nāṣir-i Khusraw." *Encyclopedia of Religion.* New York: Macmillan Publishing Corp., 1987. 312-13.

308. "Shi'ism: Ithnā 'Asharīyah." *Encyclopedia of Religion.* New York: Macmillan Publishing Corp., 1987, 260-70.

309. "In Commemoration of Louis Massignon: Catholic, Scholar, Islamicist and Mystic."
   a. *Presence de Louis Massignon.* Paris: Maisonneuve & Larose, 1987, 50-61.
   b. *Traditional Islam in the Modern World*, 253-72.

310. "Introduction." *Islamic Spirituality: Foundations*, (ed. S. H. Nasr) xv-xxix.

311. "The Qur'ān and the Foundation of Islamic Spirituality." *Islamic Spirituality: Foundations*, 3-10.

312. "God." *Islamic Spirituality: Foundations*, 311-23.

313. "The Cosmos and the Natural Order." *Islamic Spirituality: Foundations*, 345-57.

314. "*Sunnah* and *Ḥadīth*." *Islamic Spirituality: Foundations*, 97-110.

315. Response to H. Küng's "Christianity and World Religions: The Dialogue with Islam as One Model." *Muslim World* 77, No. 2 (April 1987): 96-105.

316. "Islam and the Question of Violence."
   a. *Faith* (Harvard University) 1, No. 1 (May 1987): 8-10.

b. *Al-Serāt* 13, No. 2 (1987): 26-29.

317. Review of *The Arabs in Europe*, by G. Crespi. *American-Arab Affairs* 21 (Summer 1987): 140-41.

318. "Islamic Science and Western Science: Common Heritage, Diverse Destinies."

a. *MAAS Journal of Islamic Science* 3, No. 1 (January-June 1987): 11-20.

b. *The Revenge of Athena*. Ed. Z. Sardar. London: Mansell, 1988, 239-48.

319. Foreword to *Our Philosophy*, by Allāma Muḥammad Bāqir al-Ṣadr. Trans. S. Inati. London: KPI, 1987, ix-xi.

320. "Ra's al-Ḥusayn." (Poem.) *Al-Serāt* 13, No. 2 (Autumn 1987): 3-4.

321. Foreword to *The Qur'ān in Islam*, by 'Allāmah Ṭabāṭabā'ī. London: Zahra Publications, 1987, 9-13.

322. "Evolution: A Metaphysical Absurdity." (Extract from Man and Nature.) *Critique of Evolutionary Theory*. Ed. O. Bakar. Kuala Lumpur: The Islamic Academy of Science and Nurin Enterprise, 1987, 41-50.

323. Review of *Islam and the Destiny of Man*, by G. Eaton. *Middle East Studies Association Bulletin* 21, No. 2 (December 1987): 231-33.

324. "Science Education: The Islamic Perspective."

a. *Muslim Education Quarterly* 5, No. 1 (Autumn 1987): 4-14.

b. Proceedings of the International Symposium of Science,

Technology and Spiritual Values: An Asian Approach to Modernization. Tokyo: Sophia University and the United Nations University, 1987, 235-50.

c. "تدريس العلوم من منظور اسلامى"، المؤتمر العالمي الخامس للتربية الاسلامية، الجز الثانى، قاهره، ١٩٨٧، ص ٣١_٤٥. (A)

325. "A. K. Brohi: In Memoriam." *Islamic Quarterly* 31, No. 4 (Autumn 1987): 270-71.

1988

326. a. "Echoes of Infinity." (Interview). *Parabola* 13, No. 1 (Spring 1988): 24-35.

b. "Ecos do Infinito." *Thot* 51 (1989): 18-23. (I)

327. "Islamic Studies in America."

a. *An Independent Institution in a Free Society: Essays in Honor of Lloyd Elliot*. Ed. R. French. Washington, D.C.: The George Washington University, 1988, 140-58.

b. *Echoes of Infinity: Essays in Religion and Philosophy*. Ed. A. Sharma. New York: Unity Press, 1991, 153-67.

c. *Muslims and Islamization in North America: Problems and Prospects*. Ed. Amber Haque. Beltville, Md.: Amana Pub. 1999, 257-71.

328. "Islam and the Problem of Modern Science."

a. *MAAS Journal of Islamic Science* 4, No. 1 (January-June 1988): 45-57.

b. *Muslim Education Quarterly* 5, No. 4 (1988): 35-44.

c. *Aligarh Journal of Islamic Thought* 1 (1988): 9-23.

d. *An Early Crescent: The Future of Knowledge and the Environment of Islam*. Ed. Z. Sardar. London: Mansell, 1989, 127-39.

e. "Islam i problem moderna znanosti." *Islamska Misao* (January 1991): 24-31. (BSC)

f. "İslâm ve modern bilim sorunu." *İslâmî Araştirmalar* 5, No. 2 (1991): 77-82. (T)

329. Preface to *Irshad: Wisdom of a Sufi Master*, by Shaikh Muzaffer Ozak al-Jerrahi. New York: Amity House, 1988, vii-x.

330. a. "*Wujūd* and *Māhiyyah* in Islamic Thought." *The Iwanami Lecture Series: Heritages of Wisdom and Thought* 4 (Tokyo, 1988): 204-44. (J)

b. "Existence (*wujūd*) and Quiddity (*māhiyyah*) in Islamic Philosophy." *International Philosophical Quarterly* 29, No. 4 (December 1989): 409-28.

c. *Iqbal Review* (October 1989-April 1990): 161-94.

331. "The Spiritual States in Sufism." (Taken from *Sufi Essays*.) *Sufism: An Inquiry* 1, No. 1 (1988): 12-17 and 1, No. 2 (1988): 12-20 and 51-52.

332. a. "Ibn Sīnā." *Dictionary of the Middle Ages*, Vol. 2. New York: Scribners, 1988, 302-7.

b. *The Islamic Intellectual Tradition in Persia*. Ed. M. Aminrazavi, 66-75.

333. "Intelektualni i historijski uzroci krize susreta modernog čovjeka i prirode." *Zivot*, No. 7 and 8 (1988): 127-47. ("The Intellectual and Historical Causes," from *Man and Nature*, 51-80. (BSC)

334. "Filozofija i teorija islamske medicine." *Kulture Istoka* (Belgrade) 18 (October-December 1988): 32-33. ("The Philosophy and Theory of Islamic Medicine," from *Science and Civilization in Islam*, 219-29.) (BSC)

1989

335. a. "Mystik und Rationalität im Islam." *Geist und Natur*. Ed. H. P. Durr and W. Zimmerli. Munich: Scherz Verlag, 1989, 221-41. (G)

b. "Vielleicht kann der Western auch einmal von anderen lernen." "Mystik und Rationalität im Islam." *Frankfurte Allgemeine Zeitung* 6, No. 2 (January 1989). (Summary of above.) (G)

c. «تصوّف و تعقل در اسلام»، نامهٔ فرهنگ، سال سوّم، شمارهٔ چهارم، شمارهٔ مسلسل ۱۲، زمستان ۱۳۷۲، ص ۷۳_۸۵. (P)

336. "The Teaching of Art in the Islamic World." *Muslim Educational Quarterly* 6, No. 2 (1989): 4-10.

337. "Penultimate Judgements." *Temenos* 10 (1989): 257-64.

338. "From Poem to Narrative in Sufism."

a. *Sufi: A Journal of Sufism* 1, No. 2 (Spring 1989): 6-10 and 1, No. 3 (Autumn 1989): 5-11.
b. *Iqbal Review* (Summer 1989): 3-28.
c. *The Iwanami Lecture Series: Heritages of Wisdom and Thought in the East*, 1. Tokyo, 1989, 283-316. (J)
d. *Sufi Essays* (new edition), 171-89.

339. a. "La crise spirituelle de l'homme moderne." *llem Congrès International de la Famille La Fecundite de l'Amour*. Bruxelles: Les Editions Europeennes S.A., 1989, 29-36. (F)
b. "De geestelijke crisis van de moderne mens." *ııde International Congres van Het Gezin*. Bruxelles: Les Editions Europeennes S.A., 1989, 29-37. (FL)

340. Foreword to *St. John of the Cross: Alchemist of the Soul*, by A.T. de Nicolàs. New York: Paragon House, 1989, ix-iv.

341. "Studies in Islamic Philosophy after Ibn Rushd: 1955-1970." *Al-Serāt* 15 (1989): 39-45.

342. "Being Muslim in America." (Transcription of a talk.) *Islamic Horizons* (September 1989): 32-35.

343. "Studies in Sufism in the 1950s and '60s." *Hamdard Islamicus* 12, No. 2 (Summer 1989): 3-9.

344. Foreword to *What is Civilization?*, by A. K. Coomaraswamy. Ipswich: The Golgonooza Press, 1989, VII-IX.

345. «در گذشت زین العابدین رهنما»، ایران نامه، سال هفتم،

شمارهٔ ٤، تابستان ١٣٦٨، ص ٧٢٣_٧٢٩. (P)

1990

346. Response to "Transcendence and Distinction: Metaphoric Process in Ismā'īlī Muslim Thought," by A. Nanji. *God and Creation: An Ecumenical Symposium*. Ed. D. B. Burrell and B. McGinn. Notre Dame, 1990, 316-21.
347. Review of *Allah Transcendent: Studies in the Structure and Semiotics of Islamic Philosophy, Theology and Cosmology*, by I. R. Netton. *Journal of Islamic Studies* 1 (1990): 150-51.
348. "İslâm bilimi nedir?" ("Islam and the Rise of the Islamic Sciences," *Islamic Science: An Illustrated Study*, 3-12) *İslam Bilimi Tartișmalari*. Ed. M. Armagăn. Istanbul: İnsan Yayınlari, 1990, 27-38. (T)
349. "Dasein heißt Danken." *Universale Religion* (November 1990): 6-9. (G)
350. "Islam and the Environmental Crisis."
    a. *İslâmî Araștirmalar* 4, No. 3 (July 1990): 155-74. (T)
    b. *Islamic Quarterly* 34, No. 4 (1990): 217-34.
    c. *MAAS Journal of Islamic Science* 6, No. 2 (July-December 1990): 31-51.
    d. "L'Ultima guerra alla natura di Allah." *Arancia Blu* 2, No. 4 (April 1991): 16-20. (Summary.) (I)

e. "Islam i driza životne sredine." *Izraz* (Sarajevo) (April 1991): 287-95 and (May 1991): 372-81. (BSC)

f. *Spirit and Nature*. Ed. S. C. Rockefeller and J. C. Elder. Bonton: Beacon Press, 1992, 83-108.

g. *Kesturi* 1, No. 2 (1991): 26-47.

h. "Sacred Science and the Environmental Crisis: An Islamic Perspective." *Islam and the Environment*. Ed. H. Abdel Hakem. London: Ta Ha Publishers, 1998, 118-37.

351. "The Prophet and Prophetic Religion." (Excerpts from "The Prophet and Prophetic Religion: The Last Prophet and Universal Man," *Ideals and Realities of Islam*, 6792.). *The World Treasury of Modern Religious Thought*. Ed. J. Pelikan. Boston: Little, Brown and Co., 1990, 158-68.

352. "Izucavanje filozofije" *Islamsko misao*, No. 142 (Sarajevo, 1990): 33-41.

1991

353. "Introduction." *Islamic Spirituality: Manifestations*, xiii-xxviii.

354. "Prelude: The Spiritual Significance of the Rise and Growth of the Sufi Orders." *Islamic Spirituality: Manifestations*, 3-5.

355. "Sufism and Spirituality in Persia." *Islamic Spirituality: Manifestations*, 206-22.

356. "Spiritual Chivalry." *Islamic Spirituality: Manifestations*, 304-15.

357. With J. Matini, "Persian Literature." *Islamic Spirituality: Manifestations*, 328-49.

358. "Theology, Philosophy and Spirituality." *Islamic Spirituality: Manifestations*, 395-446.

359. "What is the Meaning of Life?" *The Meaning of Life*. Ed. D. Friend. Boston: Little Brown and Co., 1991, 62.

360. "Kur'an: Božija riječ, izvor znanja i djela." (From *Ideals and Realities of Islam*, 41-66.)

a. *Kur'an u Savremenom Dobu*. Ed. E. Karić. Sarajevo, 1991, 27-56. (BSC)

b. *Glasnik VIS-a* 2 (Sarajevo) (March-April 1986), 198-216. (BSC)

361. "Spirit and Nature: A Homily based on the Quranic Verses." *Quranulhuda* (February 1991), 8.

362. a. "Religion and the Environment: An Oriental Overview." *Indian International Centre* (Spring 1991), 113-28. (Summary of Lecture given at a Conference at the Indian International Centre, New Delhi, November 1990.)

b. "Religion and the Environment: A Crisis." *Studies in Tradition* (Spring 1992): 30-42.

363. "Tradicionalni islam pred najezdom zapadnog modernizma i sekularizma." *Islamska Misao* 145 (January 1991): 6-18. (Interview) (BSC)

364. "Qu'est-ce que la science islamique" *Passerelles* 3 (1991): 48-55. (Translation of "What is Islamic Science?" from *The Islamic Philosophy of Science*.) (F)

365. "Le *mawjūd* et le *wujūd* dans la tradition orientale." *Penser avec Aristote*. Ed. M. A. Sinaceur. Paris: UNESCO, 1991, 525. (F)

366. "Les commentateurs arabes." *Penser avec Aristote*. Ed. M. A. Sinaceur. Paris: UNESCO, 1991, 757-60. (F)

367. "The Harmony of Man and Nature." *Families for Tomorrow*. Ed. J. Bogle. London: Grace Wing Books, 1991, 12-20.

368. "Islam and Modern Science." *Journal of the Pakistan Study Group* (Fall 1991): 5-19. (Transcription of a lecture given at Massachusetts Institute of Technology.)

369. a. Preface to *Ruba'iyyat of Omar Khayyam*. Trans. A. Saidi. Berkeley: Asian Humanities Press, 1991, xxi-xxiv.

b. "Omar Khayyam: Philosopher-Poet-Scientist." *The Islamic Intellectual Tradition in Persia*. Ed. M. Aminrazavi, 222-25.

370. «ایران و فرهنگ جاوید آن»، (با مختصر تغیری متن فارسی ایران پل فیروزه). (P)

a. (الف.) اقبالیات، ۱۳۹۸_۱۳۹۹، ص ٤٣_۷۷. (P)

b. (ب.) ره آورد، شمارهٔ ۲۸، ره آورد پائیز ۱۳۷۰، ص ۸_۲۰. (P)

371. «نگهی دیگر به هنری کربن»، ایران نامه، سال نهم،

شمارهٔ ٤، پائیز ١٣٧٠، ص ٤٤٧_٤٨١. (P)

372. Review of *The Feathered Sun*, by F. Schuon. *Aries*, No. 12 and 13 (1990-91): 62-64.

373. Review of *The Sufi Path of Knowledge*, by W. Chittick. *Aries*, No. 14 (1991): 40-41.

374. Review of *Symbol and Archetype: A Study of the Meaning of Existence*, by M. Lings. *Aries*, No. 14 (1991): 64-65.

375. "Tariqah-duhowni put I njegovi kur'anski korijeni." *Islamska misao*, No. 146 (Sarajevo, 1991): 30-41.

1992

376. a. "Oral Transmission and the Book in Islamic Education: The Spoken and the Written Word." *Journal of Islamic Studies* (Oxford) 3, No. 1 (January 1992): 1-14.

b. «نقل شفاهی و کتاب در تعلیم و تربیت اسلامی: کلام ملفوظ مکتوم»، ترجمهٔ فاطمه ولیانی، مجلّهٔ تحقیقات اسلامی، سال ٧، شمارهٔ ١، ١٣٧١، ص ٢١_٣٧. (P)

c. "İslâmi eğitimde sözlü aktarim ve kitap: yazilan ve konsuşulan söz," *İslâmi Araştirmalar* 6, No. 3 (1993): 181-88. (T)

d. *The Book in the Islamic World*. Ed. George Atiyeh. Albany: The State University of New York Press, 1995, 57-70.

377. a. "What is Tradition?" *Studies in Tradition* 1, No. 1 (Winter 1992): 3-27. (From *Knowledge and the Sacred*, 65-92.)

b. "Que es Tradicion?" *Caminos,* segunda epocha, No. 11, (Spring 1998): 33-51. (S)

c. "Kas yra tradicija," trans. A. Beinorius, *Liaudies Kultūra* 5 (1995): 51-60. (LN)

378. "Time (*kâla*): The Moving Image of Eternity."

a. *Avaloka* 6, No. 1 & 2 (1992): 69-94.

b. *The Need for a Sacred Science*, 25-42.

c. *Concepts of Time Ancient and Modern*. Ed. K. Vatsyayan. New Delhi: Indira Gandhi Centre, 1996, 515-26.

379. "Persian Sufi Literature: Its Spiritual and Cultural Significance."

a. *The Legacy of Mediaeval Persian Sufism.* Ed. L. Lewisohn. London: Khaniqahi Nimatullahi Publications, 1992, 1-10.

b. *Sufi: A Journal of Sufism* 12 (Winter 1991-92): 9-15.

c. "جنبه‌های روحانی و فرهنگی ادبیات صوفیانهٔ ایران زمین"، ترجمهٔ حسین کاشانی، صوفی، شمارهٔ چهاردهم، بهار ۱۳۷۱، ص ۱۶_۲۱. (P)

380. Foreword to *The Principles of Epistemology in Islamic Philosophy*, by M. Ha'iri Yazdi. Albany: The State University of New York Press, 1992, VII-XIII.

381. "İslâm Birliği: İslâm'in Gerçekleşmesi İdeali ve Engeller." (With

English summary "Islamic Unity: The Ideals and Obstacles in the Way of its Realization") *İlim ve Sanat* 32 (Mayis 1992): 12-15.

382. Foreword to *Persian Influence on the Development of Literary and Sufi Tradition in South Asia*, by K. A. Nizami. Bethesda: The Foundation for Iranian Studies, 1992, 15-16.

383. Foreword to *Classification of Knowledge in Islam: A Study in Islamic Philosophies of Science*, by O. Bakar. Kuala Lumpur: Institute for Policy Research, 1992, xi-xv.

384. "Islam in the Present-Day Islamic World: An Overview." (From *Traditional Islam in the Modern World*) *Studies in Tradition* (Autumn 1992): 33-51.

385. a. "The Significance of Islamic Manuscripts." *The Significance of Islamic Manuscripts*. Ed. J. Cooper. London: Al-Furqan Islamic Heritage Foundation, 1992, 7-17.

b. «اهمية المخطوطات الاسلامية»، در «اهمية المخطوطات الاسلامية اعمال المؤتمر الافتتاحي لمؤسسة الفرقان»، لندن ١٤١٣/١٩٩٢، ص ٢٩_٤٢. (A)

386. Review of *The Way and the Mountain*, by M. Pallis. *Temenos* 13 (1992): 259-61.

387. «در گذشت خسرو مستوفى»، ايران نامه، سال دهم، شمارهٔ ٤، پائيز ١٣٧١، ص ٧٨٧_٧٨٨. (P)

388. «پاسخ آقای دکتر نصر» (پاسخ به نامهٔ خانم فرنگیس یگانگی)، ره آورد، پائیز ۱۳۷۱، ص ۳۰۲_۳۰۳. (P)

389. پیشگفتار (برای شمارهٔ مخصوص)، ایران نامه، سال یازدهم، شمارهٔ ۱، زمستان ۱۳۷۱، ص ۳_۹. (P)

390. «عرفان نظری و سیر و سلوک در تصوّف»، ایران نامه، سال یازدهم، شمارهٔ ۱، زمستان ۱۳۷۱، ص ۱۲۱_۱۲۸. (P)

391. "The Islamic View of the Environment." (Summary of a talk given at the University of Wisconsin). *Human Values and the Environment.* Report No. 140. Madison: University of Wisconsin Academy of Sciences, Arts and Letters, 1992, 47-49.

392. Review of *Mensch und Tier vor dem König der Dschinnen: Aus den Schriften der Lauteren Brüder von Basra*, edited and translated by A. Giese. Hamburg, 1990. *Journal of the American Oriental Society* 112 (1992): 723.

393. "The Rasā'il of the Ikhwān al-Ṣafā': Their Identify and Content." *An Anthology of Islamic Studies*. Ed. Issa J. Boullata. Montreal: Institute of Islamic Studies, McGill University, 1992. (Extract from *An Introduction to Islamic Cosmological Doctrines*, 25-43).

1993

394. "Traditional Art as Fountain of Knowledge and Grace." (From *Knowledge and the Sacred.*) *Studies in Tradition* 2, No. 1 (Winter 1993): 22-46.

395. "The Rise and Development of Persian Sufism." *Sufi*, No. 16 (Winter 1993): 5-12.

396. a. "Islam." *Our Religions*. Ed. A. Sharma. San Francisco: Harper and Row, 1993, 425-532.
   b. *Islam, Religioni A Confronto* (Venice: Neri Pozza Editore, 1996), 575-718. (I)

397. "Islamic View of the Universe." *Islamic Culture*, Vol. I: Foundations of Islam. Ed. Z. Ansari. Paris: UNESCO. (in press)

398. "Islamic Cosmology." *Islamic Culture*, Vol. IV: Islamic Science. Paris: UNESCO. (in press)

399. "İslâm geleneğini yeniden keşfetmek," (Interview with İlhan Kutluer), *İzlenim* (Mart 1993), 32-36.

400. "İslâm sanatının manevî kaynakları ve sembolizmi üzerine," (interview by Akif Emre), *Dergâh*, no. 36 (1993): 12-13. (T)

401. "فلسفه، روشنفکری و بحران تمدن معاصر"، مصاحبه با ماهنامهٔ فرهنگی و هنری عاشقانه، مهر و آبان، شمارهٔ ٤٣_٤٤، ١٣٧٢. (P)

402. "Reflection on Man and the Future of Civilization."

a. (Summary), *Al-Noor* 3, No. 27 (September 1993): 6-7.

b. *Dialogue* (October 1993): 4-5.

c. (Full text) *Islamic Studies* (Islamabad) 32, No. 3 (Autumn 1993): 253-59.

d. «تأملات حول الانسان و مستقبل الحضارة،» آفاق الاسلام، العدد الاول، السنة الثانية، اذار ١٩٩٤، ص ٦٨_٧٥. (A)

403. "Mukaddime," *Tarihi, siyasi, ilmi, irfani ve ahlaki Boyutlariyla islam'da Şia* by Allame Tabataba'i. Istanbul: Kevser, 1993, 9-12. (T)

404. "Islam, Islamic Science and the Environmental Crisis," *Eco-Justice* 13, No. 4 (Autumn 1993): 8-9 and 22.

405. "Modern Dünyada din" Haşimi Rafsancani, Cevad Bahoner and Seyyid Hüseyin Nasr, *İslam Öncesi Cahiliyye ve Günümüzde Din Gerçeği*, Erzurum: İhtar Yayıncılık, 1993, 147-68. (T)

406. "The Rise and Development of Persian Sufism," *Classical Persian Sufism: From its Origin to Rumi*. London and New York: Khaniqahi Nimatullahi Publications, 1993, 1-18. *The Heritage of Sufism, I*. Oxford: Oneworld Press, 1999, 1-18.

1994

407. Foreword to Laleh Bakhtiar, *Moral Healer's Handbook: The*

Psychology of Spiritual Chivalry. Chicago: Kazi Publications 1994, vii-viii.

408. "Seyyed Hossein Nasr on 'Islam and Music'," *Harvard University Center for the Study of World Religions News* 1, No. 2 (Spring, 1994): 1, 3, 4, 5, 10, 11.

409. "The One in the Many," *Parabola* (Spring 1994): 12-19.

410. "What is Islamic Science?"

  a. "İslâmî Bilim Nedir?" *İslâmî Araştırmalar* 7, No. 1 (Winter 1993-94): 1-12.

  b. *MAAS Journal of Islamic Science* 10, No. 1, (January-June 1994): 9-20.

411. "To Live as a Young Muslim in America." *Islamic Horizons* (September 1994): 6-8.

412. Foreword to George B. Grose and Benjamin J. Habbard, eds., *The Abraham Connection: A Jew, Christian, and Muslim in Dialogue.* Notre Dame: Crossroad Books, 1994, xxii-xxv.

413. Interview with Robert Siegel, ed., *The NPR Interviews 1994.* New York and Boston: Houghton Mifflin, (1994), 163-67.

414. a. (الف.) «گفت و شنود با سیّد حسین نصر» (مصاحبه با منصوره شیوا کاویانی)، مجلّهٔ کلک، مهر و آبان ۱۳۷۲، شمارهٔ ٤٣_٤٤، ص ۱۷۷_۱۹۷. (P)

  b. (ب.) خلاصه در کیهان (لندن) شمارهٔ ٤٩١، ۲۷ ژانویه

۱۹۹٤، ص ۹، و شمارهٔ ٤۹۲، سوّم فوریه ۱۹۹٤، ص ۹. (P)

415. «فلسفه و بحران جهان کنونی»، ره آورد، شمارهٔ ۳٤، فصلنامه تابستان و پائیز ۱۳۷۲، ص ۱٦_۲۹. (P)

1995

416. Review of A.M. Schimmel, *The Mystery of Numbers*, New York and Oxford: Oxford University Press, 1993, in *The Journal of Religion* (Chicago) 75, No. 1 (January 1995): 162-63.

417. Foreword to Shaykh Muhammad Hisham Kabbani, *The Naqshbandi Sufi Way*. Chicago: Kazi Publications, 1995, xxi-xxiii.

418. "Ṭabāṭabā'ī, Muḥammad Ḥusayn," *The Oxford Encyclopedia of the Modern Islamic World*. Ed. John Esposito. New York: Oxford University Press, 1995, 161-62.

419. "Philosophy," *The Oxford Encyclopedia of the Modern Islamic World*. New York: Oxford University Press, 1995, 328-33.

420. a. Review of R. Guénon, *Fundamental Symbols: The Universal Language of Sacred Science*. Cambridge: The University Press, 1995, in *Parabola* (Summer 1995): 93-94.

b. *Iqbal Review* 37, No. 1 (April 1996): 151-53 and again in 38, No. 1 (April 1997): 158-59.

421. "The Islamic World-View and Modern Science."

a. *Islamic Quarterly* xxxix, No. 2 (Second Quarter 1995): 73-89.

b. *Constech* 7, No. 1 (March 1996): 7-22.

c. "جهان بینی اسلامی و علم جدید"، ترجمهٔ ضیاء تاج‌الدین، نامهٔ فرهنگ، سال هشتم، شمارهٔ دوّم، شمارهٔ مسلسل ٣٠، ١٣٧٧، ص ٤٨_٥٩. (P)

422. "Comments on a Few Theological Issues in Islamic-Christian Dialogue." *Christian-Muslim Encounters*. Ed. Yvonne and Wadi Haddad. Florida: University of Florida Press, 1995, 457-67.

423. "Islam, Tradition and the West" (interview), *Gnosis*, No. 37 (Fall 1995): 50-55.

424. Review of Syed Nomanul-Haq, *Names, Natures and Things: The Alchemist Jābir ibn Ḥayyān and his Kitāb al-aḥjār (Book of Stones)*, *Isis* 86, No. 3 (Sept. 1995): 475.

425. Foreword to Muhammad Abdul Rauf, *Imam 'Alī Ibn Abī Ṭālib: The First Intellectual Muslim Thinker*. Alexandria: al-Saadawi Publications, 1995, xi-xiii.

426. Préface to Titus Burckhardt, *Principles et méthodes de l'art sacré*. Paris: Editions Dervy, 1995, 1-4. (F)

427. "Le cosmos comme théophanie," trans. P. Laude (from *Knowledge and the Sacred*). *Connaissance des Religions* (Jan.-June 1995): 68-85, (July-Dec. 1995): 7-24.

428. "Spirituality and Science: Convergence or Divergence?"

a. *Sophia* 1, No. 2 (Winter 1995): 23-40.
b. *Journal of Islamic Science* 12, No. 1 (Jan.-June 1996): 3-12.
c. *Iqbal Review* (October 1996): 3-12.

429. Review of J. L. Michon, *Lumières d'Islam*, *Sophia* 1, No. 2 (Winter 1995): 23-40.

430. "Ibn Arabī y los Sufies" (trans. of chap. III, *Three Muslim Sages*), *Postdata* (Murcia, Spain), No. 15 (June-August 1995): 8-29. (S)

431. "Principi Islamske Arhitekture I Savremeni Urbani Problemi," *Sumejja*, November 1995, Broj 13, Sarajevo, p. 19; trans. into Bosnian as "The Principles of Islamic Architecture and Contemporary Urban Problems" from *Traditional Islam in the Modern World*, 239-50.

432. "Islamska Etika Rada." *Sumejja* (November 1995), Broj 14, Sarajevo, 18-19; trans. into Bosnian as "Islamic Work Ethics" from *Traditional Islam in the Modern World*, 35-46.

433. "The Subjective and Objective Dimensions of the Study of Religion: A Panel Discussion with John Hick, Robert Segal, S. H. Nasr and Arvind Sharma." *Religious Traditions* 18-20 (1995-97): 81-108.

434. «جهان اسلام در دوران جدید» (اخذ از راهنمای جوان مسلمان در دنیای متجدد)، روزنامهٔ همشهری، سه‌شنبه ۲۷ اردیبهشت ۱۳۷۳، سال دوّم، شمارهٔ ۴۰۱، ص ۶، و

چهارشنبه ۲۸ اردیبهشت ۱۳۷۳، سال دوّم، شمارهٔ ۴۰۲،
ص ۶. (P)

1996

435. *History of Islamic Philosophy*. Ed. S. H. Nasr and O. Leaman. London: Routledge, 1996.
   a. "Introduction," Part I, 11-18.
   b. "The Meaning and Concept of Philosophy in Islam," Part I, 21-26.
   c. "The Qur'an and *Ḥadīth* as Source and Inspiration of Islamic Philosophy," Part I, 27-39.
   d. "Ibn Sīnā's Oriental Philosophy," Part I, 247-51.
   e. "Introduction to the Mystical Tradition," Part I, 367-73.
   f. (i.)"Mullā Ṣadrā: His Teachings," Part I, 643-62.
   (ii.) «تعالیم ملا صدرا»، ترجمهٔ حسین علی شیدان، اطلاعات، ۲۹ تیر ۱۳۷۸، ص ۶، ۳۰ تیر ۱۳۷۸، ص ۶، و مرداد ۱۳۷۸، ص ۶. (P)

436. "The First Prophet: An Interview with Seyyed Hossein Nasr" (Interview by Gray Henry). *Parabola* XXI, No. 1 (Spring, 1996): 13-19.

437. "The Relation Between Religions in the Shadow of the

Environmental Crisis." *World Faiths Encounters*, No. 13 (March 1996): 3-18.

438. "The Prophet as the Exemplar Par Excellence" (chap. III of *Ideals and Realities of Islam*). *Ḥadīth and Sunnah: Ideals and Realities* Ed. P. K. Koya. Kuala Lumpur: Islamic Book Trust, 1996, 253-78.

439. a. "Metaphysical Roots of Intolerance: An Islamic Interpretation." *Philosophy, Religion and the Question of Intolerance*. Ed. M. Aminrazavi and D. Ambuel. Albany: SUNY Press, 1996-97, 43-56.

b. «مبادی مابعدالطبیعهٔ و تلقی اسلامی در مقولهٔ مدارا و عدم مدارا»، ترجمهٔ هومن پناهنده، کیان، سال هشتم، شمارهٔ ٤٥، بهمن و اسفند ١٣٧٧، ص ٣٨_٤٦. (P)

c. *Iqbal Review* 37, No. 1 (April, 1996): 1-16.

440. "A Conversation with Seyyed Hossein Nasr." Hugh Hewitt, *Searching for God in America*. Dallas: Word Publishing, 1996, 75-96.

441. "L'arte della transformazione spirituale interiore seconda Evola." Preface to Julius Evola, *La Tradizione Ermetica*. Rome: Edizione Mediterranee, 1996, 15-21. (I)

442. Review of Titus Burckhardt, *Chartres and the Birth of the Cathedral*, in *Sophia* 2, No. 1 (Summer 1996): 92-95.

443. "Sufism, Creativity and Exile: An Interview with Seyyed Hossein Nasr" (Amirah El-Zein). *Jusoor*, 1996. Bethesda: Kitab, 131-58.

444. Preface to Whitall N. Perry, *Challenges to a Secular Society*. Oakton: The Foundation for Traditional Studies, 1996, 5-6.

445. "Divine Beauty: The Qur'anic Story of Joseph and Zulaykhā." Bill Moyers, *Talking About Genesis: A Source Guide*. New York: Doubleday, 1996, 149-54.

446. "Conversations." Bill Moyers, *Genesis: A Living Conversation*. New York: Doubleday, 1996, 219-47; 319-47.

447. "To Live in a World with No Center and Many." *Cross Currents* 46, No. 3 (Fall 1996): 318-25.

448. "Revival of Islamic Medical Tradition." *The Journal of IMA* (Islamic Medical Association of America) 28, No. 4 (Oct. 1996): 153-59.

449. "Islam and the West: Yesterday and Today." *The American Journal of Islamic Sciences* 13, No. 4 (Winter 1996): 551-62.

450. "Religious Art, Traditional Art, Sacred Art: Some Reflections and Definitions," *Sophia* 2, No. 2 (Winter 1996): 13-30.

451. «یگانگی عمل و نظر معماری در سخن متفکران معاصر»، مجلهٔ آبادی، سال پنجم، شمارهٔ ۱۹، زمستان ۷٤، ص ٤٦، ٤٩. (P)

452. a. (الف.) «رویارویی تمدنها و سازندگی آینده بشر»،

ره آورد، شمارهٔ ٣٦، تابستان ١٣٧٣، ص ٦_١٦، کلک، شمارهٔ ٦٠، اسفند ١٣٧٣، ص ١٢_٢٤. (P)

b. (ب.) در «نظریه برخورد تمدنها: هانتینگتون و منقّدانش»، ترجمه و ویراستاری مجتبی امیری، تهران، مؤسسهٔ چاپ و انتشارات وزارت امور خارجه، ١٣٧٤، ١٢١_١٤٠. (P)

453. «فلسفه و بحران تفکر در ایران و جهان معاصر»، دیدارها، به قلم شیوا کاویانی، تهران، انتشارات فکر روز، ١٣٧٤، ص ١١_٢٧. (P)

454. *UXXII stolječu očekujemo sukob vjere i neujcre* (We expect a clash between faith and unbelief in the 21st century), interview with Enes Karić, Preporod Sarajevo: May 1996.

1997

455. Foreword to Sajjad S. Haider, *Love, Virtues and Commandments: An Interfaith Perspective*. Chicago: Kazi Publications, 1997, vii-viii.

456. "Islam and Music: The Legal and Spiritual Dimensions." *Enchanting Powers: Music in the World's Religions*. Ed.

Lawrence E. Sullivan. Cambridge: Harvard University Press, 1997, 219-35.

457. "Perennial Ontology and Quantum Mechanics: A Review Essay of *The Quantum Enigma* by Wolfgang Smith," *Sophia* 3, No. 1 (Summer 1997): 135-59.

458. Foreword to Muhammad ibn 'Abd Allāh al-Kisā'ī, *Tales of the Prophet. Great Books of Islamic Civilization*, No. 1. Chicago: Kazi Publications, 1997, (repeated in other volumes of the series).

459. "Islamic Aesthetics" in Eliot Deutsch and Ron Bontekoe, eds., *A Companion to World Philosophies*. Oxford: Blackwell, 1997, 448-59.

460. Review of Peter Kingsley, *Ancient Philosophy, Mystery and Magic: Empedocles and the Pythagorean Tradition. Journal of Islamic Studies* 8, No. 2 (July 1997): 242-44.

461. "Incantation of the Griffin (Sîmurgh) and the Cry of the Eagle: Islam and the Native American Tradition." *Sophia* 3, No. 2 (Winter 1997): 35-44.

462. "El cosmos coms teofanía" (trans. of chap. 6 of *Knowledge and the Sacred*). *Axis Mundi* 2 (1997): 71-86; 3 (1998): 6-99. (S)

463. "Islamic Unity: The Ideal and Obstacles in the Way of its Realization." *Islamic Studies* (Islamabad) 36, No. 4 (1997): 657-62.

464. "Kur'an- Božija Riječ, Izvor Znanja i Djela" (Chap. II of *Ideals and Realities of Islam*) Enes Karić, ed., *Kur'an u Savre menom*

Dobu, vol. I. Sarajevo: El Kalem, 1997, 67-92.

465. "Moderni nacin zivota" *Muallim*, No. 53-54-55, Sarajevo, 1997.

1998

466. "Dr. Seyyed Hossein Nasr on Spirituality in Islam," *The Muslim Magazine* 1, No. 1 (Jan. 1998): 12; 68-69.

467. Preface to S. J. Ashtiyani, H. Matsubara et. al, *Consciousness and Reality: Studies in Memory of Toshihiko Izutsu*. Tokyo: Iwnanmi Shoten, 1998, xi-xv.

468. a. "The Quranic Commentaries of Mullā Ṣadrā," S. J. Ashtiyani, H. Matsubara et. al, *Consciousness and Reality*. Tokyo: Iwanami Shoten, 1998, 45-58.

b. (ب.) «تفاسیر ملا صدرا بر قرآن»، بخارا، ۱، مرداد و شهریور ۱۳۷۷، ترجمهٔ حسن لاهوتی، ص ۲۲_۳٤. (P)

c. *The Transcendent Theosophy of Ṣadr al-Dīn Shīrāzī*, New Edition, 123-35.

469. Feature Review of Roshdi Rashed, *Les Mathématiques Infinitésimales*, 2 Vols. London: Al-Furqan Foundation, 1996, in *Isis* 89, No. 1 (March 1998): 112-13.

470. "Mystical Philosophy in Islam." *Routledge Encyclopedia of Philosophy*. London-New York: Routledge, 1998, 616-20.

471. "Frithjof Schuon (1907-1998)." *Sacred Web* No. 1 (1998): 15-17.

472. "What does it mean to be human?" in F. Franck, J. Roze, and R.

Connolly, eds. *What Does It Mean to be Human*. Nyack, N.Y.: Circumstantial Productions and UNESCO, 1998, 96-103.

473. Foreword to Shaykh Muhammad Hisham Kabbani, *Encyclopedia of Islamic Doctrines: Beliefs*. Mountain View, Calif.: As-Sunna Foundation of America Publications, 1998, xi-xiv.

474. Foreword to A. K. Saran, *Traditional View of Man*, Varanasi: Cultural Institute of Higher Tibetan Studies, 1998, xvii-xxviii.

475. "Islamic-Christian Dialogues: Problems and Obstacles to be Pondered and Overcome." *Muslim World* 1x-xxviii, No. 3-4 (July-Oct. 1998): 218-37. (same as book #55).

476. "Vie et doctrine de Ṣadr ad-Dîn (Mullâ Ṣadrâ)" (from *Islamic Life and Thought*), *Aux Sources de la Sagesse* 5, No. 18 (1419/1998): 61-92.

477. Preface to Ibn Qayyim al-Jawziyya, *Medicine of the Prophet*, Trans. P. Johnstone. Cambridge: The Islamic Texts Society, 1998, xvii-xxii.

478. "In Memoriam: Frithjof Schuon--A Prelude." *Sophia* 4, No. 2 (1998): 7-13.

479. Review of J. L. Michon, *Le Shaykh Muhammad al-Hâshimî et son commentaire de L'Echiquier des gnostiques* (Sharh Shatranj al-'ârifîn), Milan: Arché, 1998, *Sophia* 4, No. 2 (1998): 265-66.

480. "Hakim Muhammad Said." *Islamic Studies* 37, No. 4 (Winter 1998): 565-66.

481. "Soruşturma." *İslâmiyât, Şeriat Dosyasi* 1, say 14 (1998): 299-301. (T)

482. «زبان فارسی و هویت ملّی»، گلستان، سال اوّل، شمارهٔ ۱، بهار ۱۳۷۶، ص ۲۵_۴۲. (P)

483. «چرا مولانا و چرا اکنون؟»، گلستان، سال اوّل، شمارهٔ ۲، تابستان ۱۳۷۶، ص ۹_۱۱. (P)

484. "Can Science Dispense with Religion?" in *Can Science Dispense with Religion?* M. Golshani, ed. Tehran: Institute for Humanities and Cultural Studies, 1998, 157-74.

1999

485. "Toward the Heart of Things," (pp. 83-104 of *Man and Nature*), *Parabola* 24, No. 1 (1999): 40-48.

486. "The Spiritual Significance of Jerusalem: The Islamic Vision." *Islamic Quarterly* XLII, No. 4 (1419/1999): 233-42.

487. "Separation from God: An Interview with Seyyed Hossein Nasr." *Parabola* (Winter 1999): 59-66.

488. "Preface: What Attracted Merton to Sufism?" in Rob Baker and Gray Henry, ed., *Merton and Sufism*. Louisville: Fons Vitae, 1999, 9-13.

489. "Prayer" in Elizabeth Roberts and Elias Amidon, ed., *Prayers for a Thousand Years*. San Francisco: Harper, 1999, 129.

490. "El Shiismo," (Trans. of Appendix III of *Shi'ite Islam*), *Revista*

Islámica Kauzar vi, No. 23 (April 1999): 7-8. (S)

491. "Homage to Huston Smith," *Sophia* 5, No. 1 (Summer, 1999): 5-8.

492. a. "Frithjof Schuon and the Islamic Tradition." *Sophia* 5, No. 1 (Summer 1999): 27-48.

b. Frithjof Schuon et la Tradition islamique. *Connaissance des Religions*. Hors Série (1999): 123-39. (F)

493. Review of A. K. Coomaraswammy, *Hinduism and Buddhism*, *Sophia* 5, No. 1 (Summer, 1999): 209-211.

494. "'Our Religions in a Religiously Plural World" in Arvind Sharma and Kathleen Dugan, eds., *A Dome of Many Colors*. Harrisburg, Pa.: Trinity Press International, 1999, 57-65.

495. "Religion, Globality and Universality," in Sharma and Dugan, *A Dome of Many Colors*, 152-78.

496. "Recollections of Henry Corbin and Reflections upon His Intellectual Significance," *Temenos Academy Review* 2 (Spring 1999): 34-45.

497. Foreword to *The Visual Islamic and Traditional Arts, The Prince of Wales's Foundation for Architecture and the Building Arts*, London, 1999, 6-8.

498. *An Anthology of Philosophy in Persia*, vol. 1, with M. Aminrazavi. New York: Oxford University Press, 1999.

a. Prolegomena, xxiii-xxx.

b. "Introduction to Early Islamic Philosophy," 85-88.

c. "Introduction to Fārābī," 91-93.

d. "Introduction to Abu'l-Ḥasan 'Āmirī," 135-36.
e. "Introduction to Ibn Sīnā," 195-98.
f. "Introduction to Miskawayh," 274-75.
g. "Introduction to the Independent Philosophers," 351-53.
h. "Introduction to Bīrūnī," 374-75.

499. "The Place of the School of Isfahan in Islamic Philosophy and Sufism." *The Heritage of Sufism*, III, ed. L. Lewisohn and D. Maryam. Oxford, 1999, 3-15.

500. "The Perennial Voice of Islam: An Interview with Seyyed Hossein Nasr," (Interview by Lucian W. Stone, Jr.), *Kinesis* 25, No. 2 (Fall 1999): 5-26.

501. «اسلام در غرب (اروپای غربی و امریکا)»، دائرة المعارف بزرگ اسلامی، جلد هشتم، تهران ۱۳۷۷، ص ۵۸۱ـ۵۸۸. (P)

502. «عرض و طول تاریخ فلسفه اسلامی و استاد سید جلال‌الدین آشتیانی»، خرد جاویدان، جشن نامهٔ استاد سید جلال‌الدین آشتیانی، به کوشش علی اصغر محمد خانی و حسن سید عرب، تهران، نشریهٔ فرزان، ۱۳۷۷، ص ۱۱ـ۱۹. (P)

503. «معضلات تجدد و فرهنگ اسلامی ـ جنبشهای احیا گرانه اسلامی»، گفتگو در همشهری، چهارشنبه ۱۲ آبان ۱۳۷۸،

ص ۹، و یکشنبه ۱۶ آبان ۱۳۷۸، ص ۹. (P)

504. «اسلام و موسیقی» (بر گرفته از کتاب «هنر و معنویت اسلامی»)، گاهنامهٔ ایمان، سال ششم، شمارهٔ ۱۲، تابستان ۱۹۹۹/۱۳۷۸، ص ۲۴ـ۲۹. (P)

INDEX

(by Lucian W. Stone, Jr.)